GOVERNMENTAL REORGANIZATIONS

Cases and Commentary

Edited by

FREDERICK C. MOSHER

A Joint Project of

THE INTER-UNIVERSITY CASE PROGRAM, INC.
Syracuse University, Syracuse, New York

and

THE INSTITUTE OF GOVERNMENTAL STUDIES
University of California, Berkeley

Published for The Inter-University Case Program, Inc., by

The Bobbs-Merrill Company, Inc.
A Subsidiary of Howard W. Sams & Co., Inc.
Indianapolis · New York

Dedicated to the Memory
of
EGBERT S. WENGERT
Colleague on the Board of the Inter-University Case Program;
Colleague on its Research Committee;
Colleague in the Study and Teaching of Political Science.

Printed in the United States of America
Library of Congress Catalog Card Number 66-27884

FIRST PRINTING

Preface

This study has had the dual sponsorship of the Institute of Governmental Studies of the University of California at Berkeley and the Inter-University Case Program, Inc. (ICP). It also has had dual aims. From the start of the venture, nine years ago, these dualities have focused on the director of the study, Frederick C. Mosher, a board member of the ICP, occasionally a staff member of the Institute of Governmental Studies, and a professor of political science at Berkeley. Thereby hangs a short tale that will help the reader understand better the contents of the volume.

During a meeting held at Cornell University in the summer of 1958, the Executive Board of the Inter-University Case Program, to quote from its minutes,

> ". . . agreed to encourage Mr. Mosher, with the assistance of Mr. Waldo and others, to undertake the production of a cluster of cases in the public management-organizational behavior area. While the field of concentration of this Committee may be the budgetary process, reorganization, or any other aspect of the area, the Board would look with favor on an effort by this Committee to design its case cluster *primarily for scientific research purposes,* and, if the members of the Committee so decide, *for the purpose of systematically exploring or validating hypotheses about administrative behavior.*"

Italics were not used in the original minutes, but those phrases were big news for the ICP, not least for board member Mosher, who was then in Italy. The ICP had been in existence almost ten years, counting its 1948 origin as the Committee on Public Administration Cases by political scientists from Cornell, Harvard, Princeton, and Syracuse. It had published upwards of sixty cases, including the ground-breaking collection, *Public Administration and Policy Development* (Harcourt Brace, 1952), so brilliantly introduced and edited by the late and rare Harold Stein. Some 70 universities participated in the Case Program, which was governed, then as now, by an inter-university board of political scientists.

At almost every meeting of this inter-university directorate since the publication of the Stein casebook, board members had discussed and debated a succession of possible experiments at attempting to make clinical case studies (widely acknowledged to be useful for teaching and for the initial exploration of previously unknown or unappreciated areas of government administration) more valuable in terms of scientific theories about political science and organizational behavior. For us, therefore, the June 1958 decision to initiate the experimental study, of which this volume is the product, was important but certainly not impetuous. Its immediate antecedents were discussions of communications from three members who had participated in the previous years of board deliberations about this general topic. One came from the late E. S. Wengert. The second came from Dwight Waldo (then Director of the Institute of Governmental Studies) in the form of a draft essay written after conducting a second-semester graduate seminar on methodological aspects of the public administration case study in the Political Science Department at Berkeley.* The third and possibly the decisive communication was a letter that had arrived some months earlier from Professor Mosher in Italy, indicating that on his return to the University of California he would be willing to take responsibility for supervising the preparation of a collection of cases on some aspect of administrative behavior. The upshot of the 1958 meeting was a decision that, in addition to the seven other clusters then being launched under a five-year Ford

---

* A revised version of the Waldo essay appears in E. A. Bock, editor: *Essays on the Case Method* (Brussels, International Institute of Administrative Sciences, 1962). Professor Wengert's communication was partly incorporated in an essay, *Some Thoughts on the Uses of Cases of the Inter-University Case Program,* 1961, obtainable in mimeographed form from the ICP central office, Syracuse University.

Foundation grant, an eighth cluster, under Professor Mosher's direction, was to aim at using cases primarily for systematic scientific research and, therefore, at the companion objective of contributing to substantive scientific knowledge about some important hypothesis or theory concerning administrative behavior.

One reason the ICP board had not acted earlier to launch an experiment of this type was the unavailability, for the direction of such an enterprise, of a man who embodied scholarly and scientific standards of the highest order along with an immense personal experience of the realities of actual government administration at federal, state, and local levels. When Professor Mosher's letter from Italy indicated his availability, all of us felt in our bones that he was the ideal man for this assignment, one who commanded respect, not to say admiration, over a wide spectrum in public administration, from practitioners, at one extreme, to theorists and researchers at the other. We believed he could bring this experiment off successfully, if anyone could, and we hastened to act while he was still too far away to register a change of mind.

To work with Professor Mosher in the design of the cluster, a Research Committee was appointed from among serving or former ICP board members. It included:

Frederic N. Cleaveland, University of North Carolina
Herbert S. Kaufman, Yale University
Frank Sherwood, University of Southern California
Dwight Waldo, University of California at Berkeley
E. S. Wengert, University of Oregon

By the winter of 1959-1960, the Research Committee, having decided that several other widely accepted hypotheses concerning organizational behavior were unresearchable, agreed to concentrate on the process of administrative reorganization, specifically upon the so-called participation hypothesis. The committee also discovered a chasm between the financial resources ICP could provide and the great amount of planning, case writing, and analysis that would be required to carry out the project. At this critical moment, the Institute of Governmental Studies of the University of California at Berkeley agreed to contribute a very substantial amount to the project, and it became a joint venture of the Institute and the ICP.

The Institute and the ICP have sought to support this experiment unstintingly, without in any way intruding on Professor Mosher's ultimate responsibility or limiting his freedom of action. Professor Mosher's colleagues at Berkeley and on the ICP board have contributed judgments and comments on drafts of the research design, on drafts of his analytical chapters, and on drafts of some of the cases prepared specifically under his direction primarily for this project.* But without slighting the contribution of case writers, committee members, colleagues, government officials, and all the others who helped and supported along the way, it should be stated that this study is in considerable part the product of Professor Mosher's talent, energy, and responsibility. For the six years it has taken to carry out this project (including a twelve-month interruption while Professor Mosher served as staff director of the [Herter] Committee on Foreign Affairs Personnel), he has been its head, heart, and soul. Almost everything of consequence in this volume comes from him or bears his mark.

Professor Mosher has deliberately refrained from including a chapter that analyzes what this experiment has shown about the use of case studies or similar clinical studies for systematic scientific research. We believe that we cannot evaluate the methodological side of this experiment fully until we are in a position to estimate how successful it has been on the substantive side—i.e., how much it has contributed to scientific knowledge about administrative reorganization in government organizations and about the participation hypothesis. We cannot make an overall judgment on the latter question until we learn the views of the several types of social scientists interested in the substantive subject matter. We are, therefore, more than usually interested in securing the critical assessments of readers of this volume, and we would be grateful if readers not preparing reviews for publication would take the trouble to write personal communications.

While assessments of the methodological implications of this experiment will be prepared and published at a later date, one statement can be made now from the perspective of the Inter-University

---

* Three cases in this collection were edited and published by the ICP before this project began: *The Transfer of the Children's Bureau* (CPAC #21), *Personnel Problems in Converting to Automation* (ICP #44), and Professor Mosher's own study, *Reorganization of the California State Personnel Board* (ICP #32). *The Reorganization of the U.S. Public Health Service* (ICP #89) was prepared by an ICP staff member under joint supervision. All other cases were prepared for this collection under Professor Mosher's direction.

Case Program. The ICP hopes to undertake, or to participate in, more experimental studies with this combination of methodological and substantive objectives, hopefully in areas near the highest point of intersection of the respective curves of political science significance and systematic clinical researchability. We will try to pursue this purpose (when suitable talent is available) concurrently with our other work of preparing clinical studies for the purpose of discovering and exploring operationally significant aspects of the governmental process not yet fully discerned or appreciated by teachers, theorists, or practitioners.

In his introduction, Professor Mosher acknowledges his gratitude to the case writers, the members of the Research Committee, the staff of the Institute of Governmental Studies, and the many government officials who contributed data. For the Inter-University Case Program, I reiterate these thanks. I wish to register, once again, appreciation to Dwight Waldo for his efforts at initiating and succoring this venture, and to the Institute of Governmental Studies for making it possible. The ICP's own financial contribution came from a grant from the Ford Foundation and from annual fees from over 70 participating universities. Three of the earlier cases in this book were prepared with funds from the Carnegie Corporation of New York, which supported the Case Program from 1948 to 1956. The Maxwell Graduate School of Syracuse University has contributed the ICP central office to this inter-university effort since 1963. Carol Melling, Marian Natelson, and Bonnie J. Bienkowski read the galleys.

Finally, I wish to acknowledge the contributions of the political scientists who have served on the ICP board, out of whose continuing discussions this enterprise evolved, and on whose voluntary exertions the nature and quality of our inter-university collaboration depends. Their names are listed below.

Edwin A. Bock
President, Inter-University
Case Program, Inc.
Professor of Political Science,
Maxwell Graduate School,
Syracuse University

January 1, 1967

BOARD MEMBERS OR TRUSTEES OF THE CASE PROGRAM 1948–1967

Contents

Preface by EDWIN A. BOCK iii

Introduction by FREDERICK C. MOSHER ix

Part One CASE STUDIES OF REORGANIZATIONS

A. *Agencies Engaged in Services to the Public and Regulation Procedures*

1. *The Reorganization of the Public Health Service* *by* EDITH T. CARPER 3
2. *Health Centers and Community Needs* *by* MARIANA ROBINSON 61
3. *A Wildlife Agency and Its Possessive Public* *by* JOHN R. OWENS 103
4. *The Transfer of the Children's Bureau* *by* E. DREXEL GODFREY, JR. 149
5. *Personnel Problems in Converting to Automation* *by* JAMES R. BELL *and* LYNWOOD B. STEEDMAN 166
6. *Reorganization and Reassignment in the California Highway Patrol* *by* PHILIP O. FOSS 185

B. *Agencies Engaged in Research, Development, or Education*

7. *The Demise of the Ballistics Division* *by* EVELYN GLATT 217
8. *The Coming of Age of the Langley Porter Clinic* *by* MARIANA ROBINSON 251
9. *The Regionalization of Business Services in the Agricultural Research Service* 301
   a. *The Decision to Regionalize** *by* LYNN W. ELEY 306

* A revised version of the ICP case originally published as: *The Decentralization of Business Services in the Agriculture Research Service.*

b. *A Business Office for the West*
by GERALD W. BUSH 336

C. *Agencies Engaged in Management and Services within the Government*

10. *The Guardians of La Loma*
by MARGARET G. OSLUND 361
11. *The Reorganization of the California State Personnel Board*
by FREDERICK C. MOSHER 397
12. *Architects, Politics, and Bureaucracy: Reorganization of the California Division of Architecture*
by ERNEST G. MILLER 441

Part Two ANALYTICAL COMMENTARY
by Frederick C. Mosher

I. Organizations in Public Administration 475
II. Organizational Change 493
III. Participation and Reorganization 515

Appendixes

I. Bibliographical Note Concerning Case Materials in Public Administration and Politics 537
II. Selected References Relevant to the Participation Hypothesis 538
III. Guidance to Case Writers 540

INTRODUCTION

THE ICP CASE AND ADMINISTRATIVE RESEARCH

The use of case studies as a tool for the enlargement of knowledge about the administration of government is a relatively recent phenomenon.[1] And the value, the purposes, and the appropriate style of such cases are still objects of debate and experimentation. The project of which this volume is the product was conceived as an experiment in a somewhat different use of the case method. It may therefore be desirable to sketch, as background for this report, certain features of the evolution of cases in public administration.

The first systematic effort to produce administrative cases in government was undertaken by the Committee on Public Administration of the Social Science Research Council during the late 1930's. Between 1940 and 1944, that committee, through its Special Committee on Research Materials, produced and published 100 case reports. The cases were primarily concerned with managerial problems and decisions in areas such as administrative organization, coordination, budgeting, personnel, field-office relationships, public relations, etc. Those cases were brief (normally limited to eight pages), structured according to a predetermined outline, and specifically enjoined from dealing with "questions of major policy concerning the substance of the service being performed."[2] The purposes of these studies were three: "(1) to provide useful guides to administrators faced with such (similar) problems; (2) to furnish useful material for critical consideration by students; and (3) to promote the development of a true science of administration."[3] This third objective, which the Special Committee regarded as "perhaps most important of all," depended upon the accumulation of case reports to provide material "by which the validity of generalizations about administrative relationships and the administrative process can be tested."[4] Some of the guiding committee regarded case studies as the principal hope for the development of a "true science of administration."

The products of this first initiative toward public administration cases were disseminated primarily among teachers and students in public administration. They undoubtedly had substantial influence upon the teaching of the subject. But they made no perceptible progress in the direction of their third goal—the building of a science of administration. Few formulations or generalizations were drawn from the case material; and there was little, if any, systematic effort to formulate or illuminate general hypotheses in or through the cases.[5] The case program and its sponsoring committee were terminated in 1945, before any systematic work had been undertaken toward this objective. More important, interest in this kind of case enterprise waned because of a broadening and quite different understanding of what comprises public administration. After the war, students in the field increasingly emphasized questions of public policy and its determination as parts of administration and, as a corollary, de-emphasized managerial techniques. At the same time, there was increasing concern with the human and behavioral aspects of organization and administration, reflecting the emerging influence of the so-called behavioral sciences. This trend, too, moved away from the emphasis in the earlier cases upon organizational mechanics. Indeed, the direction of the entire discipline during the years following World War II was toward a redefinition, a re-understanding of what constitutes public administration.

The second major initiative for case studies in public administration was in the vanguard of this movement and as such can be viewed in part as a

---

[1] Some other social science disciplines have used one or another form of case study for many years; and in a few, cases have been at the core of the study of the discipline. Compare, for example, the study and teaching of business administration, clinical psychology, cultural anthropology, law, psychiatry, social welfare, and sociology.

[2] Public Administration Service, "Case Reports in Public Administration," a Statement by the Special Committee. Chicago, 1940, p. iv.

[3] *Ibid.*, pp. iii, iv.

[4] *Ibid.*

[5] At least there is little published evidence of such effort. However, it is entirely possible and even probable that individual scholars utilized such materials for their own teaching and research.

reaction against the earlier type of case. A seminar group at Harvard's Littauer School in 1945 began the production of cases which would take account of the new trends in public administration thinking. Two years later, a broader base was established for the production of cases through the establishment of the Committee on Public Administration Cases (CPAC), which engaged a small full-time staff in 1948. The CPAC was further broadened into a full-scale organization of nationwide scope when it became the Inter-University Case Program (ICP) in 1951. The new style of cases was quite different from the old, and deliberately so. The new cases aimed to illustrate the complexity of public administration rather than to find simple rules; they focused upon decisions in matters of policy and program and, with some exceptions, avoided technical and managerial subjects; they ranged the whole spectrum of politics and administration in virtually all functional fields and at all levels of government up to and including international organizations; they were selected and written with the aim of telling a story with style, movement, and comprehensiveness, and they were not constrained by requirements of consistent format or length. Each case was intended to stand on its own feet as an independent, literary contribution to the understanding of public decision-making.

Since their inception, the primary objective of the CPAC-ICP cases has been the production of a body of materials to enrich the teaching and the study of public administration and related fields. In this, there can be no doubt that they have been successful; it is doubtful that any development since World War II has had a greater impact upon pedagogy in public administration. Furthermore, the cases demonstrated and emphasized some facts of administrative life that the founders of the program wished to have brought to the attention of students and practitioners in the field. They showed that policy and political elements inhered in administrative process and decision. They demonstrated the tremendous variety, scope, and importance of administrative decisions in our national life, as well as the myriad of variables that enter into the shaping and carrying out of those decisions. They made it clear that an important element of administrative performance—perhaps *the* important element—is the art of negotiation.

It is probably true that the cases produced during the first decade of the CPAC-ICP programs provided a basis for understanding public administration that was broader and more profound than those that preceded them. But beyond providing a broader basis, they did not conspicuously contribute to the development of a "true science of administration," if indeed such a science may be made to exist. Some of the very features of the cases that made them valuable for teaching purposes inhibited their utilization for systematic research. Case writers were discouraged from articulating hypotheses, from structuring their cases according to theoretical designs, and from drawing conclusions or formulations from their stories. Further, there was no systematic effort to analyze the completed cases in order to formulate generalizations. The cases themselves were not preselected on the basis of any plan, either as to subject matter or as to study design. In fact, there was a bias in the reverse direction. There was an effort to obtain variety, broad coverage of governmental subject matter, and occasionally, unusual or unique character; this meant, therefore, the avoidance of repetition in subject matter and of enforced consistency in method and style. In the language of ICP's own governing board,[6] the cases were "targets of opportunity"—the products of the happy convergence of significant administrative stories with students and writers capable of describing them with insight and style.

Potential Research Applications of the ICP Cases

The failure of the cases to produce or test systematic generalizations about administration gave rise to a growing restiveness among some scholars in the field, including some on the governing board of ICP itself. This concern did not necessarily reflect criticism of the case method as it had been developed nor deprecation of the contribution the cases had made and were making to the study of the field. Rather, it was grounded in a belief—or a hope—that the case method might produce a great deal more if it were more disciplined and focused. Some felt that the program had effectively accom-

[6] As its name indicates, the ICP serves about eighty universities, including most of those with graduate programs in public administration. It was incorporated in 1963 and since that time has been located at, and attached to, The Maxwell Graduate School of Citizenship and Public Affairs at Syracuse University, which has encouraged it to continue its inter-university character. It is governed by a President and a rotating board of twenty trustees, mostly professors from its subscribing universities.

plished its original objectives and should move on to what they believed were logical next steps. This latter point of view gained momentum during 1956, when the foundation grant underwriting the program was approaching termination. At that time the ICP was, in effect, confronted with the alternatives of expanding and developing new goals (in the pedagogic, research, or operational uses of case studies) or of going out of existence.

Evidence of ferment about the systematic research use of cases appeared from time to time in journal articles and reviews. For example, in 1952, Professor Egbert S. Wengert, in a review generally favorable to the ICP cases, commented: "Unlike scientific data the cases do not provide students with an opportunity to develop or test some well-defined hypotheses."[7] Three years later, Professor Herman M. Somers wrote:[8]

> They [the forty-six cases to mid-1954] have no designed relationship to one another, methodological or substantive, and the totality of the series is rather formless. . . .
>
> Yet it seems doubtful that much further progress will be made toward these goals [the three aims of ICP] without some attempt at ordering the content of the cases as a basis for comparative analysis and increasing the opportunity for generalization.

In 1958, Professor Herbert Kaufman criticized the program more sharply:[9]

> On these propositions and questions, many of which antedate the case program, the cases shed little light. Instead of helping us to validate the former and answer the latter (which *only* the case method can do!), they enlarge the number of untested declarations and unresolved questions with which our discipline already abounds. And this, I submit, is derelict. . . .
>
> But it does seem to me that we cannot go forward if the ICP continues to operate as it has.

The proposals for changing the orientation of the program aimed in general toward a somewhat greater emphasis upon the potential scientific research contribution of the cases and relatively less emphasis upon their purely pedagogical use.[10] These suggestions may be grouped in four rough categories: First, it was proposed that one or more scholars systematically study the case materials already published with the aim of drawing from them "systematic formulations," "principles," and "laws," or, alternatively, establishing that such generalizations could not be drawn from the cases. The second proposal contemplated that the bulk of future cases be focused on certain subject-matter areas, in the effort to develop more intensive understanding of selected phases of administration. This would constitute a substantial reversal of the "target-of-opportunity" approach and would make the cases potentially more useful as exploratory research—the search for hypotheses in areas of more nearly finite dimensions. Third, it was suggested that scholars from other social science disciplines be invited to participate in the planning and supervising of case studies, partly in order that their knowledges, perspectives, and methodologies might enrich the public administration cases. Fourth, it was proposed that at least a few cases be planned and developed with a view toward testing the utility of this kind of case method in building and illuminating hypotheses about administrative behavior.

During the late 1950's, ICP initiated steps in most of these directions. Its program after 1957 provided for the allocation of most of its resources to cases in specified subject-matter areas—"clusters"—rather than in the "target-of-opportunity" category. Clusters were set up in such fields as: urban planning, government regulation of business, overseas operations and comparative administration, executive leadership, and administrative-legislative relations. Each cluster was planned with the aid of a committee of scholars specialized in the subject, and several of these committees co-opted scholars from related disciplines. Finally, ICP established, in 1959, a Research Committee to experiment with utilization of cases of the ICP

[7] "For the Teacher of Public Administration," *Public Administration Review*, XII (Summer 1952), 197.

[8] "The Case Study Program: Where Do We Go From Here?" *Public Administration Review*, XV(2) (Spring 1955), 118.

[9] "The Next Step in Case Studies," *Public Administration Review*, XVIII(1) (Winter 1958), 56-57. It should be noted that all three professors quoted above have at one time or another served on ICP's governing board. There have been a number of unpublished papers by board members relating to the same problem, and it has been fodder for frequent debate in the board meetings for some years.

[10] There was disagreement among the scholars as to whether or not the educational and the research values of the cases are compatible with one another. But there was no doubt that a stronger research orientation would require some changes in approach —for example, in the selection of subjects for the cases.

type as a tool of disciplined empirical research. This book is the outcome of the efforts of the Research Committee.

It should be noted parenthetically that the selective history sketched above focuses only upon those developments, concerning the systematic research use of cases, that led up to the research project herein concluded. The use of cases and case materials for all purposes has grown rapidly in recent years through the efforts both of ICP and of other agencies and authors.[11] There have been a number of case series and casebooks in politics and public administration in addition to those of ICP. And cases have been relied upon extensively in studies and books reflecting both pedagogic and research objectives.[12]

INCEPTION OF THE STUDY OF REORGANIZATION AND PARTICIPATION

In the light of the brief history reviewed above, this effort may appear to be a reversion to the earlier work of the Committee on Public Administration of the Social Science Research Council. True, the objective was similar, but, beyond that, the differences far surpass the likenesses. The research instrument of the ICP, the case, is of a species entirely different from the prewar case. And the Research Committee has relied upon the ICP understanding of the case and what it comprehends as that understanding evolved during the years after World War II. All research effort must rest on some underlying assumptions, and those on which this work was based bear little resemblance to those widely held during the war years. The ICP cases seek to lay emphasis upon considerations largely excluded in the earlier ones: the interrelationship of process with program and purpose; the impact of role, personality, and group; the impact of political factors; the dynamics of change rather than the statics of before and after.

The Research Committee of ICP met on a number of occasions in late 1959 and in 1960. Its discussions were devoted principally to the finding and selection of a suitable problem area and process that would provide basically comparable foci for cases in various places, and to the determination of a hypothesis that would be meaningful and significant in all those places, as well as transferable elsewhere. A great many possibilities were explored, and the discussants were impressed, perhaps more than they had been previously, with the lack of precision in language and definition in the existing literature. Even from the works commonly considered "scientific" they could draw out few propositions that avoided ambiguity and that were testable. The basic process and variable ultimately chosen for study seemed reasonably finite and concrete, but even with these the project has had difficulties.

A *first* step in reaching a feasible determination on the objects for study is the definition of certain boundaries within which the study is to be conducted. The field, potentially almost unlimited in dimension, was restricted to some degree by the type of research tool to be used—the administrative case as it has been developed in the Inter-University Case Program. An ICP case is first of all a history, usually limited to a relatively brief span of time in months and years. It is a story of action or, at least, of potential action. While the story has always an antecedent history and also a subsequent succession of events, one assumes that the story itself can be studied and described as having a beginning and an end. These cases tend to be concerned with action that is out of the ordinary, not simply a repetitive process. This is another way of saying that a typical ICP case study involves a significant change or at least an effort to bring about a significant change, even if the effort was frustrated. It is not simply a description of the ordinary and the routine. The cases, then, deal with actions that cumulatively constitute the process whereby change is made, or, conversely, whereby it is avoided or frustrated.[13]

The target of most ICP cases is the *decision,*

---

[11] For a thoughtful series of essays on the uses, features, and limitations of the case method in public administration, see *Essays on the Case Method in Public Administration*, Edwin A. Bock, ed. (Brussels: International Institute of Administrative Sciences, 1962). The essays by Bock and James Fesler are particularly pertinent to the current project.

[12] Appendix I contains a brief bibliographical note with reference to some of the more recent books of cases or drawing upon case materials.

[13] In the language of the computer technologists and many management scientists, such decisions are *unprogrammed*, i.e., they are nonroutine, as opposed to the *programmed* decisions. Some scholars have urged that more attention be given to routine and repetitive phenomena through the case method.

or the series of related decisions, to do something or not to do it, or to do something else. Complex situations usually involve a number of different decisions made by different persons and groups, related and sometimes in conflict with each other, sometimes carried out over a considerable period of time. Decision-focused cases fall into three reasonably finite parts: the situation and the developments leading up to basic decision; the basic decision itself (or the basic decisions themselves); and the events and decisions following upon the basic ones. The decision cases are therefore limited to historical developments in which significant and identifiable decisions were, in fact, made. Among other things, this signifies that the primary focus of this kind of case study is upon events, sequences, actions, and the strategies and perceptions of the principal actors.

The scope of the present study was further confined by the area of social activity to which the uses are directed. Like other ICP cases, these are cases in public administration. They deal with agencies of government, normally of some size, operating under the aegis of politically designated and responsible officers in areas of public concern. They concern organizations, not small or primary groups nor whole societies. The organizations are legitimately established and are so recognized, and they perform functions toward purposes other than, or in addition to, their own internal welfare. As administrative organizations, they operate within a formal structure characterized by vertical hierarchy and horizontal differentiation of kinds or places of work or both. As public organizations they operate with some degree of legal and political responsibility and, necessarily, some degree of political responsiveness. Most of them have frequent contact with a sector or a substantial portion of the citizenry, and all are dependent in some degree upon public support.

The Research Committee made several key decisions that should be indicated here. It decided at an early date that its cases should be directed to the general area of administrative organization and management of government organizations in the United States. Foreign government experience was excluded because it would introduce variables of culture and history that would overcomplicate comparisons at this infant stage of research. The organization-management orbit was chosen deliberately to avoid the basic non-comparability in substance of differing program and policy considerations in different fields. It was felt that decisions to build a nuclear submarine, or to pave a street, or to change the rules on reductions-in-force would have too many divergent variables to permit the drawing or testing of generalizations. On the other hand, all sizable administrative organizations in governments have an organizational structure and require management. It has long been contended by some that their operations, whatever their missions, are in accord with common principles or rules, so far as internal management is concerned. The relevance and usefulness of some of these rules were precisely what the Committee aimed to explore.

Secondly, the Research Committee, seeking a kind of process common in all types of government organizations, decided to investigate the process of reorganization. Formal reorganizations of government agencies are relatively frequent and are normally concrete and discernible when they occur. Those that are, in fact, implemented bring about changes in power relationships, roles, working relationships, and behaviors, for a few or for many people. They are, in short, visible, definable, and perceived by those immediately concerned and often by a great many others. A governmental reorganization has a further advantage for purposes of case study in that it is a dramatic experience for the organization concerned and often a traumatic one for a few or a great many of its members. Its initiation always suggests the possibility of change. When this occurs, even if change is later staved off, existing and possibly latent drives, dissatisfaction, tensions, and insecurities that otherwise might only be sensed or guessed may be brought to the surface. Reorganizations may reveal a great deal about organizations not easily discernible under more normal circumstances.

The Committee chose as its focus reorganizations of the middle range: that is, those that applied to, or were attempted for, individual departments, bureaus, or divisions of governmental jurisdictions. Sweeping changes in the form of government or in its basic institutional structure and jurisdiction-wide organization surveys, after the style of the various "little Hoover Commissions," were generally avoided.[14] On the other extreme, changes in activities at the working level in small, individual

[14] One of the cases in this volume, "The Guardians of La Loma," is, in part, an exception to this policy. It began as a jurisdiction-wide study, but its later phases dealt with particular agencies of the government.

units were likewise ruled out.[15] The Committee did not contemplate cases descriptive of small-group behavior, although intra-group relationships would surely be involved. It may be noted that objective, non-prescriptive research on this intermediate range of public organizations has been sparse. The small group has been the object of a great deal of study in recent years and, on the other extreme, forms of government and the revision of governmental institutions have been for many centuries the principal fare of legal and political scholars and philosophers.

The *third* major decision of the Committee was that the principal variable in connection with the reorganization stories would be the impact upon projected reorganizations of the *participation,* in decision-making and in implementation, of affected persons. Concern with the problem of participation in decision-making has had a considerable history in the fields of political science, psychology, sociology, anthropology, and others.[16] Much recent research and literature in social science has been addressed to the hypothesis that persons and groups are more likely to modify their behaviors in desired directions if they participate in the decisions as to what the changes will be and how they will be made. Because reorganization involves the changing of human behaviors, studies of reorganization processes should provide built-in laboratories for the appraisal of the impact of varying degrees and kinds of participation (or its complete absence) upon their consequences.

Objectives of the Research Project

The Committee thus determined upon a program to develop a series of case studies involving reorganizations or attempted reorganizations in a variety of government organizations, having as their major focus the consequences for the reorganization of participation in decision-making. In this effort, it had four principal objectives:

(1) To experiment with the usefulness of case studies of the ICP type as tools of disciplined, empirical research in public administration.

(2) To explore and gain new or refined insight and develop new hypotheses as to regularities and variables in reorganization processes in governmental agencies.

(3) To explore the applicability and the validity of the participation hypothesis in public administration, as indicated by its impact upon projected reorganizations.

(4) To add to the growing library of public administration materials a number of case studies that are of value for teaching in this field.

The first three of the purposes stated above may be described as research goals; the fourth is pedagogical. It was the belief of the Committee that research and pedagogical objectives need not necessarily be incompatible. And it was its hope that each case, while contributing to the research objectives of the entire project, would stand on its own feet as a meritorious and useful contribution to general knowledge in the field.

The Research Committee was aware that organization and its management are complex subjects composed of many interrelating forces and factors. Any attempt to separate out and study any single variable (such as participation) as though it were completely independent and unaffected by many other variables would be doomed to failure. Indeed, part of the value of the case studies, as distinguished from other kinds of research, lies in the comprehensiveness with which the cases treat many of these interrelating factors. Obviously, in different organizations participation would assume different meaning and different significance and would take on different forms. In studying the participation hypothesis, the Committee was not striving for a slavish pursuit of a single narrow concept. Rather, it sought from its case writers whole stories about reorganizations, but with a primary focus on the workings of participation in the particular and unique setting of each case. It encouraged the examination of interrelationships of participation with other significant elements of the organizational situation. It specifically invited attention to such elements as: the current and precedent leadership pattern; the relationships growing out of previous internal decision processes; the nature of the personnel involved as to education, personality types, tenure, group relationships, etc.; the external relationships of the organization; the social and political "climate" within which the organization was operating, especially at the time of the reorganization; and others. It was the aim of the Committee to explore the reorganization-

---

[15] Several of the cases did entail significant changes at the working level, but the considerations that entered into such changes went well beyond and above any single operating unit.

[16] See Part II, Chapter III.

participation relationship in the context of a variety of situations and a variety of types of organizations, taking into account as many of the major variables as had a significant impact.

CONDUCT OF THE RESEARCH

Definitions of Terms

A first essential in any research project is a specific, understandable, and operational definition of terms. As indicated earlier, the development of definitions that meet such specifications is no small challenge in a field that has customarily been loose and careless in its terminology. Some of the definitions used for the current project were necessarily arbitrary and do not exactly conform with other usages of the terms.

Organization and Reorganization. As indicated earlier, the focus of the study was to be upon middle-level administrative organizations of government, operating within the framework of an official hierarchy, under formal and informal controls, and subject to outside influences and controls.

> *Organizations:* official governmental administrative agencies, legitimately established; the term comprehends their structures, purposes and functions, personnel, assignments of responsibilities and activities, resources, communications, and operating procedures. The term is here employed to emphasize *actual,* as distinguished from merely official or formal, structure and operating practices. It comprehends what has sometimes been referred to as "informal organization"—the system of accustomed relationships and interactions carried on within organizations.

> *Reorganizations,* as considered in this study, are purposeful (intended) changes in purpose, functions, procedures, assignments, and relationships in organizations. For the purposes of these cases, reorganizations, or intended reorganizations, must be sufficiently substantial to involve a clearly recognizable change in the roles, relationship, and behaviors of some or of a great many people. They do not include: changes in program or activity that do not importantly modify structure and relationships; normal, expectable or routine changes (such as seasonal changes); changes brought about accidentally; and minor changes to which the organization can readily adapt itself.

The process of changing organization normally involves a series of steps at each of which participation may occur. The rational "model" of this sequence is suggested below, but only to indicate the difficulty of applying a given hypothesis to a total reorganization process. The model is itself a gross oversimplification.

(1) Inception
- (a) identification and recognition of problem
- (b) initiation of idea for change or for consideration of change

(2) Study and development
- (a) study (or survey) of situation and problem
- (b) development of proposal or alternative proposals
- (c) testing of proposals (in some instances)
- (d) recommendations

(3) Action decision
- (a) review and consideration of proposals
- (b) formal decision

(4) Implementation
- (a) communication of decision
- (b) study of specific steps to give it effect (in some instances)
- (c) making of changes in behaviors, relationships, etc.
- (d) follow-up

Goals. Administrative organizations cannot be understood nor evaluated apart from the objectives that they endeavor to achieve. Similarly, reorganizations are intended to accomplish purposes of one kind or another in addition to and beyond the modification of organizational structure. This is another way of saying that reorganization is an intermediate objective toward something else. It is normally a means, not an end unto itself.[17] In order to appraise the effectiveness of any effort to reorganize, one cannot escape consideration of the

---

[17] Though change "for its own sake" sometimes contributes to the motivation for reorganizing. Furthermore, it should be noted that the means-ends relationship is by no means a one-way street or indeed a street at all. Ends modify means, and means modify ends. There are abundant illustrations in the cases that follow in which ends were changed during the planning and implementing of reorganizations, often as a consequence of the process itself.

objectives of reorganization as seen by those responsible for decision to reorganize. In other words, in the analysis of individual reorganizations, we attach greatest importance to the goals as they are perceived by those officers who have primary responsibility for initiating a reorganization process and for decisions to reorganize.

Goals are defined as ends or objectives deriving from the application of a system of values to an area or field of activity. For purposes of analysis, they may be classified in three rough categories:

> *Organizational goals*, as stated in law or other legitimizing documents and as interpreted and perceived by the management of the organization concerned. (Organizational goals are always an approximation or an amalgam, since no two persons view them in exactly the same way.)
>
> *Group goals:* the ends sought by face-to-face groups of persons or clusters of such groups. (Likewise not precisely definable.)
>
> *Individual goals:* the ends sought by individuals within or connected to the organization.

Reorganization constitutes a willful disturbance of an existing situation, and therefore it must itself be motivated by strong goal feelings. These may be classified according to the same three categories as those described above. They may also be classified along another dimension, as follows:

> *Stated goals:* the ends *asserted* to be sought by reorganization, as stated by the responsible officials. (These may and in many cases do vary, depending upon to whom the assertion is made—e.g., the press, an interest group, a legislative committee, one's superiors, one's immediate colleagues, one's subordinates, or the student [the case writer].)
>
> *Unstated real goals:* the unarticulated ends of the decision-maker. (These constitute a dangerous area for the student. The decision-maker himself may not be aware of some of his own underlying goals, and the case study hardly provides opportunity for psychoanalysis.)

The real goals, whatever mix of organizational, group, and individual they might be, and whether or not they are stated, constitute the principal yardstick against which to assess the degree of *effectiveness* of a reorganization effort. A reorganization may be *structurally effective* in the sense that formal organization, allocation of power, distribution of functions, and internal relationships are modified in accordance with intent; and it may, at the same time, be *substantively effective* or *substantively ineffective,* depending upon whether the underlying goals are in fact achieved. The ultimate test, of course, is that of substantive effectiveness. But the measurement of effectiveness can seldom be a precise operation.

Participation. For purposes of these case studies, participation is defined as:

> The taking part, formally or informally, in the making, or the influencing, of decisions of an organizational character by individuals and groups potentially affected by the consequences of such decisions, other than by the officials in whom is vested formal authority and responsibility for such decisions.

It may normally be assumed that the responsible executives in a bureau or department, and sometimes other individuals, such as the chief executive or legislators, would normally share responsibility for decisions affecting organizations, whether or not the decision-making process has a participative flavor. The concern in this research effort is with the participation of others who might or might not be involved, but who do not formally *have* to be involved. Potentially, participants might include some or all of the following:

(a) subordinate and intermediate supervisors of the organization concerned;
(b) employees of the organization, organized or unorganized;
(c) officials and employees of other public organizations whose work, relationships, and status may be affected by the change;
(d) clientele, interest groups, and representatives outside the government;
(e) legislatures, legislative committees, and individual legislators;
(f) interested and influential political and civic leaders.

This is obviously a broader interpretation of "participants" than the one commonly used in literature and studies concerning participation. The primary emphasis in these cases, as in earlier studies of participation, is laid upon "inside" participants—i.e., (a) and (b) above. However, the involvement of "outsiders" is often of great importance in government, and their omission, or the consideration of them merely as "external" forces, would appear unrealistic. The extent to which the same hypotheses about participation apply is one of the targets of the research.

The participation hypothesis as stated below depends in part upon the awareness or lack of awareness on the part of the participants that they are, in fact, taking a real and influential part in the decision process. For this reason, it is useful to distinguish between *felt participation,* in which the individual is aware of his participating function, and *latent participation,* in which the reverse is the case—a person takes part in influencing a decision without being aware that he is doing so. There is also a third category in which persons are given to believe that they are participating but, in fact, are exercising no real influence upon decision. This is here called *pseudo-participation.*

The Participation Hypothesis

Concerning the interrelation of participation and the process of reorganization in administrative agencies of governments, the following hypothesis was formulated:

> Government reorganizations involving intended changes in individual behaviors and relationships are more effective, both structurally and substantively, when the persons whose behaviors are expected to change take part in the process of reaching decisions as to what the change will be and how it will be made.

Further, it is hypothesized that participation will enhance reorganization effectiveness primarily through two mechanisms: first, by reducing resistance to change among the participants, or, more positively, by increasing their motivation to make reorganization successful in accomplishing its intended goals; and second, by providing information and ideas to the planners and deciders, thus contributing to modifications (potential improvements) in the content of the reorganization proposals.[18]

The central hypothesis may be amplified and conditioned by consideration of three subsidiary hypotheses. First, it would appear that participation would be more relevant to persons and groups who will be, or who will expect to be, most directly and severely affected by the reorganization, and vice versa. It is possible that participation of persons on whom the impact will be nil or remote would be completely immaterial or, in some cases, have a negative effectiveness. For example, some reorganizations that may appear to the outsider quite drastic involve only changes in titles and box-shifting in the organization chart and have little or no effect upon the behaviors of middle- and lower-level personnel. In such cases, participation is significant primarily for the upper administrative personnel and perhaps for some outsiders. This may be stated as follows:

> *Sub-hypothesis No. 1:* The effectiveness of participation in contributing to reorganization goals by different persons and groups depends directly upon the degree of expected impact of projected reorganizations upon the behaviors of those persons and groups.

There is normally some degree of divergence between organizational goals, on the one hand, and group and individual goals, on the other. There may also be some degree of complementariness among the three categories of goals. The expected impact of a projected reorganization upon goal accomplishment as the goals are perceived and evaluated by potential participants cannot fail to influence the way participation affects the reorganization itself. This may be stated as follows:

> *Sub-hypothesis No. 2:* The effectiveness of participation in making a reorganization effective is enhanced where the anticipated effect of the reorganization as perceived by the actual or potential participants is to decrease the divergencies, or increase the complementariness, between organizational goals, on the one hand, and group and individual goals, on the other.

We have indicated above that reorganization involves a number of stages that are more or less identifiable. Participation in one form or another may occur at any or all of such stages. The kind and degree of impact upon the process will vary, depending upon which stages are characterized by participative processes. The case studies endeavor to direct attention to the effects of participation at each stage. Some guidance may be drawn by deduction from the central hypothesis: In general, participation is more effective the earlier it starts.[19]

---

[18] The two mechanisms may roughly be described as "affective" and "cognitive," respectively.

[19] Mary Parker Follett wrote: "Participation is not part of the process [of coordination]; it should begin with the beginning of the process." *Dynamic Administration,* Henry C. Metcalf and L. Urwick, editors (New York and London: Harper and Brothers, 1940), p. 223.

This idea may be stated:

Sub-hypothesis No. 3: The earlier in the process of reorganization that participation begins, the more effective it is toward increasing motivation favorable to reorganization or, conversely, reducing resistance to change.

The Choice of Cases: Problems of Sampling

The resources available to the Research Committee were limited. Clearly, it could not undertake a mammoth series of studies which could offer statistical support of its findings. Rather, its field of study had to be confined to a relatively small, finite number of instances, selected with some care to provide a representative sample of a variety of situations and reorganizations. The Committee sought cases that would represent:

varying degrees of structural and substantive effectiveness, from slight, or none, to complete;

varying degrees of participation in the reorganization process, from none, to comprehensive.

Within the broad ranges described above, the Committee sought cases representing a wide variety of types of situations and organizations. Specifically, it looked for reorganizations or attempts to reorganize from most of the categories shown below:

by level of government
- federal agencies: both headquarters and field
- state agencies: both headquarters and field
- city agencies

by types of function
- service agencies in social and economic fields
- agencies concerned with natural resources and physical development
- regulatory agencies
- police agencies
- revenue agencies
- internal management and control agencies

by degree and nature of political exposure
- agencies in sensitive political areas, subject to continuing political, party, interest group, and/or legislative surveillance
- agencies relatively protected from outside intervention in fields of slight political sensitivity

by types of personnel involved
- agencies operating in highly technical, professionalized fields
- agencies employing relatively unprofessionalized personnel
- agencies operating with a highly developed career personnel system
- agencies operating without such a career system

During the planning stages, the Committee, its staff, and some of its case writers learned of and explored, on a preliminary basis, more than fifty different reorganizations. The initial number of possibilities was whittled down to nine. To these have been added four earlier ICP cases that appeared particularly relevant to the participation-reorganization problem.[20] In these thirteen cases,

[20] The four cases previously published by the Inter-University Case Program were: *The Transfer of the Children's Bureau, The Reorganization of the California State Personnel Board, Personnel Problems in Converting to Automation,* and *The Decentralization of Business Services in the Agricultural Research Service.* The last of these is substantially revised herein from the original. It may be noted that a number of other ICP cases have dealt with public reorganizations, and a few might have qualified for this volume. One might mention, for example, Frank T. Adams, Jr., *The Gainesville School Problem* (No. 15, 1953), Peter Bart and Milton Cummings, Jr., *The Transfer of the Kansas State Civil Service Department* (No. 31, 1955), Arch Dotson, *Production Planning in the Patent Office* (No. 6, 1952), Thomas H. Eliot, *Reorganizing the Massachusetts Department of Conservation* (No. 14, 1953, rev. 1960), Irving F. Fox and Isabel Picken, *The Upstream-Downstream Controversy in Arkansas-White-Red Basins Survey* (No. 55, 1960), Herbert Kaufman, *The New York City Health Centers* (No. 9, 1952, rev. 1959) and *The UN Publications Board* (No. 11, 1952), Grant McConnell, *The Steel Seizure of 1952* (No. 52, 1960), Glendon A. Schubert, Jr., *The Michigan State Director of Elections* (No. 23, 1954), and Albert A. Blum, "Birth and Death of the M-Day Plan" [published in Harold Stein (editor), *American Civil-Military Decisions* (Birmingham: University of Alabama Press, 1963).] There are also substantial data about the political and administrative leadership aspects of reorganization in S. K. Bailey, *The Office of Education and the Education Act of 1965* (No. 100, 1966). The ICP is also preparing a collection of studies on the Kennedy reorganization of the U.S. foreign aid program and a study of a later (1965-1966) reorganization of the U.S. Public Health Service. All ICP case monographs are now published by the College Division, The Bobbs-Merrill Company, Inc., Indianapolis, Indiana. A free Index and Summary of all published ICP cases is available from the publisher.

the nature of the "spread" in terms of governmental jurisdiction and functional area is:

BY JURISDICTION	
Federal, Washington	3
Federal, Field	2
State, Headquarters	5
State, Field	1
City	2

BY FUNCTION	
Public Health	2
Social Service	2
Mental Hygiene Institution	1
Research	3
Wildlife Management	1
Architecture	1
City Administration and Finance	1
Police	1
Personnel	1

There is a wide scatter along the dimension of political exposure, ranging from very little in *The Reorganization of the California State Personnel Board* to very much in *The Guardians of La Loma.* There is also reflected a variety of types of personnel systems and types and degrees of personnel specialization.

Preparation of the Case Studies

During the spring of 1960, the Research Committee and its staff actively pursued case possibilities and, at the same time, enlisted a number of scholars to study case situations and write case reports. Mindful of the considerable difficulty that the Committee itself had experienced in clarifying and establishing a research design for the project, several measures were taken to ensure that the case writers, once they had been launched on independent research, would be thoroughly conversant with and would adhere to a common set of concepts, terminology, and hypotheses. First, the study of the Langley Porter Clinic was initiated as a pilot case to test the adequacy of the preliminary planning and the instructions for case research. Then, early in the summer of 1960, all of the writers who had been engaged joined in a two-day meeting to discuss the problems, the methods, and the substance of several cases on which exploratory work had already begun. Subsequently, each case writer was provided with a memorandum of guidance for his field research and the preparation of his case narrative.[21] Each was requested to write, in addition, an analysis of his case, as it related to the overall design of the project and to the theoretical assumptions involved. This contribution, while not a normal responsibility of ICP case writers, was intended to aid in the development of the analysis contained in the second part of this volume.

Early drafts of all the cases were reproduced and distributed among all members of the Committee for comment and criticism. Subsequent drafts of all the cases tentatively selected for publication were similarly distributed among members of the ICP Board of Trustees, so that all the contributions to this project have indeed traveled a rocky road of review.

This research program has exemplified a consolidation around a central theme and objective of the efforts and wisdom of a number of people—nine case writers, seven members and three assistants of the Research Committee, twenty-one members of the ICP Board of Trustees, and, of course, the President and the staff of the ICP itself. The ICP Board and the Research Committee consists almost entirely of professors of political science, most of whom have concentrated much of their study in the field of public administration. In most instances, the case writers were professors or advanced graduate students of political science. All have studied in this field, and several had prior experience in the exacting task of writing cases. Most of the cases written in conjunction with this project can "stand on their own feet" as independent contributions to the field, and some have been separately published.[22]

Commentary and Analysis

With regard to some but not all of the cases, it appeared desirable to append an editorial note that would relate the events of the case to the central themes of the project—that is, reorganization and participation—and underline certain events and sequences that might otherwise escape the reader's notice. A few of these editorial comments also

[21] See Appendix III.

[22] *The Coming of Age of the Langley Porter Clinic, Reorganization and Reassignment in the California Highway Patrol, A Wildlife Agency and Its Possessive Public,* and *Reorganization of the Public Health Service* have been published by The Bobbs-Merrill Company, Inc., for The Inter-University Case Program, Inc. *The Guardians of La Loma* will be published by 1967. *The Demise of the Ballistics Division* has been published by the Institute of Governmental Studies, University of California, Berkeley.

undertake to draw attention to factors and situations of significance beyond the localized context of the cases themselves. They are, in a sense, a bridge between the cases and the more generalized analysis of the cases as a group.

The penultimate step of the project was to analyze all the cases together in relation to the project's initial research goals, and to draw such conclusions and generalizations as the data warrant. This analysis is presented as Part II of this volume. It may appear to overpass the initial target of the project; only the last of the three chapters is focused specifically upon participation. The other two chapters were written in part to provide a base and perspective from which to examine the validity of the participation hypothesis in large organizations, and in part to present in an orderly way some of the findings from the cases about organization and organizational change which might add to our understanding of these subjects more generally. In a sense, they are an instance of what Robert K. Merton described as the *serendipity pattern.* "Fruitful empirical research not only tests theoretically derived hypotheses; it also originates new hypotheses. This might be termed the 'serendipity' components of research, i.e., the discovery, by chance or sagacity, of valid results which were not sought for."[23]

In another respect, the analysis appears to undershoot the target of the project. I have undertaken no evaluation of the case method as a research tool in these pages although this was an original goal of the ICP Research Committee. I expect that this task will be undertaken at a later date by others, as well as myself, who are still so closely identified with the project through protracted "participation."

The authors of these cases and I are, of course, initially indebted to the participants and observers in the cases themselves who gave us so much of their time, energy, and information and thus made the cases possible. Beyond them, a very great many hands and minds contributed to this book: the case writers, who not only produced the cases but contributed greatly to my own work through written analytical essays about their cases, and through their suggestions, through review, and criticism of the analytical sections; the members of the Research Committee and the Trustees of the ICP, who devoted many hours to planning, discussing, and reviewing over several years, and offered many helpful comments and suggestions on the individual cases and the analysis; the staffs of ICP and of the Institute of Government Studies at Berkeley. I should like to express my particular gratitude to five research assistants who helped me over the years and have since moved on to other and perhaps greener pastures: Mrs. Mariana Robinson, Mr. Gerald W. Bush, Mr. Kenneth Hanf, Mrs. Helga Moeller Christopherson, and Mr. Larry G. Ludwig.

While extending my thanks to all who have contributed to this undertaking, I of course retain my full responsibility for the accuracy as to fact and interpretation of this Introduction and the analytical sections.

FREDERICK C. MOSHER

Berkeley, California
September 1966

[23] *Social Theory and Social Structure*, revised and enlarged edition (New York: The Free Press of Glencoe, 1957) p. 103. The quotation was drawn from an earlier work by Merton, "Sociological Theory," *American Journal of Sociology*, 1945, 50, 469n.

Part One

CASE STUDIES OF REORGANIZATIONS

A. AGENCIES ENGAGED IN SERVICES TO THE PUBLIC AND REGULATION PROCEDURES

EDITH T. CARPER

The Reorganization of the Public Health Service

EDITH T. CARPER

The author of *The Reorganization of the Public Health Service* is a former member of the staff of The Inter-University Case Program. At present she works for a private corporation in Washington, D. C.

CHRONOLOGY OF KEY EVENTS

1948, 1954	Previous studies and organizations of the Public Health Service occur
April 1959	Health Subcommittee of the House Appropriations Committee requests study of organization for environmental health activities
Late 1959	A panel of the Public Health Service recommends consolidation of environmental health activities
Mid-December 1959	Surgeon General Leroy Burney decides to have a self-study of the Service
January 4, 1960	Study Group begins work
February 9, 1960	First summit meeting discusses report of "mission phase" of the study
February 11, 1960	Group begins "organization phase" of the study
March 8, 1960	Burney tells Health Subcommittee of the House Appropriations Committee of his willingness to use his administrative authority to create a major environmental health unit in the Service
March 28, 1960	Second summit meeting discusses organization recommendations of report
March 31, 1960	Budget Bureau's "little summit" discusses proposals of report
April 15, 1960	Study Group is formally disbanded
April 25, 1960	PHS staff is told of reorganization study
May 5, 1960	Draft bill incorporating reorganization is sent to Budget Bureau
May 10, 1960	Arnstein task force on mental health is established
May 27, 1960	Budget Bureau approves draft legislation
June 7, 1960	Burney directs to Secretary of Health, Education, and Welfare a formal request for authority to go ahead with administrative reorganization
June 7, 1960	Final report of Study Group is issued
June 14, 1960	Senate subcommittee opposes transfer of National Institute of Mental Health's training programs
June 20, 1960	Department of Health, Education, and Welfare authorizes administrative reorganization
July 7, 1960	Arnstein task force reports
Fall 1960	Felix, Director of National Institute of Mental Health, is named chairman of a study group on future relocation of mental health activities
January 16, 1961	Burney is replaced by Luther L. Terry

PRINCIPAL CHARACTERS

Margaret C. Arnstein, Chief, Division of Public Health Nursing, Bureau of State Services; member, study group; chairman, mental health task force

Leroy Burney, Surgeon General, Public Health Service, 1957-1961

Paul Caulk, Executive Officer for Administration, Office of the Surgeon General, 1951—

Burnet M. Davis, member, study group; Deputy Chief, Division of Hospital and Medical Facilities, Bureau of Medical Services

Robert H. Felix, Assistant Surgeon General and Director of National Institute of Mental Health

James Fogarty, member of the House of Representatives and of the House Appropriations Committee

Donald J. Galagan, member, study group; Assistant Chief, Division of Dental Public Health

Harold M. Graning, member, study group; Regional Medical Director of PHS, New York Region

Harry G. Hanson, member, study group; Assistant Surgeon General

Lister Hill, U.S. Senator, member of Senate Appropriations Committee

James M. Hundley, chairman, study group; Special Assistant for International Affairs, National Institutes of Health

James Kelly, Director of Financial Management, Department of Health, Education, and Welfare

Harold J. Magnuson, member, study group; Chief, Occupational Health Branch, Division of Special Health Services, Bureau of State Services

Rufus E. Miles, Jr., Director of Administration, Department of Health, Education, and Welfare

Thomas D. Morris, consultant to the study group

John D. Porterfield, Deputy Surgeon General, Public Health Service, 1957—

Wallace S. Sayre, consultant to the study group

James A. Shannon, Director, National Institutes of Health

William H. Stewart, member, study group; Chief, Division of Public Health Methods, Office of the Surgeon General

Luther L. Terry, Surgeon General, Public Health Service, 1961—

INTRODUCTION

"So damn your eyes,
Reorganize!
No, nothing can stop the Service Task Force."*

In 1960 the Public Health Service (PHS), the principal health agency of the federal government, faced acute growing pains.

The direction the PHS would take during the next decade turned on the answers to certain political questions, principally the extent to which the federal government should extend health care and protection to specific population groups.

Subsidiary questions concerned the nature and extent of the government's responsibility for increasing the supply of doctors, nurses, and other health workers; building new medical schools; fostering a system of health insurance; policing such health threats as air and water pollution; combating specific diseases such as polio; and treating such disturbances as alcoholism, drug addiction, and juvenile delinquency as health problems rather than as breaches of public order.

If Congress were to order the government to take on a larger share of any of these duties, the PHS would have to be reoriented, take on new functions and burdens, and prepare to enter fields hitherto barred. During 1958 and 1959 there was much public discussion of these questions, and in 1959 Congress considered legislation to provide health care for aged persons.

In 1960 the PHS set out to study itself with a view to reorganizing to meet accumulated problems and anticipated future responsibilities. The instrument it chose for the study was a task force of experienced, knowledgeable PHS people. The task force, or Study Group, as it came to be called, was given a twofold assignment: (1) the challenging and imaginative task of planning for 1970, totally disregarding the inherited organization structure and legal prohibitions; and, (2) the practical job of planning the reorganization. The latter meant that the group would have to take account of established precedents, vested interests, personal and organic relationships, and going political imperatives.

* Refrain from a skit given at a Public Health Service Christmas party in 1960. The performers were billed as the Surgeon General's Ad Hoc Players, the oldest established permanent ad hoc task force in the world.

History and Functions of the PHS

The PHS was the oldest of the five major units of the Department of Health, Education, and Welfare (HEW), a Cabinet agency created in 1953. Other major units of this loose confederation (see Figure 1) were the Social Security Administration (including the Children's Bureau), Food and Drug Administration, Office of Education, and Office of Vocational Rehabilitation. The PHS mission—necessarily imprecise—was to protect and improve the health of the nation.

The PHS had begun as the Marine Hospital Service in 1798, when Congress passed legislation authorizing the federal government to provide medical care and service "for the relief of sick and disabled seamen." The law provided a system of prepaid health insurance, with twenty cents a month deducted from each seaman's wages. Since the funds were administered by the local collector of customs, the Hospital Service was placed in the Treasury Department. Medical care for seamen remained the agency's basic function for the next seventy-five years.

In 1878 the growing concern of the state and federal governments with preventing the introduction of epidemic diseases led to congressional passage of the first quarantine act. It embodied an important departure for the Hospital Service, since it authorized the agency to investigate the origin and causes of epidemic diseases, especially yellow fever and cholera. In 1890 domestic quarantine was added to the Hospital Service's responsibilities.

In 1912 the designation of the U.S. Public Health Service was adopted. The Service took on broadened responsibilities in the next few years, including investigation and research, improvement in methods of public health administration, and interstate control of sanitation and communicable diseases.

Developments of far-reaching significance occurred in 1935 with passage of the Social Security Act. It authorized the Service to initiate grant-in-aid programs to help state and local health departments "in establishing and maintaining adequate public health service, including the training of personnel for state and local health work." During the next twenty years grants were made to establish

FIGURE 1:
DEPARTMENT OF HEALTH, EDUCATION, AND WELFARE—1960

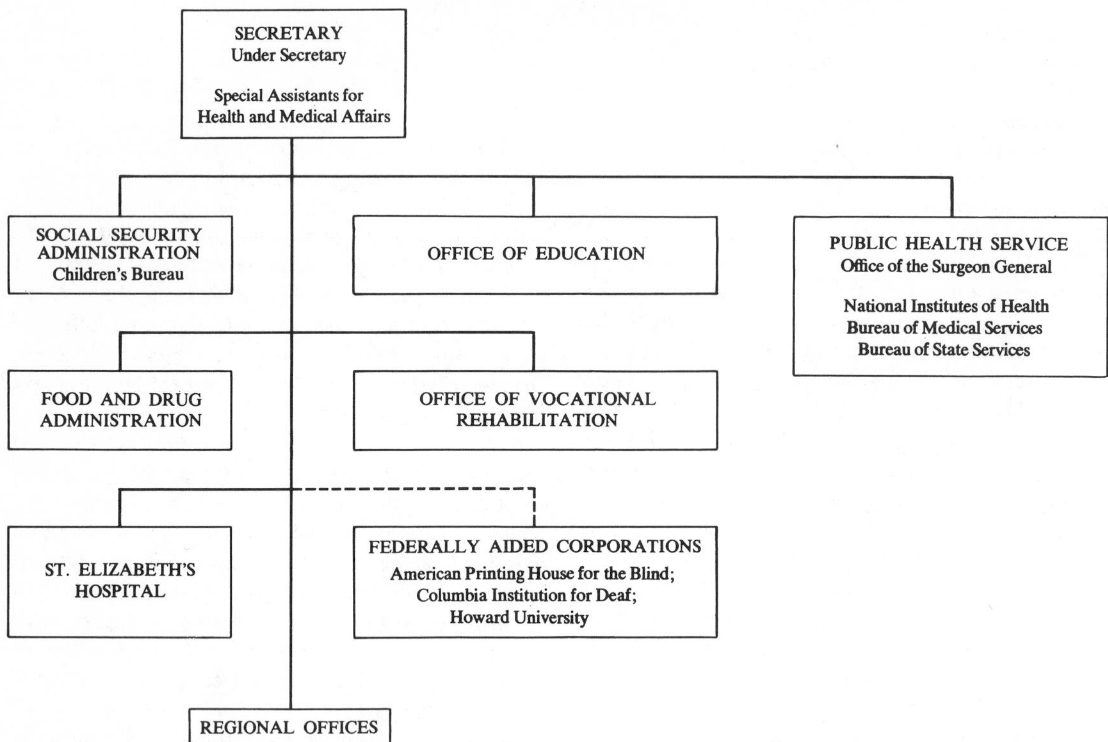

and maintain proper sanitation facilities; to improve general public health services, including industrial hygiene and mental hygiene; and to provide control measures for cancer, venereal disease, and tuberculosis. Other activities financed by grants-in-aid included state and local programs for employing and training personnel, purchasing supplies and equipment, providing appropriate facilities for care and treatment of designated illnesses, and loan of personnel for temporary duty. An intricate network of relationships with client agencies in the states grew in the wake of these programs. In 1939, as part of President Roosevelt's program for the reorganization and consolidation of federal services, a Federal Security Agency was created to bring together most of the health, welfare, and educational services of the federal government. One of its components was the PHS.

A vast enlargement of PHS functions occurred after World War II. Twenty-three new programs were launched; some by administrative action, others by legislation. Among them were increased emphasis on research in diseases grouped by categories, such as heart disease and cancer; a program of federal grants-in-aid to states for hospital construction (the Hill-Burton Hospital Construction Act); a water pollution control program; air pollution control studies; and a grant program for construction of medical research facilities. Other responsibilities were acquired by the PHS by the transfer to it from other federal agencies of the National Office of Vital Statistics (in 1946), the Indian Health Program (in 1955), and the National Library of Medicine (in 1956).

In terms of function, the most substantial increases in PHS duties after 1945 came in four areas: research, facilities construction grants, beneficiary care, and environmental health. The latter covered a vast array of activities designed to safeguard the environment. These activities dealt with pollution of air and water, the growing dangers of radioactivity, occupational health hazards, and the problems accompanying the development of large urban areas. The range of PHS beneficiaries was widened to include (in addition to the original merchant seamen) Indians, some dependents of military personnel, the Coast Guard, the prison population, drug addicts, and—on paper—some federal employees.

The PHS, along with other units of the Federal

Security Agency, became a component of the Department of Health, Education, and Welfare, which was created in 1953. By this time performance of the Service's mission brought it into contact with a number of other federal departments and agencies concerned with medical treatment and threats to health, principally the Veterans Administration, Defense Department, Food and Drug Administration, Atomic Energy Commission, and International Cooperation Administration.

Organization of the PHS

In 1960, when the PHS reorganization study began, the agency had 26,430 full-time employees. It administered a program of $1,013,600,000. Only a little over one-quarter of the budget went for direct PHS operations; the remainder was allocated to states and to agencies and institutions outside the federal government for construction, study, research, planning, disease control, demonstrations, and tests. The chief officer was the Surgeon General (SG), a physician selected by the President from the Commissioned Corps of the Service; his appointment was ratified by the Senate. The Commissioned Corps (the Corps) dated from 1890, when Congress had provided quasi-military status for Service personnel by authorizing commissions and uniforms. Physicians who had entered the Service after that had formed the nucleus of the Corps. They had exercised a strong influence on the organization and direction of the agency; identifying their interests with those of military medical officers, they had established a personnel system different from that of any other civilian health organization in the world. Of the 1960 PHS employees 1,666 were members of the Regular Commissioned Corps; 2,150 were members of the Reserve Corps; and 22,614 were civil service personnel.

The existence of the Corps, and its long hold on key jobs, had long been accepted as a fact of life in the PHS. The underlying assumption in job assignment, rotation, training and advancement, since the Corps was founded, was that Corps people were better fitted for responsible supervisory positions than civil service personnel. Consequently, Corps people—physicians, dentists, pharmacists, nurses, scientists, and engineers—had always held a substantial majority of key management posts.

The dual personnel system reflected advantages as well as disadvantages. The Corps had been effective in recruiting young physicians. Career development was enhanced through mobility and the opportunities for diversified training. Finally, the traditions and *esprit* of the Corps were valuable assets. The civil service system also offered certain advantages. It permitted free movement of personnel between the PHS and other agencies. It also provided certain flexibilities of appointment at the senior levels that the Commissioned Corps did not.

On the other hand, the two systems inevitably generated tensions. Friction resulted merely from the existence side by side of two sets of people hired under different systems and accorded different prestige, pay, and rank. The fact that Corps officials dominated supervisory posts in the Service set a ceiling on the promotional possibilities of civil service personnel. And there was almost no interchange of personnel between the two systems.

The Service was organized into four bureaus (see Figure 2). Three were operating bureaus: the Bureau of State Services (BSS), the Bureau of Medical Services (BMS), and the National Institutes of Health (NIH); the fourth was the Office of the Surgeon General (OSG).

Bureau of State Services

BSS had the widest spread of functions among the Service bureaus. Its principal mission was to assist states and communities in the development of adequate public health services and in the maintenance of a healthy environment. In addition it had such diverse functions as responsibility for Arctic health programs, occupational health, accident prevention, and administration of public health nursing and dental public health. The newest increment of activities in BSS related to safeguarding the environment from air and water pollution and radiological poisons.

Its bureau chief believed that supervision and control of BSS were difficult, given its range of activities. In fiscal 1960 the BSS's budget was $119,487,000, and it had 4,452 persons on its staff.

Bureau of Medical Services

BMS was the largest bureau in terms of personnel, with over 12,000 employees, almost half the personnel of the Service. It was responsible for providing medical, dental, and hospital services to

FIGURE 2: U.S. PUBLIC HEALTH SERVICE—1959

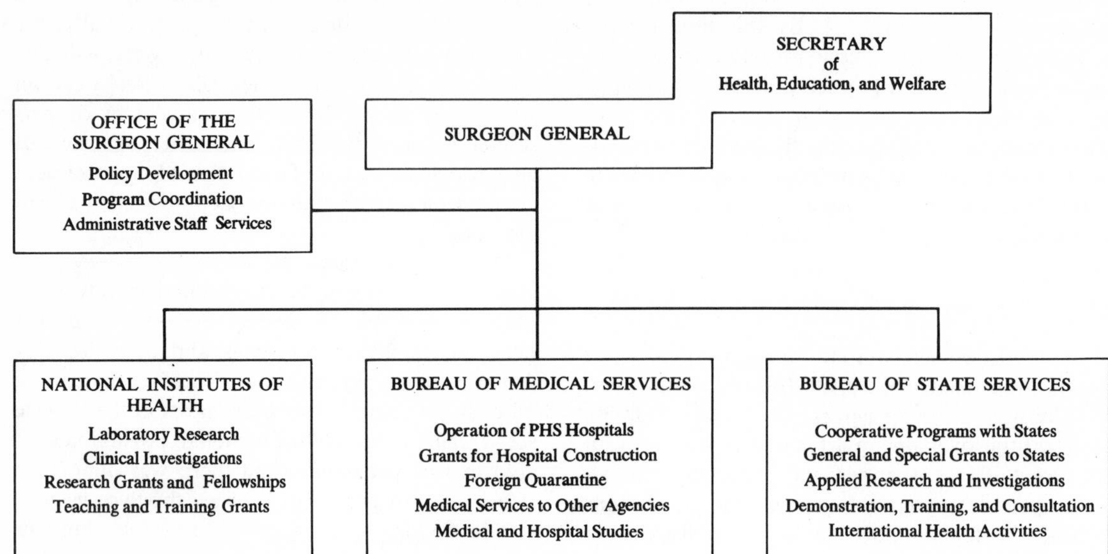

federal beneficiaries designated by Congress to receive such care, including Coast Guard personnel and federal prisoners. It administered the federal portion of the hospital and medical facilities survey and construction program (the Hill-Burton Act), the foreign quarantine laws, and the Indian health program. A Division of Hospitals operated twelve general hospitals, two neuropsychiatric hospitals, one tuberculosis hospital, one leprosarium, and twenty-five full-time clinics. The BMS budget for fiscal 1960 was $304,607,000.

Office of the Surgeon General

The OSG provided central management services for the PHS: coordination of planning and evaluation of programs; centralized responsibility for budget, personnel, and management; and responsibility for long-range planning. Although not an operating bureau, it had, from time to time, housed direct program operations, especially new programs and those of direct concern to either the Secretary of HEW or the Surgeon General.[1]

The Deputy SG was by law chief of the OSG, which was a small bureau in terms of both money and manpower. In fiscal 1960 it had 1,025 employees and a budget of $11,665,000.

The headquarters staffs of these three bureaus—BSS, BMS, and OSG—were "downtown" in the heart of Washington. PHS offices were distributed among two large office buildings and a covey of "temporary" structures that housed HEW.

National Institutes of Health

The center for PHS research activities was the NIH, an organization that was both a bureau and a field activity. It occupied a 300-acre tract in Bethesda, Maryland, a suburb of Washington. After 1937, research activities had been concentrated in Institutes that were set up to study specific categories of disease. In 1945, research as a Service activity took on a new emphasis and importance, although PHS had carried on basic research for over fifty years. In addition to seven categorical Institutes (for the study of cancer, heart disease, mental illness, dental disease, arthritis and metabolic diseases, neurological diseases and blindness, and allergy and infectious diseases), NIH maintained a fourteen-story, 500-bed hospital, enabling the PHS to combine laboratory and clinical research. NIH also conducted intramural research in the various laboratories at Bethesda, conducted limited field testing of research findings, and supported research and research training in nonfederal medical institutions.

As the categorical Institutes grew and flourished, NIH began also to emphasize extramural research. Around 1945 a program of grants and

[1] Included under the OSG umbrella in 1960 were the National Library of Medicine and other miscellaneous units.

fellowships was launched which by 1959 had come to account for more than two-thirds of the NIH budget.

The spacious grounds at NIH, the physical separation from Washington, the existence of Institutes dedicated to probing for knowledge of specific diseases—all lent support to an image of NIH as a university. Thus each of the categorical Institutes became "colleges," and employees referred to NIH as the "campus" or the "reservation."

The visibility of units devoted to study of the great killing and crippling diseases, plus the fact that Congress itself had called for establishment of six of the seven Institutes, was reflected in generous appropriations for NIH. In 1950 NIH funds had amounted to $52,146,000; by 1960 they totaled a little more than $400,000,000, an increase of more than 700 per cent. The partiality of Congress for NIH had been accentuated during President Eisenhower's two terms, when the House and Senate Appropriations Committees, under Democratic leadership in every Congress save one, regularly had voted NIH more money than the Administration had requested. NIH's 1960 budget was $421,655,000; it had 8,288 employees. (See Figure 3.)

The physical location, the popularity of medical research, and the generous appropriations had served to foster something of a separationist tendency on the part of NIH. Office jokes among "downtown" people often referred to the independent office of NIH or to the hope of making NIH a Public Health Service bureau some day.

The Climate for Reorganization

The basic internal structure of the 1960 Public Health Service described above—the four bureaus —had been prescribed in 1944 by Congress in the Public Health Service Act. Two subsequent reorganizations in 1948 and 1954 had been designed to bring about greater efficiency but had not basically altered the 1944 structure. However, to persons with supervisory responsibility for PHS, both in the Service and in the Department of Health, Education, and Welfare, the vast enlargement of Service functions after World War II indicated the need for a major overhaul. The new programs, the increase in research, the growing number of beneficiaries—these alone had created problems of management. Occasionally new functions had been allocated to a bureau at a pace it was unable to absorb. Also, the new functions had grown unevenly; some had flourished, others had not.

Service officials cited other problems as well: the dispersion of environmental health activities; the unwieldy size of the BSS and the ill-assorted groupings within it; and the expansion of the BMS and its seemingly unrelated activities. Many top PHS leaders felt strongly that the concentration on research during the previous fifteen years had produced spectacular results but that the time had arrived for the Service to try to put some of the findings into practice. The preoccupation with research, they felt, had delayed the application of research results to disease and health problems and, in their opinion, constituted an abdication of PHS responsibilities.

FIGURE 3:
BUDGETS OF THE BUREAUS OF THE PHS—1945–1960

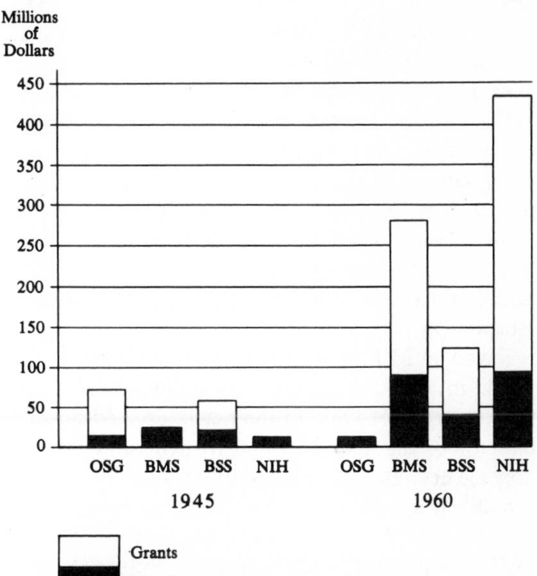

Finally, the fact that the bureau structure was prescribed by statute immobilized the Surgeon General. He lacked authority to alter the Service structure to keep pace with rapid change.

Dramatis Personae

Five people figured especially prominently in the PHS study group and reorganization story. Three were in the Service; two were members of Congress.

The Surgeon General, Dr. Leroy Burney, was

born in Burney, Indiana, in 1906. A graduate of Indiana University, he received his M.D. in 1930 and in 1932 earned a public health degree (M.P.H.) from Johns Hopkins University. Commissioned in the regular corps of the PHS in 1932, he returned to Indiana in 1945 to serve for nine years, first as secretary, later as commissioner, of the state public health service. He was recalled to Washington in 1954 with the rank of Assistant Surgeon General and became deputy chief of the BSS.

When Surgeon General Leonard Scheele resigned in 1956, Burney was named his successor. He was selected for the post by the Secretary of HEW (Marion Folsom) and the Secretary's Special Assistant for Health and Medical Affairs (Dr. L. T. Coggeshall). Burney assumed his duties as SG in August 1956 during the congressional recess. His appointment was confirmed by the Senate in January 1957, and his four-year term began on the date of his confirmation.

Deputy Surgeon General John D. Porterfield, like Burney, had once been a state health officer (Ohio, 1947-1954). Born in Chicago in 1912, he was the fifth generation of physicians in the Porterfield family. He had interned at the PHS Marine Hospital in San Francisco in 1938-1939 and had received an M.P.H. degree from Johns Hopkins in 1944. In 1954 he accepted an appointment from the Governor of Ohio to the newly created post of director of the state's mental hygiene and correction agency. Because the position was considered a political appointment, Porterfield resigned from the Service. After Burney's selection as SG in 1956, he persuaded Porterfield to return to the PHS. Porterfield was made Deputy SG on October 1, 1957.

Burney and his deputy had first met in the late 1940's. Both had been elected to offices in the professional group called the Association of State and Territorial Health Officers. Within the PHS the two men worked well together and shared responsibilities in a balanced, somewhat personal way. Burney's particular program interest was international health, and he was able to combine it with his ambassadorial functions as PHS chief. Since these duties required him to be away from Washington much of the time, the internal management responsibility devolved on Porterfield, who was also chief of the OSG bureau. Porterfield's special OSG program duties were medical care organization and financing and medical mobilization in event of national emergency.

In personality the two men tended to complement each other. Dr. Burney was a quiet, somewhat aloof, cautious person who wanted all the returns in before making a decision. Porterfield, simultaneously outspoken and disarming, had had his political insights strengthened by the mental hygiene job in Ohio. Burney knew he could rely on his deputy's friendship and counsel; he felt certain that Porterfield had no ambition to succeed him or to assume greater responsibility.

The *Study Group Chairman, Dr. James M. Hundley*, was a Hoosier, like Burney. A cool, capable person, firm but not aggressive, he was a nutritionist assigned to NIH. He had entered the PHS in 1940 and was a commissioned officer holding the rank of medical director (equivalent to Navy captain).

Two persons outside the Service exercised a strong influence on the course of the reorganization. They were *Senator Lister Hill* (Democrat, Alabama) and *Representative John Fogarty* (Democrat, Rhode Island). They chaired, respectively, the Senate and House subcommittees on PHS appropriations, and both had long taken an interest in health matters.

Hill, a doctor's son, had been named in honor of the celebrated British physician, Sir Joseph Lister. Legislation sponsored by Hill in 1946 (the Hill-Burton Hospital Construction Act) had resulted within twelve years in the initiation of 4,624 construction projects for hospitals and other health facilities in every corner of the United States. The program, amounting to around $104,000,000 annually, was administered by the Division of Hospital and Medical Facilities in the BMS.

Hill favored an accelerated medical research program, and his interests, influence, and alliances with private organizations and voluntary associations were partly responsible for the massive growth of NIH during the 1950's. Hill was chairman of both the substantive and appropriations Senate subcommittees that dealt with PHS.

John Fogarty, a onetime bricklayer and former president of a bricklayers' union in Providence, R. I., had come to exercise a decisive influence on PHS affairs during his thirteen years on the Health Subcommittee of the House Appropriations Committee. Elected to Congress in 1940, he was originally assigned to the old Naval Affairs Committee. When he won a spot on the Appropriations Committee in 1947, he chose the Health Subcommittee and in 1949 was named its chairman.

Like Hill, he was especially interested in accelerated programs of medical research. Fogarty's particular concerns were studies of cancer and heart disease. He was also interested in mental illness and had been instrumental in pushing PHS programs for psychiatric training of general practitioners.

THE REORGANIZATION STUDY IS LAUNCHED

The story of the PHS reorganization study actually began in 1959. Although some PHS personnel had previously wanted an overhaul of the agency, in that year two factors contributed especially to the urgency of a reconsideration of the federal government's health responsibilities. One was the drive initiated by organized labor for a federal program of medical care for the aged. The other was the congressional prodding for increased PHS activity in environmental health—abating air and water pollution and safeguarding the environment from radiation poisons.

The health problems of elderly persons had begun to receive increased attention following proposals made by the AFL-CIO that the federal government adopt a system of health insurance for the aged to be financed by Social Security. The unions sponsored mass meetings around the country in 1958 and 1959 to call attention to the plight of the elderly, besieged by chronic diseases and long-term illnesses at a time when they were least able to pay the bills for hospital and medical care. In 1959 a Democratic congressman, Representative Aime Forand of Rhode Island, introduced a bill for medical care for the aged to be financed under the Social Security system, and committee hearings were held.

The Eisenhower Administration failed to take a public stand on the Forand approach, but the rising tide of public concern forced PHS to a consideration of the problem. Regardless of what stand the administration might take, the Service had to be prepared to furnish expert knowledge about medical economics—judgments dealing with the quality and quantity of medical service available under a government-sponsored plan and alternative ways of "delivering" medical care to the 8,000,000 persons who might qualify by 1965. The Service had begun to compile data on medical economics but was not adequately prepared to answer some of the questions expected to arise during the 1960 congressional session. The congressmen wanted expert information on the relationships between such things as the various methods of financing medical care and the quality of care that would result under each system.

Congress also evinced strong interest in 1959 in problems of "environmental health." Representative Fogarty gave voice to the concern by making a formal request that the Service study environmental health problems and suggest better organizational arrangements to meet current needs. The request was embodied in the April 1959 report of the Fogarty Health Subcommittee of the House Appropriations Committee.

At that time the PHS conducted environmental health programs in all three operating bureaus, but the bulk of the activity was in the BSS. The Service had acquired heavy responsibilities in environmental fields during the prior decade, beginning with the first Water Pollution Control Act of 1948. Its environmental programs, grouped loosely with other major public health activities, were dispersed in several divisions: Engineering Services, Water Supply and Pollution Control, Radiological Health, and the Communicable Disease Center. In addition, environmental health played an important part in three programs of the Division of Special Health Services—accident prevention, medical aspects of air pollution, and occupational health.

The appropriations structure for financing these BSS programs was poorly mated to the BSS organization. Environmental health programs were financed from four different items: assistance to states; communicable disease activities; environmental health activities; and grants for waste treatment facilities.

The other two operating bureaus of PHS also were concerned with a miscellany of environmental health programs. In BMS three divisions (Foreign Quarantine, Indian Health, and Hospital and Medical Facilities) conducted environmental health programs. In NIH, because its categorical form of organization focused primarily on disease entities, research on environmental influences tended to be concentrated on specific disease problems. Thus, research related to environmental health was carried on in each of the seven Institutes and in two divisions, Biologics Standards and General Medical Sciences.

In response to the request that Representative Fogarty had incorporated in the Appropriations Report, the PHS called together a panel of experts in sanitary engineering and public health problems. After studying the problems, the panel members in late 1959 recommended a consolidation of environmental health activities. The Service leaders, faced with a decision on what the final recommendations should be, deferred action for the moment. The question was whether the report should call for a new bureau devoted to environmental health activities or whether it should propose a thoroughgoing study of the Service, with a view to regrouping all activities on a more rational basis.

The winds blowing from Capitol Hill indicated the urgency of a reorganization. Drs. Burney and Porterfield, as well as representatives of HEW, feared that Congress might prescribe a reorganization of environmental health activities unless the Service did it first. Both men were also concerned about where the PHS "was going" and for this reason, during the autumn of 1959, they called together bureau chiefs and top staff men to devote some time and thought to long-range problems. Several meetings were held in October and November during which routine, day-by-day problems were excluded and the PHS directors devoted themselves to serious discussion of the agency's mission and organization. The concensus of these meetings was that a Service-wide study should be conducted to serve as the basis for a reorganization from top to bottom.

Added Impetus for Reorganization

The idea that the PHS should be reorganized gained momentum during the autumn of 1959 among officials of both the Service and HEW. In fact, at least six persons decided, independently or in concert, that a major reorganization, preceded by an intensive study, was due. The following paragraphs describe how some officials came to hold their views.

Dr. Porterfield was joined in his campaign for an early reorganization by one of the top staff men in the OSG, Dr. William Stewart, who headed the Division of Public Health Methods. Stewart had served as a member of the PHS secretariat for the panel that conducted the environmental health study. These two, close friends who worked well together, wanted the Service to commit itself to an immediate study and reorganization, and they wanted the environmental health report to Congress to carry the commitment. In the early stages of the draft report to Congress, before the SG openly voiced his hope for a reorganization, Drs. Porterfield and Stewart met informally with Representative Fogarty. Fogarty applauded their ideas about a general reorganization and offered to give the ideas another congressional push—by incorporating a request for a reorganization study in a committee report if necessary. (As it turned out, Fogarty's help was not necessary.)

These developments happened to coincide with a plan that the PHS executive officer had nurtured for several years. He was a career civil servant named Paul Caulk, who since 1951 had been one of the SG's principal administrative officers (Executive Officer for Administration). Caulk had long felt the need for an overhaul of the Service. He was concerned over the administrative disorder that resulted from the ragged growth of some functions and the drying up of some of the earlier important PHS efforts. He had unsuccessfully pressed his idea for a PHS self-study with Dr. Burney's predecessor. The fact that his office had the administrative management function and had instituted a number of management studies, using both internal management staff and private management consultant firms, reinforced Caulk's feeling about the need for a Service-wide study. Caulk was disenchanted with management consultant companies as instruments for bringing about needed organization changes. They were "outsiders" with limited usefulness, he felt. They descended on an organization, "surveyed," and proposed many desirable reforms, but they left without developing any impetus for pushing those reforms through. Without a continuing force for change, Caulk felt, many reforms died on the vine.

Beginning in 1956, Caulk had renewed his effort to persuade the new SG, Dr. Burney, of the need for a self-study. Burney put the matter aside at that time. Day-to-day problems crowded in on him, and he was often away from his office, attending conferences on international health. Finally, late in 1959, under pressure from both Dr. Porterfield and Caulk, Burney extended his general approval. Before doing so he consulted with and secured the agreement of two important HEW representatives, Rufus Miles, Director of Administration; and James Kelly, Director of Financial Management.

As a matter of fact, both Miles and Kelly had clearly foreseen that if the report to Congress proposed creation of a "major organizational entity" for environmental health functions, a host of auxiliary problems would arise. The question of how far the environmental health report should go in committing the Service was discussed at a meeting of Burney, Porterfield, Miles, and Kelly on December 11, 1959. The four considered the alternatives. The report might simply recommend a consolidation of the bulk of environmental health activities, with no other changes. Or it might go further and suggest postponing any changes until a thorough study could be made, with a view to regrouping all Service activities on a more rational basis.

The governing idea was that the environmental health units could not be regrouped without throwing the Service out of balance. This factor loomed especially large in the minds of Miles and Kelly, and they were surprised at what they interpreted as the SG's failure to realize that a major new entity for environmental health activities would have jarring effects on the rest of the Service. They therefore threw their support to the plan for an immediate, all-embracing study, with proposals for a reorganization to follow, based on findings of the study.

After getting positive recommendations from Caulk, Porterfield, and Stewart, the SG agreed that the job should be done by the Service itself rather than by a management firm or by the HEW Office of Administration.

Planning for a Study Group

Burney and Porterfield turned over to Caulk the general planning for the study. Caulk, with his deputy, Lyman Moore, worked out plans in regular staff meetings of his own staff with the executive officers of the three operating bureaus. Caulk proposed a fifteen-man Study Group representing the professions and the administrative staff. The bureau executives considered this an unwieldy number for an action group and suggested five persons. They did not concern themselves with what forces the five should represent. Dr. Burney decided on a Study Group of eight members.

Work plans for the Study Group were devised by Caulk and his staff. They called for the study to be carried out in two phases, the first to decide what the Service should be doing ten years in the future—the Service "mission"—and the second to plan the organization to carry out the mission. One reason for projecting the plan a decade in the future was to ensure that even the most sensitive and delicate problems would be included in the survey. Caulk had been disappointed in a previous organization proposed for the PHS when the then Surgeon General had ordered a Service-wide study but at the last minute had placed certain areas "off limits" as far as permitting change was concerned. At the end of the first phase, the Study Group was to present the mission statement to the SG at a review session. Once Burney and his advisers—the bureau chiefs, deputies, and chief professional officers[2]—had agreed on the mission, the Study Group was to plan the organizational structure. This plan, too, was to be reviewed by the SG and his advisers. The two sessions of the SG's review committee came to be known as "summit meetings."

In response to Burney's request that he put his plan in writing, Caulk wrote a memorandum, dated December 17, 1959, embodying his ideas.

> I recommend setting up a Surgeon General's Committee on Organization to consist of six or eight carefully selected individuals picked because of their knowledge and ability rather than representing any categorical or organizational interest or because of their place in the supervisory hierarchy.
>
> Membership on the Committee should include field representation but should exclude bureau chiefs, deputy bureau chiefs, and chief professional officers, because this is the group that should be called upon to advise and counsel with the Surgeon General on the recommendations or proposals made by the committee to the Surgeon General.

Caulk's memo included these other suggestions:

(1) The PHS should retain two "recognized" topflight management consultants to guide the study group in making its decisions. The makeup of the group—medical, health, and sanitary engineering people with no experience of management—made it important to provide some source of balanced, professional advice on organization and management.

---

[2] There were three chief professional officers, one for dentistry, one for engineering, and one for nursing. Their functions included some formal obligations to advise the SG on matters affecting their professions and many informal duties whose definitions were never realistically confined in a job description. The offices of chief dental officer and chief sanitary engineering officer had been created by statute in 1942 as a result of lobbying efforts by professional societies. The SG had created the post of chief nurse officer.

(2) The committee, as its first assignment, should define the present and future mission of the PHS. As its second task, it should develop an organizational form to carry out that mission "without regard to existing legislation, existing distribution of functions, or existing supervisory hierarchy." Finally, the committee should prepare to effectuate the recommendations through the required administrative and legislative changes.

(3) The committee members and their supporting staff, which should consist of "the very best talent we have in the area of management analysis," should be detached from their regular tasks for the duration of the study. Caulk believed the project, including the drafting of legislation, could be completed in the first five months of 1960.

Caulk proposed that three members of his staff, all management specialists (Allen Moore, Robert Seater, and Norma Robinson), be assigned as staff to the committee, with Allen Moore as Chief of Staff.

(4) The Surgeon General should issue an announcement to all PHS personnel about the formation and purpose of the committee to "create the right climate for the work of the committee and to pave the way for acceptance of its efforts." Caulk also wanted the SG to call for ideas and suggestions from all PHS officers or employees, because "Such information is essential to prevent misunderstanding and reduce the apprehension which a study of this sort is bound to create among many persons."

Naming the Members

Drs. Burney and Porterfield, Paul Caulk, and Lyman Moore selected the members of the Study Group and the staff. The proposed members were checked with the bureau chiefs, and the general terms of reference, charges, nature of assignment, and deadlines to be met were agreed upon just before Christmas of 1959.

Caulk had suggested five criteria for selection. Study Group members should have: (1) demonstrated ability; (2) outstanding achievements; (3) perspective and breadth of outlook (in general, most committee members should have moved around on their assignments so that they would be free of any long-term identification with a specific program of interest); (4) a large segment of their career still ahead of them; (5) combined headquarters and field experience.

The members chosen were: Dr. James M. Hundley as chairman, Miss Margaret Arnstein, Dr. Donald Galagan, Dr. Harold Graning, Harry Hanson, Dr. Harold Magnuson, Dr. William Stewart, and Dr. Burnet Davis. (See Appendix I for biographical sketches.) All eight were members of the Commissioned Corps of the Public Health Service. All were professional program people (five physicians, one dentist, one nurse, and one engineer). The only one who had ever had any part in planning a reorganization was Hanson.

The criteria for membership particularly influential in the selection of members were the ones that called for wide experience throughout the Service, breadth of outlook, and a settled future career in the Service. The Caulk planning group wanted to be sure the members would "live" with the organization they helped to create. These criteria almost inevitably called for strong representation of Commissioned Corps members, since Corps personnel practice accented wide experience from bureau to bureau and from activity to activity. The purpose was to maintain a nucleus of trained medical and public health personnel who knew the Service from top to bottom.

Under Caulk's original plan, the Study Group would have been larger, with some outstanding management people on it. Had this come about, civil service personnel would have been represented.

Caulk was overruled on his candidate for head of the Study Group's staff, and instead of Moore, the Surgeon General assigned Joseph Murtagh, a statistician, who was Assistant Chief, Office of Research Planning, at NIH. Murtagh, a civil service employee, had joined the PHS in 1947 with the Division of Hospitals. He had been in the NIH job since 1956. Several factors favored Murtagh. He had had wide experience throughout the Service and was well versed in the intricacies of program management analysis. His candidacy had been proposed by the NIH bureau chief as one means of "representing" NIH, and he was acceptable to Dr. Hundley. Moore had only recently joined PHS.

The secretary assigned to the Study Group was Mrs. Margaret West, a member of the staff of the Division of Public Health Methods, who had served on many medical study commissions, including President Truman's Commission on the Health Needs of the Nation (1952) and the second Hoover Commission (1954).

The Caulk planning group created several liaison teams. Two departmental representatives, David Stanley (of Management) and Edward Rourke (of the General Counsel's Office) were to keep the Secretary of HEW abreast of the Study Group's thinking, and a member of Caulk's staff (Lyman Moore) was to provide him with information. No formal links with the Surgeon General were provided, since Hundley was to be in close and frequent touch with both Drs. Burney and Porterfield. Plans were made for Hundley to attend the SG's weekly staff meetings.

THE STUDY GROUP WORKS ON THE STATEMENT OF MISSION

During the 1959 Christmas holidays the various members of the Study Group (the Study Group on Mission and Organization of the Public Health Service) were notified of their assignment. Dr. Hundley was in his office at NIH when he got a call from the SG. Relations between the two were cordial; they were on a first-name basis but were not close personal friends. Burney summoned Hundley to a meeting "downtown" to be held December 28. Hundley's only information was that it was an important meeting, called "for the good of the Service." He mentioned the call to the NIH director, who told Hundley he had been tapped to head a committee to study the PHS and to recommend measures for its reorganization. Similar calls from the Surgeon General's Office went forth at the same time to the other members of the group and to the bureau chiefs.

The Study Group members gathered in the Surgeon General's office on December 28. Most were puzzled about why they had been called together. A few minutes later they met in the SG's private office for coffee and sandwiches.

In a brief speech Dr. Burney told them of their assignment. The project, he said, was one to which he attached the utmost importance, and he had selected them as the persons who would do the very best job possible for the Service. He said he would support their recommendations fully and wished them luck in their assignment.

The members' reactions varied: some felt honored, others amazed. Some were astonished at the selection of Hundley as chairman. He was an unknown quantity to the downtown people. Also, they were worried about having to shed their regular responsibilities completely for three months—especially in the three and one-half days allotted.

Miss Arnstein turned impulsively to her bureau chief when she learned that she was to serve on the reorganization committee. She scribbled a quick note asking (1) if the planning committee knew that she was untrained in organization matters and did not put much stock in organizational forms anyway; and (2) whether she should offer to "resign." Her chief wrote a quick answer: yes to the first question, no to the second.

On Monday, January 4, 1960, seven[3] Study Group members and five staff assistants gathered to begin their three-month assignment. They were quartered in the "penthouse" of the main HEW building in Washington. The penthouse, located one and one-half floors above the general offices, was a self-contained unit. With the committee members detached from regular duties and sealed off in the penthouse, they operated in something of the fashion of a jury.

The first order of business was a thorough digest of the Study Group's assignment as embodied in the Surgeon General's written charge. It was dated January 4 and had been prepared by Caulk.

"The general responsibility of your group is to make a critical appraisal of the mission and organization of the Service and to make appropriate recommendations to me." The SG set forth the task in two phases: defining the mission of the Service for the present and for 1970, a task that was to occupy five weeks; and developing an organization plan for the Service, also in five weeks. The final three weeks of the term were to be reserved for revising, redrafting, and preparing the organization proposal for final clearance by HEW and the Bureau of the Budget.

The SG suggested certain procedures but emphasized that the members were to use their initiative and imagination. He suggested a study of published materials and interviews of key PHS personnel. He offered these thoughts on interviewing:

---

[3] Dr. Graning, regional director of the New York area, was not able to join the committee until several weeks later.

> You will want to interview selected program and administrative officials to supplement the written materials available and to secure opinions and suggestions from those whom you feel will have a constructive contribution to make. Time probably will not permit field interviewing, but the group should feel free to arrange for field personnel to come here for interview by the group.

The final portion of the SG's charge was his estimate of the importance of the task.

> I strongly believe that this is the single, most important and challenging task facing the Service at this time. This assignment to you is a stimulating one; your responsibility is without question grave. I know you can meet the test. I shall await with keen interest your recommendations.

Plan of Work

Some of the members hoped to go to work immediately. All seven were experienced PHS people, with an average of twenty years of service behind them. With this background, they should have been able to reach early agreement on some part of the PHS mission—so ran the view of Joe Murtagh, the Chief of Staff, and Mrs. Margaret West, the secretary. With Dr. Hundley's assent, these two had met beforehand and had worked out a study plan. It called for splitting into subcommittees and apportioning the work to get the job done in the most expeditious manner possible. Hundley was concerned at the prospect of trying to come to hard decisions with such a large group, eight members and a staff of five. "I couldn't see how any effective action could be achieved through the committee principle with a group as large as 13 people," he said, "not counting secretaries, part-time staff and consultants. The obvious solution was to break the group up into several smaller working sub-groups, each with specific assignments."

However, the plan for working in subcommittees was not entirely acceptable. The members were too wary at the outset to accept the idea and were uneasy about delegating authority to work parties. They preferred to work as a body on what they rated as the important parts of the assignment, but they did agree to separate into study sections to conduct research projects. Several of the participants knew each other and had worked together, for example, Dr. Stewart and Mrs. West. The hard core of the members were "downtown" people—Drs. Galagan, Magnuson, Stewart, and Davis, and Miss Arnstein. So was Mrs. West of the staff. Hundley and Murtagh were NIH men.

Nobody, of course, was an unequivocal "downtown" or NIH representative. Three of the members had been deliberately selected to speak for their professions—Galagan for the dentists, Hanson for the engineers, and Miss Arnstein for the nurses. Graning represented "the field." Magnuson had worked a great deal in the occupational health area and had associated with both management and union people; his outlook was not that of the ordinary doctor-bureaucrat. In a sense each member of the Study Group represented several constituencies.

The Study Group began by agreeing to consider the health problems and needs of the nation, their trends, and their probable dimensions in the future. The group would then consider what the PHS was doing about them, what it should be doing, and what it might be expected to do over the next decade.

This first assignment was carried out in the three processes: research and study, interviews of PHS personnel, and discussion and deliberations. These activities went on concurrently. First, the group worked out plans to assemble and digest the reports and studies of the PHS made during the prior decade and staff studies made of component parts of the Service. The chairman allotted research topics and problems to various subcommittees. Most assignments were of short duration and called for reports to be turned in within a few days. There was no distinction in subcommittee work between Study Group members and Study Group staff.

Service-Wide Notification

The Caulk suggestion for informing the employees about the reorganization study was carried out to the letter. The SG issued a general bulletin on December 29 addressed to all PHS employees. The notice, which was prominently posted, informed employees that an eight-member group had been constituted to plan the future Service mission and the organization to carry it out.

The notice also contained a general plea for employee cooperation and invited "ideas or suggestions for the consideration of the group."

Shortly afterward Dr. Hundley amplified the SG's bulletin with a memorandum directed to division chiefs, Institute directors, regional medical directors, and officers in charge. This memo, dated

January 7, 1960, listed some of the materials the Study Group was culling for past criticisms and suggestions and asked the officers addressed to pass along any new suggestions or plans from themselves or their staffs.

The Hundley memo said:

> The Study Group, for obvious reasons, would welcome your assistance in summarizing such views particularly with respect to repetitive suggestions. However, any individual should feel free to forward his own views directly to the Study Group. We are prepared to maintain confidentiality when so requested.

Suggestions and opinions on a wide variety of subjects immediately began to flow in to the Study Group. However, the people who responded represented the managerial echelons rather than the rank and file.

Consultants

Caulk had proposed that two consultants—recognized authorities in public administration and organization and management—should be retained to give expert "outside" advice and consultative service. From a list of five, he selected Wallace S. Sayre, professor of public law at Columbia University, and Thomas D. Morris, an official (Director of Management Planning and Assistant to the President) of the Champion Paper & Fiber Company of Ohio. Sayre was chosen to provide advice on general organization theory and principles of public administration applicable to the problems of the PHS. Morris was to help the group plan its own work during the organization stage. He was rated a methodology expert, based on both his experience at Champion Paper and a previous job with the management firm of Cresap, McCormick & Paget, which had worked with the Navy, the Tennessee Valley Authority, and other government agencies.

Initially, the members resisted the idea of bringing in consultants. Dr. Hundley felt that the group did not have the time to brief outsiders to the extent necessary to fill them in on Service problems. A few days after work began, Hundley reported to Caulk that the group thought it a mistake to bring in consultants.

Caulk tried to reassure him. He explained that the consultants would be able to give the group expert professional advice, guidance, and balanced judgment on organizational problems. He reiterated the importance of having the counsel of "outsiders." Finally, he told Hundley that Sayre and Morris had already been chosen and that Sayre would arrive in Washington shortly to meet the group. At that time, said Caulk, Sayre would tell the group something about general principles of organization.

The Caulk planning group had proposed to pay Sayre and Morris as "consultants," but both refused to accept compensation.

On his first appearance, Sayre was introduced by the Deputy Surgeon General. His "lecture" was a general one in which he touched on the problems confronting any large organization that sets out to reorganize. He discussed (1) the dangers of introversion in a self-study and (2) the importance in the free-wheeling mission stage of getting the views of various "publics": Congress, the American Medical Association, the AFL-CIO, clientele groups, professional organizations, voluntary associations, and the like.

Hundley explained the time limitations and said the group had a wealth of "public" advice it could tap from the many advisory committees that served PHS. The members of these advisory bodies, he pointed out, represented the widest possible source of advice: medical school faculty, private practitioners, research specialists, state and city health officers, representatives of foundations, and officers of voluntary health organizations.

Sayre sat with the group one more time during the mission stage.

Interviews

After the first two weeks, when health problems and needs had been scrutinized, the group turned to interviews. The members selected carefully some sixty key PHS officials. The entire group conducted important interviews; occasionally, subcommittees conducted others. The entire group interviewed the chief of the Indian Health Division, the three bureau chiefs, Dr. Porterfield, and Dr. Burney. Only one outsider was interviewed—the director of health services for the Office of Civil and Defense Mobilization. No members of the Service's various external advisory committees were questioned.

On January 29 Burney and Porterfield were interviewed. Burney assured the group of his faith and support. He said he attached immense importance to the job they were doing and repeated his firm intention of carrying out their proposals. He observed that he had authority to make many changes if there should be a hitch with respect to legislation and committed himself to effecting whatever changes he could, the Secretary of HEW willing. If he had any differences with the Study Group, he said, he would "talk them out" at the first "summit meeting."

Recommendations to Congress on Environmental Health

Meantime, by mid-January the SG had decided what to recommend to Congress in the report on environmental health. The drift indicated that a major organizational unit should be devoted to environmental health, but the report was purposely vague about the form the new unit should take. Any specific statement could have tied the hands of the Study Group. The report concluded:

> The need for a high-level organizational unit to carry out the environmental health mission of the Public Health Service is apparent, not only for the purpose of improving the effectiveness of internal PHS activities, but also for strengthening overall relationships and coordination with other Federal agencies.
>
> . . .
>
> Establishment of environmental health as the theme of a major high-level organizational unit of the PHS poses difficult questions with respect to the assignment of precise functions. Such a unit should include the activities of the Service relating to air pollution, water supply and pollution, and general sanitation, which are primarily or exclusively environmental health activities. Less apparent is the proper administrative location of functions in which environmental health is a major concern but which have personal health aspects, such as radiological health, accident prevention, occupational health, and Arctic health research. Other areas in which environmental health is significant are communicable disease control, mental health activities and foreign quarantine.

The report contained a notification to Congress that the Service was conducting a thorough study of its mission and organization in order to fulfill its obligations in environmental health and other areas. The study was promised by May 1, 1960.

Sensitive Questions

In general meetings the Study Group devoted a good deal of time to soul-searching and to pressing the SG or the Deputy SG for clarification of issues, problems, and responsibilities. It received clear instructions on some questions; on others it was left to feel its way.

The members were especially puzzled about stating the Service mission in two areas, delegated functions and functions shared with other agencies. The latter category included maternal and child health responsibilities (shared with the Children's Bureau), radiological safety (the Atomic Energy Commission), and international health operations (International Cooperation Administration). When the group sought clarification, it was told only that it should make recommendations on how the PHS could improve working relationships with these agencies. It was realized from the start that the Study Group could make only generalized recommendations on shared functions.

The group also began to wrestle with another personnel problem. At the outset its broad charter gave it authority to make such recommendations as seemed desirable with regard both to the personnel systems and the organization for managing them. It went into considerable depth in an attempt to gauge performance of the two systems, Commissioned Corps and civil service. It also considered the organizational form a personnel office should take.

The group's decisions on two procedural matters were ratified by the SG: the report on mission should be treated as confidential, with all copies to be numbered and returned to the Study Group; and minority reports were to be discouraged but not ruled out.

Wrestling with Organization

Despite instructions to disregard the existing organizational structure, the Study Group was unable to free itself of organizational thinking during the mission stage. Questions of organization arose again and again. During interviews, each bureau chief and division head was asked what he saw as the future of the unit he headed. Some of them, apprehensive at the prospect of change, could see the future only in terms of the status quo.

Questions of mission and organization became inextricably entangled when the group sought to state mission in terms of bureaus rather than in terms of the total PHS organization. The problem became particularly prominent with BMS and NIH.

One argument centering on BMS grew out of a discussion on the Service's evolving mission. The members were unanimous in stating that public health in the future should emphasize services to people—"personal health services." Personal health services traditionally supplied by official health agencies included services related to maternity, the infant and child, and communicable diseases. Group members saw the challenge of the future in terms of prevention of chronic disease and disability and care of long-term mental and physical illness. They agreed that it was ironic that medical research had yielded promising results but that the lag between the findings of research in public health and full community application of this knowledge was so great. The Service mission, in bringing about realization of these ends, the members felt, was threefold: (1) giving vastly increased attention to supporting the training of additional doctors, dentists, nurses, health educators, social workers, physical therapists, and other health workers; (2) stimulating and supporting the construction of hospitals and facilities to supplement hospitals—diagnostic centers, day-care institutions, institutions to provide long-term care, and "halfway" houses; and (3) supplying technical assistance to state and local health departments to enable them to provide the services needed by the community.

To fulfill PHS responsibilities in the latter area, the group thought closer relationships were needed between the Service and municipal health departments. Also, more joint federal-state interest in and assistance to cities was necessary.

The concept of a dynamic program to furnish increased personal health services brought the members down to earth to a consideration of the existing structure. As they visualized it, some components from all three operating bureaus would form the nucleus of a new entity that they called a Bureau of Health Services. One of the building blocks of this new bureau should be the existing Division of Hospital and Medical Facilities, which administered the vast Hill-Burton construction program. That division constituted the largest block of the BMS in terms of both budget and popular support. It seemed clear to Dr. Stewart and the majority of the Study Group members that BMS, with its multiplicity of functions, was muddy in its aims and ineffective in its operation; building hospitals and developing additional professional resources in nursing and dentistry had little in common with treating patients. They felt that *treatment* should be set apart. Even more compelling, they felt, was the need for a new bureau to supply health services to the nation, and they wanted the Hill-Burton construction program in it.

There was some opposition among the members of the Study Group to fragmenting BMS and splitting off the Hill-Burton program. The spokesman for the opposition was Dr. Burnet Davis, Deputy Chief of the Division of Hospital and Medical Facilities since 1958. Davis, the only member of the Study Group from the BMS, thought a split would downgrade the bureau.

Each time Davis tried to tell the others how things worked "in my Division," he was jokingly rebuked. "What do you mean, *your* Division?" he was asked. The members tried conscientiously to attain objectivity and to rise above their own programs to see the Service as a whole. Each member was to be twitted, before the task was completed, for preoccupation with his own unit's program. This chastisement took effect. By the time the members reached the organizational stage, some were able to plan the extinction of their own jobs.

Many factors contributed to the process of elevating the members to the disembodied and selfless heights from which they surveyed the PHS of the future, not the least of which was the very plan devised by Caulk. He had foreseen that the members, separated from their daily work and from their fellows, would tend to rise above program and organizational loyalties. At the same time, the work plans instituted by Dr. Hundley and the staff helped to forge strong bonds among the members. Membership on the various ad hoc committees was deliberately scrambled to expose members to new ideas and suggestions.

Disciplinary measures, overt and covert, were instituted for the outspoken, garrulous, or intensely dedicated members. Dr. Davis was told to stop representing BMS; Dr. Graning, a talkative man, was frequently shushed. In fact, informal records of "filibusters" were maintained.

Of paramount importance, however, was the lack of concern on the part of each of the members for the job he held at that moment. Each was well aware that his place in the organization was secure and that if his existing job were altered or abolished, he would almost certainly get a better one.

Future Role of NIH

Organization intruded on mission once again when attention turned to the NIH. The issue reflected the conviction of the group that one PHS goal was to bring the results of research into wider use. For instance, research had demonstrated that one type of cancer prevalent in women—cervical cancer—could be cured if it were detected in its early stages and treatment begun. Other research showed fluoridation of water to be effective in reducing dental caries. Under the Study Group concept of the agency's future mission, the PHS would take the lead, without necessarily being the action agency, in putting such discoveries to use and uniting the resources of the community (physicians, public health officials, hospital staff, other health personnel, and civic leaders) to prevent and cure illness and to reduce disability.

Following their tendency to think of mission in terms of existing bureaus, the members agreed that NIH, which during the past decade had increased its activities relating to testing and field demonstrations of research findings, should be redirected toward research. In organizational terms, this meant a transfer of all disease control functions and community demonstration projects from NIH to the new bureau that would carry the bulk of PHS community health work, the Bureau of Health Services.

The Study Group members were unanimous in phrasing the NIH mission as a return to research. The Director of NIH, Dr. James Shannon, when interviewed, said he, too, supported such a redirection and was satisfied that removal of activities to apply research knowledge would strengthen his bureau.

However, one piece of this problem—the transfer of the community health functions from one of the Institutes, the National Institute of Mental Health (NIMH)—was to become a crackling controversy when the Study Group's recommendations became firm proposals.

The group members saw signs of trouble when they interviewed the Director of NIMH, Dr. Robert H. Felix, on January 23. Felix said flatly that he envisaged an expansion—not a contraction—of NIMH activities. NIMH was engaged not only in fundamental research but in three of the other four steps involved in public health work—application of knowledge, field trials, and demonstrations. He indicated that only by continuing all these activities at NIMH could advances be made in the fight against mental illness. He saw NIMH as the general staff office in the fight.

The Study Group Is Expanded

In February, at about the time drafts of its mission report were being completed, the Study Group was enlarged from eight to twelve persons. There were several reasons for expanding the membership.

Under the plan originally conceived by Caulk, the group was to number fifteen persons, with a strong quota of management appraisal specialists. However, the SG had decided on an eight-man group. Once the mission assignment was completed, it was apparent to the SG and the Deputy SG that the group could benefit from members with organization experience and judgment. By this time, too, Drs. Burney and Porterfield realized that the makeup of the Study Group might result in ill will among the 23,000 civil service PHS employees, who were not represented.

It was not anomalous to members of the Corps that only Commissioned Corps officers had been selected for the Study Group. They do not recall that Caulk pushed his suggestion for civil service representation. And for the bureau chiefs and chief professional officers—the people who had suggested the candidates—it was second nature to turn to their own kind for key assignments like membership on the Study Group.

The impetus for expansion actually came from the Study Group, and it was at Hundley's suggestion that the SG proposed that civil service people be added. The expansion served a dual purpose: It brought civil service representation and it put management experience within easy reach when it was most needed—the Study Group's organizational phase. However, Hundley's overriding aim was to bring in the civil service.

The expansion in membership did not come about as a result of criticism or pressure from civil service spokesmen.

The four new members were threaded into the group with a minimum of orientation. One was the Chief of Staff, Joe Murtagh. The other three, management people from several areas in the Service, were Sam A. Kimble, a branch chief in the Bureau of State Services; Norman E. Lindquist, Bureau of Medical Services; and Lawrence E. Ring, a member of Caulk's staff. The new Chief of Staff, chosen by Hundley, was Allen W. Moore, an information specialist who had joined the Public Health Service in May 1959. Hundley selected Moore for both his organizational competence and his lack of emotional bias toward any Public Health Service program. Caulk had favored Moore from the beginning.

DRAFTING THE MISSION REPORT

Talking, arguing, compromising, and rephrasing, the members of the Study Group finally reached a concensus on the Service mission.

The mission report was a ringing statement of purpose. It proposed a dynamic, driving, creative role for the Service that leaped the barriers of agency jurisdiction and the traditional boundaries of the federal system. It proposed new grants of authority, new programs, and new enforcement powers. However, it did not propose national health insurance.

Over 100 pages long, the report consisted of a text that spoke movingly and dramatically of Service responsibilities and made eighty specific recommendations for early implementation. The action recommendations did not immediately project the Service into areas of controversy. However, the impression gained from the text alone was that the document was a genuinely "hot" paper.

The mission document concluded that the Service had failed to achieve the role Congress had repeatedly assigned to it of providing federal leadership in civilian health and that the reason lay in Service preoccupation with its earliest assigned responsibilities, the Marine hospitals and foreign quarantine. From 1940 onward, the Service had expanded its activities and had begun to fulfill its potential. The document listed as creditable Service achievements the new and expanded programs in health research and training; hospital construction; development of professional resources in nursing, dentistry, and engineering; conservation of water resources and control of pollution; and control of environmental health hazards such as air pollution, accidents, and ionizing radiation.

The report used demographic data as one method of guiding the Service down the paths it should pursue in the next decade. By 1970, the report said, two-thirds of the U.S. population would be concentrated in metropolitan areas. The expected 1970 population of 214,000,000 would include a twenty-five per cent increase in the number of "older persons." Accidents and chronic diseases, it said, had advanced sharply in mortality rates, while communicable diseases, both acute and chronic, had diminished in importance as causes of death.

The PHS, the group said, was "destined" to play a larger role in health in the future. The battle would be on two fronts—control of technologic environment and "health services: their availability, adequacy, quality, and scope." Effective action on the first front meant acceptance and promotion of the concept that the various sectors of the environment—atmosphere, surface, waters, land, and ocean—were areas of public domain and that "private use must be limited in the public interest."

The group concluded that the Service should "mobilize for the protection of human life all of the available resources of knowledge and skill in the health services" and should seek "constantly to increase those resources in order to meet the changing health needs of all the people."

Functional Responsibilities of PHS

The Study Group delineated twelve broad areas of functional responsibility to encompass the activities the Service should carry on to achieve its objective. In each area certain activities were rated for greater emphasis or expansion in the future. The twelve were as follows:

(1) Leadership and direction in the national health scene.

(2) Research on health and disease.

(3) Improvement, support, and extension of health services, personal and nonpersonal.

(4) Development of adequate supplies of health manpower.

(5) Aid in construction of facilities for diagnosis, treatment, care, "progressive patient care," and research.

(6) Direct medical care for legal beneficiaries.

(7) International activities.

(8) Functions in support of other federal agency programs.

(9) Health statistics and program intelligence.

(10) Library services.

(11) Information and education.

(12) Administration.

Some of the recommendations for action involved no break with tradition or with current practice; others called for sharp alterations of policy. Some of the most controversial statements of mission and future function came in the section devoted to "health services." One of the Service's major missions, the group said, was "to provide, or stimulate the provision of, adequate and comprehensive health services, including definitive diagnosis and treatment of disease for every American citizen."

> The PHS must have some concern for every aspect of the total national health service effort—from the performance of the private practitioner . . . to the great national drives for the control of specific diseases such as polio . . . society is looking increasingly to government, at all levels, for more direct assistance in health matters. The PHS, therefore, should anticipate an increasing Federal involvement in the conduct of health services for people.

The group found that four factors compelled the government to expand health services: the increased cost and complexity of personal health services; increased understanding of the social and behavioral aspects of health services; the contamination of the environment; and the changing pattern of social and demographic organization.

The problems engendered by the increasing incidence of long-term illness and disabilities, the group felt, posed serious problems for the Service. "Need has developed for new approaches to housing and caring for the chronically ill and disabled. The cost of long-term care is requiring a whole new approach to financing health services." The group called on the Service to provide leadership in organizing and administering programs of medical and related health care.

Two factors led the group to call for an "area" approach to problems rather than preserving the traditional channels of state and county. One was the necessity for more integrated approaches to the problems of contamination of the environment; the other was the concentration of population in metropolitan centers straddling state and county lines. "The very emphasis on the establishment of formal Federal-State-local structure has created a fixed and unnecessarily rigid pattern of relationships which may have retarded rather than enhanced the effective development of total public health practice in this country." This structure no longer sufficed, the group concluded. It called on the Service to develop new patterns of operation designed to permit the Service to work *with* rather than *through* state agencies.

Under the heading of Manpower, after noting the increasing demand and the decreasing supply of physicians and other health personnel, the report called for additional federal assistance to provide scholarships for students of medicine, dentistry, nursing, and osteopathy; federal aid to expand existing medical, dental, and nursing schools and to construct new ones; and federal financial support to help meet the operating costs of medical, dental, and nursing schools. The last proposal, of course, represented a radical departure from White House policy and threw the Service into an area of lively dispute—the possibility of federal control of education by means of assuming *operating* costs.

Under Facilities, the group proposed that "careful planning for effective use" be emphasized rather than mere provision of construction grants. It proposed that the Hill-Burton Hospital Construction Program focus attention on the critical problem of providing facilities for coordinating health service in major population centers. This meant a redirection in emphasis, since Hill-Burton had been concentrating on satisfying rural needs.

Under International Operations, the mission report proposed a larger PHS role in the formulation and execution of health policies carried out by such other federal agencies as the International Cooperation Administration. Under current practice, PHS personnel were detailed to those agencies, but in the Study Group's judgment, because of the failure to include a Service voice in planning these activities, many of the international health programs had failed to achieve their full potential. The document called for direct PHS representation in selected locations abroad.

In the area of Direct Medical Care, the document proposed a gradual diminution of services. The group phrased this section in a deliberately provocative way in order to stimulate discussion and decision. The language went this way: The PHS hospital plants were badly deteriorated (as a result of years of Budget Bureau reluctance to see them expand or even continue); equipment was obsolete; modernization and improvements requiring vast outlays were necessary to bring them up to acceptable standards. The report also indicated that some of the arguments for continuation of the hospital system were equivocal, the main one being that the hospitals served as attractive recruiting devices for Service personnel. A further point was that the hospitals should not only be modernized to provide better care but should serve as model hospitals and demonstration units—as showcases for the best hospital care that could be provided. Short of this, the report went on to say, the hospitals should be abandoned. (Current policy on the hospitals was for their continuation at about the same level of maintenance. For at least one [the leprosarium at Carville, La.], the administration was asking for increased appropriations to finance improvements.)

The mission report was delivered on Friday afternoon, February 5, so that the Surgeon General, bureau chiefs, and HEW departmental officers could study it over the weekend.

THE FIRST SUMMIT MEETING

On Tuesday morning, February 9, 1960, thirty-three people sat down together at nine o'clock at the Marriott Motor Hotel in Virginia, just across the Potomac River from Washington, to discuss the mission report. Three blocs were represented. The first was the Study Group and its staff members. The second was the Public Health Service directorate (Surgeon General Burney; his deputy, Dr. Porterfield; the three bureau chiefs, Dr. David E. Price of the BSS, Dr. James A. Shannon of the NIH, and Dr. James V. Lowry of the BMS; the three chief professional officers; the Executive Officer, Paul Caulk; and the three bureau executive officers). The third bloc consisted of four representatives of the Department of Health, Education, and Welfare: the Director of Administration, Rufus Miles; his assistant, David Stanley; the Director of Financial Management, James Kelly; and Edward Rourke of the General Counsel's Office. The departmental representatives were present at the meeting at the suggestion of the SG. However, their presence nettled the Study Group members, who had not known in advance that they would attend.

In preparing the mission document, the members "had intentionally written a completely frank, provocative document, for family eyes only," Hundley said. Its principal purpose, as they understood it, was to stimulate thought, discussion, and —eventually—decision. By *family* he meant the PHS alone.

The striking aspect of the meeting was the absence of any plan to direct the discussion. Neither the Study Group nor the SG's review committee had a clear idea of what the meeting was supposed to accomplish. When Caulk and the bureau executive officers had provided for the two review sessions, they had envisaged decision-making forums. At the conclusion of the first summit meeting, the SG, supported by his advisers, would accept, reject, or modify the mission statement. Assuming general acceptance, the Study Group would then tackle the organization structure to carry out the mission.

However, the only guidance the bureau chiefs had was the mission document, which had been given to them to read only a few days before. They did not understand that the Study Group had been instructed to enunciate the mission without regard to existing structure or controlling laws. They saw it as a vastly impractical "cloud-hopping" exercise. They interpreted the mission in organizational terms and saw a major disruption of the Service as it then existed. They also tended to see proposals for change in terms of criticism of the way they were doing their jobs.

Director of Administration Rufus Miles and other HEW representatives were no better briefed on the mission document. They did not realize it was to be used only as the basis and stimulus for discussion. They were afraid the SG had already endorsed it in principle, that it was a basis for real action, and that its contents might be made public at any time. Miles suspected that the document might be used by some in PHS to force the administration to take a more positive stand on certain highly controversial issues that were scheduled for congressional consideration, e.g., medical care for the aged and federal aid for construction of medical schools.

The misunderstanding about the attendance of the HEW officials indicated a breakdown in communications at this stage. Miles and his associates understood that they were properly accredited participants. They believed the SG wanted their comments to be made during the open sessions. They were unaware of any resentment or surprise on the part of the Study Group members occasioned by the presence and participation of officials from an echelon even higher than the PHS Surgeon General and his bureau chiefs.

At any rate, it was a large group that immured itself in the Marriott for the discussion of the mission report—especially large for a discussion without ground rules of a deliberately provocative paper about future goals and policies. Some petty annoyances—the small quarters and faulty acoustics—added to the strain. Dr. Porterfield presided in order to leave Burney free to accept telephone calls and attend to whatever critical problems might arise back at the Service.

The meeting opened with a perfunctory formal endorsement of the Study Group's report on mission by the Surgeon General and the Deputy SG. Then, after Dr. Hundley had reported on the way the group went about its job, the presiding officer called on each reviewer, in turn, to comment on the report.

The PHS bureau chiefs were critical and resentful. One wave of critical comment ignited another; from the vantage point of Study Group members, the atmosphere soon seemed afire with reproaches. Members of the PHS directorate scored the mission document section by section. They were joined by Miles and Kelly.

Miles called the mission document defective on three counts: it did not go far enough on some levels; in other areas it was entirely too specific; and, finally, it dealt inadequately with the Service's lateral relationships.

With respect to the first problem, he said the report should have taken more cognizance of forces and trends, particularly the program implications of the gathering storm over the government's role in financing medical care for the aged. He felt that the group failed to recognize adequately the scope and importance of the subject of medical economics. He thought they should have explored much more fully the responsibilities of the Service in gathering and analyzing a vast amount of information on the interrelationships between demands for services, the alternative means and cost of providing services, the availability and efficient use of professional and technical personnel and facilities, and the sources and methods of financing.

On the second count, portions of the document took definite positions on current legislative and budgetary matters without concern as to whether the positions were in harmony with those of the administration. Thirdly, he thought the group erred in failing to take proper account of other federal agencies with health and medical responsibilities and consequently dealt inadequately with methods of achieving lateral coordination.

Kelly excoriated the group for what he called unauthorized incursions into the political arena. He emphasized that the PHS function was to give administration policy-makers the best professional advice but that the group was out of line in proposing alteration in established policy. It was a mistake, he said, to characterize PHS as the national health agency rather than as the federal government's principal arm for fulfilling its health mission. If there were to be a "Ministry of Health," Kelly said, it would be the HEW—not PHS.

Firm decisions were reached at the summit meeting on at least two questions: retention of the PHS hospitals and the Study Group's responsibility for dealing with the personnel system. As was intended, the hospital recommendation created a commotion. The Service directorate, led by the chief of BMS (the locus of the Hospital Division), sharply opposed giving up the hospitals and providing medical care to Service beneficiaries through other means.

With regard to personnel, the summit cleared the air on the group's responsibility. Initially the members had been told only that the personnel question was part of their assignment. However, the summit discussions indicated that radical alteration of the two basic systems was beyond the scope of the Study Group. The Surgeon General then instructed the group to consider only the organizational form of the personnel office and the relation of personnel practices to operating problems.

Reactions to the Summit Meeting

Most of the Study Group members agreed that the summit meeting was a shattering morale blow. They were specially disturbed at the comments characterizing the mission reports as "fuzzy, dreamy, and impractical." They had been told to cast themselves adrift from practicality and to chart the mission of the PHS during the next decade. That instruction had been incorporated in their original charge, and it had been repeated to them by the SG. Hundley believed that few people would have quarreled with the mission statement in the light of the group's charge; the only indelicacy was that the document was subject to leakage and could easily have caused political damage—by giving aid and comfort to congressional Democrats and others who were advocating a more active role for the federal government in promoting medical care—had news of it reached the press.

The Study Group knew its recommendations were at odds with the prevailing policy of President Eisenhower and the Secretary of HEW. However, it also was aware of the fact of life that policy can be, and is, made in daily administration by bureau chiefs, division chiefs, and section heads.

Furthermore, the members understood that they were only doing their job in using their best judgment to decide what the PHS mission would and should be in the ensuing decade. And finally, they said ruefully, they had not expected the departmental people to attend the summit discussions.

Many Study Group members felt that most of the criticisms were not only undeserved but picayune and provincial. Some of the critical comments had been directed at the report's phraseology, the members said; words and phrases had been wrenched out of context and distorted.

One of the members of the Study Group, Dr. Magnuson, said the group was thoroughly demoralized and dispirited after the two-day session. He felt that the reviewers had not understood the nature of the assignment, and he was disappointed at what he felt were the parochial reactions displayed by some chief professional officers and bureau chiefs. He felt with particular acuteness the existence of a wide gap between the Study Group and the working chiefs at this stage; the members had been living in the rarefied atmosphere of top-level planning for five weeks and were especially rattled to hear humdrum complaints. Magnuson feared that the work, sweat, negotiation, and imagination the group had poured into the task were to be treated as an academic exercise.

Magnuson and others interpreted Kelly's criticism as a sharp schoolmaster's rebuke to wayward pupils. Boiled down, it read: "You have been talking about political problems and you should get back to your technical competence, your professional competence. The *department* determines health policy."

Hundley characterized the summit as something of a fiasco. He too was upset and puzzled by the reaction.

> Much of the criticism seemed unjustified to us because it concerned ideas, statements, even words, picked out of context and at times by those who did not seem to understand the purpose of the document. It seemed to us that too much of the criticism was about how we said things and relatively little about the substance of the ideas presented. We were frankly astonished that our bosses seemed to have developed such narrow vision and such fixed viewpoints. As a matter of fact, the group was quite demoralized for several days after this conference. The document itself was judged to be so radioactive that all copies were recaptured and destroyed.

Hanson, who had experienced top-level action meetings before, during the years he had been PHS executive officer, was not as disturbed by the criticisms as were the others.

The department officials and the PHS bureau chiefs and executive officers were, in turn, surprised at the sensitiveness of the Study Group members. To them the summit meeting was routine. Accustomed to the bruising give-and-take of meetings at which top-level decisions were made, they failed to take account of the fact that the Study Group members were lower on the hierarchical ladder and lacked the experience of encountering such tough discussions. Moreover, some of them said later, if the report had really been written primarily to stimulate discussion rather than as an action document, why had Study Group members been upset when vigorous discussion took place?

The summit meeting, despite the bloodshed, had some positive results. The Study Group got a panoramic view of the forces it would encounter in the second phase of its work—the preparation of an organization plan. It also got some decisions on specific program activities. Finally, the blows it sustained unified the group as little else could have.

The primary purpose of staging the summit conference—agreement on the Service's mission—was not achieved. The reviewing group ordered all copies of the mission statement impounded. However, Burney and Porterfield promised to work closely with the Study Group members during the next few weeks to guide them on linking organization with mission. The reviewing group agreed that, with this close connection between the Study Group and the SG, the mission report could be recast and used as the basis for planning the reorganization.

PLANNING AND ORGANIZATION

On February 11 the Study Group members, discouraged and dispirited, gathered once more in the HEW penthouse to tackle the second phase of their job, the organization to fit the mission. A motto Dr. Magnuson had chalked on the blackboard set the tone for a half-hour postmortem of the bruising summit session. "Back to the brave new world of 1940," it read.

With catharsis behind, the group began work again.

Plans had been made earlier for a briefing at this time by the consultants. Professor Sayre, who appeared first, outlined the standard forms of organization: clientele, purpose, process or function, and place. He rated the PHS a combination of process and clientele. The members, conscious of their lack of experience in organization and aware of the magnitude of the problems ahead, listened with attention and respect. Many of the decisions they faced would be difficult ones, with choices almost evenly balanced. Sayre reminded them that if the alternatives were evenly matched, there was no best or ideal way; the decision could go either way. Only experience would demonstrate the wisdom of the choice, and by that time additional reorganization might be indicated.

Sayre spoke of factors to keep in mind in altering existing arrangements and suggested consideration of how the changes would affect relationships with clientele organizations.

He reminded them that reorganization was almost a continuous process. If one reorganization did not accomplish the desired purpose, another could be ordered. The best of organizations could be frustrated by ineffective personnel, he told them, and similarly, capable people could triumph over poor organization.

The following day the second outside consultant, Tom Morris, reporting in from Ohio, outlined various methods used by other organizations planning changes. Morris had been selected to instruct the group in methodology, to help them plan their work during the organizational phase. After suggesting several possible work plans, he proposed one he guaranteed to be workable, one he felt would serve the needs of the PHS group. The plan had been worked out by Morris and Allen Moore, who had gone to Ohio shortly before this to confer with Morris.

The plan Morris suggested involved two phases, each to occupy two weeks. During the first, the group was to make an inventory of the Service's major tasks, present and future; to identify the major organizational objectives; and to conduct whatever special studies were needed. During the second phase, the group was to split up into four work parties to devise and test alternative forms of organization.

Morris suggested that the final week be devoted to drafting a report carrying the organization plan. He demonstrated to the group a work method using cards on which some of the PHS functions were listed. The cards could be shuffled at will and arranged according to any kind of organizational pattern desired. The group agreed immediately to accept the Morris work plan (see Figure 4).

Dr. Hundley was especially conscious of the consultants' value as "outsiders" at this time. Sayre was helpful in rebuilding morale and making the members aware of the universality of their problems. Morris was able, as no insider could have been, to get agreement on a work plan that called for discipline and tight deadlines. As Hundley described it, the group accepted the consultants' "knowledge, wisdom and suggestions with a finality which would have been totally unachievable with anyone from the PHS itself, no matter how competent."

Classification of Tasks and Experimentation with Models

The group found, after completing the inventory, that 404 separate tasks were involved in carrying out existing programs, and an additional fifty tasks in future programs. The number in each program varied considerably. The hospital construction program (which then had an annual budget of $180,000,000) was described in terms of six discrete functions. By contrast, one of the Institutes at NIH (with an annual budget of $50,000,000) required seventeen tasks to describe its principal functions.

Once listed, the tasks were classified and coded according to functional area, type of operation, clientele group, interrelation with other programs, and size in terms of men or money. Each task was coded as to whether it would probably expand, diminish, or stay constant. This information was put on 3″ x 5″ cards and duplicated, so each member could have a set. New tasks and field operations were put on distinctively colored cards. The cards were then used as basic units in designing organizational models.

Concurrently, subcommittees worked on organization objectives and carried out special studies. One subcommittee studied personnel office organization; another, administrative problems capable of correction through organizational devices; a third conducted selected interviews.

Another subcommittee returned to the mission

FIGURE 4:
WORK PLAN

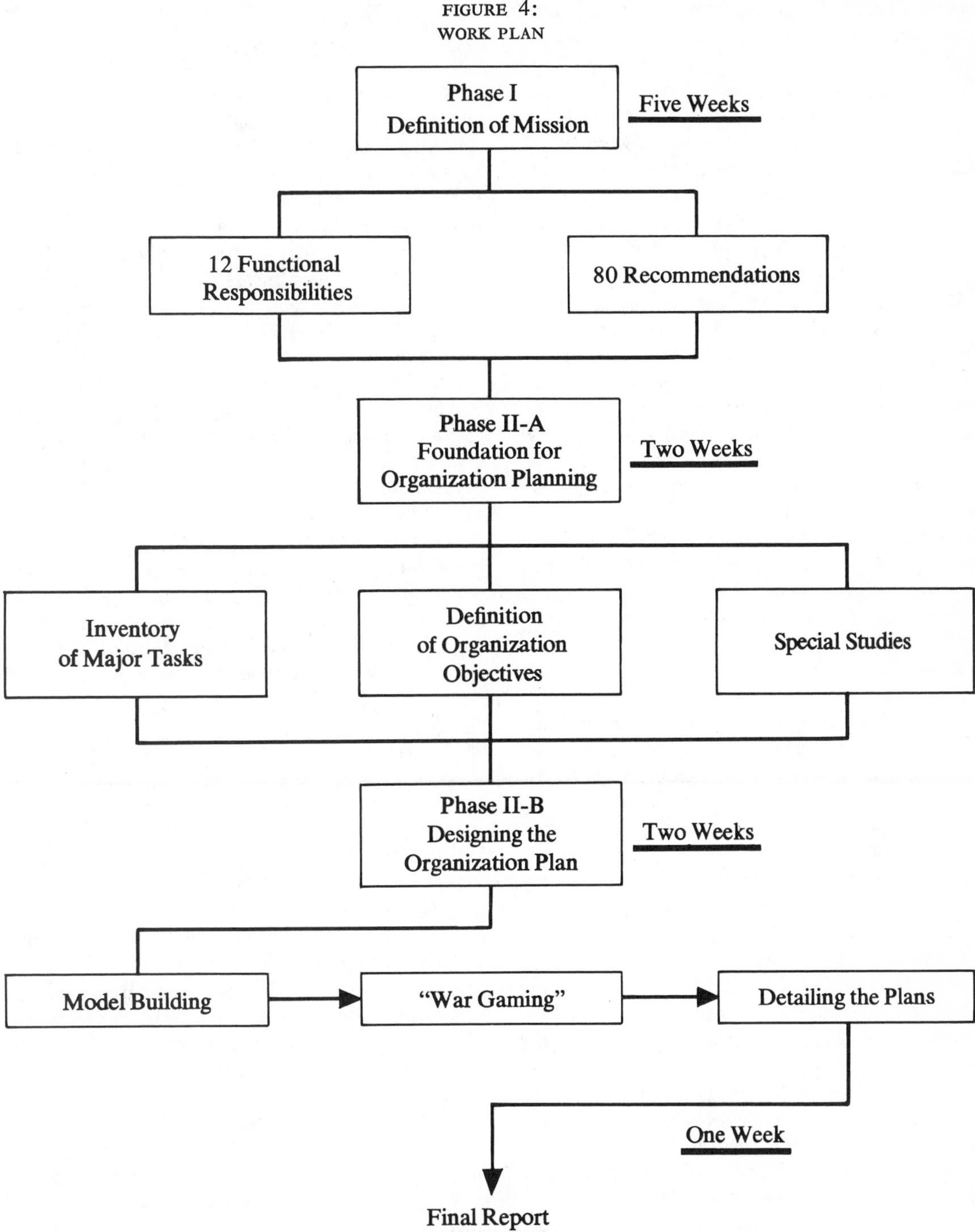

report in an effort to redefine the Service mission in the light of the comments made at the summit meeting. The final decision on the purpose to be served by the new mission statement was deferred until the second summit.

During the second stage, which Morris had designated as model-building and war-gaming, the group separated into work parties. Each was instructed to design one specified organization plan and one free-style alternate. The four assigned axes were clientele, health problem or disease category, function (the mission had been defined in terms of twelve functional areas; see page 23), and a continuation of clientele-process organization with minor alterations.

For a period, then, the group experimented with the various organizational forms, testing, altering, comparing, trying to fit together the most reasonable and workable model. No group acted as advocate for one plan or another. It was a period of open-minded experimentation.

The first form discarded was the clientele axis. Then the design according to the twelve functional areas was tossed out on grounds that the functions were too splintered. Although several members lobbied against it, the group clung for a time to the plan for organizing along the disease category axis, which called for separate units to handle every operation connected with cancer, heart disease, and so on, from earliest research to final service. Such a plan would have called for about fifteen to twenty major units, with an elaborate superstructure for each.

One variation considered was a modified functional approach that called for seven bureaus (management services, research, intelligence and information, resources, environmental health, personnel services, and medical care). Another was reconsideration of the plan for minor alterations of the existing structure. The disease category axis was "attractive," and there was a last-minute disagreement over it. It called for a flattop structure, with all of the disease category units reporting directly to the SG. Some of the group favored it, and it was discarded reluctantly. Hundley opposed it vigorously. This question was one of the few on which he took an open position. The role of chairman, as Hundley saw it, called for him to preside and to moderate but not to advocate.

As the time neared for a final choice, the members began to lay out the new organization without regard for the places they would occupy in it. By the middle of March, under two similar plans being considered, the jobs then held by six of the group members—Drs. Hundley, Galagan, Stewart, and Magnuson, Miss Arnstein, and Mr. Kimble—were either to be abolished or drastically altered.

The SG Decides to Unify Environmental Activities

At about this time the SG concluded that a consolidation of the environmental health activities was important enough to be made even before legislation was passed that would create new bureaus and give him additional administrative flexibility. On March 8, 1960, when the Health Subcommittee of the House Appropriations Committee held hearings on the environmental report, Burney told Representative Fogarty and the subcommittee members about the progress of the organization study.

Although the Administration was asking $35,000,000 for all air and water pollution functions, various nonfederal witnesses and representatives of conservation groups had convinced the Fogarty Subcommittee that an additional $15,000,000 should be appropriated to finance an expansion of those same programs. Dr. Burney said that, in the event such expanded amounts were available, he would not wait for legislative changes but would act under his administrative authority to create a major unit devoted to environmental health. Burney went on to say to the subcommittee:

> I believe the urgency of some of these [air and water pollution problems] is so great that I would be inclined to go ahead with certain organizational changes which I could make without legislative changes, without waiting for the legislation to be done, within the authority that I have at the present time. . . .

Burney also promised that he would discuss the proposed organizational changes with the members of both the legislative and appropriations committees before acting.

Burney made this loose commitment as part of a campaign to keep PHS's political fences mended. The pressures for expansion of environmental health activities reached a crescendo during the spring appropriations hearings when representatives of outside groups testified. His promise was more of a reassurance than it was a new commitment, since some consolidation and expansion of environmental health programs was a virtual certainty.

THE STUDY GROUP'S ORGANIZATIONAL RECOMMENDATIONS

The first draft of the Study Group's organization report was dated March 22, 1960. It outlined two recommended plans, both based in general on clientele orientation. Plan 1, the favorite, called for five bureaus; the alternate for six. According to Hundley, Plan 1 had only a slight edge over the alternate. In general, both plans covered only bureau structure. Even here the group allowed some latitude for staff work to develop optimal organization at the lower division level. It did not make recommendations at the branch level and below.

Within each bureau the group offered recommendations on staff functions, which were shown organizationally as offices. Most charts did not present staff functions at the division level. However, the group believed that each major division should have similar staff functions, at least in the fields of administration, program planning and analysis, and health education and information.

Plan 1 proposed increasing the number of operating bureaus in PHS from three to five. It called for Bureaus of Environmental Health, Health Services, Beneficiary Care, NIH, and National Health Intelligence, plus two other major units, a National Library of Medicine and an Office of the Surgeon General. Plan 2 differed only in proposing separate bureaus for Health Services and for Health Resources (resources were defined as manpower and facilities).[4]

In essence, Plan 1 split the current Bureau of State Services into two units—one in which the principal environmental health activities (radiological, air, and water pollution) were grouped together, and a second, the Bureau of Health Services, that would bring together in more logical form the functions relating to health services, resources, and facilities.

Health Services: A New Bureau

The Study Group members had agreed that the Bureau of Health Services would provide the principal means for reorientation of the PHS. The new unit would serve as the vehicle for bringing better health services to people by increasing the number of doctors, nurses, and other health personnel; by building more hospitals and other treatment and care facilities; by developing more dynamic education and information programs to increase the public's awareness of the new techniques and discoveries for disease detection, prevention, and cure; and by providing the stimulus to states, communities, and nonprofit agencies for improving techniques for better medical care. The last proposal involved combining existing programs dealing with public health practice, research, organization, and financing with a new grants program designed to turn up better methods of organizing and financing medical care. It meant such projects as searching for better nursing and home-care techniques and better facilities and methods of caring for aged persons and persons suffering with chronic diseases or long-term illnesses.

The Study Group had conceived of this bureau as the agency for putting into practice some of the findings turned up by the past fifteen years of research. It would bring together in one manageable entity some of the scattered functions relating to research application—the work on progressive patient care carried out by the Division of Hospital and Medical Facilities in the BMS; the heart and cancer control work done in the BSS; and some of the studies and planning then being done in the Division of Public Health Methods in the OSG.

The new Bureau of Health Services was to contain nine divisions, one of which was predestined to run into trouble. It was the proposed new Division of Mental and Social Health, an amalgamation of the Community Services Branch (from the NIMH), field studies and demonstrations from BSS, and a new Public Health Education Branch.

The chief of the new bureau would have additional staff services, including an Office of Grants Management. That office would provide central policy, scientific review, and management services for most of the scattered grant programs.

Other features of the recommended plan included:

(1) A reorientation (and renaming) of the Bureau of Medical Services, pointing it more sharply toward direct medical care of the special population groups designated as PHS beneficiaries. The reconstituted unit, the Bureau of Beneficiary Care, was to include the existing PHS hospitals, the Division of Foreign Quarantine, the Division of Indian Health, and responsibility for professional supervision of the PHS medical care programs for other federal agencies, including personnel covered in Federal

[4] The object of creating a separate unit for health resources was to give clear and exclusive focus to those manpower resources and training activities that were closely related to providing health services. The bureau would provide the setting for administration of an educational facilities construction program. It would also be the locus for a Division of Mental Health Resources to administer the mental health clinical and PHS training programs to be transferred from the NIMH.

Employees Health Services, the Coast Guard, and the Federal prison population.

(2) A redirection of NIH, to focus sharply on biological and medical research, and curtailing some of its functions relating to research application. This was to entail the separation of the disease control, demonstration, and community service programs. The NIH was to continue to support research training and research facility construction.

(3) Elevation to bureau status of the components that measured the health status of the nation, to be called the Bureau of National Health Intelligence. This unit would have five divisions: the National Office of Vital Statistics (then located in the General Health Services Division of BSS); the Division of Mental Health Services Statistics (located at NIMH); the National Health Survey (from the OSG); and two new divisions, the Division of Health Trend Analysis and a Data Processing Center.

(4) A National Library of Medicine, with expanded roles in research, training, and communications activities.

(5) Alteration of the Office of the Surgeon General to provide the SG with better arrangements for meeting his responsibilities. The somewhat idealized objectives of the revised OSG were fourfold: to augment the Surgeon General's staff resources; to enhance the importance of personnel policy and administration; to provide means for improved interdepartmental and intergovernmental relationships; and to cut down the OSG's routine operational responsibilities.

Additional staff resources were to be provided through six staff offices: Offices of Management Services; Personnel; Health Education and Information; International Health; Program Planning and Analysis; and Government Relations (which would also provide management services involved in the Surgeon General's supervision of the regional medical directors).

The redirection proposed for the OSG rested on two foundations: streamlining the duties of the Deputy SG so that he could act as a genuine deputy, or alter ego, to the SG, and allotting additional staff services to the SG.

Some of the Deputy SG's supervisory and coordinating functions would be delegated to an Assistant Deputy SG, a new post.

The organization document, developed during the last week of the war-gaming phase, presented both Plans 1 and 2, with the strengths and weaknesses of each. Within each plan there were a number of alternatives the group had considered but did not recommend. The reasons for their choices were given. Objectives and responsibilities for each organizational unit were stated. Two check lists accompanied the document. One showed each existing program and its location in the new organization. The other showed the new organization and the origin of the programs that would form it. A third appendix showed the size of the new organizational units in terms of men and money.

Sneak Previews

At this point Dr. Hundley and his colleagues, still smarting from the blows of the first summit meeting, began to search for some technique for presenting their proposals in the most favorable light possible. "We felt it essential," Hundley said, "to find a device for presenting our total plan to all key officials in a way which would clarify what the total proposal was before anyone had a chance to consider or criticize any segment of it."

Morris gave them the answer. He suggested a special visual briefing for the PHS and HEW leaders, which would present the plan to them in a logical, orderly fashion. What he proposed was a sophisticated version of the "before and after" technique. Two charts would be used throughout the briefing, one showing the existing structure with a text that pointed up its deficiencies, the other showing the proposed new organization with a text that described its virtues. Only when the briefing was completed were copies of the organization plan to be distributed.

The group accepted the plan and enlisted the aid of one of the SG's speechwriters to work on the text. The showings took place March 22-23 in separate sessions of about two hours each for the SG, the PHS bureau chiefs, and the top leaders of HEW and one of each of the top echelon from the three operating bureaus.

The visual briefing furnished the occasion for giving the PHS and departmental hierarchy their first intelligence on the proposed new organization. The tight security arrangements the Study Group had been maintaining were deliberately tightened during the second phase because, as Hundley said, "We didn't want anybody to react to some fragment of the plan, without understanding what the plan in its entirety was." Not even the SG knew the contents of the organization document.

When the preview session began, the audience saw the charts by means of two color transparency projectors. On one was flashed a word chart that stated tersely the objectives for each new organizational unit. While this remained on the screen, a brief word chart listing the principal problems of the existing organization appeared on the second screen. Then, while the "problems" chart remained, the scene in the first projector shifted to a diagram of the existing PHS, showing by means of distinctive colors the various organizational entities whose unification was proposed. The purpose of this one was to display forcefully the scatter of existing programs. This "scatter" chart was retained, while on the second screen appeared a word chart describing the new organizational unit. This remained in view, while a traditional organization chart of the proposed new structure was projected on the first screen.

As Morris and the staff people saw it, the sequence of presentation, bureau by bureau, was very important. The presentation began with an outline of the new Bureau of Environmental Health, since a new unit for those activities seemed inevitable. The next chart showed the BSS, from which most of the environmental programs were to be taken. The denuded BSS was then given unity and form by an indication of the new programs and units that would be added to it. This sequence was designed to give an impression of inevitability to the proposals. The presentation ended with plans for the OSG, the "superstructure." Its form seemed almost predestined, in view of the proposals for the operating units.

The group imposed a parlor gag rule at the showings. Questions were forbidden during the chart projections. At the end, questions of only one kind were permitted, those designed to clarify *what* the group proposed, not *why*. At the conclusion of each briefing session, the reorganization document was distributed. Each official had nearly a week to study it before the second summit meeting.

A great deal of work went into these presentations to make the plan attractive. Hundley rated them an unqualified success. "Not everything we proposed was applauded but the lucidity of our presentation was."

Consultants' Role

As the planning phase ended, the Study Group members took occasion to reflect on the part played by the outside consultants. They concluded that they could not have done the job without the consultants. Each had provided a vital service. Sayre, who had sat with the group through some half-dozen sessions, had played the role of detached observer. He refused to make any substantive judgments. Instead, he listened to the discussions while the group searched for solutions and occasionally helped the members see where their plans might be leading, and what reactions might be expected from other levels of government or from clientele organizations and interest groups. Morris's contribution had come principally during the organization phase. He had worked out the study plan before coming to Washington, and he met the group several times on Saturdays to consult on the progress of the work. By the time the Study Group had finished its work, he had joined the staff of the Budget Bureau in Washington. Both consultants were "irreplaceable," Hundley said.

The last item remaining before the second summit meeting was a decision from the SG on what he wanted the meeting to accomplish. The Study Group hoped it would be a forum at which the various Service points of view would emerge, points of view that would furnish the SG the guidance and opinion he needed to make decisions. Burney confirmed their hope, saying he wanted the consensus of the group to come out at the meeting. He would make his decisions later.

REVIEW AND ACCEPTANCE OF A REORGANIZATION PLAN

On March 28, thirty-three persons gathered once again at the Marriott Motel for the second summit conference. The participants were the same people who had reviewed the mission document some six weeks earlier. This time the presence of the departmental representatives was sanctioned officially and unofficially.

Members of the Study Group took their places with the relaxed air of seasoned veterans. The greater part of their work was behind them, and they had survived the first summit. Nothing that followed could be worse, they reasoned. They believed they were as capable as anybody else of making the "right" decisions on PHS organization.

Finally, they had done everything possible to load the scales in favor of their reorganization plan. They were poised and confident.

As the meeting opened, Dr. Hundley rose to outline the discussion rules. First, the group was to discuss the concept of each new bureau. Once there was general agreement, the group would consider division structure, the details of whether a particular function should have division status, whether the division was properly located, and so forth. Thirdly, staff office functions were to be discussed, and, lastly, implementation.

Dr. Burney presided, but Dr. Porterfield acted as chairman. The second summit was being held, Porterfield said, to get views and opinions from the hierarchy of the Service. The plan being presented was to be attacked and defended mercilessly, but, he added, the participants were not going to have the opportunity to vote for or against it. Dr. Burney spoke only once or twice as the PHS chief. Most of the time he was an interested, alert spectator, and he observed parliamentary procedure with fine punctilio.

The discussions proceeded smoothly along the prescribed paths. There were no acrimonious arguments, no blocs or factions. The group was "integrated." In every case but one, the various reviewers—the bureau chiefs, chief professional officers, and others—made their comments as individuals. However, Dr. Shannon spoke for himself as Director of NIH and in addition reported the views of some of the Institute directors and other NIH personnel, particularly Dr. Robert H. Felix, Director of the National Institute of Mental Health. (Dr. Felix did not rely exclusively on his chief; he made plans immediately to discuss the proposed NIMH transfers with the executive director of a nongovernmental national mental health organization at an early luncheon at a Washington club. (See page 49.)

The HEW men offered advice and personal opinions on the proposals. Their concerns were generally with the contiguous boundaries the Service had with other areas of government. James Kelly of the Office of Financial Management asked whether the group had translated the proposed organization into budget items. They had not, he was told. He then proposed that the SG name a committee soon to make arrangements for funding the new organization. He hoped the new system would come closer than the existing one to funding by bureau.

One member of the Study Group (Murtagh) made this comment: "Needless to say, we would like to preserve the money-drawing power of the categorical identification[5] and still proceed for maximum decentralization of responsibility for administration. In other words, we would like to work out an appropriation structure which will allow us to have our cake and eat it."

Another departmental representative, Edward Rourke, asked whether the Study Group had proposed that any function then exercised by PHS be turned over to another agency of government. He asked particularly about the possibility of shifting the regulatory program of the Biologics Division, which ensured the safety and purity of serums, vaccines, and antitoxins, from NIH to the Food and Drug Administration, a separate regulatory agency in HEW. Some thought had been given in the past to a transfer, Rourke said. Hundley answered that the group had touched briefly on it but had decided against a transfer, because the Biologics Division did not carry out its regulatory functions in the same spirit or manner as the Food and Drug Administration.

The reviewers leafed through the proposals and quickly came to agreement on the general concept for two bureaus, Environmental Health and Beneficiary Care.

Discussion grew lively when the reviewers turned to the question of the new organizational arrangement for health manpower and health services. They asked what plans had been made for locating programs not yet authorized or for a considerable enlargement of programs then existing in only rudimentary form. Among these were aid to medical education by a program of grants for construction of medical, dental, and nursing schools; medical insurance; and medical care for the aged.

The Study Group had proposed that aid to medical education, when and if it were authorized, should be located in the Bureau of Health Services rather than with the existing research facilities construction program at NIH—a possible alternative. Burney, acknowledging the NIH know-how and experience, asked Dr. Shannon's advice on the proper locus. Shannon laid no claim to the program.

On medical economics, Hundley assured the reviewers that the Study Group had concerned

[5] The reference was to potent private organizations that supported congressional appropriations for research in specific fields such as heart disease, cancer, muscular dystrophy, mental health, etc.

itself only with determining the proper location for studies of medical care organization and financing. He explained that the group believed the Service should build up competence and knowledge of medical economics. The location of a studies unit in the Bureau of Health Services did not mean that the Service was using this opportunity to seek enactment of legislation providing for medical insurance.

The problems of the aged, which often took the form of chronic diseases, had become a strong political force, one reviewer noted. He suggested that this increasing "visibility" meant that some organizational entity should be created. Hundley explained the Study Group's conclusion that services to the aged should be treated as a staff office because the federal government rendered a variety of services to the aged that cut across a multiplicity of federal agencies.

The conferees indicated that they leaned toward one bureau for both health services and health resources—Plan 1.

National Institute of Mental Health

The discussion, which continued throughout the day, turned several times, almost inevitably, to the problem that had already developed as the group's most sensitive proposal—transfer of NIMH functions. The matter ceased to be a talking point when the reviewers reached the proposal for a Bureau for National Health Intelligence, for it was on the decision of the NIMH Biometrics Branch that the bureau concept for health intelligence functions hung.

The Study Group had recommended that the statistical activities of the Biometrics Branch concerned with national measures of mental illness and the patient population of mental institutions be transferred from NIMH to a Division of Mental Health Statistics in the new bureau. The group had also recommended, in line with its proposals that NIH should concentrate more exclusively on research, that three other NIMH programs (nonresearch training, community services, and so-called Title V project grants) be transferred to other PHS units. The changes would mean a cut of about fifty per cent in the NIMH budget.

Dr. Shannon, chief of the NIH bureau, was torn between his accord with the "logic" of splitting off some of the NIMH functions and sympathy with his Institute director, Dr. Felix, who wanted to preserve intact an orderly, well-functioning mental health operation. Shannon considered a transfer of NIMH's community services functions inevitable, but at the same time he gave notice that he was going to allow Felix to wage his own campaign for continuity. He told the conferees he had promised to speak for Felix in the meeting, but he asked the SG and the Deputy SG to give Felix some consideration before making up their minds.

Dr. Shannon summed up the dilemma. For one thing, NIMH was doing a good job in community services. Dr. David Price of BSS, agreeing readily, said he was unprepared to support wholeheartedly any takeover of these NIMH activities. On the other hand, said Shannon, the effects must be considered of this "intense preoccupation with the training of service personnel . . . on the development of the other functions of the Institute."

> And I think that there is a definite, at least I so interpret it, preoccupation of top management in the NIMH with problems that are very pressing, that are urgent, but nonetheless are practical and somewhat removed from the overall mission of NIH.

Some of the bureau chiefs supported continuation of the mental illness statistics function at NIMH. Dr. Lowry of BMS, who had served from 1947 to 1954 as chief of the Community Services Branch of NIMH, praised highly the work of the Biometrics Branch. One of the Study Group members, trying to put the proposal in focus, explained carefully that it was not proposed that the Biometrics Branch be stripped, but that only one activity, the census of mental institutions—a function acquired from the Census Bureau—would be transferred out and grouped with other national health statistics. The function of the Biometrics Branch concerned with experiment design would be left at NIMH.

Shannon explained that the statistical function was Dr. Felix's most intimate concern. "I think this would require very extended negotiations . . . to determine that which was straightforward service as opposed to that which was program-based or oriented." Shannon went on to explain the importance, as he saw it, of mental illness statistics to program. Fifty per cent of all hospital beds in the nation was occupied by mental patients. "The studies are continuously modified to bring out changes in the composition of that group. This is the most important single factor to mental health programs in the country," he said.

Dr. Burney gave notice of his neutrality. As a

general principle, he felt it proper to follow recognized administration and organization principles, but "there are times when it's wise to be inconsistent. . . ." Although the community service activities in heart and cancer were working well outside NIH and although he supported the Study Group's recommendation for transfer of the Field Investigations and Demonstrations Branch of the National Cancer Institute to the new community service bureau, he indicated that he would not necessarily favor transfer of similar NIMH functions.

The immediate effect of the discussions of NIMH's statistical activities was to downgrade the proposal for a Bureau of National Health Intelligence. The consensus of the meeting was that centralized intelligence activities should be launched with only two functions—the National Health Survey and the National Office of Vital Statistics. Final decision on the Biometrics Branch of NIMH was, of course, deferred.

Office of the Surgeon General

The organization of the Surgeon General's Office involved another problem area, the position of the chief professional officers. The Study Group had been divided for a time about whether or not to recommend their abolition. The members eventually concluded that it was prudent to retain them and to recommend that they continue to serve approximately the same functions. The group was unable to agree on criteria for creating chief professional officers for other professions—toxicologists, epidemiologists, social workers, and others—that were pressing for similar organizational recognition.

The chief professional officers, aware that their status was uncertain, had spoken during the early interview sessions about the importance of their functions in recruiting, in representing the Service with their professions, and in providing high-level supra-bureau advice to the SG.

The conferees at the summit meeting agreed with the Study Group's concept of the OSG as a staff function divorced from operations. Only Burney voiced a dissent; he said he would reserve judgment on how much of international health he would continue as an *operating* function of the OSG.

However, the conferees, particularly the departmental men, called the Study Group to task for failing to make final recommendations for the organization of the OSG. The criticism was directed to two points. One was the fact that supervisory duties were not specifically apportioned among the four persons in the top executive box (SG, Deputy SG, Assistant Deputy SG, and Executive Officer); the other was that the proposed arrangement overloaded the SG by requiring some twenty-five people to report to him. On the latter point, Rufus Miles spoke fervently of the importance of spelling out the duties and responsibilities of the persons holding top staff jobs immediately beneath the SG and the Deputy SG—"staff vice presidents," he described them. He said the functions these people exercised should not be defined in terms of line functions.

> Their proper mission really is to relate to functions which cut across the bureau structure, so that you have a kind of warp and woof, you have your key staff people concerned about problems that are common to the several bureaus which, therefore, require a different kind of perspective than that which any particular bureau chief may have.

Dr. Hundley defended the group. He said members deliberately refrained from spelling out details of the division of labor in order to give the SG freedom to apportion the responsibilities himself.

The reviewers ratified the Study Group's recommendation that the regional medical directors, who represented the SG in the regions, should continue to have direct access to him. The Study Group, by providing direct links from the regional directors to the SG, in effect legitimized the existing working arrangement. The regional offices were then administered by the BSS, and the formal channel was to the SG through the chief of the BSS.

Informing the Bureau of the Budget

Before disbanding, the conferees discussed the time and manner of presenting the plans to the Budget Bureau in the Executive Office of the President. The bureau, of course, was concerned in two respects: it had to pass on legislation and it required details on what the new organizational structure meant in terms of staff, money, and overhead. Until this time, the bureau knew only the general scheme for conducting the study. On February 25 the Study Group had discussed with Budget Bureau representatives the general plan for conducting the study and for drafting plans for the reorganization.

The majority of the conferees, including Dr. Burney, favored an immediate conference with full disclosure of the working plans and the various alternatives being considered. They believed it was an important psychological move to bring in the Budget Bureau as early as possible—even *before* HEW clearance. One participant, R. W. Bunch, a bureau executive officer (civil service) and an alumnus of the Budget Bureau, summarized this line of reasoning. He thought it the better part of wisdom, and fairness, to take the agency along in all the plans, even before decisions were made, "because once decisions are made, there is no point in briefing them on what you had as your background material."

One bureau chief (Shannon) opposed early notification. He argued that the Budget Bureau men, concerned over details, cautious in reaching decisions, and painfully slow in acting, should be brought aboard only after HEW clearance. He proposed that the Secretary of HEW negotiate directly with the Director of the Budget. Caulk reminded the conferees that the PHS, at the time the Study Group was formed, had agreed to brief the Budget Bureau at the appropriate time, and argued that the "appropriate" time was immediately. The unanimous desire for legislation tipped the scales in favor of early presentation.

After two days of open discussion and a consensus in some areas, the summit meeting broke up. There was widespread agreement that the Study Group had "produced" a smash success. Departmental representatives who had viewed the gathering with some misgivings were among those who turned in rave reviews. They agreed that although the first meeting was handled poorly, the second was carried off imaginatively and successfully.[6] Dr. Hundley considered the meeting a "success" and said that general approval of the group's organizational concepts emerged from it.

The summit settled two broad questions: Plan 1, with one bureau to house health services and health resources, was accepted; and health intelligence functions were grouped together but were not considered important enough for bureau status. It remained for Burney to confirm these decisions.[7] (Formal HEW and Budget Bureau approval, of course, had to be secured.)

Post-Summit Decisions

The following day, March 30, Study Group members gathered once again at the penthouse to assess the impact of the summit and to press for answers to the stream of remaining questions. Two hours later, Porterfield joined the group and proposed that he and Hundley close in on the SG for some decisions.

Burney was ready. Once Plan 1 was accepted in broad outline, there remained a series of decisions affecting the location of specific units. After asking for Hundley's recommendation, Burney made a series of decisions governing the location of several divisions.

Burney saw the NIMH situation as a potentially dangerous one. If he supported the Study Group and pushed the NIMH reforms, he could expect Dr. Felix to resist, and there would be a family fight. His term as SG was drawing to a close. The question of whether he would be reappointed for a second four-year term would be decided in January 1961 by the man who would succeed President Eisenhower. The situation discouraged any unnecessary disturbances with NIMH and its strong allies among professional and citizens' groups active in the mental health-psychiatry field.

For the moment, then, Burney instructed Porterfield and Hundley to get Felix's views and to try to come to terms with him. These two met with Felix in a series of conferences in early April. Although the meetings produced no firm agreements, Hundley was instructed by Dr. Burney to draft the Study Group's final report in terms of a transfer of the NIMH community services functions.

Congress Speaks on NIMH

While these intramural negotiations on NIMH were taking place, efforts at exercising control were going on in other areas. All during March and April, the House and Senate Appropriations

[6] A subsequent self-study conducted by another HEW unit, the Office of Education, employed the same general method for presenting its recommendations on reorganization to its "Board of Directors." Stanley recommended the procedure, based on the success of the PHS at the second summit.

[7] Departmental people objected to the PHS habit of calling these actions of the SG "decisions." Real "decisions," they felt, required the assent of the Secretary of HEW, since the statutes involved the Secretary in the establishment, dissolution, or transfer of PHS organizational units down to the division level.

Committees had been going over the PHS budget proposals for 1960-1961.

The Senate subcommittee, which was chaired by Senator Hill, followed its long custom of interesting itself in the minutiate of NIH organization, and it offered the PHS planners a tip. "The committee is definitely opposed to any efforts to transfer the clinical training programs of the NIMH to any proposed overall training division of the Public Health Service." The committee argued that the training programs were an inseparable part of the NIMH battle against mental illness.

> Since the inception of the Institute in 1948, these training programs have been an integral part of a united comprehensive offensive against mental illness. Planning for the clinical training of psychiatrists, general practitioners, psychologists, and others, is, because of the nationwide scarcity of psychiatric personnel at the present time, probably the most important single mission of the Institute.

The committee's report (Senate Committee on Appropriations, Departments of Labor and HEW, and related agencies) was dated June 14, 1960, but the information it contained was part of general currency before then. The Subcommittee on Labor-HEW had a small staff. The section expressing opposition to transfer of training functions was drafted by Mike Gorman, a crusader for improved mental hospitals and director of a voluntary association in the mental health area.

The Budget Bureau's Review

Meanwhile, negotiations were going forward with the Budget Bureau. The Burney-Caulk desire for early consultation prevailed, and around March 31 the Budget Bureau was given a "little summit," which included the visual briefing, a copy of the organization document, and an opportunity for discussion and explanation.

The PHS, HEW, and the Budget Bureau had to decide what form the authorization of reorganizations should take. It was theoretically possible for the desired changes to be achieved by means of a reorganization proposal that Congress could vote for or against but not alter. Presidential authority to submit such reorganization plans had been extended. However, the reorganization plan route was rejected because, for one thing, it would involve clearance by another set of congressional committees (House and Senate Government Operations) rather than the Service's legislative committees. The former did not include PHS's congressional supporters, Representative Fogarty and Senator Hill. Another argument for straight legislation was that the proposal contemplated amendments to other PHS laws, and it was inappropriate for these matters to be handled in a reorganization plan. The decision to attempt straight legislation posed problems for the framers of the bill. Proposed legislation would have to have a positive appeal for Congress, whereas presidential reorganization plans would take effect in the absence of negative action (within sixty days of submission) on the part of Congress.

The Budget Bureau's man for PHS estimates was Hirst Sutton (chief of the Labor and Welfare Division), a career employee who had spent a good many years at the Budget Bureau in the Office of Organization and Management. His professional interest led him to probe deeply into the whys and wherefores of the organizational arrangements. Sutton and his colleagues had long felt frustration over the limits that existing law put on the Surgeon General's freedom to create new organizational forms for developing needs, and for several years they had pressed the PHS to break out of the statutory bonds. Naturally any plan for additional flexibility was welcomed at the Budget Bureau.

However, a snag in the negotiations developed. The 1944 public health statute (Public Health Service Act, 58 Stat. 682, 42 USC 201) had consolidated and revised existing public health laws. That law declared that the Service consisted of four bureaus, which were listed by name—the OSG, NIH, BMS, and BSS. It authorized the Surgeon General to assign, distribute, or transfer functions among them but forbade any changes at the division level or above without the HEW Secretary's concurrence.

Other provisions of law and amendments of the basic statute dipped deep into the PHS to prescribe certain forms of organization. Some housekeeping laws also referred to bureaus or other units. One such provision was a section applicable to personnel, the well-known Section 208(g) of the Public Health Service Act, that enabled the PHS to employ scientists and other specialized technical people at supergrade positions. It allowed 150 supergrade positions and specified that 115 were to be employed in one bureau, NIH. The elaborate crisscrossing of statutory references to bureaus, divisions, and other units constituted an intricate tapestry that depicted past and present political tensions and adjustments.

The PHS people thought complete flexibility was desirable, but they did not consider it a likelihood. Therefore they argued that it was sheer folly to think, as the men of the Budget Bureau did, of trying to get an open-end bill through Congress. They pointed out additionally that the current session of Congress was already well advanced; that the term would undoubtedly be a short one because of the coming presidential election; that a bill asking only for organizational flexibility lacked appeal; and that in view of the preoccupation with NIH of the Senate's legislative and appropriations committees on health, it would be wise to capitalize on NIH appeal by listing the bureaus by name, starting with NIH, and continuing with the new ones to be created.

The Budget Bureau team indicated a reluctance to approve such language on grounds that it was too binding and that the nomenclature of the new bureaus was sloppy. Sutton argued that it was faulty logic to seek organizational flexibility in a piece of legislation that spelled out the bureaus by name, one by one.

There was an impasse for a week or so, during which the top PHS officials, supported by the department's Assistant Secretary for Legislation, tried to bring Sutton and his colleagues around to their point of view. Both HEW and the PHS agreed on the form the legislation should take, and departmental clearance was given in a routine fashion.

At length, the two groups agreed on a draft form proposed by the PHS that would combine open-end flexibility with a statement that the PHS would consist of the major units then in existence. This meant the draft would refer to the OSG, the NIH, the BMS, and the National Library of Medicine and "such other bureaus or other constituent units as the SG may find appropriate. . . ." It would not list the BSS, since that bureau was to be split in two, and it would not list the new bureaus to be created. A draft bill incorporating this agreement was forwarded to the Budget Bureau on May 5.

Agreement still had to be reached on other matters to be covered in the legislation, among them a proposal for raising the number of general grade officers in the Service, and it was not until May 27 that the Budget Bureau gave its formal assent to the draft. Approval was carried in a letter dated May 27 from Budget's Assistant Director for Legislative Reference to the Secretary of HEW.

The Study Group continued to work as a body until April 15, when it was formally disbanded. During that time the members were engaged in refining the proposals, planning for legislation, drafting the final report, and recommending key officials to head the new structures. After April 15 the task of drafting the final report was left with Dr. Hundley and the staff. The report was, of course, reviewed by the members on completion.

It was not until the end of April that the reorganization plan was unveiled for the PHS rank and file. The reviewers at the second summit had suggested that the two-day session of the big brass might indicate to employees that major changes were being considered and that it was important for morale reasons to present the reorganization plans to personnel throughout the Service. The talk was in terms of two large meetings, one for PHS people downtown, the other for NIH people at Bethesda. However, at that time Dr. Shannon had cautioned against calling a meeting at Bethesda until some firm decisions had been made about NIMH; temporizing, he had said, would injure morale among NIMH employees.

On April 25 Burney and Hundley called the PHS staff downtown to a meeting in the large HEW auditorium to explain the reorganization plans. There the two men discussed the plans that had been made and the hope for early implementation. The following day they went to Bethesda to present the plan to employees of NIH.

Plans for Legislation

The Surgeon General had originally hoped that the work of the Study Group would culminate in legislation, and his timetable provided that the proposals would be cleared with HEW and the Budget Bureau by May 1. They would be then ready for transmittal to Congress. Two factors were involved in Dr. Burney's thinking.

The first was the assumption that the PHS might be under pressure from Capitol Hill to unify environmental health activities in a hurry. The Fogarty Subcommittee was determined—according to word reaching PHS—to bring about a consolidation of the environmental units and it might have taken matters into its own hands. It could have done this either by ordering its own form of reorganization (possibly by creating a new institute at NIH) or by consolidating all the budget items on environmental health functions for the coming fiscal year.

The second was the conviction of the PHS directorate, based both on management concepts and on the hope of riding the psychological momentum, that the entire reorganization should go through as a continuous process rather than piecemeal.

Although the time was not ripe for presenting the legislation formally to Congress, Burney conferred informally with various key members of the House near the end of April before going abroad for international health meetings. He devoted a good part of two days (April 20-21) to conferences with both Democratic and Republican members of the House Interstate and Foreign Commerce Committee (Oren Harris, chairman, Democrat; John Bennett, ranking Republican; Paul Schenck, Republican; Kenneth Roberts, chairman of the Commerce Committee's Health Subcommittee, Democrat) and a member of the Health Subcommittee of the House Appropriations Committee (Melvin Laird, Republican).

Liaison at the top between the PHS and Capitol Hill dropped off during the first three weeks in May when Burney was outside the country. The Deputy SG was almost wholly occupied during that same time with the various highly publicized and controversial bills providing health care for the aged on which the Ways and Means Committee was conducting hearings.

Burney returned to his desk at the end of May. He concluded, after conferences with Representative Oren Harris on May 31 and with Senator Lister Hill's secretary on June 1, that the possibility for legislation that session was dim. It was at this time—May 27—that the Budget Bureau gave formal approval to the proposed legislation, and the PHS was free to send to Congress its suggested bill draft.

Despite discouraging prospects for passage of the legislation, HEW took the step of forwarding bill drafts formally to Congress. "Dear Mr. Speaker" and "Dear Mr. President" letters were sent to the House and Senate on May 31. A few days later, identical bills were introduced in the House by Representatives Harris (H.R. 12590) and Bennett, the ranking Republican on the House Commerce Committee (H.R. 12250).

Senator Hill, the logical sponsor in the Senate, chose not to introduce the legislation. His stated explanation was that he was unwilling to sponsor a Republican administration bill. However, Hill had serious reservations about the effect of the reorganization, particularly on NIMH, and wanted more time to find out what was involved. His committee had already reached a conclusion that the NIMH clinical training programs should not be transferred.

There was no action whatever on the legislation in the House or the Commerce Committee. There was no push or drama in the bill itself, and Representative Harris could see no reason to schedule hearings. After a legislative statement that the PHS "Shall consist of" the Office of the Surgeon General, NIH, BMS, and National Library of Medicine, the bill delegated authority to the SG to create such other bureaus or constituent units as he found appropriate.

Request to the Secretary of HEW

Burney then decided (as he had previously indicated he might) to go as far as he could within the limits of his administrative authority and thus "to accomplish many of the major purposes of the reorganization in the near future." On June 7 he directed to the Secretary of HEW a formal request for authority to go ahead with administrative reorganization. Burney outlined the advantages in moving ahead.

> It would also enable us to regroup existing programs and functions so that final reorganization would be achieved easily when legislative authority is obtained. This would permit me to designate the key officials to be responsible for new groups of functions and these officials could assume the administrative burdens of preparing detailed functional statements, job descriptions, budget estimates, etc., for their respective enterprises. It would also avoid the uncertainties that result from delay and, at the same time, take advantage of the momentum and enthusiasm generated within the Service by the excellent work of the Study Group.

After reminding the Secretary that Miles, Kelly, and Stanley of his staff had participated in a number of the deliberations of the Study Group and had generally endorsed its findings, the SG asked the Secretary for permission to abolish, transfer, or create the new divisions as recommended by the group.

The SG went on to explain that he was not requesting blanket approval for all changes. Actual implementation of the organizational arrangements entailed drafting functional statements, new job descriptions, delegations of authority, and other administrative details that would be submitted to the Secretary as plans matured.

The SG notified the Secretary that some decisions were still up in the air.

> We are not, at this time, requesting your approval for all of the changes we may ultimately wish to make. Revisions in the structure and functions of the Office of the Surgeon General are still under study. . . . These include certain operating divisions, staff offices, and transfer of several programs from the National Institutes of Health, especially the National Institute of Mental Health. Several special task forces are now working out detailed plans. We will transmit our proposals in these areas at a later date.

On June 8, Miles and Stanley met with Dr. Burney and his staff. They told Burney that approval would be forthcoming but explained that the Secretary's assent did not constitute approval *ipso facto* of any organizational change proposed.

Following this, Miles drafted a brief memo to the Secretary endorsing the proposals for change and recommending that the Secretary accord the SG permission to proceed. The Secretary wrote a seven-line memo June 20 granting permission.

> I congratulate you [he said] on the fine job done by your Study Group on Mission and Organization of the Public Health Service. They have produced a report of impressive scope in a relatively short time.

The Final Study Group Report

On June 7, the Study Group had issued its final report with a printing of 10,000 copies. Some 7,000 of these copies were distributed.

The final report proposed the following arrangement of bureaus and divisions (see Figure 5).

1. BUREAU OF ENVIRONMENTAL HEALTH

This bureau emerged virtually unscathed in the post-summit deliberations. The final proposal called for six divisions. Five incorporated functions and responsibilities of existing organizational units (water pollution, radiological health, air pollution, occupational health, and general environmental health services—made up of programs dealing with safety of milk, food, shellfish, and other perishables in interstate commerce). The sixth division incorporated a new service—a research unit to conduct studies on the effects of economic, social, and political organization on environmental health.

2. BUREAU OF COMMUNITY HEALTH

This title replaced that of Bureau of Health Services, which the Study Group had used.

The other five divisions were formed by regrouping scattered activities and programs and upgrading others that had previously existed in rudimentary form. They were:

(1) A Division of Community Health Practice, a new enterprise whose way had to be paved by a task force. The report proposed that it have "unique" responsibilities for studies and action programs designed to unify and integrate general health services delivered through public and private channels. Other proposed functions included an expanded and intensified program of studies on medical care organization and financing; responsibility for general health grants, public health manpower activities, school health, and migrant labor; and concern with health problems in metropolitan areas.

(2) A Division of Communicable Diseases. This incorporated the functions of the Communicable Disease Center in Atlanta and the tuberculosis control program.

(3) A Division of Chronic Diseases. This included responsibility for heart, cancer, and other chronic disease programs, including *field research* and all community demonstrations. The heart and cancer control programs had formerly been part of the respective institutes at NIH but had been transferred to BSS units several years prior to this. The directors of the Heart and Cancer Institutes had not opposed assignment of these application and control functions from research to operating units. The Heart Disease Control Program had been transferred as recently as 1959. The success of the transplants was one of the factors that had moved the Study Group to recommend transfer of the NIMH functions as well as those of other Institutes.

(4) A Division of Medical Resources, a new organizational unit to promote ways and means of augmenting medical and related professional manpower.

(5) A Division of Mental and Social Health, a unit to focus major attention on studies in the social and behavioral sciences and to have program responsibility for community mental health services, alcoholism, juvenile delinquency, and drug addiction.

3. BUREAU OF MEDICAL SERVICES

This proposed bureau also emerged unscathed, except for change of name, from the Study Group's earlier recommendations. (The group had called it the Bureau of Beneficiary Care.) The proposed division of Federal Employees Health Services was in the incubation stage at the time. The Study Group felt that the PHS should take a strong leadership position to create and develop federal employee health activities, but existing budgetary and policy restrictions prevented it.

4. NATIONAL INSTITUTES OF HEALTH

The Study Group's report was unequivocal in

phrasing the NIH mission as conducting and supporting biological and medical research. The report called it an error to conceive of the NIH mission in terms of activities ranging from basic research to disease control and community programs.

With this guideline, the report proposed that NIH be divested of all responsibility for disease control, demonstrations, certain types of field research, and community service programs. The report thought it proper that NIH retain functions relating to research manpower and research facilities.

The report proposed that a task force be set up to decide which programs should be transferred, since often the decision on which programs were training for research and which were training for service was a hair-line one.

5. NATIONAL CENTER FOR HEALTH STATISTICS

This unit was mauled in the post-summit squeeze. Its original five divisions were reduced to two, the National Office of Vital Statistics and the National Health Survey, and it lost bureau status. Decisions on two statistical programs, mental health statistics and hospital data (then collected by the Division of Hospital and Medical Facilities), were postponed. "Further staff study will be required to determine whether these activities should be transferred or should remain in their present organizational location," the report said.

The report proposed that data processing and health trends analysis be treated as staff services.

6. NATIONAL LIBRARY OF MEDICINE

There were no problems with respect to this office.

7. OFFICE OF THE SURGEON GENERAL

The report made no changes here despite the critical comments of Rufus Miles. Some members of the Study Group conceded that lack of time prevented them from giving sufficient thought and effort to plans for creating a more dynamic organizational form for the OSG.

FIGURE 5:
NEW ORGANIZATION OF THE PUBLIC HEALTH SERVICE—1960

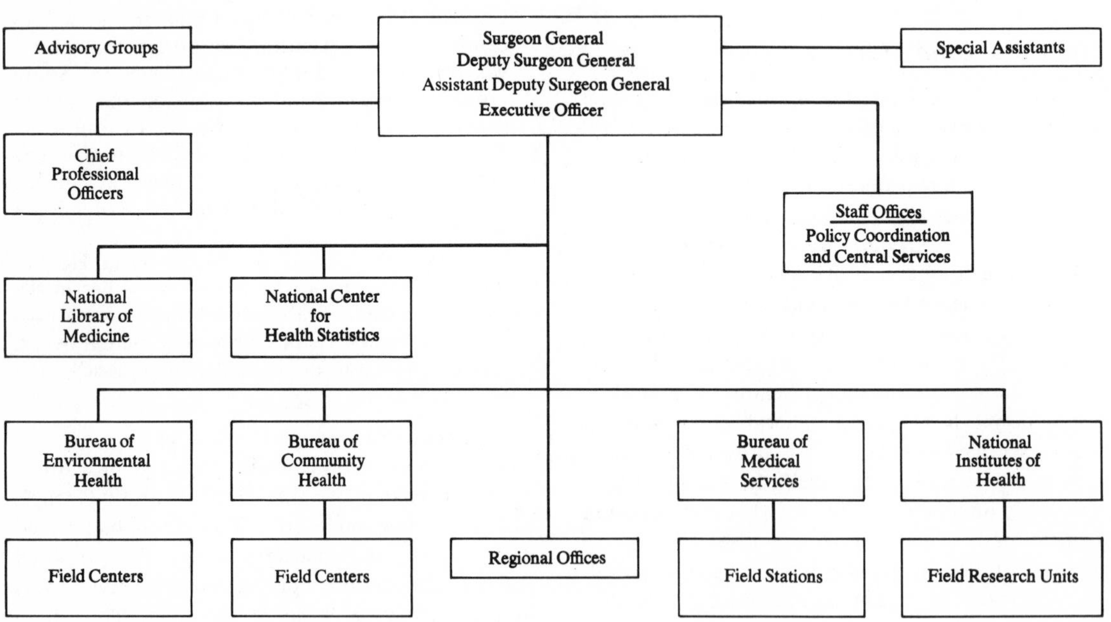

CARRYING OUT THE REORGANIZATION

With the Secretary's permission and the SG's authority and influence behind it, the reorganization began to move ahead. Burney designated Hundley to take charge of implementation and set up several task forces to plan details of the reorganizations for which the Study Group had sketched in only the broad outlines. In June, Hundley cleaned his desk at NIH and moved into an office downtown, adjacent to the SG's.

Some of the task forces were assigned jobs that required tact and diplomacy as well as organizational ability and knowledge of the Service. Others were given assignments of a more routine organizational nature. The critical task force jobs involved the establishment of new units, and as a first step the SG chose as chairman the person who would become chief of the new unit when it was activated. He thus sought to assure himself of the loyalty and understanding of the chiefs of the new units. The general formula he used for selecting the task force members had been devised by the Study Group; equal representation of the affected units and of so-called "neutrals." Burney selected the chairmen himself but consulted Hundley and Caulk on membership.

It came as a surprise to several members of the Study Group when they were chosen to head the SG's task forces on implementation. As early as the first summit meeting in February, the SG had asked the Study Group members to keep in mind the number of new positions that would open up when the reorganization proposals took effect. He had also asked them to suggest candidates to head the new units. The members had put together a confidential list of candidates, with six names suggested for each office. They had not listed their own names. The SG made his selections from this list and went beyond it only in choosing members of the Study Group for new assignments. (The SG selected the bureau chiefs who, in turn, selected the division chiefs, with the "consent" of the SG. The SG formally appointed them.) Five members of the Study Group (Hundley, Arnstein, Galagan, Hanson, and Magnuson) were to move upward to larger responsibilities in the Service.

There were only two deviations from the pattern of having the chief-designate of a new unit serve as chairman of the task force on implementation. The task force that consolidated the two dental units[8] was headed by the chief dental officer, and the task force that consolidated the two nursing units[9] was headed by the chief nurse officer. Thus, the SG continued to rely heavily on the chief professional officers. These two task forces were the first ones created and the first to report.

The initial memorandum paving way for creation of the dental task force was dated May 20, 1960. Dr. John W. Knutson, the Chief Dental Officer, was named chairman; and the task force of six persons included Dr. Donald J. Galagan, a Study Group member. There were no serious problems involved, and no opposition was raised. The task force brought in its report June 26. Dr. Galagan was chosen to head the merged divisions on August 1, and by September 1 the new Division of Dental Public Health and Resources officially came into being.

The new Division of Nursing Resources enjoyed a similarly smooth genesis. The task force reported on June 30; the new chief, another Study Group member—Miss Margaret Arnstein—was chosen August 8, and by September 1 the new division was operational.

Other task forces, with the following assignments, were activated in June and July after the SG was authorized to go ahead with reorganization:

(1) To create a new division in the Bureau of Environmental Health to handle general environmental services (milk, food, shellfish, and other perishables in interstate commerce).

(2) To create a new division in the Bureau of Environmental Health to handle environmental economics and organization.

(3) To create a new Division of Chronic Diseases in the Bureau of Community Health.

(4) To create a new Division of Mental and Social Health in the Bureau of Community Health, the basic unit being the Community

---

[8] Division of Dental Resources (BMS) and the Division of Dental Public Health (BSS) into the Division of Dental Public Health and Resources in the new Bureau of Community Health.

[9] Nursing Resources Division (BMS) and the Public Health Nursing Division (BSS) into the Division of Nursing Services and Resources in the new Bureau of Community Health.

Services Branch of the National Institute of Mental Health. (In this instance, too, the plan of having the chief-designate serve as task force chairman was modified. Miss Arnstein was chosen to head the task force to plan the new Division of Mental and Social Health, but the SG had no thought of naming her division chief.)

(5) To make detailed plans for the organization of the OSG.

(6) To study the field study, demonstration, and control activities of NIH and to decide which portions were appropriate for transfer to the Bureau of Community Health.

Implementation

Much of the implementation proceeded routinely. Some units were consolidated, others abolished at the operational level without agitation or dislocation.

Other proposals made by the Study Group caused grave disturbances of existing relationships, and painstaking diplomatic negotiations were involved before they could be brought into effect. In some cases the repercussions were so violent that changes were postponed. The prime example was the reorganization of the NIMH. That story will be told in the next chapter of this case study.

The SG had assured the Study Group and the Health Subcommittee of the House Appropriations Committee that he would go to the limit of his authority in carrying out the reorganization. He moved promptly to put some of the proposals into effect, particularly those that Congress had already informally endorsed. Although Congress adjourned without granting the SG authority to create new bureaus, Burney did the next best thing. He divided the BSS into two parts, comprising the major groupings of activities in environmental health and community health. He created, in effect, two common-law bureaus, functional entities that would assume legal status and grace once their existence was confirmed by law (see Figure 6). The "Bureau" of Environmental Health was the first to take shape. Two existing units, one on water supply and pollution and another on radiological health, were upgraded to provide the nucleus. The air pollution functions were combined in September to form one of its divisions; and at the same time the occupational health program, which had been a branch in BSS, was transplanted and upgraded to division status. Dr. Magnuson, who had been chief of the old branch, became the new division chief.

The "Bureau" of Community Health was slower to acquire operational status and assume new functions. Its first components were the Divisions of Nursing and of Dental Services and Resources. The Division of Hospitals and Medical Facilities was transferred to it November 20, 1960 (from BMS).

New Chiefs

The chief of the BSS, Dr. David Price, left that post in the fall of 1960 to become Deputy Director of NIH. He was succeeded by his deputy, Dr. T. J. Bauer. Bauer was slated to head the Bureau of Community Health when it was formally designated, and his principal deputies were to be Dr. A. W. Christianson as deputy chief and Richard W. Bunch as executive officer.

The chief-designate of the Bureau of Environmental Health was Dr. Robert J. Anderson, formerly a deputy chief of the BSS. His top aides were to be Harry G. Hanson (a Study Group member) as deputy chief and Lyman Moore (formerly Paul Caulk's deputy and liaison man with the Study Group) as executive officer.

In November 1960 Dr. Hundley became a permanent member of the downtown family when he was elevated to the rank of Assistant Surgeon General in the OSG. His areas of responsibility included implementation of the reorganization and supervision of the regional offices and of international health matters. The position was a new one.

A SPECIAL PROBLEM: NIMH

The PHS had first attacked mental disturbances by creating a Narcotics Division in 1929 to conduct research on drug addiction and to operate a hospital for the care of addicts. During the 1930's the division, then renamed Mental Hygiene Division, broadened its activities to include survey and consultation service to mental hospitals and consultation on community mental health programs. Two hospitals were established, one at Lexington, Kentucky, and another at Fort Worth, Texas.

FIGURE 6:
PUBLIC HEALTH SERVICE—1960

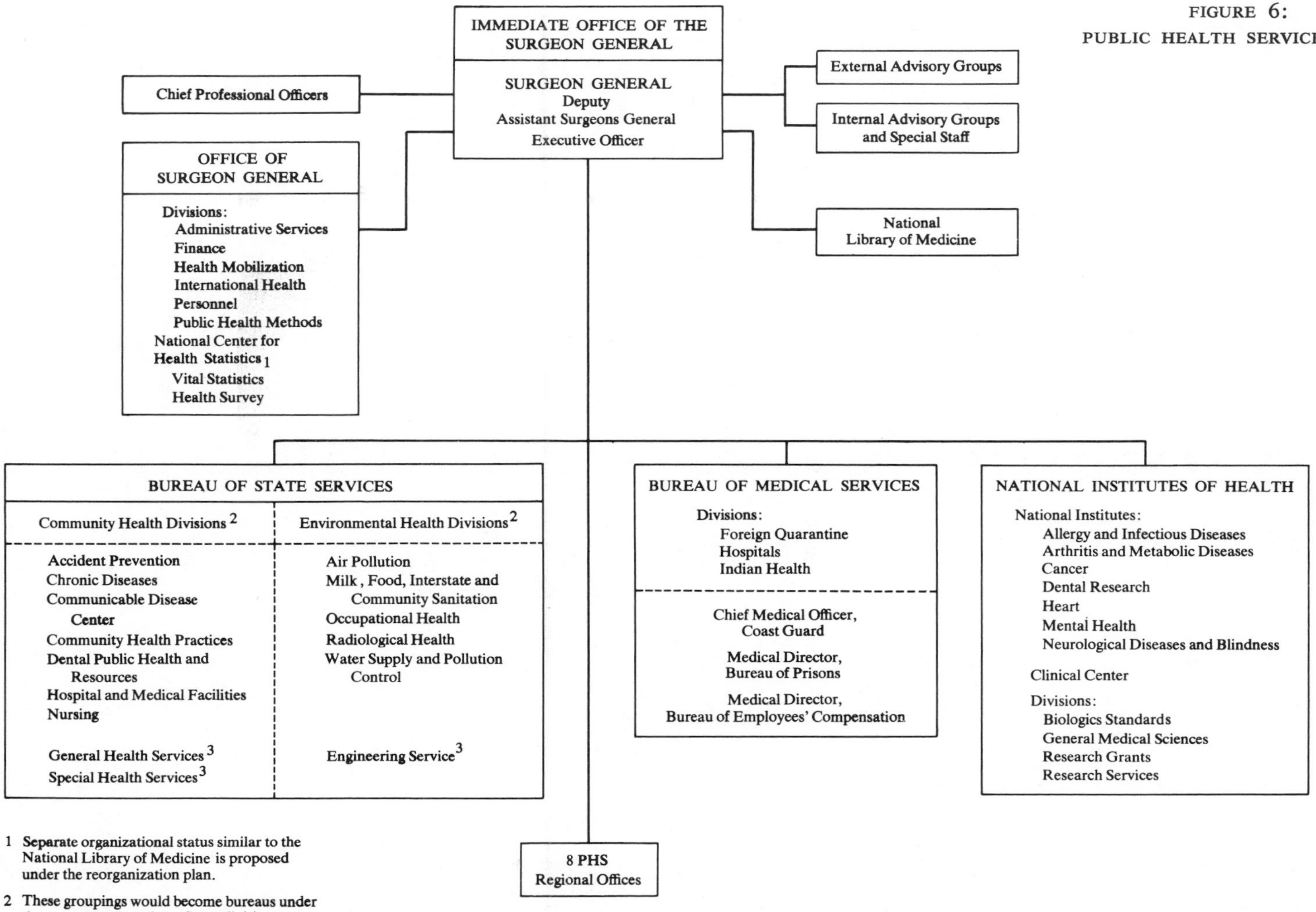

IMMEDIATE OFFICE OF THE SURGEON GENERAL

SURGEON GENERAL
Deputy
Assistant Surgeons General
Executive Officer

Chief Professional Officers

External Advisory Groups

Internal Advisory Groups and Special Staff

National Library of Medicine

OFFICE OF SURGEON GENERAL

Divisions:
Administrative Services
Finance
Health Mobilization
International Health
Personnel
Public Health Methods
National Center for Health Statistics [1]
Vital Statistics
Health Survey

BUREAU OF STATE SERVICES

Community Health Divisions [2]
Accident Prevention
Chronic Diseases
Communicable Disease Center
Community Health Practices
Dental Public Health and Resources
Hospital and Medical Facilities
Nursing

General Health Services [3]
Special Health Services [3]

Environmental Health Divisions [2]
Air Pollution
Milk, Food, Interstate and Community Sanitation
Occupational Health
Radiological Health
Water Supply and Pollution Control

Engineering Service [3]

BUREAU OF MEDICAL SERVICES

Divisions:
Foreign Quarantine
Hospitals
Indian Health

Chief Medical Officer, Coast Guard
Medical Director, Bureau of Prisons
Medical Director, Bureau of Employees' Compensation

NATIONAL INSTITUTES OF HEALTH

National Institutes:
Allergy and Infectious Diseases
Arthritis and Metabolic Diseases
Cancer
Dental Research
Heart
Mental Health
Neurological Diseases and Blindness

Clinical Center

Divisions:
Biologics Standards
General Medical Sciences
Research Grants
Research Services

8 PHS Regional Offices

1 Separate organizational status similar to the National Library of Medicine is proposed under the reorganization plan.

2 These groupings would become bureaus under the reorganization plan. Some divisions not listed but recommended by reorganization plan are still under consideration.

3 To be abolished as reorganization progresses.

In 1944 Dr. Robert H. Felix came to Washington to head the Mental Hygiene Division, a unit of the BMS. Previously he had been clinical director and then executive officer of the Lexington hospital; clinical director of the medical center for federal prisoners at Springfield, Missouri; and senior medical officer of the U.S. Coast Guard Academy. His training, orientation, and experience had emphasized treatment and services to victims of mental disorders.

Felix, born in 1904, was a Kansan, the son of a physician. An energetic person, engaging, talkative, and affable, he was determined to make mental illness as strong a concern to the public as it was to him. His geniality was sometimes mistaken for pliability. However, he was ambitious, and he wanted to see the techniques of psychiatry teamed with the resources of medical and biological sciences to alleviate mental illness.

It was not long before Dr. Felix made his mark in Washington. As soon as he got settled in his new job, he began to push his case. He wrote extensively on mental hygiene problems, he joined organizations, and he made speeches. He took an active part in such professional organizations as the American Psychiatric Association, the American Psychological Association, the National Association for Mental Health, the American Public Health Association, the National Medical Correction Association, the Association of Social Workers, and the National League of Nursing Education.

With support from some of these groups, Felix was able to block a reorganization proposed during the mid-1940's for the Division of Mental Hygiene. Plans had been made for the division's hospitals to be transferred to the Hospital Division of BMS and for its modest training programs to be transferred to a general training division. When he learned about the proposals, Felix alerted the professional associations and organizations, which in turn raised enough of a hue and cry with Congress to cause the reorganization to be dropped. The episode was instructive to Felix: he had not injected himself into the fight; rather, he had set in motion a successful commando operation, carried out primarily by professional societies, citizens' groups, and congressmen interested in mental health.

Soon afterward, Felix seized the initiative in expanding Service activities in mental health. He had long nourished the hope of establishment of a major research unit at NIH devoted to mental illness. He had the backing of the American Psychiatric Association, which since 1940 had advocated an increase in the PHS commitment to research in mental illness. In 1945 he set about launching the idea by drafting a legislative proposal. Federal Security Administration officials encouraged him and put him in touch with one of the legislative draftsmen in the General Counsel's Office. The result was a workable legislative draft that received the blessing of the SG.

Felix himself took the draft to Capitol Hill and left it with the chairman of the House committee concerned with health matters (Percy Priest, chairman of the Interstate and Foreign Commerce Committee). Felix learned from the newspapers soon afterward that Priest had introduced his bill in the House without altering a word of the draft.

Felix's efforts in the Senate were equally successful, and the result was the National Mental Health Act of 1946. A fruitful era of cooperation, association, and friendship began during this time between Senator Lister Hill and Dr. Felix.

The Mental Health Act authorized the construction of buildings and facilities, to be known as the National Institute of Mental Health, to serve as the focal point of research, experimentation, and advanced or specialized training, and as a clearinghouse for information on psychiatric disorders. It also established a National Advisory Mental Health Council to help the SG plan and develop a national mental health program, including recommendations on grants-in-aid for research projects. The Service was authorized to provide training, instruction, and demonstrations in the field of mental health and to make grants to the states for this purpose. The charter of the NIMH was sweeping; the 1946 act set for the Institute the goal of improving the mental health of the nation.

Dr. Felix became the director of the new Institute, which was opened in April 1949 on the "reservation" at Bethesda. The job then rated the rank of eagle, or Army colonel.[10] Establishment of NIMH was the realization of a great dream for Felix. As he described it, the Director of NIH (R. E. Dyer) "believed" in NIMH possibilities and "gave me my chance." Felix took advantage of the opportunity; he developed research and training programs, created a laboratory for intramural research, and projected greater plans for

[10] By 1957 NIMH activities had expanded to the point where the directorship carried star rank. On March 5, 1957, Dr. Felix, along with the director of the National Cancer Institute, was elevated to Assistant Surgeon General (a rank equivalent to rear admiral, lower grade).

the future. "My concern was to have an integrated program," he said.

Intimations of Change

Dr. Felix put up his guard when he learned that a study of the entire Service was being made in 1960 with a view to reorganization. He was disappointed that the job was being compressed into so brief a time span, feeling that three months was too short. Two other factors contributed to his malaise. One was his previous experience of sweeping reorganizations, and the other his estimate of the men and women chosen to do the job. He feared that the concept that had controlled the earlier reorganization was again the prevailing view—that like activities should go together. On the second count, he knew everybody in the Study Group well and thought all of them were biased against mental health programs. He said they were not happy about the extraordinary growth of NIMH and the wide spread of its activities.

The Study Group first came to grips with NIMH during an interview with Felix on January 23. On that occasion he was asked, as were the others interviewed, what he saw as the future of his unit. In the background was the fact that the Heart and Cancer Institutes had recently been divested of community demonstration projects. Felix replied in forthright fashion that he saw no reason to make any changes at NIMH. He explained that the diversity of the programs there had fostered the first and only comprehensive federal attack on the problems of mental illness. These programs included, in addition to laboratory and clinical research, collection of mental health statistics (Biometrics Branch); community services, including technical assistance and formula grants to the states (Community Service Branch); and large training programs both for clinical service and for research. Although the Study Group had witnessed resistance on the part of several bureau chiefs and division heads who were reluctant to face the prospect of a reordering of their units, the group considered Dr. Felix unusually stiff. (The Study Group people by this time had shed the first stages of insularity and were ready to take an olympian view of the Service. Feeling that they had "freed" themselves from their own program moorings, they found Felix obstinate in his refusal to acknowledge that better organizational arrangements were possible or that mental health could be served better through any other arrangement. The Study Group encountered the same resistance to change when it interviewed various branch chiefs at NIMH. Dr. Morton Kramer, chief of the Biometrics Branch, was adamant, as was Dr. Raymond Feldman, head of the Training Branch.)

The next encounter between Felix and the Study Group occurred at the sneak preview given the NIH people on March 23. This was a large meeting—with the seven Institute directors, their staffs, and others—about 150 people. One of the Study Group members tipped Felix off at the entrance to the auditorium. "Bob, you're going to flip when you hear this," Felix was told. He was also told that it was useless to protest or to fight the decision, which had the force and prestige of being unanimous. (However, according to Felix's intelligence reports, there had been a division among the Hundley group although the recommendation had emerged as a unanimous one.)

Felix was angry and aroused to the boiling point. Frustrated by the house rules barring explanations, he had to rely for information on the Study Group's draft report, numbered copies of which were distributed to top staff at NIH after the preview. He got no comfort from the report, which said:

> It is proposed to transfer to other units of the PHS the nonresearch training programs of the various Institutes, the Community Service Program and Title V project grants of the National Institute of Mental Health, the Field Investigations and Demonstrations Branch of the National Cancer Institute, and the statistical activities of the Biometrics Branch of the NIMH concerned with national measures of mental illness and the patient population of mental institutions.

Felix said he could not learn whether the transfers would be made immediately or spaced out gradually. It was not made clear, he maintained, that the SG had yet to act on the NIMH proposals—that they were indeed only "proposals." He concluded that time was short, that with the prevailing attitude "downtown," he had to act fast—had to drop a blockbuster in order to gain time.

(It was within the realm of possibility that when the community service and other functions were shaved off NIMH, the Institute directorship would no longer have carried star rank. Only one other Institute director had star rank. However, the Study Group never considered transferring or "demoting" Dr. Felix. On the contrary, it thought of suggesting his name for two jobs, Institute director and chief of the proposed Division of Mental and Social Health.)

Dr. Felix's Attitude

Dr. Felix's position on the proposed separations was this: He was willing, even anxious, to get BSS, or an equivalent *service* branch, to take over some of mental health's community service operations—but only when the time was ripe. He believed transfers should take place gradually so that the new functions could become engrafted onto the new structure without dislocation. For ten years he had tried without success to interlard various service programs in the field with behavioral science and mental health concepts—to imbue professional workers and the community with *"mens sana in corpore sano"* ideas. He had crusaded—successfully—to get psychiatric field personnel to take advanced public health training; some six or eight NIMH regional psychiatric consultants had taken masters' degrees in public health during the 1950's. "I tried to get every regional psychiatric consultant trained in public health," he said.

In 1958 Dr. Felix had participated in a special conference—called at his insistence—with the seven regional medical directors in order to trade information, experience, and plans for mental health activities. Felix had explained plans in the making to push mental health aspects in programs like alcoholism, chronic diseases and aging, juvenile delinquency, and school health. He had also sought to learn how NIMH could be helpful in the regional programs of public health.

Felix had unveiled for the directors a new career development plan under which NIMH would lend mental health personnel to various public health programs in the field. The plan—still on the drawing board at that time—had involved giving advanced psychiatric training to Service personnel and possibly to outsiders also, later commissioning them into the Service. These people would then move into various operating programs as the psychiatric members of the team. The regional directors had been enthusiastic about the plans.

Felix had experienced no difficulty "communicating" with the regional medical directors. He said they understood mental health concepts and wanted to cooperate in plowing them into operating programs. He enjoyed no such understanding among the PHS people "downtown." The void was far greater than the eight miles that separated NIH from headquarters. Felix claimed there was a feeling of uneasiness among the people downtown about psychiatry, an uncertainty that it was a discipline ranking equally with clinical medicine, a feeling that psychiatry still had to come out of the woods and free itself of mumbo-jumbo. The headquarters people were civilized, of course. They did not denounce psychiatry and psychotherapy techniques. Rather, or so it seemed to Felix, they revealed their uneasiness in a plethora of psychiatrist jokes and other protective, reassuring mannerisms. He also felt that he was an outsider with the downtown people; as an NIH man he was inadmissible to their clique.

Dr. Felix was aghast at the Study Group's plans, which he interpreted as meaning the summary removal of half the Institute's programs. As he interpreted it, the divestiture involved about half of NIMH's budget but "functionwise, it would have put us out of business." Actually the proposed transfers involved about forty-five per cent of the NIMH budget. His objection, he said, was that the group would wrench off at the roots vigorous, growing programs that were anatomically and physiologically a part of NIMH. He favored all due deliberate speed.

The Felix Memorandum

The day after the sneak preview Felix sat down with his top staff to draft a letter of protest. He intentionally wrote a shocker, calculated to halt precipitate action. Felix felt he had to do this to gain time to marshal his arguments to the SG. He took a calculatedly extreme position, one he did not wholeheartedly embrace.

The letter—eight single-spaced pages—went out March 25 to the SG, with copies to Executive Officer Paul Caulk, Dr. Hundley, and Dr. Shannon. The letter resisted each change the Study Group had proposed, arguing, program by program, that each should remain at NIMH.

Felix was critical of the total reorganization plan, which concentrated too heavily, he said, on functional clusters. Such a concept applied to NIMH "on a somewhat arbitrary basis will destroy the integrity and effectiveness of the mental health activities of the Service now mediated through the NIMH."

> An analysis on a point by point basis shows the disastrous results of this dismemberment of a presently integrated approach to a major health problem that appears to require, even more than other areas, integration of effort in all areas of approach: research, training, service, control.

Felix concluded with a warning to the SG that the plan to strip down NIMH to a research institute and to distribute its operating programs to other bureaus was at odds with the mental health organizational trend elsewhere. The trend was characterized by the establishment of separate departments in state governments for mental health and the increasing recognition of mental health problems and organization of units to cope with them by other groups—planning officials, schools, and industry. Apropos of these developments, Felix continued:

> These groups need both at the State and Federal level representation of mental health that is visible, understandable, easily approached, and organized in such a way as to give counsel, guidance, and prompt action from one over-all source to promote implementation of their presently adumbrated responsibility. It would be a bit comical, if it were not so destructive of these developing interests, to contemplate the efforts of individuals seeking these clarifications to get help from the PHS if it were organized as proposed with discrete punctiform representation in a variety of bureaus.
>
> Literally, the schools, industry, community planners and the like need a one-stop service. . . . It is contended that the NIMH can and does provide this kind of assistance. It should be permitted to continue to do so.

Felix carried on his resistance campaign with a frontal assault and a flanking movement as well. Taking stock of his resources, he concluded that he was not empty-handed. He could rely on support from the many professional and lay organizations with which he was associated. In addition to being affiliated with dozens of national organizations, and state chapters as well,[11] he was scheduled to be elevated to the presidency of the American Psychiatric Association in May. He thought this professional recognition might aid him in his campaign. He moved directly to argue his case with the SG, and he asked friends and allies in private life to fight the plans. Immediately after dispatching the letter, he requested an appointment with the SG. Burney, who was planning a trip abroad, asked Porterfield and Hundley to talk with Felix.

Felix began his flanking movement with an intimate luncheon in early April at the Cosmos Club, a distinguished town club for writers and scientists. His guest was a veteran combat fighter on the mental health front, Mike Gorman, Executive Director of the National Committee Against Mental Illness. Gorman was an energetic, dynamic ex-reporter (and Phi Beta Kappa), long associated with the crusade for improved mental hospitals. He had pioneered in the establishment of a mental hygiene commission in Oklahoma, and he brought to national attention the sorry state of mental hospitals by publishing several graphic stories in various national magazines. In 1948 he had received a special Lasker award for his efforts on behalf of mental health. In 1952-1953 he had served as chief writer for the President's Commission on Health Needs of the Nation.

The organization he ran, the National Committee Against Mental Illness, was formed in 1949 largely to give Gorman a Washington base. Its principal sponsor and angel was Mrs. Albert Lasker, who also served as co-chairman. Largely a paper organization, it distributed to state governors, state mental health officers, and others an annual fact sheet on statistics of mental illness and scope of various state and local mental health programs.

One of its principal functions was to arrange for the regular appearance of psychiatrists and prominent private citizens to testify on behalf of a so-called "Citizens' Budget" before the congressional appropriations committees. This troupe, which had begun its appearances in the early days of the Eisenhower administration, requested increases over the administration's budget for mental health research funds. A congressional favorite himself, Gorman also appeared regularly as a witness in behalf of additional funds for NIMH.

As the luncheon progressed, Gorman's alarm mounted over the plan to carve up NIMH. He indicated that his influence was not inconsiderable, that he would do whatever he could to keep NIMH from going under the knife, and that he might try to pass along some of this information to members of Congress.

The Meetings Downtown

The SG had pointed out at the second summit that he had an open mind on the proposals for NIMH. Anxious to avoid dissension and an open break with Felix, he ordered a series of meetings

---

[11] American College of Physicians; American Medical Association-American Bar Association Joint Committee on Narcotics; American Psychological Association; American Psychopathological Association; American Public Health Association; Association for Research in Nervous and Mental Diseases; National Association for Mental Health; Maryland Mental Hygiene Society; and Maryland Public Health Association—this is a partial list of his memberships.

between Felix and the organization architects downtown. He was also influenced by protests from one other Institute director at NIH. The director of the Cancer Institute told Burney that the changes proposed for NIMH were too sudden and too harsh.

At the first meeting with Porterfield and Hundley, Felix amplified the objections outlined in his letter to the SG. Felix talked fluently, eloquently, emotionally. He spoke of the violence that hasty action would bring and compared the act of transferring NIMH functions to wresting living tissue from the human body. Felix made it plain that he was unwilling to preside over the dismemberment of an organization that had grown fortyfold under his leadership. He asked if his offer to retire would be accepted and, later, allowed information to get around in professional organizations and universities that he might be available.

Felix argued for leaving NIMH alone for the present but making plans for gradual separation. He made two suggestions: postponing any action until the task force reports were in, and assigning immediately an NIMH liaison official to BSS to survey the state of readiness of BSS for mental health operations. "I proposed taking the very best person I had at NIMH and assigning him to BSS. He would be administratively responsible to BSS and professionally responsible to NIMH." Felix offered to include him in the NIMH budget. BSS, under his plan, would assign a senior officer to NIMH to spot the programs that should be transferred.

Porterfield told him his views would be taken into consideration in reaching a final decision. According to Porterfield, Felix, comporting himself like a proper civil servant and gentleman, said he would abide by the decisions made at the top. Then—defying the rules of the game—Felix went immediately to his influential friends, including members of Congress, and poured out a story of dismemberment of mental health. At least that was the way it appeared to the Deputy SG.

These meetings took place in the spring, at the time the Study Group's final draft was being prepared. Final decision on NIMH functions and several narrow decisions on both reorganization and implementation could not be made without further study. The SG planned to act after getting the task force reports.

Felix felt he had another ally in the task forces —a structural or mechanical ally rather than a personal one. All committees, he said, are by their nature delaying devices and divided bodies. "I was sure the creation of the task forces was a blessing," he said. "The more people who were brought in to help reach a decision, the greater were the chances that they would neither agree among themselves nor with the Hundley people."

A Special Mental Health Task Force

One of the first task forces to be created was a seven-member body to report on the organization of mental health activities. To head it, the Surgeon General selected Margaret Arnstein, who had been a member of the Study Group. The members were chosen by Dr. Hundley and Miss Arnstein jointly according to the Study Group formula—two members from the donor unit, two from the receiving unit, and two neutrals. The NIMH representatives were Curtis G. Southard, chief of the Community Services Branch, and John A. Clausen, a sociologist engaged in behavioral research. Clausen soon afterward left to accept an academic post and was replaced by Richard H. Williams, a sociologist and chief of the Professional Services Branch of NIMH. The members from the receiver agency were Leslie W. Knott, chief of the Special Health Services Branch of BSS (the unit that had accepted the heart and cancer community demonstration programs and would be the locus of similar activities in mental health) and E. H. Guthrie, a BSS program director. The neutrals were Lyman Moore and Evelyn Flook, who acted as the task force secretary. Moore at one time had been NIMH executive officer.

The Arnstein task force received its charge on May 10. It was given two duties: (1) to study the Community Services Branch, the Biometrics Branch, and other pertinent NIMH activities and recommend to the SG which should remain at NIMH and which should go; and (2) to set forth criteria and concepts for allocating programs and responsibilities between the NIMH and the rest of the PHS in the future. It was ordered to report by June 30.

A week passed during which tensions mounted. The result was that the charge was modified. When the task force met for the first time on May 18, Dr. Porterfield told them that the range of conclusions open had been extended to include an option of *no change* as well as recommendations for transfer of any or all of the activities originally mentioned by the parent Study Group. Consequently, the Arnstein task force was to accumulate technical information and delineate the main factors to be considered in helping the Surgeon General to make up his mind.

Miss Arnstein interpreted the change as further evidence that the pressures from Dr. Felix and his friends had been too great to allow the proposed changes to be made. She had expected that the task force would have rough sledding but was surprised that the SG now allowed for the possibility of continuation of all the community service, statistical, and training activities at NIMH.

The group met whenever the members could get together. It was in session about five full days all told. The members interviewed the people affected and studied PHS documents and congressional committee hearings. They interviewed Shannon and Felix; headquarters and field people at NIMH; a regional medical director; the chief-designate of the proposed Bureau of Community Health; some BSS personnel; and the director-designate of the National Center for Health Statistics.

The NIMH field staff people were the least committed to existing organizational arrangements. They worked with individuals and groups in the community and interacted with BSS personnel. They were indifferent as to whether they belonged to the NIMH or to a service-oriented bureau.

The issuance of the Study Group's report on June 7 brought some coherence to the "negotiations" being conducted between the SG and Dr. Felix. At least the Study Group's recommendations were a matter of public record. The report stated firmly that NIH's disease control programs, demonstrations, community service activity and field research would have to go. It recommended task forces to decide which activities should remain at NIH and which should be transferred. With regard to the special problems at NIMH, the report said that special task groups would study mental health activities but "it seems clear that community service programs and most if not all 'demonstrations' [at NIMH] must be transferred to the Bureau of Community Health." The report hedged on biometrics. "Possible transfer of certain statistical activities . . . , particularly those concerned with national measures of mental illness and the patient population of mental institutions, is still under consideration."

Problems for the Arnstein Task Force

The Surgeon General's advisers hoped that the NIMH decisions could be reached after the Arnstein group had studied the programs and made a recommendation for the future of each activity on its merits. They were disappointed.

In June two events occurred that demonstrated the difficulty of reaching a dispassionate decision. The first was the report of the Senate Appropriations Committee that expressed the committee's unyielding opposition to transfer of the NIMH training activities. The report, which appeared June 14, burst like a bombshell over the PHS, shattering shell fragments over several areas. There was general agreement that the report halted all action for at least the time required to assess its meaning and strength. The Arnstein task force was immediately affected, and Miss Arnstein's first reaction was that the committee caveat in effect killed it off. She immediately checked with the Surgeon General. "Should we disband the Task Force?" she asked.

Dr. Burney was uncertain what course to take. He felt intuitively that the language in the Senate report might well have been bootlegged to the Appropriations Committee. Nevertheless, the report was legitimate, and the voice was that of the U.S. Senate. He decided to get some advice from HEW.

The Secretary gave him a free hand by ruling, in effect, that the PHS could take any action it chose. The Secretary told Burney he could disregard the committee altogether—that he could make any decision he felt would benefit the Service.

Miss Arnstein was notified that the task force should continue to work as if nothing had happened. It was to complete the assigned task—of providing the SG with technical information and criteria on which to base his decision. Its independent judgment would give the SG not only information but additional support for whatever course he decided to take.

The second event was a stern injunction from the National Mental Health Advisory Council, NIMH's statutory advisory group. This fourteen-member body was composed of six medical and scientific leaders in the mental health field, six leaders in public affairs, and one liaison representative each from the Defense Department and the Veterans Administration. Its principal function was to pass on the applications made to NIMH for grants in research, training, and community services. However, it was also empowered to advise the SG on all Service matters relating to mental health.

When the Advisory Council gathered on June 20 in Bethesda for its regular spring meeting, Dr. Burney appeared to discuss mental health in the context of total PHS programs and, especially, to present the reorganization proposed for NIMH. The council members displayed a lively interest and asked so many questions that Burney promised to send Hundley out the following day to fill them in on the Study Group's thinking.

The upshot was that the Advisory Council went on record as being "strongly apprehensive" over transfer of any NIMH functions. Members said they would notify the SG of their further reactions after they had studied the plan. They indicated a belief that NIMH's growth and prosperity were due to its "integrated" program.

Soon after this, letters from the council members expressing varying shades of opposition to NIMH reorganization began to reach the Surgeon General. Some members expanded their comments to cover other areas of the reorganization plan. One council member, Dr. Eli Ginzburg, a social scientist and director of the Institute of Human Resources at Columbia University, expressed the view that the PHS was too large to be reorganized across the board. He said reorganization should take place piece by piece, unit by unit. (He evidently did not understand that implementation was proceeding in just that fashion.) He favored strengthening Service work in environmental and community health, but "my prejudice is very definitely against as thorough-going a reorganization as is contemplated in the Final Report." He continued:

> Yours is pre-eminently a service whose effectiveness depends upon Congressional enthusiasm, widespread support from the scientific community and the quality of the staff that you can attract and retain. I do not believe that the Study Group weighed adequately the losses on these three fronts incident to the reorganization which they propose.

He expressed definite opinions on the NIMH plans.

> I feel *very strongly* that it would be a fundamental error to divide training functions; and to move the statistics unit. I would also question as of this moment even the desirability of moving Program V. I do believe the NIMH could profit from correlating community health programs in mental health more closely with other programs of community health. My preference would be to have NIMH assign a strong group to work in the Bureau of Community Health.

The letters from Advisory Council members happened to coincide with a flow of mail that reached Burney from other sources at about this time—late June and July—opposing reorganization of NIMH. Some correspondents opposed any alteration, some opposed one or another part of the plan. A few persons approved the transfer, but (PHS people said) the correspondence ran three to one against change.

The correspondents were professional people with a special interest in mental health—state mental health commissioners, professors or department heads in university psychology and psychiatry departments, and some former members of the National Mental Health Advisory Council. A number of these letters went also to the Director of NIH, Dr. Shannon.

Two letters carried special weight with the SG and his advisers. They were from directors of mental hygiene departments of New York and California, the states with the largest and most extensive mental hygiene programs. Dr. Paul H. Hoch, the New York commissioner, expressed the view that if psychiatric services were distributed among bureaus having a wide spread of functions, "psychiatric services would be designed on policy-making levels by people who have very little or no psychiatric experience. This surely does not lead to very effective planning in this complicated field."

Hoch went on to say, with respect to NIMH:

> If the NIMH were to have no other functions but research, then other aspects of psychiatry will have no focal point of organization. I do not believe that the new Division of Mental and Social Health will fulfill these functions effectively.

Dr. Daniel Blain, the California director, wrote an NIMH testimonial:

> An excellent job has been done by the NIMH. There has been widespread satisfaction and growing public support, as witnessed by the rapidly increasing annual appropriations by Congress. These funds have been widely used by NIMH under its outstanding Director with the aid of an excellent staff and strong advisory councils. One would need to have very good reasons for changing the organization of such a valuable and far-reaching program. In short, the five major functions that are now so successfully integrated within the organization of the NIMH would suffer both from being divorced from one another and from being carried out without the over-all knowledge, specialized supervision and still needed leadership of persons with particular skills and experience in this newest, though big-

> gest, area of concern in the whole field of public health.
>
> I hope that further consideration may be given to accomplishing your excellent objective without breaking up this fine and successful operation. It fills a unique need and deserves special consideration. It is ironic that just as NIMH is coming into a place of great importance in the national picture, it should be deprived of its broad and unified approach.

Meantime, the Arnstein task force was continuing its examination of criteria to guide the SG in determining which, if any, NIMH activities should go to the new bureau. On June 15, when the task force members interviewed two of the principal figures involved, Dr. Shannon and Dr. Felix, they found what seemed to be significant changes in the attitudes of both.

Shannon, who at one time had spoken eloquently of the need to turn the NIMH prow more squarely in the research direction, now expressed doubt about transferring some programs. He told the task force he believed a "good share" of NIMH activities properly belonged in the new Community Health Bureau. They should not necessarily be transferred right away, but neither should they be left for the indefinite future. Shannon said also that the biometrics activities should not be moved at all and that he had some doubts about the Title V grants in community health services.

Felix had not altered his views; he had simply changed tactics. He told the task force that he actually supported the proposals but still opposed the timing. He was able to visualize the possibility of a mental health division in the Community Health Bureau, but only after a suitable transition stage. He saw the transition as a period in which persons professionally trained in mental health—psychiatrists, psychologists, social workers, nurses, and so forth—would be seeded throughout the new bureau to create a hospitable atmosphere for mental health operations. He opposed transfer of any program or activity from NIMH to the new bureau at that time. (Miss Arnstein and the task force members were aware of Dr. Felix's eight-page screed in which he had summarily rejected the possibility of change at NIMH. They interpreted his willingness to consider future changes as a mellowing.)

Miss Arnstein was particularly conscious of group processes after the stint with the parent Study Group. She saw that her task force was concentrating almost exclusively on NIMH and the reactions of a tightly knit group of people, many of whom had initiated programs, had nurtured them along in the lean years when funds were low and support negligible, and now were reluctant to see them transferred to another organizational matrix. After two weeks she was able to get her colleagues to turn their attention to the structure proposed for the new Bureau of Community Health. This served to change their attitude. They decided that the bureau could not properly function without the mental health community services functions.

Once again the task force bogged down when the members realized that this conclusion meant that some NIMH functions must be moved. For a time the members returned to their hesitations, anxiously repeating the doubts and dire warnings expressed by many NIMH branch chiefs. Transfer of any going activity would be unwise and impractical, because mental health would languish in the community health setting; the morale and *esprit* of the professional psychiatric people would sag when they were separated from their fellows. The Bureau of Community Health setting would be restrictive and unimaginative in comparison with the crusading, activist environment of NIMH. Most important, the money would be harder to get once the disease category identification was dropped —the visible, saleable, popular "mental health" label that, along with "cancer" and "heart disease," served to pry loose congressional funds so easily.

Findings of the Arnstein Task Force

The task force members eventually composed their differences and issued a report on July 7, 1960. Two principles were adduced, in the light of the parent Study Group's deliberations and decisions: (1) mental health as an entity was an essential element of the new Bureau of Community Health and should be incorporated from the start, and (2) mental health was an element of several major PHS programs, particularly some that would be in the new Bureau of Community Health.

The task force then proposed establishment of a Division of Mental Health in the Bureau of Community Health. This, of course, was in line with the recommendation of the parent Study Group for establishment of a Division of Mental and Social Health. The task force altered only the name, suggesting that "social health" had unfortunate connotations.

The task force considered several alternative

ways of getting a new division in motion: (1) setting it up by fiat and allowing it to do its own recruiting; (2) assigning key NIMH people to the new division and allowing them to work out plans for staffing; and (3) transferring specific NIMH organizational units (the Community Services Branch would go *in toto*) to the Division of Mental Health. Discarding these, it came up with what Miss Arnstein called an organizational monster—the establishment "as soon as practicable" of a division that would be administratively responsible to the chief of the Bureau of Community Health and professionally responsible to the director of NIMH. The principal agent for change under the plan was the director of NIMH, who with the cooperation and approval of the chief of the Bureau of Community Health, would be responsible for the development, staffing, and funding of the division.

Dr. Williams filed a minority view. He opposed the new division and suggested a plan of trial development of various mental health activities in the new bureaus without specific organizational goals.

One other task force charged with conducting across-the-board studies had special significance for NIMH. The parent Study Group had concluded that only training activity related to research should continue as an NIH function. Training for nonresearch functions and for service should be transferred to other bureaus. The parent group called for the establishment of a special task force to categorize the existing NIH training programs and to develop standards for locating such programs in the future.

That task force recommended that NIMH be divested of its service training programs and training for other nonresearch functions.

The Surgeon General Hesitates

The Arnstein task force report did not hasten action on NIMH, and the decision continued to hang fire throughout July. Burney proposed further meetings between Felix and his chief lieutenants, Porterfield, and Hundley; and he and Felix met on two occasions. At one of the meetings, NIH Director Shannon accompanied Felix. Shannon told Burney that he had changed his own views about altering NIMH. The changes might do serious violence to mental health activities by alienating some influential members of the profession. Another consideration, he said, was the possibility that operations at NIMH might be imperiled, because some key staff people were so upset about the proposed changes that they were preparing to resign or to move on to other opportunities.

In August the SG called a meeting of the PHS bureau chiefs and HEW representatives to present to them the various plans and recommendations that had been made by the task forces on implementation. Burney was ready with his decision on NIMH.

He was guided by two considerations. One, of course, was his reluctance to offend the members of the Senate who presided over health policy and funds. His own future as SG was enmeshed with this consideration. Furthermore, the arguments that unfolded in the wake of the Study Group's recommendations indicated to Burney that the case for redirecting NIMH was not open-and-shut. Many sound, cogent arguments favored the status quo. It seemed to Burney that despite the Study Group's logic, three ill effects might result if he endorsed its proposals. His endorsement might alienate important outside groups, especially the National Mental Health Advisory Council and the American Psychiatric Association, which Felix then headed; it might jeopardize some program operations at NIMH; and it might result in the loss of Dr. Felix to the Service.

Burney announced at the meeting that additional planning and study would be given to NIMH operations before any changes were made. For the present, he said, he had decided to follow a suggestion advanced by Dr. Felix to assign a senior NIMH staff member to BSS. This person would not have a definite assignment, but would, in effect, cruise around BSS and prepare the ground for eventual transfer of some of the NIMH activities.

The SG announced also that a committee with long-range goals in the area of mental health would be established and that its work would also lay the foundation for relocation of mental health activities in the future. This committee of advisers would report to the SG on what the Service should be doing in meeting national needs, not in the area of mental health as such, but in the application of mental health concepts, skills, disciplines, and approaches to health programs having other disease or health conditions as primary targets. Also it would estimate the number of trained personnel necessary to do the job. The committee was to be made up of twelve persons representing state health officers, state mental health officers, the National Mental Health Advisory Council, and three neutral persons to give scientific coverage and balance.

As autumn advanced, Felix and his staff at NIMH settled down once more to their exciting and wide-ranging work in mental health. The crisis was over. The problems were being studied. Felix was named chairman of the committee of twelve to advise the SG, and one of his branch chiefs, Dr. Richard Williams, was designated chief of the committee staff. The committee's budget was assumed by NIMH.

Felix was prompt to name an advance agent for the BSS assignment. He chose a psychiatrist and pediatrician, Dr. Mabel Ross, a person whom he trusted and admired. He described her as capable, tactful, and imaginative, ideally suited for an assignment that was not clearly mapped.

Assessment

Dr. Felix clearly emerged as the master strategist and tactician. The Surgeon General's decision to rely on the recommendations of the committee of twelve put off for the indefinite future any changes at NIMH. Felix's faith in the inherent delaying characteristics of committee action was amply justified.

Felix had several factors on his side; his own personality and adroitness in the political area were not the least of them. He also had the advantage of a tight shop, with high *esprit* among his staff, and effective working relationships with client groups. And, as always, it turned out to be more difficult to alter than to maintain the status quo.

Finally, Felix could point out to the PHS chiefs that the very arguments advanced for altering NIMH were brushed under the rug in the recommendation for the new Bureau of Environmental Health. The blueprint for that bureau called for a unit that combined research functions with operational responsibilities and a host of other diverse activities—all under one roof. Where, Felix had asked, was the concept for functional groupings? What happened to logic?

Nevertheless, with all of Felix's resources, the reorganization of NIMH might have taken place if the SG had shared the Study Group's conviction that the benefits to be realized from a change would outweigh the dislocations predicted by Felix and his friends. But Dr. Burney, as he had indicated at the second summit, attached more weight to the fact that NIMH was doing a good job than to the orderliness of an organization chart. His feeling that mental health activities should not be tampered with was strengthened when the protests began to flow across his desk and the dicta to issue from Capitol Hill. Dr. Porterfield shared the Study Group's views but was unsuccessful in his effort to influence his chief.

NIMH in 1961 continued to enjoy congressional bounty, with an appropriation of $100,000,000—about thirty-three per cent higher than the funds it was awarded in 1960.

FINALE

Any assessment of the "success" of the PHS reorganization must take account of the change in national administration in 1961. The new Democratic President, John F. Kennedy, campaigned on a promise of serious attention to medical problems and endorsed the principle of Social Security financing for medical care of the aged. In the interval between the election and inauguration, the President-elect designated a number of task forces to lay down plans for the new Administration, including one on health policy. Another evidence of his concern for vigorous social legislation was the fact that he named a close associate and early supporter, Abraham Ribicoff, as Secretary of HEW. Ribicoff, former governor of Connecticut, was one of the first Cabinet appointments announced.

Early in February the new Administration sent to Congress a comprehensive health program spearheaded by the plan to help older persons meet hospital costs through Social Security. The plan called for federal assistance to persons over sixty-five to meet hospital, but not medical, bills. The President also requested Congress to authorize federal scholarships for medical and dental students; to provide funds to help build medical and dental schools and nursing homes; to create a new Institute at NIH in child health; to increase funds for medical research and vocational rehabilitation; to strengthen community service and facilities for better care, especially of the chronically ill and aged; and to control air and water pollution through consolidation of existing functions and expansion of research programs.

These proposals adhered closely to those made by the Kennedy medical task force, but they also resembled to a remarkable degree the proposals the Hundley Study Group had made. There was no coordination between the two bodies, although, of course, the Hundley task force report was available to the Kennedy planners. The Study Group had foreseen expanded Service programs in community service and facilities, with emphasis on care for the chronically ill and aged; in aid to medical education; and in control of air and water pollution. It had created new organizational units to foster their development.

To some observers, the principal change the Democratic administration wrought in the Service was not in the area of new programs. Rather, it was in imparting a sense of buoyancy and determination to press for congressional approval of programs that earlier administrations had offered but not urged. The new President and the Secretary of HEW fostered an increased emphasis on and awareness in finding better ways of organizing, delivering, and financing certain services, especially in the area of community health services and facilities. "The ability to afford adequate health care is to no avail without adequate health facilities," Kennedy said in his health message on February 9, 1961. ". . . our communities need additional help to provide those services where everybody can use them." He proposed grants to improve the quality of services in nursing homes; to develop organized community home-care health services for the aged and chronically ill; to develop health service information and referral centers; to train additional personnel required for out-of-hospital health services; and to assist in meeting the cost of studies and demonstrations of new and improved means of providing out-of-hospital care.

Early in the administration the President asked Congress to authorize a new bureau for community health "to ensure maximum Federal attention to the rapid development of this program." He also requested a new bureau for environmental health. And, although Congress did not act promptly, the two common-law bureaus continued to function as separate operational entities. In fact, for practical purposes they were statutory bureaus. The 1962 PHS budget was presented to Congress in terms of environmental health operations and community health operations, and the chiefs-designate of the "bureaus" supported the budget requests before the House and Senate Appropriations Committees. Dr. Hundley characterized the reorganization as an accomplished fact. To him, the plan in its broad outlines was accepted and functioning by 1961 when the budget requests went up to Capitol Hill.

The health planners' hope for improvement in three areas was not realized—strengthening the organizational arrangements for handling personnel, integrating and unifying the various splintered programs of information and education, and devising a practical method of unifying training programs and centralizing grants.

The SG Is Replaced

Dr. Leroy Burney was a casualty of the change of administration in January 1961. It was a strange turn of fate. The SG had taken no controversial positions in the reorganization, and the entire Study Group process had been brought to a conclusion without any noticeable lasting damage to agency morale. However, President Kennedy named a new Surgeon General on January 16.

The office of Surgeon General has not usually been thought of as a partisan political office and most occupants have served two or more four-year terms. Dr. Burney's term expired in January 1961. The President decided to replace him immediately despite conflicting advice. One group of advisers urged on him the importance of replacing Burney, of naming not necessarily a "Democratic" SG but a new one who would reflect the character, temper, and spirit of the new Administration. Another group, conceding that Burney was identified as a Republican, believed he should be replaced but suggested that the President defer acting for six months or so in order to avoid the impression that partisan politics entered into the selection of the SG.

President Kennedy, rejecting the waiting period, named a new SG on January 16. He chose an NIH man, Dr. Luther L. Terry, who was assistant director of the National Heart Institute. The selection, made by dipping down into the second level of command of the Commissioned Corps, caused some surprise. Terry, 49, a native of Alabama, had entered the Service in 1942. His middle name, Leonidas, had been given him as a tribute to the famous surgeon, Dr. Leonidas Hill, who was the father of Senator Lister Hill of Alabama.

What did the reorganization amount to? First, the end sought by the PHS directorate was realized. The Service's wide and diverse activities had been rearranged into more logical, orderly groupings. The new arrangement—in the view of officials of HEW and of the PHS—would enable the PHS to carry out its present mission and assigned tasks in a better way and would, at the same time, provide the basic organizational structure for assuming new functions and responsibilities in the future. The reorganization of itself did not involve new programs, but the Study Group members cherished the hope that the new organization might result in a sum greater than its parts.

The reorganization had other beneficial results. The very exercise of self-study was a valuable one. Also, the process served to identify a number of new leaders within the Service, i.e., the Study Group members.

The educational process extended beyond the Study Group itself into ever-widening circles. The two summit meetings, involving as they did the top command of the PHS, brought to the Service leadership an awareness and knowledge of emerging health problems and their organizational implications that no other mechanism could have provided.

Finally, the reorganization effort created in the PHS an atmosphere receptive to organizational change that could not have been achieved by having an outside agent make the study.

APPENDIX I: ORIGINAL MEMBERS OF THE STUDY GROUP

Dr. James M. Hundley, chairman. Hundley was 45. Most of his twenty years in the PHS had been devoted to his professional specialty, nutrition, and to international health matters. He had joined the NIH staff in 1944 and had served there most of the ensuing years. His interest in nutrition had led to a two-year assignment with UNICEF in 1958. At the time he was selected to head the Study Group, he was special assistant for international affairs at NIH. He considered himself a research man; he had had no previous experience with organizational matters.

Margaret C. Arnstein. Miss Arnstein, 56, had a richly diversified background in nursing. A graduate of Smith College, she had received her nurses' training at Presbyterian Hospital in New York City. Subsequently she was awarded an M.A. at Columbia and an M.P.H. degree at Johns Hopkins. Before World War II, she had worked in public health nursing in New York and had taught courses in public health nursing at the University of Minnesota for three years. During World War II, she was chief nurse of the Balkan Mission of UNNRRA. In 1946 she had joined the PHS and at the time of the study was chief of the Division of Public Health Nursing, BSS. She considered organization and management as outside the realm of her experience or competence.

Dr. Donald J. Galagan. Galagan, 46, was assistant chief of the Division of Dental Public Health in the BSS at the time of the study. A native of Iowa, he had graduated from the University of Iowa College of Dentistry in 1937. His specialty was dental public health.

Dr. Harold M. Graning. Graning, 48, was, at the time of the study, regional medical director of the New York region of the PHS.

Harry G. Hanson. Hanson, 51, was an Assistant Surgeon General in 1960. He was a sanitary engineer, a graduate of the University of Minnesota. He had been awarded the M.S. degree at Harvard in 1940. From 1936 to 1942 he had worked with the North Dakota State Department of Health and had been director of the Division of Sanitary Engineering when he left to join the PHS. From 1948 to 1952 he had been executive officer to the SG.

Dr. Harold J. Magnuson. Magnuson, 47, had attended the University of Southern California and had received his M.D. and M.P.H. degrees at Johns Hopkins. He had interned at the Los Angeles County Hospital and had joined the PHS in 1941. He had also taught courses in the medical schools at the University of Southern California, University of North Carolina, Johns Hopkins, and George Washington University. His program interests were venereal disease control and occupational health. In 1960 he was chief of the Occupational Health Branch, Division of Special Health Services, BSS, a post he had held for four years. Possessed of a healthy sense of humor and a genial disposition, he was to enliven many of the Study Group's sessions. A talented artist, he often was able to reduce tension at the sessions by producing a pertinent cartoon.

Dr. William H. Stewart. Stewart, 39, had received his M.D. at Louisiana State University in 1945. Before joining the PHS in 1951, he had been in private practice in Louisiana and had been resident physician in pediatrics at Charity Hospital, New Orleans. His early PHS assignments had been in control activities in heart disease and he had been assistant director of the National Heart Institute at NIH from 1956 to 1957. He was chief of the Division of Public Health Methods, a staff arm of the SG, when the study was begun.

Dr. Burnet M. Davis. He was 49. At the time of the study he was deputy chief of the Division of Hospital and Medical Facilities in the BMS, a post he had held since 1948. A native of Massachusetts, he was graduated from Harvard in 1932 and received his M.D. at Harvard in 1937. After attending Oxford University as a Rhodes scholar, he had been assistant resident at Massachusetts General Hospital in Boston from 1940 to 1941. After joining the PHS in 1942, he had been detailed as an observer to the British Ministry of Health from 1947 to 1948. His other time in the PHS had been devoted to Indian health matters, international health, and program responsibilities in the BSS. Davis was an intense, dedicated man who considered organizational arrangements of less importance than program content.

EDITORIAL COMMENTS

The Public Health Service, and in fact the field of public health itself, has been in a state of explosive development ever since World War II. This has been a result partly of vast changes in the emphasis and scope and even in the definition of public health work. In a sense, public health has been a victim of its own success. Its substantial conquest of the majority of the traditional communicable diseases such as tuberculosis, smallpox, and typhoid fever, and its work in some of the traditional fields such as sanitation, meat and dairy inspection, has relegated these areas to a relatively routine status. At the same time, new challenges, new standards, new knowledge, new technology, and new popular demand have given rise to tremendous areas of activity hardly dreamt of thirty years ago. These include research work; exploration and prevention of such diseases as cancer, heart disease, and many others; and the emergence of federal leadership in such areas as hospital construction, mental hygiene, and atomic medicine.

The PHS reorganization of 1960 described in the preceding pages may appropriately be viewed as one of a series of efforts to bring a large and very old organization up to date with the vast changes in responsibility that had occurred and that could be foreseen in the future. It may also be observed as an example of an agency's effort to adapt itself to rapid and accelerating growth in size. And the strategy of undertaking the reorganization at that time was clearly to take advantage of congressional interest and pressure with regard to one functional area—environmental health—to obtain support for a much broader readjustment of the entire agency. The complexity and difficulty in such an undertaking in so volatile and dynamic a field, with so many vying interests both within and outside, are clearly reflected in the case.

To these were added the difficulties of the competing viewpoints of a wide variety of personnel within the agency. The Public Health Service had traditionally been governed by a relatively small corps of commissioned officers, within which the group of physicians contributed an inner "elite." But the bulk of the growth in size had arisen from the employment of large numbers of civil servants, including many scientists and other professionals. At the time of the case, the civil servants outnumbered the regular commissioned officers by about fourteen to one. Furthermore, among both the commissioned and civil service personnel were a large number of various kinds of specialists with differing education and differing orientation. They included, for example, non-specialized physicians, specialists in almost every field of medicine and public health, sanitary engineers, nurses, hospital administrators, dentists, psychiatrists, and scientists in virtually every field of social and life science.

The membership chosen for the Study Group apparently reflected a careful effort to provide representation from as many of the important specialist groups as feasible. Its initial composition included individuals oriented to research, to hospitals, to sanitary engineering, to occupational health, to heart disease, to dentistry, to nursing, and to administration of field programs. But there were some conspicuous omissions: psychiatrists, administrators, and representatives of the civil service (since the entire initial group were commissioned officers). The latter two omissions were later corrected at least in part by the addition of four new members of the Study Group, but the omission of psychiatrists remained and may have contributed to the later difficulties with the National Institute of Mental Health. It is interesting that the two topics that proved the most difficult were the personnel systems in general, from which the group's jurisdiction was withdrawn, and the NIMH, concerning which all action was postponed. In both cases, the stalemate gave rise to new study groups and new sets of recommendations. The "case-within-a-case" concerning the NIMH is a nice illustration of the mobilization of individuals and groups outside the agency, including congressmen, professional organizations, state officials, and private citizen groups to protect the integrity of a subagency against what it viewed as dismemberment.

This reorganization process reflected at some stages efforts to elicit participation by officers and employees. The Study Group itself was composed entirely of officers *within* the agency and, as indicated above, was broadly representative of many different specialists. On the other hand, the Study Group members deliberately avoided any active and responsible representation; they did not propose to check with any of their constituents, nor undertake to keep the others in the agency systematically informed. Furthermore, they did their best to grow beyond any parochial, specialist point of view, apparently with some success. The "summit meetings" were, of course, examples of participation by the top officers of the agency and representatives of HEW, but they were used by the Surgeon General primarily to inform him, to measure the "climate," to gain acceptance, and to help him decide what he should and could do. The basic decisions were clearly his. The various meetings, invitations for suggestions, task force investigations, and discussions apparently had somewhat the same purposes, particularly during the implementation stages. It is worthy of note that except in the case of NIMH, there was little response to invitations for suggestions and criticisms. Apparently participation was not particularly sought by the employees at middle and lower levels.

MARIANA ROBINSON

Health Centers and Community Needs

MARIANA ROBINSON

The author of *Health Centers and Community Needs* and *The Coming of Age of the Langley Porter Clinic* received a B.A. degree from Swarthmore College. She has served as a Public Administration Analyst, Bureau of Public Administration, University of California at Berkeley, and, most recently, has been a consultant to San Joaquin County Local Health District on a two-year administration study, *Forty Years of Public Health in San Joaquin County*.

CHRONOLOGY OF KEY EVENTS

1948	Fife-Hamill Memorial Health Center—the first community health center—opens in Philadelphia
1949-1950	Philadelphia Health and Welfare Council conducts survey of the city's health resources
1950-1951	Reeves, Director, Department of Public Health, begins implementation of survey recommendations: opens health centers, encourages generalized operations, begins generalization of nursing services
January 1952	Dixon is appointed Commissioner of Health by Mayor Clark; adopts 1949 survey recommendations as his policy base
1952	Miss Hall, Director, Public Health Nursing, carries out an almost complete merging of nursing services
October 1952-1954	Dixon called on leave; Ingraham, Deputy Commissioner, is named Acting Commissioner
1953	Purdom is appointed Director of Environmental Sanitation; two spring pilot projects in decentralization of programs to health centers are begun
August 1954	Ingraham issues report on city health center administration
April 1955	Ingraham issues second report on activities capable of decentralization to community health centers
April 1957	Hanlon is appointed to fill new position of Director of Public Health Services
May 7, 1957	Hanlon transfers district directors, staffs, activities to his supervision
May 15, 1957	COOLS committee is formed by Hanlon
August 1957	COOLS committee issues report on plan for decentralization
January 1958	Managing Director and Health Commissioner agree to decentralization plan
February 3, 1958	Hanlon issues first orders implementing plan
June 1958	Interdisciplinary team appraises success of decentralization in a single district
February 1959	Co-op Council established to work out procedures for implementation of orders
March 1959	Co-op Council establishes procedures for scheduling clinics
May 1959	Community Nursing Services is established through merger of Visiting Nurses Society with city's public health nurses
July 1959	Commissioner Dixon resigns
1961	Public Health Services unit changes its name to Department of Community Health Services
Fall 1961	Hanlon meets with top staff on "program, priorities, and organization"; establishes five task forces to facilitate further decentralization

PRINCIPAL CHARACTERS

Alfred S. Bogucki, M.D., M.P.H.; District Health Center Administrator, 1950-1957; Director, District Health Operations, 1957-1961; Director, Epidemiology, 1961–; member of COOLS committee and Co-op Council

James P. Dixon, Jr., M.D.; Commissioner of Public Health, 1952-1959

Madelyn N. Hall, R.N., M.A.; Director, Division of Generalized Public Health Nursing, 1951-1960; Deputy Director, Community Nursing Services, 1960–; member of COOLS committee and Co-op Council

John J. Hanlon, M.D., M.S., M.P.H.; Director, Public Health Services (later, Community Health Services), 1957–

Adele S. Hebb, Personnel Officer, 1952-1957; administrative assistant to Hanlon, 1957–; member of COOLS committee and Co-op Council

Norman R. Ingraham, M.D.; Chief, Division of Venereal Disease Control, 1950 (and earlier)—1952; Deputy Commissioner, 1952–; Acting Commissioner, 1952-1954, 1959-1960

Paul W. Purdom, M.S., M.G.A.; Director, Division of Environmental Sanitation, 1953–; member of COOLS committee and Co-op Council

Rufus S. Reeves, M.D.; Director, Department of Public Health, 1944-1952

Alexander Witkow, M.D., M.P.H.; Director, Division of Preventive Medicine, 1955-1958; Director, District Health Operations, 1956-1957; member of COOLS committee

FOREWORD

At the beginning of the 1960's, the Philadelphia Department of Public Health was widely regarded as one of the finest municipal health agencies in the United States. It had not always been so regarded; this excellence was the product of a vigorous political reform movement in the late 1940's and early 1950's that had succeeded in bringing a highly professional service into the city government. The new professionals in public health brought with them the values, the concepts, the ideals of their field that were currently popular in the thinking and practice of their several specialties.

One such concept, already nearly half a century old, was that of local, or "decentralized" health services, physically housed in a number of "centers" throughout a municipality, each providing programs individually tailored to the needs in its particular area.

The story that follows is the account of a twelve-year effort to translate this concept into a successful action program; that is, to institute a system of district health centers with enough delegated administrative authority to provide for flexibility in program and genuine response to local community needs. This study describes the effort and the ideal behind it. Philadelphia's efforts to decentralize its health program operations had not entirely succeeded by early 1962. Both the department as a whole, and those programs within it designated "public health services," had undergone repeated reorganizations during this time; frequent change had become part of the Public Health Services' way of life, along with discussion, self-study, and planning. Implicit in its most recent review of progress and unresolved problems (late 1961) was the expectation of further changes, as the staff explored ways to achieve more effective decentralization.

PENN'S "CITY OF BROTHERLY LOVE": THE BEGINNINGS

Like many of Philadelphia's contemporary institutions, the City Department of Public Health has a long history and tradition; its roots are two and one-half centuries old. From the early 1700's various regulations were instituted sporadically for the control of sanitary conditions and of contagious disease. In the final decade of that century a Board of Health was established to administer the city's growing public health functions, which by then included responsibilities for the care of patients with dangerous contagious diseases and for the "sick poor." In 1904 a Department of Public Health and Charities was established to administer the functions of the Board of Health. This department was split in 1920 to form the present Department of Public Health and the Department of Welfare. (The latter retained responsibility for the medical care of the special groups it served.) Thus, by tradition, public health in this city has had a strong emphasis upon medical care and a close association with welfare activities.

Stimulus for the development of city health programs came mainly from Philadelphia's medical community and voluntary health and welfare groups. From the early eighteenth century, Philadelphia has been a leader in the medical field, establishing the first medical school and the first hospitals in the New World. It has continued to be a major medical center, with abundant and excellent resources. This excellence has been for the most part confined to private institutions and voluntary agencies that were supported by influential members of the community. Philadelphia's citizens concentrated their efforts primarily in private agencies, neglecting public programs. Thus, in spite of (or perhaps because of) the strength of private health and welfare programs, the city never developed comparable public health services.

There was, therefore, an extreme contrast between the private, professional sphere and the political-public sector in regard to health care. Leadership came entirely from the private groups, with the city government yielding reluctantly to sporadic pressures to improve the quality of public health services only to the extent that it seemed politically expedient.

For many decades before 1952 Philadelphia experienced one-party local government, with attendant political patronage, occasional corruption, and open scandals. The political conservatism and apathy traditional in Philadelphia were largely responsible. Those public servants who were able and honest could do little or nothing in the face of the indifference, mediocrity, and patronage that permeated the city government. Late in the 1940's, however, Philadelphia began to stir from its long political sleep.

At that time, the Department of Public Health was divided into two principal units, a Bureau of Hospitals and a Bureau of Health, comprising all other public health programs in communicable disease and sanitation. It is with these programs of the former Bureau of Health that this story deals. When Dr. Rufus S. Reeves took office in 1944, as Director of the Department of Health, it was regarded in the most tolerant view as "weak." As part of a local government that was at best mediocre, at worst corrupt, its leadership was severely limited in what it could accomplish. Reeves, however, was interested in developing better programs for the city and set out to accomplish what he could. One of his major objectives was the establishment of a system of health centers throughout Philadelphia.

Reeves Promotes Health Centers

The health center concept had emerged in the field of public health before the First World War.[1] While there were a variety of versions of this concept, the common principle in all was a physical plant, located in an urban area, providing health services appropriate to the particular needs of the area. The original concept went further: health centers should be administered by a health officer with authority and responsibility to direct the activities of all the professional and specialized people working in the center. The purpose was to provide integrated, coordinated health programs, which, it was believed, could best be achieved through multidisciplinary teams. This administrative form was early labeled "horizontal." The philosophy behind the concept reflected a shift from

[1] See: H. Kaufman, *The New York City Health Centers,* Inter-University Case Program No. 9 (Indianapolis: The Bobbs-Merrill Company, Inc.).

limited regulatory and control functions toward a broader goal of positive programs in prevention and in protection of the public health.

Health centers were not new in Philadelphia, but those that had been established up to that time were either privately operated or stimulated and partially supported by private foundations. The city had its own specialized clinics, scattered randomly throughout the city, for diagnosis, referral, and treatment of tuberculosis and venereal disease; it conducted dental clinics and child and maternal health clinics, called "health centers." In addition, it had one "consolidated" health center at 20th and Berks Streets, established in 1941 with support from the Rosenwald Fund with special stipulations: it was to be administered by a Negro and to serve primarily the largely Negro community in which it was located. This center provided under one roof a variety of health services, each conducted by a specialized professional division in the central office of the Health Department.

In Philadelphia, one of the leaders in promoting health centers was Dr. William Harvey Perkins, Dean and Professor of Preventive Medicine at Jefferson Medical College, and member of the Public Health Committee of the Health and Welfare Council. He envisioned a "health maintenance clinic" housed in district health centers throughout the city. Partly through his efforts, a demonstration health center was opened in 1948, with voluntary agency funds, as the Fife-Hamill Memorial Health Center.

In accord with this concept of public health practice, Reeves developed plans for a single large city health center, to cost between $1,000,000 and $2,000,000. But the mayor and the City Council rejected this proposal on the grounds that such a project would be very costly, would serve only a small part of the population, and was politically undesirable. They proposed instead that Reeves plan for ten centers in ten city districts, for the same amount of money, and Reeves decided to proceed on this basis. By buying sites in old buildings that could be converted to serve as health centers, he could at least launch a city-wide health center program. Each center would cost around $25,000 for the site, with $75,000 and upwards available for renovations. Funds from the city were made available, and in 1948 seven such sites were purchased.

At the time Dr. Reeves was developing his plans and purchasing sites, however, there was no idea in the Department of Health of going beyond the housing together of those specialized services already being conducted. Such an arrangement was thought of as "decentralization" of public health services, but it lacked the philosophy and administrative form conceived by the inventors of the idea, in which *generalization* and *delegated authority* were cornerstones. Confusion over the meaning of the term "decentralization," as applied to health centers, entered the discussions early and persisted for years.

Reeves Requests Public Health Survey

Dr. Reeves made a second decision that would profoundly affect public health programs in Philadelphia for years to come. Under his leadership the Department of Public Health and the City Planning Commission formally requested the Health and Welfare Council of Philadelphia to conduct a survey of the city's public health resources. The essential purposes were "(1) to afford information and guidance for the city in its program of District Health Centers and (2) to study and make recommendations respecting the administrative functions and operations of the Department of Public Health."[2] Dr. Perkins was appointed chairman of the Executive Committee, which secured as directors of the survey Dr. Carl E. Buck, Professor of Public Health Practice at the University of Michigan, and Dr. Roscoe P. Kandle, Field Director of the American Public Health Association. Financing was provided by a contract with the city, but additional contributions came from the Philadelphia Tuberculosis and Health Association and the Division of Medical Service of the Board of Public Education. Many other agencies and individuals contributed services to special phases of the survey.

Through the medium of this survey project, which continued for about one year, virtually all of Philadelphia's very considerable health and welfare resources were brought together, and the collective knowledge and viewpoints of these groups were focused upon the public health problems of the city. The document, published in 1950, became the foundation for Health Department policy in the development, organization, and administration of its public health services.[3]

---

[2] Philadelphia Public Health Survey 1949, p. *v*. Hospitals were *not* included as part of this project.

[3] The Health and Welfare Council of Philadelphia had fifty-six member agencies in its Health Division; of these, fourteen primarily concerned with public health are listed in Appendix I, p. 99. The Survey Executive Committee, Technical Advisory Committee, and Consultants are listed on pp. 99-100.

"PUBLIC HEALTH IS ONE OF THE SOCIAL SCIENCES": THE 1949 SURVEY

The survey staff carried out its mission in accordance with a statement of objectives formulated by the Executive Committee:

A. To identify the most significant health problems. . . .
B. To indicate the extent to which problems are being met. . . .
C. To suggest ways by which public and voluntary agencies . . . may individually and jointly further the efficiency of their operations. . . .

The survey report filled 241 pages and made 192 specific recommendations. These covered both immediate steps to be taken and others that would admittedly take several years to institute. The survey was, in effect, a long-range plan for development and sweeping changes in the total public health program of Philadelphia. Those proposals that had most significance for the future direction of the Health Department fell into three main categories: (1) Reorganization, upgrading, and expansion of the department; (2) Generalization and consolidation of five of the city's public and voluntary public health nursing services into a single service; (3) Establishment of nine city health districts, each with a health center, administered at the community level as semiautonomous units.

Organization of the Department of Public Health

At the time of the survey, the Health Department had a Director, an Assistant Director, and a Chief Clerk. The Director was required by law to be a qualified physician, but he did not need to have any real training or experience in public health. The Department had two bureaus, one for hospitals and one for health. A City Board of Health was composed of three physicians, one being the Director, as an ex-officio member. A secretary of the Bureau of Health acted also as secretary of the City Board of Health.

The Bureau of Health was made up of "some 10 or 12 divisions or services all responsible solely to the Director or Assistant Director," each more or less autonomous, and with no machinery for coordination other than through the Director.

The survey noted that in the entire Bureau of Health there was only one full-time physician, "an astounding situation for a city the size of Philadelphia."

The medical programs were conducted by separate divisions of Child Hygiene, Communicable Diseases, Venereal Disease Control, and Tuberculosis. Each of these had its own specialized nurses as an integral part of the division. Environmental sanitation was carried on by three divisions: Milk, Livestock, Meat and Food; Housing and Sanitation; Air Pollution Control (a recently added program, with its own Departmental Board). Each of these also had its own specialized personnel in the field. There was a Division of Laboratories and a Division of Vital Statistics. There were no divisions of public health nursing, mental health, or health education; no programs in nutrition, adult health, industrial hygiene, or accident prevention; and there was almost no use of medical social workers. The bureau operated twelve "so-called" health centers, but most of them were specialized in maternal and child health; none of these qualified as true, comprehensive health centers. While much of the bureau's work was found good, the survey criticized the need for more qualified personnel, the inadequate salaries, and the total lack of coordination of programs.

Finally, the bureau lacked any division of local health services, such as was usually found in large city health departments. Such a unit "carries the direct responsibility for the total public health services for the *people*. It is the place where the actual needs of a specific group of people . . . are related to the many special programs, services, and resources of the department."

At the time of the survey, the budget of the Bureau of Health was $1,700,000. This amounted to only twenty-nine per cent of total Department expenditures; most of the remainder was expended by the hospitals.

The survey recommended an expanded Board of Health, with some nonmedical representation, a requirement of qualification in public health for the Director, and a reorganization of the Department, with the addition of new services. The proposed new organization chart provided for a new Bureau of Mental Health. Within the Bureau of Health, related functions would be grouped under directors. A new Division of Preventive Medicine would include sections of Maternal and Child Health, Public Health Dentistry, Disease Control (by combining acute communicable disease, venereal disease, and tuberculosis), and Accident Prevention. A new Division of Environmental Sanitation would similarly combine Air Pollution Control; Housing and Sanitation; and Milk, Livestock, Meat and Food, and redistribute these in four sections, with a new fifth section of General Sanitation. A new Division of Public Health Nursing was recommended. Business administration, the old Division of Laboratories, an improved Statistics and Records section, and new sections of Health Education, Nutrition, and Medical Social Work would make up a new Division of General Services. Lastly, a new Division of Health Center Administration was recommended.

Public Health Nursing

Public health nursing in Philadelphia presented unusually complex problems. The Department of Public Health had no generalized public health nurses. All of its nurses were functionally specialized in the four divisions of public health medicine: Child Hygiene, Communicable Diseases, Tuberculosis, and Venereal Disease Control. The public school system had its own nurses.[4] Among the voluntary agencies were several carrying on nursing activities, the largest and oldest being the Visiting Nurse Society. Founded in Philadelphia in 1886, it was highly respected, had a fine reputation for the quality of its services, and was supervised by a board that included some of the city's influential citizens. The visiting nurses, operating out of five area offices, provided bedside care and instruction as part of a generalized nursing program. Theirs was the only city-wide generalized nursing service.

The Starr Centre Association provided, in a limited area of the city, the only other generalized nursing service. This was a nonofficial project, but the Visiting Nurse Society and the City Department of Public Health participated in it. Other small nursing units rendered specialized services to limited areas, mainly in child health and tuberculosis. The survey identified ten nursing groups in all, employed by six agencies, operating in the field of public health.

The major recommendations made were to combine and generalize all but one of these—the exception was the public school nursing service—within a single organization, under a board with representatives of both the official and the voluntary groups. This was admittedly a long-range objective. The survey recognized that financial support from voluntary sources was declining, while tax monies from state and federal sources were increasing. The Visiting Nurse Society had reached its peak in numbers of nurses in 1939 and led all agencies until 1943, but there had been a steady decline through the 1940's. The surveyors' objective was to provide a city-wide, generalized, public health nursing service. For immediate implementation, the survey recommended establishment of a Division of Public Health Nursing within the Department, raising of the qualifications for city nurses, and institution of a program of complete generalization. To head this division it recommended that a highly qualified public health nursing administrator be secured.

The surveyors recognized that there was, "unfortunately," considerable emotional heat clouding the issue of generalization versus specialization. "Among Philadelphia's leaders in public health are those who have long been devoted to the cause of specialized nursing, and one can only respect them for their steadfast and absorbing interest in their own programs." Among nursing leaders they found a "remarkable unanimity of opinion on the basic concept of a combined, generalized service." Less agreement was found among school nurses and medical and other administrators. The surveyors attributed this lack of agreement to a belief that specialized nurses were more efficient for their own programs, to emotion in favor of specialized nurses, and to a background of therapeutic medicine, with the traditional subordinate relationship of nurses.

Health Center Administration

Sporadic experiments with health centers had been made as early as 1914, when Dr. Samuel McC. Hamill opened the second health center in the United States, to provide child health care. The Babies Hospital had been opened in South Philadelphia in 1912, and the Starr Centre Association

[4] Nurses for parochial schools were paid out of the Department's budget but were nominally responsible to the Division of Medical Services of the Board of Public Education.

had been formed as early as 1905. The recently opened Fife-Hamill Memorial Health Center, most closely approaching the surveyors' concept of what a health center should be, was an evolutionary growth of the former Babies Hospital and the Philadelphia Child Health Society. The city's own program then included the one consolidated health center opened in 1941, the many specialized clinics, and the Department's plans to open seven new centers.

Twenty years before the 1949 survey, but unremarked in the survey report, Dr. Haven Emerson, former Commissioner of Health in New York City (1915-1917), had directed a "Philadelphia Hospital and Health Survey." Tucked away in its 844 pages were three brief paragraphs recommending that Philadelphia be divided into ten districts, based on census tracts, each with a "district health building or Health House." The purpose was to decentralize so far as practicable the field and family activities, to bring the protective services "as close as possible to the homes of the people," and to adjust "the quantity and quality of health work more appropriately to the diverse groups of the community according to race, economic, housing, density, and other factors. . . ." Dr. Emerson had begun to establish such a system of centers in New York during 1915-1917. A political change had swept him out of office, and his plans for district centers disappeared without trace.[5]

A like oblivion had overtaken his recommendation to Philadelphia in 1929. The surveyors in 1949 made no mention of his earlier proposal. But in 1961, a few recalled that he had once advocated ten health districts for the city.

As the survey work progressed, it had become evident to the project staff that there were at least three varieties of interpretation of the "health center" concept among Philadelphia's health and welfare groups. One was a facility associated with and supplementing hospitals; a second was a facility for teaching medical and other professional students; the third was a facility with varying amounts of preventive and medical services planned to meet the needs of particular local groups of people. The surveyors felt that these divergent views must be reconciled if any progress was to be made and, accordingly, arranged for a two-day workshop with leading representatives from all the city agencies most concerned, covering a "broad cross-section of the social sciences most closely related to public health." Of the seventy-five who attended, fifty-eight participants were Philadelphians, and seventeen came from outside the city.

The results of this workshop were summarized and were appended to the survey. In substance, the consensus reportedly reached was a clear victory for the integrated, community-oriented health center, with a health officer invested with sufficient authority to direct his own "teams" in his district; in short, the "horizontal" method of health district administration.

The summary stated:

> The conference reemphasized that Philadelphia is a group of communities each with its own characteristics and as dissimilar as different cities. Participants thought in terms of a *community health center* which they defined as follows: "A COMMUNITY HEALTH CENTER INVOLVES A PHYSICAL PLANT AND SERVES AS A FOCUS FOR A PROGRAM OF BASIC HEALTH SERVICES CARRIED OUT BY A QUALIFIED STAFF SERVICING *ALL* THE PEOPLE OF A DESIGNATED AREA."[6]

Continuing that no health center in Philadelphia approached this definition, the survey made clear that:

> There would be a single designated area of responsibility, but the services pertinent to *all* the population would be included. The basic concept is of a *team* of qualified public health workers who will be planning and providing services for a clearly designated unit of population. . . . The techniques of planning and providing such services are those of public health administration and epidemiology as contrasted to the provision of medical care to individual patients.

The city's Consolidated Health Center at 20th and Berks, housed in a converted police station, fell short in several important respects, although it was unquestionably making a great contribution in providing services in maternal and child health, venereal disease, tuberculosis, and dentistry. But the director's position was only nominal; he was in no sense a district officer. The center was under the central office direction of the Division of Child Hygiene. All of the services provided were directed separately by their divisions at headquarters and operated "independently with reasonable cooperation but little coordination and less integration."

---

[5] Kaufman, *op. cit.*, pp. 3-4, 6.

[6] Italics and capital letters in the original.

Moreover, there was no *single* district served,[7] no public health program related to a unit of population, no sanitation services related to the center. The services related to clinic attendance, and not, for example, to *all* infants in the area served.

The survey noted that the Department of Public Health was expecting to extend this administrative design to future centers by assigning their supervision as an extra duty to one of the division chiefs in venereal disease, tuberculosis, and so on.

The survey found some of the sites already purchased unsuitable for future development as health centers, in terms of proximity to natural community centers and good transportation facilities. In developing alternative recommendations, the surveyors endeavored to project future population shifts within the city limits and to anticipate variations in population characteristics of individual areas by age groups and other indices. Health services would need to be tailored to specific community needs.

The survey recommended that the city be divided into nine districts, based on census tracts, each with a health center. These districts were mapped and described in the document. The average population in a district would be about 200,000. Fife-Hamill Memorial Health Center and Starr Centre should become part of the city system. A new Division of Health Center Administration should be established in the Bureau of Health, and a full-time head with public health training, experience, and outstanding administrative ability appointed to direct it. Each center should have a qualified health director, directly under the head of Health Center Administration, with authority and responsibility for development of a total public health program for his district. The entire staff of the center should be responsible to this district health director, with the bureau's specialized program chiefs establishing policies and standards and providing technical supervision for their respective programs.

The survey urged that community health committees of local citizens be developed where they did not already exist, in order that the district health officer and his staff might maintain a close relationship with the community served.

Among the priorities for immediate action, listed at the end of the survey, was the following: "Sincere adoption by the Department of Public Health of the concept of decentralized, generalized health center services." The surveyors observed that "development of the health centers according to the concept developed at the conference . . . will depend fundamentally on acceptance and support of this concept by the public health administrators and their staffs."

[7] Meaning that areas covered by different programs were not identical in their boundaries.

Reeves Initiates Change

The Philadelphia Public Health Survey of 1949 was published in March 1950. Even before this date, the Department was moving to implement some of its recommendations. A position of Director of Health Center Administration was established (supported by federal funds) to head a new division in the Bureau of Health. This was filled by Dr. Melville J. Aston, a retired naval hospital administrator, who assumed his duties on May 5, 1950. On May 10, Dr. Reeves, Director of the Department, appointed Dr. Angelo M. Perri, Chief, Division of Communicable Diseases, as chairman of an advisory committee to study and report on the Department's decentralized consolidated health center program. Other members were: Dr. Norman R. Ingraham, Chief, Division of Venereal Disease Control; Dr. Pascal F. Lucchesi, Superintendent and Medical Director, Philadelphia General Hospital; and William J. Wolf, Secretary, Bureau of Health. Dr. Aston shortly began meeting with this committee. Dr. Reeves asked that a report be prepared "covering our objectives involving the establishment of the horizontal type of organization suggested," together with recommendations as to the best manner of changing over to the new form. "Proper lines of direction and supervision should be 'spelled out.' " Dr. Reeves also asked for a step-by-step program to accomplish these ends.

Two health center administrators were appointed in 1950, paid out of federal funds. One of these was Dr. Alfred S. Bogucki (who was later to play a leading part in the effort to decentralize program authority to district administration). The Department's budget for 1951 provided for health center administrators and clerks to staff Aston's new division. A position of Director of Generalized Public Health Nursing was also established, to be supported initially by federal funds.[8]

At the end of 1950 there were five so-called

[8] Federal support for this position and those indicated above came from a grant to the state, allocated to the city and disbursed from a special account. Employees supported by the funds were paid in the same manner, and conformed to the same personnel regulations, as all other city employees.

Consolidated Health Centers operating, and the Perri committee had recorded its agreement on a gradual change-over to "horizontal organization." By the time the committee next met in October 1951, the City Planning Commission had developed a ten-district map of the city, based on census tracts, that was tentatively adopted. Miss Madelyn N. Hall, newly appointed director of the nursing services, outlined her plan for beginning a gradual program of generalization of the public health nurses in a limited area. She had selected part of the district (now No. 7) in which Dr. Bogucki was then the health administrator.

By the fall of 1961, time was running out for the city's Republican administration. The forces for political change had been gathering strength for several years, fed by public indignation over repeated disclosures of corruption, embezzlement, and extortion in the city government. Finally aroused, the voters, supported by more than 500 leading civic groups, had adopted a new Home Rule Charter in April 1961. Soon Joseph S. Clark, Jr. would be elected the first Democratic mayor of Philadelphia in sixty-seven years, swept into office by a powerful reform movement. Dr. Reeves and Dr. Lucchesi, who had both promoted health centers, were very near the end of their years of service with the Health Department.

"A COMMUNITY HEALTH CENTER . . . SERVING *ALL* THE PEOPLE": THE CLARK ADMINISTRATION

Mayor Clark had campaigned on a platform that included a ten-point program of extensive improvement and expansion in the city's public health programs. Radical improvement of programs in public health for Philadelphia's citizens was, however, only one item in Clark's long agenda of reforms. He hoped to galvanize the local economy, attract new business to increase the tax base, clear slums, launch urban renewal, and provide far more and better services for the city. His philosophy of administration was to pick the best professionals he could find and encourage them to develop their own policies and programs. The new mayor retained few former city administrators at top levels, and neither Reeves nor Lucchesi was among them.

Philadelphia's new Home Rule Charter provided the framework for such administration. It replaced a "weak-mayor" system with a "strong-mayor" form, reducing the power of the City Council. It provided for firm financial controls and strict accountability. A reorganized civil service system was expected to eliminate both patronage and discrimination. A new position of Managing Director was established immediately under the mayor, with oversight of ten city departments, of which Public Health was one. Review of policies and objectives, help in formulating operating and capital budgets, review of proposed annual budgets, together with provision of management services, were major functions of the Managing Director's Office. But the flavor and character of the new administration stemmed from Clark and his like-minded aides; they were modern, professionally trained reformers who thought of themselves as "generalists."

The efforts in the Department of Health were but one part of this vigorous movement of reform and expansion in city government. The changes from 1952 on were comprehensible only as a part of this larger political scene; the substance of specific changes within the Department was determined by new policies, formulated under new leadership, and supported by the Clark administration.

As in the choice of many of his other principal administrative leaders, Clark went outside the regular career ranks of Philadelphia and beyond the limits of the city itself in his search for a new Commissioner of Public Health. He selected Dr. James P. Dixon, Jr., then head of Denver's Department of Health and Hospitals. Dr. Dixon held a degree in hospital administration from Columbia, was a Diplomate of the American Board of Preventive Medicine and Public Health, and had had successful experience in both hospital and public health administration. For Deputy Commissioner, he chose a local official, Dr. Norman R. Ingraham, then Chief, Division of Venereal Disease Control. Ingraham, cautious, meticulous, and practical, complemented Dixon's broad, bold, intellectually advanced but sometimes hazy concepts of health administration.

The new Health Department administration accepted as its underlying goals the same basic objectives that had been proposed in the 1949 survey. As indicated earlier, these may be categorized in three broad classes:

(1) To strengthen the overall performance of public health services: through improving the caliber and quality of leadership and operative personnel; through expansion of existing programs; and through enlargement of functions in accord with the best professional thought in the field.
(2) To integrate the public and private nursing services into a single, generalized service.
(3) To provide for decentralization to community centers of the management as well as the operation of health services.

Like the rest of the administration of which he was a part, Dixon moved fast and aggressively toward the first two of these objectives soon after he took office. On the third he intended from the start to develop plans through participative discussion and study with his staff. Changes were rapid and even dramatic during the first ten months of his stewardship—changes in personnel, in leadership, in budget, and in organization structure. Then, in October 1952, Dixon was drafted for a two-year duty with the U.S. Public Health Service. Ingraham was designated Acting Commissioner during his absence and efforts continued in the same directions, though with somewhat less of a headlong pace. By the time Dixon returned in the fall of 1954, the Department of Public Health was entering a period of consolidation. It is interesting that, during the Clark term, progress toward the first and second objectives listed above was very substantial; but the Department in 1957 was still far short of its goal of decentralization. The efforts toward the three goals interrelate, and it is useful, therefore, to review briefly the steps and the problems of each.

General Enlargement and Improvement of Health Services

During his first few months, Dixon began a series of organizational changes designed to better equip the Department for larger responsibilities. He established two Deputy Commissioner positions, one for program, one for administration. Under the latter, he assigned two offices—a fiscal office and a personnel office. He set up a Departmental Council of top personnel which thereafter met with him frequently. He projected a new Division of Mental Health. He hired a number of new people to top professional posts, and subsequently Ingraham brought in still more. More professional personnel were hired and assigned to each of the district offices. Salaries were increased to make possible the bringing in and keeping of better people. And a number of new professionals were employed to head sections and divisions in the headquarters.

One of the new professionals of Dixon's administration was Paul W. Purdom, hired as Director of Environmental Sanitation at the beginning of 1953. Purdom, who was to play a leading role in the decentralization controversy, was a Southerner in his mid-thirties with a disarming, relaxed manner that concealed for a time his capacity to exert considerable influence on those around him. A graduate of Georgia Institute of Technology, he held a master's degree in Engineering (Sanitary) from the University of Michigan and a certificate for a Public Health Short Course at Vanderbilt. He had worked as a public health engineer in several state and local health departments in the South, and in the U.S. Public Health Service. He had also served with the U.S. Engineers. In 1953 Purdom was among those strongly opposed to decentralization.[9]

Purdom, on his arrival in Philadelphia, had found the environmental sanitation program, in his own words, "utterly ineffective." During his first year, he reorganized his division, established a new personnel system, established new qualification standards for new recruits, and instituted in-service training programs. During its first two years, the division reorganized and enlarged, acquiring such new functions as air pollution control, radiation protection, and occupational health. Standards of performance in the older functions were rapidly raised. These included such diverse activities and such diverse occupational specializations as: meat and animal inspection; environmental health, including inspection of water supply, waste disposal, sanitation, barber shops, control of noxious birds and rodents; industrial sanitation. During those first two years, the Division of Environmental Sanitation drafted entirely new regulations and standards in accordance with a new health code and a new

[9] By 1961, Purdom seemed to be reaching the top levels of his profession: he held an M.G.A. (Master of Government Administration) and would soon receive a Ph.D. in Political Science from the University of Pennsylvania; he had received several awards and honors, was a Diplomate of the American Academy of Sanitary Engineers, officer and member in numerous professional organizations, and author of several articles.

air pollution code, trained its personnel in accordance with them, and undertook a program for educating the public to the new requirements.

The Merging of the Nursing Services

The changes in the nursing services were no less substantial and no less rapid. A few days after he took office, in January 1952, Dixon issued an administrative order transferring all the nurses in the Bureau of Health to the new Division of Generalized Public Health Nursing, and made the Director, Madelyn N. Hall, responsible to the Commissioner. Thus Miss Hall, who might have been placed within the Division of Health Center Administration, was given division-chief status, partly to strengthen her authority in carrying out the merger of nursing services. At the time Miss Hall had accepted the job of directing and generalizing the Department's public health nurses, she had been working for five years in Plainfield, New Jersey, which had a completely generalized nursing service. She had grown up in Philadelphia, where she had spent two years at the Babies Hospital in South Philadelphia, and had later taught at Abington Memorial Hospital School of Nursing, near the city. In 1950 she had been elected president of the New Jersey State Organization for Public Health Nursing.

When Miss Hall took over the Department's nursing services, she found that the specialized nurses in each medical division did not even know each other. Each group had its own salary scales and personnel practices. There were about 135 nurses, of whom fewer than five per cent, in Miss Hall's opinion, were qualified for the jobs they were performing. There were then approximately 700 clinic sessions a month, of all varieties, distributed throughout the city. These clinics were staffed in part by the public health nurses; the Department also employed in its clinics graduate nurses who did not perform the field work done by public health nurses. There was no in-service training, nor provision for curricular training.

Miss Hall set her own standards of qualifications and performance before the city had time to establish its new civil service system, following Clark's election. She proceeded gradually with generalization, taking one district at a time, over a period of several years. Since the specialized nurses lacked an adequate concept of the whole family or of the whole person, she undertook to indoctrinate them with the philosophy and practice of public health nursing. A program of in-service training was established.

Miss Hall drew heavily upon her experience in Plainfield, adopting the methods she had learned there. She found that the nurses did not oppose the change as much as others in the Department. The physicians were all opposed, however, and rumor had it that she would never last.

Miss Hall was tough-minded and forthright in expressing strongly held views in direct disagreement with her opponents. With Dixon's backing and authority equal to theirs, she held her own and "kept on speaking terms with them." She was told occasionally that she was being "too blunt," but, looking back after the events, she was not sure that there was anything else she could have done in the circumstances.

The rapid consolidation and strengthening of the nursing services inevitably produced grounds for conflict with other parts of the health program. In her efforts to build a strong nursing institution, Miss Hall exercised vigorous supervision and control. Those nurses who did not resign[10] or were not fired as incompetents (a small number) would accept direction only from within their own unit. They were developing an *esprit de corps*, pride in their profession, and a loyalty to Miss Hall that had never before existed in Philadelphia's public health nursing services. No longer "handmaidens" to the physicians, and in some instances lacking respect for the competence of the medical people they served with, they did not readily accept outside direction, especially when orders ran counter to, or were not part of, the duties and procedures prescribed by their own division. By the physicians they were regarded as uncooperative.

A report from district No. 7 during this period commented that the nurses "controlled" the clinics. The epidemiologist felt that his functions were usurped. Moreover, the central medical sections were dealing directly with the clinics and the nurses, bypassing him. A few months later a district health administrator confirmed that "At present clinics are . . . under the supervision of the nurses on a day-to-day basis."

Decentralization

In spite of obstacles and resistances, the efforts toward consolidated nursing services, like those

[10] Prior to Miss Hall's arrival, annual turnover in nursing had been about fifty per cent. It continued at this rate during Miss Hall's first year, then declined.

towards general expanding and improvement of health services, were enterprising and even bold; and their accomplishments were impressive. In contrast, the moves toward decentralization and the establishment of relatively autonomous community health centers were hesitant and faltering.

A number of "health centers" had already been set up at the time the new administration took office. But these were centers only in geographic terms. Each had a director but only in name. The directors were coordinators of service activities at the centers. The operations were budgeted, staffed, and supervised from the central offices of the Department, and there was little evidence of community programs as such. The discussions of the Perri committee, which had been established in 1950 by Dr. Reeves to develop a real health center program, had produced nothing beyond tentative adoption of district boundaries and a statement recommending decentralization of real authority to the district administrators.

Under the new administration, funds were made available for the construction of new, specially designed, health center buildings on a long-range basis. Dixon, for strategic reasons, pressed for this building program early in his administration of the Department. Those renovated centers then in use would gradually be replaced; eventually, the city would have ten district facilities. But as the new health centers were opened and staffed, however, they were administered "vertically," in the same way the 20th and Berks Consolidated Health Center had been operated for over a decade. Each program division ran its own show; the district health administrators were not much more than caretakers in their buildings.

The underlying issues were organizational rather than physical and geographic. The attack on these issues during the first three years of the Clark administration consisted of studies, discussions, reports, memoranda, and two inconclusive pilot projects, and rather little else. After the spring of 1955, the subject was virtually dropped for a period of nearly two years.

That the effort to decentralize was determined and sincere cannot be questioned. Beginning in 1953, the district directors began holding frequent sessions to discuss means of furthering decentralization. Considerable effort was invested in research on administration of public health in other large cities. In the spring of 1953, following a departmental conference on the subject, month-long pilot projects were undertaken in two districts to test the feasibility of decentralizing preventive medical services. But, though some felt they were successful, they were dropped. Toward the end of 1953 Mr. Bright M. Dornblaser, then Secretary of the Board of Health, circulated a proposal to govern the administrative relationships between the central and district office staffs.

In the spring of 1954, Dr. Ingraham held a series of thirty conferences on the subject with his top staff. In August of that year he issued a report on "District Health Center Program, Summary of Conferences to Define Administration," summarizing the consensus of the senior staff at that time. It was followed by a memorandum, asking the "collective thinking of the district staff." Significantly, the Ingraham memo continued:

> The Department of Public Health is committed to the generalized district health center program. It is not committed, at this time, to any particular pattern of developing or administering such a program.

Ingraham's report noted that almost no specific elements of administration gleaned from studies elsewhere were applicable to the Philadelphia situation, and went on:

> Unfortunately, no acceptable standard practice has been developed for urban district health center administration. Past programs have demonstrated more the weaknesses than the strengths of the district health center concept in large cities. . . . This is the tremendous challenge with which we are faced. There must be regional autonomy in programs designed to meet community needs, without loss of the efficiency to be gained from uniformity and standardization. . . .

The solution of the problem would depend upon a flexible approach, "with a certain amount of intelligent trial and demonstration, and with active participation and the best thinking of *all the members of the staff.*"

The Ingraham report placed responsibility for decisions as to which programs could be delegated to the districts with the central program directors. The determining factors in such delegation were three: (1) the competence, experience, and training of the district staffs; (2) the need for maintaining uniform standards of performance; (3) the quality of record-keeping in the districts and the channels of communication between the districts and the specialized units.

The report dealt with basic principles, rather than with details of organization and procedure.

It did propose dual lines of communication and supervision.

Full decentralization was described as an ultimate objective that might require five years or so to achieve; the chief obstacles were the necessary training of personnel to assume responsibility in the districts, and the development of adequate records and statistics to evaluate district programs. Ingraham ended by urging that responsibility be increasingly delegated by central divisions to the districts to the greatest extent possible.

Temperate as the report was, advocating change with "all deliberate speed," it was clear in stating the Department's ultimate objective of generalized, decentralized district administration.

Following his return in late 1954 from the Public Health Service, Dr. Dixon reentered the discussions with a statement declaring it to be the policy of the Department to decentralize to the maximum extent consistent with sound public health practice. He directed Ingraham to prepare an inventory of all public health programs, which would "serve as a basis for decision by the Commissioner with the advice and consultation of the Departmental Council for defining those programs which are to be administered on a decentralized basis." Accordingly, in January of 1955, Ingraham directed all the program divisions and offices to prepare inventories of their activities, classifying them as appropriate for decentralized operations or, if inappropriate, to give reasons. He prepared a report in April 1955 on the basis of these inventories, staff conferences, and individual consultations. This report seemed to uncover more problems than it settled: it had been found that a definition of the Department's overall objectives was needed, since the program directors apparently did not all have the same basic objectives; the proposed administrative structure itself, circulated in January, had been questioned, making necessary a collateral study in administrative practice; concern had been evident over a definition of channels of communication, and methods of supervision of the field operation.

Ingraham reported that the nursing division felt that generalization was so recent that program definition was not sufficiently matured to make decentralization possible without loss in quality of program. Moreover, the preventive medical programs with which the nurses worked were not sufficiently stabilized as yet for decentralization of nursing to be practicable. Environmental Health, too, had unique problems: much of its work was too highly specialized to be delegated to district administrators; most of its programs were not related to families, but to businesses and industries; some of the field men ("sanitarians") worked in more than one district. A decentralization of some, but not all, programs would result in field men reporting to both central and district offices, since the men were now generalized. Moreover, the necessity to enforce uniform standards city-wide would always exist.[11]

Finally, Ingraham noted, "After study both of our own practice and of experience elsewhere, the staff as a whole has come to realize that the differentiation between technical supervision and general supervision is artificial and impractical of definition and application." There would have to be a single line of supervision, either technical or administrative, with advice available from the other.

The report undertook to supply a definition of the objectives of the Department (as essentially the protection, preservation, and promotion of health, with programs focused on the family); proposed that the position of Director, Division of Health Center Administration, be reconstituted as Assistant Deputy Commissioner of District Health Programs; and outlined a new proposal for administrative structure. The central concept of this was that all programs would be formulated in the central office by a Council for District Public Health Programs, which would include all the disciplines, and related directly to an interdisciplinary team in each of the ten health districts. Thus all programs, central and district, would be under the same leadership. Miss Hall, Mr. Purdom, and Dr. Linden, Director of Mental Health, had prepared a diagram of this pattern as members of an ad hoc committee appointed by Ingraham to develop an acceptable pattern for the decentralization. But "the district program directors were not in favor" of this pattern of administrative structure.

Thereafter, no further discussions of decentralization were recorded for nearly two years.

---

[11] Throughout the early years of discussion of decentralization, both Purdom and Miss Hall expressed to Ingraham their view that an important block to decentralization was the lack of competent specialized supervisors to assign to the health districts. Said Ingraham, "Such qualified intermediate supervisors were almost totally lacking in the years 1954, 1955, and 1956." Ingraham felt that competent intermediate personnel were a prerequisite for successful decentralization.

The Resistance to Decentralization

Resistances to decentralization were sufficiently strong, during the entire term of Mayor Clark, to counter the pressure from the top to decentralize power and control to the districts. The principal opposition stemmed from the program directors in headquarters. The health center concept assumed an aura of virtue, but only as an idea. In any discussion of how to implement the idea—i.e., who would recruit, assign, and direct personnel; who would develop and supervise programs; who would allocate funds and other resources—the professional people in headquarters invariably found excellent reasons for retaining their control.

The district health administrators did not enjoy prestige equal to that of the division directors, nor the respect and confidence of others in the Department. In their "caretaker" roles, whatever their abilities, they had little opportunity to display leadership and competence. Some were holdovers from the previous administration and shared in the opprobrium attached to it. In general, probably only the Commissioner's office (including Dr. Ingraham), the district health administrators, and a very few others genuinely wanted to institute any real delegation of authority to the districts during Dixon's first few years.

The drive toward decentralization suffered a basic inconsistency if not an outright conflict with the other objectives of the new administration. The merger and the generalizing of nursing services under strong central leadership and the simultaneous raising of standards of personnel and performance in nursing could hardly be accompanied by a decentralization of authority and control to the districts. Miss Hall and many of the nurses understandably resisted it. Likewise, the infusion of new, strong, professional leadership in the various functional programs of public health could hardly contribute to enthusiasm for immediate decentralization of authority and responsibility for operations to district directors. Thus, Purdom, the new Director of Environmental Sanitation, was among the most vigorous and articulate opponents of decentralization during these years. At the time of Ingraham's inventory, he stated that none of his activities could be decentralized. And following Ingraham's later report, he wrote to Dixon, complaining, among many other things, that division

CHART I : DEPARTMENT OF PUBLIC HEALTH [ORGANIZATION AS OF 2/20/56]

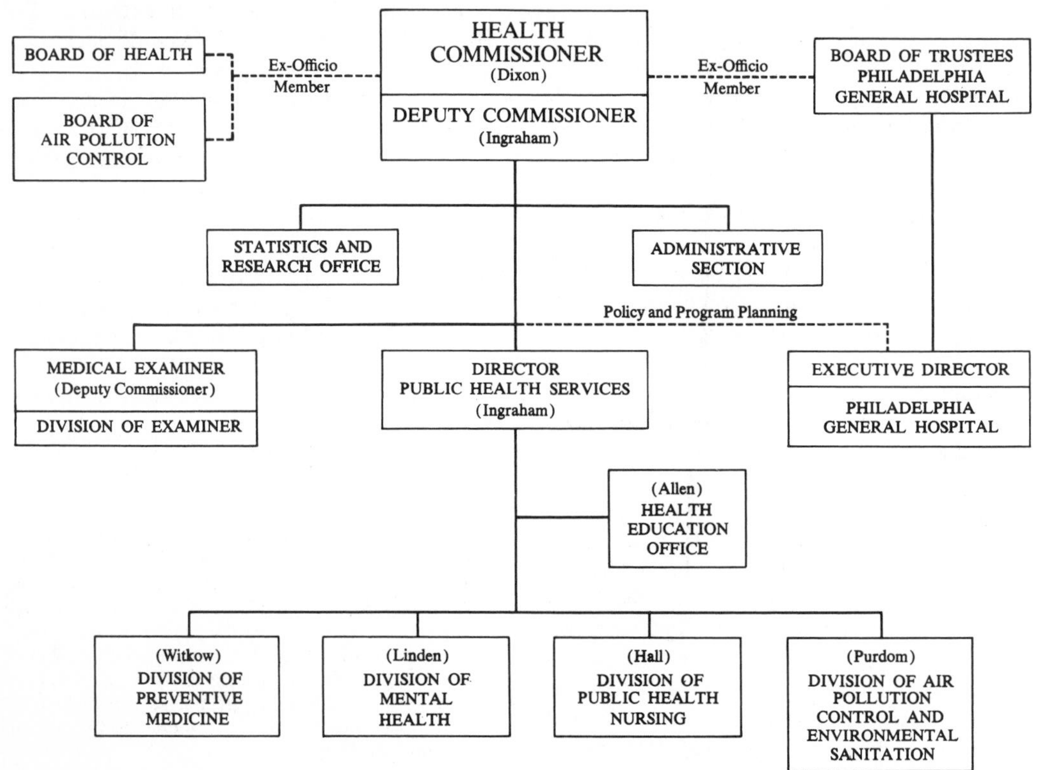

directors like himself who did not favor decentralization had been placed on the defensive by being forced to justify their opposition.

. . .

In the fall of 1956, Mayor Clark ran for and was elected to the Senate of the United States. He was succeeded as mayor by Richardson Dilworth, his closest political ally in the early reform movement and a member of his administration. Clark could look back upon a period of momentous change in Philadelphia, not least in the field of public health. But the idea of community health centers remained an idea. As the calendar opened upon 1957, the idea seemed to be resting at dead center.

However, during the latter part of the Clark administration, Dixon had made a number of organizational and personnel moves that were apparently designed to facilitate later efforts. In the fall of 1955, he had filled the position of Director of Preventive Medicine by the permanent appointment of Dr. Alexander Witkow. Then, in early 1956, he had transferred the personnel of the Division of Health District Administration to the Division of Preventive Medicine. Dr. Aston, who had been Director of the former organization, was relieved of that assignment and made a special assistant to the Commissioner. Shortly thereafter Dixon issued a new organization chart representing (in his own words) the culmination of four years of experimentation. Changes and refinements were later made, but the major divisions at the top were to remain stable.[12] The Department would consist of three principal compartments: the General Hospital, Public Health Services, and the Medical Examiner (which had been incorporated in the Department in 1954); each would be headed by a single director. For the unit of Public Health Services, line responsibility thus passed from the Commissioner and his Deputy to a new position of Director of Public Health Services. All of the program divisions and the Health Education Office were placed under this new Director.

The most significant change for the future of decentralization was the establishment of this position. Ingraham was made temporary Acting Director during the interim until a new man could be found and employed—an interim that was to last more than a year.

[12] See Chart I.

"COMMITTEE ON ORGANIZATION OF LOCAL SERVICES": HANLON PUSHES DECENTRALIZATION

As noted above, the creation of the position of Director of Public Health Services was viewed by Dixon as a major step in preparing for the decentralization of community health services. The appointment of Ingraham to this post was only temporary; during the intervening year Dixon sought a public health administrator with unusual qualifications to fill this crucial position. He felt that the candidate must be of recognized stature and competence, but also be strongly oriented toward social or behavioral sciences. He must possess an ability that Dixon considered rare among public health administrators—the acute perception of human values in organization and the ability to deal effectively with them. He believed he had located such a man in Dr. John J. Hanlon, widely known and respected as an administrator, scholar, and teacher in public health. Dr. Hanlon had served in county, city, state, federal, and international positions; he had taught at several universities and was the author of a textbook, *Principles of Public Health Administration*, regarded by many in the field as a "bible" of public health philosophy and practice. At the time Dixon approached him, Hanlon held positions with both the U.S. Public Health Service and U.S. State Department, as Chief, Public Health Division, U.S. Foreign Aid Program. Dixon felt that a man of his stature and prestige, together with his known sensitivity for human relations factors, could provide the effective leadership needed in the Public Health Services division.

Dr. Hanlon, who "would never have dreamed" of accepting any position in Philadelphia before the Clark-Dixon era, was gradually persuaded by the interest and challenge of the job Dixon offered. He believed, also, that the momentum of the reform administration would afford him support in carrying out whatever changes he might want to initiate. He accepted and assumed his new duties on April 1, 1957.

The stage was set for Hanlon's arrival in two ways. First, early in 1957, discussions of decentralization were renewed among the staff. Ingraham prepared another report on its possibilities, as did Purdom. And in March Ingraham appointed an ad hoc committee to study and make recommendations on an overall pattern of district administration. Purdom was made chairman of this group, with Miss Hall and Dr. Witkow as members. Second, just before Hanlon's arrival, Dixon ordered certain additional organizational changes, most of which would have the effect of enlarging the responsibilities of the Director of Public Health Services. Thus, the personnel office, the fiscal office, and the statistics and research office were transferred to it; a Director of Administration was established in the office of the Commissioner; and the Dental Health Section in the Division of Preventive Medicine was elevated to divisional status, becoming the fifth professional division under the Director of Public Health Services. The organization as it existed when Dr. Hanlon arrived is shown in Chart II.

Dr. Hanlon Takes Over

The new Director of Public Health Services was a man of personal charm and warmth, with an unassuming, direct, and informal manner. Both perceptive and "permissive," he preferred to create a climate and the settings for resolutions of problems rather than to rely primarily on executive orders. He openly accepted the presence of conflict among people, viewing it as inevitable and even necessary in organizations. He insisted only that his staff also recognize and deal openly with conflicts and that, despite these, it get on with the job of formulating and producing health services for the city.

As it developed, not everyone altogether liked this rather unusual "leadership style." Some of the staff would have preferred firmer and more constant direction, perhaps especially for colleagues. It was, however, the "style" Dixon had sought. Moreover, as an internationally recognized authority in the public health field, Hanlon commanded the respect of everyone.

As Hanlon became acquainted with his organization, he concluded that health services in the field were uncoordinated and inadequate to the needs of the city: a "galaxy of miscellaneous activities." The strength of the various programs seemed to be very uneven. He observed that many of his staff seldom, if ever, met. He believed that the only way to

CHART II: DEPARTMENT OF PUBLIC HEALTH [ORGANIZATION AS OF 3/25/57]

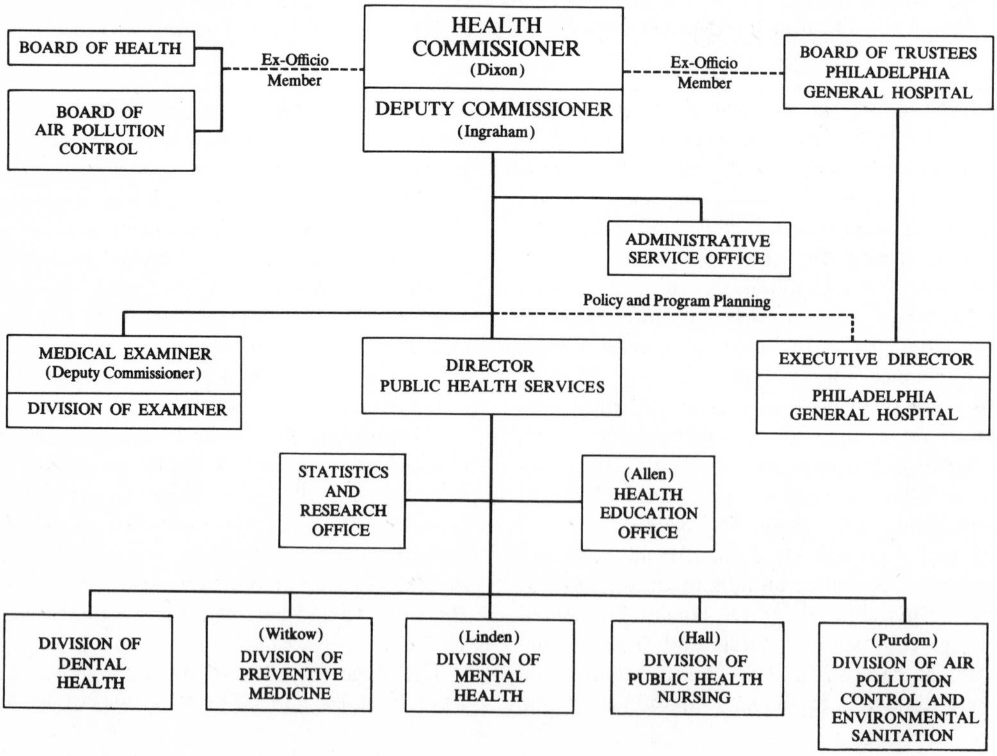

achieve integrated, effective programs was to develop a much closer meeting of the minds, by bringing people physically together and having them talk with each other.

Following this perception of the situation, Hanlon developed three main policy objectives: to pull the organization together, to equalize the strengths of the program divisions and offices, and to "decentralize" authority for operations to the districts.[13]

Hanlon's first few weeks were spent in conferences, staff meetings, attending the Ingraham-appointed ad hoc committee meetings on district organization, and visiting health centers. By May he was ready to move. On May 7, he transferred the district health directors, their staffs and activities, from the Division of Preventive Medicine, under Dr. Witkow, to his own direct supervision. He held his first conference with all the district health directors and continued to meet with them weekly. With the central office staff, he met biweekly.

He observed that every central division was bypassing channels for district administration, both in headquarters and in the districts, dealing only with personnel in its own programs. As he saw it, Purdom, Director of Air Pollution Control and Environmental Sanitation, and Miss Hall, Director of Public Health Nursing, were strong leaders; and both opposed decentralized district operations. They also directed the real core of the district programs; any attempt to decentralize would stand or fall on the attitudes and performance of these people. He therefore decided to give them responsibility for developing plans for the change. Moreover, since these two "stood to lose the most, they would be able to contribute most" to thinking through the formulating plans.

A decision was reached in the May 15 staff meeting that a standing committee be formed to "explore and recommend specific steps to be taken in order to carry forward as rapidly and smoothly as possible the decentralization of functions, staff, and programs of the Public Health Services of the Department of Public Health." (The exact means of reaching this decision is obscure, but Hanlon clearly had determined that it should be done.) In effect, this was a reconstituted and enlarged ad hoc committee with a new and far more specific charge. The members of the earlier Ingraham-appointed committee—Purdom, Miss Hall, and Dr. Witkow—continued on the new one; and Purdom, by common consent, continued as chairman. Two others were added: Dr. Alfred S. Bogucki, a district director, to represent the district point of view; and Mrs. Adele S. Hebb, the Personnel Officer, to provide an administrative perspective and to assist on managerial matters.[14]

Bogucki had impressed Hanlon as a potentially strong leader among the district directors—able, driving, and demanding of his subordinates. One of the earliest district directors, appointed in 1950, his long-held sympathy with the idea of decentralization was well-known. Miss Hall's first pilot project in generalizing the nurses had been located in his district. Likewise, his district had been one of those that had participated in the pilot project of decentralized medical services some years earlier.

Mrs. Hebb had joined the Health Department as Personnel Officer at the time of Dixon's appointment. Following the reorganization in 1957, she became responsible to Hanlon. Dixon and Hanlon both regarded her as very able, and Hanlon increasingly relied on her as a personal assistant. She was young, attractive, hard-working, with a quick, driving energy and a ready wit.

The new committee thus included the directors of the three professional divisions most involved in the health activities of the districts—environmental, medical, and nursing. Two of these, Purdom and Hall, had been among the vigorous opponents of decentralization, while the third, Witkow, favored it.

The COOLS Committee

At the first meeting, the committee adopted Purdom's suggestion that it be named "Committee on Organization of Local Services"—hence,

[13] Dixon did not ask Hanlon to carry out this last plan but rather gave him a free hand to work out his own ideas. Hanlon observed retrospectively that it was very difficult to trace the birth and spread of the idea. The concept of community-based health centers had been floating around for a long time; they were thought to be the best means of meeting the special problems found in large urban areas. Hanlon had known well Dr. Carl E. Buck, coauthor of the 1949 survey. But, despite the long history of ineffective effort to carry out decentralization in Philadelphia, Hanlon was allowed to make his own policies and independently chose "decentralization."

[14] Hanlon never considered himself a member of the committee, but the minutes revealed that he was considered a member by at least some of the others. His absences were faithfully recorded.

WARREN WILSON COLLEGE LIBRARY

"COOLS." Purdom had prepared a phasing schedule. The members first adopted the concept of providing programs for people as a unifying principle behind the entire report. The first recorded decision was that major responsibility for program planning lay with the central office. COOLS met weekly at first; later, more often. Purdom reported frequently in staff meetings, and each committee member consulted informally with his own unit throughout the deliberations. Thus information reached the rest of the staff members by several routes, and their own views were expressed during the course of the project.

Retrospective accounts of the nature and temperature of these meetings varied somewhat. One member said that no consistent blocs were visible, that while arguments were often sharp, divisions of opinion changed with each issue. But the more generally accepted view was that, in the main, there were two blocs, though these were not invariable on all specific issues. Purdom and Hall were lined up against extreme decentralization of authority, while Witkow and Bogucki wanted near-autonomous district administration. Mrs. Hebb was somewhere in the middle.[15]

Madelyn Hall remembered some of the sessions as contentious to the point where "very hot" better suited the committee than "COOLS." Issue by issue, the committee argued and fought and eventually reached compromises. Purdom recalled that on at least one occasion, faced with an impasse and the possibility of a minority report, an hour's recess was called. When the group reconvened, it was able to continue.

The sharpest conflicts revolved around who would assign, supervise, discipline, and evaluate personnel working in the health districts: the central offices or the district directors. There were other issues, such as control of research projects in the districts, vacation scheduling, and so on. All of the hotly contested points stemmed, as might be expected, from the one crucial question of how much real control would be delegated from the central divisions to the district administration.

For the first two months of its life this committee, like those before it, seemed in danger of getting nowhere. Arguments were prolonged, with Dr. Witkow, especially, holding out after the rest were ready to agree. But Hanlon would not let this project break down, nor would he let it continue interminably. On July 23 he attended the COOLS meeting and told the group to abandon the effort to work out all the necessary new procedures in detail and to present instead a statement of principles. He requested a completed report not later than August 15. Under this pressure, the committee stepped up its pace, meeting almost daily in both morning and afternoon sessions, and began to resolve the major issues. It presented a second interim report at a general staff meeting on August 7 and the final report on August 15.

After seven years of abortive efforts, the Public Health Services had at last evolved and agreed upon a plan for decentralization to the districts.

Some of the section heads still held grave misgivings about the wisdom of this change, but they had taken part in the informal discussions all along; their views had been heard. Moreover, these individuals were mainly in preventive medicine and environmental sanitation. Their own chiefs were members of COOLS and were committed to support of the plan. Hanlon, of course, was known to be strongly behind decentralization. The district health directors were in favor of any plan to increase their authority in the districts; some felt their district administrative positions were so negligible that any change at all would be for the better.

Purdom's own attitude had begun to change as early as 1955. As time had passed, he had gradually realized that with complete operating responsibility at the central level, his division had no time for long-range planning; it was constantly busy directing daily operations. Another consideration affected his thinking: as long as the district health directors were not involved in any of the division's programs, they remained uninformed and indifferent. Purdom saw that he needed increased community interest and support for more effective environmental health programs; cooperation from the district health directors in their communities was essential. In consequence, he was more inclined to regard some decentralization as potentially constructive and even necessary for the long run, rather than as threatening to his programs. Finally, by 1957, he had had over four years to reorganize and strengthen his division, train personnel and generalize the sanitarians, develop competent supervisors, and establish uniform enforcement procedures with

[15] Throughout the work of this committee, the minutes recorded almost exclusively the decisions taken, without any indication of the process leading to them or of the views expressed by individuals. The material presented here has been drawn from interviews with four of the five members four years later. Dr. Witkow had left the organization.

high performance standards. Miss Hall had had a little longer to overhaul and generalize the nursing services. Keeping close, strong control in their own hands no longer had the same compelling urgency as in preceding years.

Bogucki regretted some of the compromises he had made, but he supported the report as a whole. Every member of COOLS had, in fact, either yielded ground or been genuinely persuaded to a change of opinion; all, however, supported the outcome of their work.

The COOLS Report

The COOLS report first stated the basic principles observed in its deliberations as follows:

(1) Service to the people is the reason for the existence of Public Health Services.
(2) Services should be rendered from sources as close as possible to the persons or groups who need them.
(3) Decisions should be made at the lowest *feasible* level.
(4) Integration of the staff and operational units should be accomplished.

As had been reported to the staff in May, the concept of "program" was used to provide a unifying principle, from which a "total definition of respective responsibilities could be logically and systematically drawn." The committee developed this definition of "program":

> A program includes the planning, development, execution, and evaluation of activities directed towards the accomplishment of objectives of Public Health Services or of any subdivision thereof.

Responsibility for the development and planning of programs, together with an assessment of operational requirements and plans for meeting such needs, was assigned to the central office. However, "Consultations with the district personnel would ordinarily be held at this time." Any program ready for implementation must be considered in terms of overall priority goals of the relevant division, the Public Health Services, the Department of Public Health, and the City of Philadelphia. Setting of such priorities was declared a responsibility of the Director of Public Health Services.

Responsibility for the execution of programs was divided between the central and district offices, with three categories indicated:

A. Central activities with central responsibility.
B. Field activities with central responsibility.
C. Field activities with district responsibility.

Generally, activities falling under the following designations were reserved to the central office:

(1) Research and development.
(2) Broad supporting action to department (for example, the Laboratory).
(3) Socially limited problems (for example, radiation control, problems of certain special groups).
(4) Emergency programs of short duration (for example, a special polio "crash" program).
(5) Activities requiring extremely specialized personnel, where efficiency, cost, and lack of demand for services in a district would otherwise necessitate waste of resources.

The districts were assigned responsibility for program execution for those activities that were related to people or intimately involved them, and where programs were ongoing and recurrent, with well-established standards of performance, techniques, and execution.

The Director of Public Health Services was declared responsible for designating field activities to be conducted as a district responsibility.

The report next turned to a consideration of personnel management. The committee had developed a "suitable arrangement of relative responsibility . . . in accordance with the above principles as a means of translating them into action."

> . . . It is agreed that personnel, once assigned to a district for performance of duty in an activity of the district, are under the jurisdiction of the district director. He is responsible for their assignment and supervision and for the evaluation of their performance.
>
> *Supervision will be exercised by him in cases of groups of specialized personnel through intermediate assistants who will be termed in the rest of this report the "district technical representatives."*

These district technical representatives were distinguished from central office consultants and field supervisors not permanently assigned within one district. The report then went on to elaborate and qualify its central statement.[16]

Evaluation of program effectiveness was the

[16] For a summary of the details of this section, with the division of responsibilities, see Appendix II.

primary responsibility of the central office. However,

> It is the responsibility of the district director to coordinate and to maintain the maximum efficiency of his executory portion of the program and to govern and evaluate the performance of the personnel involved. It is the responsibility of the central office to routinely evaluate programs, not only city-wide, but on a district basis.

Development and enforcement of ordinances, regulations, and standards were vested in the central office as a primary responsibility; but in many instances it would be desirable to delegate this to district personnel.

The COOLS report next discussed the development of "a system which will insure the continuity of planning, development, execution, and evaluation." This system of administrative procedures dealt with "such subjects as communication within the Public Health Services and with persons and agencies outside of it; the actual keeping of records and statistics, and with community relations." To ensure "a fully informed corps of workers" that "must exist as the foundation on which can be built the smoothly coordinated and integrated operation of Public Health Services," staff meetings both of technical staff and of multidisciplinary staff, and at several levels, were recommended.

The report stated that the districts were the "eyes and ears . . . as to community needs, and the proper agents to report to the department proposed expenditures for personnel time, materials, equipment, and capital facilities to meet those needs." The central offices, however, "have the responsibility for the formal preparation of the budget, which includes coordination, resolution of competitive needs, and determination of the possibility of accomplishing the total projected need of the city." The committee recommended that a system of accounting be set up that would show expenditures on a district basis.

It was recommended that:

> there should be established a position in the Office of the Director of Public Health Services to coordinate the activities of the district directors. It is further suggested that there be created a committee to consider and develop organizational procedures as they are required.

The report also suggested the formation of advisory committees to consider the following: (a) priorities in programs, (b) planning evaluation, and (c) programs to be decentralized. It further recommended that frequent meetings of district directors and office and division directors be held, since free discussion of problems that might arise in adjusting to the plan was necessary to successful resolution.

The committee members observed that:

> The aims of this study and report will not reach final fruition unless all personnel within the Public Health Services strive to reach two objectives: first, that the district director and district technical supervisors attain such standards of capability that all will have confidence in their discretion, and their judgments will be highly regarded by central technical divisions; and secondly, and conversely, the personnel of central offices must also attain the high standards of competency in program design through which district personnel would hold their judgments in high esteem and carry them out in confidence.

The COOLS committee concluded with the hope that it had "achieved in its recommendations the blueprint for a balanced, smoothly functioning, coordinated, integrated unit of an essential department of this city."

Hanlon Develops a Climate for Change

During the summer, before the report was presented, Dr. Hanlon had introduced the staff to "brainstorming." He had prepared the staff in advance with information on the purposes of such sessions and what was expected of the participants. The focus for discussion was to be "program." Accordingly, on July 10 and 11, nineteen division directors, staff officers, and district directors took part in all-day brainstorming. A profusion of ideas on program was garnered, but also important in Dr. Hanlon's mind was bringing together, for the first time, all the central division directors and the district health directors. Questionnaires were returned anonymously following this event; they indicated that the staff had been very favorably impressed with the novel experience: the overall evaluation score was "excellent," 16; "good," 3. Comments noted the valuable ideas that had emerged, but equally significant were such observations as these:

> Freedom of expression—wealth of ideas—informality—working together. . . .
>
> Finding out that we really can work together despite inbred differences in approach.
>
> Spirit of camaraderie and cooperation. . . .
>
> Getting . . . to know other workers better.

> Free and open discussion with complete airing of views. . . .
>
> Ability to meet with people from all disciplines. . . .

A second brainstorming session was held on July 24, with "priorities" the subject for discussion. Hanlon was continuing his efforts to develop mutual acquaintance with increasing understanding, in the unusually free atmosphere peculiar to brainstorming.

Among his concurrent measures to raise the morale and status of the district directors was involving them increasingly in the planning and evaluation aspects of the agency. He also arranged for some of them to cover his office occasionally, when he had to be away.

The Plan Is Approved

During the fall following the COOLS report, implementation of the plans for reorganization was delayed by discussions with the Health Commissioner's Office, and with the city's Managing Director.[17] The proposed reorganization required the establishment of at least one new position, that of the Director of District Operations, recommended by COOLS. Dr. Hanlon finally got the go-ahead for his reorganization from the Managing Director, and on February 3, 1958, he issued P.H.S. Order 1 covering the general overall aspects of the reorganization, together with six additional implementing orders. Three more were issued later in the month.

P.H.S. Order 1 implemented the COOLS proposals in brief, general terms. It did not differ significantly from the recommendations, although not all of them were carried out, and Hanlon incorporated some ideas of his own. The crucial change to decentralized administration was formally made in these words:

> . . . primary responsibility and authority for the execution of field activities is assigned to the district health directors who with their staffs constitute the Operations function of the Public Health Services. It necessarily follows that all Public Health Services personnel working in a Health District are responsible to the district health director.

P.H.S. Order 3, of the same date, made specific assignments of all field personnel (except those who would, as agreed in the COOLS report, remain under central office direction) to the supervision of the several district health directors.

Hanlon divided the various divisions into two categories, designated as those conducting "programs," and those providing "service" for all or several "program" divisions. The service divisions were: Public Health Nursing, Health Education, and the Laboratory, elevated from section to division status. The program divisions were slightly changed and renamed: Air Pollution Control and Environmental Sanitation was renamed Environmental Health; a new Division of Health Protection was established, and the section of Maternal and Child Health was transferred to it to form a nucleus for future expansion; Preventive Medicine, from which this transfer was made, was renamed Disease Control; Mental Health and Dental Health were unchanged.

All of these eight divisions, said Hanlon, provided "professional direction." To coordinate these professional services, Hanlon recommended a new position of Director of Professional Services, responsible to him.

The second major functional area was "operations," to be carried out in the districts. For purposes of overall operating direction, Hanlon established the position of Director of District Health Operations.

The third major grouping was "management services."

Hanlon concluded his order with the following observations:

> In any healthy and dynamic organization, working toward a common objective, divergencies of judgment are bound to occur. Where these develop within any of the major functional groups (Professional Directions, Operations, or Management) they should be resolved insofar as possible within the major group. Where, for any reason, this is not possible, or when divergencies develop between the major functional groups, they should be brought to the Director of Public Health for resolution. In general, it is anticipated that free and open communication among all elements of our organization will form the basis for mutual support and confidence in achieving integrated public health services.

---

[17] In all the earlier efforts to develop decentralization plans, the Health Commissioner's Office had been intimately involved and had provided leadership. With the advent of Hanlon in the new position of Director, Public Health Services (in effect, a new level inserted in the administrative structure), this close, continuing involvement was lost. This, in turn, reduced involvement with the Managing Director's Office.

CHART III: ORGANIZATIONAL CHART—PUBLIC HEALTH SERVICES, EFFECTIVE 2/17/58

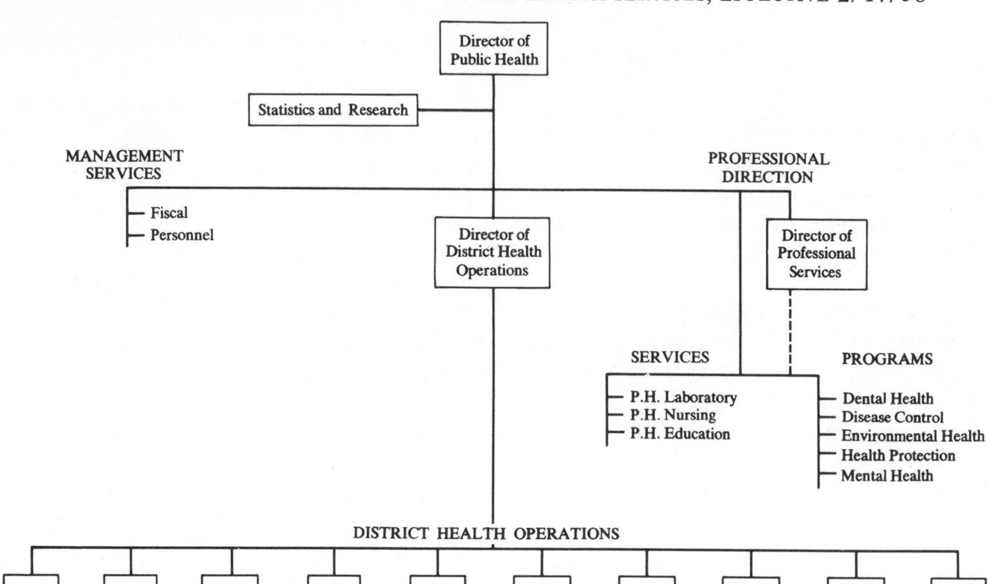

A new organization chart was appended to P.H.S. Order 1.[18]

Order 2 made three appointments, in an acting capacity: Dr. Mary K. Bazemore, Director of Health Protection (new); Dr. Bogucki, Director of District Health Operations, and Dr. Carl C. Janowsky, Director of Professional Services. Dr. Bazemore, a pediatrician, had worked in the Department's child health conferences (clinics) since 1937 and, more recently, had served as acting director of child health.

Dr. Janowsky, like Bogucki, was a District Director, having served in this capacity in district No. 6 since joining the Health Department in 1955. He also had a strong orientation toward community-based health services, but otherwise the two were very dissimilar. Janowsky was reserved, unassuming, and studious; Bogucki, driving and authoritative, expecting strict conformance with the high standards he set for himself as well as subordinates. As early as the previous August, Hanlon had discussed the possible new assignments with these men, whom he regarded as outstanding among the district directors. Bogucki, Hanlon felt, would give the district directors firm, positive leadership during the transition; he would also be able to hold his own among the central division directors, as the organization began implementing the drastic changes decentralization would entail.

The several other implementing orders issued by Hanlon dealt with details of procedural changes in payrolls, appointments, discipline, personnel evaluation, and the like.

The Public Health Services of the Department, after eight years of talk, study, and maneuver, finally were embarked upon decentralization of program operations to the ten health districts. The plan and the consensus in the agency had been reached through a process of participation, under Hanlon's leadership. But no one in this diverse, highly specialized organization had ever experienced the decentralized administration now formally in effect; it would not be easy for any on the staff—even those most eager for this change.

18 See Chart III. This chart was devised for internal use only and was never officially approved.

"TO MEET COMMUNITY PUBLIC HEALTH NEEDS": DECENTRALIZATION BEGINS

Over the next three-and-a-half years, the Public Health Services tried to fulfill its objective of decentralized administration. It encountered many obstacles, some within, others outside, the organization. Under Hanlon's leadership, the internal "climate" became increasingly free and open. Staff members were, for the most part, well-educated, knowledgeable, and sophisticated. They were also outspoken, and much of the conflict generated by attempted change and by the effort to coordinate the work of many disciplines was frankly expressed. Hanlon succeeded in bringing together the key staff members so that they grew to know each other well as time passed. Not all of the distances, however, could be eliminated: the geographical dispersion of people and programs necessarily continued, and the divergence of viewpoints inherent between highly specialized disciplines, though modified, remained.

During this early implementation period, reliance was placed chiefly upon informal and ad hoc mechanisms for meeting and solving the inevitable problems attending decentralization. Aside from the order itself and the personnel shifts described above—particularly the designation of Bogucki in the new post of Director of District Health Operations—there was little in the way of formal and systematic machinery to implement the objectives during the first several months. Most of the district directors continued in their posts, and some of these assignments antedated even the arrival of Dixon. There were no training programs to better equip them or their assistants for their expanded responsibilities.

District Evaluation

Progress toward decentralization was uneven and marked by the emergence of problems. One of the duties of the central divisions, under the reorganization, was evaluation of district programs and services, and accordingly, in June 1958, an interdisciplinary team of nine made the first appraisal of a single district, No. 4, at the request of its District Health Director, Dr. Bazemore.

The team gathered much useful information on the programs and needs of this district. It also pinpointed the confusion and uncertainty that apparently were endemic in the Public Health Services following reorganization. The team recorded that it was:

> concerned with confusion expressed regarding procedures and communications within the health district office and between the district office and the office of district health operations. . . . District health director should review appropriate existing orders and procedures with the district staff and seek clarification from the Director of District Health Operations. . . .
>
> The committee observed in general that the various disciplines were operating as independent units. . . .

The team recommended that regular district staff meetings be held, that the district director assume continuing responsibility for seeing that his staff understood the current policies and procedures, and that the district staff be informed by the district director of the need for keeping the director aware of developments and problems in district programs.

Under the heading "Coordination with Central Divisions and Offices," the report stated:

> The team observed areas of uncertainty in relationship between the district staff and central units. Specific areas in need of clarification are:
>
> (1) Responsibilities of the district health director to District Health Operations, and to the program and service units respectively, particularly in relation to the expansion or contraction of operations which affect program within the district.
> (2) Communications from the central units to the district director regarding contemplated program action by the central units relating to the district.
> (3) Development and interpretation of central office standards and indices to enable the district health director to carry out operations in accordance with program intent.
> (4) The scope and content of activities and operations for which the district health director is responsible.
>
> The team will bring the above items to the attention of the appropriate central units for resolution.

This team report had historic interest; the problems being discussed three years later in this agency were essentially the same (although not in the same degree) as those observed by the team: confusion over authority and procedures; lack of adequate communication and coordination; a strong tendency for central offices to bypass the district directors; and uncertainty on the part of district directors in their new roles.

The report uncovered a formidable difficulty in attempting to implement decentralized administration: the need to inform and to orient the district staffs in the new system. No one below the level of district director had directly participated in discussions and planning for decentralization. The district staffs were accustomed to reporting either to field supervisors or to the central offices. Now they were expected to change their methods, and, in effect, be responsible to both the district administration and the technical supervisors. As the team report indicated, however, neither the central offices nor the district directors were themselves clear about carrying out the new plans.

Concrete implementation of the report recommendations rested on several factors. For one thing, the new system required making a distinction between *technical* and *administrative* supervision and accountability (a similar distinction had been labeled "impractical of definition and application" by some of these same planners just two years earlier). Second, both the COOLS report and P.H.S. Order 1 were hedged with exceptions and blurred with vague or overlapping areas. They both admittedly relied for effectiveness on two principal administrative factors: (1) development of appropriate communications, cooperation, and coordination; (2) resolution of any conflict, either where it first occurred or by appeal upwards to the Director of Public Health Services. Third, where explicit and detailed new procedures had been prepared and circulated, the entire staff was expected to abandon the old ones and adopt the new.

It was up to the district directors, said the team, to accomplish the change-over in their staffs. But the directors, too, were confused and unsure of their authority and, as noted, were lacking in support from the central divisions, which were still bypassing them.[19]

P.H.S. Order 1 was, in effect, an attempt to replace the simplest administrative form—direct line supervision—which the agency had always had, with one of the most difficult, highly complex forms. It required, first, coordination in the central offices for every field program in which more than one service or discipline was involved, and, second, consultation with districts in advance of program changes. It required coordination in communications and supervision, through at least two parallel channels (technical and administrative) to the districts. Within each district, it again required coordination "horizontally" among disciplines, supporting services, and so on. It also required a similar process in reverse, from field to headquarters.

[19] No formal training program for the position of district health director was ever instituted. The agency relied upon basic qualifications and informal, on-the-job experience.

The reiteration of exhortations to "follow procedures" was not very effective in the face of confusion, overlapping authorities, habitual methods, and ingrained attitudes. The established informal system also tended to perpetuate the old ways. None of the directives issued could by themselves alter the status and power structure within the agency. Such authority as has been formally vested in the districts could be no more effective in practice than the amount of authority the central divisions chose to delegate and the amount the district directors were willing to exercise. This shift in the locus of real authority was, in June 1958, conspicuously lacking.

The Co-op Council

It was perhaps partly in response to the persistence of problems like those identified in the survey that Hanlon, in February 1959, established a committee "to consider and develop organizational procedures as they are required." Such a committee had in fact been proposed in the report of the earlier COOLS committee. Hanlon had in mind a staff council, to serve in an advisory capacity, "for the joint consideration of plans and solutions to problems in the operation of total Public Health Services program." There was an obvious need for more integration and coordination, which was openly recognized. Hanlon was acting partly in response to the expressed needs of people within the organization, who wanted very specific direction in implementing the new system.

Hanlon appointed Purdom as director, "with specific responsibility in the areas of intra-organizational relationships, resolution of problems of internal procedure affecting agency performance, and coordinated planning for the execution of programs." Hanlon delegated authority to Purdom "to decide, authorize, and direct any appropriate actions. . . . relating to these areas." Appointed to serve initially on this council were: Bogucki; Dr. Donald A. Cornely, Chief, Maternal and Child Health; Dr. Thomas W. Georges; Miss Hall; and Mrs. Hebb.[20] The group was directed to meet regularly and frequently. The new council was speedily dubbed Advisory Council for Coordination of Operations—"Co-op Council."

One problem that had proved especially trouble-

[20] Four of these had served on the COOLS committee: Purdom, Bogucki, Miss Hall, and Mrs. Hebb; all four were still on the council two-and-a-half years later, while other staff members served in rotation.

some was the scheduling of clinic sessions in the districts, and it was to this the Co-op Council first addressed itself. Before decentralization was effected, the program specialists had controlled the establishing, operating, shifting, or canceling of clinics. But now the district directors were supposed to have major responsibility for operations and for representing the special needs within their districts. In one instance, as an example of this problem, a morning tuberculosis clinic was canceled by the central division. This cancellation had a significant effect upon the public health program in that particular district, for the morning clinic had served an area with numerous "skid row bums" among whom the incidence of tuberculosis was much higher than in the general population. These men could be found on the streets and brought to the clinic for examination only in the morning; by afternoon they had dispersed and could not be located. In this case, by the time the issues were worked out, the clinic could not be rescheduled; the time of the nurses and clerks needed for the clinic operation had been absorbed into other programs.

The Co-op Council, after consulting with program division directors, section chiefs, district directors, and district supervisors, issued a directive in March setting up detailed procedures for any change—expansion, contraction, or important procedural alterations—desired by either the central or the district staffs. Consultation was obligatory in all instances, with the central offices retaining authority for final decision on the *number* of clinics and the district directors having final authority on the *timing* and *location* of clinic sessions held in their districts. The Director of District Health Operations was to be brought in in every case where budget and personnel changes were involved; where these were not, he was only to be notified. The directive made clear that the procedures referred only to formal communications; informal contacts were strongly encouraged.

Following study and reporting by a council-appointed task force, Purdom issued a directive, in August, on policies and procedures for staff development. Details covered eight pages. The main divisions of responsibility made were: overall coordination and general orientation, the Personnel Office; in-service, specialized training, the functional divisions and offices; on-the-job training, the immediate line supervisor.

The Co-op Council became an established institution in the Public Health Services. It met fairly regularly and continued to take up problems emerging in the change-over to decentralized administration, issuing statements and directives from time to time. The procedures set forth were necessarily lengthy and involved, since so many people were now concerned in every step of program planning, operations, evaluation, and so on. The council clearly had authority delegated from Hanlon to promulgate the procedures; ensuring compliance was another matter. In an operation now become so complex, when coordination obviously did break down somewhere, responsibility often could not be pinpointed. In any case, as a group of peers, the council itself could scarcely undertake enforcement. Hanlon did not provide direct day-to-day supervision, since he was far too busy. He was consistently refused a deputy, or a director of professional services, by the city; and his formal "span of control" comprised about thirteen people. Hanlon's policy, moreover, was to provide his subordinates a free and supportive atmosphere and to expect them to work out their problems cooperatively. He was available for resolving conflicts brought to him; in other words, the exceptional cases. The void that staff members increasingly felt was the lack of any mechanism, either executive or advisory, for ensuring continuing coordination on a daily basis. Lacking this, plus the presence of confusion and noncompliance with both the spirit and the word of the orders, conflict and a rather high level of frustration were evident among the staff.

The Changing Context of Decentralization: 1958–1961

The efforts to realize a true decentralization during these first three years were attended, and in some instances complicated, by changes in the context of the Public Health Services and in its relations with other agencies of the city government. Among these, one of the most important derived from the changing *atmosphere and the support within the city government*. The earlier Clark period of exuberant expansion and reform was over. The convergence of professional and political forces that had supported Dixon's efforts during his first four years flagged and gave way to forces that placed emphasis on efficiency and control. Increasingly, Public Health Services found itself on the defensive in dealing with City Hall. Moreover, it became apparent that it also lacked a strong political constituency. The difficulties and obstacles experienced by the Public Health Services reflected the general city government movement away from positive support for expansion and improvement toward a stabilization of programs and a leveling off of expenditures.[21]

For these reasons Hanlon encountered increasing difficulty in getting support for new or expanded programs in the City Council, in the Health Department's own Administrative Services Office, and especially in the Managing Director's Office. Much of the trouble between Hanlon and the Managing Director's Office apparently stemmed from a marked divergence in their respective organizational philosophies. As an administrator, Hanlon was considered to be somewhat unconventional in a technical sense. Nonetheless, Dixon, who was not himself concerned with administrative methods as such, believed that "once you have picked a good man who is providing good programs, you let him run his own operation in his own way, and give him leeway to carry out his own ideas." The city's Managing Director, however, did not share Dixon's views on allowing leeway; he distrusted Hanlon's kind of administration. As a result the Managing Director kept unusually tight control over the personnel and funds of the Public Health Services, reviewing even the smallest requested changes. In this connection the method of budgeting was a mechanism of centralized control and a contributing factor to increasing rigidity. While the City Council appropriated lump sums to the various departments, the Managing Director's Office allocated funds and controlled expenditures of the departments on a line item basis. Changes in allocations of individual items required approval "all the way up." Hanlon's own flexibility was thus hampered; he was permitted very little discretion in the use of his agency's resources after the annual budget had been authorized. But more than this: the existing budgetary system and practices made it infeasible if not impossible to delegate much in the way of budgetary control to the health districts.

During the three years under discussion, the building program for new district health centers, which had been authorized and begun earlier, proceeded, and a number of centers were opened. But operating expenditures (about $5,000,000) and the working force (about 850) remained virtually constant from 1958 on. All new undertakings and expansions during this period sought their financial support from federal and state funds. An example of Hanlon's difficulties stemming from budgetary limitations was his inability to obtain funds for his proposed new position of Director of Professional Services; eventually, in 1958, he gave up and dropped it.

Another major development during this period was the establishment, in May 1959, of the *Community Nursing Services* (CNS) through the merger of the Visiting Nurse Society (VNS) with the city's public health nurses. Earlier, most of the smaller voluntary nursing services had been combined with the Health Department, and this was the final step. It was the culmination of nearly a decade of formal consideration and the fulfillment of a major recommendation of the 1949 survey. It was also a "first" in this country: while a few smaller urban communities had accomplished the merging of voluntary and public nursing agencies, no large city comparable to Philadelphia had done so successfully. The legal and formal arrangements were unusual; the new Community Nursing Services was composed of two agencies, each with its own nurses, payrolls, personnel regulations, and so on. The agreement was made between the City of Philadelphia, "acting through its Department of Public Health," and the VNS. The controlling body was a board of fourteen members, half appointed by the mayor and half by the VNS. The Health Commissioner (or his designee) was required to be a member of the CNS Board. There were to be two advisory committees: the Medical Advisory Committee, of which the Director of Public Health Services (or his designee) would be a member; and the Program Committee, to be chaired by the Director of Public Health Services. An executive director, responsible to the board, was to be the chief officer of the CNS.

To ensure that the new head of CNS would have had no personal involvement in the years of discussion, nor be identified with either Philadelphia agency, the directorship was filled from outside the city. Miss Dorothy Wilson, then Director of the New Haven Visiting Nurse Association, was appointed; she assumed her new duties in September 1960.

By this time, the nursing services in district No. 9 were fully integrated, and the CNS began op-

[21] At the start of his administration, Clark had obtained substantial increases in the city tax rates to finance a greatly expanded program of services. Philadelphia, however, was faced with urban decay and an economy in serious trouble. Taxes could not be increased repeatedly; in consequence, there was a leveling off after the early sharp rise in city expenditures.

erating under its new name. The city's public health nurses, only recently generalized under Miss Hall's direction in the course of a several years' program, were embarked once more on a major organizational change that would involve performing new duties. For the visiting nurses, it was also a drastic upheaval. They felt threatened with the loss of their indentity, traditions, and a proud history of service much older than that of the city nurses. As the smaller group, they feared being overwhelmed in the new organization.

The merging of operations, which would take several years to effect, put the nursing services under unusual stress. At the same time, the structure of the new CNS, under a semi-independent board, meant that the merged nursing services were not formally under Hanlon's executive direction, nor even Department of Public Health direction. In effect, while the city had gained increased nursing resources for expanded services through the merger, it had also relinquished some of its authority over its own public health nurses to a board, half of which was appointed by a voluntary agency over which the city had no formal controls.

As merging proceeded, the nurses gradually became indistinguishable in functions[22] and in uniforms, yet each continued to be employed by one or the other agency, with funds for the visiting nurses still coming from private sources. Such a situation obviously imposed additional strains on the pattern of decentralized supervision at the district level. The district directors still had presumed operating control of and responsibility for supervision of the nurses; but a separate channel of authority and responsibility over the nursing services in general stemmed downward from a board, itself outside the Health Department and, indeed, outside the city government.

In the new CNS, Miss Hall became Deputy Director for Service and Education. Mrs. Marian Shand Andrews, Director of the VNS (and formerly of the Starr Centre Association) was appointed Deputy Director for Personnel and Citizen Participation.

There were a number of other *organizational and program changes* during the period; but none of these marked any significant shift in the philosophy of decentralized operations, and none approached, in its significance, the establishment of the Community Nursing Services. The name of the Public Health Services was changed, in 1961, to Community Health Services (CHS). The name of the division headed by Dr. Witkow was successively changed from Preventive Medicine to Disease Control and then to Epidemiology to recognize a "broader professional concept of its current and developing program." Dr. Witkow himself resigned in 1958 and was replaced by Dr. Janowsky, whose acting position of Director of Professional Services was abandoned. A new section of Adult Health was added in the Division of Health Protection, again reflecting the changing and enlarging importance of medical technology and the shifting emphasis to chronic diseases such as cancer, heart disease, and diabetes. Lacking local funds, this program relied heavily upon volunteer efforts and federal grants. Another significant addition was the appointment of a cultural anthropologist to Hanlon's staff to explore ways of making the organization more effective.

Perhaps the most significant change of all, however, was the *resignation of Dr. Dixon* as Commissioner of Public Health in July 1959 to become president of Antioch College. He was succeeded the following year by Dr. Eugene A. Gillis. In view of the important role played by Dr. Dixon in this case study, it may be useful here to review briefly his record and accomplishments.

By the time Dixon left Philadelphia, at the end of seven-and-a-half years, he had developed a city health department some thought second to none in the United States. The major accomplishments in the public health services unit of the Department, during his administration, had been the improvement of its professional personnel, the expansion of its programs, the generalization of public health nursing, the groundwork for decentralization of program operations, the construction of new health centers, and the merger of public health and visiting nurses. Of the 1949 survey recommendations, approximately eighty per cent had been put into effect.[23]

His relations with the private medical community and with the Health and Welfare Council had been mixed. By the socially conservative organized med-

---

[22] One major difference in traditional functions of public health nurses and visiting nurses was that the latter had always provided bedside care, whereas public health nurses did not. Both groups, once merged in the CNS, would have to learn and perform the activities of the other, as well as those they already knew.

[23] This figure was based on a departmental study and affirmed by an officer of the Health and Welfare Council.

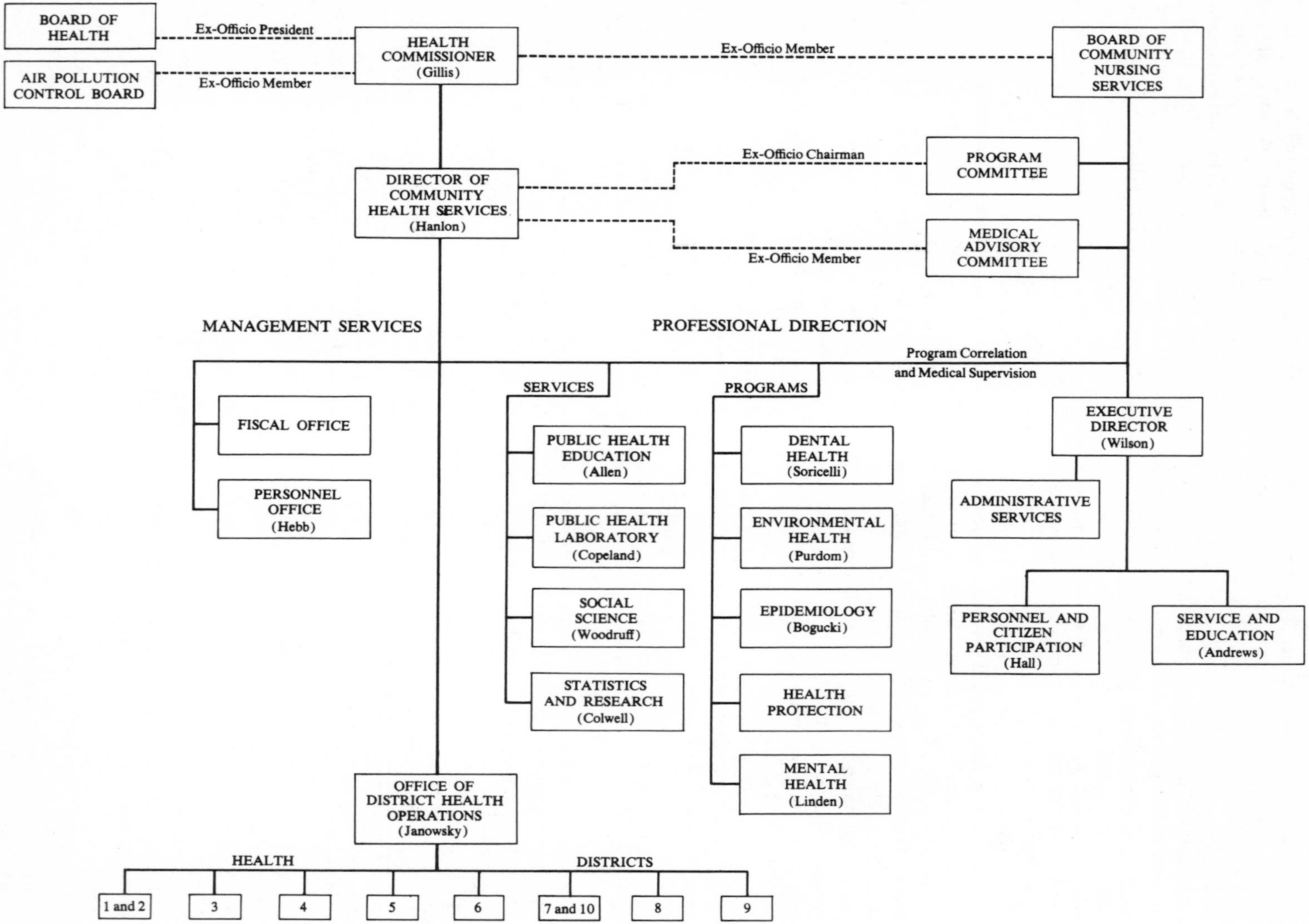

CHART IV: PHILADELPHIA DEPARTMENT OF PUBLIC HEALTH COMMUNITY HEALTH SERVICES, EFFECTIVE 2/6/61

ical groups, he was considered too radical; but he was respected. As head of a highly professional agency, Dixon did not rely for direction and advice upon the private and voluntary groups, as had his predecessors; but he cooperated with them. He viewed them, in fact, as a more stable community resource over the long pull than political vicissitudes would allow the city government to be. For this reason, he had deliberately tried to root elements of the public health program to some extent in the private community—most notably the Philadelphia General Hospital, which he had formally tied into two medical schools,[24] and the Community Nursing Services.

"BEHOLD! I HAVE SET BEFORE THEE AN OPEN DOOR":[25] COMMUNITY HEALTH SERVICES, 1961

The study on which this report is based was conducted in the fall of 1961, twelve years after the 1949 report from which most of the changes in Philadelphia's public health program stemmed, four years after the COOLS report, and more than three-and-one-half years after the order directing decentralization was issued. Over the twelve-year period, the changes in the health program as a whole had been enormous, almost revolutionary. The programs had been vastly enlarged and expanded. The budget for public health services had grown almost threefold, from \$1.7 million to \$4.7 million. The agency's personnel had increased from . . . to 874.[26] A large number of highly qualified professional people in a great variety of specialized fields had been recruited, and many of them were widely recognized as national leaders in their fields. Public health in Philadelphia had been transformed from a relatively limited, financially impoverished, and professionally inadequate program to a status of eminence among public health programs in the nation.

The extent to which the program of decentralization had contributed to these attainments was less clear. Indeed, the extent to which real decentralization had occurred in the terms conceived by its early advocates was in 1961 a matter of wide difference of opinion. The objective of decentralization was the subtlest, the most difficult, and probably also the most profound, in terms of changing the nature and the image of public health, of all the objectives of the reform movement. The assessment of the degree to which it had been successful and of the degree to which it had actually happened is approached, in the paragraphs that follow, from three standpoints: first, the different professional programs involved in public health; second, the districts and their directors, presumed recipients of decentralized powers and responsibilities; and finally, the opinions of the officers and personnel involved within the agency.

24 See Robinson, Mariana, and Silverman, Corinne, *The Reorganization of Philadelphia General Hospital,* Inter-University Case Program No. 47 (Indianapolis: The Bobbs-Merrill Company, Inc.).

25 Revelations 3:12, quoted in Community Health Services Annual Report 1960. This biblical phrase was attributed to the Quakers of Philadelphia as a "motto" frequently used. The report suggested it was appropriate to the new health centers, symbols of a new way of life for Philadelphians.

26 Filled positions; 933 were authorized.

Professional Health Programs

In 1961 the degree of decentralization among different health programs varied widely. A number of the different sections remained completely centralized in headquarters offices, with little or no participation by the districts. In most cases, these remained centralized by design and also by necessity; they required highly specialized personnel and /or facilities, and it would hardly have been feasible to subdivide the limited resources among the districts. Thus the *Laboratory* remained almost completely centralized, as did *Adult Health,* which was too small a section for decentralization. Likewise, the *Division of Statistics and Research* was centralized; there were no statisticians in the districts. And the work of the *consulting social scientist,* Dr. Woodruff, could hardly be divided among a number of districts.

There was a wide scatter of practice among those programs that might have operated either on a central or delegated basis.

The Division of Environmental Health had one sanitarian supervisor in each of the eight health centers. These men directed forty-four sanitarians and sanitarian aides in the ten districts. Purdom was encouraging as much decentralization as possible to the districts. He had taken steps to enlist the district directors in the division's program and was preparing to decentralize more activities to the districts. A very successful move had been to turn over to the district directors the conduct of hearings on violations of sanitary regulations found in their districts. These hearings were informal and preliminary to legal proceedings by the city, in those cases where violators persisted in failing to meet standards. One value in this delegation, in the opinion of the division, was that the district directors, as physicians, were regarded by the public with a respect that lent increased prestige to these hearings. It was also a method of enlisting the interest and involvement of the district directors in the environmental health program. Special demonstration projects in rat-control carried out in selected neighborhoods met with enthusiastic response on the part of some district directors who participated.

All of the engineering and other highly specialized activities in veterinary medicine, entomology, chemistry, air and radiological pollution, occupational health, and so on were centrally directed, in the main. Portions of some of these, however, were decentralized to the districts in a geographical sense: sanitarians investigated complaints of such things as restaurant odors, for the air pollution section, and rats, for the engineering section. Inspections of schools were carried out on a district basis by sanitarians and engineers. Plans for further decentralization of activities included inspections of swimming pools and private dumps.

Of the three sections in *Epidemiology*, *Venereal Disease*, under Dr. Lentz, was least decentralized. Dr. Lentz, who served half-time with Community Health Services, had worked in the Health Department for twenty-one years. The program of this section was highly regarded, and its administration was smooth; "no one ever worried about it." Everyone was concerned, however, about the rise in incidence of venereal disease. Since 1955, after a long decline following the war, venereal disease had nearly doubled in the population each year. The highest rate of increase was among teen-agers. The incidence of gonorrhea was much higher than that of syphilis, and its control and cure much less effective. But syphilis, by far the more dangerous, was preventable and curable. The main job of this section was to educate the public and to find the carriers and contacts for treatment in the clinics. Clinics were conducted in only three of the district centers. Dr. Lentz would have preferred that all this work be centralized in a single district, partly to simplify control in case-finding and treatment. Bogucki, however, was insisting that more, not less, decentralization be instituted, and wanted venereal disease clinics in five of the centers. This section, by now, "always remembered" to contact the district directors about its programs.

The *Tuberculosis Section* was decentralized, under Dr. Samuel C. Stein, who also served half-time. There were six supervisors for nine of the districts. Dr. Stein had set up a registry system to provide real record control on patients' histories. Work in tuberculosis had changed radically in the 1950's. New drugs had cut the mortality rate drastically, but incidence had declined only moderately. The disease was far from stamped out, although this was now theoretically possible. Of those with tuberculosis, few now needed hospitalization; most moved freely among the public. The problem was to find the cases, keep them under treatment and/or supervision, and to protect contacts, especially children in the family of a patient.

Tuberculosis clinics were conducted in all the district centers, which all had complete X-ray equipment. One mass-screening unit was housed in district No. 1, for use in compulsory examinations of certain classes of workers such as food handlers, and for special mass-screening projects. Control of tuberculosis in Philadelphia was lagging behind the U.S. as a whole, with higher rates: 2,224 reported cases and 256 deaths, in 1960.

The *Communicable Disease Section*, headed by Dr. Sylvan M. Fish, was still mainly a centralized operation. There were only three physicians working in the field, and they reported to the central office. Reports of cases were also made to the district in which they occurred. In any outbreaks of disease, Bogucki's practice was to delegate responsibility for handling them to the appropriate district health director. All follow-up of enteric disease[27] cases was completely decentralized to the district centers.

The *Division of Epidemiology* had a corps of disease control inspectors, all men, working in all the districts but under central supervision. Of the twenty-one inspectors, eleven were assigned for training by the U.S. Public Health Service; these worked only in the venereal disease program. The ten city employees, however, carried out field activities for the whole division. All were college graduates; ninety per cent of the field work in venereal disease control was done by these disease control inspectors, the rest by the public health nurses.

---

[27] Communicable diseases of the gastro-intestinal tract, such as typhoid, dysentery, etc.

The division had, as yet, only one "director of clinics and epidemiologist" position, in district No. 1. The lack of such district positions may have presented some difficulty in effecting further program decentralization.[28] Bogucki had adopted a policy of issuing memos regarding district programs jointly with Janowsky, in order to emphasize to central and district staffs that decentralization was in effect.

The *Maternal and Child Health Section* under Dr. Cornely operated on a largely decentralized basis. Over 3,000 clinic sessions a year were held. This section also inspected hospital and other nurseries and provided consulting services in pediatrics. Dr. Cornely was concerned, however, over one of the highest infant mortality rates in the country: 32.4 per 1,000 live births, in infants under one year of age. Greater efforts were being made to reach those women who otherwise did not receive any prenatal care, since it was among these cases that the maternal and infant death rate was highest.

The program of the *Division of Dental Health* was, for the most part, still centralized, although the Director, Dr. David A. Soricelli, was strongly in favor of decentralized operations. The work of this division was one of the old and extensive operations. Over thirty dental clinics, including one in each district health center, were conducted throughout the city, some located in the schools. The division treated 20,000 children, up to eleven years of age, each year. But one-third of all the city's children, 100,000, were eligible for the free dental care provided by the Health Department; only about twenty per cent of the real need was being met by the program. Soricelli was unable to establish dental supervisors in the health centers, and lacking these, he could not readily decentralize operations. He and his two assistants spent a high proportion of their time in daily supervision, with too little time for the planning and research they felt was desirable. Dentistry, moreover, was somewhat separate and specialized, making it difficult to integrate with the other programs. Soricelli found it hard to interest some district health directors or to involve the nursing services in his clinic program.

Dr. Linden's *Division of Mental Health* was attracting national attention in his field, as an example of what a city mental health program could accomplish. Much of the division's work was carried on cooperatively with other agencies, both public and private,[29] and outside the district centers. There were special programs for older people and for alcoholics. Linden had established a registry of cases and published a manual and directory of community facilities and resources. By now, a city-wide system for handling all mental cases, by referrals for treatment or hospitalization, was in operation. A referral center was operated on a twenty-four-hour basis. A large proportion of the division's own work was done with disturbed children—mainly preschool age—as a primary preventive measure. There was a minimum of decentralization to the districts; mental health teams of three conducted a total of 156 hours per week of consultation and evaluation in five of the centers, on both a regular and an occasional basis. These teams also went out on emergency calls. Linden hoped eventually to expand and decentralize the program further by establishing teams in every center and enlarging the teams.

Public health nurses of the CNS made 128,000 home visits in 1960.[30] Health District nurses worked in all of the medical programs (but not in dentistry). Community Nursing Services, Miss Hall believed, were more decentralized to district operations than any of the other programs in Community Health Services. Every center had a supervising nurse, and some had assistant supervisors. There were also three field supervisors, responsible to the central office, who covered all the districts. Miss Hall realized that not everyone agreed that nursing was the most decentralized of all the divisions, but she felt that substantial delegation of authority had been effected. There was, however, close consultation throughout the CNS, and constant technical guidance.

Health Education, under William A. Allen, carried on both centralized and decentralized activities. There were now five health educators, in five district centers, to carry on community educational work and to take part in district programs. Their functions were mainly those of liaison be-

[28] Epidemiology had not been given the "green light" to develop as early as had environmental health and nursing. Its turn came in 1961, but by then city policies no longer supported expansion in public health services.

[29] One of these was the Pennsylvania Department of Public Welfare. In this state, mental health was part of this department, and Dr. Linden had been State Regional Director for Mental Health, in the Department of Public Welfare, from 1955 through 1957, concurrently with his city appointment.

[30] This figure does not include home visits by VNS nurses. The first combined report was made in 1961, when a total of 194,564 home visits were made by CNS.

tween the community and the district center. Allen felt that his service program had suffered from being spread too thin among many demands. He anticipated that recently established priorities for five programs would permit more substantial accomplishments where the needs were greatest. He hoped for the eventual establishment of two or more health educators in each district, to increase program effectiveness.

The Health Districts and Their Directors

It was the job of Dr. Janowsky, as Director of District Health Operations, to supervise and coordinate all district operations. He met with all the district directors every two weeks. He had authority to make determinations among competing district needs, to provide for supplies and equipment, and, in emergency, to transfer personnel as required. He was also the liaison between the districts and the central offices. All proposed program changes of consequence were supposed to be discussed with him while they were still in the planning stage, and all administrative matters were supposed to be channeled through his office. The degree to which these organizational and procedural prescriptions were actually obeyed varied considerably among different types of programs, as suggested above. They also varied among the districts, depending in part upon the nature of the district and its problems, in part upon the confidence commanded by the different district directors. In fact, a crucial factor of any delegation program such as that pursued in Philadelphia depended in substantial degree on the caliber and the esteem of the district directors upon whom new powers were intended to devolve.

For the most part, the persons who filled the district director positions were the same people who held the jobs before the reorganization; and the new appointees were basically similar in their qualifications. In the main, they commanded less prestige, less pay, and less status than the various professional directors in the headquarters.[31] Of the eight district directors in 1961, all were physicians and all but two held the graduate degree of Master of Public Health. Four of them had worked in the Health Department for eleven years or more, the longest service record being twenty-four years. They ranged in age from thirty-four to sixty-four years. Four were forty years old or younger, and four were over fifty. Among them were three women, and four were Negroes.[32] Most of them had specialized or practiced in other fields of medicine before becoming district health directors.

Their characteristics as district directors also varied substantially. They ranged from vigorously aggressive and outspoken to relatively passive; all of them "spoke up" to some extent, however, for Hanlon's influence had made this agency highly articulate. The particular backgrounds of the district directors to some extent influenced their emphasis and involvement in the health centers: for example, a pediatrician was likely to find the child health conferences of special concern to him because of previous years of concentration in this field.[33]

There is insufficient evidence to generalize about the degree to which the district directors had "taken command" of the health programs carried on within their jurisdictions or about the extent to which they had identified their local offices and programs with the communities and the unique problems of their communities. It should be observed, however, that the districts the directors served showed wide variations in population, in health characteristics, and in health problems. They varied in population from 96,545 (in No. 1) to 265,238 (in No. 9); their infant death rates ranged from 18.8 (in No. 10) to 44.7 (in No. 4); their overall death rates spread from 8.1 (in No. 10) to 19.2 (in No. 1). Some of the districts were predominantly Negro (eighty-one per cent in No. 5), and one (No. 6) had a large Puerto Rican population. The health problems thus varied widely among the districts. Each was to some extent unique unto itself. This fact alone lent support to the health center concept, which was designed to tailor each community program to the characteristics and the problems of the people it served.

[31] It may be significant to note that two of the district directors, Bogucki and Janowsky, had been selected as divisional directors in the central office, suggesting a line of promotion for the most capable of the district personnel. But it is perhaps equally significant that these reassignments from the districts were in fact viewed as promotions.

[32] Both were more readily recruited for the positions than white males, apparently because of the advantages afforded by equality of opportunity without discrimination, and regular hours, especially valuable to women with families.

[33] This was denied by one health district director, formerly a specialist.

CHART V
ORGANIZATION OF A TYPICAL DISTRICT HEALTH CENTER, 1961

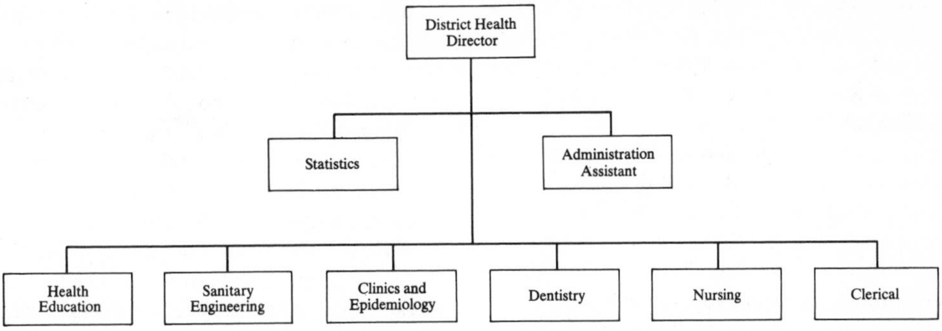

One expression of outside professional opinion concerning the success of district decentralization was made by representatives of the Health and Welfare Council. While paying tribute to the great improvement in health services in the previous decade, they expressed concern about what they regarded as inadequate meeting of community needs, as reported to them by people in voluntary agencies. They regarded the district programs as insufficiently flexible and found community education and contact inadequate. They did not feel that the Health Department was receiving the kind of support it needed from the city government. One individual speculated that Hanlon was possibly more of a philosopher of public health than an administrator.

Self-Evaluation

There was no question in the minds of most staff members that, in terms of programs and services provided to people, reorganization had improved the effectiveness of the agency, or at least not detracted from it. Most believed that overall health services were better than they had ever been.

The staff was fully and openly agreed that, so far, its decentralization plans, orders, and procedures had not been completely effected. Beyond this point, however, there were many shades of opinion.

These views ranged from, "Decentralization? There isn't any," to, "We have come a long way; we need just a little more now, to make it really effective. We don't want complete decentralization, we need to have the central offices set standards and give technical direction." Hanlon's own estimate was that in three-and-a-half years, CHS had achieved about fifty per cent of the amount of decentralization it had tried to implement. Why it had not moved faster, he was not quite sure.

Purdom, in connection with his academic work, had made a study of informal communications in his own division that year, as a test of a research design for a later extensive study. Its findings were not reliable, in his opinion; the study had been too brief and was distorted also because of special circumstances. The findings had indicated that, by a tremendous margin, communications between his central sections and the districts were going directly through technical channels rather than through the district operations office and the district directors. Even allowing for its unreliability, this study was at least suggestive of a tendency to bypass district administrative channels.

Many opinions about the lag in decentralizing operations were held among staff members. One opinion frequently heard was that hardly any two people in the agency interpreted "decentralization" in the same way. One COOLS committee member remarked, "We got a consensus down on paper, but there are nearly as many concepts of the meaning as there are people." Many staff members mentioned that there was still a lot of vagueness and confusion, although, they added, it was much better now than earlier. Common, also, was the opinion that, "It's all there, in the COOLS report, Hanlon's orders, and the Co-op Council procedures. If everyone would just carry these out, it would work. But they don't."

"People," some said, "forget to go through proper channels." Program planning and operations were a major point of difficulty, and consequently of conflict, in the agency. Some observed that you could not really separate the two very well, they were so interrelated. Central office planners were frustrated and annoyed, apparently because there were now so many people to be consulted; and if this was not done at the right time, with the right people, the program might be blocked or delayed, or, at the least, irritations created among the staff. One staff member said about another division, "I usually get good cooperation from them. But I am not always sure whom to see first, and I wouldn't dare make a mistake!"[34]

One of the clearest divisions of viewpoint was that between the central offices and district directors. Some representative statements of headquarters personnel were: "We've given them the authority, but they don't exercise it." "They don't take on as much responsibility as we wish they would." "We can't get them really involved in our program." "Some are interested, but others are indifferent."

On the other hand, various district directors observed:

> They don't let us run operations, really. They're delighted to delegate the irksome details, the administrative dirty work. But when it comes to program, they run it.
>
> Some of the district directors don't really want any more responsibility. And in this organization, if you don't use your authority, someone else will.
>
> They plan things without consulting us. Usually, we can work it out somehow, at the last minute, but we ought to be brought in much earlier. There is staff morale to think about.
>
> They planned a program, so I talked to the staff and they were ready. Then they called it off at the last moment, and I didn't even know it. I heard from one of the nurses. They made us look like idiots to our staffs.
>
> They asked for recommendations, so I prepared them. Then I was overruled at the last moment, and we had to revise all our preparations. Then, when it was over, there was criticism of our district. I'd told them we wouldn't be able to use that much stuff; but they wouldn't listen, and I was blamed for an inadequate job.
>
> They don't know enough about the districts; they hardly ever come around.

One district director reported, of the personnel evaluation procedure,

> I made one, and the nursing supervisor signed it. But then the nursing service took it to Hanlon, and I got called in. I didn't mind about changing it—that was O.K.—but I found out how much authority I really had.

As Purdom commented, "Probably the chronic feeling of both field and central offices, that each does not really understand the work of the other, still persists—and probably always will."

Typical observations on coordination were: "There isn't anyone to take care of this, and resolve the conflicts. Hanlon's too busy, and he leaves a lot of it to Adele [Mrs. Hebb]. But she isn't a professional,[35] she's not competent to decide about technical programs in our work. The Co-op Council doesn't deal with this sort of thing." "Hanlon's a swell guy, but he's very hard to see." "I wish he'd do a lot more by executive direction. A lot of time is wasted around here in committees." Miss Hall: "People don't realize they should take their administrative questions to Adele, and their technical problems to John [Hanlon]. That's the way it's supposed to be done."

Preparing for Further Change

To continue and further implement decentralization, Hanlon arranged, in the fall of 1961, to have the top staff hold a series of meetings on "Programs, Priorities, and Organization." Participants included the section heads and various assistants, and the top management officers of the agency. In all, fifty-two staff members took part in the study meetings.

Proceedings at the first general session were "off-the-record." In general, the problems raised and discussed were those that have been indicated —the difficulties in communication and coordination; vagueness and confusion over authorities and procedures; the lack of some administrative mechanism for continuous resolution of competing or conflicting program demands. This last problem received attention from several divisions, in the form of a variety of recommendations for a "coordinator," a "deputy director," and "advisory committee," or simply more executive decisions by Hanlon. It was recognized by some speakers that Hanlon lacked the time necessary to fulfill this coordinating function continuously, but at the same time, it was argued that a "coordinator" would not be able to carry out the function, for if he served in an advisory capacity, he would be ineffective; if he had delegated authority, this would be in con-

[34] This quotation and most of the following ones are paraphrases.

[35] Mrs. Hebb had no advanced degree, although she had taken graduate courses.

flict with Hanlon's formal role as Director of CHS. Hanlon's own comment was that he was, in fact, the program coordinator, but there were limits on his available time. As for a "deputy," he regarded all of his division heads as "his deputies for their own programs."

The issue of decentralized district administration was prominent among the problems aired. The district directors wanted to be given more authority, while some of the division directors wanted them to exercise more authority and assume greater responsibility. In the course of this discussion, Hanlon voiced his personal philosophy: along with the traditional concept of delegation of authority and responsibility, confidence and respect must also be accorded, if an organization such as theirs was to operate successfully; this was his own practice.

The effect of the city government's unwillingness to increase the agency's funds further was another of the problems raised. Some of the staff were discouraged, others urged greater efforts in meeting this challenge through improved allocations of resources within CHS.

The discussion at this meeting was frank, open, and at times very spirited, characterized occasionally by both heat and humor. While an outsider found it remarkably outspoken, a long-time staff member commented afterward, "They were pretty repressed today; I wonder why?" But frank as it was, some of the most sensitive issues in the organization were not referred to in the meeting. They were voiced informally in limited groups, but were too deep-going, too "loaded," to be mentioned at this time and place.

One week later, five task forces appointed after the general session held their first meetings. In task force No. 1, on "Strengthening District Administration," after an hour or so of discussion of specific problem-areas, the group reached a fundamental question stated by a participant: "What *is* decentralization?" Another crucial, though intangible, factor was implicit in the statement of one of the district directors, "I need to feel that people have confidence in me."

Between these two meetings, one of the top administrators observed, "My hope is that these meetings will make people think about our problems, and, as a result, will have a better idea of what we are trying to accomplish, and carry it out more effectively. But what worries me is this: suppose we do develop better arrangements and procedures, and then we find it still doesn't work. Then what?"

Hanlon, in the first general meeting, had summarized his own philosophy of conflict, and the nature of a dynamic, highly professionalized, and diverse organization such as theirs:

> I think that when you put any two human beings together, at some point there is inevitably some disagreement, some misunderstanding, gripes, and so on; the hope being that along with this comes a certain amount of mutual respect, love, trust—some of the finer things of life, and that one will kind of offset the other.
>
> Well, we compound that by dealing with not two people, but a whole group of people; if they are alive and conscious, this compounds it further; if, beyond that, they are ambitious and sincere about what they are doing, you reach an almost impossible state in terms of really trying cooperation.
>
> There are bound to be gripes in a group as large as this, in a program as complex as this; there are bound to be misunderstandings—we'd be strange indeed if there were not. In fact, if there were not, it would mean that we weren't trying to do the job, that we didn't give a damn; therefore, if we didn't give a damn, we wouldn't have any gripes, we wouldn't be bumping up against each other and hurting each other's shins. So that this is to be expected.[36]

The above story of Philadelphia's Community Health Services, and its efforts to institute a decentralized administration for the district health centers, was far from complete by the end of 1961. But, in any case, no one foresaw an interruption in the continuous change to which this agency in over a decade of repeated reorganization had become accustomed. The one possibility that apparently never entered into any agency discussion and thinking was that of no further organizational or program changes. While the vigor, dedication, and search for solutions continue, many shins might be hurt; it seems probable, however, that unless the political trends in the city become too adverse in succeeding years, Philadelphia will be a beneficiary in constantly improving health services "for *all* the people."

---

[36] Taken verbatim from the recording.

HEALTH DISTRICTS OF PHILADELPHIA DEPARTMENT OF PUBLIC HEALTH, 1961

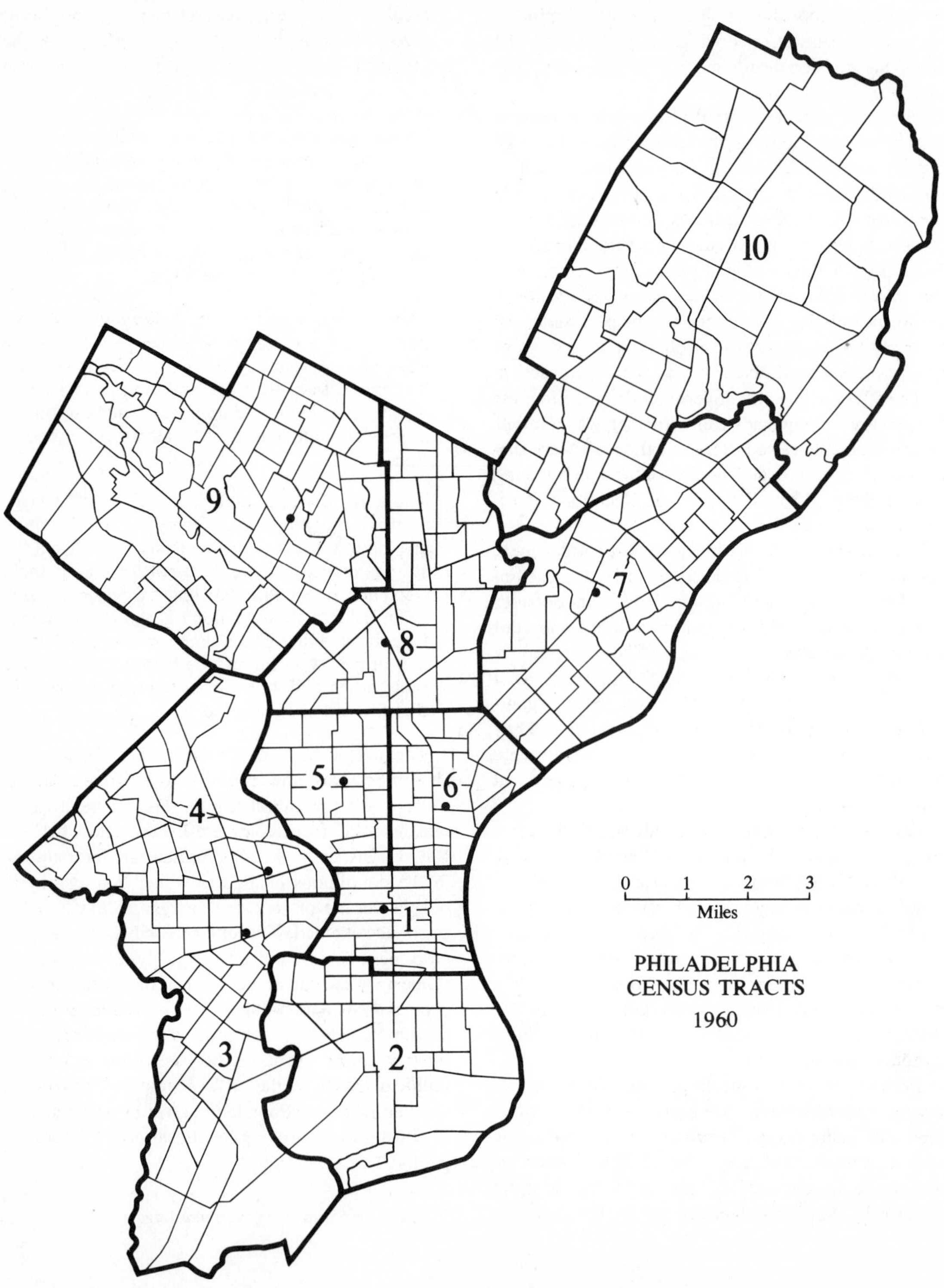

APPENDIX I:
PUBLIC HEALTH VOLUNTARY AGENCIES
Philadelphia, 1948

Visiting Nurse Society of Philadelphia
Starr Centre Association
Henry Phipps Institute (tuberculosis)
Philadelphia Mouth Hygiene Association
Fife-Hamill Memorial Health Center
Community Health Center (Federation of Jewish Charities)
Philadelphia Tuberculosis and Health Association
American Cancer Society (Philadelphia Division)
Philadelphia Heart Association
Philadelphia Child Guidance Clinic
Philadelphia Society for Crippled Children and Adults
National Foundation Infantile Paralysis
Cerebral Palsy Society of Philadelphia
Philadelphia Metabolic Association

Philadelphia Agencies Sponsoring the Public Health Survey, 1949. Health and Welfare Council of Philadelphia, official reporting agency.

Co-sponsors: The Department of Public Health
The Philadelphia Tuberculosis and Health Association
Division of Medical Service, Board of Education

Executive Committee

Chairmen: Wm. Harvey Perkins, M.D., Dean, Jefferson Medical College; Health Division, Health and Welfare Council (served part of time)
J. L. T. Appleton, D.D.S., Dean, University of Pennsylvania Dental College; Philadelphia County Dental Society

Members: Clyde E. Arbegast, Health Division, Health and Welfare Council
Edmund N. Bacon, Executive Director, City Planning Commission
John B. Dawson, Director, Health and Welfare Council
Theodore Fetter, M.D., Philadelphia County Medical Society
Julia L. Groscop, R.N., Health Division, Health and Welfare Council
Ruth W. Hubbard, R.N., Public Health Nursing Service
Raymond F. Leonard, Executive Director, City Planning Commission
Harlin G. Loomer, Senior Planning Analyst, City Planning Commission
Pascal F. Lucchesi, M.D., Supt., Philadelphia General Hospital
Harold M. Mayer, Ph.D., Chief, Planning Analysis Division, City Planning Commission
Robert B. Mitchell, Executive Director, City Planning Commission
Hubley R. Owen, M.D., Director of Medical Service, Department of Public Education

M. Fraser Percival, M.D., Philadelphia County Medical Society; Commissioner, City Planning Commission
Rufus S. Reeves, M.D., Director, Department of Public Health
C. Rufus Rorem, Ph.D., Executive Secretary, Hospital Council of Philadelphia

Technical Advisory Committee

Chairman: Harlin G. Loomer, Senior Planning Analyst, City Planning Commission

Medical Consultant: Pascal F. Lucchesi, M.D., Superintendent, Philadelphia General Hospital

Members:
Marian Shand Andrews, Executive Director, Starr Centre Association
Clyde E. Arbegast, Health Division, Health and Welfare Council
Margaret Bishop, Statistician, Department of Public Assistance
Julia L. Groscop, Health Division, Health and Welfare Council
Ethel Jacobs, Research Assistant, Health Division, Health and Welfare Council
John B. McCann, Registrar, Vital Statistics, Department of Public Health
Robert Sigmond, Research Associate, Hospital Council of Philadelphia
Tina Weintraub, Research Assistant, Bureau of Municipal Research

Citizens Committee: Frank J. Chesterman, ex-President, Bell Telephone Company of Pennsylvania, chairman

Consultants on Special Phases

Russell E. Teague, M.D., Senior Surgeon, U.S. Public Health Service
Louisa J. Eskridge, M.P.H., Secretary of Public Health Division, Public Charities Association of Pennsylvania
Helen E. Weaver, R.N., Consultant in Nursing Activities
Franklin M. Foote, M.D., M.P.H., Executive Director, National Society for the Prevention of Blindness, New York
Ernest S. Tierkel, V.M.D., M.P.H., Assistant Chief, Veterinary Public Health Division, U.S. Public Health Service, Montgomery, Alabama
Elberton J. Tiffany, M.D., Bacteriologist-in-charge, Immunology-Serology Division, Communicable Disease Center, Atlanta, Georgia

APPENDIX II:
SUMMARY OF PERSONNEL PROVISIONS IN THE COOLS REPORT

Absolutely reserved to central office control were: establishment of qualifications and duties of a class of personnel, recruitment and employment of all persons, establishment of performance standards for a class. Determination of city-wide needs for personnel and for distribution of personnel in a class on the basis of availability and need were also designated as central office activities, together with review of and decision upon requests for specific types of personnel that came from a district director.

However, in meeting the needs for personnel for the execution of programs or portions of programs carried on in the district, it was "incumbent upon the district director to initiate all requests for district personnel for ongoing program."

Before assignment of technical supervisory personnel to a district, "there will be discussion between the director of the technical division and the district director as to the suitability of the assignment."

As a general rule, assignment of personnel within a district would be the responsibility of the district director and his technical supervisors. But whenever a technical division made suggestions to the district director about the type of assignment (as for training purposes), deviations from the suggestions must be fully justified by him by reason of emergency or other special situation, "although the district director has the final authority in the assignments."

Planning and management of in-service training were the responsibility of the central office, but district supervisory personnel would be consulted as to the timing of the training. Persons in pre-assignment training would remain under central office jurisdiction.

Technical standards of performance, once established by the central office, became the responsibility of the district director to enforce.

Performance ratings were made the responsibility of "direct line operational supervisors." The report continued:

> When a "generalist" (such as a district director) is either the rater or reviewer of an employee in a more specialized discipline where there is a central office counterpart, in making the rating he must avail himself of consultation with a central office representative. Where there is a divergent [sic] between such a rater or reviewer and the central technical division, it must be resolved by joint conference with the Director of Public Health Services before the rating is given to the employee.

Discipline of employees was made a "dual responsibility": all general administrative aspects of job performance were under the jurisdiction of direct in-line supervision; all matters pertaining to professional performance usually, and in serious situations always, required consultation with the technical division. Where agreement on action

APPENDIX III:

SUMMARY OF HEALTH DISTRICT CAPITAL PROJECT AND RELATED DATA AS OF SEPTEMBER 26, 1961[a]

Stage of develop-ment	*Health district number*	*Area served*	*Population*	*Bldg. square footage*	*Cost per square foot: Land*	*Cost per square foot: construct.*	*Total cost*[b]	*Comple-tion date*
Completed	1	S. Cen. Phila.	96,545	73,300	$6.08	$21.96	$2,202,630	5/31/60
Fully Financed	2	South Phila.	200,974	24,690	3.23	23.53	862,639	2/1/63
Completed	3	West Phila. So.	203,984	33,255	3.17	19.63	839,758	4/1/60
Projected	4	West Phila. No.	197,228	22,000	8.82	23.00	777,000	5/31/64
Fully Financed	5	No. Cen. Phila. W.	192,319	24,130	5.28	21.14	761,769	11/30/62
Completed	6	No. Cen. Phila. E.	154,894	23,768	6.43	18.94	797,783	6/30/58
Projected	7	NE Phila.	253,655	22,000	5.56	23.00	825,000	After 1967
Projected	8	No. Phila.	233,707	22,000	6.00	23.00	825,000	After 1967
Completed	9	NW Phila.	265,238	18,344	2.72	23.30	547,209	4/1/58
Projected	10	Far NE Phila.	202,241	22,000	—	23.00	618,000	5/31/67

[a] Both cost figures and dates of completion were later revised.
[b] Estimated cost as of September 26, 1961, except for Health District No. 9 which is actual cost.

could not be reached, the Director of Public Health Services was to make a final decision.

Certain special cases of personnel management were reserved to the central office.

Vacation schedules were another instance of "dual responsibility," with the district director having primary responsibility. He was to determine schedules where there were several in a class in a district, but where this was not the case, the central office was to handle the scheduling. (Temporary transfers between districts might be required.)

EDITORIAL COMMENTS

This "Philadelphia Story" apparently constitutes one of the better examples of participation in decision-making on reorganization and its implementation in a large public agency. Dr. Dixon and Dr. Hanlon both made clear, by intent and practice, their faith in the participative principle in the attempt to bring about decentralization of public health activities. And the work of the COOLS committee and its successor, the Co-op Council, was illustrative of the participative device. Initial review of this case leads one to vigorous support of the hypothesis that participation contributes to the acceptability of change and, therefore, to its effectiveness. How else than through membership on the COOLS committee might the most influential and powerful leaders in the agency have been brought to support decentralization? The committee included the two most vigorous and outspoken opponents of decentralization, Miss Hall and Mr. Purdom, who was in fact its chairman. Both swung full circle.

But a more penetrating examination may lead to a modified conclusion: that participation may have delayed, obstructed, and perhaps even prevented the real accomplishment of decentralization. According to the author of the case, Dixon's principal objectives were the same as those of the 1949 report: improving and expanding the public health program in general; integrating and improving the public health nursing services; and decentralizing operations and operational control to the districts. On the first two of these he moved very fast, immediately after taking office, and in neither instance was there any evidence of employing participative devices. They appear, in their many ramifications, to have been "command decisions." In both cases, he was eminently successful. Only in regard to the decentralization did he insist upon staff participation and decision. This was followed by years of argument and procrastination; the decision ultimately reached was incompletely carried out. Twelve years after the 1949 report that laid the basis for future efforts, decentralization was judged, at best, partial; at worst, ineffective.

Further consideration leads one to question the complete validity of either of the above conclusions. The events of the case at least suggest that Dixon gave his first priority to the two objectives of improving the service in general and integrating the nursing service. Decentralization was a third but no less important goal. Whether or not intended, it is possible that participation served as a device for delaying decentralization until the agency was prepared for it. Further, as suggested in the case itself, general strengthening of the service and merging of the nursing services were not consistent with simultaneous decentralization of powers to districts; in some ways, they were antithetical. One can hardly build up quality, prestige, and status at the center and at the same time delegate power away from the center. It would appear that the various participative mechanisms employed in Philadelphia served purposes somewhat different from those associated with the participation hypothesis. They kept the idea of decentralization alive, kept the personnel thinking about it, what it would mean, how it could be brought about; and they forestalled action for some years until the leadership judged the agency capable of positive action.

Delaying the decentralization, however, had the further effect, whether or not anticipated by Dixon and the other top officers, of making it more difficult to accomplish. The early, yeasty period of the Clark administration, with its hospitality for change, its relatively free budgetary situation, and its joining of political with professional drives toward common ends, had passed. By the time of Hanlon's arrival, the temper of City Hall had changed. Budgets as well as organization and central controls had stabilized and hardened. In short, the honeymoon was over.

Crucial to a projected delegation of this kind are

the quality and the strength of those to whom added responsibilities and powers are to be assigned. It is, therefore, particularly significant that little effort was evidenced to change, upgrade, or reeducate the top personnel in the districts. This contrasted with the determined efforts, and their clear results, to strengthen the personnel at headquarters. Even after the decentralization order was issued in 1958, there was no program to train, replace, reassign, or otherwise improve leadership at the district level. In spite of efforts by Hanlon to improve the prestige of the district directors within the Department of Health and to bring them into departmental discussions, the confidence of officers in the headquarters in the district leadership remained low. This must certainly have discouraged delegation of powers.

Two other obstacles to decentralization should be noted. First, budgetary stringency and the difficulty of delegating budgetary initiative and control to the districts impeded the delegation of true program responsibility. Second, the continuing centralization of discretion in headquarters on matters of personnel, recruitment, assignment, etc., deprived the district directors of a nearly indispensable tool of management, if they were to assume full responsibility for operations in their districts. In regard to both budget and personnel, the Public Health Department of Philadelphia was subject to city-wide rules and practices that restricted its own freedom of action. This type of limitation, common to most public administration, makes delegation such as that sought in this case a particularly difficult goal.

JOHN R. OWENS

A Wildlife Agency and Its Possessive Public

JOHN R. OWENS

The author of *A Wildlife Agency and Its Possessive Public* received a Ph.D. degree in Political Science from the Maxwell School of Citizenship and Public Affairs, Syracuse University. He is an Associate Professor of Political Science at the University of California at Davis.

CHRONOLOGY OF KEY EVENTS

1951	Division of Fish and Game receives departmental status in reorganization
September 1951	Gordon is named Director of Department
1952	Five regional offices are established; Department adopts a staff-line organization
1955	Office of Legislative Analyst conducts an administrative survey of the Department
September 1956	Either-sex deer hunt controversy focuses criticism on Department
January 1957	Fish and Game Commission and Department request an increase in license fees
May 1957	Senate Fish and Game Committee holds hearings on license bills; compromise bill includes provision for management survey of Department; Resolution 126 defines scope of management survey and assigns it to Joint Legislative Budget Committee
June 1957	Legislature enacts license bill with provision for survey and concurrent resolution defining scope of survey
October 10, 1957	Contract for survey is awarded to Booz, Allen, and Hamilton (BAH); Legislative Analyst designated to oversee the work for the Joint Legislative Budget Committee
February 1958	BAH begins study of departmental program costs and license system
March 15, 1958	Swift, wildlife specialist, begins work
April 15-June 15, 1958	Specialists conduct review of departmental wildlife management programs
July-August 1958	BAH conducts field work on departmental organization-administration
December 1958	BAH report presented to Joint Legislative Budget Committee
January 1959	Department begins evaluation of BAH report
January 1959	Governor announces dismissal of Gordon
March 1959	Gordon presents first departmental evaluation to revenue subcommittee; Fish and Game Committee delays hearings on BAH report
April 1959	Warne takes over as Director; orders new evaluation of BAH report
December 1959	Senate Interim Committee on Fish and Game holds hearings on organizational-administrative recommendations of BAH report
March 1960	Senate Interim Committee rejects BAH organizational proposals
June 1960	Department makes final report to Fish and Game Commission on action taken on BAH report

PRINCIPAL CHARACTERS

Arthur Breed, Chairman, Joint Legislative Budget Committee

George Difani, President, California Wildlife Federation

Seth Gordon, Director, Department of Fish and Game, 1951-1959

Henry Grafe, Executive Secretary, Senate Fish and Game Committee

J. Doyle Gray, Project Director for Booz, Allen, and Hamilton study

William Hurst, BAH accountant

Andy Kelly, Chairman, Fish and Game Commission

G. W. Philpott, President, Sportsmen's Council of Central California

Alan Post, Legislative Analyst, Joint Budget Legislative Committee

William Powell, Resident partner, BAH

Walter T. Shannon, Deputy Director, 1951-1960; Director, 1960–, Department of Fish and Game

Ernest F. Swift, Executive Director, National Wildlife Federation

William Warne, Director, 1959-1960, Department of Fish and Game

INTRODUCTION

In July 1957, the California Legislature authorized the expenditure of $100,000 for a "study of the existing and future programs and plans" of the California Department of Fish and Game and the Fish and Game Commission. The Legislature specified that the survey be made by a private management consulting firm. After some deliberation, a legislative committee awarded the contract to Booz, Allen, and Hamilton (BAH) of San Francisco. BAH undertook a year-long survey of the agency, and in December 1958 the firm presented to the Legislature a comprehensive report, containing more than 250 conclusions and recommendations on the policies, program management, and administrative organization of the Department and Commission.

The story of the BAH investigation offers an interesting case history of the dynamics of a management survey of a government agency. The story is complicated because the participants included not only the fish and game agency and the private management survey firm but also the Legislature and organized sportsmen. Within the Fish and Game Department and Commission there were complicated and long-standing problems involving politics, policies and programs, organizational and administrative practices, and controversial agency leadership.

The part played by the Legislature in bringing about the survey was equally complex. Acting on behalf of the Legislature were its Joint Budget Committee, special interim committees, and the Legislative Analyst (an officer of the Legislature), who were all concerned with the agency's performance and the results of the survey. In addition, there were articulate and powerful sportsmen's groups, divided among themselves, powerful beyond their numbers, and highly influential in forming public opinion toward the agency. Finally, there was Booz, Allen, and Hamilton, a national management agency with its own team of management specialists plus a group of experienced fish and game technicians from various states who were especially recruited for this survey.

This case study analyzes the mechanics and describes the results of a management survey of a public agency. Beginning with an analysis of the Fish and Game agency and its clientele, the story moves to the crisis that led to demands for the management survey and then describes the survey process itself. The last portion deals with efforts to implement the final report.

THE DEPARTMENT OF FISH AND GAME AND ITS CLIENTELE

California is exceptionally well-endowed with wildlife resources. More than 1,000,000 deer, the largest herd in the United States, roam most of the state's 50,000,000 acres of wildlands. Bears are abundant and European wild boar are present. Smaller game—including dove, quail, pheasants, chukar partridges, sage hens, squirrels, and rabbits—are available in quantity. Each year 6,000,000 to 7,000,000 waterfowl winter in California. Lakes and streams abound with warm water and anadromous fish, and the long ocean coastline extending more than 1,000 miles provides easy access to tuna, rockfish, salmon, shellfish, and kelp—the latter a versatile seaweed used in products as diverse as ice cream and shoe polish.

In terms of aesthetic pleasure and recreation, these wildlife resources have incalculable value to millions of Californians. The state's large and growing population has substantially increased sporting and commercial demands on available fish, birds, and game animals. Every year more than 2,000,000 people purchase fishing and hunting licenses. Commercial fishing is a half-billion dollar industry.

California has imposed regulations to prevent depletion of these rich resources. Responsibility for managing the uses and protection of fish and wildlife is in the hands of the Fish and Game Commission and the Department of Fish and Game, an agency that has existed in one organizational garb or another since 1870. The Department's fundamental objective, conservation, was restated by the Legislature in the Wildlife Conservation Act of 1947. "The preservation, protection, and restoration of wildlife within the State of California," the Legislature declared, "is an inseparable part of providing adequate recreation for our people in the interest of public welfare." The lawmakers said further that it was state policy to "acquire and restore to the highest possible level, and maintain in a state of high productivity, those areas that can be successfully used to sustain wildlife and which will provide adequate and suitable recreation. . . ."

Thus stated, the three goals of preservation, protection, and propagation of wildlife resources have guided the Department's activities and procedures. In working out practical policies to implement these goals, the agency has encountered serious controversy. In attempting to regulate such popular recreational activities as hunting and fishing, the agency has been beset by difficulties resulting from the uneven distribution of wildlife resources from north to south, varied and often competitive policy demands among sportsmen, and close legislative scrutiny of the agency's affairs.

The regulatory power of the state over fish and game evolved slowly. From admission to statehood in 1850 until 1870, regulation of fishing and hunting fell principally to local governments. Occasionally the California Legislature fixed closed seasons for trout and certain game animals, but it stated no comprehensive wildlife policy, and enforcement remained in the hands of local authorities. In 1870, a growing awareness of the need for more effective state action resulted in the creation of the three-man State Board of Fish Commissioners, the forerunner of the present Fish and Game Commission and Department.[1] The Legislature assigned modest powers to the Commission, and its operations remained limited, with appropriations averaging about $3,000 per year.

After 1900 the progressive movement focused public attention on conservation, and the strength and duties of the Commission grew. In 1907 and 1913 the Legislature assured effective statewide wildlife conservation with the passage of hunting and angling laws that were designed to protect game birds, fish, and animals. Under the 1907 statute, funds to support the Commission's broader activities came from the hunters and anglers themselves. All fines and license fees went into the Commission's fish and game preservation fund for the support of the agency. In the first year, fines and fees garnered $118,000, an amount that exceeded total appropriations for all preceding years.

The Commission's enlarged responsibilities hastened organizational changes. In 1915 the Legislature created a second agency, the Department of Commercial Fisheries, thus separating commercial from sport fishing. At the same time the Fish and Game Commission created new bureaus to administer its additional duties, and commissioners individually took administrative responsibility for separate districts. The Department's confused and haphazard growth compelled a major reorganization in 1926. The guiding aim of this change was to minimize the Commission's administrative responsibilities and to confine its work to policy questions. Henceforth civil service personnel performed the day-to-day operational duties. A more fundamental reorganization occurred in 1927, when the State Legislature created the Department of Natural Resources and transferred all wildlife activities to it.

The Legislature's purpose in creating the Department of Natural Resources was to provide a consistent form of departmental units within the state government, with a director over each department and a chief executive officer over each division. In its attempt to bring wildlife management under an integrated natural resources program, however, the Legislature stirred the hostility of organized sports groups that insisted on autonomy for the fish and game agency. Impressed by the sportsmen's demands, the lawmakers modified the structure of the Department of Natural Resources to allow the Fish and Game Division to continue under the control of a three-man commission appointed by the Governor. The commissioners in turn had appointed an executive secretary, a non-civil service employee, to serve as chief executive officer of the Division.

Thus the California Legislature had created an anomalous situation in which the Fish and Game Division functioned under a politically appointed commission that drew its duties from the state fish and game code but was responsible to the director of the Department of Natural Resources. To complicate the relationship still further, the Fish and Game Division had retained its specially earmarked revenues from the fish and game preservation fund. Thus the Fish and Game Division had occupied a unique place in the state structure, and in time this confusing situation provoked a clash between the virtually independent Division and the director of the Department of Natural Resources. In 1936, an attorney-general's ruling settled this controversy

[1] The title of the Commission and Department has undergone a number of changes. No attempt has been made to catalogue these changes, and its present title is used throughout this case.

in favor of the fish and game agency. The ruling ended any effective control by the director of Natural Resources over fish and game affairs; and thereafter the Fish and Game Division, still nominally a part of the department for fiscal purposes, functioned in fact as an independent unit.

The Division's independence increased. In 1940 California voters approved a constitutional amendment creating a five-man Fish and Game Commission with staggered six-year terms. The Governor appointed the commissioners; his appointees were subject to Senate confirmation and removable only by a majority vote of the whole Legislature. (None were ever so removed.) The 1940 amendment also permitted the Legislature to delegate fish and game regulatory powers to the Commission. The Commission and various organized sportsmen urged public support for the amendment on the ground that it would remove wildlife affairs from politics, in this case from the Governor's control. The amendment deprived the Governor of his customary removal power, conferred on the commissioners terms longer than the Governor's, and effectively prevented the Governor from bringing about policy changes with new appointments.

In 1945 the Legislature, pursuant to the provisions of the 1940 constitutional amendment, conferred regulatory powers on the Commission, giving the agency plenary powers to promulgate rules and regulations having the force of law over hunting and sport fishing. In so doing, the lawmakers recognized that it was impractical to concern themselves each year with the details of fixing bag and creel limits according to fluctuating game supplies. The Commission's regulatory powers, originally granted for two years, did not extend to commercial marine fishing. Despite occasional controversy, each Legislature has extended these regulatory powers.

During the late 1930's and 1940's the fish and game agency's internal power structure had bordered on chaos. Practically speaking, the agency was a confederation of bureaus lacking any effective top management control. Troubled by these problems, in 1947 the commissioners invited the Department of Finance to make an administrative analysis of the agency's operations. The principal recommendation of the resulting study urged the commissioners to concentrate on policy-making and to leave actual agency management to an administrative head. The commissioners rejected the proposal and drafted their own reorganization plan under which they retained administrative control of the agency. The Legislature, with the endorsement of some organized sportsmen, rejected their plan and later intervened to compel reorganization.

The Organization of the Department

The 1951 Fish and Game Reorganization Act, named after its principal sponsor, Senator Charles Brown, authorized the establishment of an independent Department of Fish and Game, thus separating the agency from the Department of Natural Resources. The latter continued to control resource programs in the areas of beaches and parks, forestry, oil and gas, mines, and soil conservation. The act did not provide a detailed organizational structure for the agency but directed the Department of Finance and the director of the new Department to prepare jointly an organizational plan drawn on a regional basis. The new plan, received and approved by the Legislature in 1952, provided a line and staff organization and decentralized fish and game functions to five regions, each to operate a composite fish and game program in accordance with policies and programs laid down by the Commission and the director. This was the basic organizational structure of the Fish and Game Department at the time Booz, Allen, and Hamilton made its survey. (See Exhibit I.)

The Fish and Game Reorganization Act charged the Commission with the formulation of general policies and regulations pertaining to fish and game matters. Members of the Commission were appointed by the Governor and received per diem compensation for their services. There was active competition for these jobs, and the task of selection was complex. Party affiliation was an important consideration in appointment, and the Governor consulted various sportsmen's groups on each candidate. Most of the appointees were well-to-do businessmen actively interested in hunting and fishing but with no expert knowledge of conservation. The Commission had a geographical balance with representation from different regions and resource areas.

The Commission was responsible for setting annual fish and game regulations. By law the Commission held public hearings in January, February, April, and May to hear and consider the recommendations of interested parties. The Commission depended heavily on the Department for technical information in formulating policy, since its staff

EXHIBIT I
PRESENT ORGANIZATION STRUCTURE

Governor
State of California

Fish and Game Commission — Five Commissioners

General Policy

Department of Fish and Game — Director

Wildlife Conservation Board — Three Members Plus Participation by Three Senators and Three Assemblymen

Marine Research Committee — Nine Members

Administrative Division — Administrative Officer

Staff Operations Division — Deputy Director (Exempt Position)

Conservation Education Division — Conservation Education Director

Inland Fisheries Branch — Chief, Inland Fisheries Branch

Water Projects — Water Projects Coordinator

Game Management Branch — Chief, Game Management Branch

Wildlife Protection Branch — Chief, Wildlife Protection Branch

Marine Fisheries Branch — Chief, Marine Fisheries Branch

Marine Resources Operations — Marine Resources Manager

Region I Northern Region — Regional Manager

Region II Sacramento Region — Regional Manager

Region III Bay Region — Regional Manager

Region IV San Joaquin Region — Regional Manager

Region V Southern Region — Regional Manager

Typical Organization for the Five Regions

Business Management — Business Service Officer

Inland Fisheries Management — Fisheries Management Supervisor

Game Management — Game Management Supervisor

Wildlife Protection — Wildlife Protection Supervisor

consisted only of an executive secretary and clerical help.

The Fish and Game Department's structure in 1952 became a staff-line organization. The director, appointed by the Governor, served as chief administrative officer. He served at the pleasure of the Governor but was responsible for administering the Department according to general policies set by the Commission. In 1951 Governor Earl Warren had appointed Seth Gordon of Pennsylvania to head and reorganize the newly established Department.

Under the director, line officers included a deputy director and five regional managers, who were responsible for operations within their respective districts. The Marine Resources Operations at Terminal Island operated independently of the regional structure, but the manager of the installation had the same line responsibility as the regional managers to the Sacramento headquarters. The deputy director, appointed by the director and exempted from civil service, served as chief of operations. On his shoulders rested the responsibility for the day-to-day supervisory tasks; he was the focal point for successful coordination and programming. In the absence of the director, the deputy assumed control of the agency. Gordon's deputy was Walter T. Shannon, a professional civil servant of many years, who began his career as a U.S. Forest Service employee. At the time the Fish and Game Department came into existence, Shannon was assistant chief of the Wildlife Protection Bureau in charge of warden training.

An administrative officer and a conservation education officer served as immediate staff and reported to the director. The former, in charge of the Administrative Division, had the task of organizing, directing, and coordinating the administrative and business management activities of the Department. In 1952 Gordon hired Harry Anderson from the Department of Finance to fill this job. The conservation program officer was responsible for developing, directing, and coordinating educational, public information, and public relations programs. Robert Calkins, a newspaperman, held this position.

All but one of the pre-1952 bureaus were reconstituted into staff branches. The chiefs of these branches (Game Management, Inland Fisheries, Wildlife Protection, Marine Fisheries, and, later, Water Projects) became part of the deputy director's program staff. They had no direct control of field personnel or property in their respective fields of activity. They advised the deputy director in wildlife management matters and were responsible for recommending program direction and research.

The 1952 reorganization divided the Department into five regional administrative units with offices at Redding, Sacramento, San Francisco, Fresno, and Los Angeles (see map). A regional manager, a civil servant responsible to the deputy director, headed each office. The regional manager directed the field operations with a staff of supervisors for wildlife protection, inland fisheries, and game management, each representing the Department's basic functions. These supervisors in turn directed the fieldmen carrying out the wildlife management work. Each region had a business services officer in charge of license and other administrative work, and there were education officers in two regions. The Department was organizationally decentralized, most of its activities being carried on in the field.

Two other agencies, organizationally separated from the Commission and the Department, played a vital role in fish and game affairs. Under the Wildlife Conservation Act of 1947, the Legislature had established the Wildlife Conservation Board, including the president of the Commission, the director of the Fish and Game Department, and the director of the Department of Finance. Three members of each house of the Legislature had served as advisers to the board. The board's principal duty had been to acquire land and make capital investments in projects that would protect, propagate, and restore wildlife. To finance these activities the Legislature had earmarked pari-mutuel funds (license fees placed on horse racing) for the board's use. The Legislature had appropriated these funds separately, and up to 1957 the board had received a total of $13,350,000. About seventy per cent of this sum financed the building of fish hatcheries and waterfowl areas; the remainder was used for other capital outlay improvements.

In 1947 the Legislature had created the Marine Research Committee, loosely joined with the Fish and Game Department for administrative purposes, to coordinate research on the development and improvement of marine fisheries of the Pacific Ocean by various state and federal agencies. Of the nine-member committee, the law stated that five must represent commercial fish processors, at least one must represent organized sportsmen's groups, and another must represent organized labor. Neither the Commission nor the Department had exercised any control over the committee. The committee's main purpose had been to aid research

REGIONS OF THE DEPARTMENT OF FISH AND GAME

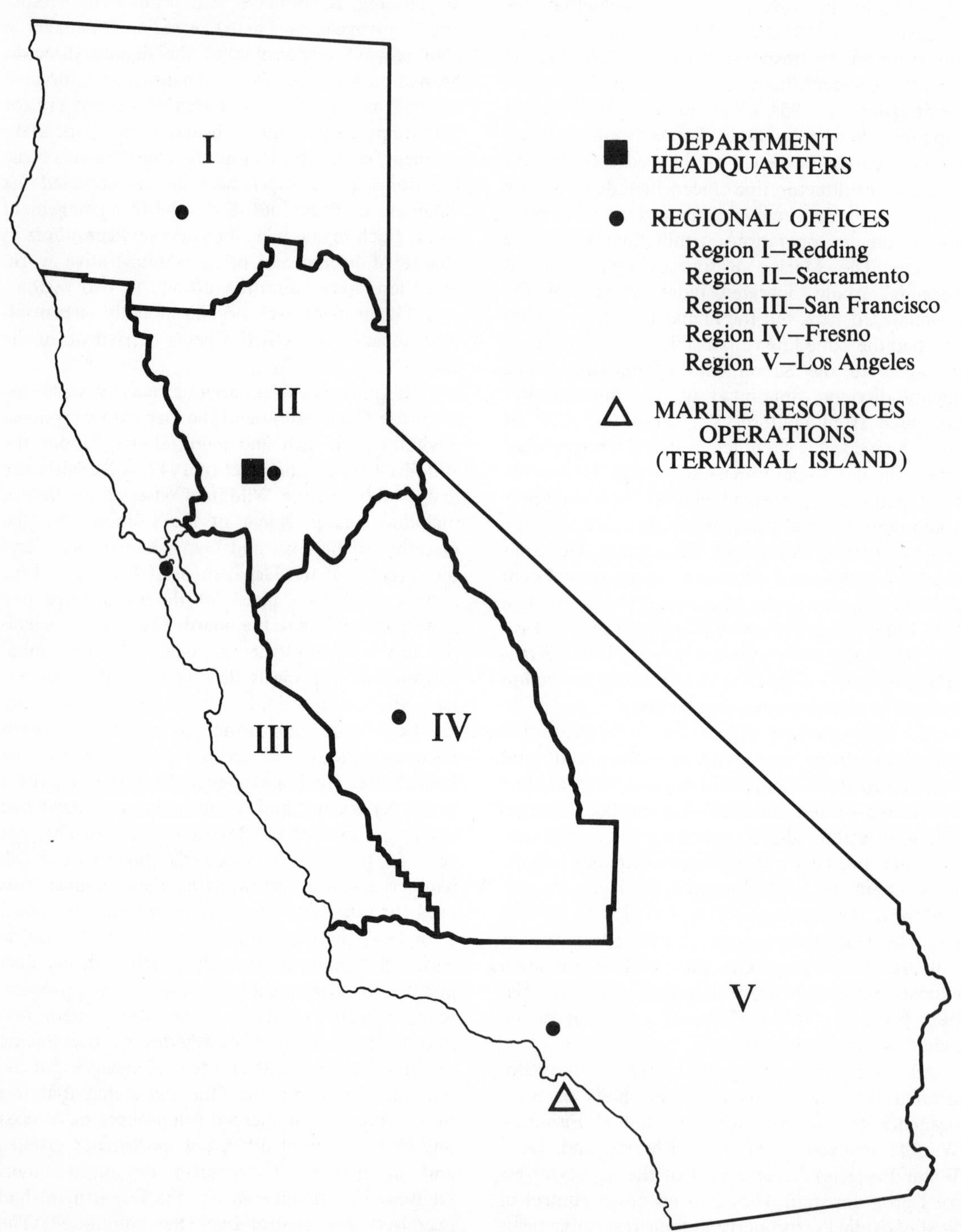

affecting commercial fishing, and its work had consisted almost entirely of contractual research projects conducted by Scripps Institute of Oceanography, the United States Fish and Wildlife Service, the Department of Fish and Game, and others. Financial support for the committee came from a special privilege tax on fish dealers and packers.

The Wider World of Fish and Game

In contrast to many relatively self-contained and little-known state agencies, the Commission and the Department of Fish and Game performed their duties in the face of extraordinarily complex forces that were, in the broadest sense, political in nature. Among the forces that directly shaped the agency's policies and the scope of its work were relations with the Legislature and relations with sportsmen's organizations, protectionists, and the general public.

The agency's unusual dependence on clientele goodwill stemmed from its special financial structure. With the exception of capital funds coming from the Wildlife Conservation Board, the Department received almost all of its revenue from license fees paid by individual sportsmen. As a result, sportsmen had a proprietary feeling toward the Fish and Game Department. Because they paid for its operations, they assumed that the principal purpose of the agency was to serve their needs. They assumed also that they should have a powerful voice in formulating policy and directing activities.

The Department held that the resources administered by it belonged to all the people but readily conceded in principle that the sportsmen should have a strong voice in the Department's operations. Yet in practice the Department faced the problem of determining who was qualified to speak for the sportsmen. Each year the Department sold more than 2,000,000 hunting and fishing licenses. Assuming that some sportsmen bought both, there were an estimated 1,500,000 individual licensed sportsmen. Of these only a small number took an active interest in fish and game legislative or administrative matters. This small number included the people who joined sportsmen's clubs.

Sportsmen's clubs in California by 1957 had a total membership of 125,000, or less than ten per cent of the total license buyers. Only a portion of the club members actively participated in club meetings or in making club policy toward fish and game matters. These activists were on the whole enthusiastic and dedicated people who gave generously of their time to sporting matters. Nevertheless, they constituted only a small portion of the licensed sportsmen, and at times they confused their own interests with those of all sportsmen. The Department was aware that the club leaders often spoke more for themselves than for the sportsmen they represented and that their demands did not necessarily reflect the needs or desires of the sportsmen or of the general public.

The Department's task of determining what sportsmen wanted was further complicated by the fact that the sportsmen's organizations could never agree upon basic policies. Many clubs had organized into regional councils, each representing the particular sporting interest predominant in the area. Over the years there had been efforts, often with the encouragement of the Fish and Game Department, to form a statewide association among the councils. In 1954, after several unsuccessful attempts, the California Wildlife Federation was organized as an affiliate of the national body. The Federation consisted of nine councils representing 640 clubs with a total membership exceeding 100,000. After 1954 the Federation was the only statewide organization in existence.

The loosely knit Federation did not succeed in uniting all the councils behind a single statewide fish and game policy because the interests of sportsmen in different parts of the state were too varied. Thus, in the north a regional council catered to deer hunters, while a council near the ocean concerned itself with ocean fishing. The local councils did not want the Federation to have extensive powers, fearing that it would subordinate local sports interests to a broader statewide policy. As a result of the differences of opinion prevailing among organized sportsmen, there was no single group that spoke for all sportsmen in California.

Somewhat bewildered, the Department of Fish and Game listened to a multitude of voices urging it to act in many different and at times contradictory ways. Meanwhile, the sports groups played off one Department program against another, each feeling that its interests should be paramount. As an example, one may cite the competing claims made on the Department by two such diverse groups as the Sportsmen's Council of the Redwood Empire and the Inland Council of Conservation Clubs of San Bernardino and Riverside Counties. The former group represented sportsmen living in one of the richest resource areas of the state. This area ranged from the ocean shore above San Francisco north and west to the majestic redwood forests. Contained in it were lakes, rivers, and streams abounding in fish of every description, and game habitat for virtually every species known in the state. Endowed with this abundance, the sportsmen of the Redwood Council sought only to maintain and improve the natural wealth they already possessed. They were content to have the Department place primary emphasis on range management, deer habitat, and water pollution control programs. The Inland Council, on the other hand, represented sportsmen in an area stretching from Death Valley, south across the Mojave Desert, to the Mexican border. In this resource-starved area the sportsmen depended more on the works of man than of nature. Fishing was possible only if the Department stocked the waters with artificially raised trout, and the best hunting depended on game birds raised on state farms. While the members of the Inland Council fought for more artificial propagation programs, those in the north viewed such programs as expensive demands on the limited resources of the Department.

Disagreements also existed among various conservation groups over the goals of conservation itself. The Department was basically committed to the scientific management of wildlife resources. Conservation to the Department meant more than the simple protection of fish and game against human destruction. It involved the management of the resources through scientific means to ensure an optimum sustained yield for more extensive use by an increasing number of people. Most professionals in the field of wildlife administration shared this viewpoint, but some groups in the state took issue with it.

The conservation groups fell along a continuum extending from absolute protectionists on one extreme to intemperate consumptionists on the other, with the majority of the sporting groups falling in between. The absolute protectionists tended to view fishing and hunting with suspicion. In their eagerness to protect the state's resources against human destruction, they often clashed with the Department over such things as the deer management program or the classification of song and game birds. A spokesman for one of these groups, Charles Bull of the Northern Counties Wildlife Conservation Association, summed up their philosophy in these words:

> By providing, arranging for, and engaging in promotion of hunting and fishing, the Department of Fish and Game is not acting in the interest of the majority of the people. . . . The majority of the people are not willing to accept the present policies of this governmental agency. These policies, which reek of commercialism and encourage the use of a great public resource as a harvestable commodity and a mere plaything for a small minority of shooters and other commercial interests, can no longer be tolerated by morally honest citizens.

The protectionists alone were not particularly powerful, but at times agricultural and sporting groups from resource-rich areas joined forces with them. Although there was no agreement in matters of principle, these groups found common cause in their desire to limit the use of their resources by outsiders.

On the other extreme, the Department had to contend with groups advocating an almost uncontrolled use of wildlife resources. While these groups realized that the resources needed to be protected against wanton use, they stressed high consumption in place of abstinence and retrenchment. As the state's population increased, the number of sportsmen eager for recreation grew and pressure on the resources mounted. Some of these sportsmen, with little understanding of conservation concepts, acted as if the wildlife wealth of the state were unlimited. When forced to face this limitation, they turned in anger on the Department and its management policies. They had paid their license fees, and they expected the Department to provide adequate fish and game. If the natural supplies were inadequate, then the Department should remedy these deficiencies by artificial propagation. Resort owners, who depended on the recreation trade and commercial interests, often allied themselves with the consumptionists.

The Department's difficulties with its clientele groups soon generated public controversy over fish and game matters. Many of California's 700 newspapers had a hunting and fishing column serving principally as a vehicle of information. But these columns also served as sounding boards for local complaints against fish and game programs. On the whole the Department received more newspaper space than any other state agency except the Governor's office. Legislators were quick to respond to loud, public complaints from sportsmen. Every lawmaker had sportsmen in his constituency, and many were sportsmen themselves. In and out of the capital they shared the average sportsman's conviction that they were experts on fish and game matters. Some legislators often agreed with the sportsmen that the fish and game agency, being financed by license fees, should serve the needs of the sportsmen.

THE SEEDBED OF DISSENSION, 1954-1956

Implementing the New Organization

Early in 1952 the California Legislature approved the Finance Department's plan for the internal organization of the Fish and Game Department in the hope of dispelling the operational difficulties that beset the agency. Despite widespread confidence that these changes would cure many of the Department's difficulties, additional problems arose during 1954, 1955, and 1956, and hostility toward the Commission and the Department continued among sportsmen and legislators. New problems sprang essentially from the financial and policy difficulties that confronted the Department during a period of growth and extensive internal change and culminated in the legislative authorization of the Booz, Allen, and Hamilton survey.

The task of implementing the 1952 reorganization plan fell to the newly appointed Director, Seth Gordon. Gordon had come to California in 1949, as a special consultant to the Wildlife Conservation Board, to supervise a major study of the state's wildlife needs. Through this work he had become well-known and eventually had received appointment as Director of the Department.[2] The change-over to the new organization was not a simple administrative task because it involved a shake-up of the Department from the top to the bottom. Gordon's job was to implement a reorganization plan aimed at unifying five relatively independent bureaus into a single Department. This was to be accomplished simultaneously with the Department's change from a functional-line to a staff-line organization and with its move toward decentralization of operations to the newly created regions.

The establishment of a unified Department presented a formidable challenge to Gordon. Under the old organization the bureaus had operated as autonomous units and the executive officer of the Commission, nominal head of the Department, had been unable to provide Department-wide leadership. Practically speaking, administrative direction had bounced among different Commission members, the executive officer, and various bureau chiefs. The executive officers' competence had varied, turnover had been high, and because of the commissioners' views, the officers' powers had been uncertain. As a result of this confusion over central control, power had passed to the bureau chiefs, and the agency had tended to become a confederation of bureaus. The bureau chiefs, civil service employees, often had shown a reluctance to accept the executive officer as head of the agency. Some bureau chiefs had ignored him and had dealt directly with members of the Commission and occasionally with the Legislature. In addition, the bureaus often had competed with each other for funds, personnel, and equipment. The absence of firm top management to coordinate bureau activities and to enforce an overall policy became apparent when the five major bureaus each divided the state into many separate districts and managed their domains with little attempt at coordination.

Gordon faced serious problems in converting the Department from a functional-line organization into a staff-line organization. The bureau chiefs, who had controlled the agency, lost their line authority, and the bureaus became headquarters staff branches. The once-powerful bureau chiefs had to learn to become planners and advisers to the director rather than doers. The new line of operations went from the director, to his deputy, to managers appointed in each region. These newly recruited regional managers exercised direct control over regional activities, and the functional supervisors (wildlife protection, game, fisheries) reported to

[2] Gordon began his long and distinguished career in wildlife administration in 1913 as a game protector in Pennsylvania. By 1919 he had risen to administrative head of the Pennsylvania Game Commission. In 1926 he had been conservation director of the Izaak Walton League and had served as president of the American Game Association. He had been a founder and the first administrative head of the American Wildlife Institute, the foremost professional association for wildlife management. In 1936 Gordon had returned to the Pennsylvania Game Commission as Executive Director and had served a total of twenty years before retiring to do consulting work.

them rather than to the old bureau chiefs. The abolition of the straight-line relationship from the field to headquarters bureaus created considerable friction within the organization. The functional people found it difficult to break their contacts with the bureau chiefs. The regional setup also made the Department highly decentralized, thus creating new problems of coordination and control for the director.

Another source of friction, which made the transition to the new organization difficult, was the long-standing conflict between the wardens and the biological specialists. This enmity can be traced back to the important changes in methods of wildlife management brought about by federal grant-in-aid programs. The federal government, through the Pittman-Robertson and later the Dingell-Johnson laws, encouraged in the states the development of more scientific methods of resource management. These programs offered federal support funds for research projects aimed at providing the necessary factual information for improved wildlife management. The emphasis on research brought into the Fish and Game Department a new breed: biological specialists trained in the universities to apply scientific information to wildlife problems. Previously the wardens had dominated the Fish and Game Department; but as the scientists gained prominence in the organization, the wardens increasingly resented them. The wardens felt that their extensive practical experience made them as knowledgeable about fish and game as did the book-learning of the biologists. The wardens, too, resented the fact that the Department recruited the biologists at a higher level and gave them higher pay.

Along with these changes, the 1952 reorganization required the departmental headquarters to move from San Francisco to Sacramento. In the process the headquarters office lost a large percentage of its clerical staff, because many refused to move from the Bay area to the Central Valley. Moreover, Gordon had to recruit new personnel to handle the accounting and service functions formerly performed for the agency by the Department of Natural Resources. The post-1952 organization, with its expanded responsibilities, called for a sizable increase in personnel; new employees had to be recruited and trained to fit into the organization. By 1954-1955 the agency had 836 positions—an increase of 111 over 1949-1950. The greatest portion of the increase, 80, consisted of administrative jobs.

Financial Difficulties Cause Criticism

The introduction of new programs, the great expansion of facilities, and the inevitable squeeze caused by the rising price level plunged the Department into financial straits. Between 1952 and 1957 the annual percentage increases in departmental expenditures over the preceding year were 16%, 6.9%, 5.9%, 3.8%, 7.7%, and 22.9%. The Department repeatedly called attention to the situation but met its increased expenditures by dipping into a large reserve fund accumulated from license fees collected during the war years when it had operated below capacity. In 1951 the reserve fund had exceeded $6,000,000. By 1957 it dropped below $3,000,000. In 1956-1957, with overall expenditures amounting to $9,500,000, the Department's budget estimated a record deficit of over $1,000,000.

Sportsmen and members of the Legislature's Fish and Game Committees paid close attention to the Department's financial plight. In 1953 the State Senate created an Interim Fish and Game Committee to oversee the reorganization plan and to resolve previous criticism. As the agency's financial status weakened, however, the Interim Committee acted as a "watchdog" over the agency. In 1954 the Senate Interim Committee noted that "continual deficit spending" would lead eventually to a request for larger revenues and perhaps higher license fees. The committee urged that "every effort should be made to curb departmental spending" even if it meant "reduction or deletion of some customary services" and especially those of "the least necessity to the operation" of the agency. The committee singled out the conservation education program, including educational films and information bulletins, out-of-state travel budget, and newly requested positions as examples of nonessential services. On the whole, the recommended reductions had been moderate. The Legislature accepted some, and the relative increase in departmental expenditures in 1954 was smaller than in the preceding year.

But these moderate reductions of services did not resolve the Department's financial difficulties, and the organized sportsmen became increasingly critical of the management of the Department. They had accepted the 1952 reorganization plan as a panacea for all their earlier frustrations. Advocates of reorganization had argued that a drastically reformed agency would operate more "efficiently and economically"; that the decentralized field structure would bring the Department closer to the sportsmen and make it more responsive to their interests. But to an increasing number of sportsmen, these advantages appeared less and less apparent, and dissatisfaction grew.

Sportsmen began to complain that they were not getting their money's worth from the Department. They charged that the departmental organization was becoming big and unwieldy and that too much money was being spent on administrative overhead. They felt the regional offices had too many administrators, managers, and supervisors engaged in shuffling papers and attending meetings and too few people actually involved in providing better fishing and hunting. They asked that less money be spent on automobiles, travel, printing, postage, telephones, and telegrams. They questioned, too, whether the reorganization had solved the problems of duplication and competition between divisions, game men and wardens, and scientists and practical fieldmen.

In addition, some sportsmen argued that the Department was spending too much money on useless research projects that had little practical application to fishing and hunting. One club spokesman voiced the objections of his group to departmental research, saying it opposed the "wanton waste and expense of having biologists, or whatever name they try to call themselves," doing such research projects as "measuring the length of tuna" or studying the "lovelife of the oyster." The research resulted, he charged, in pamphlets and books so technical "that the sportsman, or any other layman, could not get anything out of them." He demanded an end to such projects "even if it means the elimination of the soft berths of these scientific students." The only research these sportsmen wanted were practical studies that assured a plentiful supply of fish and game.

To some extent the sportsmen's criticism of the agency reflected information they had received from dissatisfied departmental personnel. Many of the tensions felt within the Department quickly passed along an active grapevine from the employees to sportsmen and legislators. Old-timers who still resented the abolition of the bureaus would readily report any hint of organizational difficulties under the new setup. Departmental people who objected to the new authority of the regional administrators were quick to report what they thought were examples of bureaucratic inefficiencies. The most active informants were the wardens, who harbored the greatest sense of grievance against the new organization. They felt that too many departmental decisions rested on the findings of the scientists, who failed to make use of the wardens' knowledge of the practical side of the problems. The old organization provided some security for the wardens against the threat of the scientists, but they felt they had lost this protection with the abolition of the bureaus.

Sensitive to the political implications of hunting and fishing, some legislators began to raise questions about the internal operations of the Department. Some legislators received complaints from disgruntled sportsmen and discontented departmental employees, and they circulated this information among their colleagues. Gordon and his staff were aware that some departmental personnel were undermining the agency by expressing their dissatisfaction to outsiders. They grew increasingly apprehensive about the effect of these complaints on the Department's public image and attempted to silence internal criticism. One legislator charged that the Department was really attempting to conceal information and had ordered personnel not to communicate with members of the Legislature. This accusation heightened suspicion of the Department.

Director Gordon, in vigorously defending his leadership of the Department against what he considered unwarranted criticism, inadvertently became the center of the spreading controversy. Some critics accused him of being an empire-builder, a spendthrift, a political maneuverer, and a person more interested in building a bigger rather than a better agency. They felt Gordon was presenting himself as the peerless fish and game expert, and some sportsmen came to feel that he was patronizing them when they presented what they considered to be valid criticisms of the Department. These critics concluded that Gordon was principally responsible for the Department's shortcomings.

Policy Conflicts—Artificial Propagation Programs

The Senate Interim Committee's 1955 report reflected the sportsmen's mounting criticism. Taking note of the growing dissatisfaction among hunters and fishermen and of the demand by one sportsmen's group for a "complete investigation" of the Fish and Game Department, the committee cautioned against an investigation lest it turn into a "witch-hunting probe made up mainly of smoke screens and headlines with scant foundation or valid information." Though the sportsmen had stressed organizational matters in their criticism of the Department, the Senate Interim Committee shrewdly perceived that, in fact, much of the criticism stemmed from disagreements over departmental programming. The committee recognized that the difficulties of the Department were not only due to the internal problems created by the reorganization but also resulted from sportsmen's differences with the Department over the emphasis placed on certain high-cost programs. The committee, therefore, had concerned itself less with Gordon's management of the Department and more with the programs and policies that underlaid the Department's financial difficulties.

The 1955 report urged the "injection of austerity-mindedness into the Department's financial thinking," and it pointed to programs where economies could be made without hurting the Department's principal tasks. The report singled out for special criticism the programs in artificial propagation, conservation education, and biological research—the very programs embodying many of the fundamental objectives toward which Gordon thought the agency should move. The committee pointed to the artificial propagation program of catchable trout as a good example of the need for "austerity-mindedness."

Compared with other fishing states, California had moved slowly in developing a catchable trout program. At first, regulation of supply had depended entirely on bag limits and closed seasons, but later the state had tried to increase fish supplies by planting newly hatched fry and fingerlings. Research gradually had demonstrated that planting of small fish would not always increase the productive capacity of a stream. Beginning in the 1930's, with the development of more advanced hatchery operation, it had been possible to raise fish of catchable size and plant them in streams. This so-called artificial propagation of fish had permitted more extensive fishing and less rigid controls and had gained great popularity among fishermen, especially among trout anglers. As the popularity of the program grew, pressures on the Department mounted. Legislators, particularly from resort areas and Southern California, pushed for more rapid expansion of the production of catchable trout. California's hatchery installations, however, were fairly antiquated and only a limited number of catchables could be produced.

In 1947 a dispute had developed in the Legislature over the disposition of pari-mutuel funds; and as part of a compromise settlement, the Legislature had allocated a certain percentage of these funds for use by the Wildlife Conservation Board, created at the time. Thus funds had become available for extensive improvements in wildlife installations. The board had decided that, in order to plan properly the expenditure of these funds, it would be necessary to undertake a study of existing facilities, and had hired Gordon to do the job. After a detailed survey, Gordon had recommended, among other things, that extensive modifications be made in the hatchery system so that the production of catchables could be increased. He had called for the closing of numerous small, uneconomical plants and for the construction of larger, more centralized facilities. The board had accepted these recommendations and had inaugurated a capital improvement program. Shortly thereafter Gordon had been appointed Director of the newly reorganized Department, and under his direction the Department had increased the production of catchable trout as planned by the Wildlife Board. By 1957 Gordon had raised catchable trout production to 7,750,000, a threefold increase from 1947; and the Department was spending between fifteen and twenty per cent of its total budget on the program.

Though "Saturday fishermen" seeking quick and tangible results were delighted with the catchable fish program, the more experienced anglers, especially those in clubs, grew resentful toward it. They were disdainful of the Department's efforts to furnish fish to the amateur or "meat" angler who measured his pleasure only in terms of his bag limit. They believed the catchable program was needlessly expensive and that it was being emphasized at the expense of other programs aimed at the development of the natural supply of fish. Also, some sportsmen argued that the Department was pushing the program because of political pressures, particularly from Southern California—an area less favorably endowed with a natural supply of fish. Increasingly, Director Gordon was caught in the cross fire between the friends and foes of the catchable trout program. The 1955 report of the Senate Committee reflected the view of the opponents of the program: "It appears to your committee that the primary danger of the continued expansion of hatchery production is that the improvement of natural propagation is likely to suffer." Natural propagation, the committee complained, "had assumed to a large extent the role of a neglected step-child."

In 1955 two investigations of the Department of Fish and Game were authorized. The State Senate reappointed its Interim Fish and Game Committee and allocated $15,000 for a continuing study of the Department. At the same time the Department, hoping to neutralize criticism of its management, requested an exploratory administrative study by the Office of the Legislative Analyst. Two specialists spent nearly five months in preparing a report dated January 1956. The investigators restricted themselves to organizational matters and did not attempt to evaluate Department policies. The major conclusion of the Legislative Analyst's report was favorable. The investigators had been satisfied that the Department was "reasonably well organized and is operating satisfactorily within the established policy frameworks set by law and the annual budget." The report went on to say, "It would appear that the evolution of the present organization from its highly criticized ancestor . . . bears out the optimism of those who sponsored the present structure and is a credit to the team that has put it into effect." However, the report continued, "Conversely, but to a lesser degree, there are distinct areas in which organizational and management improvements could possibly be made in the department." It listed the following:

(1) The director does not have a chief deputy over all activities and personnel and thereby is in the position of having to resolve and coordinate routine staff and line conflicts and interests personally, thus depriving himself of time which probably could more profitably be spent on overall matters of policy, planning, field inspection, and major decisions.

(2) The department has been slow to install and effectuate a common and consistent staff organizational pattern at the operational level in the regions, so that, while each regional organization is similar, there are significant variations.

The report concluded that a "full-fledged management study of all phases of the operations of the department is not needed at this time."

Either-Sex Deer Hunt

Hopes within the Department that the Legislative Analyst's findings and the budgetary restrictions imposed by the Legislature would dispel criticism of the Department among sportsmen collapsed when disaster befell the first statewide either-sex deer hunt in the fall of 1956.

California had moved slowly in developing a deer management policy. Game management research had demonstrated repeatedly that animal populations with a high reproductive capacity, unless regularly pruned and harvested, soon overtaxed limited food resources and suffered starvation. Advocates of game management insisted that the harvesting of the annual surplus of both does and bucks resulted in healthier herds and better nutrition for the young. California game laws from 1887 forward had permitted only the hunting of male deer. In 1950, conforming to developments in other western states, the Fish and Game Commission departed from this tradition and adopted a deer policy that proposed the "harvest of all surplus animals, of either sex, over and beyond what the range can carry in healthy conditions." This policy was based upon a statewide survey by a team of specialists of the University of California, headed by Dr. A. Starker Leopold.

Because of protests by some hunters and antihunting humanitarians, the Commission was slow to authorize the shooting of does. In order to allay the fears of those who objected to the deer management policy adopted in 1950, commissioners repeatedly, in statements to the public, stated that their first obligation was the welfare and perpetuation of the wildlife, not the wishes of the hunters. Another reason for the Commission's slowness to activate its own deer policy was the arduous, time-consuming steps required by the law. The commissioners were not free to act on the recommendations of others but had to hold public hearings in the affected areas.

The commissioners agreed with the Department that the safe way to control the number of hunters in any given area where surplus deer were to be removed was to issue a limited number of permits, for which a fee would have to be collected. This suggestion was widely discussed with the leaders of sportsmen's groups, but many objected to the extra fee and opposed any control plan that might ultimately lead to "telling hunters where they could or could not hunt for antlered bucks."

After adopting its either-sex deer policy in 1950, the Commission authorized a limited number of hunts in a few local areas, but it was not until 1956 that the Commission permitted the first general hunt. For the 1956 hunting season, Director Gordon recommended to the Commission that it adopt regulations permitting the taking of antlerless deer in specific counties or parts of counties. The Department made this recommendation after months of careful field work by trained employees and after consultations with organized sportsmen's groups, ranchers, and other interested parties. Among the important groups that endorsed the either-sex portion of the deer seasons, without control permits, were the California Wildlife Federation, the Associated Sportsmen of California, the Sacramento-Sierra Sportsmen's Council, and the Farm Bureau Federation. Of course, some groups, especially conservation groups dedicated to protectionist objectives, continued to oppose the recommended hunt.

The possible problems, and the limitations within which the Commission could act, were discussed fully at two public regulatory meetings of the Commission. Between those meetings the several commissioners held public hearings throughout the state prior to the meeting at which the Commission declared an either-sex deer season in thirty-three counties or parts of counties. The action permitted the taking of either-sex animals during the last three days of both the early and the late seasons.[3] The idea of issuing control permits was dropped because of the widespread opposition.

Despite strong opposition the Commission's decision remained unchanged. Under the law the Commission was actually powerless to change the regulations once they were formally adopted and promulgated, unless it made a finding that its original decision would jeopardize the future of the deer herds. In several counties local sports groups induced their County Board of Supervisors to adopt resolutions requesting the Commission to withdraw its antlerless deer hunting regulations for those counties. Subsequently the County Supervisors Association of California unanimously adopted resolutions condemning the hunt and requesting the Commission to revoke the either-sex deer regulation. No action was taken by the Commission on this request.

At the end of the late season (October 26-28) weather conditions concentrated hunters in some of the lower elevations, leading to a heavy kill of antlerless animals in these areas. Many hunters gathered for one last chance at a kill. In all, more than 111,000 animals were taken, about 40,000 of them being antlerless. Some hunters were shocked at the large numbers of carcasses of does and fawns taken from the range. In addition, they were dismayed by the danger of hunting accidents and the purportedly extensive damage to personal and private property.

Despite the fact that the game managers reported no herd had suffered basic damage, smoldering opposition to the Fish and Game Commission's deer management program exploded into a major controversy. Few raised their voices in defense of the Commission or Department; but sportsmen's clubs (even some that initially had favored the program) and hitherto neutral newspapers heaped criticism on Director Gordon and the Commission. Letters from angry citizens filled newspaper columns, and the fish and game columnists added their denunciations of the "monstrous slaughter" and the "Seth Gordon Massacre of 1956." Some criticized the either-sex deer hunts in principle, others argued that the Department had mismanaged the hunts and thus mutilated the deer herds for many years to come. One writer condemned Gordon's wildlife management policies as "concepts of a butcher shop." "Doe hunters are not sportsmen—they're meat hunters," another charged. "Fish and Game wants to commercialize on our game." There were a few loud demands for Gordon's resignation, for drastic reductions in the Commission's plenary powers to promulgate regulations, and for the development of "more local level management." Some northern sportsmen charged that the Commission had capitulated to pressures from Southern California and urban sportsmen for unrestricted deer hunting at the expense of northern game resources. Farmers and ranchers added their objections because of damage by hunters to private property. "Hunters endanger property owners," one rancher complained. "I am completely disgusted with shooting from vehicles, shooting from roads, night hunting, and shooting near buildings. Ranchers in self-defense have to hire enforcement deputies to protect themselves." The degree of emotionalism was unusual. Stories of wounded fawns left to die by hardhearted hunters too ashamed to bring them in stirred up feelings of disgust and horror. An angry letter to a newspaper imaginatively argued that "hunters who killed a doe and put the meat on the table before their children would be starting the youngsters on a life of crime and surely would lead them inside the gates of San Quentin Prison." Individuals and protectionist groups dedicated to halt all hunting in

[3] California regulations provided for an early (August-September) and a late (September-November) deer season. Hunting during the early season was restricted to areas along the coast and in the late season to inland counties.

California added their voices to the cacophony of criticism.

At a meeting of the Commission in Sacramento the following February the entire situation was reviewed. While it was concluded that no deer herd had been seriously damaged, it was agreed that the unexpected storms at the end of the inland season had concentrated the hunters in a most unfavorable way and that misconduct on the part of a small minority called for special consideration in relation to any future either-sex hunts. The Commission released a statement indicating that no further general hunts for the taking of antlerless deer would be considered until such time as the Commission was given authority to control the number of hunters in a given area at any given time.

THE LEGISLATURE INITIATES THE SURVEY

Late in 1956 Gordon and the Fish and Game Commissioners decided it was time for the Department to make some crucial decisions about its future. Preliminary work on the budget for fiscal 1957-1958 indicated that there would be a deficit of over $1,185,000 ($910,000 if the Legislature refused requested salary increases). The Department would be presenting a deficit budget to the Legislature for the sixth successive year, and though the Department had been able to write off previous deficits by drawing on its reserve fund, such a solution could not continue indefinitely. With the anticipated deficit for 1957-1958, the reserve fund would drop to $2,000,000. Gordon realized that this was dangerously low for an agency that depended on the variable income from license fees.

License Increase Proposal

The alternatives facing Gordon and the Commission were obvious: the Department had to cut back programs or request additional revenue through a license fee increase. Either action presented difficulties and invited opposition. At the request of the Commission, the Department had undertaken a study of the situation and made a report to the Commission in late 1956. The report recommended increased license fees to offset the anticipated deficit and attributed the department's financial difficulties to the increasing demands placed on it by an ever-growing population and the rising costs due to inflation. To make the requested increase in fees more palatable, the report recommended a program of expanded activities that could be undertaken with more funds. Perhaps as a challenge to possible opposition to the recommended increases, the Department also offered a detailed plan for possible cutbacks in existing programs. In the words of the report, "These reductions are not recommended . . . they should be made only if no additional funds are provided to offset added costs of inflation."

After considering the Department's report, the Commission publicly announced on December 20, through its chairman, Andy Kelly, that it was seeking a boost in the price of hunting and fishing licenses. Kelly argued this was the only reasonable course of action and that organized sportsmen favored the decision. However, the largest association of organized sportsmen in the state, the California Wildlife Federation, was not among those favoring license fee increases. Shortly after Kelly's announcement, the Federation, meeting in Fresno, voted to oppose an increase in license fees as proposed. The Federation also indicated it would oppose the biennial bill to extend the plenary powers of the Commission to set bag and season limits. At the same time, the United Press polled 120 legislators and discovered that they opposed a license fee increase by more than two and one-half to one.

The Commission's decision to request fee increases raised the further questions of which fees were to be increased and by how much. Gordon and the Commission were fully aware of the feeling among some sportsmen that the major departmental programs should be made to pay their own way. If additional revenues were needed, they should come from those sportsmen who benefited the most from the programs responsible for the Department's deficit, such as the artificial propagation program for trout and pheasants. Hitherto the Department had opposed fixing fees according to separate programs or a cost accounting approach because the Department was responsible for the protection of all wildlife, not just revenue-producing species. The Department prepared a bill calling for an across-the-board fee increase and persuaded Senator Charles Brown, an old friend of the Department, to introduce it in the upper house. The bill recommended the following fee increases—angling licenses from $3 to $5, hunting licenses from $3 to $5, commercial licenses from $10 to $25, deer tags from $1 to $2, and pheasant tags from $1 to $2.[4] The schedule was to provide the Department with $4,400,000 in new income, which was enough to meet the deficit.

Meanwhile, in the lower house, Assemblyman Thomas Erwin presented a different formula for the license increase. Assemblyman Erwin's bills rejected any increase in the basic license fee and substituted in its place a two-dollar stamp for trout and an increase in pheasant tags from one to two dollars. Erwin's bills assumed that the artificial trout and pheasant propagation programs largely caused the rising costs of the Department and that they should pay their own way. In defense of his proposal, Assemblyman Erwin said, "The sportsmen who don't fish for trout or hunt pheasants object to paying increased license fees to support these two programs. And I don't blame them. Now, for those who do fish trout or hunt pheasants, this increase isn't unreasonable." Both the Brown (S.B. 325) and Erwin (A.B. 2627, 2628) bills were referred to the Fish and Game Committees in their respective houses.

Because the bills involved revenue matters, they were sent to the Financial Subcommittee of the Senate Fish and Game Committee, and in May deliberations began. The subcommittee membership consisted of Senators James Cobey, George Miller, and John Murdy, none of whom were considered by the Department to be particularly unfriendly. Senator Murdy had been recently put on the full committee in order to give representation to Southern California. His interest focused chiefly on ocean fishing, and he tended to follow the advice of the Ocean Fish Protective Association, the major sportsmen's organization for ocean anglers. Senator Miller came from Richmond, in metropolitan Contra Costa County; and though a person of power in the State Senate, he was not very interested in fish and game matters. The strong man on the subcommittee was Senator Cobey from Merced, in the Central Valley. He had an active interest in fish and game and some fairly well-developed views on policy.

Various people appeared before the subcommittee to give testimony for and against the bills. Gordon represented the Department and Kelly, the Commission. Senator Brown and Assemblyman Erwin, authors of the bills, also testified. George Difani, of the California Wildlife Federation, appeared for his organization; and James McCormick represented the Associated Sportsmen of California. Sam Grosch appeared for the Sacramento-Sierra Sports Council, and L. C. Vanderlop for the State Chamber of Commerce.

All parties agreed that the Department was in financial difficulty and that some action had to be taken to remedy the problem. However, the unanimity ended there. Gordon and Kelly, speaking for the Fish and Game agency, strongly defended the principle of an across-the-board increase in fees and urged the enactment of the Brown bill. They argued that the Erwin bill would not provide enough revenue to keep the Department at adequate program levels and that the burden of additional fees should be distributed among all sportsmen. Objections to the Department's position commanded little agreement among the sportsmen. Difani summed up the confusion among the sportsmen:

> California Wildlife Federation is partly in support of this bill [Brown's bill]. San Diego and other "have not" areas favor the Brown bill. At the California Wildlife Federation meeting they agreed to compromise on a $4.00 fee, but this has since been abrogated by some councils. Skin divers oppose any increase. Ocean Fish Protective Association opposes any ocean fish licenses increase. California Game Improvement Association opposes any increase. Southern Council favors a $1.00 increase except for deer tags. Central Council favors the Brown bill except for deer tag increase. Associated Sportsmen's Council opposes a general fee increase. North Central Council favors a $1.00 increase.

Many of these differences were based on the internal divisions among the various sporting interests—between Northern and Southern California, between ocean and inland anglers, between catchables and natural trout anglers, between hunters and anglers, and so on. On the one hand, sportsmen from the south, or as Difani had said, from "have not" areas, depended heavily on artificial propagation programs and therefore opposed any license increase aimed primarily at them. On the other hand, sportsmen from areas where the natural supply of fish and birds was more plentiful felt that less emphasis should be placed on artificial propagation. They felt that these programs absorbed too much of the Department's resources and that they

---

[4] A tag is a permit authorizing the individual who legally killed the animal to keep the meat.

should be made self-supporting. McCormick, of the Associated Sportsmen of California, supported the Erwin bill, saying: "Artificial program expansion should be geared to a pay-as-you-go basis. We want no general license increase until the artificial program is self-sustaining."

Furthermore, the sportsmen were reluctant to provide additional funds to the Department without knowing how these funds were to be spent. Each sporting interest felt that additional funds should be used for programs it favored. Difani, speaking for the California Wildlife Federation, said:

> We agree to oppose any larger scale increase until specific future plans are outlined in detail. We feel the department can affect future economies in existing programs. . . . We realize that some source of additional revenues must be provided, but we do not want to write a blank check for any larger amount over and above the deficit.

Difani and Philpott

After completion of hearings on the Brown and Erwin bills, the subcommittee had to devise compromise legislation that would be acceptable to all parties. The subcommittee agreed that the Erwin bill would not provide enough revenue, that it would only provide stopgap relief, and that if it were enacted, in a few years another effort would be made to raise fees. The subcommittee agreed to accept the Brown bill; but to appease the bill's opponents, the subcommittee modified the fee schedule. It recommended a four-dollar rather than a five-dollar hunting license and rejected the Commission's recommendation for a universal five-dollar fishing license. In its place, the Federation recommended a five-dollar all-purpose sport fishing license, a four-dollar general fishing license for all species except trout, and a three-dollar license for ocean fishing only.

The subcommittee's recommended fee schedule was close to what the Commission had requested. It provided a little more than $3,200,000 in new revenues and permitted the Department to operate in the black. After having made these concessions to the Department, however, the subcommittee attempted to placate the critics of the Department by inserting the following provision into the Brown bill:

> . . . to provide an appropriation not to exceed $250,000 for a complete study of the policies, plans, and programs of the Department of Fish and Game and the Fish and Game Commission. This study would be made either by the legislative analyst or a contracting agency selected by him.

The decision to include this provision in the license bill came as a surprise since there had been no consultation between the Department and the Legislature on the matter. Gordon privately objected to the inclusion of the study in the license bill because he felt the Department was being forced into accepting it in order to obtain the increase in license fees. He believed, further, that there had been too many investigations of the Commission and Department over the years and that the "objective" ones, particularly the study by the Legislative Analyst, had proved that the Department was well-managed. He felt that this new investigation was politically motivated and that certain sportsmen would never be satisfied with the policies or management of the agency until they were able to dictate what the Commission and the Department did.

The individual singled out by people in the agency as having been most responsible for this action by the Legislature was Difani. He was a semi-retired building contractor, with an almost professional interest in fish and game, who had been active for many years in sportsmen groups. He served as the state representative to the National Wildlife Federation, had been instrumental in establishing the California affiliate in 1954, and had been its first president. He served as a legislative advocate for various sporting groups and had developed close contacts with legislators active in the fish and game area. In 1957 he was serving as the executive secretary of the California Federation and was representing it before the Legislature. Though the Federation paid Difani for expenses incurred in this work, there was no salary attached to the job and much of his labor went without compensation.

When Difani had been President of the California Wildlife Federation, he had become acquainted with G. W. Philpott, who at the time was President of Sportsmen's Council of Central California. Philpott was trained as an accountant but became a writer of a daily wildlife column for various newspapers. Difani and Philpott had on their own, over the years, conducted various studies of the operations and policies of the Department of Fish and Game. As the financial difficulties of the Department mounted, both Difani and Philpott grew increasingly critical of the agency and its leadership.

Their objections to the agency and its leadership were diverse; some had to do with policies, such as the artificial propagation programs, and others concerned internal management matters. Eventually Difani and Philpott had concluded that the only way to check on the agency was to have a survey by an outside consulting firm. As an accountant, Philpott believed the Department needed a cost accounting system to control allocation of funds. He felt that an outside management firm specializing in such work could provide the desired system. As early as 1954 Philpott had written to the Senate Fish and Game Committee requesting that an outside management survey be made of the Department, and this request kept recurring. However, the Legislature at the time, through its interim committees, had been engaged in its own investigations and had not responded to his requests.

Difani, as the lobbyist for the California Wildlife Federation, had taken a very active part in the legislative deliberations over the license bills. When the subcommittee accepted the license increase, Difani had been in a position to argue that some check had to be made on how the Department was to spend the additional funds. He had agreed with Philpott that the task could be best performed by making a management survey of the Department. Moreover, he had stated that the California Wildlife Federation had enough votes in the Legislature to kill any license bill if some provision were not made for a survey. It was a matter of conjecture whether the California Wildlife Federation had had the necessary votes to defeat a license bill, or even whether Difani had been reflecting accurately the views of all units of the loosely knit Federation, but the subcommittee apparently had respected Difani's view. Also, committee members had felt that they could not refuse to authorize such a survey, since it was to be paid for by the sportsmen through their license fees.

In addition to these considerations, the subcommittee had been impressed by the evident conflict over policies among the sportsmen and between sportsmen and the agency. For years fish and game affairs had been one of the most controversial items of the legislative agenda, and at that moment the Legislature was embroiled in an acrimonious debate over fish and game policy—specifically, the matter of either-sex deer hunting. Opponents of antlerless hunting were seeking legislation to limit the power of the Fish and Game Commission over deer hunting. The debate over this proposal was particularly bitter and showed clearly how divided were opinions over fish and game matters.

The full Fish and Game Committee made some modifications of the subcommittee's bill. The full committee reduced the appropriation for the survey from \$250,000 to \$100,000 and added a provision further restricting the Department's use of the money from the new fees. This provision, establishing what became known as the "frozen fund," provided that, "Fifty (50) percent of all revenues attributable to the increase in license fees . . . shall not be available for expenditure unless and until specifically appropriated by the legislature." The provision further evidenced the Legislature's distrust of the agency, for it compelled the Department to get approval from the Legislature for any program changes that involved use of the frozen fund. The Legislature authorized as the first expenditure from the frozen fund the \$100,000 for the survey.

In late May 1957 the State Senate debated the bill, endorsed it overwhelmingly by a vote of 27 to 1, and then sent it to the Assembly. The measure ran into no serious opposition in the Assembly, though some minor changes were attempted. At one point the Assembly Fish and Game Committee amended the bill to provide that a special joint interim committee, instead of the Legislative Analyst, be authorized to choose the management firm or firms to make the survey of Fish and Game. However, in order to avoid a possible clash over the survey among certain legislators likely to be on such a committee, it was agreed to leave the decision in the hands of the Legislative Analyst. During the Assembly proceedings, Senator Cobey heard a rumor that Gordon was attempting to get the provision for the survey dropped from the license bill. He immediately contacted Assemblyman Erwin and told him the Senate would not support a bill without provision for a survey; it would have to be a package deal. Finally, the license bill passed both houses and received the Governor's approval. The Department obtained additional revenue but at the price of undergoing another survey.

Scope of the Survey

The license bill did not specify the scope of the proposed survey. A rider to the bill provided for an appropriation of funds and delegated responsibility for granting the contract to the Joint Legislative Budget Committee and the Legislative Analyst. In mid-May 1957, when the passage of the license bill seemed certain, the Fish and Game Subcommittee turned its attention to the prospective survey.

The overall goal of the survey was to study the programs and policies of the agency, but the programs and what policies to be studied were not defined. Harry Grafe, Executive Secretary of the Senate Fish and Game Committee, was assigned the responsibility of drafting a resolution outlining more detailed objectives of the survey. Grafe consulted Difani and other representatives of the organized sportsmen. But their advice was of limited value because in general the spokesmen represented their own separate parochial interests and lacked a common perspective on the statewide problems of fish and game.

Grafe was concurrently drafting the final 1957 report of the Fish and Game Interim Committee. He had played an important role in the investigations of earlier Fish and Game Interim Committees. As a result, he had fairly strong opinions on what was wrong with the agency.

The 1957 report of the Interim Committee contained one of the most severe condemnations of the fish and game agency ever made by a legislative committee. The highly critical nature of the report was summed up in the following indictment leveled against the Commission and Department:

> Our committee files are studded with caustic complaints against the commission, the department, and key personnel of this agency. According to investigations undertaken by this committee, there appear to be incidents in which the commission and the department did not act in the best interest of the people. . . . Such reprehensive conduct can not be condoned and unless there are immediate sincere assurances that there will be no repetition of these actions, legislation should be enacted as a future preventative.

The report stated that the results of all this dissatisfaction "took the form of a lack of confidence [in the Department], and your committee received from a multitude of sources the same two-ply appeal: replace the director, and revoke the plenary powers [of the Commission]." Specifically, the report criticized the policies and program management of the Commission and Department in the areas of artificial propagation, big game management, predatory animal control, conservation education, use of federal grant funds, and internal business procedures.

Following publication of the report, the Department voiced vigorous exception to many of the findings. It maintained the report was unfair and reflected more the personal opinions of Grafe than the feelings of the full committee. According to the Department, two of the original signers of the report said they disagreed with many of its conclusions and that Grafe had obtained their signatures on the report by subterfuge.

The report served as Grafe's guide when he drew up the resolution defining the scope of the survey. He took the findings of the Interim Committee and drafted a resolution from them. To satisfy those who wanted other matters investigated, the resolution stated that the survey should include but not be limited to these matters. The specific survey objectives, as outlined in Senate Committee Resolution 126, were as follows:

> (1) An evaluation of the artificial propagation programs of the department . . . with the aim of establishing levels of emphasis and expenditures for these programs in relation to the emphasis and expenditures that should be accorded improvement of habitat and natural conditions.
>
> (2) A review of the methods and procedures of administration of the department both on the headquarters and regional levels to determine if general business functions are operating with all possible efficiency and to ascertain if there is a possibility of effecting any consolidation of regional administrative operations.
>
> (3) A survey of the conservation education activities of the department with the aim of evaluating the function of this branch and the publications and printing of the department.
>
> (4) Consideration of the effectiveness of the department's use of funds received under the Pittman-Robertson Federal Aid in Wildlife Restoration Act and the Dingell-Johnson Federal Aid in Sport Fish Restoration Act to determine if the best possible utilization is being made of these funds.
>
> (5) A survey of predatory animal control, particularly existing duplicating activities. . . . [The failure to mention specifically in the resolution the deer management program is explained by the fact that the Legislature dealt with the matter separately. Late in the 1957 session the Legislature enacted the Busch law, which provided new procedures for regulating deer hunting and also permitted a county's Board of Supervisors to

modify or veto any antlerless season within its county as proposed by the Fish and Game Commission.]

Choosing the Management Consultants

With the legislative adoption of Senate Committee Resolution 126, the responsibility for implementing the survey passed to the Joint Legislative Budget Committee. This committee, established in 1941, provided the Legislature with its own independent source of fiscal and research information. The Office of Legislative Analyst had been created to provide the Budget Committee with a trained staff of fiscal and management specialists. The office had a staff of about forty people and was headed by the Legislative Analyst, who was appointed by the Budget Committee and served as its secretary.

In August 1957, in the name of the Budget Committee, Alan Post, the Legislative Analyst, began a preliminary investigation of management firms that could carry out the survey of the Department of Fish and Game. Though Post was acting as an agent of the committee, he had to make some judgments as to legislative intent. Senate Committee Resolution 126 set forth broad guidelines about the goals of the survey and left most of the procedural detail to the committee and the Legislative Analyst.

As Legislative Analyst, Post was fairly well informed on fish and game matters. Members of his staff took part in the annual preliminary budget hearings between the Department of Finance and the Fish and Game agency, and in 1956 his office had conducted a management survey of the agency. As far as Post was concerned, the initial impetus for the new survey stemmed from disagreement over policy objectives, and managerial problems were only of subsidiary importance. Post's interpretation of legislative intent was that the Legislature wanted a completely objective, expert analysis of programs and policies of the Commission and Department. In effect, the Legislature was buying an expert appraisal of controversial programs by specialists outside the Department, which could be balanced against the judgment of professionals within the agency. This assumption guided his actions.

The first decision Post faced concerned the question of whether the survey should be broken down according to program and administrative management phases and different firms be employed to do each job. He realized that wildlife experts would be needed to do the program analysis and that a firm specializing in this area might not be prepared to handle the management study. On the other hand, he might locate the right firm to do the administrative study, but it would not have the experts necessary to evaluate the programs. At this early stage, when he was considering the employment of a firm specializing in wildlife management studies, he consulted with Director Gordon. He knew that the Department had a list of such firms and wanted to make use of it. Also, he was interested in knowing if the Department had any deep-seated antagonism toward any person who might be employed as a specialist to examine the agency. Gordon gave him the list and raised certain objections to some people on it. Gordon, at this time, was still dubious about the need for the survey; but Post's action led him to feel that the Department would be consulted on whatever was done.

After some thought, Post decided that it would be better to have a single firm responsible for both aspects of the survey, primarily because he felt that if two contracts were granted he would have to coordinate the activities of the two firms. He believed that it would be best to keep his office out of the picture in order to avoid questions on the impartiality or objectivity of the survey. He knew that some sportsmen had attacked his 1956 management study of the agency as a whitewash, arguing that any internal governmental division could not make an objective study of another.

Having decided to use only one firm, Post proceeded to canvass the field for possible firms to make the survey. The choice finally narrowed to two: the Stanford Research Institute, a large research organization with home offices in California, and Booz, Allen, and Hamilton (BAH). Post had had some experience with BAH in a highway division management study, which also had been initiated by the Legislature's directing the Legislative Analyst to employ an outside consultant. Post believed that either firm could put in the field, in association with its regular personnel, a team of wildlife management experts to make the program studies. Both firms were approached and asked to submit a prospectus outlining the ways they would handle a survey of the Department of Fish and Game. By late September the proposals of each were in the hands of Post, and on October 10 the Joint Legislative Budget Committee met.

The Chairman, Senator Arthur Breed, called the Budget Committee to order with nine of its fourteen members in attendance. He announced that the main purpose of the meeting was to consider the proposed study of the Department of Fish and Game and to execute a contract or contracts for such a study. He explained that representatives of various organized sportsmen's groups and of the Fish and Game Commission and Department were in attendance to give expression to the purposes and overall scope of the study. Brief statements would be welcomed from anyone present about whether there were additional matters to be considered beyond those contained in the resolution.

Breed asked Post to summarize his preliminary work and to explain why BAH and Stanford Research were invited to present proposals. Next, William Hosken, representing Stanford Research Institute, outlined his firm's proposal emphasizing an ecological approach to the survey. The Stanford proposal aimed at an analysis of wildlife resources and the future development of these resources in a state with an exploding population and changing agricultural, commercial, and industrial needs. The proposal concentrated on long-range problems and did not emphasize more immediate policy issues. Hosken stated that most of the work would be done by Stanford's Division of Economic Research, and if specialized consultants were needed, they could be drawn from Stanford University.

Breed then called on William Powell, the resident partner in the San Francisco office of BAH, to review his firm's proposal. Powell's explanation of the scope of the study stayed close to the objectives contained in Senate Committee Resolution 126, and he indicated the agency would recruit outstanding specialists in the wildlife management areas to do the program studies. Overall control of the survey would be the responsibility of Powell, and a senior associate of the firm would be in charge of the field work. Then, significantly with respect to later developments, the prospectus emphasized the following methods of BAH procedure:

> Our analysis and development of recommendations would be based on work done jointly with the commission and the department. We are unwavering in our adherence to the strict concepts of professional objectivity in consulting. We are also unwavering in our belief that our consulting should produce practical results. It is our experience that the best results are produced in a cooperative, open-minded environment in which client and consultant combine their knowledge and experience and jointly and concurrently arrive at the conclusion. Thus, our reports are confirmatory as to conclusions and recommendations and working documents for carrying them out. They contain no surprises.

After the representatives of the management consulting firms completed their presentations, some discussion followed, and finally the chairman called on any witnesses to come before the committee to present their views on the survey. Most of the volunteer witnesses spoke for the particular interests of the groups they represented. Herbert Davis, representing the commercial canners, advanced the proposal that the survey examine the feasibility of establishing a division of commercial fisheries in the Department of Natural Resources. Charles Bull, Chairman of the Northern Counties Wildlife Conservation Association, spoke out against the existing game management program in the Department and felt that serious study should be made of it. Dr. E. L. Dryden, representing a Southern California sportsmen's association, spoke out against the deer program and characterized the conservation policy of the Department as the "willful and negligent destruction of fish and game." Difani stated that he hoped this would be the study to end all studies. He felt the Wildlife Management Institute of Washington, D. C., could do a very competent job and recommended that the institute be invited to submit a proposal before the contract was awarded. He stated, however, that no matter who did the job it had better be an objective one, and that the sportsmen did not want just another whitewash job of the Department. Another witness said that his only purpose was to be sure that a completely independent survey would be made by an outside consultant. Another wanted to be certain that the conservation education program was studied to see if it was anything more than a propaganda machine to further fish and game policies.

At the conclusion of the testimony, ballots were passed out, and the committee voted the contract to BAH.

BAH CARRIES OUT THE SURVEY

BAH was one of the oldest and largest management consulting firms offering services to business and government. It had been founded in 1914 by Edward Booz, who had felt that the Taylorism of his day placed too much emphasis on products and procedures and neglected the study of the purposes and people of an organization. The firm was organized on a national level, with offices in principal cities, including a western regional office in San Francisco. A distinctive feature of the firm's organization was that a partner had responsibility for each study undertaken. The firm employed about 250 full-time professionals and had been subdivided into six functional fields: manufacturing, sales, finance and accounting, engineering and research, personnel, and general management. BAH had concentrated primarily on private business consulting, but in 1955 it had established a special division in the field of public administration to handle the growing volume of business with public and semipublic agencies.

Immediately after obtaining the contract in October 1957, BAH began preliminary work on the study. Powell was in control of the survey. He had been in charge of the highway division study and was known in Sacramento, particularly in the Legislative Analyst's Office. J. Doyle Gray, a senior management specialist, became full-time project director and was assigned major responsibility for the field work. Subsequently, an accountant, William Hurst, joined the team to handle the systems and procedures analysis in finance and accounting areas. At this preliminary stage, Powell and Gray arranged a series of meetings with people outside the Department—primarily members of the Fish and Game Commission, representatives of the organized sportsmen, and staff people in the Office of the Legislative Analyst. The objective was to gather background information on the agency from people not directly involved in day-to-day operations, both friends and critics, so that the objectives of the survey could be defined more clearly. How satisfied were people with the general operations of the Department? What did people object to and why? How did they feel about the policies and programs mentioned in Senate Committee Resolution 126? What did they feel needed to be investigated in these areas? What other problems needed to be looked into? With such probing questions, Powell and Gray sought to get a picture of the agency and its problems. They wanted, also, to check individual reactions to a number of people who had been suggested as possible candidates to direct the wildlife management phase of the survey. The firm's offices throughout the country solicited from informed sources (U.S. Fish and Wildlife Service, sporting publications, national sportsmen's associations) the names of wildlife specialists capable of doing the job. Before hiring anyone BAH wanted to be certain the persons were acceptable to all interested parties.

Restrictions on Survey Procedures

The first meeting arranged was in Sacramento with the Legislative Analyst. Post outlined his conception of the survey, placing great emphasis on the importance of maintaining complete objectivity in its conduct. He told Powell that he believed the survey had been initiated because of genuine disagreement over policy and program objectives, and that these differences existed within the Department at various levels, between the Department and sportsmen, and among sportsmen. These differences had bred an atmosphere of suspicion and hostility, and a thoroughly objective study of policy matters was needed to clear the air. He noted that some sportsmen were dissatisfied with the organization of the Department, but he felt that the 1956 administrative survey done by his staff had indicated that the Department was reasonably well-organized. Post also said that every effort should be made to penetrate the lower echelons of the agency, to talk to as many field people as possible, and to assess their attitudes and opinions on the programs and operations of the Department.

Post cautioned Powell on the controversial nature of fish and game affairs and pointed out that any contact with the top management of the agency would have to be handled with care. He made it clear to Powell that BAH's client in this particular instance was the Joint Budget Committee, not the Department of Fish and Game. Any work done for the Joint Committee was to be treated as confidential unless released by authority of that committee. This meant that none of the final conclusions or recommendations of the survey were to be revealed to the Department before they were presented to the Joint Committee. BAH would, of course, work with the agency to collect the necessary factual information, but the agency was not to have the customary client relationship to the survey. Post felt that any hint of departmental influence on the survey would lead some sportsmen to challenge the survey and brand it as a whitewash. He noted that some sportsmen already had criticized him for consulting with Director Gordon immediately after the Legislature had authorized the survey.

Powell and Gray were not enthusiastic about these instructions. They had not anticipated, prior to the granting of the contract, that such restrictions would be imposed on BAH. They pointed out that these procedures were not in accord with the normal methods that BAH liked to follow in any survey. They said they were accustomed to working on the same side of the desk with their clients. It was their experience that recommendations were most successfully implemented when they were worked out in a cooperative environment in which client and consultant jointly arrived at the conclusions. Post understood that these procedures might create problems, but he felt that under the circumstances they were necessary. Powell and Gray reluctantly agreed to follow Post's instructions because the firm had committed itself to the contract.

The controversial nature of their assignment became increasingly apparent when Powell and Gray discussed the survey with leaders of the organized sportsmen and members of the Fish and Game Commission. The Commission had remained officially silent about the survey, despite the fact that the legislative resolution authorizing the survey referred directly to the Commission and to policy matters under its jurisdiction. The members of the Commission interviewed showed no great enthusiasm for another investigation of Fish and Game. But they felt that the survey aimed at the Department rather than the Commission. They admitted that the Commission had come under fire because of the either-sex deer program, but the Legislature had taken care of this problem by its recent action permitting local option on these hunts. They knew, however, that there was hostility toward the Department, because sportsmen had come to them with complaints about the Department and about Gordon's leadership. It was their contention that the survey was a departmental matter, and they intended to stay out of the picture as much as possible.

Powell and Gray interviewed a number of club leaders and questioned them on the survey. Difani, in a brief conversation with Gray, indicated areas he thought needed to be investigated and named people to be interviewed, including wardens. Difani repeated the warning he gave at the October meeting of the Joint Budget Committee—that if there were a hint of collusion between the Department and the survey team, he would do all that he could to blow up the survey. As far as he was concerned, the sportsmen had initiated the study to investigate Gordon's leadership of the Department, and this could not be done objectively if Gordon exercised control over the work.

Other sportsmen voiced dissatisfaction with Gordon personally and argued that some of the Department's difficulties were due to his behavior. They respected Gordon as a conservationist, but they felt he sometimes lacked the skill to handle his critics or to sell a controversial program to the sportsmen. He was a strong-willed person who could be impatient with people who disagreed with him, and had antagonized legislators, commissioners, and sportsmen in this manner. Moreover, they questioned his skill as an administrator. Some of the sports leaders felt the Department was top-heavy with administration and the organization was not geared to a state with a population of 20,000,000. These people were interested in a survey of the organization as well as programs and policies of the agency.

Also, some of Gordon's critics refused to differentiate between the policy-making responsibilities of the Commission and the director's administrative duties. They realized, of course, that by law the Commission was responsible for making departmental policy; but they charged that, in fact, Gordon dominated the Commission and it readily accepted his recommendations. For this reason critics held him ultimately responsible for those policies they disliked. They argued that the Commission, a lay body paid on a per diem basis with no staff of its own, lacked the technical knowledge to do much more than accept what Gordon and his experts recommended. For example, they insisted that for years Gordon had personally advocated either-sex deer hunting and that he had induced the Commission to incorporate in its 1956 regulations provision for a general either-sex hunt.

At this early stage Powell consulted briefly with Director Gordon to ascertain his views on the man to direct the wildlife phases of the survey. BAH wanted a person of recognized authority who would be acceptable to the involved parties—the Legislature, sportsmen, and Department. Finally, BAH decided that the most satisfactory candidate was Ernest F. Swift, the executive director of the National Wildlife Federation. Powell met Swift in Washington in December and offered him the job. Swift was one of the nation's leading authorities on wildlife administration. He had served for many years in the Wisconsin Conservation Department, starting as a warden and eventually becoming director in 1947. In 1954 he had left this post to serve briefly as assistant director (game management) in the U.S. Fish and Wildlife Service, and in 1955 he had assumed the duties of executive director of the National Wildlife Federation. He was well-known and respected by professionals in the wildlife field, and as an officer of the National Federation he had worked in close association with the leaders of the state group. He appeared to fit perfectly the job specifications.

Swift agreed to head the survey and made arrangements with the National Wildlife Federation for a leave of absence. He notified Powell that he could commence work on March 15, 1958, and that he would stay as long as was necessary to complete the wildlife phases of the survey. He would personally handle the investigation of the wildlife protection and conservation education programs and help BAH integrate its organizational and administrative findings with the program studies. He would be responsible for locating the other wildlife management specialists, for preparing a preliminary outline of their responsibilities, and for coordinating their activities. Powell assured Swift that BAH was undertaking this assignment on a constructive and cooperative basis and that the final report would be a "confirmatory document in which there would be no surprises." He warned Swift, however, that relations with top management of the Department would have to be handled carefully so as to avoid any charges of bias from the sportsmen.

Meeting with the Department

The actual field work for the survey began in the early months of 1958. In February Powell contacted Gordon and arranged a meeting between the top staff of the agency and the BAH team. Attending the meeting were Powell; Gray; Hurst; and from the agency, Gordon; his deputy, Shannon; Anderson, the administrative officer; and Caulkins, head of conservation education. The aim of the meeting was to inform Gordon and his staff about BAH's plans and procedures and to elicit their full cooperation in the survey. Powell outlined the standard approach of BAH to a management study, stating that the general objectives of the survey had been laid down by the Legislature and within these guidelines BAH would examine and evaluate the agency.

In discussing the way BAH would go about its job, Powell emphasized the importance of an harmonious working relationship between the survey team and the agency. He acknowledged that technically BAH's client was the Legislature and that its ultimate responsibility was to this body. However, he said the work would be done in the Department, and top management's cooperation would be needed if the survey were to succeed. He outlined briefly the steps BAH would take in collecting information and said that the firm would follow "normal" procedures in its investigation. Aware of doubts about the need for the study, he attempted to reduce top management's fears by assurances that this survey would be handled much the way other surveys were done by the firm. But Powell either overstated his point or expressed himself in terms ambiguous enough to lead to misinterpretation. Gordon and his staff came away from the meeting with the impression that the final report would be reviewed by the Department before it was presented to the Legislature.

This meeting led to some changes in the attitudes of Gordon and his staff toward the survey. Gordon from the very beginning had been on the defensive, feeling that those initiating the survey had done so in part to criticize his leadership of the Department. Gordon realized too that in employing an outside consultant the Legislature intended that neither he nor his staff should be closely associated with the survey. However, after the meeting with Powell, Gordon hoped the agency would be consulted at some point on the recommendations being made. Such consultation at least would provide an opportunity for him to advance his views.

Moreover, the appointment of Swift and the other specialists who were to work with him encouraged Gordon and his staff to feel that the Department's operations would be reviewed by people experienced in such work. Swift chose a panel of experts known in the Department. The experts he chose and the areas they were assigned to study were:

SMALL GAME I. T. Bode, retired director, Missouri Conservation Commission

BIG GAME J. Burton Lauckhart, Chief of Game Management Division, Washington State Department of Game

MARINE FISHERIES Milton James, Research Coordinator, Pacific Marine Fisheries Commission

INLAND FISHERIES C. J. Campbell, Chief, Department of Basin Investigation, Oregon State Game Commission

Bode had known Gordon for many years. Similarly, James was, in a technical sense, an employee of Richard Croker, branch chief of Marine Resources. Croker, at the time, was serving as Chairman of the Pacific Marine Fisheries Commission, James's employer, and James had to be released by the chairman in order to work for BAH.[5] It would have been rather difficult, of course, to find anyone who was completely unknown to the Department, since the field of fish and game administration was limited to a relatively small number of people. The fact that the specialists chosen were known in the Department and respected as competent professionals helped to reduce some of the anxiety Gordon and others bore toward the BAH survey. They felt that if the Department had to be investigated it could best be done by professionals whose practical experience made them aware of the many problems faced by such an agency.

Collecting Information

Following the February meeting, Powell and his co-workers were ready to begin their detailed investigation of the Department. Powell decided to delay work on the administrative organization of the Department until the specialists completed their studies of the wildlife management programs. Swift, still in the process of putting together his team of experts, did not complete the task until late March.

In the meantime Gray and Hurst studied the license administration procedures and the system of management controls utilized by the Department. Hurst took major responsibility for the evaluation of the system of management controls and spent most of his time working in the accounting section of the Sacramento office. He discovered early in the course of his investigation that the annual budget was the primary means of the director's control over the wildlife program. He found, however, this control was of limited use to the director because the budget provided information on expenditures by functions and classes rather than by specific wildlife programs and sub-programs. He realized that the agency had run into trouble with sportsmen over the matter of the emphasis placed on particular programs, and in order to evaluate such criticism, revenues and expenditures needed to be broken down according to these programs.

With this objective in mind, Hurst undertook an analysis of the Department's 1957-1958 revenues and expenditures to provide a basis for evaluation of programs and to test the feasibility of developing a system of management controls. He talked extensively with all top management personnel, particularly the branch chiefs, in order to ascertain their views on ways of developing a cost accounting system. He encountered a great deal of opposition from those he interviewed. Some people objected to his method of classifying wildlife species and to his allocation of costs according to such a classification because they felt this procedure ignored the basic conservation responsibilities of the agency. Others complained that cost accounting was based on the incorrect assumption that the level of programming in a particular area should be determined by the revenues received from those benefiting from such a program. As one branch chief said, "This guy came in here with the crazy idea that you could put a dollar value on every fish in the ocean." But Hurst persisted in his efforts and eventually developed an accounting system that he felt permitted the allocation of estimated departmental expenditures with respect to the major species of wildlife. This analysis of estimated revenues and expenditures formed an integral part of the final BAH report.

While Hurst worked on this task, Gray investigated departmental procedures for the sale of hunting and fishing licenses. Some 3,900 private agents, generally businessmen commissioned by the Department, sold the bulk of the licenses issued annually to sportsmen. For these services the agents received a five per cent commission. The management of this license system entailed a considerable administrative effort for the Department, and Gray was particularly interested in knowing if there were some opportunities for cost reduction through work simplification and some centralization of administration. In order to check the operation of the license system, Gray selected, according to volume of business and location, about five agents in each of the five fish and game regions and interviewed them. He was convinced by his findings that the license procedures could be simplified and that the commission paid to the agent could be reduced from five to two per cent.

Work of the Wildlife Specialist

Meanwhile, Swift established headquarters in Sacramento in the Legislative Analyst's Office and began work. He spent about one month, before any of the other specialists arrived, outlining their assignments. He defined their duties, indicated

[5] This appointment was cleared with Assemblyman Vincent Thomas, who was a member of the Pacific Marine Fisheries Commission and a party very interested in the survey.

major problem areas to be investigated, laid out a field itinerary, and suggested the names of people to interview. In doing this he had to seek the advice of staff people at departmental headquarters, since, as an outsider, he lacked information on the details of the substantive programs of the agency. Also, he received advice on the survey from staff members in the Legislative Analyst's Office who were familiar with the Department. Swift knew Difani because of his connection with the state Federation, and Difani stopped by the office frequently to discuss the survey.

The specialists arrived in the state at different times during the months of April and May. They worked under Swift's direction and as a group had little contact with BAH. They were all informed by Powell that their findings and conclusions were to be treated as confidential; he emphasized that they were working for the Legislature and not the Department and that they were not to release any information to the press on the survey without their client's review and approval. In their investigation they were to penetrate to the lower echelons of the organization and talk to professionals and sportsmen outside of the Department.

The specialists, other than Swift, spent little time in the headquarters office because most of the wildlife programs were highly decentralized. Each specialist began his assignment with discussions with the branch chief and members of his staff and then moved on to the regional and field organization. Their contacts with Gordon and other headquarters personnel were rather limited. Swift spent more time with the headquarters staff, particularly during the early phases of his work. He met with Gordon a number of times, and they visited a couple of field installations together. Gordon was always cooperative and apparently felt that Swift and his aides could be trusted to do a satisfactory job.

The full survey team (the specialists and the people from BAH) met as a group only once—in early May to evaluate the progress of the survey up to that date. Since Swift's team of experts still had not completed its field work, it was not prepared to draw any conclusions on what had been discovered so far. Powell discussed the writing of the individual reports by the specialists and presented a tentative outline of the organization of the final report. He indicated that the bulk of the report would deal with management programs and that a couple of chapters would cover organizational and administrative matters. Powell presented for discussion some of BAH's tentative findings on the administrative setup in the Department.

The specialists traveled extensively. After visiting the regional offices, they accompanied a program supervisor into the field to interview operating personnel. Having departmental personnel chauffeur the specialists into the field displeased some sportsmen, and they eventually complained to the Senate Interim Committee on Fish and Game. They charged in a letter to the committee that another whitewash of Fish and Game was in the making because BAH investigators apparently were working hand in glove with departmental personnel. The writers doubted that BAH investigators could obtain objective information from wardens who were being interviewed in the presence of a warden supervisor. The committee, having no jurisdiction over the study, forwarded the letter to the Legislative Analyst, who in turn asked Powell to investigate the complaint. Thereafter, BAH exercised even greater caution in its relationships with departmental personnel and made greater efforts to gather opinions from people outside the Department. In every area visited, the investigator sought out local sports leaders, club members, professionals, and other interested persons.

By June 15 all the specialists, except Swift, had completed their field work and had left the state to write up their findings. They spent an average of six weeks working on the program surveys, including the time spent writing the reports. Swift reviewed the reports, then Powell and Gray gave them a careful line-by-line criticism. Each specialist reworked his report in the light of this criticism, and the reports were incorporated in the final survey report under the name of the author. With one exception the complete contents of these reports were not seen by any departmental personnel before submission to the Legislature. In one case the specialist revealed the major findings and conclusions of his report to a branch chief. He did so out of personal friendship, even though he realized that his actions might be questioned.

BAH Studies the Organization

As the specialists approached the end of the wildlife program analyses, Gray and Hurst, assisted at times by Powell, directed attention to the administrative and organizational setup of the Department. The information flowing in from the program studies, with its rich details on the functional operations of the Department, aided Gray in planning the work on the organizational aspects of the survey. Initially, the men viewed the formal organization, paying particular attention to the highly decentralized nature of the agency and to the effectiveness of the line and staff arrangements. They made an extensive review of the administrative policies, plans, and procedures at the Sacramento headquarters and at the five regional offices. Swift's responsibilities also extended to organizational matters, and he identified problems for further analysis and study.

During these investigations, BAH men interviewed all the top-level administrators as well as a large number of the field managers. Gray did most of the interviewing at the headquarters office, spending at least an hour with the director, his deputy, and the administrative officer, the conservation education director, and all the branch chiefs. This was a fact-gathering process. BAH wanted information on how the organization operated, and departmental officers were treated as sources of information rather than as confidants.

After this extensive review of the Department, Powell and Gray concluded that major organizational and administrative changes needed to be recommended. In late September, they evolved a reorganization plan aimed at remedying what they believed to be the major weaknesses of the existing organization. The principal elements of the plan involved some changes in the top organization of the Department, a reduction in the number of regions, and further decentralization of management operations to newly established district and sub-district offices. Moreover, they concluded that the Department had gone too far in the direction of functional specialization of field personnel and that this was the cause of much duplication and conflict in the field organizations. They decided, therefore, to recommend that the generalist classification in the agency be adopted and that basic field work be performed by individuals trained to combine law enforcement with fisheries and game management.

Realizing that such changes would greatly affect the organization's lower echelon, the survey team deemed it desirable to test the feasibility of these ideas by more extensive interviewing in the field. Gray consulted with the Legislative Analyst, and upon Post's recommendation the Joint Budget Committee agreed that $15,000, set aside from the original $100,000 authorization, could be released for a more intensive survey of field personnel. Gray devised a program for the field survey and interviews were held with representative wardens, patrol captains, and game and fisheries people in each region. The interviews were designed to find out more about the actual work of the field people, to be certain that the training of personnel along generalist lines was possible.

Writing the Report

By early November BAH completed the field investigation and began to work up proposals for the final report to be submitted to the Legislature in December. The team had originally projected two chapters on administration but later found that seven chapters were necessary to do the job. Powell was anxious to obtain Swift's reaction to the proposals on administration and asked him to come to the coast in November to go over the chapters as they were being drafted. Earlier in the year, Swift had written and submitted to Powell two chapters containing his views on departmental organization and administration. There had been a dozen or so recommendations contained in the chapters, but they had been fairly general in nature and had involved no major changes in the existing organization. For example, he had recommended more headquarters staff meetings, the adoption of a departmental manual, and an improved inspection system to ensure more effective central control over regional operations. Since Swift's concern with organization was related to the work BAH was doing, Powell had proposed that BAH draft the chapters on organization and administration and, in the process, incorporate Swift's material into them. Swift had agreed to this arrangement provided that he could have a chance to review BAH's work.

When Swift was given these chapters to read, in November, he was surprised by the drastic organizational and administrative changes BAH was preparing to recommend. For example, he did not expect to see the generalist recommendation in the form it appeared. He had earlier discussed with Powell the idea of adopting a plan used in Wisconsin that allowed for the rotation of personnel between jobs at certain peak-load times during the year. He thought such a system would permit more effective use of personnel and help reduce some of the friction among the functional people. However, Swift's plan did not involve the development of a new position (i.e., the generalist) but merely encouraged the transfer of personnel, regardless of their specialization, to high priority jobs during rush times. Though Swift was not in full agreement with BAH's ideas, he felt that he was in no position to challenge them, and he went along with the recommendations.

It had been agreed in the beginning that the final report would be a joint enterprise and that not only Swift but the other wildlife consultants would be given an opportunity to review the chapters authorized by BAH. However, as the December deadline approached and the number of chapters on administration grew, BAH was rushed in the process of clearing the chapters with the specialists. Nevertheless, all of the specialists read the chapters and agreed to support the recommendations contained therein.

While the final report was being prepared, Post received a telephone call from Gordon inquiring about the progress of the study. Gordon asked if he was going to have an opportunity to review the conclusions and recommendations before BAH presented the report to the Legislature. Post replied negatively but said he would inform Gordon when the report would be made to the Joint Budget Committee. This news upset Gordon, who felt that, in view of Powell's original plan, it was unfair and improper for BAH to report to the Legislature before the Department had an opportunity to review the report and react to some of its conclusions. Further, he said, the Department had made no effort to interfere with the course of the investigation, conceding that this was in accordance with the Legislature's wishes; but he felt that at some point before final submission of the survey to the Legislature, the Commission and Department should be consulted. Post sympathized with Gordon but added that he was simply following legislative intent as he understood it.

The Report—December 1958

On December 8, 1958, BAH transmitted to Chairman Breed of the Joint Legislative Budget Committee the report on the survey of the Department of Fish and Game. Four days later the Budget Committee met to receive the report and to hear some discussion of it by representatives of BAH. Post notified Gordon of the meeting and invited him and his top management staff to attend. At the meeting the committee presented Gordon with four copies of the report. This was the first time anyone in the Department had seen it. Powell, Gray, and Swift attended the meeting. The latter two spoke briefly about the report, highlighting some of its major points. There was little other discussion since the committee felt that its responsibility was not to make recommendations on the report but simply to receive and transmit it to the Legislature for further action.

The report in multilith form comprised some 600 pages, weighed eight pounds, and contained eighteen chapters. More than one-third of the report, the seven chapters written by the wildlife specialists, concerned the functional programs of the Department. The remainder, written by BAH representatives, covered organizational and administrative matters. In all, the report offered some 250 recommendations regarding the programs and operations of the Department and Commission's policies.

Most of the recommendations related to functional programs, and in general these recommendations did not seriously challenge the policy direction of the agency. The resources specialists had agreed that the wildlife management programs were operating satisfactorily, and the proposed changes generally aimed at more efficient execution of these objectives. The report declared, "As a general conclusion it can be said that, in the opinion of our survey team, the Department's concepts of wildlife management, with few exceptions, are sound and up-to-date." The report noted, "Our quarrels are not so much with what should be done as with why it is not being done."

On the question of artificial propagation versus improvement of natural habitat, the report recommended that the artificial propagation programs be held at the present levels. The cost of the catchable trout and pheasant programs could be cut appreciably by reducing the number of hatcheries from fourteen to seven and consolidating all pheasant production to two game farms. It recommended greater emphasis on the development of natural habitat for hunting through land improvement programs, the construction of access roads, and the acquisition of more public lands for recreational use. Proposals were advanced to increase the fish-producing capacity of reservoirs, lakes, and streams to take precedence over increased hatchery production of trout. The report endorsed the deer management program of the agency, including either-sex deer hunts, but recommended that surplus females be harvested on a controlled basis. In virtually every chapter of the report, there were recommendations calling for expanded and improved information, education, and public relations programs so that the Department could more effec-

EXHIBIT II
RECOMMENDED ULTIMATE TOP LEVEL ORGANIZATION STRUCTURE

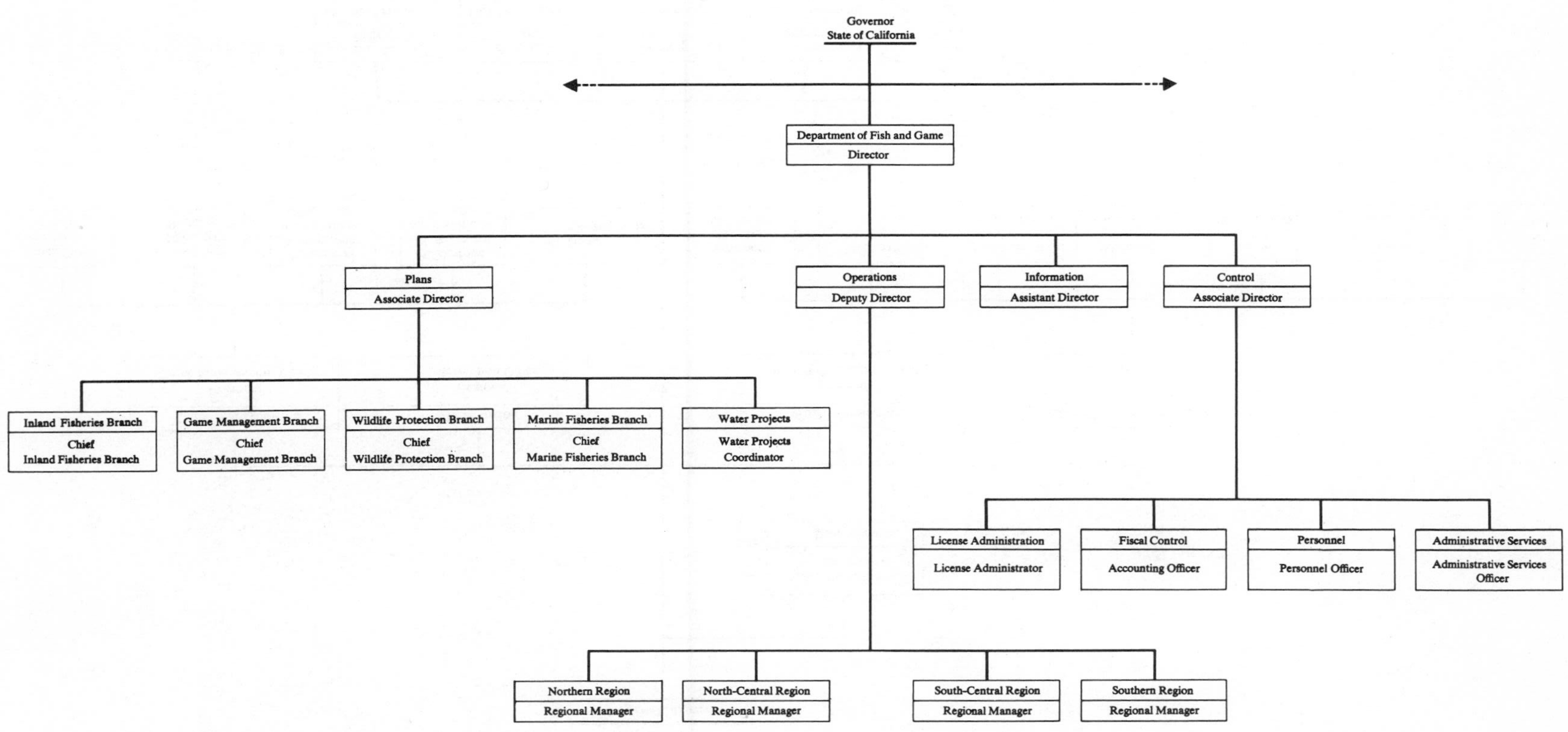

EXHIBIT III
RECOMMENDED ULTIMATE REGIONAL ORGANIZATION STRUCTURE

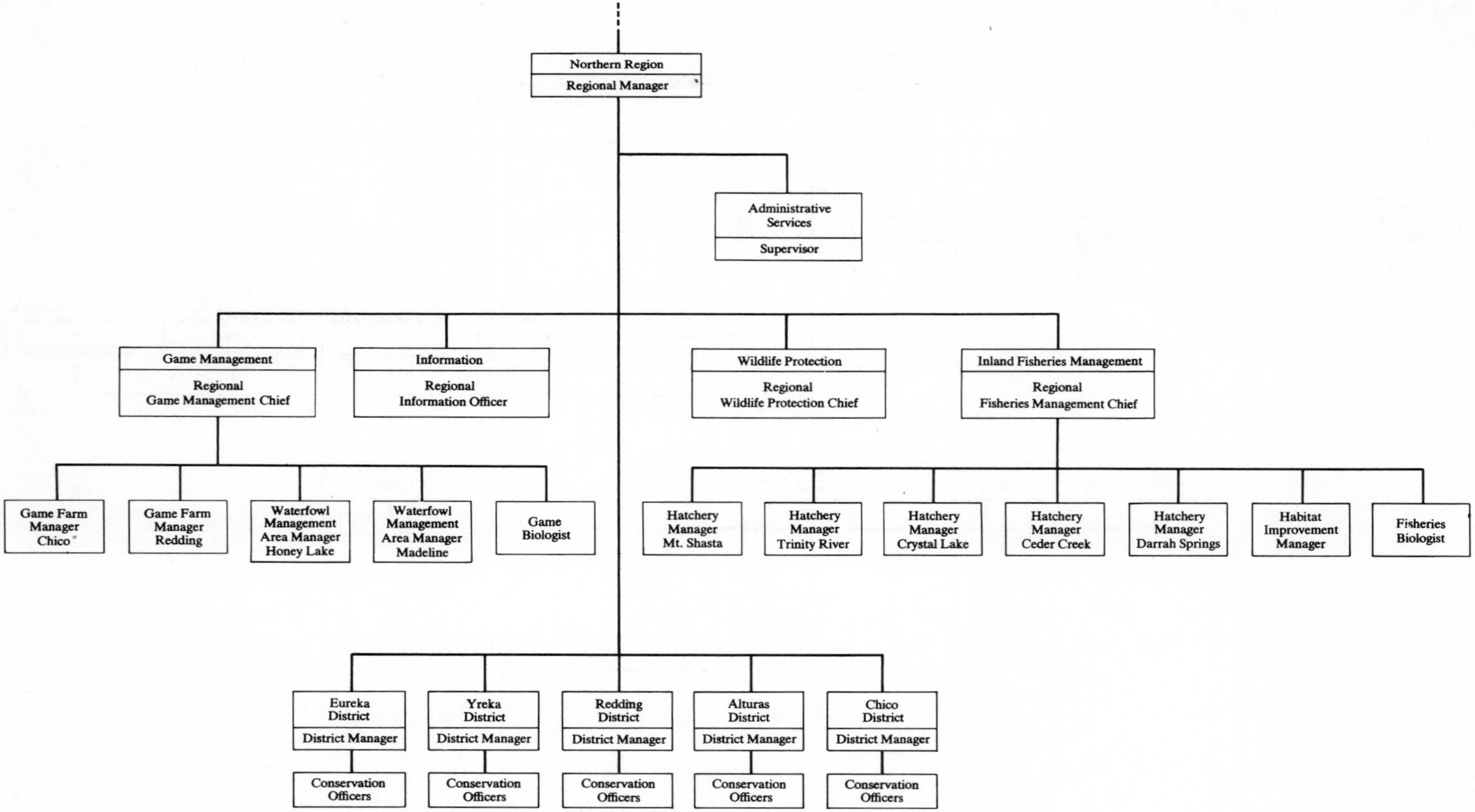

- Northern Region — Regional Manager
  - Administrative Services — Supervisor
  - Game Management — Regional Game Management Chief
    - Game Farm Manager Chico
    - Game Farm Manager Redding
    - Waterfowl Management Area Manager Honey Lake
    - Waterfowl Management Area Manager Madeline
    - Game Biologist
  - Information — Regional Information Officer
  - Wildlife Protection — Regional Wildlife Protection Chief
  - Inland Fisheries Management — Regional Fisheries Management Chief
    - Hatchery Manager Mt. Shasta
    - Hatchery Manager Trinity River
    - Hatchery Manager Crystal Lake
    - Hatchery Manager Ceder Creek
    - Hatchery Manager Darrah Springs
    - Habitat Improvement Manager
    - Fisheries Biologist
  - Eureka District — District Manager
    - Conservation Officers
  - Yreka District — District Manager
    - Conservation Officers
  - Redding District — District Manager
    - Conservation Officers
  - Alturas District — District Manager
    - Conservation Officers
  - Chico District — District Manager
    - Conservation Officers

tively communicate and sell its policies and programs to the public.

The more critical and therefore more controversial aspects of the report involved the recommendations covering organizational and administrative matters. As the report stated, "We derived from our analysis of the wildlife program the major conclusion that the greatest opportunities for improvement lie in the areas of administration *per se* and in the effect of administration on departmental unity and public relations."

The report's basic conclusions regarding organization and administration were that the Department needed greater unity of purpose, effort, and action and that it needed to do a better job of informing the public on all factors bearing on conservation problems. "There is a lack of unity in the department itself," the report stated, "and department people in the field often do not agree with department's action, nor do they agree among themselves." "And without unity within," the report continued, "unity without is difficult to achieve." In order to accomplish more effective departmental unity, the report called for an overhaul of the top management staff. (See Exhibit II.) BAH recommended the creation of the position of associate director for planning, whose responsibility would be "to develop and to keep current a unified long-range, say ten-year, plan for the department, and a unified short-range plan for the year immediately ahead." He would report to the director, and all the present branch chiefs would report to him. This arrangement would reduce the workload of the deputy director and permit him to concentrate on the coordination and direction of field operations.

Further changes in the top management structure called for the upgrading of the administrative officer to the position of associate director for controls, and of the conservation education director to assistant director for information. The associate director for controls would be responsible for implementing a set of management controls, including a cost accounting system by program, which would permit more effective management of operations by the deputy director. The information officer, reporting to the director, would have the duty of furthering the understanding and acceptance of the plans and operations of the Department both internally and externally. Thus, the report stated, "We believe planning and controlling by program will not only be effective but will provide a means for open, factual appraisal and understanding by the sportsmen and other interested groups."

The report recommended changes in the field organization leading to further decentralization of functional activities. (See Exhibit III.) It proposed the creation of twenty-two district offices in the state, each with a staff of ten to twelve people. The offices would be headed by a director who would have line responsibility to the regional manager. The field (district) office would become the basic unit of the organization with responsibility for law enforcement, basic wildlife management activities, fact gathering, and conservation education. The more specialized functions, such as research and installation management, would continue under the control of the regional and headquarters offices. The state would be divided into four regions, with the San Francisco office being closed and its functions transferred to the Sacramento region. The functional supervisors in the regional offices would be divested of supervisory authority, and business service and license administration functions would be centralized to the state headquarters office. The intent of these recommendations was to move the basic operation of the agency closer to the user, while at the same time centralizing supporting services.

One of the most drastic changes proposed by BAH called for the creation of generalists, rather than functional specialists, to carry out the basic field tasks in the districts. The generalist concept envisioned the development of a field staff consisting of people broadly trained to perform a combination of fish and game duties. There no longer would be wardens, or unit game managers, fisheries managers, or other specialists at the lowest level. Instead there would be "conservation officers" with the qualifications and authority for carrying out all law enforcement responsibilities, basic fish and game management work, and conservation education. The districts would be divided into sub-districts with a conservation officer acting as "Mr. Fish and Game." Those operations of the agency calling for more specialized and technical attention would be assigned to regional headquarters staff personnel. The report stated that the adoption of the generalist concept would improve departmental unity because "every fieldman would have responsibility for and interest in the full department programs and not only for a functional part of the programs."

IMPLEMENTING THE BAH REPORT

After Post had informed Gordon that top management would not be permitted to review the BAH report before it went to the Legislature, Gordon and his staff had grown increasingly apprehensive about its contents. At the meeting of the Joint Budget Committee they listened to Gray's summary of the report, and what they heard did not please them. As far as they could determine, the report was simply another attack on the Department and its leadership. None of the highlighted recommendations particularly surprised them because many had been considered for adoption by the Department at one time or another. They felt that the report unduly condemned the existing organization and administration of the Department, and they disagreed strongly with many of the proposed remedies. They believed that many of the recommendations would not have been made if the investigators had properly consulted with management before arriving at their conclusions. Gordon and his staff realized, nevertheless, that they would have to be cautious in their reactions. The report was the property of the Legislature, and this body would have the final word on what was to be done with it. Furthermore the report had cost the Department $100,000 and contained the thinking of some competent technicians. Gordon believed the Department should make every effort to reap all possible benefits from it.

Immediately following the acceptance of the report by the Joint Budget Committee, Gordon called a meeting of his headquarters staff to determine what action should be taken on the report. The headquarters staff members agreed that the Department must formulate some immediate reaction to the report and inform all departmental personnel of this position. They knew that some of the recommendations, particularly those calling for a drastic shake-up of the field organization, would be upsetting to some people and would be likely to create more morale problems in the Department. It was agreed that an evaluation of the report should be undertaken by headquarters personnel, and Gordon assigned to each branch chief the responsibility of evaluating relevant sections of the report and commenting on each recommendation for implementation. Gordon also decided to send a letter to all departmental employees reassuring them about the report and including a copy of the conclusions and recommendations. In the letter Gordon stated that "the report was not a directive to the department at this time" and that "it would not become an action program unless and until those who control the agency with policy decisions and allocation of funds take action to put any of the recommendations into effect." He stated further, "If changes are called for in the future which will affect certain employees, it is our intention to inform everyone concerned well in advance to avoid possibility of any personal hardships." He ended by saying "that the report generally indicated that Fish and Game is now doing a good job in California, and the recommendations made were submitted simply as areas which, in the opinion of those who made the study, might be further improved." He sent a letter with similar information and a summary of the recommendations to sportsmen's and conservation organizations.

Gordon Is Dismissed

While the headquarters staff worked on this preliminary review, an important development took place. On January 12, 1959, Edmund Brown, the newly installed Democratic Governor, announced to the press that he would not retain Seth Gordon as Director of the Department of Fish and Game. Though the Governor's decision was not directly related to the report, it cannot be completely divorced from the controversial events surrounding the survey. During the autumn campaign, before the BAH report had been completed and made public, the Governor had decided to replace Gordon. In the course of the campaign the Governor had promised some influential sportsmen and legislators (including Difani) that, if elected, he would appoint a new director. These people had never been satisfied with Gordon's leadership of the Department. They were the ones who had lobbied effectively for the BAH survey, and they reasoned that Brown's commitment was simply additional insurance against the continuation of fish and game policies and practices that they opposed.

The Governor's decision did not surprise Gordon. He felt, however, that he had been handled unfairly, although the Governor also replaced other department heads. Gordon revealed the depth of his feelings in a speech given before the convention of the Associated Sportsmen of California on January 17, shortly after the news of his dismissal. Along with summarizing his ten-year record as director of the Department, he had this to say to the sportsmen:

> Fish and game officials traditionally have been the whipping boy for those ambitious souls who try to grab the public limelight by tearing down fish and game efforts to build themselves up. These critics have helped to keep fish and game on the perpetual hot seat. . . . Fish and game will continue in constant turmoil in California until those who are unselfishly concerned with the future of the resource rise up and demand that fish and game administration be given a *good, long, letting alone.* [Gordon's italics.]
>
> I regret to say that in no other part of the nation have fish and game commissioners and administrators been so persistently harassed and hamstrung by needless restrictions, investigations, and limitations in their operations as in California.
>
> And nowhere else has there been such a consistent lack of solid organized support at critical times from the very civilian groups that should be aiding, and working closely with, their fish and game people. The tendency has been to look the other way and let the official family take all the bumps.

Though the announcement to remove Gordon appeared in mid-January, it took the Governor another two and one-half months to find a replacement; and Gordon continued as director until April 1, 1959. In late January Gordon called a departmental meeting of headquarters and regional staff people to consider the work being done on the report. The branch chiefs reviewed the various recommendations dealing with functional programs; although they took exception to some, they felt that, on the whole, the work of Swift and the other wildlife specialists supported what the Department was doing. At the meeting, the regional managers reported having difficulty with some personnel because of the proposed changes in the field organization. The managers felt that the Department should hurry along with a full evaluation and come to some conclusions about the report. Gordon concurred and ordered the regional staffs to evaluate the report and each regional manager to assess the attitudes of field personnel, particularly toward the administrative and organizational recommendations. Subsequently each regional manager held training sessions with fish and game personnel and solicited their views. In some regions, questionnaires were sent out requesting all employees to give their reactions to the report and to comment on the generalist plan, on organizational and other recommendations affecting their duties, and on whether the report reflected realistic savings for various functions.

This depth evaluation revealed diverse reactions to the BAH report. A majority of the people had not read the report nor even a summary of its main points, but there had been a great deal of discussion, and most people had formed opinions. Generally there was agreement that the Department needed more long-range planning, that objectives and goals needed to be clarified, and that public relations needed to be strengthened. A majority of the people, nevertheless, felt the existing organization was adequate and could, with procedural improvements, achieve the necessary unity to do the job at hand.

There were strong feelings, both pro and con, about the generalist concept. Few employees felt that the generalist plan would improve operations, but there were some who were prepared to accept it. More people disagreed with the idea as stated in the report and thought that its adoption would affect the quality of work. They also thought that over a period of time individuals would drift back to specialty work, according to interests and abilities. The most violent reaction came from wardens who feared the plan would take away their hard-won separate identity as law enforcement officers. Some wardens opposed the plan, fearing they could not compete with the more scientifically trained personnel on a generalist civil service examination. Also, the wardens had a separate retirement system that they would have to surrender if the plan were adopted. The Department had to give serious consideration to the wardens' objections because wardens were a powerful force in the agency. They had strong grass roots connections with local sports clubs and were organized into a protective association that could act as a lobby for their interests.

The Gordon Evaluation

On the basis of the extensive review, the headquarters staff drafted a preliminary report and evaluation of the BAH survey. Gordon had intended to leave this evaluation for his successor, but a Senate Finance Subcommittee announced that it would not act on the Department's budget until it received a report on what was being done to implement the BAH recommendations. In response to this demand, Gordon sent the recently completed departmental evaluation to the Legislature in early March. The Legislature thus provided Gordon an opportunity to state his objections to the BAH survey before he left the Department.

The Department's evaluation was generally critical of the BAH report. It began by noting that many of the recommendations on a given subject were widely scattered, often contradictory, and sometimes in error, thus making it very difficult to analyze the report. "Regrettably," the evaluation stated, "the management consultants did not discuss any of their proposed conclusions and recommendations with the department in a preliminary way in an effort to eliminate obvious errors and contradictions." This situation was complicated even more by "the fact that BAH, when recently asked for conferences to obtain further definition and explanation of their recommendations, stated that they could not provide such additional help because funds had not been provided for that purpose." The Department then declared that the "recommendations made in the report sections written by the wildlife experts . . . appear generally sound." But the Department added, "These recommendations . . . were picked up and appear to have been revised, and in some cases expanded, in the other sections prepared by BAH people, without subsequent consultation with the wildlife experts." In short, the Department was accusing BAH of distorting the substantive findings of the wildlife experts to support the firm's management recommendations. This accusation was made by Gordon because he had learned from Swift that although the specialists had consented to BAH's administrative recommendations, they had little to do with developing the proposals and were not in full agreement with all of them.

On the basis of its analysis the Department counted 229 recommendations in the BAH report. Commenting on each recommendation, the evaluation noted:

> As of March 1, 1959, more than half of the recommendations are fully or partially in effect. Specifically 78 are completely operative, while 64 are partially so. In this latter category, the extent to which they are operative has largely been controlled by unavailability of money or personnel to extend the activity involved. Eighty-seven recommendations are not in effect. Some of these are indefinite, incomplete, or contradictory with other recommendations in the report. Thus about one-third of the recommendations are not in effect and two-thirds are partially or fully in effect. [See Table I.]

Many of the recommendations listed by the Department as being implemented dealt with activities that were being performed by the Department before the BAH report. The recommendations had

TABLE I

Box Score of Recommendations' Status

	Total recommendations	*In effect*	*Partially in effect*	*Not in effect*	*Would save money*	*Would cost more money*
Marine resources	20	5	3	12	1	7
Water projects	6	1	4	1	0	4
Inland fisheries	37	18	1	18	5	9
Wildlife protection	12	5	6	1	0	3
Game management	70	22	28	20	10	3
Conservation education and teamwork	31	17	7	7	0	7
Training	12	3	1	8	0	2
Planning	10	3	7	0	0	0
Department organization	8	1	0	7	1	2
Management control	19	3	6	10	0	12
Cost reductions	4	0	1	3	6	3
TOTALS	229	78	64	87	23	52

called for continuing and improving each activity. Therefore, these recommendations were in a sense self-implementing and did not involve any drastic changes beyond improving what the Department already was doing. Approximately one-third of the recommendations, according to the Department's estimate, involved new approaches or radical departures from existing practices. The evaluation stated that these "preliminary studies do not convince us that the great bulk of them are either desirable or undesirable." The evaluation continued that "an analysis of the recommendations not in effect, from the standpoint of cost only, based on department records and experience rather than on BAH estimates, shows . . . in most cases savings would result from a reduction in public service, curtailment of existing programs, or abolition of existing personnel on full-time jobs." From this the Department concluded that "the hasty initiation of many of them would result in confusion and needless waste of fish and game funds." But the Department added, "There appears to be enough good, basic value in the report as a whole to justify taking adequate time for complete analysis and planning."

The evaluation report then proceeded to present in greater detail departmental comments on some of the more important BAH recommendations. The evaluation called the generalist concept a far-reaching recommendation involving extensive personnel changes and needing further study. The reorganization of the Department's top staff "appears to be a subject which most appropriately should be referred to the new director for his recommendation. . . ." About the proposal to decentralize the field functions into twenty-two district offices, the Department agreed that this could be done but only at a much greater cost than BAH estimated. Centralization of license distribution and business services at headquarters could be accomplished, but it would result in only small savings at the expense of service to the license-buying public. A cost accounting system might be desirable, but it would be expensive and "would add an additional load of paper work on field personnel, thus reducing the time they could devote to the job for which they are employed." The evaluation noted a significant contradiction between the recommendation calling for improved field public relations and the recommendation to close the San Francisco office in the second heaviest populated area of the state.

The report charged BAH with making many unrealistic and contradictory recommendations regarding the closing of certain hatchery installations. The recommendations to close "hatcheries such as Mt. Shasta and Hot Creek, which are the principal source of fish eggs, . . . for economic savings, are completely unrealistic if the trout hatchery and salmon planting programs are to be operated anywhere near their present levels, as recommended." Both hatcheries provided brood stock needed to maintain the fish production in the other hatcheries.

There were only three general areas in which the Department conceded immediate action should be taken to implement the recommendations. The Department agreed that the pheasant breeding program should be on a pay-as-you-go basis, that the game farms should be consolidated, and that three high-cost fish hatcheries could be closed. The report noted, however, that the Department had attempted in the past to close some of these game and fish installations but had had to rescind the order because of the violent public and legislative reaction in the affected areas.

Powell received a copy of the Department's preliminary evaluation of the survey. He felt the Department's evaluation was a bit too optimistic about the number of recommendations implemented, realizing that a number of recommendations merely called for improvements in existing activities. But the decision about whether the improvements were being made rested entirely with the Department, and he questioned whether it was the best judge of the matter. Moreover, Powell was displeased by the fact that the Department had rejected most of the organizational recommendations made by BAH and hoped that when the new director was appointed some effort would be made to implement them. But he was most disturbed by what he believed to be unfair criticism of BAH's survey procedures. He wrote a letter to the Senate Finance Subcommittee registering his objections to certain remarks made in the evaluation, and pointing out that "it is our normal practice to review in detail with the organization being surveyed all our conclusions and recommendations before they are submitted in a final report." But, he added, in this case, "it was the feeling of the legislative analyst that this practice might reduce the degree of objectivity attributed to the report by interested sportsmen's groups, and it was at his urging that we did not conduct preliminary reviews." Powell went on to say:

> Having been unable to review the report with the director and his staff prior to submission, we

> felt that it would be helpful, and thoughtful, if we reserved a portion of our budget to permit us to do so after submission. On January 22 we wrote the director asking for advance warning as to the timing of the review. . . . [but] we had not had a reply by mid-February when the committee decided to terminate authorization for additional expenditures.

He insisted that BAH had acted under instructions and in good faith with regard to the procedures employed in the survey.

The New Director and the Report

Governor Brown, after a prolonged search and extensive consultations with legislators and sportsmen, appointed William Warne as the new Director of the Department of Fish and Game because of Warne's reputation as an administrator. He had served for twenty-two years in the United States Department of Interior, and though he was not a fish and game expert, he had earned a top reputation as an administrative troubleshooter.[6] Though this was Warne's first assignment in state service, he was a native Californian and was acceptable to local sporting groups. No other changes occurred in the top management of the agency, for Warne decided to retain Walter Shannon as his deputy. When the Governor had discussed the directorship with Warne, he had made no particular mention of the BAH report; therefore, Warne had not come into the Department with the idea that his assignment was to implement its recommendations. The Governor had told Warne that he wanted the bickering and controversy over fish and game matters ended and that it was Warne's responsibility to "calm things down" in the Department.

Warne's first impressions of the Department shocked him. Of all the government agencies he had stepped into, this department was the most demoralized. It seemed to him that the long years of strife had taken their toll and that the Department had lost confidence in itself and its mission. It was completely defeated, defensive, and uncertain about what needed to be done and was afraid to act for fear of offending its adversaries. Warne concluded that the first order of business was to build up morale and restore self-confidence. He knew he could not do this if he made any drastic changes in the agency. With this outlook he approached the BAH report.

Shortly before taking command, Warne had received a copy of the preliminary evaluation of the BAH report prepared by Gordon for the Senate Finance Subcommittee. After reading the report, Warne was convinced that some of the language was intemperate and unobjective. He felt that the evaluation only added fuel to the controversy between the Department and the Legislature; consequently, he rejected it and ordered a reexamination of the BAH report. The Department began another review, evaluating the work previously accomplished and further analyzing work in progress or pending. The new review revealed that the Department had made substantial progress in carrying out those recommendations that it had favored and could implement on its own initiative. Other recommendations had been favored by the Department but required legislative or Commission approval. On a number of controversial items nothing had been done because of disagreement over the desirability of the proposals. Among these were the recommendations calling for major organizational changes, the acceptance of the generalist concept, the closing of certain fish and game installations, and modifications in the artificial propagation programs. These recommendations received further evaluation by headquarters and regional staffs, and on the basis of the findings Warne was able to formulate his own views.

Warne Acts on the Report

Warne determined that the Department had no reason to oppose certain recommendations calling for improvements in wildlife management programs that could be advantageous to the growth of the Department. Therefore, when the Department prepared its budget in the summer of 1959, it used BAH recommendations to support increases in expenditures and personnel. The Department's proposed 1960-1961 budget, as finally presented to the Legislature, requested a ten per cent increase in expenditures and seventy additional positions. Although not all of this increase could be attributed

[6] Further evidence of Warne's talent as an administrator was that the Governor later shifted him from one difficult assignment to another. He remained in Fish and Game for only nine months, then became director of Agriculture and afterwards became director of Water Resources. Under a newly adopted plan establishing a number of Cabinet-level super agencies, with policy-advising responsibilities over broad areas, the Governor later appointed Warne as Resources Administrator, thus giving him some authority, unspecified, over the Department of Fish and Game and all other resource agencies.

to the BAH report, a good portion was related to it. For example, the report called for an expanded water projects program and more pollution control in lakes and streams, and the budget requested fifteen new positions to carry out these proposals. Warne decided that something also needed to be done about the controversial catchable trout and pheasant programs. New policies were developed for both these programs and presented to the Fish and Game Commission, which eventually approved them. These policies closely followed BAH's suggestions. The catchable trout program went on a pay-as-you-go basis; that is, the Department placed a ceiling on expenditures to match the revenues available through the sale of trout stamps. Since revenues and expenditures were pretty much in balance at the time, no cutback was necessary in the existing program. The Department announced plans to close all but two game farms and to discontinue raising mature birds. The 1960-1961 budget reflected a greater emphasis on natural habitat improvement projects.

Warne did not consult with BAH regarding any part of its report, but he did talk to Swift, who told him that the wildlife specialists had not agreed with all of BAH's organizational proposals. Warne realized there were good reasons to go slowly in implementing what appeared to him to be drastic organizational changes. He did not want to demoralize the agency further. However, he agreed with part of BAH's criticism. He knew that the Department lacked unity, that conflicts and duplication of effort existed among the various functional specialists, that there was no effective long-range planning, and that the Department's public relations were poor. He concluded, however, that existing problems could be remedied by less drastic means than the major reorganization proposed by BAH. He felt that through extensive procedural, rather than organizational, changes the Department could be shaped into a more effective working unit. More on the basis of his own administrative experience than on the advice of BAH, he set out to improve the administration of the Department. He brought his administrative know-how to bear on the daily routine of the agency by doing such things as holding more frequent staff meetings, insisting on more accurate reporting, and tightening headquarters inspection of regional operations. He traveled extensively throughout the state, visiting practically every fish and game installation, trying to build up morale and bring about more unity in the organization. He struggled to improve relations with the sporting public and the Legislature and to make every employee conscious of his public relations responsibilities.

Moreover, Warne agreed with the Department's opposition to the generalist recommendation. The trend in fish and game administration, he felt, was toward greater specialization, and the adoption of the generalist plan would be a step backward. He knew that three or four states had adopted a somewhat similar plan, but all of these states had less diversified wildlife resources than California.[7] He believed that many of the frictions among various groups in the agency could be reduced through means other than the development of generalists. The wardens breathed sighs of relief when they learned the new director supported their views.

The Fish and Game Commission remained officially silent while the Department worked on the BAH report. It took no action to study the report, nor did it attempt to force the Department to implement the report.

Gordon and others in the Department resented the inaction of the Commission, both during the survey and after its completion. They felt that many of the problems of the Department resulted from wildlife policies laid down by the Commission and that the Commission should have assumed responsibility for policy decisions.

The Commission, on the other hand, viewed the survey as being primarily an investigation of administrative-management matters; in the past, it had been severely criticized for interfering in these areas. One purpose of the 1952 reorganization had been to end such interference. Since that time the Commission had made every effort to avoid entanglement in what it considered to be purely departmental affairs. It had acted with such caution that in 1955 it had refused to either approve or disapprove the Department's budget on the grounds it was the duty of the Department to prepare the budget and the responsibility of the Legislature to approve it. An opinion of the state's attorney-general had been necessary to disabuse the Commission of this notion. Therefore, much of the disagreement between the Department and Commis-

---

[7] A comparable proposal had been made by the Massachusetts Baby Hoover Commission for the Department of Conservation. Opposition to the generalist concept contributed to the failure of the reorganization plan. See: Thomas Eliot, *The Massachusetts Department of Conservation,* Inter-University Case Program No. 14 (Indianapolis: The Bobbs-Merrill Company, Inc.).

sion over the BAH survey and report was founded on different views about the separation of policy and administration.

Some sections of the report, however, dealt directly with the organization of the Commission. The fact that the Commission chose to disregard the recommendations contained therein can be explained to some extent by the hostility of the Commission's executive secretary. BAH had recommended that his position be abolished.

Legislative Consideration of the Report

Legislative consideration of the BAH report came very slowly despite the fact that Legislative Analyst Alan Post had endorsed the report almost immediately after it had been presented to the Joint Budget Committee. In his *Analysis of the Budget* presented to the Legislature in January 1959, Post referred to the recently submitted BAH report. He noted that time had not permitted a thorough analysis of all recommendations, but his office had followed the progress of the study from its inception and had reviewed the recommendations contained in the final report. He went on to say, "In general, we are in accord with recommendations made in the survey and believe that the recommendations with respect to reorganization can be put into effect for improvements in operation." Post concluded, however, that the Department should be given full opportunity to review the survey and should respond within a reasonable time, by report to the Legislature, about action that could be taken on each recommendation. On the basis of Post's suggestion the Senate Finance Subcommittee studying the fish and game budget had requested and had received from the Department the evaluation of BAH's report prepared under Gordon's direction. Because this evaluation was so highly critical of many of BAH's recommendations, and because a new director was soon to be appointed, the subcommittee made little use of the BAH report in its review of the Department's 1959-1960 budget.

Since the Joint Legislative Budget Committee refused to recommend any specific action, the responsibility for dealing with the BAH report fell to the Fish and Game Committees of the State Senate and Assembly. In March 1959 both committees considered holding hearings on the report and wrote to Powell and Swift asking them to appear before the committees to amplify information contained in the report. Powell agreed to come, but he incensed the committees by demanding a fee for testifying. He intimated that BAH's responsibility ended with the submission of the report and that the normal professional fee would be charged for any additional services rendered. Swift replied rather evasively that he was very busy and doubted whether his testimony would be of any value. Actually, Swift had deep reservations about testifying because he was suspicious of the motives of some members on the committees. He feared they were primarily interested in prying from him the names of individuals interviewed during the course of the survey rather than in discussing the substance of the report. He had read news stories implying that some legislators maintained the report was biased because Swift and the other specialists had based their findings on information collected only from friends of the Department. Moreover, these legislators had complained that the consultant who wrote the portion of the report dealing with game management had in the past appeared before committees to support and sell the deer management program of the agency. Swift did not intend to reveal the identity of people interviewed and wanted to avoid any fight over the report. He was not forced to testify because the committees decided to delay hearings until later in the year.

Even before these hearings were held, it was becoming increasingly apparent to observers in the Department that few legislators were enthusiastic about the report and some were openly hostile. Some of Gordon's opponents lost interest in the report after the Governor's announcement of his dismissal. They had supported the survey in the beginning, hoping that it would provide the evidence for a case against Gordon's leadership. But the Governor's action made this unnecessary. Some legislators were convinced that the report was a whitewash and that the Department played a more influential role in the survey than it publicly admitted. They cited as evidence the fact that the report lacked any widespread criticism of the wildlife management programs of the Department. Legislators from the Bay area were appalled by the recommendation to close the San Francisco regional office. All in the San Francisco delegation were prepared to fight this suggestion, and since this proposal was related to the one advocating the establishment of district offices, the latter came under attack too. Also, among the strongest supporters of the original survey proposal were legislators who came from areas in which BAH had recommended the closing of fish and game installations. Their constituents had developed a proprietary interest in these installations, and they were ready to oppose any attempt to take away what "belonged" to their people. The wardens, too, had friends in the Legislature who were prepared to defend them against the onslaught of the generalist. Consequently, there were few legislators who were interested enough in the report to come forward and defend it and demand legislative action on it.

During the regular 1959 session the Legislature enacted a statute imposing a system of cost accounting on the Department of Fish and Game. However, it was doubtful that the BAH report had been responsible in any way for this legislation. The motivating force behind the bill was Assemblywoman Pauline Davis, Chairman of the Assembly Fish and Game Committee, who had advocated cost accounting for the Department long before it appeared as a recommendation in the BAH report.

As the end of the legislative session approached, the Fish and Game Committees still had not held hearings on the report. Realizing that something needed to be done, the Legislature authorized the establishment of interim committees to look into the BAH report.

Committee Hearings

In December 1959 the Senate Interim Committee held public hearings. The committee focused its attention on the proposed reorganization of the internal structure of the Department—those recommendations involving district, regional, and headquarters organization; the generalist concept; and the centralization of fiscal and business services. All of these recommendations were ones on which the Department had taken no action. One month later the Assembly Interim Committee conducted hearings on the broader subject of the "costs of various services and programs" of the Department, including an appraisal of BAH's findings on the subject. Both committees subsequently issued reports. The Senate Interim Committee's report dealt specifically with the BAH survey, but the Assembly's report only referred to it in passing. In part, the Assembly Interim Committee's neglect of the survey resulted from its wider interest in departmental costs. But this neglect also indicated the lack of any great enthusiasm for the report and a generally unsympathetic attitude on the part of the committee toward many of BAH's recommendations. To some extent the Assembly Interim Committee's attitude resulted from Chairman Davis's active opposition to the report. She believed that many of the recommendations came from the Department and that the report was being used to advance its interests.

Representatives from BAH, the Department, and sportsmen's groups appeared at the hearings of both committees and presented their views. J. Doyle Gray, appearing for BAH, stoutly defended the firm's recommendations for the reorganization of the agency. By this time Powell and Hurst had resigned from BAH. Both Warne and Shannon argued that such a complete reorganization was unnecessary. An exchange of comments during the Assembly hearing among Gray, departmental representatives, and members of the committee clearly showed that no one was completely satisfied with the clearance procedures employed during the survey.

While presenting some figures from the report dealing with departmental expenditures for various functional programs, Gray was interrupted by a member of the committee who asked where he had obtained this information. Gray replied that it came from the Department. Warne immediately interposed, saying that although the Department had supplied the basic data, he did not agree with the interpretation or conclusions drawn by BAH. Another committee member commented, "It seems now this is a rehash of Fish and Game and not an unbiased report." Gray retorted, "We did not work with the Department of Fish and Game on a cooperative development of any of our conclusions [or] a cooperative development of any of our recommendations." He said that because this was a completely independent report, the Department disagreed with the analysis, conclusions, and recommendations. "They never had the opportunity to discuss them with us . . . [and] we feel that we made a very penetrating analysis here, although it certainly is true the department is in no position to understand our conclusions completely."

The testimony of the representatives of the sportsmen's clubs varied in emphasis and differed in detail, but little support was shown for the BAH recommendations under discussion. Few clubs had bothered to take any action on the report. When asked if his group had taken any action, the president of the San Diego Wildlife Federation replied that the report "is pretty deep and most of these men are not auditors; they are just sportsmen of all lines and they don't feel that they can actually make any recommendations." However, among those clubs that had taken some action, there was practically complete opposition to the organizational and generalist recommendations.

Considering the important role the California Wildlife Federation had played in initiating the BAH survey, its position on the report was most revealing. The Federation was represented by its President, Eddie Bruce, and its Executive Secretary, George Difani. Under direct questioning both admitted that within one year's time the Federation had not taken any definite action on the report. The Federation was caught in its usual dilemma. Bruce candidly admitted, "We encompass the entire state of California and the opinions are diversified so much that we cannot actually come to a concrete understanding. . . ." Difani said that in his opinion, based on some discussion with its directors, the Federation would oppose any attempts to implement the generalist recommendation of the proposed district organization.

A few months after the hearings the Senate Interim Committee issued a report containing its conclusions on the BAH recommendations for internal reorganization of the Department of Fish and Game. The committee noted that the recommendations on organization constituted only a small portion of the total report and that a large number of the other proposals, according to the Department, had been put into effect or progress was being made on them. As Warne stated during the hearings, "a great majority" of the recommendations had been acted upon by the Department, and the results had been worthwhile. But the committee report continued, "The present line and staff organization, with some minor refinements, is sufficient to support the type of organization desired by the legislature, sportsmen, and departmental employees." The committee felt that the initiation of the organizational changes proposed by BAH would involve major plant and personnel revisions and that "it would be advisable to first test the workability of the department's present organization and approach the alleviation of problems as identified by BAH through the process of modifying administrative rather than organizational controls."

The committee also rejected the substitution of the generalist for the specialist classification and advanced some modest proposals for improving departmental administration. It recommended increasing the line authority of the deputy director over sub-directors—to make him truly second in command—and placing planning responsibilities in his office. It called for the establishment of a new associate director to be in charge of regional operations and for the development of headquarters controls over warden assignments in order to allow interregional transfers during peak-load periods. In addition, the committee suggested the Department undertake a review of administrative policies and directives in order to make certain they were understood and supported by departmental employees. Finally it proposed that the Department initiate a general training indoctrination program to acquaint employees with the objectives and interdependence of each function, with the goal of achieving unity of effort.

The Senate Interim Committee's rejection of BAH's organizational recommendations ended the possibility of their implementation. Other than BAH, no one was left to push for their adoption. The Department was opposed to the changes, the sportsmen were either indifferent or in opposition, and the interested legislative committees refused to advocate any action.

Conclusion

Following the legislative hearings, the Department presented to the Fish and Game Commission a final evaluation of the BAH report. This analysis, made one-and-one-half years after submission of the report, summed up the action taken in the following manner: Twenty per cent of the recommendations had been fully implemented, thirteen per cent had either been rejected by the Department or by other control agencies, forty-five per cent were listed as having some progress made on them, and twenty-two per cent were listed as having no progress or change. Most recommendations in the last category referred to practices that the Department felt it had effected before the proposals were made. As far as the Department was concerned, this analysis was the final action it intended to take on the report. Warne left the Department for another post in state government, and his Deputy, Walter Shannon, was made Director. Since Shannon had been intimately involved in departmental action on the report, he shared the Department's feeling that all had been done that was possible and that little further action could be taken. The only exceptions were those recommendations favored by the Department but for which the Legislature had refused necessary funds or personnel. Although future action was still possible, it seemed unlikely that anything further would be done on the BAH report.

Reactions about the outcome of the BAH survey remained mixed. There were some people who felt the report brought about improvements in the Department that could not have been achieved in any other way. For example, the Legislative Analyst was "very happy with the results and would do it all over the same way." As far as he was concerned, the purpose of the survey was to gain an objective appraisal of critical program and management issues in order to end the constant wrangling among the agency, the sportsmen, and the Legislature over these matters. He felt this had been done and the result was a study "so complete and respectable—from all viewpoints—that the clamor subsided, the funds have been used as needed, the programs have gone on, and peace and quiet have prevailed." Moreover, he believed that the Department had implemented a good percentage of the recommendations and that internal departmental improvements had mitigated the need to implement many of those remaining. His view was shared by others.

On the other hand, there were people whose attitudes toward the survey ran from mild disappointment to outright disapproval. BAH was naturally disappointed because so few of its organizational recommendations had been put into effect. The firm felt that the restrictions placed by the Legislative Analyst on the survey procedures adversely affected the results, and it had second thoughts about the wisdom of conducting a study under similar circumstances. There were some sportsmen and legislators who wondered whether the state had received its money's worth from the survey. Some argued that all the Department needed was a new director. Others felt the report was merely a whitewash of the Department, cleverly used to support departmental expansion. Gordon as well as Shannon believed that a great deal of money had been spent to achieve some limited results.

On the legislative side, the survey helped to lessen uninformed and, at times, irresponsible criticism of the agency's wildlife programs. Before the survey, no matter how hard the agency had tried to defend and justify its operations, there were powerful forces in the Legislature and among sportsmen that had refused to believe the agency was doing a good job in most program areas. The survey's findings provided authoritative support for most of the programs. This evidence, coming from outside and unbiased experts, could not be as easily disregarded by departmental critics as that coming from the Department or some other state agency.

The survey also helped to bring about changes in some program areas where improvements were needed—especially in the controversial artificial propagation programs. It appeared to be true that the emphasis on these programs had been too great, at least for the money resources available to the agency. Probably all parties shared some of the blame for this. The Commission, Wildlife Conservation Board, Department, sportsmen from "have not" areas, and legislators had all played a role in expanding these programs. The survey, however, provided the impetus to the Department and Commission to modify these policies and to bring the programs more in line with the overall objectives of the agency.

On those parts of the survey that dealt with organizational-administrative matters, less was accomplished. The major organizational recommendations were never implemented. Some changes came about in the administrative operations of the Department, but it was a matter of speculation whether these were attributable to the survey or to new departmental leadership. There appeared, also, to be less criticism among the sportsmen about the administration of the Department, partly because Shannon was much less controversial than Gordon. Also, there was the realization that it would be some time before any more money would go into a study of the Department of Fish and Game.

When this study was written (1962), the agency was in a period of relative calm, but the potential forces of dissension still existed. The state's population was expanding at an explosive rate. Sporting activities were increasing in popularity, and pressures on the resources kept mounting. Sportsmen were no more organized or united than before. In fact, a few northern councils had just split off from the California Wildlife Federation, charging that southern interests dominated the group.

E. DREXEL GODFREY, JR.

The Transfer of the Children's Bureau

E. DREXEL GODFREY, JR.

The author of *The Transfer of the Children's Bureau* received a Ph.D. degree from Princeton University. He has been a foreign affairs analyst for the U. S. government since 1957.

CHRONOLOGY OF KEY EVENTS

1912	Children's Bureau is founded
1935	Hearings on Social Security Act raise question of autonomy of Bureau
1939	Roosevelt considers transferring Bureau to newly created Federal Security Agency (FSA)
December 1945	Reorganization Act is enacted
January 1946	Miss Lenroot, Chief, and Dr. Eliot, Associate Chief, Children's Bureau, discuss with Parran, Surgeon General of Public Health Service, and Altmeyer, Commissioner of Social Security Administration, the possibility of Bureau transfer to FSA
January-February 1946	Budget Bureau circulates requests for recommendations on reorganization
March 1946	Interested agencies confer on reorganization proposals; Office of War Mobilization and Reconversion recommends against transfer of Children's Bureau of FSA
May 16, 1946	Reorganization plans are sent to Congress
May 16-July 16, 1946	Labor Department, Industrial Division, Children's Bureau officials confer on location of child labor research personnel if Children's Bureau is transferred out of Labor Department
June 3, 1946	Miss Lenroot sees the President, hoping to stave off transfer
July 3, 1946	Labor informs Miss Lenroot that all personnel of Industrial Division will remain in Labor Department
July 3-16, 1946	Miller, Administrator of FSA, and Miss Lenroot protest to Budget Bureau over retaining of child labor research personnel in Labor Department
July 12, 1946	Miller informs Miss Lenroot that Children's Bureau will be transferred
July 15, 1946	Miss Lenroot and Dr. Eliot lodge a futile protest with Miller and Altmeyer over transfer of Bureau
July 16, 1946	Reorganization goes into effect

PRINCIPAL CHARACTERS

Arthur J. Altmeyer, Commissioner, Social Security Administration, Federal Security Agency, 1946-1953

Dr. Martha May Eliot, Associate Chief, Children's Bureau, 1941-1949

Oscar Ewing, Administrator, Federal Security Agency, 1947-1952

Katherine F. Lenroot, Chief, Children's Bureau, 1934-1951

Watson Miller, Administrator, Federal Security Agency, 1941-1947

Dr. Thomas Parran, Surgeon General, Public Health Service, 1936-1948

INTRODUCTION

Government agencies, or more precisely, the human beings of which they are composed, can never be indifferent to organizational proposals that will affect them. Bureau chiefs, and other officials in comparable positions, habitually desire to acquire or retain autonomy; this desire arises naturally from a feeling that they need to control means if they are to accomplish ends. Thus the achievement or maintenance of autonomy is defended as an essential element in the achievement of statutory objectives. The soundness of this view in any particular case is inevitably a matter on which disagreement can arise. Also deeply concerned are the heads of the agencies destined to acquire new bureaus or other units. Their concern usually is expressed in terms of the need for coordination and integration as a means for better execution of a whole group of related programs, with consequent increase in social utility. These contentions are also human and fallible.

Some problems of stress in the governmental fabric are avoidable, or at least foreseeable *ab initio;* more commonly, they are a by-product of underlying social and governmental change that can hardly be planned for on a step-by-step basis. Thus, for example, an agency is established to carry out a new and specialized function; in the course of time the government undertakes much broader responsibilities in related fields, and some of those responsibilities overlap the work of the established agency. This intrusion raises questions: Should the now old pioneer agency absorb the new activities? Should its functions be merged into a new structure? Or should some other form of accommodation be sought?

It is the problem of the President and his advisers to resolve questions of this character: to balance the relative values of autonomy, with its attendant vigor, against integration, with its attendant opportunity to achieve the reinforcing effects of coordinated operation; to weigh the desirability of preserving a going concern against the utility of establishing a fully rationalized structure. In dealing with these questions, many factors besides theoretical managerial virtues must be taken into account, and the final decision can hardly be satisfactory to all concerned. On a smaller scale the President's problem is duplicated by the administrator's problem when he plans a reorganization of his agency, so the recurrent tensions and difficulties can be studied on both levels. And the process of change does not have a clear-cut beginning and end. The filing of an executive order in the Federal Register does not complete the transfer process, nor indeed does the issuance of a group of orders "establishing," as they are apt to say, the organizational situs of the newly acquired unit. Adjustment is gradual.

THE CHILDREN'S BUREAU

This study offers the reader an opportunity to observe one agency, the Children's Bureau, during a period of proposed, and later actual, transfer from the Department of Labor to the Federal Security Agency. The events are unique but not uncharacteristic; they are paralleled though never precisely duplicated by other governmental transfers. For the sake of clarity, the actions and reactions of the Children's Bureau officials are treated in more detail than the actions and reactions of the officials of the other agencies concerned. This highlighting of the Children's Bureau in the account does not mean that its officials were "right" or the others "wrong"; it is essentially an attempt to sharpen the issues. Each reader will reach his own conclusions as to where the path of true wisdom lay.

As has been suggested above, this history of a governmental reorganization reveals a familiar set of difficulties; the special characteristics of the case can be largely attributed to the special qualities of the Children's Bureau itself, the only agency in any modern democratic country organized exclusively on a population age group basis—an admirable administrative device in the eyes of the Bureau's particular friends, an anachronism (today) in the eyes of many of the groups that support a broad federal welfare program.

Growth of the Bureau

The Children's Bureau was founded in 1912, a product of the social reform movement that also created Theodore Roosevelt's Bull Moose rebellion and Woodrow Wilson's New Freedom. Many men worked for passage of the organic legislation, but the movement was one in which women played a particularly active role; it was almost inevitable, therefore, that the chiefs of the Bureau should have all been women. From the beginning the Bureau has looked for support to women's organizations and organizations in which women play a major part. The original statute granted authority solely for research in the fields of child health, welfare, and working conditions. Action in the welfare field by the federal government in the form of grants was improbable and regulatory action in this field was unthinkable in 1912; even research in the area was a pioneering venture for the government at that time and was politically possible only because of the special symbolic status of children. It is perhaps difficult today to appreciate the impact on opinion that the passage of the legislation had then; but the reader must remember that the political climate and the accepted interpretation of the Constitution have undergone striking changes in the intervening years.

The first notable accretion of responsibility came to the Bureau during the 1920's, when it was authorized to administer grants-in-aid to support state maternal and child welfare programs; but this authority lapsed after a few years. Then, with the coming of the New Deal, the Bureau shared in the government's extensive new aid and regulatory activities. In 1935, with the passage of the Social Security Act, it was made responsible for the administration of certain social security grant-in-aid programs to the states, embodying technical advisory service to, and authorization of state programs in, maternal and child health, crippled children's treatment, and child welfare. With the large appropriations necessary for the federal share in financing these state programs, and the active participation of the Bureau in their operation, these new responsibilities soon overshadowed the more traditional functions of the Bureau. But the Bureau still expended a great deal of time and energy publishing its highly popular manuals on child and infant care and development.

In 1938 the child labor enforcement duties of the newly enacted Fair Labor Standards Act were added to the Bureau's responsibilities. Actual inspection was done by the Wage and Hour Division of the Labor Department, but planning, administration, and statistical reporting were handled by the Children's Bureau. War activities were highlighted by administration of the Emergency Maternal and Infant Care (EMIC) plan for wives and babies of enlisted servicemen.

Characteristics of the Bureau

Certain characteristics of the Bureau are particularly worth noting. The Bureau was originally set up in the Department of Commerce and Labor, and it was assigned to Labor when that department was split off in 1913. The Bureau Chief long enjoyed a close relationship with the Secretary of Labor, being directly responsible to him. This in itself is not unusual for Bureau heads in the federal administration, but successive chiefs worked hard to develop a tradition of discretionary independence for their unit, and their success was reflected in and supported by the relationship with the Secretary. Under the administration of Secretary Frances Perkins, which began in 1933, this independence was stoutly maintained, and the Chief also enjoyed the position of personal staff adviser to the Secretary on many broad social and public welfare problems. The warm friendship between Miss Perkins and the Bureau Chief, Miss Katharine Lenroot, was without doubt largely responsible for this development. It was a natural development from the identity of interests and backgrounds of the two women, both long trained in social welfare work. These close personal ties, added to Mrs. Roosevelt's interest in child welfare, made access to the White House for the Bureau Chief a relatively simple affair. There were no apparent formal changes in arrangement under Miss Perkins' successor, Judge Schwellenbach, who took office in 1945 after President Roosevelt's death. The new Secretary was content to give the Bureau a free hand within its own sphere of activity, and Miss Lenroot continued to serve as a staff adviser. Thus, though the relationship between the two was official rather than personal, the Bureau's internal solidarity was maintained. The somewhat unusual record of continuity of tenure at the head of the Bureau had done much to build up strong feelings of institutional loyalty. In 1950 the Chief was only the third person to hold that office since 1912.

The nature of the Children's Bureau's outside support has been an element of strength and, in this instance, of weakness as well. Originally it was a central focus for the attention of welfare organizations and for women's organizations like the General Federation of Women's Clubs. By the time of the New Deal in 1933, the welfare movement had broader horizons. The new relief activities of the federal government, and later its social security program, had a wider appeal and far more diversified support than the Children's Bureau. The new agencies established to carry out the new programs were now the pioneers; inter-agency tension was an inevitable development, and the organizational and functional discrepancies between the new and the old were bound to cause difficulty. The realignment of forces was clearly capable of affecting the future of the Children's Bureau.

THE EMERGENCE OF DOUBT

The wisdom of the independent organizational existence of the Children's Bureau and also of its location in the Department of Labor has been questioned periodically by many congressmen and public administrators. In 1930 the idea of consolidating its activities with the functions of other government agencies was first raised publicly at a convention of state public health and child welfare officials meeting in Washington. During the hearings on the Social Security Act in 1935, the question was raised even more insistently. The Bureau wished to share in this dramatic new action program, to go beyond its research function; but doubt was expressed in more than one quarter as to whether the grant-in-aid features of the bill should be divided among several government agencies: the Public Health Service, Office of Education, and the new Social Security Board were to administer the big security programs under the act. In view of this decision, was there a place for separate welfare programs administered by the Children's Bureau? After the law was passed, demands began to be made in the Congress and elsewhere for the centralizing of welfare activities in one federal agency on the grounds of logic, effective relations with the states, and administrative efficiency. When these appeals met with no success, they subsided temporarily—at least as official public utterances. However, evidence of such demands appeared in 1939, when President Roosevelt gave consideration to a proposal to transfer the Bureau to the newly established Federal Security Agency (FSA); for reasons of his own, he decided not to make the move at that time.

During the war, and with the institution of the EMIC plan, referred to above, the representatives of organized medicine began to launch an attack on the content of the new program. They embodied their criticism in the form of pointed requests to transfer the health activities of the Children's Bureau to the U.S. Public Health Service, perhaps because it was considered by the American Medical Association a more "controllable" body, though thoroughly respectable reasons for the transfer were cited. Again nothing resulted directly from this effort, but it was becoming unmistakably clear to Bureau officials that a number of forces were hostile to the continued existence of the Bureau with all its new powers intact, and at least to its retention by the Department of Labor. Perhaps the Bureau officials failed to note that the validity of a special child welfare program became debatable when the government instituted a general welfare program for all population groups.

Action Under the Reorganization Act of 1945

With the enactment, in December 1945, of the Reorganization Act of 1945, which provided that any reorganization plan of the President's not defeated by both houses of Congress within sixty days of its introduction would become effective immediately, rumors and speculations on presidential plans began to circulate through the government. Aware of considerable sentiment in the Office of the Federal Security Administrator, the Budget Bureau, and the United States Public Health Service for the transfer of the Children's Bureau to the Federal Security Agency (which was fast becoming the federal focus for health and welfare activities), Miss Lenroot and her associate chief, Dr. Martha Eliot, decided in January 1946 to discuss the matter with the Surgeon General of the Public Health Service, Dr. Thomas Parran, and with the Social

Security Board Chairman, Arthur Altmeyer, both of whose units were constituent members of FSA. Dr. Parran indicated a strong desire to see the Bureau's health activities committed to the Public Health Service; this was no surprise to the Children's Bureau officials, who had heard the plan proposed many times in the past. A few weeks later Altmeyer called on Miss Lenroot and told her that he had decided to urge that in the event of transfer, the Bureau should come under the aegis of the Social Security Board. He maintained that this location would be best suited for preserving the organization's identity and functions intact. He expressed the view that if the Bureau came into the FSA in an independent, isolated position, its functions might be taken over by the other constituent units. Miss Lenroot objected because under Altmeyer's plan the Bureau would drop into a lower hierarchical position than it occupied in the Labor Department and she feared that the move would reduce the Bureau's effectiveness in defending the interests of children. The discussion with Altmeyer ended inconclusively.

While these preliminaries were proceeding, the Budget Bureau, vested with a continuing statutory responsibility for governmental reorganization, had been circularizing all government departments with a request for their recommendations on reorganization needs. The FSA suggested the transfer of the Children's Bureau to its authority. This proposal was well received in the Budget Bureau, which believed that all the government's welfare programs should be administered by the FSA; it also believed, as a matter of sound administrative practice, that the Federal Security Administrator should have the authority to ensure a far firmer integration of welfare activities than he had been granted previously. To the Budget Bureau, the Reorganization Act offered a greatly needed opportunity to secure a more functional and effective alignment of government activities. The Budget officials were also well aware of the demands from state welfare and health administrators to consolidate the federal agencies with which they had to deal in connection with grant-in-aid health and welfare programs. With these matters in mind, reorganization plans were prepared for the President but were not disclosed to the interested agencies. This secrecy was standard operating procedure under the Reorganization Act and was approved by the President. Reorganization plans in their nature involve the destruction of autonomy, possible degradation in the hierarchic scale, and other consequences naturally abhorrent to unit heads. Success in securing congressional approval therefore is assumed to be largely dependent on the avoidance of any development of public opposition during the preliminary stages. Such at least is the major though not sole rationale for the operating procedure.

In late March 1946 another conference was held on the possible transfer of the Children's Bureau, this one attended by representatives of all the interested agencies. The Budget Bureau had suggested to the Office of War Mobilization and Reconversion (OWMR) that that agency might be interested in some of the reorganization proposals for government welfare and health activities which the Budget was considering for proposal to Congress in the event of passage of the Wagner-Murray-Dingell National Health Bill. OWMR at this time was closer to the President than was the Budget Bureau and exercised some general oversight over the President's legislative program; the two agencies worked fairly closely together, however. After this conference the deputy director of OWMR submitted an informal report to the President, not circulated among the participants, recommending against the transfer of the Children's Bureau to FSA. However, a change in the top personnel of OWMR occurred soon thereafter, and the report and its recommendations were forgotten. The one significant effect of the conference was its disclosure of the various agency attitudes.

By this time the lineup of forces, sentiments, and conflicting attitudes was beginning to emerge. On the one side was the Children's Bureau, headed by a resolute chief who was well known for her integrity and forthright defense of children's interests and for her identification of those interests with the interests of her Bureau as such. The crusading vigor with which Miss Lenroot had pushed forward the children's programs for which she was responsible had ruffled a few groups in the country; and there were other organizations whose backing, for a variety of substantive or tactical reasons, was no more than lukewarm. But Miss Lenroot had managed to maintain continuing public support for the Bureau. Further, her position of relative independence in the Labor Department, plus the fact that her father had been for a long period a popular member of the Congress, strengthened her hand in dealings with that body. On learning the rumors about transfer, Miss Lenroot was not particularly displeased with the predicted separation of the Bureau from the Labor Department. She believed, however, that the loss of prestige entailed in transfer to the Federal Security Agency, which did not enjoy Cabinet status, would weaken the Bureau, and therefore the Bureau's programs. Even more threatening was the possibility of loss of function and with it a breakdown of the Bureau's efforts to build up an organization equipped to handle all children's problems save education. Miss Lenroot now was taking the positive position that she would gladly take the Bureau to a Department of Health, Welfare, and Education (a creation often planned in Congress and elsewhere), if it could be assured parallel status with what would be the other major constituent agencies in such a department; and she realized that the Federal Security Agency would become that department, if it were established.

Those directly responsible for the preparation of the Reorganization Plan affecting the Bureau were the officials of the Budget Bureau. These officials looked on the scattering of federal health and welfare activities as a disorderly and inefficient arrangement; to them the logic of the original creation of FSA required a full concentration of all related activities within that agency. Furthermore, they could see no justification for retention of children's health and welfare activities in the Department of Labor. Indeed, to them the Children's Bureau was somewhat of an anachronism, and its continued role in the grant programs questionable; a transfer to FSA was an essential step if rationalization of the whole structure was ever to be undertaken.

Independent support for the transfer came from state welfare and health departments which had to negotiate with a number of different federal bureaus in connection with grant-in-aid programs which the states often administered from one central office; the organizational divisions tended to make more painful difficulties that arose in any event from a federal program and fiscal arrangements that differed from their own. The American Public Welfare Association, of which many state officials were members, was beginning to apply heavy pressure for consolidation. Also allied with them was the U.S. Public Health Service, which favored a consolidation of the administration of programs for maternal and child health and crippled children with its other health programs; presumably it was not averse to the prestige and power advantages that would accrue, but its arguments were not necessarily unreasonable. The same attitude was true to a lesser degree of the Social Security Board in respect to the child welfare program.

Miss Lenroot consistently met these sundry arguments by pointing out (1) that any undercutting of Children's Bureau identity would be a serious mistake because children are politically powerless and need special protection; and (2) that cooperation and coordination of grant-in-aid administration had been improving all along, with Public Health, in perfecting joint state budget reports, and with the Bureau of Public Assistance in the Social Security Board, by synchronizing the areas and coverage of regional districts. Both the state officials and U.S. Public Health Service officers answered these points by contrasting the relative amounts of grant-in-aid moneys handled by the two bodies. Children's Bureau funds for this purpose were only a small fraction of what was dispensed by Public Health, and yet the two sets of programs had to be separately sponsored at the federal level. The conference at OWMR had provided a sounding board for most of these conflicting views, so Miss Lenroot was well aware of them.

Reorganization Plan No. 2

A few weeks later, on May 16, the three 1946 Reorganization Plans were sent to Congress with an accompanying message. Prepared by the Bureau of the Budget in careful observance of the established procedure, the plans had been kept a closely guarded secret until the night before transmittal, when they had been released for publication. That part of Plan No. 2 which referred to the transfer of the Children's Bureau to the FSA contained the customary broad and hence rather enigmatic language:

> . . . All *functions* of the Children's Bureau and of the Chief of the Children's Bureau except those transferred by subsection (b) of this section [the child labor responsibilities], all functions of the Secretary of Labor under Title V of the Social Security Act [the grant-in-aid programs] . . . and all other functions of the Secretary of Labor relating to the foregoing functions are transferred to the Federal Security Administrator and shall be performed by him or under his direction and control by such officers and employees of the Federal Security Agency as he shall designate, except that the functions authorized by Section 2 of the Act of April 9, 1912, [the basic investigation, research, and reporting functions] . . . , and such other functions of the Federal Security Agency as the administrator may designate, shall be administered, under his direction and control, through the Children's Bureau.

Only one thing was clear: the Administrator of the Federal Security Agency would have broad discretion to decide the whole future shape of the Bureau. He was given no specific plan of arrangement, and under the grant of power he could reduce the Bureau to a small research unit by transferring its operating functions to other units of the agency.

This paragraph was the result of a deliberate decision on the part of the Budget; it did not seek the dissolution of the Children's Bureau, but it was anxious to leave the way open for dissolution at some future date if such an action became advisable. Aside from this consideration, the vesting of the basic powers in the FSA head was based on a broad principle that the Budget applied in all such situations, even when no specific future reassignment of functions could be foreseen. It can be reasonably assumed that this section of the Reorganization Plan would have been the same even if no one had ever suggested the dissolution of the Children's Bureau. Two successive Presidents—Roosevelt, and now Truman—had fully subscribed to the general doctrine of vesting full discretionary authority in each agency head; and both, it may be noted, believed in the administrative wisdom of transferring the Children's Bureau to FSA, even though President Roosevelt had stayed his hand for other reasons.

The FSA Administrator's potential power to reassign Children's Bureau functions was, of course, looked on by the Children's Bureau as an immediate peril. Dr. Eliot, in the absence of Miss Lenroot, who was attending a three-day semipublic convention on children's affairs in New York, immediately relayed the vital facts of transfer to the Bureau's officials, and a period of cautious but intense maneuvering began. Simultaneously a host of the Bureau's friends, including Edith Abbott, sister of Grace Abbott, the previous chief, representatives of the General Federation of Women's Clubs, and labor union legislative agents began to protest against the proposed transfer. (Parenthetically it may be noted that labor's objection was probably based less on concern for the Bureau than on general opposition to any reduction in the authority of the Labor Department.)

On her return to Washington, Miss Lenroot was faced with a difficult decision. Threatened, as it seemed to her, by what might amount to a mortal blow to her organization, which was proposed by her ultimate superior, the President, she must choose a course of action that would serve the best interests of the country as a whole. If she decided to fight the transfer she had assurances of strong support. Miss Abbott, Miss Lenroot's close personal friend, was organizing an emergency committee to save the Children's Bureau. Moreover, the President was dealing with a most altogether contented Congress, and reorganizations were notoriously unpopular, since by definition they impinged on vested interests. Perhaps Miss Lenroot could win the struggle, but she feared that by so doing she would weaken a sector of the fabric of executive loyalty and responsibility, without which the federal administration would approach impotence. In terms of the Bureau itself, for her to resign and attack from the outside would remove from the area of effective government action a veteran and successful fighter for the interests of children. Such a move might also easily dissipate a purposeful and long-nurtured *esprit de corps* within the Bureau. On the other hand, to let the Reorganization Plan go through in its present form might lead to the dismemberment of the Bureau by the Federal Security Administrator, who would be fully empowered to dispose of its varied functions throughout the FSA. To Miss Lenroot this was a grim possibility, especially since the same Reorganization Plan provided for retention of the Industrial Division, charged with child labor responsibilities, by the Department of Labor. Miss Lenroot did not oppose this latter proposal as such, but feared that this divestment, together with others of a more serious nature, would leave the Bureau with little to do.

Under the circumstances Miss Lenroot felt that there was only one avenue of action open and that was to seek a solution within the general situation in which she and the Bureau had been placed—suddenly, as it seemed to her. Accordingly, about ten days after the reorganization message had been sent to Congress, she arranged an interview with Watson Miller, the Federal Security Administrator. She asked him for specific assurances that the Bureau would not be broken up. He refused to commit himself except to say that he would consult her before making any definite move. Meanwhile she had been making attempts to put her case to the President through the intercession of one of the White House Assistants, Edwin A. Locke. The secrecy of the planning and the sudden shock of the presentation of the Reorganization Plans without any previous consultation with the agencies involved still rankled with Miss Lenroot. She believed an interview with the President would accomplish two things: (1) get across the Children's

Bureau point of view, which had not been formally presented to the Reorganization Plan writers (although they were obviously cognizant of it); and (2) persuade the President to amend the wording of Plan No. 2 slightly so as to preserve the integrity of the Bureau.

There was presumably little chance for success in the latter venture because, under the Reorganization Act, Congress was authorized to accept or reject the plans in their original form. Any amendment by the President was the legal equivalent of a new submittal with a new sixty-day period. The withdrawal of the plan and submission of a new one would almost certainly have been taken by the public and the Congress as an indication of domestic difficulties within the administration and would have endangered the possibility of avoiding congressional disapproval. Conceivably Miss Lenroot was not fully aware of this legal and political obstacle.

Armed with a draft of proposed amendments, Miss Lenroot finally secured an audience with the President on June 3. His office meanwhile had received many protesting letters from interested groups demanding that the Bureau be kept intact. Mr. Truman turned down Miss Lenroot's request for amendments in the Reorganization Plan but assured her that the children's interests would be safeguarded. She then asked if he would not issue instructions to Miller to preserve the present status of the Bureau. When he refused commitment on this issue also, she asked for a letter of assurance that would mollify the women's groups clamoring for preservation of the Bureau. The conference ended with some hopeful remarks from the President on the feasibility of the last proposal.

The letter, drafted in the Budget Bureau, finally arrived on June 10. Although it restated the original refusal of the President to trespass on the ultimate discretion of the FSA Administrator, it did contain some significant remarks:

> . . . I am asking the Federal Security Administrator to discuss with me any plans for any major reorganization affecting the basic operations of the Children's Bureau before such plans are put into effect.

And in closing:

> I am fully confident that the Bureau will have its interests well protected and that it will, indeed, be strengthened.

A copy was sent to the FSA Administrator. Miss Lenroot immediately released the letter to the press along with a statement heartily endorsing the President's sentiments. Miss Abbott telegraphed the information to the leaders of the movement to preserve the Bureau's integrity. The following day, they, too, dropped their attacks, and the air calmed. The situation had now stabilized.

Miss Lenroot interpreted the letter as a sufficient protection of the Bureau's inviolability and existing organizational status—though it could have been read, and was presumably intended to be read, rather as an assurance that the Bureau's activities would be preserved under whatever form of organization was adopted. Relying on her optimistic interpretation, Miss Lenroot now dedicated herself to the difficult administrative tasks of actual transfer without worrying about dismemberment. Still disappointed that she would no longer be operating within a department, she was, nevertheless, able to recognize the move as a long step towards making the FSA into a department. At neither the House nor the Senate hearings on the Reorganization Plan did she appear, nor did any of the groups that had been fighting the transfer, although some people testified against the proposal on other grounds.

FSA ORGANIZATIONAL PLANS

The center of activity now shifted to the deliberations going on within FSA. The Reorganization Plan had purposely given the FSA Administrator wide authority to make flexible disposition of the units assigned to him. The Social Security Board had been abolished and its powers given to the Administrator. In addition he was supplied with two new assistant administrators who were to be used to head up large blocs of constituent units within FSA. When the Reorganization Plan was sent to Congress and the initial hostility to its intent was building up, the Budget Bureau soon sensed that many of the results it wished to see realized might be blocked if vigorous action were not taken. It seemed necessary, as a matter of protection, for the Administrator to settle his internal reorganization schemes with dispatch and finality.

In the Children's Bureau the original concern

had been for retaining intact the numerous functions of the Bureau. These fears later proved to have been well founded when Budget, Public Health, and FSA memorandums written for the Administrator disclosed proposals for transfer of grant-in-aid activities to other units. The fight to forestall this originally had so occupied the Children's Bureau that Miss Lenroot assumed that her difficulties were over when she received the President's letter. In her mind (though presumably not in the President's) the statement that the Bureau would have its interests protected meant not only that it would preserve all its functions but also that it would be transferred into the same relative position that it had held in the Department of Labor. Furthermore, she had obtained the promise from Watson Miller that he would consult her before setting in motion any large-scale moves. In the intervening weeks she had had some brief contacts with Miller on the administrative phases of the transfer, but no discussion of the general location of the Bureau within the FSA. She was aware, of course, of Social Security Board Chairman Altmeyer's opinion on where the Bureau belonged, but in view of her long friendship and pleasant working relationships with him, it did not occur to her that he would take any major steps without informing her.

If Congress were to reject the Reorganization Plan, it had to do so by July 16, for by law the plan went into effect on that day. On Friday, July 12, as the time limit was approaching and acceptance appeared likely, Miller finally sent for Miss Lenroot. Miller had decided to plan his reorganization of FSA without consulting Miss Lenroot, because he feared that his purposes might be defeated if the Children's Bureau had the time and opportunity once again to muster public sentiment in its behalf. He now asked her how she would like to be under Altmeyer's supervision. While she was recovering from the shock, he produced an organization chart that pictured a new Social Security Administration as one of the four principal groupings of operations within the FSA. Altmeyer was to be the Commissioner of Social Security and have under his direction the Bureaus of Old Age and Survivors' Insurance, Unemployment Compensation, and Public Assistance, and the Children's Bureau. The first three were the operating units of the old Social Security Board and had been created by executive order to carry out the responsibilities of the Social Security Act. All power and authority had rested previously with the Social Security Board as it would now with the commissioner, subject, of course, to the overall supervision of the FSA Administrator. Grouped parallel to the new Social Security Administration in the chart were the Public Health Service, Office of Education (which had fewer employees than the Children's Bureau), and a catchall unit known as the Office of Special Services, comprising a number of smaller agencies. Thus the Children's Bureau was to occupy a lower position in the hierarchy than it had before, subordinate to a commissioner within the FSA, and with no immediate contact with the Administrator. Even more crushing to Miss Lenroot was the realization that the Bureau would not be coordinate with the two other units with which she had worked for so long, Public Health Service and the Office of Education.

Miller urged his plan on Miss Lenroot with the argument that state officials were eager to have a greater measure of program coordination at their level—something which the Social Security Administration would be able to do for the states by allying the Public Assistance, Unemployment Compensation, and Children's grants under one authority. He warned that state pressure was strong and convincing. Miss Lenroot realized that her situation was delicate because of the recent public campaign against dismemberment of the Bureau, which had aroused misgivings and some resentment in both FSA and the Budget Bureau. She felt that she could not come to a decision immediately, so she asked the Administrator to give her until Monday to think it over.

Over the weekend Miss Lenroot and Dr. Eliot reviewed their position. The Bureau's bargaining strength had diminished as a result of the semipublic attack on the Reorganization Plan. They realized that White House, Budget, and FSA officials suspected that they had manipulated strong pressure forces to obtain assurances from the President. Time was now short, and they already had capitalized to a great extent on their influence. Despite these considerations the two Bureau officers were convinced that this plan for their unit would mean inestimable harm to the Children's Bureau programs. They believed that their programs were dissimilar to the others under the proposed Social Security Administration because they were selective, project-type programs aimed at developing an area's resources in certain services, as opposed to the direct individual financial payments authorized by Public Assistance and Unemployment Compensation. Furthermore, they looked with suspicion on the preponderance of upper bracket officers with a social insurance orientation in the Social Security hierarchy, and they feared that this philosophy would be inimical to the Bureau's interests, which were based on different precepts of public and social welfare. Another unattractive prospect was the simple administrative difficulty of having to clear through the commissioner's office for all outside contacts—a procedure never hitherto necessary in the relatively independent atmosphere of the Labor Department; what would be involved as a practical matter in such clearance was, of course, still unknown. To yield to the proposal of the FSA Administrator would undoubtedly ease the whole transfer problem, but they were sure that adoption of the plan would weaken the Bureau's program and prestige and the morale of the Bureau's personnel.

The two chiefs drew up a memorandum summarizing their objections and suggesting instead that the Bureau be placed temporarily in a coordinate position with the other four branches of FSA. They further pressed for the naming of an agency committee to study the whole organizational pattern of the FSA and its relationships with the Children's Bureau and to make recommendations that would be submitted to the President for final action. They felt justified in requesting a presidential decision on the basis of the assurances in the President's letter of June 10.

On Monday, July 15, Miss Lenroot and Dr. Eliot again called on the FSA Administrator to present their memorandum and to offer oral objections to his plan. He received them in the company of Altmeyer and presented them with a *fait accompli.* The plan would stand as he had outlined it, and Altmeyer was to receive all the powers inherited by the Administrator under the Reorganization Plan—that is, all Children's Bureau responsibilities save the original functions of basic investigating and reporting. In the face of strong objections from the two chiefs the FSA Administrator explained that he could not now change his mind because he had already shown the proposal to some congressmen, who had wanted certain assurances before deciding to cast their vote against the resolution that would disapprove the Reorganization Plan. The Children's Bureau officials were deeply disturbed because they felt that they were being foreclosed from presidential protection. Altmeyer scoffed at the idea of taking such a matter to the President, and Miller insisted that no changes could be made.

In desperation the two women changed their attack and demanded that all authority to administer the grant-in-aid programs be delegated to the chief of the Bureau. Miller and Altmeyer both balked at this because they wished to retain authority in order to have a free hand with their operating units. Miss Lenroot promptly threatened to resign if she could not have decisive authority over program administration. Miller became concerned and conceded the point abruptly, and thereby something of a poor situation was salvaged. The commissioner of Social Security would still retain the authority of ultimately approving or disapproving state plans for grant-in-aid programs, but under the compromise arrangement he would not direct day-to-day operations of the subordinate Bureau.

Miss Lenroot's and Miss Eliot's decision to oppose the subordination of the Children's Bureau to the Social Security Administration had the subsequent effect of making more difficult the development of harmony within that organization. But at the time, of course, they did not know the strength of the proposal they were fighting. When it became evident that final congressional acceptance of the whole Plan No. 2 might turn on the adoption of the structural form devised by the Administrator, they realized there was little point in taking their objections to the President. Under the circumstances they could seek only the maximum amount of independence possible for them within the Administrator's plan. With this in mind, Dr. Eliot asked agreement from Altmeyer that her relations with the Public Health Service be carried on without channeling through the commissioner's office. He indicated that this arrangement would be acceptable.

The immediate results of all these adjustments were not happy. The Reorganization Plan became effective the next day, and the Children's Bureau occupied a somewhat anomalous position. It became a subordinate unit anxious for more freedom, and suspicious, at least temporarily, of the motives of the commissioner and the FSA Administrator. The actual mechanics of transfer were in no way eased by these circumstances.

LATER DEVELOPMENTS

Within the next few months a series of new developments took place. The Children's Bureau found itself integrated more closely within FSA, and especially within the Social Security Administration. One of the first moves of the Administrator was to order the removal of the "U.S." before the name of the Bureau. An inconsequential act in itself, and a not unusual symbolic manifestation of the attempt to secure central direction and control (the same problem later arose with both the Public Health Service and the Office of Education), it was interpreted by Bureau officials as a psychological weapon in the battle against their institutional identity. As foreseen, the chief of the Bureau was not called into any staff meetings at the Agency level, except those demanding the services of a technical expert on a specific question. This exclusion was in keeping with the Administrator's plan of administration adopted at the same time as his plan of reorganization. He equipped himself with a personal staff for policy advice and used the heads of the four constituent units as advisers on operational matters. For the most part, however, the integration efforts of the Administrator, at least as viewed by the Children's Bureau, appear to have resulted in annoyance and irritation rather than in the establishment of effective cooperation between the Bureau and the other units. They included efforts to define the channels of authority under the three-level system of administration (Administrator-Commissioner-Bureau Chief) by FSA directive; and they also included such quite different matters as car pooling, and the establishment of uniform housekeeping practices. Also required by directive was a two-level clearance before many official actions could be taken: ultimately the commissioner's office undertook to proofread all Bureau documents (in addition to the mandatory FSA clearance) before their circulation or public release. At the same time, larger matters of substantive policy integration were discussed at frequent conferences, but, from Miss Lenroot's standpoint, with almost no substantial result.

Meanwhile, the Office of the Commissioner of Social Security was growing into what a congressional committee later described as an "elaborate superstructure" of bodies whose efforts were dedicated largely to coordinating the operations and policies of the subordinate bureaus. In itself, this was a logical attempt by the commissioner to make effective his new authority and responsibility. It was, however, carried out in the face of inevitable suspicion from the Children's Bureau, which had never fully accepted the thesis that all its activities could be geared in completely with other Social Security functions.

The commissioner also tried to secure adoption of an orientation philosophy for his staff based on the idea of a "whole Social Security program"; under this philosophy, the operating units would be carrying on functional assignments designed to contribute to the overall program of security covering all phases of life. This was, of course, in conflict with the old Children's Bureau theory that it should be responsible for the development of the "whole child." Logically, the concept of the "whole Social Security program" would seem to preclude any organization based on an age-group segment of the population.

The situation did begin to ease, however, with time and the march of events. Congress soon started a sharp curtailment of the growth of the Office of the Commissioner which greatly reduced the effective powers of that office. As the commissioner's office lost functions, the operating bureaus gained some. With the appointment of Oscar Ewing, in August 1947, as FSA Administrator, the Office of the Administrator became more significant. An active program of integration was undertaken at the top level. Regional offices of almost all the FSA constituent units were consolidated throughout the country. The new reorganization produced much turmoil, but the Children's Bureau was left in peace. Nevertheless, in 1949, the effects of the rude original introduction to the FSA were still apparent in the overall spirit of the Bureau. Resentment and even resignation of the higher officers had largely given way to a wary expectancy of things to come from above.

The Industrial Division

One other problem of lesser importance arose during the period of transfer which occurred simultaneously but was not connected with the happenings in FSA. This was the separation of the Industrial Division and its retention in the Labor Department. This unit had been created some years earlier to study and advise on problems connected with child labor and youth employment. After the passage of the Fair Labor Standards Act in 1938, there was added to these research and state advisory duties the responsibility of administering the child labor provisions of the act. As already noted, Miss Lenroot at no time actively opposed the retention of the Industrial Division by the Labor Department, because she realized that its enforcement job was a logical complement of the work of the Wage and Hour Division of the Labor Department.

The wording of the Reorganization Plan itself was an invitation for a good deal of confused and rather heated haggling over who should go with the Bureau and who should stay with the Industrial Division. The pertinent parts read:

(a) The Children's Bureau in the Department of Labor, exclusive of its Industrial Division, is transferred to the Federal Security Agency.

(b) The functions of the Children's Bureau and of the Chief of the Children's Bureau under the Fair Labor Standards Act of 1938 . . . are transferred to the Secretary of Labor. . . .

Another portion of the Reorganization Plan, however, reserved to the Bureau all its basic functions under the original 1912 statute, including the mandate: ". . . to investigate and report upon all matters pertaining to the welfare of children and child life among all classes of our people, and shall especially investigate the questions of infant mortality . . . employment. . . ." Thus, there was some conflict within the Reorganization Plan. Although the Industrial Division, with its responsibilities for assisting the Wage and Hour Division in tracing down child labor law violators and persuading the public against violating the act, was clearly to be left behind, there was considerable doubt whether the child labor research functions should be. These latter were research activities into the general problem of child labor in the United States, its prevalence, characteristics, possible dangers, and so forth, which the Bureau had carried on under its original statute; but of course they were also relevant to work performed under the Fair Labor Standards Act.

Under the Budget Bureau's original transfer scheme, the Industrial Division was to retain the research personnel assigned to it; but Miss Lenroot took the position that she could not carry out her functions under the basic law without these persons. During the sixty-day interregnum between the transmittal of the Reorganization Plan to Congress and its effective date, several conferences were called by the Secretary of Labor with Miss Lenroot and Miss McConnell, the Division Chief, to discuss where the Industrial Division should be placed within the Labor Department. During these discussions the problem of personnel arose, and Miss McConnell tried to persuade Miss Lenroot that it would be best to leave the Industrial Division at full strength. She argued that to strip it of research personnel would so weaken its effectiveness that it could neither carry out its job adequately nor expect much sympathy from congressional economizers. On July 3, the Labor Department's solicitor informed Miss Lenroot that under his interpretation of the language of the Reorganization Plan, all personnel of the Industrial Division should remain in the Labor Department.

Miss Lenroot decided to make one more effort, and shortly before the Reorganization Plan became law interested Watson Miller in supporting her stand. At this point the Estimates Division of the Budget Bureau called a hearing on the various schedules of personnel and funds scheduled for transfer to FSA that had been submitted to it by the Labor Department. The Budget officials made it quite clear that their intent had been to keep the Industrial Division at full strength in Labor. This was a difficult decision for Miss Lenroot to accept gracefully. It would mean that almost no research on child labor could be carried on by the Children's Bureau. If anything happened to the isolated Industrial Division, all Children's Bureau activity in the child labor field would be at an end, because the Bureau itself had no additional research funds (though conceivably the Wage and Hour Division might carry on the work as part of its general research program). On the other hand, Miss Lenroot felt that there might be some justification for the view that a strong Industrial Division, if it must be separate from the Bureau, had a greater chance of success than one weakened at the outset. Miss Lenroot was concerned also by the opposition of Miss McConnell, who had lined up her division solidly behind her. Finally Miss Lenroot decided to acquiesce in Budget's proposals. Miller, however, sent one more letter to the Budget urging that the matter be reopened. There was no response.

The subsequent history of the Industrial Division has been painful. It has been decimated by congressional appropriation committees. Transfers and reductions within the Labor Department have greatly reduced its effectiveness. Meanwhile, no additional research funds have been made available to the Children's Bureau itself. Consequently, while two organizations are legally authorized to carry out research in the field of child labor, both are unable to do so.

IN PERSPECTIVE

Viewed as a whole, this history of the Children's Bureau's transfer to the Federal Security Agency is not abnormal or even unusual. Concern about hierarchical position and organizational integrity is inherent in concern about program: it is a rare administrator who is both devoted to what he is trying to accomplish and able to agree that the job can be better done by someone else and in a totally different way.

Almost equally normal is the nature of the settlement: it was a compromise in which the Children's Bureau retained almost full control of its grant-in-aid programs, but subject to the goodwill of the Federal Security Administrator; and it lost ground hierarchically and organizationally. As with many compromises, no one was fully satisfied.

From the standpoint of the participants, the struggle was largely conceived in personal terms; almost all of them—Miss Lenroot, Mr. Altmeyer, Dr. Parran, Miss McConnell, the Budget Bureau officials—had a sense of dedication and a feeling of moral rightness. To each of them, the opponents seemed wrong-headed, or insensitive, or ill-informed, or power-seeking. But the observer, reviewing the events, can see them in a larger perspective. The Children's Bureau had a philosophy that was a normal outgrowth of the reform wave of the second decade of the century; FSA and the Budget Bureau were impelled by beliefs that sprang naturally from the respective and allied social and administrative reform movements of the fourth decade. Organizational preference was deeply related to principle and program approach: "the whole child"; "the whole Social Security program"; "the full discretion of the agency head." The jurisdictional dispute was a perhaps inevitable outgrowth of this deeper conflict, though its form and intensity were affected by personalities and institutional loyalties; and a conviction of the rightness and importance of one's program is not unrelated to both.

EDITORIAL COMMENTS

The transfer of the Children's Bureau from the Department of Labor to the Federal Security Agency was but one of a long series of episodes that led to the establishment of the Department of Health, Education, and Welfare in 1953. In a larger sense, it contributed at least slightly to the then growing philosophy, which is now widely accepted, that the national government has a continuing responsibility and a legitimate concern for the well-being and the betterment of the nation's citizens, not as farmers or laborers or businessmen but simply as human beings. Its historic significance was perhaps most importantly symbolic, for the transfer itself involved no accretion of federal powers or activities. It was one of many moves to bring under a single canopy, and hopefully under unified direction, the variety of federal activities directed to improving the lot of American citizens. The underlying argument of the case between treating the problems of individual categories or age groupings of the population and treating the "whole" man and woman from "womb to tomb" appears no nearer resolution in our infinitely elastic system of administration. We do both. The children, the physically handicapped, the minority races, the aged, the veterans, the farmers, the women, the underprivileged, and many other identifiable groupings are the objects of separate federal programs and organizations. But there are also sweeping programs that apply to virtually all or vast numbers—unemployment and old age insurance, highways, parks and recreational facilities, and many others. In spite of the dire fears of its leaders, and perhaps because of the assurances they wrung from their new superiors, the Children's Bureau does not appear to have suffered over the long pull. It continues today, seventeen years later, to perform most of the functions it had in 1948, and it has acquired some new ones.

The foregoing case study was written many years before the current project was begun[1] and represents a somewhat different focus than most of the other cases in this volume. Principal emphasis in this story is upon the top-level, political-administrative features, and it contains somewhat less information than the others about the internal processes and actions. There is little discussion, for example, of studies leading to the reorganization, although some, however secret, must have been made. A major reason for including this case in this collection is that it provides the only example of the workings of the reorganization plan system of the national government whereby the President initiates a reorganization proposal that goes into effect unless the Congress vetoes it.[2] From the standpoint of the participation hypothesis, a most interesting aspect of this case is the application of the doctrine of official secrecy concerning presidential reorganization plans until they are transmitted to Congress. The secrecy requirement is obviously selective in application, since some individuals must be apprised of Budget Bureau intentions. In this case, it is quite clear that Miss Lenroot and her associates in the Children's Bureau were not aware of the content of the plan, even though they knew that the idea of the transfer was under consideration. Secrecy in such a determination must surely constitute the extreme antithesis of participative decision-making.

The decision itself was unpalatable to the leaders, the employees, and the supporters of the Children's Bureau, and it appears probable, as the author of the case suggests, that the manner in which it was reached and promulgated made it even less digestible. From that point on, negotiations were conducted in an atmosphere of suspicion and nearly open hostility, not without the threat of outright rebellion against the President. Clearly, the change entailed costs in terms of the morale of the Children's Bureau, and these might have been a great deal more severe had not the Bureau's leadership determined to make the best of what they considered a most unhappy situation.

Like other treatments of history, case studies do not reveal with certainty what would have happened had people behaved differently than they did. The evidence here suggests that the absence of participation intensified the resistance to the reorganization. But we do not know that it would have been more acceptable had there been free consultation and discussion, or, indeed, whether there would have been any reorganization at all under these circumstances. One Budget Bureau official some years later said (quite unofficially): "This was the only way it could have been done. We knew from prior experience that they would never agree to the transfer, and we also knew that if they had enough warning they could beat us in Congress. It was the right thing to do and this was the time to do it."

The transfer of the Children's Bureau posed certain problems of efficiency and more important problems of governmental role. But its most interesting aspects concerned politics and ethics, with regard both to the ends sought and the means employed. The issues that confronted the President and the officials of the Bureau of the Budget, the Federal Security Agency, and the Children's Bureau were dominantly political and ethical. The two terms are closely intertwined; and they are most significant variables in the processes of government reorganization and the role of participation therein.

[1] It actually antedates the Inter-University Case Program, having been originally published by its predecessor organization, the Committee on Public Administration Cases, in 1949. It is here republished unchanged.

[2] Temporary legislation authorizing reorganizations of this kind has been in effect most of the time since 1939, although the conditions and terms of congressional veto and certain other limitations have varied. It may be recalled that in the 1960 reorganization of the Public Health Service, described in the first case in this volume, the reorganization plan device was considered but not utilized.

JAMES R. BELL

LYNWOOD B. STEEDMAN

Personnel Problems in Converting to Automation

JAMES R. BELL

received a Ph.D. degree in Political Science from the University of California at Berkeley. He is Professor of Government and Coordinator of Public Administration Curricula at Sacramento State College.

LYNWOOD B. STEEDMAN

received a B.A. degree from the University of California at Berkeley. He is Assistant Director, Administration, California Department of Employment.

CHRONOLOGY OF KEY EVENTS

1951	Remington Rand conducts a survey of tabulating section procedures in the Department of Employment
January 1954	Bashline, Chief, Tabulating Section, reviews IBM electronic computer manual
February 11, 1954	Bashline sends memo to Burkett, Director, Department of Employment, suggesting conversion to IBM electronic data processing machines
Mid-February 1954	Burkett initials the memo
March 1954	Bashline and Steedman, Personnel Officer, meet with employees, announce decision to install electronic equipment
April 1954	Steedman appoints Departmental Personnel Committee to work out solutions to the problems of conversion
May 1954	Tabulating section employees form a committee to make recommendations to the Departmental Committee on personnel matters
August 12, 1954	Collins, Training Officer, prepares memo to Bashline indicating policies agreed to by the Departmental Personnel Committee for transferring employees to vacancies in other sections
September 1954	Bashline attends IBM school
October 1954	Seven employees attend IBM school
October 1955	Student workers begin conversion of card records to tape
December 1955	Tabulating section moves to new building
March 27, 1956	First claims are processed on EDPM

PRINCIPAL CHARACTERS

Walter S. Bashline, Chief, Tabulating Section of the California Department of Employment; member of the Departmental Personnel Committee (DPC)

William A. Burkett, Director, Department of Employment

Edgar Collins, Training Officer; after May 1954, Personnel Officer, Department of Employment; member of DPC

George Feinberg, Representative of California State Employees Association; member of DPC

Vernon Graham, Chief, Accounting Section, Department of Employment; member of DPC

James H. Kipp, Fiscal Officer, Department of Employment; member of DPC

Garvin Price, Tabulating Section, Department of Employment; member of DPC and member-representative of the Department of Employment chapter of the California State Employees Association

George Roche, Chief, Research and Statistics, Department of Employment; member of DPC

Charles Root, Legal Section, Department of Employment; member of DPC

Lynwood Steedman, Personnel Officer; after May 1954, Chief of Administrative Services, Department of Employment; member of DPC

Larry Streit, Representative of California State Personnel Board; member of DPC

THE SETTING

On the mall in Sacramento there stands a new government building—two blocks long, six stories high—one of the largest office buildings on the Pacific coast. Completed in January 1956 for the California State Department of Employment, the building was one element in a two-year decision-making, problem-solving process that started with a decision to convert conventional punch card and electric accounting machine processes to the newly developed electronic data processing machines. This case briefly describes that decision and goes on to describe how the Department of Employment sought to cope with the personnel problems that were expected to result from greater automation.

The California Department of Employment was created in 1935 to administer the California unemployment insurance law and the State Employment Service. It employs 4,000 to 6,000 persons depending on workload. It has over 150 offices in the various communities in California. The Department has five main functions:

1. It operates the California State Employment Service, available to California's 5,400,000 workers.

2. Its representatives aid communities in industrial development and assist employers seeking plant locations.

3. It accepts claims for Unemployment and Disability Insurance and pays benefits to eligible claimants, as provided by California law and various federal laws.

4. It collects Unemployment Insurance payroll taxes from 280,000 employers subject to the California Unemployment Insurance Code, and through these employers it collects Disability Insurance taxes from the wages of 3,500,000 employees.

5. The California Unemployment Insurance Appeals Board of three members hears appeals from actions taken by the Department under the provisions of the Unemployment Insurance Code.

In short, the Department is a large agency; it has thousands of employees, hundreds of offices, and literally millions of customers. Much of its work is highly organized and routinized through procedures manuals. Modern business machines are relied upon to "keep the records" of the millions of citizens who deal with the Department and who expect it to process their claims and accounts promptly and accurately. In 1937 the Department of Employment installed IBM punch card electric accounting machines (EAM) to maintain its voluminous records, to perform accounting operations, and to prepare statistical reports.

Each weekday a tour is conducted for visitors to the new Employment Building. Mechanization of clerical processes is evident everywhere. The tour proceeds through the tabulating section past a few pieces of conventional (EAM) tabulating equipment—sorters, collators, and the like—and past a large group of key punch operators. Shortly the tour stops at a large plate glass window. Through this window in a large room are seen a number of tall cabinets with glass fronts, behind which it appears that home movie film is being wound from one reel to another. Only occasional motion can be observed. At a large control panel sits an operator. Two or three other persons are in the room, but there is no hustle and bustle, no obvious machine operation, no noise—only a few flashing lights at the console. This is the new electronic data processing machine (EDPM) room. The guide explains that the room was specially designed for the sensitive electronic equipment. Humidity, temperature, and dust are controlled within narrow limits. The floors are of special wood construction; and a unique exhaust system carries off the extraordinary volume of heat generated by the electronic equipment. The guide presses a button and the automation story is completed by a recorded voice carried through a loudspeaker overhead. It says:

> You are now viewing approximately a million dollars' worth of the most modern electronic data processing equipment. This equipment is rented by the Department of Employment from the manufacturer.
>
> The equipment consists of a series of machines which can be interconnected for different jobs. The basis of its improvement over methods previously used is that it maintains records on tape instead of tabulating cards. Machines which use cards operate at ranges from 100 to 200 cards a minute, but information for the *new* tape equipment can be read into it and written out of it on tape at the rate of 15,000 digits a second. . . .
>
> It can do 237,000 additions a minute, 50,000

multiplications or 24,000 divisions a minute. The equipment also can provide true or false answers about the information it records at the rate of 434,000 answers a minute. . . .

Sometimes electronic equipment of this kind is called a "mechanical brain." Actually, it isn't a brain of any kind. You might say, though, that it is a wonderfully complicated robot which will do the bidding of a man's brain much faster than he and hundreds of others with him possibly could do it. The persons who operate this equipment are its brains. These persons are highly specialized technicians trained by the Department of Employment.

But no permanent employees were laid off because of the installation of this equipment. Permanent employees affected were transferred to other jobs in the Department of Employment or elsewhere in state service where they are needed. [Emphasis added.]

THE DECISION TO INSTALL EDPM

The story began back in January 1954 when a local representative of the International Business Machines Corporation left on the desk of Walter S. Bashline, chief of the tabulating section, the first edition of the manual for IBM's new 702 electronic computer.

In those days the Tab section presented an entirely different appearance from that just described. The Tab machine room was filled with dozens of pieces of conventional electric accounting machines operated by as many as 100 operators during a shift. Stacks of trays filled with hundreds of thousands of punch cards stood beside the machines and filled every vacant space in the room. The cluttered physical appearance was made worse by the continuing "clackety-clack" of the machines, each grinding out its specialized task with the punch cards. If the Tab room today conveys an impression of inactivity, the Tab room of 1954, to the outsider, was a roaring bedlam.

In spite of a visitor's impressions of noise and confusion, Tab's operations in January 1954 were running smoothly as usual. Bashline had been chief of the tabulating section since 1938. He had a national reputation as a pioneer in the application of machines to unemployment insurance operations.

The manual that the IBM man dropped on his desk in January 1954 was not Bashline's first acquaintance with the new "electronic brains." Since 1951 he had followed closely the development of electronic data processing equipment and had pondered about its application to Department of Employment operations. In 1951 the Remington Rand Company had made a limited survey of tabulating section procedures and had suggested the use of its Univac equipment, but in Bashline's view, the new electronic equipment available in 1951 offered little advantage over his conventional electric accounting machines. The lack of a high speed printer remained a barrier to successful use of electronic equipment in the state's social insurance programs.

But in 1954, Bashline's review of the new IBM manual caused him to believe that EDPM now *could* be used to replace much of his conventional tabulating equipment. The manual described a new printer that could write 450 lines a minute. The more Bashline studied the matter, the stronger became his conviction that conversion to electronic equipment would be feasible.

In spite of his increasing confidence, Bashline knew this was no matter for snap judgment. It was a decision involving an annual equipment rental of over $600,000. Scores of people, thousands of dollars in supplies and forms, and numerous other factors demanded consideration. A decision of this magnitude was not ordinarily arrived at without extensive fact-finding and months or even years of analysis.

But an extraneous element intervened to force a decision at the earliest possible date. If EDPM was practicable it was urgent that a decision to convert the Tab operation be made immediately. In 1949 plans had been made to erect a new building for the Department of Employment, and the first contracts were let late in 1953. The building was designed with space allowance of 77,255 square feet for the tabulating section, assuming the continued use of conventional tabulating equipment. Electronic equipment would require 35,000 square feet less, but it would require unique design features and special cooling equipment. Although construction was to begin at once, there was still time to revise the building plans to accommodate the EDPM. A delay in constructing the new building could result (1) in a significant increase in construction costs, or (2) in overbuilt and unsuitable facilities for the tabulating section. To rebuild the Tab room for electronic equipment at a later date would cost at least $200,000.

With this pressure on him, Bashline began an intensive study of available electronic equipment. He worked in almost complete secrecy. Few of his staff members were consulted. Together with technicians and engineers from two major business machine companies he made a complete review of equipment, processes, running time, costs, and savings. In five weeks, working day and night, Bashline made his decision. He would recommend that IBM's electronic data processing machines be installed. He needed to secure only the concurrence of the director of the Department.

The director of the Department of Employment was William A. Burkett. He had been appointed to the non-civil service position in November 1953 by Governor Goodwin J. Knight, shortly after Knight had assumed office. On becoming Director, Burkett promised sweeping changes in the policies and practices of the Department. Shortly thereafter, Burkett announced a "Ten Point Program" to the staff and the public. One of the most important points was: "We will insist upon strict economy in all operations. Unnecessary procedures, forms, manuals and reports burdening the claimant, employer and the Department will be eliminated." In this climate Bashline's proposal, with its "conservative" estimate of $17,000 savings per month, was likely to be favorably received. (The $17,000 a month savings figure was calculated on the basis of an assumed workload volume and the machines and personnel required to perform the various tasks involved. While electronic equipment rented at a substantially higher rate, speed and a need for fewer personnel were compensating factors.)

Bashline submitted to Director Burkett a memorandum, dated February 11, 1954, in which he recommended conversion to IBM 702 electronic data processing machines. To offset a substantial increase in rental costs, he estimated there would be a reduction of 150 persons in the tabulating section, chiefly in the machine group.

Relying on Bashline's judgment and sensing the opportunity for significant economies, Burkett initialed the memo. In a few short weeks an administrative decision had been made—or rather, forced by the new building—which, under ordinary circumstances, would have been preceded by months or possibly years of study.

The implications of the decision were many. Once construction had begun on the redesigned Tab facilities in the new building there could be no turning back. There was, at the time, no comparable high-volume data processing electronic unit in the country for direct comparison. The Department would be pioneering, though it would have the full technical support of the leasing company, which had a vested interest in making the California installation a model of success. There were many uncertainties; no one knew how long it would take to train EDPM personnel; the ability of IBM to meet the projected installation date was assumed, but by no means guaranteed; no one knew how long the EAM operation would have to continue while EDPM proved itself; and, of course, there was no operating experience against which to check the accuracy of the estimates and calculations upon which the decision had been based.

The consequences of failure seemed grave. If all data regarding California workers and employers—their accounts and claim records—were converted to magnetic tape and the system then failed, the snarl of millions of accounts that might result horrified the imagination. Benefits could not be paid promptly when due, California's employers would not know their correct tax rate, unemployed persons would go without needed benefits, and the state's economy might sag without this "extra spending power."

Some slight reassurance on the validity of the decision was to come within a few months. The decision to use IBM equipment brought complaints to the Governor's office. The decision was questioned in state administrative circles and by a competing firm. Bashline's conclusions, however, were subsequently confirmed in separate studies by the United States Bureau of Employment Security, the California Department of Finance, the Legislative Auditor, and by Price Waterhouse and Company. Price Waterhouse, in fact, confirmed as reasonable Bashline's revised estimate that savings would be $35,000 a month, or $420,000 a year.

Implications for Personnel

Little thought had been given to the effects of Bashline's decision on the employees. A great deal was made of the projected savings of $35,000 per month based upon the assumption that about 170 jobs would be abolished. Bashline actually projected his staffing for 1956 at 264 people as against 437 in 1955 under the old system—a reduction of 173 people, mostly tabulating machine operators and some general clerks and file clerks. He assumed that layoffs would be necessary when the new 702 machinery was installed. The truth of the matter was that Bashline's time had been so taken up by his intensive study of machine processes that he had had little time to consider the personnel problems of the conversion.

Was this then the extent of the Department's concern for the workers to be displaced? Was layoff the only practicable plan for carrying out the personnel adjustment that would come with automation? If so, how would this news be given to the employees? What would be their reaction, and, most important, would there be early mass resignations of employees seeking new jobs? If mass resignations occurred, how could the tabulating section continue to operate efficiently? There was, on the other hand, no question but that Director Burkett's reaction would be stern if a significant operational failure occurred, particularly on the heels of his widely publicized announcement that he would bring real economy and efficiency to the Department.

THE PERSONNEL OFFICER BEGINS TO PLAN

The man who started to worry about the effects of automation on employees was Lynwood Steedman. Steedman had worked in the Department since it began and had been personnel officer since 1944. During this time he had seen the agency grow from less than 1,000 people to over 6,000 in the immediate postwar period. He had also seen the reverse. Sharp budget cuts had forced several layoffs, some of as many as 300 people. Recently almost 200 employees had been downgraded or transferred as one phase of Burkett's economy program. Although Department layoffs had never affected the tabulating section, the agency as a whole was "gun-shy": no one knew where a layoff would strike next. Recruitment was difficult because of the agency's reputation for layoffs.

Another layoff would be a disastrous blow to employee morale, Steedman felt. He had recently launched a widely publicized program for a "stabilized work force." This plan was calculated to eliminate future layoffs caused by workload reduction or budget acts. Director Burkett had endorsed it, and the entire management group had put a lot of time and effort into it to ensure its favorable psychological effect on the employee group. Steedman, who had worked closely with the new director since his appointment a few months earlier, appeared to enjoy Burkett's full confidence.

Bashline advised Steedman in February of the decision to convert to electronic equipment and told him some of the implications. Steedman was shocked. Here was a situation that would result in the displacement of some 170 employees. Steedman's immediate reaction was that a layoff must be avoided. Conversion to EDPM was scheduled to start in March 1956. The personnel officer believed he would have to begin at once to develop a long-range program to absorb the employees who would be displaced.

Trying to Imagine the Alternatives

Steedman and his assistant, Fred Williams, tried to lay out the alternatives. They found that EDPM was so new that the potential personnel problems it involved could not be clearly identified. Only after discussing the EDPM program with many people in other sections did a set of problems and possibilities emerge in Steedman's mind. At the outset even the number of employees affected was not easy to determine.

A first step was to identify the persons in the tabulating section who were likely to be discharged. Bashline supplied Steedman the following data from his budget estimates:

Staff as of March 1954	390
Estimated staff for fiscal 1955	437
Estimated staff for fiscal 1956 prior to EDPM conversion	448
Estimated staff for balance of fiscal 1956 after EDPM conversion	282 to 264

The number of redundant posts resulting from conversion would be between 166 and 184. Higher workloads had been estimated for fiscal 1955 and 1956, and if these materialized, additional personnel would have to be hired and trained on the EAM system only to be laid off after the conversion. Taking all these factors into account, the number to be affected was set at 166, consisting of the following groups:

Classes	*1954*	*1956*	*Surplus*
Tabulating machine operators	106	153	124
Junior and intermediate clerks	75	90	27
Senior and higher clerks	15	15	15
TOTALS	196	258	166

Steedman decided for planning purposes to use the higher figure of 184 to provide for all contingencies.

A reduction of staff by 184 in something less than two years ordinarily would not be difficult. Jobs would simply be left vacant after people had quit or been transferred or promoted. Normal attrition could not, however, be relied upon in this case. All of the regular tabulating operations had to be kept going full blast until the conversion and, in addition, key personnel would have to be drawn from the EAM operations to be trained for the EDPM system. It appeared then that only after the actual switchover to EDPM could the surplus staff be laid off or reassigned. These necessities offered little hope that the stabilized work force policy could be preserved. Steedman sought the views of other management people in the Department and in the state service generally. When all the conditions were laid before them they invariably came to the same conclusion—layoff was the only practicable alternative.

The time that Steedman could devote to the personnel problems of the EDPM conversion was limited by other demands then being made on the personnel officer by Director Burkett. But gradually during the next few weeks Steedman and his staff shed their defeatism and became convinced that the personnel problems of conversion could be licked. They saw three elements necessary for a good solution: (1) The Department must set forth a clear and firm program. (2) The program must be practicable. (3) It must appeal to the employee group. The personnel officials believed that they could successfully reconcile (a) their responsibility to the director to maintain an efficiently staffed organization with (b) their responsibility to protect the interests of employees.

Out of the innumerable discussions with the management group and among themselves the personnel officers developed a four-step plan:

1. Employees were to be advised soon of the new electronic program and the reduction in positions that would occur.
2. An inventory would be made of jobs that would become surplus upon conversion.
3. An advisory committee would be established.
4. The specific personnel problems of the conversion were to be identified and solutions developed by the personnel staff and the committee.

As for step number one, the decision to tell the employees, the problem was: Tell them what? It would be impossible to answer the multitude of questions that were bound to arise. For example, it was estimated that a large number of positions would be surplus, but the specific numbers by classes and work groups were still unknown. New EDPM skills had to be learned, but the employees to be selected for training were not yet identified. No definite plan of personnel readjustment had been worked out. Was a little information better than none? Would the employees be satisfied with broad generalities? Amazingly, to date no leak had occurred. No rumors were circulating, and there was really no immediate necessity to inform the employees.

Meeting the Employees

The point of view prevailed, however, that Tab employees were entitled to know what was known by top management. Late one afternoon in March 1954 a meeting was held of both day and night shift employees. Bashline announced the decision to introduce electronic equipment. The group was stunned. Only a few questions were directed to Bashline so he turned the meeting over to Steedman, who said it was agency policy that every effort would be made to transfer surplus employees to jobs commensurate with their ability and at the same pay level. He said the Department accepted as its responsibility the proper placement of all permanent employees. He admitted, however, that a layoff was a real possibility. Gradually the group came to life. A drumfire of inquiries was directed at Steedman and Bashline. Surprisingly to both men, the questions tended to seek information about the effect on the group and the Department, rather than the effect on the individual employee. This was indicative of the strong group feeling within the tabulating section. Over the years these employees, as a group, had had separate office parties, had entered teams in athletic leagues separate from the rest of the Department, and in many other ways had shown strong cohesiveness.

Steedman announced that an advisory committee would be established to work out solutions to the numerous problems. Various interests would be represented on the committee, including the state civil service agency and the employee organization. The employees were requested to put further questions in writing and address them to the advisory committee.

On the whole, Steedman considered the meeting a success. The employees had been cooperative, and nothing had been said that heralded a crippling mass exodus to other jobs. Perhaps, to the employees in March 1954, ultimate conversion in January 1956 seemed a long way off. Then, too, the jobs to be affected by the conversion had not yet been specifically identified.

Shortly thereafter step two was initiated. An inventory was taken of the jobs affected. The number of persons who would be displaced was identified by class. These estimates were more specific than previous ones. The group was again divided into three general categories:

1. Tabulating machine operators	84
2. Junior and intermediate clerks	51
3. Senior and higher level clerks	12
TOTAL	147

Turnover rates for these classes of employees within the Department were examined and projected. The numbers of machine operator positions in other state agencies in Sacramento were determined, and their turnover rates were analyzed and projected. There was little encouragement in the fact that in recent years fewer than eight operators per year had separated permanently from the Department of Employment.

Problems and Conditions

Now the problems to be solved were beginning to emerge clearly, as well as some of the key conditions that affected the choice of solutions:

1. The agency must continue to function effectively. Director Burkett had pledged this to the public in his ten-point program. Regardless of transition, the tabulating section must maintain its level of performance and later live up to Burkett's expectations for the future. Burkett would not tolerate any major failures in putting EDPM into operation. The consequences of a failure in conversion could ruin the Department.

2. Since a going organization had to be maintained, large separations of experienced employees could not be risked. The EAM operation had to be kept running full scale while key staff was trained for the entirely different EDPM operation.

3. The two-year advance notice given to employees could be a curse instead of a blessing if the employees were not convinced that their best interest lay in "sticking it out" and that their welfare would be safeguarded by the Department.

4. The conversion to EDPM would not be slowly brought about but would occur within a period of three months in early 1956. Normal attrition could not be relied upon.

5. The machine operators were highly skilled personnel. In the departmental training program they had learned to operate all machines and because of their skills they were in great demand in private industry and in other state and governmental organizations. On the other hand, few, if any, trained machine operators were available in operators, and incidentally arranging a temporary work to replace those who might leave the Department.

6. Bashline's problems were multiplying daily. While he was charged with the job of running the tabulating section as usual, he was also learning more about EDPM himself, planning the new installation and the training for "programmers"[1] and operators, and incidentally arranging a temporary organization to convert the information from 23,000,000 punch cards currently in the files to the magnetic tapes used in EDPM.

7. A strong employees' organization, the California State Employees Association, would vigilantly guard the rights of employees. Fortunately this organization had a reputation for cooperativeness. Steedman had on a number of occasions worked closely with its general manager in solving difficult personnel problems.

8. The California civil service law contained a requirement that employees displaced by new machines should have the opportunity to learn to operate such machines. This section had seldom been applied. In addition, California's strong civil service system presented inflexibilities that restricted the range of solutions. For example, a multiplicity of narrow classes made up the state structure. To move from one class to another usually required passing an examination. Out-of-class assignments were rarely permitted and then only for "rotational training purposes." The whole civil service system was vigilantly policed by the State Personnel Board.

9. Costs would have to be carefully controlled, not only because of the budgeting system of the agency, but because of the "economy" commitments made by the new director.

[1] A "programmer" is one who prepares the instructions that the electronic machines carry out.

Even after the employee meeting and after several weeks of discussion, personnel planning was still in the stage of bringing to light the potential difficulties. The answers, in terms of a constructive program, were still lacking, as is shown by a letter Bashline directed to Steedman, after the employee meeting, in which he spoke of two problems needing early attention:

> The first of these is Department of Finance approval of the proposed [new Tab] organization, and Personnel Board approval of the classification level of the [proposed] staff shown on the attached chart. The second problem relates to the ultimate disposition of approximately 155 people, representing the difference between the fiscal 1955 level and the estimated permanent staff for 1956. . . . It seems to me that the earlier we can tell them what class will be considered comparable for layoff purposes . . . the more chance these people will have to prepare themselves for the change.[2]

Bashline's main concern appeared to be his proposed organization and staff planning for some two years hence. He identified as an attendant problem the ultimate disposition of the surplus employees. He appeared to consider layoffs necessary. So far, there were no developments that would lead to any other conclusion.

[2] Due to changes in current and estimated workload, the estimates of surplus personnel varied from time to time. The estimates ranged from 150 to 184 people. In a department of this size the workload fluctuates widely as economic conditions change.

WORKING OUT SOLUTIONS

Late in April, the promised advisory committee was appointed. It was called the Departmental Personnel Committee, and its members were selected by Steedman. He was able to get the director to send a letter to each member advising him of his appointment and emphasizing the importance of the Committee's work.

In addition to Bashline and Steedman, the members were: Edgar Collins, training officer; James H. Kipp, fiscal officer; Vernon Graham, chief of the accounting section; George Roche, chief of research and statistics; Charles Root, legal section; and Garvin Price, tabulating section. Kipp, Graham, and Roche were heads of sections employing large clerical staffs. Collins was included in the Committee because significant training problems had been identified already. Root was to advise on legal matters pertaining to possible personnel actions. Price was to represent the tabulating section employees and was also a member of the Department of Employment chapter of the California State Employees Association. The State Personnel Board (California's civil service agency) was asked to select a representative (it selected Larry Streit), as was the California State Employees Association (which designated George Feinberg, one of its staff representatives).

The Committee was to be more than advisory. Formally, its recommendations were subject to approval by Burkett. In fact, however, Steedman and Bashline enjoyed the director's full confidence, and if they concurred in the recommendations, the recommendations became Department decisions. In this respect the personnel officer carried line authority.

The Committee members, by participating in discussions and by endorsing recommendations, bound themselves and their units to work for their acceptance. The Committee was also a communications device for keeping all interested sections informed and for affording their leaders a forum.

One of the Committee's first acts was to endorse the policy that the Department would earnestly seek all means of averting a layoff. This was an important commitment for Kipp, Graham, and Roche, the consequences of which they did not immediately perceive.

Shortly after the first meeting, the Department of Employment notified the State Personnel Board and state agencies generally of the availability of workers who were to become surplus. The State Personnel Board agreed to supply no names of new eligibles to state agencies if the Department of Employment had surplus workers in the same class. Eligibles would be certified only after agencies had had an opportunity to interview Department workers and had declined to accept them.

An Error?

Steedman and Bashline went further: all tabulating machine operators, not merely those who might be surplus, were made available for transfer within the state service. A meeting to announce this policy was held in June. Some state agencies appeared to doubt the good faith of this offer of scarce skilled operators, and their questions indicated they were looking for the "gimmick." A number of them did, however, avail themselves of the opportunity. IBM notified its western offices of the prospective surplus of EAM machine operators. In spite of the opportunities that rapidly became available, few Tab operators accepted job offers. It is not clear why. It may have been that with the conversion nearly two years away, they felt little urgency in making a change.

At the time, these hurried decisions to make personnel available to other agencies seemed "the right thing to do." They later appeared to Steedman as poor decisions—parts of an uncoordinated pattern of action triggered by a desire to avoid a layoff at all costs, but wrong from an operational point of view. The reluctance of employees to take other jobs "saved our necks," as Steedman put it later. By offering its skilled personnel wholesale, the Department was inviting a mass exodus that might have crippled its ongoing EAM operations.

These more or less abortive efforts to bring about staff readjustment, then, simply emphasized that there was as yet no systematic plan for readjustment. The Committee continued to meet, to argue, and to discuss alternatives. May and June went by and no scheme had been formulated to which all could agree and which would still accomplish the basic administrative objectives: maintain a full-scale EAM operation; supply personnel to convert the cards to magnetic tape; supply personnel for EDPM training; and, finally, avoid a last-minute layoff at conversion.

Bashline's Idea

Up to this point the Committee had considered only solutions that contemplated shifting Tab employees to outside organizations or within the tabulating section itself. Outside shifts were small, and concentrating only on the tabulating section inside the Department amounted, in fact, to reliance on attrition. Finally Bashline thought of an idea that seemed promising. He suggested that Tab personnel ought to be considered for posts in other sections of the Department. He proposed that as vacancies occurred in any part of the Department he be permitted to transfer to them those employees from his own section whose jobs would not be affected by EDPM. Into the Tab vacancies thus created he could then transfer surplus machine operators. The interesting feature of this proposal was that permanent, non-surplus staff would be transferred out of Bashline's section to other units of the Department to make room in Tab for those employees, particularly machine operators, who would become surplus. Some members of the Committee observed that under this plan Bashline would have complete say as to when the people were to be transferred. Delays and complications in the receiving sections were bound to follow if Bashline could not release people at the time vacancies occurred. The advantages to Bashline were apparent. The entire Department would become involved in the personnel problems of EDPM conversion and to a greater or lesser degree would become committed to its success. In addition Bashline would have in his own section trained machine operators for emergency use before conversion time. There were three elements in Bashline's plan:

1. Clerical vacancies throughout the Sacramento office of the Department would be filled by clerks transferred from permanent jobs in the control and files groups of the tabulating section.
2. Clerical vacancies thus created in the control and files groups would be filled by tabulating machine operators. These operators would ultimately, after conversion, be available for transfer to other state agencies; would be available for jobs outside state service; or would be available for transfer to other job classifications in the Department. In the meantime these operators-turned-clerks could be turned back to EAM machine operating in case of emergency before conversion.
3. The tabulating machine operator positions vacated by transfer of regular operators would be filled by temporary employees, probably college students for the most part, who could be trained rapidly to operate one type of machine rather than all types as ordinarily required.

There were other advantages for Bashline in this plan. The machine operators knew the work of the Tab section and could quickly learn the related work in the control-files groups. Also this "double transfer" could be effected gradually or rapidly depending on Tab's operational needs. Finally, vacancies that would be occurring in several hundred clerical jobs throughout the Department would provide a broader opportunity for personnel transfers than would the tabulating section alone.

After consultation with his superiors, Streit, the Personnel Board's representative on the Committee, said that his agency would refrain from raising questions about the "out-of-class assignment" of machine operators to straight clerical work in the control-files groups. It was conceded by all that a thorough classification survey should be made after the conversion had been completed.

Bashline's proposal met strong opposition from Graham (accounting section), Kipp (fiscal section), and Roche (research and statistics). Implicit in their objections was the unvoiced thought, "Why should our operations suffer just because Bashline decided to install EDPM?" The three men insisted that they have a voice in setting the conditions for persons to be transferred into their sections. Bashline argued that some of his people were naturally of more value to him than others and that, during this critical period, he needed great flexibility in work assignments. He was adamant. Finally, after extended discussion which led only to each side digging more firmly into its prepared position, Steedman settled the issue, in effect by fiat. Both he and Bashline felt that in this matter what seemed to be Department interests should prevail over narrower section interests. The EDPM program *had* to succeed; it was the Department's program; Director Burkett's standing would be affected if there was a serious delay in conversion. They both knew that Burkett would agree with their view if the question were put to him. For this reason Steedman was able to step out of his staff role and make a top management decision in favor of Bashline's program. Kipp, Graham, and Roche recognized the departmental considerations and accepted the decision with good grace. Actually, the issue was not one of major importance to either group. To Bashline it could hardly have been vital because a short time before he had offered to transfer his people—surplus and permanent ones alike—to other state agencies. The other three section heads were standing on the usual administrative prerogative, freedom to select one's own staff. It seemed unlikely, however, that they would acquire through the forced transfer method new employees who were worse—in fact they were likely to be better—than those selected from the outside. They had been fighting to avoid operational problems which were unlikely to occur.

This decision to involve all clerical jobs of the Department in the personnel readjustment plan for Tab operators meant that the Committee no longer was relying on chance. As Steedman saw it, the agency itself could now administer and control the transfer program, speeding it or slowing it as required by operational needs. If the tabulating section needed fewer jobs in other sections than were falling vacant, new employees could always be hired from the outside. If more jobs were needed than were available within the Department, the Department could again offer to transfer personnel to outside agencies. Tabulating machine operators who wished to do so could remain with the Department, seek a new career in another type of work, and preserve the stake they had built up in the state's employee benefit program. In the meantime their services would be available to the Tab section in emergencies. Also, this program would convince employees that the Department was sincerely trying to carry out its "no layoff" policy.

Who Will Go First?

Even though they saw the possible disadvantages to themselves and their sections, Kipp, Graham, and Roche, having accepted the decision, now went a step further. They volunteered to begin at once to build up a supply of vacant jobs for Bashline's use by appointing only temporary clerks to fill current vacancies. The "temporaries" could be released without notice when their jobs were needed for the clerks to be transferred from the control-files groups.

How was the transfer program to be carried out? Everyone in the Department was aware of the great importance to employees of established, publicized standards in personnel actions, standards to apply in transfer, rehiring, day versus night shift assignments, geographical locations, and the like. These were touchy subjects in an agency that had seen violent staff readjustments due to layoff. Steedman could see the same old controversies and clashes arising: Who would have to be the first to leave the control-files groups? Which operators would be the first to leave the machines and become clerks? If "hassles" of this kind arose, Tab's work would be disrupted and so would that of the sections that were to receive the clerks. In addition, disgruntled employees could upset the whole plan, which was rather delicately balanced at best.

To cope with these touchy problems of implementation, the Committee decided to rely on the employee group itself. Tabulating section employees were asked to form a representative committee to make recommendations to the Departmental Personnel Committee on the method and order of transfer. (The former committee is referred to below as the employees' committee to distinguish it from Steedman's top-level Committee.)

Late in June 1954, the Committee had submitted a questionnaire to employees of the tabulating section who were likely to be affected by the conversion. Information from this survey was made available to the employees' committee, which also interviewed many of the affected workers. The employees' committee then made a general recommendation to Steedman's Committee.

In August Steedman's Committee released a statement on the transfer program over the signature of the personnel officer. The essence of the plan was that seniority in the Department would be the controlling factor in determining the "order of transfer." (In May of 1954, Steedman had been promoted to chief of administrative services. His position as personnel officer had been filled by Collins, formerly training officer. Steedman continued to head the Committee and retained responsibility for the final solution to personnel problems involved in the conversion.) The policy letter reflected suggestions made by Tab section employees and other persons affected. It was well received and not unexpected because there had been wide participation in the development of the procedures it promulgated:

STATE OF CALIFORNIA
DEPARTMENT OF EMPLOYMENT
Interoffice Correspondence

To: W. S. Bashline
From: Edgar A. Collins
Date: August 12, 1954
Subject: Policy for Transferring Clerks from the Control Group and the Files Group of the Tabulating Section

Following are the policies agreed to by the Departmental Personnel Committee for transferring clerks from the Control Group and the Files Group in the Tabulating Section to vacancies in other sections:

1. Service lists [seniority lists] by class for all clerical classes affected will be prepared. In determining service-list order, the total months and days of service in the Department shall be credited, except service prior to a six months' break in service.
2. a. As permanent intermediate level [journeyman clerk] vacancies occur in other sections, the Personnel Section shall select the employee to be transferred from the three employees highest on the service list interested in and qualified for the job.
   b. As permanent vacancies at the senior level [first supervisory level clerk] and above occur, the Personnel Section shall refer the three employees highest on the service list interested in the job for interview. The section shall select one of the three employees referred.
3. The Chief of the Tabulating Section shall determine the earliest date on which the employees can be released for transfer. In the event that the receiving section must fill the position earlier than the employee can be released from the Tabulating Section, the position shall be filled by the receiving section on a limited term basis.
4. If there is no one on the service list interested in transferring to any given vacancy, the Personnel Section shall determine whether anticipated vacancies are such that the position shall be filled by (1) selecting the person to be transferred on an involuntary basis from the last three names on the service list, or (2) filling the position through some other method.
5. Cases that are not precisely covered by the principles expressed herein will be resolved through joint consultation of the Tabulating Section, the Receiving Section, the Personnel Section and the employee or employees involved. The solution arrived at will be based on the principles set forth herein.

/s/ Edgar A. Collins

When the time came, those Tab employees who normally would not have been affected by EDPM but who were now subject to transfer to make room for "surplus employees" did not make any significant objections. They were, however, active participants in suggesting policies and methods on who should be transferred first.

THE CONVERSION

Although a "paper plan" had been developed to avoid a layoff, Bashline's operating troubles had just begun. The "no layoff" plan had to be carried out amid major operational and training problems:

1. The training of key men—programmers and console operators—for EDPM operations would have to begin at once. These people would have to be taken from their key spots in the EAM operations. Bashline had to balance the need to train EDPM operators with his need to retain competent

supervisory staff in the continuing EAM operations.

2. Twenty-three million cards from the wage and claim files had to be converted to tape for use in EDPM operations. Temporary help would be employed and trained for this, but supervision must come from the regular supervisory ranks of the tabulating section.

Bashline attended IBM programming school throughout September 1954. On October 4 the first programming school began for his regular staff. Seven key people were drawn from the supervisory staff to attend the school full-time for nearly one month. They returned to begin programming operations for the EDPM system, and nine other supervisors were then sent to the school. These sixteen formed the nucleus of the EDPM supervisory and programming staff. For all practical purposes their services were lost to the ongoing EAM operations.

The absence of the key people sent to programming school and of those who were transferred permanently to the development of EDPM programs left the supervisory ranks for EAM operations dangerously thin. Temporary help could not be used in the key spots, and overtime was the only answer. Bashline himself put in over 1,000 hours overtime during the next twelve months. Key supervisors worked 714 extra hours in 1955 and over 4,000 overtime hours in 1956.

The conversion of 23,000,000 card records to tape was arranged to be done solely with temporary help. It was scheduled for late 1955, and in October of that year the Placement Office of Sacramento State College was called on to supply college students to man four five-hour daily shifts. Thirty students received eight days' training, and on November 1, 1955, they started to convert the mountain of cards under the direction of two regular supervisors who were actually learning this new operation themselves.

Meanwhile, after a slow start, the planned readjustment of tabulating machine personnel progressed rapidly. Much to the surprise of the personnel staff, there was at first a reluctance to leave the section on the part of those destined to become "surplus." Their philosophy seemed to be, "Let's stick around and see what these electronic gadgets can do."[3] However, after the novelty and the shock of the prospective change wore off, there was a marked acceleration in transfers.

Steedman set up a personnel "status board" in his office. In October fourteen permanent clerks were shifted from the control and files groups to other sections in the Department. Because of the "squeeze" on the tabulating staff, only eight machine operators could be moved to the control-files groups to replace them. The other six jobs were filled by temporary employees. Steedman had added to "surplus" on the status board fifteen machine operators who were on military leave with absolute rights to return. Since they would return gradually, and some not at all, it was hoped they would simply fit into the readjustment scheme along with all the others.

As the months wore on, thirteen machine operators transferred to other state agencies; ten others accepted jobs with private concerns or with federal agencies. Meanwhile, temporary staff, largely from Sacramento State College and Sacramento Junior College, was rapidly being added to fill the many vacancies created by the "planned turnover." These people were trained for one week on one machine and then assigned to production jobs.

This "forced attrition" from the tabulating section continued throughout 1955. In May 1955, the midpoint in the program, the board in the personnel office showed a total of eighty-four temporary employees at work: sixty-three machine operators, seven clerks, and fourteen key punch operators temporarily assigned to clerical work. It was Bashline's good fortune that the Department workload was lower than had been anticipated —fewer employees were required than originally budgeted. If this had not been the case, serious operational difficulties might have arisen, for the personnel readjustment plan was working almost too well. It had to be deliberately slowed.

As things went, however, wage records were kept, claims were processed just as before—the work went on "as usual" while the Department was tooling up for the EDPM system. Test runs of some of the EDPM programs had begun in April 1955 at the IBM testing center at Poughkeepsie, New York, and had been repeated on Bank of America equipment in San Francisco in August. The conversion of the punch card records to tape proceeded normally. By December 1955 the six men trained for programming had reached some degree of consistency in their EDPM operations.

In December 1955 the Tab section moved into

---

[3] One thing they would do, so rumor had it, was to render sterile the employees who worked around them. This report, denied by IBM and the Department, soon ran its course.

the Department's new building and prepared to begin the EDPM operation parallel to the conventional EAM system which remained in the old building. Then a freak accident occurred to upset the entire plan for a gradual conversion. A key piece of electronic equipment dropped from a fork-lift while being unloaded from an airplane in San Francisco. It was demolished, and no replacement was available. One had to be built. One full month was lost. The plan for a parallel operation had to be revised, for meanwhile, in the regular Tab section in the old building, matters had become desperate. Since early fall many temporary workers had been leaving to return to school or in anticipation of the end of their temporary jobs. Trained staff was now so scarce that the EAM operation could not be continued. Bashline had no choice but to begin the EDPM operation at once without overlap and without the extensive trial runs and experimentation that had been planned.

On March 27, 1956, the old EAM operation was terminated and the first claims were processed on EDPM. The last of the temporary workers were separated, and the remaining permanent personnel —now many fewer than Bashline would have liked —transferred to the electronic equipment.

The Department's commitment to the employees had been fulfilled: not a single employee had been laid off. Everyone who wanted a job was retained, either by the Department of Employment or by some other state agency. (In 1958 some of these former Tab employees were still seeking transfers back to that section.)

Conclusion

In retrospect, the officials involved in the EDPM conversion felt their experience suggested certain conclusions. For one thing, it seemed clear that with a favorable labor market such as that existing in 1954-1955, a large employer could, with sufficient advance planning, make a "no layoff" commitment and keep it, *provided* certain conditions were present: employees would have to be willing to take other kinds of work; the personnel system would have to be flexible so that the strict letter of job classification could be ignored for a time, at least; the employer would have to employ and train temporary help to continue the old operations while preparing for the new ones. The last condition suggested that the complexity of the supplanted operation was a key variable in determining the degree to which temporary help could be rapidly and economically trained.

Was the conversion process a success? Steedman gives an unqualified "yes"; Bashline a "yes, but." Both men feel the "no layoff" policy raised morale at a time when the Department's reputation among employees left much to be desired. Bashline qualifies his answer when he recalls the many operating problems that attended the conversion and that were, of course, complicated by the personnel decision.

The crux of the problem was a lack of time. Bashline says now: "I would never again attempt a conversion of this magnitude within the narrow time limits of this one."

Was EDPM worth it? Did the savings materialize? Two studies, both about one year apart, have been made to analyze the savings. In both of them the Department of Employment made the original findings and they were validated by "experts" in the state fiscal agency, the Department of Finance. The first study showed that in the fiscal year 1957-1958 there were savings of $159,986. Subsequently, higher workloads were estimated and a new calculation was made. This study showed wage savings of $460,455 annually.

From the standpoint of efficiency, EDPM has resulted in improvement in the speed and quality with which claims are processed. The machines, in the view of Department officials, have turned out to be more accurate than the employees were.

PHILLIP O. FOSS

Reorganization and Reassignment in the California Highway Patrol

PHILLIP O. FOSS

The author of *Reorganization and Reassignment in the California Highway Patrol* received a Ph.D. degree from the University of Oregon. He is currently Professor and Chairman, Department of Political Science, Colorado State University.

CHRONOLOGY OF KEY EVENTS

October 1946	Report of International Association of Chiefs of Police on California Highway Patrol is submitted to Senate Interim Committee on Government Reorganization
1947	California Highway Patrol given departmental status upon separation from the Department of Motor Vehicles
March 1953	Senate Finance Subcommittee conducts study of Patrol organization and operation
May 1953	Management Analysis Section of the Department of Finance examines organization of the Patrol
1958	Commissioner Caldwell and Deputy Commissioner McDonald retire
February 1, 1959	Office of Legislative Analyst issues report on organization and management of the Patrol
March 1959	Crittenden becomes Commissioner
July 6, 1959	Crittenden discusses with Johnson, Departmental Secretary to the Governor, the possibility of reorganization; asks Finance's Organization and Cost Control Division to study the Patrol
July-August 1959	Farmer of OCC examines the Patrol
September 1959	Farmer works out tentative reorganization plan and meets with Senior Staff
September 1959	Crittenden decides to make reorganization effective December 2, 1959
October-November 1959	Luethje and Donaldson, career field Patrol officers, plan implementation of reorganization
October 1959	Patrol inspectors meet in Los Angeles
December 2, 1959	Reorganization becomes effective

PRINCIPAL CHARACTERS

Fred Bly, Assistant Commissioner; Commander, Field Operations Division (before reorganization); Chief of Staff (after reorganization)

Bradford M. Crittenden, Commissioner, California Highway Patrol

D. T. Donaldson, Stockton District Commander; member of team to plan implementation of reorganization

Elton W. Farmer, Administrative Analyst for Organization and Cost Control Division, Finance Department

D. S. Luethje, Inspector; Bureau Commander for Technical Services; member of team to plan implementation of reorganization

THE CALIFORNIA HIGHWAY PATROL

In 1959 California motorized vehicle registrations stood at seven and one-half million. Vehicle miles traveled totaled sixty-eight billion. The annual statistical report of the California Highway Patrol for that year declared:

> Third among the Nation's States in total land area . . . second most populous of the entire fifty . . . but far and away the Nation's leader in total traffic problems by every known standard of measurement . . . this was California in 1959.
>
> Within the borders of the Golden State are to be found the most diversified conditions and terrain available to any traveler, wherever he may go. On any given day California's millions of resident drivers will be joined by more motorists traveling more miles than in any other state in the Union.[1]

Another of the Patrol's publications further indicated the size of its task:

> This vast army of drivers, as it operates more vehicles more miles, also experiences greater accident exposure and is involved in more accidents which, tragically, kill and maim more people than in any other state.
>
> It is the job of the California Highway Patrol to regulate this flow of traffic with the goal of providing for efficient and accident-free movement for all California highway users.[2]

In the process of regulating highway traffic the Patrol not only made arrests for speeding and reckless driving but also engaged in a wide variety of other functions. A considerable portion of a patrolman's time was taken up with such activities as giving directions to confused motorists; changing tires for helpless ladies; providing emergency transportation and traffic control at the scene of accidents; notifying farmers of broken-down fences or livestock on the highways; emergency transport of medical supplies to outlying communities; escorting hazardous trucking loads; traffic direction and control when highways had been washed out or had become otherwise hazardous; escort and protection of visiting dignitaries; direction of traffic at times of high concentration (state fairs, national conventions, and the like); and appearances in the courts.

The Patrol was responsible for the periodic inspection of school buses and the weighing and inspection of trucks suspected of being overloaded or in an unsafe condition. It also devoted considerable attention to auto theft investigation.

During the first three decades of the century traffic regulation on California highways was considered to be the responsibility of county governments. Traffic officers were appointed by county boards of supervisors, county sheriffs, or district attorneys—often on the basis of political influence. During this period there was little consistency in traffic regulation or enforcement methods among the various counties, except that traffic officers were ordinarily expected to apprehend enough violators so that fines would more than equal salaries.

In 1915 a state Motor Vehicle Department was created to assist county and city governments in working toward statewide uniformity in highway traffic regulation. Because of the limited number of personnel allocated (ten in 1919), the Motor Vehicle Department was not primarily involved in direct enforcement activities, although one of the first inspectors of the department, Inspector Fred Leber, does recall arresting the driver of a 1916 Dodge for speeding. The department sought mainly to improve and standardize traffic regulation and enforcement throughout the state by instruction and assistance to local enforcement agencies.

Establishment of the Patrol

The passage of the California Vehicle Act in 1923 laid the groundwork for the formation of the present highway patrol. The old Motor Vehicle Department was abolished, and a new Division of Motor Vehicles was established in the Department of Finance. The act authorized the appointment of *state* traffic officers, who would directly engage in enforcement activities. Responsibility for highway traffic regulation was thus transferred, in theory, from local governments to the state Division of Motor Vehicles. In actuality, the counties retained

---

[1] California Highway Patrol, *Annual Statistical Report 1959* (Sacramento: State Printing Office, 1960), pp. 102–103.

[2] California Highway Patrol, *1959 Annual Report* (Sacramento: State Printing Office, 1960), p. 5.

considerable influence because they could "join" or abstain from entering the state system at the discretion of the county supervisors.[3] The counties that joined the system entered into a contract with the chief of the Division of Motor Vehicles which stipulated, in part, that appointments of personnel would be made from lists submitted by the county board of supervisors and that patrol officers could not serve outside their county of appointment more than one week without the consent of the board of supervisors. This system of dual control, or "home rule on the highway," persisted until the passage of the California Vehicle Act of 1929.

The 1929 act created the present California Highway Patrol in the Division of Motor Vehicles, which by this time had been moved to the Department of Public Works. Traffic officers from the old "contract counties" were blanketed into the Patrol and given permanent civil service status. The remaining counties were offered the privilege of "joining," and by 1932 the last remaining county, Los Angeles, had been integrated into the Patrol. New Patrol officers were required to take a civil service examination, but only those persons recommended by county boards of supervisors could compete in the test. This provision continued in effect until 1936. The prohibition against moving an officer out of his county of appointment was technically still in effect in 1961.[4] In actuality, the statute had been nullified by the practice of making statewide appointments only; that is, new members of the Patrol were appointed to the Patrol Academy rather than to a particular county. Successful graduates were assigned from there on the basis of manning requirements, although personal preferences were taken into account.

While direct local control of Patrol personnel ended in 1936, local groups continued to exert an influence on the Patrol through their senators and assemblymen in the State Legislature. Some legislators considered the patrol unit in their district to be partially under their jurisdiction and expected the Patrol to provide them with personal taxi service—sometimes all the way to Sacramento. Other legislators assumed a paternal interest in particular patrols and attempted to exert their influence in such matters as the nonenforcement activities of patrolmen, the rank of officers, and the assignments of Patrol personnel.

Officers appointed prior to 1936 continued to serve in the Patrol for many years afterward, and a considerable number of them were still active and occupied key positions in 1959, when the reorganization of the Patrol that is the subject of this study took place. By custom, law, and because of operational needs, patrol officers were seldom moved to different localities except at their own request. Thus they tended to form close ties and allegiances with local political organizations and influential persons, regardless of the method by which they were originally appointed. These ties were further strengthened by the close cooperation with local governments and law enforcement agencies needed for effective traffic control.

The Division of Motor Vehicles was divorced from the Department of Public Works in 1931 and became a separate department. Sixteen years later, in 1947, the Patrol was, in turn, separated from the Department of Motor Vehicles to become the new *Department* of the California Highway Patrol.

Organization and Characteristics

The organizational structure of the new Department of California Highway Patrol closely followed the recommendations set forth by Franklin M. Kreml, Director, Traffic Division, International Association of Chiefs of Police, in his *Report on the California Highway Patrol* to the Senate Interim Committee on Government Reorganization in October of 1946. The state was divided into three geographical areas, designated Coastal Zone, Valley Zone, and Southern Zone. The zones were further subdivided into districts, and the districts into patrol areas, with the latter roughly following county lines. Zones, districts, and patrol areas were headed by patrolmen with ranks of supervising inspector, inspector, and captain, respectively.

The Patrol, a semi-military organization, was organized along traditional military lines, with staff and line functions rather clearly delineated and defined. As in many other law enforcement agencies, military designations of rank (sergeant, lieutenant, captain, commander) were used, and insignia of rank was worn on uniforms. Effective officers were sometimes referred to as "good soldiers." General

---

[3] California's county supervisors had the same general functions as did county commissioners in other states.

[4] State of California, *Vehicle Code*, as amended through 1959, Sec. 2255: "No member of the California Highway Patrol, appointed to serve in any county, shall be assigned by the commissioner for service outside the county for a longer period than one week, except:

(a) Pursuant to a request by the employee for a transfer.

(b) As may be necessitated by temporary traffic emergencies. . . ."

FIGURE 1:
ORIGINAL THREE ZONE ORGANIZATION

Source: Department of Finance, Organization and Cost Control Division, *Management Survey for the Department of the California Highway Patrol,* Survey 1060.1

FIGURE 2:
NEW SIX ZONE ORGANIZATION

Source: Department of Finance, Organization and Cost Control Division, *Management Survey for the Department of the California Highway Patrol,* Survey 1060.1.

directives were issued as formal "orders." Physical fitness, grooming, and appearance of uniforms and equipment received considerable emphasis. Because much of a patrolman's work involved emergency situations, many of them hazardous, the maintenance of a high order of discipline was considered necessary.

No prior police or traffic experience was required for appointment to the Patrol, and no uniformed personnel were appointed above the entry (traffic officers) level. Applicants for appointment as traffic officers were required to have an education equivalent to the completion of the twelfth grade, to be in good physical condition, and to pass an examination consisting of a written test, an oral interview, and a physical performance test. Successful applicants then underwent twelve weeks of training in the California Highway Patrol Academy. The entrance salary (1960) was $481 per month, with a maximum of $584 in the grade of traffic officer. Patrolmen had to spend two years in grade before they were eligible to take a promotional examination. They could retire at the age of fifty, while the minimum retirement age for most other state employees was fifty-five. For most employees the state retirement system provided, after thirty years of service, benefits of approximately fifty per cent of the highest three years' salary. Patrolmen, however, could retire with the same benefits after twenty years of service, but their contributions to the retirement fund were substantially higher than those of other employees. Patrolmen, or their survivors, also received special benefits for disability or death incurred in "line of duty."

By 1960 the Patrol numbered some 2,600 uniformed patrolmen and 800 "civilians." Promotional possibilities for uniformed personnel were somewhat limited because of the "flatness" of the organizational pyramid. The uniformed positions budgeted for 1960 were:

Assistant Commissioner	1
Supervising Traffic Inspector	7
Traffic Inspector	14
Traffic Captain	58
Traffic Lieutenant	72
Traffic Sergeant	200
Traffic Officer	2,237

Appointment, promotion, and separation of personnel, both uniformed and "civilian," were governed by regulations of the State Personnel Board, which administered the California civil service system and performed a function roughly comparable to the United States Civil Service Commission at the national level. Only two positions in the Patrol (Commissioner and Deputy Commissioner) were "exempt" from the state civil service system. The Commissioner was appointed by the Governor, and the Deputy by the Commissioner. All of the top uniformed positions in the Patrol, both line and staff, were filled by promotion from within the ranks; there was no lateral entry. All promotions were awarded in accordance with scores obtained on promotional examinations consisting of both written and oral tests. As with some other organizations with linear promotion systems, and consequent organizational "inbreeding," the Patrol had the advantages of consistency and predictability of behavior and high standards of competence, discipline, and devotion to duty,[5] coupled with some of the rigidities such a promotion system engenders and a tendency for members to equate "the good of the service" with the good of the public.

Uniformed patrolmen differed sharply from most other government employees in that their loyalties and identifications were, of necessity, restricted to the Patrol rather than also being directed toward a profession or an occupational group. Skills and experience gained in the Patrol were not readily transferable to other agencies and occupations. California highway patrolmen did not think of themselves primarily as policemen—they were *traffic officers* and considered themselves to be much superior to city policemen in both integrity and competence.[6] Because of this "elite group" feeling, the lack of opportunity to utilize acquired skills in other activities, and the lack of opportunities to transfer out, the turnover rate in the Patrol was one of the lowest in the state service. All these factors, plus the tight, military discipline considered necessary in an emergency-oriented organization, tended to create a singularly complaisant and malleable personnel force.

Possibly because enforcement activities have been centered around legal codes, patrolmen have tended to take a formalistic and legalistic approach to problems and to explain or rationalize problem solutions in the same manner. They could, therefore, accept orders and regulations with fewer reservations than was usually the case in other agencies.

---

[5] According to Inspector Fred Leber, who entered the Patrol in 1921, "We have the finest Patrol in the world and it's a part of me."

[6] One zone commander said, "I suppose we are generally considered to be the most effective traffic regulatory agency in existence."

One of the "images" held by patrolmen was that successful supervisors of uniformed personnel were decisive, hard-driving individuals who could be rough and tough but who were fair and above-board in their dealings with subordinates. This image may have been substantially correct, but successful supervisors were also apt to be extremely knowledgeable about the characteristics, preferences, and personal lives of their people. Such knowledge and understanding was more easily acquired in the Patrol than in most other government agencies because of the stability of personnel and the tightly knit character of the organization. Because of this stability and close association, supervisors became exceedingly adroit in managing the personnel assigned to them and in effectuating changes with a minimum amount of opposition.

Non-uniformed personnel were utilized mainly in clerical, equipment maintenance, supply, and other support and administrative services positions.

THE ELECTION OF 1958 AND A NEW COMMISSIONER

The election of 1958 brought about an abrupt change in the political climate of California state government. The Democratic Party elected its first Governor since 1942 and won a majority in both houses of the Legislature for the first time since 1888. Not only had the Republican Party dominated the State Legislature for almost three-quarters of a century, but, because of various peculiarities in California politics, incumbents were more likely to be reelected than in most other states. As a consequence of this stability in the Legislature, and to some extent in the Governor's office, administrative policies had been fairly consistent and predictable. The long tenure of individual legislators and of one party had also encouraged administrative departments to work closely with the Legislature and with the local interest groups represented in it.

The election of Democrat Edmund G. (Pat) Brown to the governorship in 1958 to succeed Republican Goodwin J. Knight resulted in the retirement of Highway Patrol Commissioner Bernard R. Caldwell and Deputy Commissioner Ross McDonald and the appointment of a new Commissioner—Bradford M. Crittenden. Both Caldwell and McDonald were career police officers who had come to the Patrol after many years' service with the traffic division of the Los Angeles Police Department.

The New Commissioner

Commissioner Crittenden took office on March 16, 1959. He had been district attorney and assistant district attorney of San Joaquin County and had considerable experience in cases involving the State Vehicle Code. Personally acquainted with many patrolmen, he was generally considered to be a "friend of the Patrol." Governor Brown had also been a district attorney and had served as state Attorney General prior to his election to the governorship. The two men had worked together frequently, and their association extended back over several years. Crittenden's appointment was not "political" in the sense of rewarding a party "regular"; he was a Republican. (Governor Brown appointed other Republicans to state government offices and retained some Republican executives who were appointed during previous administrations.)

Crittenden had "never been a cop" and thought of himself as a public administrator rather than as a policeman. He had not been indoctrinated with traditional "police" methods and attitudes and was receptive to experiment and innovation. However, long acquaintance with the Patrol and respect for the competence of its members caused him to proceed carefully in instituting changes.

As a district attorney, Crittenden had been accustomed to "holding all the reins" and personally supervising the work of subordinates. He apparently wished to work the same way as Commissioner of the Highway Patrol. This approach to public management was in consonance with the administrative philosophy of Governor Brown. Brown expected and intended that his appointees would actively direct the agencies they headed. Furthermore, Brown was determined that positive action be taken to reduce highway traffic accidents. He had campaigned on this issue and after taking office had used his influence with the Legislature and with other state agencies to encourage action designed to reduce the highway accident toll. Thus the political climate of March 1959 was particularly favorable for a new Commissioner who wanted to "run his own show."

Shortly after his appointment, Crittenden moved to fill in the gaps in his understanding of Patrol activities by making a series of field trips. He visited every Patrol office in California, including some ninety field offices. Informal meetings were held at each stop, and the men were encouraged to express their ideas about Patrol organization and activities.

The fact that the new Commissioner was willing to go to the trouble of visiting field offices "to get acquainted" left a favorable impression with field personnel. They were generally pleasantly surprised at his knowledge of their particular operation. As a result of his frequent field trips, his interest in the details of local operations, and his methods of dealing with subordinates, Crittenden became "popular with the troops."

The Patrol in 1959

Crittenden found a highly dispersed organization, with some ninety field offices scattered over the third largest state in the United States. The distance from El Centro patrol office in the South to the Yreka office in the North was farther than from New York to Chicago. The Patrol was dispersed still further geographically: each officer, while he was patrolling the highways, spent much of his time miles away from his patrol office and from direct supervision.

Along with this dispersed geographical organization there was, however, a considerable degree of centralization of decision-making in the headquarters office in Sacramento. A complaint to the Commissioner from a citizen in the Bakersfield area, for instance, would go to the Bakersfield Patrol Area office for investigation. After completion of the investigation a report would be forwarded to the district commander and from him to the zone commander, to the Commander of Field Operations, to the Deputy Commissioner, and finally to the Commissioner for final disposition. At any point along the route, the report could be returned for revision or correction.

Centralized decision-making provided consistency and specialized expertise, but these benefits were thought to be at least partially offset by the loss in time and clarity in moving information and decision into headquarters from the far-flung field and back again. These communications difficulties were further complicated by the many clearance points along the way. A simplified version of this communication channel is depicted below.

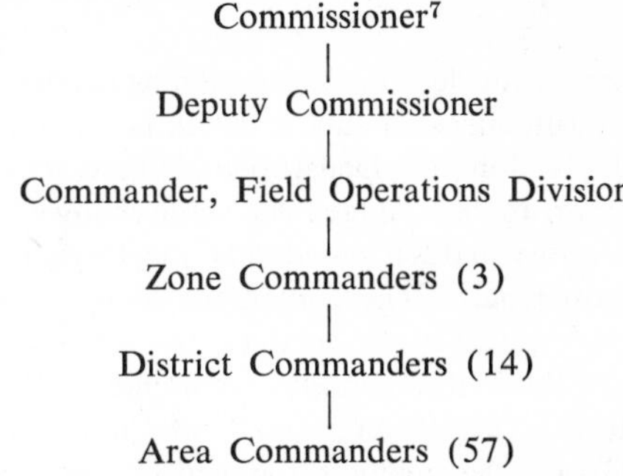

Certainly not every communication that originated with an area commander needed to move all the way to the Commissioner. Nor was every communication from the Commissioner intended to reach every area commander. Nevertheless, some communications *were* intended to move through all the command levels.

According to one story, Commissioner Crittenden once issued a statewide directive that was so variously interpreted as it passed down through the hierarchy that its meaning had become altogether different by the time he next encountered it on a remote patrol office bulletin board. The Commissioner was even more concerned, however, with the upward movement of communications. Newly appointed to head an established agency, he felt somewhat insulated from his career subordinates. To Crittenden this insulation seemed especially objectionable because of the Governor's desire that his appointees assume actual operational control over their agencies.

After some weeks on the job and after his extensive field visits, consultations with staff personnel in Patrol headquarters, and conferences with individual legislators and with Governor Brown, the new Commissioner came to the conclusion that some organizational changes in the Patrol might be desirable. Such changes would have as their immediate objective the improvement in speed and clarity of communications, the shortening of command lines, and the increased participation of the Commissioner in the operational activities of the Patrol.

---

[7] These were *position* titles. Civil service grades were: Commissioner and Deputy Commissioner—exempt; Commander, Field Operations Division—Assistant Commissioner; Zone Commander—Supervising Traffic Inspector; District Commander—Traffic Inspector; Area Commander—Traffic Captain.

THE TECHNIQUES OF PLANNING FOR CHANGE

Once having decided that something needed to be done, Crittenden, on July 6, 1959, consulted with Charles W. Johnson, Departmental Secretary to the Governor. Johnson agreed that some changes might be desirable and suggested that the Organization and Cost Control Division of the Department of Finance[8] be asked to conduct an organizational study of the Patrol. Johnson accompanied Crittenden to the Organization and Cost Control Office (OCC) and personally introduced him to Marvin L. Blanchard, head of the Division.

As an immediate result of this conference, Elton W. Farmer, Administrative Analyst for OCC, was assigned to study the organizational structure of the Patrol. Farmer had some eight years' experience as a personnel officer for the California Department of Corrections. He had also worked as a personnel analyst for the State Personnel Board and in that capacity had conducted an extensive salary study of the Highway Patrol. He had previously completed organization studies for OCC of the California State Police[9] and the Department of Alcoholic Beverage Control.

Farmer first reviewed the organizational structure of the Patrol with the Commissioner. In the course of this discussion Crittenden pointed out some specific problems and problem areas in Patrol operations. He also outlined the objectives he hoped to achieve. Farmer then carried on the same kind of discussion with Assistant Commissioner Fred Bly and with a few other persons who had intimate knowledge of the Patrol. According to Farmer, these conversations had some orientation value, but they were conducted mainly to identify problem areas so that the scope and objectives of the study could be clearly defined. By thus identifying, defining, and limiting, the study was reduced to manageable proportions in time; the analyst could proceed with fairly definite purpose; and the work of the analyst could be better supervised. In a meeting with the top staff of the Patrol on July 13 it was agreed that "priority should be given to the organization of the department's top structure, number of levels of field command, and the placement of staff and service activities in headquarters' divisions."[10]

Earlier Recommendations for Change

After the study plan had been approved by his supervisor in OCC, Farmer reviewed two previous reorganization proposals that had been submitted in 1953. In March of that year a Senate Finance Subcommittee had undertaken a study of Patrol organization and operations. According to the subcommittee's report, its survey team had "visited every Patrol office in the State of California." The subcommittee had reported that failure to delegate authority was lessening the effectiveness of the Patrol; that excessive paperwork and reporting were required from the field, hampering supervisory activities; that power to take disciplinary action, which was retained in the Sacramento headquarters, should be delegated to the field; that there was insufficient observation of field officers by top-level personnel; and that the morale of the organization was generally low.[11] The subcommittee had also proposed a new organizational structure in which fifty-nine separate squad areas would report directly to one chief inspector, thus eliminating both zone and district levels. This recommendation had not been adopted.

In May 1953 the Management Analysis Section (predecessor of OCC) of the Department of Finance had also conducted an organizational survey of the Patrol. In its report to Commissioner Caldwell it had recommended that the Commissioner be

8 The Department of Finance had general supervision over the financial activities of California state government and was the Governor's staff agency for carrying out his management policies. Budgeting, management analysis, auditing, purchasing, building maintenance, and printing were centralized in this department. The Organization and Cost Control Division of the Department of Finance provided consultation services to state agencies in organization and methods, policy development, records management, accounting systems, and related activities.

9 The California State Police organization was concerned mainly with the protection of state-owned buildings and other properties and had no connection with the California Highway Patrol.

10 Department of Finance, Organization and Cost Control Division, *Management Survey for the Department of the California Highway Patrol,* Survey 1060.1 (Sacramento: Department of Finance, 1960), p. 1.

11 California Legislature, Senate, Finance Subcommittee, *Report on the California Highway Patrol* (Sacramento: State Printing Office, 1953), pp. 1-2.

made directly responsible for field operations and that the Commander of the Field Operations Division (then called Chief of the Patrol) be made a staff officer to the Commissioner. Zone commanders would then report directly to the Commissioner. The report had also recommended that zone commanders be given more authority and responsibility and that the "field should participate more actively in solving management problems."[12]

Commissioner Caldwell also had given some attention to several informal reorganization proposals. One of them would have eliminated the district commands and increased zone commands from three to seven. No significant action had been taken on any of these reorganization proposals, apparently because Caldwell had considered the political atmosphere to be unfavorable for any drastic changes. However, some of the same ideas appeared in the reorganization plan of 1959.

Farmer next reviewed the recommendations of the Legislative Analyst.[13] In his report of February 1, 1959 on the proposed 1959-1960 budget, the Legislative Analyst had been especially critical of Patrol organization and management practices. He had criticized budgetary procedures and personnel policies, especially with respect to distribution of personnel and the nonenforcement duties assigned to traffic officers, and had recommended that the Patrol budget be reduced by $623,568. The Legislative Analyst also had recommended a reorganization that would have eliminated the three zone commands entirely and reduced the number of district commands from fourteen to eight.

Farmer Examines the Patrol

Farmer's next step was to study the current organizational structure of the Patrol and the functions of each unit. (See Figure 3.) In 1959 the principal line functions were still carried out in a Division of Field Operations through the zone, district, and area commands. The state was still divided into three geographic zones, each headed by a zone commander. (See Figure 1.) These zones were further divided geographically into a total of fourteen districts, which were, in turn, subdivided into fifty-seven area commands.

Staff and auxiliary services were organized into a Technical Services Division and an Administrative Division. Technical Services included Research and Development; Public Information; Special Services (Auto Theft and Felony Files, Commercial Vehicles and School Bus, Auto Equipment Engineer and Laboratory); Communications; and Training. The Administrative Division contained Accounting, Personnel, Office Services, Supply and Motor Transport. (See Figure 3.)

Farmer then compared the organizational structure and function assignments of the Patrol with those of highway patrols in other states and state police organizations and with some of the larger city police forces. The structures of other California state agencies with substantial field forces (Motor Vehicles, Fish and Game, Forestry, Disaster Office) were also reviewed and compared with that of the Patrol.

In the course of Farmer's study numerous questions arose. Some could be answered by referring to the State Vehicle Code or by consulting the operations manual published by the Patrol. Others could be answered only by questioning of Patrol officers. Most of these preliminary inquiries involved questions of fact, but as the interviews progressed, the "why" questions tended to become more frequent. Still other questions could be answered only by direct observation of a particular activity.

In the process of inquiry and observation, Farmer visited twenty-five field offices in various parts of the state. In his discussions with field personnel Farmer was mainly interested in obtaining detailed knowledge of Patrol operations and of attitudes of Patrol officers. Personnel consulted in the field were not asked to submit reorganization suggestions, nor were they notified that a possible reorganization was pending, but many of them were probably aware through the "grapevine" that some changes were in the offing.

As the study progressed, Farmer began to develop preliminary and tentative reorganization possibilities. His general procedure was first to define a problem, determine its major causes, and then work out a set of tentative, alternate "solutions." He then "tested out" these possible solutions by informal consultation with those persons most likely to have detailed information and representative

---

[12] Department of Finance, Management Analysis Section, *Department of the California Highway Patrol—Organization of the Top Structure* (Sacramento: Department of Finance, 1953), pp. 2-4.

[13] The California Legislature employed a Legislative Analyst mainly to assist in determinations on budget requests from the executive departments. In studying budget requests, however, the Legislative Analyst was inevitably drawn into considerations of organization and management.

FIGURE 3:
DEPARTMENT OF THE CALIFORNIA HIGHWAY PATROL

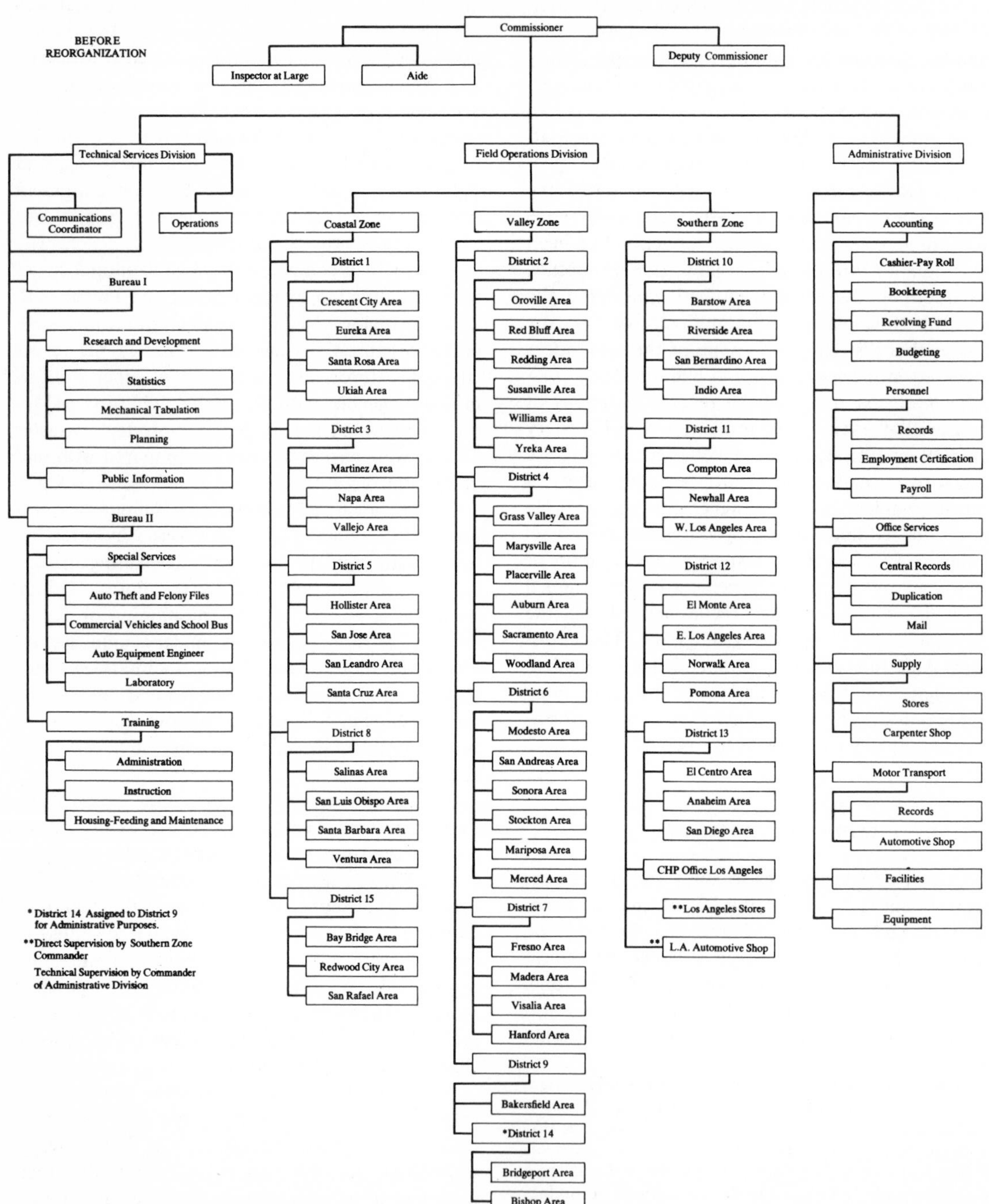

attitudes. Thus many people were consulted on specific proposals in the form of questions such as: "What would happen if . . .?" "How would this affect . . .?" "How would it work to . . .?"

A Tentative Reorganization Plan

By September 1959 Farmer had worked out a tentative reorganization plan that he believed would accomplish the Commissioner's objectives with a minimum amount of disruption. This plan was submitted to Assistant Commissioner Fred Bly for its first review as a whole.

Bly generally approved Farmer's proposals, which were submitted next to the Commissioner. Crittenden was also generally satisfied with the reorganization plan, but he deferred action until it could be considered by the Senior Staff at its regular monthly meeting. At that time the Senior Staff consisted of the commanders of the Field Operations Division, Technical Services Division, and Administrative Division; the commanders of the three geographical zones; and the Inspector-at-large. The Senior Staff consisted, thus, of the four top line officers, the heads of the two staff and auxiliary organizations, and one member of the Commissioner's personal staff.

The reorganization proposal was brought before a meeting of the Senior Staff in late September 1959. Farmer was present to explain and clarify possible ambiguities and to defend his proposals. At this point Crittenden felt the plan was sound and workable, but he would not have pushed its adoption if the Senior Staff had voiced strong objection or had pointed out operational difficulties that would have jeopardized its successful operation. The Commissioner's role in the staff meeting was to listen to objections and suggestions and evaluate them and, at the same time, to try to gain the acceptance and cooperation of his senior commanders for the reorganization proposals. Probably because of the Commissioner's obvious acceptance of the plan's general outlines, there was little discussion of whether or not it should be adopted. Most of the discussion was directed to questions of how the plan might best be implemented. There was, for example, considerable discussion of the location of boundary lines for proposed new geographical zones. Since no serious objections emerged in the Senior Staff meeting, the Commissioner accepted the Farmer reorganization proposals with only minor modifications.

The reorganization proposals were next accepted, without opposition or exceptions, by the Governor's Departmental Secretary, the Department of Finance, the Legislative Analyst, and the State Personnel Board. Personnel immediately concerned were then notified of the impending changes.

The reorganization was pronounced in effect on December 2, 1959 by Patrol Headquarters General Order 110.1. (See Appendix II for the full text of the general order.)

THE REORGANIZATION PLAN

Prior to the reorganization, the line function of the Patrol had been directed (by custom) by the Deputy Commissioner.[14] According to Farmer's survey report, "Although not shown on organization charts as such, the review and decision authority exercised by the individual formerly occupying

[14] Deputy Commissioner McDonald denies this informal assumption of authority. According to McDonald:

"Your comment, 'at the time of the reorganization the line functions of the patrol were directed (through custom) by the Deputy Commissioner,' is completely erroneous.

"If you will observe the organization charts of the previous administration you will note that the Deputy Commissioner's position was definitely not another level of command.

"His principal duty was Chief of Staff. He was available at all times to the division commanders for consultation on controversial matters, to reconcile differences between division commanders, to assume the duties of Commissioner in his absence, to be alert to all phases of the operation and thereby keep the Commissioner informed of matters critical to the administration, to hold pre-staff conferences for the purpose of resolving problems and presenting findings to the Commissioner for final approval. Most personnel matters, appointments, punitive action cases, injury cases and appealed controversies were considered by the Deputy Commissioner for recommendations to the Commissioner. Routine appointments and other routine personnel matters were directly acted upon by the Deputy Commissioner. All such matters of major concern were submitted directly to the Commissioner for his decision.

"Even these personnel activities did not constitute

the Deputy Commissioner position has made it another level." However, in September 1959, the position was vacant and had been since the retirement of Deputy Commissioner McDonald the previous March. After McDonald's retirement, Crittenden, with the help of Assistant Commissioner Fred Bly, directed the line operations of the patrol. The customary and traditional chain of authority in line operations, however, went from the Commissioner to the Deputy, to the Commander of the Field Operations Division, to the three zone commanders, to the district commanders in each zone, to the area commanders in each district, and, finally, from the area commanders to patrol sergeants and patrolmen.

Changes in Command Levels

Farmer proposed the elimination of the two positions of Deputy Commissioner and Commander of Field Operations, an increase in zone commands from three to six, and the elimination of all fourteen district commands. (See Figure 4 and Figure 2 for, respectively, the proposed new organizational and zone structures.) In effect, he proposed to flatten the hierarchy by eliminating three levels. Thus, he thought, communications, both into and out from headquarters, would be expedited and the possibility of misinterpretation reduced. By eliminating the positions of Deputy Commissioner and Commander of Field Operations from the hierarchy, the Commissioner would have direct contact with zone commanders and could become, in fact, the operational director of the Patrol. The essentials of the reorganization of line activities are depicted in the comparative chart in the next column.

Farmer and the persons with whom he consulted believed that organizational problems could not be solved simply by eliminating positions, if those positions had previously served any useful purpose.

another level of command as they were specifically delegated to the Deputy Commissioner and handled directly from the personnel section to Deputy Commissioner.

"On numerous occasions when the Commissioner was busy or away from the office temporarily, the Deputy did make decisions on routine matters presented by the division-heads, but rest assured the division commanders were directly responsible to the Commissioner, and I doubt that anyone questioned this." Letter from former Deputy Commissioner Ross R. McDonald, dated September 15, 1960. Quoted with permission of the writer.

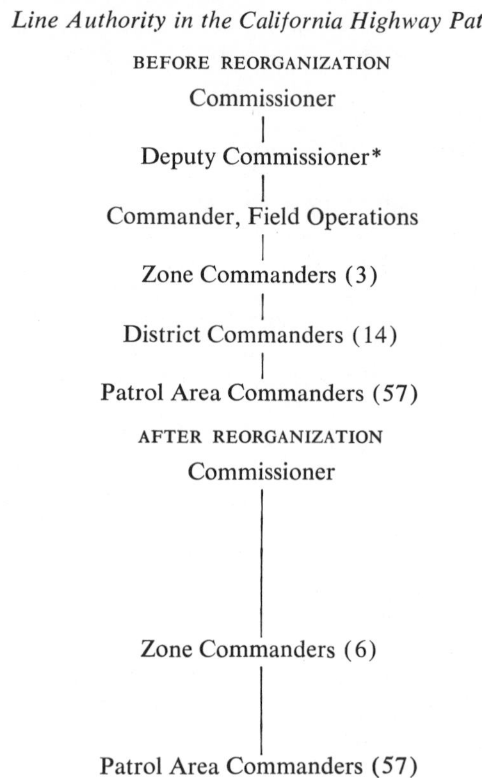

* The Deputy Commissioner appears in this position because he sometimes assumed these line responsibilities. He did not appear in the command line on organization charts. This was an informal, but nonetheless real, assumption of authority and responsibility.

Removing the two high-level positions would thrust additional, direct responsibilities upon the Commissioner. To meet these operational responsibilities, the Commissioner's personal staff was to be enlarged by adding an executive assistant, a public information officer, and a special representative. To meet statutory requirements and for budgetary reasons, the special representative was to be called officially "Deputy Commissioner," although he was not to be responsible for any operational activities, nor was he to act as Commissioner in the latter's absence. He was to function primarily as the Commissioner's representative and as liaison officer with the Legislature and with other agencies, both public and private. The executive assistant was to perform the usual duties of an administrative assistant. The public information officer was to carry on the customary functions of that office. Of these three

FIGURE 4:

RECOMMENDED ORGANIZATION, DEPARTMENT OF THE CALIFORNIA HIGHWAY PATROL

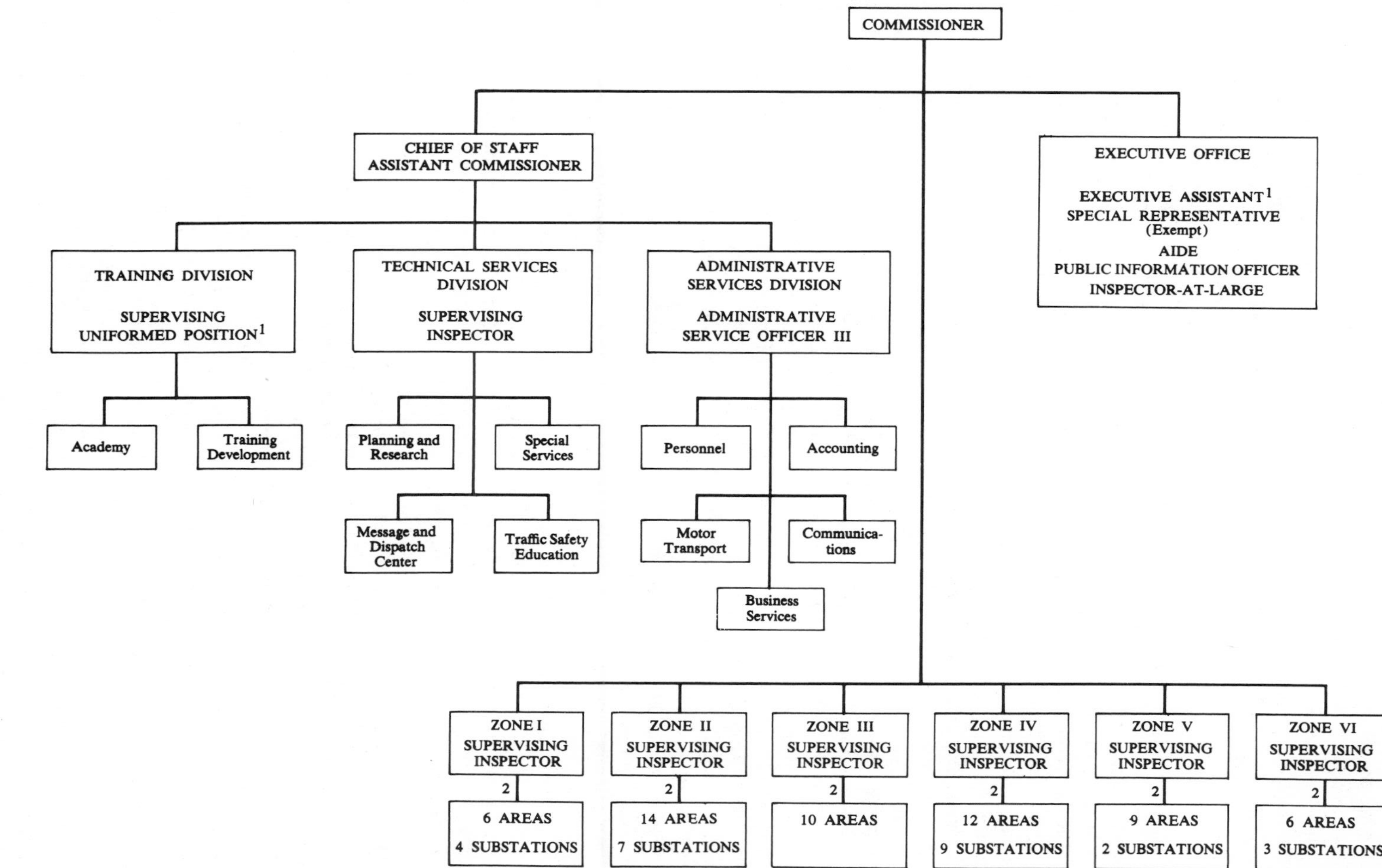

1 Classification to be determined by State Personnel Board

2 Number of Areas and Substations are those existing within proposed geographical zones. Area organization not within scope of study.

Organization and Cost Control Division
Department of Finance
January, 1960

aides who were to work directly under the Commissioner, only one, the Deputy Commissioner, was exempt from civil service appointment requirements. The other two were career employees. The reorganization thus did not increase the number of exempt positions.

Changes in Staff Functions

In 1959 commanders of staff and auxiliary services reported directly to the Commissioner. Farmer believed that if the Commissioner were to function effectively as the chief line officer of his organization, he had to be relieved of much of the work involved in directing and coordinating staff functions. At the same time, it was necessary to establish a position for an individual who could assume command in the Commissioner's absence, if the Deputy Commissioner's post was eliminated. The creation of a new position of chief of staff seemed to offer a solution to both problems. This officer, who would hold the civil service grade of Assistant Commissioner, would assume command of the Patrol in the Commissioner's absence, thus becoming second-in-command. Heads of staff and auxiliary services would report to him.

The transfer of the public information officer from the Technical Services Division was proposed to allow closer contact and control by the Commissioner in departmental news releases and other public relations activities. It also was intended to facilitate and expedite the handling of requests for information from various news-gathering agencies.

An important change was the creation of a third unit, a separate Division of Training. It would give increased status and influence to the training activity, and it was proposed on the assumption that increased decentralization would require increased training (and indoctrination) if decisions were to be consistent and predictable and if policies were to be carried out with uniformity.

Other staff and auxiliary functions were reorganized to some extent. Four sections of the Administrative Services Division—Facilities, Office Services, Equipment, and Supply—were to be combined into one section, Business Services, under the direction of a business services officer. This change was intended to reduce the span of attention of the commander of the division and to provide better coordination among the four sections concerned.

Proposals for Decentralization

One of the objectives of the reorganization was greater decentralization of decision-making to the field. Such decentralization was considered desirable for more expeditious disposal of problems, greater familiarity with local situations, and the improvement of relations with the public. It would also reduce the workload in the Commissioner's office. According to Farmer, ". . . decentralization is essential if the Patrol is to continue to function effectively in view of its expanding size and the increasing complexity of traffic enforcement."

A considerable number of activities formerly carried on in headquarters were to be delegated to the zone offices. A few examples of such delegation follow: most citizen complaints were to be investigated and disposition made in the zone where they originated; requests of patrol officers to engage in outside employment were to be decided at zone headquarters; approval for public appearances of officers representing the Patrol was to be given at zone level. In addition to such specifics, the Commissioner was to give zone commanders general authority to act on most matters except those involving policy decisions.

Elimination of the district commands meant that decisions formerly made at that level would have to be made either at zone headquarters or in the patrol areas. The assignment of automotive and motorcycle equipment and the supervision of scale and weight activities involving some sixty persons) were to be transferred to zone commands. In addition, some other former district functions, such as temporary assignment of personnel, policy clarifications, and legal interpretations, were assigned to the various zone commands. District functions of a more local character—coordination of "blood runs" (emergency transport of blood plasma), arrangement for motor vehicle repair, policing of local emergency situations resulting from floods, fires, storms, and the like—were to become the responsibility of the patrol area captains. Actually, some of the former district functions had already been transferred to the patrol areas during the years immediately preceding the reorganization. With the development of more effective radio and telephone communications, the increased personnel and responsibilities of the patrol areas, and the development of better trained and more capable patrol area commanders, the district offices had lost much of their *raison d'etre*.

The decentralization, then, was twofold—from

headquarters to the various zone commands, and from the districts to the patrol areas. In the process, however, some functions of the district offices were to be moved up to zone commands rather than down to the patrol areas. These exceptions notwithstanding, the overall effect of the reorganization would be increased delegation of responsibility to field commanders.

The reorganization planners recognized that real decentralization to the field would inevitably lead to inconsistencies in both policy and routine matters. They believed, however, that such tendencies would be more than counterbalanced by the elimination of three command levels, by improving the operations manual, by the establishment of field inspector positions at zone level, by increased emphasis on training, and by the systematized, lateral transfer of information among zones.

Relationships Between the Reorganization Proposals

The primary objectives of the reorganization, as stated in the Farmer report, were (1) to expedite communications and minimize the possibility of their distortion and misinterpretation; (2) to decentralize a considerable amount of decision-making to field offices; and (3) to improve the training program.[15] The principal *implicit* objective of the reorganization appears to have been to make the Commissioner, in fact, the operational director of the Patrol.

[15] Farmer's report stated: "A primary need . . . is to strengthen communications between the policy-making and execution levels of the Patrol.

"The growth of the department has brought out the need for increased decentralization of authority . . . to field commanders. Major field commanders should be delegated full responsibility, with corresponding authority, for final decision and action within established policy. . . . The proposed structure will facilitate the delegation of authority for decisions downward in the organization.

"The training and development of patrol employees plays such an important part in equipping the California Highway Patrol to perform as a progressive and effective traffic enforcement agency that divisional status is being recommended for this function. It is not intended merely to lift the present academy staff out of the Technical Services Division and call them a Training Division. The program . . . should encompass a much broader range . . . including, in addition to cadet training, the in-service training of non-uniformed traffic officers, supervisory and leadership training for supervisors and commanders . . . [and] the training of enforcement officers from other state agencies and local jurisdictions. . . ."

Happily for the reorganization effort, most of these objectives complemented each other. In fact, many of them could be effected by eliminating the positions of Deputy Commissioner, Commander of Field Operations, and District Commander. The removal of these three command levels was expected to accelerate the movement of communications and reduce the possibility of misinterpretation. According to Farmer, "The excessive number of command levels now existing between the traffic officer and the Commissioner has weakened communications between headquarters and the field. . . ." Elimination of the three command levels would also cause zone commanders to report directly to the Commissioner and tend to make him the actual chief line officer of the Patrol.

The abolition of the three command levels could not be undertaken without making other adjustments in the organizational structure. These necessary adjustments provided additional opportunities for advancing the objectives of the reorganization. If the Commissioner were to assume additional line functions, he would need to have more people on his personal staff and/or to be relieved of non-operational duties and routine operational functions. Both of these changes were incorporated in the reorganization plan. The Commissioner received additional personal staff; he was relieved of some responsibility for coordinating staff activities by the creation of the position of chief of staff; and routine operational functions were decentralized to the field. Decentralization would speed up the decision-making process and eliminate the need for much previous "communicating," but it also would increase the possibility of inconsistent behavior and tend to make field units more susceptible to local pressures. These tendencies were to be counteracted by the establishment of inspector positions at zone level and by increased emphasis on training and indoctrination through the creation of a new and separate training division. Also, subservience to local pressures was to be counteracted by shortening the command line.

The elimination of the district command level would increase the span of control of the zone commanders. Decentralization from headquarters to the field would add still other duties to the zone commander's office. To accommodate these additional responsibilities the number of zones was increased from three to six, so that the geographical area and total personnel assigned to each zone commander was cut approximately in half. Zone commanders were also to be assisted by the former district commanders, who would function as inspectors. (See Appendix III for a description of the proposed duties of field inspectors.) Increased emphasis on inspection would also counteract tendencies toward inconsistency and lack of uniformity. Roving inspectors would aid in keeping zone commanders better informed of activities in the field. Finally, the inspector positions provided an opportunity for utilizing the experience and leadership skills of the former district commanders.

Further decentralization to the field was accomplished by moving the point of decision from district down to patrol level.

"REDUCING THE COSTS OF CHANGE"

The Farmer reorganization proposals, as noted previously, were accepted, with minor modifications, by the Commissioner and the Senior Staff in September 1959. The next step became what has been called "the tactics of execution: reducing the costs of change."[16] During the next month the general reorganization plan was explained to headquarters personnel by the commanders of the three staff divisions and, in the field, by the three zone commanders. At this point, division and zone commanders were merely explaining and forewarning employees of a *fait accompli*.

The substantial reorganization set forth in the Farmer plan could not be accomplished overnight simply by the issuance of a general order. Personnel would be needed to fill the new staff positions in the Commissioner's office and in the three new zone commands. Personnel and equipment would have to be transferred from the original zones to new zones. Personnel, buildings, office equipment, and motor vehicles of the fourteen district offices would have to be disposed of in some manner. Functions and responsibilities of the various offices would have to be planned so that the sequence of changes would permit the transition to be accomplished with the least possible confusion and disruption of enforcement activities.

Primary responsibility for planning the change-over was given to inspectors D. S. Luethje and D. T. Donaldson. Luethje was a bureau commander at headquarters, and Donaldson—brought in from the field to work on this particular assignment—was a district commander in Stockton. Both men had experience in the Patrol in both staff and operational assignments and both were probably personally acquainted with several hundred patrol officers. Luethje was President of the California Association of Highway Patrolmen.[17]

During October and November 1959 Luethje and Donaldson devoted full time to planning the details of the change-over. This planning involved not only the procurement of detailed information and the making of decisions but also the drafting of new regulations, orders, personnel actions, and the like.

Personnel Actions

In effectuating the reorganization no one was separated from the Patrol; no one was reduced in grade; and few, if any, persons were transferred to another position or location against their wills. (See Appendix I for information about the position changes, education, and length of service of all executive officers involved in the reorganization.) Additional opportunities were opened for patrol officers by the creation of three new supervising inspector positions to be assigned to new zone commanders, and by the new positions of executive assistant to the Commissioner, assistant to the chief of staff and commander of the new Training Division. Assignments to these new, upper-level positions and the elimination of district offices started a chain reaction that resulted in over 100 personnel actions. Most of these reassignments were simply transfers in grade from the former district offices to zone or patrol area offices in the same locality. Other personnel actions were promotions or transfers to more desirable positions or locations. This aspect of the reorganization was considered to be

[16] From Herbert A. Simon, Donald W. Smithburg and Victor A. Thompson, *Public Administration* (New York: Alfred A. Knopf, 1950), p. 451.

[17] The California Association of Highway Patrolmen was established originally as a benevolent organization to secure benefits for the widows and children of deceased patrolmen. It later became interested in other matters, such as retirement pensions for patrolmen. The association has refrained so far from any attempts to influence departmental policy and was not involved in the reorganization in any way except that its president happened to be assigned to help plan details of the change-over.

crucial to the success of the plan. It is described below in detail.

Deputy Commissioner. This position was left vacant until July 1960. The vacancy forced zone commanders to break old habits of referring matters to the Deputy Commissioner and caused them to solve problems at the local level (an objective of decentralization) or to refer them directly to the Commissioner. Thus, the newly appointed Deputy Commissioner (in actuality the Commissioner's special representative) would not be plagued with operational problems but would be able to devote his time and energies to legislative liaison and other external affairs of the Patrol.[18] (It will be recalled that the Deputy Commissioner was "exempt" from civil service and was appointed by the Commissioner.)

Commander, Division of Field Operations. Prior to the reorganization, the Commander of the Field Operations Division was in charge of enforcement activities on the highways and directly supervised the three zone commanders. Fred Bly, the Field Operations Commander, also held the rank of Assistant Commissioner—the highest civil service grade in the Patrol. The potentially troublesome staffing problem created by the proposed replacement of the Field Operations Commander with a chief of staff was solved by the appointment of Assistant Commissioner Bly to the new position. No change in location or salary was involved, but, by relieving the Deputy Commissioner of operational responsibilities, the Assistant Commissioner (and new Chief of Staff) became the number two man in the Patrol. In the event of absence or disability of the Commissioner, the Assistant Commissioner (rather than the Deputy) now assumed command. A further difference was that the Assistant Commissioner assumed command only when the Commissioner was out of the state. Under the previous arrangement the Deputy Commissioner "took over" whenever the Commissioner was absent from the Sacramento headquarters. This change made the number two man considerably less important and influential than he had been in the past.

[18] Proposed duties of the Deputy Commissioner as outlined in the Farmer report were: "represents the Commissioner on matters of a special nature usually related to the external affairs of the department; represents the Commissioner before the Legislature and follows legislative activities which affect the department's program; prepares or reviews and recommends on traffic enforcement rules and regulations."

District Commands. The fourteen districts were eliminated in the reorganization plan. Their commanders, who held the rank of inspector, were all key men with many years of service in the Patrol. Commissioner Crittenden proceeded with great care in determining the new positions to which the fourteen inspectors might be assigned. (For details of the reassignments of the former district commanders, see Appendix IV.) Three new positions as zone commanders would be available under the new six-zone plan. Zone commanders carried the rank of supervising inspector—one step up from the rank of inspector. These new positions were filled by the three inspectors who received the highest scores in a promotion examination. (This examination consisted of a written test and an oral examination before a board composed of the Commissioner, an officer of the State Personnel Board, and a private citizen.)

The new zone commanders were D. J. O'Connell, H. G. Amborn, and A. F. Dillon. In all three cases the new assignment resulted in a change of location—but it was also a promotion. O'Connell had been a bureau commander in the Technical Services Division with headquarters in Sacramento. He was assigned to command Zone III in San Francisco. Amborn, who had been Commander of District 5 in Oakland, was assigned as Commander of Zone IV at Fresno. Dillon, former Inspector-at-large for the state (working from Sacramento headquarters) was assigned to be Commander of Zone I at Redding.

These new zone commanders could not object to the reorganization, because they had been promoted in the process. But two of them had come from headquarters, and only one (Amborn) had been promoted from the ranks of the now defunct district commanders. The other thirteen still had to be placed. A meeting of all patrol officers holding the rank of inspector was held in Los Angeles in October 1959. At this meeting Commissioner Crittenden explained the reorganization plan and the reasons for its adoption. He then conferred individually and privately with each inspector about the new assignment contemplated for him. In the course of these interviews each inspector was given the opportunity to voice objections and to suggest modifications or exceptions to his projected new assignment. These assignments were planned with the welfare and convenience of the inspectors and their families in mind. Transfers requiring a physical move from one city to another were avoided unless accompanied by a promotion or unless they were made at the request of the individual. Some inspectors were allowed to remain in their home cities even though their new assignments were in different, nearby cities. Others, nearing retirement, were given assignments that allowed them to continue in the same location until they were separated. In terms of position changes among the fourteen district commanders, the overall picture was as follows: one was promoted to zone commander and moved; three were promoted to senior positions in Sacramento and moved; the remaining ten were assigned as inspectors in the various zone headquarters, but none of these last required a change in residence. Salary rates remained unchanged for those inspectors who were not promoted.

Administrative personnel and traffic officers employed in the former district offices were reassigned in grade to zone or patrol area offices in the same locality or were allowed to transfer if they so desired and if an opening was available in another office.

All reassignments were thus accomplished without requiring any change in residence except for those persons who received promotions or were transferred to another location at their own request. Some of the "promotions" were admittedly in title only and did not result in increased pay or rank, but no one involved in the reorganization suffered any decrease in pay or reduction in rank.

The reorganization had no direct effect on the traffic officers patrolling the highways. Sergeants and lieutenants in some cases were asked to assume new responsibilities as a consequence of the transfer of some former district functions to the patrol areas.

Since the reorganization was accomplished without the need for any statutory changes, the possibility of controversy in the Legislature was minimized. No budget revisions or additional appropriations were required. The new zone commander positions were created at higher salary rates, but this small additional expenditure was offset during the first year by applying unused personnel appropriations resulting from normal economics unrelated to the reorganization. Revisions in class specifications (job descriptions) of the positions of Assistant Commissioner, supervising traffic inspector, and state traffic inspector were accepted by the State Personnel Board.

In the process of planning the reorganization, particular attention was given to the personalities and abilities of the individuals whose duties would be changed or who would occupy new positions. The Patrol was a relatively small, stable, career service; its administrators had to work with the personnel they had.

THE ATTAINMENT OF OBJECTIVES

The degree of improvement in speed and clarity of communications was difficult to evaluate. It was assumed from the beginning that improvement in communications could best be accomplished by improvement in organization. The leaders of the reorganization expected that the elimination of three command levels would speed up communications and lessen opportunities for misinterpretation, although the shortening of vertical communications channels might cause lengthened horizontal communications because of extended span of control.

Decentralization moves did eliminate the need for a considerable amount of communicating. Members of the Patrol generally felt that the communications system was much improved. Field commanders, especially patrol area captains, appeared to be convinced of the improved efficacy of communications in the reorganized Patrol. According to one captain, "Communications from headquarters used to go through a routine that was almost like the parlor game of Gossip, with some of the weirdest interpretations coming out at the end. Now we're only one step from the Commissioner, so we usually get it straight."

Another patrol captain said, "I think communications not only move faster and with less garbling than in the past but they don't get 'short-stopped' along the way."

A third patrol captain summed it up this way:

> Communications undoubtedly move faster than before, but the important thing is that we have been delegated more authority, so we don't have to get clearance on as many things. After all, a large part of our work is of an emergency nature, so if we have to ask somebody what to do, and then wait for an answer, it's often too late. When we do need a decision we can usually get it from

Zone [headquarters] because they also have more authority than they had in the past.

Decentralization

The objective of decentralization to the field was partially successful. However, it appears that only partial decentralization was intended. Zone commanders had authority to make decisions on nonpolicy matters, and a considerable amount of work was decentralized to the field.

Some commanders accepted this delegation of authority rather fully and others to a lesser degree. After years of reliance on headquarters for decisions, it was difficult for commanders to change habits of thinking and action overnight, regardless of stated policy. Furthermore, some field commanders were not quite sure what the Commissioner meant by "policy decisions," so they tended to feel their way rather cautiously. The actual amount of decentralization accomplished was somewhat dependent upon the personalities and experience of the various zone commanders.

If only partial decentralization was the original objective, this phase of the reorganization appeared to have been successful. As zone commanders became better acquainted with their new responsibilities and with the expectations of the Commissioner, and as the Commissioner became more familiar with the problems of his office and the personalities of his line commanders, it was anticipated that some of the uncertainties of role and responsibility would tend to disappear.

The decentralization of some of the former district responsibilities to the patrol areas at least improved the morale of the patrol area commanders. In the words of one captain, "Most of us feel pretty capable of running our own organization."

> If we're not, we should be, and they'll find it out quicker this way. Anyway, a lot of the stuff we formerly had to clear with District was strictly routine that we should be able to handle ourselves. Then other times we probably tried to second-guess the District Commander rather than decide on the merits of the case. It's a whole lot better this way.

Furthermore, area captains did not find it as convenient to "buck" difficult decisions to the more remote zone commander as they once had to the district commanders.

Patrol area commanders insisted that they had no more hesitation about contacting the zone commander than they had formerly had about consulting the district commander. The frequency of such contacts depended to some extent on the personalities involved. However, there were now fewer occasions on which consultation with a superior officer was necessary. When such a contact was necessary, the patrol area commander could be certain of reaching the zone commander or an inspector authorized to act for him. Under the old organization, district commanders frequently had been absent on field trips and not immediately accessible.

The influence of decentralization on the overall effectiveness of the Patrol could not yet be determined at the time this study was written. It was possible, however, that the zone commanders' span of control had been expanded beyond the point of maximum effectiveness. The possibility also existed that some patrol area commanders might be unable or unwilling to accept their new responsibilities.

Musical Chairs

A bonus benefit of the reorganization was the elimination of a kind of "musical chairs" sequence that occurred whenever a commander was temporarily absent from his assigned duty station. A commander's position could become temporarily vacant because of illness, vacation, assignment to special boards, or other temporary duty. When such a vacancy occurred, an officer in the next lower rank moved up in an "acting" status. He, in turn, was replaced by another officer also in an acting status. When the temporary vacancy occurred in one of the higher command levels, as many as four or five acting positions could be created by one absence. When this happened, presumably, each such position was conducted at a reduced level of efficiency because of lack of knowledge and experience. Certainly, acting incumbents could be expected to postpone difficult or disagreeable decisions if it were possible to do so. Furthermore, when the acting officer returned to his assigned position he would be disoriented and suffer a loss in momentum. Such disruptions and dislocations frequently involved separations from families and familiar surroundings with a consequent diminution of morale and effectiveness.

This problem of musical chairs was solved in the reorganization plan by the establishment of assistant or "back-up" positions at each command level (the number of command levels was also reduced).

The Assistant Commissioner (and Chief of Staff) functioned in the absence of the Commissioner. A zone inspector assumed the position of a zone commander in the latter's absence. A lieutenant acted as patrol area commander in the captain's absence.[19] Not only was the "escalator" movement of personnel eliminated, but the persons who now assumed temporary command were already familiar with the office and thus able to act more effectively. Furthermore, such assumptions of command could be accomplished instantaneously, a factor that could be of vital importance in an emergency situation.

Counteraction of Splintering Tendencies

An early fear that real decentralization would result in six different highway patrols did not materialize. Such splintering tendencies were prevented by employing several countervailing techniques. The assignment of the new zone commanders to localities other than those in which they had served previously, and the statewide orientation of these particular men, acted to limit the growth of "independent" patrol zones. Of the three original zone commanders, J. R. King was transferred from San Francisco to head the new San Diego Zone. M. L. Hewitt, Commander of the old Valley Zone, remained in the same office to command the new Sacramento Zone. He had spent considerable time in Patrol headquarters, however, and appeared to be headquarters-oriented. Probably the only zone that showed any indications of splintering tendencies was the Los Angeles Zone, commanded by R. E. Fuson—one of the commanders of the three original zones. The Los Angeles Zone had, of course, the largest complement of personnel and had more special problems than the others.[20]

Splintering tendencies were also counteracted by the shortened command line which put zone commanders closer to the Commissioner, by the assumption of direct operational responsibilities by the Commissioner, and by the use of such specific devices as the circulation of weekly reports to all zone commanders.

The increased emphasis on training and inspection was expected ultimately to minimize the centrifugal forces of decentralization, but this effect had not yet become noticeable.

Training

One of the stated objectives of the reorganization was improvement of the training program. Newly appointed traffic officers continued to undergo a three-month training period at the Patrol Academy in Sacramento before being assigned to patrol duties. Some officers could also return to the Academy for short in-service training courses. This latter program operated on a rather haphazard basis, with reference to both time and selection of officer-students, because of space limitations at the Patrol Academy. Establishment of a more orderly program was anticipated whereby all Patrol officers would return to the Patrol Academy periodically, and in rotation, for updating and upgrading training. Training of non-Patrol officers, i.e., local traffic policemen and sheriff's deputies, was also to receive additional emphasis. Tangible improvement in the training programs was yet to be accomplished, because of budgetary limitations. The success of the envisioned training activity depended, in large part, on the willingness of the Legislature to provide the necessary funds.

In addition to formal training, Commissioner Crittenden intended to promote "informal" training wherever feasible by the rotation of personnel into different kinds of duty assignments. Such a policy, of course, faced the difficulties of personal adjustments, work redistribution, loss of momentum, and loss of specialized skills. An organized cross-training program was, therefore, practical for only a few selected individuals with particular interests and aptitudes. So far, no formal program of cross-training has been established.

Reassignment

The reorganization required the reassignment of the former district commanders. All except one were removed from positions of line authority and were given staff or inspector positions. Formal reassignment did not entirely eliminate this group from command functions. Persons accustomed to

---

19 This last provision was in operation before the reorganization.

20 Assignment of uniformed personnel to the various zones on November 1, 1960 was:

ZONE		
I	Redding	148
II	Sacramento	396
III	San Francisco	534
IV	Fresno	457
V	Los Angeles	677
VI	San Diego	346

giving orders probably continued to do so, and persons accustomed to taking orders from a particular individual probably continued to do so. Nevertheless, the opportunities for issuing orders were reduced drastically. This facet of the reorganization could be considered successful in that key personnel were moved without any appreciable political repercussions or internal disturbances. The reassignment was, in some cases, a severe blow to morale, because the individual was deprived of his command even though he did not suffer any reduction in pay or rank. Furthermore, persons with years of command experience were not likely to become competent inspectors overnight—especially if their new duties were thrust upon them somewhat against their will. The possibility that some former commanders might consider the inspection function inappropriate for their particular talents and a waste of manpower was anticipated and considered to be one of the unavoidable costs of change. With the passage of time, some of the newly appointed inspectors were expected to adjust to the situation and become effective inspectors, while others might become executive officers for the various zone commanders. The eventual retirement of older, and possibly more rigid, inspectors, and their replacement by younger men for whom inspection duties would also mean a promotion, would, it was hoped, result in a more effective inspection program. The new inspector positions were not created to provide jobs for the former district commanders, but they did provide an opportunity to utilize the skills and experience of these officers. Abolition of the districts and the consequent increase in the zone commander's responsibilities made it essential that he be given additional staff assistance. This aid was provided, in part, by the new inspector positions.

Changes at the Top

One obvious result of the interposition of the new Chief of Staff was that commanders of staff divisions were moved one step away from the Commissioner. One reaction to this change within the Patrol was that, in assuming line responsibilities, the Commissioner might have put too great a distance between himself and vital staff functions.[21] The success of this arrangement would depend largely upon the effectiveness, judgment, and loyalty of the Chief of Staff.

Lastly, it is evident that the Commissioner became, in fact, the chief line officer of the Patrol. The appointment of a Deputy Commissioner in July 1960 to handle the external affairs of the Patrol was expected to lighten the Commissioner's load. In many situations, however, the statement or appearance of the Deputy would not suffice. Individuals and groups frequently insisted that their problems receive the personal attention of the Commissioner. So, while the Commissioner had attained his objective of becoming chief line officer of the Patrol, he might find that the demands of the public are so exacting as to make it physically impossible for him to discharge effectively the operational responsibilities he had now acquired.[22]

After one year of operation, the reorganization appeared to have been a qualified success in accomplishing the objectives of its protagonists. This success could be attributed to a clear understanding of reorganization objectives; a reorganization plan that considered the secondary effects of projected initial changes; detailed planning of the changeover so as to minimize the "costs of change"; the energetic support of the Commissioner; a political climate favorable to change; and the cooperation of loyal and disciplined personnel who accepted changes, not always to their personal liking, for the good of the California Highway Patrol.

---

[21] According to one former official, "This type of organization has the effect of having two heads—one directing enforcement activities and the other directing auxiliary and support functions."

[22] Crittenden noted that this possibility was recognized at the time of the reorganization; it was then decided that such problems might be alleviated by temporary additions to the Commissioner's personal staff.

APPENDIX I

EXECUTIVE OFFICERS INVOLVED IN THE REORGANIZATION OF THE CALIFORNIA HIGHWAY PATROL

Name	*Rank*	*Position* BEFORE	*Position* AFTER	*Education*	*Date of entry into patrol*
Crittenden, B. M.	Commissioner	Commissioner	Commissioner	A.B., LL.B.	1959
Bly, Fred	Asst. Commissioner	Commander, Field Operations Div.	Chief of Staff	2 years college	1925
Duryea, H. A.	Supervising Inspector	Commander, Tech. Services Div.	Commander, Tech. Services Div.	1 year college	1930
Fuson, R. E.	Supervising Inspector	Zone Commander, Los Angeles	Zone Commander, Los Angeles	1 year college	1932
Hewitt, M. L.	Supervising Inspector	Zone Commander, Sacramento	Zone Commander, Sacramento	3 years college	1930
King, J. R.	Supervising Inspector	Zone Commander, San Francisco	Zone Commander, San Diego	3 years college	1927
Amborn, H. G.	Supervising Inspector*	District Commander, Oakland	Zone Commander, Fresno	1 year college	1936
Dillon, A. F.	Supervising Inspector*	State Inspector-at-large	Zone Commander, Redding	High school	1937
O'Connell, D. J.	Supervising Inspector*	Bureau Commander, Tech. Services Div.	Zone Commander, San Francisco	3 years college	1941
Cassell, E. F.	Inspector	District Commander, Sacramento	Inspector, Sacramento	High school	1927
Donaldson, D. T.	Inspector	District Commander, Stockton	Assistant to Chief of Staff	3 years college	1936
Eagan, C. L.	Inspector	District Commander, Ukiah	Inspector, Redding	High school	1937
Ellis, O. H.	Inspector	District Commander, Santa Barbara	Inspector, Fresno	3 years college	1930
Hastings, A. R.	Inspector	District Commander, Bakersfield	Inspector, Fresno	High school	1925
Kridler, R. A.	Inspector	District Commander, Los Angeles	Inspector, Los Angeles	A.B.	1936
LaTourette, J. H.	Inspector	District Commander, San Diego	Inspector, San Diego	3 years high school	1928
Leber, F. A.	Inspector	District Commander, Richmond	Inspector, San Francisco	Elementary school	1921
Luethje, D. S.	Inspector	Bureau Commander, Tech. Serv. Div.	Exec. Asst. to Commissioner	2 years college	1941
Murray, J. J.	Inspector	District Commander, Redding	State Inspector-at-large	High school	1929
Null, H. W.	Inspector	District Commander, Los Angeles	Commander, Training Div.	High school	1941

APPENDIX I—*Cont.*

Name	*Rank*	*Position* BEFORE	*Position* AFTER	*Education*	*Date of entry into patrol*
Page, G. E.	Inspector	District Commander, San Bernardino	Inspector, Los Angeles	1 year high school	1927
Porter, K. E.	Inspector	District Commander, Fresno	Inspector, Sacramento	1 year college	1940
Sequeira, W.	Inspector	District Commander, San Francisco	Inspector, San Francisco	2 years college	1934

* Promoted from Inspector to Supervising Inspector

APPENDIX II
Department of
CALIFORNIA HIGHWAY PATROL
HEADQUARTERS GENERAL ORDER 110.1

To: ALL MEMBERS AND EMPLOYEES, CALIFORNIA HIGHWAY PATROL
Re: ORGANIZATION OF THE DEPARTMENT OF CALIFORNIA HIGHWAY PATROL

Effective June 8, 1960, this order supersedes and cancels HGO 110.1 dated December 2, 1959, and Annex A dated December 2, 1959.

A. EXECUTIVE

1. The California Highway Patrol is a Department of State government administered by a civil executive officer titled Commissioner.
2. There is an executive office consisting of a Deputy Commissioner, Executive Assistant, Assistant to the Commissioner, Public Information Officer, Inspector-at-Large and supporting staff. This office provides certain internal and external staff functions for the Commissioner.

B. ORGANIZATION

1. To provide for effective administration and control, the Department of California Highway Patrol is divided into the following Zones and Divisions as indicated in Annex A attached.
   a. *Zones*
      (1) The State of California is divided into six (6) Zones, each under the control of a Supervising Inspector, who is directly accountable to and supervised by the Commissioner.
         (a) To provide for effective administration of the Zone, State Traffic Inspectors are assigned, depending upon the size and complexity of operation in the Zone.
      (2) The Zones are comprised of geographical commands designated as Areas as follows:

ZONE I	ZONE II	ZONE III
Crescent City	Ukiah	Santa Rosa
Eureka	Oroville	Concord
Yreka	Williams	Napa
Red Bluff	Grass Valley	Vallejo
Redding	Yuba City	San Leandro
Susanville	Placerville	San Rafael
	San Andreas	San Jose
	Auburn	San Francisco
	Sacramento	Santa Cruz
	Woodland	Redwood City
	Bridgeport	
	Stockton	
	Modesto	
	Sonora	

ZONE IV	ZONE V	ZONE VI
Hollister	Ventura	Barstow
Salinas	Compton	Riverside
San Luis Obispo	Newhall	San Bernardino
Santa Barbara	W. Los Angeles	Indio
Visalia	Baldwin Park	El Centro
Bakersfield	E. Los Angeles	San Diego
Merced	Norwalk	
Mariposa	Pomona	
Madera	Anaheim	
Fresno	Lancaster	
Hanford		
Bishop		

APPENDIX II—*Cont.*

(3) Each Area Commander is accountable to and under the direct supervision of the appropriate Zone Commander.

b. *Chief of Staff*

(1) There is an Assistant Commissioner who is the Chief of Staff and is immediately subordinate to and under the direct supervision of the Commissioner. The primary function of the Chief of Staff is to act as chief advisor to the Commissioner and to direct and coordinate the general staff and field support activities of Headquarters. He will act as Commander of the Department in the absence of the Commissioner.

(a) The Chief of Staff is assisted by an Assistant to the Chief of Staff.

c. *Training Division*

(1) The Training Division is under the control of a Division Commander (Inspector) who is under the direct supervision of the Chief of Staff.

(2) The Division is composed of the following Subdivisions, the Commanders of which are under the direct supervision of the Training Division Commander.

(a) Academy

(b) Training Development Section

d. *Technical Services Division*

(1) The Technical Services Division is under the control of a Division Commander (Supervising Inspector) who is under the direct supervision of the Chief of Staff.

(2) The Division is composed of the following Subdivisions, the Commanders of which are under the direct supervision of the Technical Services Division Commander.

(a) Planning and Research Section

(b) Special Services Section

(c) Message and Dispatch Center

(d) Traffic Safety Education Section

e. *Administrative Services Division*

(1) The Administrative Services Division is under the control of an Administrative Services Officer III, who is under the direct supervision of the Chief of Staff.

(2) The Division is composed of the following Subdivisions, the Commanders of which are under the direct supervision of the Administrative Services Officer.

(a) Accounting Section

(b) Personnel Section

(c) Motor Transport Section

–1– Sacramento Automotive Shop

–2– Los Angeles Automotive Shop, which is under the direct supervision and control of the Zone V Central Services Officer, with functional supervision from the Motor Transport Section.

(d) Communications Section

(e) Facilities Section

(f) Stores and Equipment Section

(g) Office Services Section

BRADFORD M. CRITTENDEN
Commissioner

Sacramento, California
June 8, 1960

APPENDIX III

PROPOSED DUTIES OF FIELD INSPECTOR

I. *Function*

As a line assistant to the Zone Commander, the Field Inspector is charged with keeping the Zone Commander informed as to the status of field operations and with advising and assisting Area Commanders on operating problems.

II. *Duties*

A. Conducts authoritative inspection of personnel, material, procedures, and results of operations.

APPENDIX III—*Cont.*

B. Informs the Zone Commander of any unsatisfactory conditions within his area of jurisdiction which affect the following:
   1. Morale of personnel.
   2. Use or maintenance of equipment.
   3. Public reaction to departmental policies, methods or employees.
   4. Operational efficiency of units.
   5. Compliance with departmental rules and regulations.
   6. Supervision and training of personnel.
   7. Actions of employees.
   8. Adequacy of facilities and equipment.

C. Maintains satisfactory relationships with unit commanders, employees, and local law enforcement agencies.

D. Advises and assists Area Commanders in the management of their units.

E. Assists the Zone Commander in coordinating patrol activities in the zone.

F. Takes immediate corrective action when the situation demands.

G. Recommends to the Zone Commander on organization, policy, procedures and assignment of personnel and equipment when correction is needed.

H. Acts in the absence of the Zone Commander or when otherwise directed to do so.

APPENDIX IV

REASSIGNMENT OF FORMER DISTRICT COMMANDERS

The post of State Inspector-at-large, vacated by A. F. Dillon, was filled by the appointment of the former District 2 (Redding) Commander, J. J. Murray. Appointment as State Inspector-at-large was considered to be a position of greater prestige than district commander even though it did not involve any increase in pay or rank.

H. W. Null, former Commander of District 11 in Los Angeles and the junior inspector in the Patrol, became Commander of the newly established Training Division in Sacramento.

D. T. Donaldson, former District Commander at Stockton, became Assistant to the Chief of Staff in the Sacramento headquarters.

D. S. Luethje, Bureau Commander in the Technical Services Division in headquarters, was appointed Executive Assistant to the Commissioner.

The remaining former district commanders were reassigned to the new zone inspector positions.

E. F. Cassell had been a District Commander in Sacramento. He was reassigned as an inspector in the Sacramento Zone headquarters. The change in assignment thus did not involve any change in location.

K. E. Porter had been a patrol captain in Sacramento before being promoted to District Commander in Fresno. During his Fresno assignment Porter had maintained his home and family in Sacramento. He was reassigned as a second inspector in the Sacramento Zone office.

Walter Sequeira, District Commander at San Francisco, was reassigned as inspector in San Francisco.

Fred Leber, District Commander at Richmond, was reassigned as inspector in the San Francisco Zone. At the time of the reorganization Leber had approximately one year left before retirement. His new assignment did not involve any change in residence.

C. L. Eagan, District 1 Commander, with a home in Santa Rosa, was reassigned as inspector in the Redding Zone but continued to maintain his residence in Santa Rosa in anticipation of the retirement of Fred Leber and subsequent transfer to the San Francisco Zone to take Leber's place.

C. H. Ellis, District Commander at Santa Barbara, was reassigned as inspector in the Fresno Zone but continued to maintain his residence in Santa Barbara.

A. R. Hastings, District Commander at Bakersfield, was reassigned as inspector in the Fresno Zone. Hastings was scheduled to retire in June 1960 and continued his residence in Bakersfield.

R. A. Kridler, District Commander at Los Angeles, was reassigned as inspector in the Los Angeles Zone.

G. E. Page, District Commander at San Bernardino, was reassigned as inspector to the Los Angeles Zone but continued his residence in San Bernardino.

J. H. LaTourette, District Commander at San Diego, became zone inspector in San Diego.

B. AGENCIES ENGAGED IN RESEARCH, DEVELOPMENT, OR EDUCATION

EVELYN GLATT

The Demise of the Ballistics Division

EVELYN GLATT

The author of *The Demise of the Ballistics Division* received a Ph.D. degree from the Case Institute of Technology. She is a social science analyst employed by an agency of the U. S. government.

CHRONOLOGY OF KEY EVENTS

Early 1946	Formation of Ballistics Division
December 1947	Restatement of the responsibilities of Ballistics Division by Research Board
1948	PHENIX project begins (*subrosa*)
Summer 1949	First review of Laboratory operations by team from Harvard School of Business Administration
March 1950	Ballistics Committee appointed by Research Board to review the ballistics function
May 1950	Submission of Ballistics Committee report to Research Board
Summer 1950	Korean War begins
Late 1950	Dr. Lindberg becomes head of Ballistics Division
Summer 1951	Second review of Laboratory operations by team from Harvard School of Business Administration
Late 1951	Dr. Thomas, Technical Director, resigns; Dr. Black becomes new Technical Director
1952	Aeromechanics Branch is established in Aviation Ordnance Department; Lee Jackson leaves Ballistics Division to become its first Branch Head
1952-1953	Committee is appointed to study Research Department and make report to Research Board; study of Ballistics Division is included
Late 1953	Laboratory Advisory Board commends program of Ballistics Division
Mid-1954	Dr. Black resigns as Technical Director; he is succeeded by Dr. Mackay, formerly head, Aviation Ordnance Department
Early 1955	Dr. Lindberg is promoted from his position as head of Ballistics Division to become head of Test Department
Summer 1955	Dr. Henderson becomes head of Ballistics Division
Late 1955	PHENIX is announced as operational weapon
January 1956	Dr. Warner becomes head of Weapons Development Department
December 1956	Dr. Warner establishes Aeromechanics Division in Weapons Development Department
Spring 1957	Lee Jackson and personnel of Aeromechanics Branch in Aviation Ordnance Department transfer to Aeromechanics Division, Weapons Development Department; Leroy Reed joins Aeromechanics Division
April 1958	Dr. Warner is appointed head of Research Department and Assistant Technical Director for Research; Warner issues informal paper explaining his viewpoints on role of Research Department in Laboratory
May 1958	Ballistics Division is reassigned from Research Department to Weapons Development Department and becomes part of Aeromechanics Division
March 1959	Letters of "unsatisfactory performance" are issued to seven professional personnel of Aeromechanics Division

PRINCIPAL CHARACTERS

Note: All names have been changed to preserve anonymity.

Dr. R. S. Benson, Head of Ballistics Division, 1946-1950

Dr. W. C. Black, Laboratory Technical Director, 1951-1954

Dr. F. N. Henderson, Head of Ballistics Division, 1955-1958

Lee Jackson, Head of Aeromechanics Division, 1958—

Dr. Karl Lindberg, Head of Ballistics Division, 1951-1955

Dr. J. F. Mackay, Laboratory Technical Director, 1954—

Dr. C. A. Molnari, Physicist, Ballistics Division, 1946-1947

Leroy Reed, Assistant Head of Aeromechanics Division, 1959—

Dr. R. E. Sherman, Head of Research Department, 1948-1958

Dr. J. E. Thomas, Laboratory Technical Director until Fall 1951

Dr. G. B. Warner, Head of Weapons Development Department, 1956-1958; Head of Research Department, 1958-1959

THE SETTING

Introduction

The federal government, within its executive branch, maintains a substantial number of scientific and technical laboratories engaged in a wide variety of efforts ranging from agricultural research to research on, and development of, weapons systems. Government laboratories are an integral part of the established civil service system, and they function in areas also engaged in by universities and private industrial organizations. Although government agencies contract for a large share of scientific research and development services with universities, industry, and a variety of private nonprofit laboratories, most maintain some in-house capabilities for accomplishing their respective missions. The extent of use of in-house laboratories varies widely from agency to agency.

In this study we examine a small segment of one such government laboratory, a field activity of one of the military services in the Department of Defense. The Laboratory itself is one of several similar technically autonomous activities functioning in various parts of the country. Its mission is a small part of the total national defense effort, and its functions primarily support only one of the three military services of the Defense establishment. The Laboratory's military and civilian complement includes persons with a wide variety of scientific and technical skills—physicists, engineers, chemists, mathematicians, to mention a few.

The Laboratory has more than 4,000 civilian employees, of whom some twenty-five percent are professional scientists and engineers. It also employs supporting personnel representing almost every occupational category within the Department of Defense.

As an integral part of the nation's defense effort, the Laboratory engages in a wide spectrum of activities applicable to its basic mission—research, development, test, pilot production, and evaluation of weapons components and weapons systems. Over the years it has concerned itself with a variety of weapons technologies, including work on rockets, guided missiles, fire-control systems, and a number of other related areas. In pursuit of its mission, the Laboratory has also been concerned with basic and applied research in physics, chemistry, mathematics, and other disciplines, particularly as those relate to its weapons development responsibilities.

A major portion of the research program has fallen between the applied and the basic, comprising, as this area is defined in local Laboratory terminology, "exploratory" and "foundational" research. In recent years development programs have provided the major focus of effort; research, test, pilot production, and evaluation, with some exceptions, occupy supporting roles. None of the terms involved can be defined to everyone's satisfaction. Appendix I provides a partial definitional framework generally accepted within the Laboratory and most applicable to that portion of the organization with which this study concerns itself; also, in Figure 1 a schematized diagram of these definitions can be seen.

The Laboratory organization is difficult to characterize. Under the Technical Director, a civilian scientist who manages the entire technical effort, there were usually (during the period of this study)

FIGURE 1:
STAGES OF RESEARCH—FROM "PURE" TO "APPLIED"

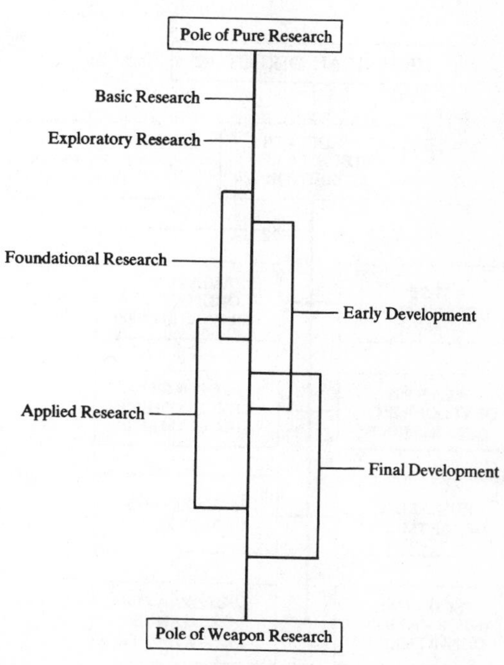

eight scientific and technical departments. As research and development laboratories usually are, this one too is a hybrid—partly functional, partly project, and partly a combination of both types. Functional organizations are basically of two kinds. Some are collections of specialists working in well-defined areas of specialization such as mathematics, atmospheric physics, and guidance and control. These groups may or may not be interdisciplinary, depending upon the area of specialization. Other functional groups are concerned with broad areas of operation such as test, engineering, and evaluation. The project-oriented group, on the other hand, is organized to solve a specific problem—the development of a rocket, for example. It includes most of the necessary skills in requisite numbers to carry the burden of the project at least through the development stages. If, as often happened, the project-oriented group required additional, specialized knowledge or test data that its own personnel did not possess, two courses of action were open to its personnel. They could turn to the specialists in the functional units in the Research Department or elsewhere, or they could recruit such persons and employ them in their own project units. Just what

FIGURE 2:
BASIC STRUCTURE OF TECHNICAL AND SCIENTIFIC PORTION OF LABORATORY—1960

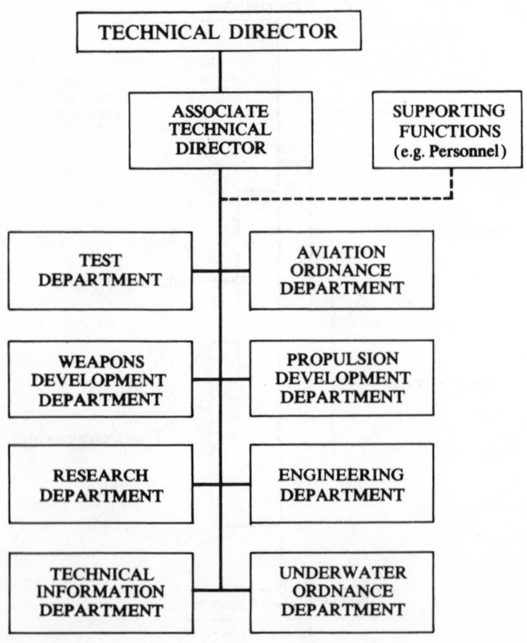

the project group encompasses depends upon the particular circumstances of the project and on the individual desires of the project manager.

Although the names, components, and sizes of the technical organizations have varied widely over the years, the broad spectrum of activity and the several patterns of organization have existed from the beginning. Each department is subdivided into divisions, and the divisions into branches; each level also represents mixtures of functional and project-oriented groups. The departments vary in size; the Research Department has traditionally been one of the smallest of the technical and scientific organizations. Figure 2 shows the current organization of the scientific and technical portion of the Laboratory.

A major problem for the Laboratory was maintaining smooth, productive relationships between functional and project-oriented units. Project men working on the problems of developing a new guided missile, for example, felt that functional units should give priority to their requests for special data; typically, they wanted quick answers to specific problems directly connected with their projects. Some scientists in functional units—particularly those in the Research Department—felt that their fundamental research studies were more important in the long run. Sometimes they regarded requests from project units as requests for too-precise answers in too short a period of time. Project men, on the other hand, were inclined to be impatient with functional units for not sharing their sense of urgency and their project-orientation and for not producing precise answers. Moreover, project men were inclined to feel reservations about the relevance and value of scientists doing fundamental research (more or less for its own sake) in a government laboratory with an important weapons development mission.

Controversies and discussions about the balance between research and development and about priorities that should be accorded functional or project-oriented units were an integral part of the process of defining the role and goals of a government research-and-development laboratory that existed to serve the nation's defense effort. They took place against a background of rapid changes in science and technology, national defense interests, and shifts of mood in Washington. They persisted because it was virtually impossible to determine the comparative long-run values of the contributions of scientists and engineers in such a variety of specialties and project areas. The technological issues are often complex and are frequently obscured by the issues of interpersonal relationships which are as much in evidence in a scientific laboratory as they are in any other human organization. There are frequently as many interpretations and conflicting views on issues of technology as there are on goals and organization. Controversies persisted also because of the freedom given to senior scientists and engineers. It was appreciated by the Technical Director and the department heads that these men needed scope if they were to be productive and, more important, if they were to be retained in government service. With its civil service pay scales, the government had to compete with universities and private industry for increasingly scarce scientific and engineering talent. The inducements that the Laboratory could offer, apart from the opportunity to work for national security, were an extensive assortment of scientific equipment and an organizational atmosphere of security and toleration. The managerial climate reflected these considerations.

The segment of the Laboratory that is the focus of this study played a small but significant role in the continuous efforts to redefine and redirect programs during a period of rapid change in technology, in technical and scientific goals, and in personalities both within and without the Laboratory.

The Ballistics Division Is Formed

This story describes the dissolution of the Ballistics Division and the steps that led to the transfer of its personnel from the Research Department in 1958. The Laboratory itself had been established late in 1944 to carry out an important wartime mission of research, development, testing, and evaluation of rockets. Emerging from the hectic pressures of the war to consider what its peacetime role should be, the Laboratory entered a period of expansion and continual reorganization, all to the accompaniment of heavy turnover in scientific personnel. Between 1945 and 1947 there was scarcely time to reduce the organizational picture to paper before further major changes took place.

The Research Board (organized during this period) played a key role in the early organization and division of work within the Laboratory. Composed of the Technical Director (as chairman) and the heads of the technical departments, the Board became the chief policy advisory group to the Technical Director. From a three-member board at its first meeting, it grew as the number of technical departments increased. In the early period of the Laboratory's development, the Research Board met at least weekly and often daily to discuss and make recommendations on problems of space requirements, organization, recruitment, funds, projects, and other areas of concern to the rapidly expanding laboratory complex. The first Technical Director, Dr. Thomas, brought his urgent problems to the Board, which gave them a thorough and sometimes explosive airing. Controversial issues were considered at a fast pace; personalities clashed and compromised (though not always) under the astute direction of Dr. Thomas. It was into this arena that the prospective organization of the Ballistics Division was introduced in an early period in the Laboratory's development.

The Technical Director and the Research Board were faced with one leaderless department in early 1946 because of the last-minute failure of a prospective department head to accept the position. Something had to be done about the headless department, which included, among other units, the whole ballistics group, consisting of about fifty persons. Without any apparent plan in mind, the department was abolished; its various sections were divided up and placed in other departments for what was called "an indefinite period of six months or more." The Research Board made no subsequent review of its "indefinite" decision.

As a result of this reshuffling, the ballistics group was moved into the Research Department and combined with the aerodynamics group already there, to form the Ballistics Division. The relationship between the two functions made this seem a reasonable move. Other reasonable alternatives also were considered, including placing the ballistics group in the Experimental Operations Department, which contained most of the test functions and operated the ranges where ballistic data were obtained. However, Dr. Molnari, who then headed the ballistics group, was opposed to its placement in the Experimental Operations Department for various reasons including a personality conflict between himself and the department head. The combination of ballistics and aerodynamics was, therefore, a compromise rationalized by functional considerations but, in part, carried out to keep peace in the organization family.

The newly created Ballistics Division consisted of sixty-five employees, including the aerodynamicists. About three-fourths of the division's personnel, throughout its life, were professional scientists and engineers. The remainder included subprofessionals, technicians, clerical personnel, and occasional journeymen. The ballistics men tended to be physicists and mathematicians by background; the aerodynamicists more often had engineering training.

FIGURE 3:
FORMATION OF THE BALLISTICS DIVISION—1946

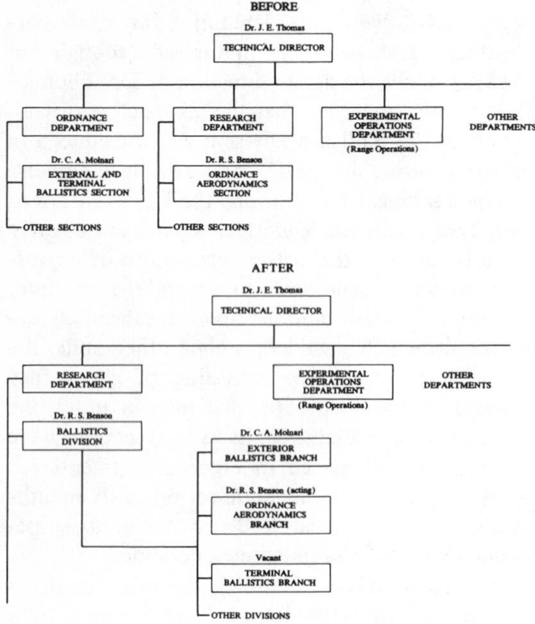

Dr. R. S. Benson was appointed the first head of the Ballistics Division in 1946. An astronomer with research interests, he had been in charge of the small aerodynamics group. Without much time to plan, he found himself the head of a division of about sixty-five people, more than four times larger than his original group, with a number of responsibilities quite far removed from research. Molnari, who was second-in-command, later characterized Benson as a scientist and distinctly not an administrator. Benson was neither interested in, nor adept at, managing a large division, according to Molnari (who was never regarded as modest in his own claims to ability in this respect). "I tried to help him in a management sense," Molnari stated, "and I took care of the management problems of the division. Benson concentrated on the scientific aspects of the work and the scientific programs, and on the necessary research tools." This was not how everyone saw it, however. According to another member of the group,

> When Benson's division was organized, an attempt was made to differentiate research from the development and operations work. But Molnari wanted to do research and get involved in aerodynamics, and Benson wouldn't stay away from development-type projects; so this differentiation, while it may have had some basis in theory, did not work in fact.

Whether it ever would have been a workable arrangement was never answered because Molnari, having mended his fences, transferred within a year to the Experimental Operations Department—the same department into which he had refused to move his ballistics group in the first place.

This left Benson to do what Molnari claimed he could not do, namely, manage the entire Division by himself. There was some subsequent support for Molnari's opinion. Benson's inability to manage the Ballistics Division successfully was noted by most of the former members of this division who felt that his failure in interpersonal relationships, both within his group and without, was his most serious problem. His desire for perfection from people and from the work they did frequently resulted in widespread disappointments and morale disturbances among the members of the Division. Reports of incidents which led to disappointments and some measure of exasperation were legion, including the time Benson assigned the same problem to two different physicists without their knowing it. Some time later, when both had arrived at solutions, he called them together and asked for results. The realization of what had happened was unnerving to the men, who were further embarrassed when asked to account for minor discrepancies. Although the men involved were juniors, this was still considered a poor way to treat professional employees. While many of the incidents reported were minor, they nevertheless had an unfavorable impact on the work and output of the Division as well as on its relationships with other departments.

The functions of the Ballistics Division, its fund support, the allocation of these funds to research, facilities, and the problem-solving services provided to the development and design engineers—all of these things were continuing sources of concern during the Benson era.

It was an unusual Research Board meeting that did not deal with at least one of the problems facing the Ballistics Division. In December 1947, the Research Board found it necessary to restate, as it had done before and would do a number of times after, the responsibilities of the Division as follows:

> They will be responsible for determining the fundamental aerodynamics and ballistics knowledge. This they will supply to the design engineers who are responsible for the specific design of weapons. The design engineers will be forced into compromises and will submit these compromises to the Ballistics Division for opinion, approval, or disapproval.

The difficulty with the Research Board's statement of purpose was that the Ballistics Division was in no position to force compromises, nor were the design engineers amenable to being forced into anything. Even persuasion was unlikely to succeed in view of the muddled relationships often existing between the Ballistics Division and the design and development personnel. The Research Board statement reflected little more than a hope.

Personnel problems of all varieties were also troublesome. The Division's size was reduced during Benson's tenure. In part, this resulted from an increasing division of labor and specialization throughout the Laboratory. In part, also, it resulted from recruitment and retention problems. Some skills were virtually impossible to recruit. Aerodynamicists, for example, could hardly be found at the salaries that a government laboratory was able to pay. Nevertheless, some physicists, mathematicians, and even a few aerodynamicists were recruited by Benson, who, it turned out, was quite vigorous and effective in this respect. Benson, however, was unable to keep some of the more talented people he recruited in his own organization for any useful length of time. Some who left the Division remained in the Laboratory; without intending it, Benson was helping to staff several other departments.

The Role of the Ballistics Division In the Laboratory

The Ballistics Division had an important role in the Laboratory's technical efforts from the beginning. As the Research Board had indicated, it was responsible for the fundamental aerodynamics and ballistics knowledge in support of the Laboratory's development programs. The Division's work was primarily theoretical, its specialized areas being exterior ballistics and aerodynamics; its organization was functional. Exterior ballistics is defined as that area of physics which studies the motion of projectiles and the conditions governing that motion in free flight. Aerodynamics is defined as the study of fluid-flow phenomena related to the motion of solids in air, including the study of disturbances generated in air by the passage of solid bodies and the motion of these bodies under the influence of air reactions. Exterior ballistics is a very old discipline; its theoretical base stems from Newtonian physics. Aerodynamics, a more recent area of inquiry, emerged with the advent of manned flight and became more significant with technological advances in the missile and spacecraft development.

As far as the development people in the Laboratory were concerned, the Ballistics Division's main function was to provide a reservoir of knowledge leading to specific answers on the ballistic and aerodynamic characteristics of whatever missile or related project they were engaged in. Such information was required in order for the development groups to proceed with design and development and with the successive evaluations and modifications of their systems. These expectations, largely ones of providing analytical support, significantly determined the direction of effort within the Ballistics Division, sometimes against the wishes of those within the group who would have preferred not to have their problems selected by the design and development people but instead preferred to pursue their own interests, whether directly related to the Laboratory's programs or not.

Developing the necessary reservoir of knowledge in order to provide specific answers to design and development questions led to several requirements: (1) familiarity with existing knowledge and the gaps in knowledge in the fields of concern; (2) development of theoretical and experimental programs to fill the gaps; and (3) performance of experiments, validation of theories, performance of computations, and development of test programs—all related to the Laboratory's development programs. It was important, further, for the Division to anticipate future directions of weapons systems and the nature of the information that would be necessary for the Laboratory to keep up with a fast-moving weapons technology.

To meet all of these requirements, or at least some of them, the Division was engaged in a series of well-defined programs. By and large, none of these could be classified as basic research. (See Appendix I for the definitions of the "research" spectrum.) A substantial number of Division programs were in the exploratory and foundational research area, with emphasis on application. The Division also engaged in development programs of its own; for example, in the area of instrumentation to provide the necessary tools for its experimental operations. Another portion of the Division's work was continuing computations, and this required the development of mathematical programs to be used in conjunction with large-scale computers. Some specific examples will serve to illustrate the kinds of programs and projects in which the Division was engaged during most of its life.

One important program in the area of exploratory and foundational research was a series of theoretical studies and systematic wind-tunnel tests of small-scale models of missiles, to provide improved aerodynamic designs. This work had specific application to the Laboratory's rocket development programs. Other experimental programs were carried out in the Aeroballistics Laboratory, the Division's major research tool. In this facility the aerodynamic and ballistic characteristics of projectile models were determined. In some cases the models were basic shapes used for research studies, in other cases they were models of specific weapons under development by the Laboratory or by outside agencies. The major part of the work in the Aeroballistics Laboratory was in the field of specific weapons.

In that part of the Division's work concerned with exterior ballistics, much effort was invested in developing programs for more sophisticated ballistic calculations on high-speed computers. These calculations included the determination of drag characteristics and trajectories of specific missiles. Not all of the data came from model studies. Some came from test firings of the actual missile under development. For a short period of time the Ballistics Division had some involvement in terminal ballistics research, i.e., studies of penetration and fragmentation. This function, however, was never fully staffed and eventually was moved to the Physics Division of the Research Department.

The scope of the various programs changed from time to time. In the early formative years much time was invested in the development and construction of research tools, most notably the Aeroballistics Laboratory. The work connected with the development of research tools was expensive and time-consuming and drew upon personnel resources which, in consequence, could not be used in other areas of work. Depending on development requirements and amounts of research funds available, work shifted to some extent between getting quick answers to immediate design problems (which the development programs paid for) and carrying out long-range experimentation (which was much more difficult to get funded). One thing was clear: The design and development people were eager for the quick answers.

Differences Within the Division

One of the major areas of disagreement within the Division centered on its proper role. There were at least three major and disparate viewpoints evident among Division members. One group held that research should be the primary function; a second considered analysis, in terms of support for the Laboratory's weapons project, the most important Division activity; and a very small third group would have preferred to see the Division include specific "hardware" projects. These widely divergent objectives influenced the organization of the Division much more significantly than occasional shifts on the formal organization charts. There was a tendency for the research-minded to group together, comprising about ten to twenty-five per cent of the Division; the analysis-minded clustered in a much larger grouping, representing half or more of the Division; the small minority who were project-oriented tended to seek friends and supporters elsewhere in the Laboratory. The remaining personnel supported the Division as a whole. This lack of a unified point of view on goals within the Division led to a wide separation between many of its personnel. Partly for this reason, no clear-cut image of the whole group ever emerged.

There were continuing frictions in the relationship of the Ballistics Division to much of the rest of the Research Department. The difficulty derived chiefly from the nature of the Division's functions, and the role played by Dr. Sherman, head of the Research Department from 1948 to 1958. Because so much of the work performed by the Ballistics Division was of a "service" type (that is, providing support for the design and development groups), other divisions in the Research Department were inclined to view the Ballistics Division as an anomaly in the Department. There was much discussion of the extent to which the work of the Ballistics Division tended to "dilute the research effort." These intra-departmental controversies were not viewed as being handled effectively by the Department head. Dr. Sherman, with a background in chemistry, was regarded by those affected as indifferent to, and unaware of, the work and problems of the Ballistics Division. In the absence of forceful, understanding leadership at the head of the Department, coalitions were formed which divided the groups within the Research Department. It was reported that divisional meetings often resulted in arguments that found the Physics and Chemistry Divisions aligned on one side and the Ballistics and Mathematics Divisions on the other. The persistence of internal frictions, and the absence of leadership to mitigate them, intensified conflict over the years of the Ballistics Division's existence. The combination of technological problems with serious interpersonal and interdivisional frictions was not conducive to effectiveness or general satisfaction in the long run.

The Ballistics Division thus found itself trapped: In the Research Department it could be criticized for not doing what could honestly be called research and, at the same time, it was looked upon by development groups as having its important supporting analysis functions diluted by research efforts that were not producing immediate solutions.

Had it been clear what the role of such a group should be in the Laboratory, some of the problems might have been less serious. However, the Laboratory itself was continuously struggling with the pains of role-definition—largely by handling the conflicts that arose on a day-to-day basis. Questions of who should support whom and where, organizationally, were aired frequently and loudly before the Research Board, but in fact each organizational unit had to find its own way, its own support, and its own rationale.

Personnel Characteristics of the Ballistics Division

The personnel of the Ballistics Division never emerged as clearly as the problems connected with the work in which they were engaged. People were largely in the background of the issues, almost unidentified as individuals. Aggressive personalities not content to be in the background all of the time left the group, thus enhancing the general anonymity of the Division. A few colorful persons did stand out, and the character of the Division tended to become identified with their personalities. In the earliest period, Benson and Molnari created much of the image of the Division in the Laboratory as a whole. Dr. Lindberg, who would later become head of the Division, was a Ph.D. mathematician with a background of college teaching experience. He had been head of the Physics Department in a small western college before he joined the Laboratory in 1947. Lindberg headed a branch of the Ballistics Division under Dr. Benson. Another conspicuous figure was Dr. Henderson, a senior scientist in the Division. Henderson was a Ph.D. physicist with some teaching and research experience at several universities, and wartime service in Army research and development laboratories. He had entered the Laboratory in 1946, a year and one-half earlier than Lindberg.

Both men had reputations for unusual behavior: Lindberg, a needler and gamesman, managed to unnerve some of the professional people in his Division; those who had difficulty responding to his supervisory characteristics withdrew from the relationship and became part of the undifferentiated image of the group. Henderson added to the stereotype of the erratic scientist; his behavior was generally unpredictable. He worked mainly alone and for the most part shunned administrative responsibilities. These men provided color but also created problems for the Division. The remaining members contributed to the group's technical output inconspicuously.

In general, the senior personnel, those who held branch head positions or nonadministrative senior positions in the Ballistics Division, had somewhat more limited academic backgrounds than Lindberg's and Henderson's. There were no Ph.D.'s among them, although several had virtually completed Ph.D. requirements. Almost all had a Master's degree, the majority in physics and mathematics. Two were engineers. All had previous experience, primarily in teaching or in government laboratories. Several of these men had been recruited from previous association with the Manhattan Project. A number of the younger men had also been associated with the Manhattan Project, which served as a valuable resource for physical science personnel when the war ended. In general, the profile presented by the senior members of the Ballistics Division was one of academic orientation and/or research experience in government or university laboratories. An occasional individual had a background of wartime industrial experience, but this was usually accompanied with wartime government laboratory experience in or out of one of the branches of military service.

The early period under Benson saw the recruitment primarily of experienced men. Few juniors came into the Ballistics Division immediately after completing their academic work. It was not really until the Korean crisis, when the recruitment efforts of the Laboratory were intensified and its staff expanded, that college graduates with no work experience began to enter the Ballistics Division. The majority of the professional newcomers in junior positions had only a Bachelor's degree; a very few had a Master's degree; none were Ph.D.'s. The Research Department as a whole had upward of seventy-five Ph.D.'s (in a total complement of less than 150); the Ballistics Division, however, varied markedly in this respect from the rest of the Department; it never had more than two or three at any one time.

The personnel structure of the Division fluctuated somewhat throughout its history, depending upon recruitment outcomes. Its size ranged from fifty to sixty-five persons. The ratio of scientists (i.e., physicists and mathematicians) to engineers was generally three to two. The ratio of professionals to all others (clerical, sub-professionals, technicians) was about three to one, making the Division a predominantly professional group. The professional personnel, on the average, were young, as was the case in all other parts of the Laboratory. The average age on entrance was approximately twenty-six years. As would be expected, the senior experienced group recruited during the early period was somewhat older than the total average—about thirty years of age on entrance. In terms of its age structure, the Ballistics Division was no different from the rest of the Laboratory.

Underlying Problems of the Ballistics Division

The early decision of the Research Board to form a Ballistics Division in the Research Department had a series of consequences that were not anticipated at the time the decision was made (and not reviewed shortly afterwards, as the Board itself had suggested should happen). In the first place, the mixture of research, development, and test functions into one relatively small division created a set of role conflicts that split the group into small and sometimes hostile factions. These conflicts were intensified within the Research Department as a whole, where there was antagonism toward a group the Department felt was "diluting the research effort." Furthermore, the analytic supporting functions in which a substantial number of Ballistic Division personnel were involved, although extremely important to the successful accomplishment of weapons programs, were nevertheless favorite targets for development groups that were never entirely satisfied they were getting the answers they needed, when they needed them, and in just the manner they wanted the service accomplished. Paying for services over which the development groups had limited control was considered much less desirable by some of these groups than having the services performed in their own units where they would have greater control over who worked on the projects, how the money was spent, and so on.

The Ballistics Division's problems of recruitment and leadership were also significant. They increased over time with changing directions and emphasis in the Laboratory. Financial support was never certain. While in fact enough money was always forthcoming to cover each year of effort, some of the Division's personnel did not believe it or want to believe it. Money for exploratory and foundational research was available, but always on the defensive in Washington. It was not possible to be sure from one year to the next what the situation would be. This state of affairs was not peculiar to the Ballistics Division. It meant, however, that there was a continuing need to seek support—a task that was distasteful to more personnel in the Ballistics Division than in other Laboratory groups. Project money was somewhat more available, but within the Laboratory it had to come from the project engineers in the development groups. This also meant a continuous process of persuasion and the building of influential personal relationships. Some members of the Division could and did do this effectively. Others could not and did not.

In summary, the Ballistics Division was confronted with a series of problems related to its several roles. In the first place, it suffered, as did other groups in the Research Department, from some lack of understanding by project managers in the Laboratory of the role of a research group that produced no hardware. It was in a position of continually having to defend itself and the funds the Division expended to individuals who could often see no relationship between the Division's work and the Laboratory's end products. Secondly, even when its role was understood, the Ballistics Division suffered from the impatience accorded to all supporting groups by the project managers, that is, a felt lack of appreciation of the Division's efforts in support of the development programs. It was the convenient scapegoat for missing deadlines. The Division also bore the brunt of the empirically oriented project manager's hostility toward theory and analysis—time-consuming efforts that could rarely be rushed. These latter differences resulted in continuing arguments over whether it was better to try something that seemed intuitively sound and possibly make a mistake or wait for the equations to be developed and solved. Finally, the Ballistics Division was troubled with its own intra-divisional personality problems. Any one of these difficulties would be a major problem for effective leadership. Without effective leadership, many of the Division's personnel felt that these problems were becoming virtually insolvable.

FERMENTATION, CONTROVERSY, AND STALEMATE

Roles and Functions Examined

The foregoing problems which developed in the Ballistics Division and in other parts of the Laboratory as well came up for consideration on many occasions, formally and informally. From late 1949 until 1958 the Laboratory made numerous attempts to resolve them. A few of the most significant efforts are described below.

In the summer of 1949 and again two years later, a group of consultants from the Harvard School of Business Administration were brought to the Laboratory to make a study of its organization and administrative problems. They raised several questions on the division of responsibility for research between the development departments and the Research Department. Among other things, they questioned whether at least fifty per cent of the work being done in the Research Department was suitably placed there. Furthermore, they found a tendency for the development departments to use the Research Department as a kind of "service" organization to do certain portions of their work that they themselves did not have time to do. The Harvard group also found communication poor between research people and those in development; they noted that these groups had failed to establish the personal acquaintanceships necessary to close collaboration. The Harvard group found considerable expression of opinion both inside and outside the Research Department to the effect that many of the research personnel were not sufficiently experienced to do foundational research of real significance or even applied research of high quality. They therefore felt that these people could be employed more effectively in the development departments on engineering assignments. These findings and considerations were drawn from the experiences of the Ballistics Division, among other units in the Research Department.

The Harvard consultants further decried their impression that individual departments placed too much emphasis on various "organizational maneuvers" to solve the problems of interdepartmental relationships. These "maneuvers," they pointed out, usually took the form of a department setting up a group of its own to do work that should be done someplace else in the organization, resulting in the growth of many little groups that duplicated each other's efforts.

As a result of their findings, the consultants recommended that the Laboratory

> gradually move in the direction of establishing a small central research department, consisting of perhaps twenty to fifty [rather than the existing 150] experienced and highly qualified scientists, to conduct the major portion of the foundational research and to do such types of applied research as can best be handled in a central department. A major portion of the applied research would then be conducted in the development departments.

They also recommended "that immediate attention be given to the problem of improving the working associations between research and development people."

Spurred partly by the statements of the Harvard consultants and partly by internal review and discussion, the Research Board in March 1950 called for an evaluation of Research Department programs and organization. A series of ad hoc committees was appointed by Dr. Thomas, the Technical Director, to review every aspect of the Research Department. A Ballistics Committee was appointed, with Dr. Lindberg as chairman, to review the entire ballistics function. Out of a membership of four, three were from the Ballistics Division, and one came from a development department. The Ballistics Committee made it clear from the outset that it would not limit its review to aeroballistics functions within the Research Department alone since these represented only one-fifth of the total effort in this area. It dealt also with similar functions being performed in several of the development departments.

After looking at the existing division of work among the several departments involved, the Committee recommended that while there was no logic in proposing that all the work be centralized and a new Ballistics Department created, the opposite extreme—to decentralize this function completely by abolishing the Ballistics Division—was equally undesirable. The Committee stated that "there is complete justification for a central aeroballistics organization, roughly of division size, relatively independent of the development program, and staffed in several key positions with the most competent aeroballisticians obtainable." The Committee also pointed out that "under the present type of departmental organization, the Research Department seems as good a place as any to append this division." The Committee endorsed the dual role of research and service for the Ballistics Division and entered a strong plea to all other departments to utilize to the utmost the experience and judgment of the central group, to keep it informed, and to provide for continuing liaison. When the Committee presented its report in May 1950, a strong statement for the status quo was once again entered on Research Board books, supported by Dr. Thomas and challenged by no one, at least in writing. Thomas himself had a very special interest in ballistics. He was a physicist who had had an extensive career in the field of ballistics research dating back to the First World War. He took particular interest in the Ballistics Division and had an intimate knowledge of its area of work. While not a supporter of centralization in the Laboratory, he nevertheless preferred to have at least one strong aeroballistics group with research capabilities, along with smaller numbers of specialists in the development departments.

Any possibility of effecting a change at this time appeared to have been effectively blocked.

At the end of 1950, Dr. Lindberg succeeded Benson as head of the Ballistics Division, under circumstances that involved a plot to oust Benson —a plot in which Lindberg himself participated. Benson moved into the anonymous, nonadministrative position of Research Scientist in the Research Department head office. Lindberg's appointment encouraged hope for improvement in the situation of the Ballistics Division, since he had been chairman of the Committee that had made a successful plea for retaining the group intact.

Three events, however—external to the Division itself—occurred to forestall any favorable changes for the Ballistics Division under new leadership. First, Dr. Thomas, the Technical Director, resigned at the end of 1951. Second, the Korean War, which had begun in the summer of 1950, was creating a series of pressures for operational weapons that directed attention toward project groups and hardware and away from the research efforts. Finally, the Laboratory had become engaged in a major guided-missile project which would produce a significant shift in technological emphasis and absorb a substantial share of its resources for many years to come.

The resignation of Dr. Thomas weakened the concept of a strong, central aeroballistics group. Subsequent emphasis by the technical leadership was to strengthen project organizations further by encouraging them to provide for their own specialists. Although there was no stated policy that indicated that central groups of functional specialists were no longer needed, the long-run existence of these groups seemed threatened in fact by the growing strength and status of the project organizations.

Changing Technology

The Korean conflict had found the country short of operational weapons. The Laboratory's attention was directed immediately to a number of "crash" development programs with emphasis on early payoffs. The mobilization of effort on development programs was rapid and effective, and long-range needs were subordinated to short-run objectives. Thus, research of all varieties remained in the background, at least for the time being. Successful results brought enthusiastic response from the fighting front. Though the dividends of earlier research were evident in a number of actual hardware accomplishments, they were nevertheless not as obvious as the finished product, for which the project groups could take credit. The impact of the Korean conflict shifted emphasis from basic and applied research *per se* toward the development of weapons and weapons systems, together with that portion of applied research directly related to these.

Technology was also beginning to change: The rocket, a major weapon during the Korean conflict, was gradually being superseded by the guided missile; technological interests in guidance and control systems were increasing; the advent of remarkable high-speed computers was reducing requirements for some technical skills and creating requirements for new ones. The impact of these changes in the Laboratory was resulting in consideration by the top technical leadership of new objectives and programs, particularly with respect to the emerging guided-missile development. It was becoming clearer that future success would depend, at least in part, upon competing vigorously in the new missile programs, and that the survival of the Laboratory would depend upon its technological successes as measured by the advanced hardware it could develop.

Under new leadership, the Ballistics Division began to redefine its role, yielding to some of the new pressures and remaining somewhat immune to others. Dr. Lindberg announced his philosophy of operation for the Division. One-third of the effort would be devoted to "service" for development departments; one-third to special projects originating outside the Laboratory; and one-third to "research" as the Division would define it. To accomplish the first of these, Lindberg attempted to build effective relationships with the development departments and met with at least partial success. Funds for the other two-thirds of the program, particularly the research portion, were becoming scarce. Most important, however, was the role of the Division with respect to a new guided missile program, the PHENIX.*

New Leadership

By 1950 the PHENIX project was already well launched, under the overall direction of Dr. J. F. Mackay, Head, Aviation Ordnance Department, and under the direct project leadership of Dr. G. B. Warner. Despite reluctance at the Washington level to support the project, and virtually without any funds specifically allocated to it, Mackay and Warner had moved ahead with speed and persistence. Aerodynamic assistance was required on the project, so attention was directed to the Ballistics Division to provide problem solutions. Although one or two aerodynamicists in the Ballistics Division had been assigned to the task, the missile project directors were generally dissatisfied with the results they were getting.

> I went to the man they had working on the project [Dr. Warner stated] to check out some figures I had been given. The numbers didn't make sense. There seemed to be obvious errors. He couldn't tell me how accurate the numbers were and he couldn't stand behind them. The guy at the next desk turned around and said they were accurate to five per cent. I didn't know who this fellow was. It turned out to be Lee Jackson. For some reason, another man had been assigned to the job but Jackson had much more insight into the problems. I instantly shifted my attention to Lee. Lee was able to answer my questions. He had a very fine intuitive feel for the problem.

Thus began a very important informal relationship.

Even with Jackson's help, Warner continued to be dissatisfied with what he regarded as the ineffective support he was getting from the Ballistics Division, so he launched a personal program to persuade Jackson to transfer to his own group. This took more time than had been anticipated. Jackson had left his position with the Laboratory in April 1951 to work in a private industrial organization on the East Coast. He gave as his reason for the departure a better job opportunity with higher salary. However, when the new job did not turn out as expected, Jackson returned, in a little less than a year. Moreover, even before he left, he had had mixed feelings about making the change Warner wanted. Looking at it in retrospect, Warner stated:

> Jackson found it difficult to make up his mind. He was torn between a series of conflicting viewpoints which made it very difficult for him to reach a decision. When he returned from his year's absence he was offered the opportunity to come to work directly for me, or, at the same grade, go back to Ballistics Division again. As far as we were concerned, we didn't care where he was. At least, let's say that was the published statement. As a matter of fact, I preferred him to be directly with us. A selfish viewpoint, if you will. But he was dedicated to the concept of a centralized aerodynamics-aeromechanics group so he went to Ballistics Division. Not more than a few months later he came back feeling that this was not going to work out, that he couldn't be as effective as I would like him to be, or as he

* Fictitious name substituted for actual project name.

would hope himself to be. And so he came over to our division and we set up another group (called the Aeromechanics Branch) which was not large and was never intended to be large. It was not intended to be a rival to the Research Department's Ballistics Division. It was intended to be solely a project group oriented toward PHENIX or a particular phase of the missile. It never numbered more than one man in actuality. There may have been more persons who showed on the charts but there was one guy only who really did anything. That was Lee Jackson himself, who was, in my opinion, one of the world's greatest workers, and one of the most capable guys in the field of aerodynamics.

FIGURE 4:
ESTABLISHMENT OF AEROMECHANICS BRANCH—1952

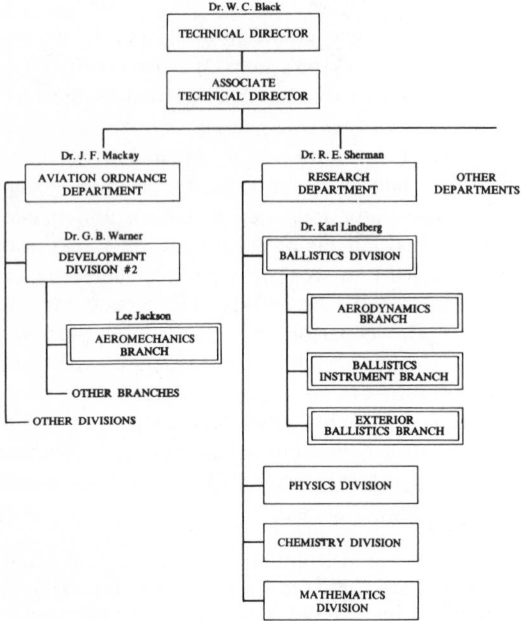

Although he moved reluctantly to the Aviation Ordnance Department, Lee Jackson found himself in a department and a division that had clearly delineated and clearly accepted goals, where the PHENIX project with which he would be associated throughout his tenure there was clearly important, and where effective leadership and support in the persons of Warner and others were clearly present. It did not take long, therefore, for his original doubts to disappear in an environment where the work was well recognized. For much of its existence the Aeromechanics Branch was one person, Jackson, and the work of the Branch involved the support of the PHENIX missile project. A few more people were added to the group as time passed, one or two of them from the Ballistics Division, but it never numbered more than six to eight people. The Aeromechanics Branch differed from the Ballistics Division not only in size but in type of personnel; all were engineers, most without an advanced degree. Jackson himself lacked even a Bachelor's degree when he became head of the Branch but was granted one in 1953, after completing his undergraduate work.

The attitude of members of the Ballistics Division toward the Jackson-Warner relationship and subsequent merger was quite different from Warner's own feelings. To the professionals in the Ballistics Division, it represented the coming together of two strongly project-oriented people. They did not agree, for example, that Jackson was dedicated to a centralized ballistics-aerodynamics group. The Jackson-Warner relationship had been viewed as an intrusion upon the way in which the Division operated and wanted to operate. Many in the Ballistics Division felt that the only reason why the PHENIX project could not work successfully with Jackson remaining in the Division was the personal orientations and philosophies of both Warner and Jackson. Several senior professionals emphasized that other important projects were carried out successfully by cooperation between the Ballistics Division and project-development groups. On the other hand, of course, was the fact that PHENIX was the most important of all the projects.

Conflicting Objectives

In the minds of many, the seeds of future reorganization of the Ballistics Division had been planted the day that Jackson moved out of the Division and joined Warner. Although Warner claimed that he was not creating a rival organization, this was widely disbelieved among Ballistics Division personnel, who viewed this development as the first really serious competition with their own organization and functions, and who resisted further expansion of ballistics work by project units. The issue was settled, at least for a short while, in early 1952, when the new Technical Director, Dr. W. C. Black, made a policy statement to the Research Board:

> The Technical Director does not approve the idea of a centralized control of Laboratory aerodynamics problems or any other technical problems. He feels it is the prerogative of the development departments to recruit their own aerodynamics talent wherever and whenever possible. The general philosophy is that the Aerodynamics Branch of the Ballistics Division shall be considered a reservoir of such talent, to be called upon by the development departments as needed, and it shall be the responsibility of the departments to obtain for themselves, either from the Aerodynamics Branch or their own aerodynamicists, competent advice on their individual aerodynamics problems.

> According to Warner, Dr. Black's statement

> . . . reflected the attempt of the leadership to get around the argument of the Ballistics Division that it had exclusive prerogatives in the aerodynamics area, which had always been a very strong argument on the part of the Ballistics Division and one of their principal weaknesses.

The philosophy expounded by Black simply ratified the existing situation.

The Ballistics Division considered Dr. Black's statement as a defeat. It moved farther and farther away from fields of inquiry essential not only to the PHENIX project but to other projects as well. There were many disagreements over levels of technical competence and areas of concentration of effort within the Ballistics Division during this period. One thing was clear. At higher levels in the organization, there was some unhappiness with the Division's programs and efforts. Moreover, the considerations raised by the Harvard consultants (discussed early in this chapter) were far from dead. The Research Department's program was reviewed again in 1952-1953 under the new Technical Director, Dr. Black. A new committee—including three men from Research but none from Ballistics—was appointed to make another study. The size of the Research Department was being questioned again, and doubt was raised as to whether the Ballistics Division should be in the Research Department at all.

Once again, but this time as Division head, Dr. Lindberg expressed in two memoranda to the Research Committee his disagreement with the Harvard recommendations; he stated that the Laboratory was no place for a small research department engaged in pure research. Such research, he stated, should be left primarily to universities. He reiterated his earlier advocacy of a strong, central aeroballistics group and urged that the work and program of the Research Department be even more closely integrated with the work of the development departments. On the basis of these views he made several proposals. He suggested changing the name of the Research Department to the Applied Research Department and expanding the Ballistics Division into three separate divisions in the new department. In the event that this proposal would not be accepted (and there was no likelihood that it would be), Lindberg recommended a minimum condition: that a central aeroballistics group of considerable size be permitted to operate either as an appendage to the Research Department (no matter how the final organization of that department would turn out), or that it be transferred intact to another department, or that a new department be formed from a combination of Ballistics and Mathematics Divisions.

At the same time that the fate of the Research Department was being reconsidered, questions were being raised in other quarters on how the general efficiency of the Laboratory could be improved. Several department heads took the opportunity to comment on the Research Department in these terms. Dr. Mackay, as head of the Aviation Ordnance Department, expressed his views in a memorandum also covering general problems within his own department:

> I feel that the Research Department is too large and too highly organized or "compartmentalized" to do effective individual research and has a considerable number of people who are primarily interested in development rather than research and could be more effectively employed in the development departments. The research activities should be confined to a few outstanding men who have definite ideas of the programs they would like to carry out with the support needed to implement these programs. They should develop sufficient leadership in their fields so that they will act as sources of information for all the development groups. The prosecution of active development programs tends to dilute the effort on research and the improvement of new techniques, and tends to confuse the picture as regards development organizations. I think the function of the Research Department should be to promote research activities throughout the Laboratory. They should never get in a position of feeling that all research should be done in the Research Department.

Dr. Mackay's comments were significant for at least two reasons as far as the future of the Ballistics Division was concerned. In the first place, it was in his department that the "competitive" group (the Aeromechanics Branch) under Warner and Jackson had developed and where the major missile program was now in full swing. In the second place, within two years he would be the Laboratory's Technical Director.

Decision and Disagreement

The immediate result of all the committee reports, statements, memoranda, and Research Board discussions was that by mid-1953 several key decisions and statements were recorded in Research Board minutes:

> Dr. Black said that the Ballistics Division would remain in the Research Department and the development departments should endeavor gradually to build up an aeroballistics staff for their own design work. The program will be reviewed in one year, at which time the increase in the number of ballisticians and aerodynamicists will also be examined. Miscellaneous job-shop type work should be looked at very critically before acceptance. Attention should be given to aeroballistic research problems in all major fields of the Laboratory's programs; namely, rockets, torpedoes, guided missiles and fire control. This above action has been directed by the Technical Director and these minutes shall be considered as authority to proceed with the action designated.

For the time being, Lindberg's approach had paid off. By making a proposal to expand the ballistics group into three divisions, he succeeded in making the existing situation appear more desirable than it had before. Although he was not successful in modifying the trend toward partial decentralization, he did succeed in keeping the Ballistics Division in the Research Department reasonably intact, even if completely divorced from the Laboratory's most important weapon project—the PHENIX. According to some of its personnel, the Division had received at least a new, if not entirely stable, lease on life. The new strength was further enhanced at the end of 1953 when the Advisory Board (a group of top-level scientists from industry and universities who reviewed and advised on the Laboratory's programs) made the following statement in its year-end report:

> The Board commends the Ballistics Division on its excellent program which appears to be well-designed to contribute to the Laboratory mission and to be well-executed.

The Advisory Board's appraisal may have correctly evaluated the existing situation, but it was not an accurate reflection of the future course of events. Several of the persons who left the Ballistics Division during subsequent years reported a deteriorating situation:

> In 1954 and 1955 I saw that the group was stagnating and people were leaving the Ballistics Division wholesale. So I decided to leave myself.

> Starting in 1954, the Ballistics Division was unable to answer the questions that the development people raised. They had been working on a backlog of theory. When this ran out, nothing was left.

On the other hand, those who agreed with the Advisory Board's commendation were represented in the opinion of one senior man, who, even though he left the Division himself, evaluated it as follows:

> The Ballistics Division was a much maligned group. Actually, the mark of their work was on everything the Laboratory had produced. But this was not seen because they were a quiet group who sat in the corner and just got their work done. They did not have the glamour of a project group, nor were they the empiricists. As a result of the environment, they got their fingers burned. Neither Mackay nor Warner understood what the group had done. All they knew was that they weren't getting answers fast enough. This was a part of the environment in which we lived. The gadgeteers were in full swing and this was all that mattered.

THE AX FALLS

New Patterns Emerge

In mid-1954, Dr. Mackay was appointed Technical Director, replacing Dr. Black, who resigned to accept a position as Technical Director of another government laboratory. The appointment of Mackay marked the climax of a very successful technical career which had begun in the Laboratory in 1946. He had won recognition for the Laboratory, particularly for the PHENIX project, which he had conceived. Warner remained with the missile project in his position of division head but assumed increased responsibilities for it, since Mackay's new position removed him from the day-to-day direction of activities; Jackson continued to occupy a key subordinate role. The leadership pattern that emerged at this time was widely regarded as reinforcing a changing technological direction within the Laboratory—change that had begun during the Korean War with the new emphasis on advanced missile systems and on the project organizations that were created to carry the development phases of these systems to completion.

New decision-making patterns were also emerging. The Research Board, which had played a key role during the Laboratory's formative period as the Technical Director's major advisory body in technical and related organizational matters, was becoming less an advisory group and more a forum to disseminate information of technical interest. The discussions and controversies that had been aired frequently in the Research Board up to this time were now taken up in other committees or in more private situations, and the Board's earlier role in the decision-making process was measurably reduced. Many department heads who were its members continued to exercise important influence on technical policy and organization, but not through the Board itself. At the same time, encouraged by Mackay, more responsibility for decisions was delegated to lower levels in the working organization; this allowed leadership to emerge in division and branch head positions and provided for differences of opinion on organizational and technical matters to be resolved well below the Technical Director's level. Such changes made it unlikely that problems affecting the future of the Ballistics Division would be brought to the attention of the Research Board, but rather would have to be resolved at levels where the day-to-day work was being performed.

The possible implications of these developments for the future of the Ballistics Division did not appear to have any appreciable impact within the Division itself. Work there continued as before, but no new ideas emerged that were relevant to the changing technology. The function of anticipating future requirements in the Laboratory and developing significant new areas of inquiry was relatively dormant. Furthermore, new patterns of leadership did not evolve to meet the requirements of increased delegation of technical responsibilities.

Those within the Ballistics Division who saw this happening and were not satisfied, either from the standpoint of the work they were doing or from the standpoint of personal advancement, began to leave the organization. A few left the Laboratory; several others transferred within it to missile-project organizations which seemed to offer a brighter future in terms of advancement and personal development. Generally speaking, two types of people left the Ballistics Division: those who felt they could best pursue their scientific and technical interests elsewhere; and those with above-average ambitions who felt they could rise more rapidly on the administrative ladder in project groups which offered more opportunity for experience in program direction. This meant that the reservoir of potential future leadership within the Ballistics Division was seriously depleted at a time when the need for strong leadership at branch and division levels was increasing. Those who remained in the Division were not individuals with either strong interest in, or capacity for, assuming the important administrative functions of developing and directing new programs or new research ventures, nor for taking part in the continuous battle for funds at the Washington level—a pursuit demanding a high order of salesmanship.

Funding for anything as esoteric as research (even of the applied variety as opposed to development programs) had traditionally been difficult to obtain, and this situation was not improving. Furthermore, there were disagreements within the Ballistics Division itself over how funds should be spent. Some preferred the largest share to be spent for research; others did not care if any research at all was conducted. The latter group assumed their role was purely of a supporting nature to the development programs. Even this group was split into two parts—those who were satisfied to support projects in the development departments and those who were so completely project-oriented that they would have preferred to have development programs in the Ballistics Division itself. When the intra-divisional conflicts subsided, research efforts emerged as the major trend in the group, much to the concern of the Laboratory management, which did not see this direction of effort as the most fruitful for the future.

In sharp contrast to the problem-ridden Ballistics Division, the Aeromechanics Branch was doing well. It was right in step with the changing patterns in the Laboratory. Furthermore, it differed from the Ballistics Division in that all of its resources and interests were directed toward a single project within a division whose total resources were also directed to the same single project. A very high *esprit de corps* characterized the work situation, and the Aeromechanics Branch shared in it. As the PHENIX project approached operational status, and as the funds for its support grew, the Aeromechanics Branch shared in this success and affluence to a degree that had never been accorded the Ballistics Division, at least for any extended period of time. The relationship between the two rival organizations was scarcely congenial. The "defectors" from the Ballistics Division were not always welcomed in their former group. This mutual antagonism was to reach a peak later, when the successful missile project was publicly announced and laurels were freely extended to all who had made contributions, however small, from every part of the Laboratory. On the day this occurred, a large sign was mysteriously hung outside the wing that housed the Ballistics Division. It said, "We had nothing whatsoever to do with PHENIX."

An event of importance to the Ballistics Division occurred in 1955. Dr. Lindberg, the Division's head since 1951, was promoted to the position of head of the Test Department. A delay in naming his successor was a circumstance that did not contribute to an improvement in the situation. The man later appointed to succeed Lindberg was Dr. Henderson, who for several years had held the position of Research Scientist in the Division. This was a senior consultant position carrying no administrative responsibilities. Dr. Henderson (as stated earlier) had a Ph.D. in physics and had been at several universities before working in Army research-and-development laboratories during the war; he had come to the Laboratory in 1946.

Unlike Lindberg, Henderson had never held a position of administrative responsibility for any significant length of time within the Ballistics Division and had not previously appeared to want one. He was, however, interested in the position of Division head, and he was the senior man there. He considered the Division chief's function a highly political one in an environment that he felt overemphasized political roles. He felt that the Ballistics Division was a stepchild much like the rest of the Research Department. Henderson further believed that the top levels were not interested in research so that the whole future situation did not appear very hopeful. His acceptance of the position was not accompanied by any change in his general attitude toward administration. He regarded the new period in the Laboratory's development as less exciting than the earlier days when he felt the organization had been "primitive but very productive." In evaluating the relationship of the Ballistics Division to the rest of the Research Department, he felt that, like all of the other divisions in the Department, it operated as a small department on its own, making all of its own decisions with little relationship to the Department head, Dr. Sherman. From his own standpoint, Dr. Henderson found this operating situation stimulating but at the same time onerous. In sum, Henderson's perspective on the role and future of the Ballistics Division did not suggest a period of renewed vigor or direction for the group; it suggested, rather, a future of strained relationships with individuals and groups both inside and outside the Division.

A New Division Is Formed

In the Aviation Ordnance Department, Dr. Warner was doing a successful job of bringing the PHENIX project closer to completion, and Jackson continued to make substantial contributions to the project's success in his position as head of the Aeromechanics Branch. These accomplishments did not go unrecognized. In January 1956, Dr. Warner was promoted from his division chief position in the Aviation Ordnance Department to the position of head of the Weapons Development Department. By this time Warner had become one of the most influential technical leaders in the Laboratory, not only because of his technical skills but also because of his fresh ideas and his capabilities as an articulate spokesman for the Laboratory and its programs in Washington, as well as locally. The expectation was that Warner would inject his ideas and philosophy into the department he now headed; that he would, in effect, shake up the established order and move on to new areas of development activity. Interested in emerging viewpoints on total weapons systems, he began to move his department in that direction, phasing out the older rocket projects, some of which were in the "clean-up" stages when he took over. Emphasis was placed on guided missiles and related areas of guidance and control and on aeromechanics. A major portion of funds was still in the hands of the Department and the PHENIX project he had left, but not for long.

In the spring of 1957, the personnel and funds of the PHENIX project that Warner had headed in the Aviation Ordnance Department were moved to the Weapons Development Department, including Jackson and the Aeromechanics Branch. Just before the move occurred, Warner singled out the Aeromechanics Branch for higher status, which would mean a step up for Jackson and several other personnel. At the end of 1956, Warner drew a new box on the year-end organization chart of the Weapons Development Department, establishing an Aeromechanics Division. When the move from the Aviation Ordnance Department took place in the spring of 1957, Jackson became the new Division head and the former members of the Aeromechanics Branch became members of the new Aeromechanics Division. In summarizing his rationale for the action, Warner stated:

> I felt that Jackson was an outstandingly capable individual among a batch of individuals who were not outstandingly capable. I took him from Ballistics Division the first time because I had a job to do. He was a man who could do it and one in whom I placed great trust. And I think that Jackson warmed to this situation and did a tremendous job, a job that surprised himself and everybody else. When I moved to the new department I still had tremendous trust in him.

What Warner meant by an outstandingly capable individual was described by a personnel analyst who had been involved in the series of organization changes:

> Warner, if he had trust in a man's technical capability, figured that was enough. He figured that the administrative side of the organization would take care of itself. Jackson fit the bill. Up to this point he had satisfied Warner in terms of his technical capability. He had shown no such ability in administration and the direction of people, at least up to this point in time.

The creation of the new division also resulted in an important reunion. Several former members of the Ballistics Division, who had joined the Weapons Development Department several years earlier in project capacities, were reunited with their former colleagues in the Aeromechanics Division. Chief among these was Leroy Reed, who became head of the Aeroresearch Branch in the new division and who was described by the personnel analyst serving the division as a very capable administrator.

Significant also was the removal of Jackson from direct association with the PHENIX project; the circle was completed with Jackson back in a service group that resembled the Ballistics Division in its organization and newly acquired personnel. Warner was sure Jackson would succeed in this new capacity, but some of his colleagues, particularly Reed, had substantial doubts.

This series of organization changes, particularly the establishment of the Aeromechanics Division, looked threatening to many of the personnel of the Ballistics Division. By this time they had come to regard Warner as a hatchet man—a man who seemed to have a habit of creating competing groups wherever he went. For his part, Warner saw a growing need in his own department for the kind of skills that the Aeromechanics group represented, and he felt he would never get the support he needed from the Ballistics Division. The requirements he anticipated were sufficient to warrant establishing a division organization of broader scope to replace the more circumscribed level of activities possible in the previous branch organization.

Several immediate problems were encountered when the Aeromechanics Division was established. One was the development of a position description for Jackson that would not appear to be in conflict with the already existing position description for Henderson in the Ballistics Division. This was done without much difficulty, although the position was established at one grade-level lower than Warner had hoped. Another, more critical problem was the

FIGURE 5:
THE ORGANIZATION STRUCTURE PRECEDING REORGANIZATION OF THE BALLISTICS DIVISION
(January 1957–April 1958)

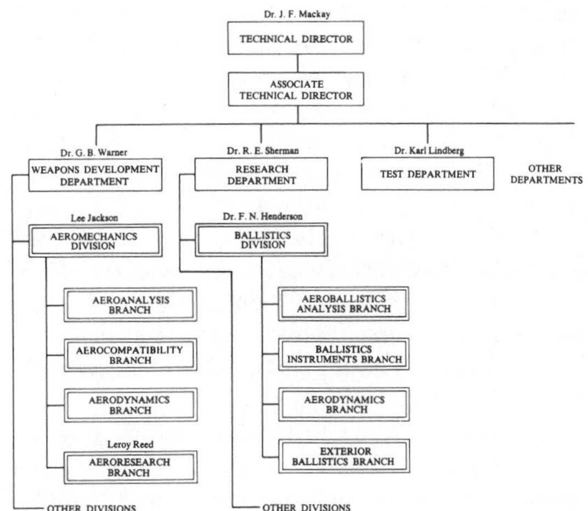

need for additional personnel in the Aeromechanics Division. If the Division were to fulfill its mission as Warner viewed it, many more people would be needed. A final problem was to develop an effective internal-organization structure.

The spring of 1957 found the Laboratory with two divisions whose functions, though not entirely alike, were very similar. The Ballistics Division was charged with the responsibility of providing consulting services and conducting foundational and applied research in aeroballistics; with developing aeroballistics design; and with conducting performance analyses on rockets, missiles, etc. Ordinarily its major customer and fund source among the development organizations would have been the Weapons Development Department. However, this no longer appeared likely when the Aeromechanics Division was established. The new division was charged with responsibilities similar to those of the Ballistics Division except that these responsibilities would be confined primarily to the work of the Weapons Development Department. Some observers within the Laboratory predicted that one of the divisions would disappear; those making such predictions left little doubt as to which division they thought would remain.

The Struggle for Dominance

The relationship between the Aeromechanics and the Ballistics Divisions was far from cordial. The personnel of the Ballistics Division saw some of their former junior colleagues promoted to positions of responsibility in the new organization. This did not improve their attitudes toward these men; few of the new leaders in the Aeromechanics Division were well regarded within the Ballistics group. Moreover, the two division heads, Jackson and Henderson—who, according to one observer, would have nothing to do with each other—did nothing to encourage better rapport. The events leading to the creation of the Aeromechanics Division suggested that little effort would be made to establish harmonious working relationships. Furthermore, it was Henderson's view that Jackson's background and personality were not suited to research pursuits, and this also tended to preclude a close working relationship between the two men and the two divisions.

Jackson had come to the Laboratory at about the same time as Henderson, but at a much lower grade-level. Unlike most of the early Ballistics Division personnel, Jackson had offered only industrial experience, and did not have a college degree. During his tenure in the Ballistics Division he had been given an "outstanding" performance rating, and later he was awarded a patent for work relating to the missile project in the Aeromechanics Branch. The very dissimilar backgrounds of these men who were now at the same level in the organization were not conducive to rapport without some effort to establish it.

It was not surprising, therefore, that a battle line was formed between the two groups in the year preceding the decision for a major reorganization. The Ballistics Division was fighting to survive; the Aeromechanics Division, to consolidate its organization. A serious problem of insufficient personnel still faced the new division, which met frustration in trying to operate with a very limited staff. The slow process of picking up a few people around the Laboratory did not help much; the Aeromechanics Division was able to get only about seven or eight men in this way. Efforts to recruit from outside the Laboratory were doubled and redoubled, but returns were negligible. The only other available source of skills and experience was the Ballistics Division itself.

Jackson and Reed, with the advice and support of their department head, Warner, became an informal team for the purpose of determining how the Aeromechanics Division could most effectively tap this only remaining personnel resource. With Warner as its unofficial head, it was a pretty formidable team. Warner had the full support of key management officials, including the Technical Director, a record of being able to get what he wanted, and an important asset in Reed. The simplest and most desirable solution, these men decided, would be to merge Ballistics Division with the Aeromechanics Division by moving the former organization out of the Research Department and into their own Weapons Development Department. When Warner made this first informal proposal at higher levels, he met with serious, and somewhat unexpected, opposition.

> For some years [Warner recalled], I had felt that the Ballistics Division was not doing any research to speak of. And I had recommended for quite some time that the Division be moved to my department. But a lot of people defended Ballistics Division on the grounds, "Well, that's just Warner trying to be an empire builder." It looked that way. The people in the Division didn't want a change. The head of Research De-

partment opposed it. The head of Ballistics Division opposed it.

I wouldn't say that Dr. Mackay was opposed to it, but he did not want to force it. His point of view was, "What do the people want to do?" My argument was that people want to do anything that a forceful leader wants them to do. They want to feel part of the thing, to feel needed, and all one needs to be is a forceful leader and to say, "This is what I want you to do" and they would be glad to do it. That's what they are looking for. Most people don't want to make up their own minds about large, abstract issues. They want the thing laid out in such a way that it's clear, that they have a niche, that they are important, that they are comfortable, etc. And they are actually willing to suffer a fair amount of discomfort to be part of a going operation and feel like they are making a contribution.

Warner felt that his own Aeromechanics Division was the "going operation," or at least had the most future promise if it could obtain additional personnel. It was, therefore, somewhat surprising to him, in view of his evaluation of the situation, that he was not able to get the kind of support from the top that he had enjoyed in the past. He had underestimated, as he himself realized, the strength of the status quo and the unwillingness of higher level management to force a resolution of issues from the top rather than have it resolved somehow at a lower level. Though the Technical Director's views—both oral and written—about the kind of Research Department the Laboratory needed theoretically supported the kind of change Warner was proposing, such opinions apparently did not mean that he, Mackay, would take any action that was highly disagreeable to some of the parties involved. The proposal did not succeed in bringing about the change suggested by Warner; but it did succeed in intensifying the controversy that revolved continuously around the role of the Research Department, and the effectiveness of its head, Dr. Sherman. Together with more significant considerations of long standing (the Harvard recommendations, and earlier Research Board studies, among others), it would lead eventually to a change in the leadership of the Research Department. Meanwhile, the more Warner, Jackson, and Reed pressed for change, the more resistance increased in the Ballistics Division.

Failure to accomplish reorganization in 1957 did not end the attempt. The Aeromechanics Division continued efforts to recruit from the outside and also to attract specific individuals from the Ballistics Division. There were few illusions, however, about the feasibility of the latter, considering the atmosphere, the relationship that existed between the two division heads, and the attitudes of former colleagues toward each other. Even the newer personnel in the Ballistics Division were well indoctrinated about what to expect in the Aeromechanics Division. Despite the aura of controversy, the Research Department was still regarded by most of its members as an organization of higher prestige than any one of the development departments. As a result, the Ballistics Division front remained solid.

Some attempts were made to revitalize the Ballistics Division, particularly in the Aerodynamics Branch, where it had suffered the most serious personnel losses. A former head of that branch who had left the Laboratory to join a private organization was about to leave his new job. He had enjoyed a good reputation while he was in the Laboratory, and there was some hope that he might be persuaded to return and rebuild the Aerodynamics Branch of Ballistics Division. However, the attempt failed because it was impossible under the civil-service pay structure to come close to meeting the salary he was offered in private employment.

In September 1957, Reed went to Washington for nine months as part of an executive-development program. He was temporarily replaced by a man from Washington who came to spend equal time in the Laboratory. This stint in and around the parent organization in Washington provided not only an opportunity for personal development but also a link between Aeromechanics Division and the officials in Washington who made the important program decisions. Through informal discussions with officials in the parent organization, Reed discovered that the existence of both the Ballistics and Aeromechanics Divisions was causing some confusion, not so much from the similarity of the functional statements describing the work of the two groups but rather from the programs that each had submitted for funding. It was difficult enough to obtain funds in this area, but to get two separate and very similar sets of programs funded was almost impossible. Aside from the merits of individual programs, those with the most articulate advocates were the most likely to receive favorable consideration. Reed was available to discuss the apparent similarities and conflicts in the work proposals of the two divisions, and he did this with the reviewing officials. According to Reed, these casual discussions resulted in an informal but strong suggestion by the Washington officials that program conflicts be resolved. It was apparent that funds sufficient to support adequately all of the programs requested would not be provided. This information was passed along to the Laboratory by Reed, bringing into prominence once again the problem of the Aeromechanics and Ballistics Divisions.

Warner Heads Research Department

Potential reconsideration was postponed in October 1957 by an unrelated event in the form of a satellite called Sputnik. The repercussions of the Soviet achievement for the U.S. defense posture now are history. It became an immediate major issue for the Laboratory; what more might the Laboratory contribute to the space effort than it had? Such new efforts involved the whole technical management group, but most particularly Warner, in whose department many of the space programs logically fell. Both at the Laboratory and in Washington, problems of organizational change and program efforts not directly related to the new considerations were overshadowed. Until conditions became more normal, efforts to move the Ballistics Division out of the Research Department, if not entirely forgotten, were at least held in abeyance.

As it turned out, the future of the Ballistics Division was not to require much more discussion and reconsideration; instead, it would be decided by Warner himself, in a new role. The issues surrounding the Research Department, which had simmered for many years and were brought into the spotlight off and on by such problems as Ballistics Division, led to some action in 1958. Dr. Sherman, for ten years head of the Research Department, resigned and left the Laboratory in April 1958. Dr. Warner was appointed by the Technical Director to succeed him. At the same time, the position of head of the Research Department was enlarged by naming the incumbent as Assistant Technical Director for Research, reporting directly to the Technical Director in this capacity. This new position of Assistant to the Technical Director for a program area was the first such job created, although other similar ones were established later for test and development department heads. These events confirmed and reinforced the influential position of Warner in the Laboratory and indicated that changes were imminent in the Research Department.

Warner represented a new type in the research role, although this kind of role was not new to him. A Ph.D. physicist, he had been an Assistant Professor of Physics at the University of California before coming to the Laboratory. But to the people in the Research Department he represented the image of the "organization man" rather than of the discipline-oriented researcher that most of them thought themselves to be. Nearly all of his previous experience in the Laboratory had been in connection with development projects, and many of the personnel of the Research Department anticipated themselves being changed from researchers to development people. Few of them had a clear understanding of what the appointment of Warner meant to the future of the Research Department.

The future of the Ballistics Division had not been a consideration in Mackay's appointment of Warner; it was too insignificant an issue as far as Laboratory top management was concerned. It was, however, pretty obvious, in view of the decision-making structure in the Laboratory, that Warner could, if he wished, carry out his long-standing plan. No one doubted that he would, but those outside the two divisions were not very concerned with the outcome. As with many other organization changes in the Laboratory, the department and division heads involved would have the final word. The members of the Ballistics Division had no illusions about the eventual outcome. They just waited for the ax to fall.

"The last brick . . . in place . . ."

To begin his program of change, Warner issued a sixteen-page informal paper on his philosophy of the role of the Research Department in the Laboratory. In addition to presenting a careful statement of his definition of research, he elaborated specifically on what he considered to be "trivial research," in the following statements:

> I suppose one could find, perhaps, examples of research individuals and groups who have frittered away their time and efforts on problems which, even if solved, would not advance man's knowledge in a worthwhile degree. In attempting to think of some pertinent examples, the following sorts of problem areas come to mind:
>
> 1. The problems have already been solved (and the researcher is ignorant of this fact) so the results will not advance man's knowledge.
>
> 2. The problems are of such nature that their solutions constitute some sort of new checks on knowledge that is already well established.
>
> 3. The problems spotlight small islands of

> slight uncertainty in the midst of a sea of certainty, so that, when answered, they promise to advance our general structure of knowledge not at all.
>
> The third (above) is truly unworthy of the whole efforts of a professional research individual or group, in my opinion, and are better left to be cleaned up by any individuals or groups who may find it necessary in the course of solving their special problems.

It was no secret that Warner considered much of the work of the Ballistics Division to fall in category three. The stage was now set for a reorganization supported by the rationale of Warner's informal statement. Since considerable discussion had occurred between Warner, Jackson, and Reed throughout the preceding year, the objectives seemed relatively clear to them. Only the details of making announcements and clearing through the necessary administrative procedures remained. Warner reported it as follows:

> As soon as I got over into Research Department I had the necessary authority to carry out the change. I made it my first major decision. The new head of my former department saw it the way I did, perhaps largely because I saw it so strongly that way. The people in Ballistics Division all knew my feelings. I brought the key personnel together and I said something to the effect that they weren't doing any research anyway, they were not in the front ranks competitive with [other government laboratories doing aerodynamics work]. Of course I said I didn't see any reason to expect that they would be competitive with these laboratories. Well, probably I sugar-coated it a little because I personally felt that one good man could do a tremendous amount. [Warner felt the situation was much worse than his statement to the group indicated.] But I put it on the basis that we were a small, poor outfit and didn't have the tools, and so forth. Since we were not doing any research here anyway, and we didn't have a lot of aerodynamically oriented people, I thought it would probably be reasonable to consolidate with the Aeromechanics Division in the Weapons Development Department. And I said that anybody who wanted to stay in Research Department could. They preferred to move.

Even though everyone in Ballistics Division was expecting the ax to fall momentarily, the way in which it happened was demoralizing to the group. None of the people in the Ballistics Division felt that there had been a real opportunity to discuss a reorganization and its potential outcome for the people involved. They knew the decision was made in advance and that nothing they could have said would have altered it. They further felt that there was little that they could say about their future relationships in the Aeromechanics Division that would affect the outcome measurably. It had not been pleasant to listen to a dissertation from Warner on their faults and failures, as "sugar-coated" as Warner thought he had made it; it was not easy for a group of professional personnel with long service in the Laboratory to accept a disagreeable change in which they had essentially no voice. One man who had listened to Warner present his decision on reorganization summarized the feelings of the group as follows:

> Warner called a meeting and told us he didn't want us. He said we would be happier in the Weapons Development Department. He left the final decision to us, but there was really no choice.

Warner himself agreed that the "choice" was somewhat unrealistic:

> It would have immediately raised the question, "Well, if I stay in Research Department, what will I do? I mean, this guy Warner, what would he have for me to do?" No, the choice was probably not meaningful. In other words there was a greater sense of belonging and security staying with the group as it moved than staying in Research Department. No one elected to stay except the division head, who wouldn't go. And he had already been given a senior scientist position.

Warner summarized his view of the reorganization in these words:

> Of course you must consider [Warner stated] that the Aeromechanics Division was also the subject of the reorganization and they had quite a bit of voice in it. Certainly Lee Jackson did. Lee had a long-term voice in it because he did much to shape my thinking. A great deal of the reorganization was brought about by the individual presence of Jackson. Had Lee not been there, I would have been very much at a loss. I would have had no one, then, in whom I had confidence. This confidence may have been misplaced, but the confidence was there and it was the triggering fact in the thing. Without that I would have been quite uninterested in having a reorganization. I would have undoubtedly kept Ballistics Division in Research Department and I would have done what I could to bring in good people.

And he went on to say:

It had been my feeling that the reorganization turned what was in fact a service organization doing rather pedestrian, service-type functions in the field of aerodynamics, and what was theoretically a research group, into a group which was both theoretically and in fact a service-type group. In other words, it was a ratification of the existing situation. It was an attempt to resolve what was obviously a built-in conflict between the mission of the Ballistics Division as it would be derived from the semantics of being in the Research Department and the actual fact of being a service-oriented group.

In the last analysis, the people in the Ballistics Division had seen the situation developing over a period of time and when I became head of the Research Department it was pretty clear that now the last brick had been put in place and that I was prepared to move. Up to that point I was unable to move and I was the only individual around who had a definite idea of what should be done, as I pictured it. The men at the top were neutral. My predecessor who opposed the change was gone, and the division head who also opposed it was no longer in a position to make his opposition stick. So it happened.

With the announcement made, the administrative detail followed in short order. On May 15, 1958, less than one month after Dr. Warner became head of Research Department, a memorandum was issued by the Associate Technical Director (the normal procedure) with the following statement:

Ballistics Division with functions, funds, facilities and personnel, is reassigned from Research Department to Weapons Development Department.

On the basis of this formal statement provided by management, some forty-two physicists, engineers, mathematicians, and other assorted professionals representing the total complement of the Ballistics Division except for the division head, ended their long association with the Research Department. Two months later, approval for the change was requested, as required, from the Washington level with the following justification:

The functions of the Ballistics Division of the Research Department will be integrated with those of the Aeromechanics Division of the Weapons Development Department. This consolidation will provide an integrated group with capability of dealing with all problems of air frames. At the same time it will relieve the Research Department of what has been to a large extent a service function and thus increase the emphasis of that department upon research aspects of the Laboratory's programs.

Approval was perfunctory. The Ballistics Division which had been the center of so much controversy over such a long period was heralded into oblivion in two succinct statements.

Post-Reorganization Problems

For the Aeromechanics Division with its newly enlarged staff, the problems associated with the reorganization were just beginning. As Warner had indicated, a good deal of discussion between himself, Jackson, and Reed had preceded the reorganization. Of chief concern was how to fit a group of forty-two people from the Ballistics Division into the Aeromechanics Division, which had about twenty people in it at the time of the reor-

FIGURE 6:
THE DEMISE OF THE BALLISTICS DIVISION
(May 1958)

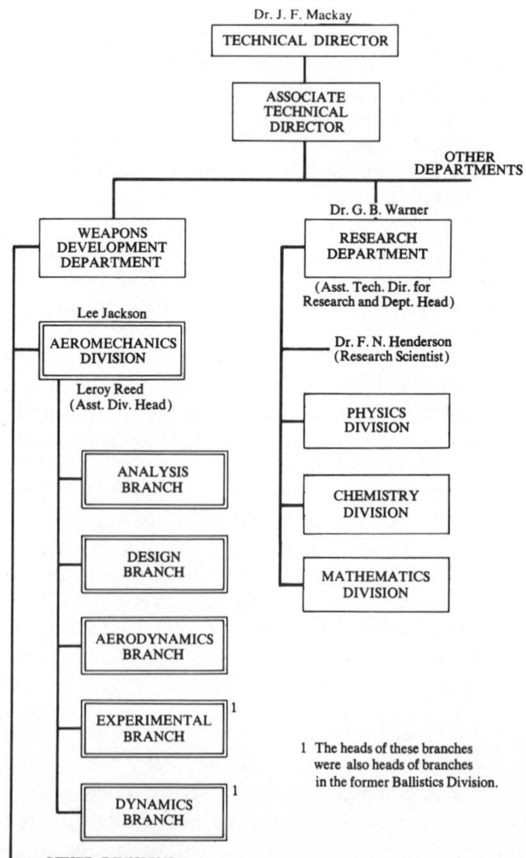

ganization. One tentative decision that was made *a priori* was not to keep all of the Ballistic Division's branches intact. It was felt that individuals could be restimulated and redirected by changing their associations and work groups. As Reed put it:

> We decided to intersperse the groups with considerable thought given to who could work with whom. We actually went down a list of people. I knew them all very well, so I could say, "Put him here," or "No, he would never work out here at all." This is pretty much how we arranged things.

This "mixing up" process, as Reed called it, involved limited prior consultation with the members of the Ballistics Division. At least the senior members of the Ballistics Division most affected by the change viewed the process of consultation as much more limited and useless in terms of its outcome than did Reed or the others in the Aeromechanics Division who were involved. Yet, the consultation did, in fact, have some effect on the immediate outcome of the reorganization.

Less interspersing occurred than Reed originally proposed. Two branches of the Ballistics Division were kept intact—the Ballistics Instruments Branch and the Exterior Ballistics Branch. Only three names were changed in the process of reorganization. The Aerodynamics Branch of the Ballistics Division was merged with the Aerodynamics Branch of the Aeromechanics Division. This left an extra branch head from the Ballistics Division for whom a consulting position was established, adding to the two already existing consultant positions that moved over from the Ballistics Division. According to Reed, this arrangement was satisfactory to the branch head concerned. There were no changes in grade, up or down, for anyone involved, and there were only minor changes in level of administrative responsibility. Reed, in looking back, felt that it had been a mistake to keep any of the old branches of the Ballistics Division intact. As it turned out, a few months following reorganization, the old Ballistics Instruments Branch, which had been renamed the Experimental Branch during the reorganization, was abolished. Its head was made a consultant with no change in grade, and the rest of the people were moved into the Aerodynamics Branch. As a result of this change one man transferred out of the Aeromechanics Division to another group in the Laboratory. He provided the following account of his reasons for moving:

> In 1957 I went on educational leave and was gone when the actual reorganization took place. I returned to the Aeromechanics Division several months after the reorganization, and to my old branch which was still intact, only now with a different name [Experimental Branch]. The branch head was on leave in Europe. I was made acting branch head on my return. I had been thinking for some time previously about leaving this group, even before the reorganization, but in talking with Jackson I was encouraged to stay. Not more than two weeks after that talk the branch was wiped out. This was a terrible thing. No one knew why or what happened and there was no discussion of it. I found myself in the Aerodynamics Branch. It was at this time I definitely decided to transfer.

By now, only one of the former Ballistics Division branches remained intact (the Exterior Ballistics group, which had been renamed the Dynamics Branch), and of it Reed remarked in retrospect:

> As I look back on it now, it was a mistake to keep that branch intact because they have been the most difficult group to integrate into the organization. If I had it to do again, I would have mixed them up as we did with all the other groups eventually.

In sum, when the situation settled down for a short while at least, the merger had resulted in a reduction of the number of branches from eight originally in two divisions, to five in the Aeromechanics Division. Two additional consultant positions had been established, occupied by former branch heads in the Ballistics Division. The internal organization structure was completed after about two or three months. The remaining steps were to get the work organized and the people moving ahead in their new roles.

THE AFTERMATH

Redirecting the Division

During the first year after reorganization the leadership of the Aeromechanics Division set out to redirect the work and the individuals doing it. Warner's philosophy, which had an impact on molding Jackson's thinking, had stressed the need for all work groups to have an "identifiable output"; Warner had felt that a major shortcoming of the Ballistics Division was that, to him, it never had it. By his definition, such an "identifiable output" did not necessarily mean a concrete piece of hardware. He made it clear that university physics departments, for example, had such an output without regard to hardware, and in so describing it, he was speaking from his earlier days as a faculty member of a university, as well as from more recent experiences with university research groups. Jackson, however, appeared to see output more in terms of projects that had tangible results more closely tied with development efforts. In planning the future direction of the Aeromechanics Division, he felt it would be necessary, in order to enlist management support, to turn to concrete projects and to move away from the general functional areas of inquiry. Among other things, Jackson wanted to prove to the people whose judgment counted in the Laboratory that his division could undertake a project, complete it, and show tangible results. His general feeling about the future success of the Aeromechanics Division was that it would have to produce hardware or it would be finished.

Reed, on the other hand, believed that the Division could succeed as a functional organization, although he conceded that it was a constant struggle to make this work out. The major problem he found was getting across to management the need for analysis and careful study; it was necessary to persuade, argue, and battle to convince people that analysis was necessary (if not glamorous) and that failures could be prevented by more careful analytic work.

These differences between Reed and Jackson caused conflicts. Reed saw Jackson attempting to change the personnel in the Division into his own image of a project-oriented individual. He further felt that Jackson was unhappy away from the close association he had had with the PHENIX project, and that all the conflicts Jackson had faced as a part of the Ballistics Division were again reappearing in the Aeromechanics Division—this time without Warner's moral support. At the same time, Jackson was just as convinced that Reed's approach would never succeed in the eyes of the Department head and the Laboratory management generally. These differences between Reed and Jackson made it impossible to confront the incoming ballistics men with a firm and unanimous concept of new goals.

The divergent views of Jackson and Reed suggested that the Division would engage in a variety of types of work during the ensuing year and would meet a variety of problems. It suggested further that, in any case, the products would be identifiable whether they were of the hardware, paper, or service variety. A portion of the work carried over from the Ballistics Division was continued, as for example, in the area of exterior ballistics. There was no appreciable change in the work direction of this group, which was the only one remaining intact as the Dynamics Branch of the Aeromechanics Division. Some major changes in effort were expected and were developed in the aerodynamics area; the Aeroballistics Laboratory, considered to have outlived its usefulness, was put on a standby basis; the consultants were expected to develop their own programs pertinent to new fields of interest in the weapons field, although still of the exploratory and foundational research variety; the work remaining from the PHENIX program in which the old Aeromechanics Branch had engaged was yet to be completed; and finally, several new projects (mostly in the nature of new weapons-feasibility studies) were added.

All in all, plans for the coming years were ambitious. Emphasis was placed on studies of significance to the Laboratory's changing technological interests and on requirements for design and analysis services. This included applied research programs in the area of aerodynamic heating, feasibility studies of missile systems (leading to development programs), and the continuation of the service-type functions for the design and development personnel of the Weapons Development Department, as well as some similar services for a few groups in other development departments. The actual nature of the work (i.e., exploratory and foundational research, service-type analysis functions, etc.) did not alter appreciably from the work previously carried on in the Ballistics and Aeromechanics Divisions before reorganization, although the kinds of problems to be investigated were expected to change in accordance with changing technological interests.

On the other hand, the environment in which the work was done was different for those who had been in the Ballistics Division earlier; it changed from the rather casual atmosphere prevailing in the Research Department to the faster pace of a development department with established deadlines that were expected to be met with as little slippage as possible. For example, when a senior scientist was assigned the task of developing an exploratory research program in a new area of inquiry within three, six, or nine months, he was expected to have something concrete to show at the end of the allotted time. Often, other programs hinged on his accomplishments. Also, commitments were made in Washington, for which the timing was of real concern. When Jackson's and Reed's expectations were not met, considerable consternation resulted. This was true also for the feasibility studies and service-type work in which the division engaged.

In attempting to step up the pace and to redirect individuals and groups into new fields of inquiry, Jackson and Reed tried to work closely with supervisors and other senior personnel. Not everyone, however, was amenable to the new environment, to new or former colleagues, or to new superiors. The unpleasantness of the time when the Ballistics Division was still in existence carried over to the new organization. Jackson and Reed met with resistance from some former Ballistics Division personnel, and sometimes their attempts to get these people moving met with no response whatsoever. This "passive resistance movement," as one man described it, was very frustrating for the division leadership and did not produce good overall morale, even among those who were attempting to move ahead with their work. Further, the project-image that Jackson was trying to create and the obviously conflicting views of Jackson and Reed led to confusion and discontent.

Before the end of the first year following reorganization, Jackson and Reed began to examine their mixed blessings. The events during preceding months had to be evaluated in terms of frustrations as well as accomplishments. A number of people still were not producing according to expectation or just were not producing at all. Most of these were former Ballistics Division people, although a very few were Aeromechanics Division personnel who had either been in the original Aeromechanics Branch or had joined the Division after it was formed. Jackson and Reed tended to deal with individual cases—rather than to examine the whole organization structure, and the relationships within branches and among individuals—to discover whether their own conflicting objectives, or supervisory and communication problems might have been responsible for the difficulties that were being encountered. Clearly, with the consultants whose work was independent of other groups within the Division, difficulties were not entirely a matter of supervision; interpersonal and performance problems were involved. For others, however, conflicting expectations and the quality of supervision did play a part but were not noted in the early considerations. In any case, Jackson and Reed had satisfied themselves that they had done all they could to help and encourage supervisors and subordinate personnel to improve output and attitudes toward work.

Performance-rating time arrived in the spring of 1959—the first since reorganization.[1] Jackson and Reed gave very serious thought to the potentialities of the rating period. Despite the resistance by some to the new environment, almost no one was leaving the Aeromechanics Division. Jackson and Reed expected, or at least hoped, that several persons would transfer within the Laboratory to an area that better suited their interests or would resign for their own and the Division's good. But this did not happen. Hints and encouragement to consider other employment were not effective, except in creating a threatening atmosphere that encouraged a few but not the expected persons to depart. The culmination of all the frustrations of the first ten months led Jackson and Reed to consider more drastic steps after their earlier attempts to improve the situation

[1]The immediate line supervisor is responsible for the day-to-day discussions of performance with the employees under his supervision. In these discussions, the supervisor will make his performance requirements known to the employee and he will establish goals to be reached. For record purposes, the supervisor completes a performance rating on all his subordinates annually.

At rating time the supervisor will summarize the regular performance discussions mentioned above. The individual receives one of three adjective ratings: "outstanding," "satisfactory," or "unsatisfactory." The great majority of ratings given are "satisfactory."

For the other two ratings ("outstanding" and "unsatisfactory") it is necessary for the supervisor to complete additional justification beyond what is required of the "satisfactory" rating. A supervisor must recommend an employee for an "outstanding" rating and substantiate this, by example, in writing. It must then be approved by his superiors.

Before an employee can be given an "unsatisfactory" rating, he must be given a ninety-day advance letter of warning. In the letter of warning, the supervisor must state exactly what the employee has been doing to warrant a rating of unsatisfactory performance. One of four courses of action must result by the end of the ninety-day period: (1) the output of the employee improves enough to warrant a "satisfactory" rating; (2) proceedings are originated to remove the employee from employment; (3) the employee transfers to another job (without reduction in pay); or (4) the employee is demoted.

by discussion and encouragement had not succeeded.

In an organization such as the Laboratory, carrying on research and development with highly specialized scientific-technical personnel, it was not easy to determine precisely that a man was not producing what he should. This was especially true of those specialists who performed foundational or exploratory research, as did some of the ballistics men who seemed problems to Jackson and Reed. Such assessments might require judgments about a man's work in a field in which he was more authoritative than others in the Laboratory.

With assistance from Personnel Department analysts, Jackson, Reed, and other supervisors within the Division prepared letters of warning to nine individuals preliminary to possible "unsatisfactory" performance ratings three months later if performance did not improve sufficiently to warrant a "satisfactory" rating. One letter (stronger and more detailed than most) included these statements:

> The quality and quantity of your work has been below that expected from one at your level. In your general area of interest you are expected to determine and recommend areas where research of fundamental interest to the Laboratory is required. After these areas are established, you are to plan and initiate and direct research programs as needed. For example, Research Program X* is a very important part of our overall Laboratory program. It took approximately six months' time before you were able to arrive at an acceptable program to contribute to Program X for our division. During this time, counseling and attempts at motivation by me and others did not appear to be fruitful, although the requirement for expediency was obvious to all concerned. Definite commitments have been made in connection with this program to headquarters. Thus far, the indications are that you have not put forth sufficient effort to assemble and use effectively the resources required to carry out this program. In view of poor performance on your part in connection with headquarters commitments on Study Y*, you should appreciate my concern at this time.
>
> As a consultant and an implied expert in aerodynamics with an extensive background in ———— phenomena, you have thus far failed to demonstrate any interest or enthusiasm in division projects or problem areas requiring competence in this area. When a problem area has been pointed out, you have shown little or no interest. You are not forceful enough in the presentation of your ideas and proposals, thereby failing to stimulate interest in your work by other Laboratory personnel.
>
> Every opportunity and assistance will be given you to improve your work performance. To achieve this necessary improvement, it will be necessary for you to demonstrate by your initiative and actions that we can with confidence expect some *early, definite* achievements in Program X research. You must also show greater interest in the work of the division. . . . Excellent opportunity for you to demonstrate the necessary improvement can be found in your conduct of Program X research, in initiating and directing other research programs, directing your creative energies toward division objectives. . . . You should define the broad areas of your responsibility that you would actually like to see work out in practice. I will be happy to discuss your draft jointly and reach an agreement as to its adequacy. Then it is recommended that you establish short-term performance goals or targets for yourself, which will enable you to achieve simultaneously both your objectives and those of the organization.

Most were written to former Ballistics Division personnel. After the writing process was completed, only seven of the letters were actually issued; several were withdrawn shortly after issuance. By the end of the ninety-day period all of the letters were, for record purposes, withdrawn, and all the individuals involved received "satisfactory" performance ratings. In view of what was hoped for by those responsible, the outcome was not as unusual as it first seemed. In the first place, it was hoped that the personnel involved would make serious efforts to improve their performance so that "unsatisfactory" ratings would not need to be issued. The procedures for processing such a rating were complex and unpleasant—a last-resort measure that supervisors generally tried to avoid. In the second place, it was expected that several of the persons would seek transfers to other parts of the Laboratory or find outside employment during the three-month period before a final rating was due. Each of the letters offered assistance to the individual to improve his performance within the Division.

During the ninety-day period that followed the issuance of the letters, reactions were mixed. In a few instances performance improved sufficiently

* Letters substituted for actual project names.

to warrant a "satisfactory" rating. In one case the improvement was described as "remarkable" by the supervisor. In another, the individual opened negotiations to transfer to another department, but nothing materialized. Not one person left the Laboratory during this period or appeared seriously to consider leaving. In the end, whether performance had materially improved or not, no attempt was made to carry through the process of formalizing an "unsatisfactory" rating. According to the personnel analyst involved, the reasons for abandoning further action were as follows:

> They [the letters] were extremely unpopular, not only with the people who received them and the rest of the old Ballistics Division group, but they were also unpopular throughout the Laboratory. And even top management appeared a little bit annoyed about it—annoyed that it had gotten to the point of a warning letter and that the knowledge of it reached other groups in the Laboratory. This was, after all, the first time we had issued letters of warning in such quantity in a single group to personnel at the grade levels involved in these cases (GS-12's, 13's and 14's). It was, of course, not the first time we had issued individual letters of warning to professional personnel. But this was more of a group situation. Furthermore, we hoped we would not have to go through with them [the 'unsatisfactory' rating procedures] because we were not sure of ourselves and we knew they would have to be studied and restudied in a long, drawn-out process.

By the time the ninety-day period was over, Jackson and Reed were still left with the problem of resolving their own conflicts and of reshaping the Division and redirecting some of its efforts. By now they realized they would have to do this by means other than the use of warning letters which had brought relatively unsatisfactory, or at best, inconclusive results.

Postscript—1960

A year and one-half after the warning letters were issued and after the problems of effectively merging two divisions into one organization were seriously faced, a number of internal changes had been made. Two new branches, many new faces, and a series of new projects had been added. Another branch was abolished, and its personnel were divided into several of the existing branches. The former Ballistics Division personnel represented a much smaller portion of the Aeromechanics Division than when they had outnumbered the Aeromechanics Division personnel two to one, just after the reorganization. The Aeromechanics Division grew from a group of twenty persons just prior to the merger with the Ballistics Division to more than ninety, making it one of the largest technical divisions in the Laboratory. Jackson and Reed held their same positions, as did most former Ballistics Division personnel, including those who had received warning letters. One of this group subsequently left the Laboratory. Warner left also, and the role that he had played in the Ballistics Division reorganization was of only historical interest.

The Aeromechanics Division had some success

FIGURE 7:
ORGANIZATION OF THE AEROMECHANICS DIVISION—1960

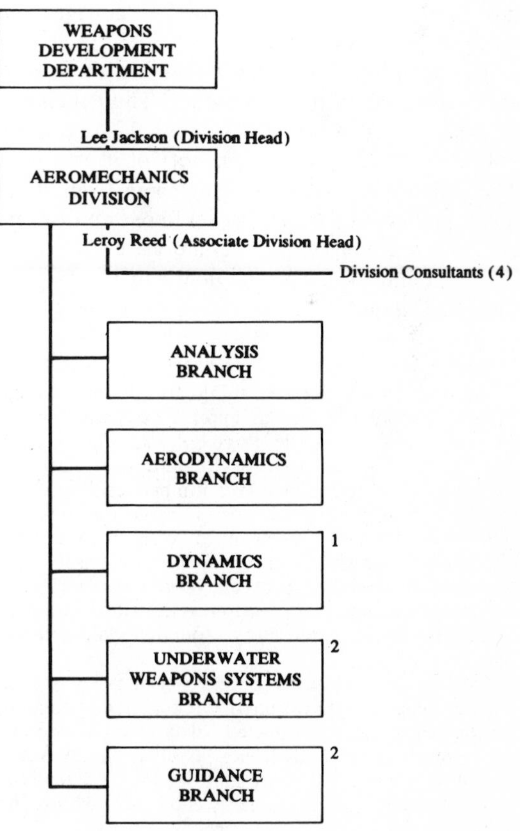

1 Only branch head from former Ballistics Division still remaining.

2 Added from another division in Weapons Development Department since reorganization. Two branches have been abolished since reorganization: Experimental Branch and Design Branch.

in its later projects, especially with some of its feasibility studies. Some said that these accomplishments tangibly improved the climate and morale in the Division. On the other hand, the funding problems which had plagued the old Ballistics Division remained as serious for the Aeromechanics Division. Some interpersonal difficulties remained, and the internal organization changes were probably not yet completed.

This much can be said about the success or failure of the 1958 reorganization: A service-type group was removed from the Research Department. Making the Ballistics Division part of a development department did not solve all the funding problems as some had thought it would, nor were all of the problems of leadership resolved. To some extent, the redirection of the group into areas of more pressing technological concern was accomplished, though how successfully no one could yet say. As things stood at the end of 1960, a meaningful appraisal of the reorganization upon which a reasonable measure of agreement could be reached was not yet possible, and in such a rapidly changing organization, it might never be.

APPENDIX I

The Laboratory's program centers around its development efforts, namely, the development of weapons and weapon components. Development programs utilize research findings whether the research is done within the Laboratory or whether it is done outside the Laboratory—at colleges and universities, for example.

The definitions presented below are those generally used within the Laboratory. The definitions of research come from an internal Laboratory publication dealing with the history of its research. The definitions of development come from statements prepared by the Industrial Research Institute and follow closely earlier definitions by the Joint Research and Development Board of the Department of Defense.

RESEARCH

Research means different things to different people. What one may consider as applied research another will speak of as design development; exploratory work may be classified as basic or fundamental. There is, for instance, no line of demarcation between basic and exploratory work. The categories merge one into the other in a continuous spectrum of research effort. It is effectively impossible, and probably inadvisable, to draw any distinct line between various categories. In this statement, however, research is classified into four categories: basic, exploratory, foundational, and applied.

Basic or *pure* research is that which is carried on without specific application in view. Fundamental in the clearest sense, it is directed solely toward widening the frontiers of our knowledge. The investigator is free to follow where his findings may lead. It is essentially a creative activity. The emphasis is on formulation and validation of theory.

Exploratory research, although without specific application, has, however, an ultimate application within an area of interest to the sponsoring organization. Research in this category draws on the findings of the more general, theoretical studies. The purpose here is to explore an area and acquire data in order to learn about the behavior of materials and the mechanisms of processes. At the Laboratory there are many programs of this kind, such as research in combustion, fluid dynamics, optics, mathematical statistics, and aeroballistics.

Foundational research is defined as that work which is undertaken with a definite end item in view. It is at this point, where research might be said to cross the line from basic to applied work, that a tangible goal appears. It is here that we find general studies of propulsion, of explosive systems, and of guidance and control problems. The feasibility studies of components or of major weapon systems are included in this category. Foundational research establishes what a proposed weapon will do, and the conditions under which it will be operating. It also identifies the most promising methods, probable design, or material for the proposed applications.

Applied research then makes use of this information; here the problems of a specific weapon are attacked with the tools provided by the research that has gone before. This applied research is the research project of industry; at the Laboratory it is generally carried on under a specific assignment when the Laboratory has accepted responsibility for designing a particular weapon.

A concrete example will serve to mark out the areas more clearly.

Basic, fundamental research in physics could be represented by the highly theoretical work of an investigator studying wave mechanics—the mechanisms of radiation. A second investigator might use the results of this basic study—largely equations—to explore the region of the near infrared.

The characteristics of this region are searched out: flux density, source strength, atmospheric attenuation, and strength and width of different band frequencies. At this point, the exact application is not specified; one may conjecture that the information has probable application to problems of search and detection. But the necessary reservoir of information about a specific physical phenomenon is increased.

The general studies of the infrared region can now be used to lay the foundation for an infrared detection system. Quantitative spectral measurements of radiation from various targets and backgrounds at different altitudes indicate the types of targets, detectors, filters, and reticles possible for such a system. Foundational research indicates the most promising material for the detector, and the optimum chopping rate for the scanner reticle.

Applied research is even more specific. It is directed toward determining responses of a prototype system to simulated operating conditions. Acceleration tests on sleds, exposure to environmental extremes, and trials of different bonding materials for the scanner cell all fall into this category.

In summary, we see the shift from the most basic, far-ranging study, through the middle ground of exploratory and foundation work, to the applied study directed toward getting definite answers to specific questions.

It is the general consensus that the most basic research can be more effectively conducted in the colleges, universities, and privately endowed research institutes. . . . Exploratory and foundational research . . . can be most productive in a somewhat different climate—one nearer to development. Although some exploratory work is essentially basic—it must be, by reason of the type of information required—there is always some possible application.

DEVELOPMENT

Development is the extension of the findings and theories of a scientific or technical nature into practical application for experimental or demonstration purposes including the construction and testing of experimental models or devices.

Early Development is the application of the findings from applied research to a specific program to the point at which the first experimental model of a product or the first application of a process is undertaken.

Final Development is that portion of a product or process development from the end of the initial development to production of the plans and specifications for the item, or to the initiation of the process including pilot plant operation.

MARIANA ROBINSON

The Coming of Age of the Langley Porter Clinic:

The Reorganization of a Mental Health Institute

MARIANA ROBINSON

The author of *Health Centers and Community Needs* and *The Coming of Age of the Langley Porter Clinic* received a B.A. degree from Swarthmore College. She has served as a Public Administration Analyst, Bureau of Public Administration, University of California at Berkeley, and, most recently, has been a consultant to San Joaquin County Local Health District on a two-year administration study, *Forty Years of Public Health in San Joaquin County*.

CHRONOLOGY OF KEY EVENTS

July 1956	Dr. Simon is appointed Medical Superintendent of Langley Porter Clinic
August 1956	Dr. Prestwood is appointed Assistant Superintendent
Fall 1956	Finance Department refuses to endorse proposed budget and recommends survey for evaluation of budget requests
February 1, 1957	Top staff of Organization and Cost Control Division (Finance Department), Finance Department, and Langley Porter meet to discuss conduct of survey
February 6, 1957	Simon introduces survey team to Langley Porter staff
April 1957	Berke, Associate Administrative Analyst for OCC, brings rough draft of report to Simon, Prestwood, and Saunders, Dean of the University of California Medical School
Late May 1957	Berke, Spencer, his assistant, and Blanchard, Acting Chief Administrative Analyst, OCC, meet with staff to discuss survey recommendations; afterwards, Simon meets with his staff and urges them to go along with the plan
June 28, 1957	Survey is published
July 1957	Berke and Blanchard, Acting Chief Administrative Analyst, OCC, meet with staff to discuss implementation of report
1958	Three staff members leave Clinic
June 1958	Miss Byron, Director, Social Work Department, shifts to full-time association with Clinic
1959	New four-story addition to Clinic is built
1959-1960	Agreement is signed between state Department of Mental Hygiene and University of California, symbolizing establishment of closer ties between them
June 1960	Prestwood sets up administrative advisory committee
Mid-1960	Prestwood feels staff is adequate in size for Clinic's needs

PRINCIPAL CHARACTERS

Klaus W. Berblinger, M.D., Chief of Clinical Services

John W. Berke, Associate Administrative Analyst, Organization and Cost Control Division, Department of Finance

Marvin L. Blanchard, Acting Chief Administrative Analyst, OCC Division, Department of Finance

Karl W. Bowman, M.D., Medical Superintendent and Chairman, Department of Psychiatry (retired, 1956)

Helen V. Byron, Director, Social Work Department

A. Rodney Prestwood, M.D., Associate Medical Superintendent and Assistant Professor, Department of Psychiatry

Alexander Simon, M.D., Medical Superintendent and Chairman, Department of Psychiatry (1956—)

George Spencer, Analyst, Budget Division, Department of Finance

S. A. Szurek, M.D., Director, Children's Service; Professor, Department of Psychiatry

Robert J. Wensel, Business Manager

INTRODUCTION

The Langley Porter Neuropsychiatric Institute was the first, and until recently the only, institution of its kind in California and the Far West. It is a small psychiatric hospital of a very special sort, dedicated primarily to teaching, training, and research in the field of mental illness. The intensive treatment program of the Institute, also a major function, serves as the foundation for the teaching and research activities. Although psychiatry is dominant within this field, it functions in cooperation with, and is supported by, the allied disciplines of clinical psychology, nursing, social work, and rehabilitation therapies. Other medical specialties also are indispensable adjuncts to the work with mental illness, such as the laboratory sciences and techniques of electroencephalography and neuropathology. All of these disciplines are represented at Langley Porter, coordinated in a many-faceted attack upon the stubborn problems of the mentally ill. In most of these disciplines, teaching, training, and research are conducted in a complex interweaving of programs that come to a focus, for the most part, at the patient-treatment level.

The Institute, usually referred to by its former name of Clinic, is staffed and operated jointly by the California State Department of Mental Hygiene and the University of California School of Medicine. It stands upon the original site alongside the medical school's new Moffitt Hospital on Parnassus Avenue, half-way up one of San Francisco's high, steep hills. From this elevation, Langley Porter looks over the city and across the Golden Gate to the magnificent hills of Marin County.

Langley Porter Clinic was born of dedicated struggle and a vision in the minds of a few men. Both potential conflict and aspirations were built in at the start, for the Clinic's two parent institutions, the medical school and the Department of Mental Hygiene, through the years have not shared entirely the same goals and hopes for it. Nor, until recently, have they agreed upon a mutually acceptable, clear division of separate responsibilities and joint cooperative functions within the Clinic. Thus, centrifugal as well as cohesive forces have characterized the growing years of Langley Porter since its establishment in 1941. There have been problems and recurring stresses; yet the Clinic has survived, grown, matured, and achieved a reputation for excellence that its founders might well consider a fulfillment of their purposes and aspirations.

The story of the reorganization of Langley Porter, which began in 1957 and was nearing completion in the summer of 1960, is set in this organizational matrix of complex functioning, multiple purposes, and dual direction. It cannot be a simple story. Nor can it be completely accurate, for much of it took place only in the minds of many people, some now dead or far away, and was never recorded for the benefit of later research. Much of the presentation here is impressionistic, relying on memories, and some of it is interpretive.

This study deals with the administrative and organizational aspects of a *process of planned change* within a publicly administered agency: why change was desired and by whom; how it was planned and undertaken; who participated in planning, deciding, and implementing change, and who did not; and, finally, what the consequences were in terms of the goals of change, and in the impact upon those affected.

Essentially, the story that follows is one of achievement, of significant, if relative, success. The study's attention to stresses, divergent viewpoints, and goals should not obscure in the reader's mind the accomplishments of a vigorous institution, staffed by dedicated, able people, working in an inherently complex, difficult, and stressful setting. Identification of such frictions in change was one of the major purposes of the research.

ESTABLISHMENT AND GROWTH OF LANGLEY PORTER CLINIC

The Langley Porter Clinic underwent a process of reorganization during the years 1957-1960, following a management survey by the Organization and Cost Control Division (OCC) of the California

State Department of Finance in the spring of 1957. This process was no superficial juggling of titles, duties, or arrangements of little boxes on organization charts, although these elements were included. It was a deep-going matter that reached back in time to deal with issues raised even before the Clinic's official founding in 1941. These particular issues had remained partially unresolved during the course of the Clinic's growth, tending to hamper the institution's full effectiveness in carrying out its mission in the mental health field. The survey and reorganization effort dealt with much more than these early conflicts; yet the many-dimensioned process of change, which affected the functioning and behavior of many of the Langley Porter staff members and of others in several related agencies, had its deepest roots in this long-ago past.

The story of the management survey and the subsequent reorganization must begin, therefore, with the founding of the Langley Porter Clinic.

The Welfare and Institutions Code of the State of California was augmented in July 1941 by an act of the Legislature to read in part:

> There is an acute neuropsychiatric hospital located on the grounds adjacent to the campus of the University of California Medical School which shall be the Langley Porter Clinic. . . . [Chap. 7 added by Stats. 1941, Ch. 963]

Langley Porter Clinic was thus formally brought into being by the sanctioning act of the state's legislators. The cornerstone of the present building had been laid in April of that year, but it was to be March of 1943 before the fledgling institution opened the doors of its permanent home to its first patients.

Behind the law's simple declaration of fact lay several years of effort, frustration, and struggle for the men who saw the need for a psychiatric institute and worked to make it a reality. Unsuccessful attempts to establish a similar institute, to be operated jointly by the State Department of Institutions (now Mental Hygiene) and the University of California School of Medicine,[1] had been made at least as early as 1937. It was not until 1939, when a new Governor appointed Dr. Aaron J. Rosanoff as the first psychiatrist to direct the Department of Institutions, that the attempt was successful. Funds for a building were appropriated that same year.

The Need, the Men, and the Goals

In 1940 California had not yet developed adequate strength in psychiatry, in terms of facilities for teaching and research and numbers of well-trained people for the care of the mentally ill. Among those who saw a great need for developing psychiatry within California, and who did most to bring this about, were Dr. Robert Langley Porter, pediatrician and Dean of the University of California School of Medicine; Dr. Aaron J. Rosanoff, Director of the Department of Institutions, which administered the large state mental hospital system; and Dr. Walter L. Treadway of the United States Public Health Service, who was assigned to the University as a consultant during the planning and negotiations for establishing the Clinic. These three men cooperated in the endeavor to create the Clinic.

Dr. Langley Porter, Dean of a medical school that then had no separate department of psychiatry,[2] wanted to develop this medical specialty, together with adequate facilities for teaching and research in the field. Porter and his colleagues in the school envisaged a psychiatric institute where several specialists in medicine, especially neurology and neurosurgery, would collaborate in a true multiple-discipline approach to mental illness. The medical school, however, lacked the funds necessary to set up such an institute of its own and turned to the state's Department of Institutions for the means to achieve this goal. It was recognized that the state mental hospitals offered immense potential resources for the study of mental illness.

In the Department of Institutions, as represented by Dr. Rosanoff, the school found an enthusiastic ally, with the backing of the Governor. As early as January 1939, in his first month as Director, Rosanoff wrote Dr. Porter: "I cannot tell you how highly I value the developing contact [of the Clinic] with the University and Medical School. I cannot help but feel that this is the beginning of a new era in the destiny of psychiatry in this part of the country." Rosanoff felt strongly that the state hospital system needed the valuable resources in teaching and research that a good university medical school could offer. He foresaw as the benefits of a joint

[1] The University of California is a state university but enjoys special status. Its Board of Regents is responsible directly to the Governor (and to the Legislature).

[2] The Department of Medicine included a small group of psychiatrists.

facility advances in the diagnosis and treatment of mental illness that would reduce the ever-increasing hospital population through more and faster cures and better methods of patient care.

Thus each institution needed the other to attain its objectives, but the objectives differed. The school primarily wanted facilities and support for teaching and research, while the Department of Institutions wanted to make use of the school's scientific resources. Leaders of both foresaw a mutually fruitful collaboration that would also improve the quantity and quality of care for the mentally ill in the state as a whole.

Negotiations proceeded from 1939 to 1941. Neither Dr. Porter nor Dr. Rosanoff was free to reach a formal agreement independently. An early contract proposed by the University's Board of Regents would have given "almost complete control" of the new institution to the medical school, with the Department of Institutions responsible for all costs of building and operation. The state's attorney general refused to countenance the proposal on the grounds that the Department could not legally relinquish jurisdiction of the Clinic or even lease a site from the University. Dr. Rosanoff apparently did not find the University's proposal personally unacceptable, but he was bound by the state's decision.

In the end, the University's Board of Regents deeded to the state the plot upon which the first building was erected, but no formal contract was entered into between the Department and the University then or for many years. The act passed by the Legislature in 1941 provided for the sole authorization for, and the conditions of joint operation of, Langley Porter Clinic.

Long after, these events were described in a letter by a departmental officer, who had been on the scene at the time, as follows:

> This agreement [offered in 1940 by the University for approval] was never signed due to the fact that it could not be approved by the Attorney General as it was a very one-sided agreement, giving the Regents all power to operate the Institute while our Department paid all bills. During this early period there was considerable conflict with the Regents and their attorneys respecting this agreement. . . .
>
> As the State could not come to terms with the Regents, Dr. Rosanoff also negotiated with the San Francisco General Hospital and with Stanford University regarding locating the Institute adjacent to their facilities. As a result of such negotiations by Dr. Rosanoff, the Regents agreed to abide by the recommendations of the Attorney General.

The tension engendered by this dispute between the medical school and the state government at the time of the Clinic's founding was to persist and influence the development of the Clinic for years.

The Law Establishing Langley Porter

The law that established the Clinic laid down the basic responsibilities and privileges of each institution but left much to subsequent interpretation. This act read in part:

> The Langley Porter Clinic shall be conducted and maintained for the purpose of treating incipient and acute mental and nervous cases.
>
> The Regents of the University of California deeded unconditionally to the Department of Institutions the land upon which the Langley Porter Clinic is constructed. The purpose of the deed of gift was to provide for the State a suitable site whereon through the agency of the Department of Institutions there might be constructed, and thereafter maintained and operated, an acute neuropsychiatric hospital unit. . . . It was the further purpose of the Regents to enable the State, through the Department of Institutions, to develop as far as possible preventive work in the field of mental disorders, and to make full provisions for the diagnosis of such disorders in their incipient and earliest stages with a view to instituting timely and more effective treatment. It was the further purpose of the Regents to insure to the State through the proximity of the Langley Porter Clinic to the Medical Center of the University of California, full opportunity for consultation with the university's personnel at the Medical Center, and to provide opportunities for the State and University of California to cooperate in prevention, diagnosis, treatment and promotion of research in the field of mental disorder, and advancement of the learning and knowledge of students of the university, and others whose work lies in the fields of surgery and medicine, and, in particular, in those branches of medical science which have to do with mental and nervous diseases and disorders. It is, therefore, the intent of the Legislature that all the facilities and services of the University of California Medical School be made available to the Department of Institutions at the Langley Porter Clinic upon the desire of the Regents of the University of California to make such facilities and services available to the department.

The law gave the University the exclusive right and privilege of rendering professional and administrative consultant services to the Clinic. The University was also given the exclusive right and privilege of providing for the Clinic, of carrying on and conducting in it such teaching services as it wished, and of supervising and administering these. It was given the same rights with regard to research. In both instances the right of the Department to carry on its own teaching and research was reserved. Finally, the Regents were given the exclusive right and privilege to make available to the Clinic, and to use and employ therein in the exercise of its other privileges and rights, any or all of the professional and scientific services and facilities of the University.

Other paragraphs of the law dealt with the inclusion of an outpatient department, the setting up of a board of trustees with no duties except the arbitration of differences between the institutions, the qualifications of the Clinic's director, and some technical points.

This law established an intricate administration, meant to function in a complex, cooperative manner, but it did not provide a clear definition of goals and activities in terms of joint and separate responsibilities. Since much of the content was expressed in discretionary language, the future development of the Clinic depended largely upon the attitudes, objectives, and goodwill in both institutions, as represented in the persons who would carry on this collaborative enterprise. Neither Dr. Porter nor Dr. Rosanoff continued long in the positions of leadership they held in 1941. Dr. Porter retired in 1941; Dr. Rosanoff retired in 1942 and died in early 1943, only a few weeks before the new Clinic building opened.

The Clinic Opens

In the summer of 1941 Dr. Karl M. Bowman was offered the directorship of the Langley Porter Clinic by Dr. Rosanoff. At the time he accepted the offer, Dr. Bowman enjoyed a distinguished reputation in American psychiatry. (He was subsequently to serve as president of the American Psychiatric Association during 1944-1946.) Since 1936 he had been clinical director of psychiatry at Bellevue Medical Center in New York and professor of psychiatry at New York University. Working in a city-owned institution and in the court clinics, as well as other public institutions, had given him experience with a governmental milieu.

Dr. Bowman assumed his duties as Medical Superintendent of the Clinic in November 1941. The medical school appointed him to its faculty, and in 1942 he became chairman of a newly established Department of Psychiatry. (Both Bowman and his successor, Dr. Alexander Simon, have held these two appointments simultaneously. The University and the Department of Mental Hygiene have been joined in the person of one man, holding two positions and receiving two salaries. This has been the case also with the Associate Medical Superintendent, who must be a medical school faculty member. All the rest of the staff have been employed by only one of the two cooperating agencies.)[3]

The Clinic building was completed and dedicated in February 1943.

Langley Porter Clinic has sometimes been referred to, even though affectionately, as a "bastard" institution or a "two-headed monster." In a sense, the young Clinic became a sort of stepchild to both its parent agencies. Those who followed Drs. Porter and Rosanoff did not regard it with the founders' spirit of dedication. As a newcomer within both larger institutions, the Clinic was subject to some degree of "sibling rivalry." The medical school was disappointed by the lack of control it had been obliged to accept if it was to have any facility at all, and some established departments within the school were envious of the comparative affluence of the new department. (The Clinic would have nearly 100 beds, while the school's own hospital at that time had only 160, shared by all departments.) The Department of Institutions, with a new director, was entering a six-year period during which it lacked aggressive medical leadership.[4] Dr. Rosanoff apparently had left behind him no legacy of vigorous support for his plans and hopes for the development of Langley Porter. Some permanent officers in the Department resented the attitudes displayed by the medical school at the time of negotiations, lacked interest in supporting either research or teaching, and tended to view the Clinic as a small but pretentious upstart, because of its connection with the University.

The third factor in this situation was Dr. Bowman himself, first Medical Superintendent of Langley Porter. Dr. Bowman, as he understood

[3] However, all Department of Mental Hygiene staff physicians are given unpaid clinical appointments to the School of Medicine.

[4] The new head, Mrs. Dora Heffner, was neither a physician nor a psychiatrist.

his job, had been brought to California to develop a department of psychiatry at the medical school and an institute for the care of acute, early mental disease, where research and teaching in several disciplines would be conducted by *both* the medical school and the Department of Institutions. He expected support from both organizations in his responsibility for development of the Clinic. He now found that this was not readily forthcoming, because of the friction between them, the lack of full acceptance and support for the Clinic and its mission, and the lack of explicit agreement on responsibility and cooperation. Bowman fell heir to the conflicts surrounding the Clinic's founding. He was suspect in both the school and the Department, each of which tended to regard him as more closely allied with the other. He belonged to them both and, therefore, to neither.

In character, Dr. Bowman was independent and outspoken, with strong convictions he did not hesitate to fight for. He offered cooperation to both the medical school and the Department but refused to be dominated by either. Finding the Department more responsive to his needs, although only with respect to the Clinic's patient-treatment functions, he soon learned to seek support for developing the Clinic more from the Department than from the medical school.

Within the Department, care of the mentally ill was a normal and major function. The Clinic received support on this basis, but Bowman's requests for support of teaching and research were consistently refused, since they were regarded as functions for the medical school alone. Within the school, Bowman fought repeatedly for the Clinic's welfare (as he viewed it) and inevitably made some enemies, as well as friends. He successfully fended off efforts of some elements in the school to take control of some of the services and wards within the Clinic. In this, he received the support of the Board of Trustees of the Clinic (which included Dr. Robert Langley Porter) and of President Robert Gordon Sproul of the University. At the time, under the state's Welfare and Institutions Code, Bowman had authority to keep control of the administration of the Clinic and insisted on doing so.

Early Development of the Clinic

The early years were a period of establishing, one by one, the functions, services, and departments needed at Langley Porter to carry out the several purposes for which it had been founded.

A special grant to the medical school from the Commonwealth Fund established three units at Langley Porter as part of the Department of Psychiatry. These were Child Psychiatry, Medical Psychology, and Social Work. Each was directed by a faculty member, who thus became an administrator within the Clinic as well as a teacher, a situation that later came to be considered anomalous in the Clinic's administrative structure.[5] During 1944-1945 these three groups developed programs at Langley Porter.

Early staff members in the Clinic[6] included Miss Corinne Parsons, Superintendent of Nursing; Mrs. Evelyn Stearns, Business Manager; and Dr. Alexander Simon, recruited in 1943 from St. Elizabeth's Hospital in Washington, D.C. to become Bowman's Assistant Medical Superintendent and member of the school's faculty in psychiatry. In 1945 Dr. Nathan Malamud joined the Clinic staff to head the Neuropathology and Clinical Laboratories.

By late 1945, two and one-half years after its opening, Langley Porter Clinic, though still relatively small and incomplete, had established most of the services and departments it would have in 1960. They included Psychiatry, Child Psychiatry, Medical Psychology, Nursing, Social Work, Rehabilitation Therapies, and Neuropathology. A library had been opened; four of the six wards were open; and about 800 patients were being treated on the Inpatient and Outpatient Services.

These accomplishments were not achieved without struggle. Langley Porter's development as an institute was impeded not only by the lack of enthusiastic support within its parent agencies but also by a lack of understanding of its mission within the state government as a whole. The Clinic was the first institution of its kind in the state, and its unique mission and needs were not fully recognized or supported. Within the Department of Institutions, the Department of Finance, and the State Personnel Board, the functions of teaching and research, together with positions in appropriate classifications to perform them, were not readily accepted as legitimate for Langley Porter. This negative attitude was partly expedient: Why should the Department of Institutions spend money for programs the University was supposed to carry on? The law establishing Langley Porter had explicitly reserved the right of the Department to

[5] It should be recalled that, under the law, the Department of Institutions, not the medical school, was to provide administration of the Clinic.

[6] These were people still at the Clinic in 1957.

carry on teaching and research at the Clinic. But, although there was good reason to believe that Dr. Rosanoff had intended to develop these functions at the Clinic with departmental support,[7] the Department refused to exercise this right. Dr. Bowman's every attempt to gain Department support was met with the question, "Why on *this* budget?"

It was established policy in the control agencies of California state government that, with very minor exceptions, no state agency was permitted to engage in *basic* research; this function was considered to be the responsibility of the University of California (and of private institutions). Within limits, which varied from department to department, some *applied* research was sanctioned.

The Clinic was for many years treated as a miniature mental *hospital,* not as an *institute* for intensive treatment, training, and research in the mental health disciplines. The various agencies of state government controlling the Clinic's funds and personnel were accustomed to think in terms of the established functions and administrative structures in the state hospital system. These hospitals had very little teaching and research, but huge populations of patients. They were custodial institutions, asylums, a situation that Dr. Rosanoff had hoped to change, in part through the leadership to be supplied by Langley Porter Clinic. They operated with a far lower ratio of staff to patient population, and with less highly trained staffs, than could a full teaching and research institution. The state government did not display much sympathetic understanding of the different mission of the Clinic, for which there was, as yet, no appropriate pattern of budgeting and staffing.

One other factor apparently entered into the Clinic's difficulty: There was, in the 1940's, recognition of a need for upgrading the entire state hospital system.[8] The California state hospitals fell far short of standards recommended by the American Psychiatric Association (as did all state hospitals), according to a survey made by the United States Public Health Service in 1943 at the state's request. The Department of Institutions not only had to keep expanding to meet population needs but wanted to improve the entire system. Within the Department as a whole, the Clinic appeared very small indeed, with a tiny portion of the total budget and only a handful of patients.

The Postwar Years

Sometime during the postwar era the Clinic's status as a "stepchild" began to change. Following World War II psychiatry entered upon a period of rapid growth, new developments in treatment, and increasing acceptance. This was in part a sharing in the general advances being made in medicine. Also, the problems of mental health were receiving increasing attention as the mounting numbers of the mentally ill outgrew hospital facilities, and public financial support was forced to increase accordingly.

In California the problem was recognized as acute in all branches of the state government where the annually soaring costs of mental illness were a matter of concern. The value of programs for developing more effective treatments and new methods of patient care was gaining greater understanding, not only for humane reasons but because of potential reductions in the enormous financial burden. The Legislature's predominant attitude had always been favorable toward supplying funds; it seldom made cuts in the Clinic's budget.

The federal government had increasing influence on state programs through its grants for teaching and research. These funds were eagerly sought by Langley Porter, although, as Dr. Bowman noted in his annual report in 1948, the Clinic was having to turn down research opportunities because of lack of space.

The Clinic itself contributed to the respect with which it was increasingly regarded. Langley Porter was acquiring stature and recognition as an institution for teaching, research, and treatment of mental illness.

In retrospect, 1945 marked the beginning of the end of Langley Porter's first major period and the start of a new era, during which trends and events increasingly favored its growth and support.

During the late 1940's and early 1950's the Clinic grew gradually in staff, students, functions, and patient-load. Its teaching and research programs also grew, but these were supported primarily from University funds and federal grants.

In February of 1946 Dr. S. A. Szurek, a psychoanalyst who had specialized in child psychiatry,

---

7 Rosanoff's dedicatory speech, read posthumously in 1943, had stressed the importance of teaching and research and made not a single mention of the patient-care function.

8 For example, only two states in the nation had a lower ratio of graduate nurses to patient population. The ratio of physicians to patient-load also was considerably below that of several other states.

came to Langley Porter to head the Children's Service. Dr. A. Rodney Prestwood, a former resident, returned from war service to the Clinic. In 1947 Dr. Charles L. Yeager became Director of the Electroencephalographic Laboratory (EEG)[9] and consultant to the state hospital system. Miss Dale Houston joined the staff the same year to conduct the occupational and recreational therapy programs. Miss Helen V. Byron was appointed in 1949 to the lectureship in social work at the medical school. In 1954 Dr. Cloyce L. Duncan (who was later to become Chief of the Inpatient Service) joined the Clinic staff.

Early in 1949 the Director of the Department of Mental Hygiene[10] resigned and was succeeded by Dr. Frank F. Tallman, who was to provide the first professional medical leadership since Rosanoff's time.

In spite of the increasing stature of Langley Porter Clinic, there was, as yet, little apparent change in attitudes within the state administration. Dr. Bowman continued to press for teaching and research supported by the state, with no significant success. Receptivity to his urging, or funds, or both, were as yet lacking in Sacramento. Possibly Bowman was not effective in persuasion, or possibly the Department considered it was moving ahead as fast as it could. In any case, Bowman's requests for support of research never reached the Legislature; the budget was cut in the Department of Mental Hygiene or in the Department of Finance.

Dr. Bowman's Administration

Dr. Bowman has been described by a long-time colleague as "wonderful to work for," for he allowed the young psychiatrists under him wide latitude to develop their individual programs of treatment. At the same time, and in conflict with this blanket delegation, he exercised a close supervision of their activities. His administrative style was personal, informal, direct, and constant. He did not usually overrule subordinates' decisions; rather he challenged them. To some, his delegation of authority seemed more apparent than real.

Bowman followed an open door policy, making himself available, as time permitted, to any staff member who wished to bring problems to him. When the Clinic had opened its doors in 1943 there had been only a handful of staff, and these few had been in frequent communication with one another and with Bowman. The unavoidable relationships of small group directness and informality became established and tended to persist over the years.

But, as the Clinic grew in size and functions beyond the effectiveness of such informal group contacts, problems of communication, coordination, and delegation of authority increased. Bowman's subordinates experienced some degree of frustration and uncertainty, for their spheres of authority and their interdisciplinary relationships were not clearly defined.[11]

Bowman's policy on treatment was one of heterodoxy. He encouraged freedom of experimentation, believing that all ideas with promise should be tried. Providing intellectual freedom for his colleagues was more important to him than any personal questions he might have about the effectiveness of some of the new treatment concepts.

The administrative structure of the Clinic presented a flat picture of organization which remained little changed throughout Bowman's tenure. New staff members and programs were simply added to the structure. All heads of departments and patient services continued to report directly to either Dr. Bowman or Dr. Simon, his assistant. Until the early 1950's residents in training were in charge of the several patient services, under the supervision of Bowman and Simon. This meant in practice that the nursing staff carried a great deal of responsibility on the wards, since the nurses were on duty twenty-four hours a day and often had had more experience than the residents. In this situation, authority in the Nursing Service was particularly strong. Beginning in the early 1950's, senior residents and chiefs of service were gradually added to the Clinic staff, providing greater depth and strength in the medical administration.

In his later years Dr. Bowman increasingly turned over the direction of the wards and administrative work to Dr. Simon. His teaching and consulting activities, moreover, frequently took him abroad for extended periods. Toward the end of his administration Bowman began to relax his leadership of the Clinic, especially in planning for the future. He wanted to leave the way open for his apparent successor, Dr. Simon. At the same

9 For recording and analysis of brain waves.

10 The Department of Institutions was renamed in 1945.

11 This interpretive synthesis is based upon uniformities in descriptions and examples given by a wide variety of staff members.

time the Department of Mental Hygiene was also waiting for a new director to take over the Clinic. In his last year as Medical Superintendent, 1955-1956, Bowman asked Simon to assume full direction of Langley Porter for all practical purposes.

The first breakthrough in state-supported research on a permanent basis came in 1956, just before Bowman's retirement, by action of the Legislature. The Department of Mental Hygiene before this time had had small research projects scattered through its hospital system[12] and a Bureau of Statistical Research at headquarters. Several temporary projects had been authorized, most notably a pilot study on intensive treatment of schizophrenics at Stockton State Hospital, and a sex-deviation study conducted at Langley Porter Clinic under Dr. Bowman from 1950 to 1954. In 1956 the Department requested funds to establish a permanent program of research—a request that was omitted from the Governor's budget. However, there was a growing concern on the part of some state legislators over the meager research in mental hygiene. The Legislature requested the Department to develop and submit a research program and budget for fiscal 1956-1957. This was done, and the Legislature authorized a special augmentation of funds to establish a Bureau of Research at Department headquarters. This action marked the first official sanction of basic as well as applied research on a permanent basis within the Department of Mental Hygiene.

When Dr. Bowman's leadership of Langley Porter Clinic came to a close in mid-1956, he could look back upon fifteen years of achievement: he had developed a psychiatric institute with a national and international reputation for excellence. His goal—to develop psychiatry within the Clinic, in the Department of Mental Hygiene, and in the medical school—had been substantially accomplished, although much remained to be done. Psychiatrists trained at the Clinic were fanning out through the state, with a substantial number going into the state hospitals and other institutions where they were badly needed.

Bowman had fought "pretty much a lone fight," especially in the earliest years. The medical school, he felt, had not had much regard for psychiatry when he first came. He thought he had received reasonably good backing from the Department but mostly opposition from the school.[13] President Sproul of the University, however, had "always supported him when it came to a showdown." Bowman was certain that he had annoyed a number of people in several state agencies—particularly the State Personnel Board and, to some extent, the Department of Finance and the Division of Architecture—because he had insisted on fighting for what he felt Langley Porter should have.

The hardest years seemed to be over, however. Langley Porter Clinic had taken its place in the profession, the community, and, increasingly, in the state capital. Slowly, both its special needs and special mission were beginning to be recognized by more people in the state government. The Clinic was increasingly providing the leavening effect, the training ground, and the research resources for psychiatry that its founders had desired.

Langley Porter in 1956

The Clinic Dr. Bowman was leaving to a successor had come nearly of age in the 1950's, despite the hindrances to its development in its first fifteen years. The new Medical Superintendent would inherit both its achievements and its problems.

Except for research supported by the state government, the Clinic was performing all of the functions for which it had been designed: treatment, teaching, and research, the latter supported by the University and by grants from federal and other sources. These functions were carried on in the fields of psychiatry, child psychiatry, neuropsychiatry, neuropathology, clinical psychology, electroencephalography, nursing, social work, and rehabilitation therapies. The Clinic had students and fellows at the undergraduate, graduate, and post-doctoral levels. Programs of teaching, training, and research were being provided for the state hospital system.

By 1956 Langley Porter had a total support budget of $1,122,406 from the Department of Mental Hygiene. Department employees at the Clinic numbered nearly 200. There were fifty-two residents, thirteen of them temporarily on rotation in other institutions. Of this total, eighteen full-time residencies were supported in the Clinic by the Department and four by the University. The average inpatient population was seventy-six; the annual

[12] The total cost of all these projects in 1954 was only $83,000.

[13] Dr. Simon agreed that there was some opposition, but not to this extent.

Outpatient Department interviews, over 18,000. Slightly over twenty-one academic and clinical faculty positions in the medical school were assigned for teaching and research at Langley Porter on a full-time basis, and around 124 part-time consultants were giving their services.

This growth had been facilitated by the improving climate for psychiatry in general, the competence of the Clinic staff, and the quality of the medical school faculty. The Clinic had profited from being in the right place at the right time: it filled a strongly felt need in the state and its immediate environment. Its services were in great demand by residents of the Bay Area, and one of Langley Porter's delicate problems lay in referring elsewhere about nine out of ten requests for admission. Occasional informal pressures exerted to gain admittance for patients attested to the high regard in which it was held. This regard was shared by the state government. Langley Porter, viewed as a small hospital, was held in high esteem by the Department of Mental Hygiene[14] and commanded the respect of the Department of Finance, the Personnel Board, the Legislature, and the Legislative Analyst.

The Legacy of Issues

Dr. Bowman's successor would assume leadership of a highly respected, ongoing, complex enterprise. He would also fall heir to a legacy of problems, both those that had remained unresolved since the Clinic's founding and those that had emerged during its growth. The most crucial of these, which were to engage the attention of those who participated in the survey process of 1957, were the following:

1. Problems stemming from dual direction by the University and the Department. The conflict surrounding the Clinic's founding and the consequent tensions had never been fully resolved; this apparently led to failure to establish explicit understandings on a division of responsibilities together with areas of cooperative functions. The Clinic suffered internally from confusion on these policy issues and from a haphazard structure of mixed personnel from each institution.

2. The failure in the Department of Mental Hygiene and the control agencies of the state government to understand and support the Clinic's special mission and leadership role in the field of mental health for the state hospital system and for California. In 1956 Langley Porter was still treated as a "hospital" in the budget and personnel processes rather than as an "institute" for teaching and research.

3. The organization and administrative processes within the Clinic, which were becoming unmanageable. The flat structure, with expanded staff and functions, was overloading the two top administrators and overburdening the business services. The Clinic was understaffed and inadequately administered.

It now fell to Dr. Alexander Simon to find solutions for these problems.

[14] One high official regarded the Clinic as "the star in the crown" of the Department.

THE MANAGEMENT SURVEY: 1956-1957

As expected, Dr. Simon was appointed in 1956 to succeed Bowman as Medical Superintendent of Langley Porter Clinic and as Chairman of the Department of Psychiatry of the School of Medicine. Simon had had thirteen years of preparation for the position he assumed. During his years as Bowman's assistant, he had become increasingly involved in medical school affairs, and it was he, rather than Bowman, who had developed closer ties with the school. He had been appointed to serve on the important budget committee and as chairman of the curriculum committee.

Long before he took over administration of the Clinic, Simon began planning the changes he hoped to carry out. During Bowman's last year, Simon initiated talks with the two senior faculty psychiatrists who were top staff members in the Clinic, Dr. Jurgen Ruesch and Dr. S. A. Szurek. Where Bowman had left staff members to work independently of each other, Simon drew these men together to discuss plans for the future. Their talks concerned changes in the teaching and training programs for the school and the Clinic. (In this same period Simon made a country-wide search for an Assistant Superintendent to replace him, finally selecting Dr. A. Rodney Prestwood, then Chief of the Inpatient Service.)

Dr. Simon had further ideas for changes at Langley Porter. He wanted to develop more adequate staffing; more programs, especially in research; and new approaches in treatment policies. He knew the Clinic's problems intimately and decided to act immediately to implement his plans once he became director.

Simon's First Budget

Dr. Simon's appointment came in July 1956, Dr. Prestwood's in August. The annual budget request was due at Department of Mental Hygiene headquarters in September. Simon felt that the best time for him to ask for more personnel and programs was at the very start of his administration. With characteristic vigor, he had started to develop a plan for reorganization of the Clinic, together with requests for new personnel and programs, several months before his appointment was formally made. He consulted with his staff and with Prestwood over the enlarged budget request. Simon approached this project with a freedom from restraint that was in striking contrast to the usual budget process in the Clinic. He asked his staff to make budget requests based not upon what they thought they could get but upon what they believed they really needed to do a good job. The Clinic staff, unaccustomed to having much voice in budgetary planning, found this a heady challenge. Requests for new personnel, together with justifications and new departmental charts, flowed into the Clinic's business office. There was little attempt at sophisticated evaluation from an administrative standpoint—that was to come later —for no one in the Clinic then was highly skilled in budgeting or administrative analysis.

Simon, at the time he became director of the Clinic, "didn't know much about budget presentation." Customarily, shortly before the Clinic's budget was due in Sacramento, Dr. Bowman had asked staff members if they needed anything. Bowman's budget had been his personal budget, and he had not always discussed it with Simon. Mrs. Stearns, the Business Manager, had done the actual work of making up the Clinic's budget. In developing the 1957-1958 budget, Simon, Prestwood, and the staff were thinking primarily in terms of people to do jobs.

Dr. Simon was engrossed in his desire to implement changes at the Clinic. In regard to budget process and the possible consequences of such a budget proposal, he commented later, "I was naive." He believed in what he was trying to do—initiate a new era at Langley Porter. He realized that this first budget, requesting very substantial increases in funds, personnel, and programs, was bound to have repercussions in Sacramento. His anxiety at the time was over the possibility of being refused or of having his plans delayed. It did not occur to him, since he was not familiar with the management analysis activities of the Department of Finance, that a survey of the Clinic was a possible consequence of his budget requests.

Simon's budget request combined a reorganization plan[15] with requests for over seventy new people, several reclassifications, and an increase in funds over 1956-1957 of about $400,000[16] (an increase of about one-third).[17] New clinical and research programs, new chiefs and more staff for patient services and professional departments, and extensive strengthening of the business and supporting functions made up the bulk of the increases.

Personnel to staff two new programs was requested. One of these was an interdisciplinary research team. The other was a day-night hospital service to provide either day or night care for patients needing less than continuous hospitalization. A clinical director was requested to assume supervision of all clinical services: adult Inpatient and Outpatient, Children's, Neuropsychiatric, and Psychology, Nursing, Social Work, and Rehabilitation Therapies. This new position was intended to relieve the Assistant Medical Superintendent of an overload of duties so that he might give more time to administration.

Chiefs for *administrative* purposes were requested for the three departments then being administered by medical school faculty members—Social Work, Children's Service, and Clinical Psychology.

A new position of hospital administrative assistant and personnel officer was asked for to relieve the Business Manager, to whom ten department heads were then reporting. Other requests were intended to strengthen further this part of the Clinic's operation.

The requests for additional personnel covered almost every facet of the Clinic from experienced

---

[15] See Appendix II, page 295. (The chart was designed to follow patterns established for the state hospitals.)

[16] These figures do not include funds and staff provided by the medical school.

[17] See Appendix I on page 294 for budgets for Langley Porter Clinic, 1941-1961.

psychiatrists to janitors, including a speech correction teacher for the Children's Service Department.

The new budget's accompanying commentary pointed out that while the professional staff and the patient-load had grown over the years, no corresponding adjustment in the size of the supporting services had been made:

> It is recognized that these requests represent a very considerable increase in our staff. In many instances they are felt to be long over-due and are recommended on the basis of raising the level of existing service and in other instances are recommended on the basis of implementing needed new services.

Particular attention was paid to the administrative and business services. After noting that the Business Manager, the Accounting Officer, the Accounting Technician, clerks, and stenographers had been working evenings, Saturdays, and Sundays for two months, the budget stated:

> No such general re-evaluation and reappraisal has been undertaken before. Our administrative staff has been largely based on estimates made in the early 1940's. At that time, income from patients' accounts was estimated at $10,000 annually, while now it runs about $150,000 annually. There is a relationship between the administrative staff necessary for an organization made up of a few clinical professional persons seeing the number of patients who provide $10,000 a year, and the present extensive and complex teaching, research and treatment organization providing services that result in $150,000 a year.

The budget indicated how, by various expedients, the new people were to be accommodated until such time as an authorized new building was completed.

This Clinic budget, forwarded to Department of Mental Hygiene headquarters, was included unchanged in the Department's budget proposal, and the whole was sent to the Budget Division of the Department of Finance. George B. Spencer, budget analyst, was responsible for reviewing the Mental Hygiene budget and making recommendations to his superior. Spencer reported that he could make no recommendations at all on the Langley Porter budget, since he had no basis on which to evaluate the large increases requested. He recommended that a survey of the Clinic be made and that, in the intervening time, action on the increases requested in the Clinic's budget be deferred.

Budget Process in California

California had a strong executive budget system. It used the line-item budget form for most of its programs. The Governor could veto individual programs passed by the Legislature but could not add to the appropriations, once passed. The Department of Finance was the Governor's principal agent for the review of budget estimates. Finance also saw itself as having the positive function of ensuring that authorized programs were carried on effectively. The Department provided consulting services in fiscal, organization, and program management. Usually it was invited in; sometimes it initiated consultation.

Two divisions carried out these activities: the Budget Division, specializing in fiscal management; and the Organization and Cost Control Division (OCC), specializing in management analysis. Since their functions were closely related, considerable consultation was necessary from time to time, and they sometimes worked together on organizational surveys.

Finance was better known for its control functions. It was the big "no sayer," viewed as "they" by most administrators with, among other feelings, anxiety and antagonism. Finance was well aware of this.

Prior to legislative review, the Langley Porter Clinic budget had three major hurdles: the Department of Mental Hygiene, the Department of Finance, and the Legislative Analyst.

After analyses of departmental budgets were made by Finance, hearings were held at which departments could justify their budgets to the Budget Division. A good deal of subsequent informal discussion also took place before Finance issued the official Governor's budget, which was then presented to the Legislature for action. To assist the Legislature, California had a Legislative Analyst with a sizable staff who reviewed the entire budget item by item and made independent recommendations to the legislators. This officer's role was conceived as that of objective public servant, outside the pressures of the political process. Lastly, legislative committees held hearings and reported their recommendations to the Legislature. Final authority resided in the Legislature, but the influence on the end-product of each step in the budget process was very great.

When Finance refused to endorse Dr. Simon's proposed 1957-1958 budget in the fall of 1956 and instead recommended a survey as a basis for evaluation of the requests, it seemed quite possible to Simon that his entire program for change and expansion was lost or at least would be delayed and severely cut back. He feared, too, that this might be a deliberate stalling device.

The Survey Is Initiated

Simon was deeply discouraged. He knew that his staff was anticipating great changes at the Clinic and that he was responsible for encouraging this hope. The staff looked to him as its spokesman and leader to bring about a new order of things. Not only were his personal hopes frustrated, but, at the very outset of his incumbency, he was put in the position of apparently failing his staff members.

But his budget had served the purpose of riveting attention upon the Clinic. George Spencer, who had recommended that the Budget Division postpone action until a study of the Clinic could be made, was concerned only with clarifying and identifying the requests within the established policy framework. As a budget expert, he realized that so large a requested increase in the Clinic's budget had to involve a very considerable expansion in the Clinic's programs, not just normal growth of those already authorized and ongoing. To him, this indicated organizational change of an extent calling for review and consultation. Without a study, especially since none had been made since the Clinic's establishment, it was impossible, he felt, to recommend any of the individual proposals. Spencer's superior, Edwin W. Beach, agreed with him and took this position with the Department of Mental Hygiene.

The Department of Finance had an additional reason for wanting to make a study at Langley Porter. A second, similar institute, also operated jointly by the Department of Mental Hygiene and the University, was being developed on the campus of the University at Los Angeles. A study of the older Clinic would help Finance very materially in developing policies on staffing, relationships between the two institutions, and so on, for the new mental health facility.

The Controller of the Department of Mental Hygiene, R. E. Conahan, felt it was time for a study to be made. Langley Porter had been supported for years somewhat "blindly" by Finance, the Legislative Analyst, and the Legislature, because the high rate of increase in mental disease had brought general agreement that the Department and the Clinic must be supported and allowed to grow. But "questions were now being asked." As the responsible fiscal officer of the Department, Conahan knew he had to be in a position to defend its programs. To him, the best method of gaining support was to have Finance make a study and find out for itself what the Clinic was. He therefore supported the request for a survey.

Dr. Marshall E. Porter, Medical Deputy Director of the Department, was concerned mainly with conserving and expanding the values embodied by Langley Porter, especially the teaching and research functions. He believed that these were vitally important for the state hospital system and for the state's progress in psychiatry generally. In this he was fully in accord with Simon, in whom he had confidence, and with Dr. Rosanoff, whom he had known and regarded with a deep and warm respect. He accepted the proposal for a study, then bent his efforts toward ensuring so far as possible that the process and outcome would help rather than harm the Clinic. Porter's concern over the Clinic study stemmed in part from experience with a recent survey of the state hospital system that had resulted in dissension and bitterness. He did not want to see this repeated in the case of the Clinic. His interest was in the medical, not the administrative, aspect of the situation. He was prepared to accept any administrative arrangements that were acceptable to Simon.

Dr. Walter Rapaport, then Director of the Department, respected Simon and supported him. But it fell mainly to Porter and Conahan, together with others within the Department, to take the active roles in the developing situation.

Agreement was reached that the OCC Division should make a study of Langley Porter. Simon himself viewed the decision to make a survey of the Clinic as a mandate. Although unhappy over the postponement of decisions on his budget, he now hoped that the coming survey would enable him to get what he had asked for.

Because new positions and reclassifications of existing positions were an integral part of Simon's budget, the state's Personnel Board and the Department's Personnel Officer, Ralph Littlestone, were included in discussions of the controversial budget. Their participation in the survey was not extensive, but their advice was needed in working out recommendations for Langley Porter, and so were their involvement and commitment in any projected changes.[18]

A series of meetings was held in January 1957 in which policies and decisions were worked out. On January 7 Edwin Beach of the Budget Division met with members of the Department of Mental Hygiene, including Dr. Simon, and a representative from the Personnel Board. Beach stated that he could not consider any specific proposals until the OCC Division completed a study of the Clinic. Moreover, Simon's organization plan differed in some respects from an organization plan for all state mental hospitals soon to be released. The whole matter could not be dealt with except as part of a total organizational plan for Langley Porter. It was up to the Department to decide upon the timing of such a study.

Two days later the Budget Division recommended in a memo to the OCC Division that it make a study; on January 28 a formal assignment of the task was made to John W. Berke, one of the OCC's management analysts.

The next day members of the Department met with Simon to discuss policy with regard to the impending survey. Plans of organization for the Clinic were considered, and Conahan, the Department's Controller, offered a chart he had developed for discussion. The following day Simon informed the Clinic staff of the study about to be made, and circulated Conahan's chart for their consideration.

On February 1 a "kick-off" meeting for the OCC study was held at the Department. It was attended by the headquarters' top officers; Dr. Simon; and, from the OCC Division, Marvin L. Blanchard, Acting Chief Administrative Analyst; Dale Lapham, Senior Administrative Analyst; and John Berke, Associate Administrative Analyst. Conahan's chart was presented for discussion. Blanchard, however, stated that, before any specific organization structure could be discussed, the first concern must be a study of the general nature of Langley Porter Clinic.

By February 5 George Spencer had been assigned by the Budget Division to work with Berke on the survey in a consulting capacity. It was thought that his experience with Department of Mental Hygiene budgets would be valuable in the Clinic study. The two men conferred with Conahan and later with Porter. Conahan discussed the study with them in terms of policy, teaching, organization, and the needed classification levels for several positions at the Clinic. He explained that the Department had not had enough time to evaluate Simon's budget and had therefore sent it along unchanged to Finance. Dr. Porter stressed the importance to the Department of Langley Porter's teaching and research functions. Training programs at the Clinic for state hospital personnel, he felt, should be supported. Langley Porter must provide leadership in teaching and research for the whole Department. Dr. Porter asked the survey team to consider this overall training need in their survey.

The Survey Team Meets the Clinic Staff

On the morning of February 6 Simon met with his staff at the Clinic. The OCC Division team was to meet with them for the first time that afternoon. At this meeting Dr. Simon explained the purposes of the survey. He indicated that the final report would be advisory in nature and not binding upon the Clinic, the Department of Finance, or the Department of Mental Hygiene. Moreover, the Department of Mental Hygiene would be consulted before any final plan was accepted formally.

The staff discussed some of the problems of the mixed functions of the Department and the medical school within the Clinic. Confusion between theory and practice was reflected in this discussion, for while Simon stated that Department policy was to leave the teaching and research to the medical school, with the Department performing the service and administrative functions, one staff member asked whether Department personnel were not also charged with research and teaching functions in addition to service. This individual, a Mental Hygiene employee, was engaged in considerable research and training, as well as in service and administration. Part of Simon's answer demonstrated the difficulty of attempting a complete separation of functions in the Clinic, for, as he stated, treatment was a necessary part of teaching and research. A little later Simon said that he would "stress to Department of Finance personnel the fact that work is distributed between University

[18] The Personnel Board exercised independent controls of its own in California state government. It set the standards, qualifications, examinations, and pay schedules for all state employees within its jurisdiction, which covered most state employees and included those in the Department of Mental Hygiene. Coordination between the Personnel Board and Finance in planning for organizational changes was essential, and consultation was customary.

and Mental Hygiene personnel regardless of who benefits by what."

At 1:00 p.m. that day, Dale Lapham, John Berke, and George Spencer were introduced to the Clinic staff. Berke recognized that this first meeting with the staff was of crucial importance, and he handled it carefully. Much of the OCC Division presentation was directed toward informing the staff of the purposes and potential usefulness of the survey and toward reassuring the group about the methods and attitudes of the survey team. It was explained that staff members would be interviewed about existing structure and functions within the Clinic and that their suggestions for improvements would be elicited. The team would attempt first to get a composite view of the mission and programs of Langley Porter and then to define areas of responsibility between the University and the Department, especially in research and training. The Clinic itself would supply the information the team needed, and the final report and recommendations would be based almost entirely upon the thinking and contributions of the staff.

The Department of Finance men tried to make clear that they were there to serve the needs of Langley Porter with their specialized skills in administration. Not only would the Clinic be helped to function more effectively, but the final report, circulated to Finance, the Department of Mental Hygiene, and the Legislature, would help the Clinic to obtain needed personnel to carry out its mission.

Few Clinic staff members present at the meeting knew enough about administrative analysis skills to appreciate how the survey might contribute to their needs. Most of them were anxious about what was to take place. The Department of Finance men were strangers from an alien profession and from a branch of state government that for years had seemed to them a formidable block to achieving some of their major objectives. They felt the survey to be much in the nature of an unwanted investigation. A few, however, dissatisfied with the Clinic's administration, welcomed the survey, hoping that it might put things to rights.

Berke was well aware that he was not yet "in." The key decision at this point was made by Simon when, following the meeting, some staff members asked him how they should behave with the survey team. Simon himself barely knew Berke and Spencer as yet. He, too, could not then foresee what might result from their activities. However, he told his staff members to be open and frank, to say whatever they honestly thought. In Simon's own words: "I was proud of Langley Porter; I had faith in its people. I felt I knew what we needed, and that our enthusiastic dedication to our jobs would be convincing. We had everything to gain by complete frankness." Thus he committed himself at the outset to a policy of full cooperation that was to prevail throughout the survey and, at the same time, sanctioned full disclosure on the part of his subordinates. The entire course of the survey, in Berke's opinion, pivoted upon this early decision of Simon's. Without it, all sorts of obstructions might have been encountered.

The Survey Process Begins

Study of the Clinic by the survey team began at once. Berke and Spencer anticipated about three and one-half months on the project. They could not spend full time on it, but whenever possible they put off other work to give three or four days each week to the survey. They moved into office space in the Clinic and sometimes spent nights in a nearby motel. The operating plan worked out between them included a procedure to handle any disagreement that might arise. (None ever did; they cooperated harmoniously until mid-March, when Spencer was reassigned. Berke completed the survey alone.)

Following the initial meeting they began discussions with Simon and Prestwood, studied documents relating to the Clinic, set up schedules of appointments with staff members and with others outside Langley Porter who had formal relationships with the Clinic. Dr. Prestwood acted as liaison with the staff, arranging schedules of appointments and transmitting other requests from the team. In general, the survey did not attempt to go below the top levels of management. Except on one point, the question of workloads in relation to numbers of employees (in a few areas), only the heads of departments, chiefs of services, and the two top officers were interviewed within the Clinic. Dr. Bowman was not among those interviewed.

The survey period was complex, with several major aspects of the process developing simultaneously and interacting one with another. A strictly chronological account of it cannot be given, for no adequate records were kept to afford a step-by-step reconstruction. Moreover, the several processes are more coherent when treated to some extent as separate developments over time. In reality, however, the survey team was conferring almost daily with Simon and Prestwood, interviewing staff members and others outside the Clinic, and talking with key people in the state government. Within the Clinic, Simon and Prestwood talked with staff members informally, and staff members, with each other. What follows is an arbitrary, though necessary, arrangement.

From their perspective of budget and management-analysis skills, Berke and Spencer found "confusion" and "inadequacy" in much of the Clinic structure and administrative arrangements. They found nothing set down explicitly on organization and functions or on the purposes of the institution.[19] In theory, teaching and research were carried on by the medical school, and patient care and administration by the Department of Mental Hygiene, but in practice this division was not observed. The team felt that Simon and Prestwood lacked a clearly defined concept of the Clinic's mission and of the roles of the Department and the medical school within Langley Porter; working out clear definitions of these, therefore, became a primary goal of the survey process and a preliminary requirement for subsequent recommendations. The team soon realized that the existing organizational structure was inadequate and that the Clinic was understaffed in terms of going functions,[20] but the task of clarification and of detailed analysis, proposals, and acceptance of these by the Clinic would take weeks of work.

Communication was a major problem. For their part, Berke and Spencer had to become familiar with a highly specialized milieu. There was no lay administration. Most of the staff did not think in administrative terms; one member later remarked, "I never thought of the Clinic in terms of administration until the survey was made." The team found that people in the Clinic did not understand the organizational structure as such and "either did not know what the situation was, or were not able to explain it." Dissatisfactions existed among the people interviewed, but interpretation of these complaints into technical administrative terms took time and patience. The team's task was one of learning, eliciting ideas, analyzing, formulating proposals, and then discussing these proposals with staff members. Spencer felt that the Clinic lacked the advantage of successful experience in preparing sophisticated budget justifications, and that without these skills it would not be able to communicate its needs in clear and acceptable terms to the relevant state agencies and to the Legislature.

As these problems became clear to Berke and Spencer, they settled down to working with the Clinic staff on technical concepts of organization and on state government practices.

Participation: Simon and Prestwood, Berke and Spencer

Berke and Spencer both saw their job at Langley Porter as one of service and education. They had, really, a double objective. They wanted to develop a plan for reorganization with Simon and Prestwood that would satisfy all four men—the team, in terms of sound management principles, and the Clinic administrators, in terms of what was acceptable and useful to them. The survey process itself, they hoped, would be the means to their second goal: developing an understanding of administration and budget process sufficiently thorough that it would endure after the survey was over and maintain the Clinic on a solid basis administratively.

They were convinced that the only "good" plan would be Simon's plan, arrived at over time through a mutual learning process. Their intent was to consult and work with both Simon and Prestwood until all four could accept some final report developed through this process. In Simon and Prestwood, they found responsive collaborators.

The two doctors had more at stake than the team. While reaching their original goals very probably remained more important to them than acquiring administrative lore, they saw the potential value of learning administrative techniques. Moreover, as they worked with the team, they realized that these "boys from Finance," representatives of that remote and frustrating "they" in Sacramento, wanted primarily to help the Clinic achieve its needs and goals and function more effectively. Simon began to see the survey process as an opportunity not only to resolve some of the Clinic's administrative problems but also to gain acceptance of his original goals for the Clinic in the Department of Mental Hygiene, the Department of

---

19 Except, of course, in the legislation establishing the Clinic in 1941.

20 In this, the team was in general agreement with Dr. Simon, who had represented the Clinic's needs for reorganization and additional staff in his budget request.

Finance, and the Legislature. Simon realized that the final report would carry weight in these places. He had a receptive audience in the team and made the most of it. A spirit of mutual enthusiasm developed among the four men. Simon and Prestwood made themselves available, and scheduled conferences were often supplemented by casual lunches together.

Thus a two-way learning process developed between the survey team and the Clinic administrators. It was by no means devoid of tensions and disagreements from time to time, but the relationship was never seriously threatened with disruption. All four were willing to learn and were strongly committed to compatible goals.

Berke and Spencer developed techniques for working with the other two men. They were alert to detect resistance to unpalatable ideas; when they encountered such blocks, they dropped the issue in question for the time being and returned to it days later. Because Simon and Prestwood were frank, issues were made open and clear. Berke and Spencer were able to learn what the real problems were and what had to be resolved. Both men believed that without these qualities of frankness and response in Simon and Prestwood, they would not be able to reach a genuine consensus, and a final report would not reflect either a resolution of real issues or a strong conviction on the part of the Clinic administrators.

Substantive Issues

Four main subjects were dealt with in the survey discussions: (1) redefining the goals of Langley Porter, and the appropriate relations among them; (2) clarifying the major areas of combined and separate functions of the University and the Department; (3) restructuring the Clinic's internal organization; and (4) providing for adequate personnel, in both numbers and quality, to carry out Clinic programs effectively. Of all these, the internal reorganization presented the most difficult issues.

Berke and Spencer accepted the thinking of Dr. Porter at Department headquarters and of Dr. Simon on the Clinic's mission: it included teaching and research as major goals, as well as treatment. They also accepted the general division of functions already existing in theory between the Department and the University, the latter primarily responsible for teaching and research, the Department responsible for patient care and administration. The new element in policy was that the Department should also support and carry on teaching and research.

The survey team also accepted some major aspects of Simon's 1956 structural plan. One of these was the provision of Department of Mental Hygiene chiefs for the three services then administered by medical school faculty people: Children's Service, Social Work, and Psychology. This change would bring practice into line with the theory of division of responsibilities between the University and the Department by placing all administration in the Department.

Since the Clinic was by now too large for its existing flat structure—with the two top administrators overloaded with supervisory and other duties—the team also endorsed Simon's request for a clinical director to head all the clinical services.

Further internal structuring and the problem of the Clinic's business services became the most troublesome issues encountered in the survey process. One of the touchiest problems revolved around the Business Manager, Mrs. Evelyn Stearns. She had been at the Clinic since its earliest days, recruited by Bowman from a welfare agency at the suggestion of the Department of Mental Hygiene. Starting as a bookkeeper, she had worked her way up to the grade of Business Manager I. As the Clinic grew in size and complexity, the business functions outgrew not only the structure and the number of employees in the Business Services Division, but also outgrew, in the view of the survey team, the skills of the Business Manager. Dr. Bowman recalled in 1960 that Mrs. Stearns, years earlier, had shown him a record of what she was supposed to know about business services: techniques of budget management, adequate controls, personnel rules and procedures, and so on. She had voiced the feeling that this was an unfair and improper expectation of her, since the business functions she performed at the Clinic were carried on by three different people in other state hospitals. But, although the problem in business services was recognized at headquarters, the state government had never been willing to upgrade the level of the business manager position.

Both Berke and Spencer felt that successful reorganization of the Clinic depended on a broader concept of business functions, which they considered a crucial foundation for operating programs and a channel of communication in the state's budget and personnel processes. The Clinic's effectiveness in getting its needs met would be only as good as its business services were effective in budgeting and business techniques. These, they believed, were not being adequately performed.

It was very difficult to gain acceptance of their views from Simon and Prestwood. Simon placed personal issues ahead of "administrative expediency." Moreover, he felt he could afford to wait; Mrs. Stearns's retirement was expected in two years or so. Both Simon and Prestwood were motivated by strong feelings of personal loyalty and an appreciation of the increasing workload and complexities she was forced to deal with.

This issue raised a very real conflict between the survey team and the doctors. Berke and Spencer, in their consulting capacity, felt they could go only "so far," but they were convinced that a change was essential for successful operation. Spencer found business control systems inadequate and was anxious lest Simon find himself in untenable positions with his future budget requests. The team believed, after investigation, that some maintenance employees in the Clinic (e.g., janitors) were not performing in accordance with acceptable standards. Justifications for requested positions in Clinic budgets were not prepared in a manner likely to be effective with the administrative control agencies in Sacramento or with the Legislature.

Berke and Spencer had to move very slowly on this issue, but eventually a compromise was reached whereby Mrs. Stearns would remain in her position until her retirement. The business functions would be restructured, with Mrs. Stearns retaining her position and grade, but supervising only maintenance and food services. A new position of business manager at a higher grade would be established to head the entire Business Division. After Mrs. Stearns retired, the position she held would be abolished. This compromise satisfied no one entirely, but it was as far as either side felt it could go within the limits of their relationship.

A Single Children's Service?

Another problem in the Clinic's organization revolved around the Children's Service and its relation to the existing adult Inpatient and Outpatient Services, which had always been separate divisions within the Clinic. The Children's Service, with both inpatients and outpatients, had always been run as a *single* unit. Under Dr. S. A. Szurek (University of California professor of psychiatry and Vice-Chairman, Department of Psychiatry) it was a tight-knit division where all treatment, training, and research programs were organized around a well-articulated body of psychoanalytic theory. The survey team concluded that, in the interest of orderly administrative arrangements, this service should be split, for *administrative* purposes only, between the Clinic's Inpatient and Outpatient Divisions. The team expected that Dr. Szurek, as the University's professor in charge of teaching and research in child psychiatry, would continue to direct all medical aspects of treatment, teaching, and research with both the inpatient and outpatient children.

Simon and Prestwood, while accepting this proposal at the time, had a wait-and-see attitude about it, as they did about some other points in the survey. They could not then foresee all the implications of what was developing in the planning and felt that recommended changes could be tried and altered if they did not seem to work out well in practice. The question of how the outpatient children would be integrated administratively with the adult Outpatient Department was not fully clarified during the survey.

Separating Administrative and Faculty Roles

The Clinic's redefined goals directly affected planning for some of the departments. A delicate problem developed around the three divisions then being administered by medical school faculty members. Both Dr. Szurek, head of the Children's Service, and Dr. Robert E. Harris, head of Clinical Psychology, were to be provided with Department of Mental Hygiene chiefs of service to relieve them of administrative work. As University faculty members with full professorships, their teaching and research activities would remain undisturbed. The third division, Social Work, was a different matter.

All three divisions would have two heads in place of one, with existing functions divided between them. Szurek and Harris performed administrative duties by necessity, not choice, and had delegated these duties to assistants as much as possible. Both men had for years requested, unsuccessfully, Department of Mental Hygiene chiefs to carry out administrative functions. In Social Work, this was not the case. From the start, Miss Helen V. Byron, Director of the Social Work Department, had viewed her role as essentially administrative. The position she held as lecturer at the medical school she regarded as something of an historical accident. At the same time, she regarded social work as a separate, essential discipline in the mental health field, appropriately represented in the medical school's Department of Psychiatry. She enjoyed teaching undergraduates and residents, yet her main interests were in the supervision and development of her department within the Clinic and in community organization. Thus she was working predominantly in the areas of administration and patient care, doing relatively little teaching and no research.

The question of how to split functions in the case of Szurek and Harris was never raised in the practical sense, because the answer was implicit in the teaching and research work they were already doing. Miss Byron, however, would be confronted with a difficult choice. She could continue in her University position (but with a vague and undeveloped role) and relinquish administration of her department to a new chief of social work, or she could resign her faculty appointment to become herself the new chief, employed by the Department of Mental Hygiene. Discussions of this change began during the survey process, and the issue of a possible change of positions for Miss Byron was foreseen. It was not until after formal acceptance of the report that this issue came to a head.

One of the problems raised during the survey revolved around classification levels of old and new positions to be incorporated in the reorganization plan. The OCC Division, in its management planning, defined the duties and organizational levels of positions to be filled, but the Personnel Board established all classifications and grade levels of jobs to perform them. During the survey the Personnel Board was called in to consult on possible new and reclassified positions contemplated for the Clinic. Two positions especially concerned Dr. Simon. He felt that the size and complexity of the business services justified a higher-level business manager than the Personnel Board would grant. The Personnel Board representative was willing to recommend a new position one grade higher than the Clinic's existing position, but not two grades higher. The Clinic was much smaller than the mental hospitals or comparable agencies, he argued, and since Business Services allegedly had not been run efficiently in the past, it was reasonable to try running it with a manager only one grade higher. Later, if this did not take care of the situation, the Board would reevaluate the position. Simon also failed to persuade the Board that he needed someone to handle personnel work because of rapidly expanding training and research programs.

Reactions of the Clinic Staff

Members of the Clinic staff looked upon the coming of Berke and Spencer with as many reactions as there were individuals involved.[21] Some were indifferent, apparently, and three years later could not recall any particular reactions to the survey situation. These were people who did not expect to be affected personally or who had little or no interest in administration as such. But many were concerned and felt anxiety about the survey. There was a general feeling of uncertainty and suspense and a sense of not knowing what was happening. Perhaps none clearly understood the nature of the survey, what it might accomplish, or how; nor, equally, what it was not intended to accomplish and could not do. One staff member summed it up: "We did not want people to come in and examine the Clinic. There was an atmosphere of suspicion—what does this mean?" While this person's observations cannot speak for the whole group, they are expressive of the general climate:

> They were awfully cagey about saying what it [the survey] meant, and this was annoying. People asked me what it meant. I did not understand well enough to know what it meant, but I couldn't see why it wouldn't work. We would have to see what happened. We felt some uneasiness, wondered what they were doing. I wished we could get answers.

The speaker was a highly intelligent person of professional status within and outside the Clinic. Some others were more worried than this individual, who, though concerned, on balance tended to expect that the survey would probably help the Clinic to get personnel to do a better job. But even so, this observer found the uncertainty difficult to live with.

Another, less easily defined element in the Clinic climate at the time was a situation of flux in relationships among some staff members, with consequent tensions, struggles, and insecurities. The survey process, injected into this atmosphere, added

21 The following account is necessarily anonymous but is based upon explicit information supplied by the staff in extensive interviews.

to anxieties already present, since the consequences of the survey for existing unresolved frictions could not be foreseen.

But reactions were not all negative, even within individual staff members who were disturbed by the survey. Some who felt substantial dissatisfactions with the status quo tended to hope that the survey and reorganization would resolve problems they were encountering in their work, insofar as they thought these stemmed from faulty administration. Lacking a clear understanding of the survey's scope and potential for change, however, their expectations at this early point—and later—were not always realistic. They did not have enough factual information to make reasonable estimates of possible outcomes.

Others, who also lacked information, had dissatisfactions but did not expect the survey to relieve them. These people did not perceive their problems as stemming from administrative structure and methods.

In sum, the Clinic people had never been surveyed before; they lacked technical sophistication in administration on which to base realistic expectations and, in consequence, felt varying degrees of hope, uncertainty, and apprehension. Neither fears nor hopes were based upon sufficient knowledge and experience.

The Survey Team: Interviews and Consultation

Early in the survey each department and service head, as well as Simon and Prestwood, was asked to prepare a job analysis of activities, with the amount of time allocated to each. The team was also provided with charts of the structure and relationships within each department and service in the Clinic. These job analyses revealed the intricacies of Langley Porter's functioning. Szurek, Harris, and Miss Byron, members of the medical school faculty, were giving large portions of their time to administration and to supervision of Department of Mental Hygiene personnel and residents. On the other hand, most of the Department-employed staff members, including all the psychiatrists, were engaged in teaching and training, and some in research work. Their teaching activities included instruction of both medical school and Department students, as well as persons from other agencies (for example, the Air Force) and foreign countries. One Department of Mental Hygiene chief made this situation clear in his analysis, saying that "the teaching, research, and routine record-reading [service function] are often purposely carried out simultaneously as a program to benefit the resident or trainee."

Berke and Spencer interviewed individual members of the Clinic staff together in nearly all cases, and some more than once. They did not, however, meet with the staff as a group more than once or twice. Their deliberate policy was not to intrude upon discussions staff members might have among themselves in their meetings. As consultants, Berke and Spencer felt there were clearly defined limits to their roles. They saw themselves as, essentially, advisers to Simon, the top administrator in the organization. Their purpose in interviewing staff members was to gather information about the functions and administrative arrangements in each department and service, the problems encountered, and opinions on what improvements were needed. It was also their purpose to impart increased understanding of the techniques and principles of administration. But they believed they could not go beyond this to deal with policy matters or to advocate any particular changes, since this would constitute an interference in Simon's relationships with his subordinates. Final decisions must be made by Simon, and he alone could undertake to gain acceptance from his staff.

During the survey, staff meetings for the most part dealt only incidentally with reorganization. (Since minutes of these meetings were revised before being permanently recorded, they have contributed little useful information. Memories in 1960 were vague. Most of the discussion that all agree took place was informal and probably off the record.) There were informal discussions between each of the top two administrators and some of the staff. Dr. Prestwood recalled that he talked frequently with Dr. Cloyce Duncan, Chief of the Inpatient Service; with Dr. Marietta Houston, Chief of the Outpatient Department (who later left the Clinic); "considerably" with Miss Helen Byron, Director of Social Work; and with others of the staff. As a long-time member of the Clinic staff, Prestwood knew these people well.

There was a marked difference between what took place between Berke and Spencer working with Simon and Prestwood, and what transpired between either of these pairs and the Clinic staff. Each staff member interviewed had an opportunity to inform the survey team, thus making contributions to an overall understanding of the

Clinic and its problems. But the planning and the decisions were reached among the four men and, in the formal sense, by Simon alone. Full and free interchange occurred at the top but stopped there. The staff participated within the limits described, and its influence was mainly individual and informal.

The "consulting role" limitations the team felt in relation to Simon's staff did not apply to the state government, where Berke and Spencer undertook to gain understanding and acceptance of the Clinic's mission. There was continuing contact with the Department of Mental Hygiene and with the Budget and OCC Divisions of Finance. There was also interchange between the Budget and the OCC Divisions among the headquarters people. The Personnel Board was asked in to consult on position classifications, both existing and projected. Thus, these agencies of state government, through Berke and Spencer, were increasingly made aware of the special goals, functions, and needs of Langley Porter. This feedback had important bearing on the course and outcome of the survey.

The Survey Is Completed

George Spencer was taken off the survey project in mid-March, although he returned at least once in the ensuing months to follow through on the work. Berke continued alone. By this time, all of the budget aspects of the Clinic's organization, operations, and expected expansion had been clarified, and all of the issues of Clinic mission and reorganization had been raised and discussed. It was later, however, that Berke, working alone, developed a definite reorganization proposal, one based upon a new image of Langley Porter that emerged from the survey process itself.

This new concept of Clinic mission was not crystallized early in the survey, even though the importance of teaching and research had been emphasized from the start. It dawned suddenly upon Berke one night; he phoned Prestwood immediately and discussed it with him in person the next day. Langley Porter, Berke realized, was neither a small hospital nor a clinic, but essentially an institute. Its primary purpose was to provide not services (as in all other state hospitals), but teaching and research in mental illness; such services as Langley Porter carried on, though equally important, were mainly in support of the teaching and research activities. Berke's perception of the real nature of Langley Porter's mission had more than semantic significance. It would establish Langley Porter as a unique facility within the Department of Mental Hygiene, materially affecting budgetary and personnel practices for the Clinic by the state's control agencies. It would also affect organization and administrative practices within the Clinic itself.

This was a crucial turning point in the survey process, and quite possibly the most important development to emerge. From this time on, the final form of the survey recommendations began to take shape, and in Sacramento a new orientation toward the Clinic was developed by Berke and Spencer.

The Survey Report Is Drafted

In April Berke brought a rough draft of the survey report to Simon and Prestwood. Each of them studied it thoroughly, making relatively minor changes, which Berke accepted. With the report completed, Simon was not sure "who had seduced whom." There was genuine agreement among the four men and outsiders that the survey and final report had been so much a product of group effort that individual contributions to it could not be distinguished. It was considered a result unique to the survey process itself.

Berke next submitted the report to Dean John B. deC. M. Saunders at the medical school for informal approval. When Berke then took the report to Dr. Porter in Sacramento, Porter knew that the Clinic administrators and the medical school had already endorsed its recommendations. His concern was only with the effects of the survey process within the Clinic. He was assured that it had gone well. Following these advance clearances the report went through normal channels in the Department of Finance.

Acceptance of the survey report in Sacramento was due largely to the effectiveness of the survey team in talking to people in Finance and others throughout the course of the survey and later on. No serious stumbling blocks were encountered. What was primarily needed, apparently, was education. People were receptive to the information relayed by the team. The general climate for mental health programs had, as noted, shifted a long way from that of the Clinic's early years. Where Bowman's efforts had had limited success, those of Simon, Porter, Berke, and Spencer were far more effective. What had seemed to be such a stubborn and frustrating block in the Clinic's earlier history virtually melted away as understanding of Langley Porter's purposes, and acceptance of their legitimacy within the Department of Mental Hygiene and state government, increased. What opposition now remained centered more on method and detail, less on principle.

Within the medical school no change of attitudes on the Clinic's goals was necessary, for the school had always viewed Langley Porter as a place to carry on research and teaching.

This was the first time that any OCC Division analyst had given a preliminary draft report to a surveyed agency for comment before presenting it to his own superior. Berke did not notify his office before giving the report to Simon and Prestwood; he had, however, conferred with his superior throughout the study. His procedure was, therefore, an event of some importance for the OCC Division itself. In Berke's view, there was nothing to lose by his innovation; unless the report he had written was acceptable to the Clinic, it was not likely to be implemented in any case.

THE SURVEY REPORT

In late May Berke, Spencer, and Marvin Blanchard met with the Clinic staff for about three hours to discuss the survey recommendations before publication. Much of the report was directed not really at them but at a wider audience.

The contents of the report reflected the several purposes that had developed during the survey process and the intent to reach a varied audience. It was, as noted previously, much more than a recommended plan of internal reorganization, although this was a primary objective. A sizable portion of the report defined the Clinic's unique mission and argued its validity for the Department of Mental Hygiene. Prominent in the appended exhibits was the table of comparison, which listed twelve points of contrast between Langley Porter Clinic and other state mental hospitals. (See Figure 1, p. 276.)

Also appended was a list of twenty-nine former Clinic residents who had taken professional positions within the Department of Mental Hygiene. Teaching, training, and research programs conducted by Langley Porter for, or in cooperation with, the Department and other state facilities were mentioned. Such information was directed primarily toward establishing a new image in the Department, the state government, the Legislature, and with the Legislative Analyst of the Clinic's special mission and the legitimacy and usefulness thereof. Few among the Clinic staff itself needed to be thus influenced or informed.

Such policy statements as were made, if accepted by those to whom they were addressed, would mark a turning point in the Clinic's history of great importance for its future. Acceptance would constitute a legitimizing sanction within state government itself. While *effecting* policy changes might in practice be impeded, the new *direction* the Clinic would take was made clear. This direction was now endorsed openly and categorically, for the first time in Langley Porter's history.

Statement of Goals

On Clinic goals, the report stated: "For both agencies it is primarily a center for training and research. . . ."

> . . . in recognition of the need for more applied research in psychiatry, the Department of Mental Hygiene has recently established a position of Research Director in the Sacramento headquarters and plans to establish research teams in two or more of the facilities under departmental direction. The Langley Porter Clinic has been tentatively selected as one of the places to establish a research team.
>
> . . .
>
> Although not primarily a service agency, the Clinic, in order to fulfill its training function, provides the best service possible to its patients since good teaching necessarily involves participation in good service.

The report undertook to clarify the division of responsibilities between the Department and the University within the Clinic. But it also clearly stated that the Department, as well as the University, would carry on teaching and research, and that these would be carried out cooperatively, not in parallel functions:

> The attitude of the Department of Mental Hygiene toward staffing for teaching and research is that the teaching and research functions are inseparable from the treatment functions.

> Therefore, it must be expected that a person employed by the Department of Mental Hygiene, although his prime responsibility may be for care and treatment, would nonetheless have some teaching and research functions which might be considered primarily University functions.
>
> . . .
>
> A clear delineation of functions in all areas between the two agencies conducting operations at Langley Porter Clinic is not possible. Training, treatment, and research are participated in by both the Department of Mental Hygiene and the University. To do otherwise would alter greatly the value of these functions to both.

This policy was, of course, already in effect at the Clinic. The survey provided authoritative endorsement for an existing situation and for the extension of it.

FIGURE 1: MAJOR DIFFERENCES BETWEEN LANGLEY PORTER CLINIC AND OTHER MENTAL HOSPITALS WITHIN THE DEPARTMENT OF MENTAL HYGIENE

	Langley Porter Clinic	*Other Hospitals*
1.	Major program emphasis is training.	Major program emphasis is treatment of patients.
2.	Staffed jointly by University of California and Department of Mental Hygiene.	Are staffed almost solely by Mental Hygiene.
3.	Can select patients in accordance with program needs.	Must accept any patients that may be committed.
4.	Deals with all types of patients (necessary to give students and residents a broad training).	May specialize. Some are primarily for the mentally retarded, others for maximum security patients, etc.
5.	Is situated in a metropolitan center.	Most are situated in rural areas or near small cities.
6.	Is expected to train personnel for other public facilities, community facilities, and private practice.	Most, except in cooperation with Langley Porter Clinic residency training program, are expected to provide training for their own personnel only.
7.	Is staffed for intensive treatment as it relates to training and research.	Are staffed for less intensive treatment, with a larger percentage of chronic cases.
8.	Provides laboratory services, skilled consultative services, and training in electroencephalography and neuropathology to other hospitals. Staff of L. P. C. travel to other hospitals in addition to their work at L. P. C. to provide these services.	Do not have as specialized professional laboratory personnel as L. P. C.
9.	Has since its inception been research-oriented even though no Mental Hygiene personnel were engaged solely in that function. It is now contemplated that a research team will be assigned to L. P. C. by the Department headquarters solely for that function as research programs and projects are designed and approved.	Were never considered research centers. Even though more emphasis is now being placed on research in the several hospitals, the degree of emphasis on research will be greater at L. P. C.
10.	Has an extensive outpatient service which admits approximately 8 times as many patients annually as the inpatient service.	The outpatient service of other hospitals is minor in relation to their inpatient service.
11.	Has a small rated capacity (95 beds) for inpatients. Its complexities arise not so much from size as from intensity of programs and variety of relationships.	Have rated capacities of 1,000 to over 6,000 beds with attendant complexities of size.
12.	Treatment teams have a three-way, simultaneous orientation to treatment, research, and training.	At other hospitals, treatment teams are primarily oriented to patient treatment.

The report outlined the "treatment team" concept—wherein teams composed of people in the major mental health disciplines combined their skills in planning and carrying out treatment programs for each patient—as the basic approach in patient care within the Clinic. The report did not attempt to deal with any administrative implications of this method of functioning. The Clinic people, however, were to be directly affected by the explicit, categorical commitment to this treatment policy as stated in the report, which again provided sanction for an already existing and growing policy direction.

Major Reorganization Proposals

A major objective of the reorganization plan was to delegate administration, to relieve the two top men. Dr. Simon carried on a multitude of activities for Langley Porter; the medical school; the University; the Department of Mental Hygiene; the School of Nursing; the School of Social Welfare; numerous federal agencies; a large number of local, state, and national professional groups; and local community interests. The Assistant Medical Superintendent, Dr. Prestwood, had some sixteen people reporting to him. The report, therefore, recommended that the day-to-day administration of the Clinic be delegated by Simon to his Assistant Superintendent and that new levels be established below this position to reduce the Assistant Superintendent's overload.

Three new positions, each to head up one of the Clinic's main functional divisions (Clinical Services, Business Services, and Research), were recommended for establishment directly under the Assistant Superintendent. The new clinical director would supervise the Psychology and Social Work Departments, the Outpatient Department, a newly integrated Inpatient Service, and the contract services. Integration of the Inpatient Service was to be accomplished by putting all adult services and the children's inpatient wards under a chief of Inpatient Services. This chief would also supervise the Nursing and Rehabilitation Services, both of which worked only with inpatients.

A new rehabilitation department was to be formed by combining the existing occupational and recreational therapy functions with physical therapy.

Social Work, Psychology, and the Children's Service would each be provided with a new Department of Mental Hygiene head for administrative purposes.

The two laboratory divisions would continue to report directly to the Assistant Superintendent.

The new Department of Mental Hygiene research functions would be carried on by an interdisciplinary team of three.[22]

The Business Services Division, in addition to a new head at a higher grade, was to have an administrative assistant, and recommendations were made for revised structure, new procedures, and reallocation of duties. The librarians of medical records and of the medical library, who were both then reporting to the Assistant Superintendent, were to report to the new administrative assistant in Business Services.[23]

The OCC Division survey proposals, while adopting parts of Simon's original 1956 plan, provided much more depth in staffing and regrouping of program services. The survey also proposed more extensive changes in Business Services than Simon had contemplated. The Assistant Superintendent was given considerably more responsibility than in Simon's plan but not more than he had been carrying.

The elements in the OCC Division plan that carried the greatest implications for changed relationships in the "middle-management" group were the one or more new levels inserted between it and the Assistant Superintendent, and the regroupings of functional services.

The Proposals Are Presented to the Clinic Staff

No minutes were taken of the staff meeting at which Berke, Spencer, and Marvin Blanchard presented the OCC Division survey recommendations, explained the rationale underlying the proposed changes, and answered questions. According to several retrospective accounts, a number of people raised questions about how the plan would affect their departments and functions. As one staff member said, "The worry in everyone's mind was not the chart, but who was going to work where and with whom." Dr. Simon expected difficulty about the Children's Service. There was no clarity about the relation of the outpatient children to the Out-

22 With two additional supporting positions.

23 For a clearer picture of these recommended changes, compare Appendixes III and IV, showing existing and recommended structure in the Clinic.

patient Department (in fact, this was not even shown on the chart). Dr. Szurek, Director of the Children's Service, raised questions about the effect on his service of having a chief from the Department of Mental Hygiene. According to some recollections, Blanchard answered to the effect that Dr. Szurek, as the senior professional person on the service, would continue to control the treatment program as he always had. The new chief would take over only administration. Blanchard made a distinction between line authority and the "authority of ideas," which Dr. Szurek would continue to exercise.

Miss Parsons, head nurse, whose service was to be placed within the integrated Inpatient Service, raised questions about coordination with other Clinic functions such as business, food, housekeeping, and so on. She was advised that she might need to consult laterally even more than through the vertical line-authority channels indicated on the organizational chart.

Miss Adams, the librarian, who had no advance information on the disposition of her department, expressed the strongest objections to reporting to an administrative assistant in Business Services. She considered this wholly inappropriate to her professional function of running a highly specialized medical library serving several disciplines in the teaching and research activities of the Clinic. Not only was a business service not competent to supervise her work, but a higher professional authority was necessary to make policy decisions, especially among the competing demands made on the library. Simon told Berke subsequently that he had not talked to Miss Adams about the plan in advance of the meeting. Prestwood later reassured her that the plan was in no way binding on the Clinic and that her problem would be worked out.

No one recalls further details of this meeting. In view of later developments it is doubtful that worried staff members were much reassured by the discussions. Blanchard was left with the impression that there were no problems in this meeting, since Berke had such a thorough knowledge of the Clinic and had conveyed so well what he was trying to do. But this was perhaps true mainly in relation to Simon and Prestwood. The staff had neither participated in the planning to the same degree nor shared in the final decisions.

After the meeting Simon met with his staff. He did not consider that the plan was a mandate; rather, it was something to be tried. He was well aware that there would be problems of adjustment, and these, he felt, must be worked out as they went along, but he was anxious to persuade the staff members to accept the report. He told them he would like it very much if they would go along with the plan and try to work it out, and he hoped that they would. Supporting the survey would help them all a very great deal with the Department of Finance; the Clinic would be able to implement its plans without having to fight for everything as it came up. "Let's give it a chance."

The decision was, ultimately, made by Simon. He realized that the reorganization could not be effected entirely by seeking full agreement from everyone. Points of possible controversy were left to be worked out over a period of time.

Attitudes About the Survey

Simon and Prestwood on the whole were well pleased with the survey. It had gone far better than they had feared it might before it was undertaken. While some compromises had been made on both sides, the final report embodied most of the main points of Simon's original objectives. The survey had become a means to facilitate the expansion and other changes that Simon had wanted at Langley Porter. Simon and Prestwood simply hoped that the proposed internal reorganization would work out. They wanted to use the plans as a base to start from, making changes as needed in the light of experience and working out new relationships among and with the staff as they went along. Thus they intended to adapt the plans to the Clinic and the Clinic to the plans, according to what, in their judgment, would seem necessary and feasible as they proceeded to implement the survey. An important factor in possible future changes would be the kinds of people appointed to new positions.

Both Berke and Spencer had found the survey project a very rewarding experience. They had been challenged by the intricate problems of administration and function at Langley Porter. The end result was gratifying because it reflected optimum achievement within the limits of the possible; they felt they had brought about a maximum acceptance of as much administrative change as the organization would absorb. Berke's gesture in submitting his rough draft to Simon and Prestwood expressed the attitudes with which he and Spencer had worked throughout: only as much as could be genuinely accepted within the organization would be effective in the long run. Neither had sought to achieve more in terms of some ideal standard of technical perfection.

There was, evidently, misunderstanding about the nature and extent of the survey that still lingered in 1960. Both Simon and Prestwood had expected a thorough, top-to-bottom survey of the Clinic. This was not done. They were under the impression that the survey was cut short for lack of time, so that only the top and middle levels of the organization were dealt with. Berke, however, denied that the survey was cut short. He said, "I simply don't believe in that kind of survey when the top organization needs so much change. This should be done first, and if necessary, a later survey can go more thoroughly into the whole organization. Anyway, I doubt whether the Clinic would have enjoyed this." Spencer felt that more orientation was needed, both at the Clinic and within the business services at Department headquarters. He regretted very much having to leave the project and would have liked to assist more in the implementation of the changes.

Some members of the staff resented the survey, while others were disappointed that more was not done. Several were left with an unfinished feeling. They had expected to spend more time with the team. One said:

> I saw Berke and Spencer about two hours, and after this interview I was very hopeful. I found they could just look at the charts of my organization and recognize at once what the problems would be. But I did not see them again. They ran out of money and time or something, and although they said they were coming back, they didn't. The next step was a staff meeting where the proposal was presented. Dr. Simon asked us to please work with it.

Another stated:

> . . . they never got back to me. The survey got cut off too soon. I didn't understand at the time, and was left with an unfinished feeling. This affected the implementation of the reorganization; the Clinic suffered a loss. More time might have made things easier. You first had a vague awareness that something was happening above you, then all of a sudden you had a new boss.

Disappointment was related in part to the expectations people had in the beginning. Staff members had a variety of dissatisfactions which they hoped the survey would straighten out. When it failed to do so, their hopes were dashed. These staff members did not understand enough about the survey either before or during the process to avoid this; without adequate and accurate information, they could only speculate, worry, or develop expectations that were not going to be fulfilled.

In contrast, Berke and Spencer had a clear idea of their roles and functions in the survey process, which might be paraphrased:

> It's part of our job to listen to people, even when we can't solve their problems. Many issues are raised that we never intend to do anything about, although we might bring them to the attention of the director. We don't consider this a part of our function. It is an internal administrative matter that should be dealt with, and must be dealt with, by the responsible person, that is, the administrator.

But this was apparently not clear to the staff at the time, although Simon and Prestwood recognized that many of these problems were their responsibility.

Management Survey 868, for the Department of Mental Hygiene, Langley Porter Clinic, was published on June 28, 1957, and forwarded to the director. The Clinic staff now waited to see what the consequences of the survey would be.

ORGANIZATIONAL CHANGE: 1957-1960

During the weeks following publication of the survey, Simon and Prestwood explored the question of how much of the recommendations for increased staff could be carried out at once. Berke and Marvin Blanchard came to the Clinic in July to meet with the staff and discuss implementation of the report.[24]

The OCC Division men advised the Clinic staff on appropriate steps to carry out the plans. Conahan, Controller at Department of Mental Hygiene

---

[24] A management survey by the OCC Division was, in effect, a suggested long-range plan and was no more binding on the state government to fulfill than on the surveyed agency to adopt. It was an advisory recommendation by experts with official status. After the Department of Finance accepted an OCC Division report in principle, the Budget Division had to decide how far and fast it could go in implementing it. Each agency budget request still had to be made in the

headquarters, conferred with Simon and Prestwood and with the Department of Finance. There were hopes at first that most, if not all, of the recommended new positions could be authorized and filled out of emergency funds, but in the end the Clinic had to make these requests in the next budget year. The day-night service had been approved already, and five positions for this service and two others for maintenance were filled. Nothing else was provided in 1957. Spencer was able to persuade the Department of Finance to establish the position of administrative assistant in Business Services immediately from the emergency fund, but the Department of Mental Hygiene did not follow through. Another year passed before any of the survey recommendations for new positions were implemented.

New Staffing Through the Budget Process

For the next budget year, 1958-1959, Dr. Simon requested all of the new positions and reclassifications recommended by the survey, together with additional supporting staff that the survey had not dealt with, a total of some 114 new positions. Twenty-three of these survived the Department of Mental Hygiene budget cuts, and Finance reduced this number to fourteen. The Legislative Analyst disapproved ten, and in the end, only four were authorized by the Legislature. The next year the Clinic did better. The final count was thirty-six new positions established by legislative action. The 1960-1961 budget added another nineteen new positions. Here, too, the budget process was responsible for substantial reductions. The Clinic had requested fifty-seven, the Department asked for twenty-four, and Finance reduced this to nineteen in the Governor's budget. The Legislative Analyst disapproved nine of these, but this time the Legislature disregarded his advice.

As of mid-1960, according to Dr. Prestwood, the Clinic had staff adequate to its functional needs for the first time. The three years of implementing the survey recommendations had provided the Clinic substantially what it had asked for in 1956, in the opinions of Simon, Prestwood, and Dr. Marshall Porter.

usual way and was examined with the same routine critical evaluation. Dr. Simon commented, "The staff was informed of this by me and by Berke, repeatedly, but continued to regard the survey as if it were to be a budget implementation."

Internal Reorganization and Staff Changes

Parts of the recommendations for administrative restructuring were never adopted, while some were tried and later abandoned. Miss Adams, the librarian, continued to report to Dr. Prestwood as she had been doing. Physical Therapy was never combined with Occupational Therapy into a department of rehabilitation therapies. Here, as with the library, the nature of the work performed influenced the administrative arrangements. The single physical therapist at the Clinic worked directly with the patient-care program carrying out medically prescribed procedures with individual patients. Her activities were not closely related to the occupational and recreational programs at the Clinic, which consisted largely of group and ward activities. For a time the physical therapist reported to the head of the Inpatient Service.

The library and Physical Therapy were small, one-person departments; administrative arrangements made for them did not have much effect on the rest of the Clinic. But what was done with the Children's Service would have far-reaching effects on the organization of all the patient-care functions. Dr. Szurek and his assistant, Dr. Boatman, successfully protested the planned splitting of their service between the projected integrated Inpatient Service and the Outpatient Department; this recommendation was never implemented.

As had been anticipated, the reorganization plan forced Miss Byron, medical school lecturer in social work, to make a hard choice. With the new Department of Mental Hygiene position of chief of social work established, she could not continue in her existing capacity unless she changed jobs and assumed this position. No overt pressures for the change were evidenced, but the inherent pressure of such an either/or choice was strong. Miss Byron chose to remain in the Clinic as the new chief and resigned from the medical school faculty. Since the job change entailed a lower salary, the Department of Psychiatry made up the difference. The formal shift in positions took place in June 1958.

This incident pointed up the change taking place within the Clinic in response to the policy shift in emphasis among the Clinic's purposes. While other factors also were important, the new and growing importance of teaching and, especially, research was being felt throughout Langley Porter. Persons who functioned primarily in the patient-care services increasingly felt the stress of this shift.

During 1958 three key staff people left Langley Porter. One was Mrs. Evelyn Stearns, the Business Manager; the other two were staff psychiatrists. It is not known to what extent the reorganization was responsible for the resignations of the physicians. Their opportunities for promotions, however, were not enhanced by the changes, and one did not receive a hoped-for appointment. Both accepted positions elsewhere. Mrs. Stearns continued in her position without any change, pending implementation of the plans, but resigned before these were effected. In her case there were circumstances other than the reorganization that very probably affected her decision. She had not been well, she was close to retirement, and shortly after leaving the Clinic, she remarried.[25] Miss Helen C. Barclay, the Accounting Officer, acted as Business Manager for about three months until a new head of Business Services assumed his duties in January 1959.

The new positions of clinical director and director of research and the higher classification for head of the Business Services Division were established in the 1958-1959 budget. All were filled by January 1959. The clinical directorship was taken by Dr. Klaus W. Berblinger, who had been approached earlier by Dr. Simon to fill an associate professorship on the medical school faculty. Berblinger, of Swiss origin, had taught at the medical schools of Duke University and the University of Maryland, where he was serving as Director of the Outpatient Department at the time Simon began negotiations with him. Before an agreement was reached, however, Simon offered him a choice between the faculty position and the post of Chief of Clinical Services at Langley Porter. Simon considered Berblinger an exceptionally outstanding psychiatrist, particularly effective in teaching, where his main interest lay. It was not Simon's impression that he had any special interest in administration. Berblinger, however, elected to take the Department of Mental Hygiene position as Chief of Clinical Services.

Robert J. Wensel, a budget analyst in Finance who had been working on Department of Mental Hygiene budgets for several years, became the Clinic's new head of the Business Services Division. He had become interested in Langley Porter through his contacts with it and wanted experience in an operating job. Dr. Enoch Callaway, III, was secured to head the Department's new research program in the Clinic. In the course of a few months, therefore, three new people were brought in to fill the top jobs in the Clinic's main functional divisions of Clinical Services, Research, and Business Services, directly under the Assistant Superintendent.

Dr. M. R. Harris, who had joined the Clinic staff in February 1958, became Chief of the Outpatient Department in December of that year, when this position was vacated by resignation. Dr. Alfred J. Gianascol, trained on the Children's Service, was picked to be Department of Mental Hygiene chief of that service, as soon as the position should be established. He was given a temporary job in the adult services until July 1959, when the new position became available.

After the arrival of Dr. Berblinger to assume his new position, the consequences of keeping the Children's Service a unit became evident. The logic of the integrated Inpatient Service, as recommended in the survey, simply fell apart. Nursing, physical therapy, and occupational therapy were carried on only with inpatients, including the inpatient children. When the hospitalized children were not made part of the Inpatient Service, it was considered untenable, administratively, for these three ancillary departments to continue to report to the Inpatient Service Chief. He would not be in a position to supervise or coordinate the whole of their inpatient work. The head nurse, especially, felt it awkward for her to report to him. On his part, the Inpatient Chief, Dr. Duncan, had had no interest in assuming administrative supervision of the inpatient Children's Service, and he now felt there was no rational basis for him to retain supervision of the ancillary departments. One by one these were taken out of the "integrated" Inpatient Service and placed under the Chief of Clinical Services.

The Neuropsychiatric and Somatic Treatment Service (later renamed Neuropsychiatric and Research Service) also was removed from the supervision of the Inpatient Chief. In practice this service was not closely integrated with the rest of the inpatient programs. It was highly specialized and much closer to the research activities in the Clinic.

Langley Porter Clinic thus went through repeated shifts as it absorbed new personnel and made adjustments in the structural pattern. By 1960, in the area of clinical programs, the organization chart resembled Dr. Simon's 1956

[25] Simon and Prestwood felt that Mrs. Stearns had done a very good job as Business Manager under the conditions with which she had had to contend. She continued to visit old friends at the Clinic frequently.

plan[26] more closely than it did the OCC Division survey plan, except that Dr. Prestwood had more responsibility than in Simon's proposal (although not more than he had been carrying). The two top positions were almost as Berke and Spencer had conceived them. The Associate Superintendent[27] was supervising the three main functional divisions of Clinical Services, Business Services, and Research; the two laboratories, as planned; and also the medical library, a deviation from the plan. The new Chief of Clinical Services, however, was supervising nine rather than the four departments and services that the survey plan had contemplated, and the contract services (as recommended).[28] The simplified comparative charts, Figures 2, 3, and 4 on pages 283-285, show the situation existing in 1957, the survey proposal, and the actual structure by late 1959. They also portray the problem of the Children's Service split.

In effect, much of the Associate Superintendent's overload of supervisory duties was delegated to the new clinical director. But the effort at further delegation downward through restructuring failed, because of the failure to integrate the inpatient programs as recommended. The main reason was the refusal of the Children's Service to be split between Inpatient and Outpatient Divisions. The clinical director, as a result of this chain reaction, now had a heavy concentration of supervisory duties that was never contemplated by the OCC Division team.[29]

Consequences of Change

The changes at Langley Porter Clinic from 1956 to 1960 were very extensive, affecting all aspects of the organization, though in varying degrees. By 1960, when nineteen new people would join the Clinic staff after July 1, completing the last stage of implementing the survey recommendations and filling the last available office and desk space, Langley Porter had moved fast and far from the institution of 1956. From just under 200 Department of Mental Hygiene employees, the staff had grown to 263. There were now fifty-six residents and fifty-eight full-time research people, three paid by the Department[30] and the rest by federal and other grants. There were thirteen academic and eleven clinical faculty positions assigned by the medical school to the Clinic on a full-time basis, and 140 part-time, unpaid consultants. The inpatient capacity of the Clinic was not greatly changed; it now had 117 beds, including thirteen for the accommodation of up to twenty-six patients in the day-night service, as compared with ninety-seven beds in 1956. The outpatient load had been 485 on June 30, 1959, and was expected to increase by 129 in the following year, to a total of 614. The number of patients seen in the Outpatient Department, too, had not shown a large increase, for in 1954 the average case-load had been 572. The real increases had taken place in the numbers of people taught and trained, in the intensiveness of treatment (time spent and numbers of people involved) in each case, and in research projects.

The Clinic's expenditures budget for 1959-1960 was $1,744,746 (actual) as compared with Dr. Bowman's last budget for 1956-1957 of $1,110,188. The Clinic's budget, however, surprisingly remained at almost precisely the same proportion of the total Department of Mental Hygiene budget—just slightly under one and one-half per cent. This stable percentage apparently reflected growth and upgrading in the Department as a whole in the same period and the fact that most of the Clinic's expansion in research was being supported by funds from outside the Department.

In 1959 a new four-story addition had been opened, providing badly needed office space, a new library, and research facilities. A research ward would be opened there during 1960.

The new Research Department was in full operation. Within the Outpatient Department a new teaching and research program in community mental health had been instituted. Studies in geriatrics, mental retardation, hypertension, schizophrenia, and a multitude of other research projects had been initiated or expanded. Thirty researchers were working on geriatrics alone.

Teaching in almost all the disciplines in the Clinic except physical therapy was being carried on at the undergraduate and graduate levels. Special courses for general practitioners and for state hospital physicians were an established part of the teaching program. Langley Porter was increasingly participating in many aspects of community mental health programs and facilities.

[26] See Appendix II.

[27] Title changed from "Assistant."

[28] See Appendix V.

[29] Dr. Simon: "Since most of these units are headed up by competent supervisory professional personnel, supervision need not be close; coordination is more important."

[30] With two additional supporting personnel.

FIGURE 2:
EXISTING (SIMPLIFIED) ORGANIZATION CHART, 1957

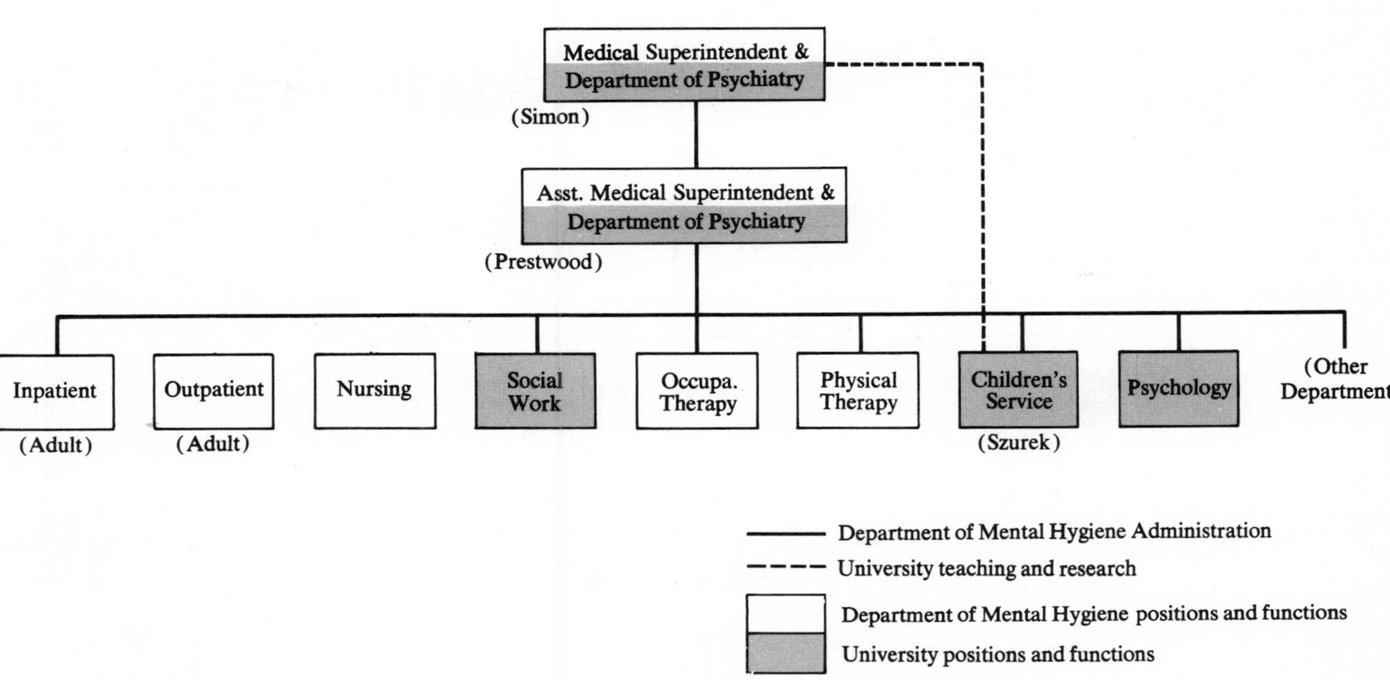

FIGURE 3:
OCC DIVISIONAL PROPOSAL (SIMPLIFIED), 1957

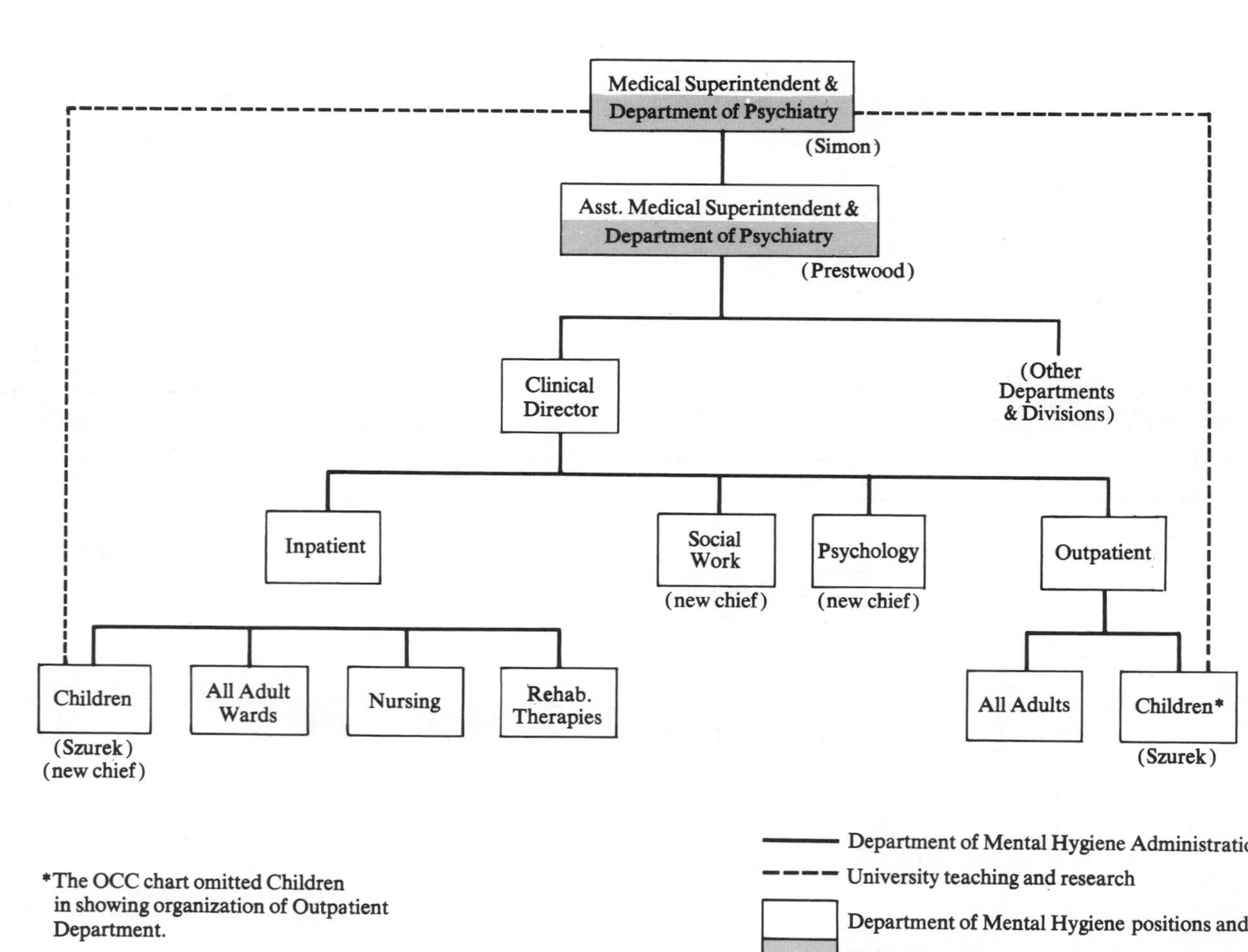

*The OCC chart omitted Children in showing organization of Outpatient Department.

FIGURE 4:
EXISTING (SIMPLIFIED) ORGANIZATION CHART, 1959

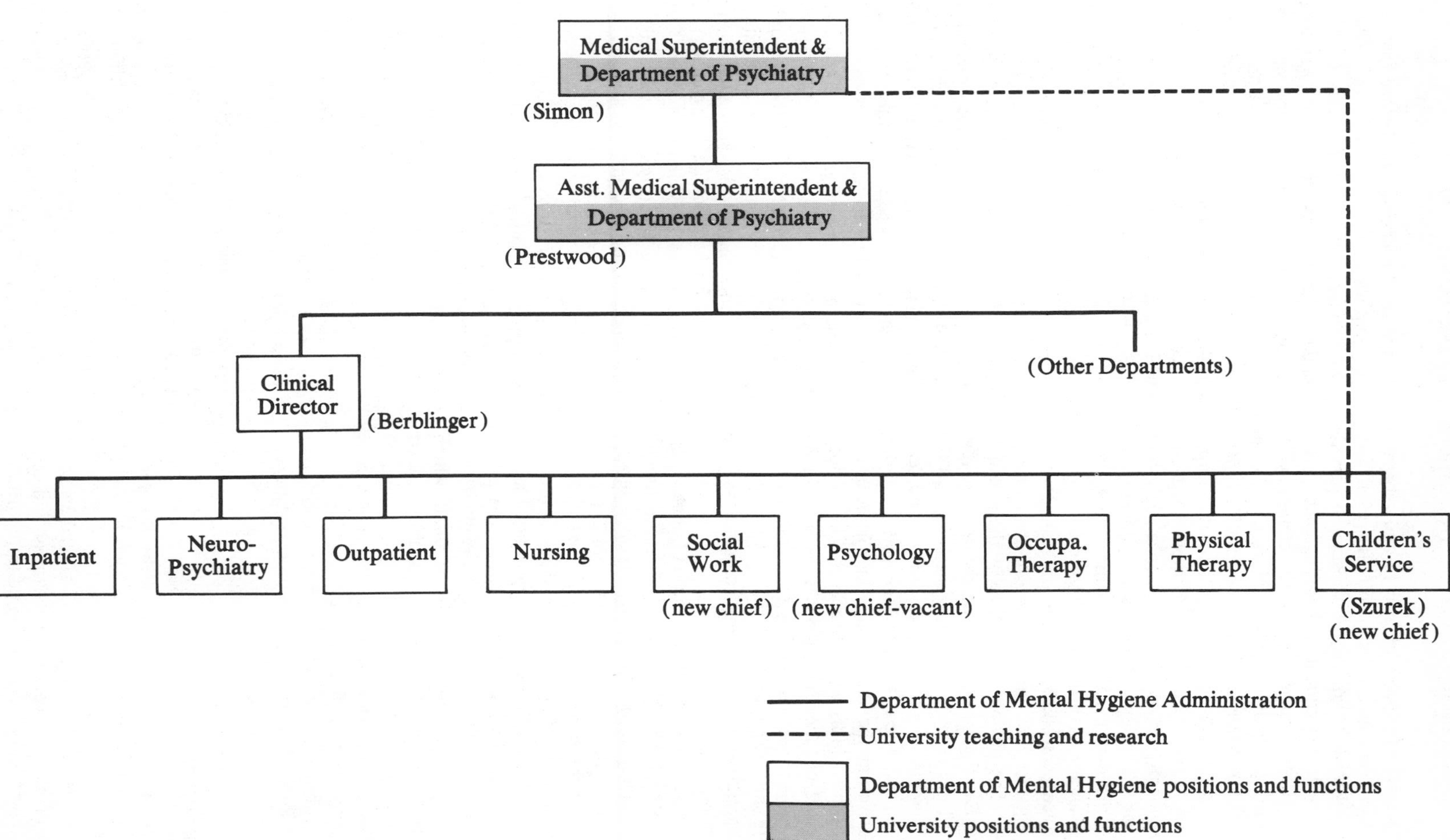

The piecemeal process of growth and reorganization had been in itself difficult, however. Key positions were left unfilled for substantial periods of time, with consequent lack of balance in the transition. Berke considered that the changes were "phased in" gradually; in his opinion, to have instituted the increases all at once would have been most unwise. Prestwood, however, felt the implementation as carried out entailed more headaches organizationally than the all-at-once approach would have. The supporting services did not keep up with the expansion in programs, which were easier to obtain. The survey had not dealt with the staffing needed to underpin this program growth; in consequence, the timing during implementation was bad. The obvious difficulties in the Business Services Division at the time of the survey were attributed primarily to poor management, and the Clinic was told to wait and see. But, despite reorganization and a new Business Manager, the spring of 1960 found the Accounting Department five months behind in its work. Much of this overload had come from the tremendous expansion in research projects. In continuing to refuse requests for more supporting personnel the various agencies in the capital were still making comparisons with the state hospitals.

The transformations taking place at Langley Porter Clinic in 1957-1960 did not all stem directly and exclusively from the OCC Division survey. This report, rather, was a vehicle and a sanction for some of the currents of change that were felt throughout the Clinic. The principal source of change was Simon himself, and the crucial alteration at Langley Porter had been his succession to the directorship. The survey was an explicit, dramatic, and conspicuous channel through which pressures for basic changes were manifested. It became *one* tool with which to carry out changes desired by Simon, both within the Clinic and in its relationships with related agencies.

It is within this context that the following account of some of the more important consequences is presented.

Communication Patterns

The substantive changes effected by the implementation process—new levels inserted in the administrative structure filled by people new to the Clinic or new in the position—disrupted habitual patterns of communication. Department and service heads who had been accustomed to reporting to Simon or Prestwood, and before that to Bowman, now reported to Dr. Berblinger, the Chief of Clinical Services, or to Dr. Duncan, Chief of the Inpatient Service. As Prestwood expressed it, "Distance occurred"; people no longer were in direct contact with the front office. Concurrent changes were taking place that were not directly attributable to the reorganization. One was Simon's discontinuance of regular, weekly, general staff meetings, which had been customary in the Clinic since the early days. Everybody came, from the housekeeper on up. These meetings, according to Dr. Simon, were rarely used for policy-making. They dealt with trivial matters and got very dull. At the same time, Simon was becoming more involved with mental hygiene activities, work at the medical school, and new teaching and research programs, while Prestwood was increasingly taking over the Clinic's internal day-to-day administration. Simon decided to call a staff meeting only when a real need for it arose.

Various other staff groups were formed, changing character after a time. In 1955 Simon had begun meeting regularly with the two other senior psychiatrists from the faculty, and later with Dr. Harris, the clinical psychologist, to discuss the medical school curriculum in psychiatry. Somewhat later, all the staff psychiatrists at the Clinic began to hold regular meetings. After a while, this body was divided into two groups, one to deal with research training and the other to deal with the regular residency training programs. After Wensel joined the staff as head of Business Services, an executive committee was formed, composed of the five top administrative officers: Simon, Prestwood, Berblinger, Callaway, and Wensel. Each department and patient service continued to hold customary regular meetings of its staff, the patient-service meetings being interdisciplinary in composition.

These were far from all of the conferences and committee meetings taking place within Langley Porter, but they were the main ones dealing with overall policy, administration, and service and department affairs. Several consequences emerged from this complex of stable and changing patterns. Whatever groups were arranged, some excluded groups and individuals tended to feel that policies concerning them were being made behind closed doors and decisions announced without appropriate participation on their part. Thus one undesirable effect was to divide the staff and create tensions.

Simon's action in putting the old weekly general staff meetings on an irregular and infrequent basis was felt as a loss by some of the staff members. Moreover, Dr. Berblinger did not set up interdisciplinary staff meetings for the heads of the patient-care services and ancillary departments who became responsible to him. As a result, except for individual reporting, there was no formalized means of communication between Prestwood and these heads, nor was there any interdisciplinary group meeting among them to coordinate programs and carry on normal administrative and other business.

While the medical staff and the head psychologist (in his capacity as a medical school professor) met together with one or another top-level group, the ancillary departments of Nursing, Social Work, and Rehabilitation Therapies, plus the physical therapist and the librarian, were not part of any interdisciplinary group meeting at their own level or above.

All of these factors together—new people, new structure, new distance from the top administrators, absence of the interdisciplinary staff meetings—produced a sense of isolation among some of the staff. Almost without exception, though in varying degrees, a breakdown of communications was felt in the patient-care services and ancillary departments, especially the latter.

The Clinic was struggling through the effects of rapid expansion. The old patterns of contact were obviously outgrown and were abandoned, but the Clinic as yet had not developed a satisfactory new system of communications to meet its new needs.

By June of 1960 Dr. Prestwood reached a decision to which he had given a great deal of thought. With all the changes going on, he said, it had taken him this long to think out what he needed to carry out his administrative responsibilities. Subject to Simon's approval, he planned to set up an administrative advisory committee consisting of himself as chairman, Wensel, Berblinger, and the heads of all the ancillary departments and patient services. This committee would have an overlap of three people with the executive committee (Prestwood, Berblinger, and Wensel). The new committee's purpose would be, in an advisory capacity to the Superintendent, to coordinate policy and to act as the Clinic's top administrative body; all existing committees would report to it. Simon would be invited to attend as the need arose, and all policy questions arising in this committee would be referred to the executive committee. This proposal was the product of considerable discussion between Simon and Prestwood, and Prestwood and staff members.[31]

The Clinic's New Image Affects Functions

The major policy change expressed in the OCC Division report was the attempt to establish a new image of the Clinic within the state government. This shift of emphasis, from the preeminence of patient care to acceptance of research and teaching as equally major functions for the Department of Mental Hygiene, was relatively successful and would continue to facilitate state support for these programs within the Clinic. In effect, Langley Porter would no longer be regarded as a service agency, a miniature state hospital, but as a true institute for research and teaching purposes. The intensive treatment program, while remaining a major and inseparable goal, would be viewed as the foundation for the expanded research and teaching functions.

This policy shift also had important consequences within the Clinic. One immediate effect was that Dr. Simon expected all department and service heads to engage in some research activities, however little. Dr. Bowman had not required this of his Department of Mental Hygiene staff. Simon changed this policy, and gradually staff members complied, some of them reluctantly.

Another consequence for some staff members engaged exclusively or mostly in patient-care activities was a sense among them that their work was no longer regarded highly as were teaching and research. This attitude was expressed in such statements as, "I think patient care is just as important as teaching and research." Especially for people who had worked for many years in service activities, the new recognition of the other major functions was a difficult change.[32]

There was more to this point than a vague feeling of discomfort. The policy change affected Clinic administration, in the perceptions of these people, who felt that teaching and research were

---

[31] By the fall of 1960 this committee was meeting regularly. Miss Helen Barclay, Chief Accounting Officer, had been included as a member of the committee.

[32] Dr. Simon commented: "Although the staff was informed that good patient care was the cornerstone of good training and research programs, some felt that patient care and treatment were being given a secondary and subservient role."

valued above patient care and given greater time and attention. One of the strongest feelings of some staff members was that those in service activities were not heard and that their problems were neglected.

One department head who complained of a lack of contact and communication with the top administration "got the impression that everybody was doing about all they could do," but added, "This has to be a matter of judgment about priorities." Regardless of the reason for it, this department head reported, problems remained unresolved.

Another staff member felt that the medical administrators insisted on their authority to make decisions, which was proper, but then neglected to make them, and added, "I need to work under someone who *is* willing, and who will take administrative responsibility. Somebody has to run the hospital; it's a full-time job."

In still another view, research functions expanded "unrealistically," outdistancing the purely administrative capacities of the Clinic in staff, procedures, skills, business services, and even in the numbers of patients needed to support the expanded teaching and research programs.

The Treatment Team Concept

The second policy change was not really new, but it received strong impetus from the change of Clinic administrators and from the OCC Division survey. This was a medical policy: the treatment team concept as a technique for treating mentally-ill patients.[33] This method relied for its effectiveness upon a cooperative, interdisciplinary group effort to develop and carry out a treatment plan for individual patients at the ward level. The difficulty experienced in functioning in this manner apparently arose from two main factors: one was the traditional responsibility of the physician in charge of the patient, who could not properly relinquish final authority for medical decisions to a team; the second was the conflict of authorities that was inherent (and either open or latent in practice) between team decisions and traditional supervisory "line" control in each of the participating disciplines. To work smoothly and effectively, the treatment team concept required some delegation of authority to each team member by his own superior. It was at this potential friction point that conflict and tension had been evidenced in the Clinic.[34]

Formerly, the professional chiefs of the ancillary services "ran" their departments from the top down. For example, as Miss Byron said, "Dr. Bowman told me, 'This is your department; run it the way you want it to be, and I'll help and support you. I don't always agree with what you do, but you take responsibility for your functions here.' " As changes were instituted under Simon, following the survey, Miss Byron refused to act as supervisor for social workers assigned to teams on special research projects, because she believed it was not appropriate for her to undertake supervision of personnel over whose activities she would have no "real control."[35]

Difficulty was most evident in, but not confined to, the departments with a strong orientation to line authority, as in Social Work and Nursing—divisions that had developed under Dr. Bowman before the modern concept of team treatment had become well-established at the Clinic and before there was enough well-trained medical staff to carry it out.[36] Miss Byron was told that the various problems she raised were not administrative or organizational in nature, but interpersonal. Miss Parsons, head nurse, felt that in dealing with many administrative problems the Clinic's administrators had placed emphasis upon interpersonal relationships to the exclusion of other elements of the problems. One staff member remarked, "The problem of line authority is treated as a psychiatric case, rather than as administrative business." "New role relationships," he said, had never been worked out among the staff of the Clinic.

---

[33] The OCC survey did not deal in any way with the administrative implications of the treatment team concept, apparently because this was an internal and technical policy matter. However, the consequences of Simon's strengthening and extending the use of this method were substantial, adding to other stresses stemming more directly from implementation of the survey itself. For this reason, the discussion of organizational change cannot ignore the impact of this "technological" change upon the organization without creating a distortion in reporting the difficulties of this period.

[34] See Appendix VI for a diagram showing how the facilities of Langley Porter came to focus in treatment teams.

[35] Dr. Simon said she never was asked to do so.

[36] It has been impossible to get any clear picture of the gradual growth of the use of this method within the Clinic. However, Simon's commitment to team treatment was significantly stronger than was Bowman's; moreover, prior to the survey and reorganization, the Clinic lacked enough highly trained medical personnel to make full and effective use of the method.

Dr. Simon observed that the treatment team concept in operation tended to blur line and staff relationships. "They say it is a line, we say it is a consulting function." The medical staff experienced annoyance and frustration at various times; they tended to feel that their authority was being challenged, as did some of the department heads.[37] But there was little indication that they were aware of and dealing with the administrative "line" and "staff" issues involved. One high-level medical administrator commented, "There are no problems in cooperation except those created by people."

There was a lack of consistency among the Clinic staff in talking about these problems, suggesting that this treatment policy was not yet fully defined and accepted, nor the issues resolved. People spoke in terms of specific conflicts and lack of cooperation, as between individuals or disciplines, but there was no clear consensus on what the policy was or on how it was to be carried out in practice at the ward level. In such a situation, some ancillary staff members either did not know, or did not accept, what was expected of them. The treatment team concept, therefore, appeared to be a strong policy direction rather than a fully understood and accepted mode of operation.[38] By June 1960 some steps had been taken toward clarification.

The relation of the OCC Division survey to this internal policy problem was twofold: the report clearly stated that the treatment team concept was the Clinic's treatment policy, and it enabled the Clinic to obtain the staff necessary to carry out the policy. While this change was mainly independent of the reorganization (although concurrent in time), it was nevertheless inextricably interwoven with the more direct consequences of reorganization and reinforced other problems encountered during the implementation period.

Business Services Improve

The reorganization of the Business Services Division and the addition of new staff, especially the new Business Manager, contributed a great deal to the more effective functioning of Langley Porter. Wensel gradually reorganized his department, established sound fiscal and business management practices, and was continuing to make further improvements. One Clinic staff member remarked, "It's wonderful! Now we get what we need." Dr. Simon stated that he had found out how much difference a good, adequately staffed Business Services could make.

Coming, as he did, directly from the Budget Division of Finance, Wensel was thoroughly familiar with budget procedures and with what was needed to provide an adequate basis for administrative policy consideration. He was able to provide an effective channel of communication from Langley Porter to the state government and the Legislature and thus to fulfill one of the objectives of Berke and Spencer. He also increasingly gave the Clinic the kind of solid support from the business function that the survey team had hoped for.

Wensel himself had undergone a change of attitudes since coming to the Clinic. As he put it, "When you are a budget analyst in Finance, you sometimes think you understand an agency, but you really don't. You only find out by working in one." Before coming to Langley Porter, he had not believed the Clinic really needed some of the increases it was asking for in maintenance staff; since working there he had "found out I was wrong. We really do need them."

New Look in Administration

By 1960 the structure and the style of administration in the Clinic were in striking contrast to those of 1956. Almost all the planned new positions had been filled. Dr. Simon was functioning as the chief link between Langley Porter and the Department of Mental Hygiene, the University, the field of psychiatry and mental illness, and the community. Dr. Prestwood was acting as chief administrator for daily operations within the Clinic. Neither man was in direct touch with patient treatment as much as he had been in earlier years. Medical responsibility had been delegated increasingly to the ward level, a change made possible by additional staffing with experienced, competent psychiatrists and by an administration more inclined to delegate decisions than Dr. Bowman had been. Personal, one-man administration in a flat administrative structure had been replaced by several administrative levels in an organization far more complex, both in depth and in new programs. At the same time, new policies were changing the Clinic's former ways of functioning, demanding new relationships. Increasing use of the treatment team

[37] A number of "incidents" were reported by the medical staff but were "off the record."

[38] This summary statement is the author's own interpretation of the situation. However, it is based upon interviews with a wide variety of staff members.

concept was requiring closer cooperation among the disciplines, concentrated at the ward level rather than at the top of the organization as formerly.

During the years of implementing the survey Simon and Prestwood developed new roles and activities just as did the rest of the staff. Theirs was now the job of policy-making, overall planning, and coordination rather than close personal supervision. As faculty members of the medical school, as well as Clinic administrators, their duties included planning and participating in teaching and research activities. Among their many responsibilities, patient-care services were only one of the Clinic's three main functions, and administration, as such, was a part-time vocation.

All of the changes at Langley Porter Clinic were as new to the two top officers as they were to the rest of the staff. Both men felt they had absorbed a great deal of administrative understanding from the survey team, but applying it in practice, under conditions of frequent change and rapid expansion, was inescapably a first experience for them. They were working things out as they went along, as they had foreseen would be necessary. Change was so frequent that, as Prestwood said about setting up some sort of administrative staff meeting, "Any plan you made didn't fit by next week." There was no ready-made pattern, no previous experience, to call on as they moved ahead into new situations.

Staff Perceptions of the Reorganization

Staff members who lived through the period of change almost without exception felt that the reorganization in general helped the Clinic a great deal, particularly in increased staffing and in providing for other needs. Most of them recognized that problems were created as well as solved, but on balance they felt that the net result had been good and that such problems as there were were moving toward solutions. A number expressed the thought that much remained to be done. They were generally enthusiastic about the improvement in the business services. But the old problem of getting from the state government the equipment, the classifications of positions, and other resources they felt they needed was still a persisting frustration, even though it was improved. Most frequently mentioned difficulties in change were the dislocation, in some cases breakdown, of established communication channels, and the need for developing new relationships with individuals and with other disciplines. Most staff members felt that these problems were gradually being worked out. One, however, thought there had been increasing chaos, administratively, for the past several years (starting before Bowman's retirement).

New people who came onto the Clinic staff, unfamiliar with the old organization under Dr. Bowman, adapted to the new order more easily than some of the older staff members, since they were not required to change familiar, established procedures and relationships. Their adjustment in the Clinic had to be total, but they had no investment in an earlier situation there.

Probably least altered in Langley Porter were the laboratories (unchanged) and the Children's Service. The Children's Service continued under the direction of Dr. Szurek in much the same manner as it always had. The addition of a new chief of service for administrative purposes was absorbed with only routine adjustment, as Dr. Gianascol assumed some of the administrative functions that Dr. Boatman, the Assistant Director, had formerly performed. Dr. Boatman regarded the survey mainly as a means of getting needed staff for the Clinic as a whole and for the Children's Service, and, in this sense, as very useful. No difficulties had been experienced in adjusting to the new Chief of Clinical Services, who provided only nominal administrative supervision.

Dr. Duncan, Chief of the Inpatient Service, had experienced repeated changes in his service when the integrated plan recommended by the OCC Division report was initiated and then abandoned and reversed, but he did not see these events as constituting any particular problem for him. His absorbing interest was in the treatment program, not in administration. Duncan recognized the frictions that had been present in the Clinic before and during the period of change, but he believed that these had moved a long way toward resolution. He felt that Dr. Berblinger had contributed a great deal to the Clinic both in teaching, in which he was particularly outstanding, and in administration, where he had given leadership and delegated responsibility to the chiefs and department heads under him.

Berblinger had had to create his own job when he came to Langley Porter. As he expressed it, he did not view his role as that of an executive with line authority or a chief of service but as that of a consultant of those under his supervision. This, he explained, resembled the French system of administration, where the highest position is regarded as embodying a consulting function. The questions of line authority and horizontal consultation, he believed, did not involve problems, unless problems were created by people. Difficulty in cooperation between services and disciplines was not necessarily inherent in organization as such, he thought, but more likely was evidence of personal problems. Berblinger pointed out that in psychiatry great importance is placed on interpersonal relations and the working out of difficulties and tensions. He felt that this could be carried too far, and that the psychiatric atmosphere of the Clinic encouraged more "acting out of feelings" than was really desirable. He encouraged the department and service chiefs under him to take responsibility for their own functions.

Miss Byron, Director of Social Work, believed that the expanded staff was badly needed at Langley Porter, especially a clinical director. She had hoped this new position would provide for continuity of patient care between the Inpatient and Outpatient Divisions. She was deeply concerned over the "lack of adequate communication," the "lack of clarity on policies," and the "lack of sufficient participation" by her department in interdisciplinary policy and program development within the Clinic. Her department was involved in all of the Clinic's programs with patients and with the community. The impact of the reorganization on this department had been especially acute for this reason. The structural changes had fragmented her functions of reporting, coordination, and planning. Where Miss Byron formerly had been able to carry these out by consultation at the top of the administration, she now found it necessary to consult with four or five different people on the various aspects of her department's work. In a memo to Dr. Prestwood in February 1960, she analyzed these problems and commented:

> Since the Chief Social Worker cannot report to the Chief of Clinical Services on all aspects of the Department's work, some aspects are unreported or handled with others on an emergency basis. . . . Top administration gets piece-meal, uncoordinated, and thus distorted reports of the Social Work Department's work. Social work does not contribute to institute program planning and evaluation. The Chief Social Worker attends no Administrative Staff, or Committee Meetings.

In the area of community work, the memo recorded that Miss Byron currently reported to, and worked with, no one. She believed she should be reporting to either Simon or Prestwood.[39] During the spring a series of meetings was held with Miss Byron, in consultation with Simon, Prestwood, and Berblinger, to try to work out satisfactory solutions.[40]

Miss Parsons, Superintendent of Nursing Services, welcomed the new medical staffing, a need she had felt for years on the wards. She was concerned, however, about problems of administration and of role relations within the Clinic. Responsible for a Nursing Service that operated around the clock, seven days a week, Miss Parsons was deeply aware of the demands and responsibilities in the patient-care functions. She felt that many of the problems she was experiencing stemmed from a "lack of coordination among all the programs" for which she had to provide nursing services. This situation was not new in the Clinic, she believed, but had been accentuated by the process of reorganization and by the rapid expansion.

Miss Dale Houston, Director of Rehabilitation Therapies,[41] had welcomed the survey and felt that, in general, the Clinic had benefited a great deal from the resulting changes. She had experienced a lack of communications during the changes, however, and felt that adjustments in the Clinic, including those in her own department, were still being worked out. She had found it easier to work out changes with the Children's Service, where ideas about what was wanted were definite, than with the other inpatient services with their greater size, diversity of program, and looser coordination. Here, reorganization had accentuated problems of communication and coordination.

Dimensions of Change

In terms of the required changes in behaviors for the top and middle administrative staff at Langley Porter Clinic, the overall dimensions of change stemming from the reorganization (in its broadest sense) were very substantial.

The major shift accomplished in the four years, 1956-1960, in terms of both substantive growth and policy redefinition, was the emergence of research as one of the primary functions in the Clinic

39 Simon commented that Miss Byron could have reported to Berblinger on all matters had she wished to, but she refused.

40 Miss Byron, however, finally resigned in October 1960.

41 A new title. Miss Houston supervised occupational and recreational therapy but not physical therapy.

for the Department of Mental Hygiene as well as for the medical school. Simon, in effect, had succeeded in moving formal Clinic policy on mission closer to the traditional academic value-system in which research and teaching are of major importance. This change was fundamental for both the state government and the staff within Langley Porter, carrying strong implications for changed functional, status, and role relationships among the Clinic staff.

Expanded staffing together with internal reorganization provided the personnel and administrative structure needed to carry out more effectively the treatment team concept as Simon's major treatment policy within the Clinic. Only incidentally stemming from the OCC Division survey, through its policy-sanctioning aspect and its facilitating function in obtaining more staff, this change also affected functioning, status, and administrative behaviors among the Clinic staff.

The first of these policy changes shifted emphasis in *what* the Clinic would do in terms of its threefold purposes; the second, *how* the Clinic would carry out its mission in treatment.

The provision of more administrative levels and sheer size—greatly increased staff, together with new programs. This growth had substantial consequences for administrative structure, for communications, and for the character and complexity of the administrative process within the Clinic. Changes necessitated by this growth in turn altered the habitual relationships, roles, and administrative behaviors of the Clinic staff.

The provision of more administrative levels and new functional groupings within the Clinic had highly significant consequences in changed relationships among the staff and "distance" from the top administrators; it also facilitated more delegation of responsibility downward.

The marked improvement in the business services served mainly to facilitate and reinforce the major policy change in Clinic mission through more effective communications with the administrative control agencies of state government. It also provided more effective support within the organization for Clinic functions.

Together with the major change from Bowman to Simon, these were the main threads of administrative change taking place within Langley Porter Clinic during the four-year period. They were perceived differently by every individual undergoing or observing them; their significance often was not realized as they occurred, but only in retrospect. Even in 1960 some of the transformations were not entirely understood in all their implications.

The impact on individual staff members varied from virtually nil to severe. While precise evaluations of the effects of individual elements of change may not be made in dealing with a total context, it can be generalized with reasonable assurance that the greatest impact of change fell upon those staff people most involved in service activities and least in research and teaching; on those formerly closer to the top administration and now further removed from it; on those most accustomed to the characteristics of Dr. Bowman's administration; on those in the ancillary services whose former control area was now impinged upon by the widening authority of the dominant medical group; and on those most strongly oriented toward line authority, with the locus of decision-making placed at the top of the organization.

Conversely, least affected were medical school faculty members; the medical group as a whole; those with strong research and teaching orientations; those least oriented toward strong line authority and top-level decisions; new staff members with no experience of the Bowman administration; and those least concerned with administrative structure and techniques.

For those who experienced the greatest change impact, the required new adaptations also were greatest. The extent to which all degrees of pressure for adaptation were met successfully by individuals depended upon individual willingness and capacity, together with the effectiveness of communications, information, and support afforded by the organization.

Perceptions of the extent and nature of the changes taking place in this period varied widely within the Clinic. Where the shifts were not understood and not dealt with effectively, uncertainty and friction ensued.

Retrospect and Prospect

The major substantive changes projected by the OCC Division survey were accomplished in the three years after mid-1957, together with substantial modifications of the survey's organization plans. Policy changes were instituted with varying degrees of success. An event of some significance took place in the winter of 1959-1960 independently of the survey but related to the same currents of change that were generated by Dr. Simon's accession as Clinic administrator. A formal agreement was signed, eighteen years after Langley Porter's founding, between the Department of Mental Hygiene and the University. The document, much shorter than the legislative act of 1941, incorporated almost identical provisions regarding the relationship of the two institutions and in much the same language. Whether the contents of this document incorporated a closer rapprochement is questionable; its formalization, however, did symbolize the establishment of closer ties between the two institutions. The real changes had been Simon himself and the leadership in the medical school and the Department. Simon had brought about a much closer integration of the Clinic with both, through his own characteristics in leadership, administration, and cooperation. At the same time, Dr. Marshall Porter of the Department of Mental Hygiene had given full support to Simon's reorganization goals, together with effective leadership within the Department and in working with the Department of Finance. Dr. Saunders, Dean of the School of Medicine since 1956, had also afforded active leadership in an effort to integrate Langley Porter more closely with the school. An important objective of his was to encourage more interchange of knowledge between psychiatry and medicine as a whole, for the enrichment of both. Joint operation of the Clinic by two agencies might never be an alliance entirely free of conflict, since they were very different in their purposes and functions, but it could be workable, and Simon to a large extent had made it so. His skills, character, and inclination, under more auspicious circumstances, had been increasingly effective, whereas Dr. Bowman had remained relatively isolated.

Drs. Simon and Prestwood were convinced of the value of the Clinic's dual direction by the Department and the University. They felt that whatever problems were inherent in this situation were outweighed by the advantages to both institutions. They believed that both were benefited by more fruitful outcomes for the Clinic, the Department, the University, and the public.

The Clinic was approaching far more closely the apparent intentions of its founders in the new emphasis upon research and teaching supported by the Department of Mental Hygiene. Langley Porter's special mission as a leader in the field of mental health, both for the Department and for the state as a whole, was now established policy for the first time in the Clinic's history. It was still encountering some resistance, for more time would be needed to make the new policy fully effective.[42] But the formal sanction of the OCC Division survey had legitimized these Clinic purposes within the state government, and the policy itself could no longer be attacked.

The effects of teaching and research—both expensive functions—are difficult to evaluate. And if the desired results are still in the form of intentions rather than a tangible product, it is even more difficult to justify these activities through a budget process in which the predominant intent is to evaluate the concrete, by cost in money terms, using the past as a base. By 1960, however, it was possible to cite some tangible results: of 1,000 psychiatrists practicing in California, 200 had had at least one year of training at Langley Porter Clinic.

It had been a very tough period for both Simon and Prestwood. Neither had any regrets, for they both held strong convictions about the Clinic's purposes, needs, and development. They had been preoccupied with the effort to get the people and programs the Clinic needed. The OCC Division survey had been very effective in facilitating this; it had also, Prestwood believed, provided the Clinic with a much better organization structure. Simon and Prestwood felt that these great gains far outweighed any problems consequent on the changes, which might remain as yet unresolved. The deviations from the recommended organizational plans, they felt, had been necessary; while the chart had "made good sense from a technical point of view, it had not in all respects made sense in terms of some of the people and the functions involved." A case in point had been putting the medical library in the Business Services Division; Prestwood believed, from a three-year perspective, that this had not been justified on the basis of the specialized function performed. But Simon and Prestwood were content. They had gained important allies in their attempt to make over Langley Porter Clinic in a new image.

For Dr. Simon the major accomplishment of the survey process had been the change in attitudes toward the Clinic within the state government. In his view, there had been no "reorganization" of the Clinic; what had in fact occurred was a great expan-

---

[42] In 1960 one high officer in the Department of Mental Hygiene asserted that only *applied* research, almost without exception, was being conducted by the Department. Yet in 1959 the report of the Legislative Analyst on the Department's budget stated that programs of both *basic* and *applied* research had been carried on since the Legislature authorized special funds for the purpose in 1956.

sion in staff and programs. In organization structure and in programs, he now had what he had wanted at the start of his administration.

With the last of the new staff due to arrive in July, Dr. Prestwood was giving increasing attention to consolidating the three-year gains through establishing smoother coordination and more effective communications within the Clinic. Problems created by the period of change, he felt, were obviously in need of resolutions. In some areas he had perceived evidence of low morale, frictions, and turnover. Prestwood knew that a new administrator coming in as head of the Clinic was hard on the staff and that the change for those who had worked under and closely with Dr. Bowman was particularly difficult. Moreover, because of the rapid growth in the profession of psychiatry, some of these people had witnessed the rise of former residents in the Clinic like himself to positions of authority over them. Prestwood realized that change takes time. "People," he said, "had to have a chance to work things through."

Prestwood recalled that in 1957 Marvin Blanchard of the OCC Division had said, "After you have established clear lines of authority, then you must facilitate collaboration across the lines."[43] Prestwood thought that perhaps Clinic officials had "sort of forgotten what they had learned about administration." Much remained to be done; further changes in attitudes were needed. Internal functioning, he observed, had not kept pace with the structural, growth, and policy changes.

The year ahead, therefore, would be one of primary attention to these problems; instituting the administrative advisory committee was one step in this program. There was a compelling reason for accomplishing this consolidation of gains: plans were afoot to build a new institute with twice the capacity of the present one, and the Clinic must be readied for this new expansion. It was time now to "get the show on the road," before the next big phase of change for the Langley Porter Clinic.

[43] Dr. Simon commented that he had emphasized this from the beginning.

APPENDIX I

BUDGETS FOR LANGLEY PORTER CLINIC, DEPARTMENT OF MENTAL HYGIENE

Year		*No. of Positions*	*Total Support Budgets*
1941-1943	(biennium)	80.0	$ 204,330 (actual)
1943-1945	"	86.0	418,019 "
1945-1946	(annual)	127.0	269,904 "
1946-1947	"	109.5	428,143 "
1947-1948	"	148.6	522,709 "
1948-1949	"	156.0	565,157 "
1949-1950	"	168.9	647,216 "
1950-1951	"	182.6	723,900 "
1951-1952	"	180.6	775,159 "
1952-1953	"	188.2	903,709 "
1953-1954	"	199.0	991,437 "
1954-1955	"	189.2	999,694 "
1955-1956	"	195.6	1,122,406 "
1956-1957	"	205.7	1,270,982 "
1957-1958	"	219.5	1,440,012 "
1958-1959	"	231.7	1,542,636 "
1959-1960	"	250.8	1,744,746 "
1960-1961	"	286.7 (estimated)	2,062,093 (estimated)

APPENDIX II

REORGANIZATION CHART OF LANGLEY PORTER CLINIC, 1956
As Proposed by Dr. Simon in Budget Request for Fiscal 1957-1958

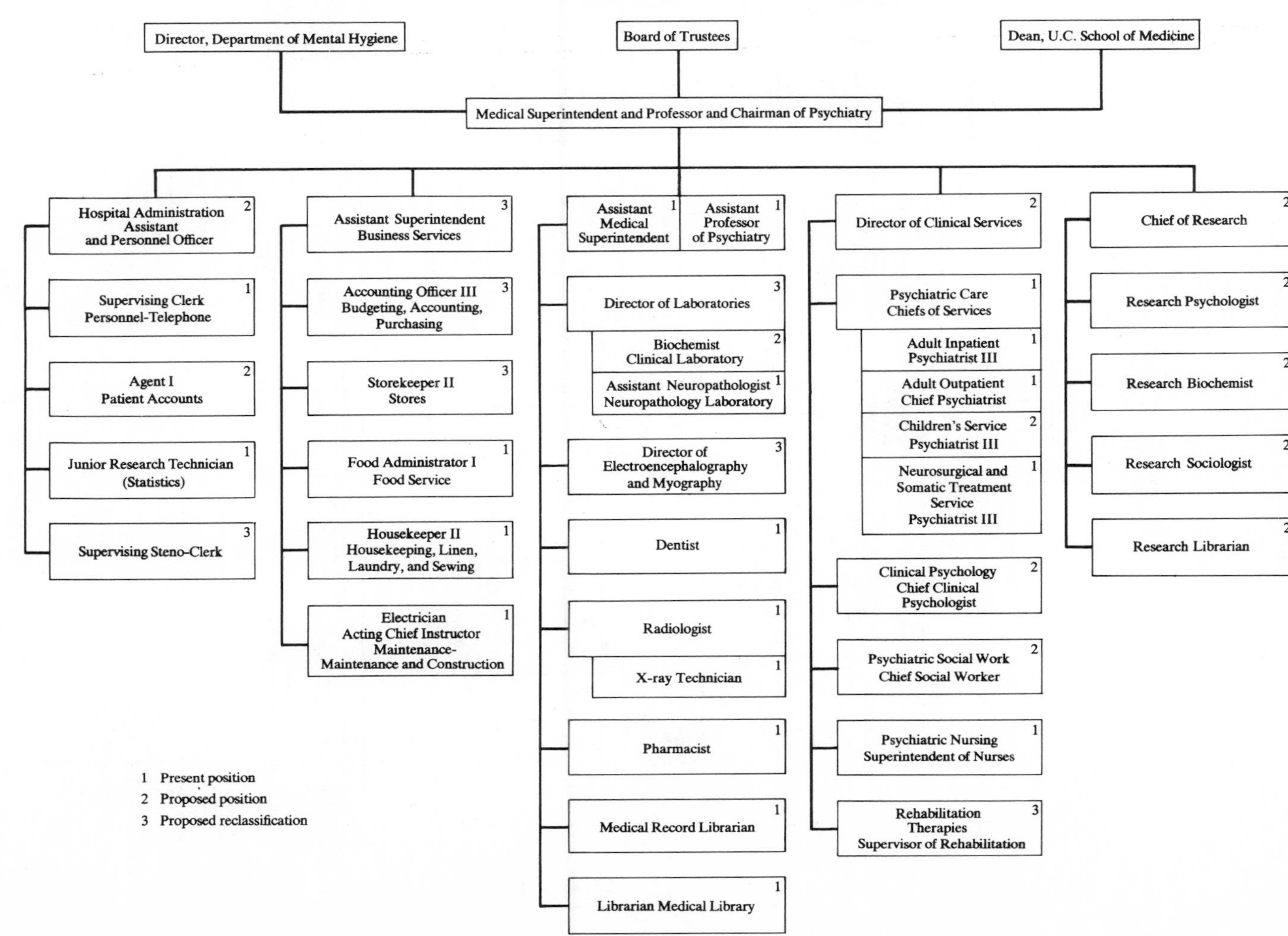

APPENDIX III

PRESENT OVER-ALL ORGANIZATION
LANGLEY PORTER CLINIC
DEPARTMENT OF MENTAL HYGIENE
1957

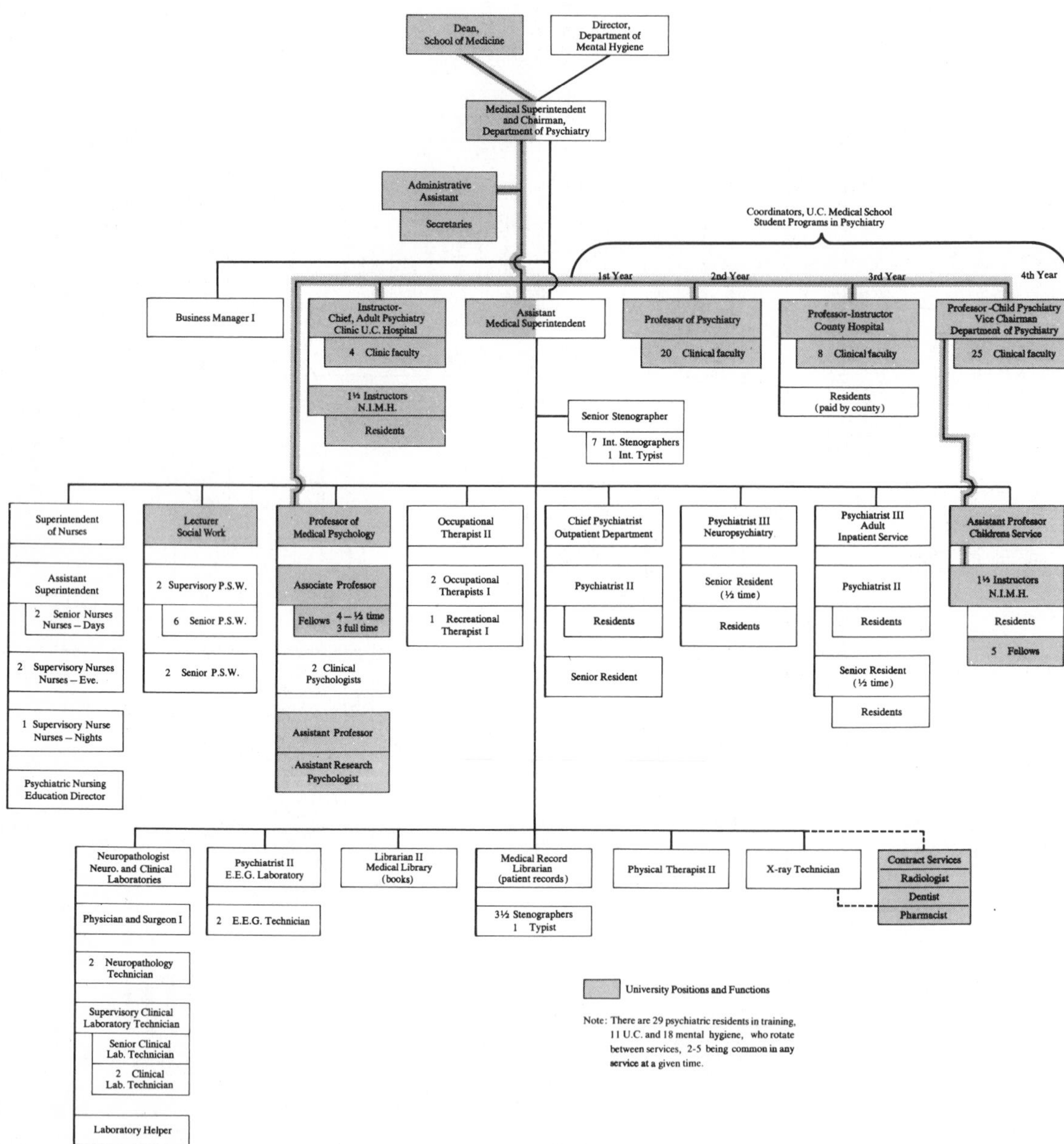

APPENDIX IV

RECOMMENDED OVER-ALL ORGANIZATION
LANGLEY PORTER CLINIC
DEPARTMENT OF MENTAL HYGIENE

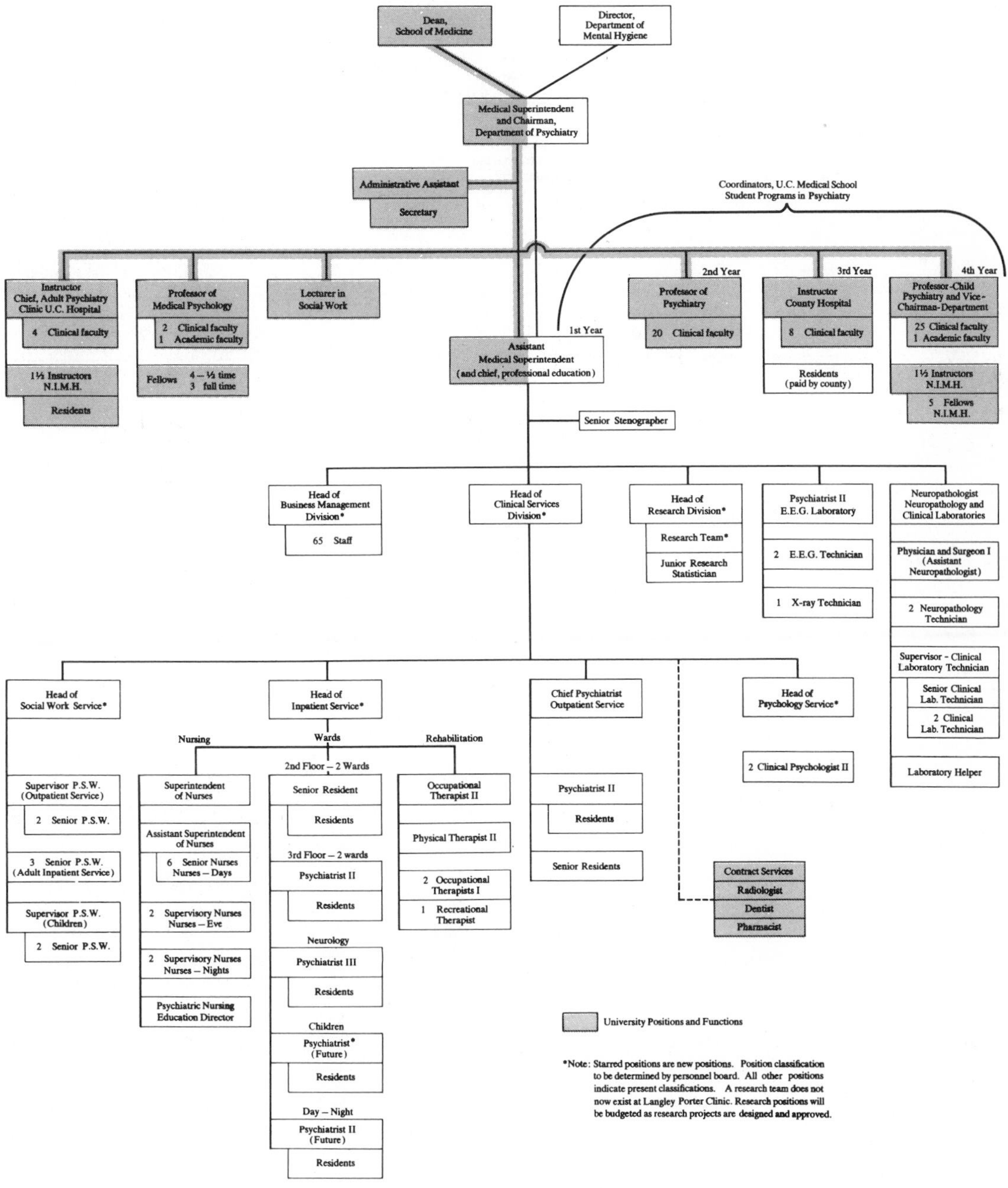

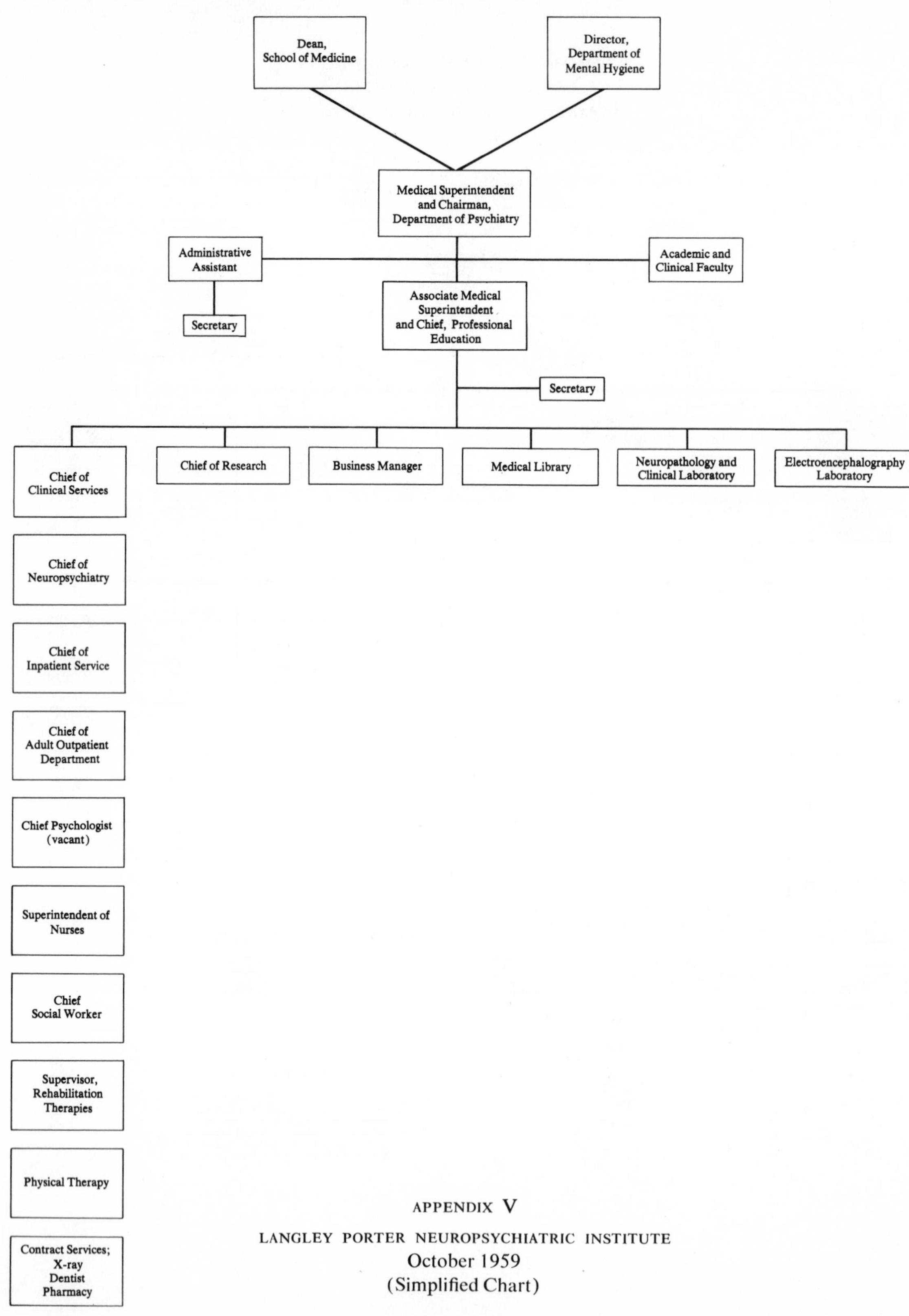

APPENDIX V

LANGLEY PORTER NEUROPSYCHIATRIC INSTITUTE
October 1959
(Simplified Chart)

APPENDIX VI

DIAGRAM INDICATING HOW THE FACILITIES OF LANGLEY PORTER CLINIC COME TO FOCUS IN TREATMENT TEAMS. THE MAJOR OUTPUT IS IN TRAINED PERSONNEL, BUT PATIENTS RECEIVE EXCELLENT TREATMENT.

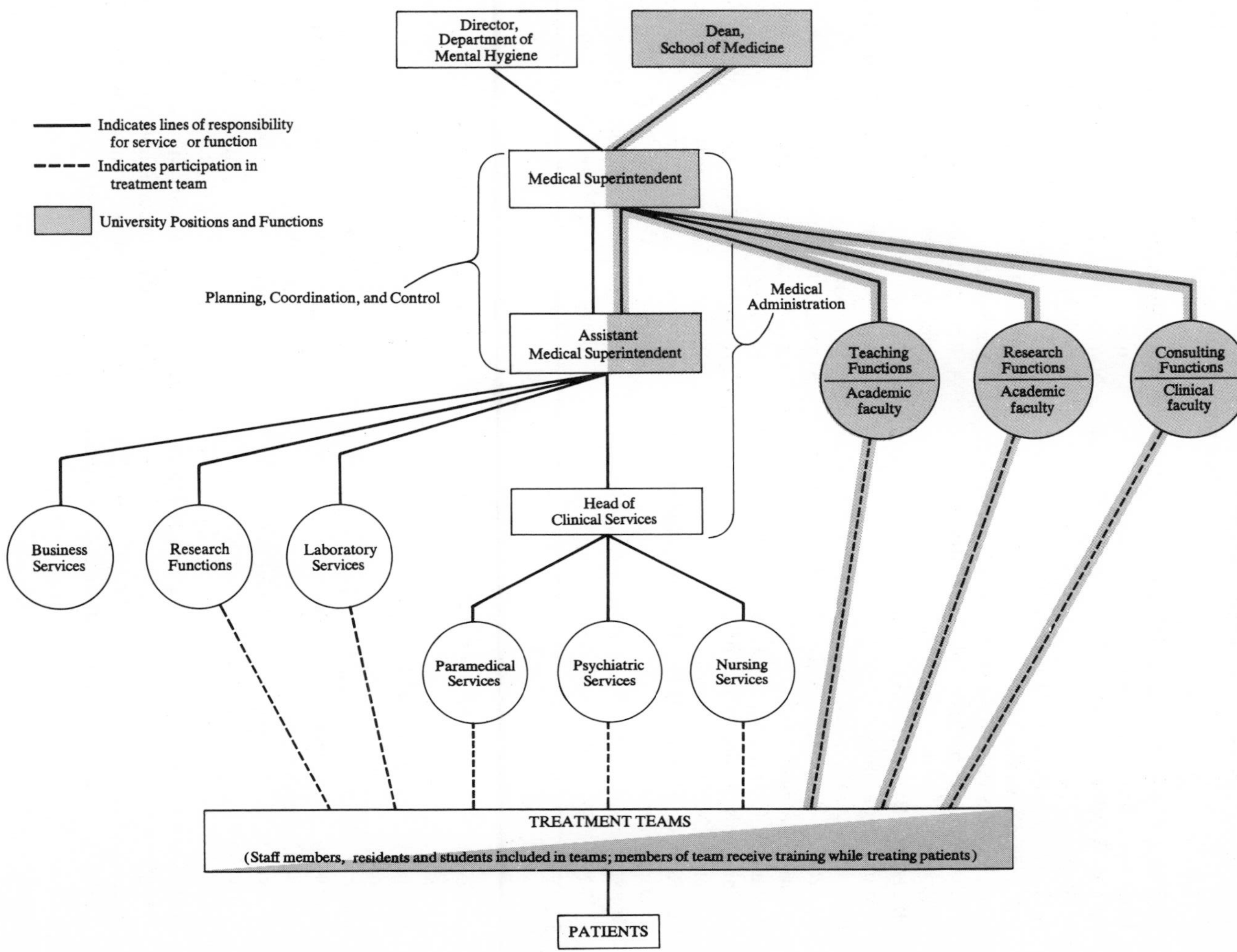

APPENDIX VII

STAFF MEMBERS OF LANGLEY PORTER NEUROPSYCHIATRIC INSTITUTE
(Mentioned in the Case Study and Interviewed)
Positions, 1960

EDWARDA ADAMS,* Medical Librarian

HELEN C. BARCLAY,* Accounting Officer

KLAUS W. BERBLINGER, M.D., Chief of Clinical Services

MALETA BOATMAN,* M.D., Assistant Director, Children's Service

KARL M. BOWMAN, M.D., Medical Superintendent; Chairman, Department of Psychiatry (retired, 1956)

HELEN V. BYRON,* B.A., M.S., Director, Social Work Department

ENOCH CALLAWAY, III, M.D., Chief of Research

CLOYCE L. DUNCAN,* M.D., Chief (Adult) Inpatient Service

ALFRED J. GIANASCOL, M.D., Senior Psychiatrist, Children's Service (Chief of Service for Department of Mental Hygiene)

M. ROBERT HARRIS, M.D., Director, Outpatient Department

ROBERT E. HARRIS,* Ph.D., Professor, Medical Psychology, Department of Psychiatry

DALE HOUSTON,* Director, Rehabilitation Therapies

NATHAN MALAMUD,* M.D., Director, Neuropathology and Clinical Laboratories

OLGA MOCHER, Director, Physical Therapy

CORINNE PARSONS,* R.N., Superintendent of Nursing Services

A. RODNEY PRESTWOOD,* M.D., Associate Medical Superintendent; Assistant Professor, Department of Psychiatry

JURGEN RUESCH, M.D., Professor, Department of Psychiatry

ALEXANDER SIMON,* M.D., Medical Superintendent; Chairman, Department of Psychiatry (1956—)

S. A. SZUREK,* M.D., Director, Children's Service; Professor, Department of Psychiatry

ROBERT J. WENSEL, Business Manager

CHARLES L. YEAGER,* M.D., Director, Electroencephalography Laboratory

* Interviewed by the survey team in 1957

APPENDIX VIII

KEY FIGURES OUTSIDE LANGLEY PORTER NEUROPSYCHIATRIC INSTITUTE

EDWIN W. BEACH, Budget Division, Department of Finance

JOHN W. BERKE, Associate Administrative Analyst (1957), Organization and Cost Control Division, Department of Finance

MARVIN L. BLANCHARD, Acting Chief Administrative Analyst (1957), OCC Division, Department of Finance

R. E. CONAHAN, Controller, Department of Mental Hygiene

DALE LAPHAM, Senior Administrative Analyst (1957), OCC Division, Department of Finance

RALPH LITTLESTONE, Personnel Officer, Department of Mental Hygiene

MARSHALL E. PORTER, M.D., Medical Deputy Director (1957), Department of Mental Hygiene

R. LANGLEY PORTER, M.D., Dean, University of California School of Medicine (retired, 1941)

AARON J. ROSANOFF, M.D., Director, Department of Institutions (1939-1942)

JOHN B. DEC. M. SAUNDERS, M.D., Dean, University of California School of Medicine (1956—)

GEORGE SPENCER, Analyst, Budget Division, Department of Finance

LYNN W. ELEY

CASE ONE: *The Decision to Regionalize*

GERALD W. BUSH

CASE TWO: *A Business Office for the West*

The Regionalization of Business Services in the Agricultural Research Service

LYNN W. ELEY

The author of *The Decision to Regionalize* received a Ph.D. degree from the State University of Iowa. Presently, he is Dean of University College and the Summer School, Washington University in St. Louis.

GERALD W. BUSH

The author of *A Business Office for the West* holds an M.A. degree from Claremont Graduate School. He is now in the Department of Political Science at Northern Illinois University and is Director of Peace Corps Training Programs.

CHRONOLOGY OF KEY EVENTS

February 1942	Agricultural Research Administration is established
July 1, 1947	Reorganization Plan Number 1 invests legal program authority in Secretary of Agriculture
June 4, 1953	Reorganization Plan Number 2 provides for functional groupings in Department
November 2, 1953	Secretary of Agriculture Benson reorganizes Department and establishes Agricultural Research Service
May 7, 1954	Acting Administrator Clarkson sends memorandum to Roberts, Administrative Assistant Secretary of the Department, asking authority to set up four regional finance offices
May 17, 1954	Roberts postpones action on request pending results of a Department-wide survey
December 15, 1954	Shaw asks Roberts for "prompt guidance" in view of desperate backlog situation
February 17, 1955	Roberts approves provisional establishment of regional finance offices and suggests that they be expanded to include other business services
March 1, 1955	Administrator announces probable locations of regional business offices
March 9, 1955	First meeting of Regionalization Work Group takes place
March 23, 1955	Spencer and Stephens meet with branch chiefs and program officials explaining plan for regional business offices
March 29, 1955	Dr. Shaw writes Copley that Western Utilization Research Laboratory will be used to house the Western Regional Business Office in Albany
April 13, 1955	Shaw decides to implement plan to have regional business managers, subsidiary work groups established
April 20, 1955	Spencer informs Copley that Adams will be Business Manager of Western Regional Business Office
Early May 1955	Shaw approves division of functions between management divisions, regional business offices, program branch offices, and field stations; meeting of business managers in Washington
May 20, 1955	Department approves division of functions; branch managers selected
May 30-31, and June 7, 1955	Orientation meetings for business managers in Washington
June 15, 1955	Employees of Western Regional Business Office move to offices
June 23, 1955	Official approval of specific regional offices is given by Department
July 1, 1955	Regional offices are formally opened
January 1, 1956	Regional offices are completely staffed

PRINCIPAL CHARACTERS

The Decision to Regionalize:

Robert B. Harris, Chief, Organization and Methods Branch, Personnel Division; member of Agricultural Research Service (ARS) Regionalization Work Group

Ralph S. Roberts, Administrative Assistant Secretary of the Department of Agriculture

Dr. Byron T. Shaw, Administrator, ARS

Raymond W. Sooy, Assistant Director, Administrative Services Division; member of ARS Regionalization Work Group

Frank H. Spencer, Assistant Administrator for Management, ARS

James A. Starkey, Director, Personnel Division; Chairman of ARS Regionalization Work Group

Edmund Stephens, Director, Budget and Finance Division, ARS

Ernest L. Struttmann, Assistant Director, Budget and Finance Division, and Chief, Finance Branch; member of ARS Regionalization Work Group

Stanley E. Williams, Director, Administrative Services Division, ARS

A Business Office for the West:

Sidney Adams, Business Manager, Western Utilization Research Branch; appointed Business Manager, Western Regional Business Office, 1955

C. E. Cooley, Head of Western Region of Plant Quarantine Branch, San Francisco; retired, 1959

Dr. Michael J. Copley, Director, Western Utilization Research Branch

EDITOR'S FOREWORD

On July 1, 1955, four regional business offices were established by the Agricultural Research Service of the U.S. Department of Agriculture. The two case studies that follow describe the series of decisions and processes leading to and from the regionalization that created those offices.

The first study is a revised version of one originally published in 1958 by the Inter-University Case Program under the title, *The Decentralization of Business Services in the Agricultural Research Service* (ICP No. 40). Its author, Dr. Lynn W. Eley, is now Dean of University College, Washington University in St. Louis. He earlier served as an analyst in the Office of Budget and Finance, U.S. Department of Agriculture (1952-1954) and as organization and methods examiner in the Personnel Division of the Agricultural Research Service (1954-1955). In the latter role he was a participant in some of the events described in the case; he served as a staff assistant to the Regionalization Work Group that was established to plan the decentralization of business services. His account is thus an "insider's" view of events as they were seen in the headquarters offices.

A substantial element in the reorganization—indeed one of its purposes—was to change the procedures and relationships of the widely scattered field offices of the Agricultural Research Service. In order to capture the field view of this process, Gerald W. Bush in 1960 undertook to develop a study of the implementation and impact of regionalization in the western states. It is here published for the first time as Case Two: *A Business Office for the West.* Mr. Bush, more recently an officer of the Peace Corps, was then a graduate assistant at the University of California.

The two case studies thus present, for perhaps the first time, two widely different perspectives—one headquarters, one field—of the same series of events in a large federal department. The introductory section that follows, "The Setting," and the closing "Postscript" may appropriately be credited to both authors, since both contributed to them. This collaboration, however, was accomplished entirely through the written word; to this date, Dr. Eley and Mr. Bush are not personally acquainted, and their work on their respective cases was entirely independent.

THE SETTING: THE AGRICULTURAL RESEARCH SERVICE

Shortly after the Battle of Shiloh, President Abraham Lincoln signed into law the "organic act" of the United States Department of Agriculture. A primary responsibility of the new Department was research. Section 3 of the Act of May 15, 1862, reads in part:

> Sec. 3. That it shall be the duty of the Commissioner of Agriculture to acquire and preserve in his Department all information concerning agriculture which he can obtain by means of books and correspondence, and by practical and scientific experiments[,] . . . by the collection of statistics, and by any other appropriate means within his power. . . .[1]

The commissioner was given responsibility for the organization of the Department. Section 4 of the act instructed him "to employ a chief clerk and 'such other persons, for such time as their services may be needed, including chemists, botanists, and entomologists, and other persons skilled in the natural sciences pertaining to agriculture.' "[2]

The first agricultural chemist in the federal government had been appointed in the 1840's; in 1854 Congress had increased the agricultural appropriation of the Patent Office by $35,000 to initiate investigations in botany and entomology.[3] During the past century the Department has experienced expansions and contractions, centralizations and decentralizations, but always research has remained a primary goal. By July 1, 1955, the Department's appropriation had increased to over $3,500,000,000 ($2,000,000,000 of which was devoted to agricultural price support operations); $89,000,000 was appropriated to the Agricultural Research Service (ARS). The Department of Agriculture had become one of the largest federal agencies. Of its 85,000 employees, about 18,500 were employed by the ARS.

Traditionally, both federal and state agricultural research programs, a $200,000,000 business, have been conducted on a project basis. In 1960, for example, nearly 15,000 research projects were being carried out at hundreds of separate locations by federal and state scientists. The project orientation and the geographical dispersion of the program inhibited communication and rendered general supervision difficult. Not only was the program conducted in relative isolation from the other agencies of the Department, but also field personnel often worked with little awareness of happenings in other branches of ARS. Most communication occurred between superior and subordinate within each project staff and within each professional field.

Dr. Byron T. Shaw, Administrator of ARS, has expressed the goals of the agency's research policy as follows:

> Co-ordination, integration, and supervision of research are necessary. But we have to face the fact that a large element of self-direction is essential for productive work by scientists. A research environment favorable to creative accomplishment by individual specialists must be provided.
>
> A scientist should be able to conduct his research in an atmosphere of free inquiry, to publish his results freely, and to take advantage of free discussion with his colleagues.[4]

The partnership of the federal and state governments in agricultural research dates from 1862 and the creation of the first land-grant universities under the Morrill Act. Coordination of this huge undertaking always presented problems. Other public agencies and private industrial organizations were often involved. In general, the federal government and ARS and its predecessor agencies attempted to concentrate on problems of national or regional scope, leaving the more restricted state and local problems to state research personnel. The major effort to avoid duplication was left to the ARS State Experiment Stations Divisions, which kept records on state projects, including those financed by state and federal-grant funds, and to

---

[1] As quoted in John M. Gaus and Leon O. Wolcott, *Public Administration and the United States Department of Agriculture* (Chicago, Public Administration Service, 1940), p. 4.

[2] *Ibid.*, p. 4.

[3] *Ibid.*, pp. 3, 4.

[4] Byron T. Shaw, "Research Planning and Control in the United States Department of Agriculture: The Experience of an Old and Well-Established Research Agency," *The Annals*, American Academy of Political and Social Science, January 1960, Vol. 327, p. 101. This brief discussion of the agricultural research setting is based in considerable part on Shaw's article, pp. 95-102.

the agency's Central Project Office, which maintained records on federal projects.

ARS carried out research in three general areas: farm production research, utilization research and development, and human nutrition and home economics. In addition, ARS had responsibility for plant and livestock regulatory programs, since these programs require research data. The objectives of all of these various programs were to promote and protect the agricultural industry and, to a lesser extent, to serve and protect the nation's consumers.

Within the function of farm production research, ARS employees worked on projects related to crops production; entomology; soil and water conservation; agricultural engineering; production economics; livestock, poultry, and dairy husbandry; and animal diseases and parasites. Utilization research and development were concerned with finding new and extended industrial and other uses for agricultural commodities and by-products, particularly those in surplus supply. Research in human nutrition, household economics, clothing, and housing was conducted by the units identified with the human nutrition and home economics area. Most of the professional researchers in this area, incidentally, were women, while most program workers elsewhere in the agency were men. The ARS Experiment Stations Divisions administered the federal-grant funds to the state agricultural experiment stations located at land-grant universities and directed the territorial experiment stations.

The regulatory programs aimed at controlling or eradicating animal and plant diseases and insect pests harmful to the nation's agriculture or its consumers. Important functions in this connection were the inspection of plants and animals being imported from abroad and the quarantine or destruction of those found to be infested with disease or pests. The Meat Inspection Division (formerly a branch) inspected all meat and meat-food products (and process or renovated butter) destined to enter interstate commerce. This work was performed as a protective service to consumers and, it might be added, to the meat packaging industry. Meat inspectors were stationed at packing plants all over the country, while plant and animal inspection and quarantine forces were located mainly at ports of entry and at major post offices. Officials and employees engaged in general regulatory work on plant or animal diseases or pests were also spread widely throughout the nation, wherever infestations of the various diseases and pests were to be found.

CASE ONE: *The Decision to Regionalize**

THE WAVES OF REORGANIZATION

January 1953–January 1954

On January 20, 1953, when Dwight D. Eisenhower assumed the Presidency, his new Secretary of Agriculture, Ezra Taft Benson, inherited a department that many Republicans and Democrats alike regarded, to quote Senator Paul Douglas, as "a loose confederation of semi-autonomous bureaus." Thirteen program agencies and seven staff offices reported directly to the Secretary.

Secretary Benson reorganized the Department during the first year of his administration. One effect of the reorganization was to strengthen the position of the Secretary and achieve greater integration of the Department's dispersed organization. Another was consolidation of related functions. By the terms of Reorganization Plan Number 2 of June 4, 1953, certain minor functions not already vested in the Secretary were transferred from the bureau level to him; six functional groupings of agencies were set up; and two additional Assistant Secretaries and an Administrative Assistant Secretary were provided to serve, along with three other secretarial officials, as heads of these agency groupings. On November 2, 1953, following the authority of the Reorganization Plan, the functions of the thirteen program agencies were redistributed, and the agencies were reconstituted.

Departmental integration under the Secretary was not one of the avowed goals of the reorganization, however. Besides seeking "to simplify and

* As used in these studies, the terms "regionalize" and "regionalization" refer to arranging the field organization on the basis of geographic regions.

make efficient the operation of the Department," the Secretary was directed by Reorganization Plan Number 2 (which had been drafted in the Department) "to place the administration of farm programs close to the state and local levels, and to adapt the administration of the programs of the Department to regional, state, and local conditions." When Benson announced the details of the proposed reorganization in October 1953, he explained that the reorganization was designed to streamline "the Department for better service to farm families and for simplified internal organization. . . . Our ultimate goal is greater decentralization to bring the program closer to farmers." On this assurance, and because many of their ideas were incorporated in consultations in the planning stage, "the big majority" of "Congressional agricultural leaders" and representatives of client groups "reacted favorably to the proposals."[5] Among the latter were members of the National Agricultural Advisory Commission, representatives of the land-grant universities, and farm organization leaders. In fact, the land-grant universities and the American Farm Bureau Federation, by far the largest and most powerful national farm organization, were enchanted with Benson's reorganization goals. They had long felt that more of the Department's research program should be administered at the land-grant universities and that all programs should be "closer to farmers." Also gratifying to them was the administration's heavy emphasis upon research to improve the production, utilization, and marketing of agricultural commodities, coupled with lowered and "flexible" price supports, as the best means to solve the nagging problems of American agriculture.

The Agricultural Research Administration (ARA), immediate predecessor of ARS, had been established in February 1942 to consolidate most of the physical, biological, chemical, and engineering research in the Department. The ARA was composed of the Office of the Administrator and seven semi-autonomous bureaus that had functioned for decades—some for nearly a century—as constituent agencies of the Department before ARA was established. (See Figure 1.) The seven bureaus had their national headquarters either in Beltsville, Maryland, just outside the District of Columbia, or in the Department of Agriculture buildings in Washington. All of them were concerned with research; three were also engaged in related regulatory work.

On January 1, 1953, ARA had 12,871 employees, only 104 of whom were in the Office of the Administrator. When Benson became Secretary, over seventy per cent of ARA employees—about 10,000 persons—were located at approximately 950 field stations, and only about 2,900 employees were stationed at headquarters. The largest unit in the agency was the Bureau of Animal Industry with approximately 4,800 employees in 271 field stations and only 727 employees in Washington.

[5] Quoted from Benson's reorganization announcement, October 13, 1953.

FIGURE 1:
AGRICULTURAL RESEARCH ADMINISTRATION, 1953

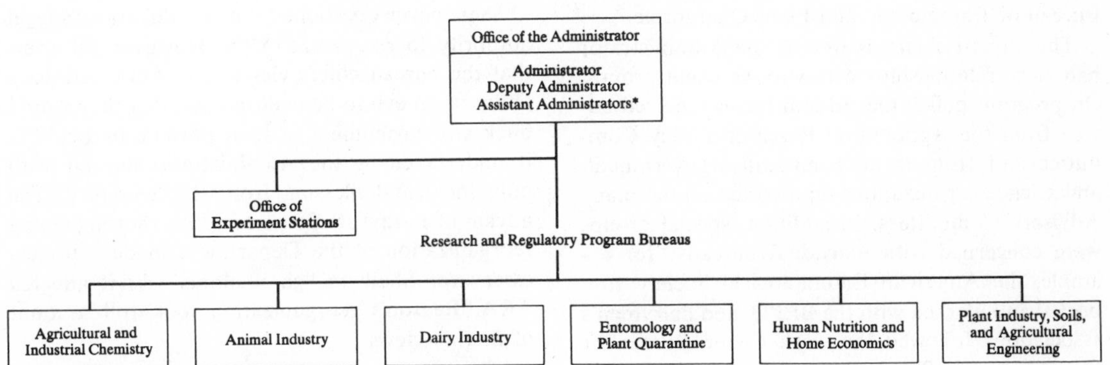

*Assistant Administrator for State Relations: Office of Experiment Stations
Assistant Administrator for Program Development and Coordination
Assistant Administrator for Administrative Management: Business Services for Office of the Administrator; Office of Operations, Agricultural Research Center (Beltsville, Md.)

Next in size were the Bureau of Plant Industry, Soils, and Agricultural Engineering (hereafter called the Bureau of Plant Industry for the sake of brevity); the Bureau of Entomology and Plant Quarantine (BEPQ); and the Bureau of Agricultural and Industrial Chemistry, including its four regional utilization research laboratories. By comparison, the remaining three bureaus—the Office of Experiment Stations, the Bureau of Human Nutrition and Home Economics, and the Bureau of Dairy Industry—were quite small.

Reorganization Plan Number 1, effective July 1, 1947, had transferred all legal authority for ARA programs from the seven bureau chiefs to the Secretary. He, in turn, had delegated this authority to the ARA Administrator. The Administrator redelegated operating authority to the bureau chiefs, retaining only the power to provide overall agency direction and to appoint and remove bureau chiefs and other top officials. Bureau organizations were left intact.

Thus, while the bureaus had ceased to exist as legal entities in 1947, their operational unity continued. Each bureau chief had effective control of the men, money, and materials connected with his program; and each bureau provided almost all of its own administrative services, even to the point of presenting its own budget estimates to the Bureau of the Budget and to Congress. The Administrator of ARA, on the other hand, maintained only embryonic staff services.

For the most part, program (or substantive) policy as well as administrative work was centralized at the headquarters level in the bureaus. Only two bureaus had been decentralized: the Bureau of Agricultural and Industrial Chemistry and the Bureau of Entomology and Plant Quarantine.

The bureau chiefs as well as the Administrator had close relationships with various client groups. On program policy the Administrator received advice from the Agricultural Research Policy Committee and from farm, commodity, government, and science organizations represented on the many Advisory Committees. In addition, special groups were concerned with individual bureaus: for example, the American Entomological Society supported and worked with the BEPQ, and dairymen's associations followed the work of the Bureau of Dairy Industry. These client groups dealt directly with the bureaus and with the Administrator to effect desired changes in programs. They "ran interference" in Congress and in the executive branch for their pet programs. Bureau officials also communicated directly with members of the congressional committees on agriculture and the subcommittees on agricultural appropriations.

Dr. Byron T. Shaw, the Administrator in 1953, had been in office for only one year; most of the bureau chiefs had held their posts for many years. Prior to becoming Administrator, Shaw had served as Deputy Administrator for three years and as Assistant Administrator for two years. Shaw had originally been a "program man," having served as a soils scientist in the Bureau of Plant Industry, and the bureau chiefs regarded him as "one of their own." Despite bureau experience, Shaw had grown to feel that a strong Administrator's Office was necessary to the ARA. He did not approve of the organizational system which permitted different bureaus performing complementary or similar functions to have different or conflicting patterns of organization and operation. Particularly disturbing to him was the lack of uniformity among the bureaus in their cooperative research arrangements with the forty-eight state experiment stations. He was unhappy about the distribution of operating authority and staff resources which left each bureau free to pursue its own ends with little regard for overall agency priorities. Further, he wanted to be able to "sell" agricultural research to Congress and the public as an entity rather than as a series of separate (bureau) packages. On a more specific level, he was concerned that research and regulation were combined in three of the bureaus: the Bureau of Animal Industry, the Bureau of Dairy Industry, and the Bureau of Entomology and Plant Quarantine. He felt that research and practice should be conducted in separate organizations with adequate liaison between them.

Shaw never questioned the Administrator's legal authority to reorganize ARA. However, he knew that the bureau chiefs viewed the Administrator's Office as an evil to be endured and that they would buck any curtailment of their powers, particularly if undertaken by the Administrator himself with only incidental blessing from the Secretary. The advent of Ezra Taft Benson and his thoroughgoing reorganization of the Department made it unnecessary for Shaw to "go it alone." As it affected ARA, Benson's reorganization took full account of Shaw's views.

The New ARS

By the terms of the Secretary's reorganization of November 1953 (implementation of Reorganization Plan Number 2 of June 1953), legal authority over ARA (now to be called the Agricultural Research Service—ARS) again was delegated to the Administrator, and for the first time he was also given authority over the Department's economic research. ARS was made one of the six agencies in the Federal-States Relations Group of agencies within the Department. Responsibility for certain projects, formerly the ARA's, was transferred to other Department agencies, and ARS received in turn responsibility for projects previously conducted elsewhere in the Department. The net effect of these inter-agency transfers was to give ARS all research and regulatory functions concerned with the production and utilization of plants, animals, and poultry (except poultry inspection) and to rid the agency of its few marketing and forestry research and control projects.[6]

Shaw announced plans, to be effective January 2, 1954, for implementing the basic outlines of the Secretary's reorganization dealing with ARS. The overall effect was to strengthen the Administrator's Office, to destroy the organizational identity of the bureaus, and to realign agency work on a functional basis. (See Figure 2.)

Shaw separated research and regulatory functions, delegating responsibility for animal and plant research programs to a Deputy Administrator for Research Programs and responsibility for regulatory programs to a Deputy Administrator for Regulatory Programs. This meant that the functions of six of the seven former bureaus were now the general responsibility of the two Deputy Administrators. The functions of the seventh former bureau, the Office of Experiment Stations, were assigned to an Assistant Administrator for Experiment Stations (later made a Deputy Administrator also), and Shaw appointed to that task the former chief of the Office of Experiment Stations.

Seven directors, five of them former bureau chiefs, were added to the staffs of the two Deputy Administrators as "sub-functional area directors." The various divisions of the old ARA bureaus were grouped into seven "sub-functional areas": crops research, farm and land management research, livestock research, human nutrition and home economics research, utilization research, crops regulatory, and livestock regulatory. Programs in the first three areas dealt with some phase of production research. All five research sub-functional area directors reported to the Deputy Administrator for Research Programs; and the heads of the crops regulatory programs and livestock regulatory programs reported to the Deputy Administrator for Regulatory Programs. Reflecting the intention to dismantle the old bureaus, the seven sub-functional area directors were deprived of line authority and became merely staff assistants to the Deputy Administrators.

What had been the divisions of the old ARA (excluding the Experiment Stations Programs) were combined into twenty-one branches and distributed among the seven sub-functional areas. Each branch was charged with direct conduct of plant or animal programs. Many of the heads of the old divisions or groups of divisions became heads of the new branches.

The net organizational effect of this reshuffling and regrouping of the old divisions of the old bureaus was a partial scattering of the functions and staffs associated with them. The old divisions of the three largest bureaus were divided among the new sub-functional areas. In the case of the other three old bureaus no fundamental changes were made, and their former divisions became the new branches of their respective sub-functional areas. No substantial change was made in the Experiment Stations Programs.

Of the twenty-one new branches, nineteen continued or established their own business offices, while one business office served both the Human Nutrition and the Home Economics Research branches, and one office served the Experiment Stations Programs. Each of the twenty-one branch business offices had an administrative officer and subordinate employees responsible to the branch chief.

The Secretary's reorganization made possible Shaw's internal reorganization of the ARS, partly because, along with all of the upheavals brought by Benson's reorganization, the relationships between the client groups and the bureau chiefs had been disrupted. Congressional relations also were disrupted since the disappearance of the old bureaus left congressmen, like the client groups, uncertain as to where to take proposals and grievances. Henceforth, the presentation of budget estimates and other appearances before the Bureau of the Budget and congressional committees would be handled by the Administrator's Office. Furthermore, the Republicans, newly in control of Congress, were initially disposed to approve of ad-

[6] Poultry inspection and marketing projects were transferred to the new Agricultural Marketing Service, while those concerned with forestry went to the Forest Service.

FIGURE 2: ARS ORGANIZATION FOLLOWING JANUARY 2, 1954 REORGANIZATION

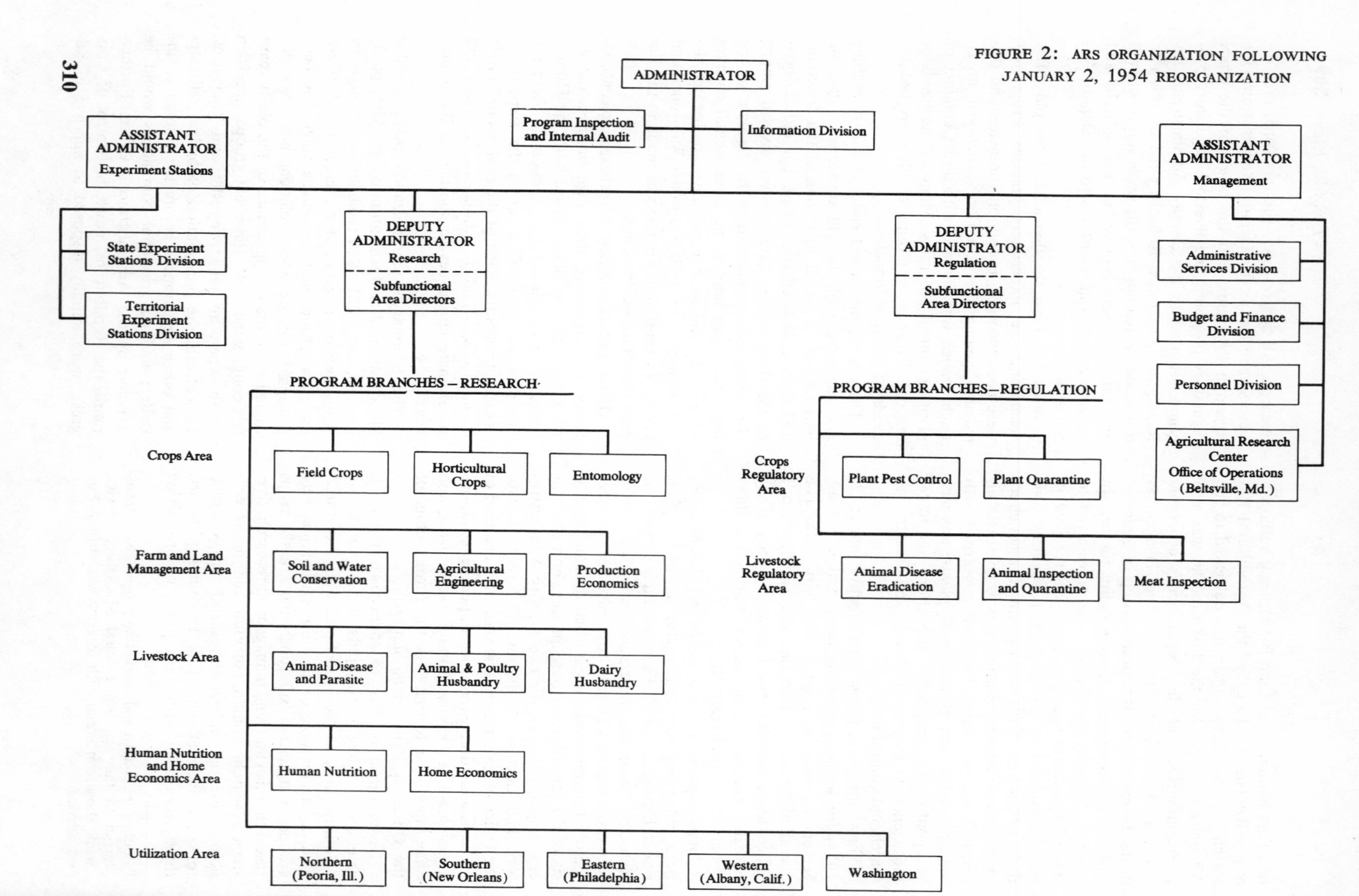

ministrative reforms, especially those that loosened ties between Democratic congressmen and agency officials carried over from Democratic administrations.

On the positive side, most congressional Republicans and some Democrats, particularly those from agricultural districts, plus the influential land-grant universities and the American Farm Bureau Federation, as well as other farm, commodity, and special groups, tended to applaud the new administration's emphasis upon agricultural research. (Later, after the administration's honeymoon period, Benson's corollary program of substituting lower "flexible" for high "rigid" price supports on the "basic" agricultural commodities would encounter mounting opposition from Democrats, the National Farmers Union, other liberals, and many farmers. But this protest would seldom find fault with the research program, which was administered by a different part of the Department.) Separating research and regulation was regarded as a long-overdue reform by client groups in both areas. While many of the special groups were dismayed to see the dissolution of old bureaus with which they had had intimate relationships for many years, they were able to swallow the bitter pill in these circumstances of increased appropriations for both research and regulation. As one measure of the expansion, by January 1955, two years after the new administration took office, total employment in ARS had increased by about twenty per cent.

In addition to transferring effective control over programs to himself as Administrator, Shaw's reorganization was designed to establish his predominance over management and business services. In delegating functions within the reorganized agency, Shaw was careful to retain clear-cut jurisdiction over the management and business services of greatest agency-wide import. Having gone so far with his reorganization, however, he stopped. After two waves of reorganization in two months, the momentum appeared to be spent, but only temporarily. Later Shaw and his advisers launched a third; this is the subject of our study.

NEGOTIATION AND DECISION

January 1954–February 1955

The first two waves of reorganization did not immediately affect the field installations; nor did they bring uniformity to the program and business operations of the agency.

Diversities in Program Organization and Behavior

The divisions of six of the old bureaus had been juggled into new groupings to form the branches of the seven sub-functional areas. Regardless of which sub-functional area they now found themselves in, the new branches maintained their old administrative and management procedures. As a result, several different patterns of branch program organization were discernible.

The officials of the three branches transferred from the old BEPQ—Entomology Research, Plant Pest Control, and Plant Quarantine—believed in decentralization and delegated as much authority as possible to the field installations.[7]

The four field utilization research branches were another distinct category. Each was a regional laboratory. The four laboratories were unique in ARS. Each was a large field station and a program branch in its own right. They were located at Albany (California), New Orleans, Peoria (Illinois), and Philadelphia. Together with the Washington branch, they had been transferred from the former Bureau of Agricultural and Industrial Chemistry.

At the other extreme were the four plant research branches transferred from the old Bureau of Plant Industry (Field Crops, Horticultural Crops, Soil and Water Conservation, and Agricultural Engineering) and the two animal research branches transferred from the old Bureau of Animal Industry (Animal Disease and Parasite, and Animal and Poultry Husbandry). The leaders of all six branches felt that no research program could be effectively administered unless the branch chief could review almost all transactions.

A fourth pattern was followed by the three regulatory branches transferred from the old Bureau of Animal Industry—Animal Disease Eradication, Animal Inspection and Quarantine, and Meat In-

[7] See Appendix I for the headquarters and field employment of each of the twenty-one program branches in January 1954, immediately after the reorganization.

spection.[8] Together, they were the largest single group in ARS. Their officials operated on the assumption that regulation must be uniform throughout the country. Hence there must be central control over the programs. But in these branches top officials identified what they considered the few key decision points and left all other matters to the field personnel. Field personnel reported to branch headquarters only about major program activities.

The other branches with some employees in the field were Production Economics Research, Dairy Husbandry Research, and Human Nutrition Research. The first had originated from outside the agency; it had been transferred from the Department's former Bureau of Agricultural Economics. The second consisted of most of the old Bureau of Dairy Industry, while the third had been part of the old Bureau of Human Nutrition and Home Economics. They all operated under a pattern midway between complete centralization and the limited decentralization practiced by the livestock regulatory branches. The Washington Utilization Research Branch, with no field employees, and the Home Economics Research Branch, with just two, had no problems of headquarters-field relations.[9]

Diversities in Program Organization Business Services

Before the reorganization, most administrative policy had been made, and all "common" business services provided, by each bureau for itself. As a part of the reorganization, Shaw had set up (under Frank H. Spencer, ARS Assistant Administrator for Management) three new management divisions: Budget and Finance, Administrative Services, and Personnel. These divisions were to help him make administrative policy and to perform most, and ultimately all, common business services for the agency. The management divisions were staffed mainly from the now-defunct bureau business offices. Spencer had previously been ARA Assistant Administrator for Management. He had had no real power over the conduct of management and business services by the bureaus; his power had centered primarily on supervising the provision of business services to the tiny Office of the Administrator.

In conceptual terms, "common" business services in ARS consisted of the more routine activities in the fiscal, administrative services, and personnel areas that had to be provided for all federal employees and agencies, including both the actual transactions and the supporting record-keeping. Preparing and scheduling employee payrolls, examining and certifying vouchers (bills) for payment submitted by employees and outside suppliers, keeping track of financial obligations and expenditures incurred, ordering and purchasing standard supplies and equipment, managing real and personal property of the agency, and processing employee appointments and other personnel actions—these were some of the common business services.

The new management divisions had to cope with the diverse operating procedures of the branches and with the resulting varieties of service required by the twenty-one branch business offices and the four field business offices. The old BEPQ had operated regional business offices located at Greenfield, Massachusetts; Gulfport, Mississippi; San Antonio, Texas; Minneapolis, Minnesota; and Oakland, California. Under the reorganization the first four had been designated as ARS Field Business Offices and put under Spencer, while the Oakland Office was closed and its functions transferred to the Western Utilization Research Branch in nearby Albany, California. These various offices took care of the bulk of the common business services of the 2,100 field employees of the old BEPQ branches—Entomology Research, Plant Pest Control, and Plant Quarantine. In addition, the 1,300 employees of the four field utilization research branches already had fully equipped business offices that provided their common business services.

Although the common business services for the remaining 10,000 employees were provided from headquarters, there was variety in the types of business services that the central management divisions were called upon to perform. For example, the five branches transferred from the old Bureau of Animal Industry prepared and scheduled their own payrolls, while most other branches relied on ARS

---

8 The Process Butter Inspection Section was also transferred from the old Bureau of Dairy Industry to the Meat Inspection Branch.

9 The two Experiment Stations Divisions, which, as has been noted, had been formed from the Office of Experiment Stations—the seventh old bureau—had no federal program really separate from the programs of the state experiment stations, and thus had no field organization in the forty-eight states. The Territorial Experiment Stations Division closely supervised and coordinated the work in the territories: Alaska, Hawaii, Puerto Rico, and the Virgin Islands; together the division employed forty-two persons at headquarters and had eighty-nine employees stationed in the territories.

FIGURE 3:

LINES OF BUSINESS COMMUNICATION BETWEEN FIELD STATIONS AND BUSINESS OFFICES PRIOR TO REGIONALIZATION

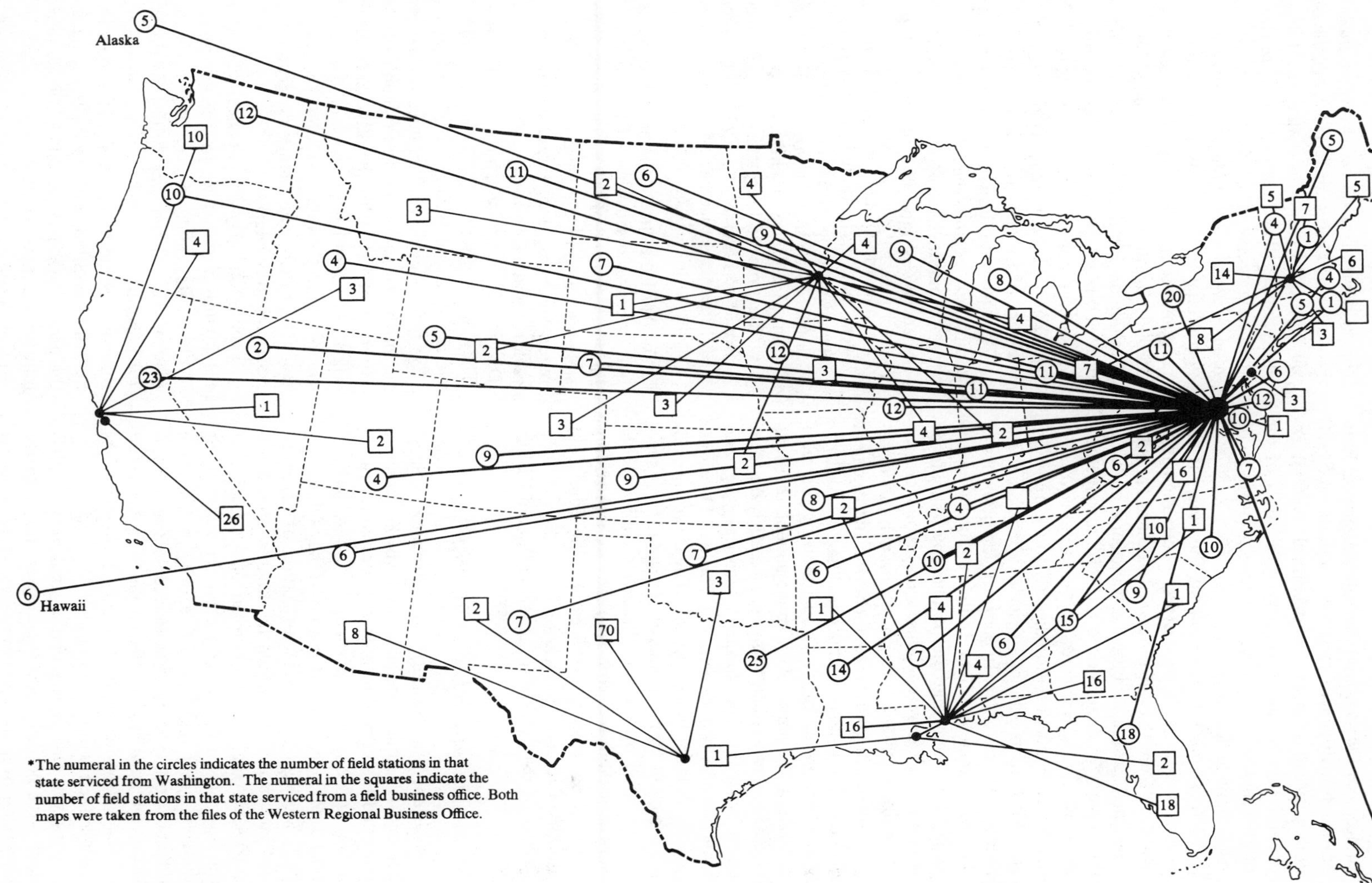

*The numeral in the circles indicates the number of field stations in that state serviced from Washington. The numeral in the squares indicate the number of field stations in that state serviced from a field business office. Both maps were taken from the files of the Western Regional Business Office.

Budget and Finance Division for this service. Four branches maintained personal property accountability records and exercised control over all expenditure documents except payrolls. Most of the other branches had these services performed by ARS management divisions.

There were also variations in the roles of the different branch headquarters. The regulatory branches from the old Bureau of Animal Industry consigned "routine" business functions either to their own field stations or to the ARS management divisions, so that a business service action typically moved from a field station directly to the appropriate ARS management division, bypassing the branch business office. In contrast, the branches of the old Bureau of Plant Industry, following the basic assumption that the branch chief should be apprised of most transactions of his branch, cleared *all* business matters through the branch office, before forwarding them to the ARS management divisions for clearance and handling.

In short, in the early period following the reorganization the three ARS management divisions under Spencer were performing, on a fairly uniform basis, virtually all business services for ten branches, the two Experiment Stations Divisions, and the Administrator's Office. They were providing some but by no means all of the business services required by the four branches from the old Bureau of Plant Industry. And they were providing virtually no business services for the four field utilization research branches and for the field employees of the three branches from the old BEPQ.

Management Division Difficulties

Assistant Administrator for Management Spencer and his three management division directors lamented the variety in branch patterns of organization and operation, particularly where business operations were concerned. In part they felt variety itself was repugnant; standardization of organization and procedures would be much more esthetically satisfying. But in a number of concrete ways the diversity of operating procedures was causing difficulty to them and (as they saw it) to ARS. One difficulty, for example, was that almost no administrative regulations directed to the branches could have agency-wide application, and most directives were loaded with exceptions.

However, the leaders of the management divisions were not in a position to press immediately for taking over the common-service-type business operations being performed by some branches and the field business offices. Most of their own employees had been transferred from the old bureau business offices, and the management divisions had not yet evolved common operating practices among their own people. They were swamped by the common services for which they already had direct operational responsibility. Several months after the reorganization of January 1954 a backlog of nearly 15,000 unpaid vouchers had piled up in the ARS Washington Finance Office. Many employees had not been reimbursed for travel and other expenses for several months. Similarly, private suppliers had not been paid for months. There were several other backlogs of serious proportions.

The program branches were soon sending in complaints. Matters had never been like this "in the good old days."

Spencer said later that he and his top advisers:

> . . . had anticipated, and in this anticipation we were not disappointed, that serious backlogs would develop in trying to service an organization of more than 10,000 people through a centralized business organization. We had decided at the time of reorganization, however, that it would be necessary to bring all [or substantially all] the parts together before we could separate them on a basis of regional operation.

By April the management staff officials had begun intensive discussions of how best to organize the finance work of ARS. The three men responsible for this problem were Frank H. Spencer; Edmund Stephens, Budget and Finance Division Director; and Ernest L. Struttmann, Assistant Division Director and Chief of the Finance Branch. They were assisted by four other officials who were considered to be part of Spencer's so-called "top management staff": James A. Starkey, Director of the Personnel Division; Stanley E. Williams, Director of the Administrative Services Division; Mark M. Kirkham, Assistant Director of the Budget and Finance Division and Chief of the Budget Branch; and Henry A. Donovan, Special Assistant to Spencer.

Then about fifty-five, Spencer had spent all of his administrative career in the Department of Agriculture. Beginning in personnel work in the Bureau of Animal Industry before World War I, by 1931 he had become business manager of the Bureau of Entomology and Plant Quarantine. He held that position until 1948, when he moved to the post of ARA Assistant Administrator for Administrative Management.

In an agency where most of the program officials had Ph.D. or veterinary medicine degrees,

Spencer's lack of a bachelor's degree reinforced his natural diffidence. His modesty and his long acquaintance with the "program official's mind" enabled him to evaluate the proposals of the management divisions (whose officials were anxious to exercise their new potency) in terms of their impact on programs and program officials. He had the respect of top program officials, and they were willing to give the management divisions a measure of operating freedom.

Spencer stated his ideas on the role of management in one of his speeches:

> The salesman of administrative management must be prepared to compromise to any reasonable extent. . . . Management must remember that operating programs have to live in a practical world and that it is not always possible to follow a particular procedure just for the sake of uniformity or because it looks good on paper.

However, he also noted that management involved something more than conciliation and adaptation:

> There are some points on which management cannot back down, even for the sake of keeping peace in the family. The doctrine of right is right and wrong is wrong is not confined to matters of morality. It is also true in the area of sound organization. Accepting defeat on a vital point in order to avoid opposition or controversy not only shows undue timidity, it defeats the very purpose for which management exists.

The second-ranking official involved in these discussions was Edmund Stephens, Director of the Budget and Finance Division. In his late forties, he had been in management work at both the agency and bureau levels. For some years before the reorganization he had served as assistant chief for administration in the old Bureau of Plant Industry.

Ernest L. Struttmann, Chief of the Finance Branch, at that time about forty-five, had been doing central staff work in the Department for ten years. He had served as agency budget officer until the reorganization and was considered a specialist on matters affecting ARS finance.

Possible Solutions

Late in April Spencer sent a memorandum on the conclusions from the group's discussions to Dr. M. R. Clarkson, Deputy Administrator for Regulatory Programs and at that time Acting Administrator. The memorandum pointed out that the group had considered the possibility of having the Budget and Finance Division handle only expenditure accounting (checks issued), with responsibility for obligation accounting (money committed but not yet paid out) decentralized to the program branches. This plan had been discarded, Spencer continued, because the Finance Branch could not "escape an overall ARS responsibility for obligation accounting. . . . There would be some unavoidable duplication between the two systems . . . and it would seem virtually impossible to defend a plan which would have fifteen or more separate accounting organizations in Washington and Beltsville."

Spencer reported that some thought had also been given to the idea "of a centralized accounting system in Washington and . . . area finance offices to handle the activities of those branches whose programs are administered on an area basis." However, Spencer and Budget and Finance Division officials had concluded that while this arrangement might be feasible, it would be more or less of a horse-and-rabbit stew arrangement inasmuch as from eighty to ninety per cent of the program activities were administered from Washington.

Once these two alternatives had been rejected, Spencer continued, he and his colleagues had been brought to the "basic question" of "whether this organization [the management divisions] should be centralized in Washington or established in area offices at various points throughout the country." They had consulted eight officials in Washington and Beltsville who were "considered representative of the program units," and all but one had "expressed some concern over the decentralization of fiscal work to area finance offices, feeling that such decentralization would lessen their ability to exercise proper control over the programs because they would not have the ready access to fiscal records which they would have with centralization in Washington." Spencer pointed out, however, that in his view "the advantage of ready access to centralized fiscal records is largely offset by the fact that such records are less current (because of delay in the receipt and posting of financial documents) than would be the reports made available through combination in the Division of Budget and Finance of reports received from the several area offices."

Moreover, he doubted "the wisdom of trying to handle at a centralized location the financial work for an organization of 13,000 people scattered throughout the United States," particularly in view of the fact that serious backlogs had already accumulated in servicing 10,000 of the 13,000 total employees on a largely centralized basis. He backed up his comment by pointing out that "Such a course also is contrary to the [decentralization] policies favored by the [departmental] Office of Budget and Finance, the Bureau of the Budget, and the General Accounting Office."

Accordingly, Spencer asserted that while he had "no desire to discount the objections of the majority of the program group consulted . . . *unless there is an overall decision that management work and program work should be organized on the same geographical basis, I am prepared to recommend that we adopt the plan of area fiscal offices.*" However,

> For organizational reasons as well as the recognized disruption of personal affairs of employees, there would not be any attempt to put this plan [if adopted] into full effect as of July 1, 1954. As a matter of fact, it would be necessary to continue for several months at least a substantial accounting and auditing staff to complete the handling in Washington of work of the fiscal year 1954. Each area finance office would begin operations on July 1, 1954, but on a basis of selective operation, and the switch-over would be made in the course of the fiscal year. For example, a start might be made with the activities of the former Bureau of Entomology and Plant Quarantine, the former Bureau of Plant Industry, and the four field utilization branches.

Over a period of time the area finance offices could assume the fiscal processing work for all the program branches, including those served by the field business offices and the utilization branch business offices in the field. Thus uniformity would be achieved. Moreover, those branches that required all operations be cleared through branch headquarters would be relieved of a heavy volume of paperwork.

Another advantage was that by freeing the Finance Branch of immediate concern for fiscal processing work, increased attention could be given to what Spencer considered its transcendent function—improving accounting policies, systems, and procedures throughout ARS.

In addition, the memorandum said, Spencer and other management division officials believed that area finance offices would contribute to better administration at the field-station level. They knew that many field units paid scant attention to ARS and departmental policies and regulations. At one large field station where administration was handled by the senior researcher on a part-time basis, all ARS issuances were simply filed in a folder by date of receipt, and, so far as could be determined, never consulted again. Having field finance offices (whose staffs would be constantly visiting and working with field stations) would make it easier to prevent such situations.

Finally, Spencer's memorandum continued, "this form of area organization for finance work would . . . call for a consideration of the treatment of personnel and administrative services activities."

> It is the current thinking that the personnel work would not be decentralized, although the present delegation of authority to the regional utilization branches and perhaps other units probably would be continued, and that there would only be a partial decentralization of administrative services work. This is because of the fact that many activities in these fields can be adequately handled on the basis of delegated authority without necessarily adopting regionalization. Furthermore, the start of an area arrangement in these fields does not necessarily have to come at the beginning of the fiscal year. A study will be made of this whole situation with a view to taking any action which may be feasible.

Decision to Establish Area Finance Offices

In a memorandum to Stephens on April 26, 1954, Spencer explained that he had just discussed the various choices with Acting Administrator Clarkson, "and he has indicated that we should go ahead with the plan to set up regional finance offices with the understanding that decisions with regard to the addition of personnel and administrative services activities to these area offices can be left until later." Stephens was asked to "take steps immediately to prepare the material necessary in securing Department approval of the area office proposal" and "to inform employees in our finance organization as well as the various [program] branch chiefs as to the plan."

Nine days later, on May 5, Spencer received a disconcerting memorandum from Stanley E. Williams, Director of the Administrative Services Division. Williams reported that, since the original decision to decentralize finance work had been made, his Administrative Services staff had discussed the idea of decentralizing administrative services functions and had concluded unanimously "that our work would be more effectively performed through the establishment of such offices." Then he listed administrative services functions that he and his division thought could be performed with greater "operating efficiency" in area offices, concluding with the comment, "we also believe that if Administrative Services and Fiscal staffs were adjacent to one another the cooperative work of the two Divisions would be expedited to a degree that would not be possible if they were separated."

Williams, then in his mid-forties, had been in ARS only since the reorganization. For years previous he had been an administrative assistant in the Office of the Secretary. His experience had principally involved service on various secretarial committees set up to investigate and report on special program and mangement problems. He had not had a great deal of experience in a "line" capacity and was inclined to leave operating matters to his more experienced top subordinates.

Two days later, on May 7, Spencer sent an answer to Williams assuring him that his memorandum was appreciated but disagreeing with his view that administrative services functions should be decentralized with fiscal functions. Spencer wrote:

> All in all—it seems to me that we should not attempt the immediate assignment of administrative services functions to area finance offices beyond the extent which proved necessary from the standpoint of fiscal functions. I do not mean that we shall not move eventually to the regionalization of administrative services functions (for I think we will) but simply that we shall have an exceedingly hard and involved job in establishing the finance offices by the early part of the fiscal year 1955 and we should not add to those difficulties unnecessarily.

On the same day, a memorandum prepared by Stephens and Spencer and signed by Acting Administrator Clarkson was directed to Ralph S. Roberts, Administrative Assistant Secretary of the Department of Agriculture, requesting departmental approval for establishing four area finance offices in the field and a Washington finance office to serve the Washington-Beltsville area. Those in the field would be located in the utilization branch laboratories at Philadelphia, New Orleans, and Albany (California, in the San Francisco Bay area), and in the Field Business Office at Minneapolis. Each office "would be equipped to handle our fiscal operations" for 2,000 to 3,000 employees, and these operations would include "preparation and payment of payrolls, examination and payment of other vouchers, maintenance of accounts, and rendition of reports." The letter went on to assure Roberts that "work on accounting systems and procedures and other fiscal staff work would [still] be done by staff in Washington reporting directly to the Chief of the Finance Branch."

In this letter Spencer repeated some of the major factors that had led to the decision to establish area finance offices. In sum, they were:

> ARA program activities were extensively decentralized with approximately three-fourths of the employees stationed outside the Washington-Beltsville area.
>
> It was desirable to pay personnel and vendors promptly.
>
> There was a need for maintaining accounting records at points nearer the scene of operations, which would provide better service to program personnel in the field and make it possible to keep fiscal records up to date.
>
> It was probable that, with an organization payrolling about 13,000 employees and handling about 180,000 other vouchers annually, sheer volume would make it extremely difficult to operate one centralized fiscal office efficiently.

Spencer proposed that the offices "begin operations on or about July 1, 1954, handling in the beginning selected program activities. . . . The full change-over would be made during the course of fiscal year 1955."

And, finally, the Department was told that there was "no urgent need" for decentralizing personnel and administrative services work, since many activities in these fields could "be effectively handled by delegated authority. . . . Should experience and study modify this concept, further recommendations will be made that these activities be assigned to area offices."

Top-management officials in ARS regarded Roberts as the key departmental figure in obtaining permission to decentralize finance activities. He was the Administrative Assistant Secretary and thus broadly responsible for internal administrative arrangements in the Department. He was also personally influential. A career employee, he had previously served for about four years as departmental budget officer and director of finance and had been elevated to Administrative Assistant Secretary shortly after Reorganization Plan Number 2 had created this position in 1953. His detailed knowledge of the Department's programs and his friendly relations with the congressional Agriculture and Appropriations Committees, established when he was budget officer, made him especially valuable to the new administration.

He was regarded by many of his fellow officials and political superiors as decisive, energetic, and competent. While he was careful to clear administrative policy proposals with his political superiors, he assumed the initiative and the main role himself.

Departmental Decision Postponed

Late in the afternoon of May 11, Roberts asked Spencer how ARS would react to a suggestion that the decentralization be postponed for six or eight months pending the results of an intensive survey of the Department's entire field organization and operations. Spencer replied that ARS would probably plan to postpone the effective date of the decentralization from July 1, 1954 to July 1, 1955, as it would not be practicable to set up finance offices in the middle of the fiscal year. He also asked Roberts to make it clear in his formal reply that the proposal was being disapproved for "overall reasons" and not because the proposal itself was unsound. He told Roberts that the Department's Office of Budget and Finance and the General Accounting Office had strongly urged the establishment of area finance offices.

On May 17 Roberts wrote to Administrator Shaw that although it was "recognized that some arrangement such as" the one proposed

> may be not only desirable but necessary to an effective handling of fiscal matters in your Service, the desirability of establishing such offices at the present time is questionable in the light of plans now being explored in the Secretary's Office for a complete survey of the field organizations of all of the Services and agencies of the Department. While it cannot be certain at this time that such a survey would result in recommendations for modifying the field pattern inconsistent with that which you now propose for the Area Finance Offices, at the same time it is quite possible that those recommendations could result in some further changes.
>
> Accordingly, your recommendation of May 7 is returned with the request that the establishment of these offices be deferred until after the Department's survey of the field organization is complete. . . .

It was not until July 22 that a Secretary's Memorandum was issued to heads of Department agencies announcing the "Field Service Review," though preliminary explorations by the Secretary's Office had been under way for several months. To lead to the study, a Field Service Review Committee was established, composed of Assistant Secretary for Federal-States Relations J. Earl Coke, Chairman; Administrative Assistant Secretary Roberts; an assistant to the Secretary; and the director of Agricultural Credit Services.

Management Division Difficulties Continue

Meanwhile harassed officials and employees of the ARS Finance Branch, particularly in its Washington Finance Office, continued working overtime. A great volume of work flowed in from headquarters, field stations, and suppliers. Finally the time required to process a fiscal document was reduced by revamping procedures and adding staff at bottleneck points. By the fall of 1954 inroads were at last made in the voucher backlog. There were now 5,000 unprocessed vouchers, whereas several months before there had been 15,000. But ARS management officials were sure that the Herculean effort required could not be kept up indefinitely. The situation was regarded as little less than desperate. Still there was no report from the Secretary's Field Service Review Committee.

On December 15 Administrator Shaw sent a memorandum prepared by Spencer to Administrative Assistant Secretary Roberts urging "that the Agricultural Research Service be given as prompt guidance as possible" on "the organization of our business activities in the field, particularly those of a fiscal nature." He was prompted to write at this time, he said, because he understood that the various task forces were completing their reports for the main Field Service Review Committee. He then reemphasized the point that "it is exceedingly difficult to handle at one point the fiscal work of an organization of 13,000 people located all over the United States and we have had some serious arrears in voucher payments. While this situation has improved appreciably we do not think it can be entirely corrected without the benefits of field business offices."

Roberts replied on December 21, assuring Shaw that he was "fully aware of the problem outlined in your memorandum." But, he added, "since action originally proposed by ARS was deferred at the request of the Department's Field Service Review Committee, I do not feel at liberty to make a decision on the matter." Any decision would have to wait at least until the next meeting of the committee scheduled for mid-January.

Early in February, Williams, the Director of the Administrative Services Division, directed a long memorandum to Spencer, this time on the subject of ARS business services organization. He began by saying that he supposed he should still classify himself "as a neophyte in ARS," since some of the management people who normally attended Spencer's staff meetings had "program experience as well as administrative background" in the organization, and all of them were "more sensitive" than he "to the interplay of forces bearing upon the situation we are discussing and are better qualified to evaluate these factors." Nonetheless, he continued,

> I would be something less than forthright and useful if I should fail to express some misgivings that are on my mind. I am fearful that we are temporizing with a situation that is potentially dangerous, if not explosive. We have had for a year a confused situation in which the Management Divisions are dealing with several different categories of unlike things. [The former Bureau of Entomology and Plant Quarantine] Branches represent one category—the Utilization Branches another. The former Plant Industry Branches are another group doing business on a somewhat different basis and the residue comprise a fourth group.
>
> Looking at ourselves from the other end of the telescope, we have a situation in which it is possible in a given locality for four field stations to be [provided business services] in four different ways—one through Beltsville, one through Washington, one through Utilization Business Offices and one through [Field] Business Offices.

Pointing out that "if no firm plan is adopted for F.Y. 1956," two years would "have elapsed without a decision as to the means of implementing the basic reorganization plan in the field," Williams asserted: "Either we shall have been declared remiss somewhere in that lapse of time or serious doubts shall have arisen that the basic reorganization plan was sound. Many people will continue to declare they were better off in the old bureaus or that there should have been a research setup on one hand and a regulatory setup on the other, or something different. . . unless there is a decision and progress toward permanence and stability."

Then he proceeded to oppose a suggestion recently made in one of Spencer's staff meetings that "it might be wise to establish only one area [business] office on an experimental basis" in fiscal year 1956. "Presumably," he added, if this suggestion were followed, "all of the present structure" would be left "in existence." Moreover, the "experimental office" would only "serve one section of the country." While "we would know whether that particular office had done well or poorly" at the end of a year, "we would not know that other offices using different staffing, serving different regions, would have done the same or a comparable job." Further, "we would continue to do business at numerous places with staffs which did not know whether they were in place permanently or temporarily. At some point indecision and suspected impermanence would wear down the effectiveness of people and lead to the loss of some who can find dependable jobs elsewhere."

Williams concluded that he was not making "a plea for any particular kind of field structure" but rather expressing "doubt that delay would be wise. . . . We as management people have an obligation to analyze our situation, adopt a plan and proceed to implement it." Doing so "will unite our people in a common effort and promote effectiveness of the research and regulatory programs."

Departmental Decision

On February 17, 1955, the Department decided to let ARS establish area finance offices. Roberts' letter, concurred in by E. L. Peterson, the new Assistant Secretary for Federal-States Relations, advised Shaw that "information developed by the [Department's Field Service Review Committee's] survey groups indicates that serious delays are occurring [in ARS] in the processing of some fiscal transactions." For this reason, he continued, "it appears desirable that you proceed at least on an interim basis to establish the four Area Offices in question," despite the fact that "the field services review committee has not completed its review of the reconnaissance survey and has not yet prepared a report."

Three conditions were attached to the Department's authorization to go ahead with decentralization:

(1) That serious consideration be given to "the desirability of extending the regionalization to personnel, procurement, and property management work." (Roberts knew that Spencer and other ARS officials were thinking of ultimately decentralizing the operational aspects of personnel and ad-

ministrative services work, and in his judgment, decentralization in one area without equivalent decentralization in complementary areas would lead to administrative chaos.)

(2) "That the plan should contemplate complete 'regionalization' of fiscal and other [business] services covered by the plan without servicing in whole or in part programs and activities across regional or area boundaries established." (By this Roberts meant that the decentralization should be of a geographical rather than a functional character. All program activities within a geographic region should be serviced from the business office located in that region, regardless of the fact that in many cases an activity would operate in several different regions. In general, program people would have preferred the latter alternative, called "cross-servicing," where a given program activity would be serviced from one business office without regard to geographic limitations. In the first case, program considerations are apparently sacrificed to administrative uniformity; in the second, administrative considerations are apparently sacrificed to program uniformity. This requirement was attached, according to Roberts, because preliminary findings from the Department's Field Service Review indicated that "cross-servicing" from the ARS Field Business Offices was without real pattern, and therefore was needlessly confusing and time-consuming.)

(3) "That a plan in sufficient detail to show operational relationships with programs and activities located in each region or an area be developed for review and concurrence of the appropriate Departmental Staff offices, and approval by the Secretary's Office prior to implementation."

PLANNING REGIONALIZATION

March 1955–April 1955

The ARS management divisions now had just over four months to clear the way for inaugurating regional business services on July 1, the beginning of the new fiscal year. It would be necessary, among other things, to make final decisions on regional business office locations and regional boundaries; to determine precisely what functions and activities would be decentralized; to select, train, and transfer personnel to man the offices; to schedule the decentralization of functions and activities; and to develop procedures to coincide as nearly as possible with the transfers of functions. Moreover, the Department's approval to all of these decisions and plans would have to be obtained before the offices could function.

There was also the problem of securing the support and cooperation of program officials. At this time most of them below the immediate Office of the Administrator were unaware of the impending regionalization. Many had even forgotten, if they ever knew, that nine months earlier Acting Administrator Clarkson had requested departmental permission to decentralize ARS finance functions. So one of the first items of business considered by Spencer and the management division directors was the necessity, "in view of the apparent impossibility to control rumors," as Spencer phrased it, for "immediately" publishing "such information as we can give and to supplement it as rapidly as possible with details as they develop."

Program Officials Told of Regionalization Decision

Accordingly, on March 1, three notices prepared by Spencer were issued to different categories of ARS officials and employees. One, signed by Spencer himself, went to "ARS Staff Engaged in Business Operations" and informed such staff of the reasons for decentralizing and outlined developing plans for handling administrative work under regionalization. The second memorandum was signed by Administrator Shaw and directed to "All Divisions, Branches, and Field Stations." It simply indicated that plans were being developed for the regionalization of business operations and named probable regional business office locations. Officials and employees also were assured that lines of program supervision would remain unchanged.

The third notice, also signed by Shaw, informed "Program Directors and Branch Chiefs" of some of the reasons for decentralizing business operations and asked for their "best efforts in helping to bring

. . . about . . . a smooth and effective transition to the regionalization." Shaw promised that "the best means of accomplishing this" would be worked out "jointly." "In the very near future," he promised, "people from the Management Divisions will be calling on Branch Chiefs, Division Directors and their Administrative Assistants" for this purpose.

Program officials did not take the news calmly. Angry complaints were soon deluging Spencer's office, so he decided to call a meeting to explain to the program officials the reasons for decentralizing.

Spencer Defends Regionalization

The meeting with branch chiefs and other program officials took place in the Secretary's Conference Room on March 23, 1955. (All branches except the four field utilization research branches were represented. Because of the time factor, the management divisions had decided to hold the meeting at once and deal with utilization branch complaints later as a separate matter. Also absent were representatives of the Experiment Stations Divisions. Management officials presumed this was because, having no field employees in the forty-eight states and only a small number in the territories, these divisions were not much concerned about regionalization.)

First Spencer sketched the background of the regionalization proposal, emphasizing that he, Shaw, and management division officials recognized that providing business services on a centralized basis had many disadvantages, particularly in the fiscal field. The Department's permission to proceed with regionalization, he added, involved observing the three conditions the Department had imposed. Those most relevant to program operations were that there be no business servicing across regional boundaries and that consideration be given to regionalizing routine personnel and administrative services as well as fiscal work.

Then he remarked that the management divisions had just created a "Regionalization Work Group" which, together with other officials from the management divisions, would explore regionalization possibilities and implications with the program branches through group conferences and individual consultations.

Next he reported on the management divisions' "present thinking" on some of the basic questions to be settled in regionalization planning. First there was the question of regional business office locations and regional boundaries. The earlier plan, he said, had been to locate the offices in Albany, California; New Orleans; Minneapolis; Philadelphia; and Washington. Now it appeared that Philadelphia would be eliminated because of its proximity to Washington. Justifying the location of two offices less than 200 miles apart to the Department, the General Accounting Office, and the Congress might prove too difficult.

Another fundamental question to be settled, he continued, was that of determining precisely what business functions would be decentralized. On the basis of preliminary thinking in the management divisions, "common" business functions would "almost surely" be regionalized. These included: (a) payrolling, voucher examination, and allotment ledger accounting; (b) general procurement and sales authority, personal property management, and records management; and (c) employment, classification, and personnel record-keeping for certain undetermined categories of employees. "Substantive" management functions "almost surely" would not be decentralized. Some of these were: (a) development of policies, procedures, and systems for all management activities; (b) approval and filing of program research contracts and other cooperative agreements with outside agencies and organizations; (c) budget formulation and execution; and (d) organization and methods analysis and employee investigations.

Spencer then indicated that nothing had yet been done about three other major questions: selection of regional business managers, decisions on the proper relationship of the regional business offices to the program branches, and development of staffing patterns and selection of subordinate personnel for the regional business offices. (Actually, Spencer had already contacted Howard C. Ameigh, Business Manager of the Field Business Office at Greenfield, Massachusetts, to offer him the business manager position for the region to be served from Minneapolis. However, because of the uncertainty regarding office locations and regional boundaries, this offer had been couched in tentative terms.)

Finally, he discussed what he termed certain "fundamentals" of philosophy and policy to be observed in the regionalization process:

> Purpose of regionalization is to expedite business operations and release time of technical staff for use in program activities.
>
> Fewer business operations would be conducted in the management divisions and program branch headquarters under regionalization.

> In general, all business operations would be conducted by the regional business offices, except:
> (a) those where time factor required handling at local field station level.
> (b) those where overall policy considerations or need for high-level decisions in either management or program areas indicated handling in Washington and/or Beltsville.
>
> Program branch control should be exercised through predetermination of routine policy and procedure, budgetary controls, etc., rather than through handling of individual cases.
>
> Field stations must be given a clear understanding of types of matters to be handled directly through regional business offices and those to be cleared through their program branch headquarters.
>
> Planning and implementing regionalization is a mutual responsibility of management and program staffs. Program branches must recognize the necessity for substantial change in existing methods of handling business operations. On their part, management divisions must recognize the need for providing a system which will safeguard program branches' control of field activities.

In closing, Spencer invited the frank reactions of program officials.

The officials from the production research branches, particularly those transferred from the Bureaus of Plant Industry and Animal Industry, immediately spoke out against regionalization. It had been apparent throughout Spencer's talk that they were restraining themselves only with great difficulty. At first the intent of their comments was obscure, but soon a clear pattern emerged. They objected to the fact that they were not consulted before the decision to decentralize had been made. Some deplored the Department's "non-cross-servicing" requirement. This, they said, would play havoc with their program organization since leaders of projects crossing regional lines would be deprived of a single reliable source of business information. They also argued that they could not retain central control of widely dispersed research programs if they were deprived of the tools that had always been considered essential for the job. Furthermore, Plant Industry branch chiefs asserted, management officials must be thinking of ultimately dismantling the Plant Industry branch business offices (which were much larger than those of other branches) in order to find additional staff to man the regional business offices, and how then, for example, were they to maintain control over the obligation and expenditure of branch funds? Or how, wondered Dr. Bennett T. Simms, Chief of the Animal Disease and Parasite Research Branch and former Chief of the Bureau of Animal Industry, would the management divisions and the regional business offices propose to handle a problem as complicated as that of the field recruitment and placement of veterinarians and other professional persons who might be in short supply in one region and overabundant in another? Since this was a real and not just a theoretical problem, he continued, he would certainly object strenuously if the management divisions proposed to decentralize professional recruitment and placement to the regional business offices. On this point, Spencer assured him that the Personnel Division was as conscious as he of the hazards of decentralizing this function and that this and other problems would be discussed in detail at the later meetings with individual branches.

Underlying Complaints

It was clear that underlying these specific objections was a general feeling of insecurity. First, the branch headquarters organizations and clientele relationships had been disrupted by the reorganization; now, little more than a year later, the branches were being asked to allow the scope and character of relationships with their own field employees to be altered. And this was being asked by the management divisions, the supposed servants of the program branches. What was to keep the management divisions from ignoring the special needs and requirements of this or that program branch in what the program people regarded as a pursuit of uniformity for uniformity's sake? Furthermore, under the present centralized setup financial reports to the branches were usually tardy and inaccurate. How then were the program operations of a branch to be run on the basis of piecemeal business information, probably even less timely and accurate, submitted from five widely scattered points? Decentralization would bring with it a hazardous and unnecessary diffusion of responsibility.

Another underlying factor had to do with pay and prestige. Throughout the history of the bureaus and the agency, bureau research officials had run the business services as well as the program functions. As a consequence many felt that their pay and prestige would be adversely affected if they were deprived of the common business services functions. Though they did not express this view to program officials, Shaw and management division officials were convinced that, as a long-range proposition, research programs of the agency would be more effective if officials responsible for directing the programs were freed of these diverting demands on their time. To Shaw, Spencer, Starkey, and others, then, regionalization presented the opportunity to take another necessary step toward organizing the agency for the best utilization of program people for program purposes. Once this was accomplished, they reasoned, good program work would bring its own pay and prestige rewards.

In addition, research officials, long accustomed to taking up routine as well as policy questions with management officials on a face-to-face basis, feared that this would no longer be possible once the management divisions delegated great chunks of their functions to the regional business offices. Many program officials, for example, knew very well that sometimes the success of a whole enterprise could turn upon such a seemingly petty matter as reclassifying a field station head's secretary.

The attending management division officials could see from this meeting that while the Plant Industry and Animal Industry research people were in substantial agreement in their opposition to regionalization, they had not agreed on a spokesman for their viewpoint or on an approach to warding off regionalization plans. But they had never before been confronted with a staunchly independent management position. In the old bureau and ARA days, not, after all, very far back, administrative people had accepted the main role accorded them: getting the personnel, supplies, and equipment desired by program operators, and providing the records necessary for program direction. "Policing" program operations was definitely a secondary role. In this situation, they had never developed the sort of professional consciousness they were now displaying.

Program people, particularly research officials, had always looked on administrative work and administrative people with a jaundiced eye. They saw themselves as being engaged in the real work of the organization and as persons of higher professional and job qualifications. Most of them had advanced college degrees, whereas, at least until quite recently, administrative workers had seldom attended college. Many administrative workers had begun their careers as sub-professional program workers. Not academically qualified to rise in program work, they had transferred to administrative work where academic qualifications were of no special consequence. Many of them progressed over a period of time to rather high administrative positions, while promotions for program people were comparatively slow. This was construed by program people as a confirmation of their impression that administrative work called for inferior ability and technical competence.

Accordingly, ARS research officials were disconcerted by the new unity and independence of the management divisions and their own lack of countervailing influence.

Officials from the animal regulatory branches had remained silent up to this point of the meeting. Finally Spencer interrupted research officials' comments to ask Dr. Miller, Chief of the Meat Inspection Branch, what he thought of the idea of regionalization. Miller replied that while he and other animal regulatory officials were not enthusiastic supporters of regionalization, they would not fight it, particularly in view of Spencer's assurance that the management divisions would be consulting program branch officials with respect to their needs and requirements.

Two days before, on March 21, in response to Deputy Administrator Clarkson's request that he try to reflect regulatory branch sentiments on regionalization, Miller had written that "except to the extent that personal contact [between the regulatory branches and management divisions] will be substituted by correspondence and telegraphic communication [between these branches and regional business offices], most regulatory programs will experience no [insurmountable] difficulty with the regionalization of administrative services [and fiscal] functioning." He was assuming, he continued, that budgeting for regulatory programs would not be performed in regional business offices and that "the existing basic relationships" between the regulatory branches and personnel and fiscal management functioning would "not be disturbed."

Most regulatory work, whether on plants or animals, was repetitive in nature. Regulatory workers were engaged mainly in routine inspection and control activities. While most of their supervisors were veterinarians, entomologists, or other professionals, many of them were nonprofessionals. Regulatory people often had a different attitude toward management than researchers had. Less questioning, the regulatory people did not care too much how ARS management officials organized to do their own work; this was a technical matter best left to experts in administration. What they did care about was being paid on time and having other business services provided expeditiously and accurately.

Spencer Replies

With Miller's pledge of cooperation, Spencer undertook to respond to some of the heated objections of research officials. He pointed out that while they had not been specifically consulted before the decision to decentralize was made, Administrator Shaw, the top program official in ARS, had been consulted and had approved. Secondly, Spencer continued, there was no intention of dismantling the program branch business offices, though it would probably be necessary to transfer some personnel from those few offices that were clearly over-staffed to the management divisions or the regional business offices. Next, he emphasized that wherever practicable the regional business offices would, at least for a time, perform the specialized business services to which some of the branches had grown accustomed. But he also served notice that the management divisions intended to work toward uniformity in providing services to program units. Then he repeated his earlier promise that the program branches would be individually consulted before final decisions were made.

The research officials who still objected evidently felt it useless to prolong the discussion, for they made no reply to Spencer's rebuttal. The Administrator held all the trump cards: all legal authority was his. And obviously Shaw approved of regionalizing.

At this point Spencer adjourned the meeting.

The meeting had brought two gains to the cause of regionalization. Program officials in some areas had been converted from tentative opposition to neutrality or, even better, lukewarm support. Spencer and his management division directors had also been given a clearer idea of the patterns of opposition, neutrality, and willingness to cooperate (albeit grudging).

The meeting made clear that opposition to the proposed regionalization was centered in the production research branches, while cooperation and support for the plans were to be found in the regulatory branches. With a single exception, all research branches with field stations, which were represented at the meeting, were opposed to, or at least disliked, regionalization. The exception, the Entomology Research Branch, was willing to give regionalization a try.[10] As of January 1955, these opposing branches had a total of approximately 3,200 field employees. On the other hand, cooperation appeared to be forthcoming from all the regulatory branches, which, with the field personnel of the Entomology Research Branch, had about 8,500 persons employed in the field.

Although the four utilization research branches did not attend the meeting, it was known to Spencer and the management divisions, though not to most program officials attending the meeting, that these branches were actively opposed to the regionalization plans. The basis of their opposition was not difficult to understand. The nearly 1,500 employees in these branches were all in the field; each branch already had its own full-fledged business office in the same building providing common business services. Each branch realized that regionalization would change this desirable situation. In effect these branches were being asked to sacrifice for the good of the agency as a whole.

The meeting might have had a different outcome if the utilization officials had been present to state their views in the hearing of branch leaders in Washington. Their voices would have been added to an opposition that was, as noted above, nearly unanimous among the research branches with field stations.

Establishment of Regionalization Work Group

On March 4, over two weeks before Spencer's meeting with program officials, Robert B. Harris, Chief of the Organization and Methods Branch, Personnel Division, and then Acting Director of the division, had prepared a long memorandum to Spencer on the subject of regionalization planning.

His main purpose, he wrote, was to urge the creation of a Regionalization Work Group, to be composed of one representative from each management division, "to undertake, coordinate and carry

[10] Two of the smaller research branches whose officials attended the meeting, the Production Economics Research Branch and the Dairy Husbandry Research Branch, clearly disliked the idea of regionalization but were unwilling to declare active opposition to what appeared to be a firm decision. On the other hand, the Human Nutrition, Home Economics, and Washington Utilization Research Branches assumed a neutral position on this issue. Only the first had as many as twenty field employees to be concerned about.

out all phases of regionalization under your supervision." Since "this will probably be a full-time job, at least on an interim basis," he went on, "the Work Group members should either be relieved of regular assignments or subordinate them to the larger responsibility of accomplishing regionalization."

Harris also foresaw the need for a so-called "subsidiary work group" within each management division, to have "responsibility for developing and carrying out [its] plans." While he thought it would be best to make each overall Regionalization Work Group member responsible for his own division's work group, he emphasized that the latter group should function "under direction of the Division Director, and all plans in their various stages [should be] coordinated with you and the Division Directors as necessary." As he saw it, "the overall and division work groups are the keys" to the planning and action phases of regionalization.

Later the same day, Harris sent another memorandum to Spencer, again making a strong plea for "coordination of effort on regionalization." "Unless coordination is exercised . . . we will have a situation in which various branches of a single division and each of the divisions will be calling upon each other and upon the same program branches for essentially the same information. . . . It seems, therefore, that action should be taken to coordinate reviews, surveys, examinations, etc., including the gathering of data by our management people." Creation of the Work Group would also mean that program branches could be asked to direct all of their inquiries to one central place.

Until he received these memoranda, Spencer had thought that overall regionalization planning should be handled within established channels, with himself and the management division directors as the prime movers. However, since he was concerned about how they could plan regionalization and continue at the same time to supervise normal operations, he was most receptive to Harris' proposal. After all, it would allow Spencer and the directors to sit on top of the planning process without having to plan each specific detail.

Accordingly, after getting the same favorable reaction from Stephens and Williams, Spencer asked them on March 8 to name their representatives to an overall Work Group. Since finance work was obviously going to be directly affected by regionalization, Stephens appointed Struttmann, Assistant Director and Chief of the Finance Branch, as his division's representative. Williams named Assistant Director Raymond Sooy because most of the Administrative Services Division's work would be affected, and only Sooy besides Williams himself could speak for the whole division.

Both Director Starkey and Assistant Director McAuley of the Personnel Division were absent on two weeks of military leave, and a permanent representative from that division could not be named until their return the following week. Meanwhile Spencer appointed Harris on a *pro tem* basis, with the understanding that Starkey might make some other designation on his return.

The next morning, on March 9, members of this "interim" Regionalization Work Group met in Spencer's office with Spencer and Donovan, Spencer's Special Assistant. Spencer told the Work Group it would be responsible for coordinating, under his direction, all of the work of the subsidiary work groups to be established in the respective management divisions and for keeping itself informed both on the progress of regionalization planning and on management division contacts with program branches and other units.

Later that afternoon, the interim Work Group convened the first of the meetings it was to hold daily during the following week. Since no one knew whether Harris would continue as a member after Starkey's return, these early meetings were largely preliminary and exploratory. One short-lived conflict did occur. Struttmann suggested that a committee representing the program branches (preferably one research official and one regulatory official) should be set up to work with the Work Group. This proposal was promptly vetoed by Sooy and Harris, who argued that such a committee might hamstring planning efforts. Besides, they went on, precisely which program branch chiefs would be considered representative by their peers of the various program points of view?

Some six weeks later, Spencer was to be told by Dr. George W. Irving, Jr., Deputy Administrator for Research Programs, that the research sub-functional area directors had come to feel that the Work Group should definitely include "a member of the research staff." In his written reply on April 25, Spencer tactfully but firmly rejected the suggestion. "This matter was considered rather carefully when the work group was set up," he wrote, referring to Struttmann's proposal and its rejection by Sooy and Harris, and

> It seemed . . . that it would be impossible for any one person to represent adequately the viewpoint of the various branches because they embrace a wide variety of organization patterns, work pro-

grams, and individual ideas. If the group had been enlarged in this way, it would have been necessary also to include representation from the control and regulatory branches and, although I think there is more similarity in the organization and operations of these branches than there is in the research field, again it would seem doubtful that any one person could function effectively. It seemed best, therefore, to consult with the branches one by one so as to make sure that each one had a thorough opportunity to present its specific problems and, in turn, to consider the overall problems with regard to the organization and conduct of business operations from the regional business offices.

Starkey and McAuley returned from military leave on March 16, and Spencer immediately asked Starkey to name his representative to the Work Group. Two days later Starkey informed Spencer that he would like to name himself but felt that Harris, as the official having overall organization and methods responsibility in ARS, should be a member, too. Spencer replied that he would be happy to have both men serve and would name Starkey as chairman.

On March 22, just one day before his meeting with program officials, Spencer formally announced to "All Divisions and Branches" the establishment of the Regionalization Work Group.

At this time in his early forties, Chairman Starkey had spent his early professional years doing personnel work in the Bureau of Plant Industry. Just prior to the reorganization he had served several years as ARA personnel officer. In this position he had actually been a sort of executive assistant to Administrator Shaw on program and personnel matters. On the basis of his experience, he was convinced that research officials would now and forever resist any move to decentralize administrative activities that did not take full account of the limitations imposed by centralization of program authority. His more recent experience confirmed his thinking that from a management point of view administrative policy-making must be performed on a centralized, nationally uniform basis.

In some ways Starkey was difficult for his colleagues and subordinates to understand. He usually discussed current agency problems in long-range policy terms they found hard to apply to concrete situations. Yet his ability to identify factors of cause and effect, to separate long-run from short-run requirements and consequences, and to "philosophize" about program objectives and methods, inspired his co-workers to try to see their own responsibilities in terms of the total institutional environment. They all thought he was a remarkable "idea" man.

Struttmann, having served in central staff work for ten years, was more inclined than Starkey to have the management divisions "go it alone" in decentralizing. However, his primary concern, as he frequently observed, was to have the regional business offices organized to handle fiscal processing work and their other functions so as to furnish the maximum service to program operations.

Sooy was regarded by his colleagues as an able operator: he knew the "ins and outs" of administrative services functioning; he could get things done. But he was also regarded as intrepidly blunt in stating his opinions to others.

Then forty-one, Harris had initially begun his career as a messenger. Shortly thereafter he became a meat inspector in the Meat Inspection Division of the old Bureau of Animal Industry. With his advancement up the program ladder blocked because he lacked a veterinarian degree, he found his way into administrative work in the bureau. By the time of the reorganization he had served as its assistant personnel officer and then as special assistant to the bureau's assistant chief for administration. He had vast knowledge and enthusiasm about the programs of that bureau and, in general, took the view that administration would be successful only to the extent that it served legitimate program needs and requirements.

Harris had an active manner. Although he was blunt and occasionally short-tempered, his associates knew that he fought for his convictions with little regard for the personal consequences.

The Regional Business Manager Issue

Beginning with its meeting on March 25, the meetings of the Regionalization Work Group for the ensuing two weeks, and many hours of Spencer's time for the week following, were taken up with one overriding issue: should business manager positions be established in each regional business office to direct and coordinate its operations? As discussion of this issue proceeded, it became clear that Work Group members differed not only on this but also on three other closely related issues. Although the disagreements within the management divisions were peripheral to the main conflict described in this study—between the management divisions and some of the program units—they affected the chances for successful regionalization. Most were at long last settled with an eye to the effects upon program units. These issues, in logical rather than chronological order, were as follows:

(1) Whether, in light of the fact that operating program authority (particularly research program authority) was predominantly centralized at headquarters, anything more than routine business services of a processing character could and should be decentralized from the management divisions (and some program business offices) to the regional business offices.

(2) Whether this problem was relevant to the decision concerning regional business manager positions.

(3) Whether the regional technical staffs—Fiscal, Administrative Services, and Personnel—should be given national direction through the assistant administrator for management or through the management division directors in their respective functional areas.

Work Group members believed that agreement on the first two of these issues had to be secured before the question of whether regional business manager positions should be established. The third issue was thought to be so intimately related to that question that neither could be considered independently.

While Work Group disagreements inevitably reflected differences in the members' personalities and backgrounds, all four members tried to keep the discussion on an impersonal level. Following the example of Chairman Starkey, they sought to examine the issues from the standpoint of "the good of the Service."

The precise manner in which the concept of regional business manager positions first came to be questioned is not fully known. Up to mid-March none of the Work Group members had questioned the advisability of having regional business managers. Shortly after his return from military leave, Starkey learned that some management division officials were considering the decentralization of certain substantive management functions as well as of common business services. Starkey looked for some dramatic means of impressing upon these officials that this was not a wise move, since research branch program authority was centralized, and since many research officials had expressed hostility to regionalization. Quite apart from the factors mentioned, Starkey was convinced that management policy affecting the operations of the regional business offices should be uniform throughout the agency and should be made in Washington.

At about the same time, Starkey became aware that the existence of business managers would place the regional business offices under the organizational jurisdiction of the assistant administrator for management; otherwise the various regional technical staffs would be controlled by the management divisions in their respective functional areas. This was the dramatic issue he sought. If there were no business managers, each central management division would continue to be responsible for consulting

FIGURE 4:

REGIONAL BUSINESS MANAGERS: THE ALTERNATIVES

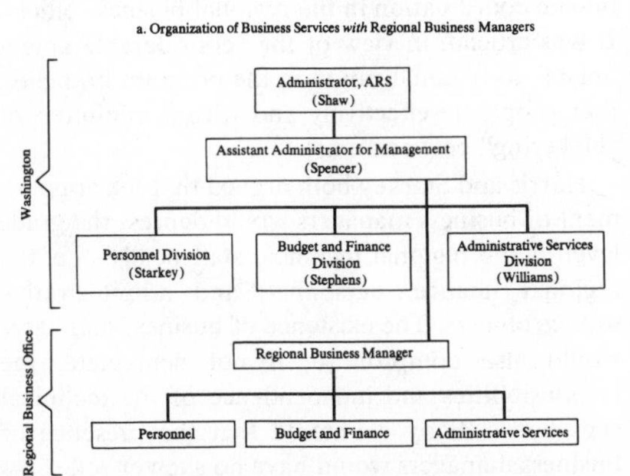

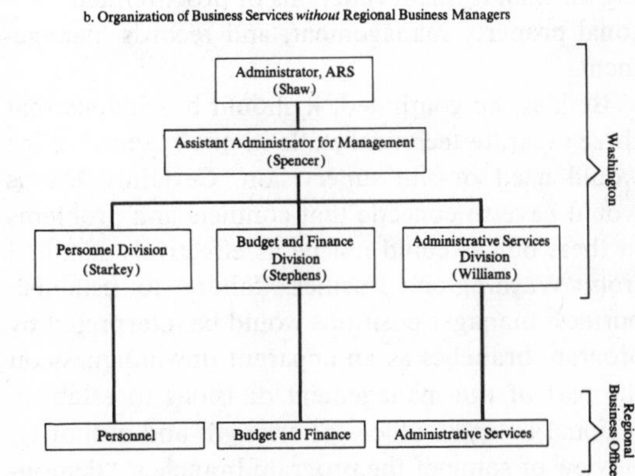

program branches about its own particular type of problem. If, however, on-site business manager positions were established, the program consultation function would be elevated to the office of the assistant administrator for management. In addition, the business managers, lacking policy-making or coordinating functions of their own, would ultimately substitute their judgments for those of their technical staffs, of the management divisions, and of Spencer. Not only would the function of consulting the program branches be elevated to the office of the assistant administrator for management, but national policies would be frustrated and national uniformity destroyed.

Starkey communicated his reservations to Harris on or about March 21 and found that Harris also questioned the necessity of regional business managers. Starkey then asked Harris to prepare a memorandum for the Work Group pointing out the theoretical disadvantages of establishing business manager positions.

Copies of Harris' memorandum were circulated to other Work Group members at a meeting on March 25. In general, Harris presented the same arguments against having business managers that Starkey had outlined four days earlier, though now the points were more sharply developed. After Sooy and Struttman read their copies, Starkey asked for discussion. Sooy said vigorously that every point seemed ridiculous. In the first place, he said, he saw no reason why management as well as routine business functions could not be decentralized, despite centralization of research program authority. Management functions had certainly been decentralized without disaster in his old bureau, the Bureau of Agricultural and Industrial Chemistry. And he knew that the Administrative Services Division had every intention of regionalizing the management functions of procurement, personal property management, and records management.

Besides, he continued, it should be obvious that three separate technical staffs in one regional office would need on-site supervision. Certainly Harris would have to concede that conflicts and problems in these offices could not be as effectively handled from Washington. Further, failure to establish business manager positions would be interpreted by program branches as an apparent unwillingness on the part of the management divisions to establish regional business offices of strength and authority. In view of some of the program branches' "demonstrated opposition to change," this could be disastrous. The very suggestion that business managers were not needed or would do more harm than good was preposterous. And to argue that the management divisions, rather than the assistant administrator for management, should direct these offices on the national level was equally outlandish, besides being subversive to Spencer's position. Obviously, if one individual, reporting directly to Spencer, were given responsibility for the entire operation at a given location, the Administrator's Office would be in a better position to exercise effective control than if three individuals, each of whom had responsibility for only a fraction of the operation, reported independently to separate people in that office.

These comments irritated Harris, and he and Sooy were soon engaged in a hot argument.

Struttmann interrupted to say that he did not care particularly what theoretical claims could be asserted on either side. He would make his decision on the basis of the answer to one question: would the establishment of business manager positions have a depressing effect on the classification grade level that the Department would be willing to approve for the heads of the regional technical staffs? If so, he would recommend against establishing business manager positions, because failing to provide a grade level high enough to attract the strongest possible technical staff heads would be "fatal" to the success of regionalization. If not, he would favor the appointment of business managers. Managers had been appointed in the two old ARA bureaus where business operations had been decentralized—the Bureau of Entomology and Plant Quarantine and the Bureau of Agricultural and Industrial Chemistry—so precedent was on this side. Then too, there would be a "real need" for on-site coordination in the regional business offices. It was crucial, in view of the "considerable antagonism" to regionalization in the program branches, that it operate effectively and with a minimum of "bickering" between units.

Harris and Starkey both argued that the appointment of business managers would depress the grade level of the regional technical staff heads—i.e. the regional finance, personnel, and administrative service officers. The existence of business managers would also compromise, if not depreciate, the responsibilities and independence of the technical staff heads. Sooy countered that the presence of business managers would have no such effect.

Starkey commented that he could not understand the position of Sooy and the Administrative Services Division. Why was it not clear to them that management functions simply could not be decentralized as long as program authority remained predominantly centralized? Could they not see that this circumstance eliminated any need that might otherwise exist for overall administrative policy-making at the regional level?

Since the arguments were becoming repetitive, Starkey suggested that the meeting be adjourned, to be resumed on the following Monday, March 28.

The March 28 meeting saw a recapitulation of the arguments advanced in the earlier session. In view of its inconclusiveness, Starkey proposed deferring additional discussion until Wednesday, March 30.

At the Wednesday session Starkey suggested that, since compromise seemed a long way off and there were many other urgent problems demanding attention, the Work Group discontinue discussing this question. He proposed that Sooy and Struttmann each prepare a memorandum presenting his views on the need for regional business managers, and that these, together with Harris' original memorandum and a memorandum listing advantages and disadvantages of each alternative to be prepared by himself, be forwarded to Spencer for study and decision.

The memoranda were sent to Spencer on April 7. Sooy's and Struttmann's memoranda repeated their oral arguments. Starkey's summary memorandum, besides listing advantages and disadvantages of the alternatives, identified a third course: establishing what he termed "regional coordinator and expediter" positions. These positions would allow the assistant administrator for management to have a direct representative coordinating "across-the-board" functions like space assignments in each regional business office. Yet, since the men in these positions would lack authority over the internal substance of regional management staff operations, this third course would not impair relationships between the regional management staffs and their respective management divisions. Moreover, regional coordinators would provide a single local point of contact for program and management staffs on business matters within any given region, a consideration that everyone concerned felt was important.

On April 8 Spencer distributed these memoranda to members of his top management staff—Special Assistant Donovan; Division Directors Starkey, Stephens, and Williams; and Assistant Budget and Finance Division Director Kirkham—and to Program Inspection and Internal Audit Director Kenneth A. Butler. His covering memorandum did not state his own preference.

On Wednesday of the following week, April 13, Spencer reported in a memorandum to Administrator Shaw that the question had been considered by the top management staff and Butler at two meetings earlier in the week, and at the end there had still been "divided opinion—some of the staff feeling that better results would be secured under Plan I [having business managers] and others under Plan II [not having business managers]. Neither group felt, however, that success or failure depended on which plan was adopted. In other words, there was agreement that we could use either plan and do a good job." Then Spencer stated that "after weighing the several considerations and giving the full weight to the views of the staff members," he would recommend adopting "the organization contemplated in Plan I." His reasons were:

> It seems highly important to have a recognized responsible head in each of the regional business offices. To do otherwise would lead to confusion among the people in the office and also in the minds of program people served by the office.
>
> Much more effective contacts can be maintained with field program offices if this is primarily the responsibility of one man. . . . This is particularly important in gaining acceptance of the idea of a regional organization.
>
> The danger of this plan causing confusion with the management divisions in Washington is, I think, not so great as it might be feared. I base this feeling on the fact that the plan was used in both the former Bureau of Agricultural and Industrial Chemistry and the Bureau of Entomology and Plant Quarantine with satisfactory results. While it is true that neither of these situations quite parallels the one we shall have, I think that overall the same principles would apply.
>
> Should the regionalization idea expand into some area of program work (and it is not unreasonable to expect this might happen), Plan I would be much better adapted to such a development than Plan II.

That afternoon Shaw called Spencer to his office and told him to go ahead on the basis of Plan I.

CONCILIATION AND ACTION

April 1955–December 1955

At about the time it was decided to have regional business managers (April 13), the subsidiary work groups began their long-prepared-for discussions with the chiefs and administrative officers of those fourteen program branches headquartered in Washington and Beltsville that had field organizations. (The four field utilization research branches were to be handled separately at a later date.) To minimize overall program management conflict and to keep program opposition unorganized, program branches were approached individually on separate occasions by the subsidiary work groups. Each work group took the initiative in these meetings by discussing management division opinions regarding the functions to be regionalized. Thus it became the responsibility of the program branch to identify reasons why certain of its business activities should remain at the branch headquarters level.

The subsidiary work groups found the leaders of the fourteen branches still maintaining the various positions they had assumed at Spencer's earlier meeting with them. The four Plant Industry and two Animal Industry research branches, in particular, opposed the whole idea of regionalization. Since they comprised the largest group of the production research branches, with over two-thirds of the field organization, their opposition posed a serious problem. They were not sympathetic to the view of the management divisions that, in effect, it was the administrator, speaking through his agents, the management divisions, who was telling the program units how their operations would be conducted.

The program branches reasoned this way: If management division-type functions performed by their branch business offices were to be transferred to the regional business offices, then probably their branch business offices would be deprived of the staff positions and funds devoted to performance of these functions. Should this occur, they would be deprived of both the authority and the facilities for effective direction and control of field operations and would be dependent upon information from the management divisions and regional business offices to run their own programs. On the one hand, the branches would be held administratively responsible for results in their program areas, while on the other, they would lack direct control of the "tools" considered essential for producing those results.

At this stage, the view of the management divisions was that maintaining duplicate or complementary staffs would be indefensible. As members of the subsidiary work groups explained to the branch officials, the units primarily involved in the transfers would be business offices of the four Plant Industry branches and the four field utilization branches. However, the work group members added, it was not possible at that time to identify precisely either the branches or the number of positions and the amount of funds involved. These facts could be determined only after the subsidiary work groups had completed their discussions and the members of the Regionalization Work Group had talked with individual branch administrative officers. Meanwhile the branch officials were assured that the management divisions would not cavalierly dismantle any branch business offices.

The leaders of the three branches of the old BEPQ—Entomology Research, Plant Pest Control, and Plant Quarantine—gave full cooperation after becoming convinced that (1) the "non-cross-servicing" requirement, to which they had objected, was a departmental requirement not of the management divisions' own making, and (2) the reassignment rights of the employees in the four Field Business Offices would be scrupulously observed in staffing the new regional business offices.

Officials of the three animal regulatory branches —Animal Disease Eradication, Animal Inspection and Quarantine, and Meat Inspection—cooperated with the management divisions throughout the discussions. Like the Plant and Animal Industry research branches and the BEPQ branches, most of their work was done in the field, and they had a major stake in regionalization. While they believed centralized common business services were better suited to the needs and requirements of their own centralized programs, they were willing to rely upon the management divisions to determine how best to organize and conduct business services in ARS. Their ready cooperation could be partially explained by the fact that, unlike the production research branches, many of their field business services were provided by on-site administrative people and, accordingly, their small branch business offices would probably not be made the subject of management division "raids."

Leaders of these branches made it clear, however, that their cooperation was based on the assumption that the management divisions were proposing to decentralize only routine business services. These officials had never cared strongly about who performed such services, as long as they were effectively performed, but if substantive management functions were to be involved, the position of these branch officials would be quite different. As they explained to the subsidiary work groups, they could not maintain control of their programs if substantive management functions were decentralized. Dr. Miller, Chief of the Meat Inspection Branch, told the Personnel Division's work group that this branch would soon be in difficulty if, for example, the function of setting overtime rates for meat inspectors was decentralized from the Personnel Division to five widely separated regional business offices. These overtime rates were charged against the private meat-packing establishments requesting the service. The industry regulated was extremely competitive; the federal force inspecting the industry was unionized nationally; and there could be explosive consequences for the whole program if regional variations in overtime rates occurred.

The management divisions were quite willing to conciliate the branches on some points. While the branches considered the points on which concessions were made as basic to their own requirements, the divisions regarded these points as of minor significance. The management divisions and, as it turned out, Administrator Shaw were willing to compromise on almost all issues but one: Spencer wrote Shaw on April 27 that "agreement" had been "brought about . . . on a number of points but [the discussions] have emphasized one basic obstacle. . . . The great majority of branches feel the necessity of retaining a large degree of control over actual business operations in the field. . . . A continuation of the present administrative operations in the branches added to the cost of a regionalized ARS business organization will, in addition to involving lost motion and a considerable degree of duplication, be very much more costly than the present system." It might therefore become necessary for Shaw "to say to a branch that in the interest of overall good management, we simply cannot permit the continuance of their present business organizations and procedures."

> The question, of course, cannot be divorced from program considerations. I think the greatest stumbling block to what we hope to accomplish is the very general feeling which runs throughout the organization that each branch, and in fact each section, has a vested interest in the funds allotted to it. This necessitates in the minds of the branch people the maintenance of actual financial records, in all cases at the branch and in some cases at the section level. Another factor is the feeling that a field man should not be bothered with any financial details. Neither of these concepts squares with the conduct of any effective program of regional business operations.

Management Division "Concessions"

There were four major management division concessions, or so it appeared to program officials. In the first place, Spencer had agreed in his initial meeting with program officials that the branches would be individually consulted with respect to their needs and requirements. However, as Shaw's directive announcing regionalization indicated, the management divisions had, from the first, intended to consult the program branches.

Second, the management divisions had decided to establish regional business manager positions and to appoint to such positions persons eminently satisfactory to program officials, largely as a means of reducing program opposition to regionalization. But Spencer favored having business managers even aside from this consideration of winning program support, and all the persons appointed business managers were competent officials experienced in handling business affairs at the operating level.

Third, the management divisions concluded from their discussions with program branches headquartered in Washington and Beltsville that substantive management functions could not be decentralized.

The fourth apparent compromise also resulted from the discussions with the branches. The management divisions agreed to schedule the assumption of functions by the regional business offices so as to cause the least possible disruption of program branch operations. Scheduling the regionalization of functions over an extended period of time suited the convenience of the management divisions as much as it did the wishes of the branches.

The management divisions did not know how far several of the program branches would go in opposing the regionalization, nor did they know how deep-seated the opposition was. Would these branches try to encourage sentiment against regionalization among the client groups, which in turn would prevail upon Congress and the Department to call off the decentralization? Or, failing this, would internal program opposition still be so strong that the Administrator would finally withdraw his support of the management divisions? He was abstractly in favor of regionalization, but would he favor it in the face of organized opposition? There was undoubtedly a point beyond which the Administrator could not afford, either for his own good or for "the good of the Service," to support staff services against the line. What was this point?

These were some of the questions that the management divisions could not answer. To their officials, perhaps the only way to aid their cause was to take the plan directly to the program branches in the hope that, at best, the branches could be educated to accept the need for regionalization or, at worst, the force of their opposition could be blunted and neutralized.

Then, too, for long-run as well as short-run considerations the management divisions could not afford to seem dictatorial. Even if program units did not seek or secure aid from their client groups, and even if the Administrator stood by the management divisions, who could say how long either of these situations might continue?

External Complaints

Actually, there were only two sources of complaint from outside the agency. Early in June, Administrator Shaw received a letter from Congressman Jamie L. Whitten of Mississippi, then ranking minority member of the House Agricultural Appropriations Subcommittee. Whitten had heard from constituents in Mississippi that the Southern Field Business Office at Gulfport was to be closed before the end of June, and he wondered what reasons ARS had for closing an office of some importance to the economy of Gulfport. Shaw wrote immediately, developing some of the background reasons for the decentralization and dealing in more detail with the reasons for closing the Gulfport office. It was much more sensible, he wrote, to locate the Southern Regional Business Office at New Orleans, a natural communication and transportation center for the ARS Southern Region. He informed Whitten that all Gulfport office employees who wished to transfer to the new office in New Orleans could do so, with ARS paying their moving expenses. This answered Whitten's query, and he dropped the matter.

The second source of complaint was the Meat Inspectors Union, the nationwide bargaining agent for the meat inspection force employed by the Meat Inspection Branch. When the officers and members heard about the impending regionalization, they flooded Washington with hundreds of letters expressing fear that their pay checks would be delayed under the new setup. They seemed satisfied with the explanation that, among other purposes, the regionalization was being carried out to speed up payrolling and other fiscal functions.

In retrospect there appeared to be several reasons why Congress and the client groups failed to challenge regionalization, even though many of the program branch officials at first had been ready to take up arms. The management divisions had consulted and partly persuaded the opposing program units, thereby neutralizing some of the hostility within the agency. Many of the interested outsiders were sympathetic to Secretary Benson's goal of adapting "the administration of the programs of the Department to regional, state, and local conditions" and, in cases where they knew about it, no doubt viewed the impending regionalization as another step in that direction. As noted previously, they were pleased with the expanded programs of agricultural research and regulation. Finally, there is a question whether, attuned to program considerations, they would have construed administrative rearrangements, chiefly affecting business services to agency personnel, as threats to their pet programs. In any event, the battle over regionalization was fought out within ARS and the Department.

The Decisions Are Approved

Early in May, Shaw approved the final determinations of the management divisions on the distribution of business and management functions between the management divisions, the regional business offices, the program branch business offices, and the field stations. The Department approved these determinations around May 20. In general, the management divisions retained all substantive management functions, while routine

FIGURE 5: LINES OF BUSINESS COMMUNICATIONS BETWEEN FIELD STATIONS AND REGIONAL BUSINESS OFFICES AFTER REGIONALIZATION

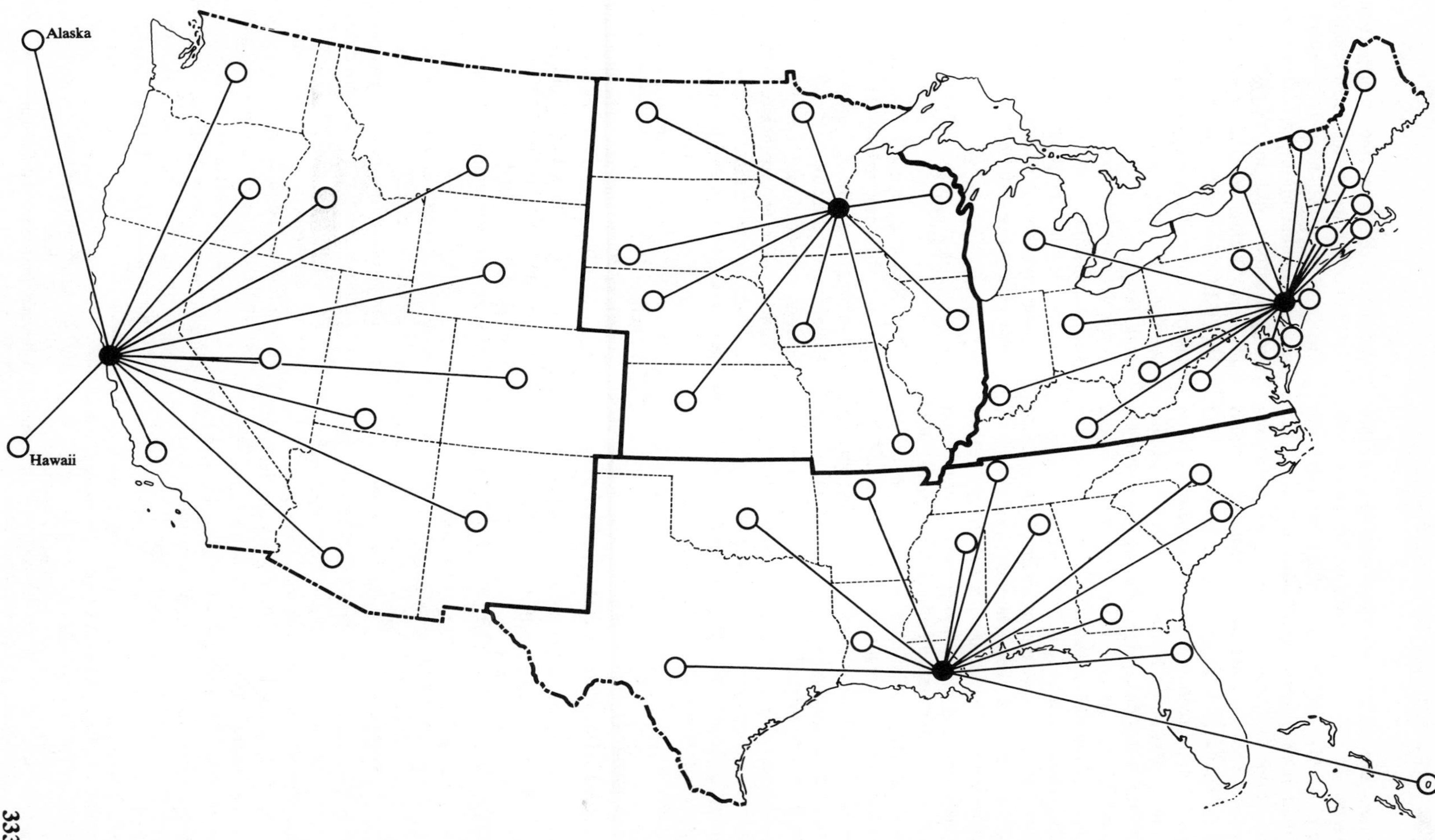

business services, largely of a processing character, were decentralized to the regional business offices. The program branch business offices were left with all their internal management and business functions except for those operational and processing functions now assumed by the regional business offices. Shaw let it be understood, however, that those functions remaining in the program branches would be performed to complement, not conflict with, the functions performed by the business offices. Finally, operations to be performed by field stations for themselves were considerably expanded on a uniform, across-the-board basis.

Thus, officials of the management divisions could boast, though none did so publicly, that the battle had been won. They had been able to regionalize business services and had succeeded in reorganizing business and management affairs throughout ARS, even in the program branches.

In discussing regionalization later, Spencer expressed his gratitude for "the fine support of administrative management by the Administrator and the Deputy Administrators. . . . Not once have the Administrator or his deputies wavered in their support of a sound program of administrative management and without that support, of course, the entire situation would have been impossible."

Office Locations and Regional Boundaries Established

Regional business office locations and regional boundaries were finally settled about May 20. By then, total employment in the agency had grown to approximately 18,500—a rise of 5,500 in eighteen months.[11] Arguing that to serve 6,800 employees in Washington-Beltsville and the Eastern Region from the management divisions in Washington would be inefficient and would mean that only slightly over half of the agency was regionalized, Spencer convinced the Department staff offices about May 15 that two locations were needed. It was decided, accordingly, to set up an Eastern Regional Business Office in the utilization branch laboratory in Philadelphia to service the 3,600 employees in seventeen northeastern states, and to service the 3,200 employees in the Washington-Beltsville area from the management divisions.

Other offices were established to serve the Northern Region at Minneapolis, serving 4,400 employees in nine midwestern states; the Southern Region at New Orleans, serving 4,600 employees in eleven states, Mexico, Puerto Rico, and the Virgin Islands; and the Western Region at the utilization branch laboratory in Albany, California, serving 2,700 employees in eleven states and Alaska and Hawaii.[12]

Finally program branches were directed to "make such administrative arrangements as are necessary to operate through appropriate regional offices without regard to whether program operations cross regional boundaries."

Business Managers Selected

By May 20 Spencer had selected the four regional business managers and cleared their appointments at the GS-13 grade level with the Department's director of finance and director of personnel. Ameigh, Business Manager of the Field Business Office at Greenfield, Massachusetts, was now officially appointed Northern Regional Business Manager. Regional Business Manager for the Southern Region was Earl D. Sharar, Administrative Officer of the Horticultural Crops Research Branch and for years associated with the former Bureau of Plant Industry. The other two Regional Business Managers were both drawn from the utilization research branches; Sidney J. Adams had been Business Manager of the Western Branch, and Paul K. Knierim had been Business Manager of the Eastern Branch.

The program officials were pleased that all of the business managers had had previous experience as administrative officers in program units. The appointment of the business managers of two of the utilization research branches also dulled the opposition that had been evident earlier in the month when the members of the Regionalization Work Group had talked with the business officers of the four utilization research branches; so did the location of regional business offices in three of the cities—Albany, New Orleans, and Philadelphia—where these branches were situated. Now the Northern Branch at Peoria was left in lonely opposition.

---

[11] Most of the increase was attributable to the large number of veterinarians hired on a fee basis under special authority beginning in November 1954. By this means the government was able to compete for their services; about 4,000 fee-basis veterinarians were employed by ARS by late May 1955.

[12] Official departmental approval was not recorded until later. Shaw requested formal approval, for the record, in a letter dated June 21; Roberts gave it on June 23.

Transfer of the Branch Business Staffs

With the locations and staffs of the offices agreed on, positions and funds directly associated with functions being decentralized to the regional business offices were withdrawn from the branch business offices. As expected, only the four field utilization branches and the four Plant Industry branches were fundamentally affected. In addition, minor positions related to payrolling were transferred from the five old Bureau of Animal Industry branches to the regional business offices. In the case of the Eastern and Western Utilization Research Branches, the transfers were primarily paper transactions, as the Eastern and Western Regional Business Offices were located in these branch laboratory buildings. Existing patterns of service were not to be significantly altered.

All of these branches, in the opinion of the management divisions, were left with sufficient business office staffs to take care of strictly internal branch requirements. The Regionalization Work Group members felt that withdrawals should be made only in the interests of overall consistency and did their best to make it clear to the branch administrative officer concerned that withdrawn positions and funds were being transferred, not discontinued, and that the business function to which the positions and funds referred would be the responsibility of the regional business offices and, above them, the management divisions. Nevertheless, officials of the Northern Utilization Research Branch and the four Plant Industry branches remained unhappy about the withdrawals. They believed that their business offices could perform the functions that had been transferred better than could the regional business offices.

About June 1, the Regionalization Work Group decided that the four Field Business Offices of the BEPQ branches would be abolished and their funds transferred on a staggered basis between June 15 and June 20. In follow-up instructions to these offices, persons who chose to transfer were advised that they would be moved at government expense to the nearest regional business office.

The Business Offices Are Staffed

Following a week of indoctrination by the management divisions, the regional business managers were dispatched to their new offices about June 1. Between then and July 1, persons were recruited from the management divisions to serve as technical staff heads in the offices. The Department allocated these positions at the GS-12 grade level, a level that proved high enough to attract experienced persons. Although many officials in the management divisions felt that more experienced people could have been attracted if the grade level had been GS-13, there were few who believed that the existence of business managers actually had a depressing effect on the grade level of the technical staff heads. By July 1, subordinate professional and clerical staff members were transferred to the new regional offices from the management divisions, the liquidated field business offices, the field utilization branch business offices, and the Plant Industry branch business offices in Beltsville. Some staff was recruited locally.

By June 24, the decentralization of functions and authorities had been scheduled, procedures had been developed for initial operation of the transferred functions, and all ARS units and employees were informed of appropriate transfer dates. Many common business functions and authorities were assumed by the regional business offices on July 1:

(1) Administrative Services—Operational matters concerned with procurement and records management.

(2) Finance—Payroll, leave, and retirement, and related accounting for all field employees of the former BEPQ branches and the field utilization research branches, and for certain field employees of all other branches except those from the former Bureau of Animal Industry; voucher examination for all units and employees; accounting for all funds other than those payrolls not yet decentralized; and fiscal reconciliations and reports relating to decentralized functions.

Remaining routine business functions and authorities scheduled for decentralization were assumed by the regional business offices at intervals between July 1 and December 31:

(1) Personnel—Classification activities for nonprofessional positions in the lower grades; employment functions, including records and reports; and operational matters concerned with employee development and safety.

(2) Administrative Services—Operational matters concerning real and personal property management, including records.

(3) Finance—Payroll, leave, retirement, and related accounting and fiscal reconciliations and reports for all field employees whose payrolls had not been decentralized on July 1.

By January 1, 1956, the regional business offices were completely staffed and in full and orderly operation. The administrative and business functions of ARS had been regionalized. The common-service-type business operations were being handled on a uniform organizational and procedural basis. Field stations of all program units had been given comparable authority and responsibility over their administrative matters. Largely eliminated were those functions performed in certain program units, which had duplicated or overlapped those provided by the management divisions and regional business offices. Except for those services provided to employees in the Washington-Beltsville area, the management divisions at ARS headquarters were freed of direct operational responsibility for business services and had the time to develop agency-wide administrative policies and procedures. These divisions retained responsibility for the so-called substantive management functions. And all branch business offices were restricted to the internal business matters of their respective branches.

CASE TWO: *A Business Office for the West*

THE GRASS ROOTS: THE AGRICULTURAL RESEARCH SERVICE IN THE WEST

Most of the work of the Agricultural Research Service is conducted in what Washington usually refers to as the "field." In ARS this word may be used literally. Much agricultural research, in fact, is beneath the field; and most of it concerns the earth and its products. ARS deals with products from a large segment of the vegetable and animal world, with the conditions that foster, prevent, or damage their growth, and with their human utilization. The subjects of its concern include a great variety of meat and vegetable products, clothing, hard goods, fertilizers, grasshoppers, soil samples, home and farm economies, and poisons.

Most ARS researchers are professionals: entomologists, veterinarians, chemists, engineers, economists, nutritionists, agronomists, pathologists, and many others. Many of them work in relative isolation at places distant from other stations. Some work on the same small piece of ground from month to month and year to year. These factors, in addition to the project approach to their work, contributed to a relatively high degree of individual autonomy from others and from other parts of the ARS organization.

Nowhere were these characteristics more marked than in the West—in those areas that were to constitute the "western region" of ARS. This region comprehended 275 field stations and 2,700 personnel in the eleven western states and the territories of Alaska and Hawaii (which had then not yet acquired statehood). The programs carried on in these 275 stations represented all but five of the twenty-one program branches of ARS and ranged in size from one man to nearly 300. By far the greater number were of the small, one- to five-man, relatively autonomous type. One of the western field researchers described the region in this way:

> Most of the ARS employees out here are of the "mud on the shoes" variety. Most of us have a plot of land, a laboratory table, or a stock yard and do our own research. Perhaps regulatory people are different—I really don't know—but those of us in research lead a rather individual existence and tend mainly to develop relationships with others in our professional field. I have friends in entomology all over the world, and we keep in close contact.

Organizationally, the lines of loyalty, of professional specialization, of communication, and of command ran directly between the field stations and the program branches in Washington (known, until 1954, as the bureaus). Until 1955 ARS had no intermediary regional organization of any kind, although a minority of the branches (and employees) handled their business affairs through regional branch business offices. There had been wide variation among the different branches in the degree to which they had delegated authority over either program or administrative matters to the field stations. But in virtually all cases the focus and the seat of authority had been the Washington headquarters office of the branch, and its relationship to its field stations was direct.

FIGURE 6:

A MAP OF THE WESTERN REGION OF THE AGRICULTURAL RESEARCH SERVICE SHOWING THE APPROXIMATE LOCATION OF FIELD STATIONS*

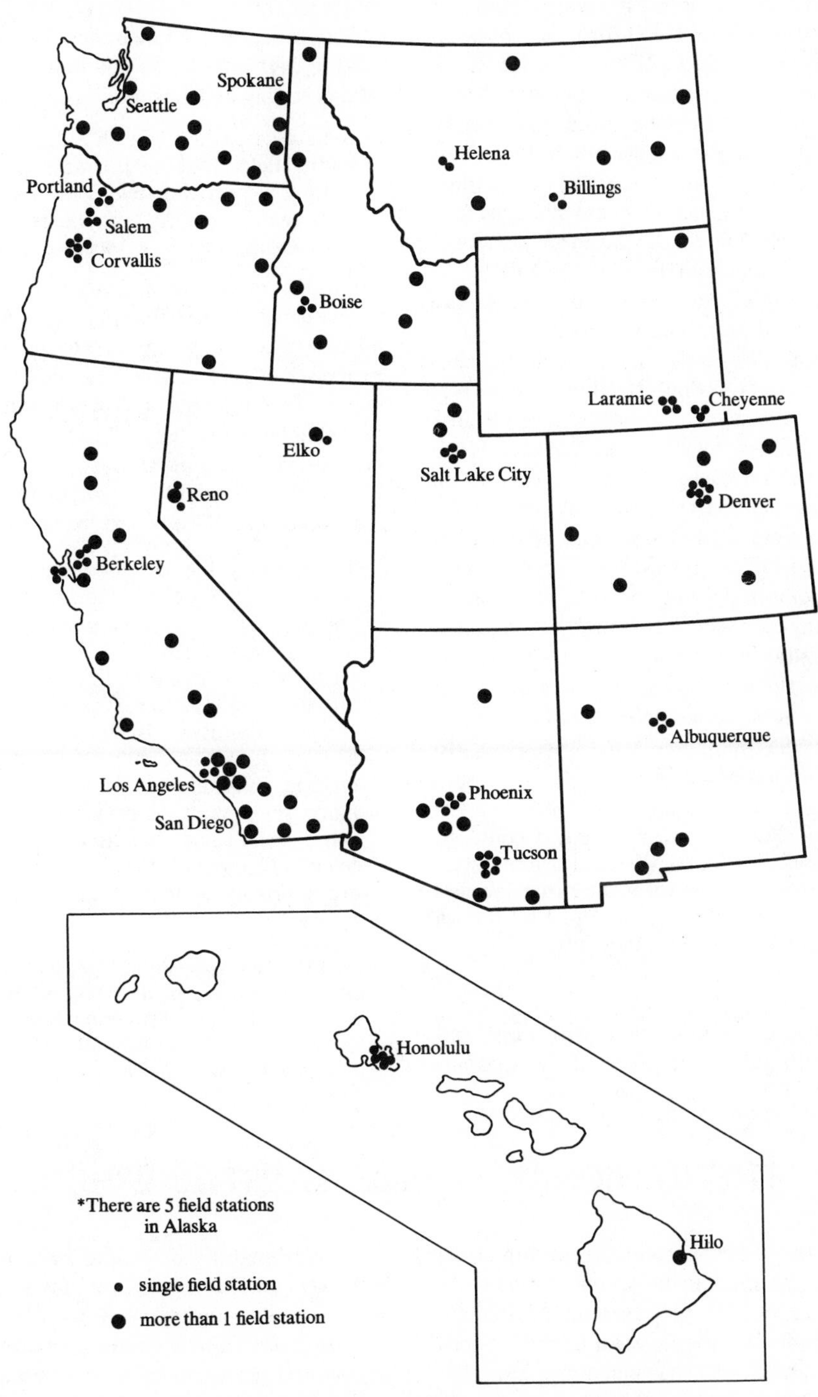

The Benson reorganization and the changes that ensued in ARS in 1953 and 1954 had not fundamentally modified the organizations, the ways of operating, the research projects, or the attitudes in the field. In the West, the most "reorganized" of the old bureaus had been the Bureau of Entomology and Plant Quarantine (BEPQ). Its forest research and control projects, and its personnel, had been transferred to the Forest Service. Each of the three remaining parts, Plant Quarantine, Plant Pest Control, and Entomology Research, had gained branch status. The impact of these changes had been most severely felt by the business personnel of the dismembered bureau. In 1947 the BEPQ had opened five Regional Administrative Offices. The office serving its western area was located in Oakland, California. As a result of the 1954 reorganization, the Oakland Administration Office was closed, and its records and authorities were transferred to the Business Office of the Western Utilization Research and Development Laboratory in Albany, California. The employees of the administrative office were offered positions in the Laboratory Business Office and various Forest Service field business offices. During the transition period a general feeling of insecurity was felt among these bureau administrative office employees. As one former employee stated, "For a few weeks late in 1953 we were out building apple carts. I, and most of the others, did not know what was going to happen next." Another stated:

> Sure I had a choice of reassignment. I could go with the Forest Service in Missoula, Montana or Portland, Oregon. I did not want either job and would have had to take a grade cut. I set out on accumulated leave to find a new job.

Eventually many of the employees of the closed administrative office took positions with the Western Regional Administrative Office of the Agricultural Marketing Service (AMS).[13] Some remained with ARS by taking positions at the Western Utilization Laboratory business office. Others transferred to the Forest Service, and a few left federal employment.

The professional researchers in the field did not hold in high repute the routines and the drudgery of day-to-day business administration. As one said:

> Believe me, when I finish a day's work, be it out in the field, looking through a microscope, or writing a journal article, I do not want to spend my evening reading complicated business directives about fancy new business procedures.

From the researcher's viewpoint, "business services" meant processing papers, and a "business office" meant a place where those papers were processed. There was at the same time, as in Washington, fear that business work and business personnel might infringe upon the decisions and the policies necessary to the accomplishment of programs. One field scientist in the Crops Research area expressed this concern in the following terms:

> The country has assigned the ARS a mission. It is the duty of the researcher to fulfill this mission. We are professional men and have professional responsibilities. In regard to business services, we all realize that they are necessary, but they are a necessary evil—a means, not an end in themselves. Business forms, procedures, and so on must be subordinate to the research mission. Business personnel, regardless of how many there may be or where they may be located, must remember that they are in existence solely to serve the program people. If the program branch is to be responsible, it must set policy.

[13] In 1954 the Agricultural Marketing Service took over the quarters of the Oakland Bureau of Entomology and Plant Quarantine Administrative Office to provide administrative services for AMS employees on a regional basis.

THE REGIONAL OFFICE IS ESTABLISHED

Rumors of the possible regionalization of fiscal affairs reached the field in the spring of 1954. As Washington had not, as yet, formulated definite plans, the rumors were vague. Most of the western field research and regulatory personnel gave the rumors only passing attention. Many of them were dissatisfied with the service they were receiving from Washington and would have welcomed any improvement. However, any favorable comment on change was always made with the qualification that *program direction* must remain with program people and not be given to business personnel.

The first authoritative, though unofficial, news of the regionalization proposal apparently reached the

West as a result of a meeting of utilization research branch chiefs in Washington late in February 1955. Such meetings, periodically held by the different program organizations with their top field officials, were usually intended to discuss current activities and to project plans for the future. In the February meeting, Dr. Michael J. Copley, Director of the Western Utilization Research Branch, was told about the regionalization proposal. (His branch occupied a large laboratory building in Albany, California.) He and the four other chiefs of utilization branches[14] also learned that Management was contemplating the use of the Western and Eastern (Philadelphia) Laboratories to house two of the new business offices. All four field branch chiefs opposed the regionalization plan in general and opposed specifically the location of the proposed new business offices in any of their laboratory buildings. They pointed out that the location of business offices in the laboratories would cause an extreme crowding of scientific personnel in facilities traditionally dedicated to research; that they were using or had plans for the use of all available floor space; and that to allocate adequate space for a regional business office would definitely hamper their primary objective, utilization research. They argued further that they had complete business decentralization (each laboratory had its own business office) and that the planned ARS regionalization, for them at least, amounted to centralization.

These arguments seemingly had little effect upon the ultimate decisions made in Washington, and there were few if any other occasions when field personnel were asked to participate in the formulation of plans. They were, however, asked to submit reports on various aspects of the proposed regionalization. This they did. They were then informed as decisions were made in Washington.

The official announcements of regionalization (described in Case One) were received in the field shortly after March 1, 1955. With only four months to go before the July 1 regionalization deadline went into effect, there was little time available to review plans with field personnel. Even a field business official like Sidney Adams, then the Business Manager of the Western Utilization Research Branch, did not participate during the early stages of planning for regionalization. He stated:

> I was informed of significant decisions as they were made. However, most of my information regarding developments of the regionalization plan, I learned in the form of informal conversations with associates in Washington.

Speaking about the program personnel (researchers) in the western states, Adams stated:

> I doubt, unless they had friends or associates in Washington, that they would have known what current progress was being made in regard to regionalization.

The official announcement of regionalization seems to have been accorded an unfriendly reception by many of the research men in the western region. One researcher recalled:

> Regionalization was just one of those things. We were not given a chance to say anything about it. Management told us on March 1 that it was coming on July 1, and that was that. Most of us had heard rumors, but like most rumors there wasn't much detail or, for that matter, accuracy. I don't think there was much anyone could have done if he had wanted to oppose it.

A researcher in the Production Economics Branch had this to say of the announcement:

> The March 1 notice did not surprise anyone. There were rumors about area finance offices and then about complete regionalization. All of us heard something, but none of us knew anything for certain. No one asked us what we would like. It is probably a good thing that we were not asked to contribute. Whenever there is change there are always some who will oppose it—just because it is change. You can't do much opposing in four months, after the fact, or at least after the announcement. I can only speak for myself, but I think that most of the field program people just accepted the announcement as an announcement of fact and waited to see what it would be like in operation. Everyone would have had something to say, but most of us had a false conception of what regionalization was all about.

From the viewpoint of the administrative personnel in the field, the process of business service regionalization had three main phases following the decision and its announcement: (1) the location of the regional business office, (2) staffing, and (3) promulgation of authorities and procedures. These processes took four months, from March 1 to June 30, 1955. Because they overlapped, each is discussed here in turn, much as the officials in the field were required to consider and deal with them.

[14] The others were located in laboratory buildings in New Orleans, Peoria, Philadelphia, and Washington.

The Albany Location

On March 3, 1955, Copley, the Director of the Western Utilization Branch in Albany, California, received from Walter Scott, Assistant Director of Utilization Research, copies of the March 1 notices with an attached memorandum stating that a decision had not been made by Management about the use of laboratories in connection with regionalization. Scott went on to say that a decision was expected soon and that he would notify Copley when it was made. Later in March Spencer sent to the Western Laboratory (Albany, California) Mackay White, of the Department of Agriculture's Office of Plant and Operations, and Charles Burdette, of his Administrative Services Division, to make a space survey of the building. Following discussions with laboratory personnel and a complete examination of the laboratory building, White and Burdette forwarded their report to Spencer without recommendation. They merely reported, in great detail, the facts of the space allocation.

On March 29, 1955, Copley received a memo from Shaw stating that consideration had been given the space survey of White and Burdette and that "we have also reviewed carefully the material submitted by Dr. Walter Scott . . ." and have "determined that the office to serve the western region can best be located at the regional laboratory in Albany, California. . . ." Shaw added that:

> I have indicated to my staff here that I feel the lobby should be left undisturbed, that a room or other appropriate space should be provided for Washington representatives' use, that an auditorium should be maintained, and that, if necessary, some utilization as business offices could be made of properly refitted windowed basement space. In providing for retention of auditorium space, I have in mind that a large conference room, which I feel is highly desirable, could be included in one end of the auditorium through the use of folding doors.

Shaw's memorandum concluded by stating that a member of his staff would be sent to "effect the necessary arrangements. . . ." On this staff member's arrival in Albany, Copley was informed that Shaw felt that 8,500 square feet, approximately one-sixth of the laboratory building, would be adequate to meet the needs of the Western Regional Business Office (WRBO).

On April 26, 27, and 28, conferences concerning the allocation of floor space were held with Copley, Adams, and Shaw's representative. Thereafter it was reported to Spencer that agreement had been reached and that the Regional Business Office would be allocated 8,161 square feet.

In response to this report, Shaw, on May 3, wrote to Copley:

> I have had an opportunity to read the report of the discussions with you last week concerning space arrangements at the Western Regional Laboratory for the ARS Western Regional Business Office which is in the process of being established. As I mentioned in my memorandum to you of March 29, I was sure you would give your full cooperation in meeting this situation and I am happy to know that your discussions were most cordial and understanding.
>
> With these space arrangements completed, it is hoped that action may follow rather promptly looking to the organization of the staff for this new business office and the inauguration of this activity.

On June 1 Copley wrote to Spencer that he and Adams had reviewed the modifications necessary for the housing of the Regional Business Office and estimated the cost to be about $26,000. Following this, authorization was granted to proceed. The funds came from Management. The matters of rent, payment of utilities, and the like were left for later negotiations between the laboratory and the WRBO.

Staffing the Business Office

At the same time that Management, Washington, was making final arrangements for housing the WRBO, it was also formulating plans about office personnel. On March 21, 1955, Spencer asked the Western Utilization Research Laboratory to make a survey of all its personnel "attached to the business office who are engaged full- or part-time in business functions."

A report was prepared by Adams; in it he discussed thirty-eight persons who were working full-time on business activities, assigning to each the percentage of time devoted to the various business activities: personnel, administrative services, fiscal, budgeting, voucher examination, etc. The report was forwarded to the Management Personnel Division on March 29.

On April 20 Spencer sent a memorandum to Copley which read in part:

> By this time Mr. Adams has no doubt discussed with you my telephone call to him this afternoon in which I offered and he accepted the job of Regional Business Manager for the western region.

This notice served as an official announcement to Copley. From the beginning of the regionalization discussions, it was generally believed that Adams would be offered and would accept the manager's job.[15]

During the first week of May, Adams was in Washington to attend a meeting of the Regionalization Work Group and Utilization Research Branch representatives. According to official documents, the purposes of this meeting were:

> (1) To identify internal management and related staff requirements of utilization research branches under regionalization.
>
> (2) To determine some common service functions to be carried out by regional and Washington offices for utilization research branches.
>
> (3) To consider administrative and other arrangements necessary to the servicing of the utilization research branches.
>
> (4) To distinguish different requirements (if any) of Northern and Eastern as against Western and Southern Utilization Research Branches.
>
> (5) To schedule transfer of common service functions from utilization research branches to regional and Washington offices.

Adams recalls that while the "size or composition of either the Laboratory or the Regional Business Office's staff" was not discussed at the meetings, he and members of the Personnel Division went over his report of the previous week. On the basis of Adams' memorandum and his informal discussions with Personnel Division, Management decided on the size of the business staff that was to remain at the laboratory. On May 24 Spencer sent the following to Copley:

> As a result of this review [the staff inventory submitted by Adams] it has been concluded that your current staff will need to be adjusted to the below listed [seventeen] positions.

Thus it was decided that the laboratory would retain a business staff approximately one-half its former size to carry out internal business matters, prepare forms to be sent to the Regional Business Office, prepare position descriptions, and the like. Twenty-one of its former business staff were to be transferred to the WRBO.

By a somewhat more complicated process the ultimate size of the WRBO staff was set at seventy-five. It was expected that as WRBO assumed broader functions, the staff would be expanded until, in December, it would reach this total. This figure, seventy-five, was determined in Washington by Management from studies of anticipated workload and "time necessary to perform functions."

By a similar process Management also set the grade level of WRBO employees. To establish a grade level for particular positions, Management, through the position classification process, first set the grade of the regional business manager at GS-13 and that of his section heads at GS-12. After this had been done, the grade levels of lower positions were established.

On the basis of Spencer's memorandum and a "go ahead" from Copley, Adams set out to staff the WRBO. His first task was to divide the laboratory's business staff.

Adams' decisions regarding these personnel were primarily predetermined by the functions performed by the employees. All the employees in the Mail, File, and Receiving units, for example, were left at the laboratory. Those who had been examining vouchers and payrolls, functions no longer to be performed at the laboratory, were assigned to the WRBO.

In dividing the staff Adams gave his assistant and his section heads an opportunity to indicate their preference. I. J. Girgich, Assistant Business Manager, chose to remain at the laboratory and assume the position of Business Manager. Girgich described the transition period in these terms:

> Adams gave me a long time to make up my mind. He kept the position of Head of Administrative Services in the Regional Office open for about six months, and I could have moved into it. However, for personal reasons, I decided to stay on at the Laboratory.

---

[15] Official public announcement of Adams' appointment was made to all other field personnel on June 9 when Shaw sent the following to "All Divisions, Branches and Field Stations": "Mr. Adams, who has an LLB degree from Columbia University, has been employed by the Department of Agriculture since 1931. Following some years of service in the Bureau of Plant Industry, Soils and Agricultural Engineering, he was appointed in connection with administrative work in the Bureau of Agricultural and Industrial Chemistry in 1941 and has since been associated with that Bureau and its successor organizations. His service has included a period as Deputy to the Assistant Chief of Bureau for Administration and as Business Manager of the Western Utilization Research Branch, which position he now holds."

Three of Adams' section heads, however, chose to follow him to the WRBO where they all assumed responsible positions at higher grades.

The laboratory's business staff did not show much concern about placement. Adams' section heads knew that there were places for them in one or the other organization. One of them summed up the general attitude: "It was nothing like 1954 during the reorganization. At least this time we knew we had jobs either with the Laboratory or with the WRBO, and in either case they would be good ones."

An employee in the receiving room of the laboratory's business office recalled that he first heard that the regional office was going to be located in San Francisco, about forty-five minutes' commuting time from Albany. "When I heard that, I did not want to be transferred. I took this job in Albany in order to avoid commuting. Later I heard that the new office was going to be in the same building. Even then it didn't make much difference to me. I knew I had a job."

There was only one reported case of dissatisfaction with the placement decisions. In this case the section head in charge of Fiscal Operations wanted very much to be transferred. However, it was decided that she should stay, primarily because of Copley's desire for an experienced fiscal accountant. When Adams met her in the hall one week before the formal announcement and informed her that this would be the case, she was disappointed. She felt that she would get "out of the stream of things" and that promotions would be slower. However, she remained and later was happy that she had because, while she did get "out of the stream of things," she also stated that: "the degree of specialization introduced at the regional level would be much more hampering than the general type of work I do at the Laboratory."

On June 7 Adams called the business staff of the laboratory together to inform them of his decisions. He stated that those assigned to the WRBO were to move to the third floor the following week and begin operations. This was the first most of them knew of their particular destiny. Adams, prior to the June meeting, had not spoken with the employees about their placement; nor had they spoken with him. The June 7 meeting was described by Adams' secretary in these terms:

> I knew where some of the others were going to be placed from papers that crossed my desk. But I did not know until the June meeting where I was going, and the others didn't know of their fate. To most of us it didn't make a great deal of difference, but that meeting in June was nevertheless quite an affair. I will never forget sitting there waiting to hear my name called. Everyone at the meeting was excited, and some were rather nervous. However, it seems that everyone except one accountant got what they wanted.

The following week the WRBO was set up on the third floor of the Western Utilization Research Laboratory. With the skeleton staff of twenty-one persons taken from the laboratory, it began operations in anticipation of its formal opening date, July 1, 1955.

Prior to the actual transfer of employees at the laboratory, Adams had contacted employees of the Management, Washington, office about transferring to the West. In late May, at the second meeting of the future regional business managers held in Washington, Adams was informed by the Personnel Division that no one on the Washington staff had requested transfer to Albany. On his return Adams sent Spencer a number of Chamber of Commerce folders describing the San Francisco Bay area. In part, the accompanying memorandum read:

> I am enclosing a few copies of a brochure describing the San Francisco Bay area. It seems appropriate to bring to the attention of members of the Agricultural Research Service in the Washington, D.C. area the splendid location and ideal surroundings in which the Regional Business Office will be established. . . .

The distribution of these, together with Adams' personal recruiting efforts among Washington employees, resulted in eighteen requests for transfer to the western office. Of the eighteen who came to California, most were younger girls with previous experience as ARS voucher examiners, clerk-typists, or payroll clerks. Adams was pleased with these Washington transfers, because they added much needed experience. In many cases the girls performed the same functions for the same research or regulatory people from Albany that they had previously done from Washington. During the first months these girls added continuity to the ARS business program. The transferees were familiar with most of the ARS forms and procedures, and in some cases were even familiar with the names and handwriting of the field research or regulatory personnel.

By July 8 Adams had twenty-two employees working in the WRBO and twenty others selected. The "twenty-two working" were the transfers from the laboratory's business office and James Hempstead, former Regional Employment Officer for the Agricultural Marketing Service in Oakland and now ARS Western Regional Personnel Officer.[16] The "twenty others selected" were mainly the Washington transfers. The additional thirty-three needed for a full staff were to be recruited from the outside during the early months of operations.

Authority and Procedures

During the first meeting of the prospective regional business managers in Washington (May 3-5), Management, Washington, began the job of introducing them to the new procedures and authorities that would be in effect under regionalization. At this meeting the managers were introduced to the two major regionalization documents: the "Distribution of Management Functions Under Regionalization and Schedule for Inauguration of Regional Business Operations," and the "Proposed Distribution of Organization and Methods Work by Organizational Unit." Together these documents set forth the responsibilities for organization and methods work of the management divisions, the program branches, the regional business offices, and the field stations. The documents dealt with more than 100 business activities. The four future managers also were oriented to the research and regulatory projects on which the program branches were working.

Since one of the main purposes of regionalization was the standardization of authorities and procedures within the ARS, the research and regulatory branches had to be informed in great detail about the new authorities and procedures. On June 24, 1955, Spencer circulated a notice to "All Divisions, Branches, Regional Business Offices, and Field Stations." Its purpose was to: "set forth the schedule and furnish other information and instructions regarding the early phases of the regionalization of business operations." On this date, the ARS became formally committed to a specific plan of regionalization. This was also the first official word the field personnel had received since March 1. June 24 was admittedly a late date, but the management divisions just had not been able to complete the discussions and reviews any earlier, and they had been unwilling to issue detailed instructions that might thereafter be subject to far-reaching modifications.

Beginning on June 24, memoranda or circulars were sent almost daily from Washington to the field stations and regional business offices explaining some detail of regionalization. One such memorandum gave the regional business offices authority to make contracted purchases and sales of $20,000 and $5,000 respectively. Another allowed them to classify positions up to GS-5. Other memoranda dealt with post-audits, personnel actions, personnel records, government supply sources, and in fact nearly all of the 112 business activities originally set forth in early May and circulated on June 24.

During the first five months of operations under regionalization, so many memoranda were sent to the field, and so many requests for clarification were received by the regional business offices and Management, Washington, that Spencer felt it necessary to issue the following statement to all ARS employees:

> I am unhappily aware of the bad impression made upon many ARS people, particularly the small field station, by the issuance of numerous memoranda containing administrative information and instructions. I cannot very well apologize for an action which is necessary, but I want to mention briefly the three general situations calling for these issuances and say why we follow the course we do in each of them. . . .

The reasons given by Spencer for the issuances were (1) the nature of the regionalization itself, (2) the need to mold one standard ARS policy out of the several that existed under the bureau setup, and (3) the need to rewrite many of the former issuances in order to keep them consistent with the new arrangement.

Adams recalled that the first few months of operations under the new procedures and authorizations were rather hectic and confusing for both the WRBO and the field stations. Much of the confusion, however, was caused by the inability of the field research and regulatory personnel to discriminate between important and unimportant issuances. A good number of the memoranda had little, if any, relevance to many of the small field stations. In many cases the field men, because of their inability to keep up with the changes, simply threw up their hands, sat back, and waited to be told by the Regional Business Office when they had made a mistake.

The new authorizations can be briefly sum-

---

[16] Prior to going with the AMS, Hempstead had been an employee of the BEPQ, in its Oakland Administrative Office. He was anxious to return to the ARS when, early in March 1955, he first heard of the impending regionalization.

marized. In regard to field procurement, the initial grant of authority authorized field station personnel to make "small-value over-the-counter purchases" with a standardized ARS purchase order form.[17]

Branches using other purchase order forms were to discontinue their use and return them to the regional offices. The field station personnel were to make any but "small-value over-the-counter purchases" through the regional business offices. An exception enabled them to make repairs up to $100 on automobiles or automotive equipment.

Management's Budget and Finance Division also introduced standardization into the field stations' accounting procedures. For this purpose it developed a system consisting of "lump sum" and specific obligation categories.[18] This was done shortly after the Benson reorganization.

On personnel actions, the field stations were instructed to "initiate them" and then forward them to the Regional Business Office for processing. The Western Utilization Research Branch, which had previously done its own hiring and classification, had these authorities withdrawn. Standard forms were also provided for part-time hiring and other personnel activities that the branches had in common.

Thus ARS Management achieved standardization of personnel and procurement authorities and procedures. However, in some other areas it had less success. For example, regulations stipulating which hires and reclassifications needed prior program branch clearance remained a matter for program determination. Some branches allowed their field station personnel to initiate all nonprofessional hires and lower level reclassifications without prior program branch approval. Thus the field station could deal directly with its Regional Business Office. Other branches, however, required that all hires and reclassifications be cleared before execution. In these cases the field man had to draw up the forms, send them to Washington for approval, and then send them to a regional business office for execution. Management naturally would have preferred to see the former procedure prevail on a standardized ARS basis, "but felt inclined," according to Adams, "to permit the various branches some leeway in the flow of such documents if they felt this was necessary in order to discharge their program responsibilities."

Thus regionalization was able to introduce substantial standardization into an organization that previously had had little.

---

[17] In the memorandum the new form was defined as: "a combination purchase order and vendor's invoice which has been designed for use in making small-value over-the-counter purchases. As the form is intended to be used where the cost of the article or service is small and for which there is an immediate need, an expenditure of an unusual amount should be fully justified by documentation of the file or otherwise. The form shall not be mailed." (AM 210.4, June 30, 1955.) Prior to the adoption of this form throughout the ARS, different forms had been used by different branches. There was also, prior to regionalization, a wide discrepancy in the purchase authority of field personnel in the different branches.

[18] In setting up "lump sum" and "specific obligation" categories within their bookkeeping systems, field stations were to allocate a portion of their quarterly allotment to each category according to the following formula. If the expenditure was of a continuing and relatively regular amount (i.e., rent, telephone, utilities, part-time employment, or the like) then an amount adequate to meet these expenditures was to be set aside in the "lump sum" category. All other funds were to be entered in the books of the field station as an open balance available for expenditures as needed. The WRBO kept its records in the same manner.

IMPLEMENTATION: ACTION, REACTION, ADJUSTMENT

Between July and December of 1955 the Western Regional Business Office took over the accounts of 275 field stations and some 2,700 program employees. On a schedule determined in Washington, the central management divisions and field stations transferred all pertinent records to the regional business offices. Thus, in an orderly manner, the field stations and their personnel came under the new ARS procedures and delegations of authority.

At first, many of the research and regulatory personnel in the western region were opposed to regionalization. This was so, it seems, because in many cases the field personnel were unaware of the true intent and purposes of regionalization and feared that it would be a hindrance to the program aspects of their work. A few were simply reacting negatively to change *per se*.

For some field stations this transfer amounted to little more than a change of address on business communications. For example, prior to regionalization, a Crops Research Branch agronomist at the University of California at Davis sent business forms and requests to Washington, D.C. Following regionalization he sent them to Albany, California. The field personnel in the western region who perceived this as the case, while perhaps holding personal opinions as to the wisdom, economy, and need for regionalization, accepted it and attempted to follow its regulations.

In some instances, however, a particular field station or branch felt that a unique need justified opposing regionalization and standardization.

The feelings of those who opposed regionalization were soon expressed in correspondence with WRBO and with program headquarters in Washington. The new procedures and authorizations in some instances left room for questioning. Some program personnel were quick to use this as an excuse to comment, question, and complain. Many of the letters received in WRBO were technical, seeking specific information on a specific topic or problem. Others were of a more general nature. They reflected a feeling of confusion and frustration on the part of the field program official.

For example, a researcher at a small field station in Montana reviewed the history of ARS from the time of the 1953-1954 reorganization, through a subsequent branch reorganization, and finally to regionalization. He concluded his well-written, three-page history with a statement of fatalism toward regionalization, a request for patience on the part of the Regional Business Office, and a request for clarification regarding his authorities and responsibilities in almost all business areas.

This correspondence was one of those referred to in Adams' July 29, 1955 "Weekly Progress Report" to Spencer. He wrote: "Numerous memoranda were received this week from field stations asking for interpretation of Administrative Memorandum 210.4 ['Procurement Functions under Regionalization']. The principal area of concern as you might well expect is the section dealing with field procurement." In August this same condition was reflected in a report to Adams from Stan Andrysek, Acting Head of Administrative Services Section in WRBO: "We are still receiving letters from the field regarding the use of 'Lump Sum' and Specific Obligation and the procurement functions under regionalization. . . ." The principal procurement problem was the inability of the field personnel to define "small-value over-the-counter."

The field stations were also having problems in areas other than procurement. A statement in the "Weekly Progress Report" of October 7, 1955, sums up the many difficulties that the field station personnel were experiencing under regionalization, and, in turn, the difficulties WRBO was having with them. In this instance Adams was referring to the problems he had discussed with the research personnel in a small field station in the state of Washington.

> I dislike being repetitious, but the problems we encountered at this station are a duplication of those we encountered elsewhere. A lack of complete understanding of the Lump-Sum Specific Document procedure [the accounting system],[19] inability to understand the allotment ledger, some questions as to the authority to purchase locally under AM 210.4, L/A employment, and wage rates.

In order to overcome this initial reluctance and general lack of understanding on the part of the field personnel, Adams immediately initiated a number of internal and external adjustments in the regional office's procedures. One of the internal adjustments that most aided acceptance was Adams' insistence that "all correspondence from the field be answered or at least acknowledged within three days." An advantage of regionalization, soon realized by the research and regulatory personnel, was that they could and did get prompt, courteous, and expert answers to their questions.

In response to letters such as:

Dear Sir:
You need your money
I need mine
If we both get ours
It will be fine
But if you get yours
And hold mine too
What in heck
Am I going to do?

Adams and the regional office found it necessary to make adjustments in the payroll procedures. To aid the meeting of payroll deadlines, conferences were held with the Treasury Department's San Francisco Disbursing Office, and near the end of pay periods employees from other sections of the regional office were assigned to the payroll section.

To further the implementation of regionalization Adams sought means to improve communications. This was a problem which, in March of 1956, Hempstead, the Regional Personnel Officer, described in this fashion: "In our fragmented or-

---

[19] See footnote 18, page 344, *infra.*

ganization with its wide geographical dispersal, there is great need for improved communications between Washington, the Regional Business Office, and Field Station." In order to improve this situation the Regional Business Office held two area conferences. The first, in Albany on September 13-14, 1955, was attended by representatives of twelve program branches; and discussions were held covering all business areas: finance, personnel, and administrative services. When regional conferences were first proposed, concern was expressed among program personnel as to who was to pay for transportation, lodging, and the like. However, from the beginning, attendance at such sessions was voluntary, and expenses were met by the program branches.

One research man stated: "At first I disliked the idea of having to pay to be brainwashed by the RBO, but it was at the September meeting that I first understood what regionalization was all about."

At the second conference held in Riverside, California, in early December of 1955, there were thirty-eight program people in attendance, twenty of whom were heads of field stations.

As plans were being made to hold a third such meeting in Arizona, instructions came from Washington to discontinue them. Adams and his staff felt that the termination of conferences was a definite loss to the western region and to the improved relations that were being built between the business and program personnel. In 1957 the business offices were able to resume regional conferences.

The purpose of "News Notes," which was sent to the field on a monthly basis starting in 1957, was to inform the field personnel of changes in policy that were of particular importance to them. The issues were not policy statements, and they did not quote administrative memoranda. They were an attempt on the part of the WRBO to inform the field personnel of such matters as dates when forms were due, information on promotions, safety rules, and the like. The field personnel welcomed these "News Notes," and it was generally felt that the publication did much to improve communications.

WRBO personnel also began a series of personal visits to the field research and regulatory stations. Adams made his first field trip in early September 1955, visiting field stations in Montana. The results of this and subsequent trips to Colorado, Arizona, New Mexico, and in time to all ARS field stations in the western region, were most beneficial. Adams said,

> If nothing else, I feel that the field trips proved to the field men that we did not have horns. But more than this, they helped the field men to understand some of the problems we were having and opened our eyes to the problems of the field by giving us a deeper understanding of field conditions.

On a more limited basis the Regional Business Office engaged in extended conferences with individual stations. For example, discussions were held with the Western Utilization Research Laboratory. Among the topics discussed in these sessions were the questions of the regional office's reimbursements and further modification of the building. It was Management's position that it should reimburse the laboratory for all "added costs"; that is, pay the increased costs of operation in matters such as telephone, utilities, mail receiving, maintenance, etc. The laboratory felt that the proper criteria of repayment would be proportioned on the basis of space used. In late 1955, Girgich, with Adams' assent, worked out a formula whereby the regional office would reimburse the laboratory for "added costs." In 1956 the Regional Business Office paid the laboratory $11,000 as its share of the cost of occupancy and use of facilities. In 1958 this reimbursement was raised, by mutual consent, to $15,000, because of increases in laboratory maintenance, personnel salaries, and costs of supplies.

The laboratory's primary contention was that it had to assume all increases in general overhead costs: for example, when the laboratory expanded its cafeteria facilities to accommodate the additional WRBO personnel, Management, Washington, on the grounds that the improvements were to the laboratory's facilities, held that the costs of such improvements should be met exclusively by Utilization Research.

The regional office and the laboratory also entered into discussions regarding the distribution of administrative work. As Adams reported to Spencer in December of 1955:

> We have undertaken a series of discussions with the Western Utilization Research Branch administrative personnel to review the procedures which we established at the inception of regionalization. The purpose of these discussions will be to determine whether further simplification

can be brought about or whether we can improve our service to the Branch. The discussion we had with the Branch administrative personnel yesterday covered Administrative Services. We covered such items as the requisitioning procedure, issuance of purchase orders and receiving reports, contracting procedures, records management, property management, the flow of work orders between the regional business office and the Branch covering such items as photographic, mimeographic, and mechanical services. We also discussed some areas of common services such as mail, and telephone and telegraph procedures. We expect to perform a similar analysis in conjunction with fiscal and personnel activities. These discussions, I am sure, will be profitable. We have already come up with several ideas in the field of Administrative Services which I am sure will be mutually beneficial.

Thus, by means of internal adjustments, "News Notes," regional conferences, and individual discussions, Adams and the WRBO attempted to speed the implementation of regionalization, to educate the field research and regulatory personnel regarding its true intentions, and to overcome their reluctance to accept the changed conditions. The adjustments were also accompanied by a series of changes in the management divisions' procedures and authorizations. Many of these changes came about as a result of suggestions from the field. First, the field program personnel informed WRBO that they could not operate effectively under a particular procedure or authorization. (In some cases copies were forwarded to program headquarters in Washington.) Second, WRBO in its reports and discussions with Management, Washington, would indicate the difficulty the field personnel were experiencing with the procedure or authorization in question and suggest a change. The final stages were Management's change of the regulation and implementation of a new one. In some cases Management, Washington, had previously formulated plans for further delegation or changes in procedures, and therefore regionalized authority according to plan. However, the former process was the more common.

The field procurement authorization was the most frequently adjusted. Because of the strong negative reaction of the field to the original purchase authorization and subsequent discussions between the business managers and Management, the field purchase authority was rewritten within one year. In June of 1956 Management granted field personnel the authority to purchase up to $500 in emergencies or for "unique needs"[20] and to $25 for "all other purchases."

At this time Management, Washington, also granted authority to the heads of field stations to mail the purchase order form to "out-of-town vendors." The matter of mailing had been a bone of contention with the field stations. Since many of the small stations were located in rural areas far from suppliers, they wanted the authority to make small purchases through the mail. This authority had been denied them in the original authorizations.

This modification in purchasing did not, however, solve the field men's problem. As one research field man said: "Whoever decided on $25.00 must have been crazy. I could have told them it wouldn't work. How can we run a place with $25.00 petty cash?"

In 1957 and again in 1958, Management found it necessary to issue new statements regarding field procurement procedures and authorizations. However, even with these additional clarifications, the WRBO and Management, Washington, continued to receive complaints. Many field stations felt they had a "unique need" and requested authority from the regional office to purchase under the "unique need" provision. In the absence of detailed criteria it became increasingly difficult for the Regional Business Office to grant or withhold the authority.

For instance, in early 1957 a small field station in the state of Washington requested copies of catalogs and a delegation of contracting authority under the "unique need" provision. Commenting on this Adams said:

> In 1957, two years after we opened, there was still wide-spread ignorance regarding regionalization and the services the regional office was to perform for the field establishments. If I had given catalogs and purchase authority to one field station I would have had to give them to all the stations. If this had been done we would have been worse off than before regionalization. The regional business office is here to perform business services for the field stations and ought

[20] By "unique needs" Management meant such things as lumber, hay, oats, etc. For example, if a particular field station had a "unique need" for livestock feed, then the regional office could delegate authority to that station to purchase locally up to $500 worth of livestock feed. However, the field station could not use the "unique need" authorization without prior Regional Business Office authorization.

to do that whenever possible. But it is hard to convince them of this.

The spring 1958 meeting of the regional business managers in Washington included considerable discussion about the possibility of a single purchase authority for all field stations. What the business managers wanted was a policy that would not admit of the many exceptions necessary under the "unique need" and "emergency" exceptions. However, no action was taken at that time.

In another area, personnel classification authority, quite a different means of extending regional authority was used. In this instance the Washington Personnel Division had shown a willingness to delegate greater authority. Hempstead recalled that at the time he was hired as Western Regional Personnel Officer, he had been informed by Personnel, Washington, that: "the Regional Officer's classification authority would be increased as his staff became more expert." In the original grants of authority the Regional Business Office was authorized to "develop position descriptions; classify GS-5 and below for all except professional positions; conduct wage surveys; and recommend wage rates to regional boards. . . ."

The first extension of authority came in August of 1956, when Management, with the concurrence of the Department's personnel director, granted the regional business offices authority to classify all positions up to GS-12 in Meat Inspection, Animal Inspection and Quarantine, Plant Quarantine, Plant Pest Control, Western Utilization Research Laboratory, and the Western Regional Business Office. In February 1958, this authority was extended to cover *all* ARS branches, and authority to classify administrative positions was set at GS-9. These increases represented primarily the philosophy of the Personnel Division. As Hempstead stated:

> I have been at times both surprised and flattered by the way the Personnel Division in Washington listens to what we have to say. We explain to it that we are having a problem because of a particular policy, and it is always ready to change. It has always shown a willingness to delegate authority to the field.

In regard to short-term, Letter of Authorization employment (L/A employment),[21] a problem of special importance to the field man, there were numerous changes after regionalization. The basic problem was described in a letter received by WRBO:

> This year because of the pressure of work due to a late spring it has been necessary to employ quite a large number of fellows for temporary work. One of the difficulties in doing this is that there are so many long forms that need to be filled out for each laborer that it seems to be rather unnecessary where one is being employed for such a short length of time. I wish that there were some way that a simplified form could be used where people are employed on a temporary basis, especially where they would be used for Agricultural labor intermittently. If this could be done I am sure it would please the people we hire as well as those of us who have to see that the forms are correctly filled out.

While the form and expression of the letters were often different, the plea was always the same, "Please simplify the L/A employment procedures." WRBO carried the brunt of this problem, since it post-reviewed all L/A employment in the western region for legality. If for some reason the hire was illegal, the Regional Business Office could not approve the payroll of the employee.

One field man stated: "The ARS L/A employment procedure is so complex that I use the funds I get from the state government to do all of my part-time hiring. The state has different procedures and they are much simpler." Another field man stated:

> I would hate to know the number of illegal hires that were made before regionalization. The Regional Business Office makes it more difficult for us to make a mistake. When Hempstead or someone up there corrects us we always get a little irritated and usually complain about red tape and so on. However, the Regional Office has always been helpful. When we make mistakes it is the first to bail us out.

Hempstead summed up the L/A employment problem in this way: "It has always been with us, and we are always seeking new ways to improve and simplify it. Washington has always been quick to implement any good ideas suggested to it, and we have adjusted the procedure many times, but the problem is still far from solved."

Throughout the regionalization, Adams had set down a basic policy emphasizing service to the field stations. Foremost among the services was getting pay checks to the field on time and expediting per-

[21] Part-time or Letter of Authorization employment is an informal hiring procedure delegated to field stations for hiring part-time, intermittent or seasonal nonprofessional persons in their local area. Authority is granted to them by the program division in their annual Letter of Authorization.

sonnel and purchase actions. This policy did much to calm the troubled waters caused by regionalization, and many comments from the field complimented WRBO on a job well done.

While Management progressively delegated authority to the regional offices, in many cases the program branches were reluctant to do the same with their field stations. According to Management, equal decentralization of authorities had to be made by both management and the program branches if the full benefit of regionalization was to be realized.

IMPACT: SOME EXAMPLES

In order to gain some indication of the impact of the reorganization upon the program operations in the field, the author interviewed a number of program directors of field stations in the West, representing a variety of ARS undertakings. Since these discussions were carried on about five years after the regionalization was ordered, they should be interpreted as retrospective and perhaps tempered by time and experience. A sample of the responses is summarized below.

The Grasshopper Control Project

The Grasshopper Control Project, a major undertaking of the Plant Pest Control Branch, was directed in the West from an office in Oakland, California. From 1947 to 1955 this operation had received business services from the Minneapolis Administrative Office of the BEPQ. During the reorganization of 1953, when BEPQ was divided, Plant Pest Control became a separate branch; but it continued to receive business services from Minneapolis. Throughout this period the bureau, and later the ARS Minneapolis Administrative Office, had allowed the field stations a great deal of latitude. In early 1955, the Department of Agriculture stipulated that, if ARS regionalized, there was to be no crossing of regional lines. As a result, the business work of the Grasshopper Control Project in the West was transferred to the WRBO in Albany.

James Dutton, a large, action-oriented man, originally trained in the law, was chief of this project group. Dutton states that he first heard rumors about regionalization early in February of 1955, but that his first official notice was the ARS March 1 notification. "Between March and July," stated Dutton, "I heard a lot of rumors, but no one asked me to comment on regionalization or made any effort to justify or explain it to me." Dutton's primary fear was that the regionalization of business services would hamper his program efficiency. In order to guarantee that it would not, he took immediate remedial action. As Dutton described the situation,

> The new plan was designed to emphasize decentralization. It did not seem to. Prior to the establishment of the five bureau administrative offices, we were as decentralized as we could get. At that time we worked directly with the Treasury Department. When they opened the Bureau of Entomology and Plant Quarantine administrative offices, we received services from Minneapolis. At that time the BEPQ regional offices were organized on a subject matter basis. This was the first step in centralization. In 1955 they decided to bring all of ARS into four regional offices. This did not indicate to us a trend toward decentralization.
>
> The Plant Pest Control Branch, and in particular the Grasshopper Control Project, has some rather peculiar needs; I wanted to be sure that Adams understood them. If we had to have regional business offices I wanted to make certain that we received the service we needed in order to realize our program objectives. I immediately set out to make certain Sid Adams understood them.

Grasshopper Control did indeed have some "peculiar needs." Its activities had many complications. Usually grasshopper control involved spraying vast areas with insecticide. In general the first step in grasshopper control was delimiting the problem area. This could vary from a few thousand acres to a few million. The second step was to obtain, in cooperation with the state government or governments involved, agreements with the landowners. In this program, the federal government, the states, and the property owners each assumed one-third of the cost of spraying. The third step was the negotiation of contracts for insecticides and spraying apparatus. Complications arose when an occasional property owner was reluctant to sign agreements even though the control job had been requested by his immediate neighbors. As Dutton stated:

> There is no purpose in spraying if you leave an area or areas in the middle unsprayed. If some of the property owners continue delaying the signing of agreements, we are never positive, until the last minute, that the spraying will actually take place. Grasshoppers continue to develop during such delays and since treatment work becomes impractical soon after the beginning of egg deposition, it is imperative that aerial contracts be invited, awarded, and the treatment begun almost immediately after the final decision to do the job. Temperature, wind, rain, etc., limit application periods to 0 to 6 hours per day, making treatment itself time-consuming and permitting further grasshopper development. Contracting officers who had grown up with other agencies were accustomed to long, formal bidding periods in contracting and had to be convinced that our work just couldn't be accomplished under that system. Bidding periods of three days and telegraphic invitations, bids, and awards are a necessity.

The conditions associated with the Grasshopper Control Project were but one reason why the Plant Pest Control Branch adopted the attitude it did. Similar circumstances were attendant to most of their other control projects.

Adams recalled with a smile Dutton's first visit to his office. "Dutton came in with three or four of his top people and started right off with 'Sid?', stuck out his hand and introduced himself. It has been 'Sid' ever since and he is still trying to educate me in regard to the necessities of Plant Pest Control work."

In the following months Dutton and Adams settled on a workable relationship. They agreed, with somewhat different emphasis, that there was need to expedite the letting of the Plant Pest Control contracts. The Regional Business Office attempted to do this as much as possible. "We have," said Dutton, "a working understanding in regard to what I have to do and what the RBO has to do. However, I feel certain that I infringe upon the RBO's area more than it does on mine. The Regional Office does a fine job and will continue to do a fine job, particularly since Mr. Adams has had his staff visit, and has personally been 'on site' to learn what we do in control operations. We too have learned what the WRBO requires and try to comply."

The Salinity Laboratory

To the Soil and Water Conservation Branch's Salinity Laboratory in Riverside, California, an office with about fifty employees responsible for research on the effects of salt in soil and water on agricultural crops, the primary disadvantage of regionalization was that it cut its procurement authorization from $500 to "small-value over-the-counter purchases." Regionalization in no way affected the size or grade level of its business staff, and it tended to expedite their personnel actions. However, while thankful for the latter, the Salinity Laboratory felt that it could not operate as effectively with the new limited purchasing authority. Regionalization, in its view, "helped a lot and restricted a little." As Walter Lansing, the Administrative Assistant at the laboratory, stated:

> We have always found the WRBO most cooperative and helpful. While the monetary restriction on purchasing has been frustrating at times, the Regional Business Office has gone all out to be of service to us in matters of procurement, property management, fiscal entanglements, personnel classifications, and employment actions.
>
> I should mention that regionalization has resulted in freeing more of my time for management functions, i.e., serving on the Laboratory Personnel Committee, plant management, safety, Health Benefits Program, personnel relations, and the like.

The Meat Inspection Branch

The Meat Inspection Branch employees welcomed regionalization. Although some of them had serious apprehensions at the beginning, these fears were soon dispelled when pay checks arrived on time and business matters received faster handling. Having had a pleasant experience with regionalization of business services within their own unit under the ARA and an unpleasant experience of centralized business operations during the interim period of 1954-1955, most of these field men were happy with the return to a regionalized business operation. However, they, not unlike the other branches, were concerned lest the new Regional Business Offices attempt to control the program aspects of their work.

At the time of regionalization the Meat Inspection Branch officials in Washington, in an attempt to expedite implementation, delegated greater personnel authority to their field stations. Feeling that regionalization would be relatively ineffective if the field stations had to clear all business as well as program actions through the central office, they delegated to the field sufficient authority to allow the stations to deal directly with the regional office on most business matters. For example, prior to regionalization field stations had to clear all nonprofessional employment first with their program chiefs and then through the central Personnel Division. After regionalization, a field station head was allowed to hire nonprofessional personnel on his own authority and deal directly with the Regional Business Office for execution.

Soil and Water Conservation

A two-man research station of the Soil and Water Conservation Branch in Southern California expressed the general feeling that the regional business office had proven its worth, but only after some time. These field men stated that they were aware of considerable apprehension in Washington among their program chiefs and felt that it stemmed from two causes: First, the program chiefs were afraid that they might lose control of the program aspects of the organization; and second, they feared that the regional office might become a "watchdog" for all ARS operations in the field and thus limit the control that program chiefs could exercise over their field stations.

However, these two researchers felt that the Regional Business Office, while definitely requiring more work of them, had relieved them of some of the minute details. To this station the one big advantage of regionalization was that they received the new standardized purchase form. Prior to regionalization, the Soil and Water Conservation Branch had used a more complicated form which entailed considerably more handling.

The feelings of the research personnel in the Soil and Water Conservation Branch were summed up by one of the researchers as:

> Fiscal and personnel affairs were relaxed and easy before regionalization. The Regional Business Office requires more of us now, but at least things are right; we have more standardization, more accountability, and probably more efficiency.

Entomology Research

The employees of a larger field establishment of the Entomology Research Branch had a somewhat different reaction to regionalization. They felt that far in the past they had had ideal working conditions. At that time (1947) they dealt directly with the Treasury Department for disbursements and payrolls. They saw regionalization as centralization, and they feared loss of control.

This field station did, in part, lose clerical help as a result of the 1955 regionalization. It seemed that regionalization was "the straw that broke the camel's back," and they were forced to put their bookkeeper on part-time. This particular office was, as they described it, "too large for a part-time girl and too small for a full-time one." Yet it was said that:

> Generally speaking, regionalization has increased our paper work. However, if this extra work has been caused by the greater accountability required by Congress or by Department executives, regionalization is justifiable. If, on the other hand, it has been added by the Regional Business Office to justify its existence, then there is no justification whatsoever for regionalization.

The Plant Quarantine Branch in Hawaii

In the case of the Western Regional Headquarters in San Francisco of the Plant Quarantine Branch, which had regionalized program management prior to the regionalization of business services, there was considerable concern regarding the latter. First, its officers felt that the change would save no money and was thus "unnecessary." Second, it would put a regional business manager in a position to control program work and, according to C. E. Cooley, at the time Head of the Western Region of Plant Quarantine Branch, "jeopardize the essential uniformity of quarantine enforcement on the national level." For these reasons, the Plant Quarantine Branch sought from the start to maintain the status quo, with particular regard to its Hawaii office.

On May 20, 1955, G. E. Hanna, Administrative Officer, Plant Quarantine Branch, Washington, sent a memorandum to Cooley in San Francisco that read in part:

> We have been advised informally that it is planned that all fiscal work now performed in Hawaii by ARS Program Branch Offices located there will be done eventually in the Albany, California, business office.
>
> In order that we may be fully apprised of the effects these proposals will have, we would ap-

> preciate having immediately, if you oppose these changes, justifications why we should continue as at present.

During the interim period 1953-1955, the field station of Plant Quarantine in Hawaii had performed some of its own fiscal services. Vouchers and payrolls were prepared and certified there, and checks were issued by the local Treasury Disbursement Office. Personnel and procurement actions, however, were forwarded for clearance from the Hawaii office to the regional branch headquarters office in San Francisco, then to the business office at the Western Utilization Research Laboratory for processing and action. Western field stations of the Plant Quarantine Branch on the mainland had received business services from the laboratory's business office in Albany since the 1954 reorganization and the subsequent closing of the BEPQ Administrative Office in Oakland.

On May 23 Cooley, described by some as "being of the old school," forwarded Hanna's memorandum to Maehler, head of the Hawaii office, stating that:

> I am inclined to attempt to justify maintaining the status quo of our fiscal operation in Hawaii. You, however, will have to supply the reasoning and the justification which we can use.

On May 26 Maehler replied to Cooley by referring to a study that had been made in 1952 of the possibility of transferring the Hawaii business office to Albany and concurred in its conclusion that:

> . . . if this contemplated change would result in delays in payment of vouchers and personnel, additional reports of a fiscal nature, a general breakdown in liaison between program, personnel, and fiscal activities, it would undoubtedly have a deleterious effect on our program work.
>
> There are certain definite as well as intangible advantages to me in being able to discuss fiscal questions and personnel problems with my administrative assistant. Other advantages in the present arrangement are the procuring of supplies through military channels, the handling of reimbursable over-time accounts, arranging for transfer of personnel and their household effects can all be accomplished more expeditiously when we can make personal contact here in Hawaii.
>
> Even if the fiscal activities are removed to the Albany office, a certain amount of preliminary assembling of payroll data, vouchers, fiscal reports, etc., would be necessary in Hawaii and the present administrative assistant position certainly would have to be maintained, even if downgraded.
>
> In spite of these facts, I would not "drag my feet surreptitiously" at any contemplated change merely to maintain the status quo. If this change is considered good for the Branch and it would improve the quality of our program work and at the same time allow a saving in administration, I'm for it.

On the basis of this report Cooley forwarded a memorandum to Hanna. In the memo he concluded that:

> Since there would be no saving in money to transfer the fiscal work in Hawaii to Albany, and because of the disadvantage of doing so, I strongly recommend that every effort be made to maintain our fiscal operations in Hawaii as now constituted.

Cooley's reaction was partly conditioned by an attempt much earlier to consolidate business services and program responsibility. A year or so after the establishment of regional administrative offices for the BEPQ, it was announced by the chief of the bureau that the chief regional administrative officer, a former program man, would be vested with discretionary powers in program areas. This general proposal was soon abandoned because of the extreme reaction it produced among program officials both in Washington and in the field. However he did retain some program discretion. While this idea was never mentioned in regard to regionalization, Cooley, not unlike other program men, feared that the incorporation of all ARS branches into a regional business office would be a step in this direction. In general, Cooley's criticism of regionalization remained unchanged even a year after his voluntary retirement from the service in 1959: "Regionalization costs more, it distracts responsible program officials with an ever increasing multiplicity of 'paper work,' it is impossible to keep as close tabs on expenditures as before, and the Regional Office is just one more layer in the cake."

Regionalization affected the Plant Quarantine Branch less than some other branches. Although its fiscal officer in Hawaii had to be downgraded from GS-9 to GS-7 because the branch lost its authorizing and certifying powers, it had to hire a full-time administrative assistant in the regional supervisor's San Francisco office. Therefore the only substantive change for the Plant Quarantine Branch was that now the Hawaii office was to be serviced by the Regional Business Office.

* * *

The Plant Quarantine Branch reaction seems to have been rather typical both in procedure and in content. The field officials, following the lead of their branch chiefs, were concerned lest they lose control of program administration. Their only alternative at this stage was to argue for the status quo. It became the duty of the field officials to provide ammunition for their Washington program chiefs to use for this purpose.

Prior to regionalization the field personnel had received a distorted and in many cases false notion of regionalization and the reasons for it. Management did, insofar as seemed appropriate to it, keep program officials in Washington informed of the purposes and progress of the plan. However, little of this information reached the field stations. Since many program officials in Washington tended to oppose the plan and looked to the field for support in their opposition, it was natural for the field personnel to pick up the attitudes of their superiors. This situation tended to make the job of the new Regional Business Office more difficult. Not only did it have to secure the cooperation of reluctant field research and regulatory personnel, but it also had to instruct them in the true nature and purposes of regionalization.

POSTSCRIPT: A LOOK BACK AT THE CLOSE OF 1963

The first months following the opening of the regional business offices were a difficult period for ARS. In summing up the first half-year of regionalization at a meeting of the business managers, Spencer made the following points:

(1) Regional business office performance in general has been good.
(2) Cooperation of field program men has been good.
(3) Acceptance of regionalization by program branch headquarters has been "spotty."
    (a) Some branches have been cooperative.
    (b) Some branches have been skeptical.
    (c) There has been some "foot dragging."
(4) Greater delegation of authority by program branches to field men is necessary to realize maximum advantage of regionalization.
(5) ARS policies and procedures must take precedence over branch policies and procedures.
(6) We are probably past the most critical period, but not yet out of the woods.
(7) Dr. Shaw, Administrator for ARS, has indicated full support for regionalization.

On January 9, 1956, Spencer addressed the finance officers of the Department on the topic "Can Work Programs and Administrative Management Live Together?" After identifying the chief purposes of regionalization, he described what he called the "questions always asked by program people of all Management proposals." They are as follows:

> First, will the procedure make more work? Second, will it cost more? Third, will it deprive program officials of any controls or prerogatives?

His presentation did not answer the first question. About the second and third, he said:

> Since reorganization and regionalization of business operations, the ratio of ARS overhead costs to total funds has decreased from 6.26 percent to 5.28 percent and that part of overhead costs chargeable to management has decreased from 3.99 percent to 3.60 percent.
>
> We have to say honestly that many management policies and procedures, particularly when a matter like regionalization of business operations is concerned, do take away from program branch officials certain controls that they have had. . . . The problem in this area, therefore, is to encourage officials at the branch headquarters to do a reasonable amount of delegating to their people in the field and at the same time to assure these headquarters officials that, by a system of budgetary control and the financial education of their men in the field, they can still keep their programs entirely responsive to their own plans and wishes. This is by no means an easy job and I am frank to say we are far from having completed it.

Program directors, branch chiefs, and other headquarters officials on the regulatory side appeared generally satisfied with regionalization; on the other hand, the headquarters officials of the Plant and Animal Research Branches were still resistant, sometimes overtly. Early in 1956 Spencer received a letter from one such official that said:

> Regional business office personnel should recognize branch and section policies. This is quite important inasmuch as regional business office personnel are in frequent contact with our field people, and unless they are thoroughly cognizant of our policies they will issue instructions not in conformance with branch and section policies.

Spencer replied:

> It seems to me more important for the branches to be in conformance with ARS policy than for the ARS regional business offices to be in conformance with branch policy. . . . If any of the instructions issued from either the centralized management divisions of the regional business offices seem to be unreasonable from the standpoint of branch operations, we shall of course be glad to discuss the matter. . . . We cannot, however, recognize the policies of any branch taking precedence over those of ARS.

At the end of one year's operations, Adams reported to Spencer on regionalization in the western region:

> Substantial progress has been made in orienting the field offices to the procedures and requirements of ARS and the regional business office. From a state of confusion which prevailed at first, we feel that the field offices appreciate our efforts and cooperate with us to the fullest extent.
>
> Despite the constant increase in workload, and the many problems of a new organization, we have, we believe, rendered the stations good service. As a result, the field establishments now accept regionalization.

Program officials stationed in the field had by this time taken notice of the prompt and accurate service provided by the four regional business offices and appreciated the periodic visits to their field stations by the business managers and other office personnel. Program officials in the western region, especially those in close proximity to WRBO, agreed that the personal service they received, and the ease with which they could pick up the telephone and talk to an expert in personnel, finance, or administrative services, were valuable. Even so, the battle was mostly uphill for Adams and his staff. It was their job to sell the program officials on regionalization. In most instances they succeeded. But as late as 1958 and 1959, some veteran field personnel still had reservations in one form or another and reminisced about "the old days" when things had seemed simpler, easier, and therefore better.

By the end of three or four more years, regionalization was working smoothly and effectively. Program people in both headquarters and the field had come to realize that the management and business staffs were seeking to serve programs, not to direct or frustrate them. Some of the program officials who had taken violent exception to regionalization had retired or otherwise left the agency; others were near retirement. Management officials had brought about further refinements in the organization and conduct of business activities. The Classification and Wage Branch of the Personnel Division had reviewed and adjusted the grade and staffing patterns in the business offices of the production and utilization research branches to ensure that these offices were similar to other branch business offices from the standpoint of staff organization and pay. The production research branches had been encouraged, with some success, to establish full-time administrative positions at large multi-project field locations. Also, the management divisions were now able to concentrate on the development, testing, and implementation of new administrative policies and procedures.

The general tendency under regionalization was delegation of more operating functions in the common business services areas. For example, as we have seen, lower-grade professional classification functions were delegated to the RBO's by the Personnel Division in 1958. In response to repeated urgings from the RBO's and the field, enlarged procurement authority was finally delegated to both groups by the Administrative Services Division in 1959 and thereafter. At the same time, substantive management functions and program authority remained predominantly centralized at headquarters.

Accompanying increased appropriations for ARS were expansions in both program and administrative staffs. As one consequence, the Western and Eastern Regional Business Offices were moved out of the utilization research laboratories in 1959. Each office was relocated in federal space near the laboratories; the Western, in Berkeley, and the Eastern, in Fort Washington.

By the end of 1963, almost a decade after regionalization had begun, the conclusion was inescapable that in the administrative area regionalization of business services was a success. Gone were the pockets of "foot dragging" resistance, as a result (1) of the departure of many of the program officials who had been most opposed and (2) of the mellowing of the attitudes of others throughout the agency. By the end of 1963, regionalization was ancient history, and there were other, more immediate events with which ARS men were concerned. Program people at headquarters and in the field had long since accepted regionalization, and many were enthusiastic about the quality of service provided by the RBO's. Despite their acceptance of regionalization of business services, however, the regionalization idea had not expanded into program areas. Formal program authority still remained predominantly centralized.

Of course, all was not sweetness and light in dealings between administrative and program staffs. Researchers could still be found, for example, who viewed administrators with suspicion, even loathing. Within limits, this would always be the case. But their animus tended to be directed against administrators in general, not against regionalization in particular.

Shaw still served as Administrator in 1963, and Clarkson had been promoted to Associate Administrator. The program branches had been renamed divisions, and their chiefs were now called directors. Several new program responsibilities had been delegated to the agency, and others had been expanded since the mid-1950's. The division engaged in research had been regrouped under two Deputy Administrators, one for Farm Research and the other for Nutrition, Consumer, and Industrial Use Research. Another new Deputy Administrator had charge of Research Planning and Coordination.

By 1962, in close collaboration with the appropriate program officials, the regional business offices were performing functions considered by most management officials in 1955 as substantive management functions that could never be decentralized while program authority continued to be centralized. The RBO's classified professional positions from the beginning grades through the lower supervisory levels without checking with the Personnel Division. Similarly, beginning in 1963, persons could be hired for professional positions through GS-13 and could be fired for good cause, without the approval of the Personnel Division.

In the area of procurement, to cite other examples, the regional business offices had authority by 1962 to procure supplies, equipment, and services in the open market of a value not to exceed $2,500; where justified by the frequency of need, to initiate blanket purchase arrangements for field stations with local vendors; and, for "control of incipient or emergency outbreaks of insect pests or plant diseases" (Plant Pest Control), to execute contracts for supplies, equipment, and services of a value not to exceed $200,000. Moreover, each regional business manager had a new duty: to carry out "a comprehensive program" of management reviews within his region. It was his responsibility "to review and evaluate the effectiveness of management of program field activities." In 1955, just a hint to the effect that the business managers would have such a management audit function would have wreaked havoc. No doubt the fact that Spencer had selected as business managers those who already enjoyed the confidence of program officials helped to set the stage, as did the responsible performance of the business managers through the years. Most of the original business managers served for the entire period to 1963, and there was also a high measure of stability among the technical personnel in the RBO's.

The RBO's were renamed Field Administrative Divisions in 1962. The business managers were given the title of director and their positions were upgraded to GS-15; many of the top staff positions in these offices were also raised. By late 1963, all payrolling functions were projected for transfer to a new, automated operation at the departmental level; when this occurred, it would be the first loss of functions experienced by the RBO's. In Washington, Spencer was now Deputy Administrator for Administrative Management, with Starkey as Assistant Administrator. The management divisions had been retitled administrative management divisions, and the Budget and Finance Division had been split into two divisions.

The Field Administrative Divisions appeared to have secure futures as 1963 drew to a close. Headquarters and field officials alike had come to accept, even appreciate, the services that these units were providing to the programs of the agency. By then, too, it was obvious that regionalization had prospered under Secretary Orville L. Freeman, Benson's Democratic successor, as it had earlier under the Republicans.

APPENDIX I:

HEADQUARTERS-FIELD EMPLOYMENT IN ARS PROGRAM BRANCHES FOLLOWING REORGANIZATION, JANUARY 1954

AREA	PROGRAM BRANCH	EMPLOYMENT *Washington Metropolitan*	*Field*	CENTRALIZATION —DECENTRALIZATION*
	RESEARCH			
Crops	Field Crops	196	868	C
	Horticultural Crops	241	360	C
	Entomology	149	696	D
Farm and Land Management	Soil and Water Conservation	147	574	C
	Agricultural Engineering	54	190	C
	Production Economics	156	72	M
Livestock	Animal Disease and Parasite	199	243	C
	Animal and Poultry Husbandry	194	254	C
	Dairy Husbandry	149	51	M
Human Nutrition and Home Economics	Human Nutrition	108	19	M
	Home Economics	85	2	W
Utilization	Northern Utilization	—	294	F
	Southern Utilization	—	394	F
	Eastern Utilization	—	286	F
	Western Utilization	—	322	F
	Washington Utilization	63	—	F
		1,741	4,625	
	REGULATORY			
Crops	Plant Pest Control	91	943	D
	Plant Quarantine	26	423	D
Livestock	Animal Disease Eradication	35	1,257	M
	Animal Inspection and Quarantine	21	478	M
	Meat Inspection	61	2,931	M
		234	6,032	
		1,975	10,657	

* KEY D: decentralized, maximum delegation to the field; C: centralized, review of virtually all actions; F: field, each field laboratory constituting a program branch; M: mixed, central control of program, but some delegation; W: Washington, Washington personnel only.

EDITORIAL COMMENTS

The issues, the arguments, and the events described in the agricultural research cases may be relatively obscure to the layman and even to most social scientists; and many of them may appear trivial. Yet these cases describe problems and processes that are part of the daily diet of many officials in the federal government. From the standpoint of the practitioner of big organizations, the reorganization in Agricultural Research Service was both representative and significant. It is interesting to observe how decisions, argued in Washington on the basis of broad administrative "principles," devolved in application into questions of how much floor space should be allocated to the Regional Business Office in Albany, California, or of how promptly an agriculturist in Montana might receive his pay check.

The central issues and tensions in the case were by no means unusual or unique:

(1) program personnel (in this instance, agricultural scientists) *versus* administrative personnel;
(2) direction and control from above (the Administrator of ARS and the Secretary of Agriculture) *versus* bureau (or, in this instance, branch) autonomy;
(3) separation of administrative activities (finance, personnel, services) from program activities *versus* their integration;
(4) standardized agency-wide procedures *versus* heterogeneous and traditional procedures;
(5) headquarters control *versus* the field.

But the dominating issue was the degree to which administration, here as in many other organizations viewed as paperwork and services, should be permitted to assume a role that might control or at least influence agency program operations. The administrative supporters of regionalization endeavored to assure the program personnel that the change would not infringe upon program decisions but rather would relieve professional workers of menial administrative detail, thus expediting work on the substantive aspects of the agency's work. And it is clear from the second case that this was the basic criterion against which many program personnel judged the regionalization.

These cases may confound students of administration about the meaning of centralization and decentralization, even though the situation in the Agricultural Research Service was quite typical in this respect. From some perspectives, the establishment of regional business offices was certainly an example of decentralization—of operations and, increasingly, of decision-making authority. One of the arguments for the move was to relieve Washington of an enormous and growing amount of actions and records on individual cases. But the reaction of some of the program branches and their field personnel was quite the opposite and understandably so. They viewed the change as centralizing administrative actions and control in regional business offices and in the Management Division in Washington, detracting from local authority, and adding to the processing of individual actions. Both views were correct. Regionalization was both centralization and decentralization, depending upon one's point of view. More important, it was a shift of responsibility and, in some degree, of authority from the program branches to the administrative line in both Washington and the field. The reader may usefully study decentralization of authority in three different channels: from the Washington Management divisions to the regional business offices; from the business offices to field stations (with Washington authorization); from the program branch headquarters (mostly in Washington) to their field stations. One of the sources of confusion to the reader of these cases is that the degrees of decentralization on administrative matters among the program branches varied widely from one to another. And the existence of two different channels for the review, approval, and processing of actions (finance, personnel, procurement, and other fields) was certain to create difficulties.

One can hardly judge the decisions in these cases to have had much flavor of participation. The basic decisions appear to have been made with no participation whatever:

(1) The decision by Shaw and Spencer to request authority for regionalization of finance offices from the Secretary of Agriculture.
(2) The decision by Assistant Secretary for Administration Roberts to withhold approval.
(3) The later decision by Roberts to encourage the regionalization of all administrative functions.
(4) The ensuing directives from ARS headquarters for regionalization.

Spencer's subordinates in the Management Division were brought into the planning of *how* the change should be done, but even for them some of the basic decisions were "givens." Participation by the program branches was minimized by design. After some argument, it was decided that they should not be members of the planning group. And there was apparently some effort to deny them an opportunity to coalesce into an opposition group. At the Washington level, the principal goal seems to have been to prevent more than the barest minimum of participation so as to forestall concerted opposition.

The field offices and their personnel for whom the changes could be expected to cause the greatest changes had virtually no voice at all. The decisions were made in Washington, and the field representatives had only minor influence in deciding how the changes would be implemented. Even during the implementation process, though information and recommendations were invited from the field, virtually all decisions were made in Washington.

It is interesting that in this large headquarters-field agency, decision authority was so much more concentrated at headquarters than in some other organizations, such as two considered in this book: the Langley Porter Clinic of the California Department of Mental Hygiene and the Ballistics Division of a research laboratory of one of the military services in the Defense Department. But in the Agricultural Research Service, there was little pretense of participation by the field and apparently little expectancy of it or resistance to the change because of it.

C. AGENCIES ENGAGED IN MANAGEMENT AND SERVICES WITHIN THE GOVERNMENT

MARGARET G. OSLUND

The Guardians of La Loma

MARGARET G. OSLUND

The author of *The Guardians of La Loma* received a D.P.A. degree from the University of Southern California. At present she is Director of Public Administration at the Illinois Institute of Technology.

CHRONOLOGY OF KEY EVENTS

1950	Mayor-designate of La Loma asks for additional compensation because job requires full-time responsibility
March 1956	Green tells Dean Nelson of city's administrative problems
April 1956	Nelson and colleagues meet with City Council at first informal luncheon to discuss city's problem
May 15, 1956	City Council votes $505 for exploratory study. Mayor formally introduces consulting team to department heads
July 10, 1956	Preliminary Report presented to City Council at informal session
August 10, 1956	City Council passes Resolution 3873, at formal session, authorizing study in depth to determine reorganization needs of La Loma city government, and appropriates $11,900 for that purpose
January 1957	Two-volume *Report of the Organization and Management of the City of La Loma* issued to City Council members
May 1957	Report becomes available by sections to city department heads; general distribution withheld
Spring and Summer 1957	Council members meet in "rump sessions" to study findings and recommendations of report
June 1957	Council drafts ordinance creating position of CAO
August 1957	Council chooses Allen as CAO after interviewing seven candidates
December 1957	Allen assumes position as CAO of La Loma; two weeks later he issues first Administrative Directive
February 1958	Allen selects Mrs. Wolfe as his private secretary; issues second Administrative Directive
April 24, 1958	Allen sends letter to City Council formally recommending creation of Finance Department
May 1958	Council passes resolution appointing Miss Henderson as Director of proposed Finance Department
June 1958	City Council passes Ordinance 1399, creating Finance Department
July 1958	Mrs. Alonso announces her opposition to Ordinance 1399
October 7, 1958	Mrs. Alonso presents petition to City Council; Council sets April 7, 1959, as date for referendum vote on Ordinance 1399
April 7, 1959	Ordinance 1399 defeated in referendum vote, 2,869 to 1,335
July 1959	Council approves appointment of Larry King as Chief of Police following Bemis' retirement
February 1960	Allen resigns to accept position as CAO of neighboring city
March 10, 1960	Becker and Committee of '60 endorse CAO plan of government
April 4, 1960	General elections held

PRINCIPAL CHARACTERS

Ronald J. Allen, First City Administrative Officer of La Loma (December 1957-February 1960)

Mrs. Wanda Alonso, Sometime entrepreneur; private citizen; dabbler in city affairs

Ferdinand E. Bemis, Chief of Police of La Loma

Joseph Green, Employee of city school system (personnel); member of the three-man Civil Service Commission; crusader for modern management methods in government

Miss Betty Henderson, City Clerk of La Loma (1952—); *ex officio* leader of city's "old guard"; long-time employee of the city, serving as Deputy City Clerk from 1927 to 1952

Alfred Kirk, Head of La Loma's Street Department

Dr. William H. Nelson, Director of the survey team; Dean of the School of Business and Public Administration, University of the West; President of Consultants Unlimited

Miss Clara Osgood, Secretary to the Mayor of La Loma and the Civil Service Commission; *de facto* Personnel Director

Lester K. Peterson, Associate Professor of Criminology, School of Business and Public Administration, University of the West; Vice President, Consultants Unlimited; expert in police field

Richard Shelton, Coordinator of survey team; Executive Secretary of Consultants Unlimited; lecturer in public administration at University of the West; expert in personnel field

Rexford A. Simeon, City Engineer of La Loma for twenty-seven years; adroit, behind-the-scenes politician

Benjamin White, Mayor-designate of La Loma in 1950 and member of City Council; Mayor of La Loma in 1957 when full study was launched; operator of small filling station

Dr. Floyd M. Winfield, Team consultant responsible for study of finance and personnel; Associate Professor of Public Administration, economist; specialist in field of public finance

James R. Winston, Long-time member of City Council; advocate of modern management practices; local real estate broker

Mrs. Marie Wolfe, Secretary to CAO of La Loma; wife of Henry Wolfe, Managing Editor of La Loma *Daily News*

LA LOMA IN THE NINETEEN-FIFTIES

Called the "balanced city," La Loma, California, comprised an area of almost three square miles with a population of 32,000. It had a large, concentrated shopping district and a number of light and heavy industrial enterprises. By far the largest part of the community was residential, though fewer than fifty per cent of those who lived in the city were property owners.

La Loma was the commercial center for a southern California metropolitan area of about 250,000 people. It was, in a sense, a bedroom community, but it differed from many of the neighboring cities in that it was rapidly becoming a community of apartments. Haphazard growth and intense land use had led to borderline blight conditions in certain parts of the city.

The nature of the population was also different; the city had a disproportionate share of older people. The "old guard" could be characterized as lower middle-class, retired property owners, merchants, and small businessmen. The remainder of the residents, mostly apartment dwellers, worked outside the city in the electronics industries and food processing plants.

Politically, the older residents of La Loma could best be characterized as conservative. There were slightly over 13,000 registered voters.[1] Of this number, approximately 4,900 were Republicans, while some 8,100 claimed membership in the Democratic Party. Despite the fact that Democrats outnumbered Republicans by almost two to one, governmental issues were approached from a conservative point of view by both groups. Voters often joined forces to put into local, state, and national office those who would reflect the conservative philosophy of La Loma's voting citizens. As in the rest of California, local elections were nonpartisan. The five-man City Council, the legislative body of the city, was composed in 1956-1960 (the period of action in this case) of three Republicans and two Democrats. However, this party allegiance dichotomy is not too meaningful in view of the pervasive conservative viewpoint of both groups.

From the time of its incorporation as a general law city[2] in 1906 up to about 1950, the city government of La Loma appeared adequate. A five-man Council served as the policy-formulating body, and the Council member designated mayor (by majority vote of the Council) handled most of the details associated with the city's business. The twelve department heads as well as other city officials dealt directly with the Council in getting approval for projects or in developing solutions to problems. To facilitate the attainment of program objectives, department heads often attempted to cultivate friends on the Council who interceded for them when necessary.

In addition to fourteen departments run by twelve department heads (two departments, Parks and Water, were under the supervision of the heads of the Streets and Engineering Departments respectively), there were nine appointive commissions and boards composed of lay citizens appointed by the City Council. These part-time bodies were established as the heads of several of the departments.[3] (See Figure 1, page 371.)

In the main, the activities of the boards and commissions were confined to those of an advisory nature, though it was not unknown for members to interfere and attempt to influence administrative decisions in the departments.

La Loma did not suffer from the problems of rapid growth common to many California cities;

---

1 The low voter registration is explained by the fact that almost one-half of La Loma residents were more or less transient apartment dwellers who had little interest in community affairs.

2 A general law city is a corporate entity that is governed by laws promulgated by the State Legislature. In California applicable laws are determined by the class or category assigned to the city. Cities do have the option, however, of drawing up individual charters to fit local needs. Such charters are usually desirable since they permit greater flexibility in meeting local problems. Once the charter is ratified by the voters in the municipality and approved by the State Legislature, it has the force of law.

3 The lay board or commission is not limited to California but probably has been used more widely there than in other states. The major rationale for creating such bodies is that agencies that might be subjected to various pressures of a public or political nature are protected by being placed under independent citizen boards. Generally, appointments are staggered in order to preclude tampering by political groups. Some boards and commissions have administrative responsibilities of an operational nature; others are confined to an advisory and/or watchdog capacity.

however, it showed a steady increase in population, industry, and business establishments over the years. The functions and activities of the city's established departments expanded in a rather haphazard fashion, and new departments proliferated as increased demands were made for services.

In 1950, 250 individuals were employed by the city. In general, employee turnover was extremely low. Average length of service for department heads was fifteen years.

Councilmen's duties were handled on a part-time basis. Most Council members were small businessmen and shopkeepers, and they lacked the financial resources necessary to devote more than part of their time to their city responsibilities. Over the years the burden of administrative responsibilities had grown to such an extent that it was almost impossible for Council members to process the work and, at the same time, continue their private business activities.

There was also a growing belief on the part of Council members that the complexities of city government were becoming such that the council did not possess the time or technical knowledge to provide the work-a-day direction and control necessary for good administration.

Another complicating factor was that the duties and responsibilities of the mayor were not precisely spelled out; the incumbent was never sure just what was his area of authority for action. The result was that the mayor often acted with limited knowledge and, in doing so, frequently aroused the ill-feeling and animosity of his Council colleagues.

PRELUDE TO THE SURVEY

In 1950 the mayor-designate felt that his administrative duties had become so demanding that he was going to have to choose between neglecting his private occupation or the city's business. He asked the city attorney to check existing laws and statutes to determine whether or not it was possible to provide additional compensation for the position of mayor. After he had collected and weighed the facts, the city attorney indicated that there was no possible way to pay the mayor for the extra time spent in that office.

In the minds of many interested in La Loma city government, the mayor's effort to find a way to increase his salary signaled a recognition of the need to improve governmental arrangements. Despite this overt recognition of the difficulties of the Council and the office of mayor, the situation continued unchanged for several years.

Inception of the Reorganization Study

A behind-the-scenes force for a reorganization study came from Joseph Green,[4] who held a personnel position in the city school system. Green was a respected member of the community who had served for years on the city's Civil Service Commission. He had expressed concern about the informal manner in which city personnel matters were handled and had asked several times for a study of La Loma's civil service. Until members of the Council began to feel personally the pinch of administrative burdens, Green's pleas were ignored.

In late 1955 the Council's irritation over the chaotic condition of city administration reached a new high. Lack of coordination among departments, inability of Council members to control department heads, and lack of planning within the departments had the Council in turmoil. Heads of departments were fighting among themselves and in some instances deliberately obstructing each other's work. Green sensed that the Council's irritation had reached a point where that body was willing to consider almost any solution that promised relief.

In March 1956, Green spoke to Dean William H. Nelson of the School of Business and Public Administration, University of the West. He described La Loma's administrative difficulties. Through his work in personnel, Green had met Nelson some years before and knew of his reputation as an organization and management consultant. When Nelson indicated interest in La Loma's problems, Green arranged to have him meet the City Council members at an informal luncheon meeting in April 1956.[5] Nelson brought with him

[4] Names of characters and locations in this case have been altered.

[5] It may be noted that this meeting and other subsequent informal meetings described in the case were technically in violation of the so-called "Brown Act" of the State of California, originally passed in 1953, which prohibits secret meetings of official bodies, except for the discussion of personnel problems. It is interesting that these violations of the law apparently never aroused criticism or comment during the course of the case.

two colleagues, Lester K. Peterson, Associate Professor of Criminology and an expert in the police field, and Richard Shelton, an expert in the field of personnel. At this first meeting, Nelson and his associates learned enough about La Loma government to make them strongly suspect that the municipality was faced with critical administrative problems.

A number of informal meetings followed, spread over several weeks, and the consultants became convinced that La Loma's problems would probably need extensive study. Nelson proposed to the Council that he and his associates do an exploratory study to determine whether a full-fledged survey was needed and what areas should be covered. If the exploratory study indicated the existence of serious problems in La Loma, the preliminary report to the Council would also include a proposal for a full survey.

Almost all Council members seem to have been convinced that some sort of study was necessary. Indeed, most opted for a full survey from the beginning. For them an exploratory study was merely a rough sketch of what was to be investigated.

The only Council member who evidenced skepticism as to the worth of a full survey, even if the exploratory study indicated the need for one, was Mathew J. McDonald, an attorney. At the final luncheon meeting between the Council and consultants, in May 1956, McDonald pointed out that he was concerned about the possibly adverse nature of the report; it might hold La Loma up to ridicule or embarrass members of the city government. He told the consultants, "If we can't make changes in the final report, we cannot go along with it." At this Nelson rose and said, "Gentlemen, . . . if those are the conditions, it is time for us to leave." McDonald's objections notwithstanding, at its next formal session (May 15, 1956) the Council voted $505 for an exploratory study.

During the initial negotiations, the Council made every effort to keep the projected study confidential. The only city employee who knew exactly what was being considered was the city engineer. (While many department heads and other officials had "friends" on the Council, members of that body were exceedingly closemouthed about the exploratory study. City employees had had no concrete information that the study was to occur, but there had been a general feeling that "something was in the wind.") Council members deliberately withheld information because they felt city employees might resist a survey, and they believed secrecy might help minimize that resistance. At the May 15 Council meeting, after funds were voted for the exploratory study, the mayor introduced the team of Nelson, Peterson, and Shelton to the department heads. He then summarized to them the purpose of the exploratory study.

In June the reason for the presence of the consultants was explained more fully by the mayor in the following memorandum:

CITY OF LA LOMA
June 12, 1956

To: City Department Heads
From: Mayor
Subj: Preliminary Survey of City Government

The City Council has unanimously approved the retention of several members of the faculty of the School of Business and Public Administration of the University of the West in their capacity as private individuals in order to make a preliminary survey of the organization, management and personnel problems of the City of La Loma. The Council feels that the growth of the City both in population and importance requires that we examine the adequacy of our governmental structure and administrative operations in order that we may be able to provide a better and more responsible service to our citizens and taxpayers.

The preliminary survey has as its objective the identification of general and specific problems within the organization and operations of the city departments which may lead to a more complete study of the organization and operations of our city government, if the results of the preliminary survey so indicate.

This study is not intended nor shall it be conducted as an investigation into the personal conduct of any city employee, but shall be exclusively concerned with the way in which our departments measure up to established standards of municipal governmental organization, administration and operation. For that purpose we have obtained the services of professional experts in the field of public management from the faculty of the School of Business and Public Administration at the University of the West. This work shall be done by these people acting as private individuals and as part of their concern for the development of good public administration in our California area and is a non-profit undertaking. Dr. William H. Nelson, Dean of the School of Business and Public Administration, shall head up the survey in association with Mr. Lester K. Peterson, Associate Professor, and

Mr. Richard Shelton, Lecturer, who are specialists in the fields of police administration, personnel management and the organization and administration of municipal government in general.

The Council feels sure that all the city employees will recognize the importance and the need for such a study and that they will cooperate fully and completely, making available to these gentlemen all data, records and files that they may need and request for the purpose of their survey.

The Exploratory Study

Shelton was approximately forty years old at the time of the survey. He had just returned from a foreign assignment and was between jobs. Nelson asked him to assist in the exploratory study and also indicated that he would like Shelton to become coordinator and project director on a full-time basis if the Council later agreed to a full survey. On June 6, 1956 (six days before the mayor's memorandum was issued) Nelson, Peterson, and Shelton began a quick initial survey. This consisted, for the most part, of informal interviews with officials and department heads, review of the city charter, and review of existing operations manuals for the various units. In the main, however, Shelton—who did most of the work—relied on the organization chart for the city. To Shelton, an exploratory survey was similar to a diagnostic study, and information could be developed in a fairly routine way.

Based on the information obtained through spot-checking city operations, Shelton drew up an organization chart and compared it with what he considered to be sound organization structure and practice. He felt that "in the process of obtaining information to draw up the organization chart, three-fourths of the problems were identified."

The major purpose of the exploratory survey was to determine just what areas of La Loma city government appeared to need attention. For this reason, the survey did not discuss city problems in depth. It was impressionistic but represented the best judgment of the consultants as to where their time could most profitably be used. Shelton compiled the information he and other members of the team had developed in a kind of "working paper," a twelve-page, double-spaced document briefly setting forth problem areas. Along with this he submitted a proposal for a full-scale study of the city administration.

Miss Henderson, the Elected City Clerk

Shelton's exploratory survey was not without problems. The most formidable of these appeared in the person of Miss Betty Henderson, elected City Clerk of La Loma.

Miss Henderson was a slim, beautifully groomed woman about forty-nine years old. She was dedicated and strong-minded about those things that she considered "right." She owned considerable property in the city and had become, over the years, the champion and spokesman for the conservative element of the city. She felt it part of her civic duty to engage actively in municipal affairs that she felt would advance the progress of the city and the welfare of the home owners who had been residents of long standing.

She did not seem to have much influence with, or support from, bankers, newspapers, or county supervisors in the area. After graduating from high school, Miss Henderson had gone to work for an attorney who specialized in municipal law. At this time (about 1926) her uncle, Scott Seward, was the City Clerk in La Loma, a position he had held since the beginning of the 1920's.

Shortly after going to work, Miss Henderson learned that her uncle needed an assistant, and she asked him to take her on as his deputy. Seward, or "Uncle Scotty" as the community affectionately called him, was a dedicated man who, on more than one occasion, had fought successfully against political corruption, graft, and spoils.

Like that of many other western cities, La Loma government in the 1920's had reflected a latter-day frontier atmosphere. Even in the early 1930's it was fairly common for citizens to attend Council meetings armed with guns and clubs in order to make their arguments more persuasive. Miss Henderson had grown up in this atmosphere, and she never lost her conviction that direct relations between citizens and those elected to represent them was the essence of democratic government.

From 1927 until 1952, Miss Henderson had served as Deputy City Clerk. When her uncle died in 1952, she was appointed by the Council to serve out his unexpired term. She ran successfully for the post at the next election and experienced no more than token opposition from then on.

Miss Henderson admired her uncle and believed that his philosophical approach to the office of city clerk and the operational methods he had established for it were "right" and "proper."

Shelton first learned about Miss Henderson while trying to form a picture of the functions of the city clerk's office. Primarily, these involved aspects of budget preparation, accounting, auditing, and certain personnel activities—chiefly the maintenance of personnel records and payroll. To Shelton, Miss Henderson seemed determined to block his every move. He found her to be suspicious, hostile, and uncooperative in providing information. Miss Henderson, on the other hand, felt that Shelton approached his study of her office in a cold, critical manner and that he did not give her a chance to explain what she was doing and why. When she tried to explain the reasons for some of her office methods, Shelton indicated, rather impatiently, that he was not interested in her explanations but simply wanted facts. Shelton, in the main, saw Miss Henderson's attempts at explanation simply as rationalizations to support outmoded and antiquated workways.

Preliminary Recommendations

The preliminary report was presented to the Council in informal session on July 10, 1956. In an introductory paragraph, the consultants were quick to point out that:

> . . . these findings attempt merely to define the major problems and needs of the City organization and operations which we have observed as a result of the diagnostic survey, and do not, at this time, represent in any sense a set of conclusions and recommendations for solution. These we would expect to furnish in the report following the more complete survey which should search deeply into the wide variety of problems which we feel exist within the city's administrative organization.

As the consultants saw it, the significant problem areas consisted of the following:

(1) Excessive departmentalization with resultant duplication.
(2) Lack of centralized administrative directions and control.
(3) Inadequate and atomized staff functions.

The report concluded with the recommendation that a more complete and thorough study be undertaken which would include the following:

(1) An intensive study into the functional activities of the departments which make up the administrative organization of the City with the view of eliminating duplication and bringing about more specialized and responsible activities.
(2) A review of the necessary staff services which should be made part of the city administrative structure, together with a listing of their proposed functions, responsibilities, and place in the organization.
(3) A position classification survey to establish up-to-date class specifications in order to make possible the installation of correct procedures for recruitment, selection, promotion, in-service training, merit rating, and the fixing of salaries, and to prepare a set of rules and regulations for the administration of the system.
(4) An area-wide salary survey to determine the prevailing compensation for the positions in the City of La Loma, in order to construct a rational and proper salary for the City and to prepare appropriate rules and regulations.
(5) An intensive study of the organization, management, and operations of the Police Department, including an evaluation of police departmental relationships with other city departments, in order to achieve the most effective possible police service.
(6) A general evaluation of the internal management and organization of the Fire Department to determine the extent to which community needs are being met.
(7) An examination of the possible alternatives which would be appropriate for the City of La Loma in order to provide administrative assistance to the City Council and bring about central responsibility for the administrative and organizational problems of the City, and to make possible the constant supervision and coordination of all functions performed by the departments.

The report also recommended a survey among citizens to determine municipal opinion of alternative types of administrative organization and the continued use of the consultants after completion of the study for hearings, appeals, and general assistance during the implementation phase.

For about one month Council members considered the report and its recommendations. In due course it became the unanimous opinion of all members that the findings in the report demonstrated the need for a comprehensive survey of La Loma city government.

In formal session on August 10, 1956, the Council passed a resolution authorizing a study in depth to determine the reorganization needs of La Loma and appropriated $11,900 for that purpose.[6] As usual, Miss Henderson was present. She expressed no opposition to the study.

The preliminary report was never published and was not available to the city's employees. Reportedly many employees were apprehensive about its contents.

[6] It appeared evident that the Council reached agreement on the need for the full study rather quickly. Between the time that body received the preliminary report on July 10 and formally approved the full survey on August 10, a draft agreement under a cover letter dated July 31, 1956, had been prepared and forwarded to the city attorney by Shelton.

THE FULL-DRESS STUDY

The contract drawn up between the consultants and the Council specified certain areas of city government for intensive study. As Nelson saw the situation, the consultants had been hired to "do a diagnosis and write a prescription." The group was not hired for a general study of the dynamics and politics of the community. Nor was an implementation study considered in these early stages of negotiation. The job of the consultants was to develop and present to the Council recommendations for reorganization. The consultants said, in effect, "With this much money, this is what we can do and no more."

At a regular meeting of Council and department heads, Mayor Ben White again formally introduced the principal members of the team. Shelton, observing the department heads at this meeting, felt that they seemed insecure and apprehensive.

Organizing the Survey

In late August, Shelton, as full-time survey coordinator, moved into the office provided in City Hall. The stated objectives of the contract between Nelson, Shelton, and Peterson, as partners, and the City of La Loma were those of analyzing "(1) Administrative assistance to the City Council; (2) General organization of the City departments; (3) Police Department; (4) Fire Department; (5) Staff services, including Fiscal management, Planning, Personnel administration; (6) Position classification; and (7) Salary survey." The diagnostic survey had also indicated that study was needed in the areas of Recreation, Public Works, and Mechanical Equipment. One of Shelton's first tasks was to hire the necessary technical experts to complete various phases of the study. He determined his manpower needs by breaking the study up into its component parts and setting up folders for each. He knew that the services of several faculty members at University of the West were available: e.g., Dr. Floyd Winfield, the finance expert. He also obtained, from the School of Business and Public Administration, a list of working administrators-practitioners who might be willing to devote some time to the specialized areas of the study.

Most of those who participated in the study did so on a part-time basis. With the exception of Shelton and one or two research assistants, the group that the project director assembled was composed of professionals who held full-time positions. Thus the research was carried out in bits and pieces as individuals found time to get away from their desks and classrooms. The consultants usually spent one half-day a week or would "run out" to La Loma for a "couple of hours" during the week.

Many segments of the study were subcontracted for a flat rate (ranging from $100 to $500 per segment); therefore, an estimate of total man-hours spent on the project is almost impossible. Nelson, Shelton, and Peterson alone reported spending a total of 723 man-hours or slightly in excess of ninety man-days on the study. Over $2,000 was paid to "outside" consultants—meaning anyone other than Nelson, Shelton, and Peterson.

For the most part, traditional techniques of administrative analysis were used by the consultants. Key individuals in each area under study were interviewed, records and manuals—where the latter existed—were reviewed, and desk audits were made.[7] Findings then were compared with what were considered to be good management practices, and recommendations for change were made on this basis. The entire emphasis was on developing facts in this precise, methodical way.

[7] A desk audit usually consists of observing work in process at a work station (desk). The analyst notes what is taking place at the desk, origin of the work flowing to the desk, where the work is sent and why.

As project director, Shelton had overall responsibility for the final report. Shortly after the study began, team members started submitting reports. Shelton edited the reports, and, as each was completed, it was read to Council members in private meetings. As Shelton saw it, the two forces that were most important in gaining acceptance of the final report were the City Council and the La Loma *Daily News*. In order to make certain that the Council understood what was being done and why, principal members of the team met with that body frequently and explained the study step by step. With the exception of the Police Department, no one other than the Council was permitted to see the individual reports. Shelton had one hard and fast rule in interviewing: "Don't discuss report content with anyone."

The research team developed its information about the operation of La Loma government quickly and with a minimum of wasted motion. Team members, with the exception of Peterson, observed the edict of the Council and revealed no more information about the study than was necessary to obtain the information needed. No information concerning the progress of the study was given to the employees, and there apparently was no informal communication between the employees and those doing the survey.

Shelton established what he considered a fortuitous relationship with Miss Clara Osgood, secretary to the mayor and the Civil Service Commission, and *ex officio* Personnel Director. He felt the relationship was fortuitous because Miss Osgood provided a direct line of communication between himself and the mayor. Shelton favored this arrangement, not because of any particular admiration for Mayor White, but because he felt it was necessary to the success of the survey.

Shelton also was interested in Miss Osgood from the standpoint of her information about employee sentiment. Many employees felt Miss Osgood was overly ambitious and disposed to take advantage of any opportunity that would contribute to her personal advancement. They often commented that Miss Osgood made a habit of ingratiating herself with her superiors by repeating what she thought they wanted to hear. Some employees felt that they could not say anything to Miss Osgood unless they were willing to have it repeated.

Miss Osgood exacted certain concessions for her

FIGURE 1: ORGANIZATION CHART
CITY OF LA LOMA, CALIFORNIA
Actual (1957)

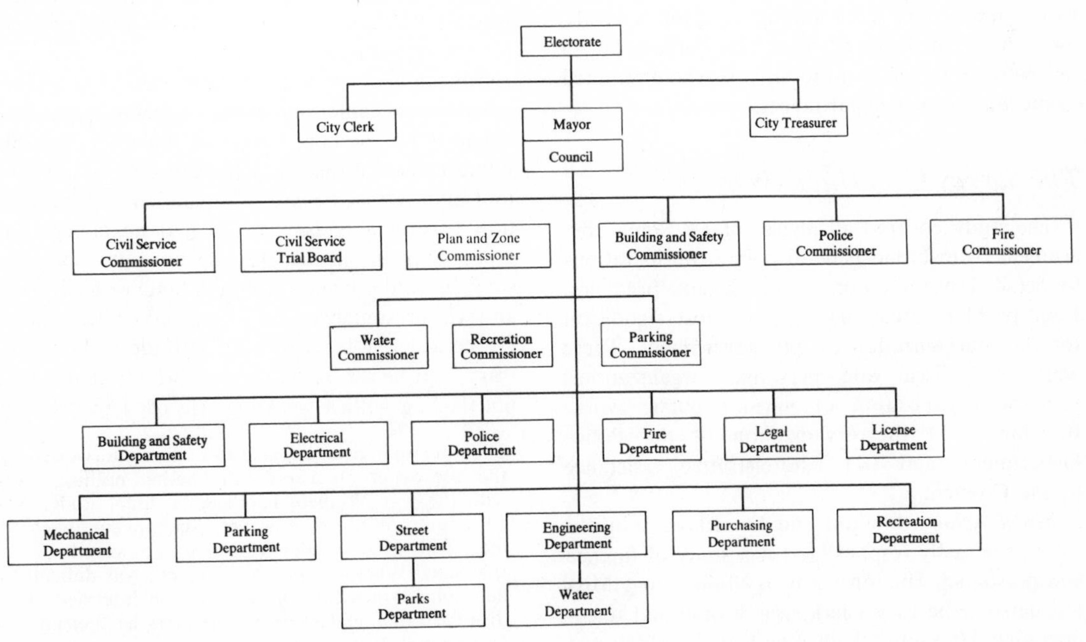

information role *vis-à-vis* Shelton. She took the study in stride but made it quite plain that she did not want her "personnel position" hurt. She was given to understand by Shelton (backed by his colleagues and the Council) that the reorganization would not affect her. If and when a Personnel Department was created, she was assured that she would become the senior personnel clerk.

For other information, Shelton relied on George Huber, who had been City Attorney in La Loma for approximately twenty years. Huber was, according to Shelton, his "consultant in guiding him along the proper path." Shelton knew the Council was critical of Huber because it felt he was old and slow in the performance of his duties. Nevertheless, he felt he "could count on his cooperation." Shelton seemed to feel that Huber was a moving force in the government, but the accuracy of this assessment was later disputed by many in La Loma, particularly the city clerk and city engineer, who told the case writer that Huber had never been considered, by persons familiar with La Loma affairs, as a major force in government.

As the study moved into its final phase in mid-December 1956, city employees became increasingly apprehensive. Those who were in a position to do so busily set about shoring up their defenses against the time when they might have to fight to preserve their positions. Such defensive tactics took the form of written justifications for maintaining the status quo and a considerable amount of informal missionary work among department heads, most of whom believed their best defense lay in presenting a united front to anyone who attempted to meddle in their departments.

The Survey Gets Under Way

The study covered all phases of La Loma government from broad general policy considerations to detailed examination of purchasing practices. Four problem areas emerged as most significant for the reorganization of city government. These were: (1) fiscal and personnel organizations; (2) the organization of various public works functions; (3) the organization of the Police Department; and (4) administrative assistance to the Council.

Fiscal Affairs. Shelton and Dr. Floyd Winfield were principally responsible for a study of finance and personnel. Shelton warned Winfield that Miss Henderson, the City Clerk, was hostile and uncooperative. He said that since he had already drawn her wrath, Winfield might as well steer clear of her and let him continue to take the heat.[8]

Winfield, a tall, spare man with graying hair and quiet manner, spent about eight hours observing the operations of the city clerk's office in handling financial affairs. He worked with the clerical personnel and the deputy city clerk in getting the information he needed. He gave Miss Henderson a wide berth.

Public Works. The public works portion of the study was handled by Malcolm Pierce (forty-five years old), a graduate civil engineer, city manager, and lecturer in public administration. Pierce spent about fifteen hours surveying the activities of the seven individual departments that dealt with public works. He used the usual techniques of interviewing key people, reviewing records and work procedures, and studying operations manuals. In his activities, he was substantially assisted by Rexford A. Simeon, the City Engineer.

Known affectionately as "Rex," Simeon held a civil engineer's license with the State of California and had been with the City of La Loma for twenty-three years. At the time of the study he was sixty-eight years old, two years from retirement.

In 1923 Simeon had moved to La Loma and had gone to work for an industrial concern. During the ensuing years in private industry he had made many friends among industrialists, businessmen, and merchants in the area. He became known and respected in the city as a man who had influence and who worked tirelessly on various volunteer projects for the community.

Simeon had lived in La Loma about ten years when he became interested in being appointed engineer for the city. He found, however, that his interest was not shared by the Council, and he was told bluntly that he was not qualified for the position (presumably because he had no college degree). Simeon felt that this was not fair, especially since he held a license from the State of California and was presumably a fully qualified civil engineer. He considered the Council's attitude rather arbitrary, and he set out to show that body that it was not dealing with a weakling. He tried to get men

[8] Shelton emphatically denied this when interviewed by the case writer. He asserted that he had nothing to do with the way Winfield handled the fiscal study. According to Winfield, however, Shelton continued to meet with Miss Henderson where necessary to "take the heat." Whether this was so or not was difficult to determine, since Shelton, also in the interview, had dismissed the incident of the city clerk as "not important enough to talk about."

into Council seats who would favor his appointment.

Simeon handpicked men for the Council, solicited funds for their campaigns from his friends, and was eventually successful in seeing his candidates elected. Immediately after the election in 1936, Simeon was appointed City Engineer.

Simeon did not like the idea of "playing politics," and he vowed to himself that once he had his job he would stop. He found, however, that the only way he could control his situation and do the things that, as city engineer, he thought should be done, was to continue operating in the political arena as he had in 1936. All of his political maneuvering was low-key and undercover. Rarely was he identified publicly as being aligned with any political element. He was privy to most Council confidences, and he usually was able to get just about what he wanted in the way of Council approval of his plans and projects. Simeon knew from the beginning that the Council was planning a study of La Loma city government.

Simeon believed that the public works function of the city was hampered by an obvious lack of coordination between departments. He was not able to control other department heads directly. Interdepartmental rivalry was rampant, and each individual stoutly guarded his domain. Through the medium of the Council, however, Simeon could bring pressure to bear on other departments and often did. As the department heads saw it, Simeon was trying to build an empire by taking over their jurisdictions. Simeon was nettled by the accusations, for, as he pointed out, he did not need or want public recognition as a kind of "city manager," because he felt he was that in fact anyhow.

Police. In his study of the Police Department, Peterson, one of the original three-man team that did the exploratory survey of La Loma, departed significantly from what apparently was standard operating procedure. When he began his study, he arranged for an office in the Police Department and announced to all police personnel that he was available to answer questions and explain what he was doing. He often visited the department at odd hours to observe operations and talk with those on duty. During the course of his survey, he talked to almost every member of the department, including clerical personnel.

From the first day of the survey, Peterson bumped heads with Ferdinand E. Bemis, Chief of Police. Bemis had some college background and, at the time of the study, had been a member of the Police Department for over eighteen years. As was the case with Simeon and Miss Henderson, Bemis believed in direct relations between the citizens of La Loma and members of their government. He was suspicious of the "experts" who were going to tell him how to run his department.

Chief Bemis had strong ideas about the functioning of his department, and he was prepared to defend them. He had arrived in La Loma in 1934, bringing with him a variety of experience gained from positions in military and civilian situations. In 1954 he had become chief of police. Once appointed, Bemis had cultivated the support and goodwill of businessmen and merchants who had more than a passing interest in matters of parking, general traffic control, and security of their enterprises. This active, vocal segment of the community affected many of the policies of the Police Department.

Bemis used the Police Commission as a source of support in protecting his own position. (According to his assistant, this is why he fought so hard to retain the commission after the consultants recommended abolishing it.) To staff the commission Bemis selected leading businessmen and merchants and issued them badges and identification cards, which became, some alleged, symbols of prestige in event of violations of law. Both Bemis and Simeon relied upon the more influential merchants in the city for support. Simeon, however, had the backing of the "old guard" and certain industrial interests who were not necessarily the backers of Bemis.

In general, it was the feeling of the community that Bemis did a good job. However, some insiders, such as Miss Henderson and Simeon, felt the work of the police chief "left much to be desired."

Peterson met Bemis' opposition head-on and dealt with Bemis in a forthright manner. As far as Peterson was concerned, the cards were on the table; he was there to change the status quo, and the police chief was there to maintain it by whatever means he could muster.

Peterson maintained an attitude of friendly objectivity and refused to allow the police chief to draw him into a battle based on an exchange of personal aspersions. Bemis voiced his objections to the study through the daily and weekly newspapers, through interviews with the press and public speeches, and through social contacts. In doing so, he attacked Peterson's reputation both as an individual and as an expert in the police field.

Peterson happened to meet Bemis over cocktails during this time. After an exchange of amenities, the police chief pointed out that he had nothing personal against Peterson and that he hoped he would understand that anything disparaging he might say about him was strictly for public consumption.

Administrative Assistance to the Council. The fourth major consideration of the study—what to do about the administrative burden carried by the mayor and Council– -became the focal point of much of the contention that arose when implementation of certain recommendations was attempted. This controversy will be described separately in a later section of this case study.

THE REPORT

The two-volume *Report of the Organization and Management of the City of La Loma* was issued only to members of the Council in January 1957.[9] Its major recommendations concerned the general administrative structure, fiscal operations, personnel, public works, and police. These are discussed below.

General Administration

To relieve the City Council of its administrative responsibilities, the study recommended that the Council take the following action:

(1) Adopt the Council-Manager plan as soon as possible by ordinance.
(2) Study the feasibility of adopting a city charter in order to provide a more permanent basis for the Council-Manager plan.
(3) Make the elected offices of city clerk and city treasurer appointive.[10]
(4) Abolish the Building and Safety, Water, Parking, Fire, Police, and Recreation Commissions.

These recommendations were in line with current thinking relative to the creation of a centralized administrative machinery headed by a "strong executive." The report pointed out that a city manager could not function properly unless he were given authority and backing from the Council and unless he also had control of the various departments and offices responsible for administrative functions. The report recommended that the Council recruit a professionally trained city manager and that he be given the authority, within civil service regulations, to hire and fire.

To further strengthen the city manager's position, and to prevent violation of the chain of command and short-circuiting of the manager, the offices of city treasurer and city clerk were to be made appointive, and a number of boards and commissions were to be abolished.[11] By thus structuring the organization of the city's government, the office of city manager would become a funnel through which all city business of an administrative nature would flow. The study also strongly recommended that the Council withdraw from direct contact with department heads, and that the city manager be recognized as the coordinating head, interposed between the city employees and the Council.

The question of whether to recommend a Council-Manager form of government for La Loma, or a variation of the plan, occasioned some discussion and even argument among the consultants.

Nelson was a firm believer in the "strong executive" approach to municipal government, and he was convinced that La Loma's interest would be best served by a city manager who, with the strong Council support that seemed to be promised, would have a rather large amount of administrative independence. Those consultants who had argued against the Council-Manager plan for La Loma believed that the city would be better off with a city administrative officer, an officer with somewhat smaller formal grants of authority.[12] Dr.

[9] Official publication of the report was somewhat ceremonial as far as the Council was concerned. As noted earlier, the Council members had been fully briefed earlier as each segment of the report had been completed.

[10] It was recommended that this not be done until the incumbents had completed their current terms in office.

[11] The recommendation to abolish certain boards and commissions aroused no particular comment when it became known, except on the part of the chief of police. The report noted in passing that most of these bodies were not particularly active at the time of the study. Abolition of the boards and commissions did become a minor issue in the 1960 elections.

[12] In California, the post of city manager customarily commands more *formal* authority, independence,

Carlton T. Marshall, who was involved in the planning phase of the study, privately questioned whether or not the Council-Manager plan was as good as its exponents claimed. Marshall believed that a city administrative officer (CAO) would be more responsive to the Council and the people. Nelson, however, stuck to his position that La Loma needed a strong executive. The report recommended the establishment of a city manager in La Loma.

Fiscal Operations

The question of fiscal organization came under close scrutiny. Winfield introduced his study by noting:

> The fiscal organization of the City of La Loma is inadequately structured to meet its present needs. It is a typical example of the efforts made a half century ago to provide protection for public funds by diffusing financial responsibility. Such an organization was necessary, both legally and practically, when cities had neither high personnel standards nor adequate accounting and auditing. These conditions no longer prevail, and the State of California has modified its legal requirements accordingly.

The fiscal organization of the city is shown in Figure 2.

Miss Henderson's office was responsible for all accounting activities for the city and for maintenance of accounting records. In addition she was responsible for preparation of all warrants, the payroll, the annual budget, and the monthly report of expenditures and revenues.

Winfield pointed out that under California law, the duties of the city clerk are primarily those of a legislative secretariat and chief accountant. In describing the operations of the city clerk's office, he noted:

> Under existing conditions, the General Ledger was entirely hand posted by the accountant, and all warrants and payroll items prepared by the deputy clerks. The lack of any accounting machines severely handicaps this office, a handicap which is clearly demonstrated by the fact that it takes an estimated two clerical man-days to type up the payroll checks and the journal.

In reviewing the city clerk's preparation of the annual budget, Winfield indicated that because Miss Henderson saw the budget strictly from an accounting point of view, she had no interest in it as a planning or management device. Thus preparation was largely a matter of "copying the figures of previous years." This comment outraged Miss Henderson when she finally saw the report, and did much to determine her general view of the document.

Winfield also examined the functions of the city treasurer, particularly his dual responsibility as Water Department auditor. Such an arrangement had a number of weaknesses, one of the most important being that, in the position of Water Department auditor, the treasurer was not only receiving cash but also had responsibility for auditing the account.

FIGURE 2: FISCAL ORGANIZATION
Official (1957)

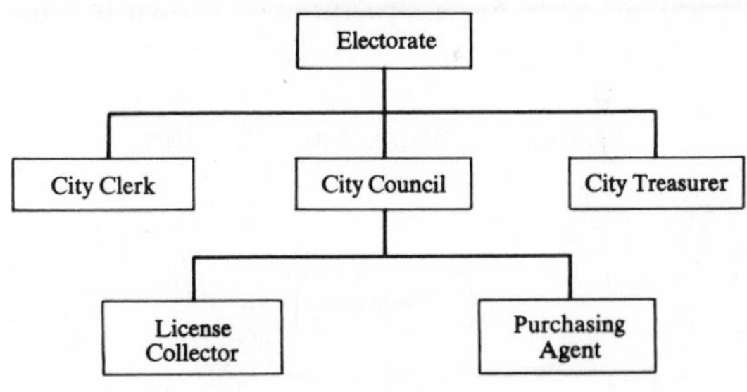

In analyzing the activities of the purchasing agent, Winfield found that:

> Owing to circumstances, he has assumed responsibility in an area in which he has no authority; he has assumed responsibility for informal pre-audit of all requisitions.

At the time of the study, the system of purchasing was so designed that, technically, all purchases were supposed to be authorized by the Standing Committee on Finance of the City Council, but the delay caused by referring purchases to that body had resulted in an informal pre-audit by the pur-

and prestige than that of city administrative officer. Although there is a good deal of variation among cities, the manager usually has more authority in hiring and firing, budget preparation, and general direction of the city's business. The CAO's, in contrast, are usually more in the nature of advisers to the Council and coordinators in regard to personnel, budget, and other matters. But in operation, the distinction is not clear-cut. Strong CAO's with the confidence of friendly Councils can assert and exercise real powers fully comparable to those of strong city managers. And weak managers, or managers operating under divided or unfriendly Councils, may find their effective powers severely limited.

chasing agent. For this reason the Finance Committee usually found itself in the position of rubber-stamping the decisions of the purchasing agent. While the system worked fairly well, this was believed to be due to the long years of experience and the special knowledge possessed by the incumbent. Even so, in assuming the audit function the purchasing agent frequently came into conflict with department heads who disagreed with his decisions.

In summarizing the fiscal operations of La Loma, Winfield reported:

> The responsibility for the financial activities of the City of La Loma is thus scattered through four offices, two elective and two appointive. It is now well recognized in both business and government that current, accurate, and complete financial data are essential to the proper functioning of the organization. Furthermore, it is recognized that this objective can best be achieved if responsibility for financial activities is centralized. The members of the City Council might well consider whether they would be willing to assume responsibility, as individuals, for the operation of a business with assets of more than $3,000,000 and which grosses $1,500,000 a year with a similarly disorganized finance and accounting section.

Winfield recommended that scattered fiscal activities be centralized in a Department of Finance headed by a finance director. As reorganized, fiscal operations were to be structured as shown in Figure 3.

FIGURE 3: FISCAL ORGANIZATION
Proposed (1957)

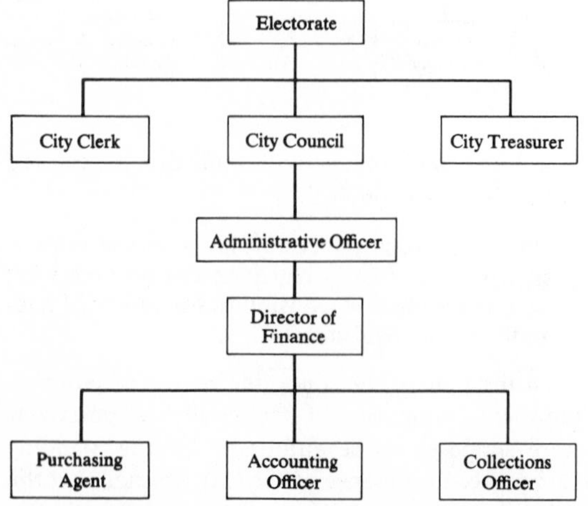

Winfield also recommended in his study that:

(1) Accounting functions in the office of the City Clerk be transferred to the proposed position of Director of Finance.
(2) The functions of preparation and collection of water bills be transferred from the City Treasurer to the Department of Finance.
(3) The City Treasurer be relieved of all responsibilities and duties relative to the Water Department; the Treasurer's salary to be reduced accordingly.
(4) The Council adopt an effective budgetary system. The term "effective" is here utilized to mean: (a) budget estimates which accurately reflect the various department heads' considered opinion of their needs for the ensuing year; (b) a final budget which is the Council's considered opinion of the optimum use of the City's anticipated income for the ensuing year; and (c) a policy of strict enforcement of the budget.[13]

Personnel Administration

Shelton himself was the principal analyst for the personnel segment of the study. He found that the system was badly in need of modernization. His recommendations included:

(1) Creation of a Personnel Department headed by a full-time Director of Personnel.
(2) Centralization of personnel activities which were divided between the City Clerk's office and the office of the Mayor.
(3) Establishment of a "positive" personnel program; e.g., improved recruiting methods, updating job classifications and descriptions, abolition of the residence requirement, and emphasis on the merit principle.

A wage and salary survey was also included as part of the study. Here Shelton found that a substantial number of La Loma employees were drawing salaries that were well above the average when compared with other cities. For the first time in the experience of the consultants they were unable to use mean salary levels as a bench mark in recommending rates of compensation.

The salary distortions were pointed out to the Council, and the team explained that a pay plan based on the middle fifty per cent of salaries re-

[13] At one point in the study, Miss Henderson is alleged to have said to Shelton, "But Mr. Shelton, we don't need all those controls; we have plenty of money."

ported for comparable cities would result in lowering the salaries of most La Loma employees.

At the start of the study, city employees had been clamoring for a raise. This demand had been set aside by the Council until the salary survey was completed. The unpleasant facts were placed before the Council by the consultants. On the one hand, salaries were much too high in comparison with other communities. On the other, to recommend realistic levels would result in salary reductions and would contribute even more to lowering morale and reinforcing negative feelings employees had expressed toward the study.

After much pulling and hauling, the Council agreed to the consultants' suggestion that salaries be pegged at the seventy-fifth percentile level. Those whose salaries were above that level would not receive increases until their salaries fell within the proposed schedules. As Marshall pointed out in retrospect, setting salaries at the seventy-fifth percentile was "politically inspired—and rather innovative. It was a means of making a concession to the employees in value-neutral terms. Anything higher than that would have caused public reaction. Thus Shelton did everything he could do to relate a rational compensation system to the political realities of La Loma. It obviously was not enough, because politics and rationality often do not go together."

In drawing up the new schedule, Shelton used the seventy-fifth percentile bench mark, but this was not, in the long run, satisfactory to the employees. They wanted more money than they were presently making, and in this they were supported by their department heads.

In summary, the Staff Services volume of the report recommended doing away with Council intervention in administrative matters by appointing a city manager. As proposed, the city manager would eventually exercise strong direction with respect to the activities of department heads, the city clerk, and the city treasurer. The city clerk was to be stripped of all fiscal functions, and the office itself was eventually to be brought under the control of the city manager. The city treasurer's job was to be cut back to the functions normal to such an office and the incumbent was to be paid the established salary for this on a one-third time basis. This office also would eventually become appointive. The purchasing agent and the license collector were to be brought under the control of the proposed finance director. Finally, a personnel director was to be appointed and given the functions then handled by the mayor's secretary and the city clerk.

Public Works

At the time of the study, public works activities were organized as shown in Figure 4.

Pierce was the principal analyst for this portion of the study. He found, as Figure 4 indicates, that what should have been a centralized public works function was splintered into seven different departments. Five of the departments had individual heads, each of whom reported directly to the City Council. The Parks Department was directed by the head of the Street Department, and the Water Department was run by the city engineer.

FIGURE 4: PUBLIC WORKS
Official (1957)

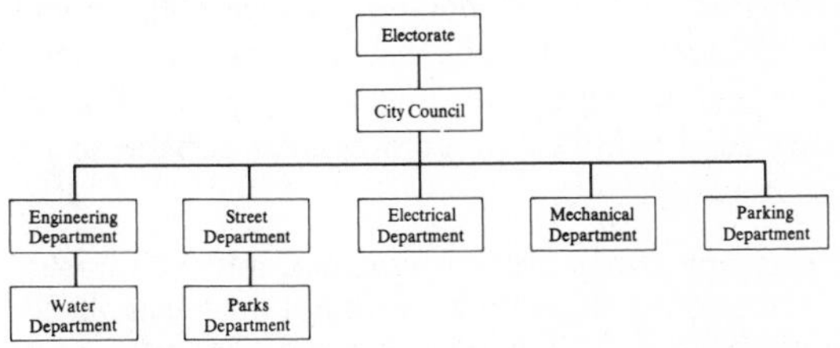

Pierce's comments were terse. He noted that spreading public works functions among several departments, all reporting to the Council, had created a situation wherein:

> Departmental activities are not tied together within the organizational framework of the City so as to provide interdepartmental control, coordination, and overall administrative supervision.

Furthermore,

> The City Engineer presently coordinates public works type construction projects because of his technical skill and abilities. The services of the Engineering Department are needed in solving problems of most of the other public works functions. The Engineering Department, therefore, is acting as a staff aide to each of the other department heads.

Pierce's recommendations were to the point:

(1) Create a Public Works Department headed by a Director.
(2) Place in that department, as divisions, the

Engineering, Street, Water, Electrical, and Parking Departments.

In summary, Pierce recommended that atomized public works functions be pulled together under a Department of Public Works and that existing departments be reduced organizationally to the level of divisions. Hierarchically, division heads were to be responsible to the director of public works, who, in turn, would report to the city manager. These recommendations were designed to alleviate some of the problems of coordination that Simeon had experienced.

Police Department

Peterson pulled no punches in describing the activities of the fifty-one-man Police Department. In his summary he said that while the department was performing all the functions considered necessary in providing law enforcement service to the community:

> its operations are not efficient, and administration of the department does not meet established standards. This means that the City pays more and receives less from its Police Department than the citizens of La Loma are entitled to in the way of police service.
>
> Poor administration of the Department has resulted from City Council involvement in detail, lack of developing positive programs by the Chiefs of Police, the shaping of policies based on citizens' complaints, both by the Council and the Chief of Police, and from undue pressures from particular citizens' groups. This has led to an over-emphasis on traffic control throughout the City, improper organization of the Department, and poor management practices.
>
> At the present time there is no functional organization in the Department. This means that the Chief of Police is personally directing all police operations with almost no delegation of authority or responsibility to ranking officers. Approximately 25 percent of the departmental personnel is assigned to traffic control work. Officers of the Department are not trained. New recruits learn their police work from older officers, and supervisory personnel must rely on common sense and experience or personal endeavor in order to carry out supervisory responsibilities.

The report went on to note that chiefs of police had, in general, used their relationship with the City Council to settle specific problems as they arose, but no effort had been made to have the Council establish overall broad policies which could then become a basis of operation for the department.

Peterson's report brought out the informal, ad hoc nature of police operations in which the police chief personally directed all activities. There was no chart that described the structure of the organization or the various functions and responsibilities of the individuals in the department. Assignment of shifts and areas to be covered were not clearly set forth; nor had there been any real effort to identify the jobs to be done. As far as staffing went, Peterson felt that there was a disproportionate number of supervisory officers.

Peterson concluded that the department was poorly managed.

> Lack of definition of function, poor organization, lack of planning and poor utilization of personnel are evidence of poor management. The present management system of the Department has evolved over a number of years, influenced by a number of factors. There has at times been considerable meddling in departmental operations by City Councilmen. Inadequately trained personnel promoted to management positions, including the position of Chief of Police, has influenced the management system. The Department has never had a manual, therefore, changes have been made, orders given, and operations carried out without real planning or direction.

Peterson made twenty-nine recommendations for reorganization of the Police Department. Among the more important were:

(1) Relationships between the Council and the Chief should be through the Manager when appointed.
(2) The position of Assistant Chief should be abolished, and the position of Administrative Assistant created and filled from the lieutenant rank.
(3) The Department should be reorganized on a functional basis with three divisions consisting of Field, Investigations, and Services.
(4) Sworn personnel should be reduced from 51 to 42.
(5) A system of control and inspection of department activities should be established, and a departmental manual, setting forth organization, policies, and procedures should be prepared.
(6) Adoption of a budget system which would

require a time schedule for preparation of the budget by all departments, including the Police Department.

In sum, Peterson recommended that the Council assume its proper functions of policy-making body for the Police Department and that the police chief work through the city manager rather than directly with the Council. He also recommended that the police chief reorganize his department on a functional basis and establish appropriate control devices. Once this was done, Peterson suggested that a series of directives be published as an operations manual for guidance of Police Department personnel. Peterson recommended a "positive" personnel program that included heavy emphasis on training. Finally, he suggested that the Council exercise control over the police chief through implementation of a performance-type budget for the department. In effect, this meant an end to the police chief's departmental autonomy.

REACTION TO THE REPORT

All in all, the research group's recommendations called for fairly drastic overhauling of La Loma's city government. If reorganized as recommended, the government would be structured as shown in Figure 5.

The report became available in May 1957, but because of apprehension on the part of Council members, no general distribution was made. Interested department heads and officials could obtain from the city clerk the sections of the report directly relevant to their own activities. No explanatory memoranda accompanied the pieces of the report that were distributed.

Very few of the city's employees (other than some department heads) read the report. Employees obtained sufficient information by word of mouth (from department heads and other officials) and from newspaper accounts to know in a general way what its implications were as far as their jobs were concerned.

Theoretically the duplicated report was a public document available to any interested citizen or employee, but the Council made sure that distribution was limited for the reasons stated. That body also made no effort to ask for comments from those whose operations were affected. Instead,

FIGURE 5: RECOMMENDED ORGANIZATION
CITY OF LA LOMA, CALIFORNIA
Proposed (1957)

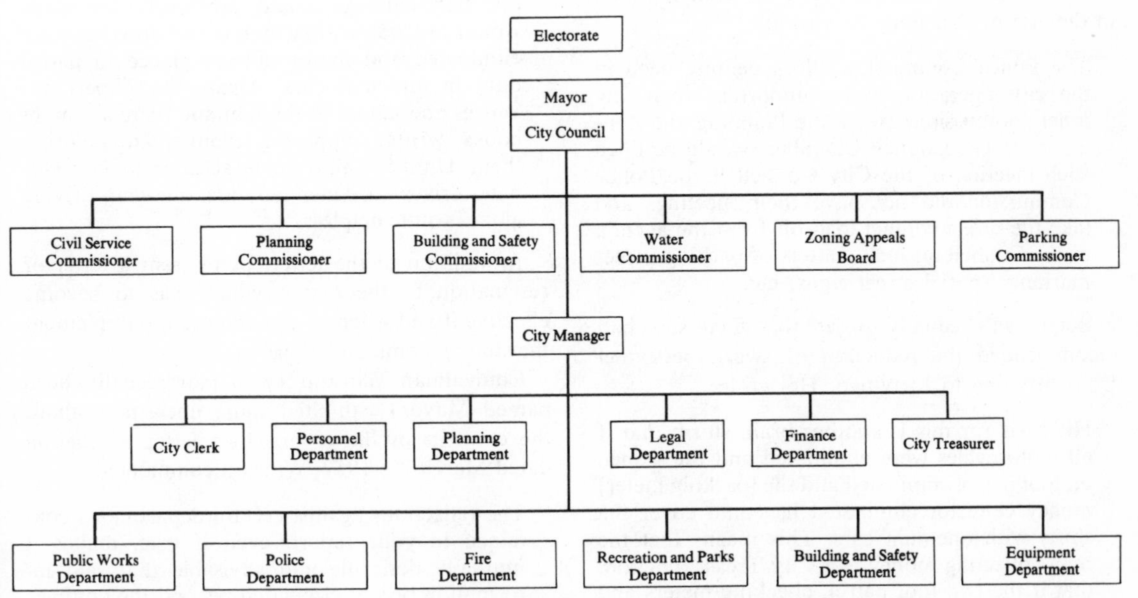

Council members continued to meet, throughout the spring and summer of 1957, in a number of "rump sessions" (usually in the home of a member) to study findings and recommendations. In these informal sessions, Council members worked out agreements about which recommendations they would accept and which they would not.

The introduction to the report pointed out that members of the team were fully aware of the need for scientific method in social research and that each analyst had made certain that

> . . . the survey of La Loma concerns itself only with facts and not with personalities.

This spirit of "scientific objectivity" was not considered admirable by those officials whose operations the report criticized. What the consultants considered objectivity and impartiality was seen by some city officials as cold-blooded detachment accompanied by a swaggering professional superiority and complete lack of sensitivity to those who were filling the positions that had been analyzed.

Peterson was the only one of the analysts who immediately made copies of his report available to a department head. Bemis, the Police Chief, lost no time in reading the report and instantly countered with a three-page, single-spaced letter which he typed himself and sent to the Council in December 1956. As far as Bemis was concerned, not a single recommendation made by Peterson was worthy of consideration.

He was particularly disturbed over the recommendation to disband the Police Commission, and in defense of that body he wrote:

> The Police Commission fills a definite need in the city operation, more important than any other commission, except the Planning and Zoning [sic]. The Council Chambers would be filled each meeting of the City Council if the Police Commission did not have their meetings and take the direct contact load off from the agenda of the Council on such matters of parking, street marking, special street signs, etc.

Bemis was equally upset that Peterson had recommended the reduction of sworn personnel from fifty-one to forty-two. He wrote:

> His basis for this is another brain storm that if all motorcycles were eliminated and the 4 men on foot patrol eliminated and the [parking meter] money collector eliminated he could cover the shifts with one-man cars. This means that the man collecting money is a City Treas. function, that if the two foot patrol, checking meters and the Blvd. and alleys, shaking doors, are taken away, he could cover the shifts. The merchants, Chamber of Commerce, etc., would ride both the City Council and the expert out of town on a rail in about one month.

The police chief was absolutely opposed to the idea of a Police Department budget. In defending his position he asked:

> Is the City Council the Administrative officers for budgeting matters in all City Dept. or should the Heads of Depts work on their budgetary matters? I can not see why we should meddle. After deciding on the special items needed for the ensuing year should we be concerned with the over-all picture?

As to the training recommendations, Bemis had certain reservations. He agreed to the need for training but pointed out:

> The cry in all small departments is "how can I spare the men from their watch." I am of the opinion that if the men were given the same schooling the Expert [Peterson] has and didn't return with more practical application the City would profit if the men stayed untrained. We manage to conduct a few courses each year in different police subjects and at each class the strain is to keep the watch covered.

Finally, Bemis blasted the recommendation for one-man patrol cars:

> This is the foundation for his entire wordy thesis. His entire program revolves around the one-man car. As stated previously his plans would not be possible unless motorcycles were eliminated and motor officers placed in patrol duty in one-man cars. Again, the Expert advances one school of thought and there are more books written opposing them than favoring them. Until the auto manufacturers make right-hand drives on American cars, one-man driving alone is quite helpless.

In addition to the letter, Bemis sent a letter of resignation to the mayor which was to become effective if and when he was required to implement the study recommendations.

Councilman Winston (who had recently been named Mayor) exhibited some uneasiness about the contents of the report. In a letter to Shelton dated March 29, 1957, Winston commented:

> The reflections against certain departments contained in your report, even if true, makes it mutually desirable and advisable that said information be not circulated beyond the confines

of the City Hall. Some of the personnel in the departments adversely affected are at the moment sufficiently incensed to precipitate an attack that can only result in damaging repercussions. Therefore, it is imperative that we be very circumspect in the premises and thereby minimize the damage that can result from unnecessary dissemination. The City of La Loma has in the past and does now enjoy an enviable reputation in the industrial and commercial world. I am sure that you will cooperate with us in perpetuating such a reputation.

In May 1957 the City Clerk was given all copies of the full report to keep on hand for future distribution.[14] Miss Henderson immediately checked the section dealing with her office and was so disturbed at the description of the way she managed her work that she became physically ill.[15] She asked Nelson to keep the extra copies at the University of the West, since she felt it was too damaging and explosive to be made available generally. She felt that the report "made me and the Office of City Clerk a laughingstock."

Miss Henderson had two reasons for feeling that the report was destructive. First, she did not feel that she had been fairly treated by Shelton; the section of the report on the method of budget preparation, for example, remained an extremely sore point with her. She maintained that when she had told Shelton she used last year's figures in budget preparation, she had thought he "was smart enough" to know what she meant. She pointed out that she did not simply repeat previous years' figures as he reported, but she did use them as a point of departure. The fact that Shelton did not understand this made Miss Henderson "wonder whether he was actually competent as an analyst."

Miss Henderson's second objection to the report centered on the planning section, portions of which had been made available to the editor of the La Loma *Daily News*.[16] In February 1957 the *Daily News* had made quite a story out of the fact that the city was faced with "blight conditions." In essence, the report stated that La Loma was on the verge of blight, that its single-family dwellings were old and decrepit, and that its population was aging. Miss Henderson felt that the newspaper story had depressed real estate values and that a number of people had unloaded their properties because of the story.

Miss Henderson was a property owner in La Loma, and she took an active and personal interest in the affairs of the community. In order to maintain property values, Miss Henderson believed, the city needed better publicity to increase La Loma's desirability as a place to live and work. She felt that the money spent on the survey had been completely wasted and could have been much better used in a city public relations program.

The consultants, on the other hand, saw nothing particularly damaging in the stories released by the *Daily News*. Most of the team felt that the *Daily News* gave them excellent coverage and that its support had helped in "selling" the study to the Council and the public in general.

Simeon had believed for a long time that something should be done to coordinate and direct the efforts of the many departments concerned with public works. He also felt that public works activities should be directed by a civil engineer; he was not opposed to the creation of the Department of Public Works. However, he did not see himself as a subordinate to a director of public works. The Council agreed that Simeon would continue to operate as an autonomous department head until he retired in 1959, even if the position of director of public works were created.

As to the Council-Manager plan in general, Simeon was undecided. He did believe, however, that city managers should be civil engineers, since those without engineering training could not possibly understand most major municipal problems.

As far as the rest of the department heads were concerned, no one particularly relished the idea of having his unit reduced to a division, though some (the head of the Electrical Department, for example) had no strong feelings about the recommendations.

The purchasing agent was completely opposed to placing his office under the finance director, and

---

14 Although the report was dated January 1957, the time the study had been completed.

15 Miss Henderson said that she became so upset when she read that part of the report dealing with the city clerk's office that she could read no further. She declared that if the rest of the report was as wrong as it had been about her office, it was probably nothing but a tissue of fabrications throughout and not worth reading.

16 Despite the mayor's apprehension about the report, information on the progress of the survey and findings of the consultants had been "leaked" to the press. At the time of the research on this case, there was disagreement about whether such "leaking" had been done by some consultants and/or councilmen who thought that publicizing some portions would make the report more acceptable.

he was not shy about saying so. The license collector felt the same way. The treasurer did not like the idea of making his office appointive, and he certainly was not in favor of reducing his full-time position to one-third time with a comparable reduction in salary.

The recommendation on salary and wages was distasteful to a number of city employees. This was particularly true for those whose salaries were above the limits recommended for the positions they filled. It struck these employees as outrageous that they might be excluded from a general pay raise (or, perhaps, two or three such raises) until their salaries fell within the recommended limits.

In February 1957 one meeting had been held with representatives of city employees to discuss salary and wage recommendations. Nelson, Shelton, the department heads, and other city officials were present. Nelson opened the meeting by explaining what the recommended salary and wage schedules were and how they had been determined. At this time the head of the Street Department, Alfred Kirk, took issue with Nelson over the recommended hourly wage to be paid laborers. He pointed out that laborers were in short supply and that he could not get men to work for the wage suggested.

This criticism was met with the comment that the wage recommended represented the seventy-fifth percentile in the rank order of wages paid for such work in other cities and should be adhered to as suggested in the report. When Kirk asked Nelson what he should do if he could not get men at that wage, Nelson simply shook his head and repeated that the recommended wage compared favorably with the average for other cities.

IMPLEMENTATION OF THE REORGANIZATION PLAN

Of all the recommendations made by Consultants Unlimited,[17] the one the Council was most enthusiastic about was that of getting an individual who could shoulder the administrative responsibilities for the city. Unwilling to establish the Council-Manager plan, the Council agreed to settle, for the time being, on a city administrative officer (CAO).

In June 1957 the Council drafted an ordinance creating the position of CAO. Consultants Unlimited had recommended a supplementary contract to cover assistance in implementing reorganization recommendations, but the Council was reluctant to spend the additional funds. However, the Council asked Consultants Unlimited to handle the recruiting for the CAO post. George Douglas, a man of wide experience in personnel recruitment, was asked to handle this phase. Douglas had acted as consultant many times for cities attempting to recruit top management people. While Shelton was nominally in charge, as project director, Douglas actually did the recruiting work.

Announcements for the La Loma CAO post were circulated in July 1957. Out of a number of applicants, seven were finally selected for serious consideration. Ronald B. Allen, then CAO and City Clerk of a small city in California, ranked third on the list. Douglas made no recommendation, but his personal preference was the man who was number one on the list. In August 1957 the Council, after interviewing the seven applicants, selected Allen. Council members were impressed by his forthright manner and general bearing.

Ordinance 1390 establishing the position of CAO was passed on August 6, 1957. It specified:

> SECTION 1. Office of the Chief Administrative Officer
>
> A. Office of the Chief Administrative Officer created. That there be and there is hereby created the position of Chief Administrative Officer of the City of La Loma, who shall be appointed by the City Council solely on the basis of his executive and administrative qualifications and ability. . . .
>
> F. Powers and Duties. The Chief Administrative Officer shall be the administrative head of the City Government under the direction and control of the City Council. He shall be responsible for the efficient administration of all the affairs of the City. . . .
>
> (2) To exercise administrative control over all the departments and divisions of the City Government except those of City Clerk, City Attorney, City Prosecutor, and City Treasurer. . . .
>
> (11) To supervise expenditures of all departments, divisions or services of the City Government: no expenditures shall be submitted or

[17] Nelson, Shelton, and Peterson formed the corporation, Consultants Unlimited, about midway through the study.

recommended to the City Council without his support or approval. . . .

(22) The Chief Administrative Officer shall act as the agent for the City Council in the discharge of its administrative functions, but shall not exercise any policy-making or legislative functions whatsoever.

In December 1957 Allen assumed the CAO post. It was understood that he would serve at the pleasure of the Council and could be relieved at any time.

The City Administrative Officer

Allen was an impressive man. Thirty-eight years old, married, and the father of one child, he seemed the epitome of the competent, capable executive. He was not a particularly tall man, but his movements and general bearing gave that impression. Allen could almost have been characterized as a "collar-ad" man. In talking with people, his narrow-eyed, direct gaze gave the impression of a keen intellect and an alert and knowledgeable attitude.

When announcement was made of Allen's appointment, speculation began to circulate about him and his background. It was generally thought, for example, that he was a college graduate who had been trained in management. When he ran into trouble, which was almost immediately, his critics often referred contemptuously to the "diplomas" hanging on the wall of his office, and pointed out that a college education did not make a manager. The diplomas were actually testimonial scrolls Allen had received from city councils for which he had worked in earlier years. Allen had finished almost all the requirements for a bachelor's degree in political science, and he took the La Loma job partly because he thought he might be able to finish his degree at a nearby college. Contrary to general belief of those in and out of La Loma city government, Allen had never had a course in "management." Whatever professional knowledge he possessed he had gained through experience as a CAO and city clerk prior to coming to La Loma.

Allen had been singularly fortunate in his former job because he had held both an elective and an appointive position at the same time. As an appointed CAO, he had often run into city problems that were troublesome and difficult to handle. When this had occurred, Allen had discarded his CAO hat and put on the hat of elected city clerk. In this manner, Allen had been able to deal with balky Councils or other hostile groups.

In the interview in August 1957, members of the Council told Allen frankly that he would face some fairly tough problems as CAO of La Loma. Winston described the reorganization study and the hostilities it had generated. Allen was warned about moving too swiftly in attempting to implement the report's recommendations. Winston told him that many of the recommendations were explosive in nature. Council members made it plain that they did not expect him to go into action immediately. He was told to take his time, to get acquainted with the city and its government, and then to begin his moves. Tentatively, the Council set a date of six months after Allen's appointment as the time to begin "phasing-in" the reorganization plan.

To Allen, what the Council said it expected and what it actually wanted from him were two different things. The Council had indicated that he was to take it easy. Nevertheless, once he was on the job Council members immediately began dumping problems in his lap. These problems were the same ones that had triggered the survey in the first place. The office of the mayor continued to be swamped administratively; there was no personnel program worthy of the name; city finances were disorganized; the public works function was uncoordinated. Members of the Council had urged him to go slowly, but shortly after he took over in January 1958, he was urged with equal vigor to do something about the chronic administrative problems of the city. To Allen the only answer appeared to be that of following the reorganization recommendations of the consultants.

The Council appeared to be somewhat uncertain as to just what it did expect from the CAO. While theoretically members of that body could intervene in the administrative affairs of the city, they appeared to take a "wait and see" approach and allowed Allen considerable discretion in attacking problems. He found himself caught between the Council, which expected solutions to problems, and those city officials who were fully prepared to fight to the last ditch to maintain the status quo.

Once installed, Allen carefully read the reorganization report and set about implementing its recommendations. His preoccupation with the report led a number of employees to comment that he had adopted it as his "Bible."

Allen's first effort was to try to channel all communications through his office. Two weeks after

Allen took over, he announced in his first staff meeting that all direct communication between department heads and other officials, and between such employees and the Council, would cease as of that date. He indicated that communications were to be put in writing and routed through his office. He went on to say that those who ignored his request would answer to him personally. Since city employees for years had dealt directly and often informally with each other and with the Council, Allen's announcement met with antagonism from subordinate city officials. His communications edict was largely ignored.

In the first Administrative Directive issued from his office in January, Allen formalized the procedure for communicating with the Council. He repeated his request that all communications be channeled through his office and pointed out that this was in conformance with Ordinance 1390 creating the position of CAO.

Allen's attempt to shore up his communication channels met a solid wall of resistance. For years city employees had ambled about from office to office, and city business had been conducted along with general conversation of a social nature.

To Miss Henderson, Allen's attempt to routinize communications was nettlesome. His insistence on the use of written communications "tied employees to their desks." They spent many hours writing out activities and actions that they could have handled in minutes through use of the telephone or by face-to-face contact. As Miss Henderson saw it, Allen was out to "channelize" the operations of city employees.

In February 1958, Allen issued a second Administrative Directive to all department heads, calling for weekly progress reports. This was considered an unwarranted attempt to "snoop" into the affairs of department heads and an indication that Allen lacked confidence in these officials. To department heads who rarely had had to account for their activities or even for how they spent the money allotted them,[18] except for sporadic Council requests for reports, Allen's call for progress reports appeared like an invasion of privacy.

From the moment Allen appeared on the scene, individual department heads began dropping into his office in an attempt to get his backing for various activities. Although it was true that department heads were hostile to the idea of a CAO, they also felt they might have to live with such an arrangement, and one way of doing so was to establish "an inside track" with Allen. The constant stream of city employees in and out of Allen's office consumed so much of his time that he had difficulty finding moments to attend to other business. He talked over his problem with Simeon, the City Engineer, who advised Allen to establish "office hours" for consulting with heads of departments and others.

In late February, Allen sent a memorandum to his department heads asking that they contact his office on Tuesday or Thursday of each week to arrange for appointments to see him. The memo added that his office was open at all times and that establishing an appointment procedure was simply a method of facilitating timing. The memorandum was coldly received by the department heads, who considered it as still another indication of the distance Allen was trying to create between their offices and his.

One of Allen's problems began early in 1958 with his search for a private secretary. Seven women applied for the position, six of whom were employed by the city. The seventh, Mrs. Wanda Alonso (a prominent figure later in the case), had worked for the city years before and was rumored to have left after some unpleasantness. In February 1958 Allen selected Mrs. Marie Wolfe, who had worked in the Building and Safety Department for fourteen years. Many in and out of La Loma government were critical of Allen's choice. Some city employees, male and female, had reservations about Mrs. Wolfe. As far as the women were concerned, this may have been due to the fact that she was an attractive, vivacious woman. Some men judged her as too aggressive and too willing to "take over." Another criticism was based on the fact that Mrs. Wolfe's husband, Henry, was then Managing Editor of the La Loma *Daily News*. Many questioned the wisdom of employing someone who could become a direct pipeline from the CAO's office to the daily newspaper. Later, employee opinion was divided as to whether or not this actually occurred. One thing was certain, Mr. Wolfe was convinced that the Council-Administrative Officer form of government was right for La Loma, and he used his influence to gain support for the plan. He was later credited with "saving" the CAO

[18] Department heads spent their funds as they saw fit. Post audit, if it could be so called, was simply checking vouchers for payment by the city clerk. Pre-audit of requests for equipment purchase was made by the purchasing agent. There appeared to be no accountability in terms of yearly programs of how funds were to be apportioned between various activities within departments and other units.

plan in La Loma on at least three separate occasions by persuading wavering Council members to defend it.

Of those who sought the position of private secretary to the CAO, one of the most disappointed was Mrs. Alonso. After Allen had made his choice, he sent her the usual form letter saying that the position had been filled. She returned the letter to him with a note across the bottom saying that she thought the least he could have done in turning her down was to have written her a "personal" letter.

In February 1958 Allen also tackled the problem of salary and wage raises. As noted previously, the survey team had found that, for the most part, employees were being overpaid in comparison with other cities' employees. The recommendation in the reorganization plan was to bring salaries in line by withholding raises from those already overpaid until their salaries fell within prescribed limits. Allen discussed the question with the Council, and that body agreed to follow the consultant's recommendation. Nevertheless, those employees whose salaries were above the established range and who consequently did not receive raises (this included some of the department heads) blamed Allen.

Creation of the Finance Department: Ordinance 1399

Allen began to plan almost immediately after he took office for the creation of a Finance Department. He believed that without centralized fiscal administration he would not be able to control city operations effectively. He was acutely aware of Miss Henderson's negative attitude toward the survey and especially toward its recommendation to remove the accounting and budgeting functions from her office. Allen had also heard, through City Hall gossip, that Miss Henderson allegedly had vowed to "get" the CAO, even before he was selected. Allen felt chances were poor that he could establish a friendly working relationship with her. Nevertheless, some means had to be found to create the Finance Department and make it operational.

After lengthy discussion, the Council members and Allen agreed that Miss Henderson posed the most serious obstacle to establishing the Finance Department. She had been outspoken in her criticism of the survey recommendations concerning the financial activities of her office, and it seemed likely that she would oppose any move to shift fiscal responsibilities to the proposed department.

Miss Henderson held an elective office, and that fact plus her potentiality for mustering public support made the Council cautious in its negotiations with her. She had earned a reputation for "standing up" to the Council, and that body wanted to avoid conflict with her.

Council members suggested to Allen that the only possibility of avoiding open resistance from Miss Henderson was to make her the first Finance Director. Allen finally agreed to this course, but only with the greatest reluctance.

Although he agreed, Allen had substantial misgivings. He doubted that Miss Henderson, as Finance Director, would accept direction from his office. If she did not, he would be no better off than under the old arrangement.

Miss Henderson was offered the post and accepted it. Allen was still not completely satisfied with the arrangement. In a letter to the Council dated April 24, 1958, in which he formally recommended that the Finance Department be created, he pointed out:

> It is essential that the City Clerk's function of Finance Officer be done through the Administrative Officer. If it is not possible to have this understood and clarified, the Council should arrange to appoint a separate department head for the Finance Department at this time.

The Council was not disturbed by Allen's letter. It felt that Miss Henderson's agreement to accept the position of Finance Director was a clear indication that she approved of the creation of the new department and that she would work cooperatively with Allen. Council members did not share Allen's apprehension, and therefore, they tended to look upon his letter as nothing more than "going on record."

In May 1958 Allen submitted to the Council a number of recommendations for reorganization. All were based on the survey. He pointed out the need to abolish the position of parking director and to establish the positions of directors of planning, public works, and personnel, and building and maintenance supervisor. Important among his recommendations was Allen's suggestion that the Council pass a resolution appointing Miss Henderson head of the proposed Finance Department. The resolution was passed and was considered a formal confirmation of Miss Henderson's prior verbal agreement to accept the position of Finance Director. (At this time the ordinance creating the Finance Department had not been drafted.) To Allen and the Council it now seemed certain that centralization of the city's fiscal operations would soon become a reality.

Having received Council approval, Allen set in motion the machinery to recruit for the recommended positions. He also drafted an ordinance establishing the Finance Department. A few days before he submitted the ordinance to the Council, he sent Miss Henderson a draft copy for comment. She read the draft but did not reply. She knew Allen often sent things to people for comment, but, as far as she was concerned, "for comment" simply meant that he wanted the document checked for accuracy rather than challenged as to content.

In formal session in June 1958, Allen proposed that the Council enact Ordinance 1399. As drafted, the ordinance called for:

(1) Centralization of the financial responsibilities of the city's organizational structure under a new Department of Finance to be directly assisted by an Accounting Officer, a Purchasing Agent, and a Collections Officer.
(2) Creation of the position of Finance Director.

The intent of the ordinance was to accomplish the following:

(1) Relieve the City Clerk's office of all accounting and budget responsibility.
(2) Install a program budget which would have to be presented and defended by the Finance Director annually.
(3) Modernize the accounting system utilizing the Automatic Remittance Control machine and two general purpose accounting machines.

Immediately after Allen's proposal, Miss Henderson quietly indicated to the Council that she was opposed to the ordinance. Furthermore, she requested that a statement she had prepared be entered in the Council minutes. The statement read:

> The proposed ordinance is authorized for General Law cities such as La Loma. This action takes the duties performed by the City Clerk and gives them to an officer who is responsible to the City Clerk and the Chief Administrative Officer. Being elected by the people the City Clerk feels that because she was elected by the people the duties of the Finance Officer should remain hers. Duties should not be removed midway during term. Fullest cooperation has been given the City Administrative Officer and this legislation is not necessary.

Allen and the Council were stunned by Miss Henderson's opposition; since she had agreed to accept the position of Finance Director, they had thought the matter settled. They interpreted her move as a deliberate attempt to sabotage their plans.

Miss Henderson did not see sabotage as her motivation for opposing Ordinance 1399. She had agreed to accept the position of Finance Director, but she believed she still had an obligation to explain to the public just what passage of the ordinance implied. She felt the public did not understand what was involved in creating the Finance Department, and she was convinced that she would not be fulfilling her responsibilities to the electorate if she did not make it clear that the proposed legislation would strip the city clerk's office of its fiscal responsibilities.

Despite Miss Henderson's opposition, the ordinance was passed. The Council and Allen had no alternative but to wait and see if sufficient opposition developed to push the ordinance to a referendum vote.[19]

[19] It was not clear why the attempt was made to create the Finance Department by ordinance. On the basis of Ordinance 1390 the Finance Department could have been created by Council resolution. The most likely reason was the fact that the survey report had recommended creation by ordinance, and since Miss Henderson had agreed to take the job, no opposition was anticipated. In general, it is considered preferable to create important departments by ordinance because an ordinance has the effect of law, whereas a Council resolution can be more easily reversed.

THE ISSUE GOES TO THE PUBLIC

During the study itself there had been little public involvement. However, in the late stages of the reorganization, public reaction became an important factor through the activities of Mrs. Wanda Alonso, a private citizen of La Loma and one of the unsuccessful applicants for the position of secretary to Allen.

Mrs. Alonso, about fifty-two and small, had dabbled in city affairs for many years. She was said to be politically ambitious. She felt that by taking an active interest in La Loma government she was fulfilling her role as an interested and public-spirited citizen whose prime objective was that of assuring good government for the city.

In 1954 Mrs. Alonso had run unsuccessfully as a candidate for the City Council. One of the main planks in her platform had been the need for what she termed a "city coordinator." In her view this official would have performed almost the same function that the CAO later did.

Mrs. Alonso had operated a couple of businesses in La Loma, but she spent most of her time keeping informed about various city activities. She had often acted in the capacity of Socratic gadfly in Council meetings. She was a close friend of Mrs. Noreen Fitzgerald, secretary to the city attorney. Since most city business eventually went through that office, Mrs. Fitzgerald was privy to almost everything of significance that occurred. Some people suspected that Mrs. Alonso knew everything that went on in City Hall because of her friendship with Mrs. Fitzgerald. Mrs. Alonso said she got information about city government activities on her own.

Most Council members saw Mrs. Alonso as a potential threat, because, in their view, she had a way of presenting half-truths or distorted facts that became embarrassing and difficult for the Council members to refute. Once having decided to challenge the Council, she developed her information and then waited for an appropriate time to drop her bombshell, usually in formal Council session. Some characterized Mrs. Alonso as a "crackpot" and "rabble-rouser," but others—for example, Miss Henderson, Simeon, and Robert Becker, President of the Chamber of Commerce—felt she was sincere and truly interested in the welfare of the city, not just in furthering her own political ambitions.

Mrs. Alonso was mainly concerned with what she considered to be a general trend toward socialism in the nation. She believed that a major aspect of "creeping socialism" was the trend toward strong executive leadership in government, particularly in the local level. She was suspicious of large philanthropic organizations such as the Ford and Rockefeller Foundations because she was convinced that projects sponsored by these foundations had as their ultimate ends socialistic and eventually communistic organization for the country. She alleged that the Ford Foundation was supporting the Public Administration Clearing House in Chicago[20] and that the Clearing House provided the direction for the International City Managers' Association. The ICMA, as far as she was concerned, was definitely socialistic, if not worse. For much of her information Mrs. Alonso relied on the *American Mercury*, a periodical that had campaigned against the Council-Manager plan for a number of years.

Mrs. Alonso's views were no doubt conditioned by a general political conservatism that some would characterize as well to the right of center. She identified herself as a Republican, but she was more extreme in the political position she verbalized than most in the city, even the so-called "old guard." It appears evident, however, that she reflected rather accurately the sentiment of many voters of the community. This group, whether Democrat or Republican, tended to espouse "direct democracy" in settling community disputes and preferred to keep government out of business as much as possible at the national level.

Those in and out of La Loma city government who were critical of Mrs. Alonso did not consider her particularly intelligent, and many believed she was secretly backed by smarter individuals who had their own political axes to grind. She had shown amazing political sensitivity at times, and many who had been forced to deal with her believed she could not generate such political astuteness on her own. In point of fact, however, there was no evidence that she relied on others for direction of her political battles.

The Referendum

Mrs. Alonso attended the Council meeting the night the Finance Ordinance was passed. She had heard that Miss Henderson was to be appointed Finance Director, and she was surprised when Miss Henderson opposed the ordinance. She mulled over the situation for several days and finally concluded that the voters should be given a chance to express their opinion.[21]

Mrs. Alonso went to the city attorney and asked what the voters could do if they did not approve

---

20 Which was, incidentally, untrue.

21 Some of those who had watched Mrs. Alonso in action before asserted, in interviews, that she seized upon Ordinance 1399 as an opportunity to oppose Allen, whom she did not like, and to align herself with Miss Henderson, a respected figure in the community.

of the ordinance. Actually, she already knew the procedure, but she wanted to see whether he would attempt to give her "a bum steer." She believed that city officials often attempted to mislead the public by giving false information on sensitive subjects. For this reason, she usually developed her own information first and then asked for the same information from public officials. In this way, she believed, she kept them "honest."[22]

Mrs. Alonso had decided before she talked to the city attorney that she was going to force the issue of Ordinance 1399 to referendum vote.[23] She consulted Miss Henderson on the matter and mapped out her campaign to gather the necessary signatures. With Miss Henderson and Mrs. Alonso spearheading the drive, friends both in and out of city government quickly volunteered their services.

In Council session in July 1958, Mrs. Alonso announced her opposition to Ordinance 1399 and asked the Council to delay action for thirty days so that the necessary petitions could be circulated.

Once Mrs. Alonso announced her intention of forcing Ordinance 1399 to a vote, she quickly organized a small group of volunteers into teams to collect signatures. Most of those involved in the effort were members of the old guard, who traditionally voted for Miss Henderson at election time and who were determined to maintain the status quo as far as the city clerk's office was concerned. Supermarkets, banks, department stores, and churches were assigned as posts and were manned in shifts. The stated purpose of the volunteers was to save "democratic" government in La Loma. Mrs. Alonso admitted, however, her most effective appeal was, "Save Betty Henderson." She believed that many who signed the petition knew only that the Council was "going to do something to Betty Henderson."

Mrs. Alonso worked tirelessly once she had her volunteers organized. She prepared and duplicated thousands of handouts explaining why Ordinance 1399 was not in the public interest; she directed and coordinated the efforts of those who were collecting the signatures; she talked with her friends and made speeches wherever she could.

Reportedly, Mrs. Alonso consulted Miss Henderson frequently during the signature collection drive. Although this was later denied by both women, Simeon, Allen, Winston, and the editor of the La Loma *Daily News*, among others, were firm in asserting that in all likelihood there had been an exchange of ideas between Mrs. Alonso and Miss Henderson.

When Simeon heard of the attempt to strip Miss Henderson's office of its fiscal functions, he also jumped into the fray and used the influence he had cultivated over the years in her behalf. He had no strong feelings for or against the new Finance Department, but he decided he would not "let them throw Betty out." In interviews later, he characterized his participation as a "whispering campaign," carried on among his friends, in which he questioned the motives of those who desired to remove the fiscal functions from the office of the city clerk.

Allen and most of the Council were convinced that the ordinance had to be ratified, but they also knew that they faced a community which, with the exception of the old guard, took little interest in the issue. Members of the business community, for example, later admitted through a Chamber of Commerce spokesman that they had not given the Council and the CAO the support they deserved. Members of the Council spoke in favor of the measure, the La Loma *Daily News* praised it editorially, and Allen launched a massive campaign to set the issue before the public by means of "progress reports," leaflets, and brochures. Allen assumed leadership in mapping out what strategy there was to gain support for the ordinance. In general, it appeared that the CAO, the Council, and the editor of the *Daily News* constituted the only real support for the legislation.

On October 7, 1958, the fruits of Mrs. Alonso's labor were presented to the Council in the form of a petition containing over 2,400 signatures. The Council agreed on April 7, 1959, as the date for the referendum vote. The battle was now joined.

Allen was determined to see the Finance Department established, and in this he had the backing of most of the Council. From the time the petition was submitted in October 1958 to the election date in April 1959, Allen fought to convince the citizens of La Loma of the need to vote "yes" on Ordinance 1399.

The La Loma *Daily News* fully backed the ordinance and in a sense pilloried Miss Henderson. Mrs. Alonso and Miss Henderson found that they could get little or no sympathetic coverage of their position. For the most part, the two women had to rely on their social contacts to make their story

[22] As indicated in an interview with the author in 1961.

[23] Under California law, those wishing to bring a contested ordinance to referendum vote had to obtain the signatures of fifteen per cent of the registered voters in the municipality concerned.

known. They spoke against the ordinance at various club meetings, and they were able to get fairly good coverage in the small weekly newspaper published in La Loma. This was not much, however, compared with the almost daily coverage in favor of the ordinance provided by the *Daily News*.

In getting commitments to vote against the ordinance, Mrs. Alonso used the same technique she had employed in getting the signatures for the petition. Her small group of volunteers distributed literature and button-holed people in their homes, on the street, and in businesses. Miss Henderson was said by some citizens to have worked closely with Mrs. Alonso in getting the campaign organized and publicized.[24]

In the election on April 7, 1959, the voters rejected the ordinance 2,869 to 1,335. Allen knew then that he was finished.[25]

Attempts to Implement Other Recommendations

About the time that Mrs. Alonso began her fight against Ordinance 1399, George Johnson, a civil engineer with previous city engineer–public works director experience, was appointed Director of Public Works for La Loma. Johnson was in the unique position of being a Public Works Director with nothing to direct. The vociferous opposition of those involved in the public works function to any effort to centralize their work had made the Council cautious in attempting to implement the recommendations of the survey. Simeon, the City Engineer, was due to retire in 1959, however, and Johnson would then take over his department. The Council took the stand that the Public Works Department would have to be organized on a piecemeal basis, since it appeared that present departments could not be brought in until their heads had either retired or otherwise vacated their positions.

With all the other pressures of his job, Allen made no attempt to force Bemis to implement the reorganization recommendations for the Police Department. The police chief had accepted, reluctantly, the elimination of the position of assistant chief and the appointment, as Administrative Assistant, of Larry King,[26] who had been a lieutenant in the department. Until Bemis retired in the summer of 1959 he made King's life "as miserable as possible."[27]

Allen was faced with an extremely complex situation, and the only way he knew of meeting it was head-on. He was convinced that implementation of the survey recommendations would ease his job. Therefore, he pressed members of the Council to pass the legislation necessary to strengthen his position as CAO.

Allen appeared to accept the fact that city employees would oppose any effort he made to disturb the status quo. For this reason, he believed nothing would be gained by involving them in his plans. The recommendations made by Consultants Unlimited were clearly stated, and it seemed logical to him that the recommendations be implemented in order to give him the authority he needed to carry out his responsibilities.

He had, at least for the moment, set aside the reorganization of the Police Department. He had also, and against his better judgment, agreed to the appointment of Miss Henderson as Finance Director. He felt that he had made as many ac-

---

[24] This statement was hotly disputed by the two women. They were unequivocal in saying it was absolutely untrue. Miss Henderson pointed out that the office of city clerk traditionally had held itself aloof where city politics were concerned, and for her to have taken an active part in the plans to defeat the measure would have been a violation of that tradition. Mrs. Alonso made the same point. On the other hand, Mrs. Alonso's landlady reported to Mrs. Wolfe, Allen's secretary, that she saw Miss Henderson entering and leaving Mrs. Alonso's apartment on numerous occasions during the campaign. As far as Allen, his secretary, and most of the Council were concerned, there was no question but that Miss Henderson cooperated closely with Mrs. Alonso in campaigning for defeat of the ordinance.

[25] Allen said he was fairly sure he was through about midway in the campaign when the community began to swing so solidly behind Miss Henderson. When the campaign first began, rumor had it that in a discussion of how the voting would go, someone pointed out that the vote of the city employees would be significant, and Allen was alleged to have said that he did not need the employee vote anyhow. Allen later denied having said this; he told the writer that he had known almost from the first that city employees actually "ran the city."

[26] King had been in city government for twenty-one years, but he was still a relatively young man. He felt the recommendations made by Peterson were excellent, and during the study he had given Peterson as much support as he could. As a working member of the police force, King was often irritated and frustrated by the way Bemis ran the department, and he was hopeful that Peterson's report would help alleviate the situation.

[27] As indicated to the author by both King and Peterson.

commodations as he could, and he saw no way that he could compromise further with department heads or other city officials if he was to accomplish his own job.

More Trouble in City Hall

After the election, Allen continued a kind of running fight with Miss Henderson. One of the survey recommendations, it will be recalled, was that the city clerk mechanize certain of her accounting operations. A team from the National Cash Register Company studied the operations of her office and recommended to the Council that it purchase two general purpose accounting machines. The machines were to do all accounting work, voucher preparation, payroll check preparation, billing, stores inventory records, and report preparation.

Members of the Council knew Miss Henderson was not in favor of using the machines, but they thought perhaps she might change her mind if she could see the proposed system in operation. Councilman Winston was able to talk Miss Henderson into a trip to a city where such a system had been installed. The entire Council went with her, and she was shown the system in considerable detail. Once through with the tour, the Council members asked her what she thought about it. She told them that she was impressed with what she had seen. Winston then asked her if she thought the system might work in her office. She said emphatically that it would not. She felt that, while such a system was fine for that particular city, that city was not La Loma, and her needs were different.

The Council dropped the discussion at that point. Therefore, Miss Henderson was completely surprised when two men walked into her office several weeks later and wanted to know what to do with two accounting machines. Despite her resistance, the Council had gone ahead with the purchase of the machines. During the following months, the Council pressured Miss Henderson to reorganize her work so that the machines could be utilized. She did not comply with the Council's request.

Once it became generally known that Miss Henderson was not using the equipment, the La Loma *Daily News* made capital out of what it considered her "unreasonable" attitude against programming her work so that it might be done by the machines.

Miss Henderson felt beleaguered. She resented the fact that the Council had bought the machines without consulting her. She also felt that Council members were not understanding or reasonable in their demands that she put the machines to work immediately. She argued that it took time to change from one system to another, particularly when work was coming in all the time and had to be kept current. She did not feel she was being uncooperative or resistant to the use of the machines. As far as she was concerned, the whole matter was distorted out of all proportion to its actual significance.[28] Throughout the summer Allen and Miss Henderson fought over the issue of programming the work of her office so that the machines could be used.

Allen worked on through the summer of 1959, but his heart was not in it. After the referendum defeat, he believed it was just a matter of time before he would have to leave La Loma, and the question of prime importance for him was where to go from there. He made little headway in his efforts to control his department heads and other officials; resistance continued, and the situation gradually became intolerable. The one bright spot in Allen's summer was the retirement of Chief Bemis. Once he was gone, Allen recommended to the Council that King, Administrative Assistant to Bemis, be appointed Chief of the Police Department. In July 1959 the appointment was approved by the Council. King immediately began to implement the reorganization recommendations made by Peterson.

By December 1959, the honeymoon was over as far as the Council was concerned. Councilman McDonald, who had probably been the most sympathetic supporter Allen had (they had become close personal friends) continued to champion the CAO. As far as the rest of the Council was concerned, however, Allen stood practically alone. Some Council members became openly critical, and the *Daily News* began to speculate about how much longer Allen would remain CAO. One Council member stated publicly that Allen would be fired if he did not have sense enough to resign. The dis-

---

[28] Miss Henderson was candid in admitting that even though she eventually switched to the machines, she did not think much of the system. She pointed out that she still had to have the same number of people in her office so that the personnel saving promised in the survey report had not occurred. Furthermore, she could not get the kind of information she needed for budgetary and other purposes, so one of her clerks had to winnow through reports and take information off the machine cards by hand. She still thought her old system was faster and gave her a good deal more information.

illusionment of the Council went beyond the immediate problem of Allen, for now the entire Council-Administrator concept was being questioned.

The growing lack of faith in the CAO form of government on the part of the interested, voting segment of the public in La Loma (mainly the old guard) gradually became known to Council members. Councilmen McDonald and Winston continued to back the Council-Administrator concept, but the other three members began to waver.

During the last few months of his stay in La Loma, Allen was approached by members of the City Council of a neighboring city, and in February 1960 he resigned his La Loma post and accepted the position of CAO for that city.[29]

General Elections

With Allen gone, public attention turned to whether La Loma wanted or needed the Council-Administrator form of government. General elections were set for April 4, 1960, and the issue of the CAO's office assumed important political dimension. As far as the Council was concerned, it had no desire to address itself to the problem of selecting a replacement for Allen; it wanted to let the whole matter cool off. At this point, however, Mrs. Wolfe and Miss Henderson came into conflict over who should open the mail coming to the vacant CAO's office. Miss Henderson insisted that in the absence of the CAO, she was legally responsible. Mrs. Wolfe was equally insistent that mail addressed to the CAO's office was no affair of Miss Henderson's.[30]

The whole issue was put to the Council. Rather than make a decision one way or the other, that body hastily passed a resolution making Johnson, Director of Public Works, the Acting CAO.

Johnson took office on February 16, 1960, and Council members began their plans for the April elections. Two seats on the Council were up for election,[31] and Mrs. Alonso decided that the time was right for her to run for one of them. She selected as her running mate a conservative Democrat, Earl Thrasher, who, along with Mrs. Alonso, had openly criticized the CAO plan. The main plank of their platform was abolishing the Council-Administrator form of government. In the campaign literature they handed out they made their position clear:

> We feel that the change in our form of government from Elective to Administrative is too costly, unnecessary and a waste of taxpayers' money. We want the office of Administrative Officer abolished because for a twenty-five month period this office cost the taxpayers exactly $56,187.40 of which $41,718.79 was for salaries.
>
> Your new Council will have to decide whether the administrative power in La Loma will be returned to elective City Council members, over whom you, the voters, have control—or whether it will be still further transferred to the appointed City Administrator, over whom you have no control. The City Manager or City Administrator type government is being urged by those who want to bring our entire country under *One World Government,* in which we give up our sovereignty as a nation. We intend to eliminate unnecessary positions created by the present Council to "aid and assist" the administrative form of government. Activate the City Commissions which have been re-established (but no members appointed . . . why?) by appointing public spirited citizens from different areas with knowledge of their area's needs.

In addition to this general type of giveaway literature, Mrs. Alonso also sent a letter to each city employee which read:

> It goes without saying that you don't need an administrative "watch dog" to evaluate or coordinate and destroy your initiative in your position or department at great expense and waste to you and your friends of the tax monies you pay each year. Whether this "watch dog" (dictator) be called Rover, or City Administrator, or Coordinator, or any other high-sounding name, it is merely a down-grading in every sense to you and your day-to-day security and responsibilities to the people of the City of La Loma.

Mrs. Alonso also organized the La Loma Committee for Good Government. Who the members of this committee were is not known, but Mrs. Alonso

[29] In case Allen should forget his experiences in La Loma, there is an elaborate, framed scroll hanging on the wall of his new office to remind him. The scroll, signed by members of the La Loma City Council, thanks him for giving so unstintingly of himself and praises him for his service to the community.

[30] Mrs. Wolfe said she had her differences with Miss Henderson, but she considered herself a friend. Mrs. Wolfe also was a friend of Mrs. Alonso and, in fact, voted for her in the 1960 election.

[31] Council members were elected for four years with staggered terms.

was the Chairman, and her home telephone was listed in the handouts urging the abolition of the Council-Administrator plan.

At this time Councilman Winston was Mayor, and his was one of the Council seats up for election. Winston continued to express his confidence in the Council-Administrator form of government, and he indicated that he would support continuation of the CAO position and other reorganization plans if reelected.

Winston, along with McDonald, realized that the CAO plan was definitely threatened unless they could counter the vote of the old guard by obtaining the active support of the merchants and businessmen in the community. In assessing past events, Winston had come to the conclusion that the business community was essentially in favor of the Council-Administrator plan but apathetic about supporting it. The old guard, on the other hand, had been active and aggressive in its attack, as attested by the defeat of Ordinance 1399.

Winston decided to enlist the support of Robert Becker, a prominent businessman in La Loma and President of the Chamber of Commerce. He felt that with Becker's influence, he would be able to arouse the business community to the point where it would take an aggressive position in support of his campaign.

Becker immediately set about organizing the Committee of '60. The purpose of the committee was to support those candidates who favored retention of the CAO plan. Becker was able to recruit a number of influential businessmen and merchants to serve on the committee, some of whom had been members of the Police Commission before it had been abolished.[32]

Winston realized that he could count on the behind-the-scenes support of Joseph Green (see page 366), but he also knew that Green was reluctant to be publicly identified in the campaign. Green felt that the city employees disliked him (perhaps partly because of his earlier chairmanship of the Civil Service Commission), and he did not want to add to the antagonism the employees already had expressed toward the CAO plan.

Simeon had withdrawn entirely from the political arena when he retired and could no longer be called upon for support.

The editorship of the La Loma *Daily News* had changed about one month prior to the departure of Allen (February 1960). Wolfe had resigned to accept another position. Nevertheless, the editor who replaced him was strongly in favor of the reorganization plan, and Winston knew that he would have the continued support of the daily newspaper.

On March 10, 1960, Becker introduced the members of the committee to the Council and read the following statement:

> Without necessarily endorsing every word or idea of the survey report, we are in broad and essential agreement with both its analysis of the situation and the needs of La Loma, and its recommendations regarding the administrative form of government for our City. In our judgment the Ordinance creating the City Administrative Officer was well drawn and can be effective in our City. We acknowledge our own failure to give the City Council and to the former administrative officer the support which they deserved during this period of adjustment to the new situation introduced by Ordinance 1399. The Council is to be commended for temporarily filling the position of City Administrative Officer. However, the duties of the chief administrative officer are much too important and demanding to be only a part-time responsibility for even the most capable of men.

The Committee of '60 also came to grips with Miss Henderson. It asked her to state publicly her position as far as the Council-Administrator form of government was concerned. She replied:

> City Administrators have a tendency to grow into "little dictators." They enjoy having everybody jump when they say "frog." An administrator is not a community man. As soon as he displeases a Council he starts looking elsewhere. Their philosophy is to create a hierarchy of appointed officials responsible to them—not necessarily to the people.
>
> The manager pleases a majority of the Council. Everyone under him has to please the manager. Under a true manager form of government the manager can hire and fire. It makes figureheads out of your department heads. They become desk people instead of being out in the field and making decisions on their own.

The committee then asked Miss Henderson whether she intended opposing those running for Council who favored retention of the Council-Administrator plan. She declared that:

> The City Clerk's Office is an office that serves no matter who is elected. Therefore we do not enter into council politics. The office does not endorse any Councilman and I intend to stand on the

[32] King had disbanded the commission shortly after he became Chief of Police in the summer of 1959.

principle. As for my candidacy for City Clerk, I intend to run on my record. You need someone who knows enough about expenditures and is not afraid to speak to the people.

On April 4 the ballots were cast. Out of a total of 5,043 votes, Mrs. Alonso received 1,009 and Thrasher, her running mate, polled 810. The incumbents, Winston and McDonald, received 3,224. Councilman Winston was somewhat surprised that Mrs. Alonso had shown so much strength at the polls. Miss Henderson retained her position as City Clerk.

AFTERMATH

The city of La Loma still had a Council-Administrator form of government as of April 1960, but the second incumbent of the CAO's office was serving in an acting capacity. He had relatively little managerial training or experience and was possibly working himself to death trying to learn the job. From all appearances it seemed that Johnson would remain the Acting CAO for some time to come. The Council had no wish to reopen old wounds by appointing a professional manager, and, for that matter, that body had no intention, at least in the immediate future, of changing Johnson's "acting" title.

Of the recommendations concerning fiscal operations, only those of a minor nature had been implemented. The city clerk's office finally was using the accounting machines, but this system had been superimposed, to some degree, upon the old one. The purchasing agent retired, and a restudy of his department had just been completed. In the main, however, the functions of the treasurer, the city clerk, the license collector, and the purchasing agent remained much as they had been before the study.

The Department of Public Works had a director (the Acting CAO, Johnson) and one department, the City Engineering Department. The rest of the departments doing public works functions remained semiautonomous units that reported to the CAO but also directly to the Council.

The recommendation to create the position of personnel director got as far as the recruiting stage, and there it bogged down. Miss Osgood was still head of Personnel and Civil Service as well as secretary to the mayor.

The Revised Salary and Wage Schedule was adopted finally by the Council but continued to be under constant attack by city employees. A second salary survey had been completed by an analyst not associated with Consultants Unlimited. It promised to be more favorable to city employees. A restudy of the Civil Service system had been completed by a professor from another university. Pending acceptance of the study, personnel matters continued to be handled as they always had been.

The most dramatic changes occurred in the Police Department. When King took over the department in 1959, he lost no time in making the changes recommended by Peterson. He was persistent and energetic in his efforts, and by the fall of 1960 he had implemented twenty-two of the twenty-nine recommended changes.

Everything considered, it seems fair to say that no more than forty per cent of the survey recommendations made by Consultants Unlimited were implemented. Even this figure is not too meaningful, since most of the changes were made in the Police Department.

By the end of 1960 Councilman Winston was still optimistic about implementing the remainder of the survey recommendations. He believed the Council had made progress in the eventual creation of the Finance Department. For one thing, the Council had been able to induce Miss Henderson to accept a redefinition of her job as city clerk. Under California law, the salary for elective positions had to be listed on the ballot. In the past the Council had simply listed the total amount paid the city clerk without distinguishing what portion of that sum applied to the functions of the city clerk and what part was compensation for other duties. In 1960, the Council set $500 per month as the amount to be paid those holding the office of city clerk. The remainder of Miss Henderson's salary, about $350 per month, was handled as an administrative expense (this amount did not appear on the ballot) and was designated as compensation for additional duties. In this way, the accounting, budgeting, and payroll functions were identified as responsibilities outside the purview of the city clerk's office.

Everyone was a little surprised that Miss Henderson accepted this arrangement. Councilman Winston felt that she did so because she could see the "handwriting on the wall." In other words, some Council members believed that Miss Henderson knew it was just a matter of time until the city had its Finance Department, and she was tired of fighting it. Also to be considered was the fact that another fight with the Council, coming so swiftly on the heels of the last one, might not have had the same impact on the public. If she lost, she would, of course, have lost the fiscal functions of her office anyway. In a sense, her control had been weakened, but she still remained in charge of the vital financial functions of the city.

When the Council passed the resolution separating fiscal functions from the office of the city clerk, Mrs. Alonso again attempted to stir up public comment. She was not encouraged by Miss Henderson, however, and she quickly dropped the matter.

With the city clerk's job precisely defined, Councilman Winston believed the Council would be able to create the Finance Department by resolution. However, despite the fact that over one year had elapsed since the 1960 elections, the emotional climate was still such that Acting CAO Johnson felt (in July 1961) that Winston was overly optimistic about the possibility of creating a separate Finance Department. He did not feel there was any possibility of centralizing fiscal operations for years to come. He felt Miss Henderson still had the power to thwart any such attempt and that the department would come into existence only after she retired. Since she was still a relatively young woman, this could mean a wait of fifteen or twenty years.

Miss Henderson believed she was right in resisting the attempt to centralize fiscal operations. From her point of view, she again had been able to beat off an attempt to tamper with the city clerk's office.

Miss Henderson saw the reorganization study as a waste of money and destructive in its impact upon city employees. The uncertainty of individuals during the study and their worries as to the outcome created an atmosphere of suspicion which was reflected in breaches of friendship and open quarrels between employees who had known one another for years. From Miss Henderson's point of view, the City Hall had been "one big happy family" and the coming of the survey team spoiled it all. In view of this she was convinced that the overall result of the study had been to reduce rather than increase employee effectiveness.

From the standpoint of those who did the survey, the report was considered an excellent example of the objective professional team at its best. As Shelton indicated, "It was an excellent survey, about the best we ever did. We wanted to publish it [as a book] but the Council wouldn't go along."

Shelton held the Council responsible for the ultimate demise of the survey. While that body favored the report, it did not follow through in the implementation phase. As Shelton put it, "The recommendations of the research group was a tender shoot needing nurture. They [the Council members] didn't save it." Shelton backed up his argument by pointing out that, "When the final report was presented, we recommended that we be involved in appeals on classification, but we were not. When the thing was done we wanted to go back in and help put this over. We felt we could help; we were never called upon."

To Shelton, a major complication was Allen. He did not know the man; he had never met him. Nevertheless, he considered him inadequate to carry through the recommended reorganization. Shelton pointed out that Allen "could have called us in to help put things over but he tried to do everything himself."

Shelton had not known—at the time of the survey—that Simeon was politically powerful, but he said later that he had "suspected" that this was so. At any rate, he felt that his team had had Simeon's support. Shelton had never heard of Mrs. Alonso, and he considered Miss Henderson as not too important to the study itself.

Shelton recognized that many of the officials of La Loma city government resented and resisted the reorganization, but he was certain that he could have done nothing to change their attitude. Given such circumstances, Shelton felt there was no alternative but to ignore those whom he knew would oppose any changes he might recommend. As Shelton saw it, the success or failure of the study depended upon the backing of the daily paper (to provide information to the public) and strong Council intervention at the implementation phase.

In retrospect, Marshall, who handled the planning section of the study, commented that: "All of us were anxious that the job be sound professionally; and I think it would be fair to say that a good product—that is, a good report—was regarded as an end in itself. It would be something we could show to future clients."

The apparent failure of the survey team to assess the possible impact of employee sentiment upon the study was understandable, according to Nelson's retrospective comments. He knew that "the city was pretty well run by the employees," and that the team had a "job" on its hands where they were concerned. As Nelson saw it, "The arch devil was the City Clerk. The problem [of employee resistance] we didn't really try to meet." As far as trying to sell the study to the employees was concerned, no effort was made other than to provide a series of hearings and an appeals procedure (on classifications and pay schedules). Nelson summed it up by saying, "We were not asked to study the political dynamics of the community."

Allen, looking back after a year away from La Loma, felt the whole episode was a nightmare. He believed that he could have acted no differently than he had. His downfall, he felt, was due to the fact that he had been caught in a political situation; and, he said, "I am an administrator, not a politician."

FREDERICK C. MOSHER

The Reorganization of the California State Personnel Board

FREDERICK C. MOSHER

The editor of this casebook and author of *The Reorganization of the California State Personnel Board* received a D.P.A. degree from Harvard University. He is presently a Professor of Political Science at the University of California at Berkeley. Between 1934 and 1949 he served in a variety of administrative capacities with the Tennessee Valley Authority, the Los Angeles City Civil Service Department, Army Air Force Headquarters, UNRRA, and the U.S. Department of State. He was staff director of the Committee on Foreign Affairs Personnel (the Herter Committee). Prior to his present position, he taught at Syracuse University and was the official representative of the University of California at the University of Bologna, Italy.

CHRONOLOGY OF KEY EVENTS

January 1952	Jane Carmack proposes a study of the problem of interdivisional communications and suggests a new organization plan
March 7, 1952	Miss Carmack's second memo
May-June 1952	Attitude study of staff
Spring 1952	Principal-Senior meetings discuss problems of communication
July 9, 1952	Chopson submits a plan for a generalist pilot unit for late summer and early fall
October 21, 1952	Memorandum announcing the pilot program
November-December 1952	Stephens prepares evaluation criteria
November 17, 1952	Pilot unit in operation
August 1953-January 1954	Evaluation conferences
October 5, 1953	Miss Groff's memorandum about her program
October 19, 1953	McKay submits a plan for a second generalist unit
November 27, 1953	Fisher announces implementation plans
January 1, 1954	Stage 1 of reorganization plan formally effective
April 1, 1954	Stage 2 of reorganization plan formally effective
July 1, 1954	Stage 3 of reorganization plan formally effective
October 1, 1954	Stage 4 of reorganization plan formally effective; formal reorganization complete
May-June 1955	"Push" to develop new pay plan for state service; inter-unit committee
October 1954-January 1955	Testing pool develops new tests

PRINCIPAL CHARACTERS

J. R. Bell, Assistant Executive Officer, California State Personnel Board

A. L. Brock, Senior Examiner, Examining Division, up to 1954; Chief, Recruitment and Examining Division, 1954—

Jane Carmack, Employee in Classification Division; participant in first pilot unit

E. W. Chopson, Senior Examiner, Examining Division, up to 1952, and 1953-1954; Personnel Management Analyst, 1952-1953; Chief, Operations Section I, 1954—

R. P. Everett, Chief, Pay Division, up to 1954; Chief, Operations Division, 1954—

J. F. Fisher, Executive Officer, California State Personnel Board

Kay Groff, Employee in Classification Division; participant in first pilot unit

R. D. Lawson, Senior Examiner, Examining Division, up to November 1952, and January-October 1954; Chief, first pilot unit, 1952-January 1954; Chief, Operations Section V, October 1954-March 1955

J. K. McKay, Senior, Pay Division, up to 1953; Personnel Management Analyst, 1953-September 1954; Acting Chief, Standards and Surveys Division, September 1954—

R. W. Stephens, Chief, Classification Division, up to reorganization in 1954; Chief, Standards and Surveys Division, to September 1954; Assistant Secretary of the California State Personnel Board, September 1954—

INTRODUCTION

The budget request of the California State Personnel Board for the fiscal year 1955-1956 stated, in typically succinct terms:

> The budget also reflects a major change in organization effective July 1, 1954. *The new organization provides for an Operations Division to handle classification, pay, and examinations on a generalist basis in lieu of three separate divisions, each specializing in its respective field for day-to-day activities.* A Standards and Surveys Division will handle the detailed classification and pay surveys. The examination unit will conduct oral interviews and establish examination standards and techniques. [Emphasis added.]

This study is an attempt to recapture the process by which this "major change in organization" came about, the reasons for it, the forces that impinged upon it, the problems generated by it.

Like other administrative reorganizations, this one covered a considerable span of time. It was announced as "effective July 1, 1954." But the first formal step had been taken in November 1952 after many months of gestation. The final formal step did not take place until October 1954. And the process was still going on as this was written in July 1955. The major phases of the reorganization covered three and one-half years, from January 1952 to July 1955.

Of primary interest in this story is the content of the reorganization—the substitution of the so-called "generalist" pattern for the traditional "functional" or "specialist" structure. The forward march of specialism and professionalism has long been an object of interest to students of western society, many of whom have noted a danger of losing the whole in efforts to lend perfection and dignity to the parts. Frequently deplored in public administration has been the shortage of generalists capable of an overall point of view. The problem is acute at the level of management where there is concentrated the responsibility for integrating diverse specialisms and for continuously relating goals to techniques.

Public personnel administration has enjoyed no immunity from this trend or from misgivings about it. Its various functional fields—examinations, classification, training, placement, employee relations, and others—have each provided the basis for occupational specialties, each relatively sufficient unto itself, each lending to a professional self-consciousness. Many feel that this segmentation impedes the performance of the total personnel job and retards the development of *compleat* personnel workers. In the past fifteen years, a number of public personnel agencies have begun grouping specialist functions to try to counteract the trend toward specialization.[1]

The reorganization of the California State Personnel Board, reflecting these anti-specialism considerations, was not without precedent. Yet it was in many respects a bold and forward-looking step. The state's civil service system, one of the oldest in the country, had been organized on traditional functional lines for many years. The reorganization was the first modern effort by a large public personnel organization to integrate within the same units and the same individuals the responsibilities for both examining and classification—two of the most important and virile personnel specialties.

[1] In 1954-1955 the Civil Service Assembly of the United States and Canada conducted a nationwide survey of generalist programs in public personnel administration. The findings of this study were summarized and analyzed in an article, "Personnel Generalist: Experience and Advice," by Lyman H. Cozad and Kenneth O. Warner, *Public Personnel Review,* July 1955. This study disclosed that, of its sample of 119 federal, state, and local personnel agencies in the United States and Canada, fifty-eight, or nearly half, operated partially or completely on a generalist basis.

THE PERSONNEL BOARD AND ITS STAFF

The two key dates in the evolution of California's civil service are August 15, 1913, and November 6, 1934. The earlier date marked the passage of the state's first Civil Service Act, a landmark to governmental reformers of that era and one of the many progressive contributions of Governor Hiram W.

FIGURE 1:

CALIFORNIA STATE PERSONNEL BOARD

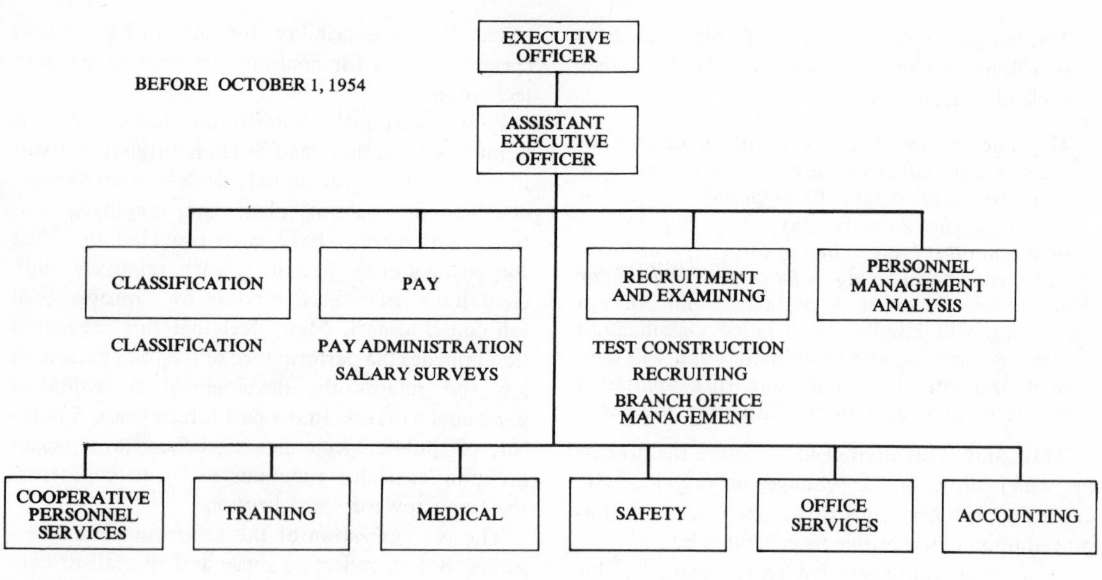

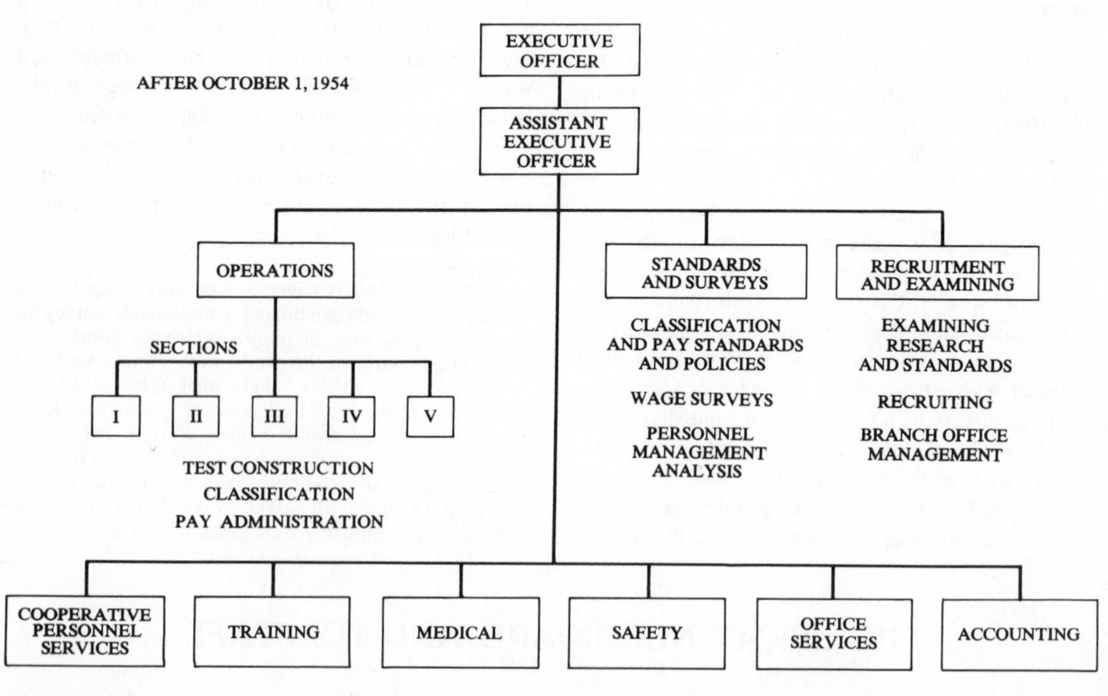

Johnson. The later date was the day on which the people of the state endorsed, by an overwhelming margin, Article XXIV of the State Constitution, which established the legal framework for the present personnel system. Both actions were conceived and adopted to counteract political pressures in the selection and management of the state service. As in many other jurisdictions, California's merit system developed as part of the popular crusade against spoils.

The 1913 legislation provided a three-man Civil Service Commission, appointed by the Governor, with powers over examining and selection comparable to those of contemporary civil service agencies. In spite of strong early appointments to the commission and the development of a competent examining staff, the commission declined in prestige during the 1920's and came itself to be increasingly responsive to political forces, particularly from the Governor's office. In 1929, by the last of several reorganizations, the commission became the Division of Personnel and Organization within the Department of Finance, then, as in 1952-1954, perhaps the most powerful of all state administrative agencies.[2] But, in the face of political inroads, the stature of the merit system continued to decline:

> Exemptions from civil service became continuously more numerous. By 1932 over half of all the state employees were either in exempt or "temporary" positions, or holding other quasi-political appointments. Violations of the Civil Service Act were common.[3]

It was this reversion toward patronage that gave rise to the new drive in 1934 to safeguard the merit system by a constitutional amendment:

> The constitutional amendment was intended primarily to correct three evils: (1) political control of the administration of civil service, (2) exemption of employees from the civil service law by either the Legislature or the Commission, and (3) the unreasonable use of temporary appointment authorizations to evade the intent of the Civil Service Act.[4]

In the best anti-spoils tradition, the constitutional amendment of 1934, Article XXIV, established an independent, virtually autonomous body. The State Personnel Board, which replaced the old Civil Service Commission, was to comprise five members appointed by the Governor with the consent of the Senate. Except for deaths or resignations, one member was to be appointed every biennium for a ten-year term. Normally, no Governor could select a majority of the Board within a single term. (The amendment did not stipulate that the Board be bipartisan, and in 1955 all the members were apparently of the same political party. Party affiliation, however, did not appear to influence their deliberations.)

The amendment reaffirmed the principles of the merit system in unequivocal terms: "Permanent appointments and promotion in the state civil service shall be made exclusively under a general system based upon merit, efficiency, and fitness as ascertained by competitive examinations."[5] It defined the "state civil service" to include "every officer and employee of this State except. . ."—and it proceeded to list a limited number of exempt positions, principally elected officers, officers appointed by the Governor with Senate confirmation, employees of the Legislature and of the Governor's office, employees of the State University and state colleges, and a few others. It locked the door against other exemptions. Further, it restricted to a period of months (now nine) the tenure of any temporary appointment. The Board received all the powers of its predecessor Civil Service Commission, and new ones were subsequently added. The Board's powers were to be exercised by an Executive Officer appointed by the Board and himself a member of the state civil service.

Neither the political sterilization of the Board nor the eradication of its subservience to the Governor were accomplished overnight. During the terms of Republican Governor Frank F. Merriam and Democratic Governor Culbert L. Olson, political forces continued to operate upon and within the Board. They contributed to the voluntary departure in 1938 of the Board's first Executive Officer, William Brownrigg, and to the dismissal in 1941 of his successor, Louis J. Kroeger. Kroeger's dismissal sparked the organization of a statewide group to defend him and to protect the merit system from the Board itself. Kroeger withdrew to a war-agency job in Washington, but enthusiasm

---

[2] For a picture of the political and administrative forces in a similar evolution in another state, see Peter Bart and Milton Cummings, Jr., *The Transfer of the Kansas State Civil Service Department,* Inter-University Case Program No. 31 (Indianapolis: The Bobbs-Merrill Company, Inc.).

[3] *Twenty-First Biennial Report of the California State Personnel Board* (1952-1954), p. 9.

[4] *Ibid.,* p. 10.

[5] *Constitution of the State of California,* Article XXIV, Section 1.

for merit system reform was once again ignited.

The picture changed two years later, following the first election of Governor Earl Warren, who apparently determined to insulate state civil service from politics. Enabled through retirements and other separations to make several Personnel Board appointments during his first years, Warren named a group of men of high, and not necessarily political, reputation. Three of these, appointed in 1943, 1944, and 1945 respectively, were still on the Board in 1955. Subsequent appointments by Warren and his successor, Governor Goodwin J. Knight, maintained a high standard, and, from 1945 to the time of this case, patronage played a minor, almost irrelevant, role in the operations of the Board. By 1952 most employees of the Board and of the rest of the state service were professional career personnel. Many department heads had "come up through the ranks," and the Personnel Board itself was increasingly called upon to set salaries, classification standards, and rules to govern the relatively few employees still in the exempt category.

The reorganization of 1952-1955, which is the subject of this study, was affected by two important conditions. One was the Personnel Board's high degree of independence. The reorganization was to be "an inside job," uninfluenced by political parties, the Legislature, or the Governor. The single formal external control over the Board throughout the reorganization was the annual budget. The way in which the reorganization was carried out was also influenced by the Board's desire to provide the best possible service to the state departments that constituted its "using agencies." It should be noted, incidentally, that while the Board endeavored to stress service rather than control in dealing with state departments, its authority to exert control in defense of the merit system was universally accepted and frequently exercised.

A second important condition affecting the reorganization was the relationship between the Board and its staff head, the Executive Officer. During the troublesome 1930's, the Board, or part of it at least, had participated frequently in staff operations—a source of many of the difficulties of the first two Executive Officers. The constitutional amendment of 1934 provided that the Executive Officer "shall perform and discharge all of the powers, duties, purposes, functions, and jurisdictions hereunder or which hereafter by law may be vested in the Board except that the adoption of rules and regulations, the creation and adjustment of classifications and grades, and dismissals, demotions, suspensions, and other punitive action . . ." required a majority vote of the Board.[6]

Following its renaissance of 1943, the Board, by tacit agreement, had removed itself from operations. Since then there has been almost complete delegation of responsibility for internal administration to the Executive Officer. The decision to carry out the 1952-1955 reorganization was his. He apprised the Board of the projected change, and the Board members had the opportunity to voice their views. Had they opposed, he would have reconsidered. But the question of his legal authority was not raised, nor had it been raised on similar issues in previous years. One Board member maintained that no one knew where the legal authority for such a decision lay and that it would probably have taken a court decision to find out. At any rate, by 1952 the Board usually met in an open session for about a day and a half every two weeks. Its calendar was prepared under the direction of the Executive Officer. Its meetings were taken up with new or amended class specifications, new or changed pay schedules, broad policy matters, and appeals. In addition to the official meeting, the Board met informally with the Executive Officer and a few top staff to discuss plans and policy questions. All Board members served part-time only, and they had few contacts with the regular staff other than through these scheduled sessions.

The Growth of the Staff

The Personnel Board's staff developed by expanding in scope, function, and size. Like other civil service agencies, the original commission had been concerned primarily with examining. The first classification plan had been completed in 1922 and had been greatly improved after a survey by a private firm in 1930-1931. A salary standardization program had been begun in 1934 and had been thoroughly revised following a survey in 1937-1938. Since that time, administration of the state salary plan has been one of the Board's principal responsibilities. An entirely new civil service law, adopted in 1937, still provided the statutory base for most of the Board's operations in 1952. Also in 1937, the Legislature gave the Board authority to provide technical personnel services on a cost basis to local governments and counties. In 1952 a separate and quite independent unit of the Board, the Cooperative Personnel Services Division, carried

[6] *Ibid.,* Section 2.

out these assignments under contract with local governments.

The postwar period witnessed sizable expansion of existing activities as well as enlargement of the Board's functions. In 1948 the Board established a Recruiting and Veterans Personnel Section. This unit was known in 1952 simply as the Recruiting Section, and it operated two field offices. The special postwar problems of pay administration were similarly recognized in 1946 by the establishment of a separate Pay Division. Also in 1946, a new office of Personnel Management Analyst was created. The Personnel Management Analyst was to develop improved personnel practices, systems, and organization structures.

Of more consequence for the reorganization of 1952-1955, however, was a vast growth in the workload of the central personnel functions, examining and classification. The increase in these duties, performed respectively by the Recruitment and Examining Division and the Classification Division, was largely a consequence of the growth of the state service.[7] Until 1930, the primary production function of the Board had been the preparation and administration of examinations. This work required six professionals in a total staff of twenty-three. Classification actions were then handled incidentally by the examining staff in what was, in fact, a generalist organization. During the 1930's, when classification became a separate division, and during the 1940's, when pay matters were extracted from classification as a third major division, examining remained by far the largest single production job of the Board. The growth of these personnel functions, rapid in the 1930's, became astronomical after the war, when the requirement that wartime appointees be replaced by permanent appointees necessitated a gigantic examining program. The number of civil service employees doubled in the 1940's. During the 1950's, staff growth leveled off, continuing gradually with the enlargement of the state service.

[7] In the rest of this study, the Recruitment and Examining Division is sometimes referred to simply as Examining.

A striking element of the Personnel Board's work in the 1950's was the staggering load of examinations. By 1955 it was conducting about 1,500 examinations a year, or an average of about six each working day. About two-thirds of these were regular written examinations, and about half involved oral interviewing by qualifications appraisal boards. The work involved in preparing examinations and in selecting, supervising, and participating in the oral examination boards was enormous. In the fiscal year 1953-1954, in the midst of the reorganization process described by this case, the Board received more than 127,000 applications for examinations, tested over 77,000 persons, and interviewed more than 16,000 competitors.

The Staff Before the Reorganization

The professional staff of the Personnel Board in 1952-1955 was largely the product of two distinct waves of recruitment. Most executive and supervisory employees had joined the Board during the late 1930's and early 1940's. For most, the Personnel Board was their first personnel job, and a few had joined it directly after leaving college. Most of these officials had studied public administration in undergraduate and graduate courses at

FIGURE 2: THE STATE SERVICE AND THE PERSONNEL BOARD STAFF*

	1930	1935	1940	1945	1950	1952	1955
Total Civil Service Employees in State (in thousands)	11	20†	25	29	50	56	60
Civil Service Commission or Personnel Board Staff, Total	23	41	142	175	319	323	339
Professional Personnel Staff, Total‡	6	17	24	23	68	69	76
Recruitment and Examining	6	10	14	14	42	42	§
Classification	†	7	10	9	16	17	§
Pay	†	§	§	§	10	10	§

* Average filled positions in the Personnel Board staff for the fiscal year, except 1955, for which are shown positions authorized in the budget. This difference accounts for much of the indicated increase in 1955.
† Figure shown is for 1936; 1935 figure is not available.
‡ Only professional staff in the three activities shown is included.
§ Figures not applicable because of organization structure.

the University of California. Relatively few, even of those in Examining, had had any psychological, psychometric, or industrial relations training. Most of the executive and supervisory officers joined one of the military services during the war and returned after discharge. The continuity and homogeneity of the senior group were thus rather striking. Virtually all were between forty and fifty, energetic, and dedicated; and all were men. Almost all top supervisory jobs were filled by promotion, assuring continuity.

On first joining the Board, men in this first wave had been assigned to the Examining or Classification divisions. Until the reorganization there was almost no movement of staff between these two divisions, so that the officials were for the most part firmly oriented to their original functional field. Later, when the Pay Division was established, a number of classifiers moved into it, and there was some later interchange between Classification and Pay. But functional or specialist allegiance remained strong. Almost none of the top officials had had significant experiences in all three functional divisions, Examining, Classification, and Pay.

The second wave of recruitment occurred after World War II, when a large number of persons was hired to meet the bulging workload. Most of the journeymen professional staff at the time of the reorganization fell into this category; a few had advanced to supervisory posts. This second wave was, of course, larger, and the men in it were younger (for the most part, twenty-five to forty years old), though it included a few older men who had had considerable outside experience, even some outside the personnel field. Most men in the second wave, like men in the first group, came from university programs in public administration. They exhibited characteristics of energy and dedication similar to those of their Seniors. Although a few, when hired, progressed through orientation programs that took them for a few months into all aspects of the professional work of the Board, all were assigned to one of the functional divisions where most remained until the reorganization. The new men, like the old, identified themselves strongly with their respective specialties and with the divisions that carried on these specialties.

The two top officials of the Board's staff were, in certain respects, exceptions. John F. Fisher, the Executive Officer, came to the Board as its first Assistant Executive Officer in 1944 and succeeded to his top post in 1947. Fisher had, a decade before, studied public administration at Syracuse University. He went into personnel work in the East and in 1939 joined the staff of the Los Angeles City Civil Service Department as head of classification. He served briefly during the war as classification director for the OPA in Washington, then returned to Los Angeles as Acting General Manager of Civil Service. At the time of the reorganization he had been with the Board a shorter time than most of his senior colleagues, and he was one of the few who had not come up through the ranks.

James R. Bell had been Assistant Executive Officer since 1947. For some years before joining the Board he worked with the Highway Department and subsequently served as personnel officer for the State Relief Administration. He came to the Board in a supervisory rank just before the war. For some years, Bell directed office services and administrative activities, and he then served as first Personnel Management Analyst before succeeding to the post of Assistant Executive Officer.

Fisher and Bell directed the staff and were responsible for relationships with the Board and with the rest of the state service. They themselves were not overtly affected by the reorganization.

At the time of the reorganization the staff was:

DIVISION	PROFESSIONAL STRENGTH*	TOTAL STRENGTH
Classification	19	50
Recruitment and Examining	41	98
Pay	10	12
Training	4	6
Medical	0	6
Office Services	0	107
Cooperative Personnel Services	7	16
Administration	4	14
	85	309
Board Secretariat and Hearing Officer	1	15
Total (Rounded)	86	324

* Includes executive, supervisory, journeymen, and trainee personnel in professional work. Does not include professional personnel in other fields such as doctors, nurses, accountants, and the like.

Only the Classification, Recruitment and Examining, and Pay Divisions were to be significantly involved in the reorganization. They included the bulk of the professional personnel and had responsibility for most of the substantive, nonclerical personnel work.

The *Classification Division* was responsible for classifying positions, developing job specifications, and servicing state agencies on all matters relating to classification. In addition, this division included a group that, every five years, surveyed all positions in all the departments. Normal classification matters were handled by two groups, totaling twelve analysts and supervisors, and were assigned on an *organizational basis* with each analyst responsible for a group of state agencies. The relatively large clerical staff consisted principally of twenty-seven people responsible for maintaining the roster of state employees. This task and all the personnel were to be transferred to the Office Services Division as a result of the reorganization.

The *Recruitment and Examining Division* was responsible for test construction, test scheduling, the management of oral boards, test research, the preparation of bulletins, review of applications, and the like. Nearly thirty examiners and supervisors, the largest bloc of professionals in the Board, engaged in this work. Most of the other professionals in this division worked for the Recruiting Section and its branch offices in Los Angeles and San Francisco. The Recruiting Section was quite independent of the rest of the division, and it was not to be directly affected by the reorganization. Much of the clerical staff was engaged in certification and the management of the Test Pool.

The *Pay Division* administered the pay plan for the state. It handled all individual requests for pay changes or new pay levels, making recommendations to the Board on each one, and it conducted at least two "community" pay surveys a year. It also was responsible for prevailing rate studies for manual and trade jobs, for overtime compensation, and for related matters. Smaller than either Classification or Examining, Pay exercised the responsibility for the state salary plan which had been delegated to the Personnel Board by the Legislature. The Board determined the salary range for every class of position within only the most general statutory guidelines, and its decisions were final. On the basis of its periodic surveys of pay levels of other employers, private and public, it annually recommended to the Governor and the Legislature the lump sums to be appropriated for salary increases. It then administered these appropriations. For this work, probably its most crucial and potentially its "hottest" assignment, the Board relied heavily upon the staff of the Pay Division.

All the divisions were hierarchically organized with a chief and an intermediate supervisory group over the operating personnel. The professional personnel were classified in two series of classes—as Personnel Analysts in the Classification and Pay Divisions, and as Personnel Examiners in the Recruitment and Examining Division. Separate classes were recognized for Engineering Examiners and a Legal Examiner. The division chiefs carried the rank of Principal—Principal Personnel Analyst or Principal Personnel Examiner. Their immediate assistants were Seniors. The journeymen operators were Associates, Assistants, Juniors, and Trainees in that sequence downward. Since California controlled its budgets on a line-item basis, the number of positions in each of these classes, especially those in the higher ranks, would be of dominating importance in the consideration of any organizational change. The major executive and supervisory titles, their salary ranges, and the numbers authorized in 1953 were:

TITLE	MONTHLY SALARY	TO BE AFFECTED BY REORGANIZATION	TOTAL IN BOARD
Executive Officer	$1,050-1,150	0	1
Assistant Executive Officer	821-1,000	0	1
Assistant Secretary to Board	821-1,000	0	1
Principal	745- 905	3	5
Senior	613- 745	9	10

The five Principals included the heads of the three divisions described above, the State Training Officer, and the Chief of Cooperative Personnel Services. Four of the Seniors supervised examining work and a fifth headed the Recruiting Section in the Recruitment and Examining Division. The Classification Division had two Seniors and the Pay Division one; another was the Personnel Management Analyst, who at that time reported directly to the Executive Officer; and the last was in Cooperative Personnel Services. With the exception of one Senior vacancy in Examining, all these positions were filled when the reorganization began.

California Government

This description of the Board, its development, and its staff has provided only small clues to the total atmosphere in which the reorganization was to occur. California's burgeoning population of the last few decades, a mobile population making ever-rising demands on government, had created a strong force for change which would not be contained either by venerable institutions or revered traditions—especially when change appeared to mean growth, improvement, or progress.

The movement for public managerial reform had found fertile soil in California. Most middle-sized cities there had already moved over to the council-manager plan. Even the two largest cities had gone far in the direction of professionalized administration. Nowhere in the United States did state and local public services enjoy higher prestige, and nowhere had public administrators developed a higher sense of professional self-consciousness.

In aspiration and performance the California State Personnel Board typified the oft-quoted California sentiment that "good government is good politics." The Board aimed at providing the best possible service to the using agencies. At the same time it treasured its independence. Maintaining a crusading spirit, it nevertheless endeavored to spread the good-government gospel through a gradual educational process rather than through the iron hand of disciplinary authority. Its staff was energetic, youthful, ambitious, and it desired to establish a preeminent professional reputation in the personnel field. At the time reorganization was first considered, the Personnel Board ranked among the largest and strongest of all public personnel agencies. One may reasonably wonder: Why did it reorganize? The program was operating well; there were no outward signs of need to change. Why, then, disrupt such an organization by an internal upheaval?

BIRTH OF AN IDEA

January-November 1952

Even in 1952 the generalizing of functions and skills was being widely discussed in the personnel world. Staff members of California's Personnel Board had participated in national professional conferences on this subject. For many years, they had talked among themselves about the potential advantages and disadvantages of a generalist form of organization. The Board's Division of Cooperative Personnel Services offered a demonstration of generalism at work; it had been organized so that each staff member worked with localities in all personnel specialties. Thus the field was already fertile when 1952 opened. And while immediate practical problems came into sharper focus that year, it is probable that they provided less of a stimulus for a generalist reorganization than did the "theoretical" and "professional" considerations, which had been under discussion for several years. These practical problems, which are described below, provoked no crises and were not particularly unusual. They provided part of the context and some of the incentive for organizational change, but they alone were not decisive.

Coordination Among the Divisions

One of the "practical" reasons for organizational change was the need for continuing cooperation and coordination among the three divisions, Pay, Classification, and Recruitment and Examining. This problem, endemic in personnel organizations organized on a functional basis, had grown more acute when the three units expanded after the war. In personnel work, many of the decisions of one functional unit affect the work of the others. Coordination of general policy at the top level is not enough; actions of the lowliest examiners and analysts require close coordination with actions of other units. In the Board, these operators had fewer regular opportunities than did their superiors for reaching meetings of the mind through arrangements such as inter-divisional staff meetings.

Some operating officials and many of the supervisory staff were aware of these difficulties. In fact, some of the initiative for organizational change came from the operating staff. In January 1952, Jane Carmack, then a junior member of the Classification Division, wrote a memorandum proposing a study of the problem of inter-divisional communications and suggesting a new plan of organization. The memo was addressed to her Senior, who forwarded it to Roy Stephens, Chief of Classification; Stephens sent it on to the Assistant Executive Officer, James Bell. The proposal elicited a good deal of discussion. Miss Carmack was asked to prepare a second memo, and this later document, dated March 7, 1952, elaborated on existing difficulties and on the new organization pattern that she had in mind.

Miss Carmack has disavowed any originality in her memoranda; they were an attempt to put down on paper ideas that had been discussed for some time by a few of the analysts in Classification. Her organizational proposal was a partial generalist plan, but it fell considerably short of the scheme that was ultimately to be adopted. She proposed that specialists in Classification, Pay, and Examining continue to pursue their specialties, but that they be brought together, organizationally and physically, in a number of groups. Each group would cover a sector of the state service. It would be headed by a Senior, who would thus have to be a generalist, and the Senior would be responsible to one of two Principals, both generalists. The Carmack proposal was apparently not seriously considered in the subsequent discussions. But the memorandum helped to trigger the self-examination and give-and-take that ultimately led to reorganization. In September 1954, after Stephens came across the second Carmack memorandum while clearing his files, he returned the document to her with the penciled notation: "For your memoirs. Look what you started."

The Carmack memoranda are particularly interesting in retrospect because they reveal what problems were seen under the old system by workers at the operating level. In her second memorandum, she wrote that the new pattern of organization was "proposed as an approach to the perennial problems of coordination and communication. These problems are more basic to the proposed study than the suggested organizational structure." Among them, she said, were:

> *Relations with the Departments:* "Departments have expressed confusion with the number of contacts required in their working with the Personnel Board Staff." "These contacts [with Classification, Examining, Recruiting, Pay] frequently require repetition by the department of information previously given to another representative." "The [proposed new] organization of our staff could reduce the number of communication channels for the department."
>
> *Coordination Within the Board:* "There would be better 'follow-through' on problems affecting more than one personnel function." "Problems of timing that occur when a staff member of one division commits the Board to work involving other divisions might be alleviated." "Departmental problems that may overlap several divisions . . ." would become the "shared problems of [one] group."
>
> *Staff Development:* "Individual staff members thus could gain broader knowledge of our total personnel management program and more effectively relate their specific specialties to over-all Board objectives and would be more aware of the total problem. . . ."

Departmental service and convenience were accorded only minor weight in the subsequent discussions, but inter-divisional coordination and staff development and morale were given central attention. Dissatisfaction with coordination was strong in Classification, and it later emerged even more markedly in Examining. The classification specialists believed that the Pay Division could hardly set the pay of a class of positions without understanding the responsibilities of, and the qualifications for, these jobs, which were determined by Classification. These data obviously affected recruitment and selection as well. Examiners had to relate their tests to the job content of positions for which the classifiers were primarily responsible; if the classifiers did not have, or did not provide, such information, duplication of field work and research was inevitable. In fact, virtually every major personnel problem of the Board involved, directly or indirectly, all three functional elements, and many also affected a fourth—recruiting. The necessity for continuing cooperation and coordination was evident; the locus of decision-making responsibility was crucial; the possibilities of conflict were many. Problems that might occur included:

> Two or more staff members of different divisions might work on the same problem from different angles without knowing that someone else was also working on it.
>
> Examinations might be announced and given needlessly, since examiners might not know of related classifications that were going to be revised.
>
> Pay proposals might go to the Board without adequate review of their implications for Classification or Examining.
>
> "Using" departments might play off one division of the Board against another.
>
> Proposed new or revised job specifications, including proposed minimum qualifications, might be sent to the Board before there had been adequate review by affected examiners.

The last example—specifications and minimum qualifications—had been a problem of long standing which assumed crucial importance during the discussions of 1952. The classifiers, the examiners felt, often merely went through the motions of coordinating "specs" and allowed only a few minutes for appropriate review by examiners. Some examiners felt that authority to give final approval to minimum qualifications should rest solely with the examiners, who were ultimately responsible for selection. Some also felt that specifications could be greatly improved if examiners were consulted in writing them. The classifiers, on the other hand, felt that the responsibility for specifications was theirs and that examiners' opinions were, at best, advisory. The question of timing, mentioned by Miss Carmack, was central to much of this difficulty. The classifiers frequently made commitments to departments as to the time when an action would go to the Board. This resulted in a number of "crash" actions, requiring rapid review by other divisions. The examiners complained that they were allowed insufficient time to consider such proposals and that too often their comments were ignored.

Problems of this kind were not unique to the Personnel Board, but they were compounded by the Board's large size. In a smaller organization employees of different divisions might have maintained daily contacts, informally resolving coordination problems before they came to a head. The size of the Board's divisions, especially its examining group, made it difficult for personal relationships to budge divisional jurisdictions. Functional divisional loyalties were strong.

The problem was further aggravated by the fact that the three divisions were organized on different bases. Classification's internal structure was on a departmental basis—each analyst was responsible for all classification matters within a group of state departments. In Examining and Pay, the basis was occupational—each analyst or examiner had responsibility for a cluster of occupational classes, the majority of which crossed departmental lines. And the clustering within Examining did not parallel that in Pay. More hampering than the jurisdictional and mechanical difficulties that these functional arrangements presented were the subtle differences they bred in outlook, in approach to the job, and, indeed, in conception of the overall mission of the Personnel Board. The departmental grouping in Classification contributed to an organizational type of outlook—a desire to service each using agency well or to control it effectively (or a little of each). The occupational view, on the other hand, saw the state service as a number of series and classes—of clerks, or social workers, or engineers—and its emphasis was upon interdepartmental relationships, upon consistency in treatment regardless of organization, and upon the logic of occupational patterns.

The Pay Division

A unique aspect of the general coordination problem was the separate existence of the Pay Division. Until 1946, pay had been the responsibility of Classification. In that year, the pay group was given divisional status coequal with Examining and Classification. The new Pay Division was staffed largely with personnel transferred from Classification. It was established partly to emphasize the importance of the function which, many felt, had theretofore been subordinated to classification. It was also a response to the tremendous need for pay studies and adjustments in the unsettled years after the war. The Board's concern to establish a logical salary alignment was shared by the California State Employees Association (CSEA), the influential spokesman for the state's organized employees. The CSEA lent vigorous support to the establishment of a separate Pay Division in the State Personnel Board, and it subsequently acted as a watchdog to protect Pay's status.

Another element that may have contributed to the establishment of the Pay Division was the desire to bring in a highly qualified man to direct pay matters and to provide him with appropriate salary and status. Carl Richey, widely known classification and pay expert, was hired as the first chief. He resigned shortly to accept another job and was replaced by Kelvin D. Sharp, who, in turn, was replaced in 1948 by R. Permin Everett when Sharp became Assistant Secretary to the Personnel Board.

Under these three leaders, the Pay Division became a highly effective organization. It blazed new trails in its field and developed an extremely advanced system for pay determination and control. Yet the senior staff of the Board felt that the permanent separate existence of the Pay Division presented something of an anomaly, principally because of the overlap with Classification. This problem was thrown into public focus by a report of the State Assembly's Interim Committee on Governmental Efficiency and Economy in the late 1940's. The Interim Committee had retained the consulting firm of Louis J. Kroeger and Associates (the same Kroeger who seven years earlier had been forced out by the Personnel Board) to make a "thorough and impartial survey" of the Personnel Board and its practices. The Kroeger study was published in its entirety by the Interim Committee in 1949. It included 157 specific recommendations, and one of the most significant of these was that the Pay Division be abolished. "We see no logic in a separate Pay Division. Much of the information required to set the salary range is identical with that which determines the classification of the job. To do this work twice imposes a double burden upon the departments, delays decision, and adds to cost." Kroeger proposed that the entire function be merged with classification and that a new unit be provided in the Classification Division "to gather and analyze salary data."[8]

In June 1949 the Assembly called upon the State Personnel Board to report on progress in implementing the Kroeger recommendations. On December 16, 1950, the Personnel Board submitted its report—as long or longer than Kroeger's original one—in which it discussed each recommendation and expressed agreement with a great many. But it rejected the proposal to abolish the Pay Division. It pointed to the dominant importance of the pay function, to the fact that seventy per cent of the state budget was spent on salaries, almost all of which were determined by the Board, and to the costliness of errors in judgment in this field. Finally, it wrote:

> In the opinion of the Board, the collection and analysis of information on which salaries must be based is still too important a function to be made the part-time responsibility of individuals assigned to a combined pay and classification division.

The Board's own position on the matter was somewhat less emphatic and unanimous than its report implied. It had given much attention to its pay responsibilities. But some Board members felt that Pay should logically be merged with Classification, sooner or later. The principal question was one of timing. The majority of the Board felt that the special postwar pay problems which had warranted the establishment of the separate Pay Division were still sufficiently important to warrant its continuation. The majority was reinforced by continuing support for the Pay Division from the State Employees Association. Another factor militating against the consolidation at that time was that it would have entailed relinquishing one position at the level of Principal—and the Board had only five of them. This was seen as a serious loss of high supervisory positions; it would require demoting one person from this level—presumably the head of either Classification or Pay—and perhaps the chain demotion of another Senior, and subsequently possibly even others at lower levels.

The Board's firm refusal inhibited further discussion at the lower staff levels about abolishing the Pay Division, and this potential argument for generalist organization was not expressed during the months that reorganization was under consideration. Yet, even submerged, it was one of the decisive background factors.

Morale, Status, and Development

Although some thought it inevitable, most Pay Division officials, even those who later became enthusiastic supporters of the generalist program, were opposed to amalgamation with Classification. The Pay Division, the smallest of the three operating units, was considered by some the "elite" professional corps of the Board. It had developed high morale. Promotion had been relatively fast. A number of its people had accepted positions as personnel officers for state departments. Its contacts with the departments were frequent, important to the departments, and at high level. Most of its work culminated in Board consideration and action, and this meant that the individual analysts had frequent contacts with the Board itself, a privilege virtually denied the examiners. Some staff members thought pay analysts were casual about intra-Board coordination. These attitudes toward the Pay Division added to the coordination problem and at the same time contributed to another of the Board's problem areas—morale.

A good deal of attention had been given for some time to the individual development of staff members. A staff personnel committee had been functioning; a grievance system had been set up; a house organ known as the *Espe Bee* was being published. The management, interested in opportunities for employees to broaden themselves and to prepare for advancement, had long favored a system for rotating personnel from one division to another. In good part, this policy emanated

[8] Assembly, California Interim Committee on Governmental Efficiency and Economy, *Partial Report of the Study of the Personnel Board and Its Operation*, p. 29.

from the members of the Board. For years they had insisted upon greater delegation of authority. Soon after Fisher became Executive Officer, the Board had practically directed him to delegate responsibility to his staff; he had been advised not to attempt to answer personally all the questions the Board might raise. Subsequently, the Board urged that the analysts concerned, not their division chiefs, present cases before the Board. Further, the Board encouraged rotation among the supervisory staff, partly so that these officials would gain broader experience, partly so that they would look at problems from an overall, organizational point of view. Under law, the Board had one position to fill that was exempt from civil service regulations, its Assistant Secretary. (The Executive Officer was the Secretary.) This job was consistently filled with career men from Recruitment, Pay, and Classification.

Efforts of management to develop temporary rotation of assignments among the operating professional personnel met with varying success. There was a good deal of rotation between Pay and Classification. In fact, for some time most of the pay analysts came from a classification background. But rotation made little headway between the Recruitment and Examining Division and the other two divisions. Most of the pay and classification analysts did not want assignments in Examining, even temporary ones. Some referred to them as "assignments to Siberia." Also, supervisors hesitated to release good men on rotation assignments; a division chief would willingly release his weakest man, but the chief of the recipient division would, of course, resist such movements.

Reluctance to move to Examining may be understood in terms of the background and leadership of that division. The oldest unit in the Board, it had been headed for many years by only two chiefs. Nova Beal had served in examining work since the establishment of the Civil Service Commission in 1914. She retired as chief of the Examining Division in 1944, and she was succeeded by Edwin A. Abeel, himself an "old-time" examiner. An engineer by training, he had joined the staff in 1931. Both he and his predecessor were strong-willed, effective leaders of unquestioned and sometimes fearsome integrity. Under them the Examining Division was an impregnable citadel against political pressure and a prodigious producer of examinations, but it was never closely integrated with the rest of the Board. Abeel, strongly oriented to maintaining production, was reluctant to rotate assignments even within his own division. After one of his men had developed into a capable journeyman in a subject matter area, he considered it wasteful to sacrifice know-how and training time for rotation to another job. Former staff members of Examining recall that Abeel severely reprimanded an associate who had asked for a rotation assignment outside the division. Thereafter, requests virtually ceased. The bulk of the professionals on the Board's staff, especially those specialists whom the "front office" believed to be most in need of a rotation program, were thus kept out of it.

The Attitude Survey

Rotation was one element of a larger morale problem that was brought to everyone's attention, and perhaps exaggerated, by an attitude study that the staff conducted during May and early June of 1952. It was apparently a coincidence that the study was made at about the same time that the generalist idea was germinating. Fisher had had the idea of making such a study for some time. He saw it as a means of improving the effectiveness of the Board and its staff. Also, Robert Gray, a Board member, was deeply interested in attitude surveys and had directed a number of them in private industry. Since no other state agency had made such studies, Fisher thought the Board might set a good example to other departments in the matter of gauging and improving employee morale.

The results of the survey—which covered attitudes toward pay, working conditions, management, status and recognition, and the like—indicated generally favorable attitudes. In a memorandum report to all staff members on August 11, 1952, Fisher stated that seventy per cent of the employee responses were favorable; fifteen per cent were unfavorable; and fifteen per cent were "don't know." The overall results were distinctly above the normal pattern of responses in industries using the same survey forms. Fisher indicated gratification at finding "the strong sense of friendliness among the people of the SPB and that a high percentage of the staff are proud to work for this agency. . . ."

On the other hand, the Executive Officer noted that the survey had pinpointed certain trouble spots including the need for "better training and more of it, better communications, better working conditions, closer cooperation between divisions, and better job instructions and performance standards." The survey indicated considerable dissatisfaction with general working conditions. (At that time the Board occupied an old building, noisy, poorly equipped, and greatly overcrowded.) The study also indicated misunderstanding and resentment between the clerical and professional staffs—a longstanding problem in this agency. Most important for the reorganization story, the survey indicated to Fisher the existence of problems among the professionals—problems about which the survey statements themselves were insufficiently explicit. Fisher asked the heads of his three principal professional divisions to take up the results of the survey in staff meetings and to attempt to identify the sources of trouble. There followed a series of conferences in Examining and Classification during August and September 1952, and reports on these meetings went to Fisher, who made them the basis of discussion meetings of all Principals and Seniors. These discussions contributed substantially to the thinking that led to the generalist reorganization.

The survey and the discussions that came after it brought to light the following problems in Examining and Classification:

In Examining the survey showed three areas in which the responses of the examiners were significantly lower than those of other professional personnel: "confidence in management"; "effectiveness of administration"; and "opportunity for growth and advancement."

The subsequent discussions among the examiners revealed that there were serious morale problems, most of which involved feelings about "status." Said a summary memorandum dated August 22, 1952:

> Members of the examining staff do not enjoy status or receive recognition comparable to technicians in other divisions; examiners feel that they are an "out group."
>
> There is some feeling also that examination problems do not receive the weight of consideration [by management] that the problems of other divisions receive.
>
> Members of the examining staff do not have either the formal or informal contacts with management above the divisional level that other divisions have.
>
> Its accomplishments are not recognized by other divisions.
>
> . . . examiners do not have occasion to participate in matters before the Board.
>
> That there is insecurity with respect to status was voiced with specific reference to contacts with the classification staff about specifications, the pay staff, the executive office, and the Board itself.
>
> General exception was taken to the fact that there is not the same chance in the Examining Division to move to other agencies or transfer to other sections as is enjoyed by others on the same grade level.

A common sentiment in Examining was, "You will never be Executive Officer if you are an examiner." It was felt that top positions in the Board went predominantly to classifiers, almost never to examiners. It was a fact that every Executive Officer in the history of the Board had had a classification background; none had been examiners. Nor, in spite of the fact that examiners had always constituted the largest number of professional employees, were any former examiners incumbent in the three ranking staff jobs of the Board.

A further thorn in the examiners' sides was the fact that the many state departments that had set up new jobs for personnel officers seemed always to hire analysts from Pay or Classification. Hence, advancement was fairly rapid in those divisions, particularly in Pay. Most of the examiners had been hired by the Board during the first two postwar years to meet emergency problems. The absence of any movement upward or out of Examining had virtually halted promotion for half a decade.

Discussions with the examiners also emphasized problems of cooperation and coordination with Classification and Pay. There were also complaints against the clerical staff and its service; it was said that the clerical tail was wagging the dog. But the basic morale problems in Examining appeared to be concerns about status and advancement.

In Classification the attitude survey indicated that "the morale of the technical staff of the Classification Division is 'average' as compared to the general industrial norm on which the inventory is based. As compared to the technical staff of the agency as a whole, it indicates that the morale in the Classification Division is lower."[9] But the nature of the complaint was quite different from that in Examining. Here was no mention of status. There was reference to some of the problems of coordination and communication suggested earlier

---

[9] From a memorandum from the Classification Division, September 19, 1952.

in the Carmack memorandum. Considerable stress also was placed upon the need for more adequate training. But most of the criticism in Classification was directed at management and supervision. Emphasis was laid upon such needs as: clearer understanding of objectives; more explicit policies and standards; assurance of support against protesting state departments; and firmer support in general, from the Executive Officer on down. Much dissatisfaction in Classification derived from the feeling that supervision was too close; that too much time was spent in reviewing details and in rewriting documents.

The difficulties of classifiers—unlike those of the examiners—could not be remedied by changes in the *form* of organization. But the awareness of these dissatisfactions and internal tensions rendered the climate more favorable to organizational change, even though morale of the staff as a whole was distinctly above the industrial average and the overall morale picture was neither desperate nor critical.

The Conception of the Pilot Unit

Exactly what the reasons were for establishing a generalist pilot unit it is impossible to say; it probably would have been impossible to identify them precisely at the time in 1952 when the decision was made. Fisher, who initiated the idea and who ultimately decided to establish the pilot unit, was later inclined to attribute the decision to three factors: (1) his decision that the time had come to merge Classification and Pay; (2) the difficulties of the rotation program; (3) the problems of inter-divisional coordination. The results of the attitude survey and of the conferences that had followed it contributed to the final decision to go ahead, but the idea had been launched before these results were known.

An important, perhaps a dominant, factor in the decision was Fisher's own predisposition. Long experienced in personnel work, both in classification and as director of personnel programs, he was thoroughly familiar with the problems of functional specialism. Even before coming to California, he had entertained the idea of a generalist personnel organization. He now wanted to give the idea a try. But in this matter, as in others, he avoided imposing a change upon his staff until it had been discussed thoroughly.

Internal communication in 1952 was accomplished principally by staff meetings. Every two weeks the Executive Officer and his Assistant met with all the Principals and Seniors on the staff. These officers likewise met with their divisional staffs on a weekly or biweekly basis. There were occasional meetings of the entire professional staff, and official announcements (usually about important personnel changes) were issued infrequently from the Executive Office. The Board was quite informal in making decisions about its internal operations, and no formal records of these meetings were kept. Informal notes were sometimes made by participants, but by 1955 these were incomplete and fugitive. For factual data, the chronicler has had to rely upon the fallible memories of participants.

During the spring of 1952 some of the problems discussed above, particularly inter-divisional coordination, were often considered in Principal-Senior meetings. They were attacked on a number of fronts: improvement of procedures (such as that for the review of specifications by examiners), review of forms, rotation of personnel, grouping of workers from different divisions in common geographic locations, and the like.

In May or June, Fisher suggested setting up a pilot unit, organized on a generalist basis, in which each analyst would have complete responsibility for all personnel functions in a segment of the state service. Response to the proposal was mixed. All three of the Principals in Examining, Pay, and Classification were opposed or at least skeptical. A few Seniors were enthusiastic, but some, perhaps the majority, were cool. Had the proposal been submitted to a vote at that time, it probably would have been rejected decisively.

Chopson's Memorandum

Fisher nonetheless pushed his proposal. He asked E. W. Chopson, a Senior Examiner then serving under Fisher as Personnel Management Analyst, to prepare a plan, or alternative plans, for a generalist pilot unit. Chopson, an enthusiastic advocate, produced a plan on July 9, 1952.[10] Indeed, he also prepared a plan for reorganizing the entire Board on a generalist basis. The latter plan was not circulated and was never seriously considered, but Chopson's proposal for the pilot unit became the basis of all further discussion on the subject, and the unit ultimately established re-

[10] Memorandum from Chopson to Fisher, Subject: Recommended Pilot Unit Assignments.

sembled in basic respects the first alternative outlined in the proposal.

Chopson's memorandum stipulated certain requirements for the proposed unit: its personnel "should all be volunteers, or people sincerely interested in trying out the plan"; they should "insofar as possible be persons with broad experience"; they should be in or near the class "which would normally be used in staffing later such units." Specifically, he thought the pilot unit should be headed by a Senior and should include two Associates, one or two Assistants, one or two Juniors, and one Trainee. These officials would be drawn as follows: three from Examining, two from Classification, and one each from Pay and Recruiting or two from Pay and none from Recruiting. Not stated was an understood requirement: each person should know the subject matter or service area that the pilot unit would handle.

Chopson further stipulated that the unit, "at least during the early phases of its operation," should have responsibility only for examining, classification, and pay. He obviously contemplated a possibility of its moving later into recruiting, training, and perhaps other fields. To remove the unit from the control of any of the functional Principals, Chopson proposed that its head be made directly responsible to the Assistant Executive Officer.

From the standpoint of timing, Chopson proposed that the unit become fully operational within fifteen days after its activation. He assumed that it would take three months to bring it to full efficiency and another three to six months to test its operation. Still another three to six months might be necessary to make changes and to evaluate the changes. "At the end of not more than one year a final decision should be reached as to whether the new organization should be adopted on an agency-wide basis or whether the project should be dropped."

Chopson calculated that if the new unit included six workers, this would comprise twelve per cent of the professional staff in the three divisions.[11] Therefore, it should assume about twelve per cent of the workload, or about 250 of the state's classes and about 6,000 of its employees. The area of coverage that he proposed comprised the Departments of Mental Hygiene, Corrections, Youth Authority, and the Division of Special Schools and Services of the Department of Education. From these he suggested expecting agricultural, clerical, and mechanical trades classes, leaving a net of 277 classes and 10,720 employees. If this grouping proved impracticable, he suggested a grouping of Agriculture, Natural Resources, and Fish and Game. For each grouping he suggested the staff members who should be assigned.

Behind Chopson's choice of the first group lay two main factors. First was the basic and as yet unresolved question as to whether the generalist unit should be structured on a departmental or an occupational basis. Some of the staff thought that the unit, and within it each analyst, should have responsibility for all personnel matters in a department or a group of departments; others favored occupational groupings which might or might not cross departmental lines. While the Classification Division was structured on a departmental basis, Pay and Examining were organized by occupation. Decision on this question was crucial to the nature of the entire generalist pattern.

But Chopson did not want his proposal to be bogged down in this argument. He therefore proposed for the new unit an area of coverage in which departmental and occupational lines were basically similar; that is, most of the classes to be covered were largely confined to a limited number of departments.

A second factor in Chopson's choice of the Mental Hygiene-Corrections group was his desire to secure the assignment of enthusiastic personnel to the pilot unit. During his work on the proposal, fifteen persons had asked Chopson if they could be assigned to the pilot unit. Three whom Chopson suggested for assignment were Robert Lawson (then on a temporary appointment as Senior in the Examining Division), whom Chopson proposed as chief of the the new unit, and Kay Groff and Jane Carmack (both in Classification), two of the most ardent advocates of generalism. All three had had experience with the occupations and departments that would be involved in Chopson's first group.

In the following months, Chopson's memorandum furnished the basis for spirited conversation but little else. It was discussed in the Principal-Senior staff meetings, in the divisional staff meetings, in corridors, and over the lunch table. Reactions were mixed, although opposition to the proposal was never well organized or well articu-

[11] In calculating this percentage he counted the five workers in Recruitment, even though he specifically opposed transferring recruiting functions at that time.

lated. William Popper, Senior Engineering Examiner, wrote Fisher early in July proposing a committee system to solve the inter-divisional coordination problem. In another memorandum to Fisher, Alden Brock, then a Senior Examiner, proposed a gradual system of grouping staff and of broadening responsibilities rather than the all-or-none technique implied in the pilot program.

Further argument ensued about the occupational versus the departmental approach. But it became evident that if Examining were to be included in the generalist program, the occupational approach was inevitable. The great majority of state employees were in classes that were employed in several different departments; in fact, the largest group, the clerical employees, occupied classes common to all the departments. This was also true of some other categories—administrative, fiscal, legal, custodial, and some trades. To have set up duplicating or competing examining systems in different units for the same classes would have been wasteful and self-defeating. In retrospect it appears that the argument for a departmental system was, consciously or not, an argument against any generalizing plan that included the examining function.

Eventually the occupational basis prevailed. In spite of Chopson's efforts at compromise, his proposal essentially accepted an occupational basis for the pilot unit. Many of the classes in the departments assigned to the pilot unit were common to the entire service, and these were excluded from the unit's responsibilities. On the other hand, the unit was given responsibility for the custodial classes, which overlapped most of the state departments.

The period during which Chopson's plan was being discussed—late summer and early fall of 1952—was also the period during which the conferences and staff meetings were held about the attitude survey. During these months the Board was handling its normal workload in normal fashion. Never did the idea of the pilot unit carry more than a minor importance in the deliberations of the staff. The delay in decision was a source of restiveness among some of the more enthusiastic supporters of the plan. It seemed that much of the original interest in and enthusiasm for the plan was being frittered away for want of quick decision. But this was a characteristic method of management in the Board. Everyone was given time to digest the idea and ample opportunity to express his views. Insofar as a meeting of minds could be reached through deliberation and discussion, this was done.

The pilot unit idea was put forth only as an "experiment." Any commitment as to future action was disclaimed. If it did not work, it would be easy to return to the old system; if it did, there would be ample opportunity to discuss what the next step would be. It is always difficult to oppose an experiment.

After a final discussion of the proposal in a Senior-Principal meeting in October, Fisher asked for a show of hands. One participant recalls that the vote came out about even. In general, the Principals of the three divisions all had reservations about it, and the Seniors were split. Members of the operating staff, had they been called upon to vote, would probably also have split but with a clear majority in favor. Their feelings, and those of many of the supervisors, would perhaps have been swayed less by arguments of principle than by personal desires to broaden their experience, to enlarge promotional opportunities, or, in some cases, to escape difficult local supervisory situations. A few felt that "it's time for a change"—whatever the change might be.

Following the vote, Fisher announced simply that he would go ahead. Thus was revealed what may have been the most crucial decision in the whole reorganization process. A few days later, Fisher told the Personnel Board that the staff was going to experiment with a generalist unit, and subsequently he informed the state departments to be serviced by the new unit.

On October 21, the following announcement was posted on the bulletin board in the Personnel Board building:

> Pilot Program for Generalist Approach to
> Examining, Classification, and Pay Activities
>
> The above program which has been discussed with members of the various technical staffs will be started on or about November 17, 1952. The program is being organized on an experimental basis to determine the feasibility and practicability of individual staff members carrying out the examining, classification and pay activities with respect to a specified group of classes. We hope to learn whether or not it is desirable to extend this generalist activity.
>
> Classes to be handled: medical and allied services; regulatory; public safety inspection; social security and rehabilitation; custodian and domestic services.
>
> Persons assigned: Bob Lawson in charge; Kay Groff; Jane Carmack; Betty Walton; Wiley Hartley.

THE TRIAL RUN

NOVEMBER 1952–OCTOBER 1953

Although Fisher's announcement stated the pilot unit's responsibilities strictly in terms of occupational classes, and although there were some important changes from the earlier proposal, the unit as it went into operation was similar to the one proposed by Chopson. The positions covered were confined to a relatively small number of agencies—Social Welfare, Mental Hygiene, Public Health Education, Youth Authority, and Veterans Affairs—many of which operated institutions. In no case did the new unit cover all positions of any department, nor even a majority of the classes in a department, but its problems were somewhat simplified by the fact that its departmental contacts were relatively limited.

The key members of the staff assigned to the unit were those proposed by Chopson, but its total size was smaller: one supervisor and four workers as against his proposal of six. In February 1953 a new member was assigned from the Pay Division, and for most of its history the pilot unit staff remained one supervisor and five operators. The staff consisted of three from Examining (Lawson, the Chief, Walton, and Hartley), two from Classification (Groff and Carmack), and later on, one from Pay (Specht).

The group was fortunate in its chief. Lawson was one of the few supervisors with experience in both examining and classification. Before he joined the Board in 1949, he had done graduate work in personnel administration and had served with civil service agencies in Detroit and Alameda County, California. Though most of his work had been in examining, he had done classification. Further, he was young, enthusiastic about the generalist idea, and determined to make it succeed. His enthusiasm was abetted by that of Groff and Carmack. Soon the entire staff was imbued with a will to prove that the new system would work—and work better.

Lawson, as the Senior in charge of the unit, assumed the responsibilities of a Principal in the three fields of pay, classification, and examining. His decisions were not subject to review by other Principals, although he called upon them for guidance from time to time—particularly in pay matters, in which he had had no experience. In examining, he largely steered his own course. He was responsible directly to Bell, the Assistant Executive Officer, but Bell encouraged him to make his own decisions.

During the period of the pilot unit's separate operation, from November 17, 1952, until January 1, 1954, the other parts of the Board continued as usual. Pay, Classification, and Examining simply lost their responsibility for the classes assigned the unit.

Preparation

None of the unit's members, aside from its chief, came with any prior training or experience in more than one functional field. Training in the other fields was, therefore, the first order of business. The mornings of the first two weeks were devoted almost exclusively to a fairly formal training program. Examining was the subject the first week. Most of this course was given by Lawson himself, but separate sessions were also conducted by representatives of the Recruiting Section and the Scheduling Unit of the Recruitment and Examining Division. The mornings of the second week were devoted to classification (three days) and to pay (two days). The sessions were conducted by various Seniors and journeymen from the two divisions concerned. The nature of the sessions is suggested by the following list of subjects covered by the Classification representatives, each having one hour for presentation and discussion:

- Document Review and Processing Transfers
- Job Survey Techniques
- Classification Plan and Principles
- Definition and Typical Tasks (in Specification Writing)
- Minimum Qualifications and Knowledges and Abilities
- Board Memoranda
- Survey Principles and Methods
- Allocation Standards

There was obviously too little time for complete coverage of the techniques of examining, classifying jobs, and making pay analyses. In fact, a considerable proportion of the allotted period was consumed in learning procedures, mechanics, and relationships. Some difficulty was encountered, for example, in the use of forms calling for signatures by one or more of the division chiefs; in general, it was decided not to develop and print new forms but to adapt the old ones to the new type of organization, giving Lawson signing authority that was comparable to that of the three Principals.

But questions of a great deal more substance also engaged the new unit during this period. There was a great deal of discussion of the varying usages of class specifications, of the differing significances of statements of minimum qualifications, and of the degree to which class requirements, determined by classifiers, had to be taken literally by examiners in the preparation of examinations and the review of applications. In general, those with examining background held for a liberal and flexible usage, with more room for discretion in the appraisal of individuals seeking employment and advancement. Though rather few solutions were agreed upon, these discussions exposed differing points of view and made one group more sympathetic to the problems of the other. Many of the problems discussed were unique to the operations of the new unit, but others were central to the whole problem of inter-divisional cooperation and understanding. As such, the discussions served as a kind of catharsis. In January Lawson wrote Fisher a six-page, single-spaced memorandum on the problems that had been discussed during the training period.

During the initial period the new unit also discussed a name for itself, bearing in mind the significance of its title should the whole Board be reorganized on a generalist basis. It arrived at "General Personnel Operations Unit," and thereafter was referred to simply as the GPOU. In this and in its other actions described above, the unit acted without direction by the Executive Office.

Although the formal training program had been completed by the end of November, a good part of the working time in December was also, in effect, training time. The members worked closely with each other, reviewed documents, and studied the groups of classes to which they were assigned. There were frequent discussions about methods and problems. Much of the necessary business was handled as a device for further training, enabling the staff to "learn by doing."

One of the first problems was to decide how work should be assigned within the unit. The group determined to proceed on a generalist basis from the start, so that each person would begin work in both classification and examining. There was further discussion of the old problem of occupational versus departmental assignments, and again it was decided to assign each individual a group of occupations and classes comparable to his prior occupational assignments, but to group the classes so as to maximize departmental concentration. The analysts were arranged in teams of one classifier and one examiner, so that they might learn from each other and review each other's work. It was agreed that the unit would not perform any work in the pay field until the Pay Division was able to assign one of its men. This occurred in February, and thereafter the unit gradually took over pay responsibilities. However, it was not until the following June that the GPOU could properly be considered a full-fledged generalist unit.

The Unit in Operation

Although the training aspects of its work continued for many months, the unit became fully operational by January 1953. The nature of its activities thereafter is suggested by its report for March, a representative month:

> prepared 15 examinations, of which four were form tests, 4 were tests provided by the American Public Health Association, one was for transfer, and 6 were regular; the regular tests involved 181 new items, or 17% of the total items in these tests; also prepared 188 other new items for future use;
>
> acted as chairmen of oral boards for 8 classes and 74 candidates;
>
> reviewed 113 classification documents;
>
> prepared 15 examination bulletins;
>
> reviewed 297 applications for examinations;
>
> conducted field trips to a state hospital and to laboratories in Agriculture and Public Health;
>
> completed a new procedure for the checking of medical licenses.

The unit was able to keep up with its schedule of work requirements—an achievement most necessary in the field of examinations.[12] Although there may have been some slowdown in classification work, the using departments made little complaint. Pay studies and adjustments for the new

[12] Under the California system, the Board has little discretion as to the timing of examinations. When a vacancy occurs for which there is no "current eligibles" list available, the department fills it with a temporary appointment or promotion. But, under the state Constitution, such an appointment must expire at the end of nine months. During that period, an examination must be prepared and administered and an eligible list produced.

fiscal year occupied much of the unit's time during June.

The analysts felt that their more intimate acquaintance with a smaller number of classes than they had handled previously provided information that made possible more adequate and quicker handling of individual actions. The knowledge they gained from pay studies, or classification transactions, or preparing examinations was, they felt, transferable. And the absence of the need for inter-divisional clearances increased the speed of the work process and added to job satisfaction. Even in its first month, December, Lawson was able to point with pride to the elimination of an examination due to the unit's acquaintance with another usable list—an accomplishment he felt would not have occurred under functional organization. The relatively high morale of the group was raised by its practice of holding informal evening staff meetings at the home of one of the members. Discussions were directed primarily at the objectives and the philosophy of the unit and at ways by which its advantages could be maximized.

The analysts of the new unit were especially eager to undertake projects for which their generalist-occupational type of organization made them especially suited. Two of them worked part-time for several months on a thorough survey of all the classes in the food service series, taking into account pay, classification, and, to a lesser extent, examining considerations. Other studies—smaller, but similarly comprehensive from a functional standpoint—were also carried out.

But the unit also had its problems. One was keeping its activities and standards up-to-date and coordinated with the policies and programs of the three functional divisions.

Another difficulty was the organization and scheduling of work. The combination of pressures and deadlines on the shoulders of a single analyst, factors that neither he nor his supervisor could control, resulted in heavy peak loads. This difficulty was partially alleviated by the team arrangement and by the flexibility that enabled assignments to be temporarily transferred among the staff.

Problems of coordination with other divisions arose, although they were of a somewhat different type than previously. Positions and classes closely related to the occupational assignments of the unit but not included in them sometimes fell "between desks." Departmental reorganizations and other developments often affected not only some of the unit's classes but also a good many classes beyond its jurisdiction.

In a six-month progress report to Fisher, dated June 25, 1953, Lawson mentioned some of these advantages and disadvantages and concluded: "It would appear that the practicality of such an organization as this has been sufficiently established. It cannot be claimed, however, that at this stage, we have demonstrated any substantial or clearcut advantages over the more conventional type of organization. We do feel that substantial progress has been made. . . ."

Evaluation

From the very beginning, the senior personnel of the Board had recognized the necessity of an objective appraisal of the effectiveness of the pilot unit. As early as July 1952 Chopson had proposed a list of objectives of the unit, which he thought would furnish a basis for appraising its effectiveness. Most of these criteria, however, were too general to permit direct measurement. Shortly after the unit was established, the Executive Office asked the heads of each of the three functional divisions to prepare a set of criteria for measuring the unit's effectiveness. A good deal of work went into this in November and December 1952, particularly by R. W. Stephens, Chief of Classification, who prepared an elaborate set of devices and indices for comparison and appraisal. These were forwarded to Lawson for comment, and subsequently Bell, the Assistant Executive Officer, called a meeting to discuss them. The criteria fell into four main categories: (1) quantity of work, (2) quality of work, (3) reaction of using departments, and (4) satisfactions of individual staff members.

But in spite of these early steps, little effort was made during the months that followed to gather data that might be evaluated systematically. The difficulties in doing so were great and perhaps insurmountable.

For *quantity of work,* the Board had no universal system of work measurement, and there was little agreement as to the work units that might be used to reflect performance. Lawson, during his tenure as the unit's Chief, tried three different methods of measuring work output and was not satisfied with any of them. Even had he been, the measurements would not have been useful for comparison purposes unless the same methods were used in other divisions. A second difficulty of quantitative comparison was that the unit's work content was not comparable with that of any of the divisions. It was like comparing the whole of a stew with the beef, onions, and potatoes that had gone into it. There was no standard time for the writing of an examination or the writing of a class specification. This problem was confounded by the fact that the classes assigned the unit were in many ways not typical—and this would undoubtedly have been true of any assortment of classes. For example, the examining load of the unit was thought to be fairly easy, because it used tests developed by the American Public Health Association for many of the medical classes. On the other hand, those in the unit thought many of the classes to which they were assigned were unusually difficult from a classification standpoint.

Comparison of *quality* was even more ephemeral. Perhaps the best device for comparing would have been a review of all or a substantial part of the work product of the unit by the Principals in the functional divisions. Variations on this method were proposed, but little was done systematically by any of the division chiefs, and the unit would probably have resented such an effort, as it was not completely convinced of the impartiality of the division chiefs toward its operations. In the field of examining, Lawson himself could make some evaluations, although his position precluded perfect objectivity; but in the other fields, he did not feel himself capable of making qualitative appraisals. Abeel, Principal in Examining, did not review any of the examining work, and no other review of completed examinations was conducted in the Board. For pay and classification recommendations sent to the Board there did exist a basis for qualitative evaluation by the Executive Office. But evaluation was not done systematically.

A further difficulty in evaluation was that the unit was still learning its job. At first, it would have been clearly unfair to compare it with the long-experienced divisions. Subsequent experience has led some to feel that it takes at least a year and a half for a unit to attain its full potential. There was little agreement during 1953 on when the unit had attained sufficient maturity to warrant a fair comparison.

Because of these difficulties, little was done in the first half of 1953 to provide a basis for objective appraisal. During the summer, however, Bell decided to evaluate the unit in order to determine its future and that of the rest of the organization. The three principal criteria upon which the evaluation ultimately rested were: the job satisfaction of the unit's employees; the reaction of the using departments; and the opinions and feelings of the principal officers of the Board's staff.

Job Satisfaction: There could be no equivocation on this criterion. Members of the unit were enthusiastic. Their reasons were set forth at some length in a memorandum written by Kay Groff on October 5, 1953. Miss Groff had been asked by John McKay, who had become Personnel Management Analyst, to write him a frank memo on her reactions to the new unit. She was then about to leave the Board in order to be married, and she dictated the memo on her last day of work. She wrote that she was "just as enthusiastic" about the unit after eleven months in it as she had been at the start, and that all of its staff felt the same way. In Classification, she had been "constantly . . . frustrated" by the way responsibilities were divided among divisions, by the time-consuming requirement of clearances, by the reliance that had to be placed upon representatives of the departments and upon the examiners for job information. She was impressed in the pilot unit by the tremendous increase in her knowledge about the jobs and classes to which she was assigned, by the usability of this knowledge in all the personnel functions, by the ease and speed of clearance, by the nearness of the Senior to advise and to act quickly on problems. She attributed part of this to the personal capability of Lawson. She felt that the increased morale and the increased knowledge about jobs were contributing to better work performance. She acknowledged certain problems of coordination but thought they were far less serious than such problems under the old organization. Finally, she expressed the hope that "even if the decision is made not to reorganize the entire board along generalist lines, that at least one or two units will be continued for the purpose of intensive review of classes in schematic groups, which is only possible in this kind of organization, and that it also be kept for the purpose of staff training."

This memo was written and broadly circulated shortly before the decision was reached to generalize the entire organization, and it may have provided a final push in that direction. But several weeks before, Bell had already become convinced that feeling within the unit was favorable. In fact, he had determined that the unit should be maintained, if only for this reason, regardless of the decision about the rest of the organization.

Departmental Reaction: In September 1953 Bell and Lawson arranged a series of meetings with the heads, the personnel officers, and certain other officials of each of the departments principally serviced by the unit. In these one- to two-hour conferences, they elicited the frank reactions of the using agencies. Fisher attended some of these meetings.

The views expressed at the meetings ranged from mildly affirmative to enthusiastic.[13] Some felt that it was still too early to express a confident judgment; some were reluctant to recommend, at that time, that the entire Board be reorganized; some wished that the unit were on a departmental rather than an occupational basis—that each department have one man to deal with. But none suggested that the old form was preferable or that the new system was not. And some officials were vigorously in favor of generalism, both as an idea and in practice. Among the advantages seen by the using agencies were:

> Personnel workers have improved understanding of jobs and of departmental problems.
>
> Personnel staff is better able to perceive relationships between jobs and classes.
>
> Staff views personnel problems as a whole, not as segments.
>
> Service, particularly in pay and classification, is faster.
>
> Strengthens position of personnel officer in the departments since Personnel Board now presents more unified front.
>
> Better solution of interdepartmental problems —analysts in position to settle such differences rather than leaving up to departments to fight it out.
>
> Makes it impossible for departments to operate with the technical divisions of the Board on the basis of "divide and conquer."
>
> Single contact with Board on any given job problem rather than several (but the obverse of this was also stated—that a number of different contacts are necessary for each department under the occupational scheme).
>
> Generalist is able to make and express a decision—the specialists are more hesitant and slower.
>
> The specialist background of staff members was at first obvious, but deficiencies disappeared in six months.
>
> The time and work of the agency on personnel problems were reduced.
>
> Qualifications of individual personnel of staff have improved as result of getting out more and seeing problems.
>
> Less buck-passing within the Board.
>
> Relationships between Board and departments are "more comfortable."
>
> May have effect of changing whole approach of Board from that previously of umpire and arbitrator to one of participant and assistant to better management.

The verdict of the departments, then, was favorable to the generalist program. But it may be noted that there was virtually no comment upon its effect on examining—still the largest single segment of the Board's workload.

Reactions of Officers Within the Board: On August 26 Bell met with Lawson, the Principals, and some of the Seniors in the three functional divisions to discuss the effectiveness of the unit. The meeting produced a fairly systematic review of most aspects of the work the unit had been doing.[14]

From the standpoint of production, both R. P. Everett, Chief of Pay, and the representatives from Examining seemed to feel that the unit had successfully carried its share of the workload in their fields. Stephens, Chief of Classification, thought it had fallen considerably short of a full job in his area. He said that regular analysts on his staff would have produced more new specifications and specification revisions. Lawson acknowledged this but called attention to the fact that many of his staff had been in a semi-training status for the first six months.

With regard to quality, Everett thought the unit had done a satisfactory job on pay, but reported that some of his staff felt the unit as a whole was not attaching sufficient importance to pay matters. There was little basis for judging the quality of examinations, since they had not been reviewed in Examining. E. V. Williams, a Senior from Classification, commented that some of the classification materials prepared by inexperienced analysts on the unit's staff were not up to normal standards, and Stephens said he saw some danger that the unit "may be drifting apart" on standards. Lawson said that his analysts felt that they were doing better jobs in their original fields.

Some expressed the sentiment that the unit's staff was exceptionally able and that not all personnel could handle this triple job. Both Stephens

[13] These comments are based on Bell's penciled notes.

[14] These comments are based on Bell's penciled notes taken at the meeting.

and A. L. Brock of Examining expressed a fear of over-specialization in regard to classes, over-identification with "special interests," and a resultant overall lack of coordination and consistency. There was little support for extending the new system to the entire staff, but representatives of both Pay and Classification felt that the unit should be continued and the experiment broadened to include another unit. Some endorsed the idea of trying out an experimental unit on a departmental basis.

Thus, staff reactions in August were mixed, inconclusive, and on balance, slightly negative. But when Bell, in early October, reported to the general meeting of Seniors and Principals on the favorable responses of the using departments, the resulting verdict was clear consensus that, for whatever reasons, the pilot unit had been a success.

REORGANIZATION

NOVEMBER 1953–OCTOBER 1954

At the beginning of October 1953, Personnel Board executives faced a choice of four possible steps:

1. Drop the pilot unit and revert to the old organization.
2. Retain the pilot unit temporarily, or even permanently, without extending the idea.
3. Keep the present unit and set up a second pilot unit, either as a further experiment or as a step in the direction of complete generalization at some unspecified future time.
4. Prepare for a complete change-over to the generalist pattern.

The first possibility was precluded by Bell's report. It would have been like saying: "We tried the idea; it worked; so we dropped it."

The second choice seemed somewhat more practicable, but the forcefulness of Bell's report militated against it. The original idea had been to give the pilot unit one year's trial. The year was almost up.

The third possibility had been suggested in Bell's meeting with the Seniors and Principals, some of whom had proposed that a second unit be set up and tried on a departmental rather than an occupational basis. For a while it appeared that this course would be followed. In September Fisher instructed John McKay, who had become Personnel Management Analyst in May, to prepare a plan for a second generalist unit. But McKay's plan, which was released on October 19, stated explicitly that its purpose was not the further testing of the effectiveness of the generalist approach. Nor was it designed to answer the "larger problem of determining the practical limits of the generalist form of organization. . . . This matter requires a great deal more study and discussion." McKay appeared to assume that the generalist idea would be extended, but that there was as yet no commitment to a Board-wide decision.

The establishment of a second unit without first deciding about the total future pattern of organization was vigorously opposed by Stephens, Chief of Classification. He held that the difficulty of operating the Board on two different organizational bases was already great enough with one generalist unit. The time had come to decide whether or not to go the full way. This view evidently was supported by others, and the choice was reduced to one of two alternatives: dropping the unit or changing the organization of the entire California State Personnel Board to a generalist pattern.

Certain other considerations probably entered into the decision and its timing. One was that in late September the Civil Service Assembly of the United States and Canada had held its annual conference in Los Angeles. One of the panel sessions had been on the subject, "The Generalist vs. the Specialist." Bell, the Board's Assistant Executive Officer, had been a member of that panel and had spoken about the Board's experience with the pilot unit. Fisher had attended the Civil Service Assembly sessions, as had a fairly large number of other staff members. The subject of generalism, and of the California experience in particular, had generated considerable attention and discussion at the conference. This focusing of national professional interest on the subject, plus the enthusiasm the Californians had developed in describing their innovation at the conference, may have contributed to a feeling of greater urgency when the Board employees returned to Sacramento.

A second consideration was that Abeel, for a

decade the Chief of the Recruitment and Examining Division, had retired during the summer of 1953. Abeel had paid little attention to the pilot unit experiment. Some staff members felt that he disliked the generalist idea and might have opposed it actively had he not been close to retirement.

A third consideration was that there still remained some of the interpersonal and supervisory problems discussed in the attitude survey conferences held many months before.

There is no record of the decision to proceed—as to exactly how or when it was reached and announced—and the memories of participants provide only vague clues. During October there was a great deal of consultation and, as in the year before, discussions were held, particularly in the Principal-Senior meetings. No special effort was made to probe staff opinions beyond the customary reports of supervisors. The decision itself was made by Fisher in close collaboration with Bell, apparently toward the end of October. The first written evidence of it occurs in the October monthly report of Personnel Management Analyst McKay, written on November 3, 1953:

> a. *As of January 1, 1954:* After detailed study and discussion it has been decided, as the next step toward a generalist form of organization, to consolidate the Classification and Pay Division staff functions. This combined unit together with Generalist Unit Number 1 would become a new Division of Operations. At the same time a Division of Technical Services would be established with responsibility for policy and standards relating to the classification and pay functions as well as the specialized services of wage surveys, departmental classification surveys, classification and pay transactions, etc.
>
> b. *As of April 1, 1954:* A Second Generalist Unit would be established on this date to undertake the technical work for the groups Agriculture and Conservation, and Regulatory and Public Safety. This second unit would report to the Chief of Operations.

Even this decision seemed somewhat tentative, and it left unanswered a number of questions about the future. (It may be noted in passing that the occupational assignments for the second generalist unit were exactly those McKay had proposed in his memorandum of October 19.)

Planning the Change

Central responsibility for developing a specific plan for change-over was assigned to McKay. During the closing months of 1953 he worked closely with the various officers principally concerned. Much of the planning process was one of negotiating, identifying the principal points at issue, and bringing to a higher level any unresolved disagreements. A number of disputed points were discussed at meetings of Principals and Seniors, and some were taken up in private meetings with Fisher and Bell. During this period McKay was seeking to maintain objectivity and thus tried to avoid taking sides.

Within the Board at this time it was generally understood that reorganization was aimed at two objectives: first, to enlarge the challenge of work to staff, thus providing greater job satisfaction and greater opportunities for development and promotion; second, to improve the quality of the personnel work from the standpoint of the Board and from the standpoint of the departments that it serviced. The second goal, it was hoped, would result in part from achieving the first. But it was also anticipated that other elements of the generalist pattern would contribute to improved performance: the approach to individual problems from a broad rather than a segmental basis; greater knowledge of the job; more direct lines of supervision and control and therefore the possibility of greater delegation of authority for making decisions; fewer requirements for intra-Board clearance, and therefore greater speed of service; and, finally, the opportunity for the development of better standards and policies by a clear-cut separation of operations from staff responsibilities.

Two possible purposes were definitely *not* considered. First, the reorganization was not viewed as a means of bringing about any basic change in the broad purposes and policies of the State Personnel Board. It was seen as a new arrangement for doing fundamentally the same things. Some anticipated that it would accelerate the trend toward greater delegation of personnel authority to the departments, but this was at most an incidental purpose. Second, the reorganization was not prompted by considerations of economy. Some hoped that there would be savings in operations which would make possible greater attention to some of the staff-type work that had been relatively neglected. But no one anticipated that any positions would be dropped as a result of the change. In fact, there was assurance that this would not be the case.

In short, Board officials hoped that by reason of the generalist plan, the Board would do essentially the same things at the same cost—but do them better than before and provide more satisfaction to those doing them.

One "formal" element of decisive importance in planning the reorganization was the budget of the Board and the positions it authorized. Early in the planning stage Fisher and Bell conferred with officials of the state's Budget Division, including members of its organization and methods section. At this meeting, they agreed that no increase in funds or in authorized positions would be sought as a result of the reorganization. (This agreement constituted the totality of Budget Division participation.) Virtually all the Board's professional positions, particularly those at supervisory levels, were filled by persons who had had several years' experience. Therefore, the reorganization had to be accomplished within the framework of the existing positions, ranks, funds, and personnel.

These budgetary, classificatory, and status considerations provided "givens" within which the new organization had to be framed. In the old organization there were three Principals, each the head of a functional division. The rank of Principal required division head responsibilities. Therefore, there had to be exactly three divisions under the new plan, each capable of supporting the classification of Principal. This might have been accomplished by dividing the operations work between two divisions, each headed by a Principal, and providing a third consolidated staff division. Since this possibility would have created difficulties of coordination between the two operating divisions, it was not seriously considered. The other possibility was that of a single operations division and two staff divisions, one for Examining and Recruitment, the other for the combined residuum of Pay and Classification.

The decision was made to proceed on the latter basis: there would be a single generalist Operating Division and two staff divisions. This meant, among other things, that responsibilities would have to be distributed among the three in such a way as to warrant divisional status—and a Principal job—in each.

Nine Senior positions were potentially involved: the Personnel Management Analyst; the chief of the pilot unit; two in Classification; one in Pay; and four in Examining, including three examiners and one head of the Recruitment Section. Unless he had a special or unusual job, such as that of Personnel Management Analyst, a Senior Analyst headed a section or group of professional workers and reported to a Principal. The head of Recruitment and Examining would need to retain the Senior in charge of recruiting and at least one other to take charge of whatever examining work was left. The head of the classification-pay staff work would need at least one Senior. The Personnel Management Analyst job was to be retained. This left, at an absolute maximum, five Seniors to head up sections in the new Operating Division. In view of the supervisory responsibilities involved in directing all operating activities, five also appeared to be the minimum. Thus, there was early agreement on having five sections in the new generalist Operations Division.

Within the basic organizational design already decided (three divisions and five sections in the Operations Division), McKay pursued his intensive study. His work was directed at the delineation of responsibilities of each division and section, the interrelationships of the units, the number and grades of positions to be assigned to each, the names of individuals to be reassigned, and the timing of the various changes.

Classification and Pay Functions

One of McKay's more difficult tasks was to determine how responsibilities should be divided between the two projected staff divisions and the generalist Operations Division. He made a detailed inventory of all the functions of the existing divisions. After conferring with the division chiefs, he prepared memoranda for the front office proposing allocations of responsibilities on which he and the divisions chiefs had agreed and stating the differences of view on disputed matters. Part of this discussion went on before the division chiefs yet knew what their new assignments would be.

The fundamental criterion in McKay's allocations was that work which applied directly to groups, classes, positions, and individuals would be assigned to the Operations Division. Developmental, research, and survey work would go to the two staff divisions, which would provide technical and advisory service to the generalists in Operations. In the fields of classification and pay, this meant that the Operations Division would have responsibility for:

The classification plan
The pay plan
Preparing virtually all classification documents for Board review (except those delegated to departments)

Providing contact and service to departments on all classification and pay matters
Developing and applying new salary scales to classes

The new Standards and Surveys Division (to be formed from the old Pay and Classification divisions) would have responsibility for:

Community wage surveys—planning, supervision, and reporting; but the Operations Division would lend personnel to participate in data collection
Special salary studies—for groups of classes as required
Studies of overtime practices, and advice to Operations Division on overtime problems
Conduct of periodic departmental classification audits
Development of classification and pay techniques—such as improved format for specifications, minimum qualification patterns, standardized terminology, work measurement techniques, improved classification and wage survey methods
Interpretation and application of the law and rules in these fields and formulation of new policies where necessary
Prevailing rate studies for manual jobs
Supervision and direction of the Board's statistical and reporting activities
Training in classification and pay for the entire agency
Preparation of the Board's reports to the Governor and the Legislature, including recommendations on appropriations needed for wage adjustment purposes
Development and maintenance of technical manuals on pay, classification, and transactions.

To this new division was also assigned the Personnel Management Analyst, theretofore responsible directly to the Executive Officer, on the grounds that his job was essentially a research function and that the Standards and Surveys Division would become the principal research agency of the Board. Another consideration was that this shift would strengthen the staff and responsibilities of the new division and its chief. For operational purposes, this officer continued to report directly to the "front office." It was decided to transfer the maintenance of the employee roster, the large clerical task of the Classification Division, to the Office Services Division.

There was little disagreement in principle with these assignments. But there were loose ends, some of which later rose to plague the divisions when they began to work under the new arrangements. For example, how were the findings and decisions of the staff studies made in Standards and Surveys to be communicated to the generalists in the Operations Division? How were the misclassifications discovered in the departmental surveys to be corrected? How many analysts, and which ones, were to be loaned to Standards and Surveys for wage surveys? The jurisdiction of the staff division, Standards and Surveys, over legal and procedural questions on individual transactions was certain to cause confusion for the operating sections, themselves presumably responsible for the transactions. One general question, which was discussed but not permanently resolved, was that of staff-line relations in assuring that standards in classification and pay were maintained by the generalists in the Operations Division. There was no provision for technical inspection or review of the operators' work by the staff unit; and it was agreed that one device that might have served this purpose, the periodic classification audit, was to be used only to correct current position misallocations without any investigation as to how they might have occurred.

Examining Functions

Little change was anticipated for the recruiting function, which would remain intact within the Recruitment and Examining Division. But the distribution of responsibilities for examining was a difficult proposition, perhaps partly because there had been so little previous understanding of Examining's activities. In theory, the allocation was quite clear. The Operations Division would take over test preparation and the review of applications; the staff division would schedule the interviewing boards, conduct research in examining, maintain the library of testing items (the Testing Pool), provide training and technical guidance on the preparation and conduct of tests, and see that testing standards were maintained and, if possible, improved.

But one difficulty arose from the fact that the Board had done little in the research and development of testing technique *as such*. It had been predominantly production-oriented. How could development of technique be divorced from the development of tests? And how could one division be held effectively accountable for technique when another was fully responsible for the tests themselves? What role could a staff division fill, and through what means, to assure the maintenance of standards in examining? This question was particularly pertinent since the head of Operations was to be a man relatively unversed in testing and since some of his Senior supervisors and operators would also have had no testing experience.

A further problem arose from the need to centralize some of the examining functions in the hands of one or two people. For example, the scheduling of examinations and of oral interview boards had to be centralized, and to maintain uniform standards it appeared desirable also to centralize the determination of passing marks and of residence requirements. Under the personnel limitations already discussed, it seemed that it would not be feasible to staff the chief of the new Operations Division with technical assistants able to perform such jobs.

After extensive study and discussions with Brock, head of Recruitment and Examining, and Everett, who by this time had become the head of Operations, McKay prepared a detailed nine-page memorandum, describing points of agreement and, most particularly, points of disagreement. This document, dated January 28, 1954, formed the basis for a meeting of Everett, Brock, McKay, Bell, and Fisher at which detailed decisions were reached about the assignment of functions. In general, these officials agreed to the allocation of research studies and developmental work to the new staff division, although they had no clear definition of what these kinds of work should consist of in practice. They also agreed that the new Recruitment and Examining Division was to prepare instructional and training material, conduct training in examining, check examinations for compliance with standards, supervise the Testing Pool, supervise investigations of applicants, and the like. Some of the key points of disagreement at the meeting are listed in the table in the next column, together with the decisions Fisher made to resolve them.

These determinations made it clear that, in addition to research and development, the examining unit in the Recruitment and Examining Division would continue to keep its hand in certain operational aspects of testing. It would continue to maintain the library of testing materials, the principal resource in the preparation of examinations; it would continue to coordinate and schedule the oral interviews for tests, a very substantial and time-consuming job. It would handle and

Functions	*Assigned To*
Handling and recommending to Board on appeals from written examinations	Operations
Handling and recommending to Board on appeals from oral interviews	Examining
Determination of need for examinations	Operations
Scheduling of examinations	Operations
Scheduling, selecting outside members, and handling correspondence on oral interview boards	Examining
Determining examination bases: open, promotional, nationwide, and the like	Operations, but Examining will determine waiver of residence
Determining promotional eligibility for examinations	Operations
Setting and approving passing marks on examinations	Operations, subject to Examining review (temporary)

make recommendations on all appeals from the oral interviews, by far the largest category of examination appeals.[15] Finally, it was agreed that for the first year its chief should review and decide upon the passing marks of individual examinations.

Assignments to the Five Operating Units

Determining the assignments of the five sections of the Operations Division was simplified by the experience of the pilot unit. The old issue of departmental versus occupational approaches was now—perhaps inevitably—decided definitely in favor of the latter. Although effort was made to align departmental with occupational groupings in the case of some sections, the occupational scheme was clearly dominant "across the board."

At this stage of the planning several requirements came into focus: (1) the distribution in

[15] The Board received few appeals from written tests, perhaps partly because its response was expected to be negative. Most appeals were handled at the staff level by deletions of items and modifications of scoring. Appeals from the oral rating boards were frequent.

terms of workload and staffing requirements should be equitable; (2) occupational assignments for each group would, where possible, have to be logically related and homogeneous; (3) the assignments should correspond as nearly as possible with the occupational divisions already developed within the functional divisions, in order to take maximum advantage of existing staff familiarity with classes.

The method of allocation employed was similar to that used by Chopson the year before—counting the numbers of different classes and of total positions in each occupational grouping and then attempting to divide them logically and also equally between the five sections. At the time, there were 2,160 classes and 56,228 employees in the state service. The pilot unit, which was to become Operations Section I, had about 300 classes and 10,600 employees in its jurisdiction. It was left largely intact but given some additional classes. McKay had already (October 19) proposed a second unit that would cover about 310 classes and 8,700 employees. A third unit was clearly indicated for the Engineering and Allied group, which already was separately handled by a small group of specialized Engineering Examiners and a Senior Engineering Examiner. A related group, Mechanical and Construction, was added to bring the totals for this section to about 550 classes and 11,800 employees. This was somewhat larger than the other projected sections, and the section had a heavy examining load. On the other hand, the majority of jobs were in the mechanical and trades fields, generally somewhat easier for classification purposes.

McKay had earlier suggested, as an alternate plan for a second generalist unit, the group of Fiscal, Management, and Staff Services. Added to these to form Section IV were the Legal group and parts of the Social Security group not assigned to the pilot unit. The totals of about 480 classes and 7,600 persons were somewhat smaller than some of the other sections, but these groups were considered most difficult for examining, classification, and pay. Personnel in many of these classes were employed by all departments and agencies, and here no specialization in departmental contacts was possible.

This left two groups (for the fifth section in Operations), the large Clerical and Allied, and the Education and Library categories. These comprised about 320 classes and 15,600 employees—most of whom were clerical. Like the fourth section, this unit would have to deal with every department and agency, and clerical positions were considered among the most difficult to classify. Also, some staff members, perhaps most of them, considered the clerical category an unstimulating, dull field in which to work.

Though there were some subsequent adjustments, these occupational assignments went into effect the following year. The basic scheme was as follows:

SECTION	
I	Custodian and Domestic; Medical and Allied; part of Social Security and Rehabilitation
II	Agriculture and Conservation; Regulatory and Public Safety
III	Engineering and Allied; Mechanical and Construction
IV	Fiscal, Management and Staff Services; Legal; part of Social Security and Rehabilitation
V	Clerical and Allied; Educational and Library

Allocating Positions

Assignment of positions to the divisions and, within them, to the sections proved more difficult. Early in the planning stages McKay attempted to make an analysis of the worker man-years and fractions thereof currently being utilized on each activity in the three divisions, and of the time required for handling the operational work for each occupational group in the state service. There were many difficulties. Complete time records were not available for all operations, and some of the figures had to be estimates or even guesses. In many cases, individuals worked on a variety of activities. Further, assignments and workloads varied from month to month during the year; in some cases, as in the periodic pay surveys, the fluctuations were extreme. And the little jobs, such as correspondence and record-keeping, which one large examining unit had been able to absorb, now loomed as a heavy burden. Another of McKay's problems was that his man-year estimates had a disturbing tendency to add up to a larger sum than the number of positions authorized. For example, his earliest analysis of the staff needs of the various occupational classes (in October 1953) showed a total requirement for the operating sections of thirty-three professional positions below the Senior level, not counting the five already assigned to the pilot unit. This would have left only twelve for assignment to the other two divisions. A later projection markedly reduced this first estimate. He proposed a total of thirty-two journeymen in the Operations Division, including six in Section I (an addition of one), five in Section II, seven in Section III, eight in Section IV, and six in Section V. This left eleven in Standards and Surveys and seven in Examining. This was approximately the breakdown finally adopted.

Staffing needs of the two non-operating divisions were not determined until much later. In June 1954 McKay worked up a detailed analysis of the functions remaining in these divisions. Discussions were held, particularly about examining, and following these discussions tentative agreements were reached. McKay's new analysis showed a total of thirty-three journeymen positions in Operations, the thirty-two indicated above and one person for the scheduling and control of written examinations. The continuing responsibilities of Standards and Surveys were expected to require ten positions, and those in Recruitment and Examining five positions, as shown in the following table.

	Working level staff requirements
Standards and Surveys	
Classification surveys	4
Personnel transactions matters	2
Wage surveys (general and special)	1.5
Personnel management research	1
Policy, standards, and developmental	.5
Prevailing rates, pay transactions, and Governor's report	.5
Special projects (overtime, fringe benefits, and the like)	.5
	10.0
Recruitment and Examining	
Investigations	.6
Oral board arrangements, deferred examinations, physical and performance tests	1.7
Oral board appeals and correspondence	.6
Test Pool supervision	.4
Application review activity	.1
Test scoring activity	.1
Test research	.2
Special projects and reports (great variety)	1.3
	5.0

This left unassigned two positions (of the grand total of fifty). Fisher, at a meeting on June 24, 1954, decided to assign one each to Standards and Surveys and to Examining for the new research work. In addition, he decided that the Operations Division should assign one analyst on a rotating basis to the examining group to work on the preparation of test materials. It already had been decided that the Operations Division would detail staff members to the Standards and Surveys Division to participate in the spring and fall wage surveys. One year later these arrangements were still unchanged.

Assigning People

The first task in assigning personnel was choosing the new division chiefs. After talking privately with each of the three Principals directly involved, Fisher decided to appoint Everett, then Chief of Pay, to head the new Operations Division. Stephens, Chief of Classification, was chosen to head the Standards and Surveys Division. Brock, who had recently assumed leadership of Recruitment and Examining, would remain in that title. Fisher's decision was announced only a few weeks before the new divisions were to start work.

The filling of the Senior positions was determined in part by the prior responsibilities and the wishes of the officials concerned. Chopson, a Senior in Examining, desired an assignment in the Operations Division. In January 1954 he traded jobs with Lawson, who had been head of the pilot unit; Lawson returned to Examining temporarily and was subsequently transferred back to Operations as Chief of its Section V when that unit was activated in October. Popper, the Senior Engineering Examiner, was the obvious choice for Section III. This left one Senior in Recruitment and Examining.

It was determined at a fairly early date that Clarence Burger, a Senior in Classification with long experience, should head Operations Section II, and McKay himself was expected to take over Section IV on completion of his Personnel Management Analyst assignment. These plans were changed in September 1954, when Stephens became Assistant Secretary to the Personnel Board, and McKay was named acting chief of Standards and Surveys. It was then decided that E. V. Williams, the other Senior from Classification, should head Section IV. As his Senior Assistant in Standards and Surveys, McKay brought in C. Heldebrant, who previously had worked in the Pay Division. After Lawson left the Personnel Board in March 1955, Section V was headed by Frank Taffet, a former pay analyst.

Many staff assignments to Operations sections were also determined on the basis of previous experience. The pilot unit became Operations Section I without staff changes. The Engineering Examiners were obviously slated for Section III. There was no systematic effort to ascertain the wishes of staff members, but all had an opportunity to express their desires, and in some cases adjustments were made. One examiner, long in clerical examining, was transferred to another operating section, partly to strengthen its examining staff and partly to give him a change and broadening of scene. The Legal Examiner, who had long had responsibility for all legal tests, asked to remain in Recruitment and Examining so that she would have no responsibilities for classification and pay matters. Her request was granted, and the preparation of legal examinations remained in Examining, though all other activities in the legal field were assumed by Operations Section IV.

Most operating personnel wanted to go to the Operations Division. In part, they sought broader experience, but even more enticing was the belief that in the new division lay the most promising road to increased responsibility and to promotion. Thus a major problem was how to keep people in the two remaining staff divisions. Discussions of a rotation program began anew, and it was agreed that such a program should be undertaken after the new organization had time to "jell."

Phasing the Change-Over

Fisher and Bell had decided at the start that the transition would be made over a period of months, thus avoiding any abruptness that might cause confusion in the office or inconvenience to the using departments. Preparatory training could then be scheduled, and the experience of the staff could be enlarged gradually. Furthermore, problems that developed during the process could be handled one at a time before they became office-wide stumbling blocks. The transition period thus served as a training period and as a "shake-down cruise."

On November 27, 1953, Fisher announced the schedule in the first two stages of change-over:

Stage 1 (Effective January 1, 1954)
1. Creation of the Operations Division, to include:
   a. Operations Section I, the former pilot unit;
   b. Full responsibility for pay and classification operations throughout the state service;
   c. Two Classification and Pay Sections, one to handle these functions for the occupations later to be assigned Operations Sections II and III, the other, those later to be IV and V; each of these sections to be headed by a Senior (Burger and Heldebrant) and to be staffed by analysts from the Classification and Pay Divisions; each staff member would handle classification and pay matters on a generalist basis for an assigned group of occupations roughly similar to his subsequent assignment.
2. Creation of the Standards and Surveys Division with the same responsibilities and staff as it would have in the future.
3. Elimination of both the Classification and Pay Divisions.
4. No change in the Recruitment and Examining Division.

Stage 2 (Effective April 1, 1954)
1. Establishment of Operations Section II in the Operations Division under Burger by transfers from Examining and from Classification and Pay.
2. The remainder of the Classification and Pay Sections would continue under supervision of Heldebrant.

The schedule for the last two stages was not announced until the spring of 1954:

Stage 3 (Effective July 1, 1954)
1. Establishment of Operations Section III by further transfers from Recruitment and Examining and from the Classification and Pay Section.

Stage 4 (Effective October 1, 1954)
1. Establishment of Operations Sections IV and V, similarly by transfers.
2. Elimination of the remaining Classification and Pay Section.
3. Heldebrant to return from his Operations Division assignment to the Standards and Surveys Division, and Williams to move from that Division to head Operations Section IV.

The schedule enabled the analysts from the Classification and Pay Divisions to benefit from a partial generalist experience for a period ranging from three to nine months before they assumed any examining responsibility. A reshuffling of desk assignments was made to enable staff members to develop familiarity with future associates as well as with the occupational groupings for which they would soon become responsible. The examiners and the analysts who were to work together in Operations sections were assigned to adjacent desks for several months before the new sections started to operate.

On December 17, 1953, Fisher sent a letter to all state agencies announcing the changes through Stage 2. This letter described the basic features of the reorganization plan and expressed the hope that better service would be the result.

After the reorganization was formally complete, on October 29, 1954, Fisher sent a second memorandum to all state agencies describing in detail the assignments of each section. The memorandum identified the proper staff members for the agencies to consult about the different kinds of personnel problems.

Formal Training

The Board could not allow its current work to be interrupted by the change-over. The pay analysts could not drop their current assignments for a month to learn how to write an examination any more than the examiners could stop examining to learn how to write specifications. Formal training sessions had to be sandwiched into the regular working day. Many of the sessions were held between 12:30 and 1:30, and the employees were asked to bring box lunches. Under these conditions training could not be very intensive. It was expected that training would continue on the job and that there would be additional formal instruction on technique and method after the Operations sections were activated.

It was necessary that the staff of each new section receive its formal training before, but not too long before, its unit was activated. This meant that training had to be carried out in four stages, each just prior to a corresponding stage in the reorganization. The first training period, held in December 1953, consisted of training in classification and pay for all analysts in the Classification and Pay Divisions as well as for members of the examining staff who would be assigned to Operations Section II. The principal topics and the instructors are shown in the next column.

Subject	*Leader*
General Introduction	Bell
Collection of Data (Pay)	Heldebrant
Analysis of Data (Pay)	Williams
Review of Typical Pay Cases (two sessions)	Heldebrant
Specification Writing*	Williams
Classification Survey of a Position*	Price
Decisions Involving Status Determinations*	Stephens
Personnel Transactions*	Thomas
Process of Establishing a New Class*	Williams
Classification Tools*	Burger
State Employees, State Agencies, and the State*	Fisher

* Relate to Classification

These one-hour sessions were conducted on about half the working days in December. During the same period the staffs of Classification and Pay also discussed problems of the new organization at weekly joint staff meetings. By early December the Personnel Management Analyst had developed a three-page bibliography of readings in classification, pay, and examining. Copies were distributed to the staff members involved, with instructions as to which items were required reading and which were "additional desirable." Each staff member was instructed to check off the items after reading them and to return the list to his supervisor when he finished.

The second training stage dealt with examining. It began late in February and ended in April. It was attended by all the classification and pay personnel who were to transfer to Operations Sections II and III.

Subject	*Leader*
Description of Examining Functions	Brock
Principles of Testing and Examination Planning	Chopson
Items—Use and Construction	Lawson
Scheduling and Recruiting Bulletin Preparation	Carney Spelbring
Application Review	Swabey
Test Pool; Consultants and Source Material	Smith
Test Assembling	Popper Taylor
Passing Marks	Brock
Performance and Physical Tests	Walton

The third training stage, in May, was substantially a repetition of the classification and pay syllabus for all the examiners to be assigned to Operations Sections III, IV and V. It was followed during the summer by the fourth and final stage—a repetition of the examining syllabus for the classification and pay personnel who were to be assigned to Operations IV and V.

In the judgment of staff leaders, the exchange of information and ideas within the various sections before and after they were activated proved as helpful as formal training. Also beneficial was the ability of the staff to collaborate on problems as they arose. Each section was organized on a team basis following the technique explored by the pilot unit. Thus each examiner and analyst, though individually responsible for a category of occupations, had a partner in his section from one of the other former functional divisions, and he could call on this partner for consultation and advice.

SHAKEDOWN

November 1954-July 1955

It was not easy for the new Operations sections to work up to full effectiveness. No longer present was the twin spur of challenge and of pioneering zeal that had fired the pilot unit in its early months. Some sections—notably IV and V— found that maintaining contact with "client" agencies was much harder than it had been before reorganization; these sections had to work with many different agencies in dealing with the personnel matters of the occupations that had been assigned to them.

Each section seemed to develop in a unique manner. Some inherited special projects and special problems. Each had a different supervisor with his own particular background, point of view, and concern for the new system. The same was true of the respective staffs.

Even Section I, the old pilot unit, did not start off at full steam. Chopson, who became supervisor of Section I, said later that it took the section eighteen months (through the summer of 1954) to achieve full effectiveness. As of July 1955, it was too early to appraise how generalism had worked out in the other sections. None had been operating more than fifteen months; two had had only nine months' experience. It was clear that in some sections the full generalist ideal would not soon become a reality. This was partly because both supervisors and staff were inclined to direct more attention to the specialist fields in which they had greater experience and confidence—and, frequently, greater interest. For example, Everett, Chief of Operations, devoted his primary efforts to pay matters for which he previously had had responsibility. Similarly, some of the Senior examiners and classifiers heading generalist sections devoted their principal attention to their former specialties and delegated to others much of the supervisory responsibility for other functions.

The perpetuation of individual functional specialisms among the staff was greatly encouraged by the pressures of work. Supervisors were reluctant to assign important rush jobs to "green hands," when time did not permit either training or close supervision. It was far easier, sometimes imperative, to use the best-trained people available. An example of this was a "big push," in May and June 1955, to develop a new pay plan for the entire state service. To supervise and coordinate this program, Everett designated a committee consisting of one representative from each Operations section. Taffett, the Chief of Section V and the only pay man among the section chiefs, was named to head the committee, and its other members were former pay men, one from each section.

Perhaps inevitably, some examiners had little inclination and small professional respect for pay and classification work. The disdain was reciprocated by a few of the classification and pay analysts. In one or two of the sections such preferences were supported and even encouraged by the supervisors, who assigned examining work to former examiners and classification work to former classifiers.

Brock, the Chief of Recruitment and Examining, supervised an analysis of the new test items developed in the Operations sections and submitted to the Testing Pool during the months from October 1954 to January 1955. Former examiners made up slightly less than half the working-level staff of the five Operations sections at that time. This group produced nearly four-fifths of the new test items—1,985 out of 2,682 multiple-choice questions and 410 out of 436 true-false questions. Only five members of the Operations Division wrote no new items and all five were of non-examining background.

By July 1955 progress toward generalism appeared to be accelerating. A former analyst, assigned to that Operations section in which generalism was thought to have made the slowest headway, was in 1955 preparing two of the most important examinations. Virtually the entire staff worked on the 1955 pay adjustments, even though leadership in that work had centered in former pay analysts. And by July 1955 most men in the Operations sections had had some experience in all three functional fields.

Reactions: Staff Development and Morale

With respect to one of its initial objectives, that of broadening the scope of the professional staff, the reorganization had already borne fruit by 1955.[16] In general the staff seemed glad for the opportunity to gain experience in other personnel fields; and it appreciated management's concern for employee development, a concern that the change-over had demonstrated. Opportunities for advancement within and without the state service appeared to have enlarged for some of the staff. (A case in point was the appointment of Lawson as personnel officer of one of the state departments; another was the 1955 examination for personnel director of Sacramento County, in which Personnel Board employees gained two of the first three places on the eligible list.) In addition, the reorganization caused greater delegation of responsibility and decision-making authority to Seniors and their operating personnel. In many cases, probably in most, this increased job satisfaction. The old complaint of the examiners—that they had no direct contact with the Personnel Board—was largely corrected. Virtually all professionals in the Operations Division were making periodic appearances before the Board by mid-1955.

The change-over to functional generalism was not without cost. Generalism focused upon individual staff members a great variety of pressures, deadlines, and interruptions. As illustrated in the accompanying cartoon (originally published as the cover sheet of the "Espe Bee," the Board's house organ), each analyst was continually forced to juggle a variety of different problems. Some, but certainly not all, complained that the accumulation of different demands interrupted the sustained con-

FIGURE 3: ESPE BEE

The Generalist

VOLUME VII FEBRUARY, 1954 No. 1

centration necessary to do a good job on any one assignment. They missed the satisfaction of doing a single job well. This reaction appeared to be strongest among former examiners who had been accustomed to a scholarly pace and to shelter from interruptions while constructing a test.

As Lawson had noted with the pilot unit, the problem of multiple pressures and interruptions was accentuated by the fact that it was so difficult to schedule or balance the workload. It was impossible to prevent peak periods when demands exceeded the eight-hour day capacity of the individual. These peaks were alleviated somewhat by flexibility in work assignments within sections and even between them. The team arrangement also helped. There was frequent detailing of individuals from one section to another to handle particular jobs.

One of the more annoying sources of interruption in 1955 was the recurring requirement that the analysts serve on, and chair, oral interviewing boards. These boards might take a man from his desk for periods lasting from one day to several

[16] Most of the material that follows is based upon meetings and interviews by the author. These included a meeting with the Personnel Board itself and individual discussions with some of its members; meetings with groups of the executives of the staff as well as individual interviews with all of them; individual interviews with the majority of supervisors in the professional divisions; and individual interviews with about one-quarter of the professional staff in the Operations Division. No claim is made as to the "scientific" validity of these observations. There has been no attitude survey since 1952. Also, the author undertook no appraisal of the reactions of the using departments.

weeks; meanwhile his normal work was either held up or handled by his team partner or by someone else in his or another section. For example, a member of Section III, normally assigned to mechanical and trade classes, had to serve on an oral board for several weeks. In his absence, an examination had to be prepared for a certain class of printers. A former classifier in Section IV, assigned to work on administrative and staff-type occupations, had to prepare the examination, even though he had had no experience with this type of position.

A further cost of reorganization was that functional generalism necessarily resulted in a greater degree of occupational specialism. Both the former examiners and the former pay analysts found that the occupational groups over which they had cognizance were considerably narrower than they had been before. The former classifiers, previously organized on a departmental basis, lost their department-wide orientation and scope. One complained that while he had once known all that was going on in a number of different state departments, he now lacked a complete picture of any department. He felt that his sources of organizational information had dried up and that with them had gone much of the interest and challenge of his job.

The reorganization did not, and could not, eliminate specialism in individual assignments. It had, it seemed by 1955, substituted one kind of specialism for another.

To some of the staff, generalism seemed to bring with it a loss of status. The examiners had complained previously of their relatively low status within the organization. But status had more than one connotation. In the eyes of some of the former examiners, the examining function had higher *professional* status than any other personnel work. A few would have maintained that examining was the only truly professional activity of the Board. Classification and pay they tended to regard as involving merely common sense plus negotiation and compromise. On the other hand, some former classifiers took the opposite line: that the first need in examining was knowledge of the requirements of the job for which the test was being designed; that once these were fully understood, putting together a selective test was easy.

Some staff members were asked in 1955 whether they thought it was harder for a former examiner or for a former classifier to become a generalist. The answers followed a consistent pattern. The former examiners thought the classifier had the harder time because he had to learn much more before he could construct a good examination. And the former classifiers thought the examiners had the tougher road since they had to acquire skills in penetrating job situations, in negotiating, and particularly in saying "no." A few, skeptical of the generalist idea, expressed the view that the two types of jobs called for different personality types: examining called for a creative, studious mind and inclination; classifying and pay work required ability in, and satisfaction from, frequent dealings with people. Still other staff members, favorable to the reorganization, discounted this argument and emphasized the wholeness of the personnel job.

By mid-1955 there were differing views about the extent to which the reorganization was aiding the professional development of personnel. Some employees, particularly from examining, questioned whether former classifiers or new trainees could be developed into truly qualified examiners within generalist units. However, others held stoutly that it was possible to develop *compleat* personnel men "from scratch" in much faster time than might have been expected. One supervisor expressed the view that a three-field generalist could be trained in about one and one-half times the period required to train a specialist in a single field.

Finally, reorganization brought morale problems to those remaining in the two staff-type divisions, Recruitment and Examining, and Standards and Surveys. The increase in the responsibility of the Operations staff resulted in some loss of responsibility for the other two divisions. In 1955 many of the non-Operations personnel looked forward to a transfer to Operations.

Reactions: The Staff-Line Problems

The reorganization resulted in a division between line and staff-type responsibilities that had not existed before. This division created new possibilities, but it also brought new problems of inter-divisional relationships. Virtually all the problems were familiar staff and line difficulties, but they were complicated somewhat because the heads of the staff and line divisions were co-equal and because the head of the line division had virtually no staff assistance of his own. The major staff and line problems are described below:

1. *How should the programs and priorities of the staff units be developed?* The principal clients of the staff units were the line sections in the Operations Division. These sections naturally expected to have some influence on the work of the

staff units. Yet there was a risk that the staff divisions would assume merely a servicing role to the line division, rather than the role of equals as implied by the structural plan. The Standards and Surveys Division at an early date undertook to develop for itself a program and priority system and to obtain from the Operations Division an expression of its views and needs. But the system fell into disuse, partly because Operations could not predict far in advance the special studies that it would need to cope with future operating problems. When it needed a study it often needed it urgently. It would not be practicable to delay a request for an urgently needed study until it could be discussed by the two division chiefs or sent to higher authority for a decision about whether or not Standards and Surveys should be asked to make the study. On the other hand, officials in the staff divisions feared that if they simply responded to the requests of the Operations sections, they would become Operations' subordinates and would forsake the functions of bolstering standards and conducting independent studies. The reorganization had left the chief of the Operations Division with no staff of his own, requiring him to lean heavily on the two apprehensive staff divisions.

2. *What may be done to assure that staff findings are communicated to the line operators and are used by them?* While they are useful, written communications have their limitations. Some time after it issued a new procedural instruction, the Standards and Surveys Division discovered that many in Operations were not following it; some had forgotten that it had ever crossed their desks. Joint meetings were held from time to time, usually with the Chiefs and the Seniors of the divisions concerned. But not all staff matters warranted such high-level meetings in a busy office; and even high-level staff meetings could not always assure adequate communication of staff advice to officials down the line at the operating level.

3. *Where is the line between "staff" and "operations"?* The work of the Transactions section in Standards and Surveys in interpreting laws and rules and applying them to individual cases was indeed very close to operations. So were the departmental classification surveys. How were the changes indicated by these surveys to be put into effect? Were the classification surveyors to act themselves, or were they simply to provide their findings to the line officials in the Operations sections? Thinking on this question in 1955 was that changes in individual allocations should be handled by the surveyors; changes in the classification plans should be transferred to the operators to handle. Questions like this one were being worked out as they arose.

But for written examinations the responsibility was unclear in 1955. Should the examining specialists prepare examining materials? A major project conducted during 1954-1955 was the development of testing materials in the manual and trade fields, and the results were highly approved on all sides. By mid-1955 the examining groups appeared to have insufficient staff for such test development work, and there had been little follow-up on the program. There were also further problems: Who should determine what kinds of test materials to develop? And who should ultimately be responsible for the content of such tests as long as the responsibility for individual tests lies in the Operations Division?

4. *Where lies the responsibility for maintaining and developing quality in work product?* The chief of the Operations Division, in 1955, had neither the time nor the staff to check work quality on any but the most important types of jobs and these did not include examinations, which amounted to nearly half the total workloads of his sections. Pre-audit by another division would have caused severe internal stresses. And the mechanics of post-auditing by another division, and making its findings effective, had not been thoroughly worked out by mid-1955. The staff divisions were reluctant to become inspectors and tended to assume that responsibility for maintaining quality lies within the line organization. In the Personnel Board, Standards and Surveys was careful to avoid letting its classification surveys take the guise of audits on the work of the operators. As of 1956, Examining had not developed a system for the post-audit of tests, nor had it mobilized its potential resources to make statistical analysis of examination question or to make studies of the validity of test results in relation to job performance.

Furthermore, in handling appeals from oral tests and in reviewing passing grades on written tests, Examining was certainly close to an inspection role. But since neither of the staff divisions was in the position to act on findings (other than communicating them to the chief of Operations), they felt that they could not assume responsibility for the quality of the Operations Division's product.

Reactions: Production

By mid-1955 opinions of supervisors and staff varied on how the transition had affected output. Some felt that increased familiarity of staff members with the occupations they handled had greatly increased productivity. Knowledge gained for one purpose could be used for other types of assignments. Thus the total output of the analyst was increased, and the greater understanding he brought to his occupational classes appeared to assure higher quality work. These persons also felt that productivity would continue to grow as job familiarity increased. They also expected that the segregation of the line from staff functions would increase productivity. Finally, a few stressed that people were working harder; the supervisors were busier, and some said the workers were spurred by greater incentive as well as heavier workloads.

On the other hand, some supervisors and workers stated that per capita quantity and quality of output in their sections was lower than before. The principal complaint was of lost time from interruptions and from repeated transfers of attention. Since much of the work had to be turned out, the principal sacrifice was in quality, not quantity. The major deficiency was felt to be the quality of examinations. A number of references were made to "cover-page" examinations—that is, old tests pulled out of the files and used again without change. One or two former examiners alleged they had to rely largely on examining materials built up over previous years, since they lacked time to develop new materials.

The overall evidence about quantity and quality was pretty thin as of mid-1955. Such clues as existed, however, did not suggest that there had been any significant changes as a result of reorganization. Throughout the transition period, the Board met its examining schedule, though apparently with increasing difficulty. The number of tests declined somewhat during 1954-1955. It was hard to say how much of this should be attributed to reorganization.

The Board completed on schedule its various pay projects, including that of June 1955. There was a noteworthy decline in the number of actions taken before the Board itself, much of it due to extraneous factors. The statistical record maintained by the Operations Division did not indicate any significant change in the speed of processing departmental requests for classification and pay actions.

As of June 1955 there had been no systematic appraisals of the effects of reorganization upon quality of output. However, some impressionistic data were available, since many classification and pay projects normally went up through channels to the Board. In spite of a few slips and mistakes, officers in the higher echelons felt that the quality of work had been maintained. Furthermore, a few broad studies were made of pay and classification of entire occupational series; under the old organizational form these probably wouldn't have been made.

Insofar as output of examining could be judged, it did not appear, overall, that there had been marked change. The new materials submitted by the Operations staff to the Testing Pool during the early period of October 1954 to January 1955 totaled only slightly under the average for the same four months during 1950-1954. During the same period, a project for developing trade tests, conducted by the Recruitment and Examining Division, produced a large number of new items, bringing the Board's total considerably higher than the four-year average. Of course, the number of new items furnished little evidence about quality.

Finally, as a result of reorganization, two new positions for performance of developmental work were created and assigned to the two staff divisions. These two divisions subsequently made significant contributions. Standards and Surveys developed manual material and conducted a survey of overtime and fringe benefit practices. Recruitment and Examining developed instructional material on oral interviewing and trade testing materials.

All in all, the results did not appear unfavorable to the new plan of organization, particularly since the period to July 1955 had been one of transition, when some decline in output was expected.

However, the maintenance and improvement of quality, in the examining field especially, appeared to present a challenging problem. No system existed for appraisal of examining work, nor even for informed scrutiny of many examinations. A large proportion of the more important pay and classification projects went up through channels to the Board; review was possible, and necessary, at a number of levels. Most examinations, on the other hand, were prepared by examiners with only general guidance from their Seniors. The Seniors approved the examinations for printing after reviewing them, sometimes in a rapid and superficial manner. No examination went above the Senior level; none was reviewed by a technician from Recruitment and Examining; and more than half of the staff analysts and the Seniors in the Operations Division had had little or no prior examining experience.

Reactions: Service to the Departments

One of the avowed intentions of the reorganization was to speed up and improve services to the users. It was hoped that it would reduce the number of contacts individual agencies would have to maintain within the Board, and that it would minimize internal clearances and opportunities for conflict among the divisions. But the decision for an occupational basis rather than a departmental basis of assignment, however inevitable, meant that every state agency had to deal with at least two different sections in the Operations Division; some of the larger departments must deal with as many as four or five.

There were offsetting advantages. The new system assured that, in any problem affecting a single series of positions or classes, an agency dealt with only one Personnel Board representative—a representative who was equipped to handle all aspects of the question. While the department head or his personnel officer might have a variety of Board contacts while handling his multifarious problems, most departmental executives and supervisors, with more restricted scope, usually found it necessary to deal with only one or two officials in the Board.

Personnel matters that cross occupational lines, and reorganizations affecting a variety of positions, raised special problems of coordination within the Operations Division. An effort at a solution was made by designating each section in Operations as primary liaison contact for specified using departments. This device was not used widely, but multifaceted problems had not been especially difficult for the Board to handle as of July 1955.

APPENDIX I:

EXECUTIVE AND SUPERVISORY OFFICERS OF PERSONNEL BOARD STAFF INVOLVED IN REORGANIZATION

NAME	RANK	POSITION BEFORE	POSITION AFTER	MAJOR OR GRADUATE (G) EDUCATIONAL BACKGROUND	MAJOR FIELD OF PERSONNEL EXPERIENCE	FIRST CAME TO BOARD
Fisher, J. F.	Executive Officer	Executive Officer	Executive Officer	Public Administration (G)	Classification; General	1944
Bell, J. R.	Assistant Executive Officer	Assistant Executive Officer	Assistant Executive Officer	Public Administration (G)	General Personnel Management	1939
Sharp, K. D.	Assistant Secretary, SPB	Assistant Secretary, SPB	Assistant Secretary, SPB	Public Administration (G)	Pay; Classification; General	1937
Brock, A. L.	Principal*	Senior Examiner	Chief, Recruitment and Examining Division	Public Administration (G)	Examining	1936
Everett, R. P.	Principal	Chief, Pay Division	Chief, Operations Division	Economics; Public Administration	Pay; Classification	1942
Stephens, R. W.	Principal*	Chief, Classification Division	Chief, Standards and Surveys Division	Personnel Administration (G)	Classification	1936
Abeel, E. A.	Principal	Chief, Recruitment and Examining Division	Retired	Engineering	Examining	1931
Chopson, E. W.	Senior	Examining Division‡	Supervisor, Operations Section I	Psychology (G)	Examining	1938

APPENDIX I—*Cont.*

NAME	RANK	POSITION BEFORE	POSITION AFTER	MAJOR OR GRADUATE (G) EDUCATIONAL BACKGROUND	MAJOR FIELD OF PERSONNEL EXPERIENCE	FIRST CAME TO BOARD
Burger, C. L.	Senior	Classification Division§	Supervisor, Operations Section II	Public Administration (G)	Classification	1936
Popper, W.	Senior	Engineering Examiner	Supervisor, Operations Section III	Engineering	Examining	1946
Williams, E. V.	Senior	Classification Division§	Supervisor, Operations Section IV	Educational Administration (G)	Classification	1943
Lawson, R. D.	Senior*	Examining Division	Supervisor, Pilot Unit†	Personnel Administration (G)	Examining	1949
McKay, J. K.	Senior*	Pay Division	Personnel Management Analyst‖	Public Administration (G)	Pay; Classification	1944
Heldebrant, C.	Senior	Pay Division§	Standards and Surveys Division	Public Administration (G)	Pay; Classification	1947

* Ranks before and after were the same in all cases except the following: Brock, promoted Senior to Principal, August 1953; Lawson promoted on temporary basis to Senior when he assumed direction of the pilot unit, made permanent Senior, June 1954; McKay, under temporary authorization in rank of Principal since September 1954, permanent rank was still Senior as of July 1955; Stephens, under exempt appointment as Assistant Secretary of SPB since September 1954, permanent rank was Principal as of July 1955.

† Lawson was Chief of the pilot unit from November 1952 to January 1954. He then returned to Examining until he was assigned in October 1954 as Chief, Operations Section V. He left that post in March 1955 to assume the job of Personnel Officer, Corrections Department.

‡ Chopson was Personnel Management Analyst, January 1952 to January 1953. He then returned to Examining until January 1954, when he was assigned as Chief, Operations Section I.

§ In 1954, Burger, Williams, and Heldebrant each served for a period as a chief of one of the combined pay-classification sections in the Operations Division prior to assuming their "after" positions.

‖ McKay became Personnel Management Analyst in May 1953 and remained in that post until September 1954, when he became Acting Chief, Standards and Surveys Division.

EDITORIAL COMMENTS

The staff reorganization of the Personnel Board in Sacramento contained rather little drama and even less political volatility. No one outside of the staff itself was particularly excited about it, and events moved slowly enough within the agency to dampen any potential volcanic eruptions. Yet, if reorganizations are measured in terms of the degrees to which they bring about changed behaviors, this must be judged a major one—perhaps the most profound of those described in this volume. It necessitated changes in the duties, the skills, the work habits, the procedures, the points of view, and the personal as well as official relationships of most of the supervisors and professional workers in three major divisions of the Board—about fifty-five people in all. It was no mere shifting of boxes on a chart.

A number of factors contributed to a somewhat special and different character of this reorganization, and most of these could be expected to add to the difficulty of bringing it off successfully. One was the very absence of pressure or compulsion from outside the agency itself. Indeed, had outside influence been effectively exercised, for example by the California State Employees Association, it would probably have opposed the change. The constitutional autonomy of the Personnel Board, plus its proud and well-established tradition of political neutrality, lent it more than average immunity from outside pressures, whether partisan, interest group, legislative, executive, or bureaucratic (from other state agencies).

Secondly, there was no dramatic event, critical failure, or change in leadership[1] to provide impetus for a reorganization. In the words of James Bell, Assistant Executive Officer of the Board: "It was not prompted by a breakdown or change in administration, but rather was a conscious, studied, experimental effort simply to see if by this type of operation a better job could be done."

Nor was the change-over forced by internal considerations. The Board had its problems before it reorganized, and some of these contributed to the desire to try the new plan. But the problems were not problems of crisis; they in no way dictated so drastic a change as that which was undertaken.

A final feature worthy of mention was the nature of the staff groups concerned, particularly their professionalization and their tenure. Personnel is one of those professional fields that has fissured into sub-professions, and the strength and individuality of each challenges the unifying force of its mother field. Each is distinctive with respect to the nature of its work, the kinds of skills it demands, the kinds of outside contacts and relationships it utilizes, and its perspective on organizational purpose. The reorganization constituted a merger of three of these sub-professions (examining, classifying, and pay) into one and thus the clouding of the distinctive identity of each. The feelings of separateness of the sub-professional groups were cemented by the relatively long tenure in the agency and in their fields of activity of most of the leaders on the staff. The majority of the top personnel had been there since the 1930's, and few of those in either examining or in classification had worked in any other personnel field.

In the light of these considerations, the bringing about of the reorganization as effectively and as noiselessly as it was done must be viewed as a considerable achievement. They probably also explain the methods and tactics that were employed —a slow, drawn-out, "low-temperature" operation. In fact, the task of readying the California staff for this reorganization, though probably not consciously conceived as such, probably began many years before 1952 with the concern about staff development and rotation. To the outsider, the movement toward change, after the idea was first broached in the spring of 1952, may appear hesitant, deliberate, and cautiously experimental. The avoidance of hasty commitment on the part of management and the lengthy discussions were probably essential. It is interesting that one of the criticisms voiced by two staff members was that the reorganization was too fast—that insufficient time was allowed for planning and adjustment. The success of the plan depended upon the understanding of the professional staff, upon the support of most of them, and upon the cooperation of all of them. It could not be dictated from above. It took time to elicit such support and to bring about change, when the scope and habits of work of all the individuals were affected.

All in all, this reorganization was achieved with a relatively high degree of participation, probably higher than in any other case in this collection. Its participative character was evidenced in many different ways: the initial sparking by suggestions from operating staff; the lengthy discussion, argument, and informal votes in staff meetings; the pilot unit and the way in which it trained itself and made decisions by itself; the attitude survey and the divisional discussions of the problems it revealed. It is noteworthy that no organized opposition ever developed within the staff. Some staff members were conscientiously opposed to reorganization, and a few felt personal threats and hurts. A few scars seem to be the inevitable consequences of major organizational change. The degree to which these pains were minimized was probably due to the skill and to the gradualness with which the reorganization was brought about. Further, the staff members—even those who opposed the principle of the reorganization—entered wholeheartedly into the program once it was decided.

The decisions of management not only to permit but also to encourage participation were made possible in part by the absence of pressure from the outside, including the Personnel Board itself. Fisher's relative freedom from outside brakes and potential vetoes enabled him to move slowly, to encourage new ideas and free discussions with confidence in his own position *vis-à-vis* the "outside." On the other hand, the absence of outside pressure probably also made participation more necessary.

With no clear-cut external pressure for change, the impetus had to be nurtured and built from within. One may ask: Was this truly manage-

[1] Although the retirement of Abeel, Chief of the old Recruiting and Examining Division, undoubtedly contributed to the decision to move ahead with the plan.

ment's decision? Or was it rather forced upon management by the staff itself? One staff member described the reorganization as a "grass-roots" movement in which the initiative and drive for change came up from below. So blunt an interpretation, however, does not seem to square with the events. There was much interest in, and support of, the generalist idea from the operating staff; and, through the variety of meetings and discussions and through the experience of the pilot unit, the staff contributed much to the shape and the timing of the change. But the initiative, the leadership, and the quiet persistence of top management were present almost from the beginning. The decisions themselves were clearly those of top management. The momentum for change came largely from the Executive Office and from the operating professional staff. The intermediate supervisory staff, with few exceptions, were skeptical or "had reservations."

Unlike a case study, which, perhaps fortunately, must come to a close, administration is an ongoing process. The ramifications of the episode described in the foregoing pages still continue and may go on for many, many years. In the decade that has followed the preparation of this case study, there have been a number of organizational changes, some of which have modified in some degree the operations of the generalist system. But its main features continue today, as do the majority of the top-level personnel who played prominent parts in this story.

ERNEST G. MILLER

Architects, Politics, and Bureaucracy

Reorganization of the California Division of Architecture

ERNEST G. MILLER

The author of *Architects, Politics, and Bureaucracy: Reorganization of the California Division of Architecture* received a Ph.D. degree from Princeton University. He is Lecturer and Director of Continuing Education, Graduate School of Public Affairs, University of Washington.

CHRONOLOGY OF KEY EVENTS

November 1957	Department of Finance releases report on its own organization, including a recommendation that the Division of Architecture be transferred to the Department of Finance
January 1, 1958	M. Gilliss appointed Director of Public Works
February 1, 1958	John Stanford, Administrative Analyst in the Department of Public Works, begins general survey of the Division of Architecture and suggests to Anson Boyd, State Architect, that an employee opinion questionnaire might be of interest to management
April 1958	Stanford conducts an employee opinion survey in Division of Architecture
April 7, 1958	Assembly unanimously passes Resolution Number 46, calling for a study of Architecture by an outside consultant
April 16, 1958	Boyd leaves on overseas trip
June 9, 1958	Gilliss, Stanford, Lindsay, and Mugford, after review of project proposals, agree that the firm of Ernst and Ernst should make the study of the Division of Architecture
June 16, 1958	Ernst and Ernst team begins study of Architecture
June 25, 1958	Boyd returns from overseas trip
July 28-30, 1958	Ernst and Ernst team discusses several preliminary conclusions with Gilliss and Stanford and with Department of Finance officials
August 15, 1958	Ernst and Ernst team meets with top-level officials of Architecture to present tentative reorganization proposals
October 1, 1958	Ernst and Ernst team present final report
December 31, 1958	Gilliss resigns as Director of Public Works to accept another position. Bradford appointed Director, and Wright, Deputy Director
January-March 1959	Wright discusses disposition of Ernst and Ernst report with Boyd on several occasions
March 26, 1959	Boyd announces in a memorandum to the Division the engagement of Ernst and Ernst to undertake the installation of a project management system
August 31, 1959	Boyd announces the new top-level reorganization of the Division to become effective September 1
December 1, 1959	Project Management Service formally established
April 27, 1960	State colleges authorized to contract with private architects for their architecture work (this amounted to half of the Division's work)
November 1961	Assembly Interim Committee on Organization holds hearings very critical of Division's actions
December 12, 1961	Boyd announces his retirement, to take effect March 31, 1962
April 1962	Legislature passes and Governor signs a bill removing the position of State Architect from civil service

PRINCIPAL CHARACTERS

Anson Boyd, State Architect, 1940-1962

Kenneth Caldwell, Member of Ernst and Ernst team

J. A. Gillem, Principal Architect, Area III (Los Angeles Office), 1948–; retained position after reorganization

C. M. Gilliss, Director of Public Works, January 1958-December 1958

H. W. Hampton, Assistant State Architect—Administrative, 1955-February 1959; Acting Assistant State Architect—Planning and Design, June 1958-February 1959; Assistant State Architect—Planning and Design, February-September 1959; Deputy Chief for Architecture and Engineering, September 1959–

C. M. Herd, Chief Construction Engineer, 1954–

H. S. Hunter, Deputy Chief, 1950-September 1959, plus responsibilities of Assistant State Architect—Administrative, February-September 1959; Deputy Chief for Administration, September 1959–

Tom Meret, Assistant State Architect—Planning and Design, Southern Area, September 1959–

P. T. Poage, Assistant State Architect—Planning and Design, January 1926—June 1958

John Stanford, Administrative Analyst, Public Works Department

FOREWORD

On June 16, 1958, three staff members of the management consultant firm of Ernst and Ernst began a reorganization study of the California Division of Architecture. The study took three months to complete, cost $16,750, and recommended numerous changes. This case is an attempt to recapture the nature and impact of that study: in its temporal context—the events that led up to it and flowed from it; in its political context—the private interests, the Legislature, and the executive branch and their influence on the course of events; and in its internal context—the people and their interrelationships within the Division itself.

THE SETTING

The California Division of Architecture is the architect for the state government of California. The Division is designated by statute as the agency that shall perform architectural services for nearly all of the many state agencies.[1]

In the broadest sense the job of the Division consists of: (1) preparing master plans for the building programs of the various state agencies after conference with each "client" agency; (2) developing preliminary building plans each year for those specific projects of each agency that are approved by the Department of Finance for inclusion in the state budget for that year; (3) completing designs and detailed plans for the projects after they are approved by the Public Works Board;[2] (4) taking bids for construction, letting contracts, and supervising the construction activity. After construction has been completed the Division recommends the acceptance of the project to the Director of Public Works, who then turns the completed project over to the client agency. (Appendix I portrays the typical "life" cycle for a one-million-dollar project.)

The range of the work of the Division reflects the diverse character of the state government, Division talents being employed for such varied facilities as educational institutions and special schools, correctional institutions, office buildings, hospitals, armories, exhibit buildings, quarantine inspection stations, fish hatcheries, laundries, chapels, and so on. The projects designed by the Division vary in size from small residences costing a few thousand dollars to vast institutional facilities housing thousands of persons and costing millions of dollars.

In addition to its primary task as architectural agent for the state, the Division is charged with the duty of approving the plans and supervising the construction of all public elementary, secondary, and junior college school buildings. This particular responsibility was lodged with the Division of Architecture by the passage of the Field Act, a legislative response to the Long Beach earthquake, which in 1933 caused severe damage to school buildings because of inadequate engineering and construction.

Ever since 1921, when the state architectural function began to approximate its present form, it had been a part of the Department of Public Works.[3] The other divisions in Public Works were Contracts and Rights-of-Way (performing the legal work of the Department), San Francisco Bay Toll Crossings, and Highways. The latter was by far the largest division, both in numbers of personnel and size of budget. The Director of Public Works is appointed by the Governor and is directly responsible to him. Normally an engineer,

---

[1] Exempted from the requirement of using the Division of Architecture are the University of California, the San Francisco Port Authority, the State Highway Department with respect to highway construction, and the Department of Water Resources with respect to projects of that department. The California State Colleges became exempt in 1960.

[2] The Public Works Board consists of the Director of the Department of Finance, the Director of the Department of Public Works, the Real Estate Commissioner, and four non-voting legislators.

[3] The entire Division of Architecture was transferred in 1963 from the Department of Public Works to the newly established Department of General Services. This was subsequent to the events described in this study but, as later paragraphs will show, not unrelated to them.

this official and his immediate staff have customarily directed most of their attention to the enormous and politically volatile problems of the highway program. This has given a degree of operating autonomy to the other divisions. At the time of this case, the Director of Public Works appointed the chief officer in the Division of Architecture, the State Architect, who, like all other personnel in the Division, was under the state civil service system.

The more than 500 professional and technical personnel in the Division include a variety of architects, engineers, building designers, landscape designers, and draftsmen. Above the architects engaged in design are project architects who have responsibility for overseeing the design and drafting work for entire projects, and above them are a few supervising architects. There are also about 200 engineers whose specialties cover the areas of structural, mechanical, civil, hydraulic, electrical, and sanitary engineering. These positions range from junior engineer to supervisor, and their duties include analyzing the building needs suggested by the character of the project site and planning the location and arrangement of the various components (wiring, plumbing, etc.) that go into a project. There are some forty specification writers who prepare detailed descriptions of the kinds of materials and equipment that are to be used in the projects. There are nearly fifty estimators whose jobs consist of estimating the costs of using various methods and materials of construction.

The whole process of architectural and engineering designing must be programmed and coordinated so that all design activities have been accomplished when the date arrives for the completion of the entire project plan. From then on contracts must be prepared and awarded, and construction activities supervised and inspected. The nearly 200 construction supervisors and inspectors work in the field at the construction sites. In addition to these activities there are the usual auxiliary administrative tasks of performing budgetary, accounting, personnel, stenographic, and clerical services for the Division.

The Division of Architecture's headquarters are in Sacramento, the state capital. There is also a principal office in Los Angeles which performs most of the same architectural design and construction services for state agencies located in the southern part of the state as those performed in the Sacramento office for the northern part. Thus there is a headquarters-field arrangement. However, the Los Angeles office is the only field office for architectural planning and design, and the northern planning and design staff is located in the same building that houses the headquarters staff.

While there are only two areas for planning and design (Northern Area with principal office in Sacramento, and Southern Area with principal office in Los Angeles), there are three areas for supervision of construction activities. Construction Area I, with principal office in Oakland, covers a coastal belt from the Oregon border to Santa Barbara; Construction Area II, with principal office in Sacramento, covers nearly all of the remaining northern part of the state with the exception of a strip east of the Sierra Nevada Mountain range running along the Nevada border; Construction Area III, with principal office in Los Angeles, covers the southern area of the state and the strip that runs north along the Nevada border. The third and somewhat unrelated general responsibility of the Division for approving and inspecting plans and construction of local school buildings is also parceled out among three geographical areas that generally correspond to the construction areas.

History of the Division to 1958

The project plans executed by the Division amount annually to more than $100,000,000 and its employees number 1,100—making the Division one of the largest architectural organizations in the United States.

Some appreciation of the growth of the Division can be obtained from Figure 1. In general, the biennial periods listed in Figure 1 represent low or high points in the numbers of technical personnel employed. The most drastic reductions in organization size came in wartime, first in 1918-1920 and then in 1943-1944, when the personnel declined to a level about equal to that of 1916-1918. A boom followed each war in response to the accumulated backlog of state building needs, raising the number of projects, the total dollar amounts of the projects, and the number of personnel in the Division. In the decade after World War II, the technical staff of the Division increased more than tenfold, from 43 to 449.

In spite of the vast shifts in size and work of the Division, there was remarkable continuity in its directive leadership. George B. McDougall, who was appointed State Architect in 1913, served in that capacity until 1938. Following his retirement,

FIGURE 1: CALIFORNIA STATE DIVISION OF ARCHITECTURE: GROWTH SINCE 1907

*Fiscal Period (biennial)**	*Average Number of Technical Personnel Employed†*	*Number of Projects*	*Amount of Work Done‡*
1907–1909	3	103	$ 2,909,000
1916–1918	42	180	3,122,000
1918–1920	28	129	3,750,000
1934–1936	86	163	6,916,000
1938–1940	160	225	11,220,000
1942–1944	43	190	1,542,000
1947–1949	155	769	58,693,000
1953–1955	449	1345	86,754,000
1958–1960	522	953	183,780,000

* The bienniums used here were selected because they are periods of greatest change in numbers of personnel.
† *Technical* refers to personnel engaged in architectural, engineering, and construction supervision and inspection tasks.
‡ This refers to the aggregate charges to the client agencies for the planning, designing, engineering, and supervisory work done by the Division for the biennial period indicated. The figures are rounded to the nearest thousand.

his Assistant, W. K. Daniels, served as Acting State Architect until June 1940. At that time Anson Boyd was appointed, and he served continuously as State Architect until his retirement in 1962. Prior to his appointment Boyd had operated a private office in Los Angeles, where he had specialized in the design of commercial and office buildings. He also had been official architect for the Los Angeles School Board. A graduate of the University of Pennsylvania School of Architecture and the Pennsylvania School of Industrial Design, Boyd spent his first professional years working for firms in Philadelphia and New York.

In 1940 Boyd assumed direction of an organization that was about to undergo a drastic reduction in staff and workload. But this contraction would soon be followed by a spectacular growth to dimensions well beyond any in the Division's previous history. The organizational strains imposed by such explosive growth gave rise to a number of efforts to make changes, some apparently effective, some not.

Boyd inherited a top organizational structure of two Assistant State Architects directly under and responsible to him. Almost all of the activities of the Division were under one or the other of these two positions. One was Assistant State Architect—Administrative,[4] with responsibility for budgeting, cost estimating, and clerical activities in the Division. The other was Assistant State Architect—Design and Planning. The responsibilities under this Assistant included architectural design, architectural drafting, specifications, and mechanical and electrical engineering. In addition, the activities related to construction supervision, structural engineering, and schoolhouse inspection were lodged in three separate sections in the Division. The chiefs of the first two of these sections reported to the Assistant State Architect—Design and Planning, and the chief of the schoolhouse section reported directly to the State Architect.

When Boyd became State Architect, Daniels returned to his position as Assistant State Architect—Administrative, a position that he had held since 1937, concomitant with his role as Acting State Architect. The occupant of the other Assistant State Architect position was P. T. Poage. Poage had been in this post since 1926, and he, as well as Daniels, had been promoted from within the ranks of the Division. Poage was a man who was well liked by the personnel of the Division, and over the years there had developed within the organization a notable degree of personal loyalty to him. At the section-head level, just below the Assistant State Architect positions, there were several individuals who had worked in the Division through rich and lean and who had become intimately identified with it. Turnover was low in the design, specifications, estimating, and drafting sections.

The Division had all along been developing a character that reflected the personalities of the men

[4] This title was "Assistant State Architect—Budgets and Fiscal" between July 1, 1956 and February 24, 1959.

who came and stayed within it. When Boyd arrived upon the scene as the new State Architect in 1940, he took charge of an agency that had functioned with little concern for how clear and rational the lines of authority were or for how neat the organization would look on an organization chart. The Division thus had its own organizational way of life, one that was hardly encouraging to any new chief who might have had ambitious ideas for rearranging things in a more orderly fashion. But Boyd's philosophy was to proceed slowly and let the organization develop much the same way that a natural organism does—by a process of gradual growth. Boyd, it seems, viewed the Division as he viewed all organizations, as a quasi-organic entity. As such, the best approach that an executive could take was to meddle with it as little as possible.

Early Organizational Changes

As the Division began its period of rapid growth after 1946, it was inevitable that organizational and operating changes would have to be made. The increasing workload, the enlargement of sections and consequent specialization of work tasks made some kind of reorganization imperative. During the period after the war and before the 1959 reorganization, there were two rather distinct kinds of organizational change. One was a period of major structural alteration and addition between 1947 and 1950; the other was a period of personnel change and reassignment between 1954 and 1958.

The schoolhouse, construction, and structural engineering sections were combined early in 1947; and the head of this new section was designated Chief Construction Engineer. Instead of reporting to the Assistant State Architect—Design and Planning, he was placed directly under the authority of the State Architect. Boyd also appointed an Administrative Assistant to make procedural analyses of operations in the Division and to serve as an "efficiency expert." In 1948 the Los Angeles office of the Division was established, and a principal architect, J. A. Gillem, was named its head. He was given supervisory authority over design, planning, and engineering activities in the southern part of the state.

By 1948 the Division's expanded staff and workload made it necessary to consider a major review and overhaul. Boyd requested the Management Analysis Section of the Department of Finance to make a study of the entire organization. (The Management Analysis Section, later renamed Division of Organization and Cost Control, existed for the purpose of making studies for any of the many state agencies with the aim of improving their functioning.) The subsequent report was emphatic in deploring the organizational inadequacy of the Division of Architecture. It asserted that "the Division of Architecture shows the effects of insufficient attention to management. Its procedures are not rapid and efficient, its lines of authority are not clear, and the work is not well coordinated." Other observations were that "strong internal management" was needed; that the regular lines of formal authority were "short-circuited" too frequently within the agency; there was a "lack of information as to what is being planned and done." The report indicated that the basic problem was the fact that the top structure of the Division of Architecture needed to be reorganized so as to promote better management practices. It noted that the Division's upper levels had not been reorganized since the time when the workload was but a fraction of what it was in 1948, and that the top executives of the Division were heavily overburdened. The report concluded that a new position concentrating on the management of the Division should be established, that of Deputy Chief, and that the Deputy Chief should have administrative authority over the entire Division. Boyd agreed with this conclusion, and the position of Deputy Chief was established in 1950. There were no basic organizational changes in the Division after 1950 until the Ernst and Ernst study in 1958. (See Figure 2.)

Changes in Personnel

The new post of Deputy Chief, established in 1950, was intended to promote administrative competence rather than architectural expertise. It is noteworthy that the first (and so far only) appointee to the position was a non-architect management specialist who came from outside the Division. This was H. S. Hunter, who, just prior to taking this position in 1950, had been on the staff of a Chicago management consulting firm. Earlier he had served as general manager of the Peninsula Housing Association of Palo Alto.

In 1954 the Chief Construction Engineer retired and was succeeded by C. M. Herd. Herd, who held a Civil Engineering degree from the University of Southern California, was appointed to the Division in 1950 as a supervising structural engineer in the schoolhouse section. Before that he had served in engineering and construction supervision positions with the Los Angeles Board of Education and with the Pasadena city school system.

In 1955 Daniels, the Assistant State Architect—Administrative, retired and E. W. Hampton was promoted to that position. He retained that post until the implementation of the 1959 reorganization plan. Hampton, who had a Master of Arts degree from the University of California School of Architecture, started his record of service in the Divi-

FIGURE 2: DIVISION OF ARCHITECTURE: ORGANIZATION CHART, JANUARY 1953
(Basic Organization Structure and Principal Officials of the Division of Architecture at Time of Ernst and Ernst Study)

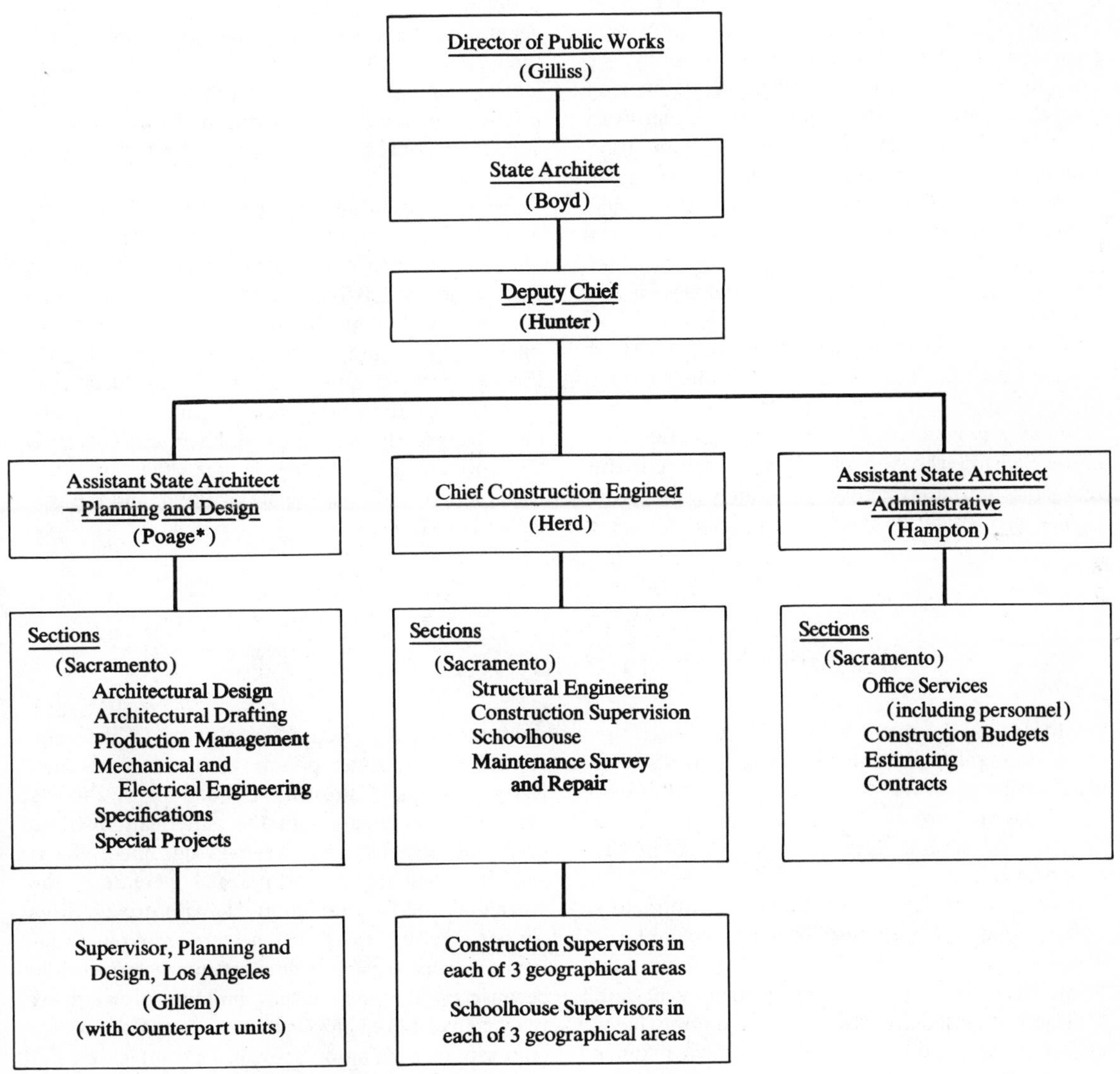

*Poage retired in June 1958, just before the Ernst and Ernst study was begun. His duties were assumed by Hampton.

sion in 1922 as a draftsman and designer. He became head of the Construction Budgets Section in 1953. Warmly regarded by Boyd, Hampton was Boyd's choice for the position of Assistant State Architect—Administrative.

The final top-level personnel change prior to the Ernst and Ernst study was the retirement of Poage in June 1958. Poage, who was then Assistant State Architect—Planning and Design, had been an Assistant State Architect for more than thirty years. His impending retirement was probably a factor encouraging the making of the organizational study of 1958, since the vacancy would provide more "elbow-room" for management to make personnel changes that might be indicated by the study. At any rate, Boyd delayed filling the position following Poage's departure; instead, he asked Hampton to serve in an acting capacity while at the same time continuing in his capacity as Assistant in charge of Administration. Later, in February 1959, he made Hampton the permanent Assistant State Architect—Design and Planning and asked Deputy Chief Hunter to carry on the responsibilities of the Assistant State Architect—Administrative.

These men—Boyd, Hunter, Hampton, and Herd—were thus the principal officials in the Division of Architecture during the period with which this case study is concerned. They were also the ones in the Division who were principally involved in the reorganization study and were among those principally affected by its recommendations. All were mature individuals with long experience in their fields of work, and most of them had extensive, high-level experience in the Division of Architecture. The "newest" among them in the Division was Hunter, who had joined eight years earlier. All except Hunter were over fifty years old, and two, Boyd and Hampton, would be eligible for retirement within a few years. All were under the state's civil service system and were protected by tenure. Boyd and Hampton were licensed architects; Herd was an engineer; and Hunter was a specialist in management who tended to believe that problems of the Division could be solved by the general application of rational procedures rather than by treating them as individual technical problems. Boyd was unquestionably the dominant figure in the Division, both by virtue of formal position and of personality; and it was clear whose would be the ultimate decision on basic issues, including, of course, organization. At the same time, Boyd was a somewhat controversial figure in Sacramento. He was the target of criticism from various sources on both the legislative and administrative sides for his free-wheeling method of operating, for not running a "tight ship," for insufficient attention to economy in his Division, for the production of generally uninteresting designs, and for alleged favoritism in the letting of architectural contracts with private firms. Hampton, the other architect, was a long-standing associate of Boyd, and the two worked well together.

THE MILIEU OF THE DIVISION: SEEDBED OF THE REORGANIZATION

Other than the client state agencies, there are three distinguishable categories of interests that are especially concerned about the operations of the Division: private interests; the legislative branch; and several agencies and officers in the executive branch.

Among the private interests, building contractors and architectural firms display particular concern over the operation of the Division. The great bulk of the state's construction is performed on private contracts awarded by the Division on the basis of competitive bids. Thus the Division's manner of operation in contract matters and in supervision of construction are understandably of great interest to private firms. Over the years the relationships between the Division and private building contractors have been relatively good. The relationships with some private architects and especially with the California Council of Architects (the state organization of the American Institute of Architects) have not been as unruffled. Occasionally when there is an unusual increase in the workload, the Division contracts with private firms for architectural work. The need to farm out architectural work has been greatest in the last decade because the number of state building projects has reached exceptional levels as a result of California's high rate of population growth. In some cases, the contracts have involved substantial fees, and certain architectural firms have received the bulk of the contract work. For example, during the period of this case, 1957-1959, fifteen contracts were let to eleven private firms, of which four firms received three-fourths of the work, each of the four receiving fees totaling over $365,000. The contract awards, though signed by the Director of Public Works, have actually been made by the State Architect. Boyd always insisted that his choices were made upon the basis of the merit and reliability of the firm, but some of those who were not selected sometimes felt that the choices reflected personal favoritism.

Legislative committees often review agency operations, and these reviews do not pass unnoticed in the private sphere. One can get an indication of the attitude of the California Council of Architects from their Sacramento Newsletter of July 30, 1954:

> DIVISION OF ARCHITECTURE: Although not scheduled to appear until the '55 Legislative Session, a report being prepared by an interim committee headed by Sen. JOHN McCARTHY, (R-San Rafael) will contain some sharp criticism of the State Div. of Architecture, headed by ANSON BOYD, long the target of attack from legislators, state department heads, and interests pushing for larger slices of state work for private architects. Nature of the criticism has not been disclosed, but it is understood the target this time will be BOYD's handling of the Division itself, plus certain extravagances in the erection of state structures.

The report referred to in this Newsletter was issued in 1955. It represented one of the more notable instances of legislative interest in the Division. In this report there were 103 specific recommendations for improving or changing the operations of the Division of Architecture. Most of these recommendations dealt with fine points of operational detail, e.g., "Change posting procedures on project ledgers to make more effective records. . . . Reduce the present volume of paper which is circulated, read, and filed within the Division. . . . Develop and promote greater use of form letters to save stenographic time and effect other economies. . . . Use Quick Copy, Ozalid, or similar processes to make inexpensive copies of letters and other material to reduce stenographic costs." But several recommendations touched upon major organizational matters. Of special interest in the area of general management was the suggestion that the Division "recast and concentrate the present organization structure to improve management control and to effect economies in operation." These recommendations were reviewed by the top-level officers of the Division, and many that were adjudged sound and practicable were implemented.

In addition to occasional review of the Division's operations by legislative committees, the Office of Legislative Analyst maintains regular oversight in its capacity as "watchdog" staff, research staff, and management analysis staff for the Legislature. The Office of Legislative Analyst is responsible to the Joint Legislative Budget Committee of the Legislature, and in performing its principal function, staff members in the Office of the Legislative Analyst attend the preliminary budget hearings (between the Department of Finance and the state agencies when the tentative budget is being prepared) and scrutinize the budgetary requests and past performance of every agency and department of the state government. Following one such review, in 1953-1954, the Legislative Analyst's Office felt that the Division was insufficiently attentive to economical operation:

> In our prior analysis we . . . pointed out the fact that there was a strong tendency in the Division of Architecture to cling to traditional and often archaic designs, methods, and materials. At this time we wish to report that while there are signs of an awakening realization of the need for more modern and more economical approaches to the problems of design and construction, we believe that there still exists in the Division of Architecture a great reluctance to change, which can only result in unnecessary burdens on the general taxpayer.

Within the executive branch itself, the Department of Finance plays an important role with respect to Architecture's operation. Two divisions, the Budget Division and the Organization and Cost Control Division, are primarily concerned with the workings of Architecture. As a staff arm of the Governor, the Budget Division is directly involved in the process of determining Architecture's annual budget: it must approve the annual state building program and any requests for new personnel positions, and it must review Architecture's fiscal record. In the Budget Division, there is a Construction Analysis Section which was established in 1953 for the purpose of supplying the Budget Chief with complete information and analysis concerning budgetary items related to the state's capital outlay program. In addition, the Construction Analysis Section has continuing responsibility for approving Architecture's preliminary plans and estimates, for reviewing working drawings, and for approving any additions to the originally approved projects.

The Organization and Cost Control Division (OCC) makes organizational and management studies of the various state agencies, either upon its own volition or at the request of an agency. From 1948 to 1958 several analyses were made of Architecture's operations. One such study, in 1948, had recommended an organizational device that was to receive major attention in later studies. The recommendation was that there be established a Project Control Unit, "to record, coordinate, and control the work of the Division of Architecture." Such a unit was essential, the report noted, in view of the increase in the postwar volume of architectural work resulting from deferred maintenance and postponed building. In response to this recommendation, a Project Control Unit was established in 1948, and the Administrative Assistant to the State Architect was given operating responsibility over the unit. Another study, in 1949, discussed before (p. 448), recommended the creation of the position of Deputy Chief and reemphasized the need to improve work flow and coordination. Still another important review of organizational structure was made by OCC in 1954. This review was undertaken at the suggestion of the Senate Finance Committee, which in turn was responding to an analysis made by the Office of the Legislative Analyst. The report contained two major recommendations. One was that the Construction Budgets Section and the Estimating Section should be transferred from the "Administrative" service of the Division to the "Planning and Design" service. (Boyd disagreed with this recommendation, believing that these two sections served as a check-and-balance function *vis-à-vis* the planners and designers.) The other recommendation was that the Project Control Unit should be removed from the jurisdiction of the Administrative Assistant and placed in the Production Management Section, the latter being a section in the Planning and Design service. The rationale for this transfer was that up to this point the Project Control Unit had not developed as a true coordination and control unit but instead was merely performing a statistical reporting operation. (This recommendation was not implemented.) The OCC report observed that "the Assistant State Architect Administrative (Daniels), it is reported, plans to retire soon. This time will be particularly appropriate for considering adoption of the organization changes recommended in this report."

Within the executive branch the office that has the closest organizational relation to Architecture is, of course, that of the Director of Public Works. In practice, the relationships between the State Architect and the Director's office have worked in favor of a rather high degree of autonomy for the Division. There appear to be three reasons for this. One is that the postwar occupants of the Director's office had never been appointed from Architecture but instead came either from the Division of Highways or from outside the Department. Thus, the tendency of most Directors was to pay greater attention to Highways. Second is that in size, in costs, and in political volatility, the highway program so far overbalanced the rest of the Public Works Department as to relegate the smaller divisions to a relatively minor and obscure position. In 1958-1959, for example, highway expenditures exceeded one-half billion dollars, against less than one hundred million spent by Architecture; and Highways' 12,700 personnel constituted ninety per cent of all personnel in the Department of Public Works, as against eight per cent in Architecture. The third reason is that the Division of Architecture and the position and authority of the State Architect were established by statute, and it was also by statute that Architecture was placed within the Department of Public Works. These facts raised some doubt about the Director's legal authority over Architecture. However, a 1958 opinion of the Department's legal staff argued that the powers vested in the State Architect could be considered to be exercised under the administrative authority of the Director of Public Works.

The Employee Opinion Survey of 1958

In 1956, the Director of Public Works appointed an administrative analyst, John Stanford, to make analyses of management operations in the divisions in the Department. During 1956-1958 Stanford concentrated upon work immediately related to the Director's office and upon the development of a management analysis program for the Division of Highways. In 1958 Stanford turned his attention to Architecture. One of his first actions was to suggest to Boyd that an employee opinion survey might help to reveal possible sore spots, as well as strong points, in the operation of the Division. Boyd found the suggestion intriguing, and he agreed. Stanford and the departmental personnel officer prepared an extensive questionnaire, which was distributed to all employees in Architecture in April 1958.

In a covering letter, Boyd explained that the questionnaire could be returned unsigned and that the administrative officers of the Division wanted to know the personal feelings and opinions of the employees so that steps could be taken to make the Division a more effective and more desirable place to work. The employees were invited to rate the Division on such matters as opportunities for advancement, supervision, in-service training, and working conditions. In addition to the questions, there was space for any comments the employee might wish to make.

Over ninety per cent of the questionnaires were returned, and while a few doubted that the questionnaire would do much good, many thought it worthwhile and expressed the hope that there would be other such efforts to obtain employee opinion. A large majority indicated that their jobs were interesting and satisfying, that they felt either "good" or "proud" about working for the Division, and that the Division did a good job. However, a considerable number reported that they received conflicting orders from their superiors in the organization (thirty-six per cent "sometimes," six per cent "usually"), twenty-nine per cent felt that their supervisors needed training in how to deal with human relations, and forty-four per cent complained of a lack of in-service training opportunities. A large proportion of the personnel made additional comments. These comments covered a considerable array of matters, from such specific concerns as the adequacy of equipment ("The tops of the drafting tables are worn out") to such general concerns as the adequacy of internal communications ("Communications should be strengthened between working levels and administrative echelons") and of top management ("Top management is weak"). In all, the number of comments that were critical far exceeded the number that were complimentary.

After the questionnaires had been tabulated, detailed breakdowns of the results were distributed to those personnel who occupied supervisory positions. No further action was taken on the attitude study at that time, but, as will be seen below, its findings were used in connection with the subsequent organization survey of 1958.

THE REORGANIZATION STUDY OF 1958

The Beginnings

In the last few months of 1957 and the first few months of 1958, there occurred a coincidence of events that focused attention on the Division of Architecture. In November 1957, OCC released a voluminous report with the title "General Management Survey of the Department of Finance." This report raised a number of eyebrows, including those of several people in the Division of Architecture. The covering letter, signed by T. H. Mugford, Deputy Director of the Department of Finance and Chief of OCC, singled out for special endorsement six of the recommendations in the report. One of these called for transfer of the Division of Architecture to the Department of Finance. Mugford made the following comment:

> The functions of the Division of Architecture being essentially the rendering of service and supervising of expenditures (in a very important field) are more related to those of the Department of Finance than to the present Department of Public Works. A number of previous surveys have recommended the transfer of the Division of Architecture to the Department of Finance. The reasons for such a transfer are even more valid today in light of the present and future capital outlay program.

Within the body of the report itself the reasoning was that because the functions of Architecture are to provide "service to and control of other state agencies," the Division should be removed from what was primarily a line agency (Public Works) and placed in the department that was primarily responsible for central services (Finance).

In addition to this, there were some key personnel changes. Poage (Assistant State Architect—Planning and Design) had already indicated his intention to retire in June of 1958. And on January 1, 1958, Max Gilliss was appointed the new Director of Public Works, the previous director having retired. Gilliss was anxious to fulfill his new responsibility by making sure that Public Works and its divisions were in the best possible operating order. Stanford, the departmental administrative analyst, was at this time making a brief reconnaissance of Architecture's organization and functions. On the basis of Stanford's findings and the results of the employee opinion survey, Gilliss felt that the Division's top-level organization could be improved. Boyd was preparing for a trip to Lebanon that would take him away from his office from April 16 to June 25, 1958. The trip was partially a vacation and partially a special assignment under a grant from the Rockefeller Foundation to draft a master plan for the campus of the American University at Beirut.

On April 3, Resolution Number 46 was introduced on the floor of the Assembly and referred to the Rules Committee of that body. The resolution was coauthored by Assemblymen Coolidge and Lindsay, but Boyd himself had drafted it and asked Coolidge to introduce it. The resolution called attention to the pressing building needs of the state and asserted that the "continuing load of planning and construction responsibilities makes advisable further careful consideration of that division's arrangement of operations and their proper place in the state government." The resolution then concluded with these words:

> WHEREAS, this study and consideration of the Division of Architecture pattern of production and management and the proper place for these in the State Government are of continuing concern to this Ways and Means Committee; now, therefore, be it
>
> RESOLVED, that it is the opinion of the Assembly of the California Legislature that the Department of Public Works, Division of Architecture, should now employ a competent firm of experts in the fields of production and management as a part of the necessary operations of the Division of Architecture Revolving Fund and to furnish this report and conclusions directly to the Ways and Means Committee not later than August 1, 1958.

Boyd would have preferred not to prepare such a resolution at all, but the cumulating external pressures and tensions had become so severe that he felt they had to be confronted somehow. Suspicious of the critical forces around him in the state government, Boyd also hoped that a study by an outside consulting firm of the Division's own choosing, sanctioned by a legislative resolution, would result in quieting some of the critics, besides staving off pressures to relocate the Division. The resolution of course came to the attention of officials in the Department of Finance and the Public Works Department, none of whom had been aware of its introduction. Gilliss had previously talked with Boyd about having an organizational study of Architecture, but this unexpected resolution raised additional questions, as, for example, the place of Architecture in the structure of the state administrative organization and the employment of an outside consulting firm. He therefore conferred with Boyd about the content and desirability of the resolution. Boyd argued that this action was necessary to offset the Finance Study, which he felt showed a set disposition by Finance to "annex" the Division at the first opportunity. He further believed that the outside consultant device was desirable on two counts: first, that an internal study within the Department might be viewed by some critics as a whitewash if they did not agree with the conclusions; and second, that a study by Finance's OCC staff could hardly be objective about the place of Architecture, inasmuch as their recent report had already recommended transfer. Thus, he argued, only a private management consulting firm could be expected to have the necessary objectivity. Gilliss reserved judgment on the resolution until he had had an opportunity to discuss the matter with officials in Finance.

Discussions between Gilliss' office and officials in Finance (John Pierce, Director; T. H. Mugford, Deputy Director; and Robert Harkness, Budget Chief) revealed that Finance had reservations about a study by private consultants. The primary reason for this was the fear that an outside consultant selected and paid by Architecture would be too solicitous of the Division's preferences. However, Finance agreed not to attempt to have the resolution killed or amended after Gilliss' office made it clear that the selection of the consulting firm would be made with great care and objectivity, and that Finance would have an opportunity to disapprove the selection of the particular consulting firm. Assemblymen Coolidge and Lindsay also indicated that they were interested in the matter of consultant selection, and Gilliss assured them that he would keep them informed on the procedures and would invite their comments before a final decision was made.

Selecting Consultants

Resolution Number 46 was passed unanimously and without debate by the Assembly on April 7 in the normal course of legislative business. Gilliss then turned over to Stanford the task of soliciting applications from various reputable management firms. Stanford prepared a statement of the objectives and scope of the proposed study, which was to accompany each letter of invitation. The statement of scope covered three areas: (1) the place of the Division of Architecture and related functions in the organization of the state government; (2) a review of top-level organization structure within the Division; (3) a review of internal operations and procedures in the Division. The statement specifically excluded the question of whether there should be greater use of private firms in performing architectural tasks for the state.

Before sending out the letters, Stanford conferred with Boyd. Boyd indicated that he was already convinced of the merits of one particular firm, but Stanford pointed out that under the circumstances the chances of obtaining acceptance of the recommendations that would emerge from the study depended greatly upon an open selection process and agreement among all concerned upon the consultants to be selected.

The letters were sent to a half-dozen management consulting firms that had offices on the west coast: Booz, Allen, and Hamilton; Cresap, McCormick, and Paget; Ernst and Ernst; McKinsey and Company; Public Administration Service; and Worden and Risberg. By the end of May all six of the firms had responded to the invitation. Stanford then made up a table of comparisons, showing such factors as the amount of the fee, the number of staff that could be immediately employed on the study, the qualifications of the staff members, and the way in which the firm proposed to go about making the study. He next conferred with Deputy Chief Hunter, who was in charge of the Division in Boyd's absence, and Hunter confirmed Stanford's judgment that Ernst and Ernst should be chosen. A subsequent meeting was held in Gilliss' office with Assemblyman Lindsay and Deputy Director of Finance Mugford. The review of the proposals at that time resulted in a general agreement on Ernst and Ernst. A contract between the Director of Public Works and Ernst and Ernst was signed by both parties and approved by the State Personnel Board and the Director of the Department of Finance.[5] On June 18, 1958, the Director of Public Works issued a news release announcing the beginning of the Ernst and Ernst survey of the Division of Architecture.

Within the Division, formal notification of the Ernst and Ernst survey was served in a memorandum of June 11 from Hunter to all heads of services and sections and to all supervisors. The announcement indicated the nature of the study and asked that the survey team be given full cooperation.

In the Los Angeles office, the general reaction to the study was one of approval and optimism. There was a widespread feeling in the southern office that it had for too long been treated as a poor cousin. Under Gillem, who was uninhibitedly vocal and forthright in supporting the needs and demands of the Los Angeles office, morale was generally high. Los Angeles personnel confidently expected that the reorganization study would result in recommendations to upgrade their office, to clarify their responsibility, and to increase their autonomy.

Down the line in the Sacramento office, there was very little reaction to the announcement of the study. No matter what kind of reorganization was instituted at the top of the structure, the specific jobs of drafting, designing, estimating, and making contracts still had to be performed. To be sure, there might be a reassignment of sections from the responsibility of one Assistant State Architect to another, or certain sections might be divided or reconstituted. But this shifting process had of itself occurred over the years, and it had not been particularly unsettling. The basic working units or groups had neither been broken up nor reconstituted.

The firm began its study on June 16, two days before the public announcement of the survey. Three men from the San Francisco office were assigned to the reorganization study: Edwin Parks, Paul Fryer, and Kenneth Caldwell. Parks was given the task of studying the construction and schoolhouse functions of the Division; Fryer was assigned to study organization and internal procedures; Caldwell, who headed the team, undertook the job of studying the relationships of the Division with other state agencies and departments, particularly as these were involved in the process of performing the planning and execution of the state's building program.

---

[5] The essential terms of the contract were as follows: (1) fee: $16,750, including expenses; (2) staff: two full-time consultants, a supervising consultant, and such part-time specialists as might be required, all under the overall direction of the West Coast Manager of the firm, plus "the entire resources of the firm" if necessary in any way in order to meet the deadline; (3) time limit: September 30, 1958, provided the award of the contract was made early in June. The complete project proposal was twenty pages in length.

At the outset, Caldwell examined the information that Stanford had obtained earlier through the employee opinion questionnaire. Caldwell was convinced of the value of the questionnaire method for obtaining information and opinions. He devised a supplementary questionnaire for supervisors in order to augment the information contained in the previous survey and to assess supervisory opinion as to the major trouble spots in the Division.

Caldwell was anxious to do as thorough a job as possible. He set out to obtain information and opinions about the process of programming state building and the operations of the Division from private and public organizations that were concerned in one way or another with these matters. He consulted officers of the California Council of Architects and of the Consulting Engineers Association. While several officers of the latter felt that relations with Architecture suffered from a general lack of coordination within the Division itself, officers of the California Council of Architects indicated no general dissatisfaction in their relationships with the Division. However, their enthusiasm for the reorganization survey was dampened by the fact that the study was to exclude the question of greater use of private architects by the state.

Within the government, Caldwell talked to the Legislative Analyst and to the assistant whose jurisdiction included the Architecture Division. In the Department of Finance he talked to Deputy Director Mugford, Assistant Director Collins, Budget Chief Harkness, and to Marvin Blanchard, Chief of the Division of Organization and Cost Control. In the Department of Public Works he conferred a few times with Gilliss, and frequently with Stanford and with Justin Ducray, Stanford's assistant. The opinions gained from these interviews tended to reinforce the previously reported evaluations of general weakness in the management of the Division. On the matter of Architecture's relationships with the client agencies, Caldwell consulted with the appropriate top-level officers in all of the state's major departments and in a sampling of the smaller agencies. He discovered that, in general, the client agencies were quite well satisfied with the performance of the Division.

Inside the Division itself, the investigation by the management team was equally thorough. In addition to the two sets of questionnaires already referred to, job and operations analysis sheets were utilized in an attempt to find out exactly who was doing what. The usual examination was made of applicable statutes, reports, statistics, operating and organization manuals, and other reports that had a bearing upon the organization's operation. The principal means of obtaining information was by individual interview. Frequent and extensive interviews were held with the top officials—Boyd, Hunter, Hampton, and Herd. Some personnel down the line were interviewed, including various people in the Los Angeles office. At no time in the course of the management survey did the firm hold group interviews. Caldwell was convinced that the individual interview method was the only way by which to gain thorough and frank information from personnel in the agency—the method of group interview, he felt, would only lead to tied tongues, at least in this situation.

How did the personnel in the Division react to the fact of the reorganization study itself? Among top officials in the Sacramento office, the study had, of course, been anticipated. And reorganization studies were nothing new. But, considering all of the circumstances surrounding the initiation of the Ernst and Ernst study, the top-level officials were in agreement in hoping that the results would clarify and strengthen the top-level management arrangements. Whether these hopes would be realized for each officer depended upon the conclusions of the study, and more distinctive reactions would come only after conclusions and recommendations had been made by the management firm.

Conclusions and Tentative Recommendations

By the end of July 1958 the management team had come to several tentative conclusions regarding the larger organizational questions under study. These were presented informally to Boyd, Gilliss, and Stanford in Public Works and to Mugford, Collins, and Blanchard in the Department of Finance. Caldwell's intent in making these informal presentations was to explain the content and purposes of the proposed tentative recommendations, to give the people who were most concerned a chance to reflect and react to them, and to avoid the possibility of overlooking any significant factor in formulating the recommendations. The reactions of the people consulted were generally favorable, though Mugford felt that the proposed increase in the authority of the Los Angeles office was undesirable from the standpoint of divisional coordination and program consistency.

Caldwell and his associates were pleased that their evaluations and the direction of their tentative recommendations had been generally accepted. Since no one had expressed strong objections, which might have jeopardized the acceptance of the conclusions of the final report, the tentative recommendations could become final recommendations.

Two weeks later, when the major organizational recommendations were more thoroughly spelled out, Boyd circulated them to his top officers, Hunter, Hampton, and Herd. He asked them to meet in his office with Caldwell and Fryer to discuss the proposed reorganization. Briefly, the recommendations called for the following changes:

(1) The abolition of the single office of Deputy Chief, and in its place the creation of two deputy chief positions, one Deputy Chief for Administration, and one Deputy Chief for Architecture and Engineering.

(2) Under the Deputy Chief for Architecture and Engineering, there would be two Assistant State Architects, one for the Northern Area, and one for the Southern Area. There would no longer be a position of Assistant State Architect—Administrative, and instead the functions of that position would be transferred to the new position of Deputy Chief for Administration.

(3) The schoolhouse function would be removed from the jurisdiction of the Chief Construction Engineer and lodged in a separate section to be headed by a chief who would report directly to the Deputy Chief for Architecture and Engineering. Furthermore, the structural engineering section would be removed from the jurisdiction of the Chief Construction Engineer and made a responsibility of the Deputy Chief for Architecture and Engineering. In addition, the construction services also would be placed under the authority of the Deputy Chief for Architecture and Engineering. All this would have the effect of abolishing the position of Chief Construction Engineer (see Figure 3).

Informal Discussion of Recommendations

At the meeting in Boyd's office, Caldwell explained the proposed top-level reorganization and presented his rationale for it. Basically, he argued, there were two primary activities in the Division: one included the "technical" (architectural, engineering) activity, and the other, administrative work. For the greatest efficiency, they should be clearly separated. In the past operations of the Division, this separation had not been consistently maintained, to the detriment of both. Architects seemed invariably deficient in administrative skill, and administrators without professional training in architecture were generally poorly qualified to make architectural judgments. Deputy Chief Hunter, who was not an architect and who had been selected for his administrative competence, had wisely refrained from exercising authority over "technical" decisions. In effect the establishment of the two new deputy positions would give organizational recognition to this distinction between technical and administrative areas of endeavor and therefore make it clearer and more effective. As to the creation of the two Assistant State Architect positions, one each in Northern and Southern California, the principal goal would be to give the southern operation the organizational status to which it was now entitled by virtue of the size of its staff, its project budgets, and the nature of the work being done there. Regarding the schoolhouse function, Caldwell argued that it should be organized separately from the main segments of the Division, since it was virtually unrelated to Architecture's regular work. Because the schoolhouse function was a relatively small one, it seemed most sensible organizationally to have the schoolhouse chief report to the Deputy Chief of Architecture and Engineering rather than to the State Architect. The structural engineering section and construction services should be placed under the Deputy Chief for Architecture and Engineering in order to improve coordination of work on projects.

Hampton (Assistant State Architect—Design and Planning) reacted favorably to Caldwell's proposals: the suggested changes made good sense to him. The problem, he thought, with only one Deputy Chief position was that the occupant had to be both an administrator and an architect, and people possessing both skills were rare. On the other hand, to create three or more deputy chief positions would merely compound the difficulties of coordination.

Deputy Chief Hunter's reaction was negative. He told Caldwell that he considered the proposed changes at the top a step backwards in that the State Architect would have to concern himself with problems of coordination that were now handled by the present Deputy Chief. As Hunter

FIGURE 3: PROPOSED BASIC ORGANIZATION OF THE DIVISION OF ARCHITECTURE
(Ernst and Ernst—1958)

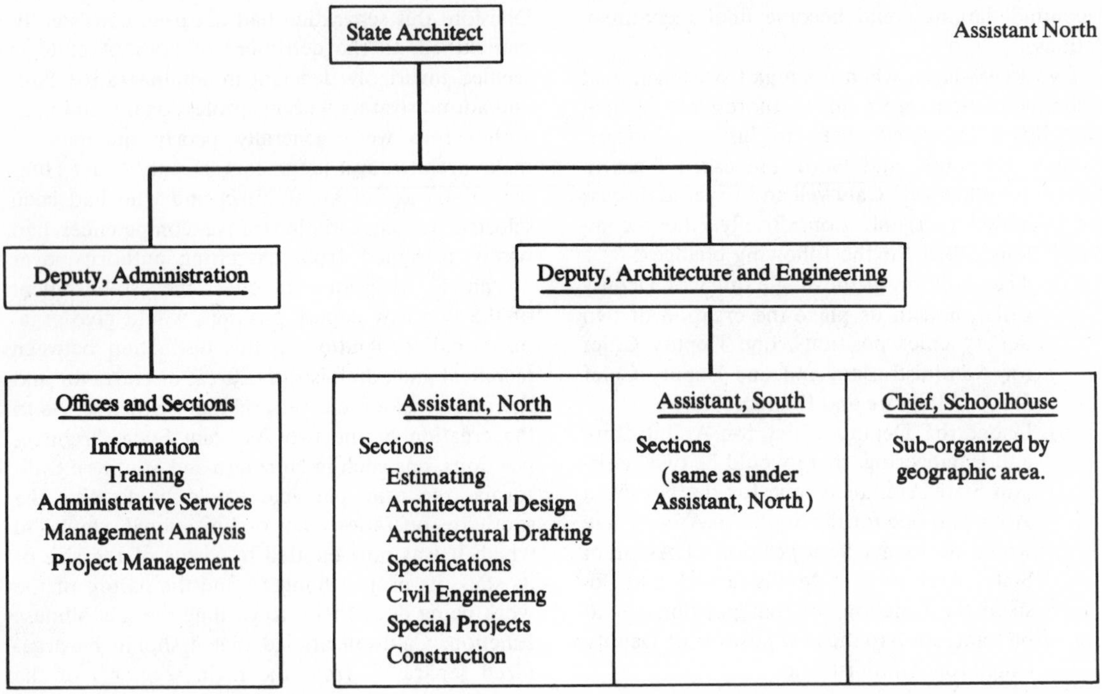

State Architect

Assistant North

Deputy, Administration

- **Offices and Sections**
  - Information
  - Training
  - Administrative Services
  - Management Analysis
  - Project Management

Deputy, Architecture and Engineering

- **Assistant, North**
  - Sections
    - Estimating
    - Architectural Design
    - Architectural Drafting
    - Specifications
    - Civil Engineering
    - Special Projects
    - Construction
- **Assistant, South**
  - Sections (same as under Assistant, North)
- **Chief, Schoolhouse**
  - Sub-organized by geographic area.

saw it, the State Architect should be concerned only with substantive policy questions and not with questions of administrative coordination.

Chief Construction Engineer Herd also reacted negatively. To him the schoolhouse and construction sections belonged together under one chief, and the difference in the kinds of work performed by engineers as contrasted with architects and designers was to him sufficient to justify the existence of a separate operation that would share equal rank in the organization with the planning and design and administrative functions.

Boyd indicated that he approved of the idea of establishing two deputy positions because he agreed with Caldwell's rationale concerning the clear separation of the technical and the administrative aspects of the Division's work.

The Final Report

The consulting team spent the remainder of the study period shaping up the final report. On October 1, 1958, the completed report was formally presented to the State Architect, the Director of Public Works, the Department of Finance, and to the Assembly Ways and Means Committee.

Caldwell and his staff felt confident that they were headed in the right direction by virtue of the generally favorable responses to their earlier preliminary conclusions and proposals. No "monkey wrench" appeared in the form of major or intransigent objections. In fact, the entire study period had been marked by cooperativeness and cordiality. The spirit of cooperation was acknowledged in the final report:

> In every presentation, the major recommendations were discussed and explained in detail. Many alternative recommendations were presented or discussed and, in a number of instances, were incorporated into the final recommendations. Sincere efforts were made by all concerned in these discussions to fully define the problem areas as well as to clarify the proposed changes. The assistance provided materially aided us in formulating or finalizing certain recommendations.
>
> We are happy to report that we received the utmost in cooperation from everyone contacted, both within and outside of State government. In

no instance did we ever receive the impression that information was being withheld or presented in such a way as to be misleading.

The final report also summarized the responses of supervisory personnel to the questionnaire that the firm had utilized. Another appendix contained excerpts from letters that had been submitted by the California Council of the American Institute of Architects and the Consulting Engineers Association of California in response to formal inquiries by Caldwell about the processes by which outside architects and engineers are selected by the state, and about the processes by which the Division reviews, approves, and supervises the plans and activities related to public schoolhouse construction. Also included were two charts showing the existing and proposed change-order procedure, and a statement of the procedures used in making the study.

The major recommendations of the report were summarized under four headings: (1) The Place of the Division of Architecture in the Organization of State Government, (2) The State Building Program, (3) Top-Level Organization of the Division, and (4) Operations and Procedures Within the Division.

Location of the Division of Architecture

With respect to the question of the proper place of Architecture in the organization of state government, the report took notice of the fact that there had been several recent studies and proposals for reorganization in certain state agencies which, if executed, would have a bearing upon the most suitable place for locating Architecture. Four "conditions" were presented as affecting Architecture's recommended location: (1) if Highways were to become a separate department, or a part of a department of transportation, and service activities were to be taken from Finance to form a department of general services, then Architecture should be made a division in such a General Services Department; (2) if Highways were to become a separate department, or a part of a department of transportation, but no changes were made in Finance's organization, then a new Department of Public Buildings should be established which would include not only Architecture but two service divisions presently located in Finance (Buildings and Grounds, and Property Acquisition); (3) if Highways remained in Public Works; or (4) if Highways remained in Public Works and service activities of Finance were split off to form a department of general services, then Architecture should remain as a division in Public Works. Quite clearly the preference in the recommendations was to leave Architecture alone unless Highways was relocated. The rationale for the preference was plainly stated in the report: "Architecture is currently functioning rather well as a Division of Public Works . . . more uniform administration of the 'State Contract Act' seems assured by continuance of the present organization . . . the large grouping of technical personnel in one department also provides for more uniform management of personnel policies . . . personnel of the Division are generally rather strongly in favor of continuing to be a part of Public Works . . . where no real advantages are apparent in a change, the status quo should be maintained."

The State Building Program

The recommendations relating to the state building program generally called for centralization of administrative responsibility over the state's capital outlay program, either in a Capital Outlay Division within the Department of Finance, or under the jurisdiction of the Public Works Board. Other recommendations under this heading called for more careful definition of the areas of responsibility of the various agencies concerned with the state's capital outlay program and emphasized the need for improving the planning of capital outlays, the timing of the annual budgeting cycle for capital outlays, and a limitation in the number of individuals who actually participate in the hearings at which the scope of building projects is considered. By and large the state building program recommendations, like those dealing with Architecture's organizational location, were directed to the State Legislature rather than to Architecture or Public Works, since the most important of these recommendations could be effectuated only by state legislation.

Top-Level Organization

The recommendations regarding top-level organization were aimed at achieving neater divisions of labor and lines of authority, clearer definitions of responsibility, and greater emphasis upon management arrangements. The specific proposals were the same as had earlier been discussed in Boyd's office. In addition, the report recommended that the position of Administrative Assistant be abolished and its functions transferred to other administrative positions in the proposed arrangement. Furthermore, two new staff positions were recommended, those of Training Officer and Management Analyst.

As a logical part of the goal of distinguishing technical from administrative operations, it was recommended that the estimating section be transferred from the administrative wing of the organization to the architectural and engineering side. The argument here was that the function of estimating is properly one of analyzing cost data for various building methods and materials and of estimating project costs on that basis. As such, the estimating function is essentially a technical one, a part of the "architectural team." However, the estimating section had in fact developed into a cost control operation rather than a service activity, and this resulted in a rivalry between the architectural designers and estimators. Occasionally it went so far that estimators advanced their own design solutions in competition with those developed by the designers. Therefore, the report concluded, if estimating were transferred from the administrative to the architectural side of the organization, a closer liaison and a more cooperative relationship were likely to develop with the design sections.

To provide an effective means for balancing and improving the project work flow, the study team recommended the establishment of a Project Management Section. This section was to be under the direct authority of the Deputy Chief for Administration, and it would have the task of controlling the planning and scheduling of all projects. Included in the new section were the following existing organizational elements: the Construction Budgets Section and the Professional Services Section (both of which were then separate sections under the Assistant State Architect—Administrative), the Production Management Section (then a staff unit in the design and planning service), and the Project Control Unit (then directed by the Administrative Assistant to the State Architect). The proposed Project Management Section was viewed by Caldwell as the key arrangement for improving the planning, scheduling, and controlling of the work of the Division of Architecture. Because the proposed Project Management Section would be a key factor in the improvement of the work of the Division, and because its establishment would constitute a major organizational and operational change, the report recommended that the development of specific organization and procedures for this section should be done by some outside firm which was broadly experienced in the development of such systems.

Operations and Procedures

With respect to operations and procedures, the firm made thirty-four specific recommendations. A few of these were intended to strengthen the authority and independence of the Los Angeles office. For example, it was urged that projects to be constructed in the southern part of the state should be designed in the southern office, that review of "change orders" on southern projects should be made in the Los Angeles office rather than in Sacramento, and that the Los Angeles project management staff should have full responsibility for administering contracts with the private architects and engineers who were used on projects in the Southern Area.

Several more recommendations were designed to clarify and make more explicit the standards and procedures to be followed in the Division, and to improve communications both within the Division and with the outside world. Other recommendations called for improving the processes of checking and reviewing plans in order to reduce delays and overhead costs.

In sum, the recommendations were designed to expedite the operations of the Division, to make it more efficient in carrying out its responsibilities, and to make more rational the allocation of responsibility and the direction of the Division's work. First and foremost, the report urged greater attention to management by separating it from technical considerations. Thus the report called for an overall planning and control section which would be the major unit on the administrative side. The report goals also included upgrading the status of the Los Angeles office and freeing it from unnecessary and burdensome interferences by the Sacramento office. But at the same time the report urged the desirability of greater uniformity of standards and procedures and improvement in coordination between the northern and southern offices, which would establish project priorities and time schedules, and allocate work in the most efficient manner possible.

Reaction to Reorganization Proposals

The optimistic expectations of Caldwell and his staff were by and large justified. With a few exceptions, the reactions of the people who received the final report were favorable. After all, the major recommendations of the final report were not much different from the tentative recommendations that had been discussed earlier with most of the high-level officials. Officials in the Department of Finance were for the most part satisfied. In many respects, the Ernst and Ernst report verified and built upon several of Finance's previous recommendations on internal organization and management. To be sure, Mugford still felt that the Los Angeles office should not be given as much autonomy as the Ernst and Ernst report proposed. And as for the transfer of Architecture to the Finance Department (which had been proposed by the OCC Division in 1957), this had stirred up enough accusations of "empire building" that the better course of wisdom appeared to be to forget it, at least for the time being. From the standpoint of the Finance Department, implementation of the Ernst and Ernst recommendations appeared to promise a more efficient and effective Division of Architecture.

Gilliss and Stanford examined the report and found it generally satisfactory, with one major exception. That exception had to do with the recommendation concerning the abolition of the office of Chief Construction Engineer and the rearrangement of these functions under the office of Deputy Chief for Architecture and Engineering. As Stanford viewed the situation, it would be one thing to create the proposed arrangement if one were establishing a brand new organization, but it was quite another matter in the case of an organization that was a going concern and in which the construction engineering and schoolhouse operations were under the direction of a capable and competent chief who had been in the Division for a long period of time.

There was no response, formal or informal, from any members of the Ways and Means Committee.

Within the top ranks of the Division itself, the reactions were much the same as they were when expressed during the meeting in Boyd's office. Boyd himself found much he could agree with but felt that some recommendations needed further reflection.

IMPLEMENTING THE REORGANIZATION

The Ernst and Ernst report was submitted just before the November 1958 gubernatorial elections, which resulted in a change in the state administration. Gilliss, the Public Works Director, accepted another appointment (as Road Commissioner for Los Angeles County) and resigned as Director of the Department before the year was out. In the brief interim before the new administration took office, action on the Ernst and Ernst proposals was deferred. On January 1, 1959, two new heads of the Public Works Department assumed office: Robert B. Bradford, Director, and James F. Wright, Deputy Director. Both were brought in from outside the state service. Bradford had been Executive Director of the Sacramento Redevelopment Agency; Wright had been an official of the New York State Department of Public Works. Wright, with the assistance of Stanford, who continued from the previous administration, assumed primary responsibility for the oversight of the Division of Architecture.

Toward the end of January, Wright contacted Boyd and discussed with him the disposition of the Ernst and Ernst report.

The reorganization proposal that Boyd thought should have first priority was the one dealing with project management. With the great growth in the Division and its work, Boyd had become convinced that the Division needed a more rational system of channeling and controlling work. He was inclined to accept the judgment of the management consultants that "the lack of a well coordinated method of planning, scheduling, assigning and controlling projects within the Division of Architecture can be considered the most serious operational problem facing the Division of Architecture." Wright approved and encouraged Boyd's decision to carry out the project management proposal and discussed with Boyd the problems involved in installing such a project management program. Because the Ernst and Ernst staff was both experienced in the design of management systems and familiar with the workings of the Division, it was agreed that another contract should be made with them for assistance in installing a project management system. On March 26, Boyd sent a memo to all employees of the Division announcing that Ernst and Ernst had been engaged to install a project management system, and that the installation process was expected to take a full year's time.

Shifts at the Top

Boyd's next task was to implement a top-level organizational arrangement in line with the Ernst and Ernst recommendations. He had earlier indicated approval of the reorganization proposed in the Ernst and Ernst report, but details of the change-over needed to be worked out. After several months of thought and discussion with his staff and with Wright and Stanford, Boyd reached what appeared to be a satisfactory organizational arrangement. On August 31 he issued a notice to the Division announcing that as of September 1, 1959, the Division would be reorganized (see Figure 4).

With two principal exceptions, the new organization chart of the Division was practically identical to that proposed in the Ernst and Ernst report. The schoolhouse and construction functions were not separated as had been recommended by the report. The second exception was that the position of Chief Construction Engineer was retained. Not only was Chief Construction Engineer Herd to retain responsibility for the schoolhouse and construction engineering functions, but he was also given rank equal to that of the two Assistant State Architects.

Boyd did not at first abolish the position of Administrative Assistant (whose functions were technically comprehended in other administrative positions, including that of the newly created position of Deputy Chief for Administration). However, his intent seems to have been to define the Deputy Chief for Administration position in the same fashion as the consultants did, and when the Administrative Assistant resigned in December 1959, the post was formally abolished.

There were no surprises in the top-level appointments that followed the announcement of the new organization structure. Hampton, who had occupied the position of Assistant State Architect—Design and Planning since February 1959, was named Deputy Chief for Architecture and Engineering. Hunter became Deputy Chief for Administration. For Hampton, of course, the reorganization constituted an upgrading in rank and status; to Hunter the change seemed a relative downgrading of rank and status. Herd remained in the position of Chief Construction Engineer, but the construction service was now under the supervisory authority of the Deputy Chief for Architecture and Engineering. Herd viewed this change as a

FIGURE 4: BASIC ORGANIZATION AND PRINCIPAL OFFICIALS, DIVISION OF ARCHITECTURE
(Effective September 1, 1959)

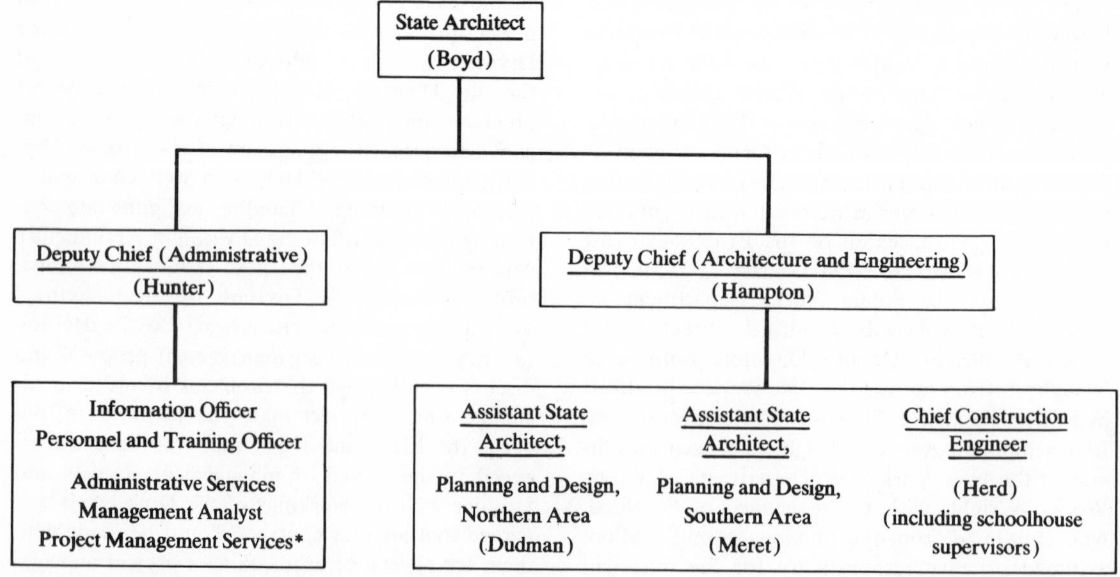

*Including Construction Budgets, Professional Services, Production Management, and Project Control Units.

drop in status and rank, for in the previous organizational arrangement, his position ranked equally with that of the top officer of design and planning activities.

Another supervisorial personnel change of particular significance took place in the Los Angeles operation. The key post there was now that of Assistant State Architect—Planning and Design, Southern Area. To this position Boyd named Tom Meret, who had been placed in charge of organizing the new Project Management Section and who had previously been head of the Construction Budgets Section in the Sacramento Office. Gillem remained as principal architect in charge of the Planning and Design Service, but he was now second-in-command under Meret.

Boyd himself viewed the implementation steps as valid and effective means to improve the operations of his Division. To Hampton the reorganization changes were sound and acceptable. Hunter was convinced of the value of the new project management system for improving the Division's operations, but with respect to the top-level organization, neither he nor Herd was persuaded that the new arrangement was the best solution.

The changes implementing the reorganization were announced either through official Division notices or through the monthly newsletter, or both. Informal communication was the other important device for passing on information. The method of announcing changes in staff meetings was not utilized.

Acceptance of Reorganization

The implementation of reorganization was, with one exception, accepted by the personnel of the Division with neither enthusiasm nor dismay. The exception was the establishment of the Project Management Section, with its central role in coordination, scheduling, and control. While many of the line personnel were able to concede the necessity for such a management service, these same individuals found the increased paperwork and reporting irksome. Some personnel were convinced that the operations of the Project Management Section were a waste of time and a hindrance to the operations of the Division, a judgment that led to the invention of the *sobriquet* "Project Manglement." The defenders of the Project Management Section pointed out that these complaints were inevitable reactions to the pains of instituting a new system of this sort. But whether or not opposition was based primarily on the newness of the system, it continued for a long time. Even after years of functioning, a few sections of the Division continued to resist the imposition of project management.

In the southern office a large part of the original optimism over the reorganization study was dampened early in the course of its implementation. Most of the initial pessimism stemmed from the fact that Gillem had been "demoted," and that the man put in charge of the Southern Area was likely to be more responsive to the Sacramento office than Gillem would have been. But after several months it became clear that Meret was as determined to promote the interests of the Los Angeles office as Gillem had been, and the pessimism over the change gradually disappeared. The architects and engineers in the southern office were also initially disturbed by a new emphasis on the shifting of personnel from the southern office to the northern office, and vice-versa, in the course of making promotions. Boyd and Hampton set forth on this course because they were convinced that it would help to improve understanding and coordination between the Northern and Southern Areas, but employees in the southern office viewed this rotation more as an attempt to keep the Southern Area "in line" than as a positive and desirable management practice.

Evaluation and Aftermath

The general reaction of those most intimately concerned was that the reorganization of the Division substantially implemented the recommendations of Ernst and Ernst. Within the Division itself the grumbling over the reorganization was generally minor enough, although project management did not win full acceptance for years.

In the other state administrative agencies directly concerned with Architecture, the reorganization was also considered successful. This was true of officials in the Public Works Department, the Finance Department, the Legislative Analyst's Office, and the State Personnel Board (which must approve new positions). Officials in both Finance and the Legislative Analyst's Office agreed that implementation of the reorganization recommendations had improved the internal functioning of the Division of Architecture. In the State Personnel Board, the stature of the Ernst and Ernst study was such that when the Division asked for new positions or for changes in existing classifications in accordance with Ernst and Ernst recommendations, it nearly always received favorable responses.

With respect to the State Legislature, the question of the success of the reorganization study and its implementation is almost irrelevant. In this arena, the reorganization question appears to have been ignored in the face of the policy question of whether the state should be in the business of doing architectural work at all, or at least whether its role should be vastly reduced in favor of more widespread use of private architects. Throughout the period preceding and during the reorganization, as noted above, Architecture had been the butt of severe criticism from private architects, many of whom wanted a larger share in the architectural work of the state. Their pressure finally culminated in legislation. In the 1960 session of the Legislature, Senate Bill 33, an act related to a master plan for higher education, was passed and subsequently signed by the Governor on April 27, 1960. A last-minute amendment to this act gave to the state colleges the authority to contract with private architects for some, or even all, of their architectural and construction work. The significance of the act becomes apparent in view of the fact that this kind of work constituted in 1960 some fifty per cent of the total workload of the Division of Architecture.[6] In the 1961 Legislature, the outside private pressures were again in evidence. The newspapers carried items such as: "The Assembly Interim Committee on Government Organization today charged four firms have received the lion's share of state contracts awarded to private architects. The committee recommends transferring the power to award the contracts from the State Division of Architecture to the State Public Works Board." On November 27 and 28, 1961, the Assembly Interim Committee on Government Organization held hearings at San Jose and Berkeley on the subject of whether state or private architects should be used for the designing of state buildings. In the course of the hearings, Assemblyman Thomas Rees urged that private architects be used, calling Boyd a "dead center architect" and a "buck passer," and asserting that the architects in the Division had not kept in step with modern concepts.

There were, to be sure, voices raised in defense of the Division in 1961, and 1962. In 1961, for example, one newspaper reported that

> State Senator John F. Thompson of Santa Clara County charges material circulated to legislators on behalf of private architecture is unfair and distorted. . . . 'I feel that under the circumstances and considering the tight fiscal control exercised by the legislature and the department of finance over the state college building program which is not exercised over the university, the Division of Architecture has done a magnificent job at San Jose and other state colleges.'

At the 1962 hearings in San Jose and Berkeley, the Chief Counsel of the California State Employees Association insisted that the Division of Architecture "is not as unimaginative as has been charged. The committee should evaluate its work in the light of the conditions under which it works and the money available to it."

Nevertheless, it seemed that pressure had built up to a peak. Two weeks after the November hearings, on December 12, 1961, Anson Boyd announced that he would voluntarily retire at the end of March 1962.[7] And on April 23, 1962, a few weeks after Boyd's retirement, the Governor signed into law an act of the Legislature that removed the office of the State Architect from the civil service; provided for appointment by the Governor, with the approval of the Senate, for a four-year term; and stipulated that the State Architect could be dismissed by the Governor "with or without cause, at any time."

One final postscript is of interest. Five years after the Ernst and Ernst report, on October 1, 1963, the Division of Architecture was moved from its old home in the Department of Public Works to a newly created Department of General Services which itself consisted very largely of the service functions of the Department of Finance. This shift was consistent with that alternative presented by Ernst and Ernst which was predicated upon the establishment of a new Department of General Services. But it was a wry reminder of the origins of the Ernst and Ernst study which seem to have been triggered by the proposal that the Division be transferred to the Department of Finance.

[6] Under the new law, the architectural design projects for state projects began to drop almost immediately. In the last few years, the amount of architectural project work that Architecture did for the state colleges amounted to a little over half of what it had been.

[7] Boyd was sixty-five when he retired. He was able to take advantage of a new law, effective January 1, 1962, which combined the State Employees' Retirement System with the Federal Social Security System, changing certain requirements and making it possible for people to retire several years earlier than the maximum retirement age of seventy and still receive the same retirement benefits.

APPENDIX I:
LIFE CYCLE OF A $1,000,000 PROJECT
Courtesy Division of Architecture

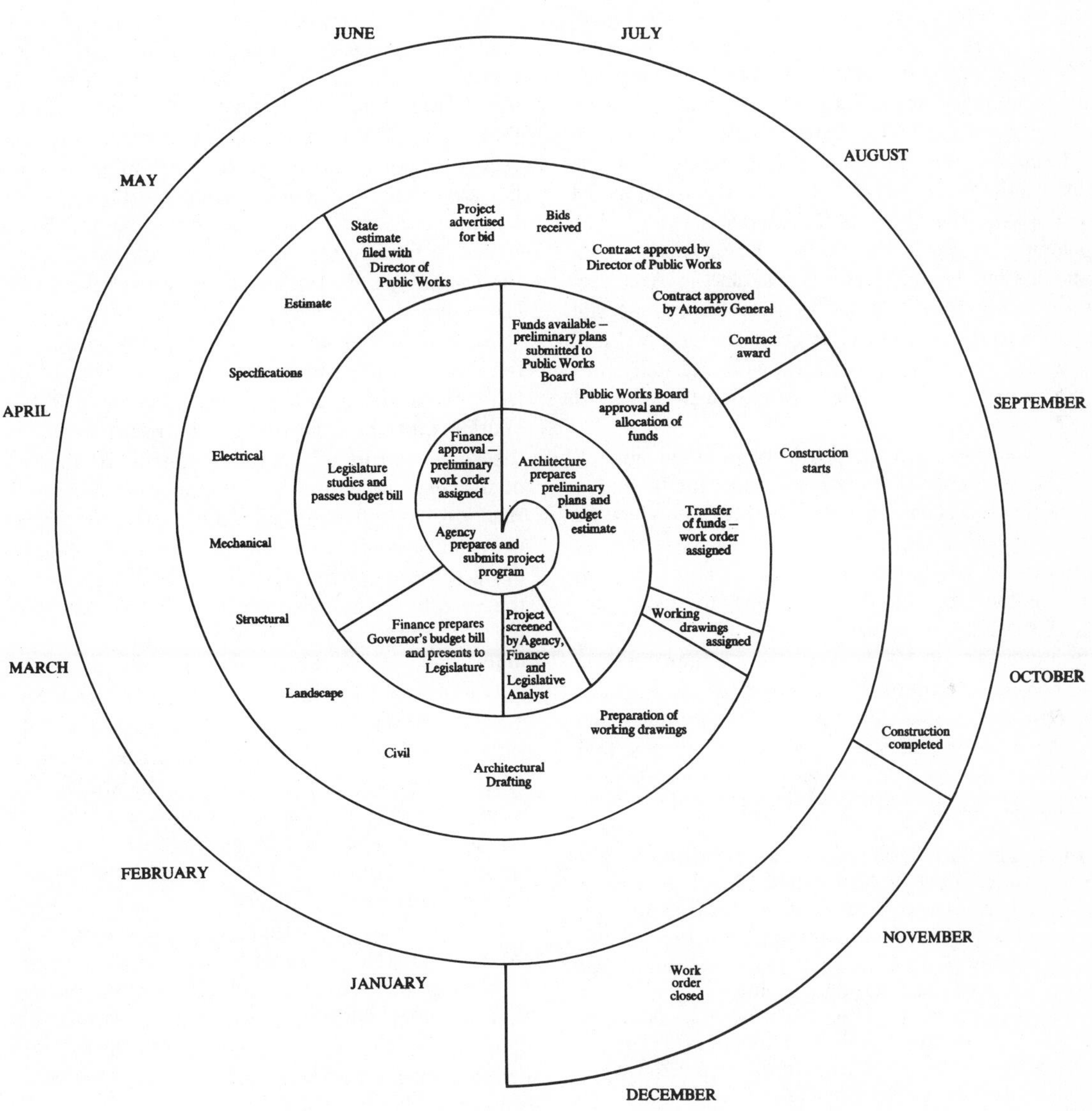

EDITORIAL COMMENTS

Scholars in public administration have for many years decried and deplored the alleged distinction between public policy and politics on the one hand and public administration on the other, emphasizing that each inheres in the other. The study of the Division of Architecture illustrates the interconnection. It was clearly focused on internal, managerial problems, but it was initiated and probably largely motivated by external, political considerations. But the case also suggests that the differentiation is useful and even necessary in the analysis of the series of events as a whole. The principal actors in the study—the consulting firm and the officials in Public Works and in Architecture—themselves concentrated on the managerial aspects to the virtual exclusion of the political and controversial. The legislators who formally authorized the study paid little attention to its report or consequences.

Viewed from the standpoint of political impact, the study seems to have been quite ineffectual—even irrelevant as the author suggests—beyond the very short range. If its basic purpose was to protect and strengthen the autonomy and functions of the Division and its chief and to discourage external criticism and attack—and the events leading up to the survey support such an interpretation —then the exercise must be judged as a failure or, at best, ineffectual. The events that followed the issuance of the report in October 1958 suggest that whatever influence the study had in the wider political scene was quite temporary:

(1) The basic structural reorganization was put into effect in September 1959.
(2) The state colleges were authorized to contract with private architects for their architectural work in 1960 (this had amounted to half the Division's business).
(3) Criticisms of the work of the Division mounted to a peak in November 1961.
(4) The State Architect announced his retirement in December 1961.
(5) The Legislature passed, and the Governor signed, a bill removing the State Architect from civil service protection in April 1962.
(6) And finally, the Division was transferred to the Department of General Services in October 1963.

Thus, within a short period of years, the Division had lost a large share of its business, its chief had retired, his position had been made a "political" one, and the Division had been moved to another department, a transfer that its chief had endeavored to avoid.

Within the narrower managerial terms of reference set for the consultant team and largely adhered to by it, however, one reaches a different conclusion. The real initiator of the reorganization, State Architect Boyd, was satisfied that the report supported his purposes of retaining substantial autonomy, particularly from the threat of the Department of Finance; of providing tools and structure for stronger control over the activities of the Division; and of other changes that gave promise of greater efficiency.

Most of the observers outside the Division—in the Department of Finance, the Office of the Legislative Analyst, the Office of the Director of Public Works, and the consultant firm itself—regarded the study and its effects as successful. At the risk of over-generalization, one might summarize their reactions as reflecting the feeling that the report provided a framework for, and generally encouraged, a more systematic, rationalized approach to the direction, the operations, and the control of the Division's work. It was an antidote for what many regarded as the somewhat loose, somewhat quixotic, somewhat episodic style of leadership of the past. From this standpoint, the subsequent development and installation of the project management system was the key result of the study. And it may be noted that this potentially powerful tool for planning and control was placed under the direction of Hunter, the only one of the leaders who was oriented to management as a specialty. Other evidences of the managerial approach were the establishment, again under Hunter, of the office of Management Analyst, and, later on, the promotion of Meret, who had been charged with organizing the project management system, to the post of Assistant State Architect in charge of the Southern Area.

Reactions among the top leaders of the Division itself were mixed, depending largely, it appears, upon the effects of the recommendations upon the position and status of each individual. In fact, one gleans from the case an almost obsessive concern with titles, ranks, and jurisdictions among a very few men near the top. Very likely, the undertones of this concern were as importantly inter-professional as interpersonal. The manifest official effects of the recommendations were to strengthen the power and position of the elite profession in the Division, the architects, through the advancement of Hampton to the status of Deputy Chief, and concurrently to reduce the power and position of the managerial specialism, personified by Hunter, and of engineering, represented by Herd. But the real effects of the change on the distribution of effective power were considerably different from what appears in the report. Herd actually lost little in the reorganization as it was subsequently directed by Boyd. And over the long pull, Hunter and the approach that he represented probably gained in effective influence through the establishment of the project management system.

Was there much participation in the case, and did it influence the course of events? Clearly there was a great deal of conversation and consultation by the consultant staff with the leaders of the Division, and, to a lesser degree, with representatives of the Director of Public Works, the Legislative Analyst, other state agencies, and even private architects. There was much interviewing with the staff, and the elicitation of staff attitudes was encouraged through the attitude study, conducted just before the survey itself, and by the later questionnaire study of supervisory attitudes and opinions. Most of this staff involvement was for the purpose of gathering data for the study rather than of sharing in the process of reaching decisions. But the relevance of participation by the staff in general was slight because of the focus of the survey on the top levels. Few would be immediately and obviously affected by the report, whatever its recommendations.

It appears that consultation with those most immediately involved was very frequent—almost daily in some cases; and the recommendations were presented and discussed in tentative form before they were finalized. From the point of view of the survey team, these various meetings and conversations probably served three purposes: they provided information as to facts, problems, and the attitudes of those in the key decision-making positions; they provided an opportunity to educate, discuss, persuade; and they furnished information as to what the "market" would accept in the way of recommendations. A large part of this consultation was with Boyd, but under the definition earlier set for this project this does not constitute participation in the usual sense, since Boyd was the principal decision-maker himself. The consultations with the other three officials of the Division—Hunter, Hampton, and Herd—do not appear to have affected the outcome very much, if at all. All responded to the recommendations pretty much in terms of their expectable impact upon them as individuals, and two of the three, Hunter and Herd, were lukewarm or negative.

One concludes that participative practices, though employed in a rather limited way, were not a particularly significant—or even relevant—element in the reorganization process. And they do not appear to have had very much influence one way or the other on the acceptance and implementation of recommendations.

Part Two

ANALYTICAL COMMENTARY

FOREWORD

The review of the foregoing case studies *as a group* suggested certain features and sequences that are common, though with some variations, to all of them. It also revealed certain distinctions among them that appear relevant to the reorganization process in general and to the participation hypothesis in particular. The likenesses led me to develop some generalizations about public administrative agencies and about their reorganization. The differences suggested certain categorizations and classifications which may be helpful to the understanding of public organizations and their change and to the making of studies about them in the future.

I should state to the reader in advance two quite different *caveats* as to the scope of the paragraphs that follow. The first is that, while Chapters I and II appear to go beyond the participation hypothesis, they seem to me essential to judgment about it. If any conclusion is clear-cut, it is that participation is *not* an independent variable. Its positive or negative effects in large organizations depend upon a great many other factors such as: the nature and purposes of the organization; the source of initiative for reorganization and the intent of the reorganizers; the orientations of the people concerned; the content of the reorganization proposed; the stages of reorganization at which participation is, or is not, practiced; and others. A more generalized treatment of these related factors is a necessary introduction to the subject of participation itself.

The second *caveat* is that the pages that follow do not purport to present a rounded, comprehensive theory of public organizations, let alone of organizations in general. This analysis is limited, in the first instance, by the kinds and levels of organizations studied and, secondly, by the focal process to which the cases were directed, i.e., reorganization. More important, stress is laid upon the features of these organizations deriving from their *public* character. A very great proportion of the lore, the literature, and the theory of organizations in general rests upon research and deduction related primarily or exclusively to private organizations or upon lower levels of organization wherein their public or private nature may be, or is, ignored. My approach and my emphasis lay stress upon differences from, rather than likenesses to, much current organizational theory.

DESIGNATION OF CASES

In the chapters that follow, references to individual cases are for convenience made in shortened form according to the following index:

ABBREVIATED REFERENCE	CASE TITLE
Agricultural Research*	*The Regionalization of Business Services in the Agricultural Research Service*
Architecture	*Architects, Politics, and Bureaucracy*
Automation	*Personnel Problems in Converting to Automation*
Ballistics	*The Demise of the Ballistics Division*
Children's Bureau	*The Transfer of the Children's Bureau*
Fish and Game	*A Wildlife Agency and Its Possessive Public*
Highway Patrol	*Reorganization and Reassignment in the California Highway Patrol*
La Loma	*The Guardians of La Loma*
Langley Porter	*The Coming of Age of the Langley Porter Clinic*
Personnel Board	*The Reorganization of the California State Personnel Board*
Philadelphia Health	*Health Centers and Community Needs*
U.S. Public Health**	*Reorganization of the Public Health Service*

* The two cases are treated in most of the discussion as one, since both concerned the same series of events.

** The "U.S." is included in the abbreviated title only for clarification. The agency is officially known as the Public Health Service.

Contents

Foreword, 471

Designation of Cases, 472

CHAPTER I *Organizations in Public Administration* 475

The Organizations in These Cases, *478*
  The Kinds of People Involved, *478*
Public Organizations as Expressions of Social Purposes, *484*
Organization as a System of Tensions, *487*
Summary, *492*

CHAPTER II *Organizational Change 493*

Incremental Change, *493*
Organizational Obsolescence, *494*
Goals of Reorganization, *497*
  Policy and Program, *497*
  Administrative Effectiveness, *498*
  Personnel Problems, *498*
  Response to Outside Pressure or Threat, *498*
The Reorganization Process, *500*
  Background of Reorganizations, *500*
  The Ignition of Reorganization, *502*
  Inception of Studies, *504*
  The Purposes of the Studies, *505*
  The Study Group, *506*
  Foci of Study, *507*
  Study Methods, *509*
  The Decisions, *510*
  Implementation, *510*
Success or Failure? *512*
Summary, *514*

CHAPTER III *Participation and Reorganization* 515

The Participation Hypothesis: Its Development and Rationale, *515*
  The Dynamics of the Small Group, *517*
  Leadership Style, *517*
  The Individual *versus* Formal Organization, *518*
  Power Equalization, *518*
Obstacles to Participation in Public Administration, *519*
Participative Devices in Large Organizations, *521*
Participation in These Cases, *522*
  By Subordinate Officers and Employees, *522*
  Participation by Superiors and Outsiders, *524*
  Seized Participation, *525*
Participation and Reorganizational Effectiveness, *526*
The Context of Reorganization and Participation, *527*
  The Time Factor, *527*
  Organizational Context, *528*
    Categories of Purposes, *529*
    Agency Autonomy-Subordination, *529*
    Accustomed Internal Compliance System and Leadership Style, *529*
    Kinds of Personnel Involved, *530*
    Personnel Systems, *530*

Participation as an Executive Strategy, *531*
The Pros, *531*
The Cons, *533*
The Participation Hypothesis and the Cases, *534*
A Concluding Note on the Study of Organizations, *535*

Charts

I–1:	Principal External Influences on the Course of Reorganization	479
I–2:	Professions and Occupations Principally Involved in the Cases	480
I–3:	Characteristics of Key Executives in Cases	482
I–4:	Examples of Organizational Tensions Relevant to Reorganization Efforts	489
II–1:	Sources of Structural Obsolescence in Organizations in the Cases	496
II–2:	Goals of Reorganization as Seen by Their Principal Initiators and Leaders	499
II–3:	Previous Studies and Reorganization Attempts	501
II–4:	Problems, Tensions, and Issues Present and Building up in the Organizations Studied; Sparks that Ignited the Reorganization Effort	503
II–5:	Characteristics of the Studies Made in the Cases	505
II–6:	Focus of Surveys in Relation to Nature of Survey Group	508
II–7:	Goals of Reorganization as Seen by Those Concerned with Implementation	511
II–8:	Estimates of Effectiveness and Costs of Reorganizations (Grouped According to Degree of Net Success)	513
III–1:	Estimated Degrees of Intra-Agency Participation at Various Stages of the Reorganization Process	524

CHAPTER I

Organizations in Public Administration

Over the last three decades there has developed among social scientists a tremendous interest in organization. Until the 1930's the study of, and writing about, what is now known as formal organization were largely the efforts of those concentrating upon business and public administration. The literature of this period usually, although not always, had a heavily normative flavor—problem-oriented and prescriptive. The splurge of interest in organization as a social phenomenon really began during the 1930's and has since achieved a focal position among most of the social sciences—sociology, social psychology, cultural anthropology, social psychiatry, and, to a lesser extent, economics and political science. In this development, the premises and approaches of the "traditionalists" in business and public administration have often been bypassed and occasionally specifically challenged.

Recent study of organization has taken primarily two forms: broad social or personality or interpersonal theory from which is deduced more specific formulations about behaviors in sectors of society; and quite specific research in individual situations, institutions, and groups, by experiment, controlled observation, and survey. Quite understandably, there has been difficulty in relating the two and a good deal of concern about it. Some of the theoretical formulations have been so broad and vague as to defy testing; and some of the research has been so confined and so narrow in scope as to make generalization hazardous. Yet it would appear that students on both ends of the spectrum have been increasingly conscious of this problem and have been increasingly successful in coping with it. Theoreticians typically refer to individual research products to verify or at least illustrate their hypotheses. And researchers frequently state the theoretical premises and hypotheses upon which they base their studies.

In all of this recent spate of theory and nonprescriptive research on the phenomenon of organization, there has been a conspicuous neglect—or deliberate avoidance—of administrative organizations in the public service, at least those of the type considered in this volume. Much of the early research dealt with organizations whose members were readily accessible and also controllable—preschool children, school children, college students, patients in hospitals and mental institutions. Studies in factories and some other types of business organizations have long been the central core of research in bureaucracy, but these have been augmented by inquiries into voluntary organizations, labor unions, political parties, etc. Studies in governmental agencies have largely been confined to legislative bodies and to personnel and activities well down the policy hierarchy and in fields in which it appears easier to measure results, such as the military, prisons, and schools. There has also been some work in institutions that might be either public or private, such as hospitals, libraries, and research laboratories. The studies directed specifically to government agencies that fall within the rubric of behavioral, organizational research have been exceptional and noteworthy—Selznick's work in TVA, Blau's in social service agencies, Kaufman's in the Forest Service, Gore's in a firehouse, and some others.[1]

The more general works on organization tend to summarize, synthesize, generalize, hypothesize, and theorize, largely on the basis of studies in nonpublic settings. A search of the bibliographies and indexes of most of the recent general books on organization reveals how very, very little the authors relied upon studies of public agencies except

[1] Philip Selznick, *TVA and the Grass Roots: A Study in the Sociology of Formal Organizations* (Berkeley: University of California Press, 1953); Peter M. Blau, *The Dynamics of Bureaucracy, A Study of Interpersonal Relations in Two Government Agencies* (Chicago: University of Chicago Press, 1955); Herbert Kaufman, *The Forest Ranger, A Study in Administrative Behavior* (Baltimore: Johns Hopkins Press, 1960); and W. G. Gore, *Administrative Decision-Making* (New York: John Wiley & Sons, Inc., 1964).

those of the types cited above.[2] Yet the majority of these works lean heavily upon a theoretical framework associated with the word "bureaucracy." And the social science usage of this term stemmed largely from observation of public agencies. The epitome of bureaucracy in the public mind, and in the thinking of a good many social scientists, is, in fact, government. There is a strong, usually implicit, suggestion in much that is written about formal organization today that the hypotheses and the findings that are applicable and verified in one bureaucratic setting may be transferred to another—as from a shoe factory to the Weather Bureau. The suggestion is sometimes made explicit, as in the preface of Rubenstein and Haberstroh's *Some Theories of Organization:*[3]

> Although the dominant emphasis is on commercial and industrial organization, the reader will appreciate that the principles discussed apply to any type of organization, including governmental, philanthropic, military, educational, voluntary, or political.

But the authors provide no evidence to support the statement and no guidance as to what are the "principles" that may be regarded as universally applicable.

The ferment of intellectual activity and the very real contributions that have been made in the study of organization have posed a dilemma for scholars and practitioners in public administration. They may challenge the applicability of knowledge developed in other contexts to government agencies, ignore it, and proceed along their more accustomed paths. Probably a good many of the more "traditional" students of politics and administration have pursued this course. Or they may, on the other extreme, go "whole hog" in the more recent approaches. This in some cases has led to virtual abandonment of their original interest in the government's business. Others have incorporated public agencies within the broader spectrum of all organizations and applied to it the conceptual and methodological tools initially developed elsewhere for a somewhat (or greatly) different subject matter. It is significant that several of the more ambitious recent works on organization were written by persons who—initially at least—were educated as political scientists—such as Simon, March, Presthus, Thompson, Golembiewski, and Gross.[4] Like other general books on organization, theirs rely heavily upon nongovernmental materials and research, but the presumption is strong that they are intended to apply equally to public administration.

Finally, those interested in public organizations may be eclectic, picking and choosing from the general literature those ideas and findings that seem to them relevant or suggestive. It is probable that a majority of the recent texts and academic studies in the public organization area include borrowings from other fields which their authors thought, or at least hoped, were relevant. But the process involves both faith and risk. There has been a paucity of empirical studies to test the applicability of such propositions and findings, developed in other contexts, to public organizations. This current project is very largely such a test: it

---

[2] For example, the bibliography of Herbert A. Simon and James G. March, *Organizations* (New York: John Wiley & Son, Inc., 1958) includes about 35 items of a total of almost 900 which focus on governmental organizations; that of Rensis Likert, *New Patterns of Management* (New York: McGraw-Hill Book Co., Inc., 1961) includes 11 out of 364 items which deal primarily with governmental organizations; and that of Amitai Etzioni, *A Comparative Analysis of Complex Organizations* (New York: The Free Press of Glencoe, Inc., 1961) includes about 140 of more than 900 items that appear to fall within the governmental area. But the bulk of these, about 115, concern somewhat specialized services—penal institutions, military units, hospitals, and education. Only about 27 may be described as "general" government, and more than half of these concern foreign governments. In fact, there is no reference to any publication about American public administration, national, state, or local, by any distinguished scholar in this field other than Herbert A. Simon and his colleagues.

A noteworthy exception, however, is Bertram M. Gross, *The Managing of Organizations* (New York: The Free Press of Glencoe, Inc., 1964). Gross' work includes an annotated bibliography of research studies in organizational behavior as reported in books and journal articles between 1940 and 1962. His own bibliographical search, of which only a portion is reported in the book, included a total of 576 items of which 77 were general government, 87 were education, health and welfare, and 51 were military.

[3] Albert H. Rubenstein and Chadwick H. Haberstroh, eds. (Homewood, Illinois: Dorsey and Irwin, 1960).

[4] Herbert A. Simon and James G. March, *Organizations, op. cit.* (and a number of other works by both authors individually and in collaboration with others); Robert Presthus, *The Organizational Society, An Analysis and a Theory* (New York: Alfred A. Knopf, 1962); Victor A. Thompson, *Modern Organization* (New York: Alfred A. Knopf, 1961); Robert T. Golembiewski, *The Small Group* (Chicago: The University of Chicago Press, 1962); and Bertram M. Gross, *The Managing of Organizations: The Administrative Struggle, op. cit.*

undertakes to evaluate, in a governmental environment, a hypothesis very largely developed with respect to small groups, industrial establishments, labor unions, and political parties.[5]

Some of the more recent books in organizational theory have laid greater stress upon likenesses and differences among organizations, and a few have been premised upon, or have at least stressed, organizational typologies.[6] In fact, the increasing concern about comparative organization with its development of more precise and sophisticated classifications of different kinds of organizations is one of the most promising developments toward a science of organization.[7] But at the present stage of the discipline, the typologies are not very helpful to the student endeavoring to translate empirical research about public administration in terms of general organizational theory. One difficulty appears to be the insufficient precision of the types, the facts that: (1) many if not most complex organizations "spill over" into two or more different classes of organizations and even more different sub-classes; and (2) many typologies group together in common classes organizations of obviously different characteristics (such as military, foreign affairs, fire fighting, and tax departments, all grouped on the basis that they service the general public).

A second difficulty arises from the facts that most large and complex organizations include a number of different levels, and that each level comprehends a variety of units with differing kinds of personnel and functions. A military department today is made up of sub-organizations which are educational, internal service, external service, religious, industrial, commercial, profit-making, eleemosynary, scientific and research, policy-making, and combat; it encompasses both the creative and the routine; it also comprehends most of the principal kinds of professions and specialists now extant, as well as most styles of administration, supervision, motivation, persuasion, and coercion currently known. It contains within itself a great variety of types of bureaucracy, and it serves and is responsive to a number of different clienteles, though it is presumably dedicated to the national interest in general. To a somewhat lesser extent, the same is true of most other very large organizations—private businesses, universities, public schools, and labor unions. Further, one may not simply class together the various sub-units of larger organizations with comparable units of other large organizations, for it is clear that the larger unit affects the characteristics of the smaller. A chapel on an army base is similar in some respects, but it is not identical, to a community church or to a chapel on a university campus. Each derives character from the larger organization of which it is a part. Clearly our taxonomy of organization must be one of considerable depth which takes into account a variety of different kinds of dimensions.

A third difficulty of recent typologies, which is of considerable concern to students of government, arises from the tendency to overlook or deliberately bypass the traditional distinction between *public* and *private* organizations of the administrative type. Clearly some kinds of organizations, such as hospitals, universities, research laboratories, fall within both public and private categories and are in many ways like to each other. Even among these, however, there are significant organizational differences arising from their public or private governments. In most governmental agencies, including most of those described in the foregoing cases, the differences from private "counterparts" are more than marginal. They relate to the systems of legitimation and current control, to history and tradition, scope, political exposure and vulnerability, legislative and executive influence, and other elements. In recent years there have been evidences that public and private administration have been moving toward each other. But there clearly remain crucial differences between them. Any student who has analyzed comparatively public and private practices in planning or in budgeting and finance or in personnel could attest to this.

In the sections that follow I attempt no general typology of organizations. Rather I seek to describe

---

[5] Although at least a part of the participation conception originated about 2,500 years ago in government, and its principal early proponent in this century in America was Mary Parker Follett, a political scientist. A brief historical discussion of the development of the participation hypothesis concept is to be found in Chapter III of this analysis.

[6] Etzioni, *op. cit.*, is very largely devoted to typological analysis, with the primary frame resting on the nature of the system of compliance.

[7] For a useful review of typologies of formal organizations, see Peter M. Blau and W. Richard Scott, *Formal Organizations: A Comparative Approach* (San Francisco: Chandler Publishing Company, 1962), Chapter Two. Blau and Scott rely principally upon a typology based upon the primary beneficiaries of organizations.

and classify some of those features among the organizations in these cases that appear to me distinctive, at least in relation to much current organizational literature. All of the organizations are public in character, but it is possible that some of the characteristics to which attention is called might apply to either public or private organizations.

THE ORGANIZATIONS IN THESE CASES

The reader of the cases in this volume cannot but be impressed by the wide variety of accustomed behaviors, decision-making patterns, and types of interpersonal relationships that are represented in the different organizations they concern. Yet all at least superficially conformed to the main features of the familiar bureaucratic prototype. They were hierarchical in their formal structure and operated within a framework of formalized division and delegation of authorities and responsibilities from top to bottom. They consisted of an agglomeration of positions (offices), each presumed to have set duties and responsibilities and to reflect rank within the organizations. The positions were in most cases defined on the basis of duties, and in almost all duties classification was the principal determinant of salary. The bulk of the personnel were employed and advanced according to some style of merit system and had protection of tenure in their agencies and grades, if not in their specific jobs. Most of the officers and top-level personnel had been with the organization for some time and could expect to remain there for some time, even though shifts in leadership at the very top were not uncommon and indeed were key events in many of the cases.

All of the focal organizations in these cases except one[8] were intermediate in a larger structure of organization. That is, they were subordinate parts of larger organizations, sometimes several echelons from the top; and they consisted of two or more levels of sub-organizations. With the exception noted above, the primary decision-making authority was vested in a single hierarchical executive, but his determinations were at least potentially subject to review and modification by his own superiors in the hierarchy. The degree of autonomy of executives with respect to internal organizational change varied considerably and was a significant condition upon the use of participative devices. (See Chapter III.) But, as shown in Chart I–3, those executives whose decisions were focal in these cases in most instances had substantial authority *vis-à-vis* their own bosses, at least on the organizational questions involved in the cases.

In most of the foregoing features, the organizations in these cases conform to the familiar bureaucratic model and also are probably representative of most sizable organizations in government. In some other respects, the applicability of any single model is less clear. For example, all of these organizations operated in a political context. Political considerations conditioned important decision-making even on such matters as internal organization, over which one might expect hierarchical officials to have dominant authority. In other words, extra-organizational forces, interests, and powers entered into decisions of this nature, even where the question at hand appeared to be purely internal. The degree of exposure to external influences as well as the principal loci of such influences varied widely among these organizations, the spectrum extending from the *Personnel Board* case, where they were effectively neutralized, to *Fish and Game* and *La Loma,* where they virtually "took over" at some stages of the proceedings. Further, it is clear from an examination of these cases that the force of external influence varied widely within the same organization at different times, with changing conditions, and with different issues. These external forces included: formal institutions within the administrative structure, such as budget and finance offices, and other departments and agencies; legislators, their committees and influential members; political party organizations and leaders; clientele groups, and other nongovernmental interests; and even the general voting public. (See Chart I–1.)

The Kinds of People Involved

Much of the literature concerning management, including that which deals with participation, has grown out of studies in industrial and other business settings. Here too there is a distinct difference

[8] The exception is the somewhat special instance of *La Loma* in which the principal decision-making unit was the city council.

CHART I–1. *Principal external influences on the course of reorganization*

CASE	*Other Administrative Agencies*	*Legislative Body*	*Outside Groups*
Agricultural Research	Adm. Asst. Secy., Agriculture	(Congress'l agriculture committees)	(Clientele of program branches)
Architecture	Finance Dept. (Personnel Bd.)	*State Assembly & Senate Committees* *Legislative Analyst*	Private architects
Automation	(Personnel Bd.) (Finance Dept.) (Other agencies in Dept.)		Calif. State Employees Assn.
Ballistics	Technical Dir. of Laboratory Aeromechanics Div. (Military Dept., Washington)		
Children's Bureau	Exec. Office of the President *Budget Bureau* Pub. Health Service (Dept. of Labor)	Congress	Health & welfare depts. in states Civic welfare groups (Labor unions)
Fish and Game	(Finance Dept.) (Fish & Game Comn.)	*State Assembly & Senate committees* *Legislative Analyst*	*Organized wildlife groups*
Highway Patrol	*Finance Dept.* (Governor's Office)		(Calif. Assn. of Highway Patrolmen) (Intern'l Assn. of Chiefs of Police)
La Loma		*City Council*	*Electorate*
Langley Porter	*Finance Dept.* Budget officer, State Dept. of Mental Hygiene UC officials (Other state mental hospitals)	(Appropriations committees)	(Natl. Institute of Mental Health) (Mental health & hygiene assns.)
Personnel Board	(Other state agencies) (Finance Dept.)	(State Assembly & Senate committees)	(Calif. State Employees Assn.)
Philadelphia Health	Managing Director's Office (Mayor's office)		(Health & Welfare Council) (Nurses' assns.)
U.S. Public Health	Officials of Health, Education & Welf. Budget Bureau	*Congressional committees*	Mental health groups State mental hygiene agencies Psychiatrists

KEY: *Italicized phrase:* a dominant influence shaping the reorganization. Phrase not italicized: influence was substantial but not necessarily decisive. (Phrase in parentheses): potential influence was largely neutralized or, for other reasons, inarticulate.

from most of the organizations treated in these cases. A large share of the industrial relations literature is premised upon a dichotomy between workers and management, as two different distinguishable classes, complementary but also in open or potential conflict. Participation has been viewed principally as a device whereby managerial powers of decision may be shared with workers that the latter may benefit through widened perspectives, greater job challenges, and better opportunities for self-actualization on the job.

Yet, in most of the cases described herein the management-worker dichotomy barely appears, at least in the terms it is discussed in industrial sociology. There are in all of these organizations numbers of lower grade workers—laborers, orderlies, clerks, typists, custodians. But only rarely do they play any significant part in the reorganization process. This is partly a matter of the level of focus: most of these cases concerned organizational change near the top of organizations of considerable size. The effects upon workers at the lowest grades would in few instances be substantial, and in many would be nonexistent.

Also significant is the fact that in the majority of these cases, the *dramatis personae* consisted of professionals, and this was true both of management and subordinates, wherever one wishes to draw the line between them. (See Chart I–2.) The professionals were not only the staff specialists; they held the key jobs in the line, and they were also the workers in the vineyard. As such they were typically well-educated, with at least a college degree, and many held advanced degrees up to and including Ph.D.'s. Some were at one time professors. Most of them were representative of professions that are widely recognized both inside and outside government—natural scientists, doc-

CHART I–2. *Professions and occupations principally involved in the cases**

CASE	*Basic Elite*	*Sub-Orientations*	*Other Line Professions*	*Auxiliary Professions*
Agricultural Research	agricultural research	various research specialties	regulatory	management personnel purchasing accounting
Architecture	architecture		engineering	management
Automation†			electronic data-processing	personnel
Ballistics	physical sciences	project (hardware) disciplines	engineering	
Children's Bureau	social welfare	social security age-group (children) enforcement (child labor)	public health	
Fish and Game	wildlife management	biologists game management fisheries management		
Highway Patrol	law enforcement			management
Langley Porter	psychiatry	patient care teaching research	library social welfare clinical psychol. nursing rehab., therapy	business-accounting
Personnel Board	personnel	classification examining pay		management analysis
Philadelphia Health	public health	community functional	nursing sanitary engineering	personnel budgeting
U.S. Public Health	public health	community functional patient care research	psychiatry nursing sanitary engineering	management statistics

* A summary table of those occupational fields principally involved in the reorganization effort *within* the agencies. This is not a census of all occupations employed in the organizations. The word "profession" is used herein somewhat loosely to comprehend occupational fields of specialization requiring recognized educational and experience backgrounds.

† *Automation* is a somewhat special instance. Most of the work involved was clerical, but the case itself involved the development of a specialized occupational field—i.e., data processing.

tors and public health officers, psychiatrists, architects, engineers, agriculturists, biologists. Others were in fields of activity striving for full professional recognition, and they viewed their own roles in professional terms—personnel officers, nurses, wildlife specialists, social workers, accountants, and policemen.

Typically in these organizations there was a single professional group which, in effect, constituted an elite corps, elite in the sense both of relatively high status and of power over the activities and personnel of the agency. The single profession from which this corps was drawn came from a similar background of training and experience and one which was, or had been, presumed to comprehend the basic substantive activities of the agency.[9] But most agencies were composed of more than one kind of profession. The representation from other professions seems to have arisen in response to three kinds of needs. First, some professionals were employed to support the substantive, line activities. These include accountants and other finance specialists, personnel officers, supply officers, attorneys and others often included under the rubrics "administration," or "auxiliary staff." Second, specialists were employed to carry on, with the elite professionals, parts or aspects of the substantive work—such as nurses in hospitals, engineers in research laboratories, and many others. Third, different kinds of specialists were added to bring to bear new skills and perspectives on substantive problems or to take care of new and added responsibilities not formerly within the purview of the agency—such as social workers in mental institutions, engineers in agricultural research agencies, sanitary engineers in public health organizations, and many others.

A related phenomenon has arisen out of the well-known tendency in our society for specialized fields or professions to fissure into sub-specializations, each bearing its separate identification, point of view, and style of operating. Under these circumstances specializations become "different" professions, and the professional structure is similar to that outlined in the paragraph above. This phenomenon is easily observable in some of the cases in this volume, such as *Agricultural Research, Personnel Board,* and *Fish and Game.*

Most of the organizations in these cases actually employed a number of different kinds of specializations, many of which may, by almost any definition, properly be considered professions. In most of them the central professional corps maintained its elite status and influence, even though there was inter-professional competition and jockeying for position. This is in interesting and significant contrast with the findings and assumptions of many students of organization that the "specialists," the experts, are "staff," whereas the line officers are presumably non-expert "generalists." An oft-quoted study by Melville Dalton of line-staff relations in several business organizations found that the staff personnel were significantly better educated, younger, more carefully groomed, and had generally higher *social* status than line officers.[10] The evidence from the cases in this volume would suggest that the line personnel were specialists, that they were on the average educated as well as, or better than, others in the organization but in different fields, and that those line officers who represented the elite organizational profession had distinctly higher organizational—and probably social—status than the staff.

A brief examination of the top executive officials who were principally involved in the cases suggests that they typically were *primus inter pares*—their equals being others in the elite profession of the agency. (See Chart I–3.) Again one is impressed by their educational attainments. Of a total of twenty-one,[11] all but six had college degrees, and one of these completed requirements for his degree during the period of the case. Three had Ph.D.'s, and five had M.D.'s; in fact, a number of them have, since the action in the cases, accepted academic posts at universities. One subsequently became a college president. Even at the time of the cases, many of these officials enjoyed eminent reputations as leaders in their professions which reached far beyond the dimensions of their agency

[9] There is an interesting and surely not coincidental parallel between the organization of many governmental agencies on the one hand and the organization of professional training and of the professions themselves on the other; public works–engineers; forest services–foresters; public health–doctors; mental institutions–psychiatrists; school systems–educators; and indeed most of the others. A cause-effect relationship undoubtedly goes both ways. Professions have been developed and recognized in response to governmental needs, expressed through organizations—as in the case of forestry. And public organizations have been shaped to some extent to accommodate the abilities and interests of individual professions.

[10] "Conflicts Between Staff and Line Managerial Officers," *American Sociological Review* 15: 342-351, June 1950.

[11] Not including any from the somewhat special case of *La Loma.*

CHART I–3. *Characteristics of key executives in cases*

CASE	*Executive*	*Position*	*Academic Degrees*	*Professional Field*	*Status of Prof. Field in Agency*	*Appointment from within or from outside of Agency*	*Autonomy vis-à-vis Superior**
Agricultural Research	Shaw	Administrator, ARS	Ph.D.	agric. research	elite	within	XX
	Spencer	Ass't Admin. for Mgmt.	none	administration	support	within	XX
	Adams	Western Business Mgr.	LL.B.	administration	support	within	X
Architecture	Gilliss	Director, Public Works	none	accounting-engineering	elite	within	XXX
	Boyd	State Architect	none	architecture	elite	outside	XX
Automation	Burkett	Director, Employment	LL.B.	no info.		outside	XXX
	Bashline	Chief, Tabulating Section	none	data processing	support	within	XX
	Steedman	Personnel Officer	B.A.	personnel	support	within	XX
Ballistics	Warner	Head, Research & Weapons Development	Ph.D.	physics	elite	outside	XXX
Children's Bureau	Miller	Administrator, FSA	none	no info.		outside	XX
	Altmeyer	Social Sec. Commissioner	Ph.D.	social security	elite	within	XX
	Lenroot	Chief, Children's Bureau	B.A.	child welfare	elite	within	X
Fish and Game	Gordon	Director, Fish & Game	none	wildlife	elite	outside	XX
	Warne	Director, Fish & Game	B.A.	administration		outside	XX
Highway Patrol	Crittenden	Commissioner, California Highway Patrol	LL.B.	law		outside	XXX
La Loma	Henderson	City Clerk	none	none			XXX
	Allen	City Administrative Officer	none	administration			X
Langley Porter	Simon	Medical Superintendent	M.D.	psychiatry	elite	within	XX
Personnel Board	Fisher	Executive Officer	M.S.	personnel	elite	within	XXX
Philadelphia Health	Dixon	Commissioner, Public Health	M.D., M.S.	public health	elite	outside	XXX
	Hanlon	Director, Public Health Services	M.D., M.S. M.P.H.	public health	elite	outside	XX
U.S. Public Health Service	Burney	Surgeon General	M.D., M.P.H.	public health	elite	within	XX
	Felix	Director, NIMH	M.D.	psychiatry	elite	outside	XX

* Judgments as to degree of autonomy within the hierarchy with regard to reorganizational decision are keyed as follows: XXX—very great autonomy; decision-maker has virtually free hand within very general guidelines; XX—substantial autonomy; decision-maker has primary initiatory authority, but it is subject to review and modification; X—restricted autonomy; decision-maker is subject to fairly specific action guide rules and careful review. A few of these judgments are inferred and untested in the cases.

or even of their jurisdiction. All but eight had training relevant to their profession; five exceptions probably considered themselves professionals through long experience in the less clearly defined field of public administration.[12] Of the group, only three were professionals in fields other than the elite profession of the agency. About half of the entire group were in the nature of political appointments, and two of the three professionals in other fields cited above were in that category. It is interesting, too, that although so many could identify themselves with the elite profession of their agency, only half can be said to have come up through the agency's ranks. The others were appointed, or transferred, to their present positions from other employment.[13]

To summarize, we have noted that the premise of the labor-management dichotomy does not appear very helpful. We are dealing in the main with well-educated men, most of whom hold important and challenging posts. The issues of job-enlargement for purposes of growth, self-actualization, and avoidance of monotony do not loom as large as they might on a production line (although they appear in some cases such as *Personnel Board).* The elite group, typically including the principal executive, represented a common professional background of training and experience and shared a common professional view of the world and of the agency which it was serving. In most cases, the agency was seen by members of the elite as complementing if not embodying the purposes and aspirations of their profession, not as its mortal enemy. Other professions and specialties, perhaps not recognized as full-fledged professions, were also employed, sometimes in very substantial number. And finally there were large numbers of workers of lesser skill, lesser status, and lesser identification with each other.

This view of the composition of the organization has implications for the way in which participation is viewed in relation to each component group. It would appear that participation in organizational decisions could be classified into three different categories, and might be expected to have a differing significance in each:

participation by members of the "in group," the elite profession of whom the executive is normally also a member;
participation by members of other professions and specialties, of whom the executive is *not* normally one;
participation by other workers.

Virtually all appointive public executives are also, in some degree, subordinates. They too have bosses. Members of organizations often view their executive as a representative before his own hierarchical superiors and the outside world rather than as their antagonist. He may view his own role similarly. When the executive is widely recognized as a leader of the profession predominant within the agency, it may be hypothesized that the confidence in him held by professional colleagues is increased and the need of participation to gain support and acquiescence in organizational change is correspondingly diminished. But such a professional identification may have exactly the opposite effect for other professionals, specialists, and workers. And it may also work the other way where there has been a sharp internal cleavage within the elite professional group into sub-specialties, and the "boss" is viewed as representing primarily only one of the sub-groups. One might logically expect, then, that participation, viewed as a device to gain understanding of and support for proposed or-

---

[12] Three of the exceptions were pretty closely linked by their prior experience to the "elite" groups. Crittenden of the *Highway Patrol* case was an attorney, but his prior experience as a district attorney was closely related to the police field. Warne of *Fish and Game* was a general administrator, but much of his experience had been in various related capacities with the U.S. Department of Interior. Although Gordon of *Fish and Game* did not possess an advanced degree, he had forty years of direct experience in the wildlife field and was widely regarded as one of the foremost specialists in that field in the country.

[13] The educational and professional attainments of this small group seem to be roughly representative of those of public executives in general, as indicated in statistical surveys in recent years. See, for example: California Commission on California State Government Organization and Economy, *A Study of Management Manpower Requirements, California State Government* (Sacramento: Commission on California State Government Organization and Economy, 1965); John J. Corson and R. Shale Paul, *Men Near the Top: Top Management in the Federal Career Service* (Washington: The Brookings Institution, 1965); Municipal Manpower Commission, *Governmental Manpower for Tomorrow's Cities* (New York: McGraw-Hill Book Co., Inc., 1954); David T. Stanley, *The Higher Civil Service* (Washington: The Brookings Institution, 1964); David T. Stanley and Associates, *Professional Personnel for the City of New York* (Washington: The Brookings Institution, 1963); and W. Lloyd Warner, Paul P. Van Riper, Norman H. Martin, and Orvis F. Collins, *The American Federal Executive* (New Haven: Yale University Press, 1963).

ganizational change, would be most important among

(1) professionals and specialists *not* in the elite profession,
(2) members of sub-specialties of professions wherein there has been internal cleavage, and
(3) other employees in those instances where their work and relationships may be seriously involved, rare in these cases.

There has, in recent organizational literature, been considerable stress upon, and also despair about, the alleged divorce and conflict between hierarchical authority and specialized competence. One book stated as its underlying thesis that "the most symptomatic characteristic of modern bureaucracy is the growing imbalance between ability and authority"—ability being associated with specialized knowledge and skill. "There is a growing gap between the right to decide, which is authority, and the power to do, which is specialized ability."[14] There may be grounds for such a concern in other than public bureaucracies and at either the lower or higher reaches of large governmental agencies. But there is rather little evidence in these intermediate-level organizations of a divorce between specialized ability and hierarchical authority. Most of the hierarchical leaders were professionals and specialists in their own right, and many had earned high prestige through previous work in the field of their specialty. That field was characteristically the same as, or closely identified with, the primary activity of their organizations. In every case but one, they endeavored to bring to bear upon their decisions information and advice from a variety of specialists, both within and outside of their organization. Indeed, the more basic problem appears to have been approximately the reverse of that quoted above: the danger that decisions with broad implications would be made by persons too narrowly specialized and on the basis of too highly specialized information. However, the problem may exist as between the heads of organizations and: their hierarchical superiors, many of whom are politically appointed or elected generalists; outside institutional control agencies such as central budget and personnel offices; and legislatures. But such offices and individuals are also specialized in fields relevant to organizational decision—in personnel or budget administration, in politics, in assessing and predicting public reactions, or in relating proposals to activities and objectives in other fields. The problem seems less one of a gap between authority and ability to decide than one of bringing to bear upon a given decision, in appropriate emphases, a vast amount of specialized information and many different points of view.

PUBLIC ORGANIZATIONS AS EXPRESSIONS OF SOCIAL PURPOSES

Much of the literature and research concerning formal organization and organizational behavior has minimized or effectively bypassed the treatment of *organizational purpose* as an important and dynamic variable.[15] This has probably been useful where the central focus of study is upon some other subject such as group structure and behavior, or role, or leadership style, or bureaucratic structure. Organization is seen more as a platform upon which human beings may be observed and studied than as a cooperative system for the accomplishment of purposes. It is interesting that Chester Barnard, in his still authoritative work on the *Functions of the Executive,* chose to define formal organization without reference to purpose;[16] yet in subsequent pages, he described the formulation and definition of purpose as one of the three basic executive functions. Many of the more recent studies, in contrast, have not accorded the continuing definition of purpose any such dynamic attribute. Some state it, or take it for granted, as a *given* in the situation (as, for example, did Peter M. Blau in his study of two un-

[14] Both quotations from Victor A. Thompson, *Modern Organization, op. cit.,* p. 6. Stress is also laid upon this thesis by Robert A. Presthus in *The Organizational Society, An Analysis and a Theory, op. cit.*

[15] There have recently been a number of distinguished exceptions, including Herbert A. Simon in a number of his publications and Bertram M. Gross, in his two-volume work, *The Managing of Organizations, op. cit.* The study of organizational purposes—or "teletics" to use Gross' neologism—is the backbone of his work and fills more than one-third of its 890 pages.

[16] His definition: "A system of consciously coordinated activities or forces of two or more persons." (Cambridge: Harvard University Press, 1938, p. 81).

identified public agencies[17]). Others have largely bypassed purpose by describing it as the product of values, which are "givens" and therefore not susceptible to scientific analysis. The object of attention thus becomes the efficiency with which purposes are carried out, which can allegedly be reduced to factual determination, rather than the purposes themselves.

Perhaps the most frequent escape from the purpose question in studies of organizational behavior has been by the route of simplification. Some studies assume that organizations are bodies which have, or are presumed to have, single uni-dimensional purposes and which produce measurable, quantitative products toward these purposes. In such studies, organizational purpose is assumed to be constant, unchanging and agreed upon. Effectiveness can then be measured objectively in terms of productivity; and other variables, such as nature of leadership or communications networks, can be tested against it. This kind of approach has characterized many of the studies associated with the Hawthorne experiments, the Survey Research Center in Michigan, the Tavistock Institute, and many others. It has also been true of investigations of the effect of bureaucratic structure upon personality wherein it is normally assumed, or established, that organizational purpose and individual purpose are in conflict.

Undoubtedly, in some kinds of simple and stable organizations, particularly those that produce measurable physical things, organizational purpose can be fruitfully stabilized, simplified, or otherwise effectively eliminated as a variable. There is no intention here of deprecating the value of those studies which have neutralized it. Yet, one fact that is abundantly clear from the cases in this volume is that purposes were a central element in these government organizations and that they were not stable *givens*. The efforts to modify the structures either derived from, or were importantly conditioned by, shifting and competing views on purpose. In a few of them (such as *Agricultural Research* and *La Loma*), the changing of purpose was not the prime object of organizational change. Even in these, however, the future control over purpose and over programs to accomplish purposes was focal. The centrality and dynamics of purposes in efforts to bring about organizational change was evident in most of the cases. Some examples are:

U.S. Public Health, in which a study of organizational structure followed after a comprehensive analysis and projection of mission, and reorganization was specifically viewed as a mechanism to bring about changes in mission;

Langley Porter, in which one of the principal products, if not the most important one, was the reaching of new understanding and agreements about the purposes of the clinic;

Ballistics, in which the underlying problem concerned the overall mission of the division in the laboratory—project-oriented or discipline-oriented;

Fish and Game, in which organization structure was viewed as essentially secondary to the kinds of programs and policies to be pursued in the future.

In these four cases, the modification of organization structure was important primarily as a means to the change of emphasis in organizational purposes. Most of the others involved purpose in some degree since all of them had to do with the locus of control over purpose definition in the future. It is apparent that any effort to neutralize organizational purpose in the analysis of these cases would be artificial and self-defeating. It may therefore be useful to set forth some of the propositions on which much of the later discussion is premised.[18]

(1) **The organizations in these cases are here understood as associations of human efforts directed to the accomplishment of purposes.** Such *organizational purposes* are seldom, if ever, identical with the individual purposes of any person working in or in contact with the organization; they are not to be confused with motivations, even though they condition, and are conditioned by, motivations.[19]

[17] *The Dynamics of Bureaucracy* (Chicago: University of Chicago Press, 1955).

[18] For reasons that should become evident in the ensuing paragraphs, the expression "organizational purpose" almost defies a clear-cut definition. "Purpose" clearly involves intent as to the future (commitment and futurity according to Gross, *op. cit.*, p. 469). Whether an organization as such can have an intent is very nearly a metaphysical question. On the other hand, individual members, controllers, and observers certainly ascribe purposes to organizations and their ascriptions may vary widely to the same organization. I draw no fine lines in these pages among such words as mission, goal, objective, end, but associate all of them within the blanket of purpose.

[19] Herbert A. Simon recently wrote: "By *goals* we shall mean value premises that can serve as inputs to decisions. By *motives* we mean the causes, whatever they are, that lead individuals to select some

(2) **Public administrative organizations are characteristically established, and their purposes defined, either in broad and general or in narrow and specific terms, outside the organizations themselves.** That is to say, they are legitimized by controlling bodies other than themselves. The administrative agencies in government normally have been established for some time in the past by their hierarchical superiors, by legislative body, by constitution or charter, by popular vote, or by a combination of these. Their purposes are, or were at some time in the past, recognized and authorized by superior agencies. Further, those public agencies that rely upon public funds that are appropriated annually (all of those in these cases) are subject to annual review of their activities and, in effect, annual renewal of their authorities by outside agencies, especially by the legislative body. The budget process is seldom sufficiently thorough and penetrating, however, to warrant consideration as a renewed legitimation, but it is a continuing reminder that agencies are creatures of authorities outside themselves. And the budget is a frequent device for amending or modifying purposes and purpose emphases.

In agencies that have a long history, the structure as well as the initial purposes for which they were established may have become obsolete in terms of developing conditions and needs. In varying degrees such agencies may have authority within themselves to modify their structures to accord with emerging emphases of purposes. But often the authorities that originally legitimized them inhibit their ability to bring about such changes.

(3) **The organizational purposes of governmental organizations are therefore presumed to be the satisfaction or elimination of needs felt or anticipated outside the organizations themselves.** That is to say, *their purposes are intended to be social.* This is not to state piously that the individual desires of organizational members do not influence the purposes of organizations. But the legitimacy of a public agency and the underlying rationale for its operations rest, except in very unusual circumstances, upon the determination of some authoritative office or group at some time that its purposes are to satisfy some social need. Indeed, any substantial influences upon organizational goals by individual members in their own interests are, in varying degrees, perceived in our society as irregular, unethical, immoral, or illegal. The point is labored here in order to make clear that, in the consideration of governmental organizations, the primary criterion must always be in terms of their effectiveness in accomplishing social purposes. Other criteria, such as the satisfactions, the morale, the development, etc., of employees, while important, must always be considered secondary to the primary one. Perhaps the principal significance of such other factors lies in the degree to which they are instrumental to effectiveness in contributing to organizational purposes. The point was nicely illustrated in the *Highway Patrol* case. Following a careful organizational study, Commissioner Crittenden determined on a basic pattern of reorganization. He then proceeded to an equally careful planning of individual assignments of his officers in order to minimize hurts and dissatisfactions that might have arisen from the plan. The organizational purposes were clearly given primary consideration; the welfare of individuals followed.

(4) **Organizational purposes are multiple in sizable public organizations; and they are complex.** Their complexity is particularly conspicuous among government agencies and especially those operating in controversial fields, where many different groups are continuously striving to modify programs in directions of interest to themselves. Even in the most staid and established agencies, however, purposes are multiple, sometimes in conflict or competition with each other, and amorphous at the fringes. No exact and final statement of an organization's purposes is ever possible; the environment within which it operates is always, in some degree, changing; its internal membership and internal relationships are changing. Outside observers can best define purposes after the fact: i.e., purposes are ultimately spelled out only by what the organization *has done.* It is easier to define an agency's overall mission in overall terms than it is to break the mission down into its constituent parts and give correct emphasis to each part. Thus the mission of the California Highway Patrol, in its most general terms, superficially appears very nearly the simplest of all the agencies in these cases: to maintain safety on the roads. But within that broad charter, how much emphasis, what proportion of its efforts and resources, should it allocate to enforcing the speed limit, to arresting offenders, to popular education about highway hazards, to helping stranded drivers, to identifying and restoring stolen cars, to catching

goals rather than others as premises for their decisions." "On the Concept of Organizational Goal," *Administrative Science Quarterly*, Vol. 9, No. 1 (June 1964), p. 3.

criminals sought by local police departments and the FBI, to providing services to legislators and other state officials, etc.? To what extent should its primary purposes be guided and even modified to avoid violating other values widely held in our society, such as those of fair play and avoidance of secrecy—important considerations in the use of unmarked cars, non-uniformed officers, and speed traps?

(5) **Organizational purposes are particularly difficult to define in those agencies operating in dynamic areas where needs, or knowledge, or technology are changing rapidly.** The sudden development of new or vastly increased health dangers resulting from atomic explosions, from smog, and from unsanitary water supplies, for example, forced a complete reevaluation of the purposes of the Public Health Service. New developments in psychiatric treatment impinged heavily upon the purposes of the Langley Porter Clinic. Among agencies operating in such volatile fields as these, organizational purposes seem to be in a continuous race to keep up with shifting needs, and this means that purposes themselves are in a state of flux.

(6) **Purposes of an organization are seldom if ever perceived in exactly the same way by different members thereof nor by others outside who have association with it or influence over it.** This is probably true to such an extent that one can doubt the existence of any real, "pure," and exact set of organizational purposes other than as a metaphysical amalgam of the purposes perceived by a wide variety of individuals, appropriately weighted according to their degrees of influence upon what the organization actually does. What, for example, are the correct emphases upon the differing purposes of the Langley Porter Clinic? Some in the Department of Mental Hygiene would probably place primary emphasis upon treatment of the mentally ill; students and some professors at the University of California would probably lay emphasis upon its use as a teaching facility; some of the scientists on its staff would give first place to research.

These cases lend a great deal of support to the idea and the importance of roles: *the perspectives on organizational purpose of different individuals in, or having to do with, organizations are heavily conditioned by the positions from which they view them.* In virtually all of the cases, differing perceptions of organizational purpose were in some degree predictable from the nature and degree of responsibility, the background, the present position, and the prospective future of the viewers. This phenomenon has enabled us, in the following section, to group and classify some predictable points of view and conflicts that are common in these organizations.

ORGANIZATION AS A SYSTEM OF TENSIONS

It is useful for analytic purposes to consider organizations that are not in the midst of basic change processes as systems of conflicting or competing forces in equilibrium. That is, the forces in one direction are approximately equal to those in the other, and any moderate change in the strength of the forces on one side will be compensated over time by an adjusment of about equal strength by the opposing forces.

The existence of such opposing forces is a continuing source of tensions within or having to do with organizations. We consider herein the existence of tensions, some of them growing out of varying views and desires as to purpose, to be universal in associative human behavior.[20] Such tensions may be, and probably are, latent at any given time; they may not be consciously apparent, even to those who are immediately involved. Further, it must be assumed that there are strong bonds in human associations working in the direction of containing tensions—i.e., preventing one set of the opposing forces from overpowering the other. These perhaps inhere in the very meaning of organizations: the pressure for continuity, stability, maintenance of the status quo, and cohesiveness. Clearly without their existence, at least in some degree, the possibility of continuing predictability in social behavior would vanish.

The equilibrium theory of organization utilized here is borrowed to some extent from the works of Kurt Lewin[21] and also, in part, from Chester

[20] A tension is here understood as a quality of a relationship among people or among identifiable groups of people centering around one or more issues on which there is underlying and continuing disagreement.

[21] See particularly his "Frontiers in Group Dynamics," *Human Relations* I (1): 5-41, June 1947; and I (2): 143-153, November 1947.

Barnard and some of his followers.[22] There is a difference, however, in that most of these works considered tensions in terms of only a limited number of dimensions—in Barnard's case, only one (essentially motivation). We here consider, in relation to any single organization, a large number of different dimensions along which counteracting forces are operating at any time. Some of these are internal to the organization itself, and the more important of these are discussed in succeeding paragraphs. Some of them are largely external to the organization but impinge upon its operations (as, in *Langley Porter,* the University of California and the State Department of Finance). Some are between the organization itself or some element of it and outside individuals and groups (as, in *Fish and Game,* the Department, the wildlife groups, and the legislative committee that stimulated the survey of the Department). This three-way classification is by no means a clear-cut compartmentation. It is not uncommon for external tensions to be mirrored within organizations and vice versa, and frequently there is a direct and continuing connection between the internal forces and their counterparts outside (nicely illustrated in *La Loma, U.S. Public Health,* and others). In fact, the interrelationship among external tensions of concern to an organization, internal-external tensions, and primarily internal tensions is one of the most important factors in the understanding of organizational development. Thus, an organization operating under heavy criticism and opposition from an articulate and strong external group often is able to develop a high sense of internal morale and cohesiveness, thus sublimating its internal tensions and presenting a united front against its outside foes.[23]

Certain kinds of tensions are common in public administrative organizations. They are exhibited at various points and levels within large-scale organizations and are also reflected between the organizations and groups and individuals outside it as well as among groups external to them. They are illustrated in greater or lesser degree in the organizations treated in the cases. (See Chart I–4.)

First and perhaps most pervasive are tensions arising from different views and desires about *organizational purposes* and degrees of emphasis among different purposes.

We have noted that the purposes of organizations are perceived differently, both among their individual members and among individuals variously associated with them outside their membership. This is true not only with respect to their viewpoints of what the purposes *actually are* at any given time but, perhaps even more, of what they think their purposes *should be.* Divergent purposes of different individuals sometimes complement and reinforce each other. Thus, for example, in *Langley Porter,* the aims of the University of California to utilize the Clinic primarily as a training center paralleled that of doctors and scientists on the staff, who sought greater emphasis upon research. On the other hand, where views of purpose conflict and compete—a situation illustrated in virtually all of these cases—tensions are created. These often underlie many of the other kinds of tensions discussed below. They focus on issues of agency *policy* and *program.*

Second are the *centrifugal-centripetal tensions* with regard to control over organizational program and operations. This may be exhibited in the pressures of an agency, or of a unit within an agency, toward greater independence and autonomy with respect to its hierarchical superiors—the agency head, the chief executive or his staff arms, the legislative body. Against it operate counteracting pressures of these legally superior agencies to exercise more effective direction over agency activities. Evidence of this kind of tension existed in almost all the reorganization cases studied, and in a few it was central to their reorganization stories. Some examples are:

> the pressures of the Ballistics Division for greater freedom (from superiors and other departments at the Laboratory) in determination of projects;
>
> the demand of the Commissioner of the Highway Patrol for more effective control over his department;
>
> the effort of the City Administrator of La Loma to establish control over finances;
>
> the contest between Altmeyer and Lenroot over the control of the Children's Bureau.

---

[22] As developed initially in Barnard's *Functions of the Executive* (Cambridge: Harvard University Press, 1938), and later in a number of works by Herbert A. Simon and his associates.

[23] This has been most dramatically illustrated by the tremendous increases in productivity and in internal cohesion of war agencies, including the military services themselves, in time of war. The performance of TVA during the period when it was under continuous attack from private power interests is another example. It is less clearly demonstrated in our cases, principally because the situations were less clear-cut and dramatic. But the apparent cohesiveness of the Ballistics Division, and the relatively unified response to external attack of the Fish and Game Division may be proper examples.

CHART I–4. *Examples of organizational tensions relevant to reorganization efforts*

						INTERPERSONNEL TENSIONS			
CASE	*Policy Program*	*Centrifugal–Centripetal*	*Expansion–Contraction*	*Professional Special-ization*	*Innovative–Customary*	*Political Career*	*Diff. Pers. Systems*	*Competition for Prizes*	*Personal Attributes*
Agricultural Research		XX	X	X	X			X	
Architecture	X	X	X	X				X	X
Automation					XX				
Ballistics	XX	X		X				X	X
Children's Bureau	X	XX		X	X	X		X	X
Fish and Game	XX	X	X	X					X
Highway Patrol	X	XX				X			
La Loma		XX			X	X		X	X
Langley Porter	XX	X	XX	X			X		X
Personnel Board	X	X		XX	X		X	X	X
Philadelphia Health	X	XX	X	X	X	X			
U.S. Public Health	XX	X	X	X		X	X		

KEY: XX—dominant tension; X—secondary tension

A third widespread type of tension is that *between pressures to maintain or, preferably, expand and enlarge program versus pressures to restrain or contract program.* Tensions of this sort sometimes accompany and give substance to the centrifugal-centripetal tensions described above, since a greater degree of autonomy offers greater assurance of program maintenance and greater promise of program expansion. Pressure toward maintenance or growth may be internal to the organization itself, arising from either sincere convictions of the importance of the program or desire for job security, prestige, advancement, etc., or both. Parallel pressures occur outside the organization from clientele or otherwise concerned interests and their representatives. Against these operate groups whose interests are seen as threatened or diminished by program maintenance or expansion (as, for instance, the view of private architectural firms that an expanded program for the California Division of Architecture would work against their interests). But probably more pervasive resistance against program maintenance or growth arises from superior elements in the administration or the legislature responsible for allocating limited resources among a variety of competing programs. That is, opposition to the growth of a single program often arises among those whose horizons and responsibilities are broader than the scope of the organization that operates the program. Tensions of this type therefore tend to complement and reinforce the centrifugal-centripetal tensions. They were present in many of the cases and nicely illustrated by:

the demands of the Fish and Game Department to raise license fees;

the efforts of the Langley Porter Clinic to gain increased appropriations (*versus* the Department of Finance).

A fourth category consists of *tensions associated with professionalism or work specialization.* We have already alluded to the often divergent views on organizational purpose that can normally be expected among professional groups within agencies, each of which normally reflects a particular kind of education and experience. Tensions of this kind may appear as (1) efforts to change emphasis in policy and programs in directions perceived as desirable by the professional group, or (2) efforts to gain positions of greater control and influence over future policies and programs, or (3) both. Similar tensions also occur between specialists within an organization and others outside, specialists or non-specialists. Private architects had different views on the "proper" purposes of the Division of Architecture than did those who worked for it; and the fishermen and hunters and their spokesmen had different views as to the purposes of the Fish and Game Department than did many of its wildlife experts. It may be noted also that sub-specialization within an organization on the basis of subject matter or of locus in the organization will often create differences in view within the same specialization. Thus a public health doctor in a district center in Philadelphia may differ in his view on public health programs from one in the central headquarters.

Finally, mention should be made of the possible tensions of a professional group of employees arising from constraints and limitations imposed upon them in the pursuit of their professional goals and standards. Such constraints may come from within the organization or from above it and from outside it—superior officers, budget and personnel officers, legislatures and laws themselves, and outside interests. Many of the cases illustrated this phenomenon—*Ballistics, Fish and Game, Children's Bureau, Langley Porter,* and others.

A fifth pervasive kind of tension illustrated in these cases is that *between the new and the old:* i.e., the innovating, disturbing, threatening, and changing versus the customary, established, secure, and predictable. All projected reorganizations, by their very definition, in some degree threaten established activities and relationships. Some persons, both in and outside an organization, may perceive a projected reorganization as a danger to themselves, or to values they associate with organizational activities and purposes, or to both. Projected innovations almost inevitably arouse fears of the damages that they may cause individuals and groups. They also are countered by positive values of conservatism, such as values of association and friendship with others through long work relationships, and values of tradition and accustomed practice. In organizations that are not actually in a process of change the forces against change are stronger than those toward change in any given direction; often the forces favoring change are so opposed to one another that neither is prepared to support a change process which might be detrimental to it.

In addition to the generalized kinds of tensions mentioned above, there is a wide variety of differing tensions, of varying importance, between the people, as individuals or in groups, within organizations. These appear, in the cases, to be more variegated, variable, and complex than the pervading personnel tensions widely described in studies of private business management. We have already noted that there is rather little evidence in these cases of a basic tension between labor and management. This may be due to a degree of unrepresentativeness in case selection; in only one of these organizations was a labor organization significantly involved in the case, and in few of them was there any labor organization at all. Another characteristic of these organizations may have worked against the development of effective labor organizations: there was no effective "management" group in the industrial sense against which labor could mobilize. The government managers were more likely to align themselves with the subordinate workers in common battle with the outside—the executive, his staff agencies, the legislature—than to place themselves in opposition to their subordinates. And the latter looked to their chiefs as representatives and advocates rather than as adversaries. The tensions in these organizations were much more virulent between differing specialized points of view running laterally or diagonally across the structure than between lower and higher levels within the structure.

Another kind of tension which has been widely studied in private business is that between the demands of personality development on the one hand and the strictures and repressions of formal organizations on the other. Such a tension does not appear to have been a very significant factor in these cases, perhaps because the focus of these studies was not upon individual personalities at the worker level. Studies directed at changes in individual work groups rather than larger organizational changes might provide a more adequate reflection.

Tensions often arise *where there are personnel appointed under two or more different systems of employment within the same organization.* One variety involves the relationship between exempt, or politically appointed, executives and career civil servants at executive and professional levels. Here the differing perspectives arise partly from the nature of appointment; partly from differences in background and specializations arising from prior experience; partly from differences in hierarchical level; but most importantly from expectations as to duration of employment in the organization. The political appointee is customarily regarded, and regards himself, as temporary. He has a stake in the organization but only for a limited period, not for the rest of his life. If he is "upwardly mobile," he wants to make a showing, which means a change and a product that will be soon visible. He will not have to "live with it" very long. Under these circumstances, desire for major change on the political side and reluctance or caution on the career side are often but not always expectable. Minor tensions of this kind were observable in several cases in which political appointments to high administrative posts were involved: *Highway Patrol, Fish and Game, La Loma,* and *Philadelphia Health.*

Another kind of tension based on personnel systems occurs *where there are two or more categories of career employees within the same organization.* Where there exists this duality or pluralism among personnel, one corps appears normally to comprehend the "elite" professionals, the possessors of the principal offices of influence and the directors of the substance of the organization's line function. Others are seen as filling supporting and subordinate positions. Tensions between corps of this kind become most virulent when there is overlapping in function, where two or more categories of personnel work together on the same things with comparable responsibilities and yet there is a difference in the way one category is treated in comparison with the other. When this is not the case and there is clear and agreed differentiation in function and responsibility, tensions of this type are lessened. Thus, the clear distinction between the nonuniformed and the uniformed personnel in the California Highway Patrol appeared to have had no significant influence upon the progress of its reorganization. On the other hand, the underlying tension between the commissioned officers of the Public Health Service and the civil service doctors and scientists in the same organization could hardly be submerged until the survey group was explicitly directed to avoid the personnel problem. Another example of tensions of this kind was the relationship between the doctor-professors of Langley Porter Clinic and the University of California, and the other professionals on its staff.

Tensions within organizations occur also from competition among individuals and among groups for "prizes" in terms of position, status, prestige, power, monetary rewards, etc.[24] Negatively, such competition may occur when one or another group or individual is threatened with demotion in these terms or, in the extreme case, when its or his survival is endangered by other competitive groups. Competition, broadly construed, underlies much of the inter-specialism tension discussed earlier. Tensions arising from intra-organizational competition warmed to a boiling point in a few of the cases:

between the Ballistics Division and the Aeromechanics Division;

between the City Administrative Officer and the City Clerk of La Loma.

Tensions among personnel may arise, or other tensions may be reinforced, by factors that at first glance seem quite irrelevant to the work situation. These are attributes ascribed to persons, over many of which they have no control, which contribute to feelings of "otherness," opposition, or jealousy among fellow workers with unlike attributes. Some of these were present in degrees of varying significance in some of the cases:

tenure in organization: the old hands *versus* the newcomers;
age: the relatively old and mature *versus* the young;
sex: male *versus* female;
racial and religious groups;
educational attainment: the relatively well educated (such as Ph.D.'s, masters, bachelors) *versus* others (high school graduates or less)
social and economic backgrounds;
differences in prior experience and achievement.

The types of potential tension in governmental organizations described above can be more or less predicted from the types of institutional settings within which they occur and from non-affective attributes of the personnel concerned. In addition to these, elements of individual personality undoubtedly contribute by adding force to them, detracting from them, or giving body to quite differ-

[24] Wallace S. Sayre and Herbert Kaufman, in their fascinating study of politics in New York City, *Governing New York City* (New York: Russell Sage Foundation, 1960), have undertaken to ascribe virtually all significant motivations and the consequent conflicts to the quest for prizes. It is contended in this analysis that such an interpretation does not explain all behaviors resulting in tensions within organizations. Unless so broadly interpreted as to lose meaning, prizes *per se* explain many but certainly not all predictable modes of organizational behavior.

ent and idiosyncratic tensions in particular cases. We do not mean to minimize the importance of personality factors but rather to emphasize that personalities must operate within contexts of organizational tensions that are, in some degree, expectable and comparable. Indeed, the effectiveness of a personality in a leadership role depends in considerable part upon his ability to sense the tensions in his organizational setting and to deal with them. The cases are rampant with instances in which different leaders worked in different ways with varying results in the same organization, even when dealing with fundamentally the same systems of tensions. (For example, Dr. Bowman and Dr. Simon in *Langley Porter.*) But for the student as well as for the administrator, it is useful—indeed it is imperative—to comprehend the nature of the tension systems and the sources of tensions that are common among different organizations.

In a democratic society and especially one in which there are so many kinds of pluralism, the existence of tensions and the possibility of their periodic eruption are inevitable. Some students have postulated that organizations operating under a high degree of tension, especially tension arising from external attack, are more effective than those in which tensions are low. Others have indicated that a purpose of cooperative organization, and a measure of its effectiveness, is the sublimation of tensions. We contend only that: tensions exist in organizations; except when the organizations are themselves considering or undergoing change processes, they are usually latent; and, as will be discussed below, they become especially significant factors in reorganization.

The kinds of tensions that have been discussed are those associated with organizations on a continuing basis; they are in a sense "givens," data about organizations prior to the initiation of a major change process. Reorganizations tend to reinforce and ignite some of them (as, for example, that between change and stability). Reorganizations also give rise to new tensions, depending in part upon the manner in which they are initiated and carried out.

SUMMARY

In this chapter we have considered some common features of the public organizations considered in these cases, laying some emphasis upon their similarity to and difference from formal organizations treated in other works. In most of their basic structural attributes they conformed generally to the bureaucratic model: hierarchy, differentiation of functions and duties, concept of "office," career personnel systems based upon merit. The organizations were, at the levels on which the cases focused, primarily composed of professionals and specialists, both line and staff, and their top executives were also professionals. In most cases, a single profession was the elite group, and it usually included as one of its members the top executive. Most of the agencies, however, employed a number of other professionals and specialists representing non-elite occupational endeavors.

Emphasis has been placed upon the analysis of organizational purposes in these organizations. They were found to be multiple, complex, unstable, and differently and competitively viewed by different individuals and groups within and outside each agency. Divergent perspectives on purpose gave rise to continuing tensions within the organizations, and such tensions complemented or existed along with other kinds of tensions, such as: centripetal and centrifugal drives for control and influence; conflicting aspirations of different specialized groups and individuals; drives for program expansion or maintenance; innovation versus conservation; and interpersonnel competition. Such tensions appear normally to be quiescent when an organization is not in a change process, but can become important issues during reorganization.

CHAPTER II

Organizational Change

An organization is a system or a cluster of interrelated systems. The principal elements of human organizations are, of course, people occupying positions which are themselves abstract conceptions of activities, relationships, and responses to be attributed to the people filling them. To the extent that the people respond in expected and approved ways, they are considered reliable, or, in organizational terminology, responsible. Without a considerable degree of such expectability and reliability, an organization could not long exist.

The concept of system itself implies a degree of continuity through time. Yet organizations exhibit, within themselves, continuous changes in activity even when the pattern of relationships is stable; and some organizations have as their *raison d'être* the initiating or the bringing about of change (such as those in *Ballistics, Langley Porter,* and *Agricultural Research*). Organizations may be relatively static within themselves, even though their work involves continuously changing activities and has to do with changing products. An organization may be a principal instrument of social dynamics and at the same time a remarkably stable system, internally resistant to change.

INCREMENTAL CHANGE[1]

Yet organizations do change, both with respect to their external relationships and to their internal configurations. In those organizations regarded as relatively stable, the changes are gradual or consist of a multitude of small incremental changes, none so great as to be construed as a reorganization—the addition of a position, the reassignment of duties, the replacement of an incumbent, a minor increase or decrease in the budget. Even when there are no changes in budget, in function, or in personnel, some degree of organizational change inevitably results from the developing and changing relationships of the people within its framework. Comparable changes must also occur with respect to clientele groups and controlling agencies—both executive and legislative.

The developing administrative organization may be compared with the developing family unit in our culture. As the children grow up, their roles, and also the respective roles of the parents and the interrelationships of all family members, change, more or less according to accepted social patterns. The changes are an hour-to-hour and day-to-day occurrence, seldom noticed by any member of the family as a change in the family system itself. The changes are apparent, however, to any observant visitor who comes periodically; if his visits are infrequent, the changes appear dramatic and extreme.

The analogy may be carried one step further. Major problems occur in families in which one or more members fail to modify their behaviors in appropriate adjustment with their changing roles in the family organization—as for example, when a growing child fails to adjust to his growing responsibilities, or when a parent continues to treat an adolescent as an infant. They occur also when one or more members fail to modify their behaviors in accordance with the changing social position of the family in its society or with its relatively increased (or decreased) economic resources. Such situations are a source of demands for major readjustments in family relationships.

Administrative organizations likewise develop

[1] Paul H. Appleby, in a typically insightful article about the first Hoover Commission report, suggested the classification of reorganizations into two types, *constant* and *episodic*. These are essentially the same as "incremental change" and "reorganization" as the terms are used herein. ["The Significance of the Hoover Commission Report," *The Yale Review* 39(1): 2-22, September 1949.]

and change through a virtually continuous succession of incremental modifications and adjustments, very few of which would warrant being called a reorganization. Most are effectual and absorbed without major disturbance to the various patterns of equilibria, described in Chapter I. But over an extended period these changes are very substantial, so much so as to impress the intermittent visitor as striking and even revolutionary. The organization members, on the other hand, may hardly be aware of them at all. Over the long pull, they cumulatively may be viewed as continuing efforts to keep the organization in tune with the dynamic situation within which it operates—i.e., the changing social needs to which it responds, its changing purposes and shifting emphases among the purposes, changing resources, and changing technology making available to it new techniques and methods. These factors may be regarded, in the main, as external to the organization itself.

In addition to these external factors, there are the dynamic internal factors deriving from the changing relationships of personnel, from emerging leadership, from the growth of individuals as they acquire experience, from the shifting interrelationships of members, etc. In this context, the developing organization is seen as a unit more or less continuously striving to keep itself in tune with its changing environment and its own changing complexion. Some organizations, operating in rather static settings and typically not exposed to political interests and cross-currents, change and develop slowly; others, in more dynamic situations, change rapidly.

ORGANIZATIONAL OBSOLESCENCE

There are, however, even in organizations that appear relatively flexible and dynamic, elements that are resistant to change and that therefore do not respond adequately to emerging internal and external conditions. A situation thus develops in which organizations become internally maladjusted; parts of them have moved rather rapidly to keep up with, or "grow with," the times; other parts are "sticky" and become increasingly out of tune with the times. Structural arrangements in formal organization may themselves constitute such frozen elements, especially when they are solidified by constitution, charter, or statutory law. More frequently, such arrangements are change-resistant because they tend to protect other elements for which a structural rearrangement would constitute a threat—such as the influence of a particular type of specialization or the power and status of a particular power center (as illustrated by a headquarters office *vis-à-vis* field offices).

Herein lies a basic rationale, and often the underlying reason, for administrative reorganizaion: to bring up-to-date, or to permit the bringing up-to-date, of those aspects of organizational operation and relationships that have suffered from "lag"—i.e., that have failed to modify themselves through incremental changes sufficiently to keep up with the changing contexts within which they operate. In fact, it may be postulated that, in a rapidly changing society, a periodic reexamination and consequent modification of organization is desirable for this purpose alone. Many organization structures, or parts thereof, originally set up in eminently rational and efficient forms in response to the needs of their times, become gradually less efficient and less in tune with the needs as the years go by. Ultimately, major modifications are necessary.

A number of different and identifiable factors may over the course of time make major structural change within an agency desirable or even mandatory. All are manifestations of organizational obsolescence. One of the most pervasive of these in a growing society is simply *growth in size,* consequent upon growth in clientele or population serviced, with or without change in nature of services or techniques.[2] It has long been observed that large organizations are, and in some ways must be, structured differently from small ones, even though they

[2] The relationship between size and structure and the dynamics of organizational growth have been the object of all too little systematic attention, either theoretical or empirical. The void is particularly gaping among government agencies. There have been a few very interesting studies in private business, including: Alfred D. Chandler, Jr., *Strategy and Structure* (Cambridge: M.I.T. Press, 1962); Ernest Dale, *Planning and Developing the Company Organization Structure* (New York: American Management Association, 1952); Ernest Dale, *The Great Organizers* (New York: McGraw-Hill, 1960); and Mason Haire, "Biological Models and Empirical Histories of the Growth of Organization," in Mason Haire (editor), *Modern Organization Theory* (New York: John Wiley & Sons, Inc., 1959).

are doing the same things. Therefore, as an organization grows within a structural framework designed for small volume, at some stages strains will appear and become increasingly intolerable until a substantial change is made in structure. For example, a growing agency, initially structured on a functional or activity basis, must frequently at some point move to a unitary structure (on the basis of clientele or geography or materials dealt with) because of multiplying difficulties of coordination and communication and the congestion of procedures (as in *Personnel Board*). Growth is certainly a reason for decentralization and regionalization of both decision-making and operating activities (as in *Agricultural Research, Highway Patrol,* and *Philadelphia Health*). The reverse process, contraction, likewise tends to make structures obsolescent, though in the opposite ways, but contractions are less frequent and are not illustrated in these cases (except, in a somewhat indirect way, in *Ballistics*).

A second factor contributing to the need for reorganization is *changes in problems and needs and therefore in organizational programs and responsibilities.* An agency may undertake (or have imposed upon it) new functions in response to emerging problems and simply tack them on within its existing framework. Over the years this often results in a skewing of its structure, complication of its internal coordination, and maladjustments among its staff. Or its leaders may perceive emerging new needs but be unable to accommodate the new activities without basic and profound changes in structure. (Both phenomena were illustrated in the cases in the public health field.) Shifts in needs and problems may work in the other direction—their gradual decline and perhaps obliteration, leaving redundant or overstaffed units within existing organizations. Shifts in program emphasis deriving from changing perceptions of needs are sometimes subtle and very gradual over the years, and a reorganization may serve not only as a response to changing needs but also as a tool to bring about changed emphases in programs. (This was probably true in *Highway Patrol,* both health cases, and others.)

A third factor contributing to a need for reorganization is a *changing philosophy as to the proper responsibilities of government* (of a particular level or jurisdiction of government) in the area of an agency's concern or in the larger arena of public activities related to that area. In our times, such changes have usually been in the direction of an expanded role of government, particularly at higher levels (as in research, the poverty program, massive involvement by the federal government in education, and international intervention). Several of the cases illustrate this phenomenon though on a less dramatic scale. (The assumption by the national government of general responsibilities in the field of social welfare was the underlying reason why the location of the Children's Bureau in the Department of Labor became anachronistic; three decades earlier, this had been its logical home. A changed view on the proper mission of the military laboratory contributed to the abolishment of the Ballistics Division. Shifting philosophies about government's appropriate role in health services were key factors in both health cases, and the emerging concept of the police function as social service and aid rather than purely disciplinary and regulatory contributed to the *Highway Patrol* case.) It may be noted that changes in viewpoints as to proper governmental role occur among members of the organizations concerned, influential officials and outsiders, and even the general public.

A fourth factor is a consequence of *new technology, new equipment, and advancing knowledge* having been or about to be adapted to an agency's work and methods, with or without change in purposes or workload. Such development may derive from research and innovation either inside or outside the agency or a combination of the two. Their effect may be to make existing procedures, existing organizational structures, and even existing personnel obsolescent. The most obvious current example of this phenomenon is the introduction of automated equipment (as in the *Automation* case, and somewhat more removed, in both *Agricultural Research* and *La Loma*).

A fifth factor is the *changing—and usually rising—qualifications of personnel* in fields of specialism used in an agency's work. This arises partly from general advances in knowledge in specialized fields and their transmission to actual and potential agency personnel through the educational system. A repeated theme in many of the cases was the need for "upgrading" personnel which meant not only raising their pay and prestige but also, in many instances, bringing their qualifications up to the rising ceilings of knowledge and ability in their fields of work. Shifting standards as to qualifications for the work were reflected in a variety of ways: toward a generalized, broader concept of the job (as in *Personnel Board, Fish and Game,* and *Philadelphia Health*); or toward better professional and educational background (as in *Ballistics*); or toward a different orientation to the work (as in *U.S. Public Health* and *Highway Patrol*).

Finally, organizations at lower levels may in effect become obsolescent because of *actions taken above them* in their department or government or in higher levels of government. These may take the form of basic policy changes or reorganizations, initiated and sometimes enforced from above, which make the current local structure obsolescent in terms of the total organizational context. Only two of the cases provided clear illustrations of this phenomenon (the regional offices in *Agricultural Research* and the *Children's Bureau,* the rationale for which in the Labor Department was severely undermined by the establishment of the Federal Security Agency). It seems probable, however, that a significant number of reorganizations are consequences of actions from above: in regional and field offices; and in state and local agencies responsive to directives, standards, and particularly grants-in-aid from higher levels of government.

This six-way categorization of factors giving rise to organizational obsolescence, and thus contributing to needs for reorganization, is doubtless incomplete; and the way I have classified the factors is not definitive since some of them interrelate with others. But the main points are clear. In a dynamic society, organizations, particularly those engaged in public services, are unable through small, day-to-day incremental adjustments and improvisations to keep themselves apace with the times on every front. There are forces, sometimes internal resistance, sometimes external and political, sometimes legal and even constitutional, which inhibit rapid response to changing demands from without. They cannot "muddle through" indefinitely. The basic sources of organizational obsolescence in the public sphere appear to be external to the agencies themselves. They are growth, consequent upon the growth in society, changing demands and needs in the sphere in which the organizations operate, and advancing knowledge, technology, professionalism, and skills. Reorganization efforts operate from a base of more or less severe organizational obsolescence, whether or not their proponents are aware of them in these terms. Such obsolescence may, I think, be considered normal; and periodic reorganization may likewise be viewed as normal and necessary. As treated in these chapters, reorgani-

CHART II–1. *Sources of structural obsolescence in organizations in the cases*

CASE	*Growth*	*Changing Needs and Problems*	*Changing Role of Government*	*New Technology Equipment, etc.*	*Changing Personnel Qualifications*	*Changes in Higher Echelons*
Agricultural Research	X			X		X
Architecture	X					
Automation	X			X		
Ballistics		X	X		X	
Children's Bureau			X			X
Fish and Game	X				X	
Highway Patrol	X	X	X		X	
La Loma	X			X	X	
Langley Porter	X	X	X	X		
Personnel Board	X				X	
Philadelphia Health	X	X	X		X	
U.S. Public Health	X	X	X	X	X	
All Cases	10	5	6	5	7	2

zation, unlike much incremental organizational change, is conscious, deliberate, intended, and planned. Unlike incremental changes, most reorganization attempts—virtually all in these cases—are aimed to upset some patterns of equilibria, to "unfreeze" the rigidities of the going concern, so that significant changes may be introduced abruptly and new equilibria may be established and integrated at different levels. Although some of the proposed reorganizations, whether achieved or frustrated, were not put forward in the terms here described as efforts to bring operations up-to-date with the times, this was a significant underlying element in almost all of them.

GOALS OF REORGANIZATION

It is, of course, hazardous to ascribe goals to individuals who initiate or sponsor reorganizations. In the first place, different persons have different goals, and one must first decide whose goals were the significant ones in each situation. In most of the cases here discussed, the initiators and backers of reorganization were fairly easy to identify. In the main, they were the top administrative heads of the organizations concerned (though in some instances their own actions were instigated from other sources). In two cases, the initiation and follow-through came from outside the organization itself: in *Fish and Game,* from the legislative committee, and in *La Loma,* from the city council. Second, the goals of the dominant party or parties, are complex and sometimes obscure. Some of the individuals themselves had difficulty identifying their own reasons, either at the time of action or later. A few years later—i.e., at the time the case investigations were made—they probably viewed their own behavior in a different light than they did when they initiated reorganization. Very likely, their interpretation in time perspective is clearer and better rationalized than it would have been at the time they took their actions. Nevertheless, happily and somewhat surprisingly, the goals of most of the dominant leaders in these cases seemed reasonably apparent in their actions and their subsequent statements; the case writers themselves were, in most instances, satisfied that they had derived an accurate and adequate understanding of the reorganizational goals of the initiators.

Most of the reorganization goals were blends of two or more elements. Those goals that were publicly announced and advertised differed to varying extents—in kind and/or in emphasis—from the goals that appeared to be "real" to the actors themselves. And the goals, even in the minds of the principal characters, changed in some cases during the reorganization process. The process was at least in part one of "learning" and consequent reorientation as to purposes and problems. This was most evident in *Langley Porter,* where the initial goal, which was quite plainly to increase the budget and thus the program, came to share importance with others, including recognition of research as a major function of the Clinic.

The principal goals of the reorganizations and the efforts toward reorganization as seen by their leaders may be classified into four main categories: (1) those having to do with changing *policy and program,* which equate with shifting of agency purpose; (2) those intended to improve *administrative effectiveness* in carrying out existing responsibilities; (3) those directed specifically to *problems of personnel,* individuals or groups; and (4) those intended to counter or respond to *pressures and threats* from outside the organization.[3] These general categories may be further subdivided into more specific classes:

Policy and Program

(1) *Shift in policy and/or in program emphasis:* as in *Langley Porter* from patient care to research; in *U.S. Public Health* to community orientation and environmental health; in *Fish and Game* to revised wildlife policies; or in *Children's Bureau* to a total welfare, rather than an age-clientele, approach.

(2) *Expansion and extension of existing programs:* as exemplified in efforts to enlarge

[3] In addition to these four categories, one somewhat special kind of goal was important in the case of *La Loma:* to relieve the mayor and council members of onerous responsibilities of city administration which they could not, or would not, carry out effectively as part-time, low-salaried officials. In a sense, of course, this falls within the general rubric of administrative effectiveness.

budgets in the *Philadelphia Health* and *Langley Porter* cases.

Administrative Effectiveness

(1) *Expanded control at top and, thus, improved coordination:* as, in *La Loma,* through the establishment of a City Administrative Officer and establishment under him of a Finance Department; or by strengthening the position of the Commissioner of the California Highway Patrol; or by bringing the Children's Bureau under the control of the head of federal welfare and health activities.

(2) *Increase in productivity and in quality of work:* as through the concentration of business services of the Agricultural Research Service, having work done by personnel trained for it, rather than by research specialists; or through giving personnel specialists in the State Personnel Board nearly complete jurisdiction over personnel activities in assigned areas of the state government in order to increase their total effectiveness.

(3) *Decentralization of decision-making and operations to points in the organization that are nearer to the problems with which it deals:* as in the establishment of regional business offices of the Agricultural Research Service; of district centers in *Philadelphia Health;* and of operations units in the Personnel Board.

(4) *Economy or the reduction of costs (total or unit) in carrying on going programs:* as in the installation of computer equipment in *Automation.*

(5) *Application of administrative principles.* Although principles of organization and management are usually advanced in terms of economy, efficiency, and coordination, it appears in the cases that they carry some independent force of their own, even when a clear-cut relationship with administrative effectiveness cannot be established. The "principles" rely heavily upon simple geometric propriety and, perhaps secondarily, upon the aesthetics of a culture which heavily values rationality. In a number of the cases, there was an eye toward clear command lines, unity of direction, and the symmetry of the "chart": as in the elimination of what appeared to be inconsistent or heterogenous activity in the Ballistics Division; or the establishment of consistent geographic areas, regardless of program locations, for business activities in *Agricultural Research.*

Personnel Problems

(1) *Enlargement of opportunity, challenge, remuneration, status, and/or welfare of employees:* as in the job enlargement implicit in generalizations of the professionals in the *Personnel Board* case. This was undoubtedly a secondary consideration in other cases, such as *Philadelphia Health* and *Agricultural Research.*

(2) *Elimination or correction of individual personnel problems.* Reorganization surveys and reorganizations themselves were sometimes utilized to bring about the separation of individuals, or substantial reassignment of individual responsibilities or influence, or the bringing in of desired individuals to high-level positions. The removal of the Director of Fish and Game may have been a principal purpose of the instigators of the survey of that Department, and problems of this sort were apparent in two or three of the other cases. It is probable that more of them occurred than appear in the cases, because this is a particularly difficult and sensitive kind of problem for the researcher to learn of and to write about.

Response to Outside Pressure or Threat

The organizational survey of the Division of Architecture was surely in part a defensive move, inspired to provide a basis for countering the proposal of the Department of Finance that the Division be transferred to that Department. The *Architecture* case was probably also inspired in part to ward off criticisms of private architectural groups. Likewise the self-survey by the Public Health Service was in part a response to the interests of congressional committees in the development of environmental health programs.

The relative frequency of the different kinds of goals which were held by the principal leaders and initiators of reorganization attempts in this volume is shown below. These have been grouped in two categories: goals that were dominant or primarily important, and goals that were ancillary or secondary.

The following is a summary of the data contained in Chart II–2:

CHART II–2. *Goals of reorganization as seen by their principal initiators and leaders*

CASE	*Policy Program*		*Administrative Effectiveness*					*Personnel*		*Response to Outside*	
	Emphasis	*Expansion*	*Centralized Control*	*Productivity*	*Decentralization*	*Economy*	*Principles*	*Opportunity—Welfare*	*Problems*	*Pressure or Threat*	*Other*
Agricultural Research		X	XX	X	XX		X	X			
Architecture							X			XX	
Automation						XX		X			
Ballistics	XX		X						X		
Children's Bureau	XX	X	XX				X			X	
Fish and Game	XX					X			XX*	XX	
Highway Patrol			XX		X		X				
La Loma			XX				X		X		XX†
Langley Porter	XX	XX						X			
Personnel Board	X			XX	X			XX	X		
Philadelphia Health	XX	X			XX			X			
U.S. Public Health	XX	X	X				X			X	

KEY: XX—primary goal; X—secondary goal
* goals as perceived by both legislators and sportsmen groups
† goal of relieving mayor and council members of burden of city administration

Classes of goals	*Occurrence of:* PRIMARY GOALS	SECONDARY GOALS
Shift in policy or programs	6	1
Expansion of programs	1	4
Enlarged central control	4	2
Increased or improved product	1	1
Decentralization	2	2
Economy	1	1
Administrative principles		6
Enlargement of employee opportunity and welfare	1	4
Individual personnel problems	1	3
Response to outside pressure	2	2

This classification is undoubtedly incomplete, since other kinds of goals certainly contribute to reorganization. We might, for example, have included as a goal of reorganization, change for its own sake; e.g., a leader instigating such a process for the purpose of stirring things up or giving the appearance of clearing up a "mess," being aggressive, etc. This may well have been a frequent motivating factor in some of these cases, especially where a reorganization proposal was made following the designation of a new chief. But it is hard to establish and seldom admitted.

The classification is necessarily somewhat arbitrary because there are many different ways in which goals might be classified. And, like other observations in these chapters, it is largely subjective, based upon the observations of the case writers and filtered into the classification, *post facto,* by the writer.[4] Nevertheless, the data are suggestive on some points. In nearly half of the cases, a major goal was to bring about significant changes in policy or program (purpose). In about one-third of them, it was to centralize control and

[4] The judgments are based upon the cases themselves, supplemented by individual analyses of the case writers which must remain confidential.

power in the head of the agency, and in some of these an ulterior or latent goal was to enable him to change or redirect agency policies in the future. Decentralization was a fairly frequent—though usually secondary—goal. As may be noted in the *Agricultural Research* case, decentralization is not necessarily inconsistent with centralizing control. It may in fact be an instrument of centralization—as when its effect is to reduce the power over staff or program specialists and enhance that of general officers directly responsible to the top officials.

It is interesting that economy was a primary goal only in the case built around the installation of automated equipment, and the increase or improvement of product—i.e., service—was a principal goal in only two cases (*Agricultural Research* and *Personnel Board*). These two goals equate roughly with economy and efficiency (or productivity), around which so much organizational literature has revolved. This probably results at least in part from the level and nature of the public organizations here studied, but it does suggest as well that many important reorganizations are aimed at expansion and enlargement of programs rather than at the traditional goals of economy and efficiency. In fact, the majority of reorganizations proposed in the cases could be expected to result in increased dollar costs.

It should be observed that in most of the cases the goals of reorganization were seen as instrumental to more basic and longer range objectives. Most of them were but one step in a long campaign aimed at changing institutions in directions that appeared desirable to their leaders. This was the case not only when the more immediate goal was to modify policies and programs but also when it was more strictly managerial in nature. It manifested itself in a broadening of the concept of agency mission (as in *Children's Bureau, U.S. Public Health,* and *Langley Porter*); or in bringing the agency closer to its public or clientele (as in *Philadelphia Health, Personnel Board,* and in a sense, *Fish and Game*); or in substituting a service for a control and enforcement orientation (as in *Highway Patrol* and *Personnel Board*). A number of the case writers referred to the desire of the agency head to "change the image" of his organization in one or the other direction, in the minds of its officers and employees, or in the view of those outside, or both.

Most of the leaders and most of the organizations in the cases in this volume were oriented toward a profession. In many of the cases, the goals may be perceived as efforts by professional people to project and further the aspirations, the values, and the standards of their professions in the public organizations that employed them. This appeared in: efforts to resist or overcome limitations imposed by the organization itself, by its superiors, and by legislators upon professional performance (as in *Langley Porter* or *Ballistics Division*); or efforts to gain appropriate professional influence, recognition, and status in dealing with other professions within the organization (as in *Agricultural Research*); or as efforts to elevate professional performance within the organization by upgrading positions and salary, entrance standards, training, etc. (as in *Philadelphia Health, Personnel Board,* and others).

One is impressed by the degree of idealism that characterized most of the hierarchical leaders in the cases—idealism about public service and idealism associated with their profession. They considered their work and that of their agency important in American society and the projection of the highest standards of professional service very nearly a moral imperative. A reorganization is but one of a number of different devices whereby that imperative may be given expression.

THE REORGANIZATION PROCESS

Background of Reorganizations

In most of the cases in which reorganization was attempted, there had been a rather extended prior history of attempts to bring about change in structure and definition of organizational purpose. Some of these earlier efforts never got beyond the stage of general proposals or trial balloons, quickly dismissed; some were seriously studied and considered; a few resulted in moderate or partial changes or compromise. (See Chart II–3 for previous attempts.)

This generalization about precedents of reorganization attempts suggests certain propositions,

CHART II–3. *Previous studies and reorganization attempts*

CASE	*Previous Studies and Reorganization Attempts*
Agricultural Research	1947 and 1953 Previous reorganizations of Department
Architecture	1948–1958 Half-dozen studies by Finance Department's Organization and Cost Control Division; 1957 study recommends transfer 1955 McCarthy's Interim Committee report 1956 Public Works Department study of Division 1958 Public Works Department employee opinion survey Yearly scrutiny by Legislative Analyst; some changes to improve management
Automation	1951 Remington Rand survey of tabulating procedures Post-1951 Bashline ponders application of EDP to the Tabulating Section
Ballistics	1949, 1951 Harvard School of Business Administration teams study Laboratory Spring 1950 Ad hoc committees to study aspects of Department called by Research Board 1952–1953 Review of Research Department by Advisory Board
Children's Bureau	1935 Hearings on Social Security Act, at which question of place of Children's Bureau comes up 1939 Roosevelt considers transfer of Children's Bureau
Fish and Game	1947 Study for utilization of grant 1952 Gordon's reorganization 1953 Senate Fish and Game Committee established to study Department 1955 Senate Fish and Game Committee surveys Department 1956 Legislative Analyst reports on Department Sportsmen's Clubs and wildlife federation conduct studies of their own
Highway Patrol	1946 Report of International Association of Chiefs of Police to Senate Committee on Government Reorganization 1953 Senate Finance Subcommittee report Finance Department report 1959 Report of Legislative Analyst
La Loma	1950 Mayor attempts to increase his salary to conform to amount of work required
Langley Porter	Unsuccessful attempts by Bowman to get support for teaching and research
Personnel Board	1949 Kroeger study for Assembly Interim Committee on Economy and Efficiency 1950 State Personnel Board reports on implementation of Kroeger report 1952 Staff attitude survey of employee morale
Philadelphia Health	1929 Philadelphia Hospital and Health Survey 1949–1950 Philadelphia Health and Welfare Council Survey 1950 Perri Committee established to implement Council report
U.S. Public Health	1948, 1954 Previous studies and minor reorganizations

which may be considered normal in going organizations:[5]

(1) That the tensions underlying reorganization efforts are already there and have been for some time;

(2) That the majority of reorganization efforts are unsuccessful or only partially successful in reducing the tensions underlying them;

(3) That the understanding of a single reorganization effort requires comprehension of the prior history in the organization concerned;

(4) That a reorganization effort is not a "one-time thing" but a step in a progressive history.

There is evidence in some of the cases that an

[5] "Normal" is used here and elsewhere to mean in all cases except those which, for one reason or another, are clearly exceptional in the circumstances surrounding the event.

extended history of reorganization efforts in response to continuing and growing tensions has a cumulative effect and that frustrations, in fact, may contribute to the tensions. This suggests further that a reorganization effort and, in fact, a successful reorganization, can best be perceived not as a single episode with a beginning and end but as a step or a stage in the development, transition, or decline of an organization.

In those instances where there had been a series of totally or substantially unsuccessful efforts to reorganize, the nature and content of the successive proposals for reorganization changed, even where the substantive problems and tensions appear to be basically comparable. This apparently reflects successive shifts in strategy and tactics and, in many cases, increasingly sophisticated understanding of what strategies and tactics are most likely to be successful. Strategy is here construed to signify the selection of the one or two or three key factors most likely to "unfreeze" the condition of resistance—the "strategic factors" in Barnard's terminology.[6] Tactics are construed as the methods and techniques employed. In the cases, shifting strategies may be illustrated by change in top leadership, or drawing upon reputable outside groups for studies, or instigating threatening action in a legislative committee.[7] Shifting tactics are most clearly illustrated in the *U.S. Public Health* case by the radically modified approaches of the Study Group to the two successive "Summit Meetings." If a "moral" may be drawn from the experiences described in the cases it might be stated: "If at first you don't succeed, try again, *but try in a different way.*"

The Ignition of Reorganization

If it is true that tensions of various kinds exist in actual or potential form in organizations at all times, and that these provide some of the bases for reorganization effort, the questions that arise are: Why is not reorganization a continuous process? Why are reorganizations episodic and occasional? And why, in some agencies, are they frequent and in others relatively unusual?

In most, if not all, of the cases in this volume, the reorganization process was preceded by a period of gradually or spasmodically growing difficulties and tensions, manifested in different ways: organizational failures (e.g., failures to meet deadlines, reflected in backlogs), pressures and criticisms from inside and outside, misunderstandings, and disputes. In some instances, these reached a point, without the introduction of any new event, at which action intended to lessen or eliminate the problems was initiated. More often, the introduction of a new element, a "spark" or a series of "sparks," set off the process, destroying the previous equilibrium and overcoming the forces resistant to change. Although the unfreezing phenomenon was often only temporary, for a period structural change was at least seriously considered. (See Chart II–4.)

It is interesting that in many instances the sparks appeared to have but a distant relationship to the processes they set off. Further, in the majority of instances they were themselves generated outside the organizations immediately concerned, and beyond their internal control. Most frequent among them were *changes in top leadership,* resulting from: an election and political turnover (in two cases);[8] or from retirement, resignation, or transfer of an incumbent and his replacement (in three cases); or from employment of a leader in a new position (in one case).[9] It is worthy of mention that in most of these instances, five of the six, the newly appointed leader was brought in from outside the organization concerned, not promoted from within. And all the appointments were, of course, made by officials *above* and *outside* the organizations immediately concerned.

In most of these cases, the change in leadership not only was followed by a reorganization process but also led to reorganizational efforts substantially in accord with the new leader's desires. That is, they were planned in terms of the goals of the new leader himself.

It is probable that, in general, the arrival of a new chief *per se* lessens resistance to change. His superior appointing officer and his new subordi-

[6] See Barnard, *The Functions of the Executive,* pp. 202-205.

[7] These are illustrated in one way or another in most of the cases and are discussed in greater length in subsequent pages.

[8] The number would be three if one were to count the reorganization of business services in *Agricultural Research,* which was really the third wave of reorganization, all sparked initially by the election of President Eisenhower and his appointment of Secretary of Agriculture Ezra T. Benson.

[9] The six instances mentioned actually are drawn from only five cases since two different leadership changes occurred at different stages in one case—*Philadelphia Health.* The first was the appointment of Dixon by the newly elected Mayor Clark; the second, the bringing in to a new position of Hanlon some years later.

CHART II–4. *Problems, tensions, and issues present and building up in the organizations studied; sparks that ignited the reorganization effort*

CASE	*Growing Problems and Tensions*	*Sparks*
Agricultural Research	backlog of work in business services; confusion and inefficiency resulting from partial measures of previous reorganization	outgrowth of an earlier reorganization which itself followed a *change in leadership*
Architecture	criticism from some quarters of Division's "product" and management; charges of Boyd's favoritism	*reaction to Finance Department study recommending transfer of Division to Finance Department*
Automation	increasing amount of work; lengthy and not always accurate claim processing	leadership change; *EDP manual; building commitment*
Ballistics	problems resulting from change in Laboratory's emphasis from research to hardware; dissatisfaction with Division service; competition with Aeromechanics Division	*leadership change*
Children's Bureau	jockeying for individual autonomy and advantage by various agencies versus deside for integration of welfare programs in one agency	*congressional passage of Reorganization Act followed by Bureau of Budget request for recommendations on reorganization*
Fish and Game	criticism of program emphases of Department and management of Department; pressures and complaints from clientele	*request for increase in license fees;* controversy over either-sex deer hunt
Highway Patrol	problems of supervision resulting from geographical dispersion of patrol offices; communication difficulties arising from centralizing decision power at faraway headquarters	change in state administrations; and resulting *change in leadership*
La Loma	problems resulting from difficulties of managing and coordinating various city programs and departments	unclear
Langley Porter	conflict on program emphases among research, teaching, and care; tension from dual direction of Clinic; overburdening of business services; overloading with supervisory work of top administrators	change in leadership of Clinic; resulting *budget request for increased appropriations*
Personnel Board	increasing difficulties of inter-divisional coordination; dissatisfaction with supervisor; inter-group jealousies	*memo from junior member of staff with criticism of Board's operation and suggestion for change*
Philadelphia Health	problems of coordination of district centers; tensions arising from attempts to upgrade certain departments	election of Mayor Clark; *appointment of Dixon and, later, Hanlon*
U.S. Public Health	confusion and lack of coordination resulting from increase in extent and scope of activities; disagreement over mission: research or application; unclear organizational lines	*congressional inquiry into environmental health program*

KEY: *italicized phrase* indicates primary spark

nates expect him to make changes. He himself, even if he does not know what changes are desirable, feels that he must make some innovations. During his first few weeks and months he is in a far more favorable position to make desired changes than would be either the long-time incumbent who preceded him or he himself after a longer period on the job. These change expectancies surrounding the new leader grow out of the situation of succession and may be quite unrelated to the respective degrees of initiative, imagination, forcefulness, or other personality attributes of the leaders themselves.

The majority of other events that led to the consideration of reorganization occurred outside the organizations themselves. They include, in three cases, actions by other agencies of the administration, such as the Budget Bureau circular requesting recommendations on reorganizations (in *Children's Bureau*), or, in two cases, actions taken or impending in the legislative body, such as an inquiry about a program (e.g., environmental health in *U.S. Public Health*). Some considerations of reorganization were in the nature of responses to proposals that originated within the organizations themselves, as when the Langley Porter Clinic requested a major increase in its budget, or when the Fish and Game Department proposed an increase in license fees. Few were generated inside the organizations except after the spur of a new leader. The best, if not the only, example of this was the *Personnel Board* case in which the process appeared to have been set off, at least in part, by a memorandum written by a junior staff member.

Inception of Studies

In all but two of the cases, more or less formalized studies were conducted prior to decision, and it is clear that many of these studies were vital in the reorganization process. In several, there were two or more studies conducted at different stages, and frequently these different studies within the same case had different objectives, different foci, and different study group organization. The principal studies considered in subsequent paragraphs are shown in Chart II–5, together with the approximate periods during which they were conducted. Each study is identified by agency and sequential number (as I, II, III), and these notations are used in the text for purposes of reference.

The usual pattern in these cases was a period of discussion, negotiation, and planning following the initial spark, a process that sometimes went on for several months. The prime object of these discussions was not whether and how to reorganize, though this could not fail to be involved, but whether and how to go about studying the matter. At this stage, the discussions and even the fact that the subject was being discussed were usually a closely guarded secret among a very few officials in the immediate circle of the principal executive. Likewise, where a survey was authorized by a legislative body, the initial talks were confined to a small circle. Secrecy was apparently aimed to prevent unrest, rumor, and, sometimes, the mobilization of opposition.

This early gestation could result in an announcement of an exploratory study to determine whether a full-scale survey was necessary and if so, what its emphases and scope should be (as in *La Loma*). More often, if the decision at this stage were to do anything at all,[10] this period was closed by an announcement of a study, including a statement of its purposes, scope, method, and who was to conduct it. In every case except *Ballistics* and *Children's Bureau* there was at least one more or less formalized, more or less extensive study prior to a substantive decision on reorganization.[11] The decision at this early stage (of whether or not to have a study, and, if so, how it should be conducted) was, of course, crucial to the events that followed. In the first place, it was an openly acknowledged recognition of the existence of problems. More often than not the cloudy outlines of organizational objectives and directions for change were stated or were implicit in the statement of the problems. For example, Dixon in *Philadelphia Health* was from the beginning clearly committed to the development of community health centers. And it is hard to imagine the City Council of La Loma failing to anticipate the recommendation of an appointive city executive—either a city manager or administrative officer, even before they authorized the exploratory study. Thus, to a varying extent, this early decision was a commitment by the official(s) who made it to make—or at least press for—subsequent changes.

The second aspect of this decision—how the survey should be conducted and who should do it—was of nearly equal importance for the sequence of future events. For, as will be discussed below, the nature and organizational role of the surveyors, the nature of their "marching orders," the scope of the investigation, and the methods to be pursued conditioned importantly the kind of recommendations that would be made, as well as the kind of

10 The cases provide no evidence as to how frequently the decision at this stage is negative—that is, to do nothing.

11 It should be noted that, in the case of the *Ballistics Division,* there had been earlier studies relevant to Warner's decision; and he apparently felt that no more were needed. With regard to the *Children's Bureau,* it is almost certain that studies were made by the Budget Bureau and within the Federal Security Agency, but these were not described in the case.

CHART II–5. *Characteristics of the studies made in the cases*

CASE	*Phase*	*By Whom Conducted*	*Time Period*	*General Focus*
Agricultural Research	I	inside staff	14 months	regionalization plan
	II	management division work group	3½ months	implementation
Architecture		outside consultants (hired by Department)	3 months (4 months to presentation of final report)	organization and management
Automation	I	responsible official	5 weeks	technical, cost analysis
	II	two representative committees	23 months	personnel implementation
Ballistics		none		
Children's Bureau		unknown		
Fish and Game		outside consultants (hired by legislature)	1 year (to presentation)	program and management plan
Highway Patrol	I	outside staff agency	2½ months	organization plan
	II	inside staff and line men	2 months	personnel implementation
La Loma	I	outside consultants (hired by council)	1 month	exploratory
	II	outside consultants (hired by council)	4½ months	organization and management
Langley Porter		outside staff agency	4 months (4½ months to publication)	administrative management, Clinic mission
Personnel Board	I	inside staff and line committee	3 months	establishment of pilot unit
	II	inside staff and line	4 months	evaluation of pilot unit
	III	inside staff and line	3 months	implementation
Philadelphia Health		inside line committee (COOLS)	3 months	decentralization, district centers
U.S. Public Health	I	internal study group (staff and line)	1 month	mission
	II	internal study group (staff and line)	1½ months	organization
	III	representative task forces	2 months (average)	implementation

reception those proposals would have. And to a substantial extent, these effects were, or could have been, predicted in advance.

The Purposes of the Studies

The manifest purposes of the studies in all the cases that contained them were to gather information, including factual data and sometimes also attitudes and ideas, and to frame recommendations for action based upon this information. In a few instances, the study group was at first given the universe of possibilities to consider (*La Loma, U.S. Public Health* I). More frequently, possibilities were circumscribed in some degree, and the work was directed to recommending how best to achieve certain predetermined objectives (*Personnel Board* I and III, *Philadelphia Health*). The studies had other purposes, some of which may have been less manifest to those studied, to outsiders, and sometimes indeed to the study groups themselves. One was certainly to create a climate of acceptance within the organization through participation in the study itself or by providing employees the opportunity to contribute information and ideas. In other words, the study could be so set up and conducted as to win support for a given reorganization through the use of participative devices (as in *Philadelphia Health* and *Automation* II). A study could also have the opposite effect—that of arousing antagonism and resistance, as it undoubtedly did in *Fish and Game.* A study can be used to bring to bear on organization problems knowledges, skills, and techniques not available within the organization, such as the skills of management analysis, a common rationale for staff and consultant surveys. And it can be designed to provide a degree of objectivity and disinterest in treating such problems, likewise an argument for outside groups.

The Study Group

Obviously all these possible purposes of studies cannot equally be served by any single survey. Some types of surveys are patently in competition with others, and some are antithetical. Complete objectivity and disinterest are hardly conducive to employee participation. And skill in managerial analysis may be obtained at the price of relative ignorance about substantive professional problems. The desired emphasis in terms of purpose to a considerable extent dictates the way in which the study is set up, the composition and structure of the study team, its *modus operandi,* and the nature of its instructions.

The structure of the team may usefully be considered on a spectrum of its relationship to and the degree of control by the organization under study—from one controlled by groups within the organization to one that is almost completely detached from it. The range here is from the completely "inside" study, where line officials in their line capacities study operations within their range of responsibilities and interrelationships; to the completely "outside" study, which is initiated, controlled, staffed, and reported upon by persons outside the control or effective influence of the agency itself. Various positions along this spectrum, with examples from the cases, are shown in the next column.

Relationships of Study Groups to Organization Studied	*Case Examples*
OUTSIDE:	
private citizen or mixed group, established and reporting to superior executive and/or legislature	
legislative committee or group responsible to it	
private consultant, engaged by and reporting to legislative body or to chief executive or his staff	Fish and Game La Loma I and II
private consultant, engaged outside of agency by superior and reporting thereto	Architecture
government staff agency without agency invitation and reporting above or outside agency	
private consultant working with agency officials on agency invitation and reporting to agency head	
government staff agency, working with agency officials on agency invitation and reporting to agency head	Highway Patrol I Langley Porter
INSIDE:	
agency staff personnel, reporting to agency head	Personnel Board I and III Agricultural Research I and II
agency line officers, temporarily relieved of operating responsibilities, with or without assistance of staff personnel	Highway Patrol II Automation II U.S. Public Health I, II, and III
agency line officers, working part time on reorganization problems concerning their particular line responsibilities	Personnel Board II
agency head, with or without assistance of his immediate aides	Philadelphia Health Automation I

Our data from the cases are obviously inadequate to validate a proposition about the effects of differing modes of setting up study groups. They do suggest some generalizations which might be pursued in later research. Studies conducted by groups near the "outside" end of the spectrum appear likely to:

be more comprehensive;
be more objective and critical in considering agency program and welfare;

lay more emphasis on structural arrangements and administrative principles;
lay less emphasis on substantive, program considerations and on personnel;
result in longer and more elaborate reports;
contain a larger number of recommendations;
require an "inside" follow-up study to consider problems of practicability and implementation;
be more imitative of other like organizations in similar fields of activities.

Studies conducted by groups or individuals near the "inside" end of the continuum are likely to:

be less elaborate and less expensive;
result in shorter and clearer reports (sometimes they are not even written);
pay more attention to the problems of political and administrative feasibility;
give more emphasis to implementation and to the probable impact of organizational changes upon the welfare of personnel;
be more focused on specific and known problems rather than covering the universe;
be easier and quicker to implement.

Outside studies which are staffed by professionals in the survey business, whether from private consulting organization or governmental "O and M" staffs, are likely to be more skilled, sophisticated, and knowledgeable in the techniques of surveys and in the general lore of organization and procedures. They are at some disadvantage, both in attempting to understand the professional and technical aspects of the agency's work and in obtaining access to information. They also have a built-in motivation to criticize and to make many recommendations; after all, their work and their employers survive on the basis of recommending changes. In contrast, the inside study may have a motivation in the opposite direction—to minimize self-criticism and prevent radical changes.

Studies conducted by outside groups, presumed to be immune to the influence or bias of officials and others in the agency concerned, have certain distinctive characteristics. When such a study is initiated primarily in response to outside criticism, the presumed objectivity of an outside group has obvious advantages, at least from the standpoint of those who initiated it. Likewise, when an administrator is reasonably confident that the basic recommendations growing out of a study will accord with his own objectives and seeks to gain support of power centers beyond the limits of his agency, the aura of objectivity provided by a reputable outside survey group may greatly strengthen his hand in his search for external support. In such a situation, the purely inside study might be useless or even negative in its impact.

It is interesting to note in Chart II–6 the relationship between the type of survey groups, "inside" or "outside," and the topics on which the surveys primarily focused—program or policy change, administrative effectiveness, or personnel welfare.

Foci of Study[12]

Study Group	*Administrative Effectiveness*	*Policy/ Program*	*Personnel Welfare*
Inside	7	2	4
Outside	6	2	0

In general, the professionals in the survey business concentrated upon organization, administrative principles, improvement and centralization of controls, etc. On the other hand, studies in which the major focus was upon employee welfare were all made by inside groups.

The only instances in which outside groups concentrated upon policy/program as well as administrative matters were *Fish and Game,* in which the consultant firm expressly engaged on a temporary basis some professionals in the wildlife field, and *Langley Porter,* in which the staff agency specialists spent many hours with the Clinic's head and his deputy.

In general, the perceptions of all the study groups, both outside and inside, of the purposes of the reorganizations under consideration were more inclined toward the administrative side than were those purposes as perceived by the officials who initiated the studies.

Goals of projected reorganization	*As perceived by* INITIATORS[13]	STUDY GROUPS[14]
Administrative Effectiveness	20	13
Policy/Program	12	4
Personnel welfare or Problems	9	4
Outside Pressure or Threat	4	0

[12] In a number of instances emphasis was divided between two different foci.

[13] See Chart II-2. Both dominant and secondary goals are included.

[14] See Chart II-5. *Ballistics,* in which no study was made, and *Children's Bureau,* about which we have no study information, are not included in the "Study Groups" column.

CHART II–6. *Focus of surveys in relation to nature of survey group*

		INSIDE			OUTSIDE		
CASE	*Phase*	*Policy/ Program*	*Administrative Effectiveness*	*Personnel Welfare*	*Policy/ Program*	*Administrative Effectiveness*	*Personnel Welfare*
Agricultural Research	I		X				
	II		X				
Architecture						X	
Automation	I		X				
	II			X			
Fish and game					X	X	
Highway Patrol	I					X	
	II			X			
La Loma	I					X	
	II					X	
Langley Porter					X	X	
Personnel Board	I		X				
	II		X				
	III			X			
Philadelphia Health		X	X				
U.S. Public Health	I	X					
	II		X				
	III			X			
Total		2	7	4	2	6	0

The studies conducted by outside groups, whether staff agencies or private consultants, tended to emphasize the before-after approach. Their recommendations concerned how things should be *after* reorganization rather than how to go about reorganizing. They were less concerned with questions of strategy and of effects on the welfare of individuals and groups in the organization and probably less well equipped to deal with such questions.[15] Characteristically, therefore, outside studies were followed by a more or less extended inside review, discussion, and further study dealing with the problems of implementation.

[15] The outside studies in these cases are not necessarily representative in this respect. Many consulting firms and staff study agencies carry out implementation studies following acceptance of their basic recommendations, and those in these cases might have been called upon to do so. In fact, in one instance, *Architecture,* one recommendation in the consulting firm's report was followed by a contract for implementation—a project management system. However, this was not dealt with at any length in the case.

Inside studies generally, though not in all cases, gave more attention to implementation and to the impact of proposed changes upon personnel. Some of them indeed were directed solely to the problems of putting into effect basic decisions already reached (such as the COOLS study in *Philadelphia Health* and *Automation* II). But the composition of the study team resulted in variations in the recommendations that were made. Studies conducted by groups of top line officials (such as *Agricultural Research* I and II, *Personnel Board* II, *Philadelphia Health*) and by inside staff officials (such as *Personnel Board* I and III) laid emphasis on problems of implementation and particularly on impact of changes upon personnel. Some of them were, in fact, exclusively concerned with implementation, the basic decisions—to reorganize and in what directions—having already been made. Likewise, those studies conducted by groups presumed to be representative of the employees concerned, but not necessarily in the line of command (*Automation* II and the task forces in *U.S. Public Health*

III) directed their principal efforts to implementation and to creating a climate of acceptance of the recommendations.

On the other hand, in two instances, inside studies were focused almost exclusively upon end results rather than implementation. In both cases it is probably correct to say that the study personnel deliberately endeavored to approach their work with the objectivity and personal detachment of outsiders. The first of these (*Automation* I) was conducted alone by the hierarchical leader. His study about the desirability of installing automated equipment was based almost solely on rational and technical criteria. The second (*U.S. Public Health* I and II) was conducted by a study group selected from among the line personnel of the agency, who presumably could bring to bear their knowledge about different aspects and problems of the different agency programs. They were encouraged not to consider themselves as representatives of their organizations or their fields but to view the problems of the agency in a completely disinterested way. Both of these efforts were succeeded by studies by inside representative groups that directed themselves to the problems of implementation.

A striking difference between the outside and inside groups was in the far greater emphasis the former placed upon their *report* as such. This was partly, of course, a consequence of the nature of the audiences. The outside surveys were usually addressed to individuals and agencies beyond the organization studied or in addition to them. Most of these reports were published or made ready for publication, even if distribution was suppressed. These documents, *qua* reports, were on the whole impressive, comprehensive, and attractive, especially those by the private consulting firms. The surveyors themselves expressed pride in their studies and the reports that grew out of them. In contrast, some of the "inside" studies resulted in virtually no reports at all but rather in memoranda, oral reports, or official implementing documents. Some were simply typewritten or mimeographed. Few were printed.

One may draw certain tentative conclusions from these observations. A study can be an important strategic instrument for an executive and also for other parties who may initiate it. It may be used primarily to inform the proponents of change about opposition, obstacles, and costs of actions or appropriate timing for actions. The executive may use it as a delaying action to gain time, as well as to gain information. (This may have been true in *Philadelphia Health.*) Initiators outside an organization may use the survey as a weapon with which to discredit and undermine its leadership or as a device to force upon an organization changes in its policies (both played a part in *Fish and Game*). In general, when an executive has a reasonably clear view of the direction in which he wishes his agency to move, and when he feels secure in his own and his agency's position *vis-à-vis* outside forces, he will rely on an "inside" study under his control. The survey itself will in most cases center upon problems of implementation and internal acceptability. If the administrator is less confident about his direction and/or insecure about his position and the strength of his agency in relation to the outside environment, he is likely to call upon an outside group to conduct a study. The outside group is particularly useful if the administrator has as a principal objective the goal to educate and convince external institutions and individuals as to the merits of the agency and of programs he wishes it to carry out. The study may thus become an instrument of executive or legislative public relations, as well, perhaps, as counsel to the executive. Finally, studies *imposed* upon agencies from the outside or from above are frequently, if not usually, conducted by outside agencies.

Study Methods

The techniques pursued by the study groups in these cases were as variegated as were the types of groups themselves. Some were conducted entirely in secret (*Automation* I and probably also in the *Children's Bureau* case). Some invited maximum employee participation (*Automation* II and *Personnel Board* almost throughout). Most could take advantage of earlier reports, memoranda, and other documentation. When there was not recent, relevant material available, the study group was likely to launch a more thorough investigation. Studies conducted by professional surveyors of organizations tended to be more systematic, more thorough, and more standardized than those by insiders. They customarily took less for granted; reviewed earlier reports and other documentation; interviewed key personnel at length; conducted desk audits; observed operations. The inside studies were less formal, and some of them were more in the nature of consultations, discussions, and negotiations than studies. They took more for granted as to the "facts" and other relevant information, as in all likelihood they had justification for doing. But they were less well equipped to relate the experience of other organizations to their own organization and to analyze organizational problems. The principal exceptions to these remarks among the "insiders" were those agencies whose personnel were in the business of dealing with organizational and administrative problems (illustrated in *Personnel Board* and *Agricultural Research*).

The Decisions

It is clear from these cases that decisions on reorganization are seldom clear-cut, one-time actions. In all cases but one (*Ballistics*) there were prior decisions that led to, or committed, or put boundaries around, the basic one to reorganize or not. In some, the basic decision was only a matter of timing or strategy, its substance having been well established and even advertised previously. And from these basic decisions flowed a variety of subsequent decisions, generally catalogued within the expression, "implementation." These subsequent decisions sometimes had the effect of negating the basic decision (as in *La Loma*). The decision that announces and orders a change in structure is subject to much prior commitment and subsequent interpretation and application. In some cases it was a fiat (*Ballistics*); in others, merely an effectuation of an earlier announced policy (*Philadelphia Health*).

These basic decisions were in all cases made by the hierarchical boss—the director or commissioner or chief. But it is impossible to generalize as to the degree to which others besides the boss entered into the decision itself. In most of the cases it appears that he leaned more or less heavily upon the advice of his immediate advisers—though not the staff in general. In some, he delayed action in order to gain more understanding and support from his agency. Normally, some weeks or months followed the receipt of a study report, for gestation, discussion, argument, and (hopefully) consensus, at least among top personnel, before the administrator acted. During this period, the chief could hardly fail to consider the impact and reactions to the proposals within his organization as well as its potential impact outside and above. But however much he relied upon consultation and advice from others (and this is not very clear in some of the cases) the basic decision to reorganize or not—and the responsibility that went with it—were inevitably his.

With a single possible exception,[16] the decisions in all of the cases in this volume were positive with respect to subsequent organizational change. In the majority, the administrators decided not to implement the parts of the reorganizational plans that appeared most vulnerable to outside attack and/or internal resistance. (The outside and inside resistances were parallel and consonant with one another in a number of cases: *La Loma, Children's Bureau,* mental health in *U.S. Public Health.*) On these most vulnerable and controversial issues, the administrators sometimes delayed decision (as in *La Loma*), or compromised (as in *Children's Bureau*), or initiated a new study (as in *U.S. Public Health*). However, in two cases (*Ballistics* and *Automation*), the basic decisions were abrupt and peremptory, at least from the standpoints of the subordinate employees affected. Both confronted situations which were potentially controversial and disruptive and in which there was little room for compromise. The abruptness of the decisions therefore can be viewed as a deliberate effort to forestall anticipated resistance and to present the probable opposition with an accomplished fact.

In two cases, *Philadelphia Health* and *Personnel Board,* the decision to proceed with reorganization was preceded by a test or trial run of the plan in part of the organization. It is probable that in both instances the decision to test involved a degree of commitment on the part of the executive to move ahead later on an organization-wide basis, even though he still could reverse himself. They constituted not only tests but also demonstrations. Particularly in the *Personnel Board* case, the relative success of the pilot unit became a powerful argument to proceed with the entire plan. And during its extended operations, it served an educational purpose for its own members as well as others on the staff who could observe it.

Implementation

In all of the cases in which a positive decision toward organizational change was made, it set off a process of implementation whereby plans could be put into effect. In most instances implementation was extended over a considerable period, and in some was still going on when the case was written. This was a stormy period in several instances, and

[16] *Fish and Game* is difficult to interpret. Changes were made, but some participants and observers contend that they were being made anyway; that is, that they did not grow out of the reorganization study.

in a few, basic parts of the reorganization plan floundered. As has been indicated, the planning and carrying through of implementation was, in virtually all cases, an "inside" job; the surveys by outsiders seldom directed much attention to the problems of putting their proposals into effect.

In about half of the cases,[17] more or less formalized machinery was established for the purpose of planning the implementation, and in a few the planning groups continued to supervise or at least advise on the implementation process, to handle special problems as they arose, and to hear and negotiate on criticisms and appeals. The cases in which reorganization was least effective, or in which the implementation ran into the gravest difficulties, were ones in which no such formalized machinery for planning implementation was provided.[18]

The mechanisms for implementation planning were characteristically groups of inside personnel—either sub-executives in the chain of command (as in *Philadelphia Health*) or a mixture of officials and representatives of subordinates (as in *Automation*), or staff personnel working rather closely with officials and subordinates in the line (as in *Personnel Board* and *Highway Patrol*). In the majority of cases, the prime focus of the implementation planners was upon the impact of the reorganization upon the personnel of the agency, both as individuals and as occupational groups. They planned and negotiated assignments and transfers; determined the responsibilities of positions; and in some instances planned training programs. (See Chart II–7.)

In general, there was more opportunity for em-

[17] *Automation, U.S. Public Health, Agricultural Research, Highway Patrol, Personnel Board,* and *Philadelphia Health.*

[18] *Ballistics, La Loma,* and *Fish and Game.*

CHART II–7. *Goals of reorganization as seen by those concerned with implementation*

CASE	*Policy/ Program*		*Administrative Effectiveness*					*Personnel*		*Response to Outside*
	Emphasis	*Expansion*	*Centralized Control*	*Productivity*	*Decentralization*	*Economy*	*Principles*	*Opportunity-Welfare*	*Problems*	*Pressure or Threat*
Agricultural Research			XX	X	XX		X			
Architecture							X			XX
Automation				X				XX		
Ballistics	X								XX	
Children's Bureau	X		XX						X	
Fish and Game*										
Highway Patrol			X					XX		
La Loma			X						X	XX
Langley Porter	X	X						X	X	
Personnel Board				X			X	XX		
Philadelphia Health	X				XX			X		
U.S. Public Health	XX						X	X		

KEY: XX—dominant goal; X—secondary goal
* Little systematic implementation

ployees to participate at this stage than earlier, either individually or through representatives, although there was a good deal of variation on this matter among the agencies. And it may be noted that participation was usually limited to the more or less immediate problems attendant upon the effects upon individuals, not to the underlying content of the organizational change.

SUCCESS OR FAILURE?

The appraisal of the degrees of effectiveness of these reorganization efforts is a difficult undertaking for a variety of reasons. It would be simpler if one needed only to distinguish between those cases in which something happened and those in which nothing happened that would not have happened in all probability anyway. Among the cases, the latter situation was most nearly approached in *Fish and Game*. In all of the others, changes were in fact made, changes that clearly flowed out of the reorganization process. All may therefore be considered to have had some *structural* effectiveness, as that term was defined in the introductory chapter. But the far more meaningful question of *substantive* effectiveness is more elusive. It involves the appraisal of results against the criteria implicit in the statement of reorganization goals. Where the goals are simple (preferably only one) and specific and where results can be objectively counted—where a clear before-after comparison is possible—such an appraisal can be made. This situation pertained in only one case (*Automation*), although in two others (*Agricultural Research* and *Personnel Board*) there was some effort at before-after comparisons of productivity and/or costs.

There appear to be roughly four kinds of difficulties in appraising reorganizations. First, the *determination of goals* against which to measure results is no easy task. It was pointed out before that goals were usually multiple and complex and that weighing them was largely a subjective matter. In a few cases, a number of different individuals had something to do with initiating a reorganization process, and the goals differed from one individual to the next. In some, important goals were apparently unstated and could only be inferred from the evidence. Furthermore, in some cases the nature or at least the relative emphases of the goals changed significantly during the course of the process. However, in most of the cases it seemed possible to identify, at least roughly, the major goals and to give them a rough weighting in terms of their relative importance.

Second, the *appraisal of results* in all but one of the cases (*Automation*) had to be qualitative and largely subjective. Again the question arises as to who is making the appraisal. Those individuals most responsible for the reorganization effort and who must therefore assume most of the credit or blame are understandably inclined to look favorably upon their efforts or at least to speak about them favorably, especially when speaking of them for publication.

A third problem concerns the *costs* incident to and arising from reorganization. All of these efforts involved costs, and in some they were very heavy—perhaps more so than the values gained. (It is doubtful that, at the time of writing the *La Loma* case, the results achieved even approached the costs incurred.) Some of the costs incurred by the contracted surveys were very direct and very definite ($100,000 for the *Fish and Game* survey). Others that could be directly attributed to the process of reorganization were less measurable but probably on the whole more substantial. They included the working time and effort applied to the process by employees, the insecurity, stress, and dissension in the staff and the concomitant temporary disruption of working relationships, temporary turnover, the costs of training and re-equipping personnel for new kinds of jobs, the temporary fall-off which occurred occasionally in productivity and in quality of product, and others. In addition, there were in some instances more or less continuing costs after the reorganization process which might or might not decline and vanish over time. These included frictions within and outside the agency, losses in some kinds of skills, and lowered morale among some workers. Costs of these kinds were certainly not "intended" in the sense that they were not a part of the goals of the reorganizers. But there were not necessarily "unanticipated" either. Many were fully expected, weighed in advance, and feared. And a good deal of the effort in the process, particularly during the implementation stages, was directed to minimizing them.

A final difficulty that should be mentioned is the matter of *time*. The consequences of most major organizational changes—and especially those aiming to modify policy and program—are often not detectable at once; they emerge gradually over the years. And sometimes reorganization efforts that appear to have failed subsequently prove to have been seeds for major changes that come later. All the cases were studied within a fairly short period after the major parts of the process, although in some the implementation was still going on. It was too early to make more than a tentative judgment about ultimate effects.

The accompanying Chart II–8 is a summation of judgments concerning the apparent degrees of success, and the costs, of the various reorganization efforts in these cases. It is based in the first instance

CHART II–8. *Estimates of effectiveness and costs of reorganizations (grouped according to degree of net success)*

CASE	*Structural Effectiveness*	*Substantive Effectiveness*	*Comment*	*Costs**
GENERALLY EFFECTIVE				
Agricultural Research	complete	substantial	major goals accomplished; still problems of relationships and delegation	moderate
Automation	complete	complete	goal accomplished; economy and morale maintained	moderate
Ballistics	complete	substantial	completely effective in terms of Research Department, but no evidence as to effects on work of Laboratory as a whole	substantial
Highway Patrol	complete	apparently substantial	but evidence of major changes thin	low
Langley Porter	moderate	substantial	changed image and even name (institute); large successive budget increases; many compromises on organization plan; overall the extra-structural gains far more important than reorganization *per se*	moderate
Personnel Board	complete	substantial	employee morale and opportunity improved; services to departments improved; little change in productivity; not entirely generalized	low
MODERATELY OR PARTIALLY EFFECTIVE				
Architecture	moderate	moderate	some formal changes made considerably later	moderate
Children's Bureau	moderate, partial	moderate	Bureau moved, but retained much of autonomy within FSA	moderate
Philadelphia Health	substantial	low, partial	community offices still relatively weak; and policy and program still centered at top; but too early to judge	moderate
U.S. Public Health	substantial but partial	probably substantial but partial	too early to judge; important areas and problems were avoided or delayed	unknown
RELATIVELY LOW EFFECTIVENESS				
Fish and Game	low	low	no significant results; Commissioner removed, but not as consequence of reorganization process	high
La Loma	low	low	established office of CAO and revamped Police Department; but little else accomplished at time of case	high

* In relation to substantive effectiveness

on judgments of the principal instigators and leaders of the efforts themselves. These were modified to some extent by judgments of others—participants and observers. Both were taken into account by the student and writer of the case study, and his analysis is the basic source of the chart. It was reevaluated by the author of these paragraphs to make it comparable with the other cases and, to a limited extent and in a few cases, modified in the light of the evidence. Although the appraisals are crude and subjective, it is doubtful that the very broad outline is far off the mark. A few reorganizations were quite clearly successful; a few were obviously failures; and the remainder fell somewhere in between—partially effective but often with high costs.

Some general observations may be made about the relative success in these reorganizations, but, for reasons mentioned below, one should hesitate before extending them to reorganizations in general. First, those directed and/or guided by persons specializing in administrative fields and those that aimed at administrative goals or concentrated on administrative problems tended to be more successful than those that aimed at programmatic changes and changes in professional behaviors. Second, those imposed upon the organizations from above or otherwise outside, which included all of those by private consultant groups as well as the *Children's Bureau* and *Ballistics,* usually met substantial opposition within the agencies concerned; and by and large were least successful. Third, a corollary of the above, those based upon studies conducted by "insiders" tended to be more successful than those that were studied by "outsiders"; but those that leaned upon outside staff agencies studying under the auspices of and in close contact with insiders (*Highway Patrol* and *Langley Porter*) were relatively successful. Fourth, those that gave major and formalized attention to the problems of implementation were generally more successful in bringing about changes than those that occurred on the more impersonal, objective, before-after approach.

These observations are suggestive for future study but little more than that. The sample is inadequate in number, even if it were truly representative. There are several reasons to question its representativeness so far as reorganization success is concerned. There is undoubtedly some warping in the *selection of cases* in the directions of success. This is a consequence of the problem of access to case research: the expectable tendency of agency officials and personnel to grant information about success stories, and their equally expectable reluctance to discuss conspicuous failures for which they have had some responsibility. That the average degree of success in these cases is relatively exaggerated is suggested in the cases themselves. Most of these reorganizations had been preceded by one or more earlier efforts which were not conspicuously successful.

The least successful of the reorganization efforts were also, at least in considerable part, the consequence of skewing in case selection. Each was somewhat unusual in that it was in effect imposed upon an agency and carried out under auspices and directions above and outside it. The objectives of these studies and/or the terms under which they were conducted may well have been atypical.

SUMMARY

Reorganizations which tend to involve substantial changes in behaviors and human relationships are slow and time-taking. They are rarely a single and simple action based upon a single and simple decision. In all the studies described herein, there was a lengthy buildup of a problem situation, up to a decade; and in most reorganizations that had any significant effect, the process of change went on—and is still going on—over a number of years. Reorganizations are the products of a great number of decisions, many of which in some degree commit the organization to future courses of action and to future decisions. They are not merely sequential; they are cumulative.

Reorganizations are here measured primarily against the goals sought by their responsible initiators. These are various and are commonly related to projected changes in agency "image," policy, and program. Rather few were based upon the traditional goals of "economy and efficiency." Most of these reorganizations relied upon formalized study and planning mechanisms and processes. The nature, the composition, the methods, and the auspices of these study groups significantly conditioned their products as well as the likelihood that their proposals would be given effect. To a substantial degree, the products of these groups were predictable in advance, at least in broad outline.

CHAPTER III

Participation and Reorganization

THE PARTICIPATION HYPOTHESIS: ITS DEVELOPMENT AND RATIONALE[1]

The roots of the participation hypothesis lie deep in western social and political philosophy. Though usually expressed in different words, its central tenets have for 2,500 years been essentially synonymous in the political realm with democracy itself. They include: the right, whether or not "natural," for the citizen to have a voice in group or social decisions affecting his destiny; the obligation that public policy pursue the community will; and the essential autonomy of the individual. The purest political expressions have been represented in such situations as the government of the Athenian city-state, the primary assemblies of Swiss cantons, the New England town meetings. Early Christianity and later the Protestant Ethic gave religious support to the integrity and dignity of the individual. North America and the United States during its first century, with their opportunities and necessities for individual pioneering, provided fertile grounds for the flowering of the individualistic spirit. Jefferson, Jackson, and Lincoln, through their pronouncements and actions, gave it support, both affective and effective.

In the political realm, the autonomy of the individual and the democratic ideal have long been the enemies of tyranny, feudalism, totalitarianism, and the "closed society." In the areas of economics and bureaucratic organization, these ideals came somewhat later—in the late nineteenth and early twentieth centuries. In fact, the emergence of the participation hypothesis was, in an important sense, the product of a collision between our political and social ideology on the one hand and the industrial revolution on the other. While we were laying increasing stress upon the integrity of the individual in his political life, the growth of large, impersonal, and authoritarian organizations in the industrial sphere was a denial of it. The individual in his economic context was treated increasingly as a cog in the machine of production. His integrity as a human being and his human uniqueness were threatened more by the economic and organizational systems than by the political system. Reactions against these trends in the late nineteenth and early twentieth centuries contributed to a variety of social movements: the Knights of Labor, the I.W.W., and ultimately to a general labor movement; the efforts to restrain organizational growth as epitomized in antitrust legislation; the beginnings of social and economic reform legislation; the cooperative movement; and efforts to introduce a variety of devices for "industrial democracy," some of them quite utopian. Underlying all of these was a basic contradiction between the operations of an authoritarian type of organizational structure, particularly in the industrial sphere, and the ideals of a democratic polity. The basic dilemma, which remains today, was how to correlate an organizational society with principles of individualism and political egalitarianism.

During the period following World War I, a number of students of and writers about our society gave vigorous voice to the ideal of democracy in administrative organizations. Among these, one of the most fervent was Ordway Tead, whose many works, beginning in 1918, expressed an ardent espousal of the individual and the principles of democracy, coupled with and buttressed by a profound religious faith, a knowledge of industrial

[1] This section is intended only as a very summary sketch to introduce the reader to the rest of the chapter. A selected bibliography of some of the major books relevant to the participation hypothesis is contained in Appendix II.

psychology, and an understanding of the realities of business management. Democratic administration[2] was a central theme and very nearly a creed in Tead's work. The ideal of democracy was central also to the books and papers of one of Tead's most influential contemporaries, Mary Parker Follett, who may properly, I think, be regarded as the godmother of the participation hypothesis in business. A student of political science, of social work, and finally of business management, Miss Follett's papers and other writings of the 1920's and early 1930's foreshadowed much of what is now nearly standard doctrine in industrial psychology and management. She wrote of the "law of the situation," of "circular response," of "integration" in decision-making as opposed to domination or compromise, of orders deriving from the situation rather than from the authority associated with hierarchy, and of "creative experience" in organization. In her time, there was rather little objective, scientific evidence upon which Miss Follett could base or support her insights, and it does not appear that her work directly stimulated subsequent investigations of social scientists in the phenomena of bureaucratic organization. Yet the current reader of Follett's papers, now three decades or more old, is startled by her presaging of much current academic thinking. For our purposes, her most important idea was that participation by employees in decision-making would contribute to more effectiveness in the accomplishment of organizational purposes.

Although there was some earlier work in some social sciences that lent support to what later became known as the participation hypothesis, notably in the emergence of social psychology and in industrial psychology, its major scientific launching pads were two, both laid in the 1920's and 1930's. The first was the studies, initiated under the direction of Elton Mayo at the Hawthorne plant of the General Electric Company near Chicago, which produced a great variety of analyses and monographs about social organization in industry, production norms, the importance of individual history in organizational performance, and the relation (or distance) between organizational, group, and individual goals in production. The second was the studies, carried out under the leadership of Kurt Lewin at the University of Iowa, of groups, leadership patterns, and change-making. Both contributed to what later became widely popularized as "human relations," as well as the recognition of social as against formal organization, and to the importance both of the small group and of the individual employee as a human being in a social setting. Further studies and emanations of the Hawthorne experiments led to a revolution in views on industrial relations. The experiments at Iowa provided the foundation of a new discipline of group dynamics. The Hawthorne experimenters were principally anthropologists and students of business; the Lewinian students and disciples were principally social psychologists. But the approaches first dramatized in the Hawthorne and Iowa studies spread into all the social sciences and contributed to the administrative and organizational aspects of what later became known as the behavioral sciences. After World War II, there were a great many studies and experiments in a wide variety of organizational contexts which amplified, or supported, or qualified their early approaches and findings, and these are continuing today. Students in this area are now a good deal more sophisticated, but their central foci of interest have not greatly changed—the individual in organization, the small group, communications, and different kinds of leadership.

It is very probable that the motivating sources of the human relations movement and of the participation hypothesis were ideological in nature. I hasten to add that this statement is intended in no sense of disparagement. Mayo, an anthropologist, was intensely concerned about the impact of the autocratic management of the factory upon the individual worker, and its consequences for the society.[3] Lewin, a refugee from Naziism, believed intensely in the freedom of the individual from oppression and suppression. Both opposed the treatment of the individual as an automaton without ideas or feelings. Their studies and many of those that followed lent pragmatic support to a profound faith: administration that took account of people as sensitive and creative human beings produced more and better than authoritarian administration, not alone for the individual employee but for the organization as well. A sizable number of studies in business and industry demonstrated the superiority of permissive and participative management practices in terms both of employee satis-

[2] This phrase also furnished the title of one of his books, published in 1945.

[3] Critics have, perhaps correctly, charged Mayo and his disciples with a basically paternalistic bias in behalf of management as against the workers. However valid the charge may be with regard to the uses of the Hawthorne studies, there seems little doubt that Mayo himself had great concern about the social and human consequences of industrial organizations.

faction and of managerial goals—i.e., productivity.

In the decades since the Hawthorne and Iowa observations, there have been a great many studies related to the participation theme. These have attracted leading scholars from a variety of social disciplines: psychology and social psychology, sociology, applied anthropology, psychiatry, and political science. Their work has ranged from general theorizing and deduction to rigorously controlled experiment, including in the spectrum survey research, observation and case recording, participant-observation, psychological testing, and others. There has also been a wide range of emphases and foci: on the small group and its leadership (the Research Center for Group Dynamics at Michigan, the Shartle group at Ohio State, and a variety of others); on supervision and styles of leadership in larger organizations and their effects upon productivity (the Survey Research Center at Michigan, the Tavistock Institute of Human Relations in London); on the worker in formal organizations (Argyris and Bakke at Yale); on the sociology of large organizations (a large number of individual scholars including Merton, Dubin, Gouldner, Blau, Etzioni, Selznick, and others); on decision-making (Simon, March, and others); and on planned change (virtually all of the above).

In view of this considerable variety of approaches to the subject, and of the increasing sophistication of students in this field, it is doubtful that any single definition of the participation hypothesis could adequately comprehend the topic. The one upon which we have principally relied in our case research was that of Herbert A. Simon of a decade ago:[4] ". . . Significant changes in human behavior can be brought about rapidly only if the persons who are expected to change participate in deciding what the change shall be and how it shall be made." Behind, within, and beyond this apparently simple and direct statement are a myriad of approaches and facets. Without undertaking any comprehensive summary of these, it may be useful to mention four emphases which seem most relevant to this study.

The Dynamics of the Small Group

It seems fairly clear that the principal source of the participation hypothesis was the small, face-to-face group—observations of it, controlled experiments on it, working through it. In general, the findings of early studies indicated that behaviors and habits could be most rapidly, most permanently, and most happily changed when decisions about the change were reached by those who were to change them in groups in which discussion was free, direction permissive, and participation encouraged. Each participant could contribute to a group decision, preferably reflecting a consensus; each would thus understand the reasons for the change; each would have a stake in making the change effective, acquired through involvement in the decision-making; each would be motivated and supported by the force and strength of the group. Studies in a wide variety of laboratory, as well as natural, settings lent support to the general finding, even though later research tended to question and qualify some elements of it.

Theory on the functioning of small groups is based largely upon situations in which persons are associated together over some period of time in face-to-face relationships. The extension of conclusions about small group behavior to larger organizations in which groups are less clearly defined, constantly shifting in membership, and amorphous at the boundaries has presented a continuing challenge. Some favor the restructuring of large organizations in such a fashion that they would consist entirely of small groups. Others have concentrated their attention and research in larger organizations upon units which, in the main, conformed to the small group prototype. In business and industrial concerns, this has meant emphasis upon the small working organization at and below the first-level supervisor or foreman. But the problem of relating findings of small group research to complex organizations—and particularly that associated with participation—remains; and it is one to which considerable attention is given in later pages.

Leadership Style

From the very beginning, studies in human relations and the behavioral sciences have emphasized the importance of the nature of leadership, the interactions between leaders and followers, the impact of leadership style upon the motivation and morale—and thus the behavior (i.e., performance) —of followers. Lewin's early studies and others that followed apparently gave scientific evidence of the superiority of democratic leadership over other types, defined by Lewin as authoritarian and

[4] "Recent Advances in Organization Theory," *Research Frontiers in Politics and Government* (Washington: The Brookings Institution, 1955), pp. 28-29.

laissez-faire, respectively. Democratic leadership is, almost by definition, leadership which encourages group discussion and decision—i.e., participation—and which involves an effective degree of delegation by the leader to his followers. It has sometimes, in fact, been called participatory leadership. A great many studies of leadership behavior in both real-life and artificial situations have tended to confirm that a democratic style of leadership contributes to follower satisfaction and morale, to less apathetic or hostile or aggressive behavior on the part of followers, to quicker adoption of changes, and to as great or greater productivity. But the findings have not been universal nor without qualifications on the matter. Perhaps most relevant for our present purposes have been the many studies conducted in private business organizations wherein leadership style has been the primary variable and it has been related to employee and supervisory attitudes, to productivity where measurable, and to such other indices as absenteeism and turnover.[5] It should be noted again, however, that most of these studies involved units of organization at the lower levels of hierarchies where something like the small-group situation could be simulated.

The Individual versus Formal Organization

A somewhat different stimulus for the participation theme derives from concern for the individual personality in the context of large, formal organization. Here the focus is upon the individual and the consequences for him of monotonous, routinized operations, of operating under a rigid system of rules, regulations, and superior-subordinate relationships, and of denying opportunities of self-development, determination of the purposes, processes, and conditions of work, and a sense of accomplishment through rewarding and creative work efforts. These consequences are seen as essentially damaging to the growth of the individual personality, giving rise to anomie, apathy, withdrawal and alienation, regression, aggression, or outright hostility, all of them injurious not only to the individual but also to the effectiveness of the organization. Among the weapons proposed for combating these tendencies are broadening and providing more challenge to individual jobs, providing opportunities for participation in decision-making, and generally relaxing the strictures of bureaucratic organization. The theme here is similar but its target is upon the personality of the worker, not upon the group nor upon the effectiveness of decisions. Participation is put forward as an instrument whereby the individual can "self-actualize" his potentialities on the job.[6]

Power Equalization

A more recent and somewhat broader interpretation of the participation hypothesis views it as a device, probably the principal device, whereby the different degrees of power and status between different levels of hierarchy may be minimized. This approach, though relying heavily on the earlier findings about the small group, leadership styles, and the needs of the individual personality, views participation in a somewhat more generalized context as an instrument for redistributing effective power within a large organization. In a sense, this view aims to correct, or at least mollify, the older, autocratic theory of organization and scientific management. In another sense, it is an attempt to adapt the small group of peers situation to larger organizations where hierarchy and authorities are important realities.

The main threads that run through the research and literature about participation may be summarized as follows:

participation in decision-making within a group or larger organization increases one's identification and involvement with the group and the organization;

it also identifies him affectively with the decision itself and motivates him to change his behavior and to make the decision successful;

it contributes to his motivation toward the accomplishment of organizational or group goals—i.e., it helps fuse group and organizational goals with individual goals;

it contributes to morale in general, and this usually contributes to more effective performance on the job—i.e., higher productivity;

a primary factor affecting "participativeness" is leadership style;

participative practices contribute to the "self-actualization" of the individual in the work situation and to the lessening of the differentials in power and status in a hierarchy.

It would be inappropriate here to undertake a general criticism of the participation theme or even

[5] See particularly various studies by the Survey Research Center and its director, Rensis Likert, and by the Tavistock Institute.

[6] On this approach, see particularly the writings of Chris Argyris.

a summary of the criticisms of others, which have been increasingly incisive in recent years. But it seems proper to call attention to certain limitations particularly relevant to the analysis of the case studies.

First, the participation idea itself stems from, and has been largely supported by, studies in small groups and in lower-level units of larger organizations that can be observed somewhat as though they were small groups. There has been rather little study of the participation hypothesis in policy-making near the top of complex organizations comparable to those considered in these cases. The content of the decisions in these cases, as well as the level to which they are directed, is considerably different from most earlier studies in this field.

Second, participation has not usually been precisely defined and, as a matter of fact, may not be precisely definable. Our own use of the term is rather loose and general. A liberal definition seems essential in view of the nature and level of organizations treated in the cases.

Third, the range within which participative decision has been encouraged and permitted in research, even in most of the artificial small groups, has been carefully circumscribed. In all but a few instances, the leaders are named, the ground rules prescribed, the scope of decision authority defined *from above.* The popular term of "democratic leadership" in administrative organizations—and even in small-group research—differs essentially from democratic leadership in a political society. In the latter, the leader is chosen by the followers and may be removed by them; and the scope of decision is unlimited except by constitution and mores. In administrative organizations, whether private or public, leadership is typically named and removable only from above, and the scope within which participative practices are possible is narrowed. This is true both in research and in practice. Participation may be only an instrument of persuasion for what superiors have already decided upon (and this has been a fairly frequent charge). It may be restricted only to the consideration of means whereby management decisions should be implemented; in fact, this type of participative decision appears to be most frequent. The literature includes rather few instances in which participation was systematically used in the reaching of major policy decisions.

Fourth, there has been a conspicuous absence of studies and literature about governmental organizations, a large and very influential segment of our organizational life. In the study of participation, this omission raises a number of questions, of which I would mention two. One is the question of relating the methodology and the ideology of organizational democracy with those of political democracy and representation. The second has to do with who the participants are or should be. Do we restrict our definition of participants to the immediate "members" of the organization who receive a wage or salary for services rendered? Or do we extend the definition to include special clienteles, interest groups, and even the general public who have an interest and frequently express it in the operations of an agency?

For political theorists and students of public administration, the democratic management thesis appears to have come almost full circle. From a base in both ancient and modern political thought, it has been revived in private and particularly industrial management, been given scientific support, and can now return to the sphere of public management. But in two important respects, the circle has not been completed. On the pragmatic plane, there has been almost no systematic observation or testing of the tenets of democratic or participative administration at the policy-making levels of government.[7] On the theoretical plane, there has been little confrontation of the problem of rationalizing political democracy, with its accompanying instruments of representation and political responsibility on the one hand, with democratic or participative administration on the other.

7 Almost all the research work in government based upon the democratic management approach has occurred in specialized and subordinate agencies where the subjects might more easily be controlled and observed—prisons, subordinate military units, hospitals (particularly mental institutions), schools, and research laboratories.

OBSTACLES TO PARTICIPATION IN PUBLIC ADMINISTRATION

There are at least four inherent obstacles to the employment of participative practices in administrative decision-making in sizable governmental organizations. The first of these arises simply from *size* and the mechanical difficulty of bringing into effective participation some hundreds or thousands of individuals who may be affected by a decision. We have already noted that much of the research and literature about participation has concerned the small face-to-face group, and there has been rather little discussion of how the alleged advantages of participation may be realized on decisions of broad range in large organizations. In fact, there seems to be some doubt as to whether the participation hypothesis can or should be applied in larger settings. If it does not apply, its potential significance in public administration is greatly diminished, since the bulk of major decisions are inevitably made on a broader scale than that within the purview of the face-to-face group. Few public administrators can have direct contact with all of their subordinates on most of their decision problems.

The problem of size is mitigated to some extent in most typical reorganizations by the fact that a substantial proportion of employees are not materially affected, and in some only a very few may find their roles, statuses, or relationships modified. According to the definition of participation used in this study, the involvement of employees not expected to be affected by a projected organizational change is not essential to a participative process. In the organizations described in this volume, the custodial, laboring, and clerical personnel were neither materially affected by the proposals nor significantly involved in the processes of change; nor were many of the operating personnel, such as the patrolmen on the road in the *Highway Patrol* case, the nurses in *Langley Porter*, the test pilots in the *Ballistics* case.

A second major obstacle to participation in administrative organizations is a simple consequence of *hierarchy*, sometimes described as the scalar principle. Hierarchy appears to be an inevitable and essential ingredient of all sizable administrative organizations. Officers at whatever level (except perhaps at the very apex) derive their authority from one or more superiors and are in some degree responsible to them for actions of their subordinates. Under such circumstances, any substantial sharing of power by a leader with his subordinates involves a certain amount of risk to himself unless he has strong confidence that they will propose and take actions that he can defend before his superiors. Complete reliance upon participative decision might not only undermine his position with superiors; it could also erode the respect and posture of leadership he holds among his subordinates. The official who is relatively strong and independent *vis-à-vis* his superiors and secure in that strength can risk participative activity which a less confident official would avoid. This is well illustrated in the two most "participative" cases in this volume: the California Personnel Board, a constitutionally independent body, gave its Executive Officer virtually complete authority to reorganize; and similarly, the Commissioner of Public Health in Philadelphia in his early years was in a position of strength wherein he could delegate substantial decision-making authority down the line. But this can also work the other way. An executive with complete confidence in his support from above can sometimes afford to forego any pretense of participation, even where some might normally be expected. This was surely illustrated in the *Ballistics* case and probably, though to a lesser extent, in the *Highway Patrol* case. He has no fear of employee resistance and need not rely upon employee support.

Many of the research studies on which the participation hypothesis was built were conducted among groups in which the hierarchical element (above the group leader) was completely absent or which were temporarily immunized from outside control. Hierarchy does not prevent the utilization of participative processes, but it does set limits within which they may be employed. These limits will vary widely among different organizations and within the same organization at different times.

A third obstacle to participation, one that is particularly relevant to governmental agencies, arises from the wide *scatter of power* to make and carry out basic decisions. This is partly a matter of hierarchy (as discussed above), partly of law (in a nation built on the concept of division of powers), and partly of politics (which may and often does involve the actual or potential influence of political parties, clientele and interest groups, legislatures and their committees, and influential individuals, employee groups, and others). The legal complexities of governmental reorganization are usually considerable and often tremendous. In agencies that are exposed to the public or a significant clientele and that operate in controversial fields, political considerations are unavoidable. Seldom can a single official, no matter what his rank, order a major reorganization of his agency without facing the prospect of review, modification, or veto elsewhere. In other words, the legal authority and the political power of any official in the realm of reorganization is normally only partial. It appears tautological that one cannot share with subordinates power that he does not have himself.[8] The responsible official must take into account not only the relative merits of a projected organizational change, but also the legal possibilities and mechanisms and the political strategies involved. On these kinds of considerations, the contribution of subordinates, however wise they may be on substantive and organizational matters, are less likely to be helpful and may often be damaging, even to their own interests. The top official can not very well share with others far from himself the basic decisions on feasibility and strategy in dealing with outside powers.

This kind of consideration is an obstacle to a participative process but not a prohibition of it. It again suggests limitations within which participative planning and decision may be carried on.

A fourth obstacle to participation in large organizations arises from the factor of *time*. The process of reaching consensus through education, study, discussion, and interaction is usually slow and laborious. While there is urgency and a necessity for decisiveness, widespread participation in decision-making is virtually impossible. On the other hand, in the absence of pressure for rapid change, participation may be not only possible but even necessary.[9] As suggested in the preceding chapter, the possibilities of organizational change are usually the result of events, such as changes in leadership, which render an organization temporarily pliable. They are customarily followed by a congealing period when significant change becomes increasingly difficult. The most propitious time for reorganization is soon after the spark, and a long delay for participative decision-reaching may dissipate the opportunity (as it apparently did in *Philadelphia Health*).

8 Though it is quite possible that one may gain greater power under certain circumstances by sharing what he already has.

9 Thus, in the *Personnel Board* case, there was no outside impetus for change and no crisis or change in leadership to spark it. Under these circumstances, one may conjecture that the extended discussions and testing were *necessary* to the adoption and acceptance of the change finally effected.

PARTICIPATIVE DEVICES IN LARGE ORGANIZATIONS

The foregoing obstacles make it clear that the application of the "pure" or group dynamics definition of participation at the level of major decision in large organizations would be severely limited at best. On the other hand, there are forms and devices which can and, in fact, have been used to achieve at least in part the presumed advantages of participation among substantial numbers of employees and others. One of these, not illustrated in these cases, is a vote, a *referendum* on proposed changes.[10] Apart from the very real practical difficulties of voting on reorganization, it would be most difficult to make a vote a truly participative process. Unless preceded by a well-planned period of education and discussion, usually laborious, expensive, and lengthy, it could hardly satisfy the basic requisites of the participation hypothesis.

A number of other devices with a participative flavor are available for reorganizations affecting large numbers of people, and most of them were to some extent utilized in some of the cases. One is a *hierarchy of meetings,* usually staff meetings, whereby the lowest levels of staff potentially affected by a proposal are reached and encouraged to express their views. These expressions are then communicated, at least in summary form, to higher level meetings and become part of the grist of decision. A good example of this was the *Personnel Board* case, but the process was used in several other cases at the implementation stage. Another, and related, device is that of *representation,* whereby one individual, usually a superior, is presumed to express and support the views of others whom he represents in decision-making consultations. The idea of representation, in fact, seems necessary to participative decision in large-scale organizations, just as it is in large-scale political democracy. Its application, explicit or implicit, is

10 There are a number of illustrations of this device in both public and private organizations. One is the vote on union affiliation, now utilized in both private and some public organizations. Another was the vote late in World War II of soldiers as to the criteria for separation from military service, which allegedly determined the point system utilized in 1945 and 1946. The various referenda of farmers on agricultural crop and price control are examples of the use of referenda in the determination of federal government policy.

illustrated in virtually all of the cases in which there was a gesture toward participation. It should be noted that representation in administrative organizations differs from that in democratic political theory in important respects. There is an assumption in democracy that the representative is chosen by those he purports to represent and is answerable to, and removable by, them. Such is not usually the case within administrative organizations, at least in formal terms. In none of the agencies in these cases were the spokesmen, the "representatives," chosen or removable by their "constituents." Yet there can be little doubt that participants in high-level, "summit" meetings often construe their missions as representing the interests of their subordinates and/or other professionals or specialists of whom they are a leader. Nor can there be doubt that in many instances such individuals are viewed by their subordinates and/or fellows as individuals who will advance and protect their views, their attitudes, and their ideas. Representation of this kind depends heavily upon the assumption that individuals in given positions and with given backgrounds will behave in predictable ways, ways that they and their followers both expect to be responsive to the views and interests of the latter.

A further device contributing to the participative nature of decision-reaching in large organizations is the *delegation* to subordinate personnel of authority and responsibility to consider, plan, and even decide on projected changes. Delegation is normally partial in the sense that each "delegatee" is granted jurisdiction over some phase or area of activity within a larger decision framework. It often, though not invariably, follows hierarchical lines; that is, the official of higher rank delegates to the next level appropriate segments of the larger decision problem. Such a process makes possible participative practices. The delegatees may, in their respective jurisdictions, elicit the views and contributions of their subordinates, or they may further subdivide and redelegate on down the line.

A final participative device is *consultation* by decision-makers or influential decision-advisers with individuals, either singly or in groups, who will be affected by projected changes. Here again, effectiveness as a participative tool depends heavily upon the expectations those consulted have as to whether their views so elicited will in fact influence subsequent decisions. And this in turn depends upon the subject matter of consultation (e.g., whether only for objective, factual information or for attitudes and prejudices, or for thoughts and recommendations) and upon the manner in which the consultation is conducted. It is entirely possible that a consultation may have a negative participative impact, e.g., when the consultant clearly disdains the views of those he is consulting.

In sum, there appear to be five principal devices whereby subordinate employees may participate in decisions in large-scale organizations: a referendum; a system of meetings of different groups, usually on a hierarchical basis with appropriate means of communication to the central decision-making point; representation; delegation; and consultation. Two or more of them may be, and often are, used in combination where there is effort to elicit participation. There is, however, no assurance that employees will participate, whatever mechanics are employed; participation depends upon the expectations of the participants, upon the style, manner, and content of the subject to be discussed, and perhaps most importantly upon whether the employees feel that their views are in fact influential in decisions. It is doubtful that any or all of these devices would satisfy the definitions of many group dynamicists who view "pure" participation as possible only in the face-to-face group. Participation of this kind, however, would be impossible in large-scale organizations. The concept used in this chapter is looser and broader, and one that is probably more difficult to practice and less definitive to study.

PARTICIPATION IN THESE CASES

By Subordinate Officers and Employees

One's immediate impression from the reading of these cases is that participation by subordinates in the agencies concerned was generally low, even according to the liberal use of the term proposed above. As indicated in Chapter II, there were in most of the cases at least two key decisions made at two different times and stages in the reorganization process: the *initiatory decision* to launch some manner of study;[11] and the *basic decision* to reorganize along certain lines or not. Both of these decisions were unmistakably made by the top man

[11] As noted earlier, no such decision occurred in *Ballistics,* and we have insufficient information about the *Children's Bureau.*

(or by a group of outside officials in those instances where a study was imposed from outside). The initiatory decision was characteristically reached in secret, following discussions with a very limited group of top officials and with officials superior to or outside the agency itself. The circle involved in discussions and consultations at the time of, or just before, the basic decisions was somewhat broader in several cases (notably *Personnel Board* and the two public health cases). And in two or three cases, there were group meetings with open and invited discussion of proposals. It is clear that this kind of participation, to the extent it occurred, was often real and not "pseudo"; that the responsible executive was receptive to comments, ideas, and criticisms and was influenced by them. But the circle of effective participants was in general a small one, consisting principally of the top line and staff officials.[12] In many instances, these participating officials behaved as though they were representing their subordinates or their professional groups and were so perceived, e.g., Miss Hall as representing the Philadelphia nurses, and Dr. Felix the mental health specialists in the *U.S. Public Health* case.

Yet, if we consider the other two important phases of the reorganization process—the study which followed the initiatory decision and the implementation which followed the action decision—it is clear that there was a good deal of participation in several of the cases. The degree to which it occurred depended in part upon the nature of the groups primarily responsible for these processes and upon the kinds of techniques they used. Many of the studies were, in fact, organization surveys involving direct contacts between the surveyors and the officers and other employees, through interviews, desk audits, informal conversations, and, in a few cases, group meetings. In the cases where these interchanges were employed solely for the eliciting of facts, it cannot be said that they involved any substantial participation. But they might also be used to assess attitudes, to invite ideas and suggestions, and to obtain reactions to ideas or tentative proposals offered by the surveyor. Or, finally, they might be used as a vehicle for thorough discussion of problems and ways of dealing with them. These uses of the survey technique were in some instances truly participative in nature and gave the individuals concerned a real sense of having taken part in the development of the plan (as was apparently true in both *Langley Porter* and *Architecture*). Or they might appear to be only substitutes for participation (pseudo-participation) and have a negative impact (as was apparently true of the effect on the City Clerk in *La Loma*).

The stage at which participation was most frequent and most consciously sought in the cases was that having to do with putting proposals into effect. In about half the cases, considerable effort was applied to bringing officers and employees into decision-making at some point in the implementation process, and in some, fairly elaborate ad hoc organizational arrangements were made (as in *Automation* II). Some participation of persons whose behaviors are to be modified is almost by definition essential in the implementing phases of reorganization. At the very least, the individuals must be informed how their own behavior is expected to change, for they must do the changing; and they presumably have at least a modicum of choice in the matter (they always have the alternative of leaving). The choices available to the scientists in *Ballistics* were reduced almost to this level: they could remain and be transferred elsewhere in the Research Department; they could take their chances by transferring to the Aerodynamics Department; or they could quit. But participation of this sort is hardly significant in terms of the hypothesis; we have judged this to exemplify a "zero" degree of real participation. The basic questions are: the degree of specification and detail of prescribed plans within which and on the basis of which employees are invited to contribute to decision-making; and the degree to which the prescribed plan remains flexible and subject to change when employee participation is invited or permitted. The broader and the more fluid are the "givens" at the time that participation begins, the greater is the effective scope of the participation process. They were apparently fairly broad in *U.S. Public Health,* fairly fluid in *Langley Porter,* narrower and more fixed in *Automation.* In *Ballistics,* the givens were solid and unshakable, and so narrow as to deny any real participation.

Most of the participation in the implementation process was pretty clearly directed to the welfare and interests of individual employees—their security, advancement possibilities, new assignments, relationships with others, duties, and status. Part of it was aimed to develop understanding of the effects and the purposes of proposed changes. And part of it was to work out details not already prescribed in the plan itself. All of these could

[12] Even where, as in *U.S. Public Health,* subordinate employees were invited to comment and criticize, there does not seem to have been much response.

CHART III–1. *Estimated degrees of intra-agency participation at various stages of the reorganization process*

CASE	*Inception*	*Study*	*Basic Decision*	*Implementation*	*Overall Judgment*
Agricultural research	0	+	0	++	+
Architecture	0	++	+	+	+
Automation	0	0	0	+++	+
Ballistics	0	none	0	0	0
Children's Bureau	0	unknown	+	+	0
Fish and Game	0	+	++*	none	+
Highway Patrol	0	+	0	++	+
La Loma	0	+	0	0	0
Langley Porter	0	++	0	++	+
Personnel Board	+++	++	++	+++	+++
Philadelphia Health	++	+++	++	++	++
U.S. Public Health	+	++	++	+++	++

KEY: ++++complete participation; +++substantial participation; ++moderate, or substantial but limited to a small number of persons; +slight, or moderate, but limited to a small number of persons; O no participation.

* The "basic decision" in *Fish and Game* is here understood to include decisions reached by the Department heads, following their and their staff's reviews of the consultant's report.

contribute to acceptance of and even enthusiasm for the reorganization; and they could operate to lower resistance to change. It would appear that here more than in any other stage of reorganization was the participation hypothesis applicable.[13]

Estimates of the degree of participation at the various stages in each of the cases, together with a "gestalt" judgment as to the extent of effective participation as a whole in each case are presented in Chart III–1. These are based principally upon the cases themselves and the unpublished analyses prepared by most of the case authors. They are, of course, subjective. A summary tabulation presented in the next column indicates that participation was rare at inception, a little more frequent at the stage of action decision, and frequent during the stages of study and implementation.

Summary of Estimated Degrees of Intra-Agency Participation at Various Stages of Reorganization

Degree of Participation	*Inception*	*Study*	*Basic Decision*	*Implementation*	*Overall Judgment*
Complete	0	0	0	0	0
Substantial	1	1	0	3	1
Moderate*	1	3	4	4	2
Slight†	1	5	2	2	6
Zero	9	1	6	2	3
Total	12	10‡	12	11§	12

* Or substantial but restricted to a small number of persons
† Or moderate but limited to a small number of persons
‡ Not including *Ballistics, Children's Bureau*
§ Not including *Fish and Game*

Participation by Superiors and Outsiders

Relatively little which might be labeled participation by individuals outside the agencies appeared in the cases.[14] Even where a reorganization was prompted or imposed from outside, there was not much of a continuing relationship. The initiators of the Fish and Game study appeared to lose all interest in the Fish and Game Department after Gordon's dismissal; congressmen, even those vitally interested in public health, showed little interest in the U.S. Public Health reorganization except where a specific protest was brought to them; and

[13] This observation is entirely consistent with the findings of research studies in business, industry, and elsewhere relative to participation. In the large proportion of such studies, participation was restricted to the decisions on means; the basic, substantive decisions were handed down to the participants from above. In other words, participation was practiced with respect to what we have referred to in these cases as implementation.

[14] To some extent this probably reflected bias in case selection, and, in a few instances, difficulties in case research.

they did not even endeavor to push through or discuss the legislation that would have legitimated the reorganization plan. The legislators and the two departments principally concerned received and approved the report on the Division of Architecture, but left the matter of giving it effect (or not) up to the discretion of the Division itself.

In that majority of reorganizations that were run from the inside, the leaders succeeded in keeping the outsiders out, and that appeared to be their intention. They usually obtained a "go-ahead" from their superiors and sometimes from other staff agencies and legislators at the start; often, when they had a firm plan, they took it to their superiors for review and approval; and then they proceeded to act. Seldom did they go beyond the government for participation and support, and some were notably successful in forestalling undesired outside intervention. Examples of potentially powerful outside groups whose influence was effectively neutralized in the cases were: the clientele groups of the program bureaus in *Agricultural Research;* the women's and welfare interests in *Children's Bureau;* the California State Employees' Association in *Personnel Board.*

There were exceptions. The basic objective of the entire *Philadelphia Health* case was that set forth in 1949 by the Philadelphia Public Health Survey, itself produced by a mixed commission of public and private leaders. The California State Employees' Association participated in planning and carrying through the personnel implementation in *Automation.* The Budget Bureau was, of course, heavily involved in the *Children's Bureau* case. And, growing out of two of the biggest stumbling blocks in *U.S. Public Health,* personnel and mental health, were two study commissions set up by the Surgeon General, each consisting largely of leaders outside the agency itself.

These various instances of actual or potential external intervention in reorganization were usually intended by the organizational leaders, insofar as they could control them, either to provide understanding and support from influential outside groups or to prevent or neutralize external interference. Whether or not they played an active part in the cases, they were always considerations, latent and potential participants.

Seized Participation

One must distinguish between participation that is freely invited by a principal executive on the one hand and participation that is threatened or forced by subordinate officers and employees, or outside interests, or both. Although the latter type appears to fit within our definition and hypothesis, it is certainly not what the students of leadership styles had in mind, and its origins and effect may be quite the opposite. It may reflect a failure, or complete absence, of "permissive" participation; it may be a revolt against leadership rather than an instrument of constructive harmony. In other sections of this chapter, we have dealt almost exclusively with participation that is invited or at least welcomed by leadership. But participation was, in effect, seized in some of the cases, and such seizure was threatened in others. Such action was an effort by disaffected officers and employees to insist that their views be heard, considered, and acted upon, utilizing available weapons and threats, for example:

> in the *Children's Bureau* case, the threat of resignation of widely respected officials of the Children's Bureau, and their earlier threat, which they suppressed, to have supporting pressure interests work on the Congress;
>
> in *U.S. Public Health,* the mobilization of mental health groups, state mental health organizations, and congressmen against the reorganization of the Mental Health Institute;
>
> in *La Loma,* the resistance of the City Clerk, which contributed to the taking of the Finance Department issue to the polls.

If participation which is forced or seized in these ways results in discussion and negotiation, as in the *Children's Bureau* case, it amounts to bargaining; if not, as in *La Loma,* it may turn into open political warfare. On the other hand, employee participation which is invited or granted by an executive is carried out within limits and subject to constraints imposed by him. The decisions to invite participation are themselves "command decisions," and the *modus operandi* and specifications for it are usually set forth or implicit in the executive's decisions to have a study and his later decision to make organizational changes.[15]

---

[15] This observation is applicable not only to empirical studies of organizational change, such as these cases. It is at least equally applicable to experimental studies in which the formal leadership, or the experimenters with the sanction of the formal leadership, set forth the conditions and the controls within which and according to which participation will be carried on. There is a presumption of hierarchical authority from the beginning.

PARTICIPATION AND REORGANIZATIONAL EFFECTIVENESS

Do the case studies in this volume support the participation hypothesis as it was stated in the introductory chapter? In very general terms the answer must be negative. While some reorganizations conducted with a considerable amount of participation were fully or moderately effective, others with little or no participation were also effective. The matrix below summarizes the individual cases according to the overall judgment on degree of participation (see preceding pages) against overall judgments on degree of substantive effectiveness (from Chapter II).

DEGREE OF PARTICIPATION	DEGREE OF SUBSTANTIVE EFFECTIVENESS		
Overall	*Generally effective*	*Moderately or partially effective*	*Relatively little effectiveness*
Moderate or Substantial	Personnel Board	U.S. Public Health Philadelphia Health	
Slight	Automation Agricultural Research Highway Patrol Langley Porter	Architecture	Fish & Game
Zero	Ballistics	Children's Bureau	La Loma

If the cases were to support the hypothesis fully, we would expect the cases to fall, roughly at least, into a diagonal line from the upper left to the lower right. Instead, they are well scattered. It is true that no instances of substantial participation were failures, but this may well be a result of distortion in case selection.[16]

The overall judgment on degree of participation is rather heavily weighted by the estimated degree of participation in the basic action decisions to reorganize and how to do it. There was little or no participation at this stage in the majority of cases. But if we examine the degrees of participation in the implementation process, not against overall effectiveness, but against estimates of employee support and resistance, it appears that there is some support for a more limited statement of the general hypothesis. Where there was substantial employee participation in implementation, there was less employee resistance. And the greatest resistance occurred in those cases in which there was no employee participation at all. (See below.)

DEGREE OF PARTICIPATION	DEGREE OF EMPLOYEE RESISTANCE		
In implementation	*Slight or zero resistance*	*Moderate or partial resistance*	*Great resistance*
Substantial	Personnel Board	U.S. Public Health	
Moderate	Automation Agricultural Research Highway Patrol Philadelphia Health	Langley Porter	
Slight	Architecture		Children's Bureau
Zero			Ballistics La Loma

To the extent that participation in implementation did, in fact, contribute to employee support for reorganization plans, the effect may have been gained through one or more of three more or less distinct processes: first, by providing a vehicle for creating understanding of the plan itself, its purposes, its necessity, and its anticipated effects, particularly where the effects can be shown to be beneficial to the employees concerned; second, by making the employees feel that they have contributed to it, thus giving them a stake and perhaps a sense of pride in making it successful (it may be noted that this effect might be achieved by pseudo-participation, *provided* that the disguise remains effective);[17] and third, by introducing into the plan modifications, specifications, and amplifications that will make it more acceptable or less threatening to groups and individuals affected. The first of these was undoubtedly a factor in all the cases in

[16] On this point, see Chapter II, pp. 493-514.

[17] Remembering, of course, that the line between real and pseudo-participation must often be unclear, even to the principals who initiate or conduct it.

which there was much participation; and where there was not (as in *La Loma, Fish and Game,* and *Ballistics*), its absence probably added to employee resistance. The second and third of these depended greatly upon the degree of generality and flexibility of the plan at the time that participative processes were begun. Employees who were brought into the reorganization process late in the game—after all the substantive decisions were made—and were given a voice only in questions on the disposition of personnel hardly gained much feeling of identification with the plan itself, although there was undoubtedly satisfaction in feeling that they had some control over their own organizational destinies. In those few cases in which participation began early (as in *Personnel Board* and *Philadelphia Health*), many individuals did feel a stake in the plans and did contribute substantially to modifications and amplifications that made them more acceptable. The case experiences tend to confirm sub-hypothesis No. 3,[18] that participation tends to be more effective in reducing resistance the earlier it begins.

[18] Introduction, p. xx.

THE CONTEXT OF REORGANIZATION AND PARTICIPATION

The paragraphs above suggest that the cases offer little support to the general hypothesis which would attribute reorganizational effectiveness to participative processes. But, as noted, there is some evidence in the cases that employee participation, particularly in the implementation phase, contributes to employee support and acceptance. Both the positive and negative findings invite closer scrutiny.

A central difficulty, which attends much scientific endeavor and is perhaps particularly troublesome in social research, is the existence of a wide variety of variables affecting a situation in addition to the one under the microscope. The great majority of these variables inevitably interact with one another; they affect each other as well as the *event* to which all contribute. It is probable that the only variables in an organization situation which may truly be considered isolable and independent are those external to the organization itself—a budget cut, an election and new leadership, technological developments, an international crisis, the business cycle, and external changes more specifically related to the service and the clientele of the individual agency. Even these, of course, may be influenced by factors internal to the organization in question, and all are modified as they are filtered through the perceptions of the organization's membership.

This nearly universal problem in social science has, in the past, been bypassed by insight and generalization through the device of declaring that, *other things being about equal,* this or that variable—viewed both as dependent and independent—contributes to such and such result. Indeed such an approach, whether or not stated, has probably been the premise of many of the great understandings about social behavior. Thus, one might in the present case state that, other things being equal, participation contributes to success in bringing about organizational change. But, in governmental organizations as well as in other social organisms, other things are never equal. The comparison of different kinds of organizations reveals extremely important variables that are never equal, as does comparison of the same organization at different times. Thus, in governmental organizations as well as in other social organizations, the "other things being equal" criterion may well be meaningless.

The Time Factor

The temper of the organization in relation to change and the environmental context within which it operates have already been treated in Chapter II. In most instances, the cathartic effect of new leadership, external criticism, etc., contributed not alone to the instigation of a reorganization attempt but also to the decisive authority of leadership—i.e., lessened the demand and the need for internal participative processes. This was illustrated in *Ballistics, Agricultural Research, U.S. Public Health,* and *Highway Patrol.* Thus, it may very well be that in those reorganizational efforts that are sparked by a crisis development, the very atmosphere of crisis militates against the degree of participation that might, in normal times, be expected and even standard. The converse was illustrated in two of the cases which were relatively participative. In *Per-*

sonnel Board, there was no crisis, no pressure from the outside; the engine of organizational change had to be fueled from within. The arduous participative processes may well have been essential to accomplishing a change. Likewise, in *Philadelphia Health,* the extended participative efforts of several years were unable to effect a significant change after the early excitement of the Clark administration had died and until the arrival of a new director reignited the possibility of reorganization.

But the atmosphere conducive to catharsis may also contain other elements favorable to participative processes, particularly when it is brought about by changes in political and/or administrative leadership. When a new leader comes in from outside the organization, he is usually not sufficiently equipped with knowledge and acquaintance to make far-reaching decisions by himself. He must call upon subordinate personnel for information and advice. And whether a new leader comes from within or outside the organization, he normally seeks the cooperation and support of his new subordinates and this undoubtedly contributes incentive for the use of participative processes in management.[19] Thus, the very conditions that make a reorganization attempt feasible are often abnormal and special to the organizational milieu. To the extent that this is true, reorganization constitutes a special case for the measurement of participative processes.

Organizational Context

When we say (as we have above) that a reorganization process is relatively participative or relatively non-participative (or authoritarian), we immediately raise the question: relative to what? If we measure the process against some absolute or abstract standard of organizational behavior, we may develop some interesting comparisons of organizational practice in different agencies. But generalized conclusions are hazardous unless one can safely assume that the basic ingredients within the different organizations are approximately equal. In spite of the fact that these organizations fall into the same general class and most of them are at about the same general level,[20] they are vastly different from one another in a great many vital respects. Comparisons with other organizations may suggest conclusions quite different from those drawn from a single agency, differences between specific practices and what may be considered its accustomed mores. Thus, the manner of reorganizing the California Highway Patrol would, in all probability, have been condemned and heavily resisted in the *Personnel Board* case. And if the Commissioner of the Highway Patrol had attempted a protracted participative process like that in the *Personnel Board* case, he might well have been ridiculed for timidity by his own people. The practices employed in both organizations were probably not too far from "normal" in the agency. Each was effective in its own context.

We lack the data in these cases to draw any confident comparisons between the process as described and what might be considered "normal" behavior in the same organization. Such analyses would be difficult to make in any case, partly because of differences in the temporal context of reorganizations, cited above, and partly because the review of general organizational problems is seldom a day-to-day, month-to-month, or even year-to-year process. Many of the personnel most importantly involved had *no* prior experience with reorganization efforts in the same agency. Further, there is reason to believe that what is normal practice on matters of organization is often quite different from what is normal practice with regard to other kinds of problems, especially those with a heavy policy or program content. Reorganization may constitute a special case, even within the same agency.

It would be useful to classify these various agencies into distinctive classes, within which comparisons about reorganizations could be made. Unfortunately, most of the organizational classifications that have been propounded are altogether too crude to be helpful; under most of these rubrics, all the organizations described in this volume would fall within one or at most two categories in spite of the obvious disparities among them.[21] The sample

---

[19] The only exception in these cases was *Ballistics,* in which the new leader had apparently already determined to destroy the organization before his arrival.

[20] See Chapter I.

[21] Thus, in the classification proposed by Peter M. Blau and W. Richard Scott, *Formal Organizations* (San Francisco: Chandler Publishing Company, 1962), p. 43, all fall within two; in that of Harold D. Lasswell in Dwaine Marvick (editor), *Political Decision-makers: Recruitment and Performance* (New York: The Free Press of Glencoe, 1961), pp. 274-275, probably two; in that of Amitai Etzioni, *A Comparative Analysis of Complex Organizations* (New York: The Free Press of Glencoe, 1961), pp. 23-67, two.

of cases is too small to attempt a comprehensive classification, but the very variety of the organizations treated illustrates the difficulty of devising a classification that would be meaningful in relation to the participation-reorganization relationship here under study. However, they do point up some of the kinds of factors that appeared to condition organizational behavior. A few of these that appeared most important in the agencies studied are discussed below. It may be noted that many agencies would fit in two or more different classes within the same set of categories.

Categories of Purposes, whether:

research (and education)—Agricultural Research, Ballistics, Langley Porter; and parts of the organizations in both *U.S. Public Health* and *Philadelphia Health;*
service to public or sectors thereof—Automation, Children's Bureau, Fish and Game, Highway Patrol, Langley Porter, U.S. Public Health, Philadelphia Health;
service to other parts of government—business services in *Agricultural Research, Personnel Board, Architecture;*
regulation and enforcement—Highway Patrol, Fish and Game, Agricultural Research, Personnel Board.

Comment: categorization by purpose appears absolutely essential to the understanding of organizational culture, but its lack of logical exclusiveness is illustrated above. Even within this crude classification, few organizations at the level here considered are confinable within a single class. And in several cases (*Ballistics, Highway Patrol, Langley Porter, Personnel Board*) a principal aim of the reorganization was to shift the purpose emphasis from one class to another.

Agency Autonomy-Subordination, legal and accustomed, whether:

completely autonomous—City Clerk in *La Loma;*
relatively autonomous but controlled at key points (usually budget)—*Children's Bureau* (until transferred), *Langley Porter, Personnel Board, Philadelphia Health, Ballistics, Highway Patrol, Architecture, U.S. Public Health, Automation;*
under close surveillance with little authority to make changes without prior approval—field business offices in *Agricultural Research.*

The organizations may also be classified according to the body or individual that exercises surveillance and control over it:

legislative body—Fish and Game, Personnel Board;
hierarchical superior (including chief executive)—*Agricultural Research, Automation,* and in varying degrees, most of others;
outside staff agency—such as Finance Department in the California cases, and Budget Bureau in *Children's Bureau.*

They may also be classified according to nature of principal tools of control, especially those controlling change, as:

budget and financial controls—virtually all the cases;
personnel controls—Agricultural Research, Automation, Ballistics, and others;
controls over program—virtually all cases;
controls over organizational structure—as field offices in *Agricultural Research, Children's Bureau.*

Comment: again the degree of agency freedom in changing itself had a clear and pervasive effect upon its reorganization process and, as already noted, upon the possibilities of true participation. But clear-cut categorization is difficult; most of the agencies would fit into two or more classes by any of these criteria. It is worthy of mention that most of the organizations had substantial freedom in changing their organizational structure, *provided* they could do it within their existing financial limitations and according to going personnel requirements. Where such modifications required explicit changes in programs and policy, they usually had to seek advance clearance from above and outside.

Accustomed Internal Compliance System and Leadership Style, whether:

highly authoritarian (relying upon sanctions for compliance)—none of these agencies;
authoritarian (in the sense that orders from on high with little advance consultation are normally expected) *but also paternalistic* (employees confident that superiors would take their interests into account)—*Highway Patrol, Automation,* and in varying degrees, most of the other cases;
democratic (changes normally made only after discussion to reach consensus, and/or much authority delegated down line)—*Personnel Board, Langley Porter;*
laissez-faire (little direction or leadership from above, and individuals relatively autonomous) —program researchers in *Agricultural Research, Ballistics.*

Comment: a difficulty here is that the accustomed style of superior-subordinate relationships often, perhaps usually, varies according to the type of question involved. This factor was particularly noticeable in some cases between program-policy matters and organizational-administrative matters. In organizations whose personnel were oriented primarily to a science or a profession, there was expectation of democratic and even *laissez-faire* practices on program matters, but also often an expectation of relatively authoritarian decisions on what they construed to be administrative matters. The program personnel, confident that the boss would take care of them on the administrative side, often preferred not to participate on questions of organization as long as their program operations would not be damaged. The important observation here is that in applying the Lewinian classification, there are different patterns in the same organization and among the same people, depending upon what type of decision is involved.

Kinds of Personnel Involved as to education, professional orientation, variety and kinds of occupational fields involved, age and maturity, and other factors, whether:

political appointees without particular background in the occupations of their agencies—a very few isolated examples;
hard scientists—*Ballistics, Agricultural Research;*
behavioral and life scientists—*Langley Porter, U.S. Public Health;*
professionals (or semi-professionals) oriented to people—both health cases, *Children's Bureau, Personnel Board, Highway Patrol;*
professionals (or semi-professionals) oriented to things (including animals)—*Architecture, Fish and Game;*
professionals (or semi-professionals) in administration—*Personnel Board* and some in *Agricultural Research, Automation,* and others;
clerical and technical—*Automation* and some in virtually all the other cases;
labor, skilled and unskilled—none of these agencies.

Comment: the kinds and orientations of people concerned have already been discussed in Chapter I. It may well be that they constitute the most significant single factor in differentiating among agencies as to administrative behavior. One might hypothesize from the cases that:

scientists and professionals in non-human subject matter are little interested in, and little sophisticated about, matters of organization and administration and unlikely to demand any voice in such matters unless their own professional pursuits seem likely to be seriously affected, positively or negatively;

scientists and professionals in human fields view administrative problems in personal and personality terms and attach rather little importance to organizational structure;

professionals in administrative fields are sophisticated in processes of organizational change but often defensive in dealing with professionals in other fields;

clerical and technical personnel view higher level management problems, such as those in these cases, as not of important concern to them except as they may directly affect their individual security and future.

Obviously, to the extent such hypotheses are true, they affect the nature and the usefulness of participative processes on particular organizational decisions.

Personnel Systems, including guarantees of security, entrance predominantly at the bottom or with lateral entry, competitive systems for advancement, allegiance with professions outside, opportunities for outside employment, etc., whether:

closed career system, with all or virtually all appointments at bottom level with progressive advancement on competitive basis to upper-level positions—most of these cases;

basically career system, but with potential transfers in and out, to and from other employers working in same occupational fields—*Ballistics, Langley Porter;*

open system with frequent appointments and withdrawals at all levels—none of these agencies except at or near the very top.

Comment: all of these agencies were effectively "careerized" with respect to the bulk of their personnel. Except at the bottom and the top, there was little expectation of entrance from the outside; there was little threat of, and great difficulty in, removal; and there was high expectation of most that they could and would remain with the agency indefinitely. There were changes at the top, and in a good many cases these were crucial to reorganization. But for the most part reorganizations had to be made by and with the people already there, and the ranking personnel, except those at the very top, had characteristically been there a long time.

This condition probably made a reorganization that would involve profound changes in behavior more difficult and the need for consensus on such changes more necessary.

PARTICIPATION AS AN EXECUTIVE STRATEGY

It has already been noted that critics of the human relations movement in recent years have focused their attack on participative devices as tools of gaining consent and on manipulating men's minds in directions desirable from the viewpoint of management. They see participation as a potential camouflage for autocracy. It is not here intended to enter into this argument, aside from observing that pseudo-participation undoubtedly exists and may have existed in some of these cases. (As explained elsewhere, the evidence is insufficient.) On the other hand, the employment of participative devices can be an entirely sincere expression of management's interest, motivated by idealistic or very practical reasons, or both. In most instances,[22] a given decision whether or not to invite or encourage participation must be made or at least sanctioned by the executive, even though his freedom of choice may be severely circumscribed by the contextual factors described above. This is true even of the experimental studies on which so much of the human relations literature has been based: someone had to authorize the experiments, set up the ground-rules, provide the resources, and set the limits.

It becomes relevant, therefore, to inquire as to the advantages and disadvantages to the executive of encouraging participation through one or another device in given situations. In the cases, and insofar as the executive could effectively influence the degree of participation at different stages of reorganizations, what considerations weighed for and against participation?

The Pros

It is clear in the first place that some of the executives in these cases viewed participation as a good in itself—an expression of democracy in administrative organization. This was probably an important, if not dominant, consideration in some of the most "participative" cases, such as *Personnel Board* and *Philadelphia Health*. Barely divisible from this idealistic consideration is a second one: the confidence that the opinions and wisdom of many minds on a problem are superior to those of one or a limited few. Such an argument appears particularly persuasive where those who might participate are deemed to be educated, intelligent, and knowledgeable individuals, and where they represent perspectives, professional orientations, and experience differing from that of the principal executive himself.

A third motivation for encouraging participative processes, related to the second, was in some of these cases the most persuasive of all: to provide the executive himself with information as to what he feasibly could do, what he should do, how and when he should do it. Viewed as such, participation is a learning device for the responsible executive, whereby he may introduce into his considerations prior to decision the knowledges, the perspectives, and the attitudes of others and perhaps of all who may be affected by his decision.

There are essentially two kinds of information elicited through participative processes: first, objective facts about the present and probable future; and second, the range and relative strengths of different points of view, affective feelings, and desires and values of the participants. Both will contribute to his assessment of feasibility and desirability of alternative courses of action, and of probable values and costs that may be expected from them.

Half a century or more ago, Frederick Taylor stated (and deplored) the fact that workers in a shop typically had more knowledge about their work operations than did their foremen. The same is no doubt as true or truer today, in spite of the earnest efforts of scientific management (and more recently of management science) to equip the managers with more objective information. It is virtually tautological in complex organizations today that the executive cannot know everything that goes on within his area of responsibility (and, if he is to avoid ulcers, should probably not try to learn it). Under such conditions, it is essential that before making decisions affecting the working behaviors of a great many subordinates he understand, to

[22] Except where participants have forced their voices to be heard.

some extent, how various alternatives will affect them and how they will probably respond to them. This is true also with regard to persons outside the organization who may be affected. Meetings and discussions, both formal and informal, interviews, desk audits, eliciting of special studies, reports, and memoranda with recommendations on particular aspects of a problem, and the carrying on of pilot or test runs all serve this educational purpose, and all *may be* truly participative in character. That is, they may all truly contribute to the substance of a decision on organization, and the contribution may be perceived both by the executive himself and by those who participated.[23] The educational purpose of participation was probably best illustrated by the extensive use of surveys and the more-or-less participative devices employed by the surveyors who themselves communicated at least part of their findings to the executives. In a more limited way, it was undoubtedly present in the initiatory and action decisions, as well as during implementation.

A fourth reason for encouraging participation by executives was to facilitate delegation of decision-making to lower organizational levels—particularly the subsidiary and derivative decisions flowing out of the more basic ones. The rationale here is essentially the same as that mentioned in the preceding paragraphs—the executive cannot know everything. At some stage in the process of carrying a change into effect, he must delegate to points nearer the operating level either formal decision-making authority (within limits and subject to ground rules and often to review and clearance) or power to share in shaping decisions. This was probably a principal reason for participation during the process of implementation in the cases, and it partly accounts for the fact that there was more participation at this stage, on the average, than at any other.

A fifth purpose of participation from the point of view of the executive was the converse of the second—as a vehicle for education, training, and enlargement of the vision of subordinate (or sometimes outside) personnel. Through participation it was potentially possible to convey the objectives and problems of the agency as seen from other perspectives and to encourage the broadening of views of individuals on their own roles and relationships. It was also possible to minimize threats to the security of individuals—not only in their perceptions but sometimes also in fact. And often it was possible to make projected changes appear to be personally advantageous to some or many participants.

A sixth purpose of the use of participative practices, intimately related to the previous one, was the traditional one: to gain the understanding and enthusiasm of those affected—or at least to minimize their resistance—by making them feel a sense of sharing power and responsibility in decision-making. The participants could be made to feel a positive stake in making the projected reorganization work—an effect nicely illustrated in the pilot unit of *Personnel Board*.

A seventh argument for participation is to gain support from the participants for the executive's position which he may use in dealing with superiors and outsiders. Such support may be valuable to him not alone with regard to the decision about which participation is invited but also with regard to other and future issues. Such a consideration may have been a factor in *Philadelphia Health* (bringing in the leaders of the nurses and sanitarians) and in *Automation* (bringing in the representatives of the California State Employees' Association).

The chances are that most or all of the above general purposes played a part in encouraging a participative style upon those few executives who, in fact, encouraged participation. It may be noted that most of them could influence the organizational climate in general, quite apart from the particular decisions at hand. They could form a precedent for future relationships and decisions (which might or might not be to the executive's long-run advantage).

Executives may employ participation for other, special purposes. The process is generally slow, certainly more so than quick decision would be,

[23] It may be noted that the reverse of this situation may occur: that a process which the executive perceived and intended as truly participative may be viewed by participants as a fake perpetrated in order to induce them not to voice objections. In fact, the reversal may have been in the cases the more frequent of the two. It appears, however, that "pseudo-participation" is itself not an operational term for this kind of research—and might well require use of the analyst's couch or of a lie detector. Seldom would a superior acknowledge it, even if he realized it; and seldom would it be safe to infer it from his actions. However, the perception by others that a participative process was not "true," whether or not the perception was itself accurate, can be a solid datum. Throughout, there is always a specter of pseudo-participation, in which the participative process serves as a camouflage covering a decision already made, and which is always accompanied by the danger, for the executive, that it may be so recognized and arouse antagonism and resistance.

and an executive may encourage it with the specific intent of delaying action until the time is more propitious or until he feels more confident about moving ahead. He may even use it to prevent action if he encourages participation when the time is ripe for decision. Decisions in which employees and sometimes outsiders have taken part and reached substantial consensus may strengthen the executive's hand in persuading his own superiors and other power centers—staff agencies, legislatures, interest groups—to go along with his plans. This was unquestionably a consideration in several cases.

Finally, participation may serve as a useful guide for internal personnel decisions—to spot those with initiative, imagination, and dedication for promotion and important reassignment and, conversely, to identify the resisters to change, the morale problems, the troublemakers, for whatever attention may be appropriate. (The author of *U.S. Public Health* specifically cited the identification of future leaders as a significant fruit of participation in that case.) It may assist the executive to bring out into the open his supporters as well as his critics and dissidents, and provide information that should be useful and in some cases indispensable for handling any given problem now and in the future.

The Cons

In view of all these potential gains for the executive from participation, one may reasonably wonder why processes conducive to participation were not more frequently employed in the cases. Against such gains operate disadvantages which may discourage and even preclude participative practices in given situations. We may cite and dismiss those instances where reorganization processes are initiated from above or outside with a purpose, perhaps among others, of discrediting an agency and its program and with it its personnel (illustrated to some extent in *Fish and Game,* where the surveyors were expressly forbidden to discuss their findings and proposals with members of the Department). Similarly, it is obvious that reorganizations initiated in considerable part as disciplinary actions against officers and employees could profit little from participative devices involving those employees—a situation illustrated to some extent in the *Ballistics* case.

A factor militating against participation was sometimes the pressure of time. Participation is usually a slow process, certainly slower than is decisive action. There was sometimes an externally set deadline for decision (such as a new building in *Automation,* or the time limit on a presidential reorganization plan in *Children's Bureau,* or an impending new budget year in *Agricultural Research*) which militated against the use of extensive participative processes. Limitations on time probably also worked against slower, participative decision in the cases of newly appointed executives who wished to take maximum advantage of their "honeymoon" periods (as in *Highway Patrol* and *Langley Porter*).

A second argument against participation from the point of view of the executive is potent when the change which he has in mind—or any change at all—can be expected to arouse resistance among influential subordinates. He may perceive participation as a means whereby such employees may mobilize resistance, utilizing whatever weapons may be available to them, within or without the organization, against his aims and even against him. Secrecy, which is the opposite of participation, was most frequently invoked where the organizational goals as perceived by the executive were obviously in conflict with individual and group goals of those who might participate—as in *Ballistics, Children's Bureau* and *La Loma.* Participation was most frequently utilized when changes could be demonstrated to help, not hurt, individuals and groups who might participate. But it was a positive threat to the accomplishment of changes where it provided opportunity to mobilize internal and external resistance.

A third factor that sometimes militates against participation is the executive's fear, sometimes well-grounded, of appearing weak, indecisive, and timid in failing to make decisions that are within his prerogative. The concern may apply to the opinions of superiors and outsiders who consider him the "boss" of his organization; it may apply to his own subordinates, to whom participation may signify lack of confidence or even incompetence, particularly where "command decisions" are customary. And it may appear to the executive himself to be a contradiction of his self-image as leader. Probably these considerations were relevant in some of the cases. The force of this factor varied widely, depending upon the culture and setting of the organization involved. The Commissioner of the *Highway Patrol* would probably have suffered criticism and even ridicule had he engaged in a long participative process; the director of *Langley*

Porter would probably have been criticized as tyrannical had he "ordered" all the changes proposed in the organizational survey. And the kinds of ultimata delivered in the *Ballistics* case might generate an academic revolution on a university campus.

Where an organizational problem can be handled only through technical analysis that requires skills not possessed by personnel who might otherwise participate, an effort to share analysis and decision would be fruitless and perhaps frustrating. (*Automation* I was an illustration of such a situation: Bashline could not have discussed the installation of automated equipment with his staff because they were not familiar with it and were in no position to advise him on it.)

An executive may be dissuaded from participative processes by doubt or insecurity as to his own decision-making power *vis-à-vis* his superiors and influential outsiders. To set off a participative process and then be unable, or unwilling, to follow through may damage the respect and standing of the executive within his organization. And where the principal issues are not substantive (i.e., in what ways to reorganize) but tactical (i.e., how to maneuver for support and acceptance of reorganization above and outside), it would normally be unwise to seek very widespread participation of employees. (As noted before, in a good many cases the executives clearly kept "close to their chests" the tactics of outside relationships—*Architecture, Langley Porter, U.S. Public Health;* and in others, like *Personnel Board,* the executives endeavored to get advance clearance from outside power centers before proceeding.)

Finally, it may be observed that some of the potential participants in these cases, especially those who were highly professionalized in fields other than administration, did not feel themselves qualified in organizational problems and did not want to participate. Like professionals in other spheres, they were uninterested in matters of administration as long as their own interests would not be damaged. Time devoted to organizational problems was time lost to the pursuit of their professional interests. And they felt confident that their superiors who had a common professional orientation would adequately represent their interests. (Examples of this attitude include: the disinterest of some of the program scientists in *Agricultural Research,* the psychiatrist-professors in *Langley Porter,* or, more specifically, the inclination of Miss Arnstein to withdraw from the Study Group in *U.S. Public Health.*) How prevalent this reluctance to participate was may only be guessed from the cases; and whether such reluctance should generally be construed to discourage participation or not is at least arguable. One might contend that participation is most needed where there is such a condition of employee apathy. But the difference between this observed situation and that which is often assumed in literature about participative leadership—i.e., that employees are eager or would be happy to participate in decision-making—is obvious. It may be that here again participation in reorganization in professionalized agencies is a special case.

It is clear from this brief recapitulation of possible *pros* and *cons* that the executive must weigh a great number of considerations in deciding whether to permit or encourage participation in any given situation. He can hardly take any single general rule and apply it indiscriminately. In a few of these cases, extensive participation would have been impossible, fruitless, or damaging (*Fish and Game* I, *Ballistics, Automation* I). In one or two, where there was no crisis and little or no outside pressure, it may have been indispensable (*Personnel Board*). But the other cases were less clear-cut, and the arguments for and against the use of participative practices had to be balanced in terms of the particular context of each situation.

THE PARTICIPATION HYPOTHESIS AND THE CASES

The cases in this volume do not support the participation hypothesis stated in the introductory chapter.[24] They suggest that there are a great many other considerations in addition to, or interacting with, participation and having a great impact upon reorganization. The cases do provide evidence that

[24] "Government reorganizations involving intended changes in individual behaviors are more effective, both structurally and substantively, when the persons whose behaviors are expected to change participate in deciding what the change will be and how it will be made."

participation contributes to employee support in reorganization or detracts from impending resistance; and in the small minority of instances where employee betterment and opportunity were an important goal of reorganization, participation was apparently useful. But most of the reorganizations in these cases were for other purposes, and it cannot be said that participation was a basic variable in determining their effectiveness.

The cases afford no evidence on sub-hypothesis #1.[25]

The cases suggest the validity of sub-hypothesis #2,[26] that participation is more effective toward reorganization when the anticipated effects appear to increase the complementariness of individual goals with reorganizational goals among participants. Participative processes were most likely to be pursued where such complementariness could be anticipated. And where individuals were likely to be hurt by reorganization, participation was generally avoided.

Sub-hypothesis #3,[27] that participation is more effective the earlier it begins, was supported in two cases, but the evidence is obviously inconclusive in view of the size of the sample.

The cases do demonstrate that participative processes are under some circumstances both possible and useful; and that, under others, they are neither desirable nor feasible. The hypothesis as a general maxim is altogether too simplified for unquestioning application in complex organizations in government.

[25] "The effectiveness of participation in contributing to reorganization goals by different persons and groups depends directly upon the degree of expected impact of projected reorganizations upon the behaviors of those persons and groups."

[26] "The effectiveness of participation in reorganization is enhanced where the anticipated effects of the reorganization as perceived by the actual or potential participants are to decrease the divergencies, or increase the complementariness, between organizational goals, on the one hand, and group and individual goals, on the other."

[27] "The earlier in the process of reorganization that participation begins, the more effective it is toward increasing motivation favorable to reorganization or, conversely, reducing resistance to change."

A CONCLUDING NOTE ON THE STUDY OF ORGANIZATIONS

Above and beyond their relevance to the participation hypothesis, the cases suggest certain observations that may be useful in future theory development and studies of organizations, particularly in the public sphere.

In the first place, the literature dealing with participation in the past has given predominant emphasis to the *affective* results of participation (and non-participation) on the feelings, attitudes, and empathy of the potential participants. Rather little stress has been given to what might be called the *cognitive* results: participation as a device to bring to bear upon problems more ideas, more different points of view, and more information from more minds in order that the decisions may be better decisions. At the level of the decisions considered in these cases, the latter types of consideration were at least as significant as the former and in some instances clearly more significant. The cognitive aspect would appear to be particularly dominant in organizations of great complexity, with a wide variety of specialisms, with broad ramifications of policy decisions beyond the organization itself, and with well-educated personnel. And these attributes characterize the bulk of agencies in public administration, at least at their upper levels. This suggests that future studies dealing with participation in these kinds of organizations should approach the topic more from the standpoint of information and problem-solving theory, less from that of social psychology.

Secondly, these cases reemphasize the difficulties and hazards involved in transferring research findings and theoretical propositions developed in one context to situations and behaviors in another one, as:

- from the small group to the large organization
- from an artificially structured and controlled experiment to a going, "natural" organization
- from private, profit-seeking organizations to public organizations
- from organizations composed of laborers or clerks to organizations of professional men.

Clearly we may gain and have gained many new ideas and insights from research and theory from the small group laboratory, private businesses, and construction gangs or bank clerks. But the simple transference of findings to a quite different context may result in faulty emphasis, and in conclusions of doubtful relevance or even of total inapplicability. Perhaps the greatest danger of this kind of analogic reasoning is oversimplification and the consequent encouragement to overlook elements in the situation that may be far more significant than the ideas "transferred." With regard to the participation hypothesis itself, many of the earlier paragraphs of this chapter were directed to other elements (beside participation) which importantly affected the reorganization process and which also conditioned the way participation operated, if it operated at all. The participation hypothesis if viewed naked and alone in these contexts might well have obscured these other elements. These hazards involved in transference appear at least as great—and perhaps not unlike—the hazard commonly associated with the case method: overgeneralizing on the basis of a single case or an inadequate sample of cases.

In a somewhat broader vein, the cases illustrate the dangers of overgeneralizing on the basis of words in our vocabulary. I have specific reference to the word "bureaucracy" and its derivatives, though other examples might be cited. There has in the past two decades been a growing literature on the topic of *bureaucracy,* now so popular an expression among social scientists; and it has included a vast amount of generalization about bureaucracies, often treated as though all were essentially alike. The organizations in these cases were all bureaucracies; all were public. But their differences by and large seem to have been more important than their likenesses. The word "bureaucracy" is about as encompassing for these different agencies as the word "mammal" is in comprehending a whale, a cow, a bat, and a man—and not much more helpful in gaining understanding about behavior.

It was noted earlier that there has been recent attention to the classification of different kinds of bureaucracy and the development of hypotheses about each class. The different classifications of organizations that have come to my attention are still too broad and encompassing to be of much aid in the development of operational hypotheses about different bureaucracies in the government. If theory about organizations at this level of classification is considered to be "middle-range"[28] it would appear that we need more research and theory at the "lower-middle" range. We need classificatory systems more complex and multidimensional than most of those so far proposed and at lower levels and sub-levels of organization. Some of the dimensions, but by no means all, along which organizations might usefully be so classified have been suggested in earlier paragraphs of this analysis. A well-developed system of organizational classification would provide a bridge between the data and insights gained through the study of individual organizations, situations, and processes on the one hand and conceptual generalization in the upper and even the middle ranges of organizational theory on the other. And this bridge should preferably be built of the foundations, the beams, and girders of real-life operating organizations than of transplanted materials and conceptual deductions from somewhere else.

The development of concepts and criteria for the classification of organizations and of organizational processes both depends upon and contributes to the study of organizations *comparatively.* I speak here not of comparisons among different nations and different cultures but of comparisons among organizations and sub-cultures within the United States alone. There is in our experience and in our current activities a vast amount of informational "ore," some of which has been tapped. But in the public sphere particularly, little of the ore has been graded, compared, classified in relation to other samples. The paucity of our interest in, study of, and knowledge about comparative public organizations in our own country contrasts paradoxically with our aspirations in the comparative analysis of bureaucracies in different nations. The case method as exemplified herein is but one of many possible research tools that might be utilized to gain greater understanding of comparative American organizational behavior.

Finally, the case studies raise again and perhaps slightly illuminate an old question which is also comparative in nature: Are public organizations different by virtue of being public and, if so, what are the underlying distinctions between public and nonpublic organizations as they affect the behaviors of their members? There is in the very existence of

[28] As suggested by Etzioni in his book, *A Comparative Analysis of Complex Organizations (op. cit.),* pp. xii-xiv. Earlier, Robert Merton had contended that the advance of sociology would depend upon the development of "theories in the middle range"; i.e., "special theories applicable to limited ranges of data . . . rather than the 'integrated' conceptual structure adequate to derive all these and other theories." *Social Theory and Social Structure, op. cit.,* p. 9.

a field of study of *public* administration an implicit assumption of a difference between it and other kinds of administration. The cases in this volume were all drawn from the governmental sphere, but the hypothesis that they were intended to assess was essentially based upon research in nonpublic administration. The cases suggest that there are basic differences between public and business organizations arising from: nature of purpose; degree and nature of political exposure; nature of legal, administrative, and political control; leadership personnel; and attitudes and motivations of employees. But such contrasts are largely inferential and indirect. Case studies of like processes (such as these of reorganizations) or other kinds of comparative studies applying to both private and public organizations would add greatly to our understanding of both public and private organizations and of what is common and what is distinctive about each.

APPENDIX I

BIBLIOGRAPHICAL NOTE CONCERNING CASE MATERIALS IN PUBLIC ADMINISTRATION AND POLITICS

A. The Inter-University Case Program, Inc., has now produced more than one hundred cases and has published five other casebooks, as follows: Harold Stein (editor), *Public Administration and Policy Development: A Case Book,* The Inter-University Case Program (New York: Harcourt, Brace and Company, 1952); Edwin A. Bock and Alan K. Campbell (editors), *Case Studies in American Government,* The Inter-University Case Program (Englewood Cliffs, N.J.: Prentice-Hall, Inc., 1962); Edwin A. Bock (editor), *State and Local Government: A Case Book,* The Inter-University Case Program (Birmingham: University of Alabama Press, 1963); Harold Stein (editor), *American Civil-Military Decisions,* Twentieth Century Fund Study in cooperation with The Inter-University Case Program (Birmingham: University of Alabama Press, 1963); and Edwin A. Bock (editor), *Government Regulation of Business: A Casebook,* The Inter-University Case Program (Englewood Cliffs, N.J.; Prentice-Hall, Inc., 1965). An ICP casebook on urban planning and development will be published next year. See also, Edwin A. Bock (editor) and others, *Essays on the Case Method* (Brussels: International Institute of Administrative Sciences, 1961).

In addition, the ICP has cooperated with and provided assistance to institutions and scholars in a growing number of foreign countries, and cases of the ICP type have been published, sometimes in casebooks, in Austria, Belgium, Brazil, Germany, Great Britain, India, Indonesia, Israel, the Netherlands, Pakistan, the Philippines, Thailand, Yugoslavia, Viet Nam, and others.

B. Cases in a variety of forms have been produced by a number of other research and educational institutions, including The Brookings Institution, the Eagleton Foundation, the National Planning Association, and the School of Public Administration of the University of Southern California. Among the recent casebooks authored or edited by individual scholars are: Richard T. Frost (editor), *Cases in State and Local Government* (Englewood Cliffs, N.J.: Prentice-Hall, Inc., 1961); Beatrice G. Markey and Nicholas G. Nicholaidis, *Selected Policy-Decision Cases,* John W. Donner Fund Publication No. 10 (Los Angeles: School of Public Administration, University of Southern California, 1960); Warner E. Mill, Jr., and Harry R. Davis, *Small City Government: Seven Cases in Decision Making* (New York: Random House, Inc., 1962); Robert J. Mowitz and Deil S. Wright, *Profile of a Metropolis: A Case Book* (Detroit: Wayne State University Press, 1960); Edwin O. Stene, *Case Problems in City Management* (Chicago: The International City Managers' Association, 1964); William B. Storm and Margaret G. Oslund, *The Politics of Administrative Behavior: A Case Book,* John W. Donner Fund Publication No. 14 (Los Angeles: School of Public Administration, University of Southern California, 1960); and Alan F. Westin (editor) *The Uses of Power: 7 Cases in American Politics*

(New York: Harcourt, Brace & World, Inc., 1962).

C. Cases are increasingly being drawn upon in the study and teaching of public administration and politics, both in general textbooks, of which the Dimocks' listed below is a prominent example, and in more specific studies and analyses, such as the following: Edward C. Banfield, *Political Influence* (New York: The Free Press of Glencoe, 1961); Marshall E. Dimock and Gladys O. Dimock, *Public Administration* (New York: Holt, Rinehart and Winston, Inc., 1964); Robert T. Golembiewski, *Behavior and Organization: O & M and the Small Group* (Chicago: Rand McNally & Company, 1962); Wayne A. R. Leys, *Ethics for Policy Decisions: The Art of Asking Deliberative Questions* (Englewood Cliffs, N.J.: Prentice-Hall, Inc., 1952); Grant McConnell, *Steel and the Presidency, 1962* (New York: W. W. Norton & Company, Inc., 1963); Richard E. Neustadt, *Presidential Power: The Politics of Leadership* (New York: John Wiley & Sons, Inc., 1960); and Nicholas G. Nicholaidis, *Policy-Decision and Organization, Theory,* John W. Donner Fund Publication No. 11 (Los Angeles: School of Public Administration, University of Southern California, 1960).

D. Mention should finally be made of the use of cases in a growing number of fields related to public administration. Cases in business administration, and particularly those produced by the Harvard Business School, of course, long antedate the ICP undertaking. A more recent "comer" in the case field is educational administration, exemplified in this regard by the individual cases issued by the University Council for Educational Administration and by Jack A. Culbertson, Paul B. Jacobson, and Theodore L. Reller, *Administrative Relationships: A Case Book* (Englewood Cliffs, N.J.: Prentice-Hall, Inc., 1960).

APPENDIX II

SELECTED REFERENCES RELEVANT TO THE PARTICIPATION HYPOTHESIS

Arensberg, Conrad M., *et al.*

Research in Industrial Human Relations (New York: Harper and Brothers, Publishers—for the Industrial Relations Research Association, 1957)

Argyris, Chris

Integrating the Individual and the Organization (New York: John Wiley & Sons, 1964)

Personality and Organization: The Conflict Between Systems and the Individual (New York: Harper and Brothers, Publishers, 1957)

Barnard, Chester

Functions of the Executive (Cambridge: Harvard University Press, 1938)

Bass, Bernard M.

Leadership, Psychology, and Organizational Behavior (New York: Harper and Brothers, Publishers, 1960)

Baum, Bernard H.

Decentralization of Authority in a Bureaucracy (Englewood Cliffs, N.J.: Prentice-Hall, Inc., 1961)

Berlo, David K.

The Process of Communication: An Introduction to Theory and Practice (New York: Holt, Rinehart and Winston, Inc., 1960)

Blau, Peter M.

The Dynamics of Bureaucracy, A Study of Interpersonal Relations in Two Government Agencies (Chicago: University of Chicago Press, 1955)

Blau, Peter M. and W. Richard Scott

Formal Organizations (San Francisco: Chandler Publishing Company, 1962)

Etzioni, Amitai

A Comparative Analysis of Complex Organizations (New York: The Free Press of Glencoe, 1961)

Modern Organizations (Englewood Cliffs, N.J.: Prentice-Hall, Inc., 1964)

Follett, Mary Parker
Creative Experience (New York: Longmans, Green & Company, 1924)
Dynamic Administration (New York: Harper and Brothers, Publishers, 1940—Collected papers)

Ginzberg, Eli and Ewing W. Reilley
Effecting Change in Large Organizations (New York: Columbia University Press, 1957)

Golembiewski, Robert T.
Behavior and Organization: O & M and the Small Group (Chicago: Rand McNally & Company, 1962)
The Small Group: An Analysis of Research Concepts and Operations (Chicago: University of Chicago Press, 1962)

Gore, William J.
Administrative Decision-Making: A Heuristic Model (New York: John Wiley & Sons, 1964)

Gouldner, Alvin W.
Patterns of Industrial Bureaucracy (New York: The Free Press of Glencoe, 1954)

Gross, Bertram M.
The Managing of Organizations: The Administrative Struggle (New York: The Free Press of Glencoe, 1964—2 vols.)

Group for the Advancement of Psychiatry
Administration of the Public Psychiatric Hospital (Report No. 46) (New York: Group for the Advancement of Psychiatry, July 1960)

Guest, Robert H.
Organizational Change: The Effect of Successful Leadership (Homewood, Illinois: Dorsey Press, 1962)

Haire, Mason (editor)
Modern Organization Theory (New York: John Wiley & Sons, 1959)

Homans, George C.
The Human Group (New York: Harcourt, Brace and Company, 1950)

Jaques, Elliott
The Changing Culture of a Factory (London: Tavistock Publications, 1951; New York: Dryden Press, 1952)

Johns, Ray
Confronting Organizational Change (New York: Association Press, 1963)

Kornhauser, William
Scientists in Industry: Conflict and Accommodation (Berkeley: University of California Press, 1962)

Lawrence, Paul R.
The Changing of Organizational Behavior Patterns: A Case Study of Decentralization (Boston: Division of Research, Harvard University Graduate School of Business, 1958)

Leavitt, Harold J. (editor)
The Social Science of Organizations: Four Perspectives (Englewood Cliffs, N.J.: Prentice-Hall, Inc., 1963)

Leighton, Alexander H.
The Governing of Men (Princeton: Princeton University Press, 1945)

Lewin, Kurt
Field Theory in Social Science: Selected Theoretical Papers (New York: Harper and Brothers, Publishers, 1951—Dorwin Cartwright edited)
Resolving Social Conflicts: Selected Papers on Group Dynamics (New York: Harper and Brothers, Publishers, 1948—Gertrud Weiss Lewin edited)

Likert, Rensis
New Patterns of Management (New York: McGraw-Hill Book Co., Inc., 1961)

Lippitt, Ronald, Jeanne Watson, and Bruce Westley
The Dynamics of Planned Change: A Comparative Study of Principles and Techniques (New York: Harcourt, Brace and Company, 1958)

Mailick, Sidney and Edward H. Van Ness (editors)
Concepts and Issues in Administrative Behavior (Englewood Cliffs, N.J.: Prentice-Hall, Inc., 1962)

March, James G. and Herbert A. Simon
Organizations (New York: John Wiley & Sons, 1958)

Mayo, Elton
The Human Problems of an Industrial Civilization (New York: Viking Press, 1960)

Priffner, John M. and Frank P. Sherwood
Administrative Organization (Englewood Cliffs, N.J.: Prentice-Hall, Inc., 1960)

Roethlisberger, F. J.
Management and Morale (Cambridge: Harvard University Press, 1941)

Roethlisberger, F. J. and William J. Dickson
Management and the Worker (Cambridge: Harvard University Press, 1939)

Selznick, Philip
Leadership in Administration (Evanston, Illinois: Row, Peterson and Company, 1957)
TVA and the Grass Roots: A Study in the Sociology of Formal Organizations (Berkeley: University of California Press, 1953)

Tannenbaum, Arnold S. and Robert L. Kahn
Participation in Union Locals (Evanston, Illinois: Row, Peterson and Company, 1958)

Tannenbaum, Robert, Irving R. Weschler, and Fred Massarik
Leadership and Organization: A Behavioral Science Approach (New York: McGraw-Hill Book Co., Inc., 1961)

Tead, Ordway
The Art of Administration (New York: McGraw-Hill Book Co., Inc., 1951)

Verba, Sidney
Small Groups and Political Behavior: A Study of Leadership (Princeton: Princeton University Press, 1961)

Viteles, Morris S.
Motivation and Morale in Industry (New York: W. W. Norton & Company, Inc., 1953)

Vroom, Victor
Some Personality Determinants of the Effects of Participation (Englewood Cliffs, N.J.: Prentice-Hall, Inc., 1960)

White, Ralph K. and Ronald Lippitt
Autocracy and Democracy: An Experimental Inquiry (New York: Harper and Brothers, Publishers, 1960)

APPENDIX III

GUIDANCE TO CASE WRITERS

RESEARCH COMMITTEE OF
THE INTER-UNIVERSITY CASE PROGRAM
AND THE INSTITUTE OF GOVERNMENTAL STUDIES,
UNIVERSITY OF CALIFORNIA, BERKELEY

I. *Introduction*

It is emphasized at the outset that the case studies for this project will be to some degree different from the previous Inter-University Case Program cases with which we are familiar. The general methodology and the decision focus are similar, and the written products will, we hope, maintain high standards of written expression and description. The writer should have an opportunity to exercise his initiative, his insight, and his style as have writers of other cases. But our cases are related parts of a single project, as previous cases have not been. They are aimed to enlarge knowledge and to test current hypotheses about a somewhat particularized aspect of public management. It is therefore important that each writer look for the same kinds of things, the applications to his particular case of similar concepts. The success of the project as a whole will depend upon the degree to which generalizations may be drawn, elaborated, or destroyed from a variety of cases.

It is imperative, therefore, that each writer study and bear continuously in mind the central ideas and foci of the project as a whole. Stress should be laid on the meanings, attached for this project, of *reorganization* and *participation.* Reorganization is construed as an intended change in individual behaviors and relationships in an organization. Its extent is to be measured in terms of the degree to which behaviors are changed or are intended to be changed, not by the shifting of titles or of the configurations of boxes on a chart. It is probable that some of the most widely publicized reorganizations involve little if any real behavioral change except perhaps at the very top level. Conversely, some of a fairly drastic nature so far as individual workers are concerned probably never show up on a chart at any time.

Understanding of this is important to the application of the participation hypothesis. The hypothesis is relevant only for the people whose behaviors and relationships are intended to be changed. It is not necessary to the hypothesis that all or, in fact, any of the journeyman workers participate in decisions at the top level which are not intended to change employee behaviors or relationships. The intelligent appraisal of the hypothesis in a specific case therefore depends upon a quite profound and subtle understanding of the nature and scope of the organizational change.

The participation hypothesis rests initially upon a psychological basis in terms of gaining support for changes from employees within organizations. We have extended it in two directions. First, we have considered as one of the potential values of participation the information and understanding gained by participants through the process itself. This may produce benefits in (1) improving and making more acceptable the substance of the reorganization plan, (2) expediting its implementation, and (3) improving the operations after installation through better understandings by persons concerned. Second, we have considered as potential participants persons outside the organization immediately concerned whose behaviors and relationships may be affected by the change. These, such as other administrative officials, legislators, and clientele, may in some cases be of considerable importance.

Researchers should not restrict their concern about participation to the decision-making step alone. It may occur at any or all of the stages of an organizational change. For our purposes it may be useful to consider these stages to include, potentially, the following five:

(1) initiation of an idea (or recognition of a problem)
(2) survey and planning
(3) analysis, negotiation, consultation leading to decision on the plan
(4) implementation—putting into effect
(5) follow-up and adjustments after installation.

Some of the case writers may wish to refer to a few works on the participation hypothesis; outstanding among those are:

(1) Chris Argyris, *Personality and Organization*
(2) Mary Parker Follett, *Dynamic Administration*
(3) Elliott Jaques, *The Changing Culture of a Factory*
(4) Paul R. Lawrence, *Changing Organizational Behavior Patterns*
(5) Kurt Lewin, *Field Theory in Social Science*
(6) Lippitt, Watson, and Westley, *The Dynamics of Planned Change*
(7) Fritz Roethlisberger, *Management and Morale*
(8) Robert Tannenbaum and Fred Massarik, "Participation by Subordinates in the Managerial Decision-Making Process," (Reprint No. 14 of the Institute of Industrial Relations, UCLA).

In addition, a few of the ICP cases already published have concerned government reorganization, even though most of them gave only incidental attention to the element of participation. Suggested cases on the reorganization theme include:

ICP Case Series 1951—

No. 14. Reorganizing the Massachusetts Department of Conservation (1953)
No. 31. Transfer of the Kansas State Civil Service Department (1956)
No. 32. Reorganization of the California State Personnel Board (1956)
No. 40. Decentralization of Business Services in the Agricultural Research Service (1958)
No. 44. Personnel Problems in Converting to Automation (1959)
No. 47. Reorganization of Philadelphia General Hospital (1954)

II. *Basic Background Information*

1. *Sponsorship.* The cases are being conducted under the guidance of the ICP Research Committee, which is itself composed of seven professors from six universities, nationwide. ICP is a voluntary academic organization whose membership consists of about 50 universities engaged in public administration educational programs. It—and this project—is supported in large part from a grant of the Ford Foundation. This particular committee's program is jointly sponsored and equally supported by the Institute of Governmental Studies, University of California, Berkeley.

2. *Objectives:* (a) to enlarge and to systematize knowledge about one important aspect of public administration; (b) to provide fresh, new, realistic materials for education and training. An incidental benefit may be (and has been) to provide persons in the organizations studied new and objective insights about their own problems and processes. It may be advisable to stress that the focus of our study is on the *process* of change and not on the *content* of change. We are undertaking no appraisal of the wisdom of proposed changes and no inspection for the benefit of any outside organizations or individuals. We are not on any muckraking expedition.
3. *Methods.* Research for the case will involve a substantial interview program with a number of people in the organization. Stress should be laid on our desire to minimize interruptions and inconvenience in the office and to schedule interviews accordingly. After a draft has been written it will be sent to the key officials for comment and criticism. We do not wish to release anything about which there is disagreement and will certainly want confirmation on any question of fact. We will welcome criticisms on matters of opinion and interpretation and will take them into account. We will also do all that is possible, within the limits of academic objectivity and honesty, to prevent embarrassment to an organization or any of its employees. We cannot, of course, guarantee to modify a case to satisfy all of its critics. (It may be pointed out that very few of the more than 50 cases so far published by ICP have raised any problem of this kind, and most of them have probably proved of benefit and favorable publicity for the organizations concerned.)
4. *Product.* Good cases will be published in a casebook on governmental reorganizations. A few may also be published separately. Authors of all cases will receive full credit in any publication. The audience for the cases will in all likelihood consist principally of scholars and students and a scattering of administrators. They do not normally have any wide public circulation. It is not normally our practice to conceal organizations and characters with pseudonyms although this has been done two or three times. For most of the cases of this committee, effective disguise is nearly impossible but it would be considered if desired and if it does not damage the fabric of the story.

III. *Preliminary Steps*

Almost all of the cases for this project will depend primarily upon information freely and informally given by officials, employees, and outsiders. It is therefore a dominating, almost unique necessity that there be a friendly, understanding, and cooperative relationship between the researcher and the individuals concerned. This relationship must be established and assured as far in advance as possible, and the preparatory steps are therefore crucial. If there is not reasonable assurance that information will be freely given, it is normally advisable to drop the case without wasting a lot of time on it.

Laying the groundwork for a case will normally include:

1. An interview with someone(s) at or very near the top of the organization. If the writer is not acquainted with him, it is desirable that he be introduced by a mutual acquaintance who preferably is well respected in the government and who is himself favorably oriented to the project. (Staff officers in O and M work or personnel may be very effective points of contact for this purpose.) This initial meeting (or meetings) should be used primarily to gain understanding and acceptance for the projected research and secondly to explore in general the nature of the organizational change to be studied. The case writer or his sponsor should at this time fully and frankly explain the background of the project—i.e., the development and use of cases in public administration and related fields, the ICP program, and the objectives of this research committee—as well as the objectives of this project, its auspices, method, timing, anticipated product, and probable disposition of product.
2. A meeting, or round of meetings, with the key personnel involved in the case, preferably arranged and presided over by the top official. This meeting would be used to explain and discuss the same things mentioned above.
3. Preliminary familiarization by the writer with the organization and, as far as possible, with the general outlines of the case itself from such documentary sources as are available—the press, legislative actions, reports, articles, budgets, etc.

4. A general overall description of the events and issues involved in the case from someone broadly familiar with it either inside or outside the organization itself. It is requested that each writer prepare and send to the chairman of the committee a brief narrative or outline synopsis of the case at a fairly early date and before he is too heavily engaged in his research.
5. The establishment of a continuing point of liaison within the organization to be studied. This should usually be some central official near the top who can schedule and arrange appointments, provide access to documents and records, perhaps provide desk space, etc.

IV. *The Body of the Research*

1. Some of the cases will take their writers into functional areas in which they have had little or no previous experience. (Cases already underway involve such variegated fields as mental hygiene, scientific research on missiles, highway police, fish and game, tax administration.) Case writing demands a fairly thorough understanding of the nature, purpose, methodology, personnel of the field with which it deals. Writers are therefore urged, where necessary, to familiarize themselves through general reading in the field of their case.
2. Although a case is focused on a single episode or a connected series of episodes, it is necessary that it be understood in the context of the organization concerned and its background. Considerable attention must be given in the research to exploration of the history, scope, evolution of purposes and functions, structure, social organizations, personnel, etc. Some of this can be gained from the written record, but more subtle understandings probably derive from personal observations and interviews.
3. *First Round of Interviews.* It is desirable:
   (a) to talk with all immediately involved in reorganization effort including, where accessible, those who have since left the organization; and talk with at least a sample of those down the line. (The people who do not feel that they were involved or concerned in the process are themselves relevant data to our study.);
   (b) at this stage, that interviews be largely open-ended; tell them about our project and its purposes and then ask them to tell about the background of the organization and the story of the attempted change as they saw it;
   (c) to leave the door open for a return visit;
   (d) to take notes, preferably during or soon after the interview, but take them before the details are forgotten;
   (e) to pick up, as you go, documentary records, notes, etc., that are available.
4. *Analysis.* After the first round it is suggested to:
   (a) review all the data gathered so far and prepare in narrative or outline a revised synopsis; discuss the case and synopsis with associates and others connected with this project, giving particular attention to the questions not yet fully answered;
   (b) prepare a list of questions on matters that are inconsistent, or unclear, or not dealt with at all.
5. *Subsequent interviews.* It is normally necessary to conduct a second round of interviews with selected personnel (and sometimes a third with a few.) These should be directed and aimed at obtaining specific information as a result of your analysis.
6. *First Draft.* The first draft should be as nearly complete as possible and probably longer than the finished product will be. The process of writing will undoubtedly reveal new questions and gaps in knowledge, requiring further research on specific points.
7. *Clearances.*
   (a) with top administrative officers.
   (b) with informants, both employees and persons outside the organization (the extent of this kind of clearance must rest largely on the judgment of the writer and the nature of the information included in the case).
   (c) with the committee and, through it, with the sponsoring agencies.

   It is probable that all of the clearances will result in some changes in the document and some of them may require further investigations. The writer should anticipate this.
8. *The Document Itself.* The case itself should be written in the style of the other ICP cases —fairly brief description of the background and setting of the case, a narrative telling the

story, a denouement, where appropriate, of what followed and resulted from the story. The case itself should not be interrupted for extended analysis or to point out the applicability (or lack of it) of various hypotheses, but it should include the information from which such analyses can be made. Like other cases, these are stories, here seen and described from a somewhat particularized point of view. But they are still stories.

Each writer is asked, in addition, to append to his case a fairly brief essay constituting his analysis and conclusions on the meaning of his case in terms of the focus of this project as a whole. The kinds of questions to be considered are suggested in Section V below, but others may also be appropriate. This document is primarily for the use of the committee and will contribute enormously to its efforts to generalize from our cases. We urge that much thought be given to it. It does not appear, at this time, necessary for these appendices to be cleared with the organizations though the writer is at liberty to do so if he wishes. We cannot at present say how much of these may be published; it is possible that the valuable ones will be published in entirety.

9. *Clerical Help.* It is hoped that writers will have access to stenographic and typing assistance, office supplies, etc., from their institutions. Where possible, drafts of cases should be reproduced in multiple copies to facilitate clearances. Writers should take up any problems on these matters directly with the chairman of the committee.

V. *Things to Look For*

1. The origins of the reorganization effort and the reasons, real and alleged, for it;
2. Previous efforts, if any, for a similar change, and their histories;
3. Who *really* made the key decisions? What considerations most influenced their decisions?
4. The devices, if any, for enlisting participation; to whom were they directed? their degree of effectiveness?
5. How far did participation go? to what extent was it influential, to what extent "pseudo"; what do the alleged participants themselves feel about it?
6. At which of the following stages, if any, did participation play a part?
   (a) the initiation of the idea
   (b) study and planning
   (c) the decision itself, including the steps immediately preceding it, such as reanalysis and negotiation
   (d) implementation and assimilation
   (e) later adjustments after installation
7. What were the objectives of the change as seen by (1) top management, (2) persons interested outside the organization, (3) various classes of employees, whether or not participants, (4) the objective student (yourself)?
8. Was reorganization effective—in form or in substance or both? Whose objectives (7 above) did it satisfy, if any? What real changes in behavior, status, relationships, program resulted? To what extent were these changes anticipated and intended, and by whom?
9. How did participation affect the reorganization process? The results? The way participants felt about the process and its results?
10. If participation was effective, in what way was it: Through overcoming resistance? By improving information and thus the content of reorganization? By generally improving knowledge, communication, and understanding? If it was not effective, what were its defects and results?
11. Aside from participation, what were the most significant other elements in the organizational, political, social climate in influencing the course and results of the reorganization?

VI. *Suggested Conceptual Approaches*

Each case study will deal with change occurring or intended in an organizational context. The nature of this particular context will have important bearing upon the change and upon participation (present or absent). Some of the major elements in this context that may be useful for understanding of the individual cases are:

1. Styles of leadership—authoritarian or democratic, or other.
2. Formal and informal or social organization, (group theory, etc.).
3. Technical or professional attitudes vs. generalist or administrative orientation.

4. Organizational goals, group goals, personal goals—coincidence and/or divergence.
5. Power, authority: formal (as legal, hierarchical, etc.) or informal (as clientele groups).
6. Communication systems, within and without the organization, not only as to adequacy and effectiveness as channels but as to success (or lack of) in transmitting *meaning*, influencing behaviors.
7. Concepts such as status and prestige, value systems, etc.